R Loire
Veso
Dijon
Bes
SWITZERLAND
R Saône
Lake Geneva
Charolles
Varennes
Geneva
Vichy
Roanne
R Rhône
Lyon
mont-Ferrand
St Etienne
Grenoble
ITALY
Valence
NOCCUPIED
FRANCE
R Rhône
Montélimar
Orange
St Hippolyte-du-Fort
Avignon
Monaco
Nîmes
Tarascon
Nice
Montpellier
Arles
Grasse
Aix
Sète
Agde
Marseille
éziers
Toulon
Golfe
Du Lion
nne
Argelès-sur-Mer
an
Collioure
Port Vendres
Banyuls-sur-Mer
Cerbère
SCALE:
Kilometres
0
50
Miles
0
50

2017

To Bernard.

Enjoy a good read!

Anonca

RAF EVADERS

RAF EVADERS

The comprehensive story of thousands of escapers and their escape lines, Western Europe, 1940-1945

OLIVER CLUTTON-BROCK

GRUB STREEET · LONDON

Published by
Grub Street Publishing
4 Rainham Close
London
SW11 6SS

British Library Cataloguing in Publication Data
Clutton-Brock, Oliver
RAF evaders: the complete story of RAF evaders, escapees and their
escape lines, Western Europe, 1940-1945
1. Great Britain. Royal Air Force – Airmen – Biography
2. Escapes – Europe – History – 20th century 3. World War,
1939-1945 – Underground movements 4. Airmen – Great Britain – Biography
I. Title
940.5′44941′0922

ISBN-13: 9781906502171

Typeset by Pearl Graphics, Hemel Hempstead

Printed and bound by MPG Ltd, Bodmin, Cornwall

Grub Street Publishing uses only FSC (Forest Stewardship Council) paper for its books

Dedication

In memory of the countless thousands of men, women, and children who, during the Second World War, voluntarily and in peril of their lives helped thousands of civilians, Allied airmen, soldiers and sailors to safety and who asked for nothing in return.

'We helped them because the airmen came to help us.
They were there to give their lives for us.'

"Michou" Ugeux, née Dumon
The Sydney Morning Herald, 23 April 1988

Contents

Dedication		iv
Acknowledgements		vi
Glossary		viii
Details of selected personalities		xii
Preface		xxv
Introduction		xxix
Chapter 1:	In the beginning: 1940	1
Chapter 2:	Marseille and St Hippolyte: 1940–1941	23
Chapter 3:	Diplomacy and evasion, Spain and Portugal: 1940–1942	45
Chapter 4:	PAT line: 1941–1942	65
Chapter 5:	By land and by sea: 1942	87
Chapter 6:	The Comet line: 1941–1942	112
Chapter 7:	Marie-Claire and other escape lines: 1940–1944	134
	Chauny escape line	148
	Dutch-Paris	152
	Bleu et Jonquille	157
	Frans Hals	158
	The Maca family	158
	Luctor et Emergo/Fiat Libertas	159
Chapter 8:	Boats, planes, more escape lines, France: 1942–1944	160
Chapter 9:	Comet and PAT/PAO lines: 1942–1943	188
Chapter 10:	Evasions: January–September 1943	216
Chapter 11:	Evasions: October 1943–June 1944	244
Chapter 12:	Operation Marathon: 1944	273
	The Marathon camps in the Belgian Ardennes	288
Chapter 13:	Evasions: June 1944–May 1945	297
	The "Ghost Train"	313
Chapter 14:	To the bitter end	325
Appendix I:	List of RAF evaders: 1940–1945	346
Appendix II:	List of Comet evaders: 1941–1944	412
Appendix III:	Sea evacuations:1942–1944	417
Appendix IV:	Marathon: 1944	423
Appendix V:	MI9, IS9, and IS9 (WEA)	427
Appendix VI:	The unusual evasion of Sergeant H.E.R. Merlin RAF	430
Appendix VII:	Operation Frankton: December 1942	433
Appendix VIII:	Statistical tables: evaders by rank; month lost; nation; type of aircraft; and place	434
Notes to Chapters		436
Bibliography		474
Index		477

Acknowledgements

To each and everyone named below, I am most grateful for their help:

Ian Adams (re his grandfather, Jack Fisher); Brian Aguiar (re his grandfather William Aguiar USAAF); Roger Anthoine (author); Ken Arnold (re Squadron Leader "Wally" Lashbrook); Dave Arundel (158 Squadron); Richard Barber (for kind permission to quote from his book); Bob Barckley (3 Squadron); Philip Barclay (419 Squadron); Mrs Peggy Barlow (re her husband Raymond Barlow, 49 Squadron); Malcolm Barrass; Kevin Bending (re 97 Squadron and Flight Sergeant C.J. Billows); John Berthelsen (149 Squadron); Jack Blandford (101 Squadron); Bruce Bolinger (Nevada City, USA, researching Tom Applewhite USAAF); Terry Bolter (77 Squadron); Geoff Bowlby (re his grandfather, Flight Sergeant Art Bowlby RCAF); Patricia Brayley (re her late husband, W.E.J. "Bill" Brayley RCAF); Fred W. Brown; John T. Brown (467 Squadron); Molly Burkett (co-author of *Not Just Another Milk Run…*); Ted Cachart (49 Squadron historian); Warren B. Carah (USA); A.E. "Ted" Church; Betty Clements (re Polish awards); Paul and Eunice Cornelius (re Reg Cornelius, 1663 HCU/10 Squadron); Ernest John Couchman (630 Squadron); Colin Cripps (49 Squadron historian); Cumbria Records Office, Whitehaven (especially Robert Baxter, archivist, and Mary Chisholm); Peter W. Cunliffe (author of *A Shaky Do. The Škoda works raid 16/17th April 1943*); Ian Darling (Canadian author/researcher, re Gordon Stacey); the late Al Day (77 Squadron); Frank Dell (692 Squadron); Robert Dixon (author, re 607 Squadron); Brigitte d'Oultremont (Belgium, re *la ligne Comète*); Linzee Druce (re Squadron Leader "Wally" Lashbrook); Alain Durier (France); Tony Eaton (re George Fearnyhough DFC); L.E. Ellingham (7 Squadron; PoW); Bill Etherington (author, *A Quiet Woman's War*); Mrs Patricia Farmer (re her husband W.W. Farmer, 10 Squadron); George Fearnyhough DFC (10 Squadron); Eddie Fell (Chairman, 158 Squadron Association, for his considerable help with Squadron aircrew information); Vítek Formánek (re Czech evaders); Richard Frost (re Mlle. Baudot de Rouville); Cecile Gemmell (re her father, Al Hagan, 77 Squadron); Jim George (re 467 & 463 Squadrons); Mrs Margaret Goddard (APC Polish Enquiries, Ministry of Defence); Tony Goodenough (re his father Reg Goodenough); Janine de Greef; F.A. Greenwell (57 Squadron); Fred Greyer (especially re his father, Capitaine D.E. Potier, Belgian Army); Mrs Winifred Hagan (widow of Al Hagan, 77 Squadron); C.L. Hallett (10 Squadron); Greg Harrison (100 Squadron historian); T.H. Harvell (514 Squadron); F.R. Haslam (207 Squadron); Frank Haslam jnr; Claude Hélias (*Conservatoire Aéronautique de Cornouaille*, Plomelin, France); Les Hood (582 Squadron); V.E. Horn (158 Squadron); Andoni Iturrioz (re evasions in the Basque region); Squadron Leader Richard James MBE (IX Squadron Association); Keith Janes (for sharing his considerable evasion knowledge); Peter Johnson (re 467/463 Squadrons); Mike Kemble (re MGB's 502 and 503); Daphne Lees (re Dutch matters); Michael Moores LeBlanc (evasion historian, in Canada); Greg Lewis (author of *Airman Missing*); Reg Lewis DFC (138 Squadron); Chris and Ann Lyth (re Elvire de Greef and family); John MacDougall (158 Squadron); Pat MacGregor (re her father, Leslie Maxwell Byrne, and crew, 158 Squadron); Elizabeth McDade (New York, re Drue Tartière); Ken McPherson (8th AFHS, re Pilot Officer Dube RCAF); Gordon Mellor (103 Squadron); Alan Mitchell (re his father Sergeant R.J. Mitchell); David Mole (former chairman of 10 Squadron Association); Diana Morgan (re her late husband, Bryan, 460 Squadron, but especially for her tireless communications work); Keith Morley (re his father, R.C. Morley); Alex Morrison (re his wife's uncle, Flight Sergeant R.F. Conroy RCAF); Jeffery Pack (author of *Love is in the Air*, and re his father J.T. Pack, 35 Squadron); Nigel Parker (former editor of *Bomber Command Newsletter*); Andy Parlour (co-author, HMS *Tarana*); G.A. Percival (2 Squadron); Matt Poole (USA, air researcher); Linda Ralph (née Smith, re her uncle, James Smith MM); Edouard Renière (Brussels, especially for help with the USAAF); Derek Richardson (author, *Detachment W*); Sheila Savage (re her father, W.E. Williams, 576 Squadron); Jim Sheffield; Roger Stanton (secretary, Escape Lines Memorial Society); Ron Stephens (co-author, HMS *Tarana*); Denys Teare (103 Squadron; friend and author, *Evader*); Tom Thackray (10 Squadron Association Newsletter Editor); Norman Thom (100 Squadron); Mary Thomas (author, *Behind Enemy Lines*); Annette Tison (*B-24.net* researcher, USA); Hubert Timmerman; Andrée Traxel (re Barney Greatrex); Wilco Vermeer (Holland, re Anton Schrader); Lorraine Denise Vickerman (re Bill Brayley); Harry Webb (640 Squadron); John A. Williams (re Pilot Officer G.B. Hall RAAF, 466 Squadron); Mrs Myra Williams (re her brother W.W. Farmer, 10 Squadron); the late Roland Williams (65 Squadron); Tom Wingham (102 Squadron); Ray Worrall (44 Squadron).

I fully acknowledge that the early chapters could not have been written without the generous assistance of Derek Richardson, author of *Detachment W*, whose permission to use material from his excellent book is most appreciated, and also of Keith Janes, who has given permission to quote from his book *Conscript Heroes* (the story of his father's time in the army and subsequent evasion). John Clinch, who has a considerable insight into affairs in Brussels and Belgium, has been a great fount of knowledge. Stefaan Calus (Bruges) has also been exceedingly generous with his time and expert knowledge of Belgian matters, as have Edouard Renière and Philippe Connart. And to Søren Flensted I owe much for sharing his great knowledge of the air war over and around Denmark, and who has a wonderfully researched website. And to W.R. "Bill" Chorley (author of the *Bomber Command Losses* etc) many thanks for all his time and research.

Thanks also to Jeff and Jacky Pack, and to Derek and Elizabeth Collett for their hospitality. Special thanks go to my wife, Diane, for sharing the run up and down the M4 and for all the hours "chained" to the (still awful) microfiche readers at The National Archives.

Finally, thanks to those at Grub Street, especially Hannah Stuart for her charming tolerance of a barrage of emails and John Davies, of course, for publishing this book.

Glossary

AASF	Advanced Air Striking Force (of the RAF).
Abwehr	The military counter-intelligence arm of the German armed forces, under Admiral Wilhelm Canaris until 1 June 1944, when he was replaced by Heinrich Himmler. The *Geheime Feld Polizei* (GFP, Secret Field Police) were the main protagonists of the escape lines.
AFC	Air Force Cross (a non-operational award).
AFRO	Air Force Routine Orders.
AMPC	Auxiliary Military Pioneer Corps.
AOC (-in-C)	Air Officer Commanding (-in-Chief).
B-17; B-24	US 4-engined heavy-bombers, respectively the "Flying Fortress" and "Liberator".
BBC	British Broadcasting Corporation.
BCRA	*Bureau Central de Renseignements et d'Action.* An organisation created by General Charles de Gaulle in January 1942 to dispatch agents to France, mainly for establishing and setting up Resistance groups.
BEF	British Expeditionary Force.
BG; BS	Bomb Group; Bomb Squadron (as used by the USAAF).
Blenheim	Twin-engined, light RAF bomber aircraft with a crew of three.
Boston	Douglas A–20. Twin-engined medium bomber used by RAF and USAAF.
Brûlé	"burnt" (French), meaning that one's cover had been "blown", exposed.
BST	British Summer Time.
Carabinero	Spanish frontier policeman.
CB	Companion of the Order of the Bath.
CdeG	Croix de Guerre (French, "War Cross". Several levels of award, e.g. Silver).
CGM	Conspicuous Gallantry Medal.
Circus	Bomber raid heavily escorted by fighters to lure enemy fighters into action.
CMG	Companion of the Order of St Michael and St George.
CO	Commanding Officer.
Convoyeur	French. One who "convoys" people, i.e. an escort.
CQMS	Company Quartermaster Sergeant.
CU	Conversion Unit, the final RAF unit before joining a front line squadron.
CVO	Commander of the Royal Victorian Order.
CWGC	Commonwealth War Graves Commission.
DCM	Distinguished Conduct Medal.
D-Day	6 June 1944, the day of the Allies' first landings in Normandy, France.
DDOD(I)	Deputy Director Operations Division (Irregular), Royal Navy.
Defiant	Single-engined, two-man RAF monoplane with four-gun .303 turret behind pilot.
DFC; DFM	Distinguished Flying Cross; Distinguished Flying Medal.
DSM; DSO	Distinguished Service Medal; Distinguished Service Order.
DZ	Drop(-ping) Zone.
E-boat	Powerful, fast German navy boat. Larger than the Royal Navy's MGBs.
Espadrille	French. A canvas shoe with a hard-wearing jute or esparto sole.
ETA	Estimated Time of Arrival.
(F)	(Fighter).
FANY	First Aid Nursing Yeomanry (Princess Royal's Volunteer Corps).
Feldgendarme	German military policeman.
FFI	*Forces Françaises de l'Intérieur*, the French Interior resistance army, created early in 1944 from a number of disparate groups in France by order of General de Gaulle in England. Placed under the command of General Pierre Koenig.
FG; FS	Fighter Group; Fighter Squadron (as used by the USAAF).
F/L; F/O	Flight Lieutenant; Flying Officer.
F/S, F/Sgt	Flight Sergeant.
GCB	Knight Grand Cross of the Order of the Bath.
Gestapo	*Geheime Staats Polizei* (German secret state police).
GFP	*Geheime Feld Polizei* (German Field Police, a branch of the *Abwehr*, q.v.).

GM	George Medal.
GMT	Greenwich Mean Time.
GOC	General Officer Commanding.
Guardia Civil	Spanish civil (as opposed to military) police.
HCU	Heavy Conversion Unit (see also CU above).
HMS	His Majesty's Ship.
HMT	His Majesty's Transport (ship). The "T" might also refer to Troopship.
IFF	Identification Friend or Foe – an RAF electronic device identifying an aircraft as friendly.
IS9 (d)	see Room 900.
IS9 (WEA)	Intelligence School 9 (Western European Area). See Appendix V.
Jedburgh	Three- or four-man teams infiltrated by the Allies behind enemy lines, mostly in France, to co-ordinate resistance with indigenous forces against the Germans. Commonly shortened to "Jed".
Ju88	Twin-engined German bomber and night-fighter – Junkers 88.
Juez Militar	Spanish military judge.
Juzgado Militar	Spanish Military Court of Justice.
KBE	Knight Commander of the Order of the British Empire.
KCB	Knight Commander of the Order of the Bath.
KCVO	Knight Commander of the Royal Victorian Order.
KIA	Killed in action.
KLM	Royal Dutch Airlines – *Koninklijke Luchtvaart Maatschappij* (literally "Royal Aviation Company").
KOSB	King's Own Scottish Borderers.
Liberté surveillée	Literally "supervised liberty", a form of controlled parole.
M., Mme., Mlle.,	Monsieur, Madame, Mademoiselle – Mr, Mrs, Miss.
Mae-west	Inflatable life-jacket named after the eponymous and well-proportioned film star.
Manchester	Twin-engined RAF bomber aircraft. Precursor of the four-engined Avro Lancaster.
Maquis	The Corsican word for scrubland, *maquis* became the name for irregular groups of French Resistance fighters – hence *maquisards*.
MBE	Member of the Most Excellent Order of the British Empire.
MC; MM	Military Cross; Military Medal.
Me109	German single-seat fighter aircraft.
Me110	German twin-engined day and (later) night-fighter aircraft. Crew of three.
MGB	Motor Gun Boat (Royal Navy). See also MTB.
MiD	Mentioned in Despatches.
MI5	Military Intelligence 5. The security service responsible for all territories of the British Empire.
MI6	Military Intelligence 6. British Secret Intelligence Service (SIS), responsible for Intelligence in the rest of the world not covered by MI5.
MI9	Military Intelligence 9. See Appendix V.
Milice, The	French para-military police force created in January 1943 from the right-wing military group *Service d'Ordre Légionnaire*, which had been established in July 1941 by Frenchman Joseph Darnand (see Selected Personalities p. xiv).
Miranda de Ebro	A town of northern Spain, some fifty kilometres south of Bilbao, on the River Ebro, that gave its name to the large concentration camp situated there. Sometimes referred to as Miranda *del* Ebro.
MT	Motor (or Mechanised) Transport.
MTB	Motor Torpedo Boat. Fast, multi-engined Royal Navy craft, usually of wooden construction.
MVO	Member of the 4th or 5th Class of the Royal Victorian Order.
NAAFI	Navy Army and Air Forces Institute.
NCO	Non-commissioned officer – e.g. sergeant, corporal.
OBE	Officer of the Most Excellent Order of the British Empire.
Oflag	Abbreviation for *Offizierenlager* – officer camp, for prisoners of war.
O/R; OR	Other Ranks. Usually below officer rank, but sometimes excluding NCOs.
OSS	Office of Strategic Services. US organisation similar to the British SOE.

P15	SIS section responsible for PoWs etc. in MI9. Comprised James Langley, Airey Neave, Ian Garrow and Captain Windham-Wright. See Room 900. (see *Secret War. The Story of SOE Britain's Wartime Sabotage Organisation*, p. 26 – Nigel West [Hodder & Stoughton, London, 1992]).
PAF	Polish Air Force.
PAO; PAT	Name given to escape line begun in Marseilles and south of France in summer 1940. From initials of Patrick Albert O'Leary. Changed from PAT at beginning of May 1942 (see *Underground from Posen*, p. 167).
Passeur, -euse	Guide, escort (literal French meaning is ferryman, -woman).
PoW	Prisoner of war.
Préfecture	(French) police headquarters.
PRU	Photographic Reconnaissance Unit, RAF.
PUF	*Presses Universitaires de France* – a French publishing company.
P.W.; P/W	See PoW.
QDM	Wireless code for a request for a bearing.
Sherwood	Codename of IS9 plan to concentrate evaders in a single spot in mid-France after D-Day.
RA	Royal Artillery.
RAC	Royal Armoured Corps.
RAAF	Royal Australian Air Force.
RAF; RAFVR	Royal Air Force; Royal Air Force Volunteer Reserve.
RAMC	Royal Army Medical Corps.
Ramrod	Fighters escorting bombers to a target; also intended to draw enemy fighters into action.
RASC	Royal Army Service Corps.
RCAF	Royal Canadian Air Force.
RCS	Royal Corps of Signals.
RE	Royal Engineers.
RFC	Royal Flying Corps.
Rhubarb	Small-scale fighter sorties against ground targets of opportunity.
RM	Royal Marine (s).
RN; RNR; RNVR	Royal Navy; Royal Naval Reserve; Royal Naval Volunteer Reserve.
RNethNAS	Royal Netherlands Naval Air Service.
RNZAF	Royal New Zealand Air Force.
ROOM 900	The number of the room at the War Office in which members of the top secret section IS9 (d) were housed. It 'did not conduct espionage, and consisted of only two or three officers and a handful of trained agents at any time during the war'. (Neave, *Saturday at MI9*, pp. 71-2). It did not begin operating until 1941. See P15.
R/T	Radio/Telephony; Radio/Telephone.
Safe house	A place of which, in theory, the enemy's counter-intelligence forces had no knowledge, and which could therefore be used as a temporary shelter for escapers and evaders.
SANF(V)	South African Naval Force (Volunteer).
SAS	Special Air Service.
SBO	Senior British Officer.
SD	*Sicherheitsdienst* ("security bureau"). The Intelligence arm of the SS (*Schutzstaffel* – protection squad). Separate from the Gestapo.
Second dickey	RAF slang for a second pilot. From the "dickey seat" in old motorcars.
Sgt	Sergeant.
SIS	Secret Intelligence Service – see MI6.
SNCF	*Société Nationale des Chemins de Fer Français* – French National Railways.
SOE	Special Operations Executive. Department created in July 1940 at Churchill's behest to 'set Europe ablaze' by infiltrating secret agents into German-occupied countries. It was originally under the chairmanship of Dalton, Minister for Economic Warfare.
Sprog	RAF slang for beginners, i.e. a crew new to operations was a "sprog" crew.
SS	*Schutzstaffel*, Nazi Black Shirts, originally formed as Hitler's personal bodyguard.

STO	*Service du Travail Obligatoire* – forced labour for the Germans.
Sûreté (Belgian)	Belgian secret service organisation.
TNA	The National Archives (formerly the Public Record Office), Kew, London.
T/Sgt	Technical Sergeant. The American Air Force had four "grades" of sergeant: Master Sergeant/First Sergeant (first grade); Technical Sergeant (second); Staff Sergeant (third); Sergeant (fourth).
Typhoon	Large, single-seater RAF fighter.
US; USA	United States; United States of America.
USAAF	United States Army Air Force(s).
V1, V2	*Vergeltungswaffe* (Reprisal weapon).
Window	Strips of metal foil cut to the width of German night-fighter radar bands.
WOP/AG	Wireless operator/air gunner.
WRNS	Women's Royal Naval Service.

Details of selected personalities

Brief details of some of the key people involved with Allied evaders, 1940-1945.

Note: (Aus) Australian; (Bas) Basque; (Bel) Belgian; (Br) British; (Can) Canadian; (Est) Estonian; (Fr) French; (Grk) Greek; (Hol) Dutch; (NZ) New Zealander; (Rus) Russian; (Sco) Scots; (Sp) Spanish.

ANCIA, Albert (Bel) – "Daniel Mouton". Born 1916. Crossed to Spain on 23/24 December 1943. Trained by IS9 to organise camps for evaders/escapers in Operation Sherwood. Parachuted into France with Jean de Blommaert on night of 9/10 April 1944. After brief stay in Paris made his way to Belgian Ardennes in May 1944 to organise setting up of camps there.

AYLÉ, Robert Constant (Fr) – "Baby". Born 4 June 1899. With his wife, Germaine, ran a safe house for Comet on the rue de Babylon, Paris. Arrested 7 June 1943. Executed by the Germans on 28 March 1944, with Frédéric de Jongh and Aimable Fouquerel at Mont Valérien, Paris.

"B" See JOHNSON, Albert Edward.

BAJPAI, Germaine Marie Lucie (Fr) – "Hautfoin", "Cramponne". Born 4 October 1894, née Flachet, at Dinan (Côtes-du-Nord). Reputed to have been married four times (including once to an Australian sailor), but was lastly married to Sirda Bajpai whose brother, Sir Girja Shankar Bajpai, was Agent General for India in Washington 1941-46. One of the three organisers of the safe-house system set up by "Jérôme" (Le Grelle) in Paris around August 1943. Also saw to airmen's welfare and guided them to and from Paris. When arrested on 18 January 1944 she had officially helped sixty-three Allied airmen, though the unofficial figure is nearer seventy-five. Died in Ravensbrück concentration camp on 4 February 1945, 'never able to forgive herself for being captured with a list of her safe-house keepers, a fact that led to their arrests.'[1]

BARBIER, Elizabeth (Fr) – Organised her own group, with forty-six helpers at one point, to assist evaders and escapers in and around Paris. Assisted Oaktree, and also Frédéric de Jongh and Comet, in 1943. She was credited with having assisted some 150 Allied airmen. She and her mother were caught on about 11 June 1943 as a result of the treachery of Jean-Jacques Desoubrie (who had also been responsible for Frédéric de Jongh's arrest on 7 June) and, after imprisonment at Fresnes, were sent to Ravensbrück, from which both emerged alive at the end of the war.

BAUDOT de ROUVILLE, Maud Olga Andrée (Fr) – Born in Paris on 14 December 1891 of a French father and an Irish mother. A nurse during the 1914-1918 war, receiving a Red Cross certificate in 1917. Assumed the *nom de guerre* of "Thérèse Martin" earlier in the Second World War when nursing British soldiers in a convent in Lille, many of whom were to end up in prisoner-of-war camps in Germany. Became involved with the PAT/PAO line there, before moving to Marseille in 1942, where she ran a safe house. Joined Françoise Dissard in Toulouse in 1943. In 1946 went to stay in Cockermouth, Cumbria with Dr John Heslop, one of her patients from Lille, but left for County Wexford, Ireland in 1947. Squadron Leader Frank Griffiths wrote that she 'lived in Cork and ran a mission to Seamen' – *Winged Hours*, p. 184.

BLANCHAIN, Francis Paul (Fr) – "Achille". Born on 21 March 1913 in Bromley, England of French parents, he had an English birth certificate. PAT/PAO line *convoyeur* in Marseille. Arrested in Limoges at the beginning of August 1942. Escaped from a police car and made his way to Marseille. Left France aboard *Seawolf* on 21 September 1942 (Operation Titania). Later, in London, married Paula Spriewald, a German of an anti-Nazi family (who had also been Pat O'Leary's "secretary" and who left on the *Tarana*). Joined the RAF in 1943, working in the photographic section until the end of the war. Commissioned in 1944. Flight Lieutenant Francis P. Blanchain BEM served in the RAF until 1947. He and Paula moved to Canada in 1958.[2]

BOULAIN, Pierre – see DESOUBRIE, Jean-Jacques.

BOURYSCHKINE, Vladimir (Rus). White Russian born in Moscow in 1913, but raised in USA. Worked for American Red Cross. An expert baseball player, he became coach to the Monaco team. Helper in the PAT/PAO line before fleeing from France in autumn 1942. Employed by Room 900, and given nickname "Val Williams" by James Langley. Volunteered to return to France to run the Oaktree line. Parachuted into France near Paris on 20 March 1943 with radio operator Raymond Labrosse. Ordered not to make contact with the compromised PAO line, nevertheless did so. Arrested by the Gestapo on 4 June 1943 while taking four evaders to Pau by train. Questioned at Fresnes and Rennes prisons. Escaped on 20 December 1943 with help of Ivan Bougaiev, a fellow Russian, though breaking a leg in the process. Sent back to England by Lucien Dumais on 26 February 1944 (Operation Bonaparte II). Locked up on suspicion of being a double agent, but released after the Normandy landings. Awarded BEM. Died August 1968.

BOUSSA, Lucien (Bel) – "Belgrave". Born 1905. Squadron commander in 1940 of Belgian Air Force's 5th Squadron (equipped with the Fairey Fox). Two combat victories. Escaped to England. Became squadron leader CO of 350 (Belgian) Squadron RAF, and scored a further five victories by end of 1943. Awarded DFC. Completed three operational tours before being trained for Operation Sherwood, leaving for France in April 1944. He and his wireless operator, François Toussaint, reached the Forêt de Fréteval via Spain on 13 May 1944. Awarded MC. He died at Cloyes on 12 March 1967, three months before a memorial was unveiled in the forest where he had done so much for the Allies.

BOUTELOUPT, Madeleine (Fr) – Courier for Comet from April 1943 between Paris and Spanish frontier. Betrayed by Desoubrie and arrested at Lille station with an evader in June 1943. Liberated by the Americans from her concentration camp. Returned home to her mother, but was so weak that she died a few days later, on 7 May 1945, aged 33.

BROUSSINE, Georges (Fr) – "Burgundy". Operated mostly in north-west France in 1943-44 on behalf of Room 900 and the French BCRA. Helped over 268 men to escape either by boat from Brittany to England, or across the Pyrenees to Spain (including Raymond Labrosse). After helping with sea evacuations and escapes to Spain from Brittany, he was sent to Normandy. Located Air Commodore Ivelaw-Chapman, shot down over France on night of 6/7 May 1944, who knew of the impending Normandy landings and whom Churchill wanted killed. Arranged for him to be kept in a safe house (which proved to be unsafe). Broussine was arrested by the Germans in July 1944, but soon escaped. He was awarded the Military Cross (British) and the Croix de Guerre (French). Later, president of the society *l'Oiseau Blessé*, formed in Paris to bring together those who aided Allied servicemen in France during the German occupation. Died on 31 October 2001 aged 83.

BRUSSELMANS, Anne (Bel) – Worked for Comet in Brussels until the line was severely interrupted by the Gestapo in December 1943. Resumed evasion line activities in the spring of 1944, together with survivors of the Michou Dumon/Maca group. Worked closely with Michou Dumon and, later, with her mother, Françoise. Was hiding forty-nine airmen in Brussels by beginning of May 1944; fifty-four in early July. Continued to work in Brussels having refused to be part of the Marathon camps. Emigrated to USA and was given citizenship of that country by President Ronald Reagan on 15 January 1987 in view of her war work. Survived, never arrested. (See *Rendez-vous 127. The Diary of Anne Brusselmans*).

CAMORS, Jean-Claude (Fr) – "Cartier", "Noël", "Gérard", "Jean Raoul", "Raoul Caulaincourt", "Philippe Wallon". Founder and chief of *réseau* Bordeaux-Loupiac. Born 27 October 1919, at Pau. Enlisted in 18ème Régiment d'Infanterie. Taken prisoner while in hospital at Châteaubriant. Escaped in July 1940. Left Marseille in a fishing boat, but on 8 April 1942 jumped into the sea near Morocco and swam for two hours to Gibraltar. Arrived in England in mid-May 1942. Joined Free French Forces on 26 June 1942, and the BCRA in October 1942. Parachuted to France in mid-April 1943 to set up escape line Bordeaux-Loupiac. Left for England in May. Reached London on 21 June 1943. Parachuted again into France on 5 July. Shot by Roger Le Neveu (q.v.) in Rennes, and died of his wounds on 11 October 1943. Some sixty airmen were helped to evade by his organisation between 23 October 1943 and 22 January 1944.

CARPENTIER, Abbé Pierre (Fr) – Priest and master-forger who ran a safe house at 13, Place du Cimetière-St Gilles, Abbeville, in northern France. Provided the Cole/Garrow/O'Leary line with false identity cards and passes. Betrayed by Cole. Arrested on 8 December 1941 with François Duprez. Deported to Germany. Imprisoned at Bochum. Condemned to death on 16 April 1943. Beheaded at Dortmund on 30 June 1943.

CASKIE, Reverend Donald Currie (Sco) – Scottish Presbyterian minister. Born 22 May 1902. Known as "The Tartan Pimpernel" (also title of his book published 1957). Forced to leave his church in Paris in June 1940, made his way to Marseille, and opened up the Seamen's Mission at 36, Rue de Forbin, Marseille, to hide British evaders and escapers. Ordered to close down the mission in July 1941. Arrested in 1943 by the Italians in the Grenoble area. Handed over to the Germans. Sentenced to death by them in Paris but a German pastor got the sentence changed to life imprisonment. In solitary confinement – not allowed to sit down during the day – he was liberated only when the Germans left Paris in August 1944. Appointed OBE (12 June 1945). Died in 1983.

CHERAMY, "Pat" (Br) – née Maud Eleanor Hawkins. Married Charles Cheramy, a French engineer, in 1940. Lived at Montauban. Charles and Pat, and their 18-month-old son, Michel, were arrested in January 1943 when German police homed-in on wireless transmissions from Tom Groome (see below). Both survived the war, Pat living through Fresnes, Ravensbrück and Mauthausen, to be reunited with her husband and son in 1945. Awarded the Croix de Guerre, Légion d'Honneur, Médaille de la Résistance, the US Medal of Freedom and the BEM (1 July 1947), she died on 26 March 1987, aged 80. She and Charles, who died in 1980, were divorced.

COACHE, Raymonde (Fr) – worked, with husband René, for Comet. Betrayed by Desoubrie and arrested in Lille in June 1943. Deported to Germany, she survived two years in a concentration camp. Appointed MBE.

COACHE, René Gustave Marie (Fr) – "Dover". Born 3 January 1904. Worked, with his wife Raymonde, for Comet. Their apartment at 71, Rue de Nanterre, Asnières-sur-Seine, a north-western suburb of Paris, was used as a safe house for evaders/escapers. Thirty men were hidden there in 1941-42. Escaped to England (crossed Pyrenees on 1 January 1943). Persuaded by Airey Neave to become a radio operator for Comet. Worked his set in Brussels but was arrested by the Gestapo on 21 April 1944. Managed to escape on 3 September 1944 from St Gilles prison, Brussels in the confusion of the German withdrawal.

COLE, Harold (Br) – Born 24 January 1903. Also called himself "Paul", "Paul Delobel", "Captain Paul Cole", "Captain Colson", "Joseph Deram". A petty criminal and "con man" before the war. Joined the army in 1939 and rose to rank of sergeant. Absconded from the BEF in spring 1940 with Mess funds. Arrested by the Abwehr in Lille on 6 December 1941. Instrumental in the arrest of Abbé Carpentier, François Duprez, and others. Married Suzanne Warenghem on 10 April 1942. Arrested in Lyons by Vichy police on 9 June 1942. Sentenced to death but saved by German occupation of Vichy France in November 1942. Worked for SS-Sturmbannführer Hans Keiffer of the Sicherheitsdienst, whose HQ was at 84 Avenue Foch, Paris. Betrayed hundreds of helpers and airmen to the Gestapo. In the spring of 1945 'walked into the headquarters of an American Cavalry Regiment in south Germany' (*Saturday at MI9*, p. 310) with Kieffer, and announced that he was Captain Mason. Given a job in US Counter Intelligence Corps, he was eventually arrested and taken to Paris. Escaped. Shot dead by French police looking for deserters in a room above Billy's Bar, Paris, on 8 January 1946. Regarded by Airey Neave as 'among the most selfish and callous traitors who ever served the enemy in time of war.' (*Saturday at MI9*, p. 311).

CRESWELL, (Sir) Michael (Br) – "Monday". Attaché at British embassy, Madrid. Did much of the difficult work of ferrying evaders and escapers around and across Spain.

CROCKATT, Norman Richard (Br) – Brigadier, CBE, DSO, MC. Head of MI9 and Deputy Director of Military Intelligence (Prisoners of War). Died 1956.

D'ALBERT-LAKE, Philippe (Fr) – Born 28 May 1909. Husband of Virginia. Comet's deputy organiser in Paris in the summer of 1944. With his wife helped sixty-five airmen to evade capture through Paris, mostly to the camp in Fréteval Forest, May-August 1944. Forced to leave Paris on 25 June 1944. Went to England via Spain. Died 10 February 2000.

D'ALBERT-LAKE, Virginia (USA) – née Roush. Born 4 June 1910, St Petersburg, Florida, USA. Went to France in 1936. Married Philippe in 1937. Arrested 12 June 1944 while escorting Allied airmen. Deported via Fresnes prison, Paris to Ravensbrück concentration camp on 15 August 1944. Liberated on 21 April 1945, weighing thirty-five kilograms (five and a half stone). Died 20 September 1997.

DAMAN, Hortense (Bel) – As a twenty-three-year old carried explosives and messages for the Belgian Resistance. Also helped Allied airmen to escape and evade near her home of Louvain (Leuven). Arrested in February 1944 and tortured for thirty successive days. Finally sent to Ravensbrück, which she reached in June 1944. Survived. Married British soldier in 1946.

DANSEY, Claude Edward Marjoribanks (Br) – "C". Born 1876. Colonel (later Sir Claude). MI6 deputy of operations to (Sir) Stewart Menzies. Removed from his post in 1944. Died in 1947.

DARLING, Donald (Br) – "Sunday". British Secret Service agent (MI6) instructed by Colonel Dansey in mid-July 1940 to go to Portugal and Spain to open intelligence links with France which, following the fall of that country in June 1940, were practically non-existent. He was also charged with opening an escape line from France to Spain for those members of the BEF who had avoided capture in the north of France and who were then congregating in large numbers in the south, especially around Marseille. Darling was empowered to offer guides a fixed fee per head for every man delivered to the British Consulate at Barcelona or elsewhere. Moved his base from Lisbon to Gibraltar on 5 January 1942. Under the title of Civil Liaison Officer of Fortress Command, he ran his one-man interrogation office until late 1943.

DARNAND, Joseph (Fr) – Born 19 March 1897 at Coligny (Ain), France. Fought in First World War and was serving in the Maginot Line in June 1940 when captured. Fled to Nice and became a leading figure in the Vichy French organisation *Légion Française des Combattants* (French Legion of Veterans) and recruited men to fight against "Bolshevism". In July 1941 he founded the right-wing group Service d'Ordre Légionnaire, which supported Pétain and the Vichy government and helped to round up Jews and to fight against the French Resistance. On 1 January 1943 the *Service d'Ordre Légionnaire* became the Milice, the Vichy secret police, with Pierre Laval (Vichy premier) becoming its president and Darnand its de facto leader. In October 1943 took an oath of loyalty to Hitler, and was rewarded with the rank of Sturmbannführer in the Waffen SS (equivalent to major in the British army). In December 1943 he became head of police and later secretary of the interior. Fled to Germany in September 1944 and joined Pétain's puppet government in Sigmaringen. Captured after the war and taken back to France, where he was executed on 10 October 1945.

DE BLOMMAERT de SOYE, Baron Jean (Bel) – "Rutland", "Kazan", "Jean Thomas". Born 1915. Started working for Comet early in 1943. *Brûlé* ("burned"), he escaped to England on 3 August 1943. Parachuted into France on 20 December 1943 to work with Commandant Potier and his Possum line. Came into contact with Jacques Desoubrie, then known as "Pierre Boulain". Returned to England again on 28 February 1944. Helped MI9 in March 1944 with proposals for Marathon camps. Parachuted back into France near Issoudun with Albert Ancia on the night of 9/10 April 1944 on Operation Sherwood. Made arrangements for the setting-up of a camp for evaders in the Forêt de Fréteval, and for Comet to provide guides to escort evaders by train from Paris. Awarded DSO.

DE GREEF, Elvire (Bel) – "Tante Go" (after her dog Go Go). Born Ixelles, Brussels 29 June 1897. Wife of Fernand De Greef, mother of Freddy and Jeanine. Comet's organiser in Bayonne/St Jean-de-Luz area in south-west France. Ran a safe house at the Villa Voisin, Anglet (near Biarritz). With her family, sent an estimated 340 Allied aircrew to Spain. Awarded George Medal. Died Brussels 3 September 1991, aged 94.

DE GREEF, Fernand Albert François (Bel) – "l'oncle". Born 11 November 1902. Husband of Elvire, father of Freddy and Jeanine. Worked as interpreter in the German *Kommandantur* at Anglet. Provided Comet with blank identity cards and rubber stamps. Provided Elvire with forged pass enabling her to warn Florentino Goïcoechea that he was to be rescued from hospital. He himself, dressed in Gestapo uniform, drove an ambulance to the hospital and ordered the Basque to be put into it, assisted by two French "stretcher-bearers". Appointed MBE. Died 19 September 1961.

DE GREEF, Freddy (Bel) – son of Fernand and Elvire, brother of Jeanine. Courier for Comet. Escaped to England in 1943.

DE GREEF, Jeanine Lambertine Angèle Marie (Bel) – Born 29 September 1925. Daughter of Fernand and Elvire, sister of Freddy. Guide in St Jean-de-Luz area. Undertook her first journey, with her mother, to Paris on 13 July 1942. Left for England in June 1944.

DE JONGH, Andrée (Bel) – "Dédée". Born 30 November 1916. Daughter of Frédéric de Jongh. Long-distance guide for the escape line later known as Comet. Delivered first British serviceman – Private Colin Cupar – and two Belgian officers to the British Consulate in Bilbao, Spain, in August 1941. Given the codename Postwoman by the British, but this was changed to Postman at her request. Arrested on 15 January 1943 but escaped. When betrayed and arrested again, in June 1943, she had escorted 218 evaders/escapers to or over the Pyrenees. Sent to Ravensbrück and Mauthausen. Survived to be liberated on 22 April 1945. Awarded George Medal (approved by HM King George VI, November 1945), and the US Medal of Freedom with Golden Palm. Died 13 October 2007.

DE JONGH, Frédéric Emile (Bel) – "Paul", "Kiki", "De Ridder". Born 13 December 1897. Husband of Alice. Father of Andrée and Suzanne Wittek. By October/November 1940 was one of those in Brussels involved with what became known as the Comet line, of which he became its effective chief. Was forced to move to Paris on 30 April 1942, where he was betrayed by Desoubrie on 7 June 1943. Arrested and executed at Mont Valérien, Paris by the Germans on 28 March 1944 with Robert Aylé and Aimable Fouquerel.

DE LA OLLA, Jean (Fr) – NCO in the French army employed in the accounts section at St Hippolyte-du-Fort prison. Persuaded by Garrow and O'Leary at Nîmes in the summer of 1941 to became a *convoyeur* for their escape line. Appointed in charge of the line in northern France after Cole's treachery was exposed in December 1941. Arrested in March 1943.

DE LIGNE, Elisabeth Marie Eulalie Hélène (Bel) – born Brussels 1 June 1908, eldest daughter of Prince Albert de Ligne. Married Guillaume de Limburg Stirum in 1932. Apart from collecting much military information of value to the Allies, she also assisted evaders and escapers to pass along the Comet line. In spring 1944 arrested whilst in the act of moving a number of RAF airmen from a safe house in a Brussels brothel. Imprisoned in St Gilles until September 1944 when she and fellow inmates were to be moved by rail to Germany, probably to Ravensbrück concentration camp. A note she had scribbled and thrown out of the wagon was passed to her father, who effected a deal allowing her to be released. Died in 1998 aged 89.

DE MENTEN DE HORNE, Eric (Bel) – Born Brussels 14 November 1914. Comet worker. Arrested 6 February 1943. Executed by the Germans at the Tir National, Brussels, 20 October 1943.

DE MILLEVILLE, Comtesse Mary (Br) – "Comtesse de Moncy", "Marie-Claire". Née Mary Ghita Lindell. Mother of Maurice, Octave and Barbé. Arrested by Gestapo in January 1941. Nine months' solitary confinement in Fresnes prison, Paris. Crossed into Spain on 27 July 1942 and reached British Consulate at Barcelona. Returned to France by Lysander on 21 October 1942. Operated from the

Hôtel de France in Ruffec (Charente département), France. Established the Marie-Claire escape route across the Pyrenees. Was hit by a car (believed driven by a collaborator) in December 1942. Discharged herself from hospital early in 1943, soon after the two survivors of Operation Frankton – Major Hasler and Corporal Sparks – had arrived at Ruffec. Using alias "Comtesse de Moncy" when arrested by German security at Pau station 24 November 1943. Jumped out of train taking her from Biarritz to Paris, but was shot in the back of head by a guard. Operated on by a German surgeon in hospital in Tours. After recovery was taken to Dijon prison in February 1944, and subjected to continuous torture. Sent to Ravensbrück concentration camp on 3 September 1944. Liberated 24 April 1945. OBE (1/1/69). Died 1986.

DE MILLEVILLE, Maurice (Fr) – elder brother of Octave and Barbé. Escorted the two "Cockleshell Heroes" to Lyons in January 1943 (they later successfully crossed into Spain). Arrested in May 1943, but released after brutal treatment by Gestapo, and after his mother had paid a ransom to Klaus Barbie, the so-called "Butcher of Lyon". Reached Switzerland in January 1944.

DE MILLEVILLE, Octave (Fr) – "Oky", younger brother of Maurice and Barbé. Arrested and died in Mauthausen concentration camp.

DE MILLEVILLE, Barbé (Fr) – youngest of three children of Mary de Milleville; sister of Maurice and Octave.

DEPPÉ, Arnold Louis Camil (Bel) – Born 15 December 1907. One of the first guides for what became known as the Comet line. Moved to St Jean-de-Luz and Bayonne in 1928 and worked for ten years for the Gaumont film company as head of maintenance of cinemas in the area from Bordeaux and Toulouse down to the Spanish border.[3] Returned to Belgium on the outbreak of war, and enlisted in the 6th Regiment of Ardennes Chasseurs. Taken prisoner by the Germans at St Omer on 23 May 1940, he escaped from a prison camp on the Rhine in August 1940 and travelled down the river to Holland. At first worked for the Martiny-Daumerie network. Introduced to Andrée de Jongh early in 1941 by his cousin, De Bliqui. Arrested on 9 April 1941 but released for lack of evidence. Arrested again, at Lille station, on 8 August 1941. Sentenced to death on 12 November 1941 on two counts – working for an escape line and for circulating the contraband newspaper *La Libre Belgique*. Death sentence never carried out. Sent to Cologne prison (where he almost died) in March 1942. Survived concentration camps at Mauthausen, Natzweiler-Struthof, and Dachau, where he was liberated by the Americans in 1945.

DESOUBRIE, Jean-Jacques (Bel/Fr) – "Jean Masson", "JJ", "Pierre Boulain". Born 22 October 1922 at Luinge, Belgium, the illegitimate son of a Belgian doctor, Raymond Desoubrie, and a Frenchwoman, Zoë Note, who abandoned her son at an early age. Betrayed hundreds of helpers and airmen to the Gestapo (including an estimated fifty of the Comet line, Frédéric de Jongh and Nothomb among them). Captured by the Americans at Augsburg on 10 March 1947, was put on trial by a French court and sentenced to death on 20 July 1949. Executed at Fort de Montrouge, Lille, on 20 December 1949. His last words were 'Heil Hitler!'

DESPRETZ, François (Fr) – City administrator in charge of housing and relief at la Madeleine-les-Lille, a northern suburb of Lille. Hid several members of the BEF. Gave Cole an identity as "Paul Delobel". Betrayed by Cole and arrested on 6 December 1941. Held in Loos prison until deported to Germany on 5 August 1942. Died of exhaustion in Sonnenburg concentration camp in April 1944.

DEZITTER, Prospère Valère (Bel) – Had many aliases, including "Captain Jackson", "The Captain", "Jack Kilarine", "Jack the Canadian", "Herbert Call", "Williams" (born in London), "Captain Tom", "Captain Willy Neper", "Major Willy", and "Professor" or "Doctor Derschied". Born in Passchendaele, Belgium on 19 September 1893 to Pieter-Jan Dezitter and his wife Mathilde, née Delbeke. Fled to Canada in 1912 after committing rape. Returned to Belgium in 1925 with the crime time-expired. Divorced from his wife Germaine Princen on 14 September 1939. Offered to work for the Germans, also in 1939, and was recruited into the Abwehr. Noted for missing end of little finger of right hand. Frequently wore gloves to hide this. Betrayed probably 1,000 of his countrymen and perhaps 500 Allied airmen by use of his false escape line. Captured in Bavaria after the war with his female accomplice Flore Dings (q.v.). Before his execution in Brussels on 17 September 1948 'he was heard howling with terror in his cell.' (*Saturday at MI9*, p. 306). Police records showed he still had an outstanding six years' prison sentence for fraud.

D'HARCOURT, Pierre (Fr) – French Intelligence. Assisted British internees in Marseille, 1941. Arrested in Paris on 9 July 1941. Two years in solitary confinement in Fresnes prison, Paris, before moved to Neue Bremm reprisal camp at the end of October 1943, and to Buchenwald concentration camp shortly before Christmas 1943. He survived to be liberated there on 11 April 1945. Born 1913, he died in 1968.

DINGS, Flore (Sp) – Born Florentine Léonarda Maria Louisa Giralt in Barcelona on 20 June 1904 of a Spanish father, Domingo Giralt, and a Dutch mother, Alida Thewes. Married Paul Stéphan

Dings, by whom she bore a son, Serge, on 29 March 1930. Lived at 27, Avenue Van Dromme, Auderghem. Began an affair with Dezitter in 1938, and became his accomplice in his treachery. Executed in Brussels on 17 September 1948.

DISSARD, Marie-Louise (Fr) – "Victoire", "Françoise". Principal organiser for the PAT line in Toulouse. Born 1880. Lived, with her cat "Mifouf", in an apartment in the centre of Toulouse, which was used as a safe house by escapers and evaders and by Pat O'Leary when he was forced to leave Marseille. In June 1943 took over the PAT/PAO line, which in effect became the *Françoise* line. Briefly arrested, with four airmen, she was able to escape, but was forced into hiding in January 1944. Actively assisted some 250 evaders and escapers to cross the Pyrenees into Spain. Awarded the George Medal. Died in 1957.

DONNY, Baron Jacques Harold Léon Florent Albert Victor William (Bel) – Born 3 March 1894. Involved with escape and evasion operations in Brussels and surrounding area in late 1941. Arrested at his house by the Germans on 1 December 1942. Condemned to death on 10 October 1943 and executed by firing squad at Degerloch, near Stuttgart, on 29 February 1944.

D'OULTREMONT,[4] Count Edouard Charles Antoine (Bel) – Born 27 September 1916. Cousin of Georges. Guide for Comet line. Escaped to England (crossed Pyrenees 6 December 1942) in December 1942 with his cousin Georges and Peggy van Lier. Appointed MBE.

D'OULTREMONT, Count Georges Albert Ferdinand Paul Marie Ghislain (Bel) – "Ormond", "Gréville", "Roméo". Born 4 April 1916. Cousin of Edouard. Guide for Comet line. Escaped to England (crossed Pyrenees 6 December 1942) in December 1942 with his cousin Edouard and Peggy van Lier. Trained by Room 900 to co-ordinate collection of evaders in Operation Marathon. Flown to France on night of 7/8 November 1943. Went to Paris and met Nothomb on 17 January 1944, the day before the latter's arrest. Appointed MBE and awarded MM.

DOWDING, Kenneth Bruce (Aus) – "André Mason". Born 4 May 1914. Came to Europe in 1938. Joined British army and was a corporal in RASC when captured at Dunkirk on 22 May 1940. Escaped from prisoner-of-war camp in France. Made his way to Marseille by December 1940. *Convoyeur* on escape line to Spanish border. Appointed chief of the escape line in northern France after denouncement of Cole. Arrested Burbure station on 9 or 10 December 1941. Deported to Germany. Executed at Dortmund on 30 June 1943. MiD (13/9/46) for 'gallant and distinguished services in the field.'

DROMAS, Etienne (Fr) – born 17 December 1911. A draughtsman employed by the French National Railways at Tergnier, he was also a reserve officer in the French Army. Called to duty in 1939. Wounded in 1940, his right leg had to be amputated. Joined the Resistance in 1942 as a captain in the FFI, and appointed commander of *Groupement B* of the 2nd Military Region, Department of Aisne (district of Laon). Used the aliases "René" in the Aisne and "Camille" in the Oise. From December 1942 to September 1944 his organisation assisted 87 airmen, 19 of whom were wounded, ten seriously enough to require surgery, and only three were captured. Was fortunate to survive a German attack on 23 June 1944 on the Maquis des Usages, when all the other Frenchmen around him were killed. Died 1999.

DUFOURNIER, Denise (Fr) – born 10 January 1915. Operated mostly in Paris as a link in the Comet line. Arrested in 1943 when Comet was penetrated. Spent next six months in solitary confinement in Fresnes prison, Paris, before transfer to Ravensbrück concentration camp. Married Scotsman James McAdam Clark in 1946. Died 1994.

DUMAIS, Lucien Adelard (Can) – "Captain Hamilton"; "Léon". Warrant Officer Class III (platoon sergeant-major) in Les Fusiliers Mont-Royal, Canadian Army. Following the Dieppe raid (19 August 1942) he escaped along the PAT line to Marseille. Assisted O'Leary until October 1942 when he was evacuated on *Seawolf*. Awarded MM (22/12/42). Agreed to return to northern France to assist in establishing the Shelburne escape line. Landed by Lysander aircraft on night of 18/19 November 1943. Directed the Bonaparte and Crozier sea evacuations from Brittany in 1944. Liberated while still in France. Awarded MC (4/8/45). Died in Montreal, Canada on 10 June 1993, aged 88.

DUMON, Andrée (Bel) – "Dédée", "Nadine", younger sister of "Michou" Dumon. Born 5 September 1922. Worked for Comet line as guide between Brussels and Paris. Arrested 11 August 1942 with her sister and father. Held at St Gilles prison, Brussels, before being sent to Ravensbrück and Mauthausen camps. Survived. Liberated 22 April 1945. Appointed OBE. Awarded the US Medal of Freedom with Bronze Palm.

DUMON, Eugène (Bel) – "Tom". Husband of Françoise, father of Andrée and Michèle. Member of the Luc-Marc intelligence service. Arrested 12 August 1942. Died in 1945 in Gross-Rosen concentration camp, Germany, aged 50.

DUMON, Françoise (Bel) – "Madame Françoise". Mother of the Dumon sisters. Arrested 12 August 1942 with Eugène and Andrée. Released a year later. Resumed evasion work and carried on with

Henri and Marie Maca (q.v.) and Mission Marathon plan until liberation.

DUMON, Aline Lili (Bel) – "Michou", "Micheline", "Lily du Chaila", elder sister of Andrée Dumon, daughter of Eugène and Françoise. Arrested with her sister and father, who had also worked for the secret organisation Luc-Marc, on 11 August 1942, but released because Gestapo considered her too young to be involved in such matters. Began working for Comet in September 1942. Forced to leave Brussels on 5 January 1944 to avoid the Gestapo and went to Paris, Bayonne, and Madrid. Though *brûlé* left Madrid on 3 March 1944, and continued to escort airmen to safety. Persuaded to return to Madrid on 10 May 1944, and reached the United Kingdom on 22 June 1944. During her time with Comet she escorted more than 250 evaders, her name becoming 'a legend amongst the airmen who had been shepherded across Brussels by the famous "Lily".'[5] Awarded George Medal, and the US Medal of Freedom with Gold Palm. Married Pierre Ugeux.

D'URSEL, Count Antoine (Bel) – "Jacques Cartier". Succeeded Baron Jean Greindl ("Nemo") as chief of Comet line in Brussels on 6 February 1943. "Burned" in June 1943. Went into hiding but continued to work for Comet. Made at least one trip to Spain to meet with MI9. Drowned on 23/24 December 1943 while crossing the River Bidassoa in the Pyrenees.[6] Aged 47.

ESCRENIER, Alphonse (Bel) – "UZH". One of the founders of Group EVA.[7] *Brûlé* in January 1944. Escaped to England in April 1944.

FARRELL, Victor (Br) – Appointed by MI6 as "Chief Passport Officer" to Geneva, Switzerland, in February 1940. He was 'an experienced SIS officer who had previously served in Budapest and Vienna',[8] and also in Prague. Provided funds to escape organisations to sustain their continued clandestine activities.

FILLERIN, Gabriel and Geneviève (Fr) – Son and daughter of Norbert and Marguerite. Helped their parents hide Allied airmen.

FILLERIN, Marguerite (Fr) – Wife of Norbert. Arrested in December 1943, and deported to Germany. Survived.

FILLERIN, Norbert (Fr) – With his wife, Marguerite, worked for PAT/PAO line in the north of France and Paris area. Lived at Renty (Pas-de-Calais). Arrested in early 1943. Deported to Germany. Survived.

FIOCCA, Henri (Fr) – Marseille businessman. Husband of Nancy Wake (see Fiocca, Nancy). Provided large amounts of cash to his wife to help escapers, evaders and prisoners in Marseille area. Eventually arrested for his involvement in clandestine activities, and executed by the Germans on 16 October 1943 after refusing, under torture, to tell them where his wife was.

FIOCCA, Nancy (NZ) – Born Nancy Grace Augusta Wake on 30 August 1912 in Wellington, New Zealand, to an English father and a New Zealand mother. Twenty months old when taken with her family to Sydney, Australia. A journalist in Marseille when she married Henri Fiocca on 30 November 1939. Helped prisoners and evaders in 1940 in Marseille by persuading her husband to provide much-needed finance. Became involved in the Garrow organisation. Was instrumental in arranging his escape from Mauzac prison on 8 (or 6) December 1942. With the Gestapo desperate to find her, she moved to Françoise Dissard's flat in Toulouse (where O'Leary was also hiding). Escaped over Pyrenees on 24/25 March 1943. Enlisted in FANY, and trained as SOE agent, codename "Hélène". Returned to France. George Medal (17 July 1945).

FOUQUEREL, Aimable Louis Augustin (Fr) – Born 3 June 1903. Former butler to Lord Dudley. His apartment on the fifth floor of 10, rue Oudinot, Paris was much used by Comet line in 1942 and 1943. Arrested by the Germans on 7 June 1943. Executed at Mont Valérien, Paris on 28 March 1944 with Frédéric de Jongh and Robert Aylé.

"FRANCO" – see NOTHOMB, Baron Jean-François.

GARROW, Ian Grant (Sco) – Captain, Seaforth Highlanders, 51st (Highland) Division. Evaded to Marseille in summer 1940 and set up a number of safe houses for fellow evaders and escapers. Established collection centres in Lille, Amiens and Rouen in the north of France before onward passage to Paris. This small organisation was to become the PAT line. Arrested in October 1941 by the French and sent to Mauzac prison. Rescued on 8 December 1942 by Pat O'Leary. Smuggled over the Pyrenees and flown from Gibraltar to England, reached 7 February 1943. Awarded DSO (4/5/43). Later lieutenant-colonel. Died 1976.

GIRALT/GIRAULT, Florentine Léonarda Maria Louisa (Sp) – see Flore Dings.

GOÏCOECHEA (or GOIKOETXEA), Florentino (Bas) – born 14 March 1898. A smuggler who took a reputed 227 evaders and escapers across the Pyrenees in sixty-six crossings. Captured by a German patrol in the Pyrenees on 26 June 1944, after being hit by two bullets in right leg, a third in the thigh, and a fourth in the shoulder. Rescued from hospital by the De Greefs on 27 July before Gestapo could question him. Awarded George Medal. Died 27 July 1980.

GREINDL, Baron Albert Marie Louis (Bel) – brother of Jean. Born 20 October 1914. Guide for

Comet line to Paris. Forced to escape. Crossed Pyrenees on 14 February 1943 with a party of American airmen, and made his way to England.

GREINDL, Baron Jean (Bel) – "Le Kas", "Nemo". Brother of Albert. Took control of Comet line in Brussels when Frédéric de Jongh was forced to move to Paris on 30 April 1942. Organised collection of evaders from Holland, Belgium and Luxembourg under cover of director of the *Cantine Suèdoise* (Swedish Relief Canteen) for children. Arrested in Brussels on 6 February 1943. Kept under sentence of death in stables at Etterbeek artillery barracks. Killed there on 7 September 1943 during a raid by US B-17 bombers on Brussels/Evère airfield.[9]

GROOME, Thomas Gilmour (Aus) – "Georges". French mother. Wireless operator for PAO line. Had been selected to work with Mary, Comtesse de Milleville, but she refused to have anything to do with him. Landed at Port Miou, France on the night of 3/4 November 1942 by Polish felucca *Seadog*. Assisted in Garrow's escape from Mauzac camp. After which he moved his transmitter to the Cheramys' house at Montauban, 55 kilometres from Toulouse, where he was caught in the act of transmitting on 11 January 1943. Taken to Gestapo HQ at Toulouse. Jumped from second-floor window to the ground, suffering only a badly sprained ankle. Re-arrested. Sent, with Pat O'Leary, to Fresnes (Paris), Mauthausen and Dachau concentration camps. Survived. Appointed MBE (26/3/46).

GUÉRISSE, Albert-Marie (Bel) – see O'Leary.

HADEN-GUEST, Elizabeth (Est) – Née Elizabeth Louise Ruth Wolpert, of Estonian origin. Became Coker on her first marriage. In 1939 married Peter Haden-Guest, third child of Leslie Haden-Guest MC (created 1st Baron Haden-Guest of Saling on 2 February 1950) and *his* second wife, Muriel Carmel Goldsmid. Reached Marseille in summer of 1940 with her young son, Anthony. Minor operative for Ian Garrow. Returned to England in 1942. Divorced Peter, who served during the war as a lieutenant in the Royal Canadian Naval Volunteer Reserve, in 1945.

HALOT, William (Bel) – "Louis Vallon", "Maurice Legrand". Born 5 September 1901. Main financier for the first British servicemen to be sent from Brussels to Spain. Arrested 28 February 1942 with his wife and daughter, Sonia (who was released). Deported to Germany on 15 August 1942. In the closing stages of the war escaped from a column of prisoners being evacuated from Flossenburg, and reached American lines near Czechoslovakia on 24 April 1945.

HOARE, Sir Samuel John Gurney (Br) – Born 24 February 1880. Former Secretary of State for Air (four times); First Lord of the Admiralty; Secretary of State for India; Foreign Secretary; Minister for Home Affairs; Lord Privy Seal in the War Cabinet. On 24 May 1940 appointed Ambassador on Special Mission to Spain, at Madrid. Flew from Lisbon to Madrid airport on 1 June 1940. In following instructions from Churchill to ensure neutrality of Spain he had difficulty approving the clandestine movement of escapers and evaders through Spain to Gibraltar. According to Darling he forbad the use of Spanish opponents of General Franco in this role, thereby obliging the 'British' to employ smugglers. Later turned a blind eye to the goings on. Appointed to the peerage in 1944 as 1st Viscount Templewood PC, GCSI, GBE, CMG. Died 7 May 1959.

HOSTE, Charles (Bel) – "Jacques". A Belgian policeman and one of the founders of Group EVA (first three letters of Evasion), a collection service of airmen evaders. Arrested in January 1944 but soon released because not considered a suspect. Unwittingly involved in March 1944 of transfer of thirty-five airmen from Group EVA to the Abwehr's false KLM line in Antwerp. Continued other resistance activities until the liberation.

ITTERBEEK, Raymond (Bel) – "Jacques De Brigaude". A member of several clandestine organisations, including the *Armée Secrète*, the *Service Zéro* and the *Mouvement National Belge*. In 1943 both his parents were arrested and condemned to death, but they survived the war. He continued organising permanent hiding places in Brussels, and accompanied a total of twelve shot down airmen from Belgium to France on their way back to the UK via Gibraltar. On 3 January 1944 he was arrested on his way by train to Lille, together with two evading British airmen.[10] Though tortured every night for three weeks, he revealed nothing. Taken back to Brussels, he was condemned to death on 27 April 1944. Deported to Germany with sixty other condemned persons a few days before the liberation of Brussels he was liberated by American troops.

JOHNSON, Albert Edward (Br) – "Albert Jonion", but known simply as "B". Born 1 September 1908. Secretary and chauffeur in Brussels to Count Henry de Baillet-Latour, President of the International Olympic Committee. Moved with the De Greef family to Anglet in 1940. Could have sailed for England but gave up his place to a French girl engaged to a Briton. Made fourteen crossings of the Pyrenees for Comet, between June 1941 and March 1943, with 122 Allied evaders/escapers. Forced to escape to England via Spain (crossed Pyrenees on 20 March 1943). Worked for the Awards Bureau in Paris in 1945. Appointed MBE. Died on 3 February 1954 in St John's Hospital, Hobart, Tasmania.

KENNY, Tom (Can) – Well-to-do businessman and resident of Marseille. Offered his help to Ian

Garrow and the PAT line in the early months. Arrested and interrogated at Fort St Nicholas, but later released.

KRAGT, Dignus (Hol/BR) – "Dick", "Frans Hals". Born 18 July 1917. British subject with Dutch father. Was dropped "blind" into Holland near Apeldoorn on 23/24 June 1943. Managed to make contact with Comet line. Responsible for the escape and evasion of over a hundred aircrew from Holland to Belgium. Coordinator for both Pegasus I and II rescue operations in September 1944. US Medal of Freedom with Gold Palm (23/7/48).

LABROSSE, Raymond (Can) – French-Canadian wireless operator to Val Williams. Landed in France on night of 20/21 March 1943 on Oaktree. Escaped via Spain to England, reached early in September 1943. Landed by Lysander aircraft on night of 16/17 November 1943 as wireless operator to Lucien Dumais on the Shelburne operations. Liberated while still in France. Lieutenant Labrosse (C.3108), Royal Canadian Corps of Signals, awarded MC (9/11/44).

LAFLEUR, Conrad (Can) – "Charles". A French-Canadian corporal wireless-operator. Escaped from Dieppe with Lucien Dumais. Returned to UK on Operation Titania (see Appendix III). Awarded MM (22/12/42). Flown back to France on 20/21 October 1943 with Georges d'Oultremont. Caught in the act of transmitting at Reims. Killed or wounded two Germans before jumping out of window. Made contact with Comet line. Escorted by Lily Dumon to Spain, and returned safely to England. Awarded DCM (15/6/44).

LANGLEY, James Maydon (Br) – Lieutenant (68294) in 2nd Battalion Coldstream Guards, he lost his left arm in the fighting around Calais at end of May 1940. Escaped from Lille hospital and reached Marseille in November 1940. Repatriated on 24 February 1941, reaching England on 17 March. Soon working in MI9, he later became head of MI9 (D) dealing with escape and evasion in north-west Europe. Used codename P15 until September 1943 (handing it over to Airey Neave) when he became head of MI9b (taking over from de Bruyne) at Beaconsfield. Promoted lieutenant-colonel and made joint head (with American Lieutenant-Colonel Richard R. Nelson) of IS9 (WEA). Married Peggy van Lier in 1944. Awarded MC (20/12/40) and MBE (29/4/41), both while lieutenant. He died in 1983.

LE GRELLE, Count Jacques (Bel) – "Jérôme", "Lewis". Born 1904. A captain in the Army Reserve when he escaped with a friend from Antwerp on 13 August 1941. Reached Spain, but arrested and spent eight months in various prisons. Reached England on 10 August 1942. Joined the Intelligence Service, but broke his spine while parachute training, and was hospitalised for a further eight months. At the end of October 1943 he was flown by a Sunderland from Pembroke Dock to Gibraltar and taken by fishing boat to the Spanish east coast near Valencia. Went to Madrid and met Michael Cresswell ("Timothy"), with whom he travelled to San Sebastián to meet Jean-François Nothomb ("Franco"). Le Grelle, now appointed to re-organise Comet's Paris/northern France sector, set up his HQ in Paris. He was arrested on 17 January 1944, with Jacques de Bruyn, who had just arrived from Brussels. They were betrayed by Desoubrie ("Jean Masson"). Tortured, and condemned to death on 27 July 1944 Le Grelle, and de Bruyn, were deported to Germany. Both were liberated by the Americans from the prison at Amberg (Bavaria) on 13 May 1945.

"LE NEVEU", Roger (Fr) – "Roger le Légionnaire" (so called because he had apparently served three years in the French Foreign Legion). Gestapo agent who betrayed countless French helpers (including Louis Nouveau and Pat O'Leary) and numerous airmen. He also fatally shot Jean-Claude Camors. Liquidated by French *maquisards* soon after the liberation of France in 1944.

LINDELL, Mary – see de Milleville.

MACA, Henri (Bel) – "Harry". Husband of Marie. Took over Michèle Dumon/Marie's "orphaned" airmen and found new homes for them after the arrests of January 1944. Continued to collect and shelter more airmen until his own arrest on 27 May 1944. Liberated in September 1944 by British forces from a Belgian concentration/torture camp. His adjutant was Marcel Van Buckenhout ("Marcus"), assisted also by Victor Schutters.

MACA, Marie (Bel) – "Germaine". Wife of Henri. Comet safe-house keeper from the summer of 1943, and guide from October 1943 until 23 January 1944, when she was "burned" and fled to Switzerland. Replaced Michèle Dumon when she left for France.

MARÉCHAL, Elsie Mary (Br) – Born 21 June 1894. Née Bell. Married Georges Maréchal in London on her twenty-sixth birthday. Mother of Elsie ("Little Elsie") and Robert (born February 1926). Worked for Comet with her husband. Their house in Brussels, at 162, Avenue Voltaire, was a safe house for fourteen airmen evaders and escapers, until her arrest on 18 November 1942. In prison at St Gilles, Brussels, with Little Elsie, before transfer to Germany on 1 January 1944. After several months at Waldheim both Elsies were transferred to Ravensbrück and, in 1945, to Mauthausen concentration camp. Both survived the war. Elsie Mary died 25 March 1969.

MARÉCHAL, Elsie Jeanette Pierrette (Bel) – Born in Koblenz, Germany, 7 June 1924. Daughter of Georges and Elsie Mary. Worked for Comet as guide and courier in and around Brussels until her arrest on 18 November 1942. Remained with her mother until liberated in 1945.

MARÉCHAL, Georges (Bel) – Born 11 December 1892. Joined Belgian Army in Folkestone, England, on 7 April 1915. Husband of Elsie Mary Maréchal, and father of Elsie and Robert. Also worked for Comet in Brussels until his arrest on 18 November 1942. Condemned to death on 15 April 1943, and murdered by a German firing squad in a mass execution in Brussels' *Tir National* on 20 October 1943.

MARSAL, Joseph (Sp/Fr) – Born in Catalonia in 1924. Moved to Perpignan as a youth. Joined French resistance. Key member of the Burgundy network, he assisted in the evasions of over 300 Allied servicemen. Died 14 December 2007.

MASSON, Jean – see Desoubrie.

MATTHYS, Gaston Charles Alex (Bel) – Born 1897. "Camille", "Christian", "Roland", "Vanesse". Policeman in Brussels. From the start of the occupation worked for the Portemine organisation, which itself became part of *Service Zéro*, an intelligence-gathering group. Joined Comet in August 1943 as head of the section responsible for housing evaders. Passed on 14 evaders to Anne Brusselmans. Involved with Service EVA as its "welfare officer", but left it early in 1944, and would have nothing to do with the Abwehr's false KLM line. Replaced Yvon Michiels as head of Comet's Brussels sector in May 1944. Played large part, with Albert Ancia and others, in the setting-up of Marathon camps for evaders in the Belgian Ardennes in the spring and summer of 1944. Forced to seek shelter in one of his own camps at Bellevaux. Never arrested.

MENZIES, Stewart (Br) – Colonel, DSO, MC (later major-general, KCB, KCMG). Head of Secret Intelligence Service (MI6) from 28 November 1939 after the death, on 4 November 1939, of Admiral Sir Hugh Sinclair.

MICHELLI, Henri (Bel) – Joined Comet in November 1941. Became adjutant for the heads of the line in April 1942. Hid several airmen himself (at least six). Set up escape lines in the Belgian Ardennes. Became chief of the Belgian sector of Comet following Frédéric de Jongh's move to Paris at the end of April 1942, but was himself arrested on 6 May 1942 and deported to Germany. Survived the war, being repatriated in May 1945.

MICHIELS, Yvon (Bel) – "Jean Serment". Member of the *Zéro* intelligence service in September 1940. Joined Comet in August 1942, becoming leader of its Belgian sector in June 1943, taking over from Count Antoine d'Ursel. *Brûlé* in May 1944. Escaped to England on 15 May 1944.

MORELLE, Charles Maurice Pierre (Fr) – "Charlie". Brother of Elvire. Born 20 January 1915. A lieutenant in a French cavalry regiment. Taken prisoner by the Germans in 1940 but escaped and became a guide for Comet. Arrested in Brussels on 8 May 1942. Sent to Dachau concentration camp, where he died on 18 May 1945.

MORELLE, Elvire (Fr) – "Irène". Sister of Charles. Born 26 August 1908. Began as a guide for Comet on 15 July 1941. Made one crossing of the Pyrenees, with Andrée de Jongh ("Dédée"), on 6 February 1942, but, returning, slipped and fractured a leg. Housekeeper and cook at a safe house at St Maur, on the outskirts of Paris, rented by the Paris section of the Comet line. Arrested in Brussels on 19 November 1942. Survived Mauthausen concentration camp. Repatriated to France on 30 April 1945. Appointed MBE.

MYRDA, Father (Pol) – Priest who helped the PAT line in south of France. Evacuated by *Seawolf* in October 1942.

NAHAS, Gabriel (Fr) – "Georges Brantès". Medical student in Toulouse. Arrested by Vichy police for dissemination of certain tracts at the beginning of the "occupation". *Convoyeur* and helper of the Dutch-Paris and *Résistance-Fer* escape lines. Escorted, among others, Brigadiers Miles and Hargest to Spain from Switzerland. Author of *La Filière du Rail* (1982).

NEAVE, Airey Middleton Sheffield (Br) – "Saturday". Born 23 January 1916. Lieutenant in 1 Searchlight Regt, RA, captured in France on 26 May 1940. Escaped from Stalag IVC (Colditz) on 5/6 January 1942. Reached Switzerland on 9 January 1942. In April 1942 went to the Nouveaus' flat in Marseille. Escaped along the PAT line. Took over P15 from Jimmy Langley in September 1943. Later lieutenant-colonel DSO, OBE, MC.[11] Murdered on 30 March 1979 by an INLA car-bomb while Shadow Northern Ireland Secretary.

NÈGRE, Gaston (Fr) – "Black marketeer" who ran a wholesale grocery store and a safe house in Nîmes. Also had large apartment in Marseille. Arrested, with Alex Nitelet, on 1 September 1942 after a supply drop near Nîmes. Rescued from Castres prison (on 16 September 1943?) with the help of a jailer, Robert, who was to pay for his part in the rescue with his life. Went to ground in Paris for the rest of the war. Ran a bar in Marseille after the war. Died in the early 1980s.

NITELET, Alex (Bel) – Born 1915. Shot down 9 August 1941, pilot officer on 609 Squadron. Lost an eye in the action. Picked up by Norbert Fillerin. Evaded via Marseille and Spain. Sent back to France by Lysander on 29/30 May 1942 to be wireless operator for PAT line. Alias "Jean le Nerveux".

Arrested by French police on 1 September 1942 after a noisy supply drop near Nîmes. (His post was later filled by Tom Groome.) In prisons at Fort de la Duchère, Lyon, and Fort de Chambaran. Released unofficially (with others) by the camp commandant on 27 November 1942. Crossed to Spain on 6/7 December 1942. Died 6 January 1981.

NOTHOMB, Jean-François (Bel) – "Franco". Joined Comet on 7 October 1942. Aged only 23 when he took over Comet after the arrest of Andrée de Jongh's father in June 1943. Escorted 215 evaders/escapers over the Pyrenees before he was betrayed by Desoubrie, and arrested in Paris on 18 January 1944. Because of his youth, the Germans refused to believe that he was the leader of Comet. He claimed that the leader had been Antoine d'Ursel, whom he knew to have drowned a month earlier. Sent to several concentration camps and survived, partly because the warrant for his execution never caught up with him. Liberated from Amberg by US troops on 23 April 1945. Awarded DSO. After the war became a missionary priest in Venezuela working with lepers. Left the priesthood, married, and had a family. He died on 6 June 2008.

NOUVEAU, Louis (Fr) – husband of Renée. Their apartment at 28A, Quai Rive Neuve, overlooking the Vieux Port, Marseille, was used as a safe house for the PAT line. Forced to move to Paris in 1942 due to attention of German security forces. Betrayed by le Neveu, was arrested in November 1942. Deported to Buchenwald concentration camp. Survived. Awarded George Medal. Died 1966.

NOUVEAU, Renée (Fr) – wife of Louis. Also survived. Appointed MBE.

O'LEARY, Patrick (Bel) – "Joseph". Born in Molenbeek, Brussels 5 April 1911. Studied medicine at the Catholic University, Leuven (Louvain), and at the Free University, Brussels. Joined the Belgian army as a doctor in the 1st Regiment of Lancers. Escaped to England from Dunkirk, May 1940. Joined British Special Operations Executive. Assumed the *nom de guerre* of a French-Canadian, Patrick O'Leary.[12] Appointed second-in-command of 'Q' ship HMS *Fidelity*, with the rank of lieutenant-commander RN. Captured on *Fidelity*'s first operation, on the night of 25/26 April 1941. Interned at St Hippolyte-du-Fort. Learned of Garrow's organisation. Escaped to Rodocanachi's flat in Marseille in June 1941. Persuaded by Garrow to join the escape line. Betrayed by le Neveu. Arrested in Toulouse on 2 March 1943. Sent to Natzweiler, Mauthausen and Dachau concentration camps. Liberated from Dachau on 29 April 1945. DSO (1942), George Cross (5 November 1946), Honorary KBE (1949). Died at Waterloo, Belgium, 26 March 1989.

PÉTAIN, Henri-Philippe (Fr) – Born of peasant stock on 24 April 1856 at Cauchy-à-la-Tour (Pas-de-Calais). After a distinguished military career became premier of Vichy France in June 1940. In August 1944 he was removed by the Germans to Belfort and Germany. Returning to France in 1945 he was put on trial in Paris and sentenced to death on 15 August 1945. Sentence commuted to solitary confinement for life by Charles de Gaulle. Imprisoned on the Île d'Yeu off the Atlantic coast. Died 23 July 1951.

PONZAN VIDÁL, Francisco (Sp) – Born 30 January 1911. Forced to flee to France during the Spanish Civil War. Continued the fight against Franco by raising funds from the traffic of evaders and escapers over the Pyrenees. Had no particular love of the British, but took many airmen across the mountains. Arrested, and shot by Germans 17 August 1944 at Buzet-sur-Tarn.

POSTEL-VINAY, André (Fr) – Agent for PAT line. Based in Paris. Arrested by two Gestapo agents at the *Café aux Deux Magots*, Paris. Tortured and put in Fresnes prison. Tried to kill himself by jumping 30 feet into courtyard. Broke many bones, but lived. Managed to escape from hospital months later and make his way to Marseille. Evacuated by felucca at end of September 1942.

PRASSINOS, Mario (Grk) – *Convoyeur* in the Marseille network. Escaped to England via Spain using the alias "Captain Forbes" in December 1942. Returned to France for SOE. Arrested. Died of typhus in German concentration camp at Schwerin in 1945. Posthumously appointed OBE.

RODOCANACHI, Fanny (Fr) – Née Vlasto. Born in Paris on 28 November 1884. Sister of Netta Zarifi. Wife of Georges Rodocanachi (married in London, 20 June 1907). Survived the war, after which moved to London. Appointed MBE. Died April 1959.

RODOCANACHI, Georges (Fr) – Born in Liverpool, 27 February 1876 of Greek parents 'who like himself were British' (*Safe Houses Are Dangerous*, p. 27). Qualified as a doctor in 1903. Refused permission to join the RAMC during the First World War. Renounced his British citizenship and became a naturalised Frenchman. Husband of Fanny. Their flat at 21, rue Roux de Brignoles, Marseille was used as a safe house by PAT line and as O'Leary's HQ. Sat on medical repatriation board in Marseille. Arrested on 26 February 1943 and sent to St Pierre prison, Marseille. Moved on 17 December 1943 to a prison at Compiègne, and then on 17 January 1944 to Buchenwald concentration camp, where he died on 10 February 1944.

ROGER, Jacques (Bel) – "Max". Assistant to Baron Jean-François Nothomb in 1943. Helped establish a new escape route near the Pyrenees with Pierre and Marie Elhorga. Executed in 1945.

SAVINOS, Leoni (Grk) – Interpreter to Greek statesman General Plastiras who lived in south of

France. Given official Gestapo pass which enabled free passage between Paris and Marseille. *Convoyeur* for O'Leary, Nouveau and others. Arrested by the Gestapo in Paris in April 1942. Fresnes prison. Released by agreeing to work for Gestapo as a double agent in the PAT line. He and his German wife, Emy, were evacuated to England on *Seawolf* on the night of 13/14 July 1942. Returned to France in 1943 to work for SOE. Appointed OBE.

SOULIÉ, Geneviève (Fr) – Born in France in 1919, to an English mother and French father. Working in a Paris bookshop when recruited by Georges Broussine. At first responsible for finding safe lodgings for enemies of Nazi Germany. Helped 136 Allied airman escape from France.

TOUSSAINT, François (Bel) – "Taylor". Born 1904. Left for England from Belgium on 2 July 1942, but was caught by the French. Escaped to Spain, but again caught and interned at Miranda de Ebro prison. Reached England in 1943 and trained as a wireless operator. Went as Lucien Boussa's wireless operator to the Sherwood camps. Later, involved in infiltrating German lines during the Battle of the Bulge (December 1944), was wounded during a night battle.

UGEUX, Aline Lili (Micheline) (Bel). See DUMON, Michèle.

ULMANN, Paul (Fr) – A French Jew married to Imelda, an American. Lived in a flat at 7, rue des Rémusat, Toulouse. Joined the PAT/PAO organisation circa July 1942. Helped with numerous evaders and escapers as they passed through Toulouse on their way to Spain, many of them staying at the safe house at 39, rue Pierre Cazeneuve, Toulouse, which had been procured for Paul and Imelda by Marie-Louise "Françoise" Dissard. Arrested with Pat O'Leary in Toulouse on 2 March 1943.

USANDIZAGA, Françoise Romaine ("Frantxia") (Bas) – Born on 29 August 1908 (née Halzuet). Married Philippe Usandizaga in August 1939. Her farm at Bidegainberri near Urrugne (between Hendaye and St Jean-de-Luz) in south-west France was a jumping-off point for Comet evaders crossing the Pyrenees. Arrested with Andrée de Jongh and three RAF airmen on 15 January 1943. Died in Ravensbrück concentration camp on 12 April 1945.

VAN LIER, Margeurite ("Peggy") (Bel) – Born 16 March 1915 in Johannesburg, South Africa, daughter of J.L. van Lier and Greta O'Reilly, herself daughter of a South African accountant. One of Comet's leading helpers. After a brief arrest in Brussels on 20 November 1942 she crossed the Pyrenees on 6 December 1942, and was evacuated to England at the end of the month with Georges and Edouard d'Oultremont. Married Lieutenant-Colonel J.M. Langley in 1944. Appointed MBE. Awarded Croix de Guerre by the Belgians. Died 20 July 2000.

VAN MUYLEM, René (Bel) – "Alfons", "Alphonse", "Donald", "Marlant", "Robert". Traitor who, from the summer of 1943, operated mostly in the Antwerp area of Belgium. Estimated to have betrayed over a hundred of his own countrymen and nearly two hundred Allied airmen. Arrested after the war in a bar at the American Red Cross centre. Sentenced to death by firing squad and shot in a baker's yard in Antwerp on 29 May 1948.

VERLOOP, Cornelius Johannes Antonius (Hol) – Born in The Hague in 1909. Sailor, private detective, joined French Foreign Legion in 1935. Soon deserted to join the German Abwehr as a V-Mann (*Vertrauensmann*). Instrumental in engineering arrest of Cole and of many Belgians.

WAKE, Nancy – see Fiocca, Nancy.

WARENGHEM, Suzanne (Fr) – Born 22 November 1921. *Convoyeuse* for PAT line. Sent by Garrow to work for Cole (before his treachery was uncovered). "Married" Harold Cole on 10 April 1942. Stubbornly refused to believe Cole's treachery until both arrested by Vichy police on 9 June 1942, when Cole admitted that he was a traitor. Brought to trial on 21 July she was acquitted of charges of espionage, and returned to Marseille in August 1942. On 30 October gave birth to a son, Alain Patrick, who died in a Marseille hotel on 23 January 1943. Re-arrested following the German occupation of Vichy France. Imprisoned at Castres, but escaped on 16 September 1943 and went to Paris. Evacuated by the Royal Navy's MGB 502 from Brittany on 15/16 April 1944. Joined SOE, as agent "Charise". Changed name to Warren. Happily married after the war in England.

WATTEBLED, Alex (Fr) – "Jacques". Worked for PAT/PAO line in Paris and elsewhere as O'Leary's right-hand man. After his arrest in early 1943, he spent eleven months in solitary confinement in Fresnes prison, Paris. Surviving several concentration camps, including Büchenwald and Flossenberg, he returned to France.

WEIDNER, Gabrielle (Hol) – sister of Johan Weidner. Born 17 August 1914. Worked for the *Réseau* Dutch-Paris until arrested by the Gestapo on 26 February 1944, betrayed by a Dutch-Paris member who had talked under torture. She died on 17 February 1945 in Königsberg, a subcamp of Ravensbrück, after the camp had been liberated.

WEIDNER, Johan Hendrik (Hol) – founder of the *Réseau* Dutch-Paris in 1943. Born 22 October 1912. Brother of Gabrielle Weidner. Arrested by the Gestapo in February 1943. Escaped from a train. Died in California, USA on 21 May 1994.

WHITTINGHILL, George (USA) – Volunteered to work for MI6 when stationed in Milan. Posted

to Lyon as American vice-consul in charge of British interests in October 1940. Helped many British servicemen to reach Spain. Recalled to the USA in October 1942.
WILLIAMS, Val – see Bouryschkine, Vladimir.
WINDHAM-WRIGHT MC, Patrick Joseph Stewart (Br) – Succeeded James Langley in Room 900 in September 1943. Like Langley, had only one arm. Awarded Bar (15/11/45) to his MC (4/8/42) for his part in the 1944 sea evacuations from Brittany.
WITTEK, Suzanne (Bel) – Daughter of Frédéric and Alice de Jongh, elder sister of Andrée de Jongh. Her husband, Paul, had three children from a previous marriage – Frédéric; Mädy; and Martin. Arrested and put in St Gilles prison, Brussels. Wrote story of Comet under pen name Cècile Jouan.
WITTON, Rosine (Br) – "Rolande". Born 23 November 1906. Lived at 6, rue de Bapaume, Arras. Helped thirty-five Allied airmen. Arrested, but survived Ravensbrück concentration camp. BEM (1 July 1947). Died in 1995.
ZARIFI, Georges (Grk) – nephew of Georges and Fanny Rodocanachi. *Convoyeur* for PAT line. Left Marseille on 22 April 1943 when the line was betrayed by Roger le Neveu and went to Toulouse. Helped to Spain, reached on 28 April 1943, by Françoise Dissard. Arrested in Spain. Six months in Spanish prisons (including Miranda de Ebro) before arriving in England. Later fought with Free French.

Preface

'In World War II, in Europe, unstinting assistance was given by brave patriots in those countries which the Germans had overrun. At risk of death, they found our airmen, hid them, tended their wounds and then led them on perilous journeys to freedom.'[13]

Lieutenant-General Carl A. Spaatz USAAF

General "Tooey" Spaatz' words succinctly sum up the story of the airmen who flew on operations from airfields in Britain, who were shot down over Western Europe[14] between May 1940 and May 1945, and who evaded capture by the Germans. There is, however, no consensus as to the number who successfully achieved this. After the war MI9, the section of British Military Intelligence that was charged with seeing to the return of evaders and escapers to Britain, published a table stating that, up to 30 June 1945, 695 officers and 1,270 other ranks of the RAF and its associated air forces had been "evaders" in Western Europe. These numbers included 'escapes from P/W camps, clandestine operations in Europe before "D" Day and operational rescues after "D" Day.'[15] Additionally, the table stated, eighteen officers and forty-six other ranks reached Switzerland without being captured.

Separate figures supplied by the Air Ministry Directorate of Manning (Manning Statistics), in respect of RAF Bomber Command aircrew alone, classified 2,868 aircrew as 'Missing now safe', but without defining that category.[16] Yet a third total was suggested by the RAF Escaping Society: '2,803 members of the Royal and Commonwealth Air Forces who were shot down during World War 2 managed either to escape from captivity or, in the majority of cases, to evade capture.'[17]

Airey Neave, on the other hand, who was employed by MI9 after his escape from Colditz Castle in 1942, suggests that while there was 'no separate total for those who reached safety from occupied France, Belgium and Holland... the fairest estimate which can be made is that over 4,000, including Americans, returned to England from these occupied countries, *before the Allied landing in Normandy in June 1944*'.[18] Some 3,000 of these he reckoned to have been airmen, the rest soldiers and sailors. An additional five or six hundred servicemen, he says, were liberated in France, Belgium and Holland as the Germans retreated towards Germany in 1944 and 1945, thus giving a rough total of 4,600 British and American evaders – 2,100 RAF airmen (including all Commonwealth air forces); 1,500 United States Army Air Force personnel; and 1,000 British soldiers and sailors. Neave's USAAF total, however, appears to be short of the mark, for the official total for American air force evaders is given as 1,380 officers and 1,312 other ranks, which raises the rough total by a further 1,200 or so to 5,800.

None of the above sources, however, defines "evader", presumably because it was felt that there was no need to do so. After all, one was either killed (or missing in action), taken prisoner of war, or returned safely from behind enemy lines having managed to avoid capture. For the purposes of this book, therefore, an evader is considered to be someone who was either able to avoid capture for any length of time *and* who returned to Allied territory without ever having been in enemy hands; or who, having been *temporarily* in captivity but having escaped, returned to Allied territory without ever being held in *permanent imprisonment within the German Reich*. "Temporarily" in this case may be taken to mean no more than a matter of days at most. There is yet another category, namely those killed either deliberately by the enemy or accidentally by other agencies while on the run and not in captivity. Sergeant J.H. Forsyth RCAF, for example, was apparently killed by a train at Chalon-sur-Saône station.

Those who succeeded in escaping from permanent imprisonment within the German Reich and achieved a "home run" (reached Allied lines) are not included.

It has not been possible in every case to determine the category into which all fell. One groundcrew member of the RAF, 518986 Leading Aircraftman John Henry Taylor, No. 6 Repair & Salvage Unit, RAF was wounded in the fighting in France on 15 June 1940 and taken to a French military hospital at Sable-sur-Sarthe. He was still there when the town was overrun by the enemy four days later. Indeed, he was still there, though in what capacity is not clear, when the Americans overran the town on 8 August 1944.

Also unclear, especially towards the end of the war when friendly and enemy lines were blurred due to the speed of the Allies' advance towards Germany, is whether or not several airmen were indeed evaders. Sergeant John Pearl, for instance, landed in woods to the east of the Rhine on the way back from Leipzig on the night of 10/11 April 1945. After a couple of days struggling through the trees he emerged on 13 April at the village of Namedy on the Rhine, barely 20 kilometres from the famous Remagen bridge. It is highly likely that the tide of war had long since swept past, but it is difficult to be sure, and his name is included in the list in Appendix I to be on the safe side. Others of his crew, though, landed in the American lines and so do not appear on the list.

Included, too, are one or two evaders who voluntarily sought refuge in prisoner-of-war camps in Germany simply to find shelter and food in the bitter winter weather of early 1945. It is a moot point whether or not those who landed in Axis-locked Switzerland should be added to the list, but thirty-one have been added because they left that country voluntarily and made their way through *enemy-occupied* France to British territory. Strictly speaking they were not evaders but internees, as were those who landed in Sweden, Spain, Portugal or the Irish Republic, but the difference is that those who "escaped" from the last four-named countries did not have to go through enemy lines.

This is not primarily an account of the escape lines that matured in Western Europe as the war progressed, but it would be fair to say that none of the thousands of evaders and escapers who managed to regain the Allied lines did so without help of some sort from the indigenous populations of the countries in which they found themselves. Fortunately for these evaders and escapers (E&E as the Americans call them) there were literally thousands of people, ordinary civilians for the most part, who were as General Spaatz said, prepared to help them in the fight against the common enemy despite the terrible risks involved. One historian has stated that by the end of 1942 the major escape lines were 'employing at the very least 12,000 helpers'.[19]

The first civilian efforts at helping were made at a time when, still suffering the humiliation of defeat, a number of people 'voluntarily assumed to retrieve the lost honour of their country'.[20] Initially, there was no co-ordinated action, no single rallying point, and Pierre d'Harcourt, a member of an old and distinguished French family, wrote that in 1940 'names like "de Gaulle" meant very little if they were known at all. Terms like "Underground" and "Resistance Movement" had not been invented because the things themselves either did not exist or were not known to exist.'[21] As another author has written, people 'were aware of the need for action. But what action? And with whom? A long time was necessary to get to know one another, to understand one another, to establish confidence and to act between men and women who had decided to react against Pétain, against the invaders.'[22]

Often the first form of resistance was the distribution of anti-German tracts and broadsheets. Very minor acts of sabotage could be undertaken, too, but usually at a disproportionate cost to the more than equal measure exacted by the savage German as a deterrent. The first opportunity, therefore, for ordinary folk to do something positive against the enemy usually came when an evader or escaper fell into their hands. They could at least feed him and clothe him, give him money if they had any, and point him in the right direction.

By and large, the first recipients of such generosity were those who had been left behind after the defeat of Belgium and France in May and June 1940, and thus it was that the people of northern France and Belgium were among the first to be caught up in the web of resistance to the invader. In Belgium, they had moved quickly, and on 1 July 1940 the famous newspaper *La Libre Belgique* was once again, clandestinely this time, published as an act of defiance.

Documents held by CEGES–SOMA[23] in Brussels, however, reveal how difficult it was to form a clandestine organisation under the very noses of the German secret police such as the *Geheime Feld Polizei* (GFP, Secret Field Police). It took one man of courage and vision, Georges Lechein, to have the idea that, for example, military intelligence that might be useful to his government in exile, and to the British, should be gathered and transmitted or sent to England. Needing someone he could trust to take documents or other objects (perhaps German shells or other pieces of ordnance) out of his country, in this case Belgium, he recruited two or three women. They in turn knew of others who wished to do something to help, and they too recruited others. Slowly the organisation, Portemine as it was to be called, expanded and within it, for reasons of security, sections and sub-sections were also formed before the end of 1940.

Portemine's members, men and women such as Albert Meeus and Henriette van Belle, were among the first to assist British escapers and evaders in Belgium on their way to England in August 1941, initially at great financial cost to the individual Belgians concerned. It was from such beginnings as these that one of the great escape lines of the Second World War – Comet – was to become established, running from Brussels through Paris to the St Jean-de-Luz area of France, and then over the corner of the western Pyrenees into neutral Spain.

As for the Germans, they sent agents of their security forces – particularly of the GFP and of the *Geheime Staatspolizei* (the Gestapo) – to the occupied countries as soon as possible. The chiefs of the GFP (Admiral Wilhelm Canaris) and of the Gestapo (SS-Gruppenführer Heinrich Müller) agreed that 'the military and political spheres of secret work should be their respective preserves; the situation in France being both military and political, both organisations considered themselves competent there.'[24]

One of the first GFP agents to be sent to France, in July 1940, was Sergeant Hugo Bleicher, later to prove a highly effective counter-intelligence agent: 'At first it appeared that we had come much too early and nobody had a proper use for us. So we sat around for a little while doing nothing.'[25] There was, of course, little for them to do at such an early stage, for it would take several months for meaningful resistance to become sufficiently co-ordinated for its results to be noticed. Certainly before the middle of 1941, however, both the GFP and the Gestapo had managed to get to grips with the first escape lines and intelligence organisations, whether "home grown" or created by outside agencies. So effective were the GFP and Gestapo to become as the war continued that 'almost every evasion line organisation had been penetrated by mid 1943… Interestingly, while the Germans were aware of these groups they allowed them to continue with their activities, meanwhile infiltrating their own [men] into the organisation in order to eventually control them…'[26]

Ruthless in their desire to eliminate all and any resistance, German security forces were to have much success over the years but, like shifting sands, somewhere, somehow, once one Resistance organisation had been damaged or destroyed another would appear to replace it. With an unending stream of proud and conquered people prepared to come forward at the risk of their own lives to help evaders and escapers, this was one war that the Germans could never win. Even as late as May 1945, with the war almost over, aircrew were still being hidden and helped in those parts of The Netherlands and Denmark that were to remain occupied until the very end.

What is so extraordinary today, well over sixty years on, is that, despite the awful toll taken by the Germans on resisters, the local population by and large bore no ill will against the men whom they had been trying to save. Sometimes the provocation to turn on the evader must have been immense as, for example, the time on 23 March 1943 when fifteen RAF Mosquitoes bombed the Batignolles company's railway locomotive repair shop at St Joseph on the north-eastern fringe of Nantes. Though twenty-four bombs scored direct hits on the works and surrounding area, they killed several of the local population, mostly workers at the repair shop. A huge and angry crowd gathered for the mass funeral at the cathedral. Their anger, however, was directed not at the British airmen but 'at the management for not providing enough air-raid shelters'.[27]

Further sorrow, not just confined to the more densely populated towns and cities, was visited upon the rural population of France, especially at the time of the Normandy landings in June 1944, when Allied aircraft roamed at will over the French countryside intent on destroying anything that moved. Polish fighter pilot Flight Sergeant W. Mrozohski was evading in the Orne *département* of France, some 20 kilometres south-east of Caen, when he saw 'a large formation of Fortresses' come over on the morning of 24 July 1944 and bomb 'Percy-en-Auge with fragmentation bombs. They were after [German] troop concentrations but during the raid Mme. Lemarechal was killed, her daughter badly injured and the house partially destroyed.'[28] What made the loss even more unbearable, if that were possible, was the fact that Madame Lemarechal and her daughter had deliberately left the house to find shelter elsewhere.

Mrozohski, who was in the house at the time, survived to witness a second tragedy before his liberation. On 10 August, now with a Monsieur Regnouf and his family at their dairy farm at Gourville, he was watching the Regnouf children, René and Jeanne, return from a field in a hay cart when, suddenly, out of the clear blue sky 'two Spitfires swooped down and shot them up with cannon fire.' René was killed, and his sister badly injured. Mrozohski was 'terribly depressed about this' but, despite Monsieur Regnouf's awful loss, his 'attitude towards me was unchanged'. It was the resolve, courage and understanding of people such as Monsieur Regnouf that the Germans could never conquer.

Regrettably, there is not room in this book to elaborate on the deeds of people such as the Lemarechals or the Regnoufs, though courage and devotion such as theirs shines through in so many examples. It is primarily a record of the RAF evaders, with much of the narrative being drawn from the contemporary reports that they made to MI9 as soon as possible after their return (see Appendix V for the composition of those reports).[29]

While these contemporaneous reports might be considered to be "best evidence", some were not altogether reliable, and there are not a few instances of two or more reports, made by evaders undergoing more or less the same evasion, innocently telling somewhat different stories. In such cases, a conclusion has been reached as to what *probably* happened, and where this occurs there will be a suitable acknowledgment. Occasionally, too, there has been a conflict between an evader's report and the account of his experiences in a later published book. Again, a balanced judgement has had to be made as to what actually occurred.

This book also draws on several exceedingly well-researched books and articles to add to the overall picture. It has not, however, been written to glorify the deeds of the participants (amazing though some of their exploits were). Nor has it been written to highlight the sacrifices made by the thousands of people of all nationalities and of all ages, male and female, who never lived to see victory. Whether their deaths were worth it or not is a moot point, and one not to be debated here, but ask any of those helpers who survived whether it was worth it or not, and scarcely one would tell you that that they would have had it otherwise. Impossible to name them all, to borrow the words of one RAF evader writing of those of his own bomber crew who perished while he lived, their 'names, I am sure, are written in that wonderful Book of Gold.'[30]

Easier to record the names of the RAF evaders, a list of them appears at Appendix I. It will be noted that a handful were shot down again and evaded again, that several more were taken prisoner of war, and that not a few, having returned to operations, lost their lives. For many of them, but by no means all, there was some official recognition of their efforts. The standard award for a "routine" evasion was a Mention in Despatches, usually in the New Year's Honours List or on the occasion of the King's Birthday, in June. The Commander-in-Chief of RAF Bomber Command, Air Marshal Sir Arthur Harris, never one to mince his words, wrote on 29 April 1942 that a 'Mention-in-Despatches is a totally inadequate and inappropriate award for a successful escape and it is my opinion that every escapee should receive an Award.'[31]

This was not to happen, but earlier in the war it was often the case that where an evasion was considered to be a little out of the ordinary an officer would be awarded the Military Cross and other ranks the Military Medal. Richard Clifford, however, as the powers-that-be doubted the veracity of his report, got nothing (see Chapter 1). In exceptional cases the DSO, MBE, CGM or DCM might be considered (though it took the RAF a while to learn that the DCM could be awarded only to the army), but whatever the circumstances each man was his own hero, and this is his brief story. It begins in the early summer of 1940, when organised resistance to the German invader was but a dream.

Throughout the book any person mentioned without any distinguishing letters after his name may, usually, be taken to be a member of the Royal Air Force. As to French place names, the *département* (more or less equivalent to a county in Britain) in which a place is located is sometimes given in brackets after its name to help with its location.

There are many gaps in both the narrative and in the appendices, and the author would be most grateful, via the publisher, for any information that might help to fill them.

Introduction

'Courage and patriotism simply are not enough when facing a superbly organised and utterly ruthless enemy.'[32]

Following the Nazis' unprovoked attack on Poland on 1 September 1939, and the British and French declaration of war on Germany two days later, the British Army was quick to respond. Within a week it had despatched several echelons to France in readiness for the expected attack on that country, and by 11 October 1939 the Secretary of State for War, Leslie Hore-Belisha, was able to tell the House of Commons 'that we have fulfilled – and more than fulfilled – our undertaking recently given to France to dispatch to that country in the event of war a British Expeditionary Force of a specified dimension within a specified time.' He added, less vaguely, that 158,000 men of the British Expeditionary Force (BEF), under General Viscount Gort,[33] had crossed to France within the first five weeks. Furthermore, he continued, they had taken with them 'more than 25,000 vehicles, including tanks, some of them of enormous dimensions and weighing 15 tons apiece or more.'

During September and October 1939, to support the BEF, the RAF had sent to France under the command of Air Vice-Marshal C.H.B. Blount OBE, MC[34] twelve mixed squadrons called collectively the Air Component of the Field Force (ACFF).[35] Also crossing the Channel was the Advanced Air Striking Force (AASF) under the command of Air Vice-Marshal P.H.L. Playfair CB, CVO, MC.[36] The AASF, ten independent squadrons of short-range Fairey Battle light bombers, formerly No. 1 (Bomber) Group, RAF was based on the area behind the Maginot Line with the idea of putting them within striking distance of German industry in the Ruhr Basin. In the event of a German attack, however, they would support the southern sector of ground operations, leaving the northern sector to be dealt with by home-based Blenheim bombers. In overall command of both the ACFF and the AASF was Air Marshal A.S. Barratt CB, CMG, MC.[37]

The following six months, a period of relative inactivity on the ground, earned the nickname "Phoney War", "drôle de guerre", or "Sitzkrieg". For the British soldiers and airmen it was just their luck that the winter of 1939/40 in France was the coldest since 1879. In January 1940 the temperature plunged to *minus* 10.8° Fahrenheit (F) at both Reims and Metz in the east of that country. Paris also experienced its coldest winter since 1838, with twenty-three days of frost in January 1940, the lowest temperature falling to 4½° (F), 27 degrees of frost. Even in Marseille, on the Mediterranean coast, 19.3° (F) of frost were recorded.

Following the defeat of Poland in September 1939, Hitler needed to secure Denmark and the North Sea coastline of Norway before he could turn on France and Britain. Shortly after 4 a.m., therefore, on the morning of 9 April 1940, an estimated 40,000 German soldiers invaded Danish Jutland from Schleswig-Holstein, while others simultaneously disembarked at strategic points on the islands of Fyen (Fünen), Laaland, Falster and Sjælland (Zeeland). Within the hour the Danish government had decided that any opposition was futile, and that evening the Danish prime minister, Thorvald Stauning, informed the nation that it was 'the duty of the population to refrain from any resistance'.[38]

In a co-ordinated attack, Norway was also invaded on 9 April. A fleet of German troopships sailed from the port of Stettin on 5 April, and nine destroyers from Bremen headed for Narvik. One of the troopships was sunk by a Norwegian torpedo boat on the evening of 8 April, but the rest pressed on, followed by a number of warships, for the Oslo fjord. The fight proper started on 9 April when a Norwegian whaling boat, the *Pol III*, with her one gun opened fire on the German squadron, which included the 10,000-ton *Blücher* (eight 8-inch guns), the 5,400-ton *Emden* (eight 5.9-inch guns), and several destroyers and other escorts. The gallant *Pol III* was sunk, but joining in the fight with her was the 1,596-ton minelayer *Olav Tryggvason* who, with her main armament of four 4.7-inch guns, damaged the *Emden* and one of the destroyers, and sank the 800-ton torpedo boat *Albatros*. Then the *Blücher*, as she came within range of the guns and torpedo tubes at Fort Oscarsborg, was set on fire and sunk. Brushing aside the fierce Norwegian resistance, however, soldiers from the German troopships were soon pouring ashore at Bergen, Trondheim, Stavanger, Kristiansund, and Narvik, inside the Arctic Circle.

Following the Norwegian government's unanimous rejection of the German ultimatum to surrender, delivered by Doktor Bräuer at 4 a.m. on 9 April, Prime Minister Neville Chamberlain quickly informed the Norwegians of British support: 'His Majesty's Government have at once assured the Norwegian Government that, in view of the German invasion of their country, His Majesty's Government have decided forthwith to extend their full aid to Norway, and have intimated that they will fight the war in full association with them.'

On 11 April Colonel Otto Ruge[39] was promoted to general and made commander-in-chief of the 25,000-strong Norwegian Army, which offered what resistance it could. Rushing over to Norway's aid was an Allied Expeditionary Force of a little over 8,000 British and French troops, followed by a further 12,000 or so, including two battalions of the French Foreign Legion[40] and four Polish battalions. Those that landed at Namsos on 15 April, without artillery or anti-aircraft defences, were compelled to withdraw within three weeks, while those landed at Narvik did not do so until 10 June. Last to leave that Arctic fastness was a small Royal Marine party under the command of a certain Captain H.G. "Blondie" Hasler, from the Royal Marine Fortress Unit, whose war, as will be seen, was far from over.

On 2 May Neville Chamberlain declaimed to the House of Commons that, thanks 'to the powerful forces which the Navy was able to bring to bear, and the determination and skilful dispositions of General Paget,[41] in command of the British land forces in the area, backed by the splendid courage and tenacity of the troops, we have now withdrawn the whole of our forces from Aandalsnes under the very noses of the German aeroplanes, without, as far as I am aware, losing a single man in the operation.'

Five days later, he was moved to further rhetoric in the House when speaking of the British troops: 'Whether in hard fighting or in stolid endurance, or in quick and skilful movement, faced as they were by superior force and superior equipment, they distinguished themselves in every respect. Man for man they were superior to their foes.'[42] Be that as it may, Admiral Sir Roger Keyes[43] was unimpressed by the short campaign, and spoke in the Commons that same day: 'It is a shocking story of ineptitude which ought never to have happened.' Within two weeks Chamberlain was gone, replaced by the charismatic and dynamic sixty-five-year-old Winston Churchill.

Sure of their victory in Norway and Denmark, the German Army then turned on The Netherlands, Luxembourg, and Belgium, at dawn on 10 May 1940. Up to this point RAF and Luftwaffe fighters had fought the occasional combat, and RAF Blenheims had carried out reconnaissance missions over German territory. Losses were few, and no member of the RAF was called upon to practise his evasion skills. Officially, for the whole of the period from 3 September 1939 to the end of April 1940 there were only eighteen RAF aircrew deaths in France and Belgium. But for the whole of May 1940 there were 236 deaths in the RAF in France, with a further sixty-four during the first seventeen days of June up to the time of the RAF's final evacuation.[44]

Responding to the Germans' westward drive the BEF advanced into Belgium with, on its left and right flanks, the French 7th and 1st Armies respectively. Thirty-eight infantry and seven Panzer (armoured) divisions of General Gerd von Runstedt's Army Group A, however, did what experts had believed to be impossible, and burst through the impassable Ardennes into France, to the south of the BEF and of the two French armies. Breaching the front held by the French 9th Army, von Runstedt's troops had crossed the River Meuse near Sedan within three days, and in a further eight days had reached the Channel coast at Abbeville. In so doing they cut off the French 7th and 1st Armies and most of the BEF in Belgium.

Only sixteen days after the attack had begun the War Office authorised General Gort 'to operate towards the coast forthwith in conjunction with French and Belgian Armies.' With the evacuation of the BEF via Dunkirk imminent Operation Dynamo,[45] the Royal Navy's codename for the evacuation, was initiated. Lasting officially from 26 May to 3 June 1940 (the "Nine Days Wonder"), Dynamo ended, officially, with an Admiralty communiqué timed at 1423 hours on 3 June 1940. The communiqué also stated that 224,585 British and 112,546 French and Belgian troops had been evacuated from Dunkirk by 222 Royal Navy ships and by 665 'other vessels'.[46] A number of stragglers were picked up during the course of the next two days, and a further 190,000 men were evacuated from French ports to the west – St Malo, Le Havre, Brest, Cherbourg, St Nazaire, and so on.

The BEF suffered 23,000 casualties (killed or missing) and lost most of its equipment, including 64,000 vehicles, 20,000 motorcycles, 2,500 guns, 7,000 tons of ammunition, 90,000 rifles, 8,000 Bren guns and 400 anti-tank rifles. In addition, 44,466 British soldiers, sailors and airmen, unable to join the evacuation, were taken prisoner.[47] Two to three thousand more managed to avoid capture, mostly in the north of France and southern Belgium. As for the Belgians, their casualties were 5,481 military personnel and 6,552 civilians killed during their eighteen days' fighting. French casualties were of the order of 60,000 killed, 300,000 wounded and around 1,900,000 taken prisoner (including five army commanders and some 29,000 officers). German losses were 27,074 killed, 18,384 missing, and 111,034 wounded.

The battle for France ended with the signing of the Franco-German armistice at Compiègne at 6.50 p.m. (5.50 p.m. BST) on Saturday, 22 June 1940. General Charles Huntziger, Minister for War in the new government,[48] signed for France, with General Wilhelm Keitel, chief of staff, signing for

Germany. Following the signing of the Franco-Italian armistice at the Villa Incisa in Rome on 24 June by Huntziger, again, for France and by Marshal Pietro Badoglio for Italy, hostilities between France and the Axis powers ceased at 1.35 a.m. on 25 June.[49]

Under the terms of the Franco-German armistice France was divided into three main areas: *la zone occupée* (the Occupied Zone); *la zone non-occupée* (Unoccupied Zone), or *zone libre* (the Free Zone); and *la zone cotière interdite* (the forbidden coastal zone). This latter zone was a wide strip of the French coastline within the Occupied Zone that ran from Belgium all the way down the Channel and the Atlantic coasts to Spain. Separating the Unoccupied Zone and the Occupied Zone was *la ligne de démarcation* (the Demarcation Line). Running from the Swiss border near Geneva it snaked westwards across France to a point a few kilometres east of Tours before turning south, and east of Bordeaux, down to the Pyrenees near St Jean-Pied-de-Port. Some 900 kilometres in length, it was policed, thinly and sometimes without too much enthusiasm, by German troops on the one side and by Vichy French police on the other. There was one further restricted area within the Occupied Zone, *la zone interdite* (the forbidden zone), a wide strip of land running from the English Channel down the border with Belgium, along the annexed zone of Alsace-Lorraine, and down to Switzerland.

While the Germans garrisoned the Occupied Zone, they left the Unoccupied Zone, basically southern France and the Mediterranean coast (see end map), to be administered by the French under Marshal Phillipe Pétain, whose pro-German government, officially formed on 2 July 1940, had been moved to the Pavillon de Sévigne in Vichy.[50]

Later, after the Germans had occupied the whole of France in November 1942 and the main areas of France were re-divided into the *Zone Nord* and *Zone Sud*, another line, marking yet another forbidden zone, was drawn a few kilometres north of, and roughly parallel to, the Pyrenees. From the Atlantic coast, immediately to the north of St Jean-de-Luz, it ran along the more major roads wherever possible, following the River Tech for the last few kilometres until reaching the Mediterranean Sea.

On 18 June 1940, shortly before the armistice and after he had managed to escape by air to England, General Charles de Gaulle broadcast a rousing appeal from the BBC in London to his fellow countrymen:

> '… The generals who for many years have commanded the French Army have formed a government. That government, alleging that our armies have been defeated, has opened negotiations with the enemy to put an end to the fighting.'
>
> '... But has the last word been said? Has all hope completely disappeared? Is the defeat final? No! Believe me, I speak with knowledge and I tell you that France is not lost... For France is not alone. She is not alone. She is not alone...'
>
> '... Now in London, I invite all French officers and men who are on British soil, or who may arrive here with or without their arms, I invite the engineers and the skilled workmen of the armament industries who are now on British soil, or who may arrive here, to get into touch with me. Whatever happens, the flame of French resistance must not and shall not be extinguished…'

On 20 June, Pétain had his say:

> 'People of France! I have asked the enemy to put an end to hostilities. The government yesterday appointed plenipotentiaries to receive their conditions. I took this decision with the stout heart of a soldier because the military situation imposed it...'
>
> '... I was with you in the glorious days. As head of the government I will remain with you in the dark days. Stand by me. The fight still goes on. It is for France, the soil of her sons.'

Although thousands of British service personnel were captured before the fighting in France and Belgium was over in June 1940, several hundred who had not been taken prisoner or who had managed to escape from German hands were now faced with the problem of how to get back to England. Some had managed to find shelter with local families, some for rather longer than others. Bandsman James H. Patching, 1st Royal Scots, stayed near Valenciennes (Nord) from 1940 until liberated by American forces in September 1944. Also trapped in France was Sergeant J.D. Vallely, 4th Border Regiment, who spent the next two years working in a shop in Verneusses (Eure). In February 1942 he joined the French Resistance and 'participated in many armed raids against the enemy and did a certain amount of sabotage work… I helped to capture a heavy machine gun from a German truck while the sentries were asleep, to mine roads, and to destroy high-tension electric cables and pylons'.[51]

Vallely also helped with the destruction of an Me109 fighter that had force-landed in the area. He and his comrades allegedly killed the pilot, Leutnant Luchou. Between February and August 1944 they also helped sixteen Allied airmen (fourteen Americans and two RAF),[52] and 'an Intelligence Service agent, Mme Simone Lecomte de Bruyne', who was wanted by the Germans. She was hidden by one of the group for three months, from February 1944, until such time as she could be handed over to Captain Douglas Higton of the British Intelligence Corps.

Some of the early evaders in 1940 were so desperate to get back that they tried to *row* across the English Channel. As will be seen in Chapter 1, one RAF fighter pilot came close to succeeding in his madcap escapade but, remarkably, at least two army officers and one Royal Navy officer *did* succeed in boating across the Channel to England.[53] The Germans had very quickly sent troops to guard the northern French and Belgian ports, and hence there were very few opportunities to find a boat that was even capable of making the crossing.

Men such as Patching and Vallely were exceptions, for most trapped willingly or unwillingly in the Occupied Zone or in Belgium did their utmost to get back, whatever the risk. Their only realistic choice was to head for British territory at Gibraltar, way down in the south of Spain. Having crossed the Demarcation Line into Unoccupied France, they then had to somehow cross the Pyrenees and neutral Spain to get there. Going to neutral Switzerland in 1940 was not a realistic option, given that it was surrounded by the Axis powers. Choices, therefore, were limited to heading to either the south-west of France and thence across the Pyrenees, or to Marseille, France's second largest city and largest port,[54] and from which it might be possible to get away by boat or ship. It was, however, nearly 800 kilometres (500 miles) from Paris and 1,100 or so (700 miles) from the Dunkirk coast to either place.[55] To get to Marseille, or indeed to anywhere in the Unoccupied Zone, one needed an authorised permit to cross the Demarcation Line. Given the considerable length of the line, however, it was not difficult to enter the Unoccupied Zone without a valid permit and without being spotted by German guards or by zealous Vichy French police in the Unoccupied Zone.

The fastest way to travel these great distances was by railway, and not a few of those who chose that form of transport received considerable help from the railway workers. Once in the south, however, a British evader still had a tricky journey ahead of him for, as a result of pressure on the French government from the German and Italian armistice commissions in Vichy, anyone caught without a proper exit visa was promptly interned.

The position of those British servicemen who had migrated to Unoccupied France in the summer of 1940 was reasonably unambiguous. In simple terms a man in uniform was likely to be arrested and interned. A "civilian", on the other hand, would not be so restrained, but would only be able to leave the country legally if he were in possession of the proper exit visas. These could only be obtained from the Vichy authorities but, thanks to pressure from the Germans, were not likely to be issued. Subterfuge was therefore the order of the day.

The position of interned British evaders and escapers in Unoccupied France was formalised by General Huntziger on 14 July 1940, when he sent an order to all commanders of the Vichy military regions that 'they should provide secure accommodation for the British soldiers present in their Divisions.'[56] The commander of the XVth Military Region, which covered the south-east of France and had its headquarters at Fort St Nicholas,[57] Marseille, chose Fort St Jean as his place of internment. Built in the 17th century, during the reign of Louis XIV, Fort St Jean before the war had been the headquarters and main recruiting centre of the French Foreign Legion, and was, with Fort St Nicholas, one of two forts guarding the narrow entrance to *le Vieux Port*, Marseille's old port.

If the position of British servicemen in Vichy France was to some extent unambiguous, then that of the French Army's *Deuxième Bureau* was not so clear-cut. After the armistice, though quartered in Vichy, it was staffed by army officers, whose duty it was to centralise and to interpret 'Intelligence for the use of the High Command. Its overt function is the presentation of Intelligence.'[58] It was *not*, however, to be confused with French Intelligence, whose role was the gathering and procuring of information by espionage and other clandestine means.

Another essential function of France's Intelligence operations was counter-espionage. During 'the first half of the 1930s the official French Counter-Espionage Service consisted of 136 special commissaries of the national police. They were attached to the Prefects of Departments... Co-operation between the commissaries and the Army was negligible.'[59] As a result of this unsatisfactory state of affairs, having become fully aware of the warlike growth of Nazi Germany, the French army created its own German counter-espionage bureau within its Special Services unit, whose headquarters were at 2 bis, Avenue de Tourville, Paris. In 1935 the head of the German section of the new counter-espionage bureau was Captain Paul Paillole, the outgoing Commandant de Robien having been posted to Sofia. Five years later, following the defeat of France, Paillole moved his small section to the Villa Eole on the Promenade de la Plage, Marseille. Entrusted by his superior officers with the creation of a cover for their clandestine activities, Paillole set up the *Entreprise Général de*

Travaux Ruraux (commonly just "T.R."), known throughout the secret service by the codename *Cambronne*.[60]

Also posted to the Marseille garrison headquarters of the XVth Military Region at Fort St Nicholas in the summer of 1940 was a young French officer, Henri Frenay: 'The windows of our vast, light-filled offices gave on to the entirety of the Vieux-Port, with a sweeping view of the Canebière... Marseille is usually a busy, gay and noisy city, but in early August 1940 it was very different indeed. A substantial portion of the French people seemed to have sought refuge in the old Phocian port, where they mingled with groups of all origins and all classes – Czechs, Poles, Belgians, Dutch and, among all these, numerous Jews fleeing Nazi persecution.'[61]

Frenay was one of the many French officers who were appalled by the changed circumstances of their defeated country. There in Marseille, he witnessed, somewhat dramatically perhaps, the arrival of 'tens of thousands' of 'men, women and children' who had been 'torn from their homes' in Alsace-Lorraine 'with only a pitifully small sum of money', and decided that France should know the truth about this upheaval. 'The need for information, for intelligence-gathering, for propaganda began slowly to impress itself on me. At the same time I was beginning to wonder just how to organize and put to work the men and women we had already recruited.'[62] Frenay set out his requirements at the end of the summer of 1940. In a nutshell, these were to get as much information on the enemy as they could, and transmit it to Britain, and to spread as widely as possible counter-propaganda against Vichy French organs, which were under German control. From these beginnings grew the French Resistance network *Combat*.

Also active in the crowded and bustling world of Marseille in 1940 was *résistant* Maurice Bertin-Chevance. Making himself known to Captain Paillole at the Villa Eole he suggested that he, Paillole, might care to meet his chief. 'Much intrigued, Paillole kept the appointment made for him, and was both amused and delighted to find that the man of mystery was none other than Henri Frenay, whom he had last met when Frenay was serving as a staff officer under Colonel Baril, Chief of the Second Bureau!'[63]

Although this liaison had little direct bearing on the world of the interned British serviceman in Marseille in 1940-41, between them *Combat* and *Cambronne* were able to identify German agents and, sometimes, even penetrate the enemy's espionage services. At the very least British internees in Unoccupied France, though most may not have known it, were not alone.

SCALE: Kilometres
0 50 100
Miles
0 50 100
IRELAND
Belfast
Dublin
Cork
Glasgow
Edinburgh
Newcastle
Liverpool
Lincoln
Birmingham
Cardiff
ENGLAND
Norwich
Bristol
London
Southampton
Portsmouth
Dover
Penzance
Falmouth
Plymouth
DENMARK
NORTH SEA
Hamburg
HOLLAND
Bremen
Amsterdam
The Hague
Rotterdam
Ostend
Calais
Boulogne
Dunkirk
Antwerp
Essen
Dortmund
Düsseldorf
Lille
BELGIUM
Brussels
Cologne
Abbeville
GERMANY
Cherbourg
Morlaix
St Brieuc
Brest
Le Havre
Rouen
Frankfurt
ATLANTIC OCEAN
Quimper
Lorient
Rennes
R Seine
Luxembourg
Paris
St Nazaire
Tours
Châteaudun
R Rhine
Nantes
Strasbourg
Stuttgart
R Loire
Dijon
BAY OF BISCAY
Limoges
SWITZERLAND
La Coruña
Bordeaux
Lyon
Geneva
R Garonne
Turin
Milan
Bayonne
Bilbao
San Sebastián
Pau
Miranda de Ebro
Toulouse
R Rhône
Genoa
ITALY
Narbonne
R Ebro
ANDORRA
Marseille
PORTUGAL
Perpignan
Figueras
Saragossa
Lérida
Lisbon
Madrid
Manresa
Barcelona
SPAIN
CORSICA
MAJORCA
Cape St Vincent
Seville
IBIZA
MENORCA
SARDINIA
Granada
Gibraltar
MEDITERRANEAN SEA

CHAPTER 1

In the Beginning: 1940

'We do not know whether we shall be able to have any British representative in the restricted region called "Unoccupied France," because that is entirely surrounded by and under the control of the enemy. But, relying upon the true genius of the French people and their judgement of what has happened to them when they are allowed to know the facts, we shall endeavour to keep such contacts as are possible through the bars of their prison.'

Prime Minister Winston Churchill,
House of Commons, 25 June 1940

The unwanted distinction of being the first RAF evaders of the Second World War most likely fell to three aircrew from two 600 Squadron Blenheims, L1514 (Pilot Officers R.C. Haine and M. Kramer) and L6616 (Sergeant J. Davis), and to three from 142 Squadron's Fairey Battle L5238 (Sergeant A.N. Spear and his crew of Sergeant J. Brookes and Leading Aircraftman R.H. Nugent). All of them were shot down on 10 May 1940 behind enemy lines. Little is known of the evasions of the 600 Squadron crews, except that Haine and Kramer were 'shot down by Me110s of III/ZG1 and crash-landed in shallow water off Overflakkee Island'.[64] Three days later they were back in England. Also shot down by Me110s of the same unit, Davis was the only survivor of his Blenheim, and he appears to have returned, presumably by sea, to Harwich. It is probable that he came back on the Royal Navy destroyer HMS *Hereward*, as did Haine and Kramer, which was also evacuating Queen Wilhelmina and her Dutch government.

Spear and crew came down near Colmey (Meurthe-et-Moselle) in eastern France, and were back on their squadron next day. Four days later, though, they were shot down again. This time Spear was the only survivor, flung clear when the tail of their Battle was shot off and the aircraft exploded. The citation for his DFM, gazetted on 31 May 1940, states that, after the tail of his aircraft was shot away on 14 May, he was 'thrown out whilst preparing to jump, but he landed by parachute in enemy territory. He was repeatedly under enemy fire but, securing a horse, he succeeded by sheer determination in overcoming many difficulties, including the swimming of a canal.' Actually, he had 'secured' two horses: 'Two American nurses in an ambulance met him and asked him what the second horse was for. His reply was typical – "Just in case this one has a break-down!" The American nurses took him in the ambulance back to their base where he stayed overnight.'[65]

Shot down on the same raid as Spear and crew on 14 May was their Squadron Leader (Flying) and *his* crew – Squadron Leader J.F. Hobler (pilot); Sergeant R.V.T. Kitto (observer); and Corporal D.J. Barbrooke (gunner). As Hobler descended in his burning, stricken Battle he could see forward elements of the German Army advancing in personnel carriers beneath them, all firing furiously at him and his crew. Crashing into some trees all three managed to get out of the Battle, but Hobler, having suffered burns, was very much the worse for wear. Kitto and Barbrooke,[66] though, helped him into the safety of the trees, out of the way of the German infantry rushing in their direction, before reaching forward French troops. Kitto and Barbrooke returned to their base at Berry-au-Bac, leaving their pilot in the hands of French doctors. They did what they could for him before sending him on his way to Berry-au-Bac, where squadron members, on entering the dining room, were greeted by the sight of a 'strange figure sitting with his back to us, swathed in bandages all over his head.'[67]

Though some ten RAF Hurricanes had been shot down on 10 May, all pilots had managed to land behind their own lines, and it was not until the following day that the first fighter pilots – Squadron Leader G.C. Tomlinson and Flight Lieutenant R.H.A. "Dickie" Lee DFC – were required to regain their own lines having been shot down behind the enemy's in Holland.[68] The citation for Tomlinson's DFC, gazetted on 11 June 1940, reads as follows: 'This officer has commanded a squadron since November, 1939. He has led numerous interception and convoy patrols, and also two raids over Holland and one over Brussels. In these raids his squadron destroyed thirteen enemy aircraft and damaged a further nine. He himself shot down one enemy aircraft and damaged another. On two occasions he was forced to land in the front lines, but by courageous endeavour he returned to his unit in both instances.'

Flight Lieutenant Dickie Lee had been slightly wounded on 10 May, but was back in action on the following day and shot down two enemy aircraft before being hit by flak himself. Having to land his Hurricane in a Dutch field near Maastricht, without further injury, he acquired an overcoat to hide his uniform, and set off for the Allied lines. Asking a Belgian the way back the man pointed him in the direction of some tanks that he said were Belgian. They were in fact German. Not realising that he was an RAF pilot, the Germans then put him in a barn with a number of civilian refugees. This was the Germans' second mistake. Finding a ladder in the barn, Dickie Lee simply propped it against a window high up in the wall and then 'just climbed out and walked four miles, got a lift from some Belgians and he was back with the squadron to fight the next day.'[69] The citation for his DSO ends: 'In his last engagement he was seen at 200 feet on the tail of a Junkers 89, being subjected to intense fire from the ground over enemy occupied territory. This officer escaped from behind the German lines after being arrested and upheld the highest traditions of the Service.'

The fog of war was quickly descending upon the dusty battlefields of Belgium and France when 79 Squadron based at Merville airfield, France, with its Hurricanes was called into action early on the morning of 11 May 1940 when, on patrol north-west of Mons, Yellow Section spotted three Heinkel III bombers. The leader, Flight Lieutenant R.S.J. Edwards, ordered the other two of his flight to carry out the standard No.1 attack and himself dived into the fray. He was hit by return fire from one of the Heinkels and his Hurricane, L2068, was set alight. Edwards managed to bale out but not before suffering severe burns to his arms. He returned to his squadron on the following day but was considered unfit for further flying.[70]

79 Squadron's fight continued and on the same day as Edwards's return Flight Lieutenant C.L.C. Roberts led Blue Section off on a patrol to the east of Brussels. With him were Sergeant A.W. Whitby (flying as his No. 2) and Pilot Officer T.C. Parker (No. 3). Sighting a Dornier 17, Roberts ordered them into line astern, but no sooner had they completed the manoeuvre than they were 'attacked from behind without warning by a large number of Messerschmitt 109s which dived down out of the cloud behind us.'[71] Blue Section had fallen into the simplest of baited traps. Being the closest to the enemy Parker was 'subjected to most intense fire', and his cockpit filled with smoke. With his Hurricane suffering a dead engine he 'tried to regain control but the controls were ineffective, so I undid the straps and, as the aircraft stalled, I stepped out and passed over the top of the rudder.'[72]

He delayed opening his parachute until he was an estimated 1,800 feet above the ground, but no sooner had he done so than he heard machine-gun fire, which he believed was being directed at him. Landing safely in an orchard in the St Trond (St Truiden) area he 'accompanied some Belgian peasants to a cottage where I was informed that I was in German occupied territory.' Belgian Henri Dehaes gave him some civilian clothes and promised to burn his RAF uniform. Joined by Martha van Brabant the three cycled along back lanes until reaching the main road from St Trond to Tirlemont (Tienen). Meeting Belgian troops retreating from the Albert Canal, Henri and Martha said goodbye, while Parker reported to the nearest Belgian HQ, north of Tirlemont. Taken to an aerodrome in the hope of getting a lift back to his squadron, Parker found that the airfield had already been abandoned. Returning, therefore, to the Belgian HQ he had dinner with a general before spending the night in an attic.

Resolving on the following day to walk the twenty or so kilometres to Louvain (Leuven), he was frequently stopped by suspicious Belgian troops, but managed to get a lift with some Belgian army transport. At Louvain he found some British troops. Suspicious, they relieved him of his revolver, but once he had proved his identity he was well-treated and taken to the HQ of 'the Second Corps of Artillery where I was interrogated about the whereabouts of the Belgians.'

Having rejoined his squadron, Parker was in the thick of the action again on 20 May, and had already flown a dawn patrol, as Blue Section leader, when all available squadron aircraft were ordered 'to fly to Arras and attack enemy bombers and armoured vehicles approaching the city.' Parker and Sergeant Alfred Whitby flew off together to Arras but, seeing no bombers, went down low and attacked enemy vehicles on the road to the east of the town, firing off most of their ammunition. Parker 'then got a bullet in engine or hit something'. Turning north he tried to gain height, but when the spluttering engine failed altogether he made a landing in a ploughed field near Thélus, and set his Hurricane on fire. Having closely avoided a second landing in enemy occupied territory he made his way to a nearby British army post, where the troops 'seemed very surprised to learn that the Germans were entering Arras.' Plans were changed immediately, and leaving the army to get on with their war Parker returned to his squadron, via Lens and Béthune, in time to fly back to England to get on with his.[73]

If 12 May 1940 was not a good day for Pilot Officer Parker, then it was even worse for 264 Squadron with its Boulton Paul Defiants. Over Maasluis, to the west of Rotterdam, Holland they were attacked by a swarm of Me109s, and four of the Defiants were shot down. One of the pilots, Pilot Officer A.E. Skelton, was taken prisoner, but his observer/air gunner, Pilot Officer J.E. Hatfield, also shot at as he descended by parachute, met up with Pilot Officer Thomas, pilot of another Defiant. In the belief that they were German spies, both were arrested by the Dutch, and nearly shot out of hand when their original captor was found to be a Nazi sympathiser. They were returned to their squadron on 14 May.

264 Squadron lost a fifth aircraft when Pilot Officer A. McLeod and Leading Aircraftman Cox

were shot down behind German lines at Zeuenbergen, Holland at around the same time as the other four Defiants were lost. Escaping to Antwerp, they were evacuated by a Royal Navy destroyer to Folkestone, and were back on their squadron by 17 May. 264 Squadron, however, continued to suffer heavy losses, and on 28 May three more of its Defiants were shot down by Me109s. This time there were no survivors, and among the dead were Pilot Officers McLeod and Hatfield.

12 May 1940 also witnessed the desperate attempt by RAF Bomber Command and the AASF to halt the advance of the German columns through Belgium. On that day alone thirty-three aircraft, Battles and Blenheims, were lost to the enemy's fighters. Sixty aircrew were killed and twenty-one taken prisoner. Only two, from a 218 Squadron Fairey Battle, evaded through enemy lines. For this and for trying to save their dying pilot, twenty-two-year-old Cornishman Pilot Officer F.S. Bazalgette, whilst under heavy machine-gun fire, Sergeant W.H. Harris and Leading Aircraftman H.B. Jones were awarded the Military Medal.

Flying Officer N.E.W. Pepper DFC, Sergeant T.E. Hyde and Aircraftman First Class Hill force-landed in their 139 Squadron Blenheim at Hoepertingen, a few kilometres east of St Trond after attacking enemy columns between Tongeren and Maastricht. Hill, injured, was taken prisoner, while the other two got safely back, Pepper 'returning in a French armoured car'.[74] Of the three, only Hill would survive the war, Pepper and Hyde being killed, still on 139 Squadron, just over a year later in the Western Desert, with Pepper by then promoted to wing commander and Hyde still a sergeant. Two more to return in an unorthodox fashion were Flight Lieutenant T.G. Tideman and Sergeant Hale, the two survivors of another 139 Squadron Blenheim. Scrambling clear of their burning aircraft, the third member of the crew was killed, but they later managed to commandeer a car left behind by German holidaymakers and to make their way back to their base at Plivot.[75]

In the chaotic conditions prevailing during the British withdrawal from France, Aircraftman Second Class Richard Clifford, attached to No. 13 (Army Co-operation) Squadron, lost contact with his squadron. By the time that he had reached the airfield at Nantes on 26 May 1940 he found it deserted and destroyed by the retreating British. He did, however, find a Hillman car in working order and, filling it with petrol and with plenty in reserve, headed off in a southerly direction. Along the way he picked up several French refugees from Paris who were heading for Bordeaux, and who were in possession of a *sauf conduit* (safe-conduct pass). At Fumel (Lot-et-Garonne, some 160 kilometres south-east of Bordeaux) Clifford and his passengers were told that there was fighting there, and so carried on to Toulouse instead, though 'Clifford had to make several detours on account of barrages on the road to Toulouse'. At Revel (Haute-Garonne), some sixty-five kilometres south-east of Toulouse, they were stopped by French police, but were allowed to proceed.

Hearing that the British were using Port Vendres (Pyrénées-Orientales) as their embarkation port, Clifford drove there as fast as he could. Reaching the port around 10 June, it was to be informed by a French Navy commander that the last of the British had left on the previous day and he was unable to offer Clifford any advice other than to 'fare as best he could'. The best he could do, as he walked through Port Vendres, was to be arrested and handcuffed by French police. He was thrown into a camp 'which contained Italians and Spaniards but managed to escape from this.' Appropriating a motorboat with the intention of either making for Barcelona or of finding a Royal Navy patrol vessel, he was arrested for the second time.

Escaping once more he gave up on Spain and walked the few kilometres to Argèles-sur-Mer, where a Mrs Davis put him up for the night. The following day he hitched a lift for most of the way to Avignon on a diesel lorry, and from there made his way to the Seamen's Mission at 36, rue de Forbin, Marseille, 'which was being run by a woman who was apparently the caretaker. At the mission there were a number of American sailors who had been torpedoed.'[76] There were also 'six or seven British soldiers' in residence whose names he was unable to remember. A fortnight later, as the mission was short of food, he decided to leave for Perpignan with one of the soldiers (whom he last saw on a stolen bicycle), but got no further than Béziers (Hérault), where he was again arrested. Escaping for a third time he reached Perpignan, and was told that he would find the British consul at le Perthus (on the Spanish border) some thirty kilometres away to the south. At le Boulou French authorities supplied him with a *sauf conduit* and he reached le Perthus without further trouble. Of the consul there was no sign.

He did, though, meet an English-speaking Czech, who suggested that they head for Switzerland. With the money that they had been given by a female Russian refugee they were able to travel by bus as far as Romans-sur-Isère, the greater part of the distance to the Swiss border. Hoping to get to Lyon they set off on foot but at Vienne, learning that there were Germans in Lyon, spent the night in a tram shed a further nine kilometres down the road. Heading now for Grenoble, they set off again via Chambéry and Aix-les-Bains until they came to Annecy (Haute-Savoie), where they asked for their *sauf conduits* to be extended. Instead, Clifford was asked why he had not been demobilised and was arrested for the fourth time. While his Czech companion was allowed to go free, provided that he did not attempt to leave the town, Clifford was 'put into a subterranean prison, where he was very badly treated' and became quite ill. Removed to some barracks, he escaped for the fourth time by climbing over the wall.

Without further interruption he walked to St Julien-en-Genevois, on the Swiss border, which lay beyond the railway line and a tangle of barbed wire. After a spot of bother with a sentry – Clifford made too much noise – he crossed into Switzerland. No one asked him for papers, and he reached the British consulate in Geneva without difficulty. Staff there made arrangements with Thomas Cook and Sons, travel agents, for his return to England via France, Spain and Portugal, and armed with legitimate papers he made the long journey back to the Spanish border. At Cerbère 'all papers were examined, passports stopped and dutiable goods declared,' but he got through Spain to Portugal, and on 26 August was flown home from Lisbon.

In the second half of 1941, while Clifford was serving at RAF Arbroath, a recommendation was forwarded by the Director of Intelligence to HQ Army Co-Operation Command ("HQACC") RAF that Clifford be awarded the Military Medal for his 'exceptional determination and skill in escaping, even when medically unfit.' HQACC, however, were not convinced, and were puzzled as to why he should have claimed that Nantes airfield was abandoned when he got there on 26 May 1940, when in fact the aerodrome was not evacuated until 18 June. Though the resident unit on the airfield, 98 Squadron (acting in the capacity of an OTU), had been sent home in May, RAF personnel had continued to maintain a depot on the airfield until 17 June when the last of them had gone home by sea: 'The recommendation, as submitted, is not therefore understood.'

On 6 December 1941 the Air Intelligence section of the RAF responsible for such matters, 'requesting that the citation forwarded… be cancelled', explained why Clifford should receive no award: 'It has been established that there is an element of doubt and further evidence has been obtained which puts part of his story in a light which, while not in any way discrediting the airman, takes his actions out of the category calling for special recommendation.'

Somewhere high in the sky over northern France, between Cap Gris Nez and Calais, Sergeant J.W.B. Phillips was on patrol in his Spitfire on 24 May 1940 when he tangled with an Me109. He shot it down, but in so doing his Spitfire was hit in the fuel tank and he, too, was forced down. Breaking a leg, he was captured by two German soldiers, and after several moves had reached the British Army's No. 17 General Hospital at Camiers (Pas-de-Calais), under the command of Colonel Robertson RAMC and Major Chappell RAMC, though all were prisoners of the Germans. It was not long before the hospital and its patients were moved, the reason being, so the Germans claimed, that the RAF had dropped leaflets stating that they were going to bomb Camiers. The real reason, the British thought, was because guns were being sited behind and above the hospital. Half the patients were therefore moved to Belgium, and the others, including Phillips, to the *Faculté Jeanne d'Arc* in Lille.

As at Camiers, the British were given the run of the hospital in Lille, the only Germans present being sentries posted around its perimeter. The patients were warned, however, by the RAMC officers not to attempt to escape, even 'going so far as to post orderlies in the grounds of the Faculté from dawn to dusk.' Two men did manage to get away, apparently, by climbing a wall but, to dissuade others from following suit, the RAMC staff told the patients that the two men had been captured and shot, though Phillips was later given to understand that the same story had been told about him after he had escaped. There was, anyway, little incentive for Phillips to remain in the hospital. Whereas the RAMC staff ate well, even being allowed into Lille to augment their rations, the patients received 'only what the Germans provided and what was left of voluntary contributions of the inhabitants. The distribution of these gifts was so badly organised that a lot was wasted.'[77]

For Jim Phillips, it was a disgraceful imbalance, and he determined to escape. Knowing that 'French civilians were allowed to visit and bring food for the patients, I decided to get in touch with someone who would be able to assist me in escaping.'[78] Writing his name and details on a piece of paper, he attached it to a piece of lead and threw it into the street, hoping that someone would find it and help him. The paper was found, and was passed to Madame Jeannine Voglimacci, the owner of a hairdressing salon at 1, rue de Turenne, La Madeleine, Lille. (Above the salon was an apartment, which was being used by a certain Sergeant Harold Cole as a "safe house"). She replied to Phillips by letter, which was 'brought into the hospital by an Irish nun'.

The courier was, strictly speaking, neither Irish nor a nun. Her name was Maud Olga Andrée Baudot de Rouville, born in Paris on 14 December 1891, the daughter of Frenchman Edouard Ludovic Baudot de Rouville and Irishwoman Susan Walters. "Ginger" Phillips, as she knew him, may have been forgiven for believing that she was a nun for, under the assumed name of Thérèse

Martin, she had been working tirelessly on behalf of all the British wounded, some 800 of them, at *la Faculté Catholique*. There she had been given the name of "the Irish Sister" by the British wounded, who told her: 'You are not the lady with the lamp but the lady with the tea!'[79] Jim Phillips was to prove to be the first of several RAF airmen whom she would help to return to England.

Assured of a hiding place in Lille, Phillips stocked up with food and wrote to Madame Voglimacci to warn her that he was on his way. On the afternoon of 27 August 1940, having changed into civilian clothing, he persuaded the RAMC orderly who was on guard duty on the gate, and whom he had previously befriended for this very moment, to let him take over. Having already made a key for the gate Phillips let himself out. A hundred metres away a German sentry watched him stroll casually to freedom. At the pre-arranged rendezvous he met a man 'who had a tandem cycle with him, and on this we rode to his place.' Phillips did not at this time stay with Madame Voglimacci, 'as she lived alone and it might have created suspicion.'

After he had been a while in Lille, and various schemes to get evaders and escapers out by boat or aeroplane had not materialised, Phillips thought about stealing a German aircraft, and 'decided to try and get a house overlooking an aerodrome, where I could watch the movements of the air personnel.'[80] During his search for an appropriate house, he met a Lieutenant Carruthers RA, who had apparently escaped from the Germans and who now wanted to share in the venture. Carruthers disappeared, and with him their plan. Sometime around the New Year Maud Baudot de Rouville met Phillips again, at Madame Voglimacci's home. She was surprised to see him still in Lille, believing that he had gone off over a month earlier. She seemed to think that part of the problem was due to the imagination of a certain Captain Murchie (see following chapter) ('Je crois que la cause en était les fantaisies de Murchie…').

Realising that he would have to make his own way out of France, Phillips obtained an identity card from the mayor of Lille and set off for Unoccupied France on 17 January 1941 with 'a young French boy',[81] crossing the frozen River Somme from the Zone Interdite into Occupied France. Very hungry when they reached Paris they discovered 'that meals were only served between 12 noon and 1 p.m. and 6 and 7 p.m. Shops were open, but they had nothing in them for sale.' Nevertheless, they were able to buy some bread before taking the train to Tours. Catching another train to Bléré (Indre-et-Loire), they were enjoying a coffee in a café when 'two gendarmes entered and told the occupants, who obviously intended to cross the line, not to hire guides as one could walk across quite easily at nightfall, taking care to avoid German patrols. There was no fixed time for these patrols, which were changed periodically.'[82] Duly warned, they crossed easily into Unoccupied France, and further trains took them, via Montpelier, to Marseille. There the two men stayed 'a week at the house of the brother of Monsieur Y in a suburb, Ste Marguerite'. Monsieur Y, a plain-clothes detective, obtained ration cards for Phillips while he was there.

Phillips called on Arthur S. Dean, former British vice-consul at Monte Carlo, now resident at the American consulate in Marseille (see this chapter below), and informed him of his plans to cross into Spain. On Dean's advice Phillips also went to the Seamen's Mission, where he met another RAF evader, Sergeant J.R. "Roy" Massey. Pursuing his plans to get to Spain, Phillips took a train to Perpignan, and caught a bus to Maureillas, in the foothills of the Pyrenees. Crossing into Spain, he was arrested by the Guardia Civil (civil guard) and put into the Castillo prison at Figueras for two weeks. Moved to Cervera (seventeen days), Saragossa (nine days), and to the notorious camp at Miranda de Ebro (ten weeks), he was eventually released and flown home by Sunderland on 13 May 1941.

Sergeant Roy Massey was one of the three survivors, but the only evader, of a Beaufort that had been shot down by flak near Vannes (Morbihan), France on 17 December 1940. He reached Marseille by 26 December, the day on which his 'family in Manchester received a telegram from Roy, saying that he was safe and well and giving his address as the American embassy'.[83] Having successfully reached Spain, Massey was almost certainly arrested and probably ended up, as most did, at Miranda de Ebro, his family being informed by the Church of Scotland in a letter dated 28 April 1941 that he was in a 'concentration camp' in Spain. His release must have been obtained soon after this date, for another letter to his family sent from the British Embassy in Madrid was dated 7 May 1941. On 22 May, now in Gibraltar, Massey sent a telegram to his parents 'saying that he expected to be home within a few weeks'.[84] On 23 May 1941 he boarded Catalina flying boat AH560 en route from the Middle East to Mount Batten, Plymouth. Departing Gibraltar at 8.20 p.m. that evening the Catalina was never seen again.[85]

Late on the afternoon of 27 May 1940 twelve Blenheims of 107 Squadron mounted a determined attack on German troop concentrations at St Omer in northern France, though their small bombs and light machine guns did little to halt the Germans, and two aircraft and six airmen failed to return. The only survivors, from Blenheim L9391, were Pilot Officer T.A. Whiting and Wing Commander B.E. Embry DSO and Bar, AFC, the squadron's commanding officer, both of whom were taken prisoner.[86]

For Pilot Officer Whiting captivity was to last for five years, but for Embry it would last only a few hours. Descending into the waiting arms of the German army, his left leg hit by a piece of the shell that had brought about L9391's demise, Embry was quickly captured, and after a short interview with the commander of XIX Army Corps, General Heinz Guderian,[87] was taken to the football pitch at Desvres (Pas-de-Calais), a holding camp for several thousand British prisoners captured at Calais.

One of the many officers at Desvres was Irishman Flight Lieutenant W.P.F. Treacy, who had been patrolling over Dunkirk and Boulogne on the afternoon of 27 May until the engine of his Spitfire was hit by ground fire and seized up. Landing 'outside Gravelines' he was instantly surrounded by flak gunners and taken to the headquarters of the attacking German forces at Oye-Plage (Pas-de-Calais). Driven to Desvres, some 45 kilometres south of Oye, he was locked up for the night in the attic of a house, and joined the other prisoners at the football stadium next day.

Marched away from Desvres in pouring rain, and locked up in Hucqueliers church for the night, Embry and Treacy decided that they would try to escape together at the earliest possible opportunity. On the march on the following day they passed a signpost to the village of Embry (11 kilometres south-east of Hucqueliers). Surely a good omen, Embry suddenly dropped into a ditch expecting Treacy to be right behind him. So surprised at the suddenness of Embry's going, however, Treacy was unable to slip away until a hundred yards or so further on and, as a result, the two failed to regain contact with each other.

Embry's plan had been to get across the River Somme but, after three days and nights, he ran into a German patrol, to whom he declared that he was a Belgian. Confident that he was British, however, the soldiers bashed him with their rifle butts and took him to a farm where he was locked in a room. Worried that the brutal soldiers were planning to finish him off Embry decided to escape. 'I banged on the door and asked for water, and a soldier brought me a drink. As he handed it to me I hit him with all my strength, and as he went down I hit him again.'[88] Rushing out of the farmhouse, he came upon two more Germans and duly 'dealt with them'.[89] There was no one else about, but thinking that he heard a car heading towards the farm he dived into the nearest available cover – a large heap of fairly dry manure – where, not surprisingly, he remained undiscovered.

Leaving his sanctuary after dark, Embry made good progress, but was then caught again. By speaking Urdu to his German captors he was able to convince them that he was Irish. They let him go, even giving him some food for good measure, and though he met more Germans he was not further detained, and reached Paris safely on the morning of 19 June. With 300 francs from Colonel Cecil Shaw, an English officer working at the American consulate, plus a further 200 francs acquired through begging, he was able to purchase a bicycle. Heading southwards, he encountered a French infantry regiment. Treated splendidly by the officers, he was taken to the general commanding the 12th Military Region, at Limoges, 'who could not have been kinder or more helpful.'[90]

Given a free railway pass by the general, who suggested that Embry should make himself scarce, he got to Brive, receiving further friendly treatment from French officers. Leaving for Toulouse on the morrow, he met Lance-Bombardier A.E. Bird RA on the train, 'and we joined forces'. They had been told at Toulouse that there was a British ship leaving shortly from Marseille, but on arrival at that port found 'that the ship had already sailed. It was a bitter blow.'[91] They overcame their disappointment when told that they might find another ship at Port Vendres (whither Clifford had also been directed). There, however, attempting to steal a Customs launch with others of various nationalities, they were spotted by police and arrested, but while being taken away Embry and Bird escaped by flinging themselves over a wall into a garden.

When news arrived that the Italian Armistice Commission were coming to the port the group of hopefuls searched high and low, but in vain, for another boat. The large, multi-national party then split up, and Embry and Bird returned to Perpignan, 'only to find that the Consul had left permanently for Nice.'[92] At the *préfecture*, in the hope of obtaining exit visas, the chief of police said that, though he was unable to help enemies of Germany, he was nevertheless able to give them the address of an Argentinian businessman – a certain Señor Ferrera – and also a written introduction to him. The affable Ferrera, a man of means, booked them into a room at the Hôtel Grand on the Quai Sadi-Carnot overlooking the River Basse. The following evening at the hotel Ferrera told Embry that early next morning, 5 July, they would find a car waiting for them, which would take them to le Perthus on the Spanish border.

After anxiously waiting an hour the car appeared. No words were exchanged with the driver or his colleague in the front seat, not even when the car reached le Perthus. As Embry and Bird got out they saw before them the frontier with its barrier and attendant police, all that stood between them and freedom. Wondering how to cross, they went to the bustling police station which, they were told, was visited three times a week by a Mr Dickens from the British consulate in Barcelona. No sooner had the man given them this information than Embry spotted a tall man with an attaché case alighting from a car. Confident that this must be Mr Dickens, Embry made himself known to the stranger, who did indeed prove to be one and the same.

The battle was far from won, however, for Mr Dickens explained that the two men would need passports to get into and out of Spain. He would see what he could do, but meanwhile Embry and Bird would have to stay at the police station. This they did for a frustrating fortnight until, by chance, they "acquired" a couple of passports. Needing an exit visa from the French they went back to Perpignan to see their friendly chief of police, only to discover that he was no longer in office and that his post was now occupied by a rabid anglophobe. Rapidly returning to le Perthus, and to more hopeless conversations with the equally hopeless Mr Dickens, they were introduced to a Mr Peters, 'who was a Gibraltern by domicile and had known service in the RFC and RAF.'[93] Peters was a very different kettle of fish, and had soon plotted their escape into Spain.

On 23 July there was a vacancy for one of them to go 'by special car'. Despite Bird's protests Embry sent the gunner first, and followed soon after in the boot of Peters' car, both arriving safely in Spain. Bird went to Portugal and was flown home from Lisbon. The wing commander had to settle for the long journey down to Gibraltar, and a longer voyage home by sea aboard the old, 1918-vintage Royal Navy destroyer HMS *Vidette*, from which he disembarked at Plymouth on 2 August.[94]

Having failed to find Embry after both had left the column, Flight Lieutenant Treacy headed south. Still dressed in RAF uniform and wearing his flying kit (but no hat), he travelled by the stars, but 'when the sky clouded over, started to walk in a circle, only discovering this at dawn.'[95] Staying at a farm at Buire-le-Sec (Pas-de-Calais) for three days as the area was swarming with Germans, he was put in touch on 4 June with Gunner Gordon Instone RA, who had been left behind in the confusion at Calais. He, too, had been held at the Desvres football stadium, and had been in hiding at a farm belonging to the Duvier family at Campagne-lès-Hesdin. On 10 June they set off for Camiers with the intention of somehow getting home by boat but, finding the coastal area swarming with Germans, returned to what they believed to be the safety of the Duviers' farm.

Their return, however, coincided with a massive German search for the crew of a crashed RAF aircraft. The Germans had taken twenty French youths as hostages, and were threatening to shoot them if the airmen were not handed over. Under such pressure Treacy decided to leave the Duvier family before it was too late. 'On 13th June, I set off alone, Instone deciding to stay as he thought he was in less danger. After three nights, I reached Crècy where I decided to make for the coast again.'[96] Returning to Buire-le-Sec, Treacy met three soldiers of the Black Watch, and on 3 July the four of them headed for the Baie d'Authie, near Berck-sur-Mer. They had just found a boat when they were stopped by four German soldiers on bicycles. Treacy and his companions pretended to be Belgian refugees, and were getting away with it until one of the Germans found a photograph with "Aldershot" stamped on the back.

At St Pol they were 'put into the exhibition grounds with a number of British troops from Camiers.' Treacy, though, had no difficulty finding a hole in the corrugated-iron wall of their "prison" and escaped for the second time. After several days he returned to the Baie d'Authie and bought a boat for 40 francs from a farmer, who helped him to launch it. With a compass and enough water to last for five days, Treacy paddled off towards the open sea during the night of 13/14 July. Warned that there were German sentries on the bridges over the river, he had taken the precaution of covering himself and the boat with hay, and had strewn yet more on the water around the boat to increase the deception. His first test came when he drifted under a bridge with two German sentries on it. They saw nothing, but further on the boat grounded. Treacy heard another sentry cock his rifle but, again, nothing more.

Now, like the tide, his luck was running out. He had had such difficulty negotiating the shallows that, instead of reaching the sea two hours before dawn as hoped, it was half an hour after sunrise when he got there. With no choice but to keep going, he was about a mile out from Berck-sur-Mer when he heard machine-gun fire. Splashes all around him indicated clearly enough that he was the target, and though two machine-gun batteries in the dunes below Berck fired at him for almost half an hour, he was slowly creeping out of range and they failed to hit him. The gunners realised this, and soon the one-sided contest neared its end as four heavier guns opened up. By now two miles or so off shore the Germans fired single shots at him for another half an hour, all falling fifty to 100 yards short, until eventually a splinter holed the boat above the water line.

The German gunners, expecting Treacy to turn around and row back towards the shore, ceased firing for five minutes, but when he did not do so they opened up a more rapid fire for a further ten minutes. Then a mist descended. At around midday, however, now some fifteen kilometres off le Touquet, Treacy was spotted by two German aircraft. The rear gunner of one of them signalled to him to return to shore, and fired into the sea to encourage him. Disregarding the Germans' invitation Treacy pressed on, but half an hour later a seaplane landed, and he was hauled off to Boulogne.

Others, however, succeeded where Treacy had failed. Second Lieutenant W.H. Dothie's voyage is worth a chapter in its own right. He was commanding a troop of six searchlights of the 1st Searchlight Battery, 1st Searchlight Regiment, RA, to the east of Calais when the German tanks arrived. In the chaos that followed he was captured on 27 May 1940. On the long, straight road from Bapaume to Cambrai, the column of straggling prisoners of war reached the village of Boursies. Seizing the moment Dothie ran down an alleyway between two houses, just as he had seen two RAF officers do some way back. He, too, was not spotted by the guards, and spent the next two weeks in the Boursies area. With only three French families left in Boursies, he had little difficulty finding shelter and food.

Once he had made up his mind to get a boat back to England, he prepared the bicycle that he had found, filled a pack with food and, on 14 June, rode off to he knew not where, but anywhere rather than Calais and Dieppe. There, he reasoned, there would probably be no boats. 'I decided to head for Brittany as from that direction I could continue either south to the Midi or turn west into Brittany according to the state of affairs in the country encountered on the way.'[97] Despite being stopped along the way by a German officer and ordered to bury a long-dead pig, he reached Brittany without any problems. At St Brieuc, on the north Breton coast, he noted that the town was crammed with refugees but, 'as it was a Sunday and everybody was out in the streets in their Sunday best,' he looked rather out of place in his 'tramp rig-out'. Encouraged by the fishing boats that he saw in the harbour, though, he walked up the coast to Binic. As hoped he discovered yet more boats.

Looting a few vital items, and with several carefully hoarded bottles of water, he made a reconnaissance of the harbour, noting a suitable boat for the crossing. On 28 June, an hour or so before midnight, he made his way 'on to the jetty where there were no houses and just got into the boat.' Laying a course for Jersey, it took him three days to get there, and out of St Helier he met two fishermen who told him that the Germans had occupied the island one day earlier. On the evening of the fifth day a good wind and favourable tides took him between the island of Alderney and Cap de la Hague. During the night he seemed to be making good progress, but daylight found him back at Alderney, a victim of le Raz de Blanchard, the strong current that runs past the Cap de la Hague. Too exhausted to do more, he returned to the French coast and beached in the Anse St Martin (St Martin's Bay). Abandoning the boat he made his way inland.

After a promise by a man from Cherbourg that he could find a boat for Dothie had turned to dust, Dothie began to ask the local fishermen for help. One of them found him two boats, one a small sailing boat, the other a motor boat. Having taken the sailing boat for a test-run and found it wanting (too small), he set off in the motor boat fuelled by three 2-litre cans of stolen petrol. 'On 31st July, I got away successfully at about 2 a.m. The sky was well overcast and in the morning when I was well out to sea, but could distinguish land, two German Army Cooperation (Lysander type) [aircraft] flew low over me and made off back in the direction of France.'[98] Fearing the worst, he carried on, but nothing happened, and the next aircraft he saw were two Blenheims flying north at low altitude. Then, late on the afternoon of 1 August, he saw The Needles on the Isle of Wight. Expecting to run out of petrol at any moment, he rigged a sail from a piece of sacking. Just in time, for soon after dark the fuel did run out, but a good south-easterly wind pushed him northwards. Sighting a patrol vessel, the *Aquamarine*, in the morning he signalled an SOS and was picked up at around 11 a.m.[99] For his exemplary evasion Dothie received the MC.

Commander R.F. Elkins RN and Captain L.R. Hulls MC, Gordon Highlanders, both captured in the fighting in France on 11 June 1940, also triumphed in the face of adversity. Managing to escape easily enough from the Germans' makeshift prisoner-of-war camp on 15 June 1940, they made their way to the coast to the north of Caen. With considerable help from a Professor Mercier of a French government research laboratory at Luc-sur-Mer who was only too pleased to help, they were able to get away from nearby Lion-sur-Mer on the night of 22/23 June in one of his sailing boats, an 18-footer with a mainsail, jib and mizzen, and an auxiliary engine. Setting off in very bad conditions – the tide was against them, as was the wind which was blowing hard – they got clear of the land without being spotted. Neither was a sailor, but they managed to rig the sails, and also start the engine, which worked intermittently throughout the crossing and was of some help. On the morning of 25 June, they sighted land, which also proved to be the Isle of Wight, but then the wind turned against them and they struggled to reach the shore. 'We had anticipated being picked up by some steamer in the Channel, but met no boat of any description. We finally sailed right into Hayling Island and ran the boat ashore there.'[100]

Following his capture, meanwhile, Flight Lieutenant Treacy was taken to Boulogne, and then to le Touquet for questioning, having been informed that he would be treated as a spy. He spent the night in the town prison with two German airmen who had been given ten days for sleeping on duty. After several further moves he found himself with three hundred wounded British soldiers at Lokeren, Belgium, halfway between Ghent and Antwerp. Their prison was poorly, though heavily, guarded, and on the night of 30/31 July Treacy had no difficulty in breaking out 'through a hole in the glass roof'. Climbing over the surrounding wall and into a convent garden, he changed into civilian clothes and made his way over the border to Genech in France, a dozen kilometres south-east of Lille. During the week that he was there he, too, heard of a scheme for returning British personnel to England by air, and moved to Bouvines, closer to Lille, from where he could see German Heinkel 111 bombers operating from Seclin airfield: 'I frequently saw them going off towards England, but never saw more than half of them come back.'[101]

During his eight weeks at Bouvines, Treacy 'heard of 561185 Sgt. Phillips of 54 Sqdn, but failed to get in touch with him.' He also heard that the air scheme had broken down, and therefore set off for the south of France on 16 October, crossing into Unoccupied France to the east of Poitiers 'on the night of the 17th, between St Julien-l'Ars and St Martin-le-Rivière. There was no difficulty as the frontier guard was a regiment just back from Norway who were very frightened and would not go into the village but lived in the woods.'[102] Avoiding internment by the French at Châteauroux, Treacy carried on to Limoges and Vichy, where the American embassy gave him 300 francs, enough to get him to Marseille.

Not to be confused with 561185 Sergeant J.W.B. Phillips, 545177 Leading Aircraftman D.L. Phillips, was also shot down during the battle for France. On the morning of 13 June 1940 Donald Phillips was manning the gun aboard a Fairey Battle when it was attacked by several Me109s. He shot down one of them but not before the Battle's fuel tanks had been pierced and set on fire. Pilot Officer A.R. Gulley tried to land the burning aircraft, but was killed when it bounced heavily into the next field. Phillips and the third crewman, Sergeant H. Berry, were both knocked unconscious and suffered burns to the face and hands. Coming round, they managed to stagger to a dressing station in a nearby château for attention, but shortly afterwards were captured by a German patrol and taken to a dressing station at another château at Vernon. 'Here we spent seven miserable days on straw in an outhouse without any attention, accompanied by several French prisoners of war, of whom two died during this period.'[103]

On 20 June Sergeant Berry was taken to the general hospital at Rouen, run by captured RAMC staff under German supervision, where he remained for three months. After three weeks at a hospital in Amiens Donald Phillips was taken by lorry with three army officers to a prisoner-of-war camp at Doullens, for a further four weeks. 'The treatment at the hospital was good and the food adequate but the treatment at Doullens was not good. We had to work and spent most of the time transporting flour in sacks from goods trains to storage houses and two or three times we had to transport heavy bombs (mostly 500 kilo bombs).'[104] Phillips had had enough of this by the evening of 28 July, when he and Private J. Witton KORR tied their homemade rope to a tree and climbed over a sixty-foot, unguarded wall. Halfway down the rope broke, and the two men dropped the last thirty feet into muddy ground.[105]

Well equipped and well prepared for their escape, they set off for Spain. Reaching Lyon after several days and finding no one to help them at the American consulate at 6, Place St Ferréol, they reported to the French military authorities, who promptly put them in prison. After two days they were sent under escort by train to Valence, where they spent a further four days in a military barracks. Their next prison was the *Camp des Étrangers* at Loriol-sur-Drôme (Drôme).[106]

Phillips and Witton were then taken by gendarmes to the Caserne Bizanet (barracks) at Grenoble, and told that they would be there for the duration. Though forced to work on the roads during the day, they were free to go into Grenoble after 6 p.m., and on one of their forays into town made contact with a Frenchman who, some nine days after their arrival at the Grenoble barracks, took them in his lorry to Lyon. With them went Captain W.G. Stuart-Menteith, 2/6th Queen's Royal Regiment, captured with the 51st (Highland) Division at St Valéry-en-Caux on 12 June but who had escaped from a prisoner-of-war column eight days later.

Heading for Switzerland, when he was at Collonges-sous-Salève (Ain), only a few kilometres from the Swiss border, Stuart-Menteith got in touch with his parents-in-law in Switzerland, and with the British Consul at Geneva, who advised him to remain at Collonges pending enquiries. Before any help could arrive from the Swiss side of the border, though, he 'was interviewed by an officer of the French *Garde Mobile* and was then removed to Grenoble, where all British soldiers in the area were to be concentrated. Here I enjoyed the *Liberté Surveillée*. I lived in the town at my own expense, reported everyday to the HQ of the *Garde Mobile*… I obtained leave to visit the USA Consul at Lyons and drew 1600 francs from him. I also got in touch with two British soldiers [*sic*], Sgt. D. Phillips, RAF, and Cpl. J. Witton.'[107]

From Lyon the three men took the train to Perpignan. On 18 September, after walking for almost forty-eight hours, they set off in the middle of the night from l'Albère, five kilometres east of le Perthus, to cross the border into Spain, but suddenly ran into a French gendarme, who opened fire. Stuart-Menteith, who was some way behind the other two, dashed into a vineyard while Phillips and Witton fled into a wood. Wandering about in the mountains for two days without food and without seeing Stuart-Menteith again, Phillips and Witton called at a farmhouse. Soon after leaving the farm, having been given both food and shelter, they were captured by Spanish police and spent several weeks in various prisons until sent to Gibraltar in a large group, some fifty strong, sometime in November 1940.

Stuart-Menteith also managed to return to England, having walked most of the way to Barcelona, only the last 8 kilometres being covered by train. He was there on 30 September, and then sent to Madrid on a Portuguese visa, leaving in an ambulance lorry for Gibraltar. At Seville, when the British consul told him that there were two British boats in port, he made his way aboard the SS *Ossian*[108] that night, and reached Gibraltar on 5 October. Four days later the *Ossian* sailed for Liverpool, where it finally docked on 29 October.[109]

When information was received at AASF HQ that an estimated 500 German tanks were said to be refuelling in the Forêt du Gault, south-east of Montmirail, 226 Squadron was one of those ordered to deal with them. It was at around 7 o'clock on the evening of 13 June 1940 when half a dozen Fairey Battles took off to do what they could to halt the Germans' armoured thrust. Flight Lieutenant F.O. Barrett (pilot), Sergeant H. Asker (observer) and Leading Aircraftman P. Kirk (gunner) were some twenty-five kilometres short of the target in their Battle when they came under heavy anti-aircraft fire. Then, with fifteen kilometres still to go, two Me109s attacked, one of them closing to within fifty metres. Though Barrett received a severe flesh wound in his right arm from a cannon shell, which also demolished his instrument panel, he bravely pressed on to the target, and bombed it. Asker and Kirk managed to shoot down one of the Me109s but the other 'continued attack at 800 yards range. Now flying very low (twenty feet) passed over village in Coulommiers area. Heavy firing from ground. Rudder controls shot away, radiator smashed, petrol and oil tanks hit a number of times.'[110] Barrett continued flying the badly damaged Battle until its engine stopped, and he made a wheels-up landing in a field.[111]

Extraordinarily, Asker and Kirk were unhurt, and the three crew ran away from the wrecked aircraft until they met some French infantry, who dressed Barrett's wounds and took him to a hospital in Provins. Here he was operated upon, but at 1 a.m. on 14 June the hospital had to be evacuated. The sick and wounded, plus the uninjured Asker and Kirk, were taken away in a convoy of seven ambulances with instructions to make for Auxerre, to the north-east. After a Dutch driver of one of the ambulances had suggested taking a quiet road to Sézanne they ran into fifty or sixty motorised German troops near Villenauxe-la-Grande. Asker and Kirk, quickly removing their RAF tunics, 'covered themselves with bandages and lay moaning. Germans looked in ambulances. No search.' Later that morning the convoy moved off, escorted by a lorry full of armed German troops bringing up the rear. Barrett and crew were in an ambulance driven by the redoubtable Ursula Lloyd Bennett and Penelope Otto.

Near Troyes, when a counter-attack was expected, the convoy returned to Villenauxe-la-Grande: 'Instructed to drive 200 yards up road and turn left. Driver Otto turned right instead and made off. Did not see escort again; her ambulance was followed by one driver Marjorie Juta.'[112] Driving through enemy territory – they saw many Germans, including fifty tanks in one field – the two ambulances managed to reach Provins again, where Barrett received further attention to his arm. The three intrepid ladies meanwhile returned to their HQ. Barrett reported that the two in his ambulance 'particularly Penelope Otto behaved extremely well throughout.'[113] When the doctors had finished with Barrett, he and his crew were put aboard an American ambulance driven 'by Miss Sheila Angus of Sloane Avenue, [London] S.W.3. and Miss Nancy Heard c/o Grindley & Co., 54 Parliament Street', who took them to their squadron's airfield at Sougé-sur-Braye.[114]

Arriving there at 3 a.m. on 15 June it was to find that 226 Squadron were already evacuating. Asker and Kirk rejoined their squadron, but their pilot continued in the ambulance until catching up with the squadron convoy 'when he was joined by F/O Summers who had injured his hand.' The ambulance made its way to La Baule hospital, where Barrett and Summers spent the night, before leaving for Southampton on 16 June. Although bombed on the way home, no damage was done to the ship or to its occupants, and Barrett recovered at the Surrey County Hospital, Guildford.

Harold Albert Asker's luck would see him safely through the war with both the DFM and the DFC. Commissioned at the end of 1941 his DFC was gazetted on 18 September 1942 in a joint citation with two others of the crew of Boston AL278, Squadron Leader J.S. Kennedy DFC and Flying Officer G.A. Casey RCAF. Their task, and that of other Bostons of their squadron, 226, had been to drop smoke bombs on a gun battery as the landing craft and launches closed in on Dieppe during Combined Operations' Operation Jubilee.[115] 'They made their run-in despite heavy AA fire, successfully laying their smoke which effectively covered an area one to one and a half miles to seaward.'[116]

Boston AL278 did not escape unscathed, nor did Casey who was hit in both thighs, while his fellow gunner, Flight Lieutenant O.G.E. McWilliams, was critically injured by a cannon shell. AL278 was repeatedly hit, and with one of its two engines out of action, Squadron Leader Kennedy flew back to Shoreham, Sussex, where he made a crash-landing. Flying Officer Asker DFC, DFM ended the war as a flight lieutenant. All in all a remarkable achievement.

On the evening of 14 June 1940, 103 Squadron despatched four of its Fairey Battles to bomb German troop concentrations in a forest south-west of Evreux (Eure). Three got away promptly, but R3916, whose engine had proved difficult to start, did not take off until shortly before 7 p.m.. Flying Officer R. Hawkins and his rear gunner, Pilot Officer F. Hugill (the only other man aboard) were alone in the hostile sky until eleven Me109s suddenly appeared. With plenty to choose from in what would always be a one-sided contest Hugill shot down one of the fighters near the target, and Hawkins, using the Battle's front gun, 'caused heavy smoke from one other aircraft'. Numbers told, however, and having been thoroughly disposed of by the rest of the enemy Hawkins and Hugill made successful parachute landings.

Frank Hugill was captured and sent to Germany for the duration of the war,[117] but Ronald Hawkins walked south 'by the stars for two nights, after which shortage of food and water eventually led to my capture on the 16th June.'[118] Very well treated by his captors he 'was taken to a temporary German prison in a disused French barracks at Vernon.' Two days later he was transferred to another makeshift prison camp, south-west of Evreux, but managed to escape 'after the second night by dodging sentries and swimming a river which bordered the prison camp.' After four or five days he reached the Channel coast at Trouville-sur-Mer (Calvados). Unable to find a boat capable of getting him back to England, he crossed the mouth of the River Seine by a small boat. Appreciating that it was too small to cross the Channel, he searched the coast between Le Havre and le Tréport (Seine-Maritime) for some appropriate vessel.[119]

Finding nothing suitable, he abandoned the idea of boating to England and, inspired by the good people of Normandy, who gave him much help and a bicycle, pedalled to Carteret (Manche), 'this being the nearest point on the French coast to Jersey'.[120] Here he arrived on 30 June. In happier days one could get a steamer to Jersey but, still determined to reach British soil, all Hawkins could find was a canvas canoe, and paddled over to Jersey. As luck would have it, the Germans had beaten him to the island by only a matter of hours, and so 'I returned to France, where I received hospitality at a farm.'[121] Finally giving up on his plan of getting a boat back to Britain he set off on 7 July for Vichy 'with a view to obtaining papers'. Once in Vichy, four days later, 'little help seemed forthcoming from the American Consulate',[122] but he did meet four British Army officers – Major W.C.W. Potts and Captain C.R.I. Besley, both 7th Royal Northumberland Fusiliers; and Captain C.D. Waters and Second Lieutenant J.D. Lennon, both RE. Inviting him to share their food, they took him to the camp where they were being interned.

Hawkins 'left the camp quickly' when he heard that the officer in charge of the camp was making enquiries about him. Reaching Marseille on 16 July he contacted Dodds and Dean at 'the unofficial British Consulate' and asked them for 1,000 francs (the sum required for a visa for Spain), but received only 340 francs and identity papers. Nevertheless, he approached several ships' captains in the harbour who, although friendly, could give him no sailing date. He did take note, though, of the German agents on board the ships that were preparing to sail.[123]

Before his papers had been prepared, Hawkins 'slept in fields or on the beach, then in a little lodging house' but, when he heard that there was accommodation at the Seamen's Mission in Marseille, he moved there on 23 July, to be greeted by the four army officers whom he had earlier met at Vichy. Potts and Besley, having arrived in Marseille on 13 July, spent their first night in a hotel before going to the mission next day, 'where the caretaker gave us the address of the British Consul.' When Waters and Lennon learnt that they were to be moved to a concentration camp further south of Vichy, they caught the next train to Marseille, on 19 July. Their escape from Vichy had not been difficult, as Captain Waters noted: 'There was no close supervision at Vichy and our opinion was that the French were glad to get rid of us because they did not know what to do with us.'[124]

The few British evaders and escapers who had arrived in Marseille by July 1940 – no more than twenty-nine officers and men – found the British consulate closed. As a reprisal for the attack by the

Royal Navy on French ships at Mers-el-Kebir on 3 July[125] the Vichy government had closed all British consular offices in Unoccupied France. Callers at the British consulate were therefore directed to the USA consulate (the USA being the nominated protecting power for British and Dominion interests in accordance with the Geneva Convention) at 6, rue St Ferréol. Here Mr Abbott, the initial US consul-general, and his successor, John P. Hurley (replaced as consul-general by Felix Cole in the autumn of 1940), had formed within the US consulate a British Interests section under Major Hugh Dodds and his deputy, Arthur S. Dean.[126] They were assisted by the former vice-consul in Paris, Geoffrey Spinney, by the former pro-consul in Marseille, Mr Wilmot, and by the chairman of the local British Chamber of Commerce, Mr Tilley.

Arthur Dean, a controversial but pivotal figure in the welfare of soldiers arriving from the north in the summer of 1940, wrote that 'all British soldiers who arrive in Marseille report to me. I listen to their stories and advise them what to do – (which is to go to the Fort [St Jean]).' What to do with the new arrivals was a delicate problem for Dean and for the diplomatic staff and, though he knew full well that 'many officers and men who have arrived here have managed in various ways to leave the country,' he himself took no part in their leaving: 'I have always made it clear that while this office is interested in the welfare of members of His Majesty's Forces, it can in no way whatsoever enter into or assist them to leave the country, which is contrary to the terms of the Armistice and would be a breach of the trust which the American Government place in British subjects employed by them.'[127]

As the American consul in Marseille was also unwilling to help in any way, shape, or form, and "surrendering" to the French at Fort St Jean was not a favoured option, evaders and escapers went to the Seamen's Mission at 36, rue de Forbin, a large, two-storey, building that could sleep up to a hundred men at a pinch. A female caretaker had been hired to look after the place until such time as a full-time manager could be appointed and permission had been received from London to re-open the premises. As it happened, the ideal candidate for the job was already in Marseille.

The Reverend Donald C. Caskie, resident minister since 1935 at the Scots Kirk in rue Bayard, Paris, had deemed it wise, in view of his well-known anti-Nazi feelings, to leave the French capital on 11 June 1940, and had arrived in Marseille a few weeks later. On 12 July, discovering that Cable and Wireless Ltd were still in business there, he sent a cablegram to his "employers", the Church of Scotland in Edinburgh, informing them that he was stranded in Marseille and would appreciate an allowance of £20.[128] Calling on Arthur Dean at the American consulate, he was offered the post of manager at the British Seamen's Mission. Having seen the weary and wounded British soldiers wandering about in the city he was delighted to accept, subject to the approval of the Church of Scotland. Making his way over to the dirty, run-down building at 36, rue de Forbin[129] on 16 July, he found three sailors standing around in the street: 'I invited them inside and we immediately set to work to get the place into order. Before I retired that night I prepared a notice. The seamen helped to pin it over the door.' The notice read: 'Now open to British civilians and seamen ONLY.'[130]

Renamed the British and American Seamen's Mission, word of what was going on there slowly but surely spread and, without Caskie having to ask for them, parcels of food and civilian clothing would appear on the doorstep overnight. And, despite his outwardly defeatist advice to evaders and escapers, Arthur Dean did what he could to help by raising funds from the richer members of the south coast community, as he later reported: 'Welfare work which began in a small way with the arrival of a handful of British soldiers from the north, has now reached considerable proportions, the number of officers and men at present at the Fort St. Jean being over two hundred. At the beginning I wrote to several friends in Monte Carlo, Nice and Cannes, asking them to send comforts, and if possible money for extra food, for these men. The response has been so generous that – even with the rapidly increasing number of men – the gifts received have been sufficient to allow something to each man. Many packages of clothing, socks, shirts, blankets, etc., also an Ambulance full of blankets, etc. from Cannes, have been received, together with sums of money totalling to date Frs 35,000.'[131]

The Vichy police in Marseille, also well aware of what was going on at the Seamen's Mission, advised Caskie that only civilians should be sheltered there. The point was not lost on Caskie, who thereafter did his best to ensure that any serviceman entering the premises changed into civilian clothes as soon as possible. Incriminating uniforms were furtively dumped into the harbour. Nevertheless, on 25 July 1940 a French detective appeared at the mission at breakfast time and announced that all officers and men were to be interned at Fort St Jean. This order, he added, was endorsed by the British consulate. Caskie, already short of funds and finding it difficult to cater for so many hungry men, was not averse to their going.

Major Potts and Captain Besley were put in charge of the officers and men by the French authorities, and escorted to Fort St Jean with no immediate prospect of escaping. Being the first two British officers to be interned there, they found themselves in the Foreign Legion officers' mess, where they were well treated by three pro-British Russian officers. The few other ranks – eighteen of them as at 31 July – were not so well cared for, but nevertheless received three meals a day and were, with funds made available by Donald Caskie, able to purchase wine, beer and cigarettes from the fort's canteen.

Life was tolerable for interned British service personnel in Marseille, largely due to an order from General Huntziger issued to the 15th Military Region on 25 July authorising a regime of *liberté surveillée*.[132] In practice, British personnel were held in custody during the day but were free to go into town between 7.30 p.m. and 10 p.m. 'provided they first gave an undertaking not to try to get away.'[133]

Captain Besley, quick to avail himself of this parole system, went to see Major Dodds at the American consulate: 'With considerable difficulty, I got him to agree to making an allowance of £1 a month for O.R.s and £5 a month for officers. I tried to discuss with him how we should escape and how he could assist us, but he would have nothing to do with it, stating that he might jeopardise his own position and thereby compromise the British civilians in Marseille.'[134] Dodds even asked him why anyone should want to escape, as they were as safe in Marseille as anywhere else. Besley's thoughts of Major Dodds are not recorded, but he did note that when a sergeant asked for a special allowance for clothing Dodds replied that, had he not thrown away his battle dress in the first place, he would not be in need of new clothes now! Unhappy at the lack of help from the British officials, Besley 'wrote to the British Embassy in Madrid, enclosing a list of the soldiers interned and asking for instructions. I received no reply, but I know the letter was received as an enclosure was sent to England.'

As a result of Captain Besley's badgering of Major Dodds the War Office in London arranged for funds to be transferred to the American consulate in Marseille which, with effect from July 1940, would enable officers to be paid a sum of £5 per month,[135] warrant officers £3, sergeants £2, corporals £1.10.0 (£1.50) and privates £1, to be paid weekly. Additionally, a one-off clothing grant of £2 per man was made. In December 1940, however, the monthly allowance was increased by £1 across the board. Feeding the "civilians" at the Seamen's Mission was also costly, and it was agreed that for each man there Caskie would be paid, at an exchange rate of 173 francs to the pound sterling, the equivalent of £4.5.0 (£4.25) per man per month – £3.5.0 (£3.25) for his board, and £1 for the man himself.

Determined to escape himself, Captain Besley tried several fanciful schemes to leave France by ship in August and September 1940, but when these came to nought he made his way overland to Spain during the first week of October, and was arrested (see Chapter 3).

Not only did Caskie act as paymaster to most British servicemen arriving at the Seamen's Mission but, with a certain amount of bribery of French police and postal workers, he was also able to send next-of-kin telegrams to the Church of Scotland in Edinburgh for onward transmission to the appropriate families. One of the first such telegrams, sent on 10 August to the parents of Sergeant R.W. Lonsdale, who had reached Marseille in the middle of October, was the first news that they had had of their son following his disappearance on 10 July 1940.

Although the general secretary of the church in Edinburgh had noted the receipt of seventy-three telegrams by the end of 1940, Caskie himself had recorded the names of three hundred and thirty-one men over that same period – twenty-seven by the end of August, a further thirty-five by the end of September, sixty-six more in October, one hundred and fifty-one in November and fifty-two in December 1940. Further news of Caskie's generosity reached official ears in January 1941, when Lieutenant C.D. Hunter, Cameron Highlanders, returned to Britain: 'It was entirely due to him that the relatives of British soldiers were informed of their arrival in Marseille. It was his own money that was used to send the telegrams to England, advising relatives.'[136]

Hawkins, Waters, Lennon and Sous-officier Mayoux (a French Liaison Officer attached to the RAF at Coulommiers), heeding the words of the French detective on 25 July, wasted no time and that evening caught a train to Perpignan 'because that was the only means of getting out of the town without having our papers checked.' Having reached Cerbère, a whisker away from the Spanish border, Hawkins and Waters on the following day prudently 'made a reconnaissance of the frontier posts in the direction of Port Bou,' itself only metres over the border into Spain. They also made a mental note of a small boat in a bay a little over a kilometre north of Cerbère. Having discovered 'that it would be impossible to pass anywhere near the frontier posts,' they rejoined the rest of the party. It was agreed that instead of going overland they would go by sea in the boat that they had spotted earlier.

Returning to the bay they found that they were too late. The boat had gone. Spending the night near the bay, therefore, they attempted to cross the Pyrenees in the morning but lost their way, and found themselves once more back at Cerbère. But not before they had been stopped by a French gendarme who demanded to see their papers. They were surprised and much relieved, however, when the policeman not only raised no objection to them being where they were but also pointed out 'the proper route to take across the mountains. The route we took lay over the foothills some miles west of the railway. The going across the mountains was comparatively hard and it took us until 6 o'clock the next morning to reach the low ground which indicated that we had arrived in Spain.'[137] Confirmation that they were indeed in Spain came as they passed 'what appeared to be an innocent looking farm.' Innocent it was not, for the "farmhands" turned out to be Spanish soldiers, who arrested the group and handed them over to the Guardia Civil.

At Figueras, where they were handed over to the frontier authorities, they demanded to see the consular official who, it was understood, lived in the area. Their wish was granted, and on 30 July consular official Mr Rapley obtained their temporary release, arranging for them to stay at a small hotel. Also brought to the hotel were two Royal Engineers, Captain P.P. Raikes and Lieutenant H.S.M. Hogg, who had crossed the Pyrenees by bicycle from Osséja on 5 August. Having been told that this was one of the easiest crossings they had covered 40 kilometres along the main road to Ribas before they were stopped by carabineros at Planolas, and were well treated. Next day they had to walk the half dozen kilometres to Ribas for questioning by the Guardia Civil, before being sent by train to Ripoll, where they were again questioned and searched by the military authorities and by the police. 'On each occasion we were asked exactly the same questions and gave the same story which substantially corresponded with the truth. We spent the night in a military prison with twelve captured Reds. Conditions were disgusting.'[138]

Moved on the following day to Figueras they were locked up in the *Prisión Cellular*, where they demanded that the British consul at Barcelona should be informed of their presence. This was done, and the vice-consul was able to visit them, bringing with him money and food. Treated no differently to the other Spanish prisoners, however, conditions in the prison were, again, 'very bad'. They were finally released on 22 August after representations had been made by the other British officers to the Spanish military authorities. A letter was then sent to the British Ambassador at Madrid and another to the British Consul at Barcelona, but no reply was received from either the embassy or the consulate.

On 22 August 1940 the six officers were taken by train to Gerona and detained in another hotel. They wrote yet again to the British Embassy, this time to the military attaché, Brigadier W.W.T. Torr DSO, MC,[139] who telephoned an encouraging reply: 'Don't do anything rash. We are working like hell to get you out.' His added hopes that they would be out in a week were not realised, and it was not until 19 September that they left Gerona by train for Barcelona. Two days later they were in Madrid and two days after that in Gibraltar.

Flying Officer Ronald Hawkins's great fortune continued when he was invited to join the mess of Gibraltar's resident 202 Squadron,[140] his army companions joining that of the RAMC. It was a fortnight before Hawkins left Gibraltar by Sunderland flying boat on 7/8 October 1940.[141] Hogg, Lennon and Waters returned by ship on 9 October, Lennon to Liverpool on 29 October, and Hogg and Waters to the raw pleasures of Barrow-in-Furness on 27 October. Major Potts escaped by boat to Casablanca and, together with twelve other ranks and four civilians, sailed from that port on 22 November aboard the Portuguese trawler *Mar Azul*, returning to Great Britain during December 1940.[142] As for Raikes, he was destined never to leave Gibraltar (see Chapter 3).

The day after the flying careers of Donald Phillips and Flight Lieutenant Barrett had come to an abrupt, if temporary, halt, so too did that of Leading Aircraftman E. G. Hillyard. The Fairey Battle in which he was flying on 15 June 1940 was forced down near Chartres by three Me109s. Badly wounded in the right arm by splinters, his two fellow crewmen – Pilot Officer Benjamin and Sergeant Armstrong – put him in a French ambulance, which took him to a hospital in Le Mans.[143] After three days at Le Mans he was evacuated to another hospital at Angers, where his right arm was immediately amputated. On this same day, 18 June, the Germans occupied Angers. Though not interfering with the running of the hospital for some reason they wrecked an adjoining chapel.

Every Sunday two governesses employed by local French families visited Hillyard. Irishwoman Miss O'Shaughnessy and Scotswoman Miss "S" both agreed to help him escape. It was not, however, until the beginning of October that he was allowed out on parole into Angers, for which he was provided with a pass 'duly stamped with the date of leave'. Later that month, when informed by one of the German medical staff that he was well enough to be transferred to a prisoner-of-war camp in Germany, he decided that it was time to leave. Altering the date on the pass, thereby in his mind not technically breaking his parole, he walked out of the hospital in civilian clothes on 21 October. Meeting Miss O'Shaughnessy at a pre-arranged rendezvous they took a bus to Miss S's house, but after two nights he moved to the home of Miss O'Shaughnessy's employers, on the Boulevard de

Palais de Justice.[144] Hillyard remained in the attic for a week, the owners of the house being totally unaware of their lodger. On 31 October, with a Frenchman whose name he could not remember, he departed by the 7.30 train 'to Tours, hoping to catch the Bordeaux express'.

As the AASF retreated in June 1940, so it lost its forward airfields, and what was left of three squadrons – Nos. 12, 103 and 226 – found temporary accommodation at Sougé-sur-Braye, forty kilometres north of Tours. On the morning of 15 June 1940 the squadrons were ordered back to England, but at noon the Luftwaffe appeared: 'Several Battles were destroyed and a shelter trench was hit and blown in.' Sergeant A.N. Dowling was killed 'and eight other casualties were inflicted on men of 12 and 226 Squadrons'[145] who were in Sougé preparing for the evacuation when the German bombs fell. Among them were Sergeant V.T. McFarlane, a regular of six years' service, who had been attached to 12 Squadron groundcrew at Sougé airfield and who was wounded in the back by a bomb splinter; Sergeant G. Roskell, hit in the fore-arm also by a bomb splinter; and Leading Aircraftman Taylor, whose right leg was blown off. The wounded were taken by ambulance to Sougé hospital, where Roskell's forearm was amputated that day. In the hospital they met a Canadian soldier, Private G. Thompson, 1st Canadian Infantry Brigade HQ, 1st Canadian Division, who was suffering from 'internal trouble'.

Two days later, with the Germans rapidly approaching, the injured were 'taken to the French Military Hospital at Sablé-sur-Sarthe, 40 kilometres S.E. of Laval.'[146] McFarlane, Roskell and Thompson decided to leave shortly afterwards, and got a lift with a French convoy to Angers. They then walked south for some fifteen kilometres, hoping to catch a boat from St Nazaire, but were picked up by another French ambulance. On 17 June they 'were admitted to a large French Military hospital in the outskirts of Nantes',[147] where an operation was performed on McFarlane on 22 June.

A few days later the Germans occupied the town and took over the hospital, but not before the three men and Driver L. Farnsworth RASC had been removed to a convalescent home in a convent in the centre of the town. It was not long, however, before the Germans, having been notified of their presence, ordered them not to leave the building. They were still in the convalescent home in September, when a French dental technician, "Monsieur B", offered to get them out. On the night of 30 September/1 October 1940 the four men escaped 'with the assistance of a young Frenchman who used to visit us. We got out of the home by climbing a wall and dropping into a cul-de-sac, whence our French friend took us to a house.'[148] They were there for a week, during which time Monsieur B procured civilian clothes and collected about 5,000 francs for them from his friends. They left with Monsieur B and two other Frenchmen and a Frenchwoman by train for Angoulême, and from there were taken into Unoccupied France on 8 October. They got as far as Perpignan, intending to cross the Pyrenees into Spain, but had insufficient cash with which to pay a guide and to bribe the necessary officials. They therefore decided to make for Marseille 'where we approached Mr Fullerton, the American Consul. On his advice we three Air Force personnel went to 36 rue de Forbin, where the Rev. Caskie looked after us during our stay in Marseille.'[149]

After two days at the mission French police took them to Fort St Jean, Marseille. Roskell was brought before a Mixed Medical Commission at the Michel Lévy hospital on 14 December and passed fit for repatriation, and both he and Thompson were back in Britain on 23 February 1941.

Sergeant McFarlane, moved to the prison at St Hippolyte-du-Fort,[150] escaped on 1 March 1941, and arrived back in Britain on 14 June 1941.

Some of the servicemen arriving at the Seamen's Mission were in need of medical attention, and Caskie was advised through his contacts at the American consulate to see sixty-four-year-old Dr Georges Rodocanachi. Caskie confided to him the perhaps obvious truth that not all those at the Seamen's Mission were civilians, but Dr Rodocanachi proved to be the sort of man not to worry about such trifling matters. One of the doctors of the Mixed Medical Commission at the Michel Lévy hospital – it was the purpose of the commission, created under the Geneva Convention, to examine British personnel to see whether or not they were fit for repatriation – Dr Rodocanachi saw this as 'an opportunity to try to find as many as possible unfit for military service.'[151] This generous man became a regular visitor at the Seamen's Mission, and a welcome advisor to, and supporter of, Donald Caskie.[152]

Those with little or no chance of being repatriated under the Geneva Convention, the lesser wounded or non-wounded, had to find their own way home, and there was a steady exodus from Marseille either on foot to Spain or by ship to the French colonies across the Mediterranean. Seven of the early arrivals had been helped on their way with false visas and identity cards supplied by the American consulate, and these false papers, usually identifying the bearer as a citizen of a neutral country such as Ireland or Sweden, enabled them 'to buy Spanish and Portuguese visas and obtain

French exit visas.'[153] The "false papers" practice continued until the Vichy French authorities, under pressure from the Germans and Italians, decided that enough was enough. By the end of September 1940, though, apart from the seven who had used false papers to get to Spain, a further forty-nine had managed to reach either Spain or Algeria. A dozen or so wounded internees remained in the Michel Lévy hospital, with seventy or so healthy ones at Fort St Jean.

Leading Aircraftman (Nursing Orderly) H.A. Morement, attached to No. 73 (F) Squadron, was to find out that not even a non-combatant was safe from torture. Wounded by splinters in his feet and abdomen as a result of enemy bombing he was left behind in Saumur hospital when his squadron withdrew to England on 17 June 1940. Five days later, now also suffering from dysentery, he was captured by the Germans and removed to a hospital at Alençon (Orne). 'There my wounds were treated moderately well, but the food was poor, consisting chiefly of bread, soup and haricot beans.'[154] Having recovered somewhat he was removed 'to a concentration camp about a mile northwest of Alençon, where both military and civilian P.W. were interned. Here the treatment was bad. Food consisted solely of soup, served in dirty tin cans, and half a slice of black bread served twice a day.' He was interrogated 'about ten times for long periods at a time, and I had my legs and arms twisted in attempts to get information from me – chiefly about aerodromes in south-east and north-east England.'[155]

On 10 August 1940 Morement escaped from the camp with Sapper L. Hartley RE. It was easy enough to hide behind some huts at evening roll call and, at around 10 p.m., lift a manhole cover and crawl along a sewer into the River Briante. They made their way to a farmhouse where, on the following day, they heard on the radio of the French collapse and German occupation. As a result of this news the two decided to go south-west 'lying up by day and walking by night.' They ate nothing but fruit and vegetables 'as we had difficulty in getting food from the French and could not buy any without tickets.' As they were still wearing their prisoner-of-war uniforms of dark-brown canvas with a yellow circle on the back, they managed to obtain raincoats from a Spanish refugee, but decided nevertheless to by-pass Le Mans and go through Tours. Finding a map of France with the Demarcation Line conveniently marked on it, they made for a crossing-point near Loches.

Asking for help when they reached Loches they were instead handed over by unsympathetic French people to gendarmes, who locked them up for the night with seven French prisoners in the military prison at Châteauroux. In the morning, instead of going to the ablution shed, they 'bolted through the main gate, and escaped in the narrow neighbouring streets.'[156] They then walked, by night only, the ninety or so kilometres (fifty-five miles) to Montluçon, receiving no help whatsoever from the French, and being forced to steal what nourishment they could from gardens. When another wall map showed them that it was 400 kilometres to Spain they opted to go to Marseille, even though it was about the same distance. Finally reaching Marseille at the end of September, they were briefly interned in Fort St Jean, receiving a much needed £2 clothing allowance.

Morement befriended a French airman, and together they hatched a plan to steal an aeroplane – a single-seater Curtiss – and make their way to either Egypt or Gibraltar. On the day that Morement set off to steal the aircraft he told Hartley that if he had not returned by 3 o'clock that afternoon Hartley was to take it that he had been successful in flying away. Hartley, however, 'left Marseilles four days later, and heard no more of him',[157] managing to stow away aboard a troopship taking French legionnaires to Oran. He was caught, but after a brief period of internment reached Casablanca. Classed as 'distressed merchant seamen', he and six others were put aboard a trawler which, when well out to sea, was intercepted by HMS *Kelvin*,[158] and taken to Gibraltar. Sailing on 7 December 1940 Hartley arrived in Scotland ten days before Christmas.[159]

When his plans to steal the aircraft fell through Morement set off for Spain, but had only got as far as Perpignan by 7 December. It had been quite a struggle for him even to get that far, for his wounds had turned septic. 'I had to give up, and reported to the French Red Cross hospital at Perpignan. The nurse on duty refused me entry on the ground that I was an escaped British P.W.'[160] Fortunately, he was admitted by the senior medical officer, on the understanding that when he was fit and well he would be handed over to the military authorities. His stay in the clean hospital was so long, with food and treatment being poor, that on 9 May 1941, still wearing his prisoner's uniform, he took his papers from the office and walked out unchallenged in the direction of Spain. It was not until three days later when he saw a signpost pointing to Barcelona that he realised that he was in Spain.

On 20 May he reported to the British consulate in Barcelona, and after two days in the 'foreign colony hospital' was sent to Madrid. The embassy doctor, having further examined him, 'sent me first to Malaga and then to Gibraltar Military Hospital.' On 6 June 1941 he sailed to Gourock (Glasgow), eight days later being 'detained in Larbert E.M.S. Hospital on repatriation'.[161]

Late on the evening of 14 August 1940, Pilot Officer George Parker (pilot), Sergeant G.H. Easton (observer), and Sergeant E. Watson (air gunner) took off from RAF Wyton to bomb an airfield near Chartres, France. Unable to find the target, Parker headed instead for the port of Le Havre but as he turned onto the new course the ailerons failed. Unable to control the Blenheim Parker ordered bombs and flares to be jettisoned, and they baled out half an hour or so before midnight. The flares ignited as they parachuted down, turning night into day. The Blenheim crashed into the ground and blew up.

Watson parachuted into a wood, and found himself 'suspended about 12 feet from the ground. After a long struggle, I managed to reach the ground and followed tracks made by tanks until I came to a road.' Sheltered at a farm for the rest of the night, on the following day the farmer sent him to the mayor of les Corvées-les-Yys (Eure-et-Loir, some twenty-five kilometres south-west of Chartres), where he was reunited with his pilot. The two airmen spent most of 15 August hiding undiscovered in the fields, 'and learnt that the Germans were searching for us by low flying aircraft and motorised troops and that a German Air Force officer had interviewed the Maire about us.'

Sergeant Easton had been found in a wood about three or four kilometres away, and re-joined Parker and Watson that night. Easton had been given a couple of Michelin maps by a schoolmaster and so, armed with these and with his and Parker's compasses, they set off south along minor roads, still wearing their uniforms, 'as P/O Parker thought we might be shot as spies if we were found in civilian clothes.' Avoiding all large towns and villages, they were walking along the railway by the station at Cloyes-sur-le-Loir (Eure-et-Loir) when shots were fired at them. 'In the ensuing scramble we dived under trucks and, although I found Sgt. Easton again, it was the last we saw of P/O Parker.'[162] The two sergeants slipped away.

Crossing the River Loire north of Beaugency by boat they reached the Demarcation Line on 7 September. The following night a farmer guided them through the German sentry posts at a point some seven kilometres west of St Aignan-sur-Cher (Loir-et-Cher) to a mill on the edge of the River Cher. The only way across was to swim. As Easton was a non-swimmer the resourceful farmer produced a large, inner-tyre tube, and a fully-clothed Watson towed Easton to the other side, where another farmer gave them shelter for the rest of the night.

Reporting to the military authorities at St Aignan, French officers gave them further assistance. One of them, a demobilised captain, not only managed to get a cable through to Watson's mother, but also supplied them with free bus tickets to Châteauroux, where they again reported to the military authorities, and 'obtained 550 frs. from a French officer and 100 frs. from a charitable organisation.' They also met two Scottish soldiers, Sergeant S.J. Fraser and Private D. McKenzie,[163] who had been there for five days. Two days later, hearing a rumour that two English soldiers who had just arrived in town had been imprisoned, the two Scotsmen and the two airmen left at once by train for Toulouse. On the journey they met a Red Cross worker who, on arrival in Toulouse, left them in a café 'while she went in search of help for us from the French Red Cross, the Portuguese Consul and the French Military Authorities'. The only help given was from the Portuguese consul – who advised them not to go to Spain.

The four men decided to go to Spain anyway and, walking by day, reached Castelnaudary (Aude), some fifty-six kilometres south-east of Toulouse, in three days. Leaving the other two at a farm to rest – Fraser had a nasty boil on his knee – Watson and McKenzie went into Castelnaudary for help from the military but, again, none was forthcoming. During their absence, however, a Frenchwoman had organised a collection among her friends and had raised a generous 270 francs for the men, which was more than enough for the bus to Quillan (eighty-six kilometres via Carcassone). There they spent the night in a café, before catching another bus to Perpignan (seventy-four kilometres), and 'immediately started to walk down the coast road towards the Spanish frontier.' Meeting two Royal Artillerymen, Drivers F. Tull and E.A. McAngus, who were also on the run, they split into three pairs.

Watson/McKenzie and Tull/McAngus went first. Meeting up again at Port Vendres (Pyrénées-Orientales), Watson and McKenzie decided to continue on foot to the frontier. Arriving at Banyuls-sur-Mer during the night, they were fed and sheltered by an Englishman. A chance encounter with a Frenchman on the following day enabled them to avoid the French police and, with the help of a map drawn by the Frenchman, they crossed into Spain and were past Port Bou when they were 'arrrested by the Spanish authorities'. Taken back to Port Bou, they were put on a train to Figueras and locked up in the Castillo de San Fernando prison, where Captain J.R. Johnson, Royal Welsh Fusiliers, was already languishing.

Vice-consul Mr J.G. Whitfield arrived from Barcelona, but 'was not very helpful and informed us that we were in Spain for the duration.'[164] They were shortly sent to Cervera by train, travelling in a cattle truck with a number of Frenchmen, ten of whom managed to break out. The others were stopped, and after five days at Cervera Watson and his group were moved to Saragossa (one night) and finally to the prison at Miranda de Ebro, where 'we remained for six weeks and five days.'

Watson left Gibraltar by ship on 19 November 1940, docking at Liverpool on 4 December, some way behind McKenzie, McAngus and Tull.[165]

Easton and Fraser, however, were caught by French gendarmes at Argelès-sur-Mer (Pyrénées-Orientales) on either 13 or 15 September (Fraser says 15) and removed to the concentration camp at St Cyprien (Dordogne) and then to one at Agde (Hérault) on the south coast. Fraser escaped on 21 October but was re-arrested at Narbonne and taken to Fort St Jean, Marseille. He left the fort on 18 December 1940 and made his way, this time successfully, into Spain. Arrested by Spanish police in Espolla, he spent the next nine weeks in prisons at Figueras, Cervera and, inevitably, Miranda de Ebro. Sailing from Gibraltar on 11 March 1941 he reached Gourock six days later. As for Easton, as will be seen, it was to be eight months before he was to return to the United Kingdom.

On its way back from operations on 22/23 December 1940 (Mannheim) Wellington IC, T2474, 75 (New Zealand) Squadron, crashed near Thérouldeville (Seine-Maritime), France, a dozen kilometres east of Fécamp and the English Channel. The rear gunner was killed, and the other five crew taken prisoner. Three of the five were uninjured, but Sergeants F.G. Willis and C. Falcon-Scott RNZAF were in poor shape, and were taken to the German military hospital at Fécamp. Falcon-Scott remained unconscious for the next two weeks, though both he and Willis were moved a week later to the Ernemont hospital at Rouen (Seine-Maritime), and then at the end of January 1941 to the Henri Martin hospital at St Quentin (Aisne).

On 3 March 1941 they were transferred to the Val de Grâce hospital in Paris: 'By then we were convalescing and studied the possibility of escaping, as we heard that we were to be taken to Germany. Two French Red Cross nurses helped us, providing us with civilian clothes and visitors' passes.'[166] Thus equipped, the two airmen walked unhindered out of the hospital on the morning of 20 April, and made their way to an address given to them by the nurses. That night they went by train to Poitiers (Vienne), and later that morning, 21 April, crossed into Unoccupied France slightly south of Fleuré (a dozen kilometres south-east of Poitiers). Arrested by Vichy police they were removed to the prison at St Hippolyte-du-Fort.

Falcon-Scott was passed "fit" for repatriation by a Mixed Medical Commission on 10 June, but it was not until 26/27 August 1941 before he was flown by Sunderland from Gibraltar to Calshot. With him were three fighter pilots who had been shot down at the beginning of July 1941 – Pilot Officer H.P. Duval, Sergeant D.B. Crabtree and Sergeant J.G.L. Robillard RCAF (see chapter 5) – and Leading Aircraftman J. Hopkins (see next chapter), who had been left behind in the evacuation of France in June 1940.

As he had not been passed fit for repatriation Sergeant Willis 'was obliged to get out of the camp and did so on 28 May, crossing the Spanish frontier on 1 June, under arrangements organised by Capt. "G".'[167] He, too, was arrested by the Spanish police and imprisoned over the next three months at Figueras, Cervera and Miranda de Ebro, reaching Gibraltar on 1 September 1941. Three days later he was flown to Oban, Scotland (see following chapter).

On the night of 28/29 December 1940 a number of assorted Bomber Command aircraft raided the dockyards at Lorient on the north-west coast of France. One of the two that failed to return was a Whitley of 78 Squadron which, flying low, was hit by flak and caught fire.[168] The pilot, Sergeant A.J. Mott, immediately ordered the other four of his crew to bale out, and all managed to do so before their aircraft hit the ground near Lanvollon (Côtes-d'Armor, in the north of Brittany), where it burnt for several hours. Four days later Sergeant John Mott saw the 'German lorries loaded with fragments [of the Whitley] which, I was told, was all they were able to collect, as French people had already ransacked the remains for souvenirs.'

The rest of John Mott's crew were taken prisoner. The second pilot, Pilot Officer J.B.T. Loudon, 'descended by parachute from a height of 1,000 feet, twisted his ankle on landing and was captured while his foot was being bandaged by a Frenchman.' The navigator, Sergeant E.W. Wilmore, was also captured on landing, but the wireless operator, Sergeant L.A. Beckett, 'landed safely from 600 feet, was given food and drink by a farmer, who later betrayed him.'[169] They were all flown to Germany on 29 December. The rear gunner, Sergeant A.J. McMillan, 'landed from 1,200 feet and went into hiding.' He managed to keep out of the Germans' clutches for almost nine months before he, too, was betrayed.

Sergeant Mott went from Lanvollon to Kérity, a few kilometres along the coast from Paimpol, in the hope, vain as it proved, that he might find a boat to take him back to England. Heading back inland he made his way to Plouézec and to Pléhédel where, on 1 January 1941, he was given a change of civilian clothing. The following day he was at St Brieuc (Côtes-du-Nord) on the north Breton coast. On 3 January a Monsieur Hevin took him to Nantes (Loire-Atlantique; population in 1939 of

179,000) and there, changing house four times, he remained until 26 September 1941.[170]

John Mott was staying with Adrien and Tantine Delavigne at 6, Boulevard Admiral Courbet when, about three weeks after his arrival in Nantes, he met up with Sergeant McMillan, who was staying with Madame Flavet and family. They managed to keep in touch with one another while their French helpers tried to find a suitable boat. Failing to find one, plans were made for the two airmen to be taken to the Unoccupied Zone of France but on 21 September, before they could be put into operation, McMillan and the Flavet family were arrested. In view of this it was decided that John Mott should be taken into Unoccupied France without delay. A guide was hastily sought, and after a fee was agreed with a Hungarian Jew known as "Rips", he and Mott 'left 6 Boulevard Admiral Courbet, on bicycles' on 26 September.

Catching a train to Bordeaux, they made their way 'to the house of a Pole called Selk'[171] at St Sulpice-de-Pommiers (Gironde), Selk escorting him into Unoccupied France on 3 October. A day later John Mott was in Toulouse, and on 12 October was taken via Ax-les-Thermes and Latour-de-Carol over the Pyrenees. He reached the British consulate at Barcelona on 15 October, and finally arrived at Gibraltar, via the British embassy at Madrid, on 14 November. Forced to kick his heels for a month while waiting to get home from Gibraltar, he had plenty to say about his enforced idleness: 'The delay in repatriating escapers from Gibraltar seems needlessly protracted. It is obvious that a special convoy cannot leave every day, but if passengers by air to UK were limited in luggage carried to 30 lbs weight per head, this would allow for more passengers per aircraft. The argument that, for safety reasons, the number of passengers per aircraft is limited since only one dinghy is carried, is easily upset by the addition of another dinghy.'[172]

It was not until 13 December that he got a lift aboard a Sunderland of 10 (RAAF) Squadron, which alighted at Pembroke Dock, Wales on the following day. He was to survive the war (having evaded for a second time) though some of his helpers would not. Adrien and Tantine Delavigne and their nephew, Maurice Cybulski, were arrested on 5 March 1942, betrayed by Rips, the Hungarian Jew. Maurice was to die in prison in April 1943 having caught a chill. In July of that year the Delavignes were released, and continued helping evaders until re-arrested on 25 January 1944. Madame Delavigne survived the horrors of Ravensbrück and Mauthausen concentration camps, and when liberated in 1945 weighed 'only four and a half stone instead of her normal ten stone'.[173] She never saw her husband again.

When Wellington R1244 developed engine trouble en route to the north Italian target of Turin on the night of 11/12 January 1941 the pilot, Sergeant S.M.P. Parkes, decided to abort the operation, and 'tried to get home on one engine'. With the aircraft steadily losing height Sergeant H.W. Bratley, first wireless operator, "bashed out" an SOS requesting a course for Manston in Kent, the nearest airfield. When R1244 was down to 4 or 5,000 feet Parkes 'told the crew to bale out, if they wished, but they remained in the aircraft. There were hills further ahead 3,000 feet high and it was impossible to go on, so I made a wheel-up landing in a field. Nobody was hurt.'[174] Parkes had brilliantly put the bomber down near Misérieux (Ain) to the east of Villefranche-sur-Saône, on the eastern edge of the Saône valley in Unoccupied France.

Given no help by the curé of Misérieux the crew – Parkes, Bratley, Flight Sergeant L.R. Willis, and Sergeants L.W. Goldingay, R. Vivian, R.W. Blaydon – 'decided to find the nearest police station'. Seeing a sign for Villefranche-sur-Saône they headed towards it, and after three hours met a *poilu* heading for Trévoux, who imparted the news that there was no *gendarmerie* at Villefranche (population 18,000) but that there was one at Trévoux (pop. 2,500) to the south. Tagging along with the French soldier, they got to Trévoux police station at about 4 o'clock in the morning, and slept for a couple of hours until woken up with bread and coffee, 'which we paid for with French money issued to us before leaving England.'

Not far from the gendarmerie, across the Rhône at Ambérieux, was a large French airfield whose Anglophile commandant, Marcel Genistat, came over to see the RAF airmen in the morning. He took Parkes with him in his car to see the burnt-out remains of his Wellington: 'On our return to the police station we had lunch, for which the Commandant paid.' It was an odd situation, for the French officers wore plain clothes, no uniforms, and on the airfield itself there were neither aeroplanes nor fuel for them, as the airmen discovered when they were taken there for the night. At no time were they searched or interrogated, except at the police station where they were politely asked for name, rank and number. The affable commandant even went so far as to say that if any of them wished to write a letter to England he would do what he could to see that it got there. Parkes's letter apparently reached Wing Commander E.A. Healy at RAF Honington, 9 Squadron's base, 'some weeks later'.[175]

The next day Commandant Genistat took the RAF men 'in the aerodrome bus to Aix-en-Provence. He said that he would have to hand us over to the military.'[176] Having got only as far as Montélimar by evening they stopped at a hotel for dinner, where a number of French diners drank their health. Arriving at Aix late at night, they spent the night in an army barracks occupied by the cadets who had been evacuated from the elite St Cyr military academy in Paris. After a second night in the barracks, Parkes and his crew were taken by a policeman to St Hippolyte-du-Fort: 'We were there for ten days and got rid of our uniform for plain clothes.'

Shortly after their arrival at the St Hippolyte internment camp, the Senior British officer, 2nd Lieutenant R.E.H. Parkinson, Royal Sussex Regiment, received a telephone call from the escape organisation saying that they were all wanted in Marseille with a view to getting them back to Britain. Parkinson was to go with them: 'We left the camp early in the morning, when it was still dark, climbing over the back gate and got to the railway station, but there ran into the police, who took us back to the camp.' Parkinson went to see the commandant, 'who was annoyed, and said that if we must escape, we must do it in the afternoon when we were normally allowed out. So we all walked out that afternoon, but this time avoided the railway station at which we had been stopped. We walked seven kilometres to the nearest village, from where we could get a train to Nîmes.'

After several delays waiting for connecting trains the five airmen and Parkinson reached Marseille. Avoiding the ticket controls at the station barrier by walking out through the kitchen and into the station yard, Parkinson took the men to the Hôtel Touring. They met Captain Murchie (see following chapter), who took them to a house whose owner was 'a sort of gangster person, who walked about with a revolver and was paid to keep us.'[177] Flight Sergeant Willis noted simply that they 'were sheltered for ten days in a flat near the harbour'.

After plans to steal a twenty-seater airliner with the help of French air force officers had fallen through, it was decided to send the six airmen off in two groups. Parkinson went first, with Willis, Vivian and Blaydon, but they were caught and returned to St Hippolyte. Next to leave, on 16 February 1941, were Parkes and Goldingay. Murchie gave them tickets for the train to Banyuls-sur-Mer, changing at Narbonne, but the plan was for the two airmen to get off the train at Collioure, two stops early: 'We had to meet a man in a café in the square at Collioure. He was to know us by a copy of a Swiss newspaper we had to carry. We met him and he took us along the road to Banyuls through Port Vendres.' They spent two comfortable days and nights in a hotel, all paid for in advance, before a guide took them 'to the frontier at the top of the mountains. He was carrying a sack, which we thought contained food. We had no food ourselves and were relying on him to give us some. At the top of the mountains, he met another man to whom he handed over the party and the sack. We thought we were going to have some food, but it turned out that the sack contained tobacco and they were smugglers.'[178] After the first man had returned to Banyuls, the second demanded his payment in advance, but the airmen said that he would be paid at the British consulate. The smuggler said nothing. Leading them down to the foot of the mountains, he went into a house telling them to keep walking and that he would catch up in five minutes. Of course they never saw him again.

Abandoned, with neither food nor money, they headed for Figueras. Captain Murchie had told them that they must not get caught within twenty-five kilometres of the frontier, the penalty for so doing being a quick return to France. If anything were to go wrong, he added, they should go to the Hôtel Paris in Figueras and ask for Joseph, the concierge. Walking along a main road they flagged down a lorry: 'All we said to the driver was "Figueras?" and he answered "Si" and took us on. We got to the hotel and walked straight into Joseph.' By luck, the vice-consul, Mr J.G. Whitfield, was in town, and Joseph arranged for him to meet the airmen. Mr Whitfield gave them each a train ticket for Barcelona and fifty pesetas. He also told them that there were two possible trains, one that night and one in the morning, but he could not say which was the less likely to have Spanish police aboard. Parkes and Goldingay plumped for the night train and decided to occupy the last compartment, the best place they reasoned to avoid the ticket collector. It was the wrong choice, for the first person they saw was a Spanish detective, who asked them for their papers. Handing over the ones issued to them by the American consul in Marseille, the detective told them to wait for him when they got to Barcelona.

The Spaniard was clearly a fool they thought, for as soon as the train stopped at Barcelona Parkes and Goldingay slipped out of the station and made their way to the British consulate. Far from being fools the Spanish police, only too aware of the nationality of the two men, had already telephoned the British consulate. Demanding that they be handed over, Parkes and Goldingay were taken to the police station. After three weeks in Lérida and Saragossa civil prisons, they were sent to the Miranda de Ebro concentration camp. Released on 28 March 1941, they were reunited with Bratley in Madrid.

Left behind in Marseille Bratley had shared accommodation with five soldiers – Lance-Sergeant J.K. Bell, Royal Scots Fusiliers; Corporal W.A. Bell, Queen's Own Royal West Kents; Driver C.F. Watkins RA; Gunner E.F. Smeed RA; and Gunner F. Castle RA – and with Sergeant G.H. Easton RAF who, on the way to Spain with his army companion, Fraser, had, as seen, fallen into the hands of French gendarmes. Going with Fraser to Fort St Jean, Easton had fallen ill on 11 November 1940 and had been in hospital until the end of January 1941, when he escaped to a house where other evaders and escapers were in hiding. These men, plus five others, left Marseille on 19 February 1941, escorted by a Spanish guide to Perpignan, which they left on 22 February in two taxis for Laroque-des-Albères.

It is probable that the taxis were supplied by François Maso, who owned a garage in the centre of Perpignan at 8, Rue Vauban. Inside the garage, with its green, wooden doors, were six or seven cars, all immobilised and without wheels. These cars were beds for any evader who was required to spend the night in the garage before being driven off in the taxis – big, black Renaults – but only after Maso's son had bought the evaders French clothing and Basque berets as necessary.[179]

At Laroque-des-Albères Bratley and party 'met another guide and then walked single file up the mountains. We slept the night in a shack and the next day continued to climb, spending the next night on top of the mountain.'[180] Crossing into Spain, they were at la Junquera, six kilometres from the French border at le Perthus, by the afternoon of 25 February. After a few hours rest they continued to Velmanya. Catching a train to Barcelona the British Consulate put them up in a hotel for the night. Due to catch an early and slow train to Madrid in the morning Bratley, who had been 'taken ill in the hotel with something like dysentery', and Easton, having sprained his ankle and having 'practically collapsed', were left behind while the other ten went on as planned.

The consul arranged for Bratley and Easton to be taken to a hospital, where they were well looked after for three days. Bratley thought that the matron was English, which no doubt helped. After a night in 'Commander Dorchy's house' (vice-consul P.H. Dorchy) they were put on a train for Madrid, where they discovered that of the ten soldiers who had left a few days earlier only Smeed and Watkins had not been arrested en route. Now reunited with Parkes and Goldingay they went on to Gibraltar, and from there, five and a half weeks later, by the *Monarch of Bermuda* to Liverpool, where they docked on 16 May 1941 after a week at sea.

Half of the Parkes crew were now home. The other half – Vivian, Willis and Blaydon – escorted by 2nd Lieutenant Parkinson, had set off from Marseille with Private Adams, Duke of Cornwall's Light Infantry (no record of him, however), and a Belgian, Alexander Halot. They waited four days at Perpignan for heavy snow in the Pyrenees to clear and for the strong winds to abate, then left by taxi with two Spaniards, one of whom was to be their guide. Half a dozen kilometres from the Spanish border all the passengers got out. The plan was for the taxi to be driven through the customs post (probably that at Bourg-Madame [France]/Puigcerda [Spain]) and for the passengers to walk around it and pick up the taxi in Spain. The plan worked well, until a gendarme spotted them getting back into the taxi. 'We believe they were searching for the second Spaniard who was wanted for murder and smuggling. The driver was arrested, but the rest of us managed to get away.'[181]

During the night of 7/8 February 1941, the two Spaniards departed, leaving the six escapers to make their own way into Spain, at Saillagouse. Here, though, Spain makes a salient into France and, without realising it, they found themselves back in France. A French farmer 'guided us from there to near Bourg-Madame, where we were all arrested by the gendarmes, who were still searching for us in the car.' Detained for a day at Bourg-Madame all their money, which 'amounted to a joint total of 2,000 pesetas, plus 750 francs each (which we had received in St Hippolyte) and 150 American dollars belonging to Halot', was confiscated. On 10 February, despite having given their parole not to escape, they were taken in handcuffs to Perpignan police station and there detained for two nights, sleeping without blankets on the hard floor. On the third day they were handed over to the Garde Mobile, 'who removed us to the military barracks. Two days later we were moved under escort to St Hippolyte (about 20 Feb).'[182]

On 1 March 1941 Vivian, Willis, Blaydon, and Sergeant V.T. McFarlane, left the prison at St Hippolyte, officially on a day out to Nîmes, but were put in touch with a Frenchman, who took them to a hotel at Port Vendres. 'Owing to some financial difficulty, guides could not be secured, and we returned to Nîmes.' Funds were brought from Marseille, and with 3,000 francs in their pockets they retraced their steps to Perpignan, but at Narbonne station Sergeant Blaydon was re-arrested by gendarmes in the waiting room.

Willis, Vivian and McFarlane spent the next four days kicking their heels in Perpignan until two more guides could be found to take them over the Pyrenees, although there was some difficulty over payment. They left Port Vendres on the afternoon of 8 March 1941, and after walking for some twelve hours reached a farmhouse near Llansá, on the Mediterranean coast. At around 4 a.m. they caught a train to Barcelona, but near Figueras a plain-clothes detective came down the train asking to see their papers. Having none the airmen were arrested. Imprisoned at Barcelona from 10 to 22 March they were, as fellow prisoner Second Lieutenant R.L. Broad was to observe, treated appallingly before being moved to prisons at Lérida, Saragossa and, ultimately, Miranda de Ebro, following the trail of Parkes and Goldingay. Released on 7 May, they left Gibraltar aboard the Royal Navy's aircraft carrier HMS *Argus* on 5 June 1941.

Sergeant Blaydon, following his arrest in the waiting room at Narbonne on 1 March 1941, was detained there for three days. After a week in Perpignan prison he was returned to St Hippolyte, but escaped again by climbing a wall on 2 April. With him were Corporal H.W.C. Surridge AMPC; Corporal Frost (no record); and Private E.J. Small, East Surreys. They were taken to Argelès-sur-Mer, and stayed the night in a café. After hiding in some woods for the day a 'guide arrived in the evening and conducted us across the Pyrenees to Figueras, which we reached about 7 April. Our guide said he could not buy us railway tickets, as we had no papers, and left us after giving us 20 pesetas each.'[183]

The following day they 'jumped a passenger train, but were arrested after about half an hour and taken back to Figueras and put in the civilian prison.' On the second day, Blaydon was removed to the military fort in Figueras, where he 'was interrogated by a German in civilian clothes who asked my name, birthplace, and age, and expressed an interest in the organisation which had got us into Spain, as too many had been getting over. I said there was no organisation and that if there had been I would not have been before him. He mentioned various names, but I denied knowing any of them.'[184]

Moved on to Barcelona, he spent three weeks at the Cervera prison and a further three and a half weeks at Miranda de Ebro before travelling back from Gibraltar with Willis and Vivian.

CHAPTER 2

Marseille and St Hippolyte: 1940-1941

Do what you can being what you are.
Shine like a glowworm if you cannot like a star.
Be a wheel greaser if you cannot drive a train.
Stay here in England if you cannot go to Spain.

Old northern rhyme

In London, once the scale of the problem in Marseille had been realised, positive steps were taken. When word of Caskie's activities reached the British Secret Intelligence Service (MI6), the head of MI6 approached Norman Crockatt at MI9 (the section set up specifically to deal with escape and evasion – see Appendix V) on 6 August 1940 to propose that a Marseille–Spain escape line be set up for evaders and escapers gathering in Unoccupied France. With the fall of France in June 1940, MI6 had been keen to establish personnel 'inside Europe obtaining information from escapers and evaders as fast as possible. To do this, MI6 first transferred officers to MI9, then it had them posted as MI9 representatives overseas.'[185]

One of these MI6 officers was Major Donald Darling ("Sunday"), who, with Crockatt's agreement, was sent to Madrid as a "reception officer" to establish 'a route to and from France, along which Intelligence could travel, as well as the BEF evaders gathered at Marseille.'[186] Before leaving London Darling had been briefed on Caskie's work at the Seamen's Mission. Estimating that he would have to evacuate 'at most some sixty to a hundred'[187] personnel after the first few had reached Spain from France by the end of August 1940, he was staggered to find them arriving in ever increasing numbers.

The maintenance of so many personnel in Marseille and the expense involved in moving them to Spain caused a serious drain on resources, and from time to time reports reached Sir Samuel Hoare, the British ambassador at the embassy in Madrid, 'about the financial situation in Marseille and requests were made for further funds.' Sir Samuel also learnt that Darling was involved in the financial support of those in Marseille and appreciated that 'he was working on similar lines but entirely independently and possibly at cross purposes with this embassy.'

It is possible that in respect of Darling's activities one of Sir Samuel's informants was a young American, Varian Mackey Fry,[188] who had arrived in Marseille in August 1940 from the USA having been sent by a group calling itself the Emergency Rescue Committee. This had been formed on 22 June 1940 to assist certain prominent political and cultural refugees, not necessarily Jewish, to escape the Nazis' clutches and to leave Europe for the Americas, funds being raised by private subscription. Given a month's paid leave by his employer, the Foreign Policy Association, Fry was appointed to go to Europe to get these people out, and flew from America aboard the Pan American flying boat *Yankee Clipper*[189] on 4 August. After refuelling in the Azores, the flying boat continued to Lisbon, with Fry arriving in Marseille on 15 August.

Anticipating that his work would be finished by 29 August, Fry had with him only $3,000 in cash (equivalent at the time to approximately 12,000 French francs) and a list of some 200 people to be rescued. He endured a short stay in 'a smelly little family-run concern, the Hotel Suisse' before booking himself into the Hôtel Splendide on the boulevard d'Athènes.[190] After a few weeks 'a French-Jewish merchant who had seen the writing on the wall' allowed Fry and his two or three assistants to use his now redundant 'office on the front of the second floor of an old building in the rue Grignan, rent free through the end of the year, and we moved in even before he had had time to move out.'[191] Here Fry set up the *Centre Américain de Secours* (American Relief Centre).

In September 1940, after plans to get one of his "names" out of France by boat had failed, Fry agreed to try to get him through to Lisbon with five others. The seven met at the Gare St Charles early on the morning of 14 September and headed for Spain, reaching Madrid with some difficulty. Whenever seats on the flight from Madrid to Lisbon became available, the refugees were sent on their way. On his way back to Marseille Fry called at the British Embassy in Madrid in the hope of persuading the British to supply a ship for the evacuation of more of his refugees. A plan had already been put to Fry by an Italian exile, Emilio Lussu,[192] for a boat to evacuate Spanish Republicans and Italian freedom fighters, as it was Lussu's opinion that it would be impossible to get all these men away to Spain by the overland route. At the British Embassy Fry was introduced to the military attaché, Brigadier Torr. 'We talked about the refugees and the remnants of the BEF in France and of [the] plan to have the British send a boat up to Cap Croisette to get them.'[193]

Torr's reply was, initially, encouraging – they had just received urgent instructions to get 'these chaps' out, and only that very morning Torr had been talking to Sir Samuel Hoare about the business – but then he told Fry that the Royal Navy would be unwilling to detach one of their ships for the men's rescue. A few days after his meeting with Torr, however, Fry was in Lisbon meeting with Donald Darling. Blunt and to the point, Darling told Fry that Torr was wrong in his belief that the Royal Navy would not detach a "cloak and dagger" vessel for such purposes, and added that Torr might have said that no boat was available either for security reasons or because 'he was such a fundamentally silly man (though kind and pleasant), that the embassy never told him anything for the sake of security.'[194]

On his return to Madrid later in September 1940 Fry had a second meeting with Torr, this time with Sir Samuel Hoare in attendance. Agreeing with Torr that the Royal Navy would not be willing to supply a vessel, Sir Samuel suggested that Fry should therefore help British servicemen cross the Pyrenees. When Fry reminded the ambassador that his duty lay with helping Lussu, Sir Samuel tempted him with an offer of $10,000. Fry accepted, and funds were made available by the British Government.

The process for getting these funds to the right persons in Marseille, necessarily circuitous, was described in a "Most Secret" minute of 7 January 1941 by "C" (the head of the SIS) to Henry Hopkinson of the Foreign Office in London: 'Reference telegram No. 1336 of 27.12.40. from Embassy, Madrid. In order to provide a further sum of money, the same procedure *previously* used should, I consider, be followed. This entails your wiring to Embassy, Washington, asking them to hand over £500 in dollars to the State Department, for transmission to Mr Hurley, United States Consul General, Marseille, with instructions that he is to give it to Mr Caskie for the maintenance of British personnel in that area. No reference should be made to Military, as it will be understood that the sum of money will be used for assisting prisoners of war [*sic*] both to maintain themselves, as well as to escape.'[195] Hopkinson, appreciating that "C" had confused Caskie with Fry, spoke with "C", who then requested that an additional £500 should be sent to Caskie, the first £500 having been earmarked for Fry.

This, though, was only part of a system that today would be called money-laundering. In the diplomatic language of the day His Majesty's Principal Secretary of State for Foreign Affairs [Anthony Eden] presented his compliments to the US Chargé d'Affaires, Herschel Johnson, on 17 January 1941 and, with reference to his letter of 28 August last, had the honour to request Mr Herschel Johnson to be 'so good as to ask the United States Consul-General at Marseille, through the United States Embassy at Vichy, to hand over to Major Dodds a further sum of one hundred thousand francs for the use of the Reverend Caskie of the mission to Seamen, in connexion with the expenses of British refugees in the Marseille district.' The Secretary of State would also be 'grateful if the United States Embassy at Vichy could be requested by telegram to hand over to the United States Consul-General at Marseille the sum of ten thousand dollars for the use of Mr Varian Fry of the American Quaker organisation for expenses of British refugees in the Marseille area.'[196]

In all but name a British agent, following his meetings with Brigadier Torr in Madrid in the autumn of 1940, Fry returned to Marseille and made contact with Captain Frederick Fitch, Royal Norfolk Regiment, who had arrived in Marseille on 8 September 1940 and who was now the senior British officer at Fort St Jean. 'Between them they organised the sending of men to the Spanish frontier in parties of two or three with instructions to give themselves up at the first police check they encountered on the Spanish side of the frontier.'[197] To assist the men in their crossing of the Pyrenees Lieutenant W. Sillar RAMC[198] was sent to Banyuls-sur-Mer, some thirty-five kilometres south of Perpignan. It was hoped that, once in Spanish hands, Brigadier Torr would be able to arrange for their release through proper channels, but towards the end of October this route to Spain was temporarily closed, only six men by then having made use of it. News of the closure was passed to Fry by another American, Dr Charles Joy, a New England clergyman of the Unitarians, who had been given the message by Donald Darling on his way through Lisbon. Darling requested Fry 'not to send any more men into Spain. Evidently Torr's plan for getting them released from prison or concentration camps wasn't working. In the future I [Fry] was to send the British direct to Gibraltar, by sea.'[199] On a positive note, though, it was recognised that Banyuls was the best starting point for the crossing of the eastern Pyrenees.

A great opportunity to use the alternative, but riskier, sea route to Gibraltar presented itself at the end of October 1940 when Leon "Richard" Ball, one of Varian Fry's operatives, met a Frenchman 'in Snappy's Bar, a favourite hangout of the British officers in Marseille'. The Frenchman put Ball in touch with the captain and crew of a *chalutier* (trawler) and a price of 225,000 francs (3,000 francs per head) was agreed for sixty soldiers (including Fitch) and fifteen refugees to be taken to Gibraltar. Ball, convinced that the deal was genuine, put it to Fry. Initially sceptical but swayed by the judgement of others, Fry handed over 'the English money to Fitch and the money for the refugees to

Ball… but only on one condition: that no money should be paid over until all the passengers were on board and the ship was clear of the harbour.'[200]

Disregarding Fry's orders Ball was persuaded to hand over the money before sailing. Neither it nor the Frenchman were ever seen again. Also never seen again was Ball, 'who vanished completely from sight.'[201] The tough British soldiers, though, got their hands on two or three of the French gang and took them back to Fort St Jean as hostages. Despite knocking six bells out of the Frenchmen, it was clear that none of them had a clue where their boss had gone. They did succeed, however, in dropping a note of their predicament out of a window into the street, where it was passed to the police. 'Perhaps because they were regarded as prisoners of war already, Fitch and the British soldiers weren't arrested.'[202] Fitch, however, testified against the crooks, who were convicted of being party to the fraud and given short prison sentences.

Another boat scheme to fail this time involved only four men – Major J.C. Windsor-Lewis, 2nd Battalion Welsh Guards, 'another English officer in the DLI and two Frenchmen'.[203] Major Windsor-Lewis had arrived in Marseille during the second week of August (see also Chapter 8) after he had reached the Spanish frontier but had been turned back. Returning to Marseille, he planned to take a ship to 'Gibraltar, Greece or Alexandria' or, failing that, to go through Spain to Gibraltar. He was advised, though, not to go through Perpignan as it 'was said to be too full of Germans'. Disappointed at finding 'that there were no boats in the harbour leaving for anywhere as all shipping was suspended', he went to the American consulate for help, hoping to be able to convince them that he was an American citizen. No sooner had he told the consul how he had been captured in Boulogne than he was told to go and see Major Dodds. 'This gentleman seemed disinclined to give me any practical assistance and pointed out that about 200 English soldiers and some dozen officers were safely housed and well looked after by the French in Fort St Jean, whom he recommended me to join.'[204]

Rejecting this unpalatable advice, Windsor-Lewis and two of his partners – Captain A.M.K. Martin and Lieutenant J. de Ceret, French Army – arranged for the purchase 'of a sailing boat, 200 litres of petrol and enough food for a fortnight' for 6,000 francs. As the boat was moored some distance away at Golfe-Juan, between Cannes and Antibes, supplies and fuel had to be carried there in relays, but a departure date was set for 27 September. On the morning before they were due to sail, however, the three and a half-ton boat was wrecked, and the two Frenchmen backed out of the operation, 'owing to the Dakar incident and the risk of their being caught'.[205] No monies were refunded to the luckless British officers, who both later crossed into Spain. Windsor-Lewis was flown back from Lisbon on 5 December 1940, while Captain Martin sailed from Gibraltar to Liverpool (8–15 May 1941).

Though *their* nautical exploits had come to an unfortunate end, during 'August, September and October five officers and twenty-five other ranks got away from Fort Saint-Jean on board boats bound for Algeria.'[206] These were opportunist escapes, as was that of Captain Derek Boileau Lang, Queen's Own Cameron Highlanders, who had escaped from St Valéry-en-Caux and had made his way to Marseille by September 1940. With the help of several French acquaintances he succeeded in stowing away aboard the French ship *Mariette Pasha*, and had reached Beirut, in the Lebanon, on 21 November. He was in British hands in Jerusalem before the year was out.[207]

In contrast was the attempt of Flying Officer Lewis Hodges,[208] who, on the day that the *Mariette Pasha* reached Beirut, stowed away aboard the *Ville de Verdun*. He, 'four Poles, two Czechs and two British soldiers'[209] were discovered when the ship was under way, bound for Casablanca, and handed over to the authorities in Oran. After a brief imprisonment they were returned to Marseille. Hodges was brought before the *juge d'instruction* and charged with taking passage in a ship without a ticket. Imprisoned as a civilian he was, however, allowed out on parole pending his trial proper.

It was not only the British who were experiencing shipping failures. The port of Marseille was controlled at this time by two unscrupulous gangs, one 'composed largely of the followers of the Corsican Sabiani, the Farinacci of Marseille', the other 'tied to elements of the dissolved trade unions'. Emilio Lussu himself was to suffer the chicanery of these gangsters through Dr Frank Bohn, an American 'involved in the illegal traffic of refugees into Spain over the Pyrenees',[210] and an acquaintance of Varian Fry, who had acquired a fishing smack capable of holding ten passengers, and had arranged for it to sail to Lisbon. His intermediary was Manuel, a member of the Sabiani gang. It soon dawned on Lussu that not only would the boat never sail but that, in all probability, it never even existed. There would be no comeback on Manuel, Marseille born and bred, 'a prominent speculator' and 'friend of influential people'.[211]

In any event, the losers in the swindle could not complain to the police as they themselves were acting illegally. Undaunted by this episode, Lussu persuaded Bohn to try to get his money back from

Manuel, and went along to add his weight to the proceedings. Whatever was said in translation by Lussu must have been convincing, 'because a good part of the money was returned that same day.'[212]

Emilio Lussu ("Monsieur Dupont") tried to get away by boat once more, and found a Belgian who owned a motor launch, *la Bouline*, also capable of carrying ten passengers and three crew 'with a bit of a squeeze'. Members of Lussu's group *Giustizia e Libertà* kept a close eye on the launch, which was moored in Marseille's Vieux-Port, after the Belgian skipper had agreed to take Emilio. It was the same old story, though, for on the appointed day Emilio was told that *la Bouline* was no longer at her mooring. The Belgian, it transpired, had had a better offer and, with twenty passengers crammed aboard each paying a king's ransom, set off for the other side. The better offer came, it seems, from Varian Fry and his organisation who wanted to add four "names" to the evacuation list. The reality was that, with these extra men aboard, there was now no room for Lussu.

Perhaps it was just as well for Lussu that he did not take passage on *la Bouline*, for off the Balearics she ran into heavy seas and strong winds. Shipping much water *la Bouline* headed back to Marseille but was picked up by a French patrol boat and towed to a small port. Those aboard were arrested for leaving the country illegally, and sent to prison.

Emilio Lussu and his partner, Joyce Salvadori (later his wife), did eventually manage to get to Spain, and to Portugal. Word of their activities reached the ears of British Intelligence, who flew them to England for "discussions". Unhappy at the lack of promises regarding Italy from the British, Emilio requested that they be returned to France. Flown to Gibraltar aboard a Sunderland from RAF Mount Batten, they and four of five other passengers then 'embarked on a small warship. It was a little grey boat with anti-aircraft guns, powerful machine-guns and a crew of thirty-five men armed to the teeth.'[213] This little grey boat, HMS *Tarana*, was to play an important part in the lives of several RAF evaders over the next few weeks (see Chapter 5). After several, stormy, sea-sick days the Duponts, as Lussu and Salvadori were calling themselves, and the other passengers transferred to a Polish-manned felucca, the *Seawolf*, a converted fishing boat, which dropped them off at a quiet point on the French Mediterranean coast of France during the second week of July 1942 to continue their own war.[214]

One of the other passengers on HMS *Tarana* was SOE agent Richard Heslop, of whom Joyce Salvadori wrote that he 'was so severely taciturn that he was difficult to classify.' Heslop, for his part, said of Lussu and Salvadori: 'Dupont wore dark glasses and a beard that he had obviously grown recently. His wife was much younger than he was – possibly in the late twenties… Dupont was a very nervous man, and I thought he would have to pull himself together if he was going to survive in France.'[216]

The failures by land and sea in and from Marseille were not a disaster by any means, for Donald Darling had been hard at work organising his own escape route, though at considerable arm's length. He recounts somewhat vaguely, no date, that he 'attempted to enlist a member of the American Jewish Aid Organisation,' and gave the unnamed man (presumably Varian Fry or one of his men) 'an envelope containing a letter written on thin paper and a large sum in blissfully slim French bank notes I had recently received from London.'[217]

Also recruited by the British as a courier was Nubar Gulbenkian (1896-1972), an Armenian who had been brought to the notice of British Intelligence after visiting his parents in Vichy. Nubar Gulbenkian's father, Calouste, a vastly wealthy oil merchant, acquired diplomatic immunity as the Iraqi minister in Paris on the outbreak of war, and followed the French government to Vichy, where he served as the Iranian minister. On 16 May 1942 he had arrived in Lisbon with his secretary. Three weeks later a certain Dom Pedro informed British Intelligence that Calouste Gulbenkian 'was now here on a six months permit with his wife and mistress, anxious to get to London. For the six months permit he had paid the Portuguese Legion Esc. 50,000,000. Parenthetically it may be stated that it looks as if he has permanently left Vichy from the quantity and description of luggage which both he and Madame have brought to Portugal.'[218]

Dom Pedro also stated that Mr Gulbenkian wished to get to London and work for the British Government 'in exchange for a guarantee that his fortune would remain intact'. He also noted that he thought that Gulbenkian would ask the same of the Germans: 'There is absolutely no doubt about it that Calouste would work for any side which gave him an advantage.'[219] Without making any recommendation the message was clear, that were Calouste Gulbenkian to go to London 'he should be very carefully watched.' In the event, he did not go to London, and lived 'until his death in a modest hotel suite at the small Aviz Hotel.'[220]

On his return to England Nubar was informed that British Intelligence seemed pleased with the information that he had brought back 'and even more pleased with the ease with which I was able to come and go from Vichy.' On the strength of this, therefore, it was decided that he 'could help to organize the escape routes for British servicemen who had managed to get away from prisoner-of-war camps in Germany and were on the run or had been shot down over France.'[221] He was given the address of a garage in Perpignan (presumably that of François Maso) where he would find "Parker", 'the man who was to look after the final stages of the escape route,' and instructed that the British Government would pay £40 for each officer and £20 for each other rank 'taken safely, from Perpignan, over the Spanish frontier', the money to be paid into a bank in England and to be collected after the war.

Gulbenkian returned to France and to Perpignan, and contacted "Parker", or Michel Parayre as he was properly named. Terms were agreed, and it was arranged that escapers and evaders would call at the garage before being taken to Spain. In the event, Parayre was unable to do much to help with the escape route, and an 'RAF officer and three sergeants who went to the garage in Perpignan to try the system out returned to Marseille the next day to report that it was non-operational.'[222] Parayre told Donald Darling after the war that 'he had been under such heavy surveillance from the Vichy French police, behind whom the Germans stirred, that he hardly dared speak to a friend in the street for fear of compromising him.'[223] At least ten men, several of whom had escaped from St Hippolyte-du-Fort (see Chapter 4), were, however, successfully passed into Spain in June 1941 via the garage.

In Madrid Sir Samuel Hoare continued to receive second-hand information of Darling's activities (possibly from a certain Mr Lea in Lisbon), but was concerned that the guides being employed by Darling unfortunately belonged, 'for the greater part if not entirely, to the wrong political party'. He also thought that 'a great number of our men would undoubtedly be arrested and the fact that they were accompanied by these "Red" guides would certainly compromise them.' Given the history between them, Darling was not surprisingly angry at Sir Samuel's ban on the use of Communists, the *de facto* enemies of the Fascist Franco regime. 'Who could be more ardent opponents of the regime,' wrote Darling, 'than anarchist guides who were later used by the Barcelona Consulate and who constantly increased their prices?', adding that the 'situation became ridiculous and continued to be so for the next two years... I was sickened by this hindrance...'[224] Sir Samuel was more phlegmatic, though still deeming it 'essential that Lisbon, Madrid and Barcelona should keep in touch, and that each should know what the other is doing and that they should pass on information.'[225]

Whatever the differences, the most practical escape route from Marseille to Spain remained that along the south coast of France to Perpignan and Banyuls-sur-Mer, and over the Pyrenees at their shallowest point.[226] Guides of whatever political persuasion (most at this time were simply *contrabandistas* or *muglaris* – smugglers) with their intimate knowledge of the mountains were essential, being paid handsomely to deliver the "parcels" (as evaders were known) safely into Spain. Sir Samuel Hoare wrote that a 'convention grew up in course of time to count an escaped prisoner the equivalent of a grand piano for the purpose of the tariff. This meant a charge of about £30 a head.'[227]

Not a few of these escapers and evaders arriving in the south of France had come from the Lille area in the north, some on their own initiative, others with the help of Captain Charles P. Murchie RASC and Sergeant Henry Keith Clayton RAF. Murchie was an old soldier who had seen service in the RFC and RAF from 1914 to 1926.[228] He was working for the NAAFI at Arras when the German push came on 10 May 1940, and he and ten other ranks were ordered to proceed to Lille on 20 May. At Vacquerie-le-Boucq (Pas-de-Calais), near Frévent, the lorries in which they had been travelling were surrounded by the Germans. 'The petrol tanks were immediately punctured by civilians, who wanted the fuel. The Germans, seeing this, set fire to the lorries and left us. The district was full of German troops, so we hid in a café in the village for nearly forty-eight hours. While we were in hiding, three of the drivers left the café. We heard shots, and later were told that three Englishmen had been killed by the Germans that day.'[229]

On the night of 21 May Captain Murchie and the rest managed to slip out of the café unobserved and make their way a few kilometres up the road to Conchy-sur-Canche. 'We remained here for two months, hiding in the house of a farmer,'[230] but living for 'most of the time in dugouts and brushwood shelters, which were constructed by myself and seven RASC other ranks who were then with me.'[231] At the end of this period, having managed to procure civilian clothing, Captain Murchie decided that the group should split up and try to reach Unoccupied France independently. Murchie departed for Lille with the intention of helping other soldiers to escape, and in September met Sergeant Clayton.

In peacetime Clayton, making use of his expertise as an agrostologist (an expert on seeds, grain etc), was secretary of a golf club near Lille, where he lived with his wife. Having joined up on 21 October 1939 and been attached to Air Ministry Works Area No. 1 (France), RAF he held the unusual rank of Acting Sergeant Interpreter. Caught up in the Germans' advance into northern France, he was wounded in the foot and taken prisoner on the morning of 22 May 1940. Escaping from a large prisoner-of-war column at the beginning of June he walked on his injured foot, without food or water, for two or three days before giving himself up. Sent by cattle truck to a camp in western Germany near Trier (Treves), he again escaped on 31 July with two French soldiers, but again suffered from a lack of food and water. Separated from the Frenchmen, he managed to reach home, on 19 August, utterly exhausted and suffering from blood poisoning.

Recovering somewhat he met up with several British soldiers trying to get home, and towards the end of September met Captain Murchie. Placing himself at the senior officer's disposal, he 'interviewed for him people about whom he was not sure, investigated aeroplane schemes, took money and false identity cards to soldiers in hiding, kept him in touch with [a] pro-British organisation, and collected the names of British wounded and dead.'[232] He also raised the not inconsiderable sum of 50,000 francs, which he gave to Murchie. Together these two men took it upon themselves to do what they could for British soldiers trapped in the north. The difficult nature of this work, even at such an early stage of the war, was underlined when, on 12 October, Clayton learnt that a soldier whom he had visited the previous day had been arrested by German police. It so happened that a senior German policeman bore a strong resemblance to Clayton, and the word was that Clayton had "sold" the soldier to the Germans. He and Murchie moved to another hiding place before heading for Paris on 15 October.

Leaving Paris on 28 October they crossed into the Unoccupied Zone the following day, only to be arrested. Clayton, able to pass himself off as a Frenchman, was released and, acting on Murchie's instructions, made his way to Marseille. There, on 2 November, he reported Murchie's arrest to Mr Dean at the American consulate before finding his own accommodation in the city. When he appeared to be showing too much of an 'interest in soldiers arriving from the north' and was suspected of being a German agent, British officers in Marseille instructed British soldiers in Fort St Jean to get rid of him. Surviving the attempt on his life, the misunderstanding was cleared up, and Clayton went to live at the fort on 26 November. Murchie was also brought there on 12 December, having arrived in Marseille some time in November.

Whether anyone was in charge of the British organisation in Marseille at this time is a moot point, but Captain Murchie, who had already been prominent in helping British soldiers to reach Unoccupied France from the north, was certainly involved, as he himself wrote in August 1941: 'From the beginning to the end of the affair, lasting from October 1940 to the end of April 1941, I concerned myself almost exclusively with the passing of officers and men from the Occupied to the Non-Occupied Zone. The method was self-developing and was simplicity itself. A guide arrived in Marseilles, bringing with him three, four or five Britishers, submitted to me a list of his expenses plus the cost of his return journey, which I settled. With this money he returned to the north of France and passed on the good word, with the result that I had at one time twenty-five such guides working. Unfortunately it eventually made my continued stay in Marseilles impossible as everyone in the north knew of my existence. I did all possible to counteract this, but the damage was done and I was forced into partial hiding and had to operate through others.'[233]

Another officer to figure prominently in the lives of British servicemen in Marseille in late 1940–early 1941 was Captain Ian Grant Garrow, 1st Glasgow Highlanders,[234] who had arrived there in October. Surrounded in the fighting near Breteuil (Eure), south-west of Evreux, on 17 June 1940 he led eight of his men through the German lines, later splitting up into three groups of three. Garrow, and Privates E. MacDonald and A. Cattrell had intended to make for the Channel Islands, but changed their minds when they learnt that they had been occupied by the enemy. Making for Spain via Unoccupied France, they were interned at Bélâbre (Indre) with several other British officers, including Captain B.C. Bradford, 1st Black Watch, and Captain Fitch, and about twenty British other ranks. The French officer in charge, Commandant Albinet, commanding the 19th Senegalese Battalion, was 'anti-British, but his treatment of us was very correct, and he looked after us very well.'[235]

As the commandant was unable to give the internees any idea as to their fate, they decided to escape, and towards the end of July left in small groups. Garrow, MacDonald and Cattrell, as before, were arrested by gendarmes at Limogne-en-Quercy (Lot) and taken to *Dépôt 602 Prisonnier de Guerre*, a château at Monferran-Savès (Gers), some forty kilometres west of Toulouse. Re-joined by Captain Bradford, the British there now totalled thirty-two – the two army officers and twenty-six army other ranks (including MacDonald and Cattrell), and four RAF personnel – Flying Officer Lewis Hodges; his rear gunner Sergeant J.H. Wyatt; Aircraftman First Class G. Hibbert; and Leading Aircraftman J. Hopkins, the last two both ground staff.

Shot down on 4/5 September 1940 Hodges and Wyatt had set off on foot from St Brieuc (Côtes-d'Armor), in the north-west of France, to Limoges 'disguised as French peasants'.[236] After a journey of some 500 kilometres they caught a train to Toulouse, and headed for Spain. Arrested at Luchon, near the frontier, on 29 September they were sent to Dépôt 602.

Hibbert and Hopkins had made a valiant, but unsuccessful, attempt to leave France following the general evacuation in June 1940. With No. 2 Section, 5 Air Stores Park, Verzenay, a few kilometres south-east of Reims, they were ordered to retire on 5 June, and left in a lorry with Corporal B. Carnell, 41 Company AMPC, attached to the AASF. At Méry-sur-Seine they were given orders to withdraw to Angers but, when their lorry broke down at St Maixent-l'École, where there was a training school for French officers, they asked the French to put them in touch with the RAF at Angers, 'but instead they put us in the guardroom. We were detained for about 24 hours, after which we got out and succeeded in starting the lorry again.'[237]

Heading for Angers, the lorry broke down again, at Chiché. Walking towards the town they turned back in a hurry when they heard gunfire and discovered that the Germans were in occupation. Returning to their vehicle, they found that the petrol had been syphoned off by French troops, who issued them with passes for Bordeaux. Joining a French army convoy they headed south with hundreds of refugees, and reached Bordeaux in time to see a British destroyer sailing off down the Gironde. On 23 June, hoping to catch up with the ship, they were given permission by French naval authorities to sail on the fishing boat *Flandre*, and had reached the mouth of the Gironde where they saw the French 8,000-ton cruiser *De Grasse* (main armament nine six-inch guns) swarming with French sailors. At that point German guns opened up and sank the *Flandre*. Swimming ashore at le Verdon-sur-Mer, they were given a lift into Bordeaux on 25 June by a French lady, who gave them food and forty francs. After a night in French barracks and a change of overalls, they headed for the Spanish border.

With a French guide they crossed into Spain from Seix (south of St Girons) on 30 June/1 July, but at Tabescán were arrested by carabineros and taken to Lérida. Escorted back to the frontier four days later, they were told to leave the country. Returning to Seix, they were arrested by a gendarme, and taken to St Girons for questioning by the Prefect of Police, who wanted to know how they had reached the south of France, how they had crossed the Pyrenees, and who had helped them. For good measure, their fingerprints were also taken. Four days later they were transferred to Toulouse and kept under filthy conditions before being sent to Dépôt 602 on 13 July.

On 18 October 1940 twenty-two of the thirty-two internees at Monferran-Savès were transferred to Fort St Jean, but the other ten escaped in small groups. Hopkins and Private Jack O'Shea, 4th Seaforths, went to Perpignan, but made the mistake of asking directions from an Italian, who turned them in to the gendarmes. After several prisons and camps, they were transferred to Fort St Jean, Marseille, in November 1940, and thence to the prison at St Hippolyte-du-Fort in January 1941. On 20 March Hopkins went before a Mixed Medical Commission, and was deemed unwell enough for repatriation. Not allowed to leave France until July 1941, he flew back from Gibraltar on 26 August.[238]

Private MacDonald and Corporal Carnell were in a group that got a dozen kilometres beyond Perpignan before being caught by gendarmes without proper papers. After three days at a camp at Agde (Hérault), they were also sent to Toulouse: 'The treatment was very bad. The food consisted of bread and bully beef, and when we asked for fresh water we were given two bottles of salt water.'[239] From Agde, Corporal Carnell was sent to Fort St Jean and then to St Hippolyte-du-Fort, before he, too, was passed "fit" for repatriation by the Mixed Medical Commission on 20 March 1941. He was in the group that sailed from Gibraltar on 4 July, and which reached Gourock eight days later.

Hibbert, who had also reached St Hippolyte via Fort St Jean, also went before a Mixed Medical Commission, on 10 June 1941, and was eventually flown from Gibraltar to Oban in Scotland on 4/5 September 1941. With him on the aircraft were Sergeant F.G. Willis (see previous chapter) and Pilot Officer B.J.A. Rennie, a South African pilot who had been flying his Hampden to Aachen on the night of 9/10 July 1941 on what was the first large-scale raid of the war on that town. A few kilometres short of the target the Hampden was caught in a cone of ten searchlights at 15,000 feet and was, as Rennie later recorded, 'then attacked by an Me109. Our controls were shot away and a petrol tank set on fire.'[240] Rennie baled out after the wireless operator and observer, but the rear gunner, already dead, crashed with the aircraft. As he descended from 5,000 feet, losing his left flying boot, Rennie saw the other two coming down, held in the beams of the searchlights, before hitting telegraph wires and hurting his ankle.

Found by some Belgians near Bilzen, a dozen kilometres west of the Dutch border and Maastricht, Rennie was told that the wireless operator, possibly hit by debris from the Hampden, had not survived, and that the observer had been captured.[241] Having to leave the Belgians when it was learnt that the Germans were looking for him, Rennie met a 'tall peasant', and tried to persuade the man to part with his shoes. When the Belgian made a grab for him, Rennie 'laid him out'. At a canal a couple of kilometres further on he ran into a German sentry. Clearly not a man to be trifled with Rennie 'had to dispose of him, leaving the body at the bottom of the canal bank in some bushes.'

His next encounter with Belgians was friendly, for they hid him in a house at Eisden, some fifteen kilometres north of Maastricht, and kitted him out in civilian clothes. Unfortunately, 'the Burgomaster's secretary was a "Bosche-Belge" so I cleared out in time to see the latter accompanied by the Germans enter the house. When they had left, my host emerged and gave me food, a map and directions to make for Hasselt.'[242] At midday on 12 July he set off westwards for Hasselt, but after twelve kilometres stopped at a hotel, and spent the night there. Accompanied by a Belgian sergeant he made his way by train to Liège, and on 15 July across the border into France. Paying a man 500 francs to row them across the St Quentin canal, they reached Paris on 17 July, where they stayed for two days before heading south-east to the Demarcation Line near Givry (Saône-et-Loire). After a close shave when they stumbled upon a German headquarters in a wood and were nearly caught, they passed an empty sentry-box ('This is definitely not a good place for crossing!' Rennie noted), before entering Unoccupied France on 19 July.

After a night in a wood near la Charmée they were caught by two gendarmes, but were released on payment of 200 francs. Walking to Tournus they caught a bus to Lyon, a train to Marseille, where they stayed briefly in a hotel, before continuing on 24 July by train to Perpignan. After five days they moved out of the town and hid up for another five days in a vineyard. Returning to Perpignan they found two guides, and left with them across the Pyrenees at 9 p.m. on 9 August, spending a night in the mountains. On 10 August they reached Vilajuiga, some fifteen kilometres from the French border, and 'stayed with the father of one of our guides', who took a message from them to the British consulate at Barcelona. Vice-consul Dorchy, 'picked us up that night in his car and subsequently arranged for our journey to Madrid.'[243] Who he was or what became of the Belgian sergeant is not known.[244]

Captain Garrow was one of those sent from Dépôt 602 to Fort St Jean on 18 October 1940. He was a 'tall commanding Scotsman; quiet and deliberate in speech and thought' who 'knew little French'. Though his 'Highland features made disguise impossible...'[245] he was persuaded to help with 'the administration and general welfare of the British internees'.[246]

Another officer persuaded to help was Lieutenant J.M. Langley, Coldstream Guards, who had also arrived in Marseille in November 1940. Wounded in the fighting in the north of France on 1 June, and suffering a secondary hæmorrhage from a compound fracture of the left humerus, he had been taken to what remained of the RAMC's 12th Casualty Clearing Station, then in the hands of the Germans, where Major Philip Newman RAMC found him 'lying in a huge pool of blood'[247] and assumed him to be dead. Jimmy Langley, though, was still alive, and it would be Newman's unpleasant but necessary duty to amputate his left arm. Within three days of the operation Langley was up and about.

Transferred to the 21st British Field Hospital, at the Faculté Catholique , Boulevard Vauban, Lille, Langley was assisted by Corporal S.F. Tachon to escape on 5 October.[248] Tachon, who had been acting as an interpreter at the Caserne St Ruth in Lille, knew several safe houses, and it was to Dr Carpentier's house at 37, rue de Turenne, Lille that Langley was sent, before reaching Paris on 17 October. Making his way to Bourges, with a view to crossing into Unoccupied France at Dun-sur-Auron (Cher), he and a French youth with whom he was travelling were put 'in touch with two persons, who took us to a little inn where, to my surprise, we found part of [a] German patrol drinking. They definitely were in the picture, and knew we were crossing. At 7.30 the Germans gave us the O.K. and we crossed in a party of twelve, which included six refugees who joined us in the inn. Actually during the crossing we were sighted by the German patrol, who shouted to us to hurry.'[249] Once safely in Marseille Langley made himself known to the French at Fort St Jean which, he noted, 'housed some fifteen British officers who were free to come and go as they wished, provided they were present at the weekly roll call on Monday mornings, and about fifty other ranks who were confined to barracks.'[250] The officers were always keen to attend roll call, as this was when the French commandant offered 'all the officers their weekly rations in bulk... These could be sold in the city black market for exorbitant prices.'[251]

One of the advantages of the generous parole system was that an officer could, if he so wished, take a room in a hotel. Not only did this offer greater freedom but it also made it much easier to go into hiding should the need arise, as it did early in January 1941. Barely a week after his arrival at Fort St Jean Jimmy Langley took a room in the Hôtel Cécile, a *maison de rendezvous*, which he shared with 'Mike Maloney, an RAF fighter pilot'.[252] "Maloney" (probably Flight Lieutenant Pat Treacy) also took a room at Les Sept Petit Pécheurs, near le Vieux Port, while Captain Murchie took a room in a hotel, though he also had an apartment elsewhere in the city. Garrow 'took a hotel room near the Gare Saint Charles',[253] but in December 1940 moved to 13, rue des Phocéens, 'the same tenement block where M. Fiocca, a member of my organisation, lived.'[254] Henri Fiocca, a successful businessman, and his wife Nancy were to prove of great help to the British in the months to come.

The liberty that was extended to officers enabled them to meet not only Donald Caskie but also others of the Marseille community who were keen to help, including 'a small, cultured, and fiercely pro-British circle, amongst whom were several Greek residents of long standing'.[255] It was in December 1940, at a tea party at the residence of a Greek couple, Monsieur and Madame Nicolopoulos, that Garrow was introduced to a certain Louis Nouveau, a forty-six-year-old exporter/importer, anglophile and anti-Pétainist. Present, too, were Tom Kenny, a thirty-year-old Canadian businessman, another man whose name Nouveau could not remember, and Lieutenant Langley.

One day in November 1940, "visiting" Fort St Jean, Treacy was talking with a group of fellow officers when a voice said: 'Hello Pat'. Turning round, he saw that it was Gordon Instone, whom he had last seen in June in northern France. Instone's story was that after Treacy had gone off on his own he had been picked up by Germans looking for young Frenchmen to deport to Germany for forced labour. Finding a steel bar in the lorry that was taking him into captivity he hit his two guards with it before jumping off, though damaging a shoulder in the process. Going back to the Duviers at Campagne-les-Hesdins, he met two Frenchmen on the run, and went with them to Paris. Leaving in September with false papers he reached Marseille on 8 November.

As with others before, he was advised to go to the Seamen's Mission, and it was there one morning that a French policeman told the assembled company 'that he was instructed by the Vichy Government on behalf of the German and Italian Armistice Commissions, who objected to our presence in Marseille, to escort us to the Fort St Jean…'[256] Being a fluent French speaker, Gordon Instone was given the job of interpreter in the French commandant's office, and was appointed as assistant to another senior British officer at Fort St Jean, Captain L.A. Wilkins, 2/5th West Yorkshire Regiment.

Treacy told Instone that he was going to get hold of an Irish passport to get home, and asked Instone if he had any plans for escaping. Instone's reply was that a scheme was being hatched to get himself and three army sergeants to Spain over the Pyrenees, but they were short of money: 'Pat promised to get two thousand francs to help me if I would agree to take two RAF sergeants with me as well… I agreed.'[257]

Towards the end of December, however, Instone heard that Fort St Jean 'was to be closed at the beginning of January [1941] and all the British internees were to be transferred to the French military concentration camp at St. Hippolyte, near Nîmes.'[258] Seizing the moment, therefore, Captain Fitch and Corporal W. West, Highland Light Infantry, escaped on 24 December. Two days later Company Quartermaster Sergeants David Lepper, 2/5th West Yorks, and M.J. McLear, 2nd South Wales Borderers; Sergeant S.T. Jackson RASC; Sergeant R.W. Lonsdale;[259] Sergeant J.H. Wyatt; and Gunner Instone followed. Bribing the guards on duty, these six men simply walked out of the fort.[260]

Catching a train to Perpignan, and a taxi to Cerbère (practically on the Spanish border), they crossed into Spain with a guide to whom they had paid a not-inconsiderable sum. Near the town of Figueras all were arrested by the Guardia Civil except for the guide, who fled the moment he saw what was afoot. After incarceration in the unwholesome prisons at Figueras, Cervera and Saragossa, they came to the end of the line – *Campo de Concentración de Prisioneros de Miranda de Ebro* (Miranda de Ebro concentration camp). Some weeks into their time at Miranda Sergeant Jack Wyatt, suffering from depression, was removed to what was laughingly called the hospital, but returned somewhat the better after a fortnight or so.

It was not until 9 March 1941 that a group of two dozen or so soldiers and airmen, including Wyatt, Lonsdale and Instone, was released. From Gibraltar, reached via the British Embassy at Madrid, they departed aboard HMT *Empire Trooper*[261] for Liverpool on 4 April. They had not gone far before the ship developed engine trouble (caused, so rumour had it, by sand having been put into the turbines by the German crew before capture) and was obliged to return to Gibraltar. They transferred to the Royal Navy's aircraft carrier HMS *Furious* and completed the voyage to Belfast, Northern Ireland on 11 April.[262]

Back in Marseille, after Captain Fitch had gone, Flight Lieutenant Pat Treacy assumed the responsibility of officer in charge of escapes with Jimmy Langley as his deputy. Varian Fry continued to act as "paymaster", while Captain Wilkins gave his support to the "escape committee". It was not long, though, before Treacy and Langley were on their way home. Having obtained an Irish passport and a legitimate French exit visa, Treacy left for Spain and Portugal on 22 January 1941,[263] and Langley, who had been passed unfit for further military duties by the board of the Mixed Medical

Commission on 4 January 1941, departed with twenty-five other repatriation candidates on 24 February, reaching Gourock on 17 March 1941.

With Langley were Private Alex Cattrell, Corporal Carnell, Leading Aircraftman J.H. Jarvis, and Sergeant A.K. Sumerson. Jarvis, RAF groundcrew, had been injured on 25 May 1940 when helping to extinguish a fire in one of his squadron's bombers. Taken to the André Gillier hospital, Troyes, he was evacuated on 18 June to the *Hôpital Complémentaire*, Lycée des Garçons, at Nîmes, and then to Marseille (14 December). Sergeant Sumerson, shot down near Sedan on 14 May 1940, suffered temporary blindness from burns to his face. When his sight had returned sufficiently he walked through the German lines but was picked up by the French and taken to Verdun hospital, where he was treated for severe burns to face, hands, right leg and back. He was evacuated via Roanne to Marseille on 1 January 1941, and medically boarded three days later.

With the return to Britain of some of the officers, Ian Garrow and Tom Kenny handled most of the escapes from February onwards, though Captain Murchie still considered himself to be in overall command with Ian Garrow as his deputy. One of the first decisions that they had to make, in January 1941, involved the young French guide Roland Lepers, whom they had met in Marseille after he had brought a small group of evaders down from the Lille area. He told Murchie and Garrow about an Englishman in the Lille area who 'had stitched together a complex network'[264] of dozens of agents willing to hide evaders and escapers. Impressed by what they had heard, the captains asked Lepers to bring the Englishman with him on his next trip, and gave him 10,000 francs to cover his expenses. Lepers returned in February with the Englishman, who called himself Sergeant Paul Cole. Satisfied with his credentials Cole was appointed chief of operations in the north, given a further 10,000 francs to keep the line going, and sent back north with young Lepers.

As anticipated, on 8 January 1941 the British military internees at Fort St Jean, Marseille now classified by the Vichy French as *Détachement W*, were moved to the prison at St Hippolyte-du-Fort, near Nîmes. The decision to move them had been made by the French authorities partly because Fort St Jean had become overcrowded but mainly because the Italians, permitted under the terms of the 1940 armistice to maintain a commission in the area, were concerned at the amount of freedom given to British soldiers in Marseille. In an attempt to make them appreciate that the move was for the best, the internees were told that conditions at St Hippolyte would be better than at Fort St Jean and also that the pay office would be moving with them.

They were housed at St Hippolyte in barracks that had been constructed in an earlier century for the soldiers who had manned the old fort to the south-east of the town. Although the barracks had lain empty for some time they had not been neglected, and the men were comfortably accommodated, each having 'an iron bedstead, a mattress and blankets'. There was also 'a library with several hundred English books provided by the International Red Cross'.[265] Food supplies, too, were as good as could be expected, and though the men had to attend three compulsory roll calls per day they were allowed out of the prison on a daily basis between the hours of 10 a.m. and 9 p.m., extended to 11 p.m. for NCOs.

Before the move Captain Garrow had had a meeting with Lieutenant Winwick Miller Hewit RA, who was to be senior British officer (SBO) at St Hippolyte, as Hewit noted: 'We decided that, in view of the number of captures at the Spanish frontier, it was desirable that we should have some organisation for assisting British escapers. We arranged that he should hide in Marseilles and arrange the organisation from outside, while I went with the troops to St Hippolyte and regulated the escapes from the inside, in addition to looking after the welfare of the men.'[266]

Ian Garrow therefore arranged with a French officer on the staff of the 15th Division that he should remain in Marseille ostensibly 'to arrange for the welfare of any British evaders who might arrive in Marseilles from Occupied France.' Moving from Fort St Jean with Hewit were two other officers – Lieutenant J.P.T. Linklater RA, and 2nd Lieutenant R.E.H. Parkinson – and forty-four other ranks, leaving over 200 others scattered throughout Marseille waiting to leave Unoccupied France.[267]

There was, though, some question over Lieutenant Linklater's loyalty. On 6 February 1941 the US consul-general at Marseille sent a telegram to London: 'Information is requested with regard to Second Lieutenant J.P.J. [*sic*] Linklater, bearer of British passport No. 292849 issued on July 24th, 1939, by the Foreign Office. Linklater was liaison officer at Czech Headquarters and is at present interned in Marseille [*sic* – St Hippolyte] with British officers, among whom he has aroused suspicions.'[268]

Lieutenant Jimmy Langley also mentioned him in his report to MI9 on his return to England: 'This man, speaking good English, represents himself as the son of the British Consul in Prague before the war, and liaison officer with the Czech division during the war in France. He appears to have plenty of money but is entirely ignorant of any British military knowledge. He went to the camp at Nimes [*sic*] and I believe he has since left for a destination not known. It is my impression and that of others that this man was working for the Germans.'[269]

This was not, however, a view that was shared by Flying Officer Lewis Hodges, who had been brought to St Hippolyte at the end of January 1941 in handcuffs. According to Hodges, Linklater 'spoke French perfectly and, on being captured after the Armistice, pretended to be a Frenchman and was put with the French in a German P/W Camp at Montargis.'[270] Hodges told the authorities that Linklater had done 'a lot of good work' at St Hippolyte, forging papers and taking men across the Pyrenees into Spain. On one occasion he and Lieutenant Hewit had taken a naval rating and a Scottish soldier to the Spanish frontier at Prats de Mollo. Showing them the way over the Pyrenees, they told them to head for Barcelona, before returning to St Hippolyte.

The truth of the matter was that John Philip Thomas Linklater, born in Prague on 18 June 1920, had immediately been registered by his parents as a British subject. He later went to Collet Court preparatory school and then to St Paul's School, both in London. As he was in France in the summer of 1939 he 'enlisted in the Czechoslovakian Army with the consent of the British Ambassador in Paris',[271] but on 19 June 1940 was taken prisoner and held at the camp at Montargis (Loiret). In February 1941 his parents were informed by the Church of Scotland that he was 'in Marseille with the Rev. Donald C. Caskie, formerly Church of Scotland minister in Paris'.[272]

Linklater and Hodges escaped from St Hippolyte-du-Fort in early April 1941 by the simple expedient of forging leave passes and walking out. From Marseille Nancy Fiocca took them by train to Perpignan, whence they took a taxi to Laroque-des-Albères, close to the Pyrenees, and walked into Spain. Arrested at Cantallóps, they were transferred to the Miranda de Ebro camp after the usual incarceration in various other, unwholesome prisons. Hodges, and another officer, were finally released into the hands of the British military attaché on 8 June 1941. Five nights later Hodges was flown from Gibraltar to RAF Mount Batten.

On 7 May 1941 Linklater was able to send a telegram in Spanish to his parents from the camp at Miranda de Ebro. Translated, it reads: 'Interned Miranda Ebro. Mobilise all for liberation. Immediate action indispensable. Greetings. John Linklater.'[273] Somehow, Jan Masaryk, foreign minister of the Czechoslovak government in exile in London, became involved and asked the British to do what they could for Linklater. Writing from the British Embassy in Madrid on 14 June 1941 to R.M. Makins at the Foreign Office, Michael Creswell was able to say that Linklater 'was released from the concentration camp last week and was sent on to Gibraltar with a party of soldiers on June 9th. The Gibraltar authorities will probably send him to the United Kingdom, and if Masaryk wants any further news the simplest course would be for him to telegraph the Governor.'[274]

Officialdom was not yet finished with Linklater for on 7 July 1941 H.M. de Groot of the War Office wrote to the Honourable H.A.A. Sankey at the Foreign Office saying that information had been received from the US consul-general in Marseille that 'one J.P.T. Linklater described as "Aspirt (*sic* – Aspirant) in the Czech forces" has received advances during the last quarter amounting to £24.'[275]

On 1 September 1941 Linklater, recipient of the Czech Medal for Bravery, was commissioned in the British Army and joined the Intelligence Corps. He was on attachment to the 1st Airborne Division in Italy when he was captured on 15 September 1943 while on a reconnaissance patrol. Four days later he and twenty-four others were on their way by train to Germany along the Italian east-coast route. Linklater and a Corporal Ialamoff, 2 SAS, both "marked men" by the Germans, had been given priority by the rest of the prisoners to escape and, despite the two guards in the cattle-truck, got out 'through the door on the evening of 25 September 1943 about approximately ten kilometres north of Pesaro'.

Joining up the two escapers walked together for a few days until reaching the village of Pieve Torina, where Ialamoff decided to stop. After a week, Linklater continued his travels, and remained at the village of Settefrati from early November 1943 to January 1944. Making his way to Rome, he remained there until its liberation in June.

Those members of Detachment W at St Hippolyte who were escape-minded, and most were, made the most of their freedom in town as others had done in Marseille. In a report made by the French commandant, it was noted that seventeen of twenty-nine escapes during the period from 15 January to 28 February 1941 were successful; in March thirty-four of fifty-three attempts succeeded; and in April sixty-three of ninety-four got away.[276] Inevitably, the French authorities, bowing under pressure from the Germans on the Franco-German Armistice Commission, decided that enough was enough, and in May 1941 the camp was wired in and guarded more strictly. This resulted in the success of only thirty-six out of eighty-nine escapes over the following three months.

Although a considerable number of internees had managed to escape, a report dated 10 June 1941 from the US consulate in Marseille noted that since July 1940 'forty-six British officers and 623 enlisted men' had arrived in Marseille. It also noted 'that of this number six officers and seventy-three enlisted men are reported as having been passed by the special medical board of revision established by the French military authorities, as unfit, and as having left the country with exit visas issued by the French government. Twenty-four enlisted men, passed as unfit by a board which met on May 15 are now awaiting here exit visas enabling them to leave France for the United Kingdom over Spain.'[277] It was also understood by the US consulate in Marseille that one officer and four enlisted men were being detained elsewhere than at St Hippolyte, and that it was reasonable to 'assume that not fewer than thirty-six officers and 284 enlisted men have succeeded in escaping from France.' It was also probable, the report added, that a small number 'may be still in Unoccupied France without the knowledge of the police and military authorities.'

Then worrying news reached the men who were still at St Hippolyte. On 6 June 1941 the US consul-general in Marseille had written to the senior British officer, Lieutenant Hewit, notifying him of a proposal from London to reduce their living allowance. It was noted that the allowance would be 'considerably lower than that which has been in practice up to this time, but, in view of the fact that no liberty outside the confines of the camp is granted now to these interned soldiers and they have little to spend their money on except alcoholic beverages obtainable in the *cantine* within the camp, it is felt that no hardship would result.'[278] The French commandant, too, was in favour of a reduction, as less money would reduce the temptation to drink too much, which all too frequently resulted in disturbances.

Lieutenant Hewit thought otherwise and in a strongly worded reply dated 14 June made it quite clear that he was 'frankly disgusted by this proposal to the pay of troops who have suffered so much... Already, news of the proposed reduction has caused hostility in a camp which has been comparatively quiet up till now. I consider that the strongest possible representations and protests should be addressed to the proper quarter.'[279]

It was, on the face of it, an odd thing for the authorities to have done. In May rumours had reached Marseille that conditions at St Hippolyte had deteriorated, and that those confined there were maltreated and underfed, so much so that the American consul, George M. Abbott, had been instructed by his embassy in London 'to call upon the commandant on May 31 and, if possible, inspect the quarters and talk to the men.'[280] Abbott noted that three officers and 238 men were confined there, and that one of the British sergeants [*sic*] had been wounded in an escape attempt on the night of 21/22 May. The man in question, Bombardier William Csete RA, had been shot in the leg after he had ignored two warning shots from a French guard, but his condition was not serious. Curiously, the guard's actions were to conform precisely with orders promulgated by General Huntziger two months later, on 22 July 1941, namely that guards were authorised to shoot on any interned British military personnel who were attempting to escape, after three warnings to halt had been given and two shots had been fired into the air.[281]

In June 1941 Captain Ian Garrow agreed with 2nd Lieutenant R.E.H. Parkinson that he should 'stay in St Hippolyte permanently to run the camp and organise any escapes. The other British officers were to attempt their escapes.'[282] These other officers, Lieutenant Hewit and Pilot Officer R.A.E. "Bob" Milton, had not, however, managed to escape by the time of 'the arrival in the camp of Wing Commander [*sic*] Whitney Straight on 9 August 1941'.[283]

Pilot Officer Bob Milton, pilot, and crew – Sergeants S.J. Houghton, J. Burridge and R.E. Griffiths – had run into an electrical storm while on patrol in their Hudson off Brest, France, on 2 April 1941. Milton made a forced landing at Maillé (Vienne), north-west of Poitiers and a long way south-east of Brest.[284] Having 'detonated the IFF, and secret papers and maps burned' the crew 'kept together and with the help of French civilians who paid for our railway tickets, made our way via Limoges to Marseille.'[285] At Marseille railway station, with no papers, they were arrested by the police and on 13 April 1941 sent to St Hippolyte.

Thought was given, meanwhile, as to how to evacuate the two hundred or so still in hiding in Marseille. With heavy winter snow blocking the smugglers' footpaths over the Pyrenees, Captain Murchie decided that the only way out for the time being was, once again, by ship to North Africa. Ten soldiers were successfully evacuated in this way, though they were caught once they had reached Algeria, and spent over a year and a half in the appalling desert camps before being liberated in November 1942, after the Allied landings in North Africa. Orders were then received from London that this route was to be closed and the one to Spain re-opened. Murchie then sent off a second party, under the command of Lance-Sergeant J.K. Bell, (see previous chapter).

Of the senior officers in Marseille Captain Murchie himself was the next to leave. The activities of the British officers in Marseille – "the gang" as they were known – had aroused the suspicions of the French authorities not least because of the 'lavish expenditure of money. This resulted in the movements of the gang being strictly watched and eventually, early in April [1941], it was obvious that the gang would have to cease operations and quit France.'[286] Murchie later stated that he had been identified by the Marseille police 'through the indiscretion of a brother officer, with the result that I was arrested daily by the French on some pretext or other.' During the second week of April, therefore, he decided that it was time to go, even though he was under 'the partial protection of a highly placed French military official'. He left for Perpignan on 15 April 1941 with Sergeant Clayton and Frenchman André Minne, a café proprietor from Lille. Minne was an unsung hero who had done much good work for Murchie as a *convoyeur*, particularly in taking men across the Demarcation Line.[287]

The three left Perpignan on 17 April, crossing the Pyrenees into Spain during the night of 17/18 April. On their way across the mountains they were 'reinforced by three other British (amongst them one Howlett, an Australian 3rd Engineer on a merchantman, who had been for five months a prisoner on various German raiders or supply ships) and also by five Belgians. The party, now numbering eleven went into hiding in some farm buildings near Figueras, and Murchie by means of two peasants sent an S.O.S. to the consulate in Barcelona asking for help to enable them to reach Barcelona.'[288]

Plans were made for the party to be conveyed to Barcelona by taxi, but at the last minute it appeared that the taxi drivers lost their nerve. Murchie then made further arrangements for the party to be taken to Barcelona on lorries taking market produce to the city, but circumstances conspired against the success of this plan too. The Spanish police were looking for 'a guide named Juan Falan who, as it transpired, was an individual very much wanted by the Spanish police not only for his contraband activities but because he had taken some prominent part in the Civil War.'[289] The guide, Juan Palou, not Falan, was, according to Murchie, 'a Nationalist soldier living in Figueras, and was involved with a big contraband smuggling organisation comprising a number of police officials, since arrested, and operating from Figueras.'

Murchie and his party were arrested by the police on 21 April and taken to the *Cárcel Modelo* civil prison in Barcelona. Captain Murchie was still wearing his British officer's uniform and was carrying a British officer's identity card. Word of their incarceration reached the Barcelona consulate, and on 3 May Vice-Consul Whitfield went to see them. Murchie and Clayton (who had given his rank to the police as flight lieutenant) 'were interviewed in the presence of a prison officer assisted by an interpreter, himself a prisoner.'[290] Whitfield learnt that the two men and Minne were 'at the disposition of the *juzgado militar*' (military court of justice) and 'had already been interrogated by a *juez militar* [military judge], on charge of "espionage"'. The other four 'appear to be at the disposition of the Gobernador Civil only'. In the difficult circumstances Murchie was able to tell Whitfield that two guides who had been sent to bring the men down from their hiding place near Figueras had been arrested.

The charges against them, however fabricated, were based on incriminating evidence that had been found on two of the party. Howlett, the Australian ship's engineer, had been found with a drawing and a description of the German Q-ship that had sunk his merchantman some months earlier. Taken prisoner, Howlett had been landed in France by the Germans, but had escaped to Marseille. Clayton, on the other hand, 'was found to have in his possession a letter from a Frenchman resident in Paris who wished to act as an "*agent double*", though no reference to this appeared in the text.' Clayton was also carrying 'some rough pencilled receipts for 75,000 French francs' which had been incurred on Murchie's authority in Marseille.

When Murchie appeared before the *Juez Militar* in May, he was asked searching questions about what he was doing in Marseille, and also if he knew the names Nouveau of Marseille and "Dr Cornet" of Brussels. After Murchie had blustered that he had 'met thousands of people and could not remember either name', the judge informed him that he thought there was nothing in the case. Three days after the military judge had examined him, Murchie was questioned by the civil authorities, the interrogator telling him that they were proceeding independently of the military. Murchie was again asked about Dr Cornet, and told that it would be useless for him to deny knowledge of the man as he was at that very moment a prisoner of the Spanish in Madrid and, furthermore, they had found on him a letter from Murchie asking the British government for funds. Faced with such evidence, Murchie did admit that he had been 'occupied with humanitarian work in Marseilles' and that he had been 'directly and indirectly responsible for the passing of some hundreds of troops from the Occupied to the Non-Occupied part of France'. Finally, he admitted that he *might* have 'asked the British government for financial support for this work'.

For his part, the vice-consul assured Murchie 'that every effort was being made to get the matter settled as soon as possible, but warned him that it would not be a very speedy matter', and he also gave the prisoners 'fifty pesetas each, a large parcel of food, clothes of various kinds, soap, toothpaste and tobacco, for which Miss Cautley had arranged.'

Early in June 1941 Captain Murchie and his party were transferred from the *Cárcel Modelo* civil prison to the fortress of Montjuich in Barcelona, leaving behind the four Belgians under Lieutenant Henri de la Bastita who was, in Murchie's opinion, 'a man capable of the most amazing indiscretions', and 'untrustworthy in other respects'. For instance, he had apparently claimed to have been 'on a personal mission from the King of the Belgians to the British Consul in Barcelona', a statement that he later retracted. Nevertheless, conditions at Montjuich were appreciably better than they had been at the *Cárcel Modelo*, where they had on occasions been left for as long as thirty-six hours without food, and had, all eleven of them, been 'herded together in a cell measuring 12′ x 6′ – without blankets'.

The British consular staff did what they could to keep up the pressure on the Barcelona authorities, but no progress was made, not even when two Barcelona civil lawyers were hired and, later, a military jurist, a cavalry officer named Nubiola, who had some influence. Murchie initially regarded Nubiola as a doubtful quantity, but changed his mind when Nubiola himself was arrested. Pressure continued to be applied until, on 15 December 1941, Murchie and party were released to Saragossa, Pamplona and Irún prisons before reaching the prison at Miranda de Ebro on 20 December, a sign that the Spanish authorities might be considering them for release in due course. Indeed, on 4 February 1942 this came to pass, and Murchie sailed from Gibraltar on 21 February 1942. Clayton followed on 4 March.[291]

Another British army officer to play a brief, but nonetheless important, part in the Marseille escape line's affairs was Second Lieutenant Richard Lowther Broad, 2nd Seaforth Highlanders, who had arrived in Marseille on 13 February 1941. Having escaped from St Valéry-en-Caux, Normandy, on 12 June 1940 with six men from his own platoon and Private George Dodd from the MT section[292] they were accommodated for several months in the Honfleur area, thanks largely to Mère Marie du St Sacrement, a Yorkshirewoman born Georgina Knapp, 'who had made a remarkable impression on the people of Honfleur who were said to be more afraid of her than of any other earthly authority.'[293] Broad and the seven soldiers were nicknamed "*Blanche-Neige et les Septs Nains*" ("Snow White and the Seven Dwarfs").

With the whole of Normandy securely under German domination, it was difficult for Richard Broad and his men to move freely in any direction but, in January 1941, they were helped on their way by 'Count Pierre d'Harcourt and a group of his Paris and Normandy friends'.[294] Pierre d'Harcourt, scion of a distinguished and ancient French family, had become involved in the shady world of intelligence gathering on a visit in the summer of 1940 to Vichy to see his father, who was himself wanted by the Germans for having published anti-Nazi tracts before the war.

As Pierre noted, it was not his 'job to help escaping prisoners', but he 'first became involved through a relative, who told me of a woman in Normandy who had been hiding some British soldiers for nearly six months. She was getting more and more apprehensive about what would happen if she could not dispose of them.'[295] Making his way to Normandy, therefore, Pierre took Richard Broad and his men, together with other desperate French men and women, across the Demarcation Line into the Unoccupied Zone but, as they did so, two of Broad's men were spotted by a German patrol. Fire was opened in the black of night, and though one of them was hit in the leg and the other (Private Osborne) in the arm both made it to safety.

Now scattered to the four winds, Broad was unable to effect a regrouping of his men in the Unoccupied Zone as he had hoped. It was only a matter of time before all were arrested by Vichy police, and escorted to the Sainte Marthe barracks in Marseille,[296] where, following the evacuation of Fort St Jean on 8 January 1941, waifs and strays were being temporarily held. They 'found themselves back in the army with a vengeance. When an NCO entered the room they had to leap to attention.' Conditions generally were bad. With no toilet facilities, the men had 'to use the prison yard which was swilled down every morning. Anyone who was seen in the yard with his clothes on at night would be shot, they were warned.'[297]

Then Broad learnt that able-bodied soldiers were to be sent to St Hippolyte-du-Fort, while those deemed incapable of bearing arms, the wounded, were to be repatriated. Broad's plan, therefore, was to escape and to arrange for his men to be hidden in the south of the town at the château of la Comtesse Lili Pastré, to whom he had been given an introduction.[298] Having discovered that wounded internees were allowed into Marseille on parole, Broad asked the commandant, Capitaine Arthur, for permission to leave the barracks on parole, but this was refused. Not letting Arthur's refusal stop him, and having found a piece of paper vaguely resembling the real parole certificates, Broad next morning 'walked towards the exit of the prison, pulled out the paper, folded it up, put it back in my pocket just as I reached the sentry and walked out of the prison.'[299]

Making his way to the château Broad found no one there, and went instead to the American consulate, where he spoke with Arthur Dean, who 'seemed quite interested in my story, but was not very helpful. This I discovered later was not his fault, but due to the fact that he was acting under the orders of a Major Dodds, who was, in my opinion, not only unhelpful, but appeared to take no interest whatever in his job or British soldiers. The American consul was equally disinterested. Comdr. Dean advised me to visit the Rev. Caskie who was in command of the Seamen's Mission.'[300]

Caskie was of little use either, telling Broad that he hadn't been in Marseille long and knew very little about the place. This, of course, was not true – Caskie had by this time been in Marseille for the best part of seven months – but he may have been wary of Broad's extremely bad identity card, 'being the ordinary French type card with the unconvincing statement' and that he was an American citizen. Nevertheless, Caskie said that Broad could stay for a short while, but that he had to be out of the mission when the French police paid their daily visit, between 7 and 8 a.m. Rather than risk being found with his poor identity card, Broad removed himself to a hotel in the city.

It was a sore point with the British officers in Marseille that some of the Americans were deliberately unco-operative. Langley was particularly harsh on the American consul-general's deputy, 'Mr Abbott, who is pro-German and loses no chance of scoffing at the British effort.' It was Langley's opinion, also, that for so long as Abbott was in the consulate at Marseille no help could be expected from the American officials. He also believed that Major Dodds and Mr Dean, however willing (particularly the latter), were 'completely handicapped by the present attitude of the American Consulate'. This consular reticence may have been due in part to the alarming discovery that the US authorities had allowed a French detective 'access to the British Consular files, which contained the names of many evaders due to arrive at Marseilles. Mr Dean was very much annoyed when this fact came to his notice.'[301]

Capitaine Arthur, meanwhile, was not amused by Broad's absence, and nor were his "seven dwarfs" when they were despatched to St Hippolyte in handcuffs, which were removed by understanding gendarmes when they got to Nîmes. Obliged to spend the night there, the gendarmes took them to a bar, and even allowed two of the Scotsmen to leave with two of the local ladies, provided that they gave their word to be at the railway station next morning. 'The smiles on the faces of the gendarmes were almost as broad as those on the faces of the two soldiers when they turned up next day.'[302]

A couple of days after his arrival in Marseille Broad had gone to the railway station to meet Pierre d'Harcourt off the train from Vichy. Waiting by the exit, his attention was drawn to a man who had just arrived. They got into conversation, and Broad discovered that he was Captain Ian Garrow, 'who acted as liaison between the prison and the consul'. When d'Harcourt did not arrive as arranged, Broad was invited for dinner with Garrow, and was introduced to Captain Wilkins and Tom Kenny. He 'also met that day another British officer called Illingworth'.[303] Garrow put him in the picture about St Hippolyte, and told him that, on instructions from Major Dodds, every effort was being made to persuade the men to go there voluntarily – with all the men in one place it would be easier to effect their escape! Garrow also told him of 'another officer, acting as their chief'. After dinner he took Broad to a café and introduced him to Captain Murchie.

Broad and Pierre d'Harcourt had missed each other at Marseille station as Pierre had arrived on another train shortly after Broad had left. Contact was, however, re-established, and Broad agreed to go with the well-connected Frenchman to Vichy where, said Pierre, something might be arranged with regard to Broad's leaving the country. On the way they went to Cannes to collect Prince Andreas Poniatowski, Pierre's uncle. Once at Vichy, it seemed to Broad that the French Intelligence officers to whom he was introduced wanted to use him as a means of restoring co-operation with their British counterparts. He had a meeting with the Vicomte de Courcy, apparently 'one of the heads of the French [Deuxième] Bureau' (Intelligence service) who said that, if Broad were prepared to help them, then he would help Broad by providing him with identity papers in the name of a French-Canadian, and offered visas for travel to Algiers, Morocco, Spain and Portugal. Broad accepted the offer, and 'though I still intended to leave with the men, I could discuss the situation with Garrow before taking any steps.' De Courcy provided him with an identity card, dated 5 March 1941.

Before returning to Marseille, Broad had a meeting in Vichy with Pierre Dupuy, the Canadian chargé d'affaires for the legations for France, Belgium and The Netherlands. Dupuy had been sent to Vichy on 2 November 1940 at the request of Lord Halifax to 'make an informal report on [the] present situation in Vichy which would be of considerable value'. Dupuy returned to England on 16 December 1940, but had been asked to go back to Vichy in February 1941.[304] At his meeting with Broad, Dupuy discussed the situation of the British soldiers in Unoccupied France and, keen to help, suggested the possibility of an evacuation by destroyer from the Marseille area. Asking Broad whether it would be possible for him to arrange this, Broad replied that it would be no problem, though how such an operation would have been carried out is not clear.[305]

Broad's next task was to go to St Hippolyte to see his men. He met some of the British officers in the town and spent the night in the prison without the French guards noticing. He spoke to his men and told them that he would return in a week's time. Back in Marseille, Ian Garrow told Broad that they were cooking up a scheme that involved 'a Swiss ship, said to be leaving within a week or so for Lisbon and Gibraltar.' The captain agreed to his ship being used for a fee of 26,400 francs. Nothing came of the deal, and the money, having changed hands, was never seen again.[306]

While in Vichy, Broad had met an American journalist, Jay Allen, who gave him a letter of introduction to an elderly American lady, Miss Margaret Palmer, who was residing at the Hôtel Splendide in Marseille. She had been, according to Allen, head of American Intelligence in Spain[307] and, should Broad and his men choose to go home via that country, might prove useful in that regard. Allen also gave Broad permission to use his room at the luxurious Splendide when he was away on business. As several German agents were also living in the best Marseille hotels, Broad decided, better safe than sorry, to move with Ian Garrow 'into a drab room in a warehouse in the Old Port. It boasted a bed, which they had to share, and a few sticks of furniture.'[308]

As 1941 wore on so, too, did the difficulties for Captains Murchie and Garrow who were trying to organise the passage of so many men to Spain. They were handicapped by the fact that they had no papers allowing themselves to travel and so they were, to all intents and purposes, confined to Marseille. Through the good offices of Pierre d'Harcourt, however, Broad was able to obtain for each of them a pass, 'renewable monthly, allowing them to remain in Marseille'. This eased the situation, but further trouble was brewing following the departure of Lance-Sergeant Bell's party to Spain on 18 February.

Word of this had reached the officers at St Hippolyte, and they were 'highly indignant', not least because Murchie had made up Bell's party from men who were lying low in Marseille. Those at St Hippolyte 'felt that as they had done as they had been asked and voluntarily gone to the camp, they should have been chosen for the trip.'[309] Their indignation had been passed on to Broad when he had gone to St Hippolyte, and he had promised Lieutenant Hewit that, when he escaped with the "seven dwarfs", he would also take any four others whom Hewit should care to name. Private Osborne still had his arm in a sling, so was unlikely to be included in the escape, but 'Hewitt [*sic*] thought he would be sent home in the next batch of *reformés*.'

Having discussed the matter with Garrow and Murchie, Broad was asked if he would include Sergeant Clayton in his party, but the latter was not keen to go and, the day before the off, persuaded Murchie that he would be of more use in Marseille, where he was 'extremely well in with all the Marseille gangsters and in consequence was able, at times, to be very useful.' Also proving useful was the American Miss Palmer. She had introduced Broad to a number of influential Spaniards who owned property on the Franco-Spanish border, and 'who agreed to escort over the border any quantity of men we liked, provided we ourselves would arrange for guides once the men reached Spain.'

Broad was able to enjoy a farewell party given by Nancy Fiocca. One of those present was Elizabeth Haden-Guest, who was awaiting papers to enable her (and her three-year-old son, Anthony) to travel to Madrid and on to England. Interned by the Germans at Besançon, she had managed to get to Marseille from Paris with her son in January 1941, and had been referred to Dr Rodocanachi when Anthony had fallen ill.[310] Broad asked her if she would be good enough to take with her a few of his personal bits and pieces, including his asthma apparatus. She and her son, Anthony, eventually left France in 1942, but too late for Broad to collect his belongings from her. At the farewell party, Broad also left details of his 'Spanish scheme with a friend of Mrs Hayden Guest [*sic*]' for her to pass on to Garrow on his return from Perpignan, whither he had gone to see the Belgian consul with his own scheme for getting men into Spain.

It was another NCO of the 2nd Seaforths, Corporal A.V. "Jock" Hubbard, who had made his own way down to Marseille from St Valéry, who revealed the plan to the "seven dwarfs". Broad would make his way to St Hippolyte in a hired lorry, with driver and mate, while the men would leave the prison at a certain hour in twos and threes, climb aboard, and hide under the tarpaulin. The plan worked without a hitch, but as the lorry made its way to Nîmes Broad was alarmed that 'the driver was somewhat erratic at taking corners' and, fearing that the men would be thrown out, ordered the driver's mate to join them under the tarpaulin. This had the desired effect on the driver, and Nîmes was safely attained. Catching the 8 o'clock train for Perpignan, they met their two Andorran guides, the brothers Olivier (the same two who had escorted Bell's party), who were to be paid from monies 'forthcoming mainly via the Fioccas'.

Making their way towards the foothills of the Pyrenees and the Spanish border they crossed into Spain near Banyuls, and caught a train near Figueras for Barcelona. Exhausted by their efforts they fell asleep, only to be woken by a Spanish official demanding passports. Having none, they were arrested, and spent several unpleasant weeks in Spanish prisons before being freed.

During their time in prison, however, Broad had a distasteful run-in with Mr J.G. Whitfield, vice-consul at Barcelona. He had written a letter to the consul-general firmly requesting that something be done at once to alleviate the conditions of him and his men and of three RAF NCOs – Sergeants V.T. McFarlane, R. Vivian, and Flight Sergeant L.R. Willis (see previous chapter) – who had been languishing in the Barcelona prison for twelve days (10–22 March). The airmen were in a particularly 'poor state of health having lived entirely on sardines, the only food obtainable from the canteen. The consul, it appeared, had given them fifty pesetas each, but had not sent in any food. They had also been without blankets in spite of the fact that they were forced to sleep on a stone floor.'

Several days after Broad's letter had been smuggled out by a Spaniard, Vice-Consul Whitfield visited Broad in the prison and 'tackled me on my letters to the consul-general, stating that he was surprised that a lieutenant should adopt such a tone to a consul-general, the equivalent of a major-general.' It was an unsavoury episode, made worse by Whitfield reminding Broad of the difficult conditions under which he and his staff were having to work.

Ever conscious of his responsibilities to his men, Broad had a further battle with consular officials after he had been released from the Miranda camp in the middle of April and had been taken to a police dungeon in Madrid. On 21 April he had discovered that there were also two soldiers in the dungeon – Lance-Corporal H.L. Forster, 9th Royal Northumberland Fusiliers, and Gunner G. Stephenson, 23 Field Brigade, RA – who, after seven or eight days existing on two watery bowls of soup per day, 'were so weak from lack of food that they were hardly able to walk.' Embassy officials had said that it was not possible for food to be sent in to them. Freed from this dungeon after three days Broad was taken to the embassy, where he protested that it was disgraceful that the two soldiers 'should have been allowed to remain as they were' and asked for steps to be taken at once to improve their condition.

Broad was not finished with the embassy staff. On the day of his release from the dungeon (24 April) a young French-Canadian, Jean-Pierre Bedard was brought in. Broad discovered, however, that he was none other than Jean-Pierre Nouveau, son of Louis Nouveau. Aware that Nouveau senior 'had been extremely good to us and, apart from any other sums of money, had to my knowledge handed to Murchie 60,000 francs to be used in aiding the escape of British soldiers in France,' Broad spoke to Lieutenant-Colonel Drummond-Wolff, one of the military attachés, about the younger Nouveau, who 'was in a bad way, half starved and was transferred to the prison hospital.'[311] Drummond-Wolff grudgingly agreed to see what he could do for the Frenchman – which proved to be absolutely nothing.[312]

On 3 May, Broad and his party, including Forster and Stephenson, were on their way south from Madrid to Gibraltar, escorted by Arthur Dean, who told Broad that he had been removed from his post in Marseille and was on his way to take up a new position in Bilbao. The party sailed on 8 May, arriving at Liverpool a week later.[313]

The Fioccas' generous donation was fortunate, for the night before Broad's plan was set in motion 600,000 francs had disappeared in suspicious circumstances from a trunk in Captain Murchie's hotel room.[314] The funds provided by Sir Samuel Hoare had all but dried up and, urgently in need of more, Murchie had obtained the loan of this large sum from a moneylender called Boris Dimitru. No one was ever arrested for the theft, but one theory was that it had been carried out by two policemen, who then split the proceeds with Dimitru.[315] Another theory was that the theft was the work of Murchie's mistress, a cashier in a local restaurant, the *Dorade*, who rather suddenly opened a restaurant of her own. Lieutenant Langley reported to MI9 on 24 March 1941 that he thought that Murchie was 'a first-class man, but has the unfortunate habit of carrying too much money on him and displaying it. He lacks discretion generally…'

When later incarcerated in Barcelona's Montjuich prison, Murchie wrote to Sir Samuel Hoare on 15 August 1941 and explained his version of events: 'My apartment was raided and robbed of a substantial sum in cash, letters, and of a camouflaged record of my cash disbursements, by parties unknown but believed to be semi-official. I was officially registered in a hotel where I had a room occupied by someone else in my name, whereas I actually lived in a small apartment registered in the name of a French girl who was also one of my operatives but had no knowledge of cash affairs. At the time of my departure this person was suspected of being one of my helpers, and was arrested and questioned several times. Immediately prior to leaving Marseilles I disclosed all the facts regarding the theft to the chief of police (a proceeding not without risk) who appeared sympathetic and vaguely confirmed my suspicions as to the parties responsible.'[316]

Lieutenant Langley had also been out and about on money-raising activities among the well-heeled British expatriates still living on the French Riviera. In Cannes, on or about 25 January 1941, he met Mr Jurgens Price, who was 'connected with the Jurgens of Unilever' and who informed Langley 'that he was in a position to advance £5,000 to the Rev. Caskie.' Langley returned to Marseille and discussed the matter with Caskie and Dean, and it was decided to accept the offer 'on the assumption that either the British Government or the Church of Scotland would pay it back as soon as possible to the account of Mr Price, National Provincial Bank, East Sheen.'

Langley returned to Cannes, was given the money in cash and, back once more in Marseille, handed over in person to Caskie 50,000 francs. The rest of the money was to follow 'by the American Ambulance, when it visited Marseille, in connection with the issuing of condensed milk to French children.' Caskie was to bank his money with the British officials at the American consulate until such time as word had been received that £5,000 had been deposited in Mr Price's bank account in England, when £3,000 would be handed over to Captain Murchie and the balance retained for the upkeep of the Seamen's Mission and for providing comforts for the men in Marseille. Langley would give the go-ahead with the words "My father is very well".[317]

The Reverend Caskie also recounts an incident involving the same amount of money. He was surprised one morning when 'a dapper gentleman called to see me. He greeted me in the hallway into the mission in quiet English…' Caskie took him into his office, where the unknown benefactor 'pulled his coat about him and without ado said, "You need money, I know. I have brought you a little contribution… It is not my money, Padre. I am a mere messenger. I come from Monte Carlo."'[318] After the man had gone, Caskie counted the money: 'It was £5,000 exactly, in French currency.'[319]

Who the man was Caskie never knew but, curiously, there was a second episode (or was it the same one?) involving a similar sum from a British expatriate. On 2 March 1941 Colonel Sawyer, an acquaintance of Major Hugh Dodds, travelled from Nice to the Seamen's Mission and handed over 850,000 francs to the Reverend Caskie. This was not the end of the matter, for Colonel Sawyer called on Major Dodds at the American Consulate and told him of the gift of money to Caskie. Dodds in turn reported the matter to the American consul-general, Hugh Fullerton, who summoned Caskie and told him that, in view of the numerous complaints from the French police about Caskie's activities at the mission, he, Caskie, must return the money from whence it came. Caskie thereupon took the money to his colleague, Pasteur Heuzy, who happened to be going to Nice, and asked him to give it back to the colonel.

Ian Garrow, for his part, turned to Louis Nouveau for financial help. Louis had made a handsome profit (some 400,000 francs) on a hundred tons of beans and, determined that it should not go into Vichy's coffers, not only arranged for a loan of 15,000 francs to be made to Garrow but also got a further 25,000 francs from 'two or three other reliable financial supporters'.[320] It was Louis Nouveau, too, who assisted in 'the transfer of several million francs held by the representative in France of Messrs. J. and P. Coates, against repayment in London.'[321] Author Helen Long is more precise: 'A French factory, *Le Fil à la Châine*, owned by the British firm M. & P. Coats [*sic*], had provided five or six million francs. Louis was sent off by Garrow to collect one million francs from a Mr Gosling, an ex-manager of the French factory at la Coquille, a small village in the Périgord district.'[322]

And Henri Fiocca, former soldier of France and now industrialist, was persuaded to part with funds by his devil-may-care wife Nancy.[323] Their lives were to change forever when they were having dinner in October 1940 at one of Marseille's finest hotels, the Louvre et Paix, on the Canebière. Nancy saw a man sitting on his own in a small bar reading an English book and, curious, discovered that he was a British officer on parole from Fort St Jean. He was invited to dine with the Fioccas, and 'they arranged to meet again next day. This time the officer arrived with two comrades.'[324] Russell Braddon says that the officer was from Newcastle-upon-Tyne.[325] If that is so, then there are three possible candidates. Captain C.R.I. Besley and Captain A.M.K. Martin both had permanent addresses there, but the third possibility, Flying Officer Lewis Hodges, recalled that he was sitting in a bar when Nancy came in – there were some Germans there – and said 'You must be British'. The Germans, hearing this, were not very happy.[326] So began the dangerous liaison with the British officers from Fort St Jean who, invited back to the Fioccas' flat, 'were well fed and provided with cigarettes and soap and other comforts to take back with them to their comrades.'[327]

Ian Garrow, one of those to enjoy the Fioccas' hospitality, saw for himself Nancy's 'contempt for all Vichy authorities', and apparently recruited her into the escape line. She needed little persuading. Also recruited into the escape line was an Australian, Corporal Bruce Dowding RASC, who is recorded as having reached Fort St Jean, Marseille on 8 December 1940. Having left his homeland in January 1938, to which he was never to return, Dowding was in Europe when the war started and joined the British army. Captured at Dunkirk on 22 May 1940, he was able to escape from a prisoner-of-war camp in France and to make his way to Marseille where, assuming the name André Mason, he was employed as a *convoyeur*, delivering "parcels" 'towards the Spanish border by train, via Toulouse and Perpignan'.[328]

Pressure had for some time been mounting on the British to close the Seamen's Mission, and there had been such a heavy infiltration of German police agents in the Marseille area that 'increased circumspection' was called for by those working for British interests in the city. It was, therefore, decided on or around 29 June 1941, with the approval of Donald Caskie, Ian Garrow and the earlier agreement of Major Dodds,[329] that the Seamen's Mission should be closed down as soon as accommodation could be found elsewhere for the twenty men living there – 'mainly Palestinians, Maltese and others having claim to British nationality or relief'. Closure was to be as soon as possible after 1 July.

Helping Donald Caskie at this time was a young Englishman, Anthony Brooks. Trapped in France when the Germans had invaded the country, Brooks had spent the intervening months assisting several British servicemen to get to Marseille. In May 1941, however, warned that he was about to be interned by the Vichy French, he realised that it was time to make use of the escape line and, once in Marseille, availed himself of the facilities at the Seamen's Mission. With Caskie frequently absent, Brooks ran the mission until he departed with a small group over the Pyrenees in June 1941.[330]

Then Donald Caskie, who was hoping to be allowed by the French authorities 'to establish himself near or in the internment camp at Saint Hippolyte', was taken away by police in a "Black Maria", like a common criminal, to a military tribunal at Fort St Nicolas. There he heard that complaints 'had been received that I was "an agitator against the State". I was warned in a friendly, but firm way that I was in danger.' They asked him a few questions, retired to consider their verdict and then, after an hour's deliberation, sentenced him to two years' imprisonment, the sentence to be *avec souris*. Asking what that meant the judge informed him 'that you will be temporarily released – put on probation... You will leave Marseilles and go to another place. I suggest Grenoble.'[332]

So another chapter in the Marseille escape line was closed when Caskie went to Grenoble. Though never far from the eye of authority, he was suddenly arrested by the Italians on 16 April 1943, and taken in handcuffs to the *caserne* on the Rue Hoche. At the end of April he was removed to a prison at Cuneo, some eighty kilometres south of Turin, Italy, where he 'remained for a couple of nights sitting on a stone floor without bedding of any kind in complete darkness'.[333] Treated appallingly by his guards, he was then moved to the Villa Lynwood in Nice, where his treatment was no better, but thankful that he was not the man whom he saw being marched endlessly at bayonet point along the passage past his cell. After four days the man was seen no more.

Caskie was not at the Villa Lynwood for long. One day in May 1943 he was moved back to Italy, to a prison in San Remo, on the Gulf of Genoa. The cruelty of his Fascist captors was manifest yet again when he was placed in a "bottle" cell: 'Shaped like a man, it is a bottle-shaped cell of stone big enough to contain one human being but short enough not to permit him to stand upright and narrow enough to restrain him from lying down.' To Caskie, it was 'the most vile instrument of torture ever devised by men. When it became unbearable a man might scream or shout and the iron door fitted deep into the walls holds the noise of his screaming from the outside.'[334] Caskie endured twenty-four hours of this abominable torture before he was released into weeks of solitary confinement.

They came for him again in July, and took him back to Marseille, where he was handed over to the Gestapo. After a few days of unexpected rest in St Pierre prison, he was transferred to Fresnes, 'the biggest and most spacious prison in Europe', on the southern outskirts of Paris, from which on 26 November 1943 he was taken to a German court in a building on the rue des Saussaies. There ten men and two women put him on trial on various charges, including spying and helping Jewish people. Caskie knew it was all up when the Germans played their trump card – the French guide Pierre, whose loyalty Caskie had doubted in Marseille in the early days. At the end of the farcical proceedings the court found Caskie guilty, and he was returned to Fresnes without knowing his sentence. Assuming that like so many others he was to be shot, he asked for another minister to help him in what would be his final hours. His request was granted, and they sent him a German pastor, Peters, who appealed so successfully to the authorities that Caskie was transferred to the Caserne St Denis on 7 January 1944. He was still there when Paris was liberated during the last week of August that year.

Not long before the closure of the Seamen's Mission, Lieutenant-Commander Patrick Albert O'Leary, a French-Canadian in the Royal Navy, had been interned at St Hippolyte. No one else there could have had any idea that he was in fact a Belgian, Albert-Marie Edmond Guérisse, a *médecin-capitaine* with a cavalry regiment who, after his country's defeat by the Germans in May 1940, had been evacuated from Dunkirk to Margate on 31 May. Sent back to France on 8 June, he had no sooner landed at the port of Brest than he and a number of other Belgian officers were ordered to make their way to the Mediterranean port of Sète. Evacuated aboard a British collier on 20 June Guérisse reached Gibraltar two days later.

Also arriving in Gibraltar on the same day was the French merchantman *Le Rhin*,[335] whose captain, Lieutenant de Vaisseau Claude André Michel Péri,[336] was 'engaged on special service for the French Admiralty and the Cinquième Bureau'. Armed 'with an *ordre de mission* and looking for a ship to take him to Gibraltar to join the British,'[337] he had taken control of *Le Rhin* while she was berthed at Marseille. With her holds filled with anything and everything upon which Péri could lay his hands, *Le Rhin* joined a convoy bound for Morocco on 18 June 1940 but, nearing the Straits of Gibraltar, Péri swung the ship towards Gibraltar. On 22 June, as she came within sight of Gibraltar, he gave the order to hoist the Royal Navy's White Ensign. It bothered him not in the slightest that he had no authority whatsoever to do this.

A forceful man capable of sudden violence, Péri was determined to fight Germany by any and every means at his disposal. He had, furthermore, a fierce dislike of anyone who showed the slightest sympathy for the Vichy government; any such sympathiser was, to his mind, a traitor to France. The true course of action, he believed, was to join the British, but on the voyage to Gibraltar he discovered that most of his crew were not like-minded. Proposing to replace the dissidents as soon as possible, his chance came when, trawling Gibraltar's bars, he managed to "persuade" a few men to sign up for his ship. So impressed were Lieutenant Guérisse and one of his fellow Belgians by his vigorous technique that they decided to sign on with Péri, who greeted them with open arms.

Guérisse was aboard *Le Rhin* on 26 June when the majority of the ship's crew mutinied – 'by the end of the night, all but six of an original crew of fifty-six had agreed to disembark'[338] – and on 27 June Péri appointed Guérisse as his second-in-command.

Resisting attempts by a visiting French admiral, Émile Muselier, to recruit him and his ship into a proposed *Forces Navales Françaises Libres* (Free French Navy), Péri instead persuaded the Royal Navy to accept *Le Rhin* into its fleet, and on 21 July 1940, flying both the Blue and the White Ensign,[339] *Le Rhin* departed for Britain for a much needed refit. An old and slow ship, capable of little more than six knots, it was not until 5 August that she reached Barry docks in South Wales. The Royal Navy liaison officer appointed to *Le Rhin*, Lieutenant Patrick Whinney, later wrote of her: 'In the normal course of events her final voyage to the scrap yard could not have been long delayed.'[340] Nevertheless, refitted she was and, renamed HMS *Fidelity* by her captain, he could now legally hoist the White Ensign. During her refit HMS *Fidelity* came under the control of Captain Slocum RN, Deputy Director Operations Division (Irregular), and, capable of little else, was earmarked for a role in SOE's clandestine operations.

Assuming the nom de guerre "Jack Langlais", Péri was given the rank of lieutenant-commander in the RNVR, the "Wavy Navy", but he noticed that, unlike Royal Navy officers, the gold lace on his cuffs was wavy as opposed to straight, and 'advised their Lordships that neither he nor his ship would fight unless Captain Langlais RN was on the bridge of the *Fidelity*. The Admiralty compromised by allowing him to wear RN insignia.'[341]

Guérisse, also given the rank of temporary lieutenant-commander RN, assumed the nom de guerre of "Patrick Albert O'Leary", Albert O'Leary being borrowed from a French-Canadian friend whom he had met while at school in England, and the first name courtesy of SOE. Another member of the crew to assume a nom de guerre was Péri's partner, Madeleine Bayard,[342] whom he had met before the war in Vietnam, where both had been engaged in espionage on behalf of the French government. She assumed the surname "Barclay" (reputedly having espied a branch of that well-known bank at Barry) and, despite strong opposition within the Royal Navy, was appointed First Officer WRNS, thus becoming the only woman to be engaged on active service during the war on a Royal Navy fighting ship. There had also been considerable changes made to the crew. Most of the disaffected were removed, and on 17 January 1941 the 'first batch of SOE-vetted volunteers arrived in Barry'.[343] Most of the French crew also assumed British names.

Early in 1941, with *Fidelity*'s refit nearing its end, Pat O'Leary and Madeleine Barclay 'were sent by SIS to Brickendonbury Hall, near Hertford, to study sabotage',[344] and then to Aston House, near Stevenage, to complete their training. Once finished, they rejoined *Fidelity*, which, with Lieutenant Patrick Whinney aboard, sailed for Milford Haven on 22 March. Leaving the ship there, Whinney handed over to Lieutenant-Commander Jasper Milner-Gibson. Continuing to Liverpool, *Fidelity* was assigned to "special services", and sailed from that port in convoy on 6 April, bound for the western Mediterranean.

Péri's orders were to undertake a two-part "cloak and dagger" operation, the first part of which required two SIS/SOE agents, E.V.H. Rizzo and Bitner, to be landed on a beach near the French Mediterranean resort of Canet-Plage, a dozen kilometres east of Perpignan. Egbert Rizzo, an elderly

Maltese civil engineer, was on his way to Perpignan on behalf of Leslie Humphreys's DF section of SOE to set up a two-way escape line over the Pyrenees, and was to seek the help of Spanish smugglers. Using the codename "Aromatic", he succeeded in setting up 'a formidable escape line, the second largest of all, known as Group Edouard or Group Troy.'[345] The other agent, Bitner, former Polish Consul at Toulouse, was to go under the cover name of "Angelica" to Lille, in north-east France, on behalf of the Polish Interallié network.[346] The second part of the operation required *Fidelity* to collect a dozen escaping Polish air force officers from the Mediterranean harbour of Collioure, near the Franco-Spanish border. The Poles' representative would be wearing a red scarf and a Basque beret.

For reasons of security, SOE had wanted *Fidelity* to arrive at Gibraltar under cover of darkness to put ashore 'some officers from SOE's Spanish section',[347] but this was not Péri's way, and he proudly brought his ship to Gibraltar on the morning of 20 April in full daylight. Final preparations for the operation were completed on 22 April, and at 10 p.m. that night *Fidelity* slipped anchor and headed east for the French coast, her crew quickly transforming her into the Portuguese SS *Setubal*. At 11 p.m. on 25 April *Fidelity* lay off the French coast between Canet-Plage and the small village of le Barcarès, a dozen kilometres east of Perpignan, and in a choppy swell launched her *berceau du marin*, a 'heavy Breton ketch... equipped with a 5 h.p. engine'.[348] Aboard were O'Leary, three French sailors with the assumed British names of Forde, Fergusson, and Rogers,[349] and the two agents, Bitner and Rizzo.

By the time that the crew had been able to start the boat's engine, the operation was already running an hour late and, with Péri becoming more and more apoplectic all the while, yet more time was lost when the boat beached on an offshore sandbank. No sooner were both agents and all their baggage safely ashore than O'Leary was steering the small motorboat south on the second part of the night's operation. *Fidelity*, meanwhile, steered a similar course, but out of sight of land. Collioure harbour[350] was some twenty kilometres away, and by the time that O'Leary had reached it dawn was not far off. All was quiet, however, and waiting for him was the man with the red scarf and beret. Of the Polish airmen, however, there was no sign. They were, said the contact, asleep in their hotel, the pick-up having been expected on the previous night. O'Leary gave him ten minutes to fetch them.

But before the contact could return, a customs officer appeared, and demanded to see the boat's papers. Having none, O'Leary had no option but to put to sea, while the customs officer alerted the French navy at Port Vendres, a few kilometres down the coast. Chugging out of Collioure harbour into what was now a near gale-force wind and a heavy sea, and with five kilometres still to make to the waiting *Fidelity*, the boat's fuel line broke. A running repair was fashioned, but no sooner had the engine been re-started than a French navy cutter was spotted bearing down on them. Unable to outrun the Frenchman the motorboat was seized and taken in tow to Port Vendres.[351]

After cross-examination by French and Italian naval officers, the four men were taken away in pairs. Fergusson and Rogers went first. O'Leary and Forde, escorted by a single guard, chose what they thought was the right moment to escape and made a dash for freedom in opposite directions. The guard made the split decision to go after O'Leary, and caught him. Taken to Fort la Malgue at the naval port of Toulon, O'Leary was reunited with Fergusson and Rogers. Forde, meanwhile, free to wander off, reached Gibraltar and England.

After a few weeks in "the brig" the three sailors were transferred to St Hippolyte-du-Fort where, after some difficulty trying to convince his fellow internees that he was indeed a lieutenant-commander RN (equivalent to squadron leader or major), O'Leary became de facto head of the escape committee. Despite the tightening of security in May, communication with the Garrow organisation in Marseille had been maintained easily enough as officers were still allowed out on parole. When O'Leary let it be known that he wished to escape, it was arranged that he would meet Ian Garrow 'in an American sympathizer's apartment in Nîmes'.[352] Informing the St Hippolyte guards that he was off to see a football match, O'Leary made his way to the rendezvous with Garrow, and told the Scotsman that he was keen to return to his ship. It was agreed that he would be helped to Marseille, but only after he had first helped Fergusson and Rogers to get away.

It was sometime in early June 1941 when Fergusson walked out of St Hippolyte wearing the uniform of a French guard, but Rogers was being assisted by O'Leary over the prison walls, 'only about ten feet in height',[353] when they were caught red-handed by a guard. While O'Leary tangled with the guard Rogers made his getaway on a stolen bicycle. O'Leary's punishment was two weeks in solitary confinement, time enough to plan his own escape and for his accomplices to saw through the bars of a downstairs room overlooking the street. One Friday in June, while other prisoners created a diversion by feigning an escape over the prison wall, O'Leary removed the last bar from the downstairs room and jumped into the street. Immediately spotted by the guards he ran off as fast as his legs could carry him, with the guards in hot pursuit. Dodging through the first convenient doorway, he found himself in a hospice for old people staffed by nuns.

The Mother Superior quickly hid O'Leary in a chest in the attic while the prison guards, sure that O'Leary was in the building, threw a cordon around it. O'Leary escaped through the underground passage that led from the hospice into a nearby vineyard, and made his way to the large fifth-floor flat at 21, rue Roux de Brignoles, Marseille, the home of Dr Georges and Fanny Rodocanachi. This generous couple had already allowed members of the escape line to use their commodious apartment as their HQ, and it was where Garrow himself had been hidden when Detachment W had moved from Fort St Jean to St Hippolyte in January that year.

Garrow persuaded Pat O'Leary to stay on in Marseille to help with the escape line but, as an officer on active service, permission was required from the admiralty in London. An appropriate message was therefore sent to London and on 2 July, after several anxious nights, the BBC broadcast the message *'Adolph doit rester'* ('Adolph may stay') confirming that O'Leary could remain in France. Though "Adolph" was the name used in these messages, O'Leary would be known as "Joseph".

CHAPTER 3

Diplomacy and evasion, Spain and Portugal: 1940-1942

'I attach a comprehensive report made at my request by the military attaché upon the many questions involved in the transit through Spain of escaped prisoners of war. Although the work connected with this question is outside the regular field of the embassy, there is no problem that has given my staff and myself more trouble or taken up more of our time.'

Sir Samuel Hoare,
British Ambassador to Spain, Madrid, 4 June 1941

'At the present moment the general policy in force here is to give preference wherever possible to British personnel, especially RAF flying personnel.'

Harold Lister Farquhar MC,
Consul-General, Barcelona, 31 December 1941.[354]

In his history of the Second World War Sir Winston Churchill summed up the British Government's attitude to Spain: 'All we wanted was the neutrality of Spain. We wanted to trade with Spain. We wanted her ports to be denied to German and Italian submarines. We wanted not only an unmolested Gibraltar, but the use of the anchorage of Algeçiras for our ships and the use of the ground which joins the Rock to the mainland for our ever-expanding air base.'[355]

Furthermore, Winston Churchill had a very low opinion of the ruler of fascist Spain, General Don Francisco Franco Behamonde,[356] calling him a 'narrow-minded tyrant' who 'owed little or nothing to us, but much – perhaps life itself – to the Axis powers.' Nor did Churchill's opinion of the general improve as the Second World War progressed, considering him to be 'entirely selfish and cold-blooded. He thought only of Spain and of Spanish interests. Gratitude to Hitler and Mussolini for their help never entered his head. Nor, on the other hand, did he bear any grudge against England for the hostility of our Left Wing parties,'[357] an allusion to those in Britain of a communist leaning who desired no more than the defeat of Franco.

As to its joining with the German-Italian Axis, Spain was totally unable to go to war again in the immediate or near future, for the country was still reeling from the effects, both physical and financial, of its bloody civil war, which lasted from 18 July 1936 to 1 April 1939. During the war an estimated 200,000 Spaniards and 10,000 foreigners were killed in the fighting itself, with some 10,000 civilians killed by bombs. 130,000 more were executed by one side or the other, and 25,000 starved, or were starved, to death. In addition, the precise figure of 271,139 is quoted as being the number of persons imprisoned during the conflict, 22,989 of whom were still prisoners by July 1944.[358] Not content with his victory, though, General Franco ordered the execution of at least a further 100,000 of his Republican enemies at, or soon after, the end of the civil war.[359]

With the onset of the European conflict only five months after the ending of the civil war the exhausted Spanish were in no position to take sides but, having coveted German armed intervention during his struggle, Franco was known to be sympathetic to the Axis powers and to tolerate the presence of German Intelligence on Spanish soil. Nevertheless, from the British point of view, it was imperative that Spain remained neutral, and it was fortunate for the thousands of escapers, evaders and refugees of all nationalities who crossed into neutral Spain from June 1940 to the late summer of 1944 that Spain *did* remain neutral. Geographically speaking, if they wished to escape German enslavement, there was nowhere else for them to have gone other than to Axis-locked Switzerland. From Spain, or from its Iberian partner Portugal, fugitives were at least within striking distance of the free world.

Not that in the greater scheme of things this was a consideration for the British Government which, given the strategic importance of the fortress of Gibraltar at the jaws of the Mediterranean, was anxious to do all that it could to ensure that Franco did not throw in his lot with Hitler and Mussolini. Accordingly the Secretary of State for Foreign Affairs, Lord Halifax, appointed Sir Samuel Hoare on 17 May 1940 as ambassador to Spain to go 'to Madrid to do there what you can to improve our relations with Spain...'[360] Within a week of his arrival in Madrid, on 1 June, Sir Samuel was reporting that nine out of every ten Spaniards believed that Hitler would win the war within three weeks, adding that the 'Germans are dug in in every direction and becoming more and more aggressive.'[361]

The strategic importance of Gibraltar was emphasised to the Germans even more after the Royal Navy had bombarded the French fleet at Mers-el-Kebir on 3 July and, in a little over a week, they had drawn up plans for its invasion. On 22 July 1940 Admiral Wilhelm Canaris, chief of the Abwehr, led a high-powered Nazi delegation in civilian clothes to Madrid, where a meeting was arranged with the Spanish minister of war to see what could be done. The Spanish minister, however, would not commit his country to the Nazi request for German troops to use Spain as the base for the attack. Nevertheless, German spies gathered what information they could on Gibraltar, and on 14 August, under the codename Operation Felix, Hitler approved the plan to attack Gibraltar as part of the overall campaign against Britain.

Another meeting took place, this time in Berlin on 16 September 1940, between Joachim von Ribbentrop, Nazi Germany's foreign minister, Italy's leader, Mussolini ("Il Duce"), and Ramón Serrano Súñer, Franco's minister of the interior (and Franco's brother-in-law).[362] Von Ribbentrop explained 'the Spanish plan for the attack on Gibraltar and Germany's participation therein, and that he was expecting to sign the Protocol with Spain bringing the latter country into the war on his return to Berlin.'[363] The Nazis misjudged Súñer, who had gone to Berlin on 19 November expecting to be treated as an ally but who had soon appreciated that his country was regarded as a minor satellite. Súñer's displeasure at being treated thus was a major reason for Spain not becoming an ally of the Axis, despite Franco's open admiration for Hitler, who finally aborted Operation Felix on 11 December 1940. It was not until 25 March 1941, however, that the British finally conceded that a German attack through Spain was unlikely.

On 17 October 1940 Súñer had replaced Colonel Juan Beigbeder y Atienza as Spain's foreign minister at the *Ministerio de Asuntos Exteriores*. Beigbeder, somewhat of an Anglophile, thereafter maintained a discreet liaison with the British ambassador in Madrid, and it was through Beigbeder that London learned that Hitler had met with Franco at Hendaye, on the French/Spanish border, on 24 October and that Franco had himself 'been alienated by Hitler's insistence that something had to be done to conciliate the Vichy authorities.'[364]

Given the relationship between Spain and Germany, Sir Samuel's already difficult task was made none the easier by the imprisonment in Spain in August 1940 of the first British military personnel to cross illegally from France. The first news that British consular staff in Barcelona had of the incarceration of these personnel was when a 'scrap of dirty paper' was smuggled out of the *Castillo de San Fernando* prison at Figueras (some twenty kilometres south of the French border). Sir Samuel at once 'demanded that a British consul should visit them', but British efforts were confounded by Súñer, who 'seemed to delight in throwing sparks into the explosive' cocktail that was 'the treatment of our escaped prisoners of war' and in 'the persecution of British subjects in Spain...'[365]

Up to at least the end of 1941 it was expected that evaders and escapers ("prisoners of war" as the British Embassy liked to label one and all) would, with or without the help of Spanish guides, cross into north-eastern Spain to the north of Barcelona. They would then, according to British consular staff, use either the 'direct method' or the 'indirect method' to pass through Spain. The former usually involved an uninterrupted journey from the frontier to the consulate-general at Barcelona, where the men were 'provided with an emergency certificate, a railway ticket, and are put on a train to Madrid with full instructions. A considerable number reach the embassy in this way and are kept there in comfortable circumstances until arrangements can be made with the Spanish authorities for their repatriation via Gibraltar.'

With the 'indirect method', on the other hand, "prisoners" were arrested on crossing into Spain and 'taken to the nearest jail. They are then taken to one of the recognised prisons… The men are transferred by the Spanish authorities to the concentration camp at Miranda de Ebro.'[366] What became a well-worn path for many illegal entrants started at Figueras, and continued westwards across Spain, via some or all of the prisons at Gerona, Barcelona, Cervera, Lérida, and Zaragosa (Saragossa), until finally reaching the concentration camp at Miranda de Ebro.

Two of several servicemen to sample some or all of these unpleasant Spanish prisons in the early summer of 1941 were a young Scottish airman, wireless operator Sergeant Duncan MacCallum, and Lance-Sergeant W.H. Batho, 23rd Field Regiment RA.

MacCallum's evasion had begun on the night of 20/21 March 1941 when his Hampden flew into an electrical storm some two hours after take-off while on its way to drop a 2,000-lb anti-shipping mine into Brest harbour. He had just obtained a wireless "fix" from Southampton at approximately 5 a.m. when they ran into the storm, which caused the mine to explode. Blown into two flaming pieces, the Hampden crashed to earth a dozen kilometres north-west of Callac (Côtes-d'Armor) before any of the four crew could bale out. MacCallum recovered consciousness surrounded by burning wreckage, and 'found that my "homing" pigeons had both been killed and their basket was blazing fiercely with the rest of the plane. I then took an axe and hacked open the remains of the upper rear cupola and escaped from the plane... I rolled myself in the grass to extinguish my smouldering flying suit and then went to a nearby farm for aid.'[367]

A search for the other three of the crew with a farmer yielded at first two dead comrades, several fields apart, who were being stripped of their valuable flying boots by French peasants. Putting a stop to that, they found the unconscious pilot, Sergeant O.B. James. His left arm was very badly injured and he was 'badly burned and his forehead was cut open'. MacCallum half carried James to a barn and dressed his awful burns as best he could. Regaining his senses James's first words were: 'Thank God you are here Mac. What are the chances of escape?'[368] For Oliver James they were not good, though MacCallum still hoped to take his skipper with him. Any hopes of moving James to safety were dashed, however, when it was learnt that German soldiers were on their way to the crash site.

James, still too weak to be moved, had to be left at the farm. Picked up by the Germans he was taken to Morlaix for medical attention, but when a surgeon found that James's left arm was so badly damaged he insisted on it being amputated. Oliver James was one of the many British wounded – 126 officers and 1,182 other ranks – who had been selected for repatriation to Britain in an exchange for similarly wounded Germans. In the autumn of 1941 the British were assembled at a holding camp – the local racecourse – at Sotteville, near Rouen, France to await repatriation.

When the planned exchange fell through, James and three other sergeants – W.J.Q. Magrath, Patterson (not identified) and A.A. Maderson – determined to escape. The senior British officer asked them to wait until Christmas, but they were not prepared to do so, and on 21 November 1941, using wire cutters appropriated from a French workman's bag, they cut their way to freedom. As arranged, they split into pairs, but Patterson and Maderson were later re-captured.

James and Magrath safely reached Paris and, seeing a notice in the window of a French Red Cross building that said that they helped prisoners of war, went in. Unsure as to whether or not the two airmen were bogus, their French helpers called on an Irish priest to question them. In a remarkable coincidence, the priest had known Northern Irishman Magrath back in Ireland! After a few days with a doctor at Nevers they stayed a few more days at another house before being taken across the Demarcation Line. They caught a train to Marseille, where they arrived on the morning of 22 December. After two nights staying at the apartment of Louis and Renée Nouveau they were escorted by members of the PAT line (see following chapter) to Toulouse (24 December) and then to Port Vendres (27 December) ready for the crossing into Spain. After a deal had been arranged with a Spanish smuggler to take them across for 1,200 francs each James, Magrath, four Belgians and two guides reached Vilajuiga in Spain on the morning of 29 December 1941.

Sailing from Gibraltar on a Polish ship the two airmen were back in England on 4 March 1942. Though recommended for the DCM both were awarded the MM.[369] Flying Officer Oliver Barton James MM, DFM was killed in action on 4 October 1943, aged twenty-three, while serving on 245 Squadron (Typhoons). Bill Magrath continued flying on a training unit as a flight-sergeant instructor, but RAF doctors later summoned him for a medical and declared him unfit for flying. Shabbily treated by the RAF, he was then reduced to the rank of groundcrew sergeant. Accepting the commission to pilot officer that he was offered Bill survived the war, though how he had lived through that day in August 1940 when he was shot down on 82 Squadron was nothing short of a miracle.

When some bright spark had the idea that Aalborg airfield in Denmark needed the RAF's attention, 82 Squadron was chosen to pay it a visit on 13 August 1940. In broad daylight and flying straight and level at 5,000 feet the thirty-nine-year-old squadron commander, Wing Commander E.C. de V. Lart DSO, led twelve Blenheim aircraft to their doom. Only one came back, but that was because the pilot, seeing the carnage ahead of him, had the good sense to realise that it was futile to press on to his probable death. Of the thirty-three airmen who were shot down twenty were killed (including Lart). The rest, Bill Magrath among them, became prisoners of war. One of the German fighter pilots involved in the massacre of the Blenheims told Bill that it had been a pigeon shoot.

Having been obliged to leave the badly wounded James to his fate, Duncan MacCallum changed out of his uniform into old French clothes and exchanged his Irvin flying jacket for the loan of a bicycle. 'Then a girl from the farm came with me to show me the way. We were only about half a kilometre from the farm when a car load of German soldiers passed us.' They met the local *sage-femme* (midwife), who took the airman in her car to her home at Callac. Whether or not it was due to delayed shock MacCallum 'collapsed and was attended by a doctor'.

When the Germans soon circulated his description, with a price on his head of 2,000 francs, MacCallum responded by shaving off his moustache and dyed his red hair a more sober colour. On about 25 March a young French woman, Marie le Roc'h, took him to Le Mans and Tours, where they caught a 'train to the station [at Reignac-sur-Indre] just before the line of demarcation where I changed into peasant clothes again.' As he and Marie were crossing the line they spotted two German patrols and were forced to lie in over a foot of water in a ditch until the danger had passed. After a wash and a change of clothes at a nearby hotel, they took a taxi to Loches, and next day a train to Châteauroux, where some of Marie's friends advised them to go to Lyon instead of to Vichy as they had planned.

Continuing by train to Montluçon, the 2 a.m. express brought them to Lyon on Saturday, 29 March, where more friends gave them food and shelter, and paid their expenses. Having to wait until Monday, 31 March, MacCallum and Marie went to the American consulate, where he gave Vice-Consul George Whittinghill 'a map with details of various German air bases in N. France, either in operation or under construction. For this he gave the girl 500 francs and I also received the equivalent of £3 as relief money', which he gave to Marie to help pay for her fare back to Callac.

The importance at this time of the American consulate at Lyon, and of George Whittinghill in particular, cannot be underestimated. When stationed in Milan in 1939 Whittinghill, an officer in the US foreign service, agreed to also work for MI6, but to make his co-operation with the British easier he was transferred to the British consulate in Lyon in Vichy France in October 1940 as the American vice-consul in charge of British interests. His role was to look after the many British and Commonwealth personnel on the loose in central France and, as time went on, to help MI9 get its agents out of France. Additionally, he was to gather whatever useful information he could and pass it on to MI6.[370]

Practical assistance included the provision of civilian clothing, false identity papers, and safe housing. Later, he provided rubber stamps with which Pat O'Leary could forge documents, and sent O'Leary's intelligence reports in the diplomatic bag to Switzerland. In return, the British consul in Geneva, Victor Farrell, provided him with funds for the support of British subjects in need.

While MacCallum stayed in Lyon with a Frenchman, plans were being made to move him to Marseille. Another American, Samuel Lewis Kresser, made suitable arrangements with Frenchman Robert le Prevost for the move, but Whittinghill was keen to retain MacCallum in Lyon as a wireless operator on behalf of the British Embassy in Geneva. So he remained in Lyon for the time being, but after a month twiddling his thumbs he was asked once again by Kresser and le Prevost to go to Marseille. This time Whittinghill agreed that it would be best if he left and so, with a *carte d'identité* provided by le Prevost, he went to Marseille and 'met the Rev. D. Caskie of the British Seamen's Mission who sent me to Perpignan.'

Travelling with him from Marseille was Lance-Sergeant Batho, who had been there since 29 January 1941.[371] At Perpignan on 4 May 1941 they were met by Bruce Dowding who, explaining how to cross the Pyrenees, advised them to give themselves up to the Spanish police when they got to Vilajuiga. They took a taxi on 6 May to Laroque-des-Albères, half a dozen kilometres from the Spanish border, arriving there at about 6 a.m. Walking into Spain they passed through Cantallóps, continuing for another six or seven kilometres before spending the night at a farm. Acting on Dowding's advice they went to Vilajuiga with the intention of giving themselves up and asked some Spaniards the way to the police station. The Spaniards, however, advised them not to do that, and suggested going to a hotel instead.

Three days later, when word of their presence had reached the ears of the Guardia Civil, they were taken away to Figueras, searched, questioned and pushed into a cell. The next day, 11 May, they were removed to the military prison on the outskirts of the town, the *Castillo de San Fernando*. On 14 May, now in Barcelona, MacCallum was able to telephone the British consul, who paid them a visit before they were taken to the prison at Cervera (eleven days). Moved on to Saragossa, they were thrown into a cell with thirteen other prisoners. Measuring only six feet by nine it 'was so small that we could not lie down on the floor to sleep. We were never allowed out of this cell for five days, and on the fifth day we were stripped and all our clothes were fumigated, and we had a bath in the yard after all our hair had been cut off. Immediately after our bath we were taken back to our cell and vaccinated and inoculated.'[372]

Shortly afterwards they were transferred to Miranda de Ebro, where they arrived on the afternoon of 30 May. Food at Miranda was bad and in short supply but, for the British at least, rations were augmented by supplies from the British Embassy at Madrid. Officially liberated from Miranda on 16 June 1941, it was not until the night of 22/23 June that the British were sent to Madrid. On 4 July MacCallum, Batho and others sailed from Gibraltar for Gourock, where they arrived eight days later.

Towards the end of 1941 Brigadier Torr, military attaché at the Madrid embassy, noted in a report dated 21 October 1941 that there was 'now a new place of detention at Figueras known as the

Comisión Receptora[373]... to which most of the men arrested north of Gerona are taken for the day and from there sent direct to Miranda via Barcelona. Through the good offices of an official in this prison, Mr Rapley is nearly always informed of the arrival of the men here.'[374] Mr Rapley, a 'consular representative who resides at Gerona', would make the forty-kilometre journey north to Figueras every Thursday to give the men money and clothes.

In view of the shortish distance between the *Castillo de San Fernando* at Figueras and the *Cárcel Provincial* at Gerona, it fell to Mr Rapley to cover them both. Again, he would be notified regularly and promptly of all arrivals at Gerona, this time by no less a person than the governor of the prison himself. 'The men are immediately visited and are given clothes and money to buy food every week.' When the time came for the prisoners to be moved on, Mr Rapley would again be notified, and would go to Gerona railway station to meet them before they set off, usually at 6 a.m., for Barcelona.

There were two prisons at Barcelona, the *Cárcel Modelo* off the Plaza España, run by the civilian authorities, and the military's *Castillo Montjuich*. In his October report, Brigadier Torr noted that there was a party of eight men at the Montjuich prison: 'Captain Murchie, who is in charge of this party, arranges for their catering and they are living under definitely better conditions than the men in the civil prison.' When any British personnel were confined in the *Modelo* (Torr in his report stated there was none) they would be 'visited regularly at least twice a week'. Every man would also receive 'two large parcels a week of fresh fruit, tinned goods, jam, fresh tomatoes, sausages, biscuits, potted meat, etc. They also receive thirty-five [pesetas] a week, which is the maximum allowed by the prison authorities. This money is handed in to the prison office and paid out to the prisoners in prison vouchers to enable them to buy extras at the canteen. Additional parcels are also sent up on each occasion to form a reserve stock of food for men spending only one or two nights at the prison en route to Miranda from the *Comisión Receptora* at Figueras.'[375]

Two British men who *were*, however, at the *Cárcel Modelo* some time in October were the Newton brothers, Henry and Alfred, who had before the war been treading the boards as The Boorn Brothers at St Jean-de-Luz but who had been arrested on their arrival in Spain a few days earlier. Their biographer, Jack Thomas, wrote of their arrival at the prison: 'Still on their leads they were dragged through the main entrance gate into a circular covered court dominated by a central watch-tower, equipped with machine-guns and searchlights. Four or five double-tiered cell blocks, each terminating in a steel gate, converged on the court like the spokes of a wheel.'[376]

It was when they were at the British Embassy in Madrid in December 1941, having been released from Spanish arrest, that the Newton brothers received the awful news that their families – wives, parents and children – had been lost at sea. Both had been married to French women, and had lived in Paris until the invasion in 1940, when they moved to the Unoccupied Zone. Alfred, who lost not only his wife but three sons, and Henry were given the full, sad story on arrival at Gibraltar. The *Avoceta* (3,442 tons), the ship in which their families had been sailing on their way from Gibraltar to England, had been torpedoed on 25 September 1941 by a German U-boat and had sunk so quickly that no one on board stood a chance.

With a bitter hatred of the enemy, therefore, they were recruited into SOE, and returned to France at the end of June 1942. After a chaotic start through no fault of their own, they tried to set up the Greenheart circuit in the Haute-Loire, but were arrested in April 1943 and sent to the notorious Fresnes prison in Paris before surviving the horrors of Buchenwald whither sent. They, Lieutenant Christopher Burney, and Squadron Leader Maurice Southgate were the only surviving British agents left in the concentration camp. On 30 August 1945 Lieutenants Alfred Willie Oscar Newton, Henry George Rodolfo Newton, and Burney were awarded the MBE. Southgate was awarded the DSO.[377]

From Barcelona the next prison on the way to Miranda was at Cervera, a little over 100 kilometres north-west of Barcelona by road. A further sixty kilometres or so west was Lérida, and another 150 kilometres west lies Saragossa, whose prison had a reputation for brutality. The final prison, 220 kilometres north-west of Saragossa, was at Miranda de Ebro, with its infamous civil war *Deposito de Concentración*. The largest of the 104 prison camps of the Franco regime, the Miranda concentration camp had been built to accommodate the enemies of fascism, and it has been estimated that in its ten-year existence some 50,000 prisoners were restrained within its walls. Originally with a capacity of 700, as many as 3,000 were housed there at the end of 1942 and early 1943 when hundreds of Frenchmen had taken to their heels across the Pyrenees in the wake of the German occupation of all France in November 1942.

When Gordon Instone was sent to Miranda early in 1941 'the place had the appearance of a disused holiday camp with a large empty swimming pool'.[378] He and the others in his party would join about 300 Poles, sixty Belgians, thirty-five Frenchmen, six Yugoslavs, twenty German deserters, 'and about fifty British soldiers and airmen... In addition, there were Dutchmen, Algerians, Armenians, Hungarians, Rumanians, Czechs and Greeks'.[379] The food was awful, as was the cold – they were nearly 600 metres (2,000 feet) above sea level – and, some five or six weeks into their time at Miranda.

By June 1941 "British" prisoners at Miranda were 'being paid at the weekly rate of: officers Ptas. 100; Sergeants: Ptas. 75; O.R.s Ptas. 50, at a rate of exchange of 46 pesetas to the £1'. The money paid to these men was largely to augment the completely inadequate Spanish army rations, and it was delivered by the embassy bus, which was usually driven by a Chancery employee, Mr Langley. In the embassy report of 2 June 1941 to London the difficulties of the distances involved in looking after the prisoners were made clear: 'It may not be realised that the concentration camp lies some 200 miles north of Madrid and Gibraltar some 500 miles to the south. Liaison with these places for the supply of food and evacuation of prisoners therefore takes a considerable time. In addition, in winter road and rail communications are frequently delayed or interrupted.'[380] And later, when the prisoners were at the mercy of a pro-German commandant, a man consumed by anti-British feelings, many an obstruction was put in the way of British Embassy staff – 'even our lorries with clothes and food were prevented from unloading their urgently required stocks of relief.'[381]

The situation in the camp was clearly in need of improvement. In November 1941 discussions were held to resolve this problem, and also on how to pass evading/escaping personnel through to either Gibraltar or Portugal. 'From time to time very special escaped prisoners of war have to be smuggled out via Portugal for reasons of security or speed.' It also seemed 'clearly desirable that this business should be in the hands of a member of the embassy staff, since he is more likely than anyone else to be able to conduct the negotiations with the minimum of risk of friction with the Spanish authorities.'[382] The man considered most suitable for the job was MI6's Michael Creswell.

At the same time steps were taken by the British Embassy to deal particularly with the problems at Miranda de Ebro, but it was not until the end of 1941 that 'new arrangements for feeding and clothing all the Allied personnel at Miranda, excluding (except for transport) the Poles, who have their own organisation' were put in place.[383] By 1 May 1942 Brigadier Torr was able to confirm that these 'arrangements have been furthered and completed since the beginning of the year and it can now be said that an efficient organisation is in being.' Each man now received, per week, an individual food parcel, plus one pound of biscuits, four ounces of sugar, and two ounces each of cheese, cocoa and tea.[384] The individual food parcel contained one tin each of bully beef, meat & vegetables, fish, and milk; plus a quarter pound of chocolate, a quarter pound of dried fruit and forty cigarettes. With the exception of the fish and dried fruit all other contents had to be brought up from Gibraltar. A clothing standard was also introduced for each man, providing him with underwear, overcoats, gloves, socks etc. Brigadier Torr was able to claim that by 30 April 1942 this standard had been 'virtually attained. It has involved the distribution of nearly 2,000 knitted garments, 160 pairs of boots, and nearly 2,000 other garments, excluding handkerchiefs and towels. The work of storing, sorting, and packing the food, and collecting, storing and packing the garments has been carried on by the ladies of the embassy and colony, for whose work no praise can be too high. Almost all of the knitted garments have been made by the knitting organisation presided over by H.E. The Ambassadress.'[385]

For the men's medical welfare, supplies were 'obtained from Lisbon or Gibraltar and introduced unofficially into the camp. Amongst the internees are several doctors who maintain an unofficial clinic for all Allied patients.' Torr was also able to report that every Allied internee had been inoculated against typhus. Such help, both medical and dietary, was not, however, available to some thirty or so Frenchmen who were interned at Miranda for 'less honourable causes' than, for example, wishing to join the Free French Forces.

It was usual for a "British" prisoner, when finally released from Miranda, to be taken to Gibraltar via the British Embassy (at Calle Fernando el Santo 16, Madrid), which would become a busy staging post over the ensuing months and years from August 1940 to August 1944. But Sir Samuel Hoare, writing to Anthony Eden on 4 June 1941, informed the minister that he had already housed large numbers of prisoners in the embassy, and added that the 'embassy building is not in the least suited as a barracks'.[386]

Nearly six months later the situation had worsened to such an extent that on 29 November 1941 he sent a note to the Foreign Office alerting them to the 'difficult and possibly dangerous situation' that had arisen at the embassy 'in view of the large number of escaped prisoners of war' that it was 'constantly housing'. He added: 'Although every corner of the building is needed for office work I have at present twenty-two men who have to live and sleep here for an indefinite time, during which I have to obtain exit permits... Living accommodation is quite unsuitable for these numbers.' He then explained that amongst the prisoners who had passed through the embassy there had been 'two cases of typhoid, one of typhus, and two of diphtheria... As we have had two diphtheria cases in the last two days I have had to take urgent action. I have therefore given instructions for several structural alterations to be made at once, and for hutments to be put up either in the garden or on an adjoining site if it can be immediately leased.'[387]

Five days later Sir Samuel was able to tell the Foreign Office in London that he had 'received plans and estimation for erection of hutment containing the minimum extra accommodation which I regard as absolutely essential, namely, one living room each for officers and men, kitchen and four bedrooms for embassy guard. Hutment will be built on the lawn since adjoining site is not available. Comprehensive estimate (including light, heating and furnishings) is the equivalent of £1,200 at the more advantageous rate of exchange... Work should be completed by the end of January [1942].'[388]

Writing from the comfort of the Palace Hotel, Rhyl, whither his department had decamped from London, a civil servant in the Ministry of Works and Buildings informed the Foreign Office on 2 January 1942 that he had been 'directed by the Minister of Works and Buildings to state for the information of Mr Secretary Eden that it is assumed that the heating, lighting and cleaning costs which will be incurred when the building is in occupation will either be defrayed by your department or by the service department most concerned.'[389]

One of those at the embassy at this time, and who was less than complimentary of his treatment while there, was Flight Lieutenant R.G.A. Barclay DFC, who commented, albeit briefly, in his diary: 'Embassy disappointing. Appalling conditions. Prisoners.'[390] Also disenchanted with the conditions that he found at the embassy after an exhausting ordeal was Captain G.F. Collie RASC. Attached to HQ 51st (Highland) Division his jaw was smashed in the fighting at St Valéry-en-Caux on 12 June 1940, and he was taken prisoner. He 'was operated on at a German field surgery in a wood near Rouen', but for ten days was unable to eat anything other than 'special diet, which was not available'.[391] After many months in various hospitals, he was moved to the Hôpital Foch in Paris in January 1942. With him were Sergeant W.H. Aston, No.1 Sub-Depot RE, one of whose feet had been amputated in Paris,[392] and Driver E. Flack, Ammunition Company, RASC, attached to 51st Division, who had also been wounded in the jaw.

They believed themselves to be 'the only British military wounded left in occupied France', and that they were there, at the *Centre Maxillo Facial*, only because their section of the German medical services was run by Czechs and Austrians who had somehow failed to mention their presence to the Kommandantur. In the spring of 1942, therefore, they decided that it was time to escape before they were found out and were sent to Germany, and so with considerable help from French sympathisers they left Paris by train on 8 April.

Arriving at Lyon on 10 April they went, as instructed, to a house at 3, rue Confort. Discovering it to be a brothel, they made their way to the home of a Frenchman, Monsieur Boudrand, who had been a patient at the *Centre Maxillo Facial* in Paris with Collie and the others. He and his family, who lived at 25, rue St Jerome, were as Collie noted 'working-class people. They kept us for two months. Fortunately we were able to pay them amply for our stay.'

After much effort on their behalf, the three soldiers were given Belgian papers and a Spanish visa by a contact whose friend worked in the passport department of the Rhône Préfecture. At the end of June 1942, though, their friend warned them to leave at once, as 'Vichy had received orders from the Germans to question all persons recently granted Belgian papers with exit visas because German deserters had used this means of escape from occupied France.' The advice was heeded and, after a month (27 June–27 July) staying in 'a château at Fanjeaux owned by M. Ricalens', they were driven to Andorra. They spent a week (27 July–2 August) in the only hotel at Soldeu (whose owner was 'very pro-British') while arrangements were made by the Barcelona consulate for smugglers to take them over the border into Spain. The crossing went without a hitch and vice-consul Mr P.H. Dorchy, who was waiting for them with a car, drove them to Barcelona.

Again by car, they were taken to Madrid on the night of 8/9 August 1942, and had been travelling for over ten hours when they reached the British Embassy on 9 August. Captain Collie was not amused by their reception:

> 'When I was there the other British escapers and evaders consisted of four RAF sergeants and a boy from 51 (H) Div (Seaforth Hrs.) who had escaped from Germany...[393]
>
> '... We had been brought from Barcelona by Mr [J.G.] Whitfield. He handed in our papers and we did not see him again. When we arrived a clerk was sent down with security certificates for signature. There was no one to receive us and to tell us where to go, and no one came to see us all day. We were left on the steps leading to the hut. Only by chumming up with the RAF sergeants did we know where

to go. Sgt Aston and Dvr Flack had to find their own beds and bedding and put them up. There is a Frenchman in charge of the hut who does not speak English or Spanish. We got no breakfast – nothing till lunch. The food was good, but the service was indifferent. The Spanish servants speak no English …

'… In the grounds of the embassy there is a building which I understood was built expressly for escaped P/W. In this room there are four bedrooms which are used principally for the embassy guard. It also contains a sitting room and a dining room used by escapers. Food is cooked in this building by Spanish women. The floor is of good quality. There is no lavatory or washing accommodation in this building. The sleeping accommodation for escapers and evaders is in another building in the grounds, known as the annex. It consists of a ground floor room with about twenty beds. The lavatory is in a cellar in another part of the annex. It is also used by Spanish workmen and is filthy. There are no facilities for having a bath in private. The washing facilities consist of two wash tubs (fitted in), which were dirty, and a bath alongside. I never saw anyone use the bath... The people passing through are supposed to keep the rooms clean.

'… They have a library which contains only three books published since 1940. All the other stuff is pre-war "throw-outs". There are no British newspapers. There is a wireless set in the billet, but it does not get London. The embassy circulates a duplicated transcript of BBC news and a copy is available.' [394]

In view of Sir Samuel's claim that the grand total of those given assistance in Spain between '1940 and the end of 1944' was more than 30,000, the odd lapse might be forgiven. Sir Samuel also wrote: 'So many of these welcome visitors appeared that we found it necessary to build an annexe in the embassy garden. Until the Germans left France, the building was never empty…'[395]

Lieutenant Airey Neave, on the other hand, left the embassy and its annexe with regret: 'Every man who passed through this strange wooden building on his way to freedom during the years of the war will remember the Ambassador, Lord Templewood, and most of his staff with gratitude.'[396]

This, then, was more or less the fate that awaited British service personnel who had crossed into Spain and been caught by the Spanish authorities. It was always a struggle for the British diplomatic staff in Spain to do their best for these personnel, particularly in the face of such Spanish intransigence, and in some instances of downright unnecessary brutality, such as that suffered by Captain Besley and a number of other British servicemen.

Arrested on or about 7 October 1940, Besley was removed to the *castillo* at Figueras after a night in the local jail at Espolla. At the *castillo* he found some forty British soldiers, most of whom were in a room so small that it was impossible for all to lie down at the same time. There was no sanitation and they were only allowed out twice during the day. Captain Besley found himself sharing an alcove under the stairs with Lance Corporal J. Llewellyn-Jones, Queen's Royal Regiment, and some fifteen foreigners. Not only was the alcove open to the elements, but they also had nothing but the stone floor on which to sleep. No blankets were provided. Washing facilities were non-existent, and soon all were suffering from lice. On the positive side, the food was not too bad.

When the time came for Captain Besley and his fellow prisoners to leave Figueras, after nine days, they were handcuffed together and removed to Cervera by cattle truck. En route, when one of the prisoners failed to hear an order from a guard, his handcuffs were tightened so severely by way of a punishment that he endured excruciating pain for twenty minutes until they were eased off. The cuffs were not removed until they had reached Barcelona, at about 4 a.m., where they transferred to other cattle trucks for the rest of the journey to Cervera, which ended at 2 p.m. that day.

Having been given a sandwich and a tin of sardines, the men were told that they would get no more food at Cervera until the morrow. At least their accommodation was better than it had been at Figueras, for now they each had a palliasse and a blanket. Sanitation was better too, but still there were no washing facilities and, as before, the men were plagued with lice and fleas, and developed scabies. Unlike Figueras, 'food at Cervera was very bad. We had chicory at 0700 hours, soup and a small loaf at 1200 hours, soup with beans or potatoes at 1900 hours. There was a canteen but they charged three pesetas for a small loaf, not much bigger than a dinner roll. Other prices were approximately double the Spanish shop prices.'[397]

A visit from Barcelona vice-consul P.H. Dorchy cheered them up. As well as giving them the news that they would soon be out, he also brought 'some woollen comforts which were very badly needed'. The men's spirits, though, were dampened by their relationship with the jailers. Already strained by the favouritism shown to French and Polish prisoners, it worsened one night when a Spanish sergeant, waving his revolver, suddenly rushed into the prisoners' room and headed straight for the toilet.

Dragging out a British sailor he accused the man of trying to escape, and 'hit him several times with his fist, knocking him to the ground and then proceeded to kick him along the room.' Whilst others looked on another sailor, who tried to help, received a similar beating. Both were then taken to a cell and 'there again were punched very badly in the face, all the time being blinded by a flashlight in their eyes.'[398] Captain Besley, who had asked to see the Spanish lieutenant in charge but had been refused, believed that it was a put-up job. A rope had been spotted hanging down from the toilet, but it had not been put there by any of the British prisoners. The sailor just happened to have been in the wrong place at the wrong time.

The British prisoners with Besley were there for nine days before again being moved by cattle truck to the concentration camp at Miranda de Ebro. Eventually released, Captain Besley left Gibraltar on 19 November, and reached Liverpool on 4 December 1940.[399]

In January 1941, shortly after Besley's release, Sir Samuel Hoare became embroiled in another particularly worrying case. He received a note from the Spanish Ministry of Foreign Affairs 'complaining that a British aviator Bob Wilson aged twenty-four, now in prison at Figueras has confessed to having been advised by the United States Consulate at Marseille to cross the frontier clandestinely… Wilson also said that his papers were false, having been bought from a Frenchman for 500 francs.'[400] This was worrying for Sir Samuel, who was concerned that 'the position of sixty-five British soldiers now in Spanish concentration camps, and others in future' might thereafter be seriously prejudiced.

His diplomacy won the day, but over the next four years Spanish official bloody-mindedness led to what Sir Samuel Hoare called 'a game of hide-and-seek' and which invariably, to his question of when would the men be released, brought the response: 'We know of no such personnel.' There would follow, said Sir Samuel, 'a request from the Spanish Government for the names, and when we gave them, a denial that any one in prison answered to them. This part of the game was played with particular zest in the autumn of 1940 in the case of Lord Cardigan...' whose full name, Chandos Sydney Cedric Brudenell-Bruce, 'provided a unique opportunity for official equivocation.'[401]

The Earl of Cardigan had made a remarkable solo evasion from Belgium through France and into Spain following his capture in June 1940. Escaping from the Germans he endured a series of nerve-wracking incidents, none more so than his meeting with a German officer who, noting Cardigan's tiredness, kindly gave him a lift in his car all the way to Troyes. On reaching Marseille at the beginning of August Cardigan learnt that a number of fellow army officers, who had drifted south as he had done, had been taken into a sort of benign imprisonment at Fort St Jean in Marseille, and determined to avoid their fate. Having further learnt that two sergeants who had 'escaped from the fortress a few weeks ago' had made their way by bicycle to the Spanish frontier, he resolved to do likewise, though aware that the two sergeants had had to return to Marseille after they had been unable to cross into Spain. Purchasing a good bicycle for 'a little over 1,000 francs'[402] Cardigan headed west one fine August day and reached Céret, south of Perpignan, with little difficulty.

After a couple of days spying out the land he headed into the mountains, where an inquisitive gendarme wondered what he was doing in such a lonely place. Cardigan and his bicycle reached Spain, somewhere near la Junquera, one of only a handful of British servicemen to have cycled into Spain during the war. There, as he made his way slowly along the main street of a village, 'a man in a green uniform with red tabs stepped out from the side of the road'[403] and signalled him to stop. After questioning he was removed to a cell in the police station at Figueras. A few days later he and several other prisoners were taken to Barcelona and then to Cervera. It was towards the end of August that he received the good news that the British consul at Barcelona had written to the prison intimating that he and the other British there could expect to be released within a very few days. Alas, it was not to be, for after a week or so at Cervera it was suddenly announced that all foreign prisoners, including some twenty British, were to be moved to 'a place called Miranda de Ebro on the opposite side of the peninsula'.[404]

It was around 10 September 1940 that Cardigan watched 'fifteen of our English contingent march out of the camp, with their shoulders back and their chins up, on their way to freedom.' He was not among them because, he was told, he had not been a prisoner long enough for his papers to have made their way through the proper channels. The days dragged by, though not as painfully as earlier, for now the Spanish jailers had at least been persuaded to recognise him as an officer and to treat him as such. Then, on or about 20 September, the word came from Madrid that he and the other British were to be released that very day. Taken to the Spanish capital at once, they had a brief rest at the British Embassy before being sent on to Gibraltar. Their arrival coincided with the reprisal bombing raids by Vichy French aircraft on the afternoons of 24 and 25 September following the Gaullist-British naval attack on Dakar on 23/24 September.

Ordered by the Pétain government, these raids were of no military value but, nevertheless, twenty-eight people on Gibraltar were killed. One of the bombs dropped on 25 September fell on the RAMC mess where Cardigan was billetted, killing Captain P.P. Raikes and Captain H.R. Trythall RA, who had also both escaped from France.[405] A third officer, Lieutenant A.G. Duff, Loyal Regiment, died on 21 October of wounds received a month earlier, while a fourth, Captain J.R. Johnson, received only an injury to a hand from falling masonry.

Though the delaying tactics employed by the Spanish in cases such as Cardigan's were infuriating and frustrating, the Spanish would always eventually admit that they were holding the men whose names they had been given, so 'that sooner or later we succeeded in freeing every British prisoner who escaped into Spain, and many thousands of Allied personnel besides.'[406] This was not done initially without considerable dialogue with the appropriate Spanish authorities. It took Sir Samuel, for instance, 'about twenty visits to the Minister of Foreign Affairs, first of all to get the principle of international law accepted, and secondly to induce the various Government departments concerned to make any movement to apply it. Eventually I got the principle accepted, but that was only the beginning of our troubles.'[407]

In simple terms, it was a principle of international law that an escaped prisoner of war was entitled to passage through a neutral country en route to his homeland. On the other hand, a belligerent who for whatever reason had *not* become a prisoner of war, if caught entering a foreign country without the proper papers, could be treated as an illegal immigrant. It was clear, from the earliest days, that the majority of British service personnel did not possess proper papers and were detained accordingly for, on 9 January 1941, the War Office notified Sir George Warner KCVO that they had heard from Sir Samuel Hoare 'that fifty-five service personnel are detained in Spanish prisons. In addition seven are at the Madrid Embassy.'[408]

The Spaniards for their part, under considerable pressure from German agents whose influence was 'rampant in many branches of the administration,'[409] were understandably keen to ensure that the several dozens of men apprehended on Spanish soil were *bona fide* escaped prisoners of war. The problem for British consular officials in Spain lay in trying to convince their Spanish counterparts that those British servicemen who *were* evaders had in fact been prisoners of war and thus could be released into British hands. The Spanish authorities, though, had their job to do and were, as the British admitted, 'fully entitled to make enquiries about each man they arrest', but the way in which these enquiries were made proved to be the reason why it took so long for those who were arrested to be released from jail.

In a report of 2 June 1941 to Anthony Eden, now Secretary of State for Foreign Affairs,[410] Sir Samuel Hoare explained the causes of the delays:

> 'In a normal case the following authorities all have to give their sanction before a prisoner can be released:–
>
> The Ministry for Foreign Affairs
> The Ministry of the Army
> The Police Department
> The Inspectorate of Concentration Camps.
>
> 'The Embassy's first application has to be made to the Ministry for Foreign Affairs, who pass it on when approved to the other departments. These are tackled in turn by the Embassy until the signed order for the release of a batch of men is obtained.
>
> 'The passage of the document through the files of four ministries or departments is never swift, and in Spain the government organisation cannot be called efficient…
>
> 'The Spanish official likes to put off till tomorrow what he could do today. In some cases he may even be pro-German or at least anti-British and therefore an unwilling collaborator.
>
> 'In any department it is customary for a document to be signed by one particular individual. At the Ministry of the Army this may be a general. The order for the release of the prisoners is prepared, finally approved and placed on his table for signature. The General may be away for a few days, in which case the document remains unsigned. When he returns he may leave it unsigned for a few more days.'[411]

A little over a fortnight later, on 19 June 1941, Sir Samuel sent his *Report on P.O.W. Situation in France & Spain* to MI9, that dealt 'entirely with the situation as regards escapes from Z.O. [Zone Occupée] in France through into Spain'.[412] Acknowledging that the most important person of all the 'British people working to organise escapes' in France was Captain Ian Garrow, Sir Samuel noted that escapers and evaders were reaching the Unoccupied Zone 'at the rate of about twenty–thirty a week' via the several organisations, including French ones 'working entirely on their own, who appear to have no contact with our people, and are being financed by benevolent Frenchmen.'

For much of 1941 evaders and escapers in France (such as MacCallum and Batho) had been told, ill-advisedly as events proved, 'to give themselves up to the Spanish police', but Sir Samuel explained in his report that on crossing the border into Spain an evader or escaper 'may either surrender immediately to the Spanish military authorities, or he may attempt to reach the sanctuary of the British Consulate at Madrid or Barcelona. If he surrenders to the military authorities he passes through a number of concentration camps, and finally is repatriated via Gibraltar after a period of about two months.' On the other hand, if the evader or escaper were to reach the Barcelona consulate undetected by the Spanish authorities 'he is then given an emergency certificate, put on the train to Madrid, and on reaching the British Embassy he is kept, and sent to Gibraltar at the first available opportunity. This procedure probably takes about three weeks.' The figures suggest that most were caught before they had reached Barcelona and would fall into the hands of the civil authorities, from whom it was 'a much harder job' to get them repatriated than if they had been arrested by the military.

One other point that Sir Samuel was keen to stress, and it was a *bête noire* of his, was the problems that arose were the escaper/evader to be caught with a "Red" guide – 'he may not only compromise the consulate or embassy officials, but also endanger the whole repatriation procedure of those who have fallen into the hands of the military authorities.'[413] All involved were walking a precarious tightrope, especially the "Red" guides, communists in the eyes of General Franco, who usually suffered unpleasantly if caught.

But two of the consular staff in particular were also playing a dangerous game – Colonel Mosley from the Barcelona consulate, and Donald Darling then working under cover of the Repatriation Office at Lisbon. Having reached Madrid in August 1940, Darling made himself known to Sir Samuel Hoare, but found that he was not welcome – there was 'extremely strong feeling in official circles in Spain against Darling due to his activities in the Spanish Civil War'.[414] Darling later wrote angrily of his treatment by the Madrid staff, and was dismissive of the ambassador's views: 'The interpretation of the prime minister's directive, in its most extreme form, was tantamount to keeping in with General Franco at the expense of our own evading personnel…'[415] In consequence, Darling was obliged to retreat to the more tolerant Portuguese capital, Lisbon. Taking an altogether different view of him there was Commander Philip Johns RN, posted to Lisbon as head of the SIS in 1941, who wrote thus of the MI6 agent: 'Very dark and tanned, tall and rather burly, he was experienced in his work and tremendously enthusiastic about it as being very much worth while. According to information which trickled through to us via the PIDE, Darling was mistakenly identified by the German SD as the local chief of our Secret Service. This suited me admirably and was obviously a great help in establishing my own cover more securely.'[416]

Given the gulf between Darling in Lisbon and the British Ambassador in Madrid, Darling made no attempt at first to inform the latter of his activities, as Sir Samuel noted:

> 'There was, of course, liaison between Madrid and Barcelona and each knew what the other was doing. But the exact nature of Mr Darling's activities in Lisbon was not known.
>
> 'Eventually contact was made with Darling and he was supplied with the nominal rolls of repatriated PoWs and lists of wounded and others in France who were reported to this embassy from time to time.'[417]

Sir Samuel was prepared to admit, however, that Darling was 'au fait with most of what is happening in France' and that he was 'also in contact with Garrow by means of the Quakers, and sundry Swiss, Americans, etc, (none of whom will ever work for anyone at Barcelona).' Darling was also in contact with Colonel Mosley but, because of the legacy of Darling's activities in the civil war, Mosley very often disregarded his advice, and only used those people whom he considered fit. Whereas the frequency of Colonel Mosley's contacts with Ian Garrow and his organisation were 'irregular', he was nevertheless passing money through to Garrow and was also 'in contact with another organisation in Toulouse. He has also a car which appears to go in and out of France, and is available to help PoWs who manage to send word that they are hiding in the frontier area.'[418]

Dealing with the many people crossing into Spain, not just genuine British service personnel, was an expensive business. Harold Farquhar, consul-general at Barcelona, in a letter dated 31 December 1941, told Anthony Eden of the work that his consulate had been undertaking in regard to these arrivals in Spain, and the cost thereof. Since 1 April 1941 Farquhar and his staff had spent an estimated 165,014 pesetas on guides and 'other expenses connected with the arrival of escapees to the consulate'; 29,860 pesetas 'on petrol, tyres,[419] etc., in respect of their journey by car to Madrid'; a further 63,665 pesetas 'in connection with the maintenance and forwarding to Portugal of certain Allied nationals whom we were instructed to assist'; and 151,033 pesetas 'on the care and maintenance of British and Allied personnel in prison'. To be fair, however, Farquhar thought that the 41,356 pesetas (£888) spent on Captain Murchie and party, who had been arrested by the Spanish on a charge of espionage in April 1941 and who 'were only transferred to Miranda on 15th December', should be deducted from the total.[420]

During the nine months of April–December 1941 staff at the Barcelona consulate-general had handled 384 'British service personnel (officers and other ranks of the BEF, RAF, RN and Merchant Service)', and 270 other personnel 'British civilians, Allied service personnel whether declaring themselves British or not, Frenchmen desirous of joining the Free French Forces, and special cases of interest to particular government departments in London'. In addition, a further 116 wounded men were repatriated 'through Barcelona' having been 'certified as unfit for further military duty by a joint Franco-German-American medical board'. Of those 384 British service personnel only eighty-three had managed to reach Barcelona 'without falling into the hands of the Spanish authorities' – forty-six army officers and other ranks; thirty-three RAF; and four RN/merchant marine – whereas the other 301 had all been 'apprehended on clandestinely entering Spain' and had been 'lodged in prison either at Barcelona, Figueras, Cervera or other civil prisons' in the area of the consulate-general's superintendence.

Farquhar did not say how many of the 384 had successfully reached the British Embassy at Madrid, but from April to July 1941 those who had reached Barcelona undetected were sent on to Madrid by train. Due to the increase in controls on the railways, however, 'this procedure was found to be unsatisfactory. The majority of the men were caught and the money expended on their railway journey was thus wasted.' It was therefore decided to drive the men to Madrid by consular car, and Farquhar was able to report that, up to the end of 1941, this method had proved successful, with sixty-four being safely delivered by this method, half of them RAF.

The work of Farquhar and his staff – particularly Vice-Consul J.G. Whitfield, and Miss Cautley[421] – was greatly facilitated by 'the excellent discipline and good behaviour of all ranks of the [British] armed forces', but the consul was not amused by 'the behaviour of the majority of would-be aspirants to the Free French Forces, whose levity and lack of responsibility have, on more than one occasion, nearly compromised this consulate.'[422] Quite apart from their dealings with the French, the consul's staff were also having to look after all sorts of personnel in the several Spanish prisons within the consulate's "parish". In June 1941 there had been a maximum of forty-six escaped personnel in prison, but this figure had fallen to only four 'genuine British PoWs' by the end of the year. They were being held in the *Cárcel Modelo* (model prison) at Barcelona together with a further twenty 'Allied personnel masquerading as Canadians'.

A nominal roll of sixteen such "Canadian" prisoners of war who were 'evacuated from Miranda on the 17/8/41'[423] throws light on this not-too-subtle and unconvincing masquerade (assumed name/real name): J. Richardson/Van de Heyden; A. Michel/Michel; R. Belpaire/Belpaire; W. Simmons/Bonnaire; P. Blancpain/Blancpain; L. Wannier/Vannier; P. Clark/Cooreman; S. Zucker/Zucker; F. Cooper/Danze; A. Anethan/de Tiege; J. Chester/Schyns; D. Green/Deheve; F. Falcon/Franchi; J. Goudchaux/Goudchaux; Hughff Ch./Bourguet; Brown/Aymard. These so-called Canadians were a great nuisance to British officials in Spain, as Sir Samuel Hoare told the Foreign Office in his cypher dated 4 February 1942:

> '1. I have received many unmistakable indications that the "Canadian" ruse cannot work much longer; the practice is now public knowledge, every foreign prisoner desiring assistance calls himself Canadian, and Gestapo is actively pressing Spanish authorities to put an end to it.
>
> '2. Over 300 men have been released under this guise since 1940 and over eighty since October, 1941. There are fifty more in camp (mostly Belgian) for whom I have applied and whose cases are outstanding, and twenty-five not yet applied for.
>
> '3. In view of the danger of prejudicing cases of genuine British personnel, if authorities make a political issue of this question, I have come to the conclusion that the only safe course is that after I have dealt with the present outstanding cases to cease claiming any more Canadians for the present…'[424]

For the meantime, though, a further report dated 1 May 1942 by Brigadier Torr showed that, while the number of British service personnel entering Spain was reducing, the number of civilians was increasing. During the four months up to the end of April 1942, of the 182 persons who were repatriated, only forty-four were British service personnel – twenty-four airmen; seventeen soldiers; and three Royal and/or Merchant Navy seamen. Of the remaining one hundred and thirty-eight, seventy-eight were described as 'formerly in Allied Forces or Merchant Navy'; fifty-one as Allied civilians; and nine as British civilians. In addition, awaiting repatriation from Madrid to Gibraltar as at 30 April 1942, were three British soldiers and twenty-four others (including nine British civilians).

One hundred and forty-four non-British personnel (including fifteen awaiting repatriation) were repatriated during the first four months of 1942: ninety-five Belgians; twenty-nine French; seventeen Poles; and three Dutch. These brought the total repatriated through Spain from June 1940 to 30 April 1942 to 1,030 – 607 British service personnel, and 423 'others'.

In an update to Anthony Eden, on 6 August 1942, Farquhar pointed out that, of the 487 persons 'who either passed through the hands of this consulate, or who were reported as having been apprehended by the Spanish authorities', only eighty-eight were British service personnel compared with 399 "other personnel". Forty of the British service personnel 'were apprehended on their clandestine entry into Spain' and imprisoned within the consulate's "parish", but the other forty-eight – nine RAF; twenty-two soldiers; and seventeen civilians – reached Barcelona without being caught.

As ever, the exuberant French taxed Farquhar to the limit. One Frenchman, by the name of Abraham Levy, had arrived with a party of British escapers – 'though how he managed to attach himself to this party remains a mystery' – but, on being invited to complete the form that would commit him to joining the Free French Forces, refused so to do, declaring that he was 'réformé' – discharged as unfit to serve. Furthermore, he expected the Barcelona consulate to get him to Mexico, advance him the necessary funds to get him there as he was almost penniless, and 'to change at a rate extremely favourable to himself a portion at any rate of all the money he had secreted on his person.'[425]

Farquhar also saw fit to mention the fact that 103 Belgians had been given some form of attention because, even though they had their own consulate in Spain, they treated the British consulate 'as a form of reception office', owing to the fact that they used 'the same transport agency as our organisation in France, and the guides profess themselves unable to differentiate between British and foreigners.' The cost of all of this to His Majesty's government was some £6,900, though Farquhar acknowledged that it could expect to receive £2,800 in refunds from Allied governments.

Observing that there had been a 'marked reduction in the number of British personnel attempting to escape through Spain, particularly RAF', Farquhar noted that by way of a contrast there had been a considerable increase in 'Allied nationals' requiring assistance.[426] He was unable to explain, though, why the number of 'genuine British personnel' arriving in Spain had fallen to a trickle, unless it was due to the possibility that, as it was now over two years since the BEF was withdrawn from France, all those who could have escaped had already done so.

He was particularly puzzled by the lack of RAF aircrew coming through – 'the valuable crews of the heavy bombers lost in recent raids over Germany, or of the fighter squadrons who fail to return from their daily sweeps over Northern France.' Again, though, the explanation might have been simply, in his view, that machines were now more important than men, though acknowledging that 'the particular efforts made by the Germans to prevent the escape of RAF personnel seems to be in itself an indication of their high military value.'[427] The answer, more likely, was that the main effort in getting airmen into Spain was then being directed over the western Pyrenees and not the eastern.

Farquhar's reference to the Belgians using 'the same transport agency as our organisation in France' suggests that he was almost certainly aware of the work then being done by the Comet organisation (see Chapter 6) which, since Jim Cromar's pioneering crossing in August 1941, had passed seventy-two "British" airmen (and ten soldiers) into Spain via the western Pyrenees by the end of 1942, almost half of the total number of airmen (149) to have reached Spain during those seventeen months.

Another worry for Farquhar was that, since the closure by the Spanish authorities of the Polish consulate (which had helped hundreds of its own people to pass through Spain) and the likelihood of the closure of the Belgian consulate, it was on the cards that the British consulate could suffer the same fate, the equivalent to his mind of 'shooting a sparrow with a 15-inch gun'. Of the opinion, therefore, that the consulate would continue in business, even if he himself were to become a consular casualty, his firm belief that the ever-increasing burden of non-British nationals crossing into Spain from France would fall upon the Barcelona staff's shoulders was to be proved correct within a few months.

On 14 November 1942 Sir Samuel Hoare sent a cypher to the Foreign Office in London informing them that, consequential upon the Allied invasion of North Africa on 8 November, the 'Germans already control the remainder of Franco-Spanish frontier from the old Demarcation Line down to Cerbere.' Although, Sir Samuel reported, there had been 'no marked increase in influx of refugees' since the total occupation of France – it had, after all, been only six days since that event – a party of 'sixteen British subjects did, however, manage to cross the frontier clandestinely two days ago and the police have allowed them to proceed to Barcelona where they are expected tonight.'[428] With the winter snows now beginning to block the high passes of the Pyrenees, a decline in the number of escapers, as in the previous winter of 1941-42, was expected. The Germans, too, were 'making a definite drive' to have all clandestine activities in and over the Pyrenees stopped.

With the prospect of few escapers arriving in Spain, therefore, Sir Samuel was now able to focus his attention on "British" subjects held in Spanish jails, particularly those at the concentration camp at Miranda de Ebro. He noted that being held at Miranda as at 15 November 1942 were 489 Poles, 400 Belgians, fifty Dutch, thirty-nine Czechs, and thirty-six Yugoslavs, plus a further 135 "British and Canadians" of whom only ten seemed to have had a legitimate claim to be British, and of those ten the only military personnel were two 'naval deserters from Gibraltar'. Of the remaining eight, two were British civilians who had lived for much of their lives in France, two more had been born in England of French parents, one was a 'seminarist from Belgium', one came from Mauritius, one was a Canadian who had lived in Spain for the last five years, and the last was a 'Cingalese pedlar who had lived in Spain for the last ten years as a gypsy and is delighted to remain in the camp in receipt of inter-Allied food and relief.' The rest were Poles (forty-one), French (thirty-seven), Belgians (thirty-five), Dutch (five), Czechs (four), Greeks (two), and one 'Baltic seaman'.[429]

The large number of Polish troops reaching Spain may be explained by the fact that over 84,000 of them had been caught in France at the cessation of hostilities in June 1940. The Poles had immediately begun to organise ways and means of getting their men out, and a Major Slowikowski, setting himself up in Toulouse as chief evacuation officer, had 'started on his own initiative immediately after the fall of France, to deal with the job of "illegal" emigration through Spain.'[430] In a matter of weeks the Poles 'had seven routes established through the Pyrenees'.

Sir Samuel, nevertheless, did what he could to "claim" these foreigners once arrested, and reckoned that forty-five of them would be released as "British". He had little hope, however, for twenty of the Poles who had 'declared themselves as possessing unmistakeably Polish names or have been registered in the camp as having been born at such places as Warsaw, Cracow or Przemsyl.' By Christmas Day 1942 though he was able to inform the Foreign Office that the numbers at Miranda 'have now risen to nearly 3,500 and parties of 200 or more keep arriving there without any warning to the camp authorities and without any preparations for their reception.' The effect of this sudden and unexpected influx was to cause serious overcrowding in a camp where the capacity, even with some degree of crowding, was now 2,000.

Despite the 'miscellaneous and (except for the Poles and Belgians) not very impressive cross-section of the population of the United Nations,' Sir Samuel could report that, in the three and a half months from 1 August to 15 November 1942, fifty-six RAF airmen and twenty-one British soldiers 'had been successful in passing clandestinely through Spain'. The total for the whole of 1942 was 116 RAF, sixty-three British Army, five Royal Navy and Merchant Marine, and thirty-one civilians (six of whom had arrived in the aforesaid period up to 15 November). Overall, in the two and a half years since the fall of France, 837 British service personnel had now passed through Spain under the watchful eye of the British consular staff, together with 990 'British civilians and foreign personnel'.

Not a few of the Poles interned at Miranda during 1942 were airmen from Polish squadrons serving in the RAF. One crew in particular, that of Flying Officer Julien Morawski (see Chapter 5), was for some reason of great interest to Polish Intelligence. Passed through to Spain by Francisco Ponzán Vidal (see below), they were arrested and ultimately interned at Miranda de Ebro. On 13 August 1942 SOE suggested to Sir Samuel Hoare 'that strenuous efforts should be made to obtain the release of the above-mentioned men for undoubtedly if we are able to do this we shall be able to establish considerable credit vis-à-vis the Polish VI Bureau whom we are in close contact with, and who are exceedingly interested in the fate of these men.'[431] It was also noted that Morawski had, for some obscure reason, given 'his name in the camp as Denise Messiter, and most probably declared himself as a Canadian.' By the time that this request had been made one of the crew, Sergeant Polesinski, was already in England. Morawski himself and another of his crew, Flying Officer Wacinski, were on their way from Gibraltar on 19 August. The fourth evader, Sergeant Wozniak, was not to leave by air until 23 September.

Francisco Ponzán Vidal, born in Oviedo on 30 March 1911, was already in trouble with the Spanish authorities by 1932. After several months in prison for his militant tendencies in the anarcho-syndicalist union *Confederación Nacional del Trabajo* (CNT, National Confederation of Labour), further involvement in the Spanish Civil War led him to flee to France at the beginning of 1939. Interned in the unpleasant concentration camp at Vernet (Haute-Garonne), he managed to escape, and organised an anti-fascist group, which undertook several guerilla operations in Spain. During one of these, the failed attempt in May 1940 to free Spanish anarcho-syndicalist militants Manuel Lozano Guillén[432] and Bernabé Argüelles from prison at Huesca, Ponzán was wounded. After several months recovering in the mountains of Spain he escaped to France again, and this time set up an escape line to help anti-fascists over the Pyrenees, the members of his organisation all being "free" Spaniards.

A link was also formed with the Marseille escape organisation, later under Pat O'Leary's direction, and also with the Comet line, though the latter did not commence operations until the autumn of 1941. MI6's man in the Iberian peninsula, Donald Darling, noted a meeting that he had 'at the grassy airport of Cintra' with James Langley, alias P15, in the autumn of 1941. The main reason for Langley's flying visit was to ask Darling for his views on the 'Spanish guides being used for the eastern end of the Pyrenean crossing whom Garrow employed, *faute de mieux*, and who at the Barcelona Consulate were constantly demanding higher tariffs.' Darling knew these Spaniards as the '*Alianza Española Democratica*, a title covering a myriad political sins... The leader of these operations was one Vidal, whose associates in Spain seemed to be as useful as they were surprising.'[433] They had created their own route over the Pyrenees, men who had used it being met at the railway station at Vilajuiga by a plain-clothes policeman by the name of Eliseo Melis.

After a number of crossings of the Pyrenees, which included several airmen evaders, Ponzán was arrested by the Germans in 1943 and imprisoned at Toulouse (possibly in the St Michel prison – see Chapter 11). When the time came for the Germans to evacuate the south-west of France, Ponzán and some twenty other prisoners were taken away on 17 August 1944 and shot dead in the Forest of Buzet (near Buzet-sur-Tarn). All the bodies were burnt to hide the evidence.

Not all airmen to reach Spain came over the Pyrenees from France. An additional burden for the British consular officials and their staffs in Spain and Portugal was the unscheduled arrival in those countries of sundry RAF personnel who had been parted from their aircraft, usually on their way to or from the Middle East and/or Malta. The first unscheduled arrival was probably that of Pilot Officer G. Bennett and crew, who were forced to put Blenheim T2114 down in northern Spain on 30 November 1940.

Then on 26 April 1941, Squadron Leader G.F. Rodney AFC and crew took off from England bound for Gibraltar in Wellington W5652.[434] Shortly after crossing the Belgian coast to the south of Ostend they entered thick cloud. When the aircraft began to ice up, Rodney was forced to climb to 14,000 feet, above the cloud, which persisted, according to the navigator's calculations, until they were barely eighty kilometres from the Mediterranean. Rodney later reported: 'When first light of day appeared, the cloud formation broke and on E.T.A. next turning point I set course on the last leg to Gibraltar. After about thirty minutes there was no sight of land, so I altered course to 280° compass in an endeavour to get a land-fall on Spain and so obtain a pinpoint.'[435]

Land was finally sighted at around 6.45 a.m. but, when it turned out to be a group of islands that the navigator was unable to identify, Rodney 'decided to break W/T silence and obtain a QDM from Gibraltar. Communication was not made with Gibraltar, but our request was answered by the Station "O9T" which the wireless operator could not identify, giving us a bearing of 285° from Gibraltar. I asked for confirmation of this bearing and received it. I then took S.O.S. procedure but Gibraltar did not reply.' Now short of fuel and suspicious of the bearings given, Rodney decided to put the Wellington down, wheels up, on one of the islands. Following a successful landing at 7.40 a.m. on Sunday, 27 April, the crew discovered that they were on Formentera, the southernmost of the Balearic Islands, some 600 kilometres north-east of Gibraltar. Spanish military authorities notified the British consulate at Palma de Mallorca of the incident.

The crew were taken by boat to Ibiza, then by flyingboat to Puerto de Pollensa, in the north of Mallorca, and by car to the Grand Hotel in Palma that same evening. On 30 April they were moved to the Mediterraneo hotel where every courtesy was extended to them, even being allowed out for a walk – provided that they were accompanied by a police officer. Then, out of the blue, tragedy struck.

During their first night in the Mediterraneo one of the crew, Sergeant C.S. Hunt, died. The autopsy revealed that indigestion had caused him to vomit and that his trachea and larynx had filled with food. Paralysis of the larynx caused asphyxia, and death. 755673 Claude Samuel Hunt, aged twenty-three, was laid to rest in Palma's municipal cemetery. The five remaining and chastened airmen were removed to the Oriente hotel at Saragossa, on the Spanish mainland.

For the British Ambassador, Sir Samuel Hoare, their presence in Spain meant yet more work for him and his staff, as weeks passed without their being able to obtain the airmen's release. A Wellington and its six crew came down in Portugal on 16 May 1941, and two more were forced down through fuel shortage having encountered an electrical storm on 20 June, one in Portugal again (Sergeant P.F. Bold and crew in X3211) and the second (Flying Officer E.I.J. Bell and crew, Z8722) in Spain.

Bell's Mark IC Wellington, having departed RAF Hampstead Norris shortly before midnight on 19/20 June 1941, ran into the storm as it was making its way down the west coast of Spain. In the darkness and with the compass thrown out by the weather Bell headed east across Spain until the

Wellington ran out of fuel some five kilometres off the Spanish east coast at Aguilas. Rescued from the Mediterranean Sea, they were brought to Albacete.

With a further three recently-arrived Blenheim airmen to deal with (Sergeant F.T.J. Bryant and crew – see below), Sir Samuel cabled the Foreign Office on 2 August 1941 that the 'three officers and eleven airmen at present detained in Spain are becoming restless, particularly Squadron Leader Rodney's party at Saragossa, as they feel it their duty to endeavour to escape. This party could probably have escaped in the beginning, but they confided their plans to their guards and are now so closely watched that this could now only be done with the connivance of the embassy by smuggling them into the building and passing them off as ordinary escaped prisoners.'[436] Sir Samuel was in no mood to rock the Spanish authorities' boat, especially when, as the 'result of another drive, we have just got a further sixty-four escaped prisoners released. We have also got the forty-nine shipwrecked officers and men at Teneriffe, and the fifty-seven naval officers and ratings off *Malvernian* released, making a total of releases to date 616.'[437] In today's parlance, he was "on a roll", and Sir Samuel was loath to add his sixpennyworth for fear of upsetting 'an arrangement that is working so well'.

Eventually, therefore, at the end of September 1941, Squadron Leader Rodney and crew found themselves on the way to Albacete, and met Flying Officer Bell and crew at the Gran hotel. Diplomatic pressure from the staff at the British Embassy in Madrid finally produced results, and from 23 March 1942 onwards the airmen left in small groups for Gibraltar, which all had reached by 11 April. Boarding ship on 27 April, they docked at Liverpool on 8 May.[438]

Sergeant F.T.J. Bryant and crew were victims of the rush to get RAF reinforcement aircraft to the Middle East and Malta to counter the build-up of Axis forces in North Africa in 1941. The only aircraft that could be spared were Mark IV Blenheims of No. 2 Group, RAF. With summer drawing on and with fewer hours of darkness the Blenheims, usually departing from RAF Portreath in north Cornwall for a refuelling stop at Gibraltar, were routed out over the Atlantic to the west of France, down the coast of Portugal, and along to the south of Spain. Needing every ounce of fuel for the estimated seven and a half hour flight, the Blenheims were fitted with extra fuel tanks. Inevitably, in the hurry of war, mechanical errors occurred.

On 24 June 1941 the air attaché at the British Embassy in Madrid was summoned to the northern Spanish town of Valladolid, some 200 kilometres from Madrid, to interview the Bryant crew who had come down a dozen kilometres north of Finisterre. They told the air attaché that their aircraft, Z6453, had taken off from RAF Portreath at 1230 GMT on 20 June with seven other Blenheims of 105 Squadron in a formation flight led by Squadron Leader D.E. Bennett to Gibraltar. When approximately 150 kilometres south of the Scilly Isles a German Dornier 17 was sighted. The formation closed up but, flying at sea level, the Blenheims were not seen. Pressing on, they were some 300 kilometres north of Cape Finisterre when they climbed to '5000 feet and assumed loose formation'.

At this point Sergeant F.T.J. Bryant ordered Sergeant D.R.C. Philip to pump fuel by hand from the extra, outer tanks into the main inner wing tanks. Shortly afterwards the port engine coughed and spluttered into inactivity. Unable to maintain height on one engine Z6453 slowly slipped out of formation, the frantic Philip all the while twiddling knobs and furiously opening and closing fuel cocks. Now well behind the rest of the formation, and down to a thousand feet, the pilot decided to try the outer tanks again. The port engine burst into life once more and the formation was regained, but then they had a similar problem with the starboard engine. When the fuel feed problem failed to go away, approximately 140 kilometres north of Cape Finisterre, Bryant asked the navigator, Sergeant P.M. Thompson, for their position and track, and what their chances were of reaching Portugal.

Thompson's reply was not encouraging, leaving Bryant with the choice of attempting a landing either in the sea or on Spanish soil. As the heavy Blenheim would not, in his opinion, stay afloat for long, he chose the latter option, and brought Z6453 down over the coast between two hills. The impact smashed the Blenheim's nose and broke its back. Though Bryant was unhurt, Thompson 'sustained slight cuts and a badly bruised leg', and Philip, thrown clear of the aircraft, 'received a blow on the head rendering him unconscious for a short period.'[439] Quickly surrounded by Spaniards the crew were unable to do much damage to the aircraft. Though the IFF was detonated and little of military value was left, Spanish officials did manage to confiscate two bags of unsealed mail.

A doctor attended to Thompson and Philip, and food was provided for the airmen, who were then led away on horseback 'to Finisterre where the pilot telephoned Mr Guyatt the British Vice-Consul' at La Coruña (Corunna).[440] Taken to La Coruña, the airmen were visited next day by Lieutenant-Colonel Enrique Matas of the Spanish Air Force General Staff, who was instructed to take the men to Valladolid. Accommodated in the Hotel de Italia Matas instructed the hotel proprietor to afford the airmen every comfort.

During what was to prove a long stay in Valladolid Spanish officials showed them 'every courtesy and in Finisterre and Corunna the ordinary people showed extreme kindness and in many cases openly expressed pro-British sympathies.' Such was not the case, though, of the citizens of Valladolid, where anti-British feeling was, as Sergeant Bryant reported, 'very strong and this rose to such an extent that some sort of lynching party was arranged for us on Christmas Day. As a result we were moved on 29 December to Soria. We remained there till we were repatriated…'[441] They finally left Gibraltar by ship on 4 May 1942, arriving at Gourock after eight days at sea.[442]

It was also a fuel problem that befell the crew of Z7366,[443] another 105 Squadron Mark IV Blenheim, flown by Sergeant G.K. Williams RNZAF. The aircraft left Portreath bound for Gibraltar just after midday on 17 July 1941, flying in the No. 2 position in a formation of four aircraft. There were no problems until 'low cloud and frontal conditions' forced the formation to climb to 10,000 feet. 'Landfall was made off the north coast of Spain and the formation flew down the coast of Portugal, some fifteen to twenty miles out to sea.'[444] Sergeant R.E. Griffin, observer, had been pumping fuel from the auxiliary tank into the main tank for an hour when the pump's mounting broke away from the fuselage, and fuel started leaking into the cockpit. At this point Williams came to the obvious conclusion that, as petrol consumption had been very high, Griffin was probably pumping in vain, and therefore made the decision to fly directly over neutral Portugal.

Leaving formation with enough fuel for an estimated further three hours' flying, he headed at 10,000 feet across Cape St Vincent in the south-west of Portugal. On course for Gibraltar, but with fuel consumption still very high, Williams decided to abort the journey and to land at Faro airfield on the Algarve coast. The wireless-operator air-gunner, Sergeant N. Kay, 'repeatedly sent out messages to Gibraltar in plain language to the effect that they were making a forced landing in Portugal, but he received no acknowledgment of his signals.'

Although the airfield was marked on their maps, they were unable to find it and Williams therefore selected a suitable stretch of beach. Just as he was turning in to land with wheels down, both engines cut, but the landing was a good one until the Blenheim's wheels suddenly sank into soft sand. Coming to an abrupt halt, Z7366 tipped onto its nose and fell back onto its tail. Though considerably shaken, cut and bruised, the three airmen set about destroying 'all maps, charts, codes with the exception of the Syko machine and the G.D. 75 which was wedged in the damaged section of the nose'. Attempts to set fire to the aircraft with flares were unsuccessful but the IFF was blown up and the wireless wrecked, though several bags of mail and packets of serum for Malta were saved.

Several Portuguese fishermen were quickly on the scene, followed by coast guards, who escorted the RAF airmen to the Portuguese naval offices in Faro. After an interpreter had been found, they were asked to give their parole not to escape, which they willingly did. Summoned to Faro, M.D.M. Falconer, British vice-consul, assured the airmen that they would be out of Portugal in no time. When the crew happened to mention that they had given their parole, his blunt reply was: 'Parole be buggered!' The forthright vice-consul was, however, able to recover some of the mail and serum, which had been deposited with the police.

The airmen remained at Faro until 23 July when they were taken under police escort to Lisbon for the night, making a full report there to Flight Lieutenant D. Cameron, assistant air attaché at the British Embassy. On 24 July their journey continued to the Atlantic port of Figueira da Foz, where they were placed in a small hotel and warned 'that if they made no attempt to escape they would be left free, otherwise they would be sent to camps at either Finisterre or the Azores.' Commander Billyard Leake arrived from the British Embassy on the following day and said that, if they could give their guards the slip, a car would be waiting at a certain spot to pick them up. To give them a decent chance it would be waiting at three different times on three different days.

It was on 31 July, the third day, that the guards' attention waned sufficiently to allow the airmen to slip away to the car. Driven back to Lisbon they snatched a quick meal at the consul-general's house before being taken to a private dock, where they boarded a Portuguese tug. They put to sea at about 11 p.m. to rendezvous with a Royal Navy corvette in international waters, but the corvette never appeared, and at 6 a.m. on 1 August, the tug returned to harbour. The three airmen were now separated and sent to stay with British residents. On the evening of 3 August, they met back at the docks and boarded the same tug, and two hours later were transferred to the freighter *Briarwood* that had earlier sailed from Lisbon and which was making for Gibraltar.[445] There they were put aboard HMT *Pasteur*, which docked at Gourock, Scotland, on 13 August 1941. Reporting to RAF Watton on 16 August they returned to RAF Swanton Morley to resume their war.

In the summer of 1941 Sir Samuel Hoare was hauled up before the Spanish minister of foreign affairs following an incident near Auamara in The Rif (Spanish Morocco), North Africa.[446] The minister, pointing out to Sir Samuel 'the gravity of this incident,' called it 'a premeditated violation of Spanish territory and a deliberate act of aggression against Spanish authority. The reconnaissance carried out by the flying boat excludes all possibility of error as regards locality.'[447] Suitable apologies made and honour satisfied, the incident was closed.

The incident in question concerned a forced landing by RAF Blenheim Z9581, but which was certainly not a premeditated violation of Spanish territory. Sergeant H.J. King (pilot), Sergeant A. Ryan RAAF, and Sergeant W.J. King, the crew of Z9581, had taken off from RAF Watton on 20 July 1941 with orders to deliver the aircraft to the Middle East via Gibraltar and Malta. All went well until, estimating their position to be approximately one hour from Gibraltar, visibility deteriorated so badly due to sea mist and low cloud that they could see no more than one mile ahead. The pilot deemed it unwise to try to land at Gibraltar in such conditions, and a signal was sent explaining their predicament.

Receiving no reply they nevertheless pressed on, but with fuel now running low. As the Blenheim climbed through the mist a reply to their QDM[448] was received at the very moment that they saw land ahead. Reckoning that they had insufficient fuel to reach Gibraltar, course was altered to the east and, making for land, they signalled their intentions. King landed the Blenheim on a cliff top: 'We immediately blew up the IFF and salvaged the first aid kit, food rations and a kit bag containing clothing. Then as the engines were still running, opened the throttles fully and let the aircraft go over a cliff. It caught fire and was completely destroyed.'[449]

Wondering what to do next, their thoughts were interrupted by the appearance over a nearby hill of a number of friendly Arabs, mostly mounted, followed by a number of armed guards, all of whom treated the airmen respectfully. When told where they had landed, they realised that they had been heading down the Atlantic coast of Morocco with nothing but thousands of miles of open sea before them. Next to appear were a Frenchman and his English-speaking wife, the latter suggesting that they should give their names, ranks and numbers, and write a brief account of their adventures. She added that she would personally deliver it to the British consul in Spanish Morocco, and also advised them to go there rather than to French Morocco.

Before they could decide what to do a Sunderland flying boat suddenly came thundering towards them over the sea. Borrowing headgear from one of the Arabs, the airmen waved vigorously at the aircraft, which circled round them before departing. The Frenchman and his wife, who had earlier gone home to fetch some food, returned with a French officer, and all were enjoying their meal when the sound of another aircraft was heard heading towards them. Soon a Fairey Swordfish biplane of 202 Squadron from Gibraltar, 'fitted with drogue towing apparatus', hoved into view.

Hand signals were exchanged between the pilot and the Blenheim crew, who all the while were gradually edging away from their guards. Then the 'Swordfish crossed the coast and circled low over our heads, [the pilot] signalling that he was going to land. The guards became very excited and shouted to us to come back. The aircraft landed just over a hillock, and came to rest on the brow of a hill, about 150 to 200 yards away from the crowd. We all made a dash towards it, zig-zagging as we heard rifle shots. The Swordfish turned and took off with three of us literally hanging on to the side. We later clambered into the rear cockpit and were brought safely to Gibraltar.'[450]

According to Sir Samuel Hoare's brief description of the Swordfish rescue, a 'pair of Moorish guards approached the wreck [of the Blenheim], but the biplane, after scaring them away with machine-gun fire and a smoke-screen, picked up the two [*sic*] members of the crashed machine and flew them away.'[451]

The gunfire was not, however, all one way for, on its return to Gibraltar, the Swordfish was found to be riddled with bullet holes. The identity of the brave and resourceful Swordfish pilot is not known. As to the rescue itself, the signals from the Blenheim appear to have been received at Gibraltar, where prompt action was taken to launch the Swordfish. The two Kings and the Australian Ryan were back at Watton on the same day as the Williams crew.[452]

If the coasts of Spain and Portugal were not littered with RAF aircraft transitting to Gibraltar and the Middle East, then they were certainly studded with them, and all incidents required some involvement by consular staff of both countries. Two Blenheims of the Overseas Air Delivery Unit (OADU) came down in Portugal on 27 August 1941, and four months later a Wellington of the same unit was forced to land at Lisbon's airport with only one good engine. The crew set their aircraft alight. On 14 February 1942 yet another Wellington, of 1 OADU, came down in Portugal, but it was to be a further six months before another transitting RAF aircraft, Wellington HX566, crashed in Spain.

Flying low in a mist along the Spanish coast between Tarifa, at the entrance to the Straits of Gibraltar, and Algeciras, HX566 had been airborne for over eight hours when it hit a hill barely 300 metres away from a Spanish coastal battery, and burst into flames shortly after 3.20 p.m. on 28

August 1942. Brave Spanish soldiers rushed over from their battery, but there was nothing they could do to save five of the crew. The sixth, however, a young American Sergeant Rodney Webber RCAF, a student from California, was pulled out of the flaming wreckage by the soldiers and taken to the hospital at Algeciras suffering from shock. On 5 October, spending a day at the military prisons at Madrid and Burgos on the way, he was sent to the camp at Miranda de Ebro. Thanks to the efforts of the British Embassy staff, he was released on 7 November. Sailing from Gibraltar on Christmas Day 1942, he was back in Scotland on New Year's Eve.[453]

At the end of 1942 British consular staff were dealing with 'the question of the release from Spain of Royal Air Force personnel, at present totalling twenty-nine (five of whom are now lodged in the embassy), who have made forced landings in Spanish territory or off the Spanish coast.'

Four of the twenty-nine were from a 10 OTU Whitley which had taken off from RAF St Eval, Cornwall on 11 December 1942 on an anti-submarine patrol. Engine trouble forced Pilot Officer F.L. Perrers RNZAF to land the aircraft, Z9437, on a beach near Cape Peñas in northern Spain. Having destroyed 'secret equipment and maps' the crew waded ashore. Arrested by the Guardia Civil, they were escorted to the nearby customs house before being taken to the town of Aviles. Though just another routine matter for the British consular staff in Spain, it all added to their workload. Ten weeks later, on 19 February 1943 Perrers and crew – Sergeants F.C. Crowe; J.F. White; and R.B. Mutum – sailed from Gibraltar for Liverpool, England.[454]

Excluding Sergeant Webber, the other twenty-four internees had come from three Wellingtons of 1 OADU lost in October 1942 and two Blenheims lost in November.[455] Not on the list, though, were eleven airmen from Liberator AL513, 1445 Flight. On its way from RAF Lyneham, England to Gibraltar on 15 December 1942, fire had broken out in one of its four engines forcing the pilot, Flight Sergeant J.L. O'Sullivan, to land in a field near Rota, on the north side of the Bahía de Cádíz in south-west Spain. None of the men on board was injured, and they were able to set fire to the wreckage of the aircraft to prevent any secrets – including their own precious logbooks – from falling into the wrong hands.

Soon picked up by soldiers, they were taken to their barracks for a feed, before continuing to Seville for the night in a hotel, where they also spent the next two nights. Flight Sergeant Bernard Clifton DFM wrote about this in a letter home: 'Most of the time we were with two Spanish Air Force officers and they were fine blokes, treated us very well. As we had no Spanish money they bought us drinks and fags. On the Friday they flew us to Saragossa and we went by bus up the mountains to this place Alhama where we are interned. But it's very nice here and we can go out in the village and up the mountains which are around this place on every side.'[456]

They stayed at the hotel Balneario Termas Pallarés in the spa town of Alhama de Aragón (some 210 kilometres north-east of Madrid), where they were well cared for by the Spanish Air Force, as many others would be after them. Nine cases of oranges were delivered to them at the hotel (no doubt courtesy of the British Embassy), but the main need of the men was for beer (of which there was none to be had, as it was out-of-season at the spa resort) and cigarettes. Spanish "fags" were awful ('rough', 'you need leather lungs to smoke Spanish fags' – Flight Sergeant Clifton), but when no cigarettes had come from the embassy a supply of Chesterfields got through for American E&E at the hotel, though two-thirds of the consignment had been filched between Barcelona and Alhama. Nevertheless, the Americans generously handed out ten each to the British.

In January and February 1943 the crew of AL513 returned to England. In July 1943 two of them, Victor Whitehall and Bernard Clifton DFM, went to India, joining 159 Squadron in Bengal. Flying operations against Japanese targets in Burma and Siam, on the night of 29 February 1944 their Liberator, BZ962, was caught by searchlights and shot down by fighters over Rangoon. There were no survivors.[457]

On 19 December 1944, by now Viscount Templewood, Sir Samuel Hoare addressed his peers in the House of Lords, London. This is an extract from his lengthy speech:

> 'I should explain that I have been abroad for nearly five years… During all this time, or perhaps I should say during the greater part of this time, Spain was practically a semi-occupied country. The German Armies were on the frontier, German influences pervaded many important sections of the national life. The Germans, for instance, had great influence in the police, they had great influence in the press, and though, as I say, Spain was not militarily occupied, for those early years of the war Spain was morally occupied. I had many instances in my own experience of this kind of non-military occupation. I had the Gestapo living in the next house looking over the wall between me and them, watching every one of my movements. I had the Gestapo constantly trying to suborn my domestic staff. I saw the Gestapo taking photographs when a mob was stirred up for the purpose of breaking the

> windows of the British Embassy. I saw what was more sinister, how from time to time the Gestapo would seize some man or woman on Spanish territory and take them over the frontier, where they might be tortured or done to death.'

This, then, was the reality facing all those in lands occupied by the Germans, that they never knew from one day to the next when they could expect the dreaded knock on the door. Even in neutral Spain, as events were to prove, airmen and others could never feel safe from the Nazi police until they had reached British territory.

CHAPTER 4

PAT Line: 1941-1942

'Ami, si tu tombes, un ami sort de l'ombre à ta place.'
Le Chant des Partisans [458]

For the hard-working embassy and consular staff in Spain, there would be no respite from the constant stream of evaders and escapers crossing from France, particularly as the French, in the summer of 1941, seemed not to take the internment of British and Allied personnel too seriously. Even though the prison at St Hippolyte-du-Fort was now well-guarded following the flood of escapes earlier in the year, opportunities for escape still existed.

After Pat O'Leary had departed for Marseille Lieutenant Hewit resumed as senior British officer (SBO) until Squadron Leader E.P.P. Gibbs arrived on 25 July 1941. Another squadron leader followed a fortnight later, Whitney Willard Straight (see following chapter), who became SBO on 18 August after Gibbs had escaped.[459] Straight was in the habit of spending the late summer days going to football matches, not to watch the game necessarily but to sunbathe. Also taking a keen interest in the football, but for a different reason, were 2nd Lieutenant Parkinson and Pilot Officer Bob Milton. They had been trying to escape for several weeks but, as they were still at the fort in September 1941, Pat O'Leary told Parkinson that he 'was to "push off" at the earliest opportunity', if he could manage it, with Bob Milton. Hewit would, as agreed, stay behind.

This was easier said than done for Parkinson and Milton were being closely watched. As no guard could be bribed and everyone knew that they were trying to escape, they tried to give the impression that they were no longer interested in escaping, but even this failed to work and guards kept a close watch on them. So, planning to get away from one of the extra-mural recreation parties, they joined Squadron Leader Straight's party. 'After about a week things were going very well. Each day we chose a site further away from the football and each day made a point of making one or more opportunities of escape and not taking them. On the day of our escape we reached the sun bathing site about fifty yards away from a sentry and as nobody appeared to be watching we walked slowly over the top of the hill and ran.'[460] As arranged, they went to Gaston Nègre's house in Nîmes, where they stayed for a fortnight, and contacted Pat O'Leary.

There they were joined by Sergeants G. Campbell and J.R. Worby, whose Wellington aircraft had come down in eastern France after one of its propellers had fallen off on the night of 10/11 September 1941. O'Leary arranged for their journey to Ax-les-Thermes (Ariège), some twenty-five winding kilometres from the border with Andorra, from where they would begin to make their crossing of the Pyrenees. After four days of waiting due to bad weather the four of them set off with their Andorran guide. 'The going was terrible, about three feet of fresh snow, which was very soft. The guide, too, turned out to be no use and after leading us up 9,000 feet of mountain, announced at the top that he had never been that way before and was lost. Rather than risk our lives in the mountains we turned back and, after a night in a cabin, took the train back to Nîmes.'[461]

A fortnight later, on 17 November and with a few more personnel added to the party, they made their way to Nîmes railway station totally unaware that also heading for the station, with an escort of gendarmes, were several of the sick and wounded men from St Hippolyte on their way to Marseille for a medical board. Parkinson saw them first, and managed to sidle off, as did everyone else except Bob Milton, who was arrested.

Parkinson, Campbell, Worby, Lieutenant Tremargat RNVR,[462] and Private W. Phillips, Gordon Highlanders, took the train to Narbonne and Perpignan, which they reached on the following day. A car took them to Laroque-des-Albères, and with a Spanish guide they began the lower crossing to Spain. 'This route was much easier, and we did not encounter snow. We walked to Figueras and went to the railway yard. The crossing took about twenty-two hours and we walked about sixty kilometres in all.'[463] In the railway yard they saw a goods train departing for Barcelona, and chased after it. Everyone except Tremargat, who was left behind, hid themselves in the wagons. At the first station past Gerona, Worby and Parkinson found themselves shunted into a siding, but were seen as they tried to board another train, and were pulled off by railway employees. Honesty being the best policy, they confessed to the station master that they were RAF airmen. It was the right thing to do, for he immediately had them put back onto the goods train, in a better hiding place, and gave them five pesetas each to pay for the fare.

With directions from the guard they reached the British Consulate in Barcelona on the evening of 19 November. Tremargat appeared next morning. Parkinson was flown back to England on 20/21

December 1941, while the others followed ten days later on the Polish ship *Batory*, reaching Scotland in the New Year.[464]

The contribution made by Louis and Renée Nouveau to clandestine matters in Marseille had, so far, been purely financial. Now, in June 1941, when an RAF sergeant in a debilitated condition was brought to Marseille, they were asked to provide shelter for him in their home. They did so without hesitation, as they were to do for dozens more over the ensuing months.

The RAF sergeant, P.R. Herbert, was second pilot of Wellington R1080 that had left RAF Wyton on the evening of 26 April 1941 bound for the Middle East. Their route took them across France to Marseille, and on down the east coast of Spain to refuel at Gibraltar. They were fifty minutes behind schedule at Marseille when south of Malaga in southern Spain and only some eighty kilometres east of Gibraltar the Wellington, having been airborne for eleven hours twenty minutes of a potential seventeen hours, ran out of fuel with the gauges indicating seventy-eighty gallons remaining. Shortly after 7.40 a.m. on 27 April Sergeant Douglas Walsh put the aircraft down in bad visibility on the Mediterranean Sea as best he could.

All the crew climbed into the aircraft's dinghy, except for Sergeant James Golding in the rear turret, who 'was apparently helpless when he climbed out and drifted away from the aircraft. Sergeant Channer very bravely jumped out of the dinghy to save him, but both were drowned in the strong sea.'[465] The four survivors – Walsh, Philip Herbert, Sergeant R.H.P. Humphris (observer) and Sergeant L. McLean (WOP/AG) – resigned themselves to their fate, drifting along with their Wellington which remained afloat for the best part of twenty-four hours. The dinghy was still going strong on 6 May when they 'were rescued by a French ship the *Menhir-Braz* (*Cargo Algerienne*), Captain Dubois, about 230 miles east of Gibraltar. The French on the boat treated us very well indeed.'[466]

The four airmen, having had virtually no food and only two pints of water during their nine-day ordeal, were in poor shape when they disembarked at Marseille on 10 May.[467] Despite their sorry state, they were hauled before members of the German Armistice Commission who were in Marseille keeping an eye on things. When the Germans, who 'hardly spoke English', had finished asking a number of questions that 'were quite absurd' the airmen were taken to the prison section of the Michel Lévy Military Hospital.

Somewhat recovered from their ordeal they were transferred to St Hippolyte-du-Fort on 9 June. Barely had they arrived when they 'saw the camp leader, Lt. Parkinson, and he arranged that we should return to the hospital the following day (10 Jun), for our Medical Board.' They were in a party of some thirty hopefuls from the prison, which included Sergeants N.J. Ingram and S.J. Houghton (one of Bob Milton's crew).

Ingram, also of RAF Coastal Command, had been shot down in a Blenheim on 13 May 1941 after information had been received that twenty to twenty-five enemy ships had been sighted off St Nazaire (France). Eight Blenheims of 82 Squadron were despatched from RAF Portreath, Cornwall, shortly after 8 a.m. on 13 May 1941 to deal with them. It was a low-level strike, and Blenheim V5997 – Sergeant F. H. Miller (pilot), Ingram (observer) and Sergeant W.E. Whiteman (air gunner) – was hit by fierce anti-aircraft fire in the port engine and controls, forcing Miller to make a landing a few kilometres inland of St Nazaire.[468]

Though badly shaken, the crew set fire to their aircraft before heading away from the scene. On the following morning, after a change of clothing and after Frenchmen had rowed them across the River Loire, they walked south. Though stopped on a couple of occasions by gendarmes, who advised them to pretend to be Algerians, they crossed into Unoccupied France on 26 May, but were arrested by Vichy soldiers and escorted to the prison at St Hippolyte.

Now, on 10 June, the party of some thirty hopeful repatriates was taken to the Michel Lévy Military Hospital in Marseille, where all were pronounced fit and all refused repatriation. Before making the long journey back to St Hippolyte an escort of some ten gendarmes took the thirty "fit" men to Fort St Marthe for lunch. When the meal was over Herbert, Houghton and Ingram casually walked out of the unguarded dining hut and strolled out of the gates without being challenged. Boarding a conveniently waiting tram, they made for the Seamen's Mission. After the Reverend Caskie had put them in touch with the Garrow organisation, they stayed for two nights at 'a farm just outside Marseille'.

Three days later, Ingram and Houghton were taken via Perpignan to Banyuls, and thence over the Pyrenees and into Spain. Catching a train at Vilajuiga, they reached the consulate at Paseo de Gracia 35, Barcelona, on 16 June. Three days later they were in Madrid and on their way home.

Philip Herbert, however, was still too weak to make the arduous journey to Spain, and was taken to the Nouveaus' apartment at 28A, Quai Rive Neuve, Marseille, where, the first of many to be hidden there, he slowly regained his strength. On 26 June, deemed fit enough to be moved to Perpignan, Pat O'Leary escorted him to Marseille station, where he was joined by Pilot Officer Marian Rytka PAF. Rytka's squadron, with two others, had been escorting eighteen Blenheim light bombers to Béthune in northern France on 21 May 1941 when German Me109 fighters put in an appearance. Rytka got one in their first attack, but was shot down himself a little further on. He eventually got to Lille (28 May), where he was sheltered by a French family for three weeks, before being put in touch with the Cole/Garrow network (see this chapter below).

Also joining him and Herbert at Nîmes were Sergeant Whiteman (of Ingram's crew) and Sapper D. Kemp, Royal Engineers' Postal Section. Under the watchful eyes of the guards, they had also strolled out of the main gate of the prison at St Hippolyte, on 22 June 1941, and had walked to Nîmes. As arranged, they met Pat O'Leary's party and, taken by car to Perpignan, were hidden at Michel Parayre's garage[469] until another guide took them by car to Banyuls-sur-Mer.

Crossing the Pyrenees on foot they reached Figueras, Spain, about twenty-four hours later and waited until dark before catching a train to Gerona, where they hoped to meet Mr J. Gardiner Whitfield from the consulate, but he was in Barcelona. On 28 June, therefore, they caught the train to Barcelona, but on the way were collared by a plain-clothes detective of the Guardia Civil. At Barcelona Herbert, Kemp and Whiteman got off first, followed by the Spanish policeman, who had expected Rytka to follow him off the train. Instead, Rytka slipped out of another door and ran off across the rail tracks. Herbert was found with £15.10.0 (£15.50) about his person and, because of that, was kept in Barcelona prison until 25 September, when he was moved to Miranda de Ebro.

Also using the Perpignan garage route at the end of June 1941 were Sergeant R.E. Griffiths (another of Bob Milton's crew); Sergeant F.H. Miller (Whiteman's pilot); Corporal W.F. Gardner, 2nd Wiltshires; Privates J. McLaren and T. Williamson, both 2nd Seaforth Highlanders; and Signalman L.R. MacDonald, Royal Corps of Signals. The first three, having escaped together from the prison at St Hippolyte on 29 June, met McLaren and Williamson, who had escaped separately, in Nîmes. MacDonald joined the group in Perpignan.

The six were then driven to the Spanish border, but became separated during the night crossing in bad weather. Griffiths, Miller and MacDonald made it safely to the British Embassy in Madrid. Gardner, McLaren and Williamson, however, having jumped a goods train, were arrested in Barcelona on 11 July, despite being in possession of emergency identification cards from the British Consulate. They joined Herbert at Miranda de Ebro.

Herbert was eventually released from Miranda on 28 October 1941, the others three days later, but it was not until 30 December that they sailed for home from Gibraltar. Rytka, Whiteman, Griffiths and Miller, on the other hand, had been back since 14 August 1941, and Kemp, with two other survivors of Herbert's crew, Humphris and McLean, on 6 October.

Sergeants Humphris and McLean had escaped from St Hippolyte on 18 July 1941: 'We hid in the kitchen until 2300 hrs and then climbed a 9 ft barbed wire fence, 6 ft of barbed wire entanglements, another 9 ft barbed wire fence and a 10 ft wall with 3 ft barbed wire fence on top.' Guides took them across the Pyrenees along with three 'British soldiers, a Russian and a Czech (both French officers)… We were all caught by civil guards south of Figueras when walking along the railway tracks by day.'[470] The guide escaped, but the rest were imprisoned at Figueras, Barcelona, Saragossa and finally, for forty-seven days, at Miranda de Ebro, where the British military attaché eventually caught up with them. They sailed from Gibraltar on 1 October 1941 aboard the battleship HMS *Prince of Wales*, and were put ashore at Scapa Flow on 6 October.

As for their pilot, Sergeant D.S. Walsh, he had to wait a year for his chance to get home. It came on 5 September 1942 when he took part in a mass breakout from Fort de la Revère, near Monte Carlo, (see following chapter), and was evacuated on 12 October from a beach near Perpignan.

It was not difficult to dislike Sergeant Harold Cole ("Paul"), as "Thérèse Martin" discovered through her many dealings with him in Lille. She found herself unable to trust him, as he was always borrowing money, or begging petrol, and never repaying it, and he talked ill of people behind their backs. She knew, too, that he had women everywhere, and was always going on a spree with them ('il avait des femmes partout et faisait la noce…').[471] He said bad things about Roland Lepers, though she knew that it was he, Roland, who did all the hard work and not Cole. So disenchanted with him was she that, in the end, she would have nothing to do with him.

To finance his wasteful lifestyle Cole was still delivering "parcels" (only a dozen were RAF airmen) to Marseille from the north of France in the early summer of 1941, for which he was being handsomely paid. It was at the Rodocanachis' flat one late July evening that O'Leary met him for the first time, and took an instant dislike to him. Ian Garrow, on the other hand, impressed by Cole's earlier success, trusted him, though he did not care for Cole's interest in the ladies, one of whom was Suzanne Warenghem. She was to fall under Cole's spell after she had met him at Le Petit Poucet ("Tom Thumb"), a 'modest undistinguished little bar' under the patronage of Monsieur Gaston Dijon on the Boulevard Dugommier, not far from Marseille's Gare St Charles.[472]

Suzanne had been keen to get to England ever since meeting a number of wounded British soldiers in late 1940. At the Val-de-Grâce hospital, near the Boulevard St Michel, Paris, she confided to Captain Geoffrey Darke RAMC, one of the captured British doctors working at the hospital, that she wanted to get to England, and was surprised to learn that he and three others – two doctors and a patient – were already planning to escape.[473] Before the four men left (they got back to England in August 1941) Captain Darke gave Suzanne an address in Marseille where, Darke said, she would find someone trustworthy to help her get across the Pyrenees. Accordingly, fired by the British officers' escape, she determined to try her luck and, for good measure, to take some of the wounded British soldiers with her.

On the warm night of 15 June 1941, with her French accomplice, Roger Pelletier, she helped Signalman Tommy Edgar RCS and Private Jimmy Tobin RAMC to escape. After ten days at the *Chantier de la Jeunesse*[474] camp at Labruguière, a few kilometres south of Castres in the Unoccupied Zone, Suzanne and the two soldiers were obliged to leave when it was learnt that 'the police were rounding up communists and aliens'[475] in the wake of the Germans' offensive against Soviet Russia, which had begun on 22 June. Suzanne and Roger at once took Edgar and Tobin to the address in Marseille that Darke had given her but, finding that it was a large apartment block, had no idea which bell to ring.[476] Giving up, she was advised to try the Seamen's Mission, but Donald Caskie, now that the police were on to him, could do no more than pass them on to Bruce Dowding, who took Suzanne and the two soldiers to a house on the Rue Paradis 'which bore an inconspicuous sign "Studios Meublés"'.[477]

After Edgar and Tobin had quickly been sent on their way to Spain, which they reached on 10 July, Suzanne Warenghem asked to follow. Her value as a *convoyeur*, though, had already been recognised, and she was persuaded to stay in France. A few weeks later, now firmly a member of the escape line, she was having a drink at Le Petit Poucet when Bruce Dowding appeared with a stranger whom he introduced as Harold Cole, usually known as "Paul". It was explained to her that Cole was the line's chief man up in the north.

One of the key links in the long chain from Lille to Marseille was the Fillerin family – Norbert; his wife Marguerite; and their three teenage children, Geneviève, Monique and Gabriel – who lived in the village of Renty, on the Aa River, a dozen kilometres south of Lumbres (Pas-de-Calais). Norbert Fillerin was 'a stalwart and active member of the line… Beekeeper, philosopher, reader of Plato, the son of a wholesale butcher, Norbert always wore workman's overalls, had perfect manners and a calm smile that radiated confidence.'[478] The family were to be kept busy over the next few months, when several RAF fighter pilots were shot down on operations over the Pas-de-Calais.

Two of those to reach Renty were poorly prepared for evasion:

> 'No money was issued to me when I set out from Gravesend and Biggin Hill. I understood that there was none left in the squadron. I have never had any compass, map or other aids to escape nor ever heard of their existence.' *Sergeant W.G. Lockhart.*

> 'No money was issued to me for my flight from Tangmere. I have had it on previous flights, but it is not always issued, apparently due to shortage.' *Flying Officer D.N. Forde.*

In spite of such deficiencies neither was caught by the Germans. Having taken off from RAF Biggin Hill early on the afternoon of 7 July 1941, Lockhart was shot down barely an hour later when a shell from an enemy fighter hit the port magazine of his Spitfire and blew off two-thirds of the wing. Jumping out at around 16,000 feet he knocked himself out on a tree at Ergny (Pas-de-Calais), while the remains of his aircraft came down at Avesnes, five kilometres away to the south. Regaining his senses, with injuries to an arm and a leg, he approached a farmer for help, but was refused. A boy whom he met shortly afterwards told him that the farmer had telephoned the Germans 'in order to collect the award of 80,000 francs… Other people, however, got me away to Renty where I stayed three weeks while my arm and leg healed.'[479]

From Renty, where he had been staying with the Fillerin family, Lockhart was taken to Lille, and met Flying Officer Forde, who had left Tangmere in his Spitfire on a sweep of northern France on the evening of 23 July 1941. An hour or so after take-off, shot down by an Me109, Forde landed by parachute close to a farmhouse near Ruisseauville (Pas-de-Calais). The Germans were out looking for him, but the wife of a farmer, who was a prisoner of war of the Germans, and her farmhands quickly hid him in the house, 'until a German car came along and then I got out of the back door and hid in hay for the night.'[480] When the Germans returned in the morning, Forde hid in a field, where he remained undiscovered for the rest of the day. That evening 'a certain person' came to the farmhouse and it was arranged that Forde would rendezvous with him in the morning 'and get on the back of his motorcycle as he came along.' Wearing civilian clothes that he had been given at the farmhouse, all went well at the rendezvous and he was taken to Blangy-sur-Ternoise, some eight kilometres down the road. On 29 July he was moved to Willems (Nord), a village a few kilometres east of Lille and a stone's throw from the Belgium border, and on 7 August into Lille itself, where he met Sergeant Lockhart.

The two airmen were then taken by a guide to the Abbé Carpentier's house at Abbeville, 'passed the sentries on the bridge with false papers and took the train to Paris, thence to Chalon [-sur-Saône], crossing the line of demarcation there on 9 August. We crossed by train with the connivance of the driver and guard who were bribed.'[481] Leaving the train, they had to cross a bridge guarded by Germans, which Forde and the guide were able to do without being stopped. Lockhart and a Frenchman with whom he happened to be walking were, however, arrested. A fluent French speaker Lockhart pretended to be a Frenchman, and was interrogated for four hours through a French interpreter. Eventually he was searched and the Germans 'found an English letter in my pocket which I had to explain away'. Having somehow got away with this, he was sent to the railway station under escort and ordered to return to Paris: 'I waited until dark and then got into a goods train which took me over the line of demarcation.'[482]

Forde, meanwhile, went on with the guide via Mâcon to Marseille, which they reached on 10 August. Lockhart was not far behind, and also got to Marseille without further interruption. On 14 August the two of them left for Perpignan, where another evader – Sergeant J. Mensik, Czech Air Force – joined the party. Sergeant Mensik had also been lost over northern France, early on the morning of 8 July 1941, baling out of his Hurricane at around 6 a.m. at Lisbourg (Pas-de-Calais), twenty kilometres south-east of Ergny and ten or so north of Blangy. Given civilian clothes at a farm he set off on foot for Paris. It took him a fortnight to get there, and eight days recovering, when he found 'a guide who took me to Bordeaux. We crossed the line of demarcation near Verdele, south of La Réole.'[483] Parting company from his guide on 2 August, Mensik made his own way to Marseille, where he stayed a further fortnight, before another guide took him to Perpignan.

Mensik, Forde and Lockhart crossed the Pyrenees with the Spanish guide whom they had met at Perpignan, but on 23 August were stopped by Spanish police and arrested. The guide managed to get away to Barcelona, but the three airmen were imprisoned at Cantallóps (the nearest village to the French border at le Perthus), then at Figueras, Barcelona, Saragossa and finally, on 7 September, Miranda de Ebro. The British military attaché was informed of their presence and eventually secured their release. Having reached Gibraltar on 10 October, first to go home two days later was the senior man, Forde, who got a seat aboard a Catalina, 'arriving at Mount Batten the same day'. Sergeants Lockhart and Mensik had to wait until 21 October, when they were also flown back to Mount Batten.

Another guest of the Fillerins that summer was yet another Spitfire pilot, Flight Lieutenant Denis Crowley-Milling DFC,[484] shot down on 21 August. On 31 August "Paul" Cole and his organisation prepared a number of evaders for another convoy south. Crowley-Milling was moved from the Fillerins, and both he and a Czechoslovakian fighter pilot, Sergeant Rudolf Ptácek, shot down on 19 August, were collected by Cole on 1 September.

Sergeant Ptácek was escorting bombers on a raid to Hazebrouck (Circus 82) on the evening of 19 August when, at around 12,000 feet, they were ambushed on the way back by four Me109s that dived out of the sun. Leaving formation Ptácek got behind one of them, and gave him four bursts. Down to some 2,000 feet he saw smoke coming from its engine, but then was himself attacked from behind by Oberleutnant Johannes Schmid, of Adolf Galland's celebrated JG 26 (the "Abbeville boys"). When a cannon shell hit his engine, which caught fire and stopped, Ptácek landed his Spitfire at 130 mph in a cornfield near Rubrouck, a dozen kilometres north-east of St Omer. He was Schmid's twenty-fourth victory.[485]

Destroying the IFF he made a corn fire under the engine before running off. From a safe vantage point he saw the fire go out but before he could go back and finish burning his Spitfire two German soldiers were already at the scene. After help from several locals he was taken to St Omer, 'where I met the nurse who had helped W/C Bader in his unsuccessful attempt.'[486]

A fluent French speaker,[487] Ptácek had no difficulty buying a railway ticket to Lille. There he went to an address that had been given to him and fellow squadron members back in England by Sergeant J.W.B. Phillips on a lecture tour following his own escape and evasion (see Chapter 1). However, Squadron Leader E.P.P. Gibbs said in his MI9 report: 'I should like to warn all escapers of the dangers of revealing the names or whereabouts of people who have helped them. Sgt. Phillips, RAF, who gave a lecture at Tangmere in June 1941 told his audience that whoever baled out in France should apply for help to No. 1 Rue Tourraine, Lille.' Gibbs added to his comment: 'I was told in France that this information got across to the Germans, who promptly rounded up the inhabitants at this address and took them away.'[488]

At the address – actually 1, rue de Turenne, la Madeleine, Lille, the hairdressing salon run by Jeannine Voglimacci – on 20 August Rudolf Ptácek was told to go away and come back later. This he did, and was taken to the flat above the salon: 'Two French officers in civilian clothes then arrived and questioned me for three-quarters of an hour, at the end of which I succeeded, with some difficulty, in satisfying them that I was not a German.'[489] Jeannine also told him that next time she would not admit anyone who did not give the correct password – "De la part de Jacques". Paul Cole added that the place was simply a rendezvous, and that no one was to be sent there.

On the train to Béthune, with Cole and young Roland Lepers as their guides, they joined three soldiers who had been hiding with French families for over a year – Corporal F. Wilkinson RE; Private P.S. Janes, 2/6th East Surreys; and Private A.C. Fraser, 4th Cameron Highlanders – and Sergeant A. Pietrasiak PAF, (shot down on the same day as Ptácek), and Polish Cadet Henryk Stachura, who had escaped from Germany. The group detrained at Abbeville and made its way to the house of the Abbé Pierre Carpentier at 13, Place du Cimitière St Gilles, where papers were hurriedly provided for the rest of their journey.[490]

Armed with their forged documents they travelled to Paris (1 September) and on to Tours (2 September). Making for the Unoccupied Zone, having changed onto a local train, they 'went about five stations farther on. We left the station in parties of two or three to walk to the river about a mile away. En route we were challenged by a gendarme, who told us we were lucky that there were no Germans about that day. A farmer met us here and took us across the bridge and then accompanied us across fields for about ten kilometres and put us on the road to Loches. From there we took a train to Châteauroux, where we arrived about 0900 hours on 4 September,'[491] and later that day they arrived at Marseille. Once through the ticket barrier they 'went down a long flight of stone stairs and along to a café where we had chocolate and long hard bread rolls. There was not enough sugar in the chocolate but it went down very well after our journey. Then we went to a barber and had ourselves made a little more respectable.'[492]

Janes, Fraser, Stachura and Ptácek were taken to the Nouveaus' apartment, while Crowley-Milling, Wilkinson and Pietrasiak went to stay with the Rodocanachis. Pietrasiak, who had hurt a leg after baling out and was still suffering from the effects of the long walk a couple of days earlier, stayed behind with Dr Rodocanachi when the others caught an early train for Perpignan on the following morning. There, the six men were taken to a garage, where 'we were received by a man who spoke not only every language that we did, viz six, but also four more. He also told us he spoke eleven more but not so well.'[493] This man, possibly Michel Parayre alias "Parker" (see Chapter 2), exchanged their French money for Spanish pesetas and, before driving them to the village of Banyuls-dels-Aspres at the foot of the Pyrenees, gave them the startling advice that on reaching Spain they should give themselves up to the Spanish police.

At Banyuls-dels-Aspres (not to be confused with the coastal town of Banyuls-sur-Mer several kilometres to the east) they waited for a guide to take them over the Pyrenees, spending the night in a café of doubtful propriety: 'Luckily the beds were good and we got some coffee in the morning which was very bad indeed.'[494] Fortified with tomatoes and wine, they set off at around 7 o'clock on the evening of 6 September. The going was hard, and within half an hour Crowley-Milling and Fraser were fighting for breath. After some four hours scrabbling over the steep and rocky terrain Janes, too, suddenly collapsed with severe stomach cramps. This happened four times altogether, giving everyone a welcome rest. Just before 1 a.m. on 7 September, in pouring rain, they crossed into Spain. Three hours later their guide left them.

Continuing their painful downhill journey they came to an old building, and managed to get a fire going to dry their sodden clothes. A Spaniard warned them that the Guardia Civil were on their way and that they should leave immediately. Trusting in the advice of the garage man from Perpignan, however, they stayed put, and realised that it was a mistake to have done so when, having been arrested, they were locked up for the night in a ghastly, bug-ridden hole, in which there were only four iron bedsteads and neither mattress nor blanket. On the morrow (8 September) they were bussed under guard to Figueras, and formally charged with entering the country without proper papers.

In the military prison they were shown to a large, bare room where, as they made the best of their lot, they were joined by two men 'who turned out to be English. Both of them had had their heads shaved and looked pretty awful, which was not surprising when we heard their story. They had spent a year in the French prison of St Hippolyte and after crossing the mountains, which took them five days, they had been whammed into the jug at Gerona.'[495] Further spells of incarceration followed, at Barcelona, Saragossa and Miranda de Ebro, where the ten of them – 'we had two French gypsies with us now, heaven only knows why'[496] – were put in a cell marked "*Tránsitos*".

On 13 September 1941, the Barcelona vice-consul, Mr J.G. Whitfield, sent a note to the British Embassy at Madrid. Its contents were sufficient for the military attaché, Brigadier Torr, to lodge a strong complaint with Captain General Kindelan on his visit to Barcelona: 'He made it clear to General Kindelan that as a soldier he felt most indignant at the unjustifiable and discourteous act of marching eight British prisoners of war, including two officers, publicly through the streets of Barcelona like common criminals with their heads shaved and in handcuffs. General Kindelan agreed heartily with the sentiments expressed by Brigadier Torr and stated that he would take the matter up personally at once with the police authorities and see that this unfortunate incident was never repeated.'[497]

Mr Whitfield's note gives more details of the indignity:

> '1. A party of eight British soldiers left Barcelona for Miranda via Zaragoza at 8.45 this morning. They included one flight-lieutenant, two sergeant pilots, two royal engineers and three infantrymen.
>
> '2. They were all handcuffed in pairs, and would remain handcuffed until arriving at Zaragoza at 7 p.m. tonight. As their wrists were already chafed following their journey from Figueras to Barcelona two days ago, it is certain that they will be in a very bad state by this evening. This order to handcuff prisoners of war has been in force for the last three months, and a sergeant of the civil guard told me, when the practice first began, that the order came from Madrid and was the result of several Belgians escaping at the station and while en route in the train. All the men's heads had been shaved in the Modelo.
>
> '3. I visited Flight-Lieutenant Crowley-Milling in the Modelo yesterday evening and saw the whole party on the station this morning. They all come direct from the north of France: one of the pilots was shot down as recently as 21st August and another on 19th August...'[498]

At Miranda Crowley-Milling contracted typhoid fever and was hospitalised for a month, but after a period of convalescence in Madrid he was repatriated by air from Gibraltar on 1 December 1941. As for the others, which now included Sergeant Philip Herbert, Corporal W.F. Gardner, Private T. Williamson, and two deserters (apparently from the King's Regiment at Gibraltar), they learnt towards the middle of October that they were soon to be released, and on 28 October this did indeed happen, though neither Henryk Stachura nor the two deserters were present to board the ambulance that conveyed the rest of the group to Madrid.

A week or so after the Crowley-Milling party had left the Rodocanachis' apartment, Sergeant Adolf Pietrasiak was moved to the port of le Grau-du-Roi (Gard), where he was joined by several Greek soldiers: 'We all went out in a fishing boat to await a ship that was to pick us up. As the ship did not arrive, the Greeks went back to Marseilles and I was taken on to Nîmes.' After a wait of some ten days, staying near the Jardin de la Fontaine, he was taken via Perpignan to the Villa Anita at Canet-Plage, where he was joined by a Polish army doctor called Gasior, Driver J. Strachan RASC, and by two airmen evaders – Flight Lieutenant A.L. Winskill and Sergeant L.M. McKee.

Flight Lieutenant Winskill had been shot down on 14 August 1941 by two Me109s, one of which he shot down. Slightly stunned on landing, he recovered to find Monsieur Caron, a French farmer, asking him if he wanted help. Replying in the affirmative, he was on his way to M. Caron's farmhouse across the field in which he had landed when a car appeared 'and two German soldiers got out and went to the aircraft. I hid in the corn and remained there till night...'[499] Winskill had had the good fortune to land near Calais, and to be picked up by Paul Cole's escape line. On 5 September he met up with Sergeant L.M. McKee, another fighter pilot, who had also been shot down on 14 August.

On 22 September they were taken to Lillers by Cole, Roland Lepers and Madeleine Damerment, where they were joined by Strachan, Gunner H. Fryer RA, and Lance-Bombardier J. Heather RA. At Abbeville the Abbé Carpentier provided them with forged papers to enable them to travel to Marseille, which they reached on 25 September. At Le Petit Poucet, Cole told them that, as they were now 'with a British escape organisation',[500] they would not be needing any money and so best to hand over all that they had got. Winskill was surprised by this request, but nevertheless did as he was asked.

A short while later, on their way to Spain (minus Fryer and Heather, who later returned to Britain), one of the group with whom they were now travelling – supposedly a Polish pilot – confessed that he was in fact a French student who had been coached, for a fee, by Cole. At this point Winskill realised that Cole was a trickster, and reported him to the staff at the British Consulate in Barcelona, only to be told that they knew all about him and that he, Winskill, was not to worry. Anyway, they added, the French student was talking rubbish (a conclusion no doubt drawn from Ian Garrow's appreciation of Cole's good work).

Towards the end of the first week of October Bruce Dowding took the small group to Perpignan, where they were joined by a Belgian pilot,[501] and handed them over to a Spanish guide, Joseph, for the next leg of the journey by train to Ax-les-Thermes. From Ax an Andorran guide was to take them across the Pyrenees, but it was not the most efficient of crossings, as Pietrasiak reported: 'We lost our way and wandered about for three days. Some of the party dropped out during this journey but later rejoined us in Andorra. Two days later we crossed into Spain. We walked for about forty kilometres after crossing the border and spent the night at a farmhouse.'[502] They continued next day, 9 October, to the town of Berga, and contacted the consulate at Barcelona, 100 kilometres or so to the south. After a night at an inn the consular car arrived and took Winskill, Pietrasiak and Gasior to Barcelona (10 October). The others of their party, including McKee and Strachan, were collected two days later, following which the three airmen and Strachan were driven to the British Embassy in Madrid, and caught up with the Crowley-Milling group.

After a few days at the embassy the group, now fifteen strong, was taken by bus to Cordoba. In it were five airmen (Winskill; Herbert; Pietrasiak; McKee; Ptácek), seven soldiers (Gardner; Williamson; Janes; Fraser; Wilkinson; McLaren; Strachan), two Belgians and Henryk Stachura, the Polish cadet (who had also caught up). From Cordoba the bus ran its drunken course (alcoholic drinks were plentiful and easily obtained along the way) to Seville, the passengers staying for one night at the Ingleterra hotel. Having somehow reached Gibraltar safely on 4 November, the bus driver, trying to negotiate an anti-tank obstacle, smashed his bus into a sentrybox, and broke the sentry's leg.

Winskill was the first to go back to the UK, on 22 November, followed by McKee, Herbert, Ptácek and Pietrasiak throughout December, the last two returning on the Polish M/S *Batory*, together with most of the soldiers.

'By June 1941, Cole was delivering anywhere from five to ten and sometimes more British servicemen at intervals of ten days to two weeks.'[503] And though he had successfully moved twelve men south in two convoys to Marseille in September 1941, he still remained an enigma to those working for the escape organisation. Flight Lieutenant F.W. Higginson DFM, had found him 'both courageous and charming', largely because of the incident that occurred on a hot July day near Tours, when Cole was escorting him to Marseille. German soldiers, demanding to see their papers, were unconvinced that Higginson's declared him to be a discharged French soldier suffering from shell shock. Ordering him to empty the briefcase that he was carrying, it was opened to reveal its contents covered by a brown, sticky substance. With great presence of mind Cole said that his simple-minded friend had defecated into the case. The Germans were satisfied with this explanation, unaware that a bar of chocolate had melted in the hot sun!

Flight Lieutenant Winskill, as seen, regarded Cole as a racketeer and a con man, but in complete contrast to Cole was one of his *convoyeurs*, Private James Smith, 5th Gordon Highlanders. Captured in June 1940, Smith had escaped and gone to ground in northern France. Working on various farms until the Germans got to hear about him, he and five others crossed into the Unoccupied Zone in January 1941, but were arrested by Vichy police. They were to be taken from Marseille to the prison at St Hippolyte-du-Fort but, with an eight-hour wait through the night for the train, they persuaded the guards to remove their handcuffs so that they could play cards. As hoped, the guards fell asleep. Seizing their chance, James Smith and Private G. Evendon jumped onto a passing passenger train, and headed back to the Lille area where, in early May 1941, Smith met Cole.

The two of them, together with two British soldiers, Mrs Gardner (a Frenchwoman married to an Englishman), and her three daughters, travelled to Marseille using documents supplied by the Abbé Carpentier at Abbeville. Cole already knew the persuasive Ian Garrow, as James Smith was to discover: '… it was agreed that I should work for him in helping to get Allied personnel to the UK and also to collect any military information I could.'[504] Garrow gave Smith money for his fare back to Lille, on about 12 May, and by the end of the month 'by the same method I escorted one Polish airman and a British soldier plus some plans of airfields and military objects to a lady known to me as "Lady Elizabeth" working for Capt Garrow.'[505] Smith then made a second journey to Marseille, towards the end of June, 'with one airman and two British soldiers and certain information', which he handed over to Cole, who was already in Marseille. It is possible that this airman was Pilot Officer Marian Rytka, shot down on 21 May, who left for Marseille from Lille on 19 June. Helped by Captain Garrow, without actually meeting him, Rytka stayed in a hotel until the time came for him to head for Spain a week later.

On 26 July 1941 James Smith was in Béthune, in the north of France, with three RASC soldiers – Private J.A. Mowat, Driver H.C.D. Simmons and Driver F. Rowe – and three RAF fighter pilots – Pilot Officer H.P. Duval, Sergeant D.B. Crabtree and Sergeant J.G.L. Robillard RCAF. The three soldiers, captured in the last few days of May 1940, had escaped easily enough. Rowe and Simmons climbed out of a window of the farm in which they were being held prisoner, while Mowat seized the chance to jump into a canal in the dark of the night. All three met up on 25 May. Hidden in a hut at Nortkerque (Pas-de-Calais), a dozen kilometres south-east of Calais, until 21 March 1941, they moved to a farm near Acquin for a week, before moving to Burbure (Pas-de-Calais). On 24 July they were taken to Béthune, and met the three pilots, who had been shot down within six days of each other over northern France.

Duval, a French-Canadian in the RAF, was on an early morning sweep from RAF Kenley on 8 July when he and his squadron were attacked by German fighters: 'I hit one which I am pretty sure went down. Another then got me as I was turning, my radiator and oil cooler were pierced, the engine stopped and I had a hole in the petrol tank. The control was jammed and I realised I would have to jump.'[506] It was time to part company with his Hurricane, and at around 6.45 a.m. he landed near the village of Tincques (Pas-de-Calais), north-west of Arras. German soldiers from Aubigny were soon on the spot, but by then Duval had been hidden by the villagers in the courtyard of an empty house. When the French told the Germans that they had not seen the airman and that the house was deserted they went away. Duval was driven to Abbeville on 9 July, taken by train to Lille on the following day, and on to Roubaix on the day after that. After a fortnight or so he went back to Lille for one night, heading off for the south of France on the following day.

Sergeant Crabtree was in his Spitfire on 3 July escorting a dozen Blenheim bombers on a Circus to Hazebrouck (north-west of Lille) when German Me109 fighters 'came hurtling in and I got separated from our main body.' Seeing a lone Spitfire about to be shot down by a pack of Me109s, he went to its assistance, shooting down one of the enemy before his Spitfire was hit in the engine. He tried to get back to the English Channel but the enemy continued to attack him, and set his aircraft on fire: 'I came down in a cornfield and hid in a hedge until dusk. I burned my parachute but kept the dinghy, intending to get to the coast.' Leaving the safety of the hedge he 'then walked smack into a German patrol of five soldiers. It was then dark. I had hurt my ankle on landing, and pretended that it was very bad and that I could hardly walk.'[507] The soldiers treated him well, and took him to a farm. Taking his dinghy, they shut him in a barn for the night and left him unguarded believing, as Crabtree had hoped, that he was incapable of walking anywhere. Squeezing through a hole in the wall of the barn Crabtree made his escape.

At a farm near Colembert (fifteen or sixteen kilometres east of Boulogne), where he stayed from 4 to 7 July, he was given civilian clothes and a bicycle and told to go to a house in Hardinghen (Pas-de-Calais), a few kilometres to the north. He stayed there for a further three days, and four more at another farm, when he was taken by bicycle to Lozinghem (Pas-de-Calais), a few kilometres west of Béthune. Despite all the attention, Crabtree was not happy: 'The man at whose house I stayed was making arrangements to help me but I did not like him and suspected him, and another Frenchman put me in touch with someone else.'[508]

On 19 July he was taken to Lillers, and met Sergeant Robillard, who had been shot down on 2 July while on a late-morning sweep in his Spitfire from RAF Tangmere: 'We encountered Messerschmitts and I was boxed in by seven of them at 6,000 feet. I destroyed three, two I saw fall and French people subsequently told me that the third had fallen. I was actually trying to collide with it when a shell shot off my port wing. The aeroplane exploded and threw me out.'[509] A few minutes after noon he parachuted onto French soil near Auchel, a few kilometres south of Lillers, and hid in a railway tunnel. He later met some Frenchmen, and was given civilian clothing at a farmhouse before being taken to Lillers. By coincidence, Simmons and Mowat had witnessed the action in which he had been shot down. They saw the wing of his Spitfire being shot off and the aircraft exploding, throwing him out. They also confirmed that he had shot down two of his assailants and that the third had indeed crashed, killing its pilot.

The six evaders took the train to Abbeville to collect their papers from the Abbé Carpentier, and then to Paris, where Robillard demonstrated his contempt for the enemy by urinating on three of the master race as they passed beneath the balcony of his safe house. It goes without saying that Robillard was stark naked at the time. The Germans upon whom the golden rain had fallen thought that he was a fellow soldier on leave having a good time.[510] Continuing to Tours and then, a dozen kilometres east, to the village of St Martin-le-Beau (Indre-et-Loire), on the north bank of the River Cher, they prepared to cross the Demarcation Line into Unoccupied France. Under cover of darkness they 'passed the German sentries who did not see us. We had intended to get to Loches that night but it was raining so we stayed hidden in a farm house during the next day, and the following night walked to Loches.'[511]

Arriving by train at Marseille on 28 July, James Smith handed over his party to Mario Prassinos. Three days later they were on their way to Perpignan and the Pyrenees, and crossed into Spain on 1

August. Dodging the Spanish police they reached Barcelona by train on 3 August, and reported to the British Consulate. Leaving Mowat behind, the other five continued to Madrid, and got to Gibraltar on 13 August. The three fighter pilots were flown back to Calshot on 26 August, but the army was in no hurry to get its men back. Simmons, Rowe, and Mowat, who had caught up his two companions by this time, sailed from Gibraltar on 1 October, making a quick passage of only five days to Gourock (Scotland).

In late August 1941 James Smith made his sixth, and last, journey south. Collecting three soldiers (Gunners F. Tuck and W. Mayes, and Signalman W. Collins) from Norbert Fillerin at Renty, a fourth "parcel", a Norwegian pilot, was added to the group at Béthune. Unfortunately, all were arrested in a routine "control" on the Paris-Bordeaux express at Orléans, when the Norwegian was exposed as a German claiming to be a deserter. Not surprisingly, he talked. Together with five others who were to be betrayed by Cole (see this chapter below) Smith was sent to a series of prisons, including Fresnes (France), St Gilles (Brussels) and Bochum (Germany). Despite never being recognised as a prisoner of war, he survived the best part of ten months at Papenburg concentration camp before being liberated by American forces at the Zuchthaus, Untermassfeld on 3 April 1945.[512]

While Smith went backwards and forwards bringing escapers and evaders to the south, Cole spent much of the time enjoying life in Marseille. By the time that Pat O'Leary first encountered Cole towards the end of July 1941, therefore, there was already much talk in Marseille of the profligate behaviour of this tall, thin Englishman. O'Leary took an instant dislike to him because 'I heard the way this man spoke to Ian [Garrow]; and the way he presented his case. To me, from the first moment I set eyes on him at the Rodocanachis', he was a nobody. No good at all. And most certainly not the sort of person for us to be in harness with.'[513]

Despite Garrow's optimism O'Leary was not satisfied that Cole was the genuine article, and decided that he should go to Lille to check out Cole's claims. In early October 1941, he and Maurice Dufour, a former employee at St Hippolyte but now a trusted agent of the escape line, went to see François Despretz[514] and his wife at their home on the rue de la Gare, Lille. They, too, were distrustful of Cole, and when O'Leary was told that none of the funds entrusted by Garrow to Cole had ever reached Despretz as intended, he had no hesitation in asking Despretz to return with him to Marseille and to repeat this alarming news to Ian Garrow.

This meeting was never to take place for three days later, now back in Marseille, O'Leary and Despretz were shocked to hear from Fanny Rodocanachi that Garrow had been arrested on the previous day, 12 October. Following the disclosure that a French detective had had access to British consular files, Garrow had taken the precaution of calling upon Capitaine Dutour (see Chapter 2), a *Juge d'Instruction* at Fort St Nicholas who was supposedly pro-British. Garrow told him that he 'was interested in the welfare of British escapers and evaders from Occupied France', though failing to mention that he was also interested in their repatriation. Dutour was most pleasant towards Garrow, assuring him that if he did not interfere with French people and kept away from the politics of "de Gaullisme" then he would have nothing to fear. Dutour even went so far as to give his *parole d'honneur* (word of honour) that if he, Garrow, were to be inadvertently arrested by the police, nothing further would happen to him were he to disclose the fact that he knew Dutour.

On his way back from the meeting, however, Garrow was stopped by detectives in the Place de la Bourse. Unable to produce an identity card, he asked them to contact Dutour. This they would not do, and took him instead to the gendarmerie, where he was searched. After the *commissaire de police* (superintendent) had also refused to telephone Dutour, Garrow was placed in the cells. Later taken to the offices of the *Direction de la Surveillance du Territoire* at 59, la Corniche, he was subjected to the formalities of the *procés verbal*. This was conducted by a commissaire from Vichy, who warned Garrow that he was not a fool. That night the prisoner was removed to Fort St Nicholas.

Some three weeks later, Capitaine Dutour called on Garrow to tell him that he had only just heard about his arrest. Garrow was also visited by two of Dutour's men, Detective Sergeants Garse and Brun. They also claimed to have had nothing to do with the arrest, though Garrow later discovered that Dutour was lying, and probably the other two as well. It was not until 7 January 1942 that Garrow had his first interview with a *Juge d'Instruction*, who said that it was a disgrace that he had been imprisoned for so long without his case having been properly investigated.

Garrow was appointed an advocate, M. Gaston Defferre, but it was not until mid-February 1942 that he had his first real interrogation before a judge, this time Dutour himself. Soon afterwards Garrow, who by this time had become severely under-nourished as a result of the awful prison diet, contracted jaundice and was admitted to the Michel Lévy hospital,[515] rue de Lodi, Marseille, where he was well treated. A month later, now recovered, he returned to Fort St Nicholas, but was no longer kept in solitary confinement. Finally, on 22 May 1942, he was 'formally arraigned, and charged with helping British soldiers to escape from German hands in Occupied France; with helping such persons to escape likewise from Unoccupied France, and with collecting and transmitting military information about German forces.'[516] The trial, almost inevitably, was a farce, and he was sentenced to three years' imprisonment and to ten years' *interdiction de séjour*. Furthermore, he was ordered to forfeit all his property.[517]

On 11 July 1942 he was transferred to the high-security prison camp at Mauzac, in the Dordogne, and put 'in a barracks with the lowest type of French criminal'. Mauzac was 'a very tough prison camp, at least as difficult as Colditz', with 'three rings of barbed wire surrounding it', and was 'very heavily guarded'.[518] Not so heavily guarded, however, that twelve agents (whose names Garrow was unable to remember) were not able to escape. Four of them were members of SOE's F Section's failed Corsican mission dropped into France on the night of 10/11 October 1941 – Lieutenant Jack Beresford Hayes RASC; Clement Jumeau; Jean Philippe Le Harivel; and Daniel Turberville. The rest, also F Section agents, had also been easily arrested – Michael Trotobas; Georges Bégué; Pierre Bloch; Francis Garel; Lieutenant George Langelaan, East Yorks; Philippe Liewer; Robert Lyon; and R. B. Roche.[519] Transferred to Mauzac in the spring of 1942 their escape was orchestrated through Madame Gaby Bloch, Pierre Bloch's wife, who got in touch with Virginia Hall (see below, this chapter) and Philippe Albert Crevoisier de Vomécourt ("Antoine").[520]

One of the guards at Mauzac was persuaded to help with the escape, and at 3 a.m. on the morning of 16 July 1942 they were let out of the camp to a waiting van.[521] The escapers were then taken to a hide-out in a forest fifty kilometres away, where they stayed for a week while false papers were prepared, leaving on 23 July in groups of two for Lyon. On 8 August the first group – Jumeau, Hayes, Le Harivel, Roche, Garel, Bégué and Bloch – set off for Spain. Arrested on a train at Figueras, they were interned at Miranda de Ebro for a while before being released and making their way to England.[522] Liewer and Trotobas followed, but were briefly imprisoned in Portugal before being flown to England on 16/17 September 1942.

As a result of this mass escape a "stool pigeon" was put into Garrow's cell, and it was only after Garrow had gone on and on about the hopelessness of ever escaping that he was 'transferred to another barracks, containing a better type of prisoner, such as French officers charged with military offences.' With the stool pigeon gone, Garrow's supervision became less strict, and he was allowed visits from his "cousin", Nancy Fiocca, who was able to bring him comforts. He also persuaded Joseph Zucaralli, Marcel Baillergeon, and Fourtin, three fellow prisoners whose work took them beyond the prison's fences, to send letters to Pat O'Leary.

The barracks to which Garrow was confined was divided into three sections – prisoners at one end, a washhouse in the middle, and *gardes nationale* (national guard) at the other end. What interested Garrow, though, was the door that led from the guards' quarters onto the parade ground and which was quite close to the camp's main gate. If, he reasoned, he could somehow procure the uniform of a guard, then it would not be too difficult to get out through the door at the far end of his hut and simply walk out of the main gate. There was, however, the small matter of the wooden partition that separated the prisoners' side of the washhouse from the guards' side.

Matters took on a greater urgency after the Germans had completed the occupation of the whole of France in the middle of November 1942, and when word filtered down that it was believed that Garrow was to be handed over to them, the matter of escaping became ever more pressing. Details of the situation were passed to Pat O'Leary, who was, from the end of November, now based in Toulouse. Through his latest wireless operator, the twenty-year-old Australian Tom Groome ("Georges"),[523] Pat contacted Room 900. Brigadier Crockatt, head of MI9 in London, made the wise decision to leave the matter of Garrow's rescue in O'Leary's hands.

One of the warders at Mauzac, a man called Peyrot, who was known to be strongly anti-Vichy and anti-German, and 'who lived at a small house near the prison camp and earned 3,000 francs a month,'[524] was bribed to co-operate. Peyrot, however, knew only too well the risks that he was being asked to run and, therefore, with his demands accordingly high, O'Leary offered him the equivalent of six years' wages – 216,000 francs[525] – with the proviso also that he would smuggle a guard's uniform to Garrow. The deal was done with 100,000 francs as a down payment, the balance payable after Garrow's escape.

But then came an unexpected setback. The guard's uniform that had already been made by Paul Ulmann, a Jewish tailor, and by his American wife, Imelda, who lived in Toulouse, was no longer usable. The uniforms had been changed following the recent German occupation of the area. Within forty-eight hours, though, Paul and Imelda had made the necessary alterations, and with the help of one of his three prisoner friends the uniform was smuggled in to Garrow on 7 December.

Pat had sent the trusted Francis Blanchain to Mauzac to make a reconnaissance, but when Francis was caught in Limoges,[526] Pat decided to travel to Mauzac himself, his papers declaring him to be the husband of Nancy Fiocca, who had herself become well-known to the Mauzac guards over the previous months. Together with Guy Berthet and Fabien de Cortes, armed with guns in case of trouble, and Tom Groome with his wireless set, Pat made his way to the farm of Jean Brégi at Lunas (Dordogne), a dozen kilometres north-west of Bergerac, in readiness for the escape. Leaving Groome behind, Jean Brégi drove the three men to the camp and, while he and Pat O'Leary stayed with the car in a nearby wood, Berthet and de Cortes positioned themselves in suitable firing positions around the gate to the camp.

That evening, 7 December, Garrow changed into the *garde nationale* uniform and, with a jemmy also provided by one of his prisoner friends, prised apart the boards in the washhouse partition and crawled through into the guards' quarters. Walking as nonchalantly as he could across the parade ground and through three separate gates, at each of which a guard was posted, he reached the main road unchallenged at about 7 p.m. and strolled south towards the village of Sauveboeuf, a couple of kilometres away. Peyrot was to cycle slowly past between 7 p.m. and 7.05 p.m. and guide the tall Scotsman to the waiting Pat O'Leary, who had been watching as Garrow strolled as innocently as he could out of his former prison.[527] As soon as Garrow and Pat O'Leary had met, Peyrot disappeared, and Garrow changed into civilian clothes.

The journey back to the farm was made without incident but, as luck would have it, Garrow's breakout had coincided with one made from Bergerac prison by six "de Gaullistes". For the next fortnight, frantic police activity in the area forced Garrow to remain in hiding until 9 December, when Pat O'Leary took him to the safe house of Monsieur Loupias in the Avenue Pasteur, Bergerac.[528] Three soldiers who had escaped from the Camp du Chambaran on 6 December 1942 – Private P.F. Inglis; Private T.F. McGlasson; and Gunner H.W. Smith – briefly met Captain Garrow at M. Loupias's house after they had been brought from Marseille to Toulouse on 22 December, and had spent five days with Paul Ulmann. Inglis reported that M. Loupias, apparently a captain in the French Army, told him 'that he had arms and ammunition stored in the house'. Inglis also formed 'the impression that the French in Bergerac are organised'.[529]

Pat O'Leary returned on 28 December to take Ian Garrow by train to Françoise Dissard's dress shop in the rue de la Pomme, Toulouse. Marie-Louise Dissard, always known as "Françoise", began her association with the PAO line in July 1942, when she had been asked to find a furnished house for Paul and Imelda Ulmann to use as a safehouse for evading airmen. By December 1942 Françoise was an important link in the PAO chain, 'enlisting guides and keepers of safehouses, and procuring civilian clothing, food, and medical supplies. Her small, dark apartment became the headquarters of the line. Agents and guides came there for information and instructions, and there she also sheltered airmen, agents in transit, and fugitives from the police.'[530] Apart from her hatred of the Germans, her other main passions in life were her cat "Mifouf" and Commandant Boutin, her nephew, who was in a prisoner-of-war camp and for whom she canned prodigious quantities of food.

After two abortive attempts to rendezvous with a guide in Perpignan, O'Leary took Ian Garrow there for the third time, on 25 January 1943, and this time met the guide. A small group of evaders and escapers – two American airmen, Technical Sergeant Erwin D. Wissenback and 2nd Lieutenant William J. Gise;[531] an RAF airman called Newton (not traced); a Frenchman and a Belgian who were unknown to O'Leary and had been added to the party by the guide – caught the train to Banyuls, where Ian Garrow said goodbye to his loyal friend Pat O'Leary. It was around 8.30 p.m. when they arrived at Banyuls, but the guide led them off at once through the Alberes hills that straddle the frontier with Spain. Once across the border, they spent the night in a wood. On 26 January they walked to a farmhouse, where they remained until dark before continuing.

They hid in a barn on the outskirts of Figueras from 4 a.m. on 27 January, again until it was dark. Once more they walked through the night and all the following morning until, in the early afternoon of 28 January, they had reached the River Fluvia, a dozen kilometres south of Figueras, which marked the boundary of the "military zone". Fording the river after dark they spent the night of 28/29 January in another barn, but before dawn were taken to a wood to await the return of the guide whom Ian Garrow had sent to Barcelona with a letter for the consul, explaining their situation. The guide returned with a message to say that the two British and only one of the Americans were to be picked up later that day. Wissenback and Gise tossed for the seat, and Wissenback won. At about 4 p.m. Garrow, Newton, and Wissenback were driven away by Mr Dorchy to Barcelona. The others were brought to Barcelona next day.

Garrow left Barcelona on 1 February for Madrid and Seville, by car. Boarding the SS *Ravens Point*,[532] he arrived at Gibraltar on 5 February. Flown back to England on the night of 6/7 February 1943, he touched down at RAF Hendon at 10.15 a.m., to be welcomed by the waiting Captain Jimmy Langley. For his 'gallant and distinguished services in the field', in other words for selfless devotion to duty in helping nearly 200 servicemen make their way to Spain, Garrow was admitted to the

Distinguished Service Order.

With Garrow removed from the organisation in October 1941, Pat O'Leary, with everyone's support, was persuaded to take over the running of it. One of his first tasks was to have a word with Cole, but he was away in the north assembling yet another large "convoy". This time, with Roland Lepers and his girlfriend Madeleine Damerment, thirteen evaders were to be brought south – seven airmen and six British soldiers, some of whom had been in hiding for months. The airmen were Squadron Leader H.E. Bufton; Flight Lieutenant R.G.A. Barclay DFC; Pilot Officer A.E.J.G. Nitelet (Belgian); Pilot Officer Oscar Hoffman Coen (American); Sergeant P.H. Bell; Sergeant W.F. Crampton; and Sergeant K.B. Read;[533] and the six soldiers were Privates Archie Neill, Andrew Pow, and Joseph Ross (all 5th Gordon Highlanders); Lance Bombardier E.W. Dimes, RHA; Sapper R. Reid, RE; and Gunner John H. Clapham, RHA.

Bell and Nitelet, both Spitfire pilots, had been wounded. Nitelet's Spitfire, shot down on 9 August, turned over on landing, as a result of which he suffered severe head injuries, including the loss of his right eye. He was rescued from the wreckage by farmer Louis Salmon, who took him to Vincent Ansel, a member of Norbert Fillerin's group. Sheltered by the Fillerin family for two months, his wounds were treated by Dr Delpierre from nearby Fauquemberges and by Dr Houzel from Boulogne. Bell, hit in the legs by a cannon shell when he was shot down by an Me109 on 21 September, also recuperated at the Fillerins' house at Renty.

Cole's plans to move the large convoy south fell through on 22 October (possibly because of pressure from Dutchman Cornelius Verloop – see below), but on 29 October, after he had sent a message to Suzanne Warenghem in Paris 'instructing her to meet him once more at the Gare du Nord with another team of "footballers"',[534] he, Lepers and Madeleine Damerment took the evaders by train to Abbeville to collect forged papers from the Abbé Carpentier.[535] Continuing to Paris, where they were joined by Suzanne Warenghem, the journey to Marseille was completed on the morning of 1 November 1941. Everyone went to the Nouveaus' fifth floor apartment on Quai de Rive Neuve, but the soldiers were soon moved to another safe house in Nîmes.

Summoned to the Nouveaus' apartment on the afternoon of his arrival in Marseille, Cole was confronted by Pat O'Leary, Mario Prassinos, Léoni Savinos and Bruce Dowding. Elsewhere in the apartment were the RAF evaders, Despretz and André Postel-Vinay, who by chance had arrived from Paris for discussions with the organisation. Accused of keeping thousands of francs for himself instead of passing them on to Despretz, Cole protested his innocence, and called Despretz a liar. Immediately, Despretz was brought into the room. Turning pale, Cole took a step towards the door but, before he could get to it, O'Leary knocked him to the floor. Abjectly confessing to the theft, Cole was locked in the bathroom while the others decided what should be done with him. Dowding thought that they should kill him, but Prassinos was aghast at the suggestion. The need for an immediate decision was taken from their hands when they heard a noise in the bathroom. Too late. The bird had flown, out of the bathroom window and in through another window into an adjacent room, before fleeing from the apartment and into the darkness of the November evening.

It was now clear to all that Cole was never to be trusted again, and Dowding was nominated to take over his duties in the Lille area. With no telling what Cole would do next, O'Leary, Dowding and Despretz headed north to pass the word that he was to be avoided at all costs. The Abbé Carpentier in Abbeville was one of the first to be warned but, dedicated to the task of providing false papers and documents, he saw no reason to stop now. Leaving Despretz and Dowding in Lille, O'Leary took the opportunity of slipping across the border to Brussels to pay a brief visit to his parents, before heading back to Marseille.

While Pat was away, Pilot Officer Oscar Coen, perhaps because he was an American and therefore a citizen of a neutral country, was separated from the others after the night in the Nouveaus' apartment, and driven to Nîmes. After staying with Gaston Nègre for several days, Nègre and another man, whom Coen had not seen before, drove him via Perpignan to the foothills of the Pyrenees. A short while later Nègre 'pulled off the narrow dirt road and told Coen they had driven as far as possible, so this was where they would part. He gave Coen a loaf of bread to put in one pocket and a flask of brandy for the other, and with an admonition not to use it all up too soon, he drove away.'[536]

As Coen and the other man climbed the lower slopes of the Pyrenees they met, to their surprise, five of the other six airmen with whom Coen had journeyed to Marseille, two of the soldiers who had also come down in the Cole group, and a few others. The five airmen – Bufton, Barclay, Bell, Crampton and Read – had left for Spain on 3 November 'with a Greek guide', breaking their journey at Paulette Gastou's Hôtel du Loge in Perpignan. On the night of 5/6 November they were driven to the foot of the Pyrenees. Now, on a very cold, moonlit night, they all crossed into Spain. After lying up for the day they made their way to Vilajuiga railway station, where the guide gave them each a ticket and told them to get off at Figueras, a short way down the line. Once again, on arrival, Coen was separated from the others and sent more or less direct to Madrid. 'The directions to the embassy were very clear, and Coen found himself standing outside the compound, in the late November afternoon sunlight, with a lump in his throat as he saw the Union Jack flying in the breeze.'[537]

"Alex" Nitelet, meanwhile, the seventh airman, had been taken to see Dr Rodocanachi on 2 November for treatment to his injured eye. A few days later he was taken across the Pyrenees near le Perthus and delivered to the British Consulate in Barcelona, where he was reunited with the other airmen who had reached the safety of the consulate early on the morning of 7 November. Bufton and Barclay 'were directed to a house owned by people called Dorchy. There they were given fresh clothes, had a bath',[538] and then shown to a comfortable bed.

After a couple of days the Bufton group were also sent on to Madrid, reaching the British Embassy on 11 November but, nine days after their arrival, Sergeant Crampton was found to be suffering from diphtheria. Four days later he was moved to the hospital at Gibraltar, where he remained until 30 December 1941. Bufton and party eventually reached Gibraltar in the small hours of 8 December. Barclay, billetted at the Bristol Hotel, was fortunate to meet the pilot of a long-range Catalina flying boat, and unofficially joined the crew as third pilot. At 4.15 p.m. on 9 December the Catalina took off with Flying Officer Barclay aboard, and touched down at Stranraer, Scotland, at 10.15 a.m. on 10 December, the first of his group to get home. Crampton was the last, flown back to England on 8 January 1942.

Pilot Officer Z. Groyecki PAF was almost certainly in the hands of the PAT line when, on about 15 November, 'a man called from an organisation and discussed plans for my getting back to England. He supplied me with identity cards for which I was able to give him photographs I had already had taken at the instigation of a man from another group.'[539]

On the night of 7/8 November 1941 Groyecki was manning the rear turret of a 300 Squadron Wellington which, on the way back from the target, ran out of fuel, probably due to a leak caused by bursting flak. Shortly after midnight on 8 November the crew of six baled out north of Lille, alert German machine-gunners firing at them as they descended by parachute and wounding three of them. They, with a fourth member of the crew, were taken prisoner, but Groyecki and Sergeant Janek Budzynski PAF evaded capture.[540]

As soon as he had landed Groyecki knocked on the door of two farms but, getting no reply from either, went back to the field in which he had landed, near Quesnoy-sur-Deûle, and went to sleep. He tried one of the farms again when it was light, and this time was taken in: 'I explained that I was a Polish officer in the RAF and was told I was quite safe. They gave me civilian clothes, food, and about 1,000 francs and destroyed my uniform, and my parachute and mae-west. I gave them my automatic pistol.'[541] That afternoon the farmer's daughter took him to a Polish café in Lille, some ten kilometres to the south. 'I did not trust the people there' and so, at about 8 p.m. walked the streets of Lille. With curfew time fast approaching (10 p.m.), a French policeman, whom Groyecki had asked for help, took him back to his house. After a stay of three nights, Groyecki was moved on to three or four other houses, until the man from the organisation called for him on about 15 November.

Now armed with an identity card Groyecki was moved to a house in the Hellemmes district of eastern Lille. Already there was Janek Budzynski, who had landed on the roof of a house near Roubaix that was occupied by German soldiers: 'As the house was only a billet, there was no guard and I was able to discard my flying kit and jump from the roof. I then made my way towards the station and swam a canal.'[542] Looked after by various Belgians, a Russian family, an Englishwoman from Lille, a Polish girl and a Frenchman, the latter took him to the house in Hellemmes where he was to stay for about two weeks.

Groyecki and Budzynski were on the move again, on 27 November, 'staying a night at a lady's hat shop in La Madeleine district of Lille'.[543] They left next day with Lance-Corporal P.H. Kincaid, 1st Black Watch, and a Belgian and a Dutchman. Joined by others along the way, the party had grown to some eleven or twelve by the time they had reached Abbeville. In the short time available the Abbé Carpentier could produce only four or five *ausweise* (passes) to get the group past the German guardhouse on the bridge over the River Somme at Abbeville. In twos and threes they went over, 'the passes being sent back after each crossing', until all were safely over. They caught a through train to Paris, on which tickets only were examined, and four or five days later journeyed to Nevers, a few kilometres north of the Demarcation Line. Driven the short distance to a spot near Sancoins, they crossed the River Allier by boat, continuing by train to Nîmes. After a fortnight or so in Nîmes, Groyecki, Budzynski and Kincaid caught a train for the Pyrenees and Spain, and were joined by Sergeant W.H. Dyer and Sergeant H.R. Wilson RCAF.

Sergeant Wilson was in a Whitley on the night of 24/25 October 1941 when it was hit by flak at around 13,000 feet over Calais. With the port engine on fire the pilot, Sergeant G.M. Porrett, gave the order to bale out. The aircraft, still with its bombs aboard, blew up when it crashed on the edge of Calais-Marck airfield, to the east of the town. Wilson's arrival on terra firma was less explosive, but he 'landed on an electric sign in front of a shop in one of the main streets of Calais.'[544] Luckily his feet were only inches from the ground and he was quickly able to disentangle himself from his parachute and harness and hide in a deep doorway. After wandering out of Calais, and back again after he had lost his way, he was given shelter by a shopkeeper and his family.

Sergeant Dyer, shot down on the night of 28/29 September 1941, landed in the middle of a wood near Romerée,[545] and hurt his ankle as he crashed into a tree. Disentangling himself from the branches and from his own flying kit he walked to a nearby house 'where I was given 100 francs and a newspaper with a map to enable me to get to Calais.'[546] Still wearing his RAF trousers and a coat that he had found, he travelled alone for seven days through Belgium to France, without any proper food, but by pretending to be deaf and dumb managed to buy apples and beer along the way. On the second day of his journey, stopping to have a drink from a water barrel beside a cottage somewhere between Charleroi and Mons, a German soldier 'taxed me with being British and asked my name and number, and where I had come from. I gave him my name and number. He left me standing inside the cottage beside a woman to whom he had been talking, and I ran off over the fields.'[547]

Arriving in Calais on 5 October Dyer sought refuge in a café, but when the time came to leave he was unable to get out of his chair. His legs had "frozen" solid. A Frenchman helped him to his home and fed him, before getting in touch with a member of the PAT line. He was taken to meet Sergeant H.R. Wilson in Calais, and told him that there was an organisation that might be able to get them home. Parting company, they were reunited a fortnight later in a house in Marles-les-Mines (Pas-de-Calais), half a dozen kilometres west of Béthune. Walking to Auchel, two kilometres west of Marles, on the following morning, they stayed there for one night before leaving for Lillers, a short way to the north. Here they stayed for another two weeks, meeting a 'Polish sergeant, whom we knew as Gustave'.[548] The three of them were taken by car to Béthune and from there by train to Abbeville, where the tireless Abbé Carpentier provided them with identity cards, which also passed the close scrutiny of the German guards on the bridge over the Somme.

In Paris, their next guide, a young Frenchwoman, made arrangements for yet another guide to take them over the Demarcation Line to Loches (Indre-et-Loire). Continuing to Toulouse the new guide put them on a train for Marseille 'and then left us, the understanding being that he was to travel first class on the same train and pick us up again at the station in Marseilles. We did not, however, see him again. I do not know whether this was accidental or deliberate. He had taken most of our money.'[549] When they reached Marseille, Dyer and Gustave went to one exit, Wilson to another 'in the hope of seeing our guide whom we had not been able to pick up at the platform barrier.' After waiting in vain for some time Wilson found that Dyer and Gustave had disappeared. He later learnt that when some policemen appeared they decided to beat a hasty retreat while the going was good. In fact they went to the address in Marseille given to them by the guide, and were sent on to Perpignan and stayed in a hotel (possibly the Hôtel du Loge).

On the morning of 5 December 1941, while Dyer and Gustave were still in bed in their hotel room, the door burst open and four or five French plain-clothes policemen charged into the room waving revolvers: 'They pocketed our false identity cards and told us to get up and dress and come with them. We were taken from the hotel singly.'[550] Once out in the street Dyer lashed out at his guard and ran off. Three men tried to stop him but he got away and, stealing a bicycle, cycled to Narbonne some sixty kilometres north. Knowing that the Frenchman who had taken him and Gustave to Perpignan was on his way again to Perpignan to see them, and that he would have to pass through Narbonne on his way, Dyer went to the station in the hope of meeting the guide. Dyer, who was delighted to meet the Frenchman as he was changing trains, told him what had happened, and they realised that they were almost certainly given away by an informer. Taken to Nîmes on the midnight train, Dyer stayed there for about eight days.

Alone in Marseille and unable to remember the address that their guide had given them while they were at Toulouse, Wilson tried the American Consulate for help. Rebuffed, he then walked the streets until he came upon 'the American Red Cross, and there was given an address which I recognised as the one we had received from our guide'[551] – 21, rue Roux de Brignolles, the home of Dr Georges and Fanny Rodocanachi. It was not until 12 December 1941, when arrangements had been made for the next stage of his journey, that he left Marseille by train for Narbonne, together with two Spaniards and a Frenchman. Meeting the other airmen, including Dyer, and Kincaid at Nîmes, they were now in the hands of 'an Englishman, who I believe had been in St Hippolyte'. The "Englishman" (possibly Pat O'Leary himself) took them via Perpignan to Port Vendres, where they were handed over to two Spanish guides. The plan, to jump off the train as it slowed down for the next station, Banyuls-sur-Mer, was accomplished without injury.

One of the guides then left them, but with the other one and two smugglers they walked to the foothills of the Pyrenees and, after a rest, crossed the mountains on 13 December. They spent a few hours in a field until, at around 5 a.m. on 14 December, the guide took them 'to a shed at a small railway station', Vilajuiga, where he left them, but not before stealing Wilson's watch. A third Spanish guide escorted them, with no identity papers, by passenger train to Barcelona.

After six days in Barcelona, Groyecki spent two weeks in Madrid before going to Gibraltar, which he reached on 5 January 1942. Wilson arrived there two days later. Groyecki was flown back to Plymouth (with Pilot Officer H.B. Carroll) on the night of 20/21 January, while Wilson returned by Royal Navy corvette on 27 January (with Wing Commander P.A. Gilchrist and Pilot Officer T.M. Gay). Budzynski and Dyer, though, remained at Gibraltar until 4 March, when they left on a six-day voyage to Gourock with eight other airmen evaders – Birk, Cox, Day, Dicks, Haley, Hutton, MacKenzie, and Warburton (see Chapter 6).

Also keen to get his hands on Paul Cole was a Dutchman, Cornelius Verloop. Born in The Hague in 1909 Verloop had joined the French Foreign Legion in 1935, before deserting to join the Abwehr, the German army's counter-intelligence bureau, as a *Vertrauensmann* (trusted agent). Head of the main *Abwehrstelle* (branch office of the counter-intelligence service) for northern France was Hauptsturmführer Karl Hegener, whose offices were located in the rue de Tanremonde, Lille, and who had under his command six German agents and 'about fifty French agents, most of them right-wing or Fascist collaborators',[552] including Verloop. The Abwehr knew Cole as "Captain Colson", and had been after him for months.

Verloop, having failed to catch him one night in June 1941, tried again on the night of 21/22 October and again failed, though he did manage to arrest some twenty of Cole's helpers in the Lille area.[553] Fortunately for Verloop, Cole was heading back to Lille after fleeing from Marseille on 1 November. Making his way to Paris, he briefly called on Suzanne Warenghem to explain that there had been 'a spot of bother in Marseilles'.[554] Hoping that no one in the north would have heard of the accusations made against him in Marseille, he decided to make his way back to the Lille area and to lie low for a few weeks. Verloop, however, was getting ever closer to the elusive Englishman and, on 6 December 1941, caught him at the house of Madeleine Deram, one of his lady friends.

Once in the Abwehr's hands Cole quickly agreed to co-operate, but for some reason did not name all of his accomplices in his thirty-page statement. That same afternoon Verloop's men raided the town hall in la Madeleine and took away François Despretz.[555] Arrests continued throughout the district, some estimates giving the total as seventy-five. Among those caught were Alfred Lanselle, the Abbé Pierre Carpentier, Désiré Didry, Bruce Dowding, Maurice Dechaumont and Drotais Dubois. On 8 December, Cole was present at the arrest of one of his former helpers at St Omer, and later that day turned up at the home of the Abbé Carpentier in Abbeville, some eighty-five kilometres to the south, with five men who, he claimed, needed passes to cross the River Somme into the Unoccupied Zone. As Carpentier began making the false papers the Abwehr burst in as planned, and the seven men, including Cole, were led away.

On 5 December Bruce Dowding, who had been staying with François Despretz, 'took a furnished room in Lille and enrolled for law studies at the university there to obtain a cover occupation.'[556] He was arrested, possibly on 9 December 1941, at the home of Madeleine Damerment, the girlfriend of Roland Lepers, and after a brief incarceration at St Omer (Nord), Loos, was deported to Germany with James Smith, the Abbé Carpentier, Dubois, Didry and Duhayon, all betrayed by Cole.[557]

Cole, for the moment his work done in the north, moved on to Paris to betray others of his organisation but, just as he had done in Lille with another of his lady friends, he now spared Suzanne Warenghem, whom he had arranged to meet at the Gare du Nord on 11 December. Instead, he was elsewhere in Paris pointing the finger not only at those who had trusted him as their leader but also, on 14 December, at André Postel-Vinay, who had given Cole his Paris address when they had met in Marseille. Three days later Postel-Vinay tried to commit suicide. He faked a second attempt in June 1942, and was undergoing psychiatric examination when, on 3 September 1942, he managed to escape via the PAO line, and to reach London by October.[558]

Cole now chose to disappear from both his German employers, and from the members of PAT/PAO who were after his blood. Having charmed his way into the Paris apartment of one of Suzanne's aunts he fell genuinely ill, with such a fever that Suzanne and her aunt were convinced that his days were numbered, but he pulled through, and was well enough to leave at the beginning of March 1942. Little is known of his activities after he left the flat in Paris but, having married Suzanne on 10 April, both were arrested by Louis Triffe of the Vichy police at one of Lyon's better hotels, the Angleterre, in June. On 21 July Suzanne was acquitted, but Cole was sentenced to death. Before the sentence could be carried out, however, the Germans had occupied the whole of France, and Cole, who was still in prison in Lyon, once again saved his own skin by offering his services to the German security forces.

Fearing that the absence of any RAF evaders or escapers during the past two months meant only one thing – that the line had been penetrated by the Abwehr – Pat O'Leary decided that he would have to find out the answer for himself, and left for Lille with Jean de la Olla towards the end of January 1942. It was mostly from the women who had *not* been betrayed by Cole that O'Leary learnt of the extent of Cole's treachery. One of these women was Maud Baudot de Rouville ("Thérèse Martin"), who arranged for Jean de la Olla to stay at the safe house of Madame Rabaud, on the Rue Barthélemy Delespaul, Lille, after he had been appointed to fill the gap caused by Dowding's arrest. It was Thérèse Martin who was to help Jean de la Olla with much of the rebuilding of the northern section, as new contacts were slowly established. She wrote that he 'was very keen, very resourceful, always ready to go, travelling everywhere, and spending the minimum.'[559]

Having left Jean de la Olla in Lille, O'Leary went to Paris to discover the extent of the problem there, staying at the *Hôtel des Empereurs*. Even though he was 'receiving messages from north and south, helping to escort airmen, interviewing agents, arranging new hideouts, continually thinking of ways and means of extending the Line,' O'Leary 'could not entirely banish Bruce [Dowding], Ian Garrow and the Abbé Carpentier from his mind.'[560] Nevertheless, the job had to go on, and several safe houses were arranged in Paris at '... the flat of Dr Schreider in the Rue Spontini, or Levêque's in the Avenue d'Orleans, or Gisele Gaudier's in the Avenue General Laperine... or perhaps simply the Hôtel des Empereurs.'[561] There was also a main rendezvous in Paris, the restaurant Chôpe du Pont Neuf, where Monsieur Durand, his wife, and Georges Croisé, a waiter, were to help many an evading airman: 'The restaurant, capacious and popular, with a reputation for hearty late-night fare, was divided into two dining rooms separated by a horseshoe-shaped bar. While German soldiers and civilians dined in the front of the Chôpe, British escapers were seated on the red-upholstered banquettes at the back by owner Eugène Durand.'[562]

Word of the Cole affair reached the ears of MI6 agent Donald Darling, who had moved from Lisbon to Gibraltar on 5 January 1942, but his boss, Claude Dansey, having failed to understand the threat posed by Cole, had ordered that he was not to be killed but to be given 'a run for his money'. To resolve the matter Darling decided to ask O'Leary to come alone to Gibraltar: 'I warned him to speak to nobody of the organisation in Marseille, by which I meant [that] the Barcelona Consulate should be kept out of details of the picture. I did not want any more meddling from that quarter.'[563] The message – 'Want to see you as soon as possible. Speak to no one'[564] – reached O'Leary when he was still in Paris. Twenty-four hours later he was on the train to Marseille and, leaving that end of the line in the hands of Mario Prassinos, made his way to Spain. Catching a train at Vilajuiga, he briefly stopped off at Barcelona. Resisting the demand by the consul-general, Harold Farquhar, to explain what he was doing there, he was driven to Gibraltar in the boot of the car of another MI6 agent, thirty-two-year-old Michael Justin Creswell ("Monday"), officially second secretary at the British Embassy in Madrid.

It had also been arranged that Jimmy Langley (agent P15) would meet with Darling and O'Leary at Gibraltar, but it was to be three weeks before Langley could get a flight from England and the meeting could be held. O'Leary produced damning evidence of Cole's embezzlement and treachery in the form of a letter written by the Abbé Carpentier when in Loos prison. This, together with O'Leary's own opinions, finally persuaded Darling and Langley that Cole was a very real threat. O'Leary nevertheless confirmed that he and his helpers were prepared to carry on with the escape line, but they needed more support from England, in the form of 'money, a wireless transmitting set, a wireless operator, arms; they foresaw combined sea and air operations carrying "parcels" away *en masse*, but this could not be done without direct contact with London or Gibraltar.'[565]

Forewarned, Langley had brought with him from England a trained radio operator, Jean Ferière (real name Drouet), though never holding out the hope that Ferière 'would make a name for himself as an intrepid radio operator. If he had had any real potential he would have been snapped up by MI6 or SOE long before I got hold of him.'[566] Nevertheless, Ferière's services were offered to O'Leary, who also formed the opinion that he would not do, but, as he was all there was, he had no choice but to take him on.

Coincidental with Cole's arrest in December 1941, there was a sudden dearth of RAF evaders passing along the PAT line. From all the aircraft lost between 7 November 1941 and 24 March 1942, only two airmen were lucky enough to evade capture – Squadron Leader J. "Whippy" Nesbitt-Dufort DSO, of 138 (Special Duties) Squadron, and Sergeant A.L. Wright, a Canadian in the RAF.

On the night of 28/29 January 1942 Nesbitt-Dufort flew his Lysander to France, but on his way back to England with two passengers 'he was forced to turn back by heavy icing and force-landed near Issoudun.'[567] He had a little over a month to wait before he was picked up by Anson R3316, 161 Squadron, on the night of 1/2 March 1942, and flown home.

Sergeant Wright was the mid-upper gunner of a Manchester of 61 Squadron, which lost three of its aircraft and twenty-three airmen, on an attack on the German battle-cruisers *Scharnhorst* and *Gneisenau* at Brest on the night of 31 January/1 February 1942. Fourteen of the twenty-three were killed, eight taken prisoner, and only Wright evaded capture. Hit by the heavy flak defending the port, Wright's Manchester was too low for the crew to bale out, leaving the pilot (Pilot Officer J.R.B. Parsons) with no choice but to land the aircraft as best he could. Wright survived the crash, and so too did the rear gunner, Sergeant R.V. Griffiths, but with a broken leg, and though Wright helped him out of the blazing Manchester Griffiths was taken prisoner.

Wright was soon found and sheltered by local Bretons. After several days he was told about an organisation headed by a French-Canadian, O'Leary, who would soon have him on his way to England by submarine. Unfortunately, the Germans arrested those that were about to help him, and he found himself trapped in Brittany. Continually moved from house to house, in mid-March he went to the Château Tréfry, home of the Comte and Comtesse de Poulpiquet, where he stayed until May, when the countess herself helped him get to Quimper. Another guide, a Jewish psychiatrist, took him as far as the Demarcation Line, where a young girl saw him across. She left him at a prearranged point while he walked on alone to a car, the driver of which, waiting to take him to La Haye-Descartes (Indre-et-Loire), was Doctor Vourc'h, one of those who had earlier helped him in Brittany. Dr Vourc'h, having had to make good his escape to Vichy France when he learnt that he was a wanted man, now took Wright to Montluçon but, failing to make contact with the next human link in the chain, escorted him to the American Consulate in Lyon.

It was still possible at that time, June 1942, for telegrams to be sent between Vichy France and England and, while he was in Lyon, Wright received the wonderful news that his wife had given birth to a son. The US vice-consul, George Whittinghill, saw that Wright was well looked after. Within a few days someone from the PAO line took him and Dr Vourc'h to Marseille, where Wright was introduced to Pat O'Leary himself. Taken to the Nouveaus' apartment, Wright 'actually arrived wearing a dinner jacket'![568]

Located more or less 150 kilometres west of Geneva, Switzerland, and some 300 north of Marseille, Lyon, in early 1942, became an essential and important link in the only organised route between these two places. It was run by Victor Farrell from the Geneva end, and by Pat O'Leary and his team at Marseille (the PAT line), though the independent contribution made by SOE's American agent, Virginia Hall, who was engaged in the setting-up of the Heckler circuit, and by Philippe de Vomécourt, cannot be ignored. Often given Czech identities, evaders and escapers were taken to Marseille and, usually, accommodated in the Nouveaus' apartment before continuing their journey to Spain. It is not clear when this link was forged, but there is some evidence, albeit slight, to suggest that, in November 1941, Sergeant J.B. Dicks RCAF was used as a guinea pig to test the viability of the route to Spain.

Three hours after taking off on the night of 28/29 September 1941 Wellington X9761 was caught by searchlights and shot down by fighters just on the Belgian side of the border with France. All six of the crew managed to bale out, three being taken prisoner and three evading capture – Sergeant H.E. "Larry" Birk RCAF; Sergeant W.H. Dyer (see above, this chapter); and Sergeant Dicks.

Calling at a nearby farmhouse, still in Belgium, Sergeant Dicks was given civilian clothes and food. Taken across the French frontier he was handed over to a bus conductor, who took him to Charleville-Mézières (Ardennes), sixty kilometres to the south. A Frenchman, realising that he was an airman, bought him a ticket to Besançon (Doubs), a further 450 kilometres down the eastern side of France, and gave him some money. On the train, however, a young lad of fourteen, again recognising Dicks as "English", took him on to Poligny (Jura), a further fifty kilometres beyond Besançon: 'There we went to a café where we met two men who said they were crossing the line of demarcation that night and offered to take me. A party of twenty of us slipped across the frontier without any difficulty. They were all French.'[569] As a result of his rapid progress Dicks had arrived in Lyon on 2 October, but there he remained for the next five weeks while his "papers" were sorted out.

In the Foreign Office files there is an intriguing "Most Secret" cypher, dated 3 December 1941, from the military attaché in Berne, Switzerland, to MI9 in England. In it reference is made to someone called "Lion", whom the attaché met at some point, and who 'believes he can pass our escaped officers through to Spain.'[570] These officers are not named, but present in Switzerland at this time were Lieutenant Chandos Blair, Seaforth Highlanders; Wing Commander P.A. Gilchrist DFC; Captain H.B. O'Sullivan, 3rd Royal Tank Regiment; Captain H.A. Woollatt, 2nd Lancashire Fusiliers; Lieutenant M.G. Duncan, Oxfordshire & Buckinghamshire Light Infantry; Second

Lieutenant A.D. Rowan-Hamilton, Black Watch; and Lieutenant H.E. Stewart, Intelligence Corps attached to the 9th Australian Division.

Captured in the desert on 7 April 1941, Stewart had escaped from the prisoner-of-war camp at Sulmona, Italy, on 30 September 1941. Blair had escaped from Oflag VB (Biberach), Germany, on 30 June 1941 by being hidden in a mattress, and had walked to Switzerland in ten days. He was also the first British officer to escape from Germany.[571] O'Sullivan, Woollatt, Duncan, and Rowan-Hamilton had also escaped from Oflag VB (Biberach), on 13 September 1941, and had all reached Switzerland by 27 September.[572]

The thirty-year-old Canadian Wing Commander P.A. Gilchrist, 405 Squadron commander, was flying Wellington W5551 on an attack on Brest (Finistère), when it was hit by fire from an Me109, killing the rear gunner, Flying Officer R.G.M. Whigham.[573] Following this devastating attack by the German fighter, communications between the crew were lost, and Gilchrist, unaware of Whigham's fate, gave the order to jump. First out was Pilot Officer W. McKay RCAF, followed by Sergeant M.H.J. Dalphond RCAF, Sergeant J.S. Paton RCAF, Gilchrist himself, and Sergeant R.H. Westburg.[574] McKay and Westburg, both wounded to some degree, were the only ones to be taken prisoner by the Germans. Gilchrist was told by one of the French farmers whom he later encountered that one of his crew had a broken leg.

As Sergeant Melville Dalphond, lightly wounded by a cannon-shell splinter in the back, parachuted down a couple of kilometres north-west of Lesneven in Brittany, he 'could see motorcycle patrols converging on the area.'[575] No sooner had he hidden his gear in a hedge, than a dozen Frenchmen ran towards him, bustled him into a nearby house, and made him change into civilian clothes. It was only just in time, for soon the Germans were knocking on the door, but they left when told that there was no one else there.

A doctor was found in Lesneven to treat Dalphond's back, which 'was swelling and very painful'. Given 2,000 francs by the generous doctor who advised him to leave the area as soon as possible, he spent the night in a house in Lesneven: 'Next morning I was put in touch with helpers by whose aid I was passed across France and eventually came in contact with an organisation by means of which I was brought back to the UK.'[576] His journey back to England was interrupted, however, when he was arrested by gendarmes and interned, firstly, at Fort St Hippolyte, and then at Fort de la Revère (see following chapter).

Gilchrist landed about a quarter of a mile from the burning remains of W5551 in a farmer's front garden, near the village of Ploudaniel, and was quickly taken by two boys and a farmhand to a wood. At nightfall three farmers arrived with food and 1,250 francs, for which he gave them an IOU, but refused the offer of civilian clothes. Heading south-east on foot for eight days and nights, he was nearly at Huelgoat (Finistère) when he met a butcher's boy, and was given a lift to Carhaix-Plouguer. A Frenchman who happened to be on holiday in the area then took him to his home in Nantes (Loire-Atlantique), where he was at last persuaded to exchange his uniform for civilian clothes. He then spent several days in the attic of a tram conductor's house, the monotony of being hidden there being relieved on 6 August, when he met two British soldiers who had been on the run since the fall of France and were now working for a farmer.

After almost two weeks in Nantes, now with false identity papers declaring him to be a deaf mute, he was given a train ticket to Angers (Maine-et-Loire), and the address of an English lady and her family who were prepared to help him. On 25 August, with her son, Gilchrist went to Tours where they met a Frenchman, who was prepared to take them to the Unoccupied Zone: 'He took us by car to Manthelan, near the frontier, and from there, accompanied by a French youth, we cycled to Vou, where we were met by the lady from Nantes and a man who had a business in Loches. This man put us up for one night in his home.'[577] They resumed their journey in the morning by bus to Châteauroux, and then by train to Lyon, where they arrived late on the evening of 26 August. Next day they went to see a man who had been recommended by the businessman from Loches, 'but he could not help, as a girl at the Swiss Legation who could have provided some kind of passports was on leave.'

Continuing to Aix-les-Bains on 28 August they went to visit another contact, who advised them to cross to Switzerland via Lake Geneva, as the frontier runs through the lake for much of its length. In the afternoon they left for Evian, on the south side of the lake, and on 29 August hired a boat with the intention of rowing across. Bad weather forced them to retreat, and though it was still stormy on the next day they tried again. They rowed to a point off Thonon-les-Bains, where Gilchrist put his young French companion ashore, having agreed that 'he had better not risk being caught by the Swiss authorities.' After a very stormy passage Gilchrist managed to cross the lake to Rolle, and made his way to Geneva.

By the time that he had reached the city, it was around 8 p.m., on 6 September, and the offices of the British Consulate were closed for the night. This came as something of a surprise, for Gilchrist had been led to believe that it was always open. Finding the front door locked, he went to the side door and tried that but a policeman, witnessing his suspicious behaviour, took him off to the city jail. The Swiss chief of police notified the British Consul of Gilchrist's arrest 'and after about four days of intermittent questioning by the Swiss military intelligence he was taken to Berne, where he was again questioned by Swiss security officials.' Swiss Intelligence then handed him over to the British air attaché (and head of British Air Intelligence) in Berne, Air Commodore Freddie West VC, who questioned him 'for several hours and found his information on his journey across France more than useful.'[578] This was hardly surprising, for Gilchrist was the first RAF evader of the war to cross into Switzerland. On 9 September, the Air Ministry notified HQ Bomber Command of his arrival there.

The Swiss authorities were well aware of the differing terms of the Geneva Convention in respect of evaders and escapers – that escapers, but not evaders, were to be given every opportunity to leave the neutral country in which they found themselves – and Gilchrist and Blair were sent to Geneva to await their prearranged departure, the Swiss turning a blind eye to Gilchrist being an evader. It was always a good idea, even in Switzerland, to do nothing that would alert Abwehr agents, who were always on the lookout for just such men, so, when Blair made the mistake of equalling the Geneva golf course record, he and Gilchrist were hurriedly sent across the border on 12 January 1942, without notifying the Swiss authorities. Safely reaching Spain, Gilchrist left for England aboard a Royal Navy corvette on 27 January, while Blair was flown by Sunderland to Mount Batten on 11 February 1942.

Before passing any of the other officers through to Spain, however, "Lion" wished to be assured that his route was working 'so as not to send others by it if it has gone wrong.' To this end, he wished to know whether or not Sergeant Dicks had got through to Spain. Once information that he had got through had been received in Berne, the attaché proposed 'to send first Stewart who can pass anywhere as a Frenchman, with Rowan Hamilton, and if they are successful to dribble the other three through.'[579] The military attaché also told MI9 that he could provide each officer with a French *carte d'identité* 'of which I have plenty of blank forms', but could not do so until he had received a set of three "mairie" stamps, 'one of which I shall keep and two of which I shall send on to Lion.'[580]

It is unlikely that Dicks would have known how much depended on his getting through when he was sent on his way on 5 November to Perpignan, and thence successfully over the Pyrenees and into Spain. There he 'jumped on a truck' that took him to Figueras, though shortly afterwards he 'was arrested at a small place nearby which I think was called St Lorenzo di Corda.'[581] After three days' incarceration at that place he was detained for a further three days in Barcelona before arriving at the prison at Miranda de Ebro on 18 November. After eight weeks, he was released to the British Embassy at Madrid, which he left on 26 February 1942 for Gibraltar, where he met up with Dyer and Birk. All three left by ship on 4 March, together with seven other airmen evaders, for Gourock, where the boat docked six days later.[582]

While the five army officers waited patiently to leave Switzerland, they were joined by Lieutenant A.M.S. Neave RA, who had escaped from Oflag IVC (Colditz) on 5 January 1942 with Lieutenant A.P.T. Luteyn, Royal Netherlands Indies Army.[583]

Once the all-clear had been given following Dicks' safe arrival in Spain, the first to attempt the route and leave for France were Airey Neave and Woollatt, who reached Marseille, and the Nouveaus' flat, by 16 April. They were then taken to the Hôtel de Paris, Toulouse, and from there escorted over the Pyrenees to Spain and Gibraltar.[584]

Next to go, some four days later, were Duncan and Rowan-Hamilton. On arrival at Marseille they were taken, contrary to orders, directly to the Petit Poucet. They should have gone to the Czech Reception Centre at 37, rue de la République (though they had been told that it was at No. 25). Victor Farrell in Switzerland was adamant that the guides from Switzerland should go directly to Le Petit Poucet, but that they should know nothing of the organisation that lay beyond – what he called a "dead line". It was apparent, however, that not only was the Czech Reception Centre no longer functioning but that the guides knew only too well that Le Petit Poucet was the real rendezvous.[585] The established procedure was then followed. On receipt of the password, *le patron* led the men to a house where Mario Prassinos would collect them and take them to the Nouveaus' flat.

After only one night Louis Nouveau took Duncan and Rowan-Hamilton, in a group that now included a Dutchman called Hecht, a Pole and two Czechs, to the Hôtel de Paris in Toulouse, run by Madame Augustine Mongelard, her husband and his mother, where they caught up with Neave and Woollatt. Duncan and Rowan-Hamilton were to stay at the hotel for ten days or so, during which period Neave and Woollatt left with Hecht and with a fifty-eight-year-old Irishman, Patrick Henry, and his thirty-two-year-old son, James, who had escaped from Paris. Before leaving the hotel,

Duncan and Rowan-Hamilton were joined by two evaders from the St Nazaire raid on 26-28 March 1942 – Corporal G.R. Wheeler, Royal Sussex Regiment, and Lance-Corporal R.W. Sims, Somerset Light Infantry, both attached to No. 2 Commando.[586]

Wheeler and Sims arrived in Toulouse with a Belgian, Gilbert Mahun, and 'tried to pass ourselves off as Belgian refugees. We asked the police where the refugee camp was, and were actually directed to the Hôtel de Paris, the headquarters of the organisation in Toulouse, but, as the Belgian said all three of us were Belgian refugees, we were turned away.'[587] Failing to find the refugee camp, they found instead a YMCA hostel with a sign saying "English spoken", and decided to try their luck there. The two sisters who ran the hostel would have nothing to do with the "Belgians", but when Sims mentioned that he and Wheeler had escaped from St Nazaire 'the attitude of the ladies (Mlles. Volattin [*sic* – Vallotton], who were Swiss) changed completely.' Having fed the men, the ladies contacted Paul Ulmann who, they understood, had already helped an English civilian to Spain.

At this time, April 1942, Paul Ulmann had yet to become involved with Pat O'Leary and his organisation, though he now 'expressed a willingness to remain and work under British auspices'[588] if he could not go with the two commandos. It was not until July 1942 that Paul joined the O'Leary organisation, after Annie Vallotton had introduced him to Françoise Dissard. When she said that she needed food for evaders, Paul admitted that he, too, was sheltering British and American airmen. Shortly afterwards, he introduced Françoise to Francis Blanchain and, later, to Alex Wattebled ("Jacques"), Pat O'Leary's right-hand man. Wattebled then asked Françoise to find a furnished safe house where Paul Ulmann could hide evading airmen. In August 1942 she found a place at 39, rue Pierre Cazeneuve, Toulouse.

While staying with the Ulmanns, meanwhile, Wheeler and Sims were offered a variety of schemes, all involving different people, to get them to Spain. One was to go with the so-called Schmidt Organisation, who would take them across the border 'from the estate of a Frenchman. This plan was regarded as dangerous because it involved going to Narbonne, where police supervision had recently been strengthened.' Another scheme was proposed by a woman who offered to take the two soldiers to Spain for the equivalent of £300. When she would not give any details of how she would make the crossing, it was decided that it would be too risky to go with her.

It was a third scheme, however, that was considered a possibility. The Vallotton sisters knew two French brothers, Collin, who 'knew of an organisation, apparently slightly connected with British Intelligence in Lyons.' It transpired that this 'organisation was spreading anti-Vichy propaganda by means of pamphlets and a newspaper called *Liberation*. It was headed by a man called M. "B" and his wife.'[589]

B's wife got promises of help in Lyon, which resulted in Wheeler and Sims being told to wait in Toulouse for instructions. B's organisation also managed to give the two soldiers 1,000 francs, and kept them supplied with food while they stayed with the Ulmanns. The Collin brothers, however, contacted a man called Francis, whom Wheeler was to meet in Toulouse: 'He is an Englishman speaking with what I took to be a North London accent. He also speaks very good French. In Marseilles he had also been three months in gaol and had moved to Toulouse.'

This was Francis Blanchain,[590] who put the two commandos in touch with the PAT line. After a night in the Hôtel de Paris, they left in the morning by train for Banyuls with Duncan and Rowan-Hamilton, who had also been 'put in charge of a Cockney called Francis'. After several delays – parties of Belgians had been given precedence – the British party left at 4 a.m. on 2 May, with a Dutchman called Decker, two Poles, and a Czech, and crossed into Spain. They met one of the earlier Belgian parties while still in the Pyrenees, and continued with them to Vilajuiga. The British party arrived safely at the British Consulate in Barcelona, where Michael Duncan passed on a message from Pat O'Leary that his organisation was no longer to be called the PAT line. From then on, O'Leary instructed, it was to be known by his three initials – PAO.[591]

Wheeler was the first of the four to reach England, in mid-May. Duncan was back in England on 12 June (Plymouth 16 June), Rowan-Hamilton on 6 July (Gourock 13 July), and Sims a few days later.

O'Sullivan left Switzerland on 23 April 1942, and on arrival at Marseille was also taken directly to Le Petit Poucet, his guide, "Richard", informing him that as the Czech Reception Centre no longer existed he would take him direct to the café. O'Sullivan was fifteen days with the Nouveaus, meeting "Joseph" (Pat O'Leary), before he was sent on his way via Narbonne to Banyuls, where he left the same night for Spain in a group that included himself, a guide, Sergeant W.H. Mills (see following chapter), Hecht (detached from the Neave/Woollatt party), and two more Dutchmen. The British personnel sailed from Gibraltar on 10 June. Mills arrived at Plymouth five days later, and O'Sullivan at Portsmouth on 19 June.

Lieutenant Stewart was the last of the escaped army officers to leave Switzerland. At 3 a.m. on the morning of 29 May two Swiss civilians collected him from the Salvation Army Hotel at Geneva, where he had been staying for the last two days, and drove him and two Poles[592] to the frontier near Geneva: 'At the frontier we crossed a stream, walked for half an hour, and were picked up by another guide who took us to his house. After breakfast and a rest of about two hours a third guide collected us and we went on foot to Annemasse.'[593] In the afternoon they caught a train to Marseille and, as instructed, went to Le Petit Poucet. Collected by Mario Prassinos, they were taken to a flat, and from there a girl took them to the Nouveaus' apartment. (The final part of Stewart's escape continues on page 88.)

CHAPTER 5

By land and by sea: 1942

... Though inland far we be,
Our souls have sight of that immortal sea ...
William Wordsworth – *Ode to Duty*

So low was his Hurricane over Abbeville airfield that when its engine was hit by a cannon shell Squadron Leader Royce ("Roy") Clifford Wilkinson DFM and Bar[594] had to pull up to all of 60 metres (200 feet) so that he could bale out. Landing safely he slipped through the approaching cordon of searching German soldiers and met a Frenchman, who told him the time of the train to Paris and what the fare would be. As it was a good walk into Abbeville and Roy was too late to catch the train he snatched a few hours sleep in an outhouse. Approaching the town early on the morning of 4 May 1942 he noticed that there 'was a guard on the barrier on a hill leading down into Abbeville, but I did not see him in time to turn aside. He came to meet me and I just glared at him and grunted, whereupon he turned back and I walked through.'[595]

Once in Paris, he had another close shave, literally this time. Sitting next to a talkative German in a barber's shop, his tried and tested grunts also seemed to work. Once shaved, he went to a café to ask for the exact location of the Demarcation Line. Taken into a back room, it was pointed out to him on a map. Advised to take the train to Chagny (Sâone-et-Loire) and to ask in the cafés there for further guidance, he spent the night in a low-class hotel (a brothel) near the Gare du Lyon, courtesy of the Madame. Arriving at Chagny next morning, 7 May, though he found it to be swarming with German soldiers, he was given directions for the line from the people in a café near the station. Setting off down the road to Buxy, he called at several farms for food and refreshment. At one near Givry he was told 'that an aircraft from the Augsburg raid had crashed somewhere in the district and that three of the crew were in hiding.'[596] He had no difficulty dodging the guard on the Demarcation Line and crossing the barbed-wire fence into Unoccupied France, but got lost as he walked further on. Fortunately he met a sympathetic gendarme at Montagny-lès-Buxy who took him 'to a large, clean café, where I was welcomed by the owner and his daughter Jeanette'.

Also arriving at the same café after crossing the line that morning were 'Mme. Duhamel, a young Frenchman Abel Henon, and a Belgian "Jean". They said they were doing secret service work on behalf of the British.' Madame Duhamel was formerly, so she said, of the French *Deuxième Bureau*. The mayor of Montagny-lès-Buxy volunteered to drive all four of them to a bus stop and to go with them to Mâcon, some sixty kilometres to the south. On the way, stopped at a control by a gendarme, the mayor told the policeman that Wilkinson had lost his papers, 'and that it was all right as he knew me. We were allowed through.' Taking them to the station hotel (possibly the Terminus) at Mâcon, the mayor told them 'to wait for a French Secret Service man'.

That afternoon a man calling himself Captain Hambert came to see them. 'He said he was French Secret Service but working for the British, and promised to help. He brought two French Air Force officials, who asked some questions about German planes.' Clearly a hotbed of intrigue, Wilkinson was also visited by another Frenchman who said that he was also doing secret service work, but for the French Air Force, and asked him 'to pass a message to Rear Admiral Marshall, Ross-on-Wye, saying that Henry and the twin sisters were all right and working for the British.'[597] As the man bore some resemblance to Wilkinson, he gave him his own photograph for an identity card.

Roy Wilkinson and his new companions were then moved to Magland (Haute-Savoie), close to the Swiss border, where Roy was billetted with the postmaster. One day he 'received a letter from Hambert on official police paper with the gendarmerie stamp saying he was afraid he could not help as he had hoped', but advising him to go to the US Consulate at Lyon. Following that advice, Wilkinson was escorted there on 22 May by Madame Duhamel, and spent the weekend with the consul, Mr Whittinghill. Also visiting the consulate that weekend was an American, Virginia Hall.

Virginia Hall's presence there was no accident. Prior to the war she had been in the US consular service until a shooting accident in Turkey in December 1933 had forced the amputation of her left foot. Having learnt to walk on her artificial limb (which she named "Cuthbert"), she was given employment at the consulate in Venice, Italy, 'where she performed traditional clerking tasks…'[598] Ambitious, Virginia wanted to climb the career ladder within the US Foreign Service, but the *sine qua non* of such advancement was the passing of two exams, one written, the other oral. Viriginia had begun this process as far back as 1929, but had not been successful by the time she had hoped to finish it in 1937. A great blow to her career prospects came when Consul General Stewart in Venice received a letter from Assistant Secretary of State Sumner Welles that effectively closed the door on any prospect of a career in the Foreign Service. In essence, the amputation of her foot excluded her, under the Foreign Service Regulations, from taking the now necessary physical exam, and that that alone was 'a cause for rejection'. As a result, the letter continued, 'it would not be possible for Miss Hall to qualify for entry into the Service under these regulations.'[599] In June 1938 Virginia transferred to the consulate at Tallin, Estonia. Realising that she now had no future in the Foreign Service, she resigned in May 1939, and moved to Paris.

In 1940 she and a French friend, Claire de la Tour, joined the *Services Sanitaires de l'Armée* and, after a short nursing course, became ambulance drivers but, following the defeat of France in June 1940, they went to Claire's family home in the Dordogne. Virginia reapplied for ambulance duties, even though these were now under German control, but when her services were no longer required in August 1940 she decided to head for England, which she reached, via Spain, in September.

Recruited by Vera Atkins, she was trained by SOE and sent to France as agent "Germaine", under the assumed name of Brigitte Le Contre, to help set up the Heckler circuit. Posing as a reporter for the *New York Post*, she arrived in Vichy on 23 August 1941, but charged with carrying out a survey of the spa town. Her report was brought back to England by Jacques de Guélis,[600] another SOE agent who had preceded her to France to prepare the ground for her. She then moved to Lyon in September 1941, initially staying at the Hôtel Grand Nouvel, one of the best hotels in the city. In June 1942 she changed her name to Marie Monin and her codename to "Philomène", continuing to work for SOE. She then learnt, in August 1942, that the Gestapo were after someone fitting her description. Worse, a new SD man, SS Obersturmführer Klaus Barbie, had recently arrived in Dijon, and he was very keen to catch her.

On 7 November the American consulate advised Virginia of the imminent Allied invasion of North Africa, and that it would be wise for her to leave France before the Germans occupied the whole of the country. She began her departure shortly after the Operation Torch landings had taken place on 8 November, and made her way by train to Perpignan, crossing the Pyrenees in a small group on the night of 11/12 November. Taken to a house where there was a wireless transmitter, she contacted London to say where she was. Adding that "Cuthbert" was being a little tiresome, she received the reply that, if he were, he should be eliminated! Arrested by the Spanish, and released from prison on 2 December, twenty-three days later 'she was having Christmas dinner with Vera Atkins and a group of friends in London.'[601]

Virginia returned to Spain in May 1943, again working for SOE but this time with D Section, not F as earlier. Not finding her duties to her liking, she asked to return to London, and in November 1943 this was arranged. For her services hitherto, she was discreetly awarded the MBE. She continued to work for SOE's F Section until switching her allegiance to the Americans' Office of Strategic Service (OSS) on 10 March 1944. With a new codename, "Diane", the Royal Navy's MGB 502 took her and Henri Laussucq, "Aramis",[602] to Brittany on the night of 21/22 March 1944 to resurrect the Heckler circuit (known as Saint by SOE), for which she would be a wireless operator. For her outstanding services thereafter she received the Distinguished Service Cross, the only one to be awarded by the United States of America to a female "civilian" in the entire Second World War.[603]

So it was, towards the end of May 1942, that Roy Wilkinson found himself travelling first class with Virginia Hall on the night express to Marseille, and to the Nouveaus' apartment, where he stayed for three days.[604] Francis Blanchain ("Achille") then escorted him to the Hôtel de Paris, Toulouse, where he stayed for twelve days. During this time Lieutenant H.E. Stewart and his party (possibly Lieutenant Marian Kozubski and Aviation Cadet Wladislaw Tucholko – see end of previous chapter) arrived, having had to leave Marseille in a hurry when there was a sudden "flap" on. Three more Poles and a Yugoslav naval airman, Lieutenant Montchilo Stanenkovich,[605] also joined the group at the same time, as did several others.

After he had been at the hotel for only two days, Lieutenant Stewart, with two Belgians, an Englishman called Napier, and a Pole who had come from Switzerland (possibly, therefore, Wladislaw Tucholko) was on his way to Spain. In the care of "Felix" (Francisco Ponzán), they left by train for Osséja (Pyrénées-Orientales), the last station before the mountains, where they were met by a second Spanish guide, who took them over the Pyrenees. Stewart recalled that 'the crossing was very strenuous, and one of the Belgians, a major, gave out, and Napier and I carried him for about four hours. After fourteen hours walking we reached the small Spanish village of Ribas,' having covered some twenty kilometres south-east from Osséja as the crow flies. Stewart spent the rest of the day in bed recovering, but on the following day the group caught the bus to Ripoll (fourteen kilometres south), and then the train to Barcelona. Two days later (7 or 8 June) Stewart was driven to Madrid, and to Gibraltar on 11 June. Sailing on 6 July he landed at Gourock, Scotland a week later.

Catching up with Squadron Leader Wilkinson in the south of France were seven Polish airmen who had been shot down in two separate aircraft – Wellingtons Z1276 and W5627 – on the night of 27/28 April 1942. As good luck would have it, all eleven aircrew survived, nine as evaders and two as prisoners of war.[606]

Z1276 was somewhere near the Franco-Belgian border on its way to Cologne when it was shot down by a night-fighter near Givet (Ardennes) in France. Pilot Officer W.P. Wasik PAF, second pilot, baled out near Fort de Charlemont, a few hundred metres west of Givet, and saw Z1276 crash 'about three miles away'. Hearing French being spoken he concluded that he was either in France or Belgium. He had in fact landed in a part of France that is surrounded to the west, north and east by Belgium and, making his way south-west, crossed the border into Belgium at Vaucelles, barely half a dozen kilometres from Givet. On 30 April a priest arranged for him to be taken to the village of Willerzie in Belgium. During his time there contact was made with "an organisation", and after fifteen days he joined another Polish evader, Flying Officer A. Szkuta PAF, who had been shot down on 5/6 May, and four Belgians. They arrived in Switzerland on 4 June.[607]

Sergeant Mieczyslaw Sierpina PAF, one of Z1276's gunners, also reached Switzerland, by 19 May 1942, but did not leave that country before 16 September 1944.

Two more of Z1276's crew – Sergeant S. Miniakowski, and Flying Officer T. Wawerski – met up at a house in Givet, but became separated when changing trains on their way to Paris. Wawerski was arrested in Unoccupied France, and was one of those to be sent from the Camp de Chambaran on 6 December 1942 to the Italian prisoner-of-war camp P.G. 5 (Gavi). Following Italy's capitulation in September 1943, he was removed by the Germans to Stalag Luft III (Sagan).

Stefan Miniakowski was also arrested in Unoccupied France, but was taken under guard to a hospital at Châteauroux (Indre). On 15 May 1942 he was transferred to the Pasteur hospital in Nice, then being used for "British" internees from Fort de la Revère. Two months later he escaped from the hospital, and was one of those to be evacuated by sea to Gibraltar (see below).

Pilot Officer Jan Fusinski PAF, Z1276's pilot, needed help when he reached Brussels: 'I asked a German officer which station I should leave from, and he gave me full directions, was very polite, and saluted me when he finished.'[608] Making his way to Lille, he met more of the enemy, this time in a café. There were 'about a dozen Germans whose regiment was going east… One went so far as to say that he would rather commit suicide.'

From Lille Fusinski went to Paris and Dijon, but to cross into Unoccupied France, on the morning of 4 May, he had to swim the River Doubs. Already weak from a lack of food, the subsequent three-kilometre walk took him the best part of two hours. A French officer helped him get to Lyon, where he contacted an old Polish friend at the Polish Administration Bureau, 'where I was given food and had my injured knee treated,'[609] and where he stayed the night. Contact had meanwhile been made with George Whittinghill, who took him next day to Marseille, Fusinski travelling under the name of Thompson. In Marseille he was taken to the Nouveaus' apartment, where he stayed for eight days, being joined on his first night there by Flying Officer Jan Wacinski and, two nights later, by Pilot Officer Julien Morawski.

The sixth crew member of Z1276, Sergeant Andrzej Malecki, made his way to the French town of Charleville-Mézières (Ardennes), just over the Belgian border. There, his dishevelled appearance attracted the attention of a gendarme, who locked him in an upstairs room of a house. Using the flexible saw hidden in the laces of airmen's boots, it took him three hours to cut out the lock and to make good his escape.[610] After walking for three weeks in the direction of Switzerland, he was helped on 21 May by some Yugoslavs at a farm near Poligny (Jura), just across the Demarcation Line, who sent him by car to Lyon. Again falling foul of the local gendarmerie, he was taken into custody but, when one of the gendarmes left the room to get a form, Malecki followed him out, and as the gendarme turned right Andrzej turned left, down a corridor, past a guard, and so to the US Consulate.

W5627, the other Wellington shot down on the night of 27/28 April 1942, came down near Charleville-Mézières. Sergeant Edward Polesinski, rear gunner, soon made contact with a French priest, who passed him on to a Polish priest in Reims (30 April). Moving to another priest in Troyes, where he stayed for a week with a Polish gardener, he was fed by 'an English lady who was looking after British refugees from northern France.'[611] Still receiving assistance from the Polish community in France, a teacher supplied him with a French identity card and 100 francs, while further help came from a 'youth who took me across the boundary near Le Creusot (15 May).' Remembering what he had been told during a lecture at his squadron, he continued to Lyon and, having been there before, made his way to 'the old Polish Consulate… They sent me to the British Consul in the US Consulate.' There he met Sergeant Malecki, and the two of them were taken to the Nouveaus' apartment in Marseille.

Travelling with them to Marseille was yet another Polish airman, Flying Officer Stanislaw Krawczyk PAF, pilot of a Wellington whose engines had been knocked out by flak on 5/6 May 1942. Krawczyk, who had been wounded by the flak, gave the order to bale out but, when Flying Officer Kazimierz Rowicki told him that he had left his parachute behind, Krawczyk unhesitatingly handed over his own lifesaver and, despite his wounds, managed to land the Wellington safely. He, Rowicki, and three others of his crew (Czekalski, Szkuta, and Siadecki) evaded capture but the sixth member, rear gunner Sergeant L. Czarnecki PAF, became a prisoner of war.

Reaching Lyon on 12 May, Krawczyk 'went to the house of a French friend (who is anti-de Gaulle, anti-English, and pro-Pétain).' After two days, the French friend put him in touch with another Pole, who worked at the Polish Bureau at the old Polish Consulate, and who gave him 'food and shelter for two weeks'.

Flying Officer Rowicki found himself abandoned in Brussels when the people who had been sheltering him were arrested. He had already been visited by Peggy van Lier, and it was she who, when meeting him by chance on 20 June, said that she would arrange his departure, but Rowicki, bored with the wait, returned to a house he had been at earlier. Nevertheless, he was still in Brussels on 26 August, when he and Flight Sergeant Arthur Fay RCAF, shot down on 11/12 August, were taken to Paris. After four days in Paris *chez* "Paul" (Frédéric de Jongh), 'chief of the "Southern Line"', Rowicki and Fay left for St Jean-de-Luz on 2 September with "Paul" as one of their two guides, and another four 'British airmen'.[612] Staying at the house of a Basque, the party set off at 9.30 p.m. on 5 September 'for a farm near the frontier, accompanied by a Basque guide and an English boy called Johnson, or "B".'[613]

Crossing the Spanish border on 6 September, however, they were spotted by a patrol of Spanish guards, who opened fire. No one was hit, and all safely reached San Sebastián, where Rowicki 'stayed for one night at a house where Paul's daughter, Andrée, was living'. He also noted that the organisation that had helped him in Brussels was called "Service Andrée". He, and twenty-one other evaders, returned to England on 30 September 1942 aboard the Royal Navy's ancient (1915) battleship HMS *Malaya*.

After three of W5627's crew had baled out, leaving only Flying Officer Julien Morawski, the pilot, and front gunner Sergeant B. Lipski aboard, Morawski stayed at the controls as he 'hoped to get the aircraft home… At last I saw it was hopeless and Sgt. Lipski and I baled out.'[614] Sergeant Lipski, however, broke a leg on landing and was captured.[615] Morawski, though, reached Lyon on 16 May, the day after rear gunner Polesinski, and also went to Marseille soon after.

Sergeant Boleslaw "Bill" Wozniak, W5627's wireless operator, was hidden for eight days in Charleville, when the man who was looking after him took him to Reims in his lorry 'hiding among champagne bottles… We were stopped outside the town by a German sentry, but the lorry was not searched.' Another man took him to Paris where he was put in touch with the PAO organisation, who also took him to Marseille.

Pilot Officer Wacinski, observer on W5627, did a lot of walking before taking a train to Paris, having been advised by some Belgians whom he had met earlier to go to Bourges to get across the Demarcation Line. Catching the train from Paris, he decided to leave it at Vierzon, though Bourges was still some way further on down the line. Walking through the town, he heard Polish songs being sung by some of his fellow countrymen, and asked them for help. They took him 'to a farm about seven kilometres west of Vierzon, where they gave me food and shelter for the night. They said that the crossing on the river Cher, west of Vierzon, was difficult. The river was deep, there were no boats, and it was being closely patrolled, as two Germans had been shot in that district recently by Frenchmen.'[616]

Next day a Frenchman showed him where he could cross: 'I waited until I saw a patrol pass and then waded through the river which was breast high at this point.' Drying out, he decided to catch a train from St Florent to Toulouse, but as he was buying his ticket a gendarme asked to see his papers. Having none, he admitted that he was an evading airman. After some hesitation, the policeman said that he could go. Dodging another control on the train, he safely reached Toulouse and, making contact with the PAO organisation, was also taken to Marseille.

These eight Polish airmen – Wacinski, Fusinski, Morawski, Malecki, Polesinski, Krawczyk, Wozniak, and Miniakowski – were all guests of Louis and Renée Nouveau at 28A, Quai Rive Neuve, Marseille.[617] Wacinski and Fusinski were the first to arrive, on 10 May, followed by Morawski two days later, then Malecki, Polesinski, Krawczyk, Wozniak and, lastly, Miniakowski on 27 June after his escape from hospital.

With Lieutenant Stewart and his party on their way to Spain, Francisco Ponzán returned to Toulouse to collect the next group from the Hôtel de Paris – Squadron Leader Wilkinson, Lieutenant Stanenkovich, Flying Officer Krawczyk and another of the Poles.

Andrzej Malecki and Edward Polesinski were sent on their own 'to report at a hotel in Osséja. At Osséja we were stopped by a police patrol, who took us with them to their station. We were put in a room and told to wait. They took our papers and food and locked it in the next room. We were then left alone and immediately broke into the next room, recovered our papers and food and left the building. We hid in bushes on the outskirts of Osséja till nightfall, when we went to the hotel we had been told of. There we found a guide who took us to a farm near the border, where we found F/O Krawczyk and six others.'[618]

Wilkinson and the other three in his party had had to wait for three days in a shelter until four others had arrived. Then they 'crossed to a village in Spain and were met by a guide, who took us on the early morning train to Barcelona. After three days a car took us to Madrid and a week later we went to Gibraltar, arriving there on 26 June 1942.'[619]

First to go back to England, on 1 July, as befitted his rank, was Squadron Leader Wilkinson. Next, five days later aboard the *Narkunda*, were Krawczyk, Malecki and Polesinski.[620] Malecki was to be awarded the Military Medal, while Polesinski was Mentioned in Despatches. Fusinski, Wacinski and Morawski returned on 19 August, after they had been escorted by Francis Blanchain to Narbonne (one night) and to Banyuls, where they remained for a week, being joined by Brigadier Roupell VC and Captain Gilbert (see below).

Wozniak, last of the eight Poles to return, did not leave Gibraltar until 23 September. He had arrived in Toulouse from Marseille early in June with Sergeant F.A. Barker, Sergeant A.L. Wright, Sergeant J. "Paddy" Prendergast, Welch Regiment (an Irishman who had escaped from Germany, and for which he was awarded the DCM), and 'two Yugoslavs'[621] – a 'major and his batman, a huge sergeant named Michel who spoke only a few words of German beside his native Slavic tongue. The major, fortunately, had a passing knowledge of French.'[622] Swelling the ranks of the party at Toulouse were four young Belgians who wished to get to England and enlist with the Belgian contingent in the RAF. After four days at a hotel near the station they were all taken to Banyuls where, on their third day there, two more men joined the group – Sergeant S.R.J. Ainger, rear gunner of a Hampden that had been shot down by night-fighters over southern Belgium on its way to Cologne on the night of 5/6 April 1942, and a 'mysterious figure who, Wright learned, was a French Intelligence agent.'[623]

Having baled out of his stricken Hampden Ainger 'came down on top of a tree about 3 kms north of Roly in a big forest.' With his 'head burned a little bit' he set off through the forest before striking a railway, which he followed for a while until meeting a Belgian farmer on the outskirts of the village of Marienbourg, south of Philippeville. After breakfast Ainger moved on. Finding some isolated houses and a loft with straw in it he went to sleep in it. 'I was woken about 1400 hours by a girl who screamed and fetched a friendly farmer and his family.' They bandaged his head, gave him more food, and summoned the local priest, who suggested that Ainger should 'hide in a hut in the village until the English invaded Belgium'. The priest, however, introduced him to a lieutenant of the gendarmerie who, after Ainger had spent eight days in the loft, put the airman 'in contact with an organisation' – the PAT/PAO line.

Moved on 11 May to Brussels, and early in the second week of June to Paris, Ainger stayed a night at 11, rue de Chateaubriand. Pat O'Leary himself ("Joseph") escorted Ainger to Dijon and thence by bus to Chalon-sur-Saône, where O'Leary left him in the hands of 'a garage proprietor'. Crossing the Demarcation Line in a party of some sixteen men, 'most of whom were simple Frenchmen' escaping from Occupied France, Ainger and two Belgians caught a train to Lyon, and then another to Montauban, where they stayed three nights at the Hôtel d'Or. Moving on to Toulouse and its Royal Hôtel de Paris for two days they met 'two men who were working with an organisation to get us into Spain. One of them was a Greek and the other passed as an Englishman.'[624] These two were almost certainly Mario Prassinos and Francis Blanchain.

With a young Frenchman (Wright's mysterious Intelligence agent) Ainger and his companions reached Banyuls on 9 June. Setting off with two Spanish guides, it took the twelve men two days on foot to reach Spain, on 11 June, the guides taking them to within twenty kilometres of Gerona. Splitting into pairs, Wozniak and Ainger walked to Gerona (14 June). Having tried in vain at two railway stations to find the train for Barcelona in desperation they asked a newsboy for help, but he probably reported them to the authorities for, within five minutes, a policeman was asking them for their papers. When one of the Yugoslavs, who had by now arrived on the scene, told the policeman that Wozniak and Ainger were British, they were removed to the police station.

Three days later they were sent to the prison camp at Gerona, where they met Barker and Prendergast, who had been caught by the Guardia Civil 'while walking through a small station before

Gerona and were taken to the police station.'[625] Suffering humiliation and privations along the way at the prisons of Figueras, Barcelona and Saragossa they finally reached, as most did, the concentration camp at Miranda de Ebro on 6 July. They had spent four days in one of Barcelona's flea-ridden prisons, without blankets, six to a small room, and were given only one mug of soup when other prisoners got two because, as the Spanish sergeant said, they were English.

After being 'interned for nine weeks and a day from 7 July', Sergeant Wozniak was released from Miranda, and in due course returned to England, on the night of 23/24 September 1942. Barker was back ten days before him, Ainger and Prendergast four days after Wozniak.

Sergeant Albert Wright, the last one home, and the only one to go by ship, had had the misfortune, along with the four Belgians, to be caught by Spanish police on a control on the train to Barcelona. Whether or not they would have got away with their papers, which declared them all to be Czechs, will never be known, for one of the young Belgians, in the heat of the moment, blurted out their true identities. Wright was thrown into a police cell at Barcelona, before being transferred to the *Cárcel Modelo*, where his hair was shaved off. He, too, eventually reached the camp at Miranda de Ebro, where he caught up with six of the original crossing party. He was released from the concentration camp on 23 September, and was one of those to return to Scotland on HMS *Malaya* a week later.[626]

Also at Miranda with Albert Wright was Stirling pilot Flight Sergeant Tom Templeman RCAF, shot down by two Ju88s on the night of 16/17 June 1942, on the way back from bombing Bonn (the secondary target, after Essen). The last to bale out, near Maubeuge, northern France, he 'broke an ankle on landing, and was rather dazed. However I walked about three miles south and then hid in a hollow tree, where I remained all day. There was a German sentry 200 yards away.'[627] Binding up his broken ankle with some fence wire, and living on the contents of his 'aid box, which was very useful', he walked for four days avoiding all roads. He got some help at a farm where the people, 'friendly but frightened', gave him food and a drink of milk, and some boiled eggs to take with him. He also had a shave before he left.

He was a short way past Guise (Aisne), a good fifty kilometres from his landing place, when he 'was arrested by a sergeant of gendarmes. It was a Sunday and my dirty clothes looked out of place. He took me to the police station and searched me.' The gendarme failed to find 400 francs and a map of the south of France tucked away in his boots but, after robbing him of several of the contents of his Aid box, gave him back the box and put him in a cell for the night. At around midnight, though, the cell door mysteriously opened. When he realised that there was no one there, Templeman slipped away into the darkness.

Despite his bad ankle, he made steady progress south, even having had to swim two canals. A short way past Troyes he was given two Michelin maps, and sold his watch 'for a very good French Army compass and 600 francs'. He was now managing some thirty kilometres a day, and despite this exercise found that the pain from his ankle was diminishing – 'but I never got my boot off until it finally wore out.' Crossing the Demarcation Line without difficulty on 5 July, despite the numerous German guards and bicycle patrols, he was clear of Montluçon when he 'got into a freight wagon on the railway,' which took him as far as Giat (Puy-de-Dôme). There a Frenchman took him to his home, cut off the boot that had by now worn out, and gave him a pair of shoes.

Taking him back to the station, he bought Templeman a ticket for Lacapelle-Viescamp (Cantal), a long way to the south, near Aurillac, but rather than risk an identity-card control after only thirty kilometres Templeman decided to get off 'at a small station and started walking south again'. Buying more Michelin maps along the way, and usually having to steal food (he was constantly being refused it at the farms at which he called), he walked on until he reached Béziers (Hérault), on the Mediterranean coast. Finding that 'there were too many holiday makers on the coast', he went inland again, until he finally crossed into Spain from near le Perthus sometime during the first week of August. But then, having come so far and having overcome the handicap of a broken ankle, he lost his footing in the dark, and fell six or seven metres into a ravine. Landing on the base of his spine, he broke his back and in appalling pain crawled to a farm in a village to the west of La Jonquera.

Given a lift on a truck that was going to Figueras, he there gave himself up to the police. No one bothered to treat him for his injuries, but he was given a grilling in what he thought was 'a Gestapo HQ.... They asked me my squadron, the operation I was engaged on when shot down, names of my crew, my means of escape and the names of the people who had helped me.' After two nights in the local prison, he was moved to Barcelona (five days), Saragossa (four days), and finally to Miranda de Ebro on 15 August. Conditions there he found much better, and a Bulgarian doctor called Abramov put him in a plaster cast, having 'created a rope noose, slung across a crossbeam as a sort of gallows'[628] so that he could apply the plaster to his patient.

Released from Miranda at the end of September, Tom was back at RAF Hendon on 6 October

1942. Perhaps it was small consolation for all the pain and suffering, but his DFM was gazetted on 4 December 1942 for setting '… an exceptionally high standard by his courageous example and extreme devotion to duty.'

Making the crossing of the Pyrenees at around the same time as Wilkinson and the others were seven soldiers – two British army officers, Brigadier G.R.P. Roupell VC,[629] and his staff captain, Captain C.H. Gilbert; two commandos, Lance-Corporal Edward Douglas, 5 Troop, No. 2 Commando and Private Victor Harding, 1 Troop, No. 2 Commando; and three escaped soldiers, Private D.R. Edwards, RAOC; Private D. Lang, AIF; and Corporal J.A. Parker, Royal Australian Engineers, AIF.

When the Germans overran the headquarters of 36th Infantry Brigade, 12th Division, on 20 May 1940, Brigadier Roupell ordered the survivors to split up into small groups and to try to join up with another British unit. He, Captain Gilbert and a French interpreter made their way to Rouen, though it took them a month of resting by day and walking by night to accomplish this. Finally coming to a halt at a farm at Perriers-sur-Andelle (Eure), where the interpreter left them, these two officers toiled as labourers for the next two years. It was not until the third week of May 1942 that they were brought, via Rouen, Paris and Lyon, to the Hôtel de Paris, Toulouse, which was, according to Roupell, 'the headquarters of the Belgian organisation'.

The two commandos, Lance-Corporal Edward Douglas and Private Victor Harding, had evaded capture following the St Nazaire raid on 26/28 March 1942, when HMS *Campbeltown* was successfully rammed into the floating-dock gates.[630] Douglas and Harding, despite the non-existence of their target, 'two 6-inch gun positions' on the water's edge, were nevertheless involved in a glorious, but ultimately futile, fight in the dock area of the port of St Nazaire. Once the commandos had received the news that all the boats detailed to get them back to England had been sunk, the expedition's commander, Lieutenant-Colonel A.C. Newman, 'ordered us to get back to England if possible, telling us not to give up while we had any ammunition left and to fight our way through the town.'[631]

This, despite many a close shave, they proceeded to do, and having reached open country wandered through it for the next three days. When they finally reached the River Loire at Langeais (Indre-et-Loire), the curé from a nearby village arranged for the ferryman to get them across, in the company of a number of German soldiers. It was not until the end of April that they crossed the Demarcation Line into Unoccupied France, not far from Ligueil. They made their way to Loches and then, with help from "an organisation", to Marseille.

Having escaped to Switzerland, Lang and Parker were escorted to Marseille on 30 April 1942. Handed over to Mario Prassinos, they stayed the night with Dr Rodocanachi, where they met Sergeant W.H. Mills. Mills had been shot down in flames by a German fighter while escorting bombers to Abbeville aerodrome on 24 March 1942. Making good his escape from the area, he had reached Paris at the end of April, but within the week had been escorted 'by Mme. Helie to Lyons to the US Consulate'.[632] Escorted by Mario Prassinos to Dr Rodocanachi's house in Marseille, he stayed there for ten days. 'While I was there two Australian soldiers, Parker and Lang, passed through going to Nimes, I believe. The day before I left Pte. Edwards arrived.'[633]

Mills moved to the Nouveaus' flat on 9 May, where he met Captain H.B. O'Sullivan (see end of previous chapter). They left for Banyuls on 10 May, 'picking up Driver Bach and a Dutch officer at Narbonne'. Joined at Banyuls by two more Dutchmen, they crossed the Pyrenees with a French guide on the night of 10/11 May and, on 13 May as arranged, another man took them to Barcelona, where they found Lance-Corporal Sims (see previous chapter). 'Next day we were taken to Madrid by the Bishop of Gibraltar in his car.'

The day after they had met Sergeant Mills, Pat O'Leary took the Australians Lang and Parker to Nîmes (as Mills had thought), where they stayed for three weeks with Gaston Nègre, at his house at 2, rue Porte de France, and were joined by Private Edwards, who had also escaped to Switzerland, from Germany. Edwards and a Belgian officer were collected by a Swiss officer early on the morning of 6 May 1942, and driven to the French border. Crawling through three lots of barbed wire they were met by a guide, who took them to the station, where a married couple escorted them by train that evening to Marseille. At the Czechoslovak Institute in the rue de la République, they were met by Mario Prassinos and taken to a house for the night. Pat O'Leary took Edwards to Nîmes on 8 May, where he joined up with Lang and Parker, and Pat then took the three of them to Toulouse on 21 May.

At the Hôtel de Paris they briefly met Brigadier Roupell and Captain Gilbert before leaving for Osséja on 22 May. They crossed that same night into Spain but, due to a misunderstanding, were stranded for twenty-four hours in the mountains when the guide failed to materialise. When he did show up, he took the three soldiers by bus to a railway station, where they caught the train to Barcelona. They reached Gibraltar on 10 June, and England a month later.

On about 25 May Roupell, Gilbert and two guides were taken to a house in Banyuls, where they met Fusinski, Wacinski and Morawski and 'the rest of the party and left to cross the Pyrenees early next morning while it was still dark.'[634] On the train from Vilajuiga, however, while Brigadier Roupell was catching up on some well-earned rest, Captain Gilbert was asked for his papers. As they were not to the liking of the policeman, he and Roupell were arrested and taken to Gerona, tied together with string from their own parcels. In handcuffs, they were removed to the police station and confined to a small cell in filthy conditions with four to six other prisoners for a week.

There was an unpleasant incident during a big church parade when one of the warders ordered a couple of Belgians to give the Franco fascist salute. One of them refused, whereupon the whole party was marched before the commandant, who ordered that they should salute everyone. When Brigadier Roupell announced that they would not do this, the whole 'party was then put into two very small cells, four in each cell', where they remained for five days. Fortunately, the British Consul in Gerona had observed Roupell and Gilbert being marched away from the railway station and had set wheels in motion for their release. While the others of the party were removed to Miranda the two British officers were released to Barcelona, and sailed from Gibraltar for Gourock on 21 July 1942, together with Sergeant W. Czekalski PAF, and Sergeants R.J. Collins, B. F. Goldsmith and W.R. Griffiths RAF (see following chapter).

Fusinski, Wacinski and Morawski were removed to Miranda. Released after four and a half weeks into the care of an attaché from Madrid, they sailed from Gibraltar aboard a Royal Navy destroyer on 19 August. The two commandos, Lance-Corporal Eric Douglas and Private Victor Harding, sailed from Gibraltar on 20 August 1942, presumably also on a warship, for they arrived at the great naval base of Scapa Flow in the Orkneys six days later.

Following the Darling/Langley/O'Leary talks at Gibraltar, it was decided that large-scale "combined sea and air operations" would take place somewhere along the Gulf of Lyons using one of the Royal Navy's "cloak and dagger" boats then operating off the Mediterranean coast of France. First though, shortly after Langley had flown back to England, Operation Abloom was put in train – Pat O'Leary and his radio operator, Jean Ferière, were be put ashore on a deserted French beach at Canet-Plage, to the east of Perpignan. Taking them would be the Royal Navy's HMS *Tarana*.

HMS *Tarana*, a 347-ton, 150-foot long vessel, had been built in Rotterdam in 1932 as a motor trawler. She had begun her working life with the French company *Societé de Grande Pêche de Boulogne sur Mer*, but in June 1940, packed with troops and refugees, she sailed from France to Southampton. Requisitioned into the Royal Navy's Auxiliary Patrol she was manned by Royal Naval Patrol Service ratings from their Lowestoft depot. Taken off patrol duties once the invasion scare had died down later in 1940, she was sent to Portland dockyard, where a twelve-pounder gun was substituted for her trawling winch on the forecastle deck. Her skipper was Lieutenant Basil Ford RNVR, with Lieutenant Douglas William Sowden RNR (First Lieutenant) and Sub-Lieutenants Henry Philip Whiting RNVR and William George Warren RNVR as third and fourth officers.

A few days after the twelve-pounder had been mounted HMS *Tarana* sailed to Camper and Nicholson's Northam yard on Southampton Water. There her crew watched in amazement as the gun was removed and she was re-fitted as a "Q" ship. Her holds were gutted, cleaned and converted into living quarters, and two two-pounder guns were also mounted beneath her forecastle, hidden by drop screens. Her arsenal was further augmented by a number of machine-guns, mostly Hotchkiss, and other sub-machine guns. Once the alterations had been completed *Tarana* sailed to Portsmouth, where her new skipper, the 'bluff and unflappable'[635] Lieutenant-Commander Edward Burling Clark RD, RNR, came aboard. Appointed on 31 December 1941 "Nobby" Clark had some difficulty discovering much about his new command, for *Tarana* was listed only in the Royal Navy's *Pink List*, a top secret publication compiled 'at regular intervals in peace and war by the operations division of the admiralty'.[636]

With her refit having been completed in January 1942 Clark was ordered to sail *Tarana*, with her full complement of thirty-three officers and men, for Gibraltar. Negotiating the Bay of Biscay in a fierce storm *Tarana* arrived at her destination on a calm sea. While her crew sorted out the mess inside that had been caused by the storm artificers from the submarine-depot ship HMS *Maidstone* fitted a three-inch gun on her deck in place of a big trawl winch.

There was surprise all round when, in the middle of February, a full captain from the admiralty – Captain F.A. Slocum CMG, OBE, RN, Deputy Director Operations Division (Irregular) (DDOD(I)) – appeared on board. Slocum, 'a small dapper man with a deceptively mild manner',[637] told Clark that his job 'would be to land agents, pick up escapers and obtain all the information he could'[638] about what was going on in France. As Slocum left the ship, so a car pulled close alongside and out got 'two civilians, laden with cases' who 'were ushered hurriedly aboard and were taken directly to the wardroom.'[639] With a cheery 'Good luck, lads' from Captain Slocum, HMS *Tarana*, now on the strength of the Coast Watching Flotilla, set off on her maiden operation, Abloom.

Abloom was successfully completed on 18 April 1942 after Sub-Lieutenant Whiting and Seaman Ron Stephens had rowed Pat O'Leary and Jean Ferière ashore. There was a moment of panic, though, when just as the seamen were rowing away from the beach to the *Tarana* Ferière turned round and cried that he wanted to go back. But he had to go on, and he and Pat O'Leary made their way to the Hôtel du Tennis at Canet-Plage, run by Madame Chouquette (real name Lebreton), who 'always had a smile for Pat in her soft brown eyes'.[640]

Departing by train for Marseille two days later, O'Leary and Ferière were concerned as to how they were to get the bulky radio set[641] through the police checks at the other end. They need not have worried, for keeping a discreet eye on them was Gaston Nègre, who saw to it that the heavy wireless set was spirited out of Marseille station with no questions asked. Gaston, the owner of an apartment in Marseille and a large house and wholesale grocery store in Nîmes, worked wonders on the black market for Pat O'Leary and the organisation.

As previously seen Langley and O'Leary had both had doubts as to Ferière's usefulness as a radio operator, fears that were borne out by the incident at Canet-Plage and by him seeming 'to lose his nerve almost on arrival' at Marseille.[642] Now without an effective radio operator, O'Leary turned to Gaston Nègre: 'Characteristically he produced an unemployed radio operator who had once worked at the airport at Nîmes: a Frenchman called Roger.'[643] Unfortunately, Roger was arrested in April, caught in the very act of transmitting – just what Ferière had feared would happen to himself – and it was not until the night of 28/29 May 1942, during the moon period, that a replacement radio operator was sent, the one-eyed Belgian fighter pilot Alex Nitelet (see previous chapter).

Having heard that SOE were planning a pick-up in France Langley had found a seat aboard an outward-bound Lysander for Nitelet. Though no longer fit for flying duties he had trained as a radio operator and was keen to return to help the escape line. The pilot of the Lysander, Flight Lieutenant A.J. Mott, put the aircraft down in a field near the hamlet of le Grand Malleray, some twenty kilometres north of Châteauroux, in Unoccupied France. When the time came to take off John Mott found that the Lysander had stuck fast in boggy ground, and was unable to leave. All attempts to destroy the aircraft by fire failed, and what was left of it was removed by the Germans and exhibited 'in their museum of captured enemy equipment at Nanterre, near Paris, until they destroyed the museum during their retreat'[644] in the summer of 1944.

Once again Flight Lieutenant John Mott found himself evading in France (see Chapter 1). This time, though, he was captured by Vichy police at la Châtre-sur-le-Loir (Sarthe), and after a few months internment in Fort de la Revère, Fort de la Duchère (Lyon), and Camp de Chambaran (west of Grenoble), he was transferred with seven fellow officers to the Italian prisoner-of-war camp, P.G.5, near Genoa, on 6 December 1942. After the Italian armistice on 3 September 1943, the Germans took over the Italian camps and removed the prisoners by train to Germany. It took John Mott and fifteen fellow officers, in a cattle truck with no guard, three and a half hours on 15 September to make a hole in the end of the truck above the buffers. As the train wound its way north from Mantua in northern Italy, the officers jumped out two at a time. Most became separated in the darkness and confusion. At the end of September John Mott found himself in anti-Fascist hands at Schio, in the foothills of the Italian Dolomites.

Here he linked up with Captain R.F. Parrott,[645] who had also dropped off the same train on 15 September, and two South African soldiers. Provided with false papers the four of them decided to make for Yugoslavia. Escorted by bus to Vittorio Veneto, a guide took them into the mountains, where a priest gave them 100 lire and directions for Caporetto (now Kobarid) in Yugoslavia. They walked without a guide for several days, 'avoiding various bands of Fascists and getting information and food from Italian women on the way' before crossing 'the plain north of Udine, which took about four days,' and contacting 'the partisans in the foothills above Cividale'.[646]

The partisans, however, were taking no chances and, treating them as if they were Germans, took them to their headquarters. Convincing the partisans of their true identities, they were escorted to a similar Slav organisation based at Caporetto, where they arrived on 5 October. Another move brought them into contact with a Major Gibbon and a Major Ballantyne, 'who said it was not possible to continue for the moment and that the partisans wished us to join in with them. We were virtually prisoners in a Yugo Slav partisan strong point.' The delay was caused by considerable German anti-partisan activity in the area, but on 7 October, when the Germans bombed the area, John Mott and Captain Parrott seized the opportunity to escape. Meeting up with another partisan group on 8 October, they heard about a Captain J.M. Ratcliffe, whom they met on the following day, whose task was to organise a band of Italian partisans into a force for disrupting German lines of communication.

Mott and Parrott remained with him until the beginning of November 1943, Parrott with his army background helping to train the partisans.

One day Ratcliffe failed to return from a sortie and, as instructed for just such an eventuality, the band broke up into small groups. Parrott and Mott had hoped to rejoin Ratcliffe at the British Military Mission HQ near Gorizia, in the Istrian province of Italy, but on the way heard that Ratcliffe had been injured[647] and, as a German alpine division was making a determined effort against the locality, decided to head for their own lines on the Dalmatian Coast. After a week or so they came across a Flight Lieutenant Carmichael and two New Zealand expeditionary force captains, A.A. Yeoman and E. Wilson, who, with thirty other ranks, had joined a partisan group some thirty kilometres north-west of Ljubljana.

Again, movement from the area was difficult due to a strong enemy presence, and the Germans' strength manifested itself on the very next day, when a fierce attack forced the partisans and their group to take to the hills. The next ten days were spent avoiding German troops who were cleaning up the area by day and night. Splitting up into ones and twos, each officer taking one other ranker, the soldiers and airmen attempted to get through to Italy. Captain Parrott was recaptured,[648] but John Mott succeeded in reaching Italy. In February 1944, befriended by the Contessa Cancellucia, he and his fellow escapers purchased a boat, which they named *Pitch and Toss*, and made a hungry and hazardous voyage to Porto San Giorgio, near Monte Cassino, just as Mount Vesuvius blew its top on 22 March 1944.[649]

Alex Nitelet, meanwhile, after John Mott had deposited him in France on the night of 29/30 May 1942, made his way to 'Louis Nouveau's flat in Marseilles but he was a very shaken man and his first message was largely indecipherable... However, from then on he was a superb operator.'[650] Always on the move, to avoid radio-detection vans, he was given the nickname "Jean le Nerveux" (John the Restless), but on 1 September 1942 he, too, was arrested in almost farcical circumstances. Attending a supply drop with Gaston Nègre and a local café owner at 'a football ground outside Nîmes', the crew of the RAF Halifax making the drop had 'had difficulty in identifying the town and did three low runs over it before spotting the reception committee's recognition signals. The roar of the Halifax's four engines woke up everyone, including the chief of the police.'[651]

The gendarmerie were telephoned by a *garde-forestier* (ranger),[652] and even though it took them the best part of two hours to answer the call they still surprised the recovery party hard at work. The police also found a telephone number on one of the party, which led them to Paula Spriewald (see this chapter, below), who was already wanted by the Vichy police. She went to ground in a flat provided for her by Mario Prassinos in La Blancarde district of Marseille.[653]

Following Nitelet's arrest a fourth radio operator, Australian Tom Groome, 'dark, young, good-looking and full of a quiet zeal',[654] would eventually take Nitelet's place. O'Leary and his helpers, now that they had a reliable radio operator, were at last able to proceed with plans to evacuate by sea the large numbers of British servicemen interned or on the run in the south of France. They would also have the opportunity to spirit away those members of the escape lines who were *brûlé*. For some months, the Gibraltar-based "cloak and dagger" boats of the Coast Watching Flotilla had been operating along the Mediterranean coast, and it was now agreed that not only could they carry agents to France but that they could also take away evaders and escapers and any others whose lives were considered to be in danger.

The vessels detailed were HMS *Tarana* and two Polish-manned feluccas, 'ex-Portugese sardine boats named *Seadog* and *Seawolf*'.[655] Some forty-seven feet in length and displacing around twenty tons, each felucca was powered by a diesel engine of doubtful ability and by a single sail, and had a normal complement of seven. *Seawolf* had already been employed by the Polish Naval Mission of the Auxiliary Patrol in the evacuation of the many Poles who, 'having fled their own country in the hope of being able to continue the fight against the hated Germans, had got as far as the south of France.' They were commanded by two formidable and experienced Polish officers, Lieutenants Marian Kadulski[656] and Jan Buchowski, who had been carrying out clandestine operations to North Africa since July 1941.[657] The Poles, described by General Sikorski as being 'too rough even for the Polish Navy',[658] were commanded at Gibraltar by Lieutenant-Commander Durski of the Free Polish Navy, 'a delightful man, who had once served with the Austro-Hungarian naval forces in the Adriatic.'[659]

It was also at this time that the Air Ministry in London were anxious to effect the return to the United Kingdom of RAF prisoners in Vichy hands. Top of its list, at his own insistence, was fighter pilot and former international racing driver Squadron Leader Whitney Willard Straight MC, DFC, 'one of the most distinguished American-born RAF pilots, known throughout the world',[660] who had been shot down in his Hurricane attacking heavily armed E-boats off Le Havre on 31 July 1941. Sent to St Hippolyte-du-Fort, he had arrived there on 9 August 1941.

Airey Neave, in MI9's Room 900, recalled that 'hardly a day passed without a call from the Air Ministry or Crockatt. What news? What were we doing about him?' So important was he, and the other pilots apparently, that Brigadier Norman Crockatt gave a direct order 'that all possible steps were to be taken to prevent their falling into German hands.'[661] A plan was therefore drawn up in which HMS *Tarana* would evacuate sundry escapers and evaders, together with a small number of Frenchmen who were *brûlé* and in danger of arrest from either the Vichy or German police, from the beach at St Pierre-Plage, near Narbonne, in southern France. Wireless messages flew backwards and forwards between Marseille, Gibraltar and London arranging the finer details of the evacuation, which was scheduled for the night of 13/14 July 1942.

First, though, Pat O' Leary and his organisation had to rescue Squadron Leader Straight from the British section of the Pasteur hospital in Nice. Straight, who had already made several attempts to escape from captivity, had been passed "fit" for repatriation on medical grounds by Doctor Rodocanachi the previous year, and was at Perpignan with eight other repatriates awaiting the journey over to Spain when the French stopped the repatriation – apparently because the RAF had bombed the Renault works at Boulogne-Billancourt near Paris on the previous night.[662] Feigning sickness, some of it genuine, Straight was removed to the Pasteur hospital on 5 June 1942, and put into the same ward as Private C.G. Knight, 2nd Dorsets, and Stefan Miniakowski (see above, this chapter).

Deputed by O'Leary to get him out, Francis Blanchain enlisted the help of a nurse, Nicole Brugère, who gave him details of the hospital layout. She also told him that, as two soldiers had escaped from the hospital on 6 June, the guard had been strengthened, and that there were now 'two armed guards permanently on duty in the ward and four gendarmes patrolling outside the hospital.'[663] On 22 June, the day of the escape, the three patients, in Whitney Straight's own words, 'managed to confuse the guards and when one of them left the building, probably to telephone for help, we followed him quietly downstairs, and when he turned left I turned right and ran. Pte Knight and Sgt Miniakowski followed me, and by good luck we all managed to avoid the second guard within the building.'[664] As arranged, Blanchain was waiting for them, and took the three men to Dr Lévy at Juan-les-Pins. After three or four days with Dr Lévy, Blanchain took them to Nîmes and to the ever-obliging Gaston Nègre.[665]

Here they met Sergeant T.G. Johnson, who had been on the run since the night of 27/28 April 1942, having come down near Dunkirk in the north of France. His evasion came to a halt in Paris, where he remained for almost seven weeks before crossing into Unoccupied France. Taken by train to Gaston Nègre's house in Nîmes he spent only one night there with Straight and the others. After the next three days and nights at the Café du Soleil he returned for a further five with the hospitable Nègre.[666]

With Johnson still in Nîmes at the Café du Soleil, the Straight party was escorted to the Nouveaus' apartment in Marseille, which they reached on 27 June. They were joined, on 7 July, by SOE agent André Simon, who had been parachuted into France in April 1942, with the rank of flight lieutenant, 'with the delicate task of extracting Daladier by Lysander, a task he was quite unable to fulfil, because his prospective passenger had no desire to make the journey.' Simon then fell into Vichy police hands in Châteauroux on 26 May, but by pure chance was recognised by a general in whose unit Simon had served a dozen years earlier. Not only was Simon allowed to go, but the general also gave him 'a message from the Vichy general staff, that they only awaited instructions about how to get rid of the Germans.'[667]

Three more men arrived at the Nouveaus' flat on 9 July – Sergeants J. Beecroft and H.P. Hanwell; and Lieutenant Anthony Deane-Drummond, RCS, who had escaped from an Italian prisoner-of-war camp.

Deane-Drummond had been in a party of thirty-eight commandos of No. 2 Commando[668] who were dropped into southern Italy on the night of 10/11 February 1941 as part of Operation Colossus. The objective of this operation was two-fold – to blow up the Apulia aqueduct spanning the Tragino gorge 100 kilometres east of Naples, which, though not a major military target, nevertheless supplied fresh water to some two million people, including residents of the distant ports of Bari and Brindisi and the naval base at Taranto; and to see if the RAF could deliver men accurately to a distant enemy target.

Accordingly, eight Whitleys of 78 and 51 Squadrons departed RAF Mildenhall on the night of 7/8 February 1941 for an eleven-hour flight to RAF Luqa, Malta. Three nights later, two of the Whitleys created a diversion by bombing Foggia marshalling yards while the other six, under the command of Wing Commander J.B. "Willie" Tait DFC, headed for the aqueduct. Five of the six Whitley aircraft successfully dropped their quota of commandos close to the target. The sixth, however, suffering navigational problems, dropped Captain G.F.K. Daley, RE, most of his small detachment of engineers, who were to provide the explosive expertise, and, unfortunately, much of the mission's explosives two hours late and three kilometres to the north in the next valley. One man, Lance-Sergeant Dennis, was drowned when he landed in a lake.

Having done what little damage they could do to the aqueduct with the limited amount of explosives that came to hand, the commandos set off overland to the mouth of the River Sele, marching some eighty kilometres away on the Mediterranean coast south of Salerno, to rendezvous with the British submarine *Triumph*. By mischance one of the Whitleys, having suffered an engine failure, chose this very spot on which to make a forced landing, thereby attracting considerable attention and forcing the captain of the submarine to abandon the rendezvous.[669] It mattered not, however, for the commandos never reached the coast. Winter conditions had forced them off the hills and onto the roads and passing through a small town they found themselves surrounded by hostile civilians and police. Rather than fire upon civilians, the commandos surrendered.[670]

John Beecroft and Henry Hanwell, the other two to arrive at the Nouveaus' flat on 9 July, had been on their way to Mannheim on the night of 19/20 May 1942 when the port engine of their Wellington, X3472, failed. Beecroft (pilot) ordered the bombs to be jettisoned but, unable to maintain height, put X3472 down in a field near Sedan in north-east France. The crew – Beecroft, Hanwell, and Sergeants S. Bradley, J.P. Love and A. Crichton – decided that they would make for Switzerland, and were within two miles of the border by nightfall on 15 June.

On 16 June a farmer took them to the Gorges du Doubs, at the point where the River Doubs forms the border with Switzerland. The only way across was by swimming. Love and Crichton, though, were non-swimmers, and were taken prisoner after leaving to find a suitable crossing place elsewhere. Beecroft, Hanwell and Bradley, meanwhile undressed, put their clothes on a log and set off across the river. With Beecroft and Hanwell alternately pushing the log, they reached the far bank, but without Bradley. Turning to look for him, Beecroft and Hanwell watched helplessly as their comrade disappeared below the surface.[671]

After a few days rest at the Salvation Army hostel in Geneva, Beecroft and Hanwell met with Victor Farrell, who advised them on their journey through France and Spain: 'Detailed instructions for Marseilles were as follows: Proceed to 37, rue de la Republique – ask for the Commandant – say we had come from "Bremen" – and ask to see M. PEO. This was to be said out of hearing of the guide or any one else.'[672]

Their departure from Switzerland was arranged for them and, with Lieutenant Deane-Drummond, they were escorted across the border into France. From Annemasse railway station their guide, Georges, took them to Marseille, where they arrived at around 6 a.m. on 8 July, leaving the station by the baggage office and a side entrance. They went to the café as instructed, but it was not until around 10 a.m. that another guide appeared, and took them 'to a flat where we met two women. The original instructions as given by Mr Farrell in Geneva were not carried out.' The two women then took the men to the Nouveaus' flat, where they stayed for two days. On Sunday, 12 July, Madame Nouveau took them to the railway station, where they were contacted by Pat O'Leary, under whose watchful eye they caught the 8 a.m. train to Narbonne. Leaving the train at Béziers, before Narbonne, they waited half an hour in the station buffet before catching a local train to Coursan. It was a two-hour walk from there to St Pierre-sur-Mer on the coast, fifteen kilometres away. 'It was dark when we arrived and we contacted six other escapers here. Among them were W/Cdr. J.W. [*sic*] Straight and Lieut. Deane-Drummond.'[673]

Now all they had to do was await the arrival of HMS *Tarana* in what would be her first evacuation for PAO, under the codename Operation Bluebottle I. Lieutenant Deane-Drummond recalled the moment:

> 'At last the day came for our departure and, in two parties, we made our way to the station and boarded a train for the west. We changed trains once at a small station [Béziers], then at about 4 p.m. arrived at our destination about fifty [*sic*] miles from Marseilles and quite close to the sea. Our guides took us along different routes, but eventually we all met at our rendezvous in a small wood a few hundred yards from the Mediterranean. In addition to those of us that had come from Marseilles, two more parties of RAF arrived at our wood before nightfall, to make a total of eight British with half a dozen French guides.'[674]

One of the RAF "parties" was Sergeant Johnson, who had been brought from Nîmes by a man he knew only as "Joseph".[675] Johnson remembers that Deane-Drummond and a Flight Sergeant Seymour were also on the train to Coursan with their guide: 'From Coursan we walked to St Pierre sur Mer and hid up outside the town for a day and a night.'[676] As they hid in the wood close to the sea, the six airmen and two soldiers were joined by Leoni Savinos and by his German wife Emy. Leoni had been arrested by the Gestapo in Paris in April 1942 with Frenchman Pierrot Lanvers but, incredibly, he had bluffed his way out of their grasp, and out of Fresnes prison, by pretending to be a double agent. Released to act as a spy for the Germans in Marseille, he and his wife were immediately placed on the evacuation list. Going with them, too, was Lanvers who, though horribly beaten by his captors, had been released thanks to yet more bluff by Savinos – if he, Savinos, were to be a good agent for the Germans surely, he argued, he would need someone to assist him, and who better than Lanvers? The Germans let him go.

Shortly after midnight, under a moonless sky, the party of evacuees, their spirits high, made their way in single file, scrambling over rocks, to the beach at St Pierre to await the boat, and spread out at 100-metre intervals 'in order to see better the light signal from the ship, which was expected at 2 a.m. During this wait some fishermen pushing a boat on a trolley passed us but did not see us.' At precisely 2 a.m. on 13 July Beecroft saw two blue flashes out to sea, the signal that they had all been so anxiously awaiting. Pat O'Leary pulled out his torch, fitted with a blue filter, and signalled back. After what seemed an eternity to those waiting on shore, though it was little more than an hour, a rowing boat appeared, with one man in it and one set of oars. He found it impossible to row back to the *Tarana* with anyone else on board, but when the rowing boat reappeared manned by Sub-Lieutenant Whiting and Able Seaman Ron Stephens matters progressed more quickly.

Observing the comings and goings from HMS *Tarana* was SOE agent Richard Heslop (see Chapter 2), patiently waiting the time to be transferred to another boat and to be dropped off on the French coast somewhere. He was amazed to see, in the third boatload of evacuees to be brought alongside, André Simon 'my friend and conducting officer from Beaulieu, and the man who told SOE I was good enough to be an agent. He was with two [*sic*] RAF officers, one of whom was Squadron Leader Whitney Straight, the racing driver.'[677]

With everyone aboard, HMS *Tarana* then headed off to meet *Seawolf*. The following day *Tarana* ran into a storm, a not uncommon feature of the Gulf of Lyon at that time of the year, but this was one of the worst ever seen: 'The seas became so mountainous and the trawler's motions so violent that at times only the upper part of the bridge seemed to be clear of the waves.'[678] Even the most hardened of sailors were reduced to seeking sanctuary below decks. It was two days before the storm abated, allowing *Tarana* to at last make the pre-arranged rendezvous with *Seawolf*, which had returned from another part of the French coast with fifty-two Poles. These were now transferred to the larger vessel, while *Seawolf* in exchange took Emilio Lussu, Joyce Salvadori, Richard Heslop together with his 'six canisters of explosives, five suitcases, two packages' and money, and "Leroy", Heslop's partner, and dropped them off along the coast towards Juan-les-Pins and Antibes.

Before *Tarana* arrived safely at Gibraltar some thirty-six hours later, however, it was all hands to the paint pot. It was the practice for the trawler to sail from Gibraltar late in the evening looking for all the world like a ship of the Royal Navy – black hull, grey upper works and flying the White Ensign – and, once at sea, to be painted to look like an ordinary fishing boat. With the shape of the funnel altered and fishing gear strewn around the decks, she flew the Portuguese flag. Now, as they neared Gibraltar, it was time for *Tarana* to be restored to her Royal Navy colours, and Lieutenant-Commander "Nobby" Clark 'announced that to-night would be "painting night". It was the thirteenth complete coat of paint that he had given his little ship in four months, and by morning we had to be a nice grey HM Trawler in all its glory with White Ensign flying… Everybody was dished out a pot of grey paint and a brush, and all night we painted, till by 4 a.m. the transformation had been completed…'[679]

After the passengers had been vetted at Gibraltar, passage was found for most of them aboard the *Llanstephan Castle*, which departed on 24 July and berthed at Gourock on the Clyde, Scotland, on 30 July.[680] The more important squadron leader was flown back to England aboard a Sunderland, together with several heroes of Malta,[681] flying on to RAF Hendon on 25 July 1942.

The *Tarana* was soon off again on another trip to the French coast, picking up a party of eight from St Pierre-Plage during the night of 15/16 August 1942 (Operation Bluebottle II), having earlier that night landed six agents near Agde (Operation Bull). In the Bluebottle II party of eight were a woman; five other foreigners (among them double-agent Henri Déricourt); and two RAF airmen – Sergeant J.E. Misseldine and Pilot Officer D.J. Perdue, who had been shot down on 1 April 1942.

Perdue was being sheltered on a farm near Ste Opportune-la-Mare in Normandy when he received a visit from the Anglophile mayor. As luck would have it, the mayor knew of an English governess in the area, and it was arranged that she should write to her brother in England letting him know of Perdue's situation. The letter eventually made its way to Switzerland in the hands of a friend of a friend, and on 10 August no less a person than Louis Nouveau arrived at the farm and announced to

Perdue that 'he had come to take me home. He had been notified from London and had got in touch with the governess who had sent him to the Mayor.'[682] Next day Louis took Perdue to Paris, and thence by train to Libourne, east of Bordeaux, for the crossing of the Demarcation Line.

Reaching Marseille by the night train on 14 August Perdue spent the night in Louis's apartment before taking another train to Coursan, one stop short of Narbonne. They walked for some fifteen kilometres to a place near the coast 'where we hid in a thicket for four or five hours. While there we were joined by Sgt. Misseldine.'

John Misseldine had come to grief on 8 June 1942 after his Spitfire was hit by a Messerschmitt 109 in a brawl over St Omer and had burst into flames, burning him in the face. After eighteen days at Aire-sur-la-Lys (Pas-de-Calais) John left on 29 June with a young Belgian, Albert Mestdagh, whom he had met at Aire-sur-la-Lys. They made their way via Paris to Tours and then across the Demarcation Line, heading for the village of Penne some thirty kilometres east of Montauban. John had been told at a lecture at RAF Kenley that in the event of being shot down he should make his way there. He 'was to find the master of the village' and 'to ask for Donald or his wife Clara.' Finally arriving at Penne, neither John nor Albert could make anyone understand what they were after. 'As we obviously were arousing suspicion, we discontinued our search and put up for the night at an inn in Penne.'[683]

It was the innkeeper who advised the pair to try contacting an American in Montauban, but when they got there they found that he had left for the USA two months previously. Further advice led them to the American Quaker Institute in the town, and from there they were put in touch with a Monsieur Cheramy, who lived at 13, rue de la Fraternité. Charles Cheramy and his English-born wife Maud Eleanor, née Hawkins but always known as Pat, were to give him shelter until 25 July. Pat, on the other hand, was not sure of Albert, and so he was placed in a local hotel.

Pat had a strong personality and was not to be put off when John turned down the suggestion that a cablegram should be sent to his home in England informing his parents that he was alive. A suitably worded cable was sent, on 9 July, as if it were news of the arrival of a baby. Unbeknownst to the occupants of Number 13 the cablegram *did* reach John's home in west London and his mother had duly made contact with the Air Ministry. They in turn had arranged for a message to be passed on to the PAT line in Marseille, with the result that on 25 July Mario Prassinos appeared at 13, rue de la Fraternité asking for John by name. Once Pat was satisfied that Mario was genuine she let him in. Wasting no time, he took John off with him on the night train to Gaston Nègre's home in Nîmes. There, in Gaston's large apartment (it had seven or eight bedrooms), John kicked his heels until he was collected on 15 August and taken, as were the others, to Coursan and St Pierre-Plage.

A week after she had left St Pierre-Plage HMS *Tarana* dropped anchor at Gibraltar, having in the meantime undergone the change from a working trawler to a grey-painted ship of the Royal Navy. Then, after a long, nine-day sea voyage, the airmen, and Déricourt, were landed at Gourock on 8 September.

Travelling back with them was Sergeant A.R. Evans, who had been shot down near the target (Dunkirk) in France on 27 April 1942. He was lucky to survive, for not only did he get hit by flak splinters in the leg and back but he was also machine-gunned as he descended beneath his parachute. As a result of bullets tearing the canopy he landed heavily, breaking a bone in an ankle. Finding help, he was sheltered locally until 26 May, when he was taken to Calais and put in the hands of the PAO line. He was in Paris on 11 July, and four days later was handed over to Louis Nouveau at a métro station, where he 'also met a Belgian, Georges Van Lear. We three went by train to Libourne. It was M. Nouveau's first trip by this route and he appeared to be very nervous.'[684] All went well, however, and the three crossed the Demarcation Line without incident. After a couple of days Evans and Van Lear were taken to Nîmes, and to the home of Gaston Nègre, while Louis Nouveau continued to Marseille.

After two days in Nîmes, Evans and Van Lear went to Toulouse, where they met "Joseph" (Pat O'Leary). A Spanish guide was arranged and, though there was a slight hiccup when the two escapers were unable to find the guide as arranged at the Latour-de-Carol railway station, the man was located further down the line at Osséja, barely two kilometres from the Spanish border. The Spaniard found another guide to take them over the Pyrenees. 'On our way we were joined by another Englishman and a Belgian.'

Another airman whose return was also desired by the Air Ministry was Flight Lieutenant F.W. "Taffy" Higginson DFM,[685] who had been brought to Marseille by Harold Cole on 2 July 1941 (see previous chapter). Arrested a fortnight later at Banyuls-sur-Mer as he was making his way to Spain, he was charged with possession of a false identity card and was thrown into Perpignan jail under the assumed name of Captain Basil Bennett RAOC. So bad were conditions there that when he was transferred to St Hippolyte-du-Fort after serving only half of his six months' sentence he had lost over two stone in weight, and was very ill. Passed by a Medical Board for repatriation he was one of the forty-three, along with Whitney Straight, whose exit visas were revoked by Vichy after the bombing of the Renault-Billancourt works in March 1942. He was moved to Fort de la Revère on 17 March, with most of Detachment W.

Sergeant Derrick Nabarro RAF, who had escaped from a German prisoner-of-war camp on 25 November 1941, wrote of his arrival at the fort, built in Napoleonic times on solid rock, with walls two feet thick:

> 'The old fort was surrounded by arc lamps and masses of barbed wire on both sides of a deep dry moat. We walked across the drawbridge. Our footsteps rang hollowly. We were led into the bowels of the fort, through three cast-iron gates, each of which was unlocked and relocked. At last we were shown into a corridor from which branched four rooms, each containing twenty beds, twenty straw palliasses and forty damp blankets… As far as concrete, barbed wire and iron bars could ensure, the fort was escape-proof. There was a deep dry moat, lit by arc lights at night. There were iron gates and heavy locks on all the corridors and most of the rooms.'[686]

Events were to prove, however, that the fort was not escape-proof. On 18 August 1942, when it was learnt that all the officers at the fort were to be transferred to Italy in a week's time, Higginson decided that it was high time to escape, and through the good offices of Father Myrda and Vladimir Bouryschkine ("Val") he was able to contact Pat O'Leary. Father Myrda, a Polish priest, was permitted access to the prison to conduct religious services, whereas Bouryschkine, born of Russian parents in 1913 and erstwhile coach of the Monaco basketball team, was appointed physical training instructor to the prisoners. Both were useful as messengers and carriers of illicit hardware – hacksaw blades and the like – and, with their help, the breakout was planned for the night of 23 August 1942. Pat O'Leary arranged for this information to be transmitted to London.

It was agreed that five airmen – Flight Lieutenant Higginson; Flight Lieutenant M.G. Barnett RNZAF; Flying Officer B.L.G. Hawkins;[687] Derrick Nabarro; and Sergeant H. I. Hickton RNZAF – would make the break at around 9 p.m., an hour before roll call, when the guards were known to be at their quietest. Under cover of a noisy concert, they would descend via a coal chute in the officers' room into the kitchen below, a drop of twelve feet or so. The top of the chute was secured by a locked grill, and there was a barbed-wire entanglement in the shaft itself. Half-inch bars secured the kitchen window. A key for the grill had been made by Sergeant M.H.J. Dalphond RCAF (see previous chapter), and the window bars would be sawn through and access gained to the moat, some twenty-five feet below, via a rope made from Red Cross parcel string. From the moat they then had to make their way through a sewer which, hopefully, would lead to the outside where their guides – the one-eyed Alex Nitelet and Tony Friend[688] – should be waiting for them. The possibility of the sewer being used as an exit from the fort had been noticed by the Reverend Caskie one day as he laboured up the hill by a stream: 'Almost hidden by a large overhanging bush, the exit to the sewer was to be seen overlooking the burn. I gazed into the fetid aperture, shone my torch and recognised its obvious route. It must come from the camp.'[689]

Flight Lieutenant Matthew Garry Barnett had been shot down near Abbeville whilst on a fighter sweep late on the evening of 31 May 1942. So badly was his Spitfire damaged that the engine fell out before he himself was out of the aircraft. He landed in a small clump of trees and made his getaway in the direction of Paris. With help along the route he crossed the Demarcation Line on the night of 5/6 June, but was arrested as he made his way to the railway station at la Réole (Gironde), south-east of Bordeaux. He was well treated and, after a half-hearted interrogation at Toulouse, was escorted by two gendarmes to Nice. 'I could easily have escaped, but I was told by them, as I had understood also from lectures in England, that escape from a French Internment Camp was a matter of no difficulty whatever.'[690] He arrived at Fort de la Revère on 11 June.

Tension mounted as the time for the escape neared, and increased even more when one of the guards wandered into the sergeants' room trying to sell bread at twenty cigarettes per loaf. He was told to clear off but, before doing so, noticed that Nabarro and Hickton were fully dressed. 'Where are you two going?' he asked. 'Off to Nice for the night!' replied Nabarro laughing. Despite the untimely interruption the escape began at around 10.15 pm on 23 August and proceeded more or less on schedule, and after one or two scares – the grill wouldn't budge easily, the barbed wire proved troublesome, a hacksaw blade snapped – the five men emerged, after an hour and a half, through the stinking sewer onto the hillside, fifty feet below the fort and two thousand or more above Monte Carlo.

Their departure was noticed within ten minutes despite the noise of the concert, and the escapers saw the fort's lights come on as they sped towards Monte Carlo. In the chaos of their descent in the darkness they took a wrong turning and found themselves too far south, at Cap d'Ail instead of Monte Carlo. In the morning Brian Hawkins, who had a good identity card, was despatched to make contact with the PAO organisation. This he successfully accomplished, and that afternoon the airmen 'were taken to Monte Carlo where we were hidden in a flat belonging to Mr Turner, a hairdresser, in London who is unaware that his flat is being used for this purpose.'[691] The flat may have been on the Boulevard de Grande Bretagne, one used by a Miss May Arathoon who, with her sister June, was to hide many escapers from Fort de la Revère.

As the whole area was buzzing with police the airmen remained in the flat for a few days, being well looked after by a Madame Guiton. New clothes were provided, and Pat O'Leary produced identity cards for them all. Also helping escapers at this time was Miss Eve Sarah Trenchard, a Scotswoman who had lived in the area for the best part of twenty years and who ran The Scotch Tea House.[692] On 28 August "Jacques" took the men to Dr Rodocanachi's flat in Marseille.

Soon after the five RAF men had gone, work began on a tunnel in the fort which was for the most part dug by the British soldiers. It started at a point where the men's bathing quarters were inset into the outer wall: 'We made a hole in this wall that came out half way down and behind an archway in the moat that hid us from the view of the sentry on a bridge over the moat. It took twenty of us a week to make the hole with spoons, knives and forks whenever we got the chance.'[693]

It was decided that the prisoners, both army and RAF, should escape in small, mixed parties and make their way to the "safe houses" in the immediate area, the addresses of which had been supplied by Pat O'Leary and his organisation. On the night of 5/6 September 1942, therefore, thirty-seven soldiers and twenty-one airmen slipped through the tunnel, among them Sgt J. Miller RAF:

> 'At Fort de la Revère at about 2000 hours on 5 September 1942 I was in charge of a party of eight in an organised mass escape when fifty-seven prisoners of war got out of the camp. The leaders were given addresses to make for. We were living in a third part of an old fort and a tunnel was dug into the disused part under the separating wall. We went through in parties at half-hourly intervals.
>
> 'My party consisted of myself, Sgt Dowty, and Sgt Cobb RAF and five army personnel, Cook, Lynes, McKay, Donnelly and Parker. Just after we had got into the disused part of the fort and across the dry moat the alarm was given. Through the night we hid in the woods, and I decided that the party was too large, so having two addresses I took Parker aside and told him to take Lynes, McKay and Donnelly to an address in Monte Carlo…'[694]

Miller and his group tried to get to their appointed address in Nice but 'were unable to cross the main highway owing to mobile patrols, and in the late afternoon we were arrested in the woods by the Garde Mobile.' Miller, Dowty, Cobb and Cook, by choosing the other address, were fated to spend the next two and a half years in prisoner-of-war camps in Italy, Austria and Germany.[695]

Sergeant C.R. Mort, leader of another group of eight escapers, also fell into the hands of the police. Following instructions, Mort and Private J.N. Luckhurst, Green Howards, made their way to the Promenade des Anglais, Nice: 'Here I was to follow it for three blocks past a certain casino and then, by various turnings, reach a house. Whilst on the promenade, my companion and I, Pte. Lockhurst [*sic*], were stopped by four civilians on bicycles. They showed us police badges and demanded our papers. As we had none they took us to the police station.'[696]

Altogether, fifteen of the twenty-one RAF escapers were caught, among them Sergeants J.W. McLarnon and R.D. Porteous RNZAF, from the same 12 Squadron crew (see Chapter 7), and spent the rest of the war in Italian and German hands. The six RAF sergeants to get away were: P.S.F. Browne RNZAF; Dalphond; A.W. Mills; Leslie Pearman; R.W.A. Saxton (of the same crew as McLarnon and Porteous); and Douglas Walsh (see previous chapter). Nineteen of the thirty-seven army escapers reached safety, though Private W. McMullen RASC was shot in the cheek and apprehended, apparently as he tried to crawl through the barbed-wire fence.

Due to the intense police activity following the break it took Mervyn Dalphond and his party six days to get to their safe house in Nice, the home of a Pole named Robert Kliks who, with his family, 'had turned their house into a reception centre for the underground railway now operating in that section of France.'[697] The massive police hunt also made it impossible for the PAO organisation to move all the escapers to Marseille immediately. It was, for example, another six days before Dalphond and his companions were taken to Marseille, where they were met by Paula Spriewald. Sergeant Leslie Pearman, though, having already been on the run for a week, was forced to wait a further three weeks at the home of Monsieur Bos de Clariale at 40, Boulevard d'Italie, Monte Carlo, before his turn came. He had escaped with Mills; Walsh; Corporal A. Howarth, Grenadier Guards, No. 2 Commando (see above, endnote 630); and Driver F. McFarlane, RASC, with instructions to go to the *Sanctuaire de Notre-Dame-de-Laghet*.

They reached the monastery on the morning of 7 September, having spent a night in the hills: 'Here, however, we received no help; we therefore remained for three days in the hills under the care of a young French farm worker.'[698] Thanks to the young Frenchman's help, they were put in touch with Pat O'Leary's group, and taken to 40, Boulevard d'Italie. While some of the others were moved on, Les Pearman stayed there until 24 September. After a further eight days in another flat, wearing civilian clothes and armed with false papers provided by PAO, Les and eleven others were moved in small groups to Marseille on 2 October 1942. Two days later, under Pat O'Leary's direction, they set off for Canet-Plage, but had a further eight days to wait before the arrival of the boat that was to evacuate them to Gibraltar.

The 213 men left behind at Fort de la Revère after the breakout were transferred north by train on 22 September to Camp de Chambaran (Isère), several kilometres west of Grenoble. On 2 October they were reunited with the eight officers from Fort de la Revère (seven airmen and Lieutenant W.M. Hewit RA) who had been moved to Fort de la Duchère, Lyon, on 25 August, accompanied by five army privates as orderlies.[699]

In November 1942, after the Germans had occupied the whole of France, Lieutenant-Commander R.M. Prior RN wrote to the local French military commander, Colonel Malraison, suggesting that the internees be released as some of them would probably be shot when the Germans got there. Having consulted with the commandant of Camp de Chambaran, Chef de Bataillon Tournier, Malraison approved the release on humanitarian grounds of nine of the officers – Captain A.R. Cooper; Lieutenant Richard Henry Heslop ("Xavier"), Devon Regiment; Lieutenant Denis Joseph Rake ("Justin"), General List; and Flying Officer E. Wilkinson ("Alexandre"), all four SOE officers; Alex Nitelet; Lieutenant A.A. Masson, Royal Canadian Artillery (from the Dieppe raid); Sergeant W.H. Allen, 19 Army Field Survey Company, RE; Sergeant H.J. Foster, 1st South Lancashires; and Lieutenant-Commander R.M. Prior, Royal Navy. Their "escape" was arranged for, and duly took place, on 27 November.

Prior and Masson made their way to the Reverend Donald Caskie in Grenoble, and on to Perpignan, crossing to Spain in early December. Heslop, Wilkinson and Cooper were taken several kilometres in a lorry before setting off on foot for le Puy-en-Velay (Haute-Loire) over 150 kilometres west. After a couple of days Cooper found the going difficult, being bothered by an old wound in the right knee, and at a sign saying 'St. Victor, 8 kilometres' they parted. Cooper asked Heslop and Wilkinson, knowing that they were making for a transmitter, to tell London 'that GB 9000 is free and will try to contact them later.'[700] Twelve years in the French Foreign Legion, and fluent in French, Italian and four other languages, Cooper made his way to Marseille, travelling for the last part of the journey with a column of Italian soldiers. He had been told by Polish soldiers at Chambaran that in Marseille the Petit Poucet café, near the Alles de Meillan, was "safe" and so went there: 'My luck was in. Sitting at a table in the right-hand corner were three men whom I recognised: Bob Milton and Lt. Hewitt, fellow prisoners at Chambaran, and one of the guards from the camp.'[701]

Milton and Hewit had also been allowed to escape from Camp de Chambaran, on 28 November 1942, as Milton noted: 'We had secured the co-operation of a French lieutenant and a French sergeant. From them we obtained the badges and stripes necessary to convert our clothes into passable imitations of French uniforms. Accompanied by the sergeant, we walked past the guard and out of the camp, where we were met by the lieutenant who took us to a house nearby.'[702] Supplied with 'civilian clothes, forged identity cards and false immobilisation papers', in early December the commandant's chauffeur drove them in his car to the railway station at St Marcellin, where they caught the train to Marseille, arriving there the day before Captain Cooper.

Rake, whom Heslop and Wilkinson erroneously believed had been responsible for their arrests in Limoges several months earlier, also made his way to Marseille, probably with the two NCOs, Allen and Foster, and with Nitelet. Allen in his report, however, mentions that he travelled with Foster, Nitelet and 'a Frenchman called Nardin'.[703] Catching the train to Perpignan, these four left on 6 December, again by train, to Villefranche, where they took the light mountain railway to Saillagouse (Pyrénées-Orientales), and crossed into Spain on the morning of 7 December.

The escape of the eleven men from Camp de Chambaran was timely for, on 6 December 1942, all the remaining officers and men were transferred to prisoner-of-war camps in Italy, the officers to Campo P.G. 5 (Gavi) and other ranks to Campo P.G. 73 (Carpi). There they remained until Italy's capitulation in September 1943, when the great majority of them were seized by the Germans and taken to camps in the Third Reich for the remainder of the war.

With so many escapers from Fort de la Revère it was planned to evacuate them from Canet-Plage on the night of 20/21 September, three nights before the full moon. Detailed to carry out the pick-up was the felucca *Seawolf* (Lieutenant Marian Kadulski, alias Krajewski), which would, in addition to the Canet-Plage operation (Titania), also be undertaking Operations Falstaff and Nectarine I and II.

With their guides, the escaping airmen and soldiers took the train to Perpignan on 19 September, Mario Prassinos looking after the Higginson party. Nabarro recorded the scene as some twenty-seven passengers alighted onto the station platform: 'Most of them were wearing new suits. At the barrier every face that turned in our direction was familiar… I tried hard to keep my features straight... Hicky coughed into a handkerchief, I could see his shoulders shaking. There were many other familiar faces – Owens was there, so was Bob Saxton.'[704]

So too were the entire crew of a 138 (Special Duties) Squadron Whitley that had come to grief on the night of 24/25 August – Squadron Leader H.A. Outram; Pilot Officer L. Wilson; Pilot Officer E.R.W. Wood DFM; Flight Lieutenant H.L. Holliday; and Sergeant G.F. Foster – and also three French-Canadian soldiers left behind after the Dieppe raid on 19 August 1942 – Privates Guy Joly, Conrad Lafleur and Robert Vanier.[705]

Lafleur and Joly were in A Company, Les Fusiliers Mont-Royal Regiment, 6 Brigade, 2 Canadian Division, and Vanier in D Company, the two companies landing at Dieppe on Red Beach only yards apart from each other. Lafleur, a printer and truck driver in peacetime, was wounded by shell fragments in his left leg, and Vanier by a bullet in the back. Though Joly was unwounded he nevertheless ended up on the same hospital train as the other two, which departed from Rouen for Germany on 24 August 1942. It did not take the three men long to decide to escape.

'Owing to the serious condition of the majority of prisoners of war, each carriage was entrusted to the care of an unarmed German orderly, occasionally assisted by less seriously wounded prisoners of war.'[706] A few minutes before midnight, therefore, they told one of the German orderlies that they would look after the sick and wounded if he wanted to retire for the night. This, the orderly was only too happy to do. Now alone in the carriage, the Canadians set about removing the three clamps that held together the concertina panels between their carriage and the next. It was the work of a moment to undo the clamps and to slip through a gap in the panel that they had made. Standing on the buffers they jumped off the train as it made its way through a wood. On the following day they were 'put in touch with an organisation' – the PAO line – and brought to Canet-Plage.

Seawolf, meanwhile, had weighed anchor at Gibraltar after dark on 11 September 1942 carrying, apart from the crew of ten, two agents (one male, one female) on Operation Falstaff. An engine failure early on the morning of 13 September slowed their progress, and on 15 September an Italian aircraft inspected the felucca, which had only just been repainted in its fishing colours. Just in case, Krajewski ordered the two agents to keep out of sight below decks, and soon after midnight on 17 September they were landed by dinghy at a spot near la Ciotat, several kilometres east of Marseille. Operation Falstaff was now completed.

Early on 19 September *Seawolf* arrived at Sormiou, just round the corner from Marseille, for Operation Nectarine I, to pick up thirty-one Poles (three of whom turned out to be British), and on 20 September collected a further twenty-five from Calanque d'En-Vau (Nectarine II). The heavily laden *Seawolf* now headed off to the mouth of the River Tet, which flows into the Mediterranean east of Perpignan, to meet the PAO party. The rendezvous at Canet-Plage was made with some difficulty, as Krajewski later reported:

> 'Since all the lights are shining on that stretch of the French coast, I based our approach to the coast – which lacks any features by which to find one's bearings in the dark – on the red light of a fishing village and "port" some 4 km away to the north.[707] At 0030 hours, moving along the coast, which was lit up almost like daytime, we noticed the flashing of a light from a point that bore some resemblance to the agreed meeting point. THEY WERE HOWEVER IRREGULAR SIGNALS. After checking the position of a fort about ½ km distant, I realised that it was one more case of unfortunate signalling from the land side. Our astonishment was all the greater when, after heaving to, WE HEARD CRIES AND SINGING AND SAW LAMPS BEING LIT among the party of people who were to be embarked. One even swam out towards us…'[708]

Horrified by this dangerous display, Krajewski was to discover, as the passengers embarked on *Seawolf*, not the fifteen persons whom he had expected but twenty-nine, who told him that his boat had been visible up to a mile off shore! His new arrivals were twenty-three Britons; four Frenchmen; one Russian ('the son of an emigrant'); and one Czech woman ('or rather "Sudeten"'). Everyone had to be accommodated on deck, Krajewski noted, 'except the woman, a wounded Canadian (from the Dieppe raid), a wounded Pole and a wounded airman (who had been carrying out Special Operations flights and had had an accident on one of his missions).'[709]

André Postel-Vinay was at Canet-Plage too. It is not recorded whether or not he recognised Sergeants Saxton and Hickton, but when these two had been in hiding in the village of Channay-sur-Lathan (Indre-et-Loire) in September 1941 'a boy went to Paris and got in touch with André Postel-Vinay (now in Gibraltar). This man was in touch with Capt. Garrow's organisation.' André arranged for the two evaders to go to Paris on 25 September. Saxton stayed at the home of Comte Pierre d'Harcourt before André escorted him and his pilot, Pilot Officer P.F. Allen, on 1 October to Vierzon. Hickton, who stayed at several houses, was also escorted to Vierzon, with fellow crew member Sergeant J.R.W. Christensen, by André three days later.

After a brief stay with Louis Nouveau in Marseille Saxton was arrested on 17 October as he tried to cross the Pyrenees. After a brief stop in Marseille Hickton and Christensen were taken by Bruce Dowding on 7 October to Nîmes, where they 'stayed for two days at the house of a rich Frenchman called Gaston Nègre.' Dowding then took the pair to Canet-Plage where, on about 10 October, they met Allen, Saxton, and Pilot Officer J. Zulikowski, a Polish Spitfire pilot who had been shot down on 28 June 1941. A week later, all posing as deaf mutes, they had got as far as Mont-Louis (Pyrénées-Orientales), close to the Spanish border, when suspicions were aroused by members of the gendarmerie. Allen, Christensen and Zulikowski managed to slip away in the confusion, but Saxton and Hickton were arrested. They were well treated and told that if they ever escaped again they should quietly call on the commandant of the gendarmerie at Perpignan (Monsieur Prum) who would personally find a guide to take them over the Pyrenees. On 20 October they were sent to St Hippolyte, and on 17 March 1942 transferred to Fort de la Revère.

Now, in September 1942, still weak and fragile after his appalling time in the hands of the Paris Gestapo, André Postel-Vinay had been accompanied to Perpignan by Georges Zarifi, who was himself to escape to Spain in April 1943. Also *brûlé* and needing to flee the country were Francis Blanchain and Paula Spriewald (possibly the 'Czech woman' – 'or rather "Sudeten"' – in Krajewski's report), who had been helping Pat O'Leary in Marseille.[710]

Carrying eighteen people more than anticipated, *Seawolf* set off soon after midnight on 21 September into worsening weather. A force four-five storm sprang up from the south, compelling Krajewski to reduce speed in the heavy swell, but it also reduced the chances of being spotted from the air by the occasional Italian aircraft. Krajewski was taking no chances, though, and altered course from the usual one between Majorca and Ibiza to one that took him between Majorca and Minorca. 'On 22 September, in pouring rain, from which unfortunately not all our passengers were able to shelter, between 0600 and 0800 hours we passed between the islands, luckily in poor visibility… On the next day we passed a large French passenger vessel, the *G.G. Grévy* going – judging by its course – to Oran; this was the second time we had met it in the same place.'[711]

The *Seawolf* was steering for 'a position thirty miles east of the south-easterly headland of the island of Formentera (Balearics)' to rendezvous at 1000 hours on 23 September with HMS *Minna* (Hickton thought that she was a destroyer) so that the passengers could be transhipped to the larger vessel. The meeting was made half an hour early, and the transfer completed in ten minutes. HMS *Minna* reached Gibraltar on the afternoon of 24 September according to Barnett, and most, if not all, of the RAF evacuees were shipped back to Scotland aboard the 31,000-ton battleship HMS *Malaya*, landing at Greenock/Gourock on 5 October.

Having been at sea for a fortnight, and having covered 1,800 miles in the process, *Seawolf* arrived at Gibraltar two days after HMS *Minna*. Krajewski was rewarded for his efforts with three weeks' leave, which he took in England, and was awarded the Polish Cross of Gallantry and Bar for his courage over the previous two years' service in the Mediterranean.

The rest of the crew of the *Seawolf* were now due for a rest, but this was not to be, for the PAO line were already mustering the remaining escaped prisoners who could not be included on Operation Titania. They were to be evacuated on Operation Rosalind, and it fell to *Seawolf* again to do the donkeywork. With Krajewski away on leave, Lieutenant Marian Michalkiewicz (otherwise known as "Lukasz" or "Lucas") took over as captain. So far as he was concerned his orders were 'to deliver a letter and two sacks of material to the British organisation in France as well as evacuate around 35 British PoWs'.[712] *Seawolf* weighed anchor at 2030 on 30 September 1942 and set course for France. By midday on 5 October she was just over sixty-five kilometres from the embarkation point and hove to for four hours, arriving at the agreed point, the southern bank of the estuary of the River Tet, at precisely one minute past midnight on 6 October.

The evacuees – including at least fourteen airmen and eighteen soldiers – were ready and waiting in an isolated house at Canet-Plage – 'Chouquette had once more hired one of the more obscure holiday villas… consisting, on the ground floor, of a dining-room, kitchen and adjoining shed, and on the first floor, of three rooms with one bed in each.'[713] Conditions in the small villa were grim, and were not made any easier by the windows and shutters having to remain closed at all times.

At 0115 hours on 6 October Pat O'Leary gave the order to leave for the beach rendezvous. He himself was first to go, with Warrant Officer III Lucien Adelard Dumais, 1st Les Fusiliers Mont-Royal, another of the Canadians to escape after the Dieppe landing,[714] who 'carried an iron bar capable of silencing anyone at a single blow'. They reached the rendezvous in good time for the appointed hour of 0200 hours, but of the boat there was no sign. Hugely disappointing, there was nothing to be done but to return to the suffocating villa.

Lukasz and the *Seawolf*, meantime, had spent three hours searching 'the coastline, continually signalling by lamp in the direction of the shore'. Seeing no returning signal, Lukasz tried again the following night, and with the same result. Deciding that it was fruitless to try any further he radioed that he was aborting the operation and returning to Gibraltar. He was on his way back when, at 1130 hours on 9 October, he received a signal instructing him to return to the rendezvous: 'On 12 October at 0015 hrs I was at the embarkation point for the third time.'[715]

After the second failure, Pat O'Leary had made the seven-hour journey back to Marseille and sent a message to London advising them of the situation: 'Pas plus de bateau que de beurre au cul.' ('No more sign of a boat than of butter on your arse.') Jimmy Langley deciphered the signal, checked the meaning with a French colleague, and burst out laughing. More messages from London followed, prompting *Seawolf* to put about and go back to France to try again on 12 October. It had been a close call. For those cooped up in the house on the beach, however, conditions had deteriorated even further. Both toilets had become blocked, and the stench was appalling. It was, therefore, with immense relief that the seventh night in the house was to prove their last.

When Lukasz yet again signalled shorewards at 0030 hours on 12 October he was grateful to receive the correct reply immediately. By 0200 hours the last of those waiting had been ferried to the *Seawolf*, and Lukasz had taken 'on board 34 British former PoWs, a Polish priest (a military chaplain called Mirda) and an officer of the French merchant navy. I left the letter and two sacks of material on shore.'[716] Conditions on board were little better than they had been in the house. It was impossible for everyone to lie down on deck at the same time, and food and water, too, became a problem because of the extra days that *Seawolf* had been at sea. Rations were reduced to 'three cups of water per man per day, three biscuits and a tin of sardines'.

Due to the boat's slow progress rations were again 'cut to one cup of water and one biscuit a day. The sardines had all gone, and now the water-barrel was taken below and locked-up.' On the following day, Dumais and several others received only half a biscuit and half a cup of water. Discovering that the full ration had been handed out, they concluded 'that a group of Scottish soldiers had been fiddling the rations, and we decided to keep an eye on them.'[717] Their fears appeared to have some substance when, at the next rations issue, Dumais and his group asked the senior officer on board – 'an RAF officer with the smallest idea of discipline' – to form the men into a line instead of the previous free-for-all. Immediately, some of the men tried to get back into the line after they had already received their rations. Lukasz, realising what was going on, went on deck accompanied by two burly Polish sailors. All the while ostentatiously fingering a gun he approached the cheats and told them that if they did not leave the queue at once they would be chucked overboard. Peace and a fair distribution of rations were restored, and the rest of the voyage was completed with no further problems.

At approximately 0800 hours on 16 October 1942 *Seawolf* passed through the gate of Gibraltar's harbour boom defences, and at 0920 hours Lukasz handed over his passengers to the local authorities. The last mass evacuation by sea of evaders and escapers in the Mediterranean was over.[718]

It was only a week or so after their arrival in Gibraltar that fourteen airmen, thirteen evacuated by *Seawolf*, were flown to Poole harbour on the south coast of England. The fourteenth airman was Sergeant R. Brown, who had been delivered to Spain by Comet. Whether or not Security Control had been overwhelmed at Gibraltar with the sudden arrival of so many personnel is not known, but the identity of each person had to be verified (often by Donald Darling) before he or she could be issued with an emergency certificate to permit their entry into England. In the event, the fourteen airmen arrived at Poole without MI5 'being able to check up on their descriptions'. Sergeant Brown was of particular concern for, by the time that he had returned to England on 19 October, MI5 had not yet been furnished with his description. MI9 had notified MI5 on 6 October that he had arrived in Madrid, and MI5 in turn had asked MI9 for Brown's particulars. Though MI9 wrote back to MI5, on 15 October, 'saying that Sergeant Browne [*sic*] had arrived at Gibraltar on 13th October', they were seemingly unable to furnish MI5 with his description by the time of his return to England.

MI5 had a good point to make: 'The information which we require is reaching us in the end, but much too late to be used for the purpose for which it is intended, i.e. checking up on the individual's identity when he arrives… It is so essential that we should check up on the identity of Service personnel returning to this country. We already have conclusive proof that the Germans are attempting to use prisoners of war to infiltrate them into this country as agents.'[719]

Another two men, ex-Operation Rosalind, who had arrived at Hendon Airport from Gibraltar on 21 October and who 'were in possession of no satisfactory papers of identity', were conveyed by Security Control transport to the Great Central Hotel at Marylebone Station, London, for further interrogation. Once their identities had been established, Corporal Arnold Howarth and Warrant Officer Lucien Dumais were released to their units. Dumais (as will be seen in Chapter 8) later returned to France to help other evaders and escapers.

Literally missing the boat by a few days were three of the crew of a Wellington that had been hit by a night-fighter and abandoned near St Omer, northern France, on the night of 16/17 September 1942. One of the crew, Sergeant H.M. James, was taken prisoner, but the other four – Squadron Leader D.B. Barnard; Pilot Officer R.E. Glensor RNZAF; Sergeants R. Forster; and A.E. Buckell – evaded capture, for the time being.

Barnard landed near Alquines, some fifteen kilometres west of St Omer, and received assistance from local farmers. On 18 September, though, he was forced to hide in a hedge while the Germans searched the area with dogs and, on being informed that St Omer was crawling with Germans, decided to make for Marseille. After a night in a farmhouse he 'was given some further clothes, lent a bicycle, and guided to a house in Renty',[720] where he met his navigator, Raymond Glensor.

Glensor had also landed near Alquines, hurting his left leg and back in the process. Calling at a house in a nearby village he was welcomed by the occupants, who proved to be Dutch refugees. Twice while he was there Germans came into the room next to the one in which he was hiding and asked if an 'English pilot' had been seen in the neighbourhood, but he was not betrayed. When a man appeared one day and asked Glensor for proof of identity, he was unable to produce his identity discs but showed him some maps. These satisfied the man who took Glensor to the Fillerins' house in Renty on the following day.

Sergeant Forster came down on a hillside near Acquin, and put on a pair of walking shoes that he had conveniently brought with him. Using his footwear to good advantage he made some distance south and, at Bayenghem, contacted 'a woman and a young man on a bicycle. I spoke to them, and they took me to a house next to the church. The occupants gave me a meal and some overalls. About 1800 hrs, two men were brought to see me.'[721] Moved to another house, he was collected on the afternoon of 22 September by the two men and driven for a few miles until they 'met two more men in cycling kit, with a spare bicycle'. Thus escorted, Forster rode to Renty, where he was reunited with Barnard and Glensor at the Fillerins' house.

At some point during their five weeks' stay at Renty, Hauptmann Gottwald, Kreiskommandant (district commander) in St Omer, had posters displayed in the neighbourhood on which he begged to address an urgent appeal to the population inviting them to collaborate in finding the four airmen fugitives. He added that for each airman handed over one French prisoner of war would be rapidly released. The fourth airman, Sergeant Buckell, was allegedly handed over by the mayor of Bayenghem,[722] but the other three, together with Mesdemoiselles Geneviève and Monique Fillerin, thumbed their noses at the Germans by posing for the camera in front of one of the posters. Squadron Leader Barnard not only acquired one of the posters but also managed to take it with him all the way back to England.[723] Forster also acquired a copy of the poster, but his was destined not to reach home.

On 21 October three French guides escorted the three airmen by train to Paris, where they were joined by 2nd Lieutenant William J. Gise and Technical Sergeant Erwin D. Wissenback (see previous chapter). They all left on 22 October by train for Dijon, and then took a bus to Chalon-sur-Saône 'in the company of a German officer'. Crossing the Demarcation Line, they caught another train to Lyon and again to Marseille, where they arrived on 23 October.[724] Glensor was then 'taken to the flat of Thérèse, a member of the organisation, and formerly at Lille'[725] and after a month or so 'was moved to a flat in Cassis, occupied by M. and Mme. Durier', some twenty kilometres along the coast. Here he was to meet Flight Lieutenant T.A. Wærner RNAF, Captain Richard D. Adams USAAF,[726] and a civilian, Walter Gosling, who was also a member of the PAO organisation. A week later they were moved back to Marseille, staying with the Rodocanachis.

As for Barnard and Forster, they had been taken to Monte Carlo, where they were met by 'Mr Friend, an Australian member of the Monaco Police… and sheltered by Miss Trenchard and M. and Mme. Giton'.[727] When the Italians "occupied" Nice in November 1942, in line with the German occupation of the rest of France, a plan was hatched to get them away by boat but, unable to procure sufficient fuel, this was abandoned. Instead, they too were moved back to Marseille, and enjoyed the hospitality of the Rodocanachis.

In the first week of December the airmen and others were moved to Paul Ulmann's safe house at 39, rue Pierre Cazeneuve, 'a modest, two-story stucco house in a quiet residential neighbourhood'[728] of Toulouse. All was set for the crossing of the Pyrenees on 6 December 1942, but the guide failed to show up. Trying again on 13 December a party of seven hopefuls set off for Banyuls and Spain with their guide – Squadron Leader Barnard; Sergeant Ralph Forster; Leading Aircraftman A.V. Bromwell; Sub Flying Officer Eric Doorly; Pilot Officer R.S. Smith (he and Doorly were Americans on 133 "Eagle" Squadron RAF); a "Captain Forbes" (Mario Prassinos); and a Frenchman by the unlikely name of Frost.

By the time of his arrival in the south of France in the latter half of 1942, 250433 Leading Aircraftman Arthur Victor Bromwell had used up several of his nine lives. Born on 6 February 1900 he had joined the Royal Naval Air Service on 22 February 1918, and had transferred to the RAF on its foundation on 1 April 1918. He was with No. 1 Servicing and Repair Flight at Boos airfield, south-east of Rouen, France when the unit was evacuated for Cherbourg on 11 June 1940. He was leading one of the withdrawing RAF convoys on his motorcycle on 14 June when, about forty kilometres south-east of Le Mans, a 'delayed-action bomb near the road exploded, causing a motor car full of refugees to skid across the road and collide with me.'[729] Seriously injured in the abdomen, he was taken to a civilian hospital at St Calais (Sarthe). The French managed to keep his nationality hidden from the Germans for five months, but on 9 November 1940 he was removed to Frontstalag 203, a German prison camp at Mulsanne (Sarthe), a dozen kilometres south of Le Mans.

Bromwell made a number of friends at St Calais, and with their help escaped from 203 at about 7 a.m. on the morning of Christmas Eve, 1940, 'by climbing a tree and dropping over the first wire fence. I climbed the second fence which was about nine or ten feet high, using my overcoat to protect me from the wire. There were machine gun posts and searchlights at the corners of the camp, but it was a foggy morning and I was not observed.' In no hurry to leave the area, he walked into Le Mans and got a bus back to St Calais: 'I went back to the hospital and remained there till 16 January 41.'

For the next eighteen months he stayed on seventeen farms in the St Calais area and was, in his own words, ringleader of a group of French railway workers 'engaged in acts of sabotage in the St Calais district… These acts of sabotage were an individual effort and were not directed by any organisation. Among the acts of sabotage we committed were the following: Sabotage of petrol dumps at Vendôme. Sabotage of stores in the forest at Vibraye. Collision between two passenger trains, one empty, at Coudrecieux on 11 Nov 41. I cut the wire of the signal and put the points across. The trains collided head on at a bend and the line was blocked for two days. Two Germans were killed and nine or eleven injured, and two French people killed and eight injured.'[730]

It was during the Vibraye act of sabotage, in June 1942, that he nearly lost his life once again. Near Vibraye he and his French saboteurs were attacked by the Germans. Bromwell hurt himself jumping off a wall, and was then hit by a bullet in his right knee. Going back to the St Calais hospital once more, he stayed there until 13 August 1942 when he left for the south with two French friends. After they had left him at Tours, he continued to Langon (Loir-et-Cher), on the north bank of the River Cher, which at that point formed the Demarcation Line between the Occupied and Unoccupied Zones. Here he was approached by a Gestapo agent who demanded to see his papers. When Bromwell showed him the identity and ration cards that he had obtained in St Calais the German went off to speak to a colleague, naïvely telling Bromwell to stay where he was: 'When he had left I ran off, hid for a little behind a hedge, and then ran down to the river. By this time there was only one German left by the river bank. I ran past him and across the river, which is low at that point.' No shots were fired at the wet and fleeing Bromwell, who made off into a wood.

After five weeks at Pellevoisin (Indre), a dozen kilometres north of Buzançais, sheltered by relatives of one of his friends from St Calais, he made his way by train to Marseille, which he reached on 26 September 1942.

This was also the day on which Bob Smith, one of the two Americans in the Barnard party, was shot down. Smith and eleven others of 133 "Eagle" Squadron were in their shiny, new Spitfire Mark IXs escorting B-17 bombers to Morlaix airfield in north-west France. Disaster struck the nimble Spitfires when the forecast wind of 35 m.p.h. from the south proved to be blowing at 100 m.p.h. from the north. Blown way out over the Bay of Biscay they ran short of fuel. Only one of the Spitfires made it back to England (crashing in Cornwall). Of the other eleven pilots, four were killed, six were taken prisoner (including Flight Lieutenant E.G. Brettel DFC, murdered after the "Great Escape" on the night of 24/25 March 1944), and only Pilot Officer R.S. "Bob" Smith evaded capture.

Though well cared for in the village of Hanvec, Bob Smith found it difficult to pass away the October days in idleness until it was time to leave in the hands of the PAO organisation. The first leg of his journey was by train down to Bordeaux and then, in the back of a truck, to Unoccupied France. Another train brought him to Lyon, where he rested for three days before completing the journey with his guide to Marseille. 'Smith soon found himself in a luxurious flat talking to a man who introduced himself as Dr Rodocanachi'.[731] After three days at the Rodocanachis' flat, Bob Smith was collected by Paul Ulmann and taken to his safe house in Toulouse.

The other American, Eric Doorly, had been shot down by an enemy fighter on 6 September 1942, near Aumale (Seine-Maritime). Baling out at 20,000 feet, his opponent followed him down to almost ground level: 'I landed in a field, unhurt, but when I attempted to pick up my parachute my adversary made a dive at me. I left the parachute where it lay, and ran into the shelter of some trees.'[732] He found help from several families before coming across the Ranson family – Madame and her two sons, Jean and Robert, who were in their late teens – late on the evening of 7 September at Aumale.

Several weeks later, it was decided that the two boys would take Eric to their uncle in Lourdes, not too far from the Pyrenees, and then take him to Spain. On 12 October, Doorly and the two boys took the train to Paris, and on to Bordeaux, where they changed for the small station of Portets (Gironde), on the banks of the River Garonne. They followed the river on foot for twenty kilometres until they reached Langon (as Bromwell had done), 'which was on the line of demarcation. Here my friends made enquiries, and found that the German patrols used dogs at night.'[733]

Crossing into Unoccupied France without difficulty, they caught a bus to Auch, where they spent the night in a hotel, but as they made their way ever south Eric Doorly suddenly became very ill. By the time they had reached Lourdes Eric had turned a sickly yellow colour, and was so ill that Jean and Robert thought he was going to die. Eventually finding their uncle's house, they learnt that he had died only three days previously. The two brothers and Eric therefore booked themselves into a boarding house, where a German-Jewish doctor happened to be in residence. He quickly diagnosed severe jaundice,[734] but with no medicine there was little that he could do but give Eric periodic enemas, and watch and wait. Gradually Eric's strength returned until, on 6 November, he was fit enough to travel to Paul Ulmann's house at Toulouse. There, standing in front of him as he walked through the door, was Bob Smith. Believing Doorly to have been killed on operations, Smith blurted out: 'My God, I thought you were dead!'[735]

They were all glad to leave Paul Ulmann's crowded house on 13 December 1942 and to head for the Pyrenees. For the train journey to Perpignan and beyond, along the branch line to Céret, they travelled loosely so as not to arouse suspicion. As the little train wound its way along the valley of the River Tech the eight men jumped off just before it reached Céret station, and made their way up the foothills of the Pyrenees. After a cold night in the mountains it dawned on them that the guide was lost, but before anyone could stop him he had taken Bromwell's compass and disappeared, never to be seen again. None of the group was in particularly good shape for such an arduous climb in winter, and with Doorly still weak from his jaundice and Mario Prassinos having hurt his leg it was decided to split into two groups.

Leaving Forster, Doorly and Prassinos in a mountain hut, Barnard, Bromwell, Smith and Frost crossed into Spain. After walking for a further two and a half days, Bromwell and Frost were beyond Figueras on 16 December when they 'were arrested by civil guards on the road to Barcelona. When we told them, in reply to their questions, that we had neither money nor revolvers, they let us go.'[736] They carried on walking, but were arrested again and sent back to Figueras. Having been advised by one of his party that it would be better if caught by the Spaniards to declare oneself to be an officer, Leading Aircraftman Bromwell promoted himself to the rank of captain.

After spells in the Barcelona, Saragossa and Miranda prisons, "Captain" Bromwell was transferred on 14 January 1943 to the officers' camp at Jaraba, from which he was released on 24 April. He left Madrid for Gibraltar on 6 May, and four days later was flown home to England. His long absence in France was not, however, well viewed by the authorities in England, and the recommendation was made on 15 May 1943 by Major Buist, one of IS9 (W)'s chief interrogators, that he should receive no award:

> 'I suggest a NIL award in the case of 250433 L.A.C. Bromwell, A.V., RAF. Although he claims to have escaped from Frontstalag 203 (Mulsanne, near Le Mans) in Dec 40, he did not leave the district until 13 Aug 42. He explains this delay by saying that during the period 16 Jan 41–Jun 42 he was engaged in acts of sabotage. My impression is that this part of his story is at least in exaggeration designed to cover up the fact that he made no attempt to get home until forced to. Langley's impression in Dec 42, to which

he still adheres, was that Bromwell had no intention of returning to the UK till after the war.'[737]

Barnard and Smith, who were some way behind Bromwell and Frost when they were first arrested, hitched a lift on a lorry to Gerona, some thirty-five kilometres past Figueras. According to Smith, they were refused help of any kind by the British Consulate there, and were forced to continue walking. By 18 December they had reached Malgrat, some fifty kilometres along the coast from Barcelona, where, filthy and unshaven, they were arrested. After questioning, they were punched and kicked into their stone cell. Three days later they were taken to Barcelona and put in the civil prison. A young Belgian who was in the prison with them managed to get a note to his consulate informing them of their predicament, and their release was duly effected. On Christmas Day the airmen were driven by a decent Spanish Air Force officer to Saragossa, and from there on 3 January 1943 they were taken to a very pleasant hotel at Alhama de Aragón,[738] picking up a further fifteen RAF personnel, before arriving in Madrid on 4 January.

Here Smith and Barnard parted company, apparently because Barnard had again become uncontrollable, a repeat performance of an incident at Saragossa when he 'had lost control of himself and, in a yelling frenzy, threatened to kill Smith for no apparent reason.'[739] Smith was allowed to continue alone to Gibraltar by bus, and was flown back to England by his fellow countrymen on a B-17 bomber. Barnard left for Gibraltar on 15 January, and sailed for Gourock five days later.

As for Doorly, Forster and Prassinos, left behind in the cold of the Pyrenees, they stumbled on as best they could over the rocky terrain until, somewhere north of the Spanish village of Espolla, the loud command 'Alto!' echoed across the valley. Halting as ordered, they were confronted by a number of Spanish police who, pointing their rifles at them, ordered them to return whence they had come, but hinting that if they 'entered Spain in an orthodox manner, the Spanish authorities' would give them passports to facilitate their journey. To make sure that they crossed back into France, the police went with them. Exceedingly hungry they spent the night in a barn in the mountains and, on 15 December, crossed back into Spain a few kilometres along the border. In the village of Rabós, a dozen kilometres north-east of Figueras, they were accosted by members of the Guardia Civil. In Rabós jail, Forster convinced their captors that they were 'genuine Service evaders' by producing the German poster that he had obtained several weeks ago in Renty.

On 17 December they were taken by train to Figueras, where all their money and Forster's poster were confiscated. Two days later they were moved to the main prison in Figueras, and were briefly reunited with Bromwell and Frost. It was not until 30 January 1943, however, that a representative from the British Consulate at Barcelona put in an appearance. Mario Prassinos was released on 2 February, four days before Doorly and Forster were taken to Barcelona and then to Miranda de Ebro. After the rigours of that prison, Doorly was taken on 11 March to the hotel at Alhama de Aragón, and on 24 March was driven to 'Madrid, and thence via Seville to Gibraltar, where I arrived the next day.' On 27 March he was flown to Hendon aerodrome.

Forster was puzzled when 'for some reason the Spaniards seemed unwilling to allow me to proceed to Alhama with F/O Doorly'. Whatever the reason, his turn came on 6 April, when he and Sergeant H.L. McBeath RCAF,[740] were driven by a Spanish Air Force officer to the hotel at Alhama. After five days they went to Madrid and, after another five days in another hotel, to Gibraltar, which they reached on 17 April. Two days later they, too, were off back to England.

As for Pilot Officer Glensor, having separated from Squadron Leader Barnard and Sergeant Forster and then been moved back to Marseille, he was escorted to Toulouse on 13 December in the company of Walter Gosling, Flight Lieutenant Wærner and three of the escapers from the Camp de Chambaran – Flight Lieutenant Bob Milton, Lieutenant W.M. Hewit, and Captain Dick Cooper. After staying with Paul Ulmann, they went by train to Banyuls, on 15 December, but without Wærner. Setting off with their guide over the lower Pyrenees, the going proved too tough for Gosling, who had to be left behind. During the night of 16/17 December they reached the highest point of the crossing, and 'waited till light to cross into Spain. There were about twenty other people congregated together for the same purpose.'[741]

Safely in Spain, they continued walking towards Figueras throughout 17 December. Having somehow got lost in the town during the night the guide eventually led them to their hiding place, but 'found that the people there were unfriendly. We therefore had to hide in a ravine. We had had very little food and no water.'[742] At around 3 a.m. on the morning of 19 December the guide hid the group in a disused brickworks near Figueras, saying that he would go to Barcelona to get help. He, too, was neither seen nor heard of again. Fortunately, Dick Cooper was a fluent Spanish speaker, and was able to persuade a smuggler who had earlier joined them to alert the British consulate in Barcelona of their predicament.

On 23 December Vice-Consul P.H. Dorchy arrived in his car, and took the "British" officers to his house in Barcelona. Six days later Cooper, Glensor, Milton and Hewit were driven to Madrid, and remained at the British Embassy until early in the New Year, when they were driven to Seville. Giving a good impression of being drunken sailors they staggered aboard a ship with a cargo of oranges, 'and were hidden that night in the propeller shaft to evade the customary search by Spanish officials.'[743]

Two days later they were in Gibraltar. They went to the British vice-consulate at La Linea at 1 p.m., 'but the Vice-Consul was taking his siesta and would not be disturbed'.

Dick Cooper, Squadron Leader Barnard, Glensor, Milton, Wærner, Hewit and others all sailed together from Gibraltar on 20/21 January 1943, and docked at Gourock five days later.[744] The last laugh, not that it was at all funny, was on the SOE agent, Dick Cooper, who had great difficulty persuading a young, one-armed RAF Intelligence officer that he was indeed a British agent.

CHAPTER 6

The Comet line: 1941-1942

'Crossing the frontier is an arduous and tricky business. The postmistress with her own haversack on her shoulders literally drives the men through this eight hour struggle. They all speak of her wonderful endurance...'[745]

'Her real name is Mlle. Andrée de Jongh. Every RAF man who has reached us through her intermediary has spoken extraordinarily highly of her courage.'[746]

Following their victory over the French and British armies in northern France and Belgium in June 1940, the German army began the task of moving many thousands of British and French prisoners to Germany. Forced to march on foot for hour after hour in hot weather, with little food or water, and 'carrying all we possessed of clothing and equipment on our backs, always tired and often hungry and dispirited, we began the awful trek, which, with little respite, was to go on day after day for a month.'[747]

Not a few, however, took the opportunity to slip away through the thin line of German guards. Four Scottish soldiers of the 4th Queen's Own Cameron Highlanders[748] – Sergeant Allan G. Cowan, Corporal Enoch Bettley, and Privates Duncan Greig and Samuel "Joe" Slavin – seized their chance to dodge the column on 4 July 1940 by diving into a wheat field near Geraardsbergen (Grammont), thirty kilometres west of Brussels. Hiding until the rest of the column had passed by, they found shelter in and around the village of Parike, some thirty-five kilometres west of Brussels.

It was not until 23 December 1940 that Bettley and Slavin were removed to Brussels, with Cowan and Greig following on 12 January 1941. For much of February Cowan and Greig stayed with Madame Marceline Deloge[749] at 100, rue Général Capiaumont, Etterbeek, Brussels. Then two more Scottish soldiers, Privates John McCubbin and Bobby Conville, both 1st Glasgow Highlanders, arrived. Their chance to escape had come at the end of July 1940 as the train that was taking them to a prison camp in Germany passed through the Forêt de Soignes, to the south-east of Brussels. Forcing open the door of their cattle truck they, and twenty-six others, jumped off with bullets whistling past their ears. An escaped Welsh soldier, Corporal Alfred Jones RA,[750] put them in touch with several Brussels families, with whom they stayed for six weeks. They were then taken to the home of Madame Ann Duchêne and her daughter Florence in the rue Sans-Souci, Ixelles, where they remained until October 1941.

With so many escaped soldiers now in hiding, particularly in the Brussels area, it was obvious to a number of Belgians, foremost among them William Halot and Roger Verhulst, that something needed to be done to keep them out of German hands, and to get them away to Britain. With the help of Arnold Deppé,[751] a number of safe houses were found in the Brussels area, among them those of Mesdames Ann Duchêne (née Hodges, from Waterford, Ireland) and Jeanne Depourque (née Monnier) in March 1941. Later in 1941 Baron Jacques Donny, a director of the large multi-national company Sofina, became involved, but he was a marked man by Paul Hollemans, a double agent, who was to betray several other Belgians over the months and years to come. Also involved at some stage was Madame Jeanie Wolf, who 'looked after the soldiers', while 'Madame Anne-Marie Bruycker-Roberts (wife of Englishman Jesse Roberts) supplied money, clothes and food'.[752]

First of the Scotsmen to tread the path to freedom was Duncan Greig, who set off on 14 July 1941 accompanied by two guides. When, however, one of them became lost and the other confessed that he did not know the way, Greig decided to press on alone. He took a train down the east of France to Charleville-Mézières (Ardennes) and Besançon (Doubs). Detraining on 15 July at Arbois (Jura) some sixty kilometres south of Besançon, he followed a crowd of people to a café where, for 150 francs, he found someone willing to take him over the Demarcation Line into the Unoccupied Zone. Two days later he had reached Lourdes, within forty kilometres of the Pyrenees, and there, as had been arranged before leaving Brussels, he waited for Cowan and Conville. 'As they did not arrive, I consulted a British civilian whom I had met in Lourdes as to the best way of getting to Spain. He put me in touch with two Belgians with whom I went by train to Cloron and Tardets, and to Licq by autobus.'[753]

The two Belgians – Willy Muelle, from Bruges, and Nestor Bodson, from Liège – were prepared to go with him across the Pyrenees, and it was at Licq-Athérey (Pyrénées-Atlantiques) that they met a French guide, Jean, who led them by the Pic des Escalier (1,472 metres/4,784 feet) and through the Forêt d'Iraty into Spain. At this point Jean handed over to a Basque guide,[754] but on 12 September, at the town of Aoiz, twenty kilometres east of Pamplona, the two men were arrested by the Guardia

Civil. Imprisoned until 30 October, the last two weeks in the prison at Miranda de Ebro, Greig was released to the British Embassy in Madrid.[755]

Sometime in late 1941 MI6 agent Donald Darling, then in Lisbon, received a visit from a Belgian, Gérard Waucquez ("Brichamart"), 'who had come clandestinely from Brussels with the intention of reaching London.' He told Darling about 'the setting up of an organisation in the Belgian capital through which it was hoped to pass evading British service personnel to Spain and Gibraltar.' Waucquez also told Darling that this 'seemingly impossible enterprise was the brain child'[756] of fifty-four-year-old Frédéric de Jongh, headmaster of a primary school in the Schaerbeek district of Brussels. Darling passed on the information to London, also with the suggestion to P15 (Jimmy Langley) that Waucquez be interviewed as soon as he arrived. The interview apparently did not take place, perhaps because Waucquez was the nephew of Hubert Pierlot, the head of the Belgian government in exile.[757] As will be seen below, Waucquez was back a few months later on behalf of SOE to help evading airmen to safety.

The "seemingly impossible enterprise" of which Waucquez spoke had arisen out of the financial need to move out of Belgium and back to Britain all those British military personnel who were being sheltered in and around Brussels following the Germans' victory in June 1940. At the same time, apart from those closely concerned with the men being sheltered, there were others in Brussels who had made it their duty to gather military information that would be helpful not only to the Belgian government in exile, and to the British Government, but which would also be harmful to the enemy.

One man who undertook the creation of a clandestine service for the provision of military information to the Belgian government in exile ('un service clandestin d'informations') was Georges Lechein,[758] who called his group Portemine. He had been on the train taking the Belgian royal family to France and to safety on 15 May 1940, but went to ground at the cavalry school at Saumur, France, before returning to Brussels in July. Looking around for suitable persons to help with his enterprise, he recruited his wife, son and father, and a Monsieur Vanderschriek. He also contacted certain members of the royal court, and a Colonel Moutier, to whom he represented himself as agent A.52, his Intelligence Service number from the First World War. Colonel Moutier, a friend of Vichy France's Maréchal Petain, was to go to Vichy itself in November 1940, where he would have been a more than useful contact, but unfortunately died soon after.

At the same time as Portemine began another group, Pavot (Poppy), was being formed in Brussels. It was led by Albert Meeus who had recruited in July among others Mademoiselle Mary Verboven. She in turn had recruited Mademoiselle Henriette Van Belle,[759] who was nursing Belgian wounded and British prisoners of war at a camp at Enghien. Early in September, when Henriette needed assistance with 'un aviateur allié blessé refugié dans un garage' (a wounded Allied airman hidden in a garage), she turned to a Madame Grangée whom she had helped during "the exodus" and whose daughter, Madame Evrard, had already been recruited into Lechein's Portemine group. Mme. Evrard then went to a Madame Michiels, who was also one of her group and who had known Lechein when they were children.

Henriette now brought Albert Meeus to Mme. Evrard's house, where both were introduced to Lechein. It is probably from this point on that Meeus and his group – including Vicky (Verboven), 26 (Meeus himself), and 46 (M. De Craen)[760] – were recruited into Portemine (which included groups 1, 2, 6, and UZH which had another group, 19, attached to it later in that month). Then, in February 1941, Henriette Van Belle introduced a certain Andrée de Jongh to Mme. Evrard, and thus to the dangerous game of resistance with men such as Roger Verhulst ("Cyrano"), William Halot ("Valon", and also Verhulst's father-in-law), Georges Hoyez, Georges Guillon, Jean-François Vandenhove, Professor Jean-Marie Derscheid, Emile Toussaint, and Englishman William Reynolds.[761]

And there were many women too. When the tide of war broke upon Belgium in May 1940, Andrée de Jongh was working for Baron Donny's Sofina company, earning a living as a commercial artist (*dessinatrice*) in Malmédy. Responding to the Belgian government's call for auxiliary nurses to help with the anticipated flood of wounded, she quit her job and returned to her family home at 73, Avenue Emile Verhaeren, Schaerbeek, Brussels. As Henriette Van Belle had done, she then nursed wounded soldiers and British prisoners of war at Bruges, and in February 1941 was recruited into Portemine.

It is not clear precisely when she became embroiled in clandestine work but, together with Arnold Deppé and his cousin Henri De Bliqui (Deppé lodged with the De Bliqui household at 25, rue de Bosnie, St Gilles, Brussels), she was one of a small *service* (the French word for "organisation") known as *l'équipe DDD*, after the first initials of their surnames. Henri De Bliqui and two others were arrested, due to the traitor Prosper Dezitter, on 9 April 1941.[762] Arnold Deppé, too, was arrested at the same time, but was released for lack of evidence and took himself off to Brittany for a month.

By March 1941, possibly as a result of the untimely death of Colonel Moutier, Georges Lechein needed to open an alternative route for passing information to the authorities in Britain, and the likeliest route was that through south-west France and on into neutral Spain. At the same time it was appreciated that if information could be passed along this route then so too could evaders and escapers, who were becoming a serious drain on their Belgian helpers' finances. Accordingly, Arnold Deppé, with his intimate knowledge of the south-west corner of France, was asked to go to his former "patch" to see what could be done about establishing a clandestine route into Spain.

In June 1941 he set off on a trial journey taking with him, but only as far as Paris, two French soldiers who had escaped from Germany – Jean Renault and Charles Morelle (of whom more later). Deppé and party called at the Café du Brabant in front of the railway station at Lille, before continuing to the Café Baroux in Corbie (Somme), a few kilometres east of Amiens, where they met Renée Boulanger ("Nénette"), a farmer's wife. Arnold Deppé had an aunt (an Englishwoman, Mrs Pybus) in Paris who could lodge them near the Gare d'Austerlitz.

Leaving the Frenchmen in Paris Deppé made his way to Bayonne, where he met Monsieur Jean Appert, secretary of the Société Genérale bank, who was known to 'to be in contact with a resistance group'.[763] Monsieur Appert, fortuitously, had already had a visit from a Belgian lady living in the area, Madame Elvire De Greef, who had made it clear to him that she was willing to help. Appert therefore gave Arnold Deppé her address and the password. Madame De Greef, her husband Fernand, and their two children, Freddie and Jeanine, aged eighteen and seventeen respectively, formerly resident in the Brussels suburb of Etterbeek, were now living at the villa Voisin in Anglet.[764] They had left Belgium in 1940, ahead of the Germans, with the intention of getting to Britain, but had been unable to get passage from Bordeaux.

Before returning to Brussels, Arnold Deppé met up with some old friends at St Jean-de-Luz and fixed up three possible routes along the Spanish border and across the Pyrenees and, most importantly, a team of smugglers to guide future escapers and evaders.[765] This news, and the fact that Madame De Greef and her family *were* willing to assist, Arnold Deppé was able to convey to his colleagues once back in Brussels.

Now all was ready for the first clandestine journey to be undertaken to Spain. Arnold Deppé was to lead the group, with Andrée de Jongh, now called "Dédée" (as she will be referred to hereinafter). They set off on 16 July with 'ten Belgians, wanted by the Gestapo, and a plump, middle-aged Englishwoman in a Panama hat. Miss Richards, as she was called, though Dédée never knew her real name, was threatened with internment.'[766] Despite the occasional hiccup along the way, the party reached Anglet. While Dédée remained with the De Greefs, Arnold Deppé shepherded the group over the Pyrenees to Spain, only to be arrested by carabineros (frontier police): 'Two eventually got through to England, one man and one woman; four got stuck in Miranda camp; and five, all Belgian officers, were handed back by the Spanish police to the Germans.' This was unfortunate, for one of the Belgian officers said more than he should have done to the Germans 'about where he had been and whom he had seen'.[767]

Following this pioneering run, a second trip was undertaken five weeks later. On 17 August 1941 a Scottish soldier, Private Jim Cromar,[768] 1st Gordon Highlanders, accompanied by Dédée and two Belgian officers, left Brussels by train for France. They were to rendezvous with Arnold Deppé and another group at the café in Corbie, but the Deppé group failed to arrive. Leaving Cromar and the two Belgians with Renée Boulanger, Dédée back-tracked to Lille, but of the Deppé group there was no trace. As something had clearly gone wrong Dédée went to Valenciennes to ask a favour of Charles Morelle, who had told her that if she ever needed him for anything then he would do what he could for her. Now she asked him to go to Brussels to find out what he could from her father, Frédéric. She, meanwhile, would escort her three charges to Spain. Charles was to bring any news to the De Greef's house in Anglet.

Hurrying back to Corbie Dédée, Cromar and the two Belgians left the Zone Interdite on 23 August, crossing the Somme into the Unoccupied Zone by Renée Boulanger's boat near the village. They continued via Paris to Bordeaux, and on to Anglet and St Jean-de-Luz. Cromar's report of his arrival in Spain is brief: '…we crossed the frontier on foot through Anglet, St Jean to San Sebastian. Our journey across was helped by some smugglers whom my three Belgian friends had contacted. We then made for Bilbao, where I visited the British Consul.'[769]

In order that she could cross the *muga* (border) into Spain Dédée, with Elvire De Greef's help, 'made contact with the smugglers of St Jean-de-Luz. The Navarrese refugee Alejandro Elizalde put her in touch with the guide Tomás Anabitarte Zapirain… Tomás Anabitarte came from the farm "Otsuene-Aundia" in Hernani (Gipuzkoa) and had taken refuge in France during the civil war.'[770] He was initially appalled at the prospect of having to make the crossing of the Pyrenees with such a fragile-looking girl, but changed his mind after she had made it over as easily as the next man.

Anabitarte left them at a farmhouse a few kilometres over the border. Refusing to go any deeper into Spain for fear of being arrested by the police, he assured Dédée that someone would come and take them to the British Consulate at San Sebastián.

Someone *did* come, Bernardo Aracama, 'an old *gudari* (Basque soldier)', another to have sought refuge in France during the Spanish Civil War, who 'had a garage in Aguirre Miramón street ... and put the group up in his house at San Sebastián.'[771] Dédée, needing to be reimbursed for expenses, made her way to the San Sebastián vice-consulate, but was told to try the consulate at 6, Calle Estación, Bilbao. There she spoke to Vyvyan Pedrick[772] who, having already heard her story from the San Sebastián office, found it hard to believe that this slip of a girl now standing before him could have come all the way from Belgium and have walked across the Pyrenees nursemaiding three men. What was more, she was now suggesting that he should reimburse her expenses and pay for all the other British personnel whom she was planning to bring in the future![773]

The expenses involved in the maintenance of evaders and escapers had been steadily mounting and if the Belgians were to pass them on to the British, then hopefully they, the British, could reimburse them for the costs incurred. An account of sorts was rendered to the British in November 1941, explaining that it cost 7,000 francs to convey a person to Spain from Belgium, a sum that included the fee for the guide to Spain and the *convoyeur*'s return train fare. As eight men[774] had already been delivered on three separate occasions, the bill now was 77,000 francs.

Quite apart from the financial aspect of the proposal, there was concern that Dédée might be a German agent trying to infiltrate the British Secret Service. After she had departed with the promise that she would return in a few weeks with three more men, a report was sent to MI6 agent Donald Darling at Lisbon informing him of this woman who wished to be supported, not least financially, in her venture by the British Government. What did he think? Darling promptly suggested 'that a German agent would hardly be likely to undertake the arduous Pyrenees crossing several times at night, in an attempt to infiltrate agents into Britain. Also, the men she had brought stated that she had made the crossing with them and they were full of admiration, to say the least of it.'[775]

Promising to return in three or four weeks with three more "parcels", as she called escapers and evaders, Dédée crossed back into France, and made her way to the De Greef's house at Anglet, where Charles Morelle arrived with the news that Arnold Deppé had been arrested by the Gestapo at Lille station, with the whole of his party. Furthermore, he added, the Gestapo had paid a visit to her father in Brussels, and were now looking for her as well. Clearly too dangerous to go back to Brussels, it was agreed that Dédée should run the French side of operations from Paris while her father, Frédéric, ran the Brussels end of the organisation. Elvire De Greef would continue to deal with the Spanish end.

Familiarly known as "Tante Go" (after her pet French bull terrier "Go Go") Elvire De Greef was the driving force, and effective chief, of the escape organisation in the south-west of France. According to a report made by a Belgian agent on 26 July 1942, on his return to England, she was an 'accountant living in Langlet [*sic*]. Often goes to Brussels to control the escape route which she is in charge of.' But another agent, reporting on 12 August 1942, said: 'Known under name of Tante GOGO. Is in charge of relay in Bayonne. Is guide between Paris and Bayonne.'[776]

She also became 'involved in numerous black market operations to obtain the best possible food', and in recruiting the necessary guides to see the evaders over the Pyrenees. And it was she who 'knew all the local smugglers and under-cover agents in the bistros of Bayonne and St Jean de Luz'.[777]

Fernand was mentioned, in the July 1942 report, as being 'a clerk in the mairie. Buys food for the escapees on the black market.' He was also an interpreter for the Germans at the Anglet Kommandantur and, as such, was well placed to help the escape line by "liberating" blank identity cards and official stamps for the production of false papers and documents.

With Arnold Deppé and Dédée now unavailable to operate from Brussels, more couriers were needed for the Brussels-Paris section. One to come forward was Jean Ingels ("Jean de Gand"), whom Frédéric de Jongh had known earlier in the war. Another was Andrée Dumon who had already worked for Frédéric carrying messages around Brussels, and who was also known as "Dédée". To avoid confusion with Andrée de Jongh, Andrée Dumon was called "Nadine", but she was nevertheless known to many evaders as Dédée! Charles Morelle continued to act as a guide over the section from Brussels to the French frontier, on which duty his sister, Elvire Morelle, was already employed.

There was a further setback for the organisation when Enoch Bettley and Joe Slavin were arrested on 14 August 1941 at the home of Madame Augusta Marioux and her daughter in Rue Bogier, Schaerbeek. Taken to St Gilles prison the Scotsmen were interrogated and beaten daily for sixteen days before being sent to a prisoner-of-war camp in Germany. Then, on 25 September, the *Geheime*

Feldpolizei raided the home of Madame Duchêne on the Rue Sans-Souci, Ixelles, where John McCubbin was staying. He tried to escape but, as he ran out of the house, he was grabbed by a passer-by who thought that he was a thief. The police opened fire. Hit by three bullets, 'one in each shoulder and one in the back of the hand',[778] McCubbin was taken to the Belgian Military Hospital with a fractured shoulder, and then to the St Pierre Hospital. He also went to St Gilles prison, as did Madame Duchêne and her daughter Florence, who had also been arrested.

This was the cue for Allan Cowan and Bobby Conville to leave Brussels. Elvire De Greef made the long journey north from Anglet to collect them, and they left by train on 14 October. The journey was uneventful as far as Quiévrain station, on the French border, where passengers were made to leave the train, walk through customs to the station on the French side, and there reboard the empty train which had, in the meantime, made the short journey into France. As the two Scotsmen made their way through customs a French *douanier* (customs official) ordered them into an office to be searched in the presence of a German feldgendarme, who was there to keep an eye on the French official. When a large number of cigarettes were found in Cowan's pockets, the French *douanier* left the office – with half the cigarettes. The two Scotsmen, who were claiming to be Flemish, remained under the watchful eye of the German policeman.

No sooner had the Frenchman left than Bobby Conville began blatantly stuffing as many of the cigarettes as he could into his own pockets, watched all the while by the German, who 'appeared highly amused and began to laugh. To Bobby's intense surprise he was allowed to leave with some of the cigarettes.'[779] Then the feldgendarme also left, leaving the door open enough for Cowan to see Elvire De Greef waving her arms furiously in the distance in a manner suggesting that he, too, should leave at once. Running for all he was worth he rejoined her and Conville, and the three of them walked hastily away. 'Suddenly there was a shout behind them. The *douanier* who had searched Alan [*sic*] was riding towards them on a bicycle, grinning broadly. He stopped and handed over to Alan the remainder of the cigarettes.'[780] He also told Elvire that, if she were to take 'birds about like that', she should empty their pockets before they got to the customs! And good luck!

At Valenciennes, a dozen kilometres down the line, Cowan remembered that they 'met, by arrangement, a Belgian girl [Dédée] who acted as our guide all the way to Bilbao. Our guide took us out of the Zone Interdite by crossing the Somme in a small boat near Villiers and then on to Amiens, Paris and Bayonne. From Bayonne we went by motor bus to St Jean-de-Luz, and crossed the Pyrenees on foot to San Sebastian, which we reached on 16 October. On 20 October we went by train to Bilbao and reported to the British Consulate.'[781] Dédée and the two soldiers were accommodated in the British Seamen's Institute in Bilbao. On 28 October Cowan and Conville were taken to the British Embassy in Madrid. Reunited with Greig, the three left for Gibraltar on 20 November 1941.

It was on this trip, on 17 October, that Dédée met Donald Darling at the Bilbao consulate. He told her 'that the British Government were vitally concerned with recovering the crews of aircraft shot down in Holland, Belgium and France,' and on behalf of MI9 'agreed to lend the money she asked for the housing and feeding of the men on the way from Brussels and the fees for the guides at the frontier.'[782] Despite the poor judgement of Colonel Claude Dansey in London ('Your summing up of the ... de Jongh situation is not appreciated and do not write further in this vein'), Dédée and the organisation were given the go-ahead, and she returned to France after four days. Conville and Cowan, incidentally, were 'convinced of her genuineness'.

At first, the Brussels-Bayonne organisation had no name, but as a result of her use of the word "parcel" to denote escapers and evaders, Dédée was given the codename "Postwoman", apparently by Donald Darling. However, she 'wished to be known as if she were a man', and her codename was duly changed to "Postman".[783] As for the escape organisation itself, it had no name amongst its members, certainly in the early months, and they referred to the line, if at all, by any one of several names – "la ligne Dédée" or "Service Andrée" – though in Belgium 'nobody was speaking about a line, neither with a name. At every stage, every member of the line was just asked to do this and that for the functioning of the passage of the airmen. They did not have a name in mind.'[784]

Flying Officer Kasimir Rowicki PAF, who was in Comet's hands in Brussels in May 1942, referred to the organisation as the "Service Andrée", after its leading courier. In August 1942 it was still known to British Intelligence as the "Andrée Escape Organisation", but on 14 January 1943 the Belgian Sûreté de l'Etat in London issued the name *Comète* in connection with Jean Greindl's forthcoming mission, Drew.[785] Flying Officer T.R. Wilby RCAF, interviewed on 28 May 1943, stated in his report to MI9: 'I cannot remember the names of the two Frenchmen who helped me in Toulouse, but I think they had something to do with the organisation "Comet".'[786] Six months later, in his letter of 29 November 1943 to a Commandant Vandermies at the Sûreté de l'Etat in London, on the subject of the secret mission to be undertaken by agents "Rutland" and "London", Captain

Charles Delloye mentions that, in the event of Rutland finding evaders to be sent back to the UK, he would be put in touch with the 'organisation belge "Comète" qui eventuallement lui remettra des évadés à évacuer.'[787] That the Service Andrée was given the appellation Comète around the end of 1942 and early 1943 is indisputable, but the jury is still out as to who so called it, and precisely when.

Once the Scottish soldiers had been escorted on their way from Belgium in the summer of 1941 the next to be taken down the line were the first three airmen of a total that by June 1944 would reach 275 – Sergeant J.L. Ives RCAF; Sergeant M. Kowalski PAF; and Sergeant S. Tomicki PAF.

Sergeant Ives had been shot down on the night of 18/19 August 1941 after his Whitley had been attacked by a night-fighter over Vliermaalroot, near Hasselt, in eastern Belgium. He stayed for four days in a wood, but developed dysentery after drinking dirty water from a field. A farmer found him on the morning of 22 August but due to a misunderstanding – he believed that Ives was a German – left him where he was. Another farmer then found the distressed Canadian, and hid him on his farm half a dozen kilometres from Diepenbeek (near Hasselt) until 27 August. On 28 August, after cycling to Hasselt, Ives caught the train to Brussels, and was taken to the house of a man who 'was one of the chiefs of the Mouvement Nationale Belge for Brussels district.' As the GFP and Gestapo were particularly active in Brussels at this time, it was necessary to keep John Ives on the move, and soon after his arrival he was taken to an apartment at 127, Chaussée d'Ixelles, the home of the Brusselmans family – Julien, his wife Anne, and their two children, Jacques and Yvonne.

The Brusselmans had been drawn into the clandestine Belgian war effort following the visit one day in September 1940 of their local Protestant priest, Pastor Schyns. Knowing that Anne's mother was English the clergyman wondered whether she and her husband might be prepared to help the score or so of British soldiers who were currently being hidden in Brussels.[787] Though surprised by that news, the Brusselmans agreed to give what help they could in the way of civilian clothing and ration cards, and they later suggested to Pastor Schyns that 'we should take in airmen if it becomes necessary, for now it seems the British are attacking the German Reich, and airmen are bound to be brought down over Belgium.'[789] It was not until roughly 30 August 1941, however, that they received their first "guest", John Ives.[790] After staying at two other safe houses, he was taken to the Gare du Midi, Brussels, on 6 November, where he met Sergeants Kowalski and Tomicki, who had been shot down in the same aircraft on the night of 5/6 August.

The two Poles landed a couple of hundred metres from the remains of their Wellington.[791] As Tomicki made his way in the direction of his comrade, shots were fired, and he threw himself to the ground. When the firing had stopped – it was the aircraft's ammunition exploding from the heat – he walked into Marche-en-Famenne and 'knocked at the door of a poor house and asked for a bed. I was taken in, but told that I could not stay there, as there were two German soldiers billetted in the house.'[792] Kitted out in civilian clothes provided by a friend of the man who had taken him in, Tomicki was then taken away by a Canadian (who had apparently been a pilot during the First World War), and stayed at his home for two nights.

After a brief spell at a farm – where he had to spend two nights in the woods as the Germans were now looking for him – he was taken back to the Canadian's house and 'met an Englishwoman who had five children. My instructions were to follow this woman, but not to speak to her. I followed her to a large house in Brussels, where I had a meal. There I was handed over to a Belgian and spent a week in his house. I then went to the home of a Belgian woman, who has since been denounced and is in prison.' He was there for the next four weeks.

Sergeant Kowalski hid in the woods for twelve hours before walking through Pessoux, also to Marche-en-Famenne, where a Belgian 'accosted me in the street there and told me that the Germans were looking for me. He took me to his house, where he gave me civilian clothes and 1000 Belgian francs collected from friends who wanted to help.' The following day he and his Belgian guide caught the train from Ciney to Brussels, and went to the American Consulate. Finding that it had been closed by the Germans, they went to the Portuguese Consulate, where they discovered 'that the secretary was attached to an organisation. My Belgian friend left me there. The Portuguese secretary took me to the house of a Belgian woman, where I stayed from 8 August till 27 September.'[793] Here Kowalski met 'a Scotsman whose name I have forgotten', and also Allan Cowan and Bobby Conville shortly before their journey south. On 27 September 1941 he was moved to a second house, but when the lady of that house became ill he moved back to the first one again on 8 October.

It was Frédéric de Jongh (using the alias "Paul") who collected Tomicki and Kowalski and took them to the Gare du Midi on 6 November[794] to meet Sergeant Ives and Elvire Morelle, who was to be their guide. At Quiévrain station the passengers disembarked as usual. 'For the airmen it was a critical moment. The instructions of Elvire and Paul ran through their minds. They were pushed and jostled towards the *douaniers* holding before them pocket-books with orange *passierscheins* or frontier passes open in their hands. They remained close to the tall, comforting figure of Elvire as they passed the *douaniers* without incident.' Safely through, Elvire Morelle spotted 'the unobtrusive figure of Dédée standing among the waiting crowds at the far end of the platform', and discreetly joined forces with her.

After crossing the Somme by boat near Corbie, for which the guide was paid 250 francs per head, they walked from the village of Hamelet to the nearest railway station, Ives noting 'a large British war cemetery' as they did so,[796] and picked up the Brussels-Paris train after it had been "controlled". At the Gare du Nord, Paris, Elvire Morelle waved goodbye. On the evening of 8 November Dédée and the three airmen crossed to the Gare d'Austerlitz and departed for Bayonne. Ives recalled that the whole train except for one carriage was reserved for the Wehrmacht and that all the 'German soldiers left the train at Bordeaux. The lights in our compartment developed a fuse just after leaving Paris and we were in darkness the whole way, a fortunate happening for us.'

At Bayonne station, where they arrived on the morning of 9 November, they were met by Jeanine De Greef and Albert Edward Johnson, an Englishman known only as "B", who introduced them to Operation Water Closet, a simple way of by-passing the police controls at the station barrier. Deviating through the station toilets they walked out through an unlocked door, which could only be unlocked from the inside, and into the street beyond. Needless to say, Johnson had a duplicate key.[797]

After spending the night with the De Greefs and having left their identity cards with Elvire, they caught an evening train to St Jean-de-Luz, where they were met by two guides, one of whom was a 'sturdy Basque', forty-three-year-old Florentino Goïcoechea. Florentino, 'a tall man for a true Basque', had like others of his countrymen 'the quality of absolute loyalty to whatever cause he had chosen'. Happily for the Comet line and its users he 'was delighted to work for Dédée and Tante Go'.[798] Florentino took the airmen on the two and a half hour walk from St Jean to the isolated farm of Francia Usandizaga at Bidegainberri, near the village of Urrugne. Lying halfway between St Jean-de-Luz and the border at Hendaye, it had the advantage that it could only be approached on foot, up a stony path.

Despite a close shave at a German roadblock, warning of which had been given to them by a passer-by, they got to the farm without mishap. The three airmen and Dédée were led off across the western Pyrenees and the Bidassoa river at 2300 hours on 10 November. Walking for five hours, they spent what was left of the night in a small shelter in Spain. Florentino returned to France in the morning, but another guide arrived early in the afternoon and took the airmen and Dédée to Irún, where they caught the train to San Sebastián. On 12 November the Spanish guide[799] took them to the British Seamen's Institute in Bilbao, then returned home. Dédée stayed on for a week in Bilbao before also returning to France.

On 18 November the three airmen were driven in the vice-consul's car to Miranda de Ebro, where a car from the British Embassy took them to Madrid. They stayed there until 7 December when, accompanied by a man from the embassy and a Spanish detective 'to whom the Poles were represented as English', they took the train to Gibraltar. Catching up with Greig, Cowan and Conville, on 30 December 1941 they sailed on the Polish motor ship *Batory* with an escort of two destroyers, docking at Gourock, Scotland, on 4 January 1942.

Sailing on the *Batory* was a total of twenty-three evaders or escapers, six of whom having been helped by Comet. Once Dédée had been given the green light by the British the Belgian countryside was scoured for airmen, though by the end of 1941 only another seven had been found – Sergeant J.L. Newton and Sergeant A.D. Day RCAF, both shot down on the night of 5/6 August; Sergeants J.W. Hutton and L.A. Warburton on 31 August/1 September; Sergeant H.E. Birk RAAF, on 28/29 September; and Sergeant G.T. Cox and Pilot Officer H.B. Carroll on 13/14 October.

On the night of 5/6 August 1941, returning from Aachen, Wellington W5421 developed such severe engine trouble that the pilot, Flight Lieutenant R.B. Langlois DFC, decided to land. Keeping a good lookout from his front turret was air gunner Sergeant Jack Newton, who saw what he thought were two rivers, but which proved to be the hard runways of the Luftwaffe airfield at Antwerp-Deurne glinting in the pale moonlight. Landing at the far end of the airfield Langlois and his crew, without interference from the Germans, set fire to the bomber, before splitting into two groups of three and heading south.

Sergeants J.W. McLarnon, H.J.E. Burrell and R.D. Porteous RNZAF 'wandered around until dawn and then hid up until the following night when we contacted a peasant who took a message into Antwerp for us to the American Consul, who unfortunately did not exist. The message, however, was received by the concierge at the consulate who contacted the Underground and they came out the following afternoon and picked us up.'[800] They were hidden in Antwerp until false papers were ready for them and, on 9 September, moved by train to Brussels.

Two days later they left for Besançon, and crossed into Unoccupied France on the afternoon of 13 September, having been told to go to a certain café where another guide would take them by bus and train to Toulouse. While at the café, a suspicious gendarme asked to see their papers. Not satisfied with what he saw and heard, he took them to the gendarmerie, where their RAF identities were established. Now under the care of the Vichy authorities, they were removed to the barracks at St Hippolyte-du-Fort, and were later transferred to the prison at Fort de la Revère in the hills above Monte Carlo.

Meanwhile, the others of W5421 – Langlois, Newton, and wireless operator Flight Sergeant R.A. Copley – were spotted by a Belgian cyclist, who told them to hide in a cornfield while he went off to Antwerp to consult a friend. Spending the night in a farmhouse, the airmen awoke to find civilian clothing awaiting them. On their way by train to Brussels on 14 August, they passed through Antwerp and Liège, where Newton had a close shave, being detained by gendarmes one evening: 'A Belgian was with me at the time. The gendarmes inspected our identity cards and, finding them unsatisfactory, took us in the direction of the police station. On the way we gave the gendarmes a push forward and ran off in the opposite direction. We were not recaptured. The gendarmes did not know my true identity.'[801]

Having separated in Brussels, Copley and Langlois were arrested on 29 September and 2 October respectively, but at a house in Waterloo Jack Newton met Al Day and Larry Birk. At the end of October, he was moved to the Brussels suburb of Ixelles, and in late November to a house in the nearby Schaerbeek district, where he was re-united with Birk and Day, and briefly met Sergeant Janek Budzynski (see Chapter 4).

In early December 1941 Comet were ready to take another group south. As Al Day had contracted pneumonia and was therefore too ill to travel, Jack Newton took his place. On 5 December, he and Birk were joined at Brussels railway station by Pilot Officer Carroll and by Gérard Waucquez.

Carroll, second pilot of a Manchester, and crew were on their way to bomb Cologne railway station on the night of 13/14 October 1941 when the aircraft was caught in a cone of searchlights as it passed Liège. Like moths to a candle four German night-fighters attacked, two of which were probably shot down by the two gunners – Pilot Officer F. Mason (mid-upper) and Sergeant A.F. Dickson RCAF (rear) – but when the starboard engine was set on fire and could not be extinguished Pilot Officer Joseph Unsworth DFM gave the order to jump. Only Carroll and the second wireless operator, Sergeant G.T. Cox, were able to get clear before the aircraft exploded.

Landing in a wood near Comblain-au-Pont, a dozen kilometres due south of Liège, Carroll watched the blazing wreckage of his Manchester fall to earth. Tom Cox landed in a tree. Leaving his parachute there he 'hurried away from the locality', but was found in the morning by some Belgians who had followed his tracks. They gave him a coat and boots and took him to St Roc [*sic*],[802] where he was hidden in the school, before moving him to Liège and where he stayed with two families for the next six weeks – one week with one family, the next with the other, and so on. Towards the end of November he was taken to Brussels, and was reunited with Pilot Officer Carroll, but returned to Liège when Carroll left for Spain.

Not sure whether he was in Germany or Belgium, Carroll had walked westwards for a while until he met a Belgian gendarme, home on leave from Brussels. The gendarme took him home, gave him food, a change of clothes, and 150 francs, and took him to Brussels (14/15 October). He 'stayed the night at a tobacconist's shop, and was taken next morning to the house of a friend of the gendarme.'[803] This friend proved most generous, as Carroll remembered: 'Although a poor man – I believe he earned only 800 [francs] a month – my host supplied me plentifully with food and clothes, being assisted by three gendarmes.' Two of the gendarmes were known to him as Omer and Henri, and the third as François Malmedy, all 'members of a Belgian organisation which had a "black list" of Belgians assisting the Nazis. People on the "black list" were being assassinated.'[804] Carroll's helpers eventually managed to get in touch with *la ligne Dédée* (Comet), and on 20 November he was moved to another address in Brussels, where Tom Cox was already in residence.

Carroll left Brussels with Jack Newton and Larry Birk on 5 December. Escorted to the Franco-Belgian border, they were met by Dédée, and crossed the River Somme at the usual point near Corbie before catching the train to Paris, and on to St Jean-de-Luz. From the De Greefs' house at Anglet, they went to Francia Usandizaga's farmhouse, where preparations were made for the crossing of the mountains. Florentino Goïcoechea would lead the three airmen, and Dédée, over the Pyrenees and into Spain, but first they had to cross the Bidassoa.

This rock-strewn river, which for the last dozen kilometres of its journey into the Atlantic between Hendaye (France) and Irún (Spain) marks the Franco-Spanish border, has its source deep in the Pyrenees. Swollen now by recent heavy rain, the group of evaders found that it was in torrent and too dangerous to ford in the dark. The disappointed men could only retrace their steps to Urrugne. Four days later it was decided to try to cross the river again. It was still in torrent, but Florentino remembered a wooden rope-bridge that they might be able to use, though it would be guarded. Finding the Spanish guards as expected, they waited until they were asleep before crossing safely into Spain, on 10 December 1941. Dédée then led the three evaders to the British Consulate at Bilbao.

Newton returned from Gibraltar aboard a 202 Squadron Sunderland flying boat on 13 January 1942, alighting at Pembroke Dock (Wales) on 14 January after a sixteen-hour flight. Carroll flew back on 20 January 1942, while Larry Birk returned by sea on 4 March 1942.

Al Day, meanwhile, was being treated for his bronchial pneumonia. Baron Donny had been unable to find him a doctor but, while in hiding at the home of Madame Depourque, Al met a man by the name of Leo, who worked at the main hospital in Brussels. Leo persuaded a Doctor Lardot to supply the necessary drugs for Al, and these did the trick, for he was well enough to leave Brussels on 21 December 1941.[805]

Two of the seven airmen rescued by Comet in the latter part of 1941, Sergeants Hutton and Warburton, were the gunners of a Wellington shot down on the night of 31 August/1 September 1941. Though their pilot (Pilot Officer J.F. Ashton) was apparently machine-gunned as he parachuted to earth, the two gunners landed safely near Diepenbeek, in eastern Belgium, (where John Ives had landed a fortnight earlier), 'and were immediately picked up by Flemish peasants, who always roam the countryside after a crash to render assistance to pilots, despite the curfew at 2300 hours.'[806] Given food, jackets and caps, they were shown the way to Hasselt. Their luck was certainly with them that night, for the bridge over the Albert Canal was unguarded and then, as they were passing through Hasselt at around 2 a.m. during the curfew period, they were seen by a gendarme, who shone his torch at them. Quick as a flash the two airmen said 'Gute nacht'. Clearly satisfied as to their identity, the policeman bothered them no more.

During the week they spent at a farm, they were told of another airman, Sergeant Harry Fraser, who had been caught in Hasselt in May 1941. Fraser had been taken to Germany, but the family with whom he had been sheltering had been shot.[807] Hutton and Warburton were taken to Brussels on 6 September, and briefly met John Ives. Two days later they were separated. Jack Hutton probably spent the next fortnight with the Brusselmans family, for an entry in Anne's diary records the arrival at their apartment of a British airman, Jack, who came from Newcastle, where pre-war he had been a bricklayer. Hutton did indeed come from the Newcastle area – Lemington-on-Tyne – and pre-war had been in general labouring.[808]

Jack Hutton and Len Warburton, reunited on 23 September, remained together until 21 December, when they left for Spain with Al Day and Tom Cox, who had been brought from Liège that same day, and successfully reached Spain on Christmas Day 1941. The four airmen were taken to Gibraltar on 4 January 1942, but it was to be eight weeks before they sailed for home.

By the end of 1941 Dédée and company had made five crossings of the Pyrenees, with thirteen men (three soldiers, ten airmen), without mishap. They took only one man across in January 1942 – Fusilier T.J. Sim, Royal Northumberland Fusiliers, on 19 January[809] – and next month only Corporal N.J. "Jackie" Hogan RASC, on 8/9 February 1942.

Hogan, a former merchant seaman, had jumped from a train taking prisoners of war to Germany as it neared Cologne, deep within Germany. Though wounded in the left hand by a bullet fired at him by one of the guards, he walked all the way to Belgium, staying in Louvain until, at the beginning of February 1942, he left for Spain with two Belgian officers, Major-Aviateur Paul Henri de la Lindi, a thirty-five-year-old Belgian airman,[810] and Lieutenant Georges Osselaer of a Belgian cavalry regiment, the 2ème Lanciers.[811]

Seriously wounded in the fighting in 1940 and captured, Osselaer was sent to a prisoner-of-war camp, from which he was released in June 1941 as *un grand malade*. His regimental ties were still strong, however, and he sent a food parcel back to one of his fellow officers who was still in captivity. Unfortunately for him and for his fellow officers, the Germans discovered 'some files for escape purposes' in the parcel and, when word of this reached the Gestapo, Osselaer had to disappear quickly.

Under the guidance of an agent codenamed "Cyrano" he and de la Lindi were taken by train from Brussels to Mons on 6 February 1942, and handed over to a man who introduced himself as "le père d'Andrée" – Frédéric de Jongh. With him was Corporal Hogan. Frédéric took them as far as the border with France, when he handed over his "packages" to 'a couple of girls one of whom was called Andrée and who was to be their guide taking them to Spain and the other girl being called Elvire who was doing the trip for the first time in order to be able to replace Andrée as guide if necessary.'[812]

On his arrival in England Osselaer gave a pen-portrait of these two "girls". Andrée (de Jongh), he said, 'is small, aged about twenty-four years, dyed brown hair. She had a bundle of documents under her arm and also a new German shell which she was taking out to send to British Authorities for inspection.' He also thought 'that she had the most extraordinary sang-froid.' As for Elvire (Morelle), she 'was very tall, blonde, slightly red hair, enormous nose and very red face; is of French nationality, about twenty-five years of age.'[813]

The small party took the overnight train, 6/7 February, to Bayonne, and stayed the night 'in a Belgian house at Langlet [*sic*] which is just on the outskirts of Bayonne'.[814] On 8 February they 'left by bus for St Jean-de-Luz, where they met a guide [Florentino Goïcoechea] who took them across the Pyrenées to a farm a couple of miles from Irun. This guide was Spanish, tall, large teeth, about forty-five years of age, with a stupid face and always grumbling. He was paid 8,000 French francs per person he took across the frontier.'[815] The farm was probably Sarobe, home to the Iriarte family – 'Manuel, Francisco, Regina and Fermina –', and 'had been a way station in the mountains along the frontier as long as anyone could remember'.[816]

The party was met at the farm by the son of the garage owner Bernardo Aracama. On 10 February Aracama senior took them by train to Bilbao, where Jackie Hogan was sent to the British Legation. The two Belgian officers went to another Belgian house, at 76, Gran Via, Bilbao, and were taken care of by Michael Creswell. They were later escorted to Portugal, by Bernardo Aracama, while Hogan made his way to Gibraltar, returning to England aboard the same ship as that on which Al Day and party were to sail. For his stirring escape and evasion Hogan would receive the DCM.

On their way back from San Sebastián, Dédée, Florentino and Elvire Morelle ran into a blizzard, in the course of which Elvire fell and broke her leg. Florentino somehow conjured up a donkey and took her to a farm at Rentéria. Bernardo Aracama was summoned from San Sebastián, and took Elvire in his car to his apartment, where she was treated by a Basque doctor.

Thanks in part to the loose-tongued Belgian officer who had talked too much in the summer of 1941, German security forces decided that they needed to investigate the de Jongh family and, while Dédée was on her first visit to the Bilbao consulate, the Gestapo and Abwehr called at their home at 73, Avenue Emile Verhaeren, Brussels. Frédéric and his family denied any knowledge of his daughter's whereabouts but, as his house was the headquarters of the escape line, he decided to transfer operations to his school in the Place Gaucheret,[817] where false identity and ration cards were already being kept.

In February 1942 German security forces intensified their search for members of the Comet organisation. Though they had failed to catch Dédée, they arrested her elder, married sister, Suzanne Wittek, and would have nabbed Frédéric, too, having put a price on his head of a million Belgian francs, but he was away in Valenciennes (a few kilometres over the border in France) 'reorganising the system of guides to Paris'.[818] He managed to avoid arrest on his return to Brussels, but so difficult was life becoming for him in the Belgian capital that he left on 30 April 1942, and went to Paris to continue operations from there.

Only six days after Frédéric had handed over the running of the organisation in Brussels to Charles Morelle and Henri Michelli, they too were arrested. He had left not a moment too soon. The new chief in Brussels was now Baron Jean Greindl ("Nemo"). He had been on the fringe of underground activities through his contact in 1941 with Peggy van Lier, who had introduced him to Jean Ingels,[819] Frédéric de Jongh's second-in-command, and subsequently to Frédéric himself and to Dédée. Early in 1942 Jean Greindl had become director of the *Cantine Suèdoise* (the Swedish Canteen), an organisation run on behalf of the Swedish Red Cross to supply food and clothing for the needy children of Brussels, but which was to provide a useful cover for his subsequent underground activities. Now, as Comet's leader, he gathered together a new and enthusiastic team, which included cousins Georges and Edouard d'Oultremont, Georges later replacing nineteen-year-old Andrée Dumon ("Nadine") who had also been picked up by the Gestapo in their summer purge.

Given the difficulties of a winter crossing of the Pyrenees and the problems with arrests Comet, as seen, were able to pass only Sim (Comet 14) and Hogan (15) into Spain throughout the whole of January and February 1942. They delivered no "parcels" in March, and only one in April, Flight Sergeant J.A. McCairns (16).

McCairns had escaped from a German prisoner-of-war camp, Stalag IXC (Bad Sulza), on 22 January 1942, and on his way through Belgium had been hidden by an SOE agent who told him about black-painted Lysanders. Taken over the Pyrenees on 27 March by Charlie Morelle (who helped his sister, Elvire, back to France on his return), when McCairns reached Gibraltar he had an interview on 20 April with Jimmy Langley, P15 of MI9. In the spirit of inter-departmental co-operation Langley passed on the gist of their meeting to SOE, who in turn informed "H" that they, SOE, were 'very interested in Sergeant McCairns as he was hidden for some time by one of our agents. He also reported a very strange message which he was supposed to take to somebody of the name of Octave.[820] This came into the hands of one of C's men and was passed on to us by the ACSS. ACSS informs us that they are not sure of McCairns, but the latter will certainly be able to throw some light on the activities of Lacquer. We should be glad if we could be informed as soon as McCairns arrives in the UK.'[821]

Back in England on 30 April, and the proud recipient of the Military Medal, Langley arranged for McCairns to become a Lysander pilot on the special duties squadrons.[822]

There was no lack of drama at RAF Dalton, Yorkshire on the night of 27/28 April 1942 when Flight Sergeant L.W. Carr and crew took off in their Halifax bomber, W7653. With its four engines pounding away at maximum boost, the undercarriage hit the airfield's boundary hedge, prompting rear gunner Sergeant G.H. "Dixie" Lee to remark: 'I don't suppose they wanted that hedge, anyway... Still, Skipper, I'd rather take a return ticket to Cologne if it's all the same to you.'[823]

This was not to be, for in bright moonlight over Belgium W7653 was attacked by an Me110 and set on fire. As the night-fighter closed in to finish off the bomber Dixie Lee 'let fly with a burst that poured squarely into the approaching German. The fighter immediately burst into a blaze and spun over, to dive earthwards.'[824] Carr gave the order to bale out of the doomed Halifax. He himself was only able to do so at low altitude, his parachute barely opening before he hit the ground near Hamois, in the Belgian province of Namur, less than a kilometre from the remains of W7653. Using his collar-stud compass he headed south for an hour and a half, away from the wreckage of his aircraft in which three of his crew had lost their lives. As he crossed a track two Belgians – Maurice Wilmet and Commandant Massinon, a senior gendarme – asked him if he were English and wanted to return to England. Answering 'yes' to both questions Carr was taken to Wilmet's house in Hamois, and while he was having a meal Massinon dutifully telephoned the Germans to tell them that there were no survivors! Later, Wilmet took Carr to a farm some five or six kilometres away, near Bormenville, where he was told that Dixie Lee had been betrayed to the Germans, apparently by a Belgian Rexist.

On the morning of 29 April Wilmet and Carr took a slow train from Bormenville to Ciney, Massinon joining them at Hamois. Changing trains at Ciney, they 'were joined by a girl aged about twenty who called herself Fernande, which was probably an assumed name. She was a representative of the organisation in that part of the country.'[825] Fernande Pirlot (alias Pochette) travelled with them third class on the express from Luxembourg to Brussels, where Massinon left them to make their way by tram to the Itterbeek suburb. Staying the night at the home of Madame Castermans, an Englishwoman married to a Belgian, Carr was taken on 30 April to the Roggeman family in Woluwe St Lambert, another Brussels suburb. Supplied with a Belgian identity card and a German passport that permitted him to travel to Bayonne in the south-west of France, he was taken by a Madame Pol on 5 May 'to a square in the centre of the city, where we were to join a party going to France. Although we waited for about an hour, no one turned up except Sergeant Shoebridge and a guide. In the absence of the rest of the party, we all went to the house where Shoebridge and Raiston were staying in the Rue de la Victoire.'[826] Sergeant R.B. Shoebridge and Flight Sergeant J.W. Raiston RCAF were two of the other three survivors of Carr's Halifax.

On 7 May 1942 the airmen heard the news that several of Comet's members had been arrested, among them its chief (Henri Michelli);[827] an unknown representative of the Belgian government in London; an unknown guide (probably Charlie Morelle); and an unknown Belgian parachutist, though 'whether this man was in the RAF or whether he had been specially landed' was not clear. Actually, the "parachutist" was SOE agent Gérard Waucquez. He and the others had been enjoying a dinner at Michelli's house, (where all the papers, false identity cards and passports for the airmen's journey south were being kept), when the Gestapo put in an appearance, led there by the traitor Flore Dings, who had befriended one of Comet's safe-house keepers, Madame Anne-Marie Bruycker-Roberts.[828] Carr was told that those arrested would be released on payment of a substantial sum of money, which the Belgians would try to reclaim from the British consul in Bilbao.

Despite the massive set-back, Comet persisted with plans to get the airmen out, and on 12 May they were moved again. Raiston and Shoebridge left together, while Carr went to the home of wireless dealer Carl Servais and his wife at Laeken. Five days later Carr heard that Raiston and Shoebridge had been arrested[829] along with their current hosts and their former hosts at the Rue de la Victoire. On the evening of 19 May Carr was collected by Peggy van Lier – 'She spoke perfect English, and I think her mother is English' – and taken to a house just outside Brussels. Early the following day, Peggy and Carr went to the Gare du Nord 'and were met by a young woman of about twenty-four called Andrée, whose father (now in Paris) used to be chief of the organisation in Brussels.'

Now in Dédée's capable hands, they caught the Brussels-Paris express, travelling second class.

The journey to Paris was uneventful, and at the Gare du Nord Carr and Dédée were met by 'a woman member of the organisation and Andrée's father, but we did not speak to them until we all met in a café near the station.'[830] After a meal in a restaurant Frédéric escorted Dédée and Carr to the Gare d'Austerlitz, where they caught the night train to Bayonne. Intending to go to the De Greef's house at Anglet, they were intercepted at Bayonne station by Elvire with the news that her house was being watched, and that they would have to go elsewhere. The three of them, therefore, caught a train to St Jean-de-Luz at midday on 21 May. Although there was a control at the station, Carr avoided it by going out through the lavatory at the back of the station, a repeat of Operation Water Closet. They had been particularly anxious to avoid any police checks, as it was understood that Spanish secret police were operating at St Jean.

Once outside the station, Carr was taken by a Basque to his house, where he was joined by Dédée and Elvire. That afternoon Albert Johnson ("B") also paid them a visit. He was, according to Carr, 'just beginning to help in the organisation' and was 'about to take over as a guide on the line'. The mountain crossing had been planned for the night of 21/22 May, but bad weather forced a postponement, and it was not until 6 o'clock on the evening of 22 May that they began the ten-kilometre walk to Francia Usandizaga's farmhouse near Urrugne. Florentino Goïcoechea arrived after dark and, shortly after midnight on 23 May, led them over the Pyrenees. After some five hours, having crossed the frontier to the east of Irún, they rested at a deserted Spanish farmhouse. They continued walking through the hills, snatching a couple of hours sleep on the morning of 24 May, before catching a tram at a small village to San Sebastián. They went 'straight to a house, the owner of which is a Spaniard who owns a garage and repairs British Consulate cars' – Bernardo Aracama again.

On 25 May Bernardo took Carr into San Sebastián, and handed him over to the consul. Driven to Bilbao, Carr spent one day there, in the seamen's hostel: 'On 27 May I was taken by car by the British vice consul's chauffeur to the British Consulate. The consul then drove me to Miranda, where Major Sir Peter Norton-Griffiths included me in a party he was taking from the internment camp.'[831] This party comprised 'a French officer, another Frenchman, a Pole, and two Belgians – all posing as French Canadians'. Leaving the British Embassy in Madrid on 31 May, in a Red Cross van, Carr arrived in Gibraltar on 1 June. Sailing on 18 June aboard the aircraft carrier HMS *Argus*, he reached Gourock five days later. For his evasion he was Mentioned in Despatches.

Due to the pressure from the German security forces, Comet's only success for the whole of April and May 1942 was Carr (17). It was a measure of Comet's resilience, however, that they got seven airmen over the Pyrenees in June. Five of the seven – Pilot Officer R.M. Horsley; Sergeants L.H. Baveystock; S.E. King; A. McF. Mills; and B.W. Naylor – were from Manchester bomber L7301 lost on 30/31 May 1942. Remaining at the controls of L7301 long enough to allow his crew to jump, Pilot Officer Leslie Manser lost his life when the aircraft plunged into the ground at Molenbeersel in north-east Belgium. His award of the Victoria Cross was gazetted on 30 October 1942.

Bob Horsley, having landed in a marshy area of Belgium, a few kilometres north-east of Bree, was able to dry his wet clothes in a farmhouse, whither taken by the farmer. The 'people told me that in the village of Bree there was an agent of the organisation. The farmer took me by bicycle to the house of a doctor in Tongerloo. There I met Sgt. Naylor and Sgt. Mills'[832] who had been 'directed separately and by different people to an isolated farmhouse near Bree, occupied by Dr and Mme. Grunnen. Only Mme. Grunnen takes an active part in the organisation.'[833] As the organisation was unable to move all three men together to Liège, Horsley was left behind while Naylor and Mills were taken to the windmill at Dilsen (the "moulin rouge", some fifteen kilometres south of the crash site) on the night of 31 May/1 June.

Departing at 4 a.m. by train to Tongeren (Tongres), Naylor and Mills were accompanied to Liège by a Mademoiselle Saul and a Dutchman ('on his way to England'). Arriving at around 8 a.m., they were looked after by no less a personage than the chief of police for District IV, Liège, Commissioner Louis Rademecker,[834] who had formed a group known as *L'Épingle Noire* (The Black Pin) from among his police colleagues and from high civil servants, customs officers, café owners and hoteliers. A branch of this group, *Jam*, functioned specifically to help evading or escaping airmen and French prisoners of war.

After the departure of Mills and Naylor, Horsley was taken back to Bree, where he met Les Baveystock and Stan King. Les had met up with Stan, who had turned an ankle, soon after they had parachuted onto Belgian soil, and they had been 'hidden by some wonderful farming people named Nijskens, who put us in touch with the Underground'.[835] On the night of 1/2 June, Horsley, Baveystock and King left the Nijskens' farm on bicycles 'accompanied by two men and a girl'. Cycling along side roads to Mechelen they had a wash and a rest before continuing to the windmill at Dilsen, reaching it at around 4 a.m. on 2 June. There a Dutchman gave his spare clothes to Bob Horsley, who 'was very disreputable'. They left not long afterwards on 'a sort of tram/train' to Tongres, where they caught the train to Liège.

The prearranged pick-up point was the church of St Denis, and there they were collected by Commissioner Rademecker, and subsequently 'met up with all of the crew'.[836] Once together, they were subjected to a rigorous examination by their helpers, the usual necessary precaution to ensure that they were not German infiltrators. Having satisfied the cautious Belgians, plans were set in train to get them to Spain, and they left for Brussels on 5 June. First to leave for the south were Les Baveystock and Bob Horsley, who had been staying together in a house opposite the Palais de Justice. Taken to Paris by Andrée Dumon on the night of 9/10 June, they were handed over to Dédée, who took them to the first floor of a block of flats at 10, rue Oudinot, in the 7th Arrondissement of Paris, where, Les remembered, 'a girlfriend of Dédée's lived… This girl was a little older than Dédée, but I did not discover her name.'[837]

Also living in a rented apartment on the fourth floor of 10, rue Oudinot was Elvire Morelle. Having broken her leg in February, she had had to follow a more sedate lifestyle, and had rented 'a huge, ugly villa at St Maur, on the outskirts of Paris, during the summer months of 1942. There the men could stay in comfort and bask in the sun behind the high garden wall. Elvire was housekeeper and cook, and Charlie, her brother, would often appear at the house, bringing a new group of airmen from Brussels.'[838] As the safe house at St Maur was some distance from the main railway stations, Elvire moved to rue Oudinot in the heart of Paris. Yet a third flat in the block, Aimable Fouquerel's on the fifth floor, was used as an overflow when the situation demanded it. Aimable 'worked as a masseur at a hospital nearby, which necessitated frequent absences at night. This capable, generous and loyal man put his flat at the disposal of the organisation. Sometimes, when there were many airmen waiting to be sent to the frontier, three of them would sleep on his large bed.'[839] And so, for 'nearly a year airmen and soldiers were hidden in these three small flats, and not a soul in the building, save the old concierge, knew the truth.'[840]

Living conveniently close to the rue Oudinot were Robert Aylé and his wife Germaine, two more Comet helpers, whose apartment on the fourth floor of 37, rue de Babylone was also used as an overflow. Rue de Babylone, near the Hôtel des Invalides, on the south bank of the Seine, 'was a street of sad, grey houses of the Second Empire. A gloomy *maison de repos* for priests overshadows the apartment house on the other side.'[841]

After an evening meal Dédée took Les and Bob to the station for the journey to the south-west. But before doing so, she told them that they would be travelling with a young Belgian, Jean Depraetre, and another airman claiming to be Sergeant H.E. "Hal" De Mone RCAF. She added that they were sure of Jean's bona fides, but they were not so sure of the airman, who seemed to know nothing of the RAF. He was, frankly, suspected of being a German. It would be up to Les and Bob to find out. If they did not get the right answers from the man, then he would be "eliminated" in the interests of security. From the replies to their questions, however, Les and Bob *were* convinced that the airman was indeed who he claimed to be. In view of what he told them, though, it was hardly surprising that Comet had been put on their guard by his lack of RAF knowledge.

Hal De Mone told his inquisitors that, having volunteered in Canada to join the RCAF as an air gunner, 'he had completed a month's air-gunnery course, but had never seen an operational aircraft, nor even sat in a modern gun turret. Neither had he flown at night.'[842] Sent over to England immediately after his short course had finished, he had barely arrived at No. 16 OTU, Upper Heyford, before he found himself on operations to Cologne manning the rear turret of a Wellington. This was the first thousand-bomber raid, when practically anyone and anything that could fly was ordered into the air by "Bomber" Harris. Attacked on the way back Hal, remarkably for a first-timer, shot down their attacker, but two nights later, on the second thousand-bomber raid, his Wellington this time went down in flames. It was little wonder that Hal knew next to nothing about the RAF.

Landing near Malines (Mechelen) a farmer took Hal home and gave him 'bread and coffee and civilian clothes'. Leaving as soon as possible, Hal followed the farmer's directions, and was walking 'along the canal towards Brussels' when he was overtaken by another farmer, who took him to a small Belgian brewery occupied by a Belgian officer. This man contacted Baron Lindon, who lived in a château across the canal from the brewery and who came over and questioned Hal 'about the RAF and about Canada. After I had satisfied him as to my identity, he said he could help me. He gave me some clothes and told me to be ready next morning.'[843]

On 3 June the officer gave Hal money for the tram fare to Brussels and told him what to say, as Hal was to travel on his own for part of the journey. Baron Lindon joined the tram on the way to Brussels, and sat opposite Hal, taking him to an apartment when they got to the city. Half an hour later another man took Hal to a large park and from there to a church, where he was passed on to a third man, to whom Hal gave his 'French money and other articles, such as my compass and my identity disc'. He was then 'handed over to a girl called Betty Christy, who I believe is English'. Betty escorted Hal to a house which he was required to leave on the afternoon of 7 June, when the Germans suddenly started searching the neighbourhood for a wireless set.[844] Betty took him to the station on the following day and handed him over to Elvire Morelle.

She escorted him to Paris, where they arrived at around 9 o'clock that evening, and it was then that he met Les and Bob. Thanks to their "all clear" he left with them, Dédée and Jean Depraetre for Spain on the overnight train on 10/11 June. At Bayonne, Elvire De Greef and her daughter Jeanine got on the train. Hal swapped his ticket with Jeanine as his 'did not go all the way'. In any case, when they got to St Jean-de-Luz Hal was not asked to produce his identity card, 'probably because I look French and was wearing a cross round my neck.' The party then walked from the station to a flat above a café and stayed the night there.

By various means the group made its way to Francia Usandizaga's farm near Urrugne, and was guided by Florentino Goïcoechea over the Pyrenees on the night of 12/13 June. After a short sleep in a barn Dédée took Bob Horsley and Hal de Mone to a café in a nearby village, where they were joined by the rest of the party some two hours later. From San Sebastián they were driven to Madrid.

Back in Brussels, meanwhile, King, Mills and Naylor were 'confined in a small bedroom all the time' at 16, Palais de Justice apartments, the home of the van Steenbeck family.[845] There they were well fed on "black market" food, and a doctor was brought to have a look at Ben Naylor, who had been hit by splinters in the shoulder, nose and toes during the attack on their aircraft. He was ready, though, for the move to Louvain (Leuven) on 17 June, as was Stan King, whose ankle had now mended: 'We had a woman guide with us, whose husband, an Englishman, was in St Jean-de-Luz.'[846] From Louvain the airmen were taken by Andrée Dumon by train to Paris, where they were met by Frédéric de Jongh, and taken to his flat.

Comet were now doing a brisk trade, for also brought to Frédéric de Jongh's flat were Sergeant Edward Siadecki PAF and Sergeant Waczan Czekalski PAF, two more Polish airmen shot down over Belgium on 5/6 May (see previous chapter). Hard on the heels of the 50 Squadron crew from Brussels, they had arrived in Paris on 19 or 20 June.

Sergeant Siadecki landed near Arbre (a dozen kilometres south of Namur) and contacted the local priest: 'He put me in touch with the owner of a castle near by, who arranged for me to be collected by people from Namur connected with an organisation.'[847]

Sergeant Czekalski and another member of his crew, Flying Officer A. Szkuta PAF, had joined forces after baling out some thirty kilometres further south of Arbre. Szkuta had been rescued by friendly Belgians, who 'rang up Philippeville, and after a time a Belgian gendarme in uniform arrived on a motorcycle, bringing with him Sgt. Czekalski.'[848] After they had had their photographs taken, the gendarme took Szkuta back with him towards Philippeville while Czekalski was left at the village of Romerée. On the following day Szkuta was collected by Monsieur Dubois, mayor of Dhuy, and driven to Floreffe, half a dozen kilometres south-west of Namur. Reunited, Szkuta, Siadecki and Czekalski were taken to Namur itself, staying three days with Monsieur Petit, a photographer and 'one of the heads of this organisation', but had to leave one day when some relations were expected who were believed to be pro-German. They went to Dhuy for five days and then to Floreffe. At some point, they were joined by Pilot Officer W.P. Wasik PAF (see previous chapter).

Meanwhile in Floreffe, ten days or so after the two sergeants had departed, plans were made to get Szkuta and Wasik to Switzerland 'with some members of the organisation who were going to try to re-organise a line. Our party left Floreffe on 21 May by car.'[849] With the two Polish officers were four Belgians – M. Petit, leader of the group; Pierre van Biest, apparently a member of the organisation; Ernest Demuyter, the celebrated balloonist, well-known airman and member of the Gordon Bennett Club; and a young man called Gaston Jadin.[850] The six men reached Nancy, France, by 11 p.m. that same day. Monsieur Petit returned north on 22 May 'while the rest of the party took a train to Belfort'. Advised by some Frenchmen on the train that it would be best to cross into Switzerland from Maîche, the group left the train at Montbéliard, and caught a bus to Maîche, some thirty kilometres south down the winding River Doubs. Here they stayed at the Lion d'Or hotel, on the rue Besançon, for five days.

Failing to get assistance from the hotelkeeper, they were put in touch with a man who offered to take them to Switzerland for 2,000 francs a head. Unable to afford the high price, a man from Soulce 'took us by car to Vaufrey. On the bridge at this town we were stopped by a German guard who told us we must have passes for this frontier zone.'[851] They went back to Maîche, and tried the bridge at Soulce on the following day. This time it was unguarded, and the five men crossed one by one. Safely over, they split into three groups, one of the Poles with each, 'and walked through the hills', spending the night in the woods before making the difficult crossing into neutral Switzerland on 4 June.

A fortnight later, with the connivance of the Swiss authorities, Szkuta and Wasik left the country, together with Flight Sergeant K.H.L. Houghton DFM and a Dutchman. Shot down on the night of 13/14 October 1941 by Major Werner Streib in the north of Belgium,[852] Houghton was on Swiss soil on 20 October, and spent the last four months of his time in Switzerland working at the British Legation. Early on the morning of 20 June 1942 Szkuta, Wasik, Houghton and the Dutchman 'were driven to the frontier, walked through a churchyard and round the back, through a stream, and over some barbed wire into France… We walked to a cross-roads where we met a man on a bicycle smoking a pipe.'[853] The mysterious stranger, probably a member of the PAO line, took the four escapers to his house, where they were later collected by a second guide and taken by train to Annemasse.

By 0630 hours on 21 June they were in Marseille: 'We went to a café in the main street near the railway station, and a guide took us to a house where we met Mario.'[854] This was Mario Prassinos, 'a suave and sophisticated Greek member of the Line',[855] who supplied Ken Houghton with Polish papers to replace the Czech ones that he had been using from Switzerland. From Mario's house they were taken that same day to Nîmes, staying for a week with 'Gaston [Nègre] – "king of the Black Market" – where they were fed as never before'.

On 29 June they were moved to Toulouse, staying for two days at the Hôtel de Paris, where they were introduced to a French guide called "Alec" who, according to Houghton, 'spoke English with a slight cockney accent.' This was Francis Blanchain, who also 'asked Houghton to deliver a message to a Mr Kirby of 286, Woolworth Road, Elephant & Castle' to the effect 'that Alec is well and doing a good job.'[856]

Ken Houghton and a Frenchman, Henri, who claimed that he was working for British Intelligence, travelled on to Osséja (Pyrénées-Orientales), close to Andorra and the Spanish border, being reunited with Szkuta and Wasik a day later. On 4 July a smuggler and his wife took them over the Pyrenees and into Spain. Sleeping in a wood for the rest of the day the smuggler took them that night to Burga, where they 'stayed a day and a night in a house above a restaurant'. At about 0200 hours on 6 July, a Spaniard and his sister, Señorita Ramona, took them over the foothills to a railway station and on to Barcelona. Henri, because of his job, insisted on being taken to the British Consulate, however risky. Houghton was much put out at Henri being given precedence, especially as the same thing had happened to him in Switzerland, 'when two RAF Sergeants who arrived well after he did were sent home long before himself.'[857]

After a week in several different houses in the poorer part of the city, they left by train for Madrid, where Wasik was arrested: 'Against the advice of the guide he had insisted on wearing an expensive watch he had bought in Switzerland. The policeman who was examining his papers remarked on the watch, speaking in Spanish to which F/O [*sic*] Wasik could not reply.'[858]

Flying Officer Szkuta and Ken Houghton departed with a guide for Portugal, but he 'left them at a point roughly half way on the journey to the Portuguese frontier. Here they waited many hours for the next guide who only turned up just as they had made up their minds to travel on alone. This guide told them to give him half an hour's start for a rendezvous arranged by himself. That was the last they saw of him.'[859] However, they made their way to Lisbon, and were flown by Sunderland to Poole on 24/25 July. Pilot Officer Wasik, however, did not return, from Gibraltar, until 7 November 1942.[860]

While Szkuta and Wasik were still at Floreffe, in May, Siadecki and Czekalski 'were sent to the railway station at Namur where we were met by a guide who had our tickets ready. He took us to Brussels and there we stayed for a week, finding shelter at two places, one of which was with the widow of a Belgian captain, and the other with the caretaker of what was apparently a gas works (?). We then went by tram to Louvain, and from there were taken by a girl called Didi to Paris. There she handed us over to a man who took us to the father of Didi (2), the original Didi. He sent us to a small grocer's shop at Asnières, where we stayed four days.'[861] Precisely when and where Siadecki and Czekalski met Naylor, King and Mills is not clear – it was either at Frédéric de Jongh's apartment or at Madame Thomas's grocery shop in Asnières, to the north-west of Paris[862] – but King and one of the Poles, probably Czekalski, were the only two *chez* Madame Thomas when, on 22 June, the party was brought together again. The others – Naylor, Mills and Siadecki – had been lodged with a Captain Violette and his wife at their house in Vincennes, on the east side of Paris. Violette was 'a wood fibre merchant who had been an interrogator in the French Army. He was a new member of the organisation and we were the first he had sheltered. We stayed till 22 June.'[863]

When it was time to take the next group of four to Spain (four being Comet's optimum number for a crossing) Siadecki and Czekalski were upset to learn that Naylor, King and Mills, who had arrived in Paris *after* them, were to have priority, filling three of the four available places. Though

Sergeant Siadecki 'regarded the preferential treatment of the British sergeants in sending them on before the Poles as being unfair, as they are all members of the same service',[864] it was nevertheless decided that *he* would accompany the three RAF sergeants, and that Czekalski would go with the next group.

Dédée took the four by train to St Jean-de-Luz on the evening of 22 June, accompanied by Elvire Morelle. They were joined at Bayonne by 'the woman who had brought us from Brussels to Paris and her husband. They brought us tickets from Bayonne to St Jean-de-Luz.' Naylor and Siadecki 'were taken by the Englishman and his wife along the esplanade on foot to St Jean-de-Luz',[865] while Mills and King stayed on the train with Dédée and Elvire Morelle. They met again at the house of a Basque in St Jean-de-Luz, and on 24 June left individually for Francia Usandizaga's isolated farmhouse, halfway to the border at Hendaye. At around 11 p.m. Florentino Goïcoechea and Dédée guided them to Spain.

After an early breakfast at a café, Dédée went to San Sebastián and returned with a car (possibly Aracama's), which took the evaders to that town. 'We were sheltered at a flat, where the British vice-consul took our personal details, and informed the embassy. At 2300 hours we were sent to the pictures with the Spanish owner of the flat. When we got out about 0045 hours (26 June) the vice-consul met us and took us to a car in which Major Sir Peter Norton-Griffiths was waiting.'[866] He took them to the British Embassy in Madrid, and on 1 July they were sent to Gibraltar. The three RAF sergeants left by the troopship *Narkunda*,[867] one week ahead of Siadecki, who was flown to England and landed only two days after them.

Sergeant Czekalski, waiting his turn in Paris, was joined by three more evaders who had been shot down between 30 May and 5 June. Collected by Comet in Belgium, Sergeants B.F. Goldsmith, R.J. Collins RAAF, and W.R. Griffiths travelled in some style to Paris on 23 June, first class in a reserved compartment, escorted by Peggy Mitchell and an unnamed man.[868] Frédéric de Jongh took Collins and Goldsmith to Captain Violette's house in Vincennes, while Griffiths and a Polish pilot officer [*sic* – not identified] were taken by René Coache to his house at 71, rue de Nanterre, Asnières. During the six days they spent there, they were joined by Privates J.M.L. Goldie and William MacFarlane, two Scottish soldiers, both 7th Argyll & Sutherland Highlanders, who had escaped from Arbeitskommando 147 (the salt mines at Unterbreizbach, near Hersfeld, Germany) on the night of 21/22 March 1942. Travelling by rail in a salt-wagon they arrived on 3 April at Hasselt, Belgium, and then spent two days in a wagon marked "Antwerp" waiting for it to leave. At the end of this period they left the wagon and started walking towards Louvain, before eventually being put in touch with Comet.

On 4 July Dédée and Elvire Morelle escorted Goldsmith, Collins, Griffiths and Czekalski by train, again first class in a reserved compartment, to St Jean-de-Luz, where they arrived at around 9 a.m. the following morning. 'In Bayonne an Englishman and two girls boarded the train and took Sergeant Collins and Czekalski through the station barrier at St Jean-de-Luz. Sergeants Griffiths and Goldsmith got out of the station through a lavatory and workmen's entrance, at which a member of the organisation met them and took them to his flat, where the party stayed for a day and a night.'[869] On the morning of 7 July they walked to Francia Usandizaga's farmhouse, while Elvire Morelle returned to Paris. That evening, Dédée and two Basque guides took the airmen over the Pyrenees and, with the help of the consular and embassy staffs, made their way to Gibraltar. Sailing for Gourock on 21 July, they arrived at the Scottish port nine days later.[870]

As for the two Scotsmen, Private William MacFarlane left for Spain at the end of July, whereas Private James Goldie followed in the next Comet group of four over the Pyrenees, on or about 17 August.

One of the evaders to cross the Pyrenees with MacFarlane was Sergeant J.T. "Joe" Pack. Shot down over Germany on his way back from Essen on the night of 8/9 June 1942, Joe landed in a marshy field near Kirchhoven, a northern suburb of Heinsberg, but only three or four kilometres from the Dutch border, and hid his parachute in a deep field drain. Finding his small issue compass to be of little use, he set off in a westerly direction by the stars. Forced to head north-west for an hour or so, he then walked unchallenged through a hamlet, but soon after dawn 'began to meet workmen on bicycles. I hid from the first few but, as any who saw me did not show any interest in me, I walked along the road.'[871]

Without realising it, he had crossed into that part of Holland that forms a narrow corridor between Germany and Belgium. After a further three hours or so he was confronted by the Julianakanaal which runs parallel to, and only a couple of hundred metres east of, the River Maas (the Meuse in Belgium and France). Unable to cross the canal, he 'hid in a small patch of fern and firs' as there were many people about. He tried to sleep, but was interrupted by three men who appeared to be surveying the canal. Plucking up the courage to speak to the men, Joe 'went up to the youngest, a man of about twenty-four… I spoke to him in English. He made a rush towards me, pointed to the sky, and asked if I was an aviator. When I said I was, he shook hands with me and called to the two others, one of whom was his father… After they had told me I was near Maeseyck they hid me in deeper shrubbery.' Having gone for help the young man returned with 'a friend, a man of about fifty, who claimed to be in the Belgian Secret Service and said he would take me to Switzerland on the back of his bicycle.'[872]

Joe's travels on the bicycle with the older man, after the younger one had produced a change of clothes, was only 'across the canal and river and round Ophoven', a small village in Belgium. He was taken to a house near the village 'where there were two oldish ladies. I was given a good meal and champagne and shelter for the night.' On the afternoon of 10 June a woman of about twenty-five brought him some better clothes and she, together with her fiancé, took him by bicycle that evening to the mill at Dilsen, home of Gertrude Moors. An English-speaking doctor arrived, and asked Joe various questions to prove his identity.

Very early on the morning of 11 June Joe was taken by tram to Liège (sixty kilometres to the south), he and his escort having been joined by two more men to protect him from fellow travellers. Taken to a church [St Denis?], Joe 'was handed over to an elderly man, who turned out to be the chief of police in Liège. I noticed he was saluted by all the policemen we passed.'[873] After ten days at 'the house of two elderly ladies', during which time he was 'provided with another suit of clothes and (by a British lady) with English books', he was taken to Louvain by the head of the organisation, Paul Schoenmaker, and then by a young Belgian 'to his flat at the Ministry of Justice in Brussels', where he took Joe's photograph. The father of the young Belgian then took him 'to stay with friends about twenty miles out of the capital',[874] Roger and Stephanie LeBlois.

On 4 July Joe was taken back to Brussels and 'given an identity card and German pass for the frontier'. Next day, he, Flight Sergeant B. Evans DFM, and Pilot Officer J.H. Watson RCAF[875] were taken to Louvain by Andrée Dumon ('our guide was a young girl'). There they took the train to Paris, but not without a spot of bother at the frontier when Watson 'kept on doing the wrong things in reply to the official's questions, but the girl passed us all off as mutes.'[876]

In Paris the three airmen 'were taken to the Hotel Luxembourg in the Latin quarter', where Frédéric de Jongh kept a room. Later that morning they were joined by Andrée and Frédéric de Jongh, when Andrée Dumon returned to Brussels. Here the three separated, Evans and Watson leaving with the de Jonghs for Frédéric's apartment, where they met Sergeant J.A.A.A.B. Angers RCAF (same crew as Pilot Officer Watson), Sergeant M. Zawodny PAF, and Private William MacFarlane. On the following day MacFarlane was moved to the Coache's house, and on 16 July, the four airmen were escorted by train by Andrée de Jongh and Elvire Morelle to Bayonne, where they were met by Elvire De Greef and Albert Johnson. Continuing to St Jean-de-Luz, they 'found the station crowded with Germans, as a number of searchlights had just arrived. It was, therefore, impossible to leave by the workmen's passage as is usually done, and we all had to walk through the Customs. Fortunately, we were neither stopped nor questioned.'[877]

The group split up and all made their way to the house of Ambrosio San Vicente, where the airmen stayed for two days. On 19 July, with Andrée de Jongh and 'two guides Florentin and Thomas' (almost certainly Florentino Goïcoechea and Tomás Anabitarte), they 'walked to a farmhouse about ten kilometres away'.[878] They left the farm at around 9.30 p.m., and were walking through a defile at midnight 'in pitch darkness and pouring rain, when suddenly from some bushes in the bracken, about three yards from the path, two German soldiers leapt out, shouting wildly, into the midst of the party, which split up in confusion.' While the others dashed forwards, Zawodny ran back down the path and Evans threw himself behind a bush. The Germans were clearly scared, and one of them fired off a shot before they engaged in a heated discussion for some twenty minutes. Only Evans was left near them, the rest having made good their escape, but he was able to slip away, too, when it began to rain even harder, the noise as he 'crawled up the mountainside' being drowned by the beating rain.

Watson made a solo crossing to Spain. He was arrested, and was not to return to England until 15/16 October 1942. The others, meanwhile, returned eventually to either San Vicente's house or to the farmhouse. They rested for a day, during which time Evans was treated for a 'twisted knee, the result of my wanderings in the mountains', before setting off once more, on 20 July. This time the crossing to Oyazun was uneventful, and the airmen were collected from San Sebastián by a car from Madrid that 'had been waiting for us for about four days'. Evans, Angers and Zawodny were flown home from Gibraltar on 18/19 August.

After Joe Pack had split up with Evans and Watson, he went to the Coache family at Asnières for a fortnight, before spending a second fortnight with Frédéric de Jongh. On 31 July, with William MacFarlane, Sergeant W.J. Norfolk and Sergeant P. Wright (from the same 76 Squadron crew, shot down on the Essen raid on 1/2 June), he left for the Pyrenees with Dédée (Andrée de Jongh) as their guide. Making their way through Spain, uninterrupted by Spanish police, the three sergeants left Gibraltar on 19 August 1942 aboard a destroyer that was protecting a slow, five-knot convoy.[879] Taking the usual route way out into the Atlantic to avoid any lurking German submarines, the destroyer reached Londonderry, Northern Ireland, six days later. The ferry took them from Larne to Stranraer, Scotland, and a train to London, where they had strict orders to report immediately to the Air Ministry.

It was a Sunday morning when they arrived at Euston station, London, and the Air Ministry was closed. So Joe Pack went home to Kent, to discover that only the previous day his mother had received a telegram from the Air Ministry telling her that her son was missing, believed killed on active service.

Shot down on the same raid as Joe Pack were Flight Lieutenant J.A. MacLean RCAF and crew. Their Halifax was damaged by flak over the target (the Krupps armament works, Essen) and finished off by a night fighter on the way home. All seven of the crew baled out over Holland, but Angus MacLean was the only one to evade capture.[880]

He was fortunate to have survived, for the Halifax was so low when he baled out that his parachute had barely opened before he hit the ground flat on his back, the Halifax crashing into the next field, barely 150 yards away, a little over one kilometre south of Zaltbommel. Apart from severely hurting his back, one arm 'had been stripped of skin and the elbow was bleeding badly. The entire arm was covered with huge purplish bruises from wrist to armpit.' He nevertheless made his way south, avoiding 's-Hertogenbosch, until he came to the River Maas near Hedel. Espying two people on a houseboat, he asked for their help. They were members of the Pagie family, 'father, mother, three girls (aged eleven, eighteen and twenty-one) and a boy of fifteen',[881] who told him that he could stay indefinitely. He left, however, on 18 July, after five weeks, and was fed into the Comet line at Brussels.

Also arriving in Brussels at the same time were Pilot Officer Geoff Silva RAAF and Sergeant A.J. Whicher, two of the crew of a Whitley of 24 OTU shot down over Belgium on their way back from Düsseldorf on the night of 31 July/1 August. Intercepted by a night-fighter, the Whitley was set on fire and blew up. Whicher had been hit in the leg by a splinter, but no sooner had he landed than two Belgians rushed up to him and carried him away. Re-united with Silva, it was not long before they had been taken to Brussels, and then by Prince Albert de Ligne 'to a flat run by two girls, both of whom we knew as Betty [Constance-Elizabeth Liégeois and Elizabeth Warnow]'.[882] Already in residence was Angus MacLean.

Moved to Paris by Georges d'Oultremont and Eric de Menten de Horne, the three airmen were taken to a block of flats and met "Kiki" (Frédéric de Jongh). While Whicher remained at Kiki's flat, MacLean and Silva went to stay with the Coaches at Asnières. A few days later all three met up again at the house at St Maur that had been rented by Elvire Morelle, escorted there by Dédée (Andrée de Jongh). 'While we were at [St Maur], Whicher's leg was treated by Elvire, who had been a nurse.'[883]

On 15 August, having been joined at the station by the Glaswegian soldier James Goldie, they left by train for St Jean-de-Luz. Also joining them at the station in Paris was Andrée de Jongh's nephew, Fred Wittek, who was escaping to England.[884] They stayed the night at St Jean, before going to Francia Usandizaga's farm in the afternoon, and being guided to Spain during the night of 16/17 August by Florentino Goïcoechea and Dédée. Everyone had to ford the icy waters of the River Bidassoa, but Whicher, because of his leg wound, was carried across on Florentino's broad back. While the others rested, Dédée and her nephew continued to San Sebastián to alert the consulate. A week later they were on their way from Madrid to Gibraltar, though MacLean, to fool the Spanish authorities as to his real identity, had to pretend to be Captain Collie, Staffordshire Regiment, absent without leave in Spain. All departed by ship for Gourock on 29 August.

September 1942 was to prove to be Comet's busiest month of the war to date.[885] Of the twenty "parcels" to reach Spain, three were Polish, including Sergeant T.J. "Teddy" Frankowski PAF, who had been shot down on the night of 27/28 August 1942. Though hit in the back by a large piece of metal and by a bullet in the arm, he baled out safely and landed near Eindhoven, Holland. On 29 August, at a farm near the crash site, he was fed and his wounds dressed. Wearing civilian clothes donated by a friend of the farmer, he set off on foot that night, and by the evening of 31 August was two kilometres from the border with Belgium. A Flemish boy promised to put him in touch with smugglers who would be crossing the border, but it was not until morning that the boy returned 'looking very frightened'. He explained that the smugglers could not take him 'as the Germans had killed three of them last night.'[886]

Despite this setback, Frankowski carried on, carefully, into Belgium on 1 September, but when the soles of his Dutch shoes began to wear through he asked for help from a group of priests whom he found working in a garden. His announcement that he was RAF brought an unexpected response from one of them: 'Wir mussen sie abgeben' – 'We must hand you over'. As this was not at all what he had in mind, Frankowski put his hand into his pocket as though he had a gun 'and, backing away, indicated to him to stay where he was. He [the priest] began to shout, and another priest came up.' By now Frankowski was 'a fair distance away, running very fast along a small canal,' and when he saw the two priests on bicycles accompanied by a policeman in black uniform he dived for cover. Then, 'soldiers on motorcycles appeared, patrolling the road slowly and looking all around.' Failing to spot him, he waited until the hue and cry had subsided before heading for central Belgium, where they spoke French and would, therefore he hoped, be more sympathetic.

Continuing south through Hasselt (2 September), he reached Rijkel on the morning of 3 September, and stayed in a house for the first time on his journey. The 'people were very pro-British and kept me for a night and a day. Among the things they gave me were socks and talcum powder for my feet.' Resuming his solitary journey on 4 September he passed through St Trond (Sint Truiden), avoiding the Luftwaffe's night-fighter base a kilometre or two south of the town. Though he could scarcely walk for the blisters on his feet, he covered some forty kilometres in a westerly direction until, south of Nethen (some ten kilometres south of Louvain), he spoke to a man at work in a field. This man also suggested that, instead of making difficulties for himself, he should turn himself in. Ignoring the advice Frankowski carried on, though desperately tired and in considerable pain.

Walking through Meerdaal forest on 5 September he had almost decided that he could go no further when 'I saw an isolated house. Here I found shelter and was put in touch with an organisation.'[887] At long last safely in Comet's grasp, he was eventually taken to a safe house in Brussels and in due course met up with three members of a Wellington – Sergeant R. "Bob" Frost; Sergeant D.C. "Dal" Mounts RCAF (an American); and Sergeant W.S.O. "Bill" Randle[888] – who had baled out of their burning aircraft over the Belgian province of Brabant on the night of 16/17 September and who were staying with the Maréchal family in a Comet safe house in Brussels.[889]

Three days after Bill Randle's arrival at the Maréchals' house, "Teddy" Frankowski and the other three airmen were on their way south. Randle (Comet 60), Mounts (61) and Frankowski (62) were taken over the Pyrenees on 29 September with Flight Lieutenant L.C. Pipkin (63), and Squadron Leader L.O. Prévot (64), a Belgian fighter pilot.[890]

Flight Lieutenant Pipkin was one of the few to evade from inside Germany. Losing a shoe as he descended by parachute somewhere near Duisburg on the night of 6/7 September 1942, he managed to find it after square-searching for forty-five minutes. Nearing the Rhine he saw two German soldiers heading towards him, and dived into the undergrowth. Discovering in the light of day that he was barely 200 yards from a camp, he also saw to his horror a company of soldiers with fixed bayonets who were, apparently, looking for him. When one of them called out 'Come here', he resisted the invitation, and waited all day before making good his escape, but it was not long before he was stopped by a German soldier, who asked him for his papers: 'He tried to take hold of my arm and, when I would not let him, a fight developed. I got the better of him, and held his head under water in a ditch beside the road till he was well out of the way. He was dead when I left him.'[891]

Crossing the River Niers without difficulty he was in Holland by the morning of 10 September, and made himself known to a farmer and his family near Reuver. A priest who had been summoned told Pipkin that everything would be all right. And so it proved, for on 11 September a guide took him across the nearby River Maas, where two men 'were waiting for me with bicycles… We cycled fast for about an hour and a half to a farm, where arrangements had been made with an organisation [Comet] to get me across the frontier into Belgium.'[892]

Another evader from inside Germany was navigator Pilot Officer P.G. Freberg RCAF (Comet 68), shot down on the night of 10/11 September 1942. The only member of the scratch crew he knew was the pilot, Flight Lieutenant L.R. Barr DFC & Bar. When the time came to bale out, Freberg was the fifth to do so: 'I left F/L Barr and two others in the aircraft.'[893] Coming down west of Düsseldorf, he headed west, avoiding a flak battery and a factory, but noted that the 'industrial area of the Ruhr valley appeared to be surrounded by a large barbed wire fence in pyramid form, the base being about 7 ft broad and the whole structure about 7 ft high.'[894] He managed to climb over this formidable barrier by using the iron supports, and in due course came to the River Maas (not far from the point where Pipkin had been). He found a small boat and, using a plank of wood as a paddle, made his way across just before the boat sank. Discovering from his escape map that he was near Nunhem he altered course south-west and walked into Belgium. After calling at a peasant's house near Kinrooi, he was taken by another man to his farm, and was now in the hands of one of the Comet-affiliated organisations.

Freberg was in the first of the three groups of four to go over the Pyrenees into Spain in October

1942. With him were Bob Frost, Sergeant W.H. Ledford RCAF, and Sergeant E.T. Heap RAAF. The other two groups of four were a mixed bag: three British army officers who had escaped from a German prisoner-of-war camp; two RAF and one Canadian airmen; and two Russian airmen, Sergeant Alexi E. Stadnik and Sergeant Pyotr K. Pinchuk, who had also escaped from a German prisoner-of-war camp.

Stadnik and Pinchuk had been shot down by flak over Berlin on 13 September 1942 and had baled out leaving the other two of their crew in the aircraft. Landing in the same field they were caught crossing a road by German soldiers. Stadnik later reported: 'The same day we were sent to a camp in Saxony. I do not know the name of the camp or its number. There were only Russian prisoners of war in the camp… We lived in a barracks, where we were rather crowded, although there was enough room to sleep. The food was not good. We had only two meals a day – soup (which was bad) in the morning and soup (a very little), some potatoes, and bread about 1500 hours.'[895] It took them little time to decide to escape.

On the night of 16/17 September, when a sentry patrolling the wire was at the far end of his beat, Stadnik and Pinchuk climbed over two barbed-wire fences, the first of which was 'about twice the height of a man, the second was not so high', and made off into the night. Avoiding large towns and walking by night they set off in the direction of Belgium, living only off the bountiful fruit plucked from trees and bushes. On 21 September they were in Belgium, and reached Namur five or six days later. Avoiding the town they carried on southwards and crossed the River Meuse at Godinne, some fifteen kilometres from Namur. They were in no hurry, but eventually came to the area around Chimay, some seventy-five kilometres to the south-west of Godinne and close to the French border. From an isolated farmhouse, given food and lodging for two nights, 'a Belgian woman who spoke Polish… arranged for a young man to take us to Namur by car. From there the rest of our journey was organised for us.'[896]

Stadnik and Pinchuk were brought to the Maréchal home in Brussels, where their ways were notably different: 'They had arrived famished and at table ate everything in sight without using knives and forks.' After they had been sent on their way to France, Madame Maréchal 'found that they had raided the larder and emptied jam pots, leaving the empties hidden in the W.C. When given new clothes, they put them on over their old ones.'[897]

Stadnik (Comet 72) was in the group that went over the Pyrenees on 15 October, with Pilot Officer L.E. Kropf RCAF (71); Sergeant M.J. Joyce (an Irishman in the RAF, from Neale in County Mayo) (70); and Flight Sergeant G.H. Mellor (69).

Michael Joyce, however, was not all that he claimed to be. After being shot down in August 1940, he had been "turned" by Luftwaffe Intelligence, and had been collaborating with the enemy ever since. In September 1942 the head of the Luxembourg Gestapo – Hauptmann (later Major) Richard Kammerich – received orders that Joyce was 'to discover the routes of escaped Allied pilots, with starting point in Luxembourg or Belgium.'[898] He was thereupon driven by Kammerich to a wood near Orval abbey, one of the suspected crossing points from Belgium into France. Joyce now realised that he had the chance to get back to Britain: 'After Kammerich left me I thought things out and realised that I had at last got an opportunity to do something in my own interests, because if I found the movement and was not caught I was OK, and even if I was caught I was all right in being able to get in touch with Kammerich.'[899]

Joyce managed to make contact with the Resistance on 28 September 1942, and was taken by car across the frontier into France on the following day. He spent the night at Carignan, a dozen kilometres west of Orval abbey, and was then driven a short distance back over the border into Belgium to a farm half a kilometre south of Muno. On approximately 12 October, he was taken to Liège, a long way north, 'where there were two ladies, Matilda and Jeannine [Ritschdorf]. There I met F/Sgt. Mellor.'

Flight Sergeant Gordon Mellor, navigator, had been shot down in Halifax PM-Q on 5/6 October 1942, a bad night for RAF Bomber Command with nine aircraft lost to German defences and as many lost in England due to severe weather or other technical problems. Warrant Officer K.F. Edwards, pilot of PM-Q, fought his way through a thunderstorm but, just as course was being set for home, a fierce attack by an Me110 left the Halifax 'badly damaged and on fire in both wings. Despite the pilot's efforts the aircraft lost height rapidly and the fires intensified and spread.'[900] Forced 'to bale out at quite a low level', three of the eight-man crew, including the pilot, were killed (one used his parachute), and four were taken prisoner.

Gordon Mellor was the only one to evade capture: 'After a very short drop I landed in trees with the parachute entangled in the branches. I tried to pull the canopy down in order to hide it but the noise disturbed some dogs at a nearby home. It was obviously time to leave. Within moments of gaining the nearby road I was abreast a group of people in front of a house watching the light in the sky in the east. Was I still in Germany? I passed the group without a challenge then followed a lane and came out on to wide open farmland and there, less than a mile ahead, was the wreck of PM-Q blazing furiously… I turned to cross a field of cabbages… Suddenly, there was someone else in the field close by… and eventually [he was] heard to move away.'[901] Years later it transpired that the other person in the cabbage field was Flight Sergeant Robert Hawthorn, the bomb aimer, who spent the next two and a half years as a prisoner of war at Stalag VIIIB (Lamsdorf).

Gordon, having put some distance between himself and the crash area, went to sleep in a small copse. Woken by the voices of farm workers on either side of him, but not discovered, he decided to make his way to Spain and Gibraltar by walking only at night: 'Food was a problem. I had the standard tin of emergency rations, which did not last for long, and rather meagre meals were of vegetables from the fields. Raw they were not very agreeable. Eventually in the strengthening daylight from the side of a valley I matched the features of a small town with the details on the map that I was carrying.' At least he now knew that he was not far from the Belgian town of Liège but, as he set off on another night march, the heavens opened. With his clothes sodden and fed up by his lack of progress he saw a chink of light coming from a house, and decided to chance his arm. Knocking on the front door, his luck was in. The Van Meeuwen family, trusting that he was a genuine RAF evader, dried his clothes, gave him some hot food, and contacted Vicaire Adons, the parish priest.

As the Van Meeuwens had a young son who might inadvertently say too much, Adons took Gordon home. The following day, having been subjected to rigorous questioning, Gordon's interrogators, satisfied that he was not a German infiltrator, gave him a coat to put over his uniform and took him by tram to Liège: 'The tram was crowded and before long I found myself surrounded by a number of German soldiers. The crush was increased when an army major boarded the tram…', but Liège was safely reached. At the home of Jeannine and Mathilde Ritschdorf, two middle-aged sisters, in the rue Waroux, Gordon met Michael Joyce. The Irishman told him that he had been a prisoner of war in Germany 'and had escaped from a locked room in a farmhouse during the night hours.' As with their Belgian helpers, Gordon had no reason to believe otherwise.

When false papers had been prepared for the two airmen, an elegant lady known to them as "The Dove" escorted them from the rue Waroux. They took the tram to Ans railway station in the north-west of the town, and caught the train to Brussels, with a number of German soldiers. They stayed at three separate addresses in Brussels over the next few days, moving between each 'during daylight hours when the streets were busy'. On the move again on 16 October, they and their escort caught the train from Brussels Midi station to Lille, in France.

At the border, as usual, all the passengers were ordered off the train to pass through customs. The case that Gordon was carrying, however, caused some interest to an official but, not understanding the questions put to him, Gordon simply shrugged his shoulders and shook his head. This seemed to satisfy the official and he rejoined Joyce and their guide for the rest of the journey to Lille and Paris, but as they waited on the platform they could not help but notice two other men who stood out like sore thumbs. They would know them later as Alexis and Petro.

In Paris Gordon Mellor and Joyce were met by Dédée, and taken by metro to Sèvres-Babylone station to meet her father and Robert Aylé. There the two RAF airmen split up. Gordon went with Aylé to his flat on the rue de Babylone, while Joyce was taken by Elvire Morelle to stay with Madame Raymonde Coache at Asnières-sur-Seine. Pilot Officer Kropf, shot down on the night of 16/17 September 1942, was already there.

Robert and Germaine Aylé seemed unconcerned by the number of French visitors to their apartment, all of whom knew of Gordon's presence. Robert was indeed so relaxed about having Gordon in his flat that he would take him out for a ride on the metro and a walk around Paris, and once they enjoyed the music of a German military band. Soon, though, it was time to move on again. Dédée and another Comet guide gathered the party of four – Mellor, Joyce, Kropf, and the Russian, Stadnik – and set off by train for the south-west of France. Someone had a sense of humour, for Gordon's papers declared him to be Jean Petit – all six feet two inches of him!

The overnight express brought them to Bayonne (17/18 October), where they changed onto the local train for St Jean-de-Luz. Accommodated in an apartment near the harbour for the night of 18/19 October, their time there was to be short: 'During the warmth of an afternoon we left the flat with two young ladies, one being Jeanine De Greef, and set forth looking like any group of young people. Crossing over the harbour bridge and along a long dusty road we reached Francia Usandizaga's farm which was to be the setting off point for our crossing into Spain.'[902]

Led by Florentino Goïcoechea and Albert Johnson the group set off after supper on 19 October into the fading light. Farmland soon gave way to stony ground and in single file they walked ever upwards, one false crest after another, until they came to open ground. The stars were bright and the moon almost full, but the airmen had little time to enjoy their beauty, for their instructions were to keep quiet and to keep up with Florentino: 'Our guide was a man of iron and keeping up left no breath for talking. He was carrying a large rucksack and in addition a large metal box on his shoulders. The struggle for height continued until it eased and the ground fell away in front of us into a deep valley to the river Bidassoa.'[903]

Descending to its banks in the moonlight, they stared at the Bidassoa's rushing waters. Having safely waded across, they climbed through some bushes, across a railway line, over the road near a custom's post and up the other side of the valley. When all were together they were told that they were now on Spanish soil. Again in single file and with the moon to light their way, they slowly descended until, as the morning mist increased, they suddenly arrived at an isolated farmhouse where they were told to await transport. Florentino and Johnson said their goodbyes and were gone, back over the hills to France.

The four airmen were taken into San Sebastián and, after food and sleep, were driven by car, arranged by the British consulate in Bilbao, to the British Embassy in Madrid. A few days later the journey continued by train and bus to La Linea and across the border into Gibraltar. The final leg of the long road home ended with a flight in a USAAF C-47 (Skytrain)[904] to RAF Portreath (England) where, on 1 November 1942, they suffered the usual customs and entry procedures. Aboard the C-47 once more they were flown to the USAAF airfield at Aldermaston, Berkshire and, after a short drive in a jeep to Reading station, a train brought them, at last, to London.[905]

Following Gordon Mellor and his companions were three army officers – Captain H.J. Fuller (Comet 73); Captain A.H.S. Coombe-Tennant (74);[906] and Major A.S.B. Arkwright (75) – all of whom had escaped from the German prisoner-of-war camp Oflag VIB at Warburg on the night of 30/31 August 1942. Also sheltered by the Ritschdorf sisters in Liège, they were escorted to Paris by Baron Jean Greindl and two other guides, where the army officers spent the night in Frédéric de Jongh's apartment. They left that evening with Dédée 'and a Belgian named François. We were joined by Sgt. Pinchuk of the Russian Air Force.'[907] From St Jean-de-Luz Dédée and Florentino took the four men over the Pyrenees, arriving in San Sebastián on 24 October.

The ultimate fate of the two Russians Pinchuk and Stadnik is not known, but their arrival in England caused some head-scratching in British Intelligence circles, the main question being whether or not they should be sent to the Royal Victoria Patriotic School in Wandsworth, London, the centre for interrogation of aliens. The MI5 officer handling the case, K.G. Younger, 'knew, of course, that in practice Soviet citizens were not sent to the R.P.S. [*sic*]', but could not remember whether MI5 'had ever given an undertaking that they would not be sent.' Younger thought that 'if an escapee arrives from Europe claiming to be a citizen of USSR, he can certainly be sent to R.V.P.S.', and ended his minute on the case with the chilling sentence: 'As soon as it is established that he [Stadnik] is what he claims to be he should presumably be handed over to the Soviet Embassy.'

One of the last airmen evaders to be taken over the Pyrenees by Comet in 1942, and a sign of things to come, was Lieutenant F.D. Hartin USAAF (Comet 80), the first of many Americans to be aided by Comet. Numbers 81 and 82 were, respectively, Sergeants R.P. Smith RCAF, and H.J. Spiller, who had been brought together through France and taken across the Pyrenees/Bidassoa route by Dédée and Florentino Goïcoechea. These two sergeants spent a jolly Christmas at the British Embassy in Madrid before they, and Sergeant W. McLean (78), were smuggled out of Spain aboard a British orange boat, that took them down the River Guadalquivir from Seville to Cadiz, and on to Gibraltar. From there, aboard an ex-French liner, they reached Gourock on 26 January 1943.

CHAPTER 7

Marie-Claire and other escape lines: 1940-1944

'When bad men combine, the good must associate; else they will fall, one by one, an unpitied sacrifice in a contemptible struggle.'

Edmund Burke (1729-1797)

Born of well-to-do parents on 11 September 1895 Mary Lindell had an abundance of what today would be called "attitude". This she amply demonstrated when she was a volunteer nurse at a hospital in Hertfordshire during the First World War. When Matron asked her why she was not cleaning a bedpan in the proper way, Mary told her not to 'ask such ridiculous questions'.[908] After a further brush with matronly authority she went to France to join the *Secours aux Blessés Militaires*, 'the aristocratic division of the French Red Cross',[909] which she served with distinction.

In 1922 she married a French nobleman, the Comte de Milleville, and bore him two sons – Maurice and Octave (Octavius, known as "Oky") – and a daughter, Barbé. When France was invaded in May 1940, Mary's husband was away on business in South America, and she was left to look after the three children, still in their teens. She decided, nevertheless, that she must do what she could to help the many wounded French soldiers. With the fighting over, she returned to the family's Paris apartment, where she further decided that she and her children would do what they could to help British army stragglers reach Unoccupied France.

Near Sauveterre-de-Béarn (Basses-Pyrénées)[910] in the south of France a friend of a friend happened to own a farm which straddled the new Demarcation Line between Occupied and Unoccupied France: 'The farmhouse was on one side, and the cowsheds on the other, with the fields stretching well into Unoccupied France… Soon Oky had piloted his first men through the farm and a brisk traffic, which was to last for years, began.'[911]

On one of his early trips to Sauveterre, Oky, still only sixteen years old, had met a retired Englishman, Major Higgins, who lived near Mauléon (twenty-five kilometres to the south) and who 'had already managed to put several escaping Englishmen over the Spanish frontier'.[912] When Oky, therefore, appeared at the Paris flat with two British soldiers, the solution for their disposal was obvious, and with his mother's approval he took the two men by train to Major Higgins. The major apparently 'knew several guides living in the foothills of the Pyrenees who were prepared to take men over, though they demanded a handsome fee.'[913]

With Oky safely back in Paris, Mary realised that the escape route could now be regularly used, and Oky and a young girl of their acquaintance, Michèle, were soon making two or three journeys each week down to Sauveterre. Mary was worried, however, that sooner or later they would be caught, though her anxiety was eased somewhat when she obtained a pass from no less a person than General Otto von Stülpnagel, Governor of Greater Paris,[914] that permitted her to drive French children into Unoccupied France to be reunited with their parents. She was also allowed to take with her a mechanic and a nurse, though the Germans were not to know that the "mechanic" would be a British officer and the nurse Michèle. For her car, the Germans also gave her many litres of petrol.

Mary was greatly helped in obtaining the pass by an old friend of hers, Colonel Cecil Shaw, who was 'a Blimpish-looking retired colonel of the 12th Lancers, about six feet tall, bald on top but with white hair at the sides and a large red nose indicating his partiality for good living. He was married to an American woman and lived permanently at the Ritz.'[915] In charge of British interests at the American Consulate, Shaw had already helped Wing Commander Basil Embry on 19 June: 'He gave me three hundred francs and strongly advised me not to attempt to leave Paris, but to go to the Salvation Army hostel in the city outskirts and remain there for the time being.'[916] This was not what Embry wanted to hear and, with the money that Shaw had given him, plus a further 200 francs raised through begging, he bought a bicycle for 500 francs and set off for Tours, and Spain.

By the time that Mary asked Colonel Shaw in July 1940 what she should do with her first smuggled British officer when they reached Unoccupied France, Shaw appears to have been aware of clandestine activities in Marseille, for he replied that the officer should make for the docks and go to the Seamen's Home run by the Reverend Donald Caskie, which he would have no difficulty in finding. He added that 'we have been able to send substantial funds to Caskie, direct from the War Office by way of an American in Cannes. Caskie is using the home as a front.'[917]

The first trip went without a hitch, and no sooner was Mary back in Paris than Colonel Shaw had another "mechanic" for her – Major James C. Windsor-Lewis, 2nd Welsh Guards, who had been captured on 25 May 1940 after his makeshift company had run out of ammunition defending the Gare Maritime at Boulogne. Many of his men were wounded, and he himself, with a flesh wound in the leg, was taken to a Casualty Clearing Station at Samer. Later moved to a hospital at Camiers he met Sergeant J.L. Axford, whose Wellington had been shot down on 31 May 1940 attacking a target at Nieuwpoort, Belgium. The two men agreed to escape together, but Axford was moved a few days later, never got the chance, and spent the next five years as a prisoner of war of the Germans.

Windsor-Lewis was also moved, to a hospital at Liège on 6 July. A week later, after the plaster had been removed from his leg, he escaped dressed as a Belgian workman, and with help from generous Belgians made his way to France: 'On reaching Paris I took the metro and got out at La Concorde intending to go to my old hotel in the Rue d'Alger. The whole city was full of Germans. The Hotel Crillon was the German Command HQ.'[918] He went to see some old friends but they had gone, so he 'turned off down the Avenue Victor Hugo and went into a small hotel where I slept the night.' On the morrow he found some friends who, though unable to put him up, gave him some money. They also gave him the de Millevilles' address, to which he went: 'M. and Mme. De M., (Mme. was a Red Cross worker), took me in and told me I could stay there as a guest of the family for as long as I wished and that in their hands nobody would find me.'

He stayed with the de Millevilles for a fortnight, until the necessary papers were in order for him to be taken south 'disguised as a French chauffeur'. It was Mary, though, who drove the car out of Paris on 8 August, stopping near Étampes to give a lift to a Luftwaffe officer, who asked to be taken to his airfield at Châteaudun. Although out of their way, Mary reckoned that with him in the car they would be able to get through the several forbidden areas without any trouble. She was right, but when they reached the officer's quarters at Châteaudun town hall the German officer insisted on taking Mary in with him. He told his fellow officers that she had been the only person kind enough to stop for him, and by way of thanking her gave her a large wad of petrol coupons which, she was staggered to find, entitled her to some 4,000 litres. She had no difficulty taking the airman to Châteaudun airfield.

After a night in a hotel at Cloyes-sur-le-Loir they drove to the small town of Ruffec (Charente), sixty kilometres south of Poitiers, to call on Madame Marthe Rullier. They visited another friend at Confolens, forty kilometres east of Ruffec, before going on to Limoges, a further fifty kilometres beyond Confolens, from where Windsor-Lewis made his way to Marseille by train, and on to a distinguished career.[919]

Some weeks later, having decided that the farm at Sauveterre-de-Béarn was too far away for the British to use, Mary motored back to Ruffec to see Madame Rullier and her husband Paul, with a view to asking them if they could help and whether they 'knew of any other farms that straddled the border.'[920] Paul Rullier suggested that they used the same two farms that were already in use for Frenchmen crossing into Unoccupied France. Farm "A", as it was known, owned by a farmer called Maxim, lay in Occupied France near Ruffec, whereas Farm "B", owned by Armand and Amélie Debreuille, was barely four kilometres away at Marvaud, St Coutant, in Unoccupied France. Satisfied that this was a workable system, Mary returned to Paris. It was not long before the escape route was operating, with her two sons and Michèle acting as couriers taking two or three men each week. Mary adopted the code name "Marie-Claire".

Security was not all it should have been within Mary's small organisation, but it was nevertheless a surprise one day when she opened the door of her Paris flat to a well-dressed German SD officer and an Austrian civilian. They wanted to know why she did so much travelling and on what authority? Able to convince them of her essential Red Cross duties, and having shown them her legal permits, they left. Suddenly, there was another knock on the door. It was the Austrian again, and he produced from his briefcase a warrant for Mary's arrest. 'Don't worry,' he said, 'I am not going to arrest you', and left saying that he would return on the morrow. He added that he knew what she was up to and would call round every Friday henceforward to check up on her. He did. Mary now knew that she was a marked woman, and was left in no doubt of this shortly after Christmas 1940 when her flat was searched by German police.

As she had long feared, Mary was taken away for questioning by the SD. They had already arrested Colonel Shaw[921] and knew the names of all her accomplices, possibly leaked by someone at the American Embassy. Denying all knowledge of them, she was nevertheless taken away to the Cherche-Midi prison in Paris, and on 6 February 1941 was court-martialled. Sentenced to nine months' solitary confinement she was removed to cell 119 at Fresnes prison on the southern edge of Paris. Then, on 9 March 1941 Maurice was arrested, in bizarre circumstances. Having obtained a gun from a common criminal, Maurice hid it in the family flat when the police had first called on his mother. The criminal from whom Maurice got the gun was himself arrested, and told the police what he had done with the gun. Maurice, too, was locked up in Fresnes, to serve a sentence of eleven months, but was removed to Troyes in due course.

On 3 November 1941 Mary was released from Fresnes. Warned by a friend that she would be arrested again as soon as fresh papers had been prepared, one of her first actions was to go to Troyes to see Maurice. She found him suffering from the intensely cold weather, against which he was inadequately protected. Unhesitatingly she gave him her own sweater, but on the way back to Paris she, too, began to suffer from the cold, and contracted pneumonia. She was hovering between life and death when the Germans came to re-arrest her. They left only when it was confirmed that she would not recover if she were to be moved.

A plan was hatched at once to get her out of Paris, and with Oky's help she avoided the German guarding her apartment block. Managing to get to another flat in Paris, it was to be some three weeks before she was strong enough to make the journey to Ruffec. Oky was to have seen her off from the railway station in Paris: 'Fortunately for her she could not know that it was to be the last time that she would set eyes on her beloved son. The Nazis took him for transportation and he was last heard of in Russia. His death has never been confirmed.'[922] Though the marriage of Mary and her husband had, to all intents and purposes, come to an end shortly after he had returned from South America in 1940, he was willing to help, and met her at Ruffec. As arranged, Mary went to Madame Rullier's house.

Deciding that it was now time to escape to England, and though she became desperately ill on the way, Mary managed to get to Lyon to obtain the necessary papers from the American Vice-Consul, George Whittinghill. He warned her that just as he had already heard on the grapevine that she was in town so the Vichy police would get to hear of her presence. Not only was she on Vichy's wanted list, but she had also been sentenced to death *in absentia* by the Germans in Paris, and so was now wanted throughout France.

After several weeks, during which time Mr Whittinghill was immensely helpful in preparing the necessary papers for her to quit France, Mary left for Perpignan and Spain with Jacques, a young Belgian fugitive. Arriving safely at the British Consulate in Barcelona, she was greeted by a delighted Harold Farquhar, consul-general, who said that he had been expecting her for over a year, having heard all about her from Major Windsor-Lewis! She made her way to Lisbon, and a flying boat took her, via Shannon (Northern Ireland), to Poole in southern England, where she arrived on 28 July 1942.

In London, summoned to Room 900 at the War Office, she met Airey Neave and Jimmy Langley, who persuaded her to return to France on behalf of SOE/MI9. They also suggested that she no longer be known as Marie but as Marie-Claire, to avoid confusion with two other Maries already in the field. Given specialist training, she was also offered the use of a wireless operator who, she was told, spoke perfect French having lived in France for some years but was in fact an Australian. Very quietly Mary said: 'And his name is Tom Groome.'[923] Dumbfounded, Jimmy Langley asked her how on earth she knew. It was Groome's passport, she replied, that George Whittinghill had let her remove from his office in Lyon before she left France! When Mary met Tom Groome she found that she did not get on with him, for no reason that she could put her finger on, but her opinion of him was settled when, on their first training flight together, he became 'violently sick'. As seen, he was sent to work for the PAO line.[924]

In London one afternoon Mary bumped into Jacques, the young Belgian fugitive, and he readily agreed to be her wireless operator. Though this arrangement was approved by Neave and Langley, Belgian Army Headquarters refused to sanction the appointment and so, when the time came for Mary to leave for France after three months in England, she went without her own wireless operator. At 2058 hours on the night of 26/27 October 1942, Pilot Officer John Bridger took off in Lysander V9353 on Operation Achilles, to land Marie-Claire and fellow SOE agent and wireless operator Ferdinand Rodriguez, plus baggage, at Thalamy airfield, a dozen kilometres east of Ussel (Corrèze) in the heart of France.

Bridger landed the Lysander without difficulty, seven minutes ahead of schedule, at 0032 hours and was away again in just five minutes. The actual evacuation of the aircraft, though, had not been without incident. In the darkness, Rodriguez had accidentally pulled the release handle of one of the stowed parachutes, which immediately filled the cockpit with its voluminous silk. Humorous though that may have seemed at the time to the two agents, less funny was the sight of their French reception committee turning up, well after the landing, totally inebriated. With all speed Mary and Rodriguez made off into the night on their own, away from the irresponsible and drunken Frenchmen.

Mary made her way to Monte Carlo to collect Maurice, and took him to Lyon, 'where Mary contacted the American Consul, who was to provide her with funds, and with a staunch supporter, Inspector Jo Deronne'.[925] Mary continued to Ruffec, having decided to set up her headquarters in the thirty-room Hôtel de France, run by François and Germaine Rouillon, at 38, Route Nationale. Barely had she settled in when Gaston Denivelle, 'her first lieutenant and an immensely courageous man',[926] told her that there were at least six airmen being hidden in the area between Angoulême and

Poitiers, and that they had been there for some weeks. They were moved as soon as possible, via the Hôtel de France and farms A and B. Then word came that a certain Abbé Pean had been looking after a further seven or eight airmen for almost two months, and was wondering whether she could help. Going at once to meet him at Châtellerault, he took her to the home of M. Goupille, who was hiding four of the airmen, and to another house where two more were in hiding. Arrangements were duly made with the abbé for the airmen to be moved across the Pyrenees.

Against Mary's advice, the abbé continued to send information back to London, resulting in his arrest and subsequent torture, mutilation and death at the hands of the Gestapo. Despite having an eye gouged out, being practically skinned alive and literally crucified to make him talk, he never revealed a single name: 'This wonderful man, who helped save countless airmen, was never, even posthumously, recognized by the British Government.'[927]

With funds running low (she had given the abbé 50,000 francs), Mary went to Lyon on 1 December 1942 not only for more money but also to see Maurice. On her way back to the Demarcation Line on a tandem bicycle with one of her French agents they were rammed, possibly deliberately, by a car whose occupants were recognised as two of the principal collaborators in the locality. Though her companion, screaming with pain, was at least alive, Mary was so deeply unconscious and bleeding so badly that it was thought that she was dead. While preparations were being made for her burial, however, she regained her senses in time to be taken to a Doctor Martinez in Loches, over fifty kilometres away. Finding her to have a broken collarbone and five broken ribs, all compound fractures, Dr Martinez ordered her to stay in bed for seven weeks or so.

It was not long, though, before the Gestapo had information that a seriously injured woman had been taken to the hospital and, when news was received that they were on their way there, Mary was hurriedly moved to the cellars. Unfortunately, in so doing, her collarbone was again dislocated. Unable to find her, the Gestapo nevertheless took away Doctor Martinez,[928] and Mary was restored to her bed.

She was still in hospital when Sergeants H.O Robertson and H.J.B. Canter, from the same crew, arrived in Ruffec on 19 December 1942. Shot down on 6/7 December 1942 in eastern France, they had been taken to Paris on 11 December, where they were helped by, among others, Henri Debussy ('either a solicitor or a law student') and Marc Rendinage, 'the proprietor of a hotel or hotels in Paris. As a number of Germans have their meals at his hotel, he was able to use a German car which he said belonged to General Stulpnagel, the Governor of Paris.'[929] Robertson and Canter stayed at his flat for three or four days, and another four at the house of a Professor Bertram and his wife, before being taken by train to Ruffec.

Sheltered from the day of their arrival by Gaston and Renée Denivelle, the two airmen reported that their host 'got in touch with a woman who spoke good English and who, we gathered, may have been organising espionage in the area (it is possible she is an Englishwoman married to a Frenchman). This woman took our numbers and names and said she would send a message to England.'[930] Mary, clearly, was not too ill to do an identity check, but she had already departed for Lyon when someone came to take Robertson and Canter back to Paris on 17 January 1943.

Just over a week later their guide, M. Nollet, a Parisian artist, led them across the Demarcation Line in daylight on 27 January. At Bergerac they spent the night in the Terminus Hotel, the owner, an elderly lady, very generously yielding her bed for all three of them 'as the hotel was full of German officers'. M. Nollet said goodbye, and on 28 January the hotel owner took Robertson and Canter by train to Toulouse, some 175 kilometres to the south. They called in at the Hôtel de Paris for a meal, following which they were 'taken to the headquarters of the organisation and met Pat [O'Leary], who said Toulouse was too dangerous.' A member of the organisation thereupon took them back to Bergerac, where they stayed for 'about ten days with a woman belonging to the organisation'. They returned to Toulouse on 6 February, spending the night at Pat's flat before leaving for Spain.[931]

Back at Ruffec, Maurice de Milleville took his mother away to Lyon after Christmas, and she was still there when he received a note from Armand Debreuille advising that there were 'two important parcels of food for him' to collect.[932] Appreciating that the parcels were evaders, Maurice went to see his mother, who told him to go to Armand and collect the men. On 6 January 1943, back at Ruffec, Maurice found two Royal Marines, Major Herbert George Hasler OBE and Marine William Edward Sparks, the only survivors of Operation Frankton (see Appendix VII).

It was not until just after noon on 18 December 1942, 'baffled, footsore and famished',[933] that Hasler and Sparks reached Ruffec. With no specific instructions as to where they should go, they wandered about the town of 3,000 souls for a while before going into the restaurant in the Café des Sports (re-named Hôtel de Toque Blanche after the war and, later, le Baroque) and ordering drinks and soup, soup being obtainable without the need of a ration card. As Hasler paid their bill, with a 500 franc note, he handed the *patronne*, Mademoiselle Yvonne Mandinaud, a note saying 'We are escaping English soldiers. Do you know anyone who can help us?'[934] Yvonne and her brother René, who also ran the café, gave them a bed for the night.

After careful questioning by members of Marie-Claire, the two marines, on the afternoon of 19 December, were taken in the back of a baker's van to a wood near Benest (twenty kilometres east of Ruffec). At dusk a guide led them over the Demarcation Line to Armand Debreuille's farm, Farm B, when Armand, 'tall, slim, intelligent-looking, in his early thirties'[935] sent the letter to Mary informing her of the two new arrivals and requesting instructions. Arriving on 6 January 1943, Maurice took them by bicycle, some twenty-five kilometres, to Roumazières-Loubert (Charente), where they caught the night train to Lyon.

When Mary first set eyes on Hasler and Sparks, on 7 January, she could not believe what she was seeing, for there stood Major Hasler sporting a large, blonde moustache (not for nothing was he known as "Blondie" Hasler), and both, for goodness' sake, were still carrying all their equipment in their haversacks! Brooking no argument, the moustache had to go, as did the marines, taken by Maurice that night to a large house in the northern suburbs of the city, where they stayed for almost a fortnight while Mary tried, without success, to re-open the line over the Pyrenees.

She now became desperately ill again and, through Maurice, 'got in touch with Mr Carter, a member of Pat's organisation,'[936] to whom they were handed over. Hasler was sent to live with M. and Mme. Bonnamour, (she being the daughter of Mr Barr, manager of Barclay's Bank, Baker Street, London). He stayed there for six days, but spent one night with Paul Reynaud, before being moved to another large house in the north of the city belonging to Mr Barr, and being re-united with Sparks. They were there for another six days, 'looked after by a young Frenchman who assists Carter', when one of Pat O'Leary's men, Fabien, arrived, in early February, to take them to Marseille.

In Marseille they 'lived in a flat overlooking the Observatory Gardens' which was 'rented by a member of Pat's organisation (Albert or Robert) and run by a French family called Markin [*sic*]',[937] and where they were joined by a Belgian fighter pilot, Flying Officer Prince Werner de Merode, shot down on 12 December 1942, and by Sergeant J.G. Dawson, who had baled out of a damaged bomber on the night of 11/12 December.[938]

On 28 February 1943 Pat O'Leary notified them that they would be leaving for Spain on the morrow, and on 1 March Hasler, Sparks, de Merode, and Dawson were taken to Perpignan.[939] Bundled into the back of a van and driven to the foot of the Pyrenees, beyond Céret, two guides led them over the lesser peaks by las Illas and Massanet-de-Cabrenys, though more than high enough for unfit men. After four days' walking they arrived at Bañolas, where they were expected, and spent 'three or four days in a hotel, seeing people who were in touch with the consulate in Barcelona.' Collected on behalf of the Barcelona consulate they were taken to Barcelona, and then on to Madrid, which they left towards the end of March for Gibraltar. De Merode departed for RAF Portreath, Cornwall on the night of 27/28 March. Hasler was flown, also to Portreath, on 2 April, while Sparks and Dawson followed by sea two days later.

Flying Officer Prince de Merode and Sergeant J.G. Dawson were recommended for, and got, nothing for their evasions, but for his part in Operation Frankton (not for his evasion) Hasler was awarded the DSO and a brevet majority. Sparks received the DSM, though not before he had been arrested at Gibraltar. A German radio transmission had been intercepted in England that said that none of the Frankton party had survived. Consequently, all were officially listed as "Missing" on 25 January 1943, and it was not until a coded message had been received from Marie-Claire on 23 February that it was known that Hasler and Sparks were definitely alive.[940] Even then, anyone claiming to be either one or the other was treated with suspicion, and Sparks was kept under guard all the way to London, where he gave the military police the slip and made his way back to Combined Operations Headquarters.

Mary, meanwhile, had gone to Switzerland, ostensibly for further treatment, but she was still without a radio operator and needed funds to run her escape line. She met with Victor Farrell in Geneva, and then went to Bern to see Colonel Henry Cartwright, the British military attaché, to whom she gave a detailed report of the Marie-Claire line. She also passed on a coded message from Hasler and Sparks, the first news of Operation Frankton to reach British Intelligence. Ignoring advice to rest in Switzerland she returned clandestinely to France, briefly calling on Maurice in Lyon. Once back at Ruffec she 'interviewed a number of airmen and took them down to Varilhes near Foix, where she handed them over to [Ferdinand] Rodriguez for the final trek to Andorra.'[941]

Returning yet again to Switzerland, she met with a sympathetic Swiss Intelligence officer. Aware of the Gestapo's interest in "the Comtesse de Milleville", and because he happened to have in his possession the 'birth certificate, marriage certificate and other papers'[942] of the Comtesse de Moncy, he advised Mary to change her name to de Moncy, which she duly did.

Then one day in May 1943, still in Switzerland, she was shocked to receive a letter saying that Maurice had been arrested and, having been interrogated by the Gestapo at the Hôtel Terminus, Lyon was now in Fort Montluc prison. Determined to effect her son's release she returned immediately to Lyon. Head of the Gestapo in Lyon since November 1942 was SS-Obersturmführer Klaus Barbie.[943] As he was known to be susceptible to bribery and also to be very fond of the ladies, Mary persuaded her daughter, Barbé, to approach him with a cash offer for Maurice's release. A sum of 45,000 francs was agreed and Maurice was released after payment had been made.[944] Though so badly beaten by the Gestapo that he was practically blinded – they beat him 'across the face with a thin, brass chain'[945] – Maurice was able to return to active service for his mother.

Mary returned to Ruffec on 9 May 1943 to find that the few couriers employed on behalf of Marie-Claire – among them at this time Armand Debreuille, Gaston Denivelle, François Rouillon (of the Hôtel de France) and Ginette Favbre – were struggling to cope with the increasing numbers of evading airmen. Mary had heard that in Foix, a hundred kilometres by road north of Andorra, 'a middle-aged Roman Catholic priest named Abbé Blanchebarbe was doing magnificent work for the Resistance'[946] and went to see him with a view to asking for his help in getting evaders to Spain via Andorra. He needed little persuading, and now the Marie-Claire line ran from Ruffec to Foix and on to Andorra. Recovered from his ordeal with the Gestapo, Maurice was now well enough to run the link from Lyon to Ruffec.

Mary also needed guides to take evaders from eastern France to Lyon. By chance Maurice had met the Vicomtesse Pauline Barré de St Venant, who fitted the bill perfectly. 'A tall, vivacious woman in her forties, she had a confident, rather domineering air. Since 1940 she had been aiding the escape of French prisoners of war and civilians from Alsace-Lorraine to the unoccupied zone. Threatened with arrest, she had fled to Lyon.'[947] Maurice agreed to reimburse Pauline, alias "Marie Odile", 10,000 francs for every airmen brought down from the Alsace-Lorraine region. Contrary to Mary's strict security rules, Pauline followed Maurice to Ruffec when he was escorting one of her airmen there, and discovered Marie-Claire's headquarters: 'Mary went white with fury, but decided to see the woman…'[948] They had a blazing row in the Hôtel de France, which reached boiling point when Pauline returned to Ruffec a second time 'after an unsuccessful attempt to open a new escape route from Alsace-Lorraine'.[949]

Marie-Claire was still functioning, with the occasional alarm, when Mary was asked if she could help Sergeant P. Whitnall RCAF, who had been shot down on 17 April 1943 and was in hiding far to the north in Normandy. Mary agreed to help and, at the end of August 1943, a girl from Lyon escorted Whitnall to Ruffec 'and thence by bicycle to a farm, about twenty-five kilometres south-east of Ruffec which Marie Claire used on her journeys'.[950] At the farm he met 'an American civilian (Haviland), who had been a member of the US Ambulance Corps'. Whitnall was there for about four days before returning to Ruffec in a truck with 'Marie Claire and another lady'. Haviland, dropped off at a railway station along the way, made his own way back to Ruffec.

Four other airmen to be brought to Ruffec at this time were Sergeants A.H. Sheppard and C.F. Trott (shot down in the same aircraft on 19/20 June 1943), Sergeant J.N. Sparkes (the only survivor of a crew on their first operation, lost on the night of 27/28 June 1943), and Sergeant J.G.F. Sansoucy RCAF, who was shot down on 14/15 June 1943 over Normandy.

At the beginning of July Sansoucy 'cycled over to Draché to see the local priest who, I was told, was connected with an organisation.'[951] Whether true or not, the man took him 'to Sepmes, where I spent six weeks at La Roche Ploquin, a château belonging to the Comtesse de Poix. During this time I was continually receiving word from my friends that in a few days I would be put in touch with an organisation and taken to Spain.' The wheels *were* grinding, albeit slowly, but it was not until the latter part of August that the priest from Draché contacted Marie-Claire at Ruffec, who arranged for Sansoucy to be 'escorted by a young girl to Ruffec'.

Wasting no more time once the party of six had been assembled Mary arranged for their departure. Sansoucy and Haviland (whom Sansoucy called de Havilland and described as 'a naturalised French American') were taken by lorry to the house of a friend of Marie-Claire, about fifty kilometres south-east of Ruffec. Travelling by train to Limoges and Toulouse, their next stop was at Le Vernet, where Marie-Claire had advised them to leave the train and walk to the planned rendezvous at Varilhes, some twenty kilometres south between Pamiers and Foix. This would avoid the German control on the train just beyond Le Vernet. As they were leaving the station, however, they were stopped by a German control. Making a note of their names and addresses the Germans let them pass.

Following them by road to Varilhes, on 9 September, were the rest of the airmen – Trott, Sheppard, Sparkes, and Whitnall – accompanied by 'Marie Claire, a police officer in civilian clothes, and the driver of the truck'. Meeting up with Sansoucy and Haviland as planned, and handed over to a Spaniard, they stayed in a shed until daylight next day, 'when the Spaniard hid us for the day beside a river.' Leaving that night, the Spaniard took them for about two kilometres before he handed over the party to a Frenchman. 'The Frenchman took us about five kilometres that night to a farm in the mountains, where we stayed two nights and three days (10–12 September) waiting for a party of Frenchmen.'[952] The farm, at St Jean-de-Verges, was a few kilometres north of Foix, and hence a long walk to the Pyrenees.

Once the French party had arrived, some twenty all told, they set off on the night of 12 September. Just short of the Spanish border, on 16 September, where the guides and all the Frenchmen left them, two guides came from Andorra to collect the party, which now included not only the RAF evaders but also a Polish family and two Polish soldiers. They arrived in Andorra on the morning of 17 September. Following the usual route via Barcelona and Madrid, the RAF evaders arrived at Gibraltar on 1 October, and all were flown back to England on 4/5 October.

The autumn of 1943 was to be a busy period for Marie-Claire, for soon after the five RAF airmen had been sent on their way, two Polish airmen arrived later in September. Sergeant P. Bakalarski PAF and Sergeant Witold Raginis PAF had come from Cracow, Poland after escaping from a working party at the Jaworzne coal mine two months earlier. Leaving on 18 August 1943, by 15 September they had reached Lunéville (Meurthe-et-Moselle), France, where they made themselves known at the gendarmerie. When Raginis told them that his parents lived in Montluçon, a wire was sent asking for confirmation of this: 'After two days, which we spent in the cells at the gendarmerie, a telegram came that my family had confirmed my identity.'[953]

On 21 September, a gendarme took them "under arrest", 'so that no questions should be asked when the train was controlled,' to *les Secours pour les Réfugiés*, an organisation working for Alsatians, at Nancy. Given false identity papers they were sent on the following day to Lyon to see Pauline Barré de St Venant, using the alias "Madame Laroche", who put them up 'for the night in the Hôtel Claridge, where she stays'.[954] Contacting Maurice de Milleville, Pauline 'told him that she had two airmen. He came and took a note of our names, ranks and numbers. He then took us to the house of the chief engineer of the [Compagnie] des Grands Travaux de Marseille, at 1, rue de Plat, Lyon.' They were there for a few days, a few more at the château of M. Devillard near Lyon, and then back to 1, rue de Plat, during which time Raginis managed to get to Montluçon to spend two days with his family. Ginette Favbre was sent to bring them back to the Hôtel de France at Ruffec, where they arrived on 4 October. After one night in the hotel, Mary took them to the house of M.Cottu, 'who is employed by the Cie. De Gaz et Electricité de Ruffec', where they stayed until 23 October.

Also on their way to Ruffec were Pilot Officer A.F. McSweyn RAAF and Driver F.G. Williamson RNZASC, and Sergeant S.J.V. Philo. McSweyn and Williamson, a thirty-eight-year-old Englishman by birth who had joined the New Zealand ASC and been captured in Crete in 1941, had escaped from Stalag VIIIB (Lamsdorf) on 19 September 1943. McSweyn had chosen the reluctant Geoff Williamson to accompany him because Geoff had lived in Germany pre-war, spoke fluent German and knew the railway system intimately. Reaching France with the help of a French worker, McSweyn and Williamson (travelling under the name of Marsden) were handed over to a gendarme at the Lunéville police station, where Bakalarski and Raginis had also been, and were also escorted in handcuffs to Lyon. Met by Maurice de Milleville and Ginette Favbre they, too, were brought to Ruffec, on 8 October.

Sergeant Philo, shot down on the way back from Milan on the night of 15/16 August 1943, had landed near Verneuil-sur-Avre (Eure), west of Paris. He had already walked a considerable distance south when, on 27 August, he asked at a farm for shelter. Directed to the Château la Boussée, just outside Azay-le-Rideau (Indre-et-Loire), M. Genechon, owner of the château, sent for the Azay postmaster. He came on the afternoon of 28 August, with a Madame Shield, widow of an American, both of whom were in the Resistance. Philo was grateful to be told to stay put, as his feet were badly blistered from his long walk. On 18 October, he left the château, and was taken in several stages to the Hôtel de France at Ruffec, where he arrived two days later: 'Marie Claire… got me new clothes and shoes and a new identity card for the frontier zone, as well as a work certificate.'

Philo's arrival was timely, for Mary was busily preparing papers for the men's departure to Spain. There was a delay, however, for the Germans had recently made the Pyrenees, including the Andorran border area, into a special defence zone, and Mary did not yet have the rubber stamp for the requisite special pass. It was not until 20 October, the day of Philo's arrival, that the airmen's papers were ready for the journey to Andorra. McSweyn was detailed to stay behind to await the arrival of more evaders/escapers, while Raginis and Bakalarski, both good German speakers, were to leave with Williamson and Philo respectively. First to go to Toulouse, via Bordeaux, on 22 October were Raginis and Williamson. José Rodriguez, a guide from the village of Urs, ten kilometres north-west of Ax-les-Thermes, took them as far as Pamiers on 23 October, the day on which Bakalarski and Philo left for Toulouse via Limoges. Arriving at Pamiers on 24 October they joined up with Raginis and Williamson. Leaving by train with their guide for Luzenac (Ariège), they walked the three or four kilometres from there to Urs, and spent the night in a cave.

At 6 a.m. on 26 October, after José Rodriguez had handed over to a French guide, Bakalarski, Raginis, Philo and Williamson began the journey over the mountains to Andorra in pouring rain. After an hour and a half the guide reckoned that they would be in Andorra by 2 p.m., but as they climbed higher up the *sentier muletier* (mule path) the heavy rain turned into a blizzard. In appalling conditions the men quickly tired, and Williamson started to lag behind, saying 'that his legs would not move any quicker on the steep slopes.'[955] The others took it in turns to help him along, trying to keep up with the guide's fast pace. At around midday they had a short rest, and lit a fire. Now a little recovered, Williamson kept up for a while on the relatively flat ground, but then again found that he could barely walk, even downhill. The guide lost his temper with all the delays, and suggested that they should leave Williamson behind. The others would not hear of it and, with Philo and Raginis holding him up on either side, moved off again. Bakalarski, now suffering from severe leg pains himself, was unable to lend a hand.

At about 4 p.m., with night fast approaching, the guide suggested that he and Raginis, the strongest of the four, should go on ahead and that he should show Raginis the route to Andorra. All agreed that this was the best course of action, and the guide led Raginis as far as the Etangs de Fontargente, very close to the Andorran border, and a dozen or so kilometres west of the border post at l'Hospitalet. Showing Raginis the track to take to Andorra, and having done his job of getting them through the German frontier patrols, the guide headed home.

Raginis plodded on alone through the deep snow in what proved to be the wrong direction. Finding it impossible to continue in the dark, he spent the night of 26/27 October in the open, at an altitude of around 2,000 metres (6,500 feet). As soon as it was light he carried on, following the River Aston down the mountains, until after five hours he saw a small hut with a smoking chimney: 'I thought I was in Andorra, but, for some reason which I cannot explain, I decided to watch the door of the hut before approaching. After about fifteen minutes I saw two German soldiers come from the hut to wash their dishes.'[956] The awful truth then dawned on him that he was still in France. Walking for a further two hours he came across a group of Spanish and French road menders: 'I went to their hut and said I was a Frenchman who had just crossed into the Zone Interdite Sud. I remained three days and three nights at this hut, as my feet and hands were swollen with frostbite.'[957]

Remembering that Rodriguez, the Spanish guide, lived in Urs, Raginis made his way there on a stolen bicycle. Rodriguez took him by train to Mérens-les-Vals, and told him to follow the main road to l'Hospitalet, a winding ten kilometres uphill. On 3 or 4 November Raginis crossed into Andorra, and in Escaldas was taken to see Dominique 'who represents the Barcelona Consulate-General'. It was arranged that he would travel to Seo de Urgel in Spain with a party of nine Poles (including Flying Officer S. Swida PAF – see Chapter 9) and two Frenchmen. They went by bus but, while some of the party continued to Barcelona, Raginis was in the group left behind. He was a week in a pensión before following to Barcelona, and eventually flying from Gibraltar to England (Whitchurch airport) on 29/30 November.

As for the three whom Raginis had left behind in the mountains, Philo and Bakalarski soldiered on with the desperately tired Williamson. They were still nine or ten kilometres short of Andorra when, at around 6 p.m. on 26 October, Williamson died. They left his body amongst the rocks somewhere near the Pic de Rulle (2,788 metres/9,061 feet).[958]

It is not known how many escapers and evaders died attempting the crossing of the Pyrenees, where the fickle weather claimed many lives regardless of nationality, but at almost exactly the same time as Williamson lost his life so too did three American airmen – 2nd Lieutenant Harold Bailey; Technical Sergeant William B. Plasket; and Staff Sergeant Francis E. Owens. They were in a group that had left Paris on 21 October 1943, with four fellow American airmen and seven French officers hoping to join de Gaulle's army. Wasting no time the crossing began on 22 October. The guide, Emile Delpy, employed by British Intelligence, was unwilling to take the evaders because of their poor condition and the prospect of bad weather, but was apparently ordered to take them anyway.

It was not long before one of the Americans, First Lieutenant Olof M. Ballinger, could go no further.[959] The others pressed on, but with German patrols seemingly everywhere progress was slow, and the group was forced to take difficult paths through the mountains. High up, a sudden and fierce snowstorm struck. Then Bailey collapsed. Plasket and Owens carried him for eight hours as far as they could until they, too, collapsed, utterly exhausted.

Delpy and his fellow guide could not allow anyone to delay their journey in the awful weather, and did all they could to get the three Americans to carry on. Even when one of the guides took out a gun and, pointing it at the head of the exhausted Owens, ordered him to get up, the airman failed to react. There was nothing to do if the rest were to save themselves, and so Bailey, Plasket and Owens were left to die in the snow, probably on 25 October 1943, at Port de Rat, Andorra. Their bodies were not found until the thaw in the spring of 1944.[960]

Ploughing on through the deep snow as night fell, Bakalarski and Philo followed the footprints left by Raginis and the guide for as long as they could. All the while the skies had been clearing and, with the temperature falling, their sodden clothes now froze. Bakalarski was leading when they 'reached a rocky mountainside, across which it took us about four hours to cover one kilometre. I was in front, and when we reached a level stretch of snow I waited for Philo. When he reached me he lay down and fell asleep. I then discovered that he had taken off his shoes and had been walking with them under his arm. I cut off his socks, dried his legs with a towel from my pack, and put a dry pair of socks and his shoes on his feet. This was very difficult, as his legs were frozen stiff. His hands were also frost-bitten. I then smacked him all over till I had revived him, and covered one of his hands with a handkerchief and the other with a sponge-bag.'[961]

Bakalarski forced Philo to keep going, and the two men carried on throughout the night, but had to retrace their steps for three kilometres when they lost their way. By the time they had reached the top of the mountains it had taken them the best part of twelve hours, a climb that should have taken little more than an hour. In daylight they studied Philo's escape map and, with the help of his compass, which he had broken when he had fallen, found the way south to Andorra. They were also able to locate a lake that the guide had told them to look for (perhaps one of the Étangs de Fontargente). Halfway down the mountain they saw Andorran guards watching them through binoculars. Avoiding them, they nevertheless followed the guards' footsteps to a road and a cottage. Directed to a second dwelling 'they were given hot milk and allowed to sleep in a hayloft'. It was 27 October. The crossing had taken two days and a night.

After a good night's rest in the hayloft they were taken to the town of Andorra on 28 October, Bakalarski going to a hotel and Philo to hospital. Released on 2 November, they crossed the Spanish frontier by bus, but were told by Spanish guards at the frontier 'to report at the police station in Seo de Urgel. A frontier guard was put into the bus with us as escort. At the police station the guard was sent away, and the police put us back on the bus again. In the centre of the town the bus driver handed us over to a Spaniard who took us to a hotel, where the "British Representative" was waiting for us.'[962] At the hotel, too, were an American airman, Kenneth Moore,[963] and five Frenchmen, all of whom were taken by car to the British Consulate at Barcelona on 3 November. First man home from Gibraltar, on 10/11 November 1943, was Bakalarski, followed by Philo on 15/16 November.

For their escapes Bakalarski and Raginis were awarded the Distinguished Conduct Medal. Philo was Mentioned in Despatches but would not live to see the end of the war. Flying on 196 Squadron with its Stirling SOE supply-droppers he was killed in action on 3 April 1945.

Two days after the two Poles, Williamson and Philo had left, three more evaders were brought from the Calvados area of Normandy in northern France to join McSweyn at Ruffec – Flying Officer M.H.F. Cooper[964] (shot down on 16 August 1943), Sergeant L.F. Martin RCAF and Flying Officer H.F.E. Smith RCAF, shot down together on 16/17 September 1943.

Cooper fell into an apple tree that, until he landed in it, had been pregnant with fruit. On 20 August he was given shelter by an elderly peasant couple, Robert and Gabriel Siroux, at Bellou (Orne), twenty kilometres or so south of Lisieux. Four days later he 'was visited by a man called M. Bordeaux, who lived at Courson. He was a member of a de Gaullist organisation and he promised to help me.'[965] Expecting to be there no more than a week at the most, it was to be five weeks before Monsieur Bordeaux returned on 20 September and took him away in a pony and trap to Fervaques, some five kilometres to the north, 'where they picked up Sgt. Martin. Continuing northwards to a farm north of Lisieux, where Flying Officer Smith had also stayed, 'we were visited by the chief of police, who arranged to have our photographs taken, and provided us with identity cards.'

Three days later, on the move again thanks to the Jean-Marie resistance network, Mike Cooper and Len Martin were taken to join Harry Smith. They were all then kept in a safe house in Villers-sur-Mer (Calvados, a few kilometres down the coast from Deauville) before being moved to the Paris area, where they split up. The two Canadians went off together, leaving Mike Cooper on his own. Within a fortnight they were a trio once more and, probably escorted by Ginette Favbre, on their way together to Ruffec, where they arrived on or about 30 October. Mike Cooper remembers their greeting at the Hôtel de France. A middle-aged, wrinkle-faced woman wearing a Red Cross uniform asked them if they had had a good journey. Then she announced: 'I am an English woman married to a Frenchman after the last war. You will know me as Marie. I have been parachuted into France with the object of getting boys like yourselves safely into Spain. I spare neither money nor effort to carry this out. You boys must trust me and obey me completely, or go away now.'[966]

Two more arrivals at Ruffec, this time from eastern France, were Captain Ralph Buckley "Buck" Palm SAAF, and Captain George Tsoucas, a forty-four-year-old Greek Intelligence officer attached to the British Special Boat Service. Tsoucas, who had been captured on the island of Rhodes on 16 September 1942, and Palm had escaped from Stalag VIIA (Moosburg), Germany on 29 September 1943 by clinging to the underside of a trailer taking Red Cross parcels to Moosburg railway station. They were told to make for the Café Rouge in the Hofmannstrasse, Munich, and to ask for a Frenchman called Phillipot. This they did, and after being sheltered by Frenchmen in Munich for almost three weeks they stowed away on a goods train, which did not leave for thirty-six hours but which finally came to a halt in a marshalling yard at Strasbourg (France) at 3 a.m. on 20 October.

At a farm at Marainviller, a short way east of Lunéville, given food and shelter, they were told to go to the *Maison des Prisonniers* in Lunéville. There the concierge put them in touch with 'the captain of the gendarmerie' (no doubt the same man who had helped the four earlier) who kept the two men 'for three days in a small room at the gendarmerie headquarters. We were given civilian clothes, photographed, and provided with false identity cards.'[967]

On 28 October the gendarme captain took the escapers to a café in the Rue Sainte Catherine in Nancy, run by Madame Salzace, where they were interrogated, and informed that a "Madame Laroche" (Pauline Barré de St Venant) would be coming for them later. When Madame Laroche failed to turn up, Palm and Tsoucas were taken by Madame Salzace's daughter, Madame Renée Havouis, to a flat next door. Finally appearing on 30 October, Pauline wanted to take the men to Paris straightaway, but their unsuitable clothes needed changing. The three left for Paris on 1 November, and 'went to the Hotel Paris Centre, the owner of which knew about the activities of Mme. Laroche.'

On 3 November Pauline took Tsoucas and Palm to Ruffec. Tsoucas was not impressed by what he saw of Marie-Claire: 'The whole village knew all about her and her private car and the trucks which she hired, and she was very indiscreet in talking English to escapers and evaders in the hotel.'[968] The story goes that soon after his arrival at Ruffec Tsoucas got into trouble when he was found cohabiting with Madame Laroche. Mary placed him under arrest and ordered Pauline to her room. There was no doubting the obvious feud and clash of temperament between the two women, as Tsoucas says: 'Marie-Claire and Mme. Laroche had a terrific row… as Mme. Laroche resented the insulting way in which Marie-Claire spoke to the French people. They quarrelled so violently that I had to separate them in the hotel.'[969]

When Maurice and Ginette had meanwhile returned from making arrangements for the rest of the evaders and escapers to be taken over the Pyrenees to Andorra, Mary (Marie-Claire) was ready to send the next group off. Having heard from the Spanish guide José Rodriguez that the Germans were actively looking for escapers and that it was very dangerous to proceed, Mary arranged for them to go by truck but, with insufficient fuel for the round trip, Mary had a word with her friend Lieutenant Peyraud, senior gendarme in Ruffec.[970] He said that he would arrange the necessary coupons but, as they could be traced back to him, he would have to leave with the party.

So it was that the truck departed Ruffec on 7 November with ten people aboard – Mary; Pauline; Henriette Rejern as driver; Peyraud; Palm; Cooper; Martin; Smith; McSweyn; and Tsoucas – bound for the railway station at St Yrieix-la-Perche (Haute-Vienne), forty kilometres south of Limoges. Mary was wearing her Red Cross uniform, part of the cover plan that she was taking a party of bombed-out refugees, deaf, dumb and shell-shocked, to a resort in the south.[971]

When the truck's rear axle broke, Mary had to persuade a farmer to lend them his truck in return for several litres of fuel. Arriving at St Yrieix half an hour after the last train had left for Toulouse, their next destination, they decided to book in at the Hôtel de la Gare and order dinner. As the motley party trooped into the dining room 'all the other customers stopped eating and sat back to watch us'. Then, to their horror, the new arrivals 'saw at one table a high ranking German officer; luckily he did not pay us much attention.'[972] His presence, though, was too much for Mary. Still wearing her Red Cross uniform with full decorations, she announced very loudly in English that she thought that all Germans were idiots.

Returning to the station on the morning of 8 November, they received a second shock, for who should be there, pacing up and down the platform, but the German officer from the hotel who was, it transpired, none other than the station supervisor. Without interruption Mary's party reached Toulouse and changed trains for Foix. Appreciating that it would be dark by the time they reached Foix, the train driver was bribed to slow the train down just before they got to Foix, to allow the party to jump off. At Pamiers station, however, a couple of stops before Foix, a man in civilian clothes rushed on to the train desperately looking for Marie and 'some RAF men, to warn them that their escape route had been discovered by the Germans and a trap had been laid at the jumping off point.'[973] There was nothing to do but to leave the train there and then, though still some twenty kilometres short of Foix.

Their informant was none other than the Abbé Blanchebarbe, whose brother was to have taken care of the party at Foix, but had been arrested. In the circumstances, Mary decided that they would all have to return to Ruffec, and try again later. The abbé, however, arranged for them to spend the night with a couple of families who lived a short distance away. In the morning they returned to Ruffec, Mary travelling alone from Toulouse by the fastest train available. When the rest had reassembled at Ruffec, Tsoucas witnessed 'another row between Marie-Claire and Mme. Laroche. The hotel owner was sick of us by this time, and we heard from the gendarmerie that they had been ordered by the Gestapo to keep an eye on the hotel.'[974] In the circumstances Mary considered that she would have to close down the Ruffec headquarters and move south to Pau. She would, furthermore, have to organise a new, circuitous route to Spain via Limoges, Toulouse, Tarbes, Pau, Oloron-Sainte Marie and Tardets-Sorholus.

Mary had orders that airmen, even NCOs, had priority over army officers, so that when Captain Tsoucas learnt that she would be sending the men to Pau in fours and that he would be in the second group, he could not resist Pauline's offer to go to Paris with her, where she would organise an aeroplane to take him back to England. So it was that Tsoucas and Pauline left Ruffec on 11 November. Mary and her organisation, no doubt thankfully, never saw him again, though within a fortnight Mary herself was to be in German hands. On the following day in Paris, Pauline put Tsoucas in touch with *La Libération*, a French Resistance organisation whose main office was in the rue d'Anvers.

Leaving Tsoucas in their ineffectual hands, Pauline went to Switzerland to ask Victor Farrell for more funds. Despite much huffing and puffing by the members of *La Libération*, when Pauline found on her return that Tsoucas was still in Paris, she decided to get him to Spain herself. They left on 19 January 1944, calling in at Tours and Châtellerault en route so that Pauline could settle up with the people who were looking after 'sixteen or seventeen British officers and NCOs in those places'. Continuing to Toulouse and Foix, intending to make use of the Abbé Blanchebarbe, they discovered that his house was now closed. 'We went to the house of Mme. Mena, where we were told that the chief of the organisation had been shot by the Germans, that the priest was in hiding, and that the whole scheme of passing escapers and evaders via Andorra was finished for the time being.'[975] Unable to continue, Pauline and Tsoucas returned to Paris a week or so later, lodging at the Hôtel Richelieu on the rue Molière, run by Marguerite Boy.[976]

Also turning up at the Richelieu was Dutch evader Flight Sergeant Reginald Overwijn, shot down at the end of November 1943. His host at 9 bis, rue de Lambert, Paris, Michel Legendre, got in touch with Madame Laroche and took Overwijn to the hotel, where Pauline noted his details. Overwijn records that he met there 'a man who said he was a member of the British Intelligence Service', presumably Tsoucas. Other arrivals at the hotel on 20 February 1944 were the seasoned evader Flying Officer H. "Bill" Furniss-Roe, and Captain Donald K. Dilling USAAF.

In his MI9 report Furniss-Roe painted a vivid picture of Pauline: 'Mme La Roche is aged about fifty, 5 ft. 8ins. or 5 ft. 9 ins. tall and of masculine appearance and looked pregnant. She has dark hair going a little grey. She was obviously the chief of the organisation.'[977] Pauline, pregnant or not, and her helpers (one of whom was Madame Alice, owner of the Coin au Bar on the rue St Diamante) had been busily gathering a number of evading airmen and was ready to move them all out of Paris at the end of February 1944. First to go, to Toulouse on 27 February, were Overwijn, an Australian fighter pilot, Pilot Officer C. Tucker RAAF, and four Americans. Overwijn, Tucker and two of the Americans had got as far as Foix 'when something went wrong and one of the [two] guides was arrested.'[978] Abandoned by the other guide in some caves for two nights and a day with neither food nor blankets they made their way back to an address in Toulouse where one of the Americans had previously stayed.

There they met Furniss-Roe, Flight Sergeant W.N. Waudby, a Typhoon pilot shot down early in January, and seven Americans, who had arrived in Toulouse on 2 March. The eleven Americans were Major Leon W. Blythe, Captain Donald K. Dilling, First Lieutenant Adolph Zielenkiewicz, 2nd Lieutenants Henry Heldman and Paul A. Marriott, Lieutenant Blaylock, Technical Sergeants Archie R. Barlow, Joseph R. Haywood and Alvin A. Rosenblatt, Staff Sergeant Charles W. Blakely, and Sergeant Alfred M. Klein.

Everyone bar Tucker, who had no boots, were assembled at the station on the evening of 2 March and caught the train for Foix, accompanied by, as Furniss-Roe described them, a ginger-bearded youth and a stutterer. Disembarking at St Jean-de-Verges, two stops before Foix, they 'were handed over to four Spanish guides, the chief of whom was named Martinez. We started walking immediately…', still a good many kilometres short of the Pyrenees, and it was not until 13 March that they arrived in Andorra, having walked for fifty-five hours during that period. Archie Barlow had had to give up through exhaustion after five or six days, and was left in a barn just above a French village on the understanding that he would not return to the village for twenty-four hours.

As the party ascended higher into the mountains they encountered deep snow, and it was here that Furniss-Roe's experience from his previous evasion stood everyone in good stead: 'I insisted on all the party removing their shoes at each halt and rubbing their feet dry. We then wrapped our feet in handkerchiefs and covered them with hay. In this way the party got very little frostbite.' After resting for six days at the Gran Café at Sant Juliá de Lòria in Andorra, Furniss-Roe, Waudby, Overwijn, and five of the Americans – Billing, Haywood, Heldman, Klein, and Zielinkowicz – walked into Spain. Stopping east of Seo de Urgel they were picked by a taxi sent by the British Consulate from Barcelona, where they arrived on 20 March.

It was a while later before Archie Barlow reached Spain, but at least he made it. As for Pilot Officer Tucker, thanks to a lack of boots, he was taken prisoner of war and sent to Stalag Luft III (Sagan), where he arrived sometime in May 1944.

Back in Paris, a few days after he had returned there from Foix, Tsoucas was taken to Montauban (Tarn-et-Garonne), fifty kilometres north of Toulouse, and was then escorted by a Pierre Dessaux to a girls' school where his mother was assistant manager. Dessaux was 'in touch with an organisation in Toulouse through George [*sic*] Nahas, a doctor of Syrian origin'.[979] A week later Pauline arrived from Paris with an officer of the Polish Secret Service, and on 21 or 22 February took them to Toulouse. There they met two American airmen evaders, Second Lieutenants Coleman Goldstein and Shirley V. Casey USAAF,[980] and their guide, who told them 'that the passage across the Pyrenees was impossible because of snow.' Tsoucas and the Pole returned to Montauban, but went back to Toulouse on 29 February 1944, and met the guide and the two Americans.

The bad weather had delayed other crossings, so that when the Tsoucas party had finally made its way to Le Pla (Ariège) on 4 March they discovered 'thirty-four Polish officers and Other Ranks who had also been held up by the weather'. The whole party set off across the mountains on 6 March in heavy snow, but trouble flared up when a Polish doctor, aged fifty or so, got into difficulties. The three guides wanted to leave him behind but, knowing that to have done so would almost certainly have led to his death, Tsoucas spoke to them. They threatened him with sticks, and one even pulled out a revolver, and for his sins Tsoucas was sent to the back of the column. By the time that they had all reached the shelter of a hut Tsoucas had frostbite to his hands, feet, ears and nose. Spain was, however, gained on 7 March, and a truck was sent to collect the group from the barn in which they had been resting for a few days.

From Barcelona (12 March) Captain Tsoucas was sent to Madrid (15 March) and Gibraltar (17 March). He remained in the military hospital there until 26 March, when he was flown to Whitchurch (26/27 March 1944). Instead of a rapid train journey to London for interrogation, he was taken to No. 298 US General Hospital at Frenchay, Bristol, where he recuperated until transferred to Westminster Hospital, London, on 18 April.[981]

The war for Tsoucas may have been over, but for Palm, McSweyn, Cooper, Martin and Smith at Ruffec it was still very much "on". They left on 12 November 1943 for the Pyrenees for the second time, after Maurice de Milleville and his father 'had opened up a new route through Pau'.[982] The tight security at Limoges having been lifted, they were able to take a train via Limoges and Pau all the way to Oloron-Sainte Marie. For most of the thirty-five kilometres or so to the Spanish border they were taken by a wheezing, wood-burning old bus to Tardets-Sorholus, where they arrived at about 6 p.m. and walked the five kilometres to Montory. Taken to a café for a meal, their French guide was joined by another, 'a huge strong man, well over six feet tall and carrying a large axe over his shoulder'.[983]

After the meal Mary left and at around midnight, in pouring rain, the two guides led them off on the next stage of the crossing to Spain. The Frenchman 'told us that our journey was only about twenty kilometres and would be easy. Because of this we took neither food nor drink with us.'[984] Heading for a house in the mountains, they walked for four hours or so through the night, by which time it was freezing hard. At the promised house, introduced to their French host and to a Spaniard, the tired men enjoyed their meal.

They were about to settle down for a good night's rest when they were told that they were leaving. Smith was already in bad shape with 'cramp in his heart', and could not go on. The guides agreed to wait until 8 a.m. before resuming the crossing. Even having rested Smith was unable to walk without assistance, which McSweyn gallantly rendered. By mid afternoon the rain had turned to snow, and within an hour and a half it was up to their knees. By this stage Cooper was also feeling the pace and, as McSweyn said, 'kept slipping back. By taking his arm I was able to get him along.' When McSweyn became exhausted from his efforts 'the two guides more or less carried him along'.

Reaching the frontier the guides admitted that they were lost and wanted to turn back, but when Palm and McSweyn threatened them with death if they did they wisely stayed with the group. Soon they struck a valley, and followed a stream downhill until they saw a small hut in the distance. One of the guides, "Buck" Palm, Len Martin and Harry Smith went on towards it. McSweyn and the others followed slowly. Then Mike Cooper collapsed. Luckily spotting him lying in the snow, the seemingly tireless McSweyn went back and dragged him along for several hundred metres until they had caught up with Harry Smith, who also helped him on to the hut. McSweyn then realised that the guide who had been with him was missing, and went back to look for him: 'By putting one of his arms across my shoulder and the other round my waist I managed to drag him along and got him to the hut.'

The hut was basic in the extreme, but worst of all there was no fire and no means of making one. Hopes were raised, however, when two Spaniards suddenly appeared. Asked if they could help, they said that they would send someone to assist them and, as they left, mentioned that there was a house about four kilometres further on down the valley. They never came back. Nor did any help. So Smith and Martin decided to press on, taking Mike Cooper with them, while Palm, McSweyn and the fitter guide would bring the sick guide with them. This poor man, alas, was frozen stiff. His arms and legs refused to work, and it was all that the others could do to get him moving. Eventually they managed to get him up and on his way, but within a few hundred metres he was dead. McSweyn, having tried unsuccessfully to dig a hole in which to bury him, wrapped him up in his groundsheet and left him there.

The rest managed to reach the house by around 8 p.m. but found it locked up. Breaking in, they were able to get a fire going thanks to the last of the fumes in Harry Smith's lighter which, having been apparently "dry" for weeks, somehow ignited. Stripping off their sodden, icy-cold clothes they dried them out as best they could. They also managed to thaw out the half-frozen Mike Cooper who, with Harry Smith, had eaten some snow, and was beginning to develop hypothermia.

On the third day, still exhausted and hungry, they were delighted to find that the snow had stopped but, when they tried to leave the hut, discovered that drifting snow had blocked the door. Beating a path through the deep, cold snow any feeling left in their fingers and toes slowly disappeared. Frostbite was upon them. Harry Smith and Mike Cooper, still the weakest, were bringing up the rear while the others trod down the snow for them. The guide said that he knew where they were, but the airmen doubted this though continuing to follow him for several more kilometres until he announced that he was going to turn upstream. This the airmen refused to do, and McSweyn took charge of the party.

Fortuitously, several horses appeared ahead of them and beat a path down the valley for the grateful men to follow. Stumbling into a Spanish sentry post near the remote village of Uztárroz, Spanish soldiers threw them into 'a filthy cell, but let the guide, who was known to them, go to a local inn. After a little bribery we were allowed to join the guide in the inn, but still under guard. The guide told us he had posted a letter to the British Consul...'[985] They were then removed to Isaba, where they 'were given a form to fill in containing purely personal details'. After Harry Smith had sold his fountain pen for fifty pesetas the police took them to a hotel where they were given a meal of potatoes.

Moved to Pamplona they spent a night in a hotel, and telephoned the British Consul in Barcelona. Their next stop, courtesy of the Spanish Air Force, was at a hotel in Lecumberri, where they remained for just under three weeks until the Spanish had finished playing their games. Leaving Len Martin behind, Smith, Cooper, Palm and McSweyn were taken away in a bus, and were flown from Gibraltar to England on 20 December aboard a Dakota. The landing at Whitchurch airport on 21 December 1943 was spectacular, for the Dakota 'ground-looped, and the aircraft was written off, but with no injury to the twenty passengers and crew'.[986]

When the others departed in the bus they strongly protested about Len Martin having to remain behind. The Spanish excuse was that he was suspected of being a Frenchman posing as an RAF sergeant and that he 'frequently talked with the French internees',[987] a number of whom were also staying at the hotel. Five days after the others had left, Len was sent to the Miranda concentration camp for a few days with Polish fighter pilot Flying Officer C. Śnieć PAF (shot down on 8 September 1943 in France). They were flown back to England on 17 January 1944.

In *No Drums... No Trumpets* mention is made of a guide, Angel Martinez, who led six airmen over the Pyrenees at about the same time that McSweyn and party were making their crossing. A second guide, jealous of Martinez's newfound wealth, demanded a cut of the business, and this was agreed: 'For the first time, Martinez was ambushed and although he and the airmen escaped, the second guide was shot. It was snowing and Martinez pushed on. When he had seen the airmen safely over the frontier, Martinez returned, but could not find his comrade, who had already been buried by the snow.'[988]

Then came the day of Mary's arrest at Pau station. She had decided to move four airmen (three American, one RAF) from Farms A and B to Pau. Henriette Rejern was given the task of fetching them but, when Mary received a telegram from Henriette that simply said 'Quite impossible to come', Ginette Favbre was sent instead. Their papers were to identify them as deaf-mutes being taken to the Institute for the Deaf at Pau, but 'Ginette forgot to include a necessary medical paper in their documents'.[989] As a result of this oversight they were caught in a routine Gestapo control on the train from Toulouse to Pau, on 23 November 1943, when one of the American airmen gave the game away. All were arrested and taken to the Maison Blanche at Biarritz for questioning. It looked bad for Ginette when the Gestapo, already sure that her boss was "Marie-Claire", found a photograph of Mary in her wallet. They could not, however, persuade her to tell them where Mary was. In the event, they did not have long to wait before discovering her whereabouts.

Wearing her Red Cross uniform Mary, unaware that the four airmen had already been arrested with Ginette, was checking all the trains arriving at Pau station on 24 November when she was picked up by the SD. Also taken to Biarritz for questioning, she maintained that she was the Comtesse de Moncy, not de Milleville, which at least caused some doubt to creep into her interrogator's mind. Once news of her arrest had reached her family, Barbé went to see the head of the Gestapo in France.[990] Using her feminine wiles she hoped that she could somehow obtain her mother's release. Rather than falling for her charms, however, the German took Barbé to the Maison Blanche in Biarritz and, peering through a doorway, asked her if the woman in the room was her mother. Barbé unwittingly confirmed that she was.

It was not long before Mary and Ginette Favbre were put on the train for Paris, but somewhere near Châtellerault Mary jumped off. Even as she did so bullets were flying. One 'pierced her cheek', while a second, 'crashing into the base of her skull, helped to thrust her towards the ground.'[991] Recovering her broken though still living body, she was taken to the Luftwaffe hospital at Tours, where the chief surgeon skilfully did what he could to save her life.

Following his mother's arrest Maurice de Milleville made his way to Switzerland in January 1944 to report to British Intelligence on "Marie-Claire's" activities. He was also particularly anxious to acquire British citizenship as his mother was, after all, English. The British, however, were not sure of this excitable Frenchman who had suddenly appeared on their doorstep with no papers and no means of identification, and were reluctant to help.

The Marie-Claire line, though shattered by the arrests of some of its key members, still had an estimated ninety-seven airmen in hiding in the Paris area awaiting evacuation. Pauline took it upon herself to continue Mary's activities, but had insufficient funds to do this, and made her way to Switzerland, where the ever-obliging Victor Farrell gave her 500,000 francs. Returning to carry on with the evacuation of the dozens of airmen in hiding, and reverting to her alias of Madame Alice Laroche, she based herself at the Hôtel Richelieu.[992] New helpers were recruited, including Nicole Lebon and Max Goldblum, a soldier of Polish origin who had escaped from the German prisoner-of-war camp Stalag IIA (Neubrandenburg). Two police detectives were also enrolled, and they, with their special passes, were able to get airmen through ticket barriers at the railway stations. She also arranged for airmen to eat black-market food at a restaurant on the rue Cinq Diamants. Once it was clear to move the airmen Nicole Lebon took them in groups of ten to Toulouse, where they were met by Robert and Germaine Thibout, and sent on to Foix and over the Pyrenees.

Running out of money, Pauline made a second journey to Switzerland. In her absence evading airmen were passed on to Françoise Dissard's organisation in Toulouse. Failing to obtain further funds Pauline returned to Paris and was introduced to one of General de Gaulle's men, Valentin Abeille ("Méridien"), who agreed to come up with the money. Both Pauline and Nicole, however, were arrested near la Madeleine metro station in Paris, as were eight others soon after, betrayed by an unknown informer. All were to die in concentration camps but, before her death, Pauline would once again meet Mary, Comtesse de Milleville.

Six weeks after her operation in the Luftwaffe hospital in Tours, Mary was transferred to Dijon prison on 15 January 1944 – Ginette Favbre was also there – and spent the next eight months in solitary confinement. Another British agent, Yvonne Baseden, joined her later in the year, having been captured after parachuting into France on 18 March 1944 for SOE's Scholar circuit. In the middle of August 1944, when the Germans evacuated Paris, Mary and Yvonne were removed to the Neue Breme camp near Saarbrücken for a few days, joining several more female SOE agents including

Violette Szabo, Lilian Rolfe and Denise Bloch.[993] Facing a long and uncertain journey deeper into Germany, they arrived at Ravensbrück concentration camp on 3 September 1944.

By some miracle both Mary and Yvonne were classified as prisoners of war which, said a Gestapo officer, meant that they would be transferred to an internment camp at Lake Constance. The move never came, and they were still at Ravensbrück as the cold winter months dragged on. Apparently there was no guarantee anyway that, even if told that one would be moving to Lake Constance, the move would ever be completed.

One day Katie Johannsen, a Norwegian woman in charge of the clothes store, received a pile of clothes which she recognised as those of Violette Szabo, Lilian Rolfe and Denise Bloch. This could only mean, she told Mary, that the three had been executed. They were reportedly shot through the back of the neck by SS-Sturmann (Lance-Corporal) Schult, though Mary believed that they had been hanged. She, meanwhile, survived by having been drafted into the sick quarters as a nurse because of her experience in that field.

Yvonne, on the other hand, became one of the many for whom there was no special treatment, and in due course was selected for extermination in the Bergen-Belsen gas chambers. When Mary heard of this she had a word with her contact in the camp's office, and Yvonne's name was removed from the list.[994] Then one day Pauline appeared in the sick quarters and came face to face with Mary. She had a slight temperature, insufficiently high under the rules for her to be admitted to the hospital, but Mary let her stay until she went off on a work detail a couple of weeks later. She came back with the other survivors in an awful state and once again begged Mary for help. With her was Ginette Favbre, still alive, but as both were suspected of having typhus they were thrown into what was called the Black Hole of Ravensbrück, there to live or die. Pauline did indeed die,[995] but Ginette was rescued by a fellow inmate, Nadadge Verdun.

Then it was Mary's turn to be helped, but from an unexpected quarter. She had contracted pneumonia and though through the worst was still seriously ill. She was seen by the camp doctor, Triter, who apparently decided to save her life because he had had an English grandmother! On 25 April 1945, the selfless, stubborn, arrogant Mary, Comtesse de Milleville, alias Marie-Claire, was led to freedom, away from the hell of Ravensbrück. Typically, before she left she bullied the *Lagerführer* into letting Yvonne Baseden and all the other British women go free, about fifty in all. Released into the care of the Swedish Red Cross they 'were driven in coaches across the ruins of Germany and then on to Sweden'.[996] At Malmö they were housed in rough and ready accommodation before being returned to Britain.

Though Mary's achievements have never been precisely quantified in terms of Allied personnel successfully passed to safety Pauline, under the guise of the "Marie Odile/Alice Laroche" line, helped some seventy-one Allied airmen – thirty-nine USAAF, twenty-four RAF, and eight RCAF.[997]

Chauny Escape Line[998]

Etienne Dromas was an ex-French soldier who 'lost his right leg while serving in the French Army in the present war', and 'lives in the Mairie in Ugny-le-Gay, where his wife is the schoolteacher… He has a secret room [in the Mairie] in which he keeps arms and ammunition.'[999] Despite the loss of a leg, Dromas, a draftsman employed by the SNCF at Tergnier (Aisne) before the onset of war in 1939, joined the French Resistance in 1942, becoming a captain in the FFI and being appointed commander of *Groupement B*, 2nd Military Region, in the Aisne Département (district of Laon). It was with the increase in air operations during 1942 that he decided to help evading airmen return to England, and to that end enlisted the help of many trusted friends in various communities to keep a lookout for evading airmen.

By 1943 he had lookouts in the area around Chauny, and at La Fère, St Gobain, Coucy-le-Château, and St Simon (all in the Aisne *département*). Other "helpers" were located further afield, around places such as Guise, Laon, and St Quentin (also all in the Aisne), and at Cambrai (Nord), Compiègne and Creil (Oise). Dromas and his lieutenants also arranged a number of safe houses for the airmen, one of them being the garage of Alfred Logeon at 24, rue Brouage, Chauny.[1000] People from all walks of life were involved – priests, mayors, farmers, teachers – though not the mayor of Ugny-le-Gay, who apparently visited the Mairie 'twice weekly', was 'a collaborator with the Germans, and is detested locally'.[1001]

The first airman to receive help from the Dromas group was Wing Commander Embling (see Chapter 9), in December 1942. It was not until over four months later, however, that the next airmen, Sergeant I.R. MacDonald RCAF and Pilot Officer G.M. Parkinson RCAF, were given assistance, after their Halifax had come to grief at Togny-et-Pont, fifteen kilometres north-west of Chauny, on the way back from Stuttgart on 14/15 April 1943. They stayed with Dr Lupanof at Flavy-le-Martel (half a dozen kilometres north of Chauny).

A couple of days later, in the early hours of 17 April 1943, a Stirling (piloted by Pilot Officer P.D. White) crashed near the village of Commenchon (Aisne), France on the way back from Mannheim. Following the rough landing the Stirling burst into flames, and though all survived they were shaken-up to some degree or other. Two of the crew, Pilot Officer D.G. Ross, suffering multiple contusions to both legs, and Sergeant R.G. Gaisford, were met shortly after the landing by a baker, M. Duboise, who directed them to the house of Madame Ansard, between Commenchon and Ugny-le-Gay. 'This woman, who was apparently a member of an organisation, had in the meantime located the remainder of our crew.'[1002] Gaisford was then sheltered by Etienne Dromas and his wife in the Ugny village hall and school.

Whether or not it was the mayor of Ugny-le-Gay who told the Gestapo that Pilot Officer White had been taken to the home of M. Duboise is not known, but 'someone must have informed the Germans, who visited the house about midday and captured him.' Ross heard later that Duboise had been closely questioned by the Gestapo, but had not been arrested. White was the only one of his crew to be taken prisoner of war (he went to Stalag Luft III), while the others, once they had received medical attention from local doctors, were passed on to the Comet line in Paris.

The task of escorting the airmen from the Chauny area to Paris was given to Mademoiselle Henri de Bizien, who told Ross that her first name was Christine, that her alias was "Marquise", and that she was the daughter of an admiral.[1003] On 13 May she took five of the airmen to Paris: the two Canadians, MacDonald and Parkinson; and Sergeant W.J. Fitzgerald RNZAF; Sergeant A. Smith; and Sergeant W.E. Phillips RCAF, three more of the White crew. On 12 May Fitzgerald and Smith, having been sheltered in Ugny-le-Gay (with the Dromas) and Cugny respectively, met up at La Neuville-en-Beine, and were taken to the waiting room at Chauny station, where they met Phillips.

Leaving Phillips at the Gare du Nord, Paris, where they had arrived at about 9 p.m. on 13 May, Smith and Fitzgerald were taken to a flat at 35, Boulevard St Cyr, Bis 5, 'owned by a married couple. The husband, who spoke English, had been a captain in the Engineers in the last war.'[1004] Smith and Fitzgerald stayed at their flat until 22 May, when they 'were moved to another house owned by a lady doctor which we believe was in the Avenue Victor, off the Champs Elysées. We stayed with her until 25 May when we were taken to a park near the Gare d'Austerlitz. Here we met Ross, Gaisford, Phillips and two guides, one of whom was called Jacques.'[1005]

Ross, Gaisford, and the rest of their crew – Pilot Officer S.F. Everiss and Sergeant J.B. Ford – had been brought to Paris on 17 May by, again, Christine de Bizien and a Madame "Bennett" or "Benetsh". Also with them was Sergeant H.N. McKinnon, who had been shot down near St Quentin on 14/15 April 1943. Ross and Gaisford went to Madame Bohn's flat at 116, Boulevard Raspail. Madame Bohn ('aged about forty-two [and] is a doctor') contacted Frédéric de Jongh ("Paul"), who arranged for the evaders to be photographed for their false identity cards at the Bon Marché.

Having assembled at the Gare d'Austerlitz on 24 May, Ross, Gaisford, Smith, Fitzgerald and Phillips were taken south on the overnight train to Toulouse by Jacques, one of the Burgundy line's guides, on what was, he told them, only his third trip. Jacques was surprised that there was no control on the train, as there had been on his other two trips. Even more surprising were the two gendarmes who shared the compartment with the evaders, and who 'seemed rather simple men'. They 'remarked that it was a great pity that there was no control as people would be able to escape into Spain. One of them handed round a photograph of a Halifax aircraft which he had known to have been brought down somewhere.'[1006]

From Toulouse the party made its way to Foix, Spanish guides leading them into Andorra on 28 May, and to Anserall in Spain two days later. On 2 June a car arrived from the Barcelona consulate, but as there was only room for three, Ross, Gaisford and Phillips went on, leaving the others to be picked up later.

It was to be a further five days before Smith and Fitzgerald were on the move again, to a farm fifteen kilometres nearer Barcelona. Their guide left them there while he returned to Andorra to collect three more evaders – Pilot Officer E.L. Gimbel RCAF; Flight Sergeant D.K. Nolan RCAF; and Sergeant F.G.A. Weight – who had arrived there via Burgundy. When the party finally left, it was some fifteen strong. The five airmen eventually sailed from Gibraltar to Liverpool on 5-11 August.

In Paris meanwhile, Everiss, Ford and McKinnon spent two days *chez* Mme. "Benetsh", when Everiss and Ford 'went to stay with Mme. Deane, near Eiffel Tower. Here we were joined by Lieutenant Wemheuer, USAAF, whom we left in Paris.'[1007] On 26 May Everiss and Ford left for Lyon by train, and met Sergeant A.C. Turner RCAF and Sergeant J. Sankey. 'The four of us were eight days in a flat in Lyons, being joined by Sergeant [G.H.] Murray, Sergeant [R.G.] Goddard, RAF, and Lieutenant Contapidis and Sgt. Minor, USAAF.'[1008]

Sergeant Alvin Clinton Turner RCAF had come a long way since leaving his job of foreman at

General Motors before joining up in July 1940 at the age of twenty-one, but all his knowledge and expertise on engines was of no avail when, as the flight engineer of Halifax DT646, 419 (Moose) Squadron, he was obliged to bale out over Holland on the night of 5/6 March 1943. Just after bombs had been dropped on target (Essen), the aircraft was hit by flak, and Turner's right eye was severely cut by splinters. The pilot, Sergeant L. Bakewell, flew on until they were over Holland, when DT646 was attacked by night-fighters and set on fire. Bakewell gave the order to bale out, and all seven of the crew took to their parachutes.[1009]

Turner jumped out of the rear escape hatch but was knocked unconscious during his descent. Regaining his senses some hours later he discovered that he was in a field, possibly near Zaandam, three or four kilometres north of Amsterdam. As his eye was still 'bleeding copiously', he used a piece of his parachute to staunch the wound. Tearing off his "wings" and left tunic pocket – leaving on his chevrons and the "Canada" shoulder patches – he extracted a compass. 'I was still wearing my flying helmet and my flying boots, over which I pulled my trousers. My flying boots were of Canadian pattern, and I was wearing a pair of ordinary walking shoes within them.'[1010] Thus equipped he headed south, but very soon came to the Noordzeekanaal, and found himself confronted by a large steel bridge which led into a large city (later identified as Amsterdam).

Walking along the canal for a time he saw three E-boats moored to the bank: 'There was a great deal of singing coming from these boats and I presumed that the German crews were occupied with festivities of some kind. Alongside the E-boats I saw two small rowing boats.'[1012] He thought that the rowing boats were chained to a steel post, but a closer inspection revealed that they were only loosely tied to it. Getting into the smaller of the two boats he allowed the current to drift him away from the E-boats until it was safe to start rowing to the far bank. Climbing ashore, he pushed the rowing boat back into the middle of the canal and continued south. 'I saw several people on the streets and a number of cyclists, but I kept to the shadows, and hid in the doorways when I thought it necessary. After about two hours the day began to break, and I found myself clear of the city.' Enjoying a long rest in a wood he continued his journey when it was dark, eventually hitting the Amsterdam–Hilversum railway line. He saw a number of German patrols but was able to evade them, grateful for the rubber soles of his flying boots.

By the evening of 7 March he had reached the outskirts of Utrecht, which he 'recognised by means of a signpost'. Walking cautiously through the streets at about 2 a.m. on 8 March 'about 200 German soldiers, unarmed, came out of what must have been a camp of some kind quite near me. I avoided them, and soon came to a number of railway lines about which guards were posted.' Still wearing his flying helmet, flying boots, chevrons and with CANADA emblazoned on each shoulder, a German suddenly flashed his torch at him and spoke to him in German. Unable to speak the language Turner could only mumble something like 'Na'. The guard came up to him and again shone his torch at him: 'He then spoke to me for some time, and I think he must have taken me for a German NCO. I replied to his remarks with some guttural noises. Finally he pointed down a railway track towards the south, and I walked on in the direction in which he indicated.'

As soon as he was out of sight of the German Alvin ran for about an hour as fast as his shaking legs could carry him. Spending the rest of the day in a haystack, he treated himself to another Horlicks tablet from his escape box, waiting until dark before walking off along the Utrecht to 's-Hertogenbosch railway line. Just north of Culemborg he came to one of Holland's myriad waterways, probably the Amsterdam-Rijnkanaal. The only way across was on the railway bridge, which was guarded by two German soldiers.[1013] Seeing no boats Alvin, 'a fairly strong swimmer', decided that he would have to swim across: 'I therefore took off my flying boots and threw them in the water, retaining my walking shoes… I took off my clothes, and tied them and my shoes in a bundle which I took upon my shoulders. I then swam across the canal.' Not surprisingly for early March the water was rather cold.

Losing his compass in the crossing, he used the one from his escape-aids box, and walked through Culemborg. At daylight on 9 March, near a farm with chickens pecking about, he hid in a haystack: 'Here I took off my clothes and dried them in the sun.' After dark he 'broke open the lock of a henhouse and stole two eggs, which I ate to supplement my diet of Horlick's tablets.' Somewhat replenished he continued walking south, with the intention of reaching Paris, having heard from various people in England that not all Dutch folk 'were sympathetic to the Allies, and I resolved not to ask for help in Holland unless it was absolutely necessary.' During the night, following the busy railway line, he reached Tricht (eight kilometres south of Culemborg), but by this time his right shoulder had become so painful that he was unable to lift his arm.[1014] He then hid in another haystack until midnight, when he decided to jump a train.

As trains were moving too quickly at this point on the line, he headed back towards Tricht, and soon after midnight boarded a stationary goods train. Moving off to the south shortly afterwards the train passed through several small towns, occasionally stopping. During one of these stops Alvin got out onto a deserted platform hoping to discover the name of the station, but failed. At another stop he suddenly heard the train guard heading for the compartment where he was hiding. Leaving quickly, he crawled under the train: 'I then remembered that I had left my water bottle in the compartment. The train then began to move off. At the next stop I managed to get back to the compartment, which was empty. The water bottle had apparently not been disturbed.' Riding his luck, and the train, for the rest of the day (10 March) he sensed that he was now heading south-east towards Germany and, when the train stopped yet again outside a small station, decided to leave it.

Once more on foot he walked until daybreak, but the pain from his shoulder had become so unbearable that he gave in and decided to ask for help. The first person he tried, a Dutch farmer, told him by sign language that he could not help, but to try a further five kilometres down the road. Still wearing his flying helmet, unshaven for several days, his tunic and face covered with dried blood, he approached another house. Taken aback by the sight that greeted them, it was a while before the occupants of the house were prepared to let him in and feed him. Shortly after his arrival a Dutchman left the house. Turner felt certain that he was about to be betrayed, but about ten minutes later the man returned with another man, who spoke English. The English speaker asked Turner a number of searching questions, particularly whether or not he had escaped from German hands or were the Germans following him? Satisfied with his answers they gave him a coat and hat, and the English speaker took him to his house, where he had a bath, a shave, and more food.

But someone in the village must have talked, for suddenly the Gestapo were there looking for him. Turner's helpers 'were very scared, and the man who spoke English took me at once into the country in a car and hid me in a haystack.' At around 7 p.m. that evening (11 March) the English speaker returned and 'drove me to a point in the country which he said was within a mile of the Dutch-Belgian frontier. He showed me an electric cable, and told me that if I followed this cable I should come to Liège. He then gave me an attaché case filled with food, and left me.'[1015] Despite the awful pain in his shoulder he walked for some seven hours, when he collapsed into yet another haystack. Around midday on 12 March, he was woken by a farmer prodding the hay with his pitchfork. The farmer spoke only Flemish, but was able to indicate on Turner's map that they were in Belgium: 'He did not offer me help.'

Still following the electric cable Turner met an old woman and a girl pushing a cart. They spoke French, and he was able to understand enough to know that they would take him to the nearby village of Barchon where he could get a tram to Liège, ten kilometres or so to the south-west. That afternoon, having arrived in Liège, he walked around for a couple of hours before deciding to go to Mons. Leaving Liège he 'passed a small restaurant, and noticed the words "English spoken here" written on the window.' Entering the Star café he asked for a cup of tea, hoping thereby to arouse the waiter's curiosity. In this he was successful, and in 'a few minutes a man who spoke English was brought to me. He took me to his house.' This man, Vandenhove,[1016] now took Turner to his house in Bessoux, a suburb of Liège.

Still in pain Turner was visited by a doctor and by a surgeon, who diagnosed a displaced vertebra in his back. They said that massage would be sufficient to restore it to its rightful place, but for now he was to rest. He was still incapacitated when the Gestapo paid the house a visit and arrested Vandenhove, for nothing more serious than blackmail. Had the Gestapo bothered to search the house, Turner too would have been arrested.

Too dangerous to remain there any longer, Turner was moved to another house. Now in contact with "Sir Charles", chief of an organisation calling itself John No. 8, he was moved to Brussels on 13 May, where he stayed with a Madame Pauli in the rue de Naples. Six days later, at the Gare du Nord, he met Sergeant J. Sankey, shot down on 14/15 February 1943, 'two Poles, a Dutchman and a girl. This girl was a nurse. She could speak no English but gave me to understand that her father and mother had been Allied agents during the last war.'[1017] For some unknown reason, they were all turfed off the Paris train by the Germans, and had to catch one on the following day.

Safely in Paris on the evening of 14 May, they found themselves in the hands of the Brandy organisation, and stayed at 'a house near, but not in, the rue de Babylone, and kept by a cook who spoke very little English'.[1018] Turner and Sankey briefly met Frédéric de Jongh ("Paul"), who was with a man calling himself by the unlikely name of Lieutenant Badger, and who was apparently 'a British agent engaged on sabotage work near Liège'. On 16 May they were moved to 'the house of an elderly woman in the rue de Clichy', leaving on 26 May for the Gare d'Austerlitz, where they met Pilot Officer S.F. Everiss and Sergeant J.B. Ford and caught the train for Lyon.

The eight airmen – Everiss, Ford, Turner, Sankey, Murray, Goddard, Contopodis and Minor – were divided into two groups for the journey to the Pyrenees. First to leave, on 6 June, were Everiss, Ford, Sankey and Turner, together with 'two Frenchmen who wanted to get to the UK'. They linked up with the other four at Lavelanet east of Foix, and reached St Paul-de-Jarrat (Ariège) together, where a further two Frenchmen joined the party.

On the night of 8/9 June they set off over the mountains with a large party of Frenchmen, some fifty all told, many of whom were armed. They reached the Andorran border at around midday on 9 June, but not before a German patrol had opened up on them with machine-guns and rifles as they were crossing a gorge. No one was hit and they safely arrived in Andorra. After two days' rest at an Andorran hotel, they walked into Spain and, hiding in woods during the day, reached Manresa on 20 June. Catching the slow train from there to Barcelona, their guide took them to the British Consulate. Everiss, Murray and Turner were flown home on 27/28 June.

Sankey and Ford returned on the *Monarch of Bermuda* with a number of other evaders, berthing at Liverpool on 24 July. Sankey and Ford, however, probably without knowing it gave Major A.J. Macphail, Security Control Officer (SCO) for the Liverpool area, a minor headache, for it transpired that contrary to Air Ministry Order A2/43 they were disembarked by the RAF embarkation officer 'without reference to SCO. This matter is being taken up locally with RAF Movement Control…'[1019] The security of the nation was paramount.

Sergeant Goddard left the British Embassy in Madrid on 24 June with two Dutchmen and an English civilian, Mr Bell. At Seville they were put on board a British collier, but as there were Spanish guards aboard, the four men were smuggled by ship's officers into the cook's storeroom, and there they remained, undetected even by the cook, until 4 July when the guards left and the ship sailed down the Guadalquivir river to Gibraltar. Goddard was back in England on 9 July.

By the liberation in September 1944 eighty-seven Allied airmen had been assisted by Dromas and his team. Of that total it is believed that only seven fell into enemy hands, four of whom were the two Canadians, Ian MacDonald and Grenville Parkinson, who were betrayed by their guide at Oloron in the Pyrenees towards the end of June 1943; Neil McKinnon; and Pilot Officer James MacDonald (sixteenth on Chauny's list), who was arrested in bizarre circumstances. Shot down on 13/14 July 1943, he was in a safe house at Perpignan when, on 30 September, 'a neighbour who was unaware of what was going on, happened to see him looking out of the window. She thought he was a thief and called the police.'[1020] Two more caught were Americans and finally, on 9 August 1944, yet another Canadian, Warrant Officer Second Class Charles G. Pallett RCAF, (seventy-fifth on the Chauny list), who had the misfortune to be in hiding in the village of Villequier-Aumont, a short distance north of Chauny, when it was surrounded and attacked by Germans.

The Chauny line continued to help airmen until May 1944 when, so intense was Gestapo pressure on the Resistance movement as a whole, the Chauny operations had to come to a halt, resulting in a logjam of evaders. After the Normandy landings on 6 June Dromas therefore 'decided to move the fifty allied airmen and fifteen Russians along with a band of Maquis (FFI) to the farm community of Ugny-le-Gay and Commenchon as a precaution… This was a temporary move and after five or six days the evaders were moved back to their former shelters in and around Chauny where possible. A few days later at a large farm in the Ugny-le-Gay and Commenchon farm area, a German patrol attacked Dromas and fifteen Frenchmen, killing all the French patriots and setting fire to the farm buildings. One of the German soldiers stepped on Dromas' head thinking he was dead. He later recovered to be the only survivor.'[1021]

Allied troops finally liberated the area on 2 September 1944, for which the six American fighter pilots shot down on 25 August in a fierce engagement over Tergnier, the last to receive assistance from the Dromas organisation, would have been grateful.

Dutch-Paris

The origins of the Dutch-Paris escape line are attributed to businessman Johan Weidner, domiciled in France but of Dutch parents, who had started an import/export textile business in Paris in 1935. Business prospered, and three years later he opened a shop in his hometown of Collonges (Ain), near the Swiss border. He was in Paris when the Germans invaded Holland in May 1940 and, remembering stories of German atrocities committed there during the First World War, tried to escape to England to join the army. He was, however, detained in Lyon, in Unoccupied France, where he noted that the Vichy government was coming under increasing German pressure to transfer Jews and other political refugees to German-controlled camps (as witnessed by Phillips and Witton – see Chapter 1).

The first consideration for Weidner and his colleagues, including men such as Arie Sevenster, consul-general at Vichy, and Gilbert Beaujolin, was to help the Jews who were being concentrated in camps in France. In 1941 Beaujolin suggested that what was needed was an effective organisation, and soon a "board of directors" was formed. Beaujolin became 'executive president of the new organisation, which they called *Les Amitiés Chrétiennes*.'[1022] At the same time, Weidner proposed the formation of a group dedicated solely to helping Dutch nationals imprisoned in French camps, though this was not easy due to their circumstances. Nevertheless, early in 1942 he decided that it was not enough just to get them out – they should be taken to safety in Switzerland. With his knowledge of the area around Collonges, only kilometres from the Swiss border, an escape line through that area seemed the obvious solution. A route from Lyon, where Weidner now had his office, to Annecy, where he had a store, was therefore established. The final stage of the journey would be completed by bus to the border and thence by foot.

Weidner still needed to be sure of the escapers' safety once in Switzerland, and when he received word that a Dr W.A. Visser 't Hooft, general secretary of the World Council of Churches, in Geneva and Johan Bosch van Rosenthal, Dutch minister in Bern, were prepared to help, he went to Switzerland himself. Both these high-ranking and influential men pledged their support for his work, Visser 't Hooft also giving him 200,000 French francs. Word of Weidner's activities was sent to the Dutch government in exile in London, and on his next visit to Switzerland Weidner was told by van Rosenthal that he would thereafter be financially supported by the Dutch.

Back in Lyon, Weidner was visited by a man calling himself Benno Nykerk, a Jewish businessman from Brussels, who wondered 'if it would be possible to establish a complete escape line running from Holland through Brussels to Paris, and then to Lyon and Switzerland, or Toulouse and Spain.'[1023] The suggestion was well received, and as 1942 wore on many trusted people were enrolled to help with the escape line, among them a young woman who had escaped from Holland, Suzy Kraay, who became a highly valued member of the organisation. She had been recommended by Herman Laatsman, chief of the organisation in Paris, who also suggested that, as their work was primarily concerned with Dutch people and the centre of the line was in Paris, they should call the organisation "Dutch-Paris". And so it became.

Gradually the line developed, and small hotels such as 'the Ibis in Paris, the Panier Fleuri in Toulouse, and the Novelty in Lyons' proved useful overnight stops for personnel on the long journey to Spain. Gabriel Nahas, a medical student at the hospital in Toulouse, was another important link in the chain, whom Weidner had arranged should 'run the new escape line in cooperation with Aarts in Toulouse'. Nahas also 'knew the rugged mountain area well. He had many contacts with guides who regularly crossed the peaks and was capable of making fast and accurate decisions, a quality necessary in operating an escape route.'[1024] Brigadier Hargest (see Chapter 10) was to form a very high opinion of him: 'The success of the Dutch escape organisation is mainly due to one young man – Dr Gabriel Nahas, who works under the alias of Dr Georges Prontas.'[1025] Hargest also reported that, since March 1943, he had sent between 300-400 persons out of France to Spain, 'using the services of a large number of young men in all sorts of positions, all of whom work voluntarily and absolutely refuse to accept any remuneration.'[1026]

Three airmen to find themselves in January 1944 in the hands of Dutch-Paris in Helden, in the south of Holland and a few kilometres south-west of Venlo, were Pilot Officer J.G. McLaughlin RAAF, and two Americans – First Lieutenant William McDonald and 2nd Lieutenant Frank McGlinchy – who had apparently been in hiding in Friesland for about fifteen weeks and had already made two unsuccessful attempts to cross into Belgium. McLaughlin had earlier been helped by a Dutch policeman and his fiancée from Venlo, and it was the policeman who, on the night of 20 January, took the three airmen in his car to Maastricht. Six nights later they were escorted to the Belgian frontier, barely one kilometre away, to catch a train to Liège and Brussels. McLaughlin reported: 'While our new guide went through the frontier gate just before the Albert Canal the rest of us walked round the back of the guard room, rejoining him on the other side.'

At the railway station, they were joined by three more Americans (McLaughlin could remember the names of only two of them – Sergeants Schneider and Elkin), and they were escorted in threes to Brussels. Here two more Americans joined the party, 2nd Lieutenant Campbell Brigman Jr USAAF, and one of his gunners, whose name McLaughlin was also unable to remember.[1027] They reached Paris at around 10 a.m. on 29 January, and were lodged in the basement of a hospital just off the Boulevard St Michel, looked after by the hospital engineer. There were eight evaders for the first two days, but then their ranks were swollen 'by five others who had been living at farmhouses on the outskirts of Paris. They were F/Sgt [G.L.] Watts; Sgt Harris, RAF (captured while crossing Pyrenees), and Top-Sgt [*sic*] Mandel, 2nd Lieut Ferrani, and 2nd Lieut Roberts, all USAAF. Roberts was also caught.'[1028]

While Ferrani was taken away on 2 February 1944 'to a doctor, being considered unfit for mountain travel', the rest left for Toulouse next day. Travelling with them from Paris were ten Dutchmen and a Belgian, Roger Bureau. Bureau, who was thirty-nine years of age and lived in Amsterdam, encouragingly told McLaughlin that Jacques, their chief guide for the journey, 'was very reliable, a good organiser, and could hold the organisation together.' "Jacques" (Jacques Rens) was one of the key figures of the Dutch-Paris organisation.

Having reached Toulouse on the morning of 4 February, eleven of the group, including McLaughlin, left a café that evening 'and, under the guidance of Pierre Felippe (aged twenty-six: a pilot in peace time), went by train to Cazères'. They continued towards the mountains by taxi on the evening of 5 February, and in the foothills were joined by the rest of the party from Paris, making a total of twenty-six. Forced to skirt round the first mountain because of a blizzard at the summit, they rested in a hut until it had blown itself out.

Felippe was leading the way 'towards a bridge over a stream at the bottom of the valley' when, suddenly, he signalled them to go back, and ran back to the hut. 'We heard a shot and realised we had been seen by a German patrol. Shortly afterwards the hut was surrounded by the patrol, and fourteen members of the party were caught.'[1029] McLaughlin and nine others – 'Bureau, Watts, three Dutchmen, Sergeant Mandel, Sergeant Schneider, Sergeant Elkin and Lieutenant Brigman' – managed to get through the cordon round the back of the hut and up the mountainside, from which vantage point they watched as the rest of the party were arrested. Having also avoided capture, Felippe took them up the mountain.

After staying in a house in Cazères until 14 February, they returned to Toulouse, to a house in the poorer part of town, but only until 16 February, when 'Edmond [Edmund Chait], the second-in-command of Jacques' came to tell them that it was time to go. That afternoon they caught the train to the station near Cierp-Gaud (Haute-Garonne), where they 'were met by an American (no name) who has been living in France for the last ten years, and an elderly guide (Charbonnet)', and were joined by Flight Lieutenant R.M. Davenport RCAF (an American), and by six more Dutchmen, who had been on the same train. These seven now brought the total to twenty-five.

Cierp was to all intents and purposes in the hands of the Maquis, and for a month they stayed high in the hills above the town. During this period all non-British/American personnel left, among them First Lieutenant Bob Krengle USAAF, who 'returned to Toulouse and was not heard of again'.[1030] The balance was redressed by the arrival of more airmen evaders, and by two Czechs. Among the new members of the party were Sergeant F.J. Page and Sergeant J.R. Vass, both RAF, and 2nd Lieutenant Ferrani (now fit enough to cross the mountains), First Lieutenant Arp, 2nd Lieutenant Sherman,[1031] and Sergeants Robert Finney and Kenneth Carson, all USAAF. 'The party which crossed the mountains consisted of five British, seventeen Americans, and seven Frenchmen, who joined us the night we started. We left by truck on sixteen March with Charbonnet as guide. This party was heavily armed, and had five sten guns. We drove for two hours before starting to walk. We crossed into Spain about 1200 hours on 19 March near Bosost.'

Early in March 1944 Dutch-Paris began assembling another large convoy of evaders and escapers at a safe house at Blagnac, on the outskirts of Toulouse. On the night of 25/26 March the party moved to Bagnères-de-Luchon, prior to beginning the long climb over the Pyrenees. One of the group, Flying Officer J.H. Watlington RCAF, whose home was in Bermuda, reported that the 'party now comprised the guide, two men of the Maquis who were armed with Sten guns, fifteen Americans, twelve Dutchmen, three Frenchmen, one Belgian, and myself.'[1032]

Taking off in his Mustang fighter from RAF Ford, Sussex on the night of 21/22 June 1943 Flying Officer Watlington failed in his primary objective – to find and destroy enemy bombers over Amiens airfield in northern France – and so targetted traffic on the French railways: 'While attacking a locomotive east of Amiens I ran into a barrage of light tracer flak and was hit in the radiator. I flew off at low level and, once out of danger, I climbed to 9,000 feet in order to bale out.' Parachuting into a cornfield, he walked to Bouelles (Seine-Maritime), and early on the morning of 23 June went to sleep in a barn. He set off again after the farmer in whose barn he had slept had fed him and given him some civilian clothes.

Rather than walk on the open road Watlington decided to walk along a railway track. Suddenly, two armed policemen jumped out from a ditch and pointed their revolvers at his head. 'Je suis anglais,' he announced, whereupon they 'put their revolvers away and took me to a field.' Producing sufficient evidence to satisfy the police that he was indeed "English", and an airman, they told him how to buy a railway ticket and what time the train left for Paris. After a night in a haystack he went to the railway station at St Saire, a few kilometres south, and made his way to Paris: 'I arrived in Paris about 2130 hours. I had no plans and wandered round small hotels some distance from the station.' Half an hour before curfew he went into a restaurant, where a woman agreed to hide him in her flat for the night.

On 25 June he went to the Gare d'Austerlitz hoping to catch a train to Toulouse but, when he saw gendarmes demanding to see everyone's papers, made his way out of Paris and, with further help from the French, caught several trains southwards. Avoiding busy stations in the large towns, as advised by MI9 in their evasion bulletins, he crossed into Vichy France at Selles-sur-Cher (Loir-et-Cher) on 28 June: 'There were two sentry boxes on the bridge, but no sentries. I continued along the road to Valençay, where a farmer let me sleep in his barn.'

Intending to get to the eastern end of the Pyrenees, he caught a train to la Chapelaude (Allier), and spent the night in a field nearby. Returning to the station on the following morning and discovering that there was no train, he loitered about the station for most of the morning. This, inevitably, attracted the attention of the stationmaster. When Watlington confessed that he was "English", the stationmaster readily agreed to help. Changing his Belgian money into French, the official also gave him directions to St Affrique (Aveyron), which was at the end of a branch line and well on the way to the Pyrenees. On reaching Merlines (Corrèze), however, Watlington discovered that there was no train to St Affrique until 4.20 a.m. on 30 June, and so booked himself into a hotel, telling the proprietor that he was British. There was, however, a slight problem, for a Luftwaffe officer, who had been on the same train as Watlington, had taken the room next to his in the hotel. Watlington therefore decided to defer his journey for a day in order to avoid meeting the officer again.

Fate was to dictate that Watlington would not cross the Pyrenees for a further nine months, until the end of March 1944. At Merlines he was put in touch with "an organisation", and that was when his troubles really began. In the meantime, he lived with maquisards, and for a few carefree weeks stayed in a château at Liginiac, the home of Max Felix de Boisson, a former governor-general of one of the French colonies. With the mountains deemed to be too dangerous to cross on account of snow, Watlington was told that he would have the chance to get back to Britain by boat. Reluctantly, at the end of October 1943, he was taken north to Brittany, but he and several other hopefuls were told by the organiser of the operation, Yves le Hénaff ("FanFan"), on 4 November that the evacuation was off. Watlington therefore spent the next few months being sheltered in Paris and in the Reims/Epernay/Châlons-sur-Marne area, until he was moved back to Brittany at the end of January 1944 for another boat attempt, also being organised by le Hénaff.

This time the boat, *le Jouet-des-Flots*, did indeed sail but due to an earlier incident sank, and many of those on board who had managed to jump ashore were captured (see following chapter). Watlington was fortunate to escape capture, and to find himself in the hands of Dutch-Paris. Now, in late March 1944, Watlington and his group took three days, in very low temperatures and at a consistently high altitude of over 2,000 metres (6,500 feet), to cross the Pyrenees, and it was not until the morning of 28 March 1944 that the weary evaders gazed down upon Spanish soil. There are several ways of getting yourself down a mountainside, but John Watlington's was probably unique. The proud owner of a fine overcoat, formerly the possession of Henri Queuille, three times prime minister of France after the war,[1033] he tucked its tails between his legs and, with a stout branch as a rudder, slid down the mountain on his backside. Understandably, at the end of the joyful descent the tail of the coat was somewhat the worse for wear.[1024]

It was at the time of Watlington's escape over the mountains that Dutchman Flight Lieutenant Bram van der Stok was on his way from a German prisoner-of-war camp. He was one of only three, out of the seventy-six who managed to escape through the tunnel at Stalag Luft III (Sagan) on the night of 24/25 March 1944, to make a "home run" to England.[1035] Thirty-six hours after escaping, travelling by train through Breslau, Dresden and Halle, van der Stok reached his hometown of Utrecht, in Holland. Resisting the temptation to visit his parents, he stayed with a friend who lived two streets away.

Six weeks later Dutch-Paris took van der Stok across the Waal and Maas rivers into Belgium. Cycling to Brussels, he stayed with a Dutch family for a further six weeks, by which time he had 'changed his cover story, and represented himself as a Flemish worker in a Belgian firm.' Salomon Chait escorted him by train to Toulouse, where he stayed at a house at Puits Verts 9 from his arrival on 26 May until his departure for Spain on 9 June. Having sold his watch to raise money for the 10,000 francs fee required for guidance across the Pyrenees, he, two Dutchmen and a guide departed by train for the Hôtel Moderne at Boulogne-sur-Gesse (Haute-Garonne). Leaving in the morning by car they stayed a further night at a farm, before driving on, on 11 June, to a second farm near Vignaut (Haute-Garonne), some twenty kilometres from the Spanish border, where they met 'Lt. McPherson and Lt. Stonebarger, both of the USAAF, F/O [H.D.] Thomas, F/Sgt [G.J.] Shaughnessy, both of the RAF [*sic* – RCAF], a French officer, a Russian, and a French girl who had acted as guide to Lt. Stonebarger, F/O Thomas and F/Sgt Shaughnessy on the journey from Paris.'[1036]

The "French girl" to whom van der Stok refers was in fact an English girl, Odette Ernest. When the three airmen were at a house at Pantin, she and a French girl, Eugènie Roby, supplied them with food, English books, civilian clothing and false ID cards. Eugènie was also making the arrangements to get them away. 'She said that the guides who were to take us over the Pyrenees had asked for

10,000 francs for each one of us. The organisation was supplying us with the necessary amount of money for our keep, but could not raise the amount necessary to get us to Spain. Odette said that she would give each of us 12,000 francs on condition that it was repaid when we reached London. She said that Mr McIrvine, 14 Chiswell Street, London, was looking after her interests over in England, and asked us to send the money to him.'[1037]

With the financial details settled, Odette escorted the three airmen by train to Toulouse on 5 June 1944. Thanks to the activities of the French Resistance they did not reach Toulouse until 7 June, and left immediately for St Gaudens. Two days later they set off for the mountains, meeting 'a party of refugees and one American, (Lt. J. MacPherson). We walked to a farm, where we remained for six days while the guides were reconnoitring for German patrols.' On 14 June 'a Scottish girl, called Nan, from St Gaudens, brought word that the Germans had ambushed our guides and killed them. She supplied us with food and contacted another guide.' It seems that the French guide "Charbonnier" (the same man as the Charbonnet mentioned above, but real name Jean Bazerque) from Boulogne-sur-Gesse was shot dead by the Germans as he was returning to the farmhouse with food.[1038]

Two days later a replacement guide was found, and the party made its way, as van der Stok says, 'approximately east of St Pé d'Ardet, through the Forêt de Cagire, east of Melles, Caneja, where we arrived on 18 June. We were apprehended by the Spanish police and all, except the two Dutchmen, declared themselves to be British. The two Dutchmen declared themselves to be Dutch.' After several stops along the way all arrived at Lérida (22 June) and made contact with the British Consul. The two Dutchmen were taken to prison while the rest, with a Spanish Air Force escort, went to Alhama de Aragón. On 5 July the British Embassy car took them to Madrid, and two days later, with a British padré for escort this time, they travelled by train to Gibraltar (8 July). The two Dutchmen, Schrijnemacher and Bleys, were apparently still in prison at Lérida. They were, as they informed van der Stok, both working for a Major Somer of Dutch HQ, and had successfully completed their mission, somehow handing over a film to the Dutch Consulate at Barcelona.

Bram van der Stok and the two Canadians were flown by DC-3 Dakota to Whitchurch airport on 10/11 July, as no doubt were the Americans.

It is estimated that over 800 Jews and over 100 airmen (this latter figure is possibly too high) were moved to safety by Dutch-Paris, but at what a price. In February 1944 Suzy Kraay was caught by the *Brigade d'Interpellation*, a special section of the French police working with the Germans, who found on her a book of Dutch-Paris names. As a result, the Gestapo were able to arrest some one hundred and fifty Dutch-Paris helpers, 'forty of whom – Weidner's sister Gabrielle included – did not survive'.[1039]

Weidner, on the other hand, did survive, but after a very close shave. On 20 May 1944 in Toulouse, he and three key Dutch-Paris stalwarts – Jacques Rens, Paul Veerman, and Dr Gabriel Nahas – were leaving le Club Restaurant when they were suddenly surrounded by five armed "civilians". While they were being searched, Nahas ran off as fast as he could down the street. The man nearest to him pointed his pistol at his back and pressed the trigger. Nothing happened. The gun had jammed and, as the man was blocking the line of fire of the others, Nahas was able to make good his escape. Weidner, Rens and Veerman, though, were taken in handcuffs to a building which Weidner recognised as the Toulouse headquarters of Joseph Darnand's Milice, that woebegotten bunch of misguided French individuals who were every bit as nasty as their Gestapo counterparts.

Ruthless and cruel they may have been, but they were also capable of making mistakes, as Paul Veerman was to discover. Left alone in a room on the third floor of the Milice HQ, he slipped out of the window, and also left Toulouse with all speed. As for Weidner and Rens, they were told that they were to be taken away for execution by the Gestapo. Fortunately, however, one of the Milice, René Brunner, was prepared to help. He agreed to move them from the fifth floor to a cell on the third, and gave them some implements for forcing open the door. He could, though, do no more for them. They would have to get themselves out of the cell. One piece of advice – do not escape between 10 p.m. and 6 a.m. – the curfew.

They opened the door within an hour, and waited for the end of curfew. No sooner was it over than they made their way out of their cell, past the sleeping guards, and out of the window to the street three floors below, as Paul Veerman had done. Breaking no bones, they made their way over to the apartment of the Abbé de Stegge as nonchalantly as they could, and there met Flight Lieutenant Bob van der Stok; Rudy Schreidmakers, a Dutch secret service agent; and Father Lodewyck, a Dutch Catholic priest, all three of whom were hoping to get to England as soon as possible. With the help of Salomon Chait this was duly accomplished. For Weidner and Rens, however, their destination was Switzerland, which they reached on 2 June 1944, and from where they continued to operate the line, though communications were to prove difficult after the Normandy invasion.

Paul Veerman was again arrested, this time in Belgium. Deported to Germany, he escaped again, but was re-captured as he was about to cross the Swiss border. He survived, though other agents were also caught, and Dutch-Paris once again 'began to crumble'. Early in August 1944 Weidner himself decided to go to London, and was picked up from an airfield "somewhere in France". He was flown back to Brussels after it had been liberated early in September 1944, by which time the work of Dutch-Paris was done.

In 1946 Weidner received the American Medal of Freedom with Gold Palm, the citation for which stated, inter alia, that Dutch-Paris, 'organised and commanded by him, successfully conveyed 112 Americans and other Allied airmen out of Holland, through Belgium and France, across the Pyrenees into Spain.'[1040] The British admitted him a Member of the Most Excellent Order of the British Empire (Military Division) (MBE).

Bleu et Jonquille

Typical of many small lines, Bleu et Jonquille (Blue and Pale Yellow) operated within a small area in and around the town of Châlons-sur-Marne (today Châlons-en-Champagne) in eastern France. It was formed, with no military or political axe to grind, by Maurice Rehheiser,[1041] a policeman in Châlons-sur-Marne. In 1942 he enlisted the help of a number of police inspectors – Emile Bourgès, René Bronne, Henri Herry, Robert Kister, André Loisy, and Joseph Menou – and in time was able to form two other units outside the town, one at Champigneul, to the west, led by Jules Rieu and his father Alexandre, and the other at Togny-aux-Boeufs, to the south, with Denis Hollender in charge. At its peak Bleu et Jonquille, whose speciality was the preparation of false papers, could call on some ninety members to help evaders of all sorts, including airmen and Frenchmen trying to avoid the STO, forced labour in Germany.

Three airmen known to have been helped by this organisation – Flying Officer A.R. Fisher RCAF; Flying Officer J.G.Y. Lavoie RCAF; and Sergeant W.E. Fell RCAF – were from Halifax LK739 which, when some twenty minutes short of the target (Berlin) on the night of 20/21 January 1944, was hit by flak in its fuel tanks. Another burst caused more leakage as they were heading for home. With only ten minutes or so of fuel left the pilot, Flight Sergeant F.F. Reain RCAF, gave the order to bale out. All seven of the crew managed to do so, landing in the area of Tilloy-et-Bellay (Marne), ten to fifteen kilometres north-east of Châlons-sur-Marne.

Flying Officers Fisher and Lavoie, independently of each other, worked their way to the west of Châlons-sur-Marne, and at Ambonnay (Marne) came into the hands of Bleu et Jonquille's Champigneul section. Sergeant Fell had reached Châlons by the afternoon of 22 January, but just before entering the town he 'saw some German soldiers on parade. I therefore turned back and walked across some fields. A girl who was coming towards me, stopped me and spoke to me. She only spoke a few words of English, but she told me her people were Welsh, and as she seemed to know who I was, I asked her if she could help me.'[1042] She agreed, and as they were walking along together they were overtaken by a man on a bicycle. She stopped him, told him who Fell was, and the man took him away.

After they had been collected by Bleu et Jonquille, Marcel Vangeluwe, a garage proprietor in Châlons, drove the three airmen, and Maurice Rehheiser, Henri Egly and René Ruttloff, two more members of Maurice's group, to Epernay railway station on 4 February 1944. The six men went to Paris and on to Toulouse. On the recommendation of André Clément, a former member of the Tritant group in Châlons which had been shut down by the Germans, they went to the house of M. Linzeau, a veterinary surgeon living in Salies-du-Salat (Haute-Garonne), a short distance from the Pyrenees. There the airmen and their escorts parted company. Taken to Spain, and on to Gibraltar, Fisher and Lavoie were flown back on the night of 1/2 May, with Fell returning four nights later.

LK739's wireless operator, twenty-year-old Sergeant W.T. Banner, the last to leave the aircraft apart from the pilot, was the first to get back to England. Landing in pitch darkness in a tree near the village of L'Epine, half a dozen kilometres from Châlons, but with no idea how far he was off the ground, he released his harness and dropped to the ground, knocking himself out for about five minutes. Having recovered his senses he ran and walked south until hiding in a hay barn. Watching the occupants of a nearby farmhouse, at dusk he 'approached the farmer with my phrases card and indicated that I was English, hungry and thirsty.'[1043] After he had been fed and watered Banner was advised to go to Châlons, but rather than go in to the town itself he skirted round it until he came to another farmhouse.

As before, he stayed hidden all day. Towards evening he asked a young woman for help but, scared by his sudden appearance, she ran off to fetch her husband. Having fed Banner the couple advised him to go south along minor roads, pointed out the bridge that he would have to cross over the river at Nuisement-sur-Coole, and gave him two Michelin maps to help him on his way. When he got to

Nuisement it was so dark that he was unable to find the bridge. Instead he went to a house that was showing lights, and was invited in by a man to whom Banner declared that he was an RAF wireless operator: 'The man immediately turned the wireless on to a station that was sending out morse signals and asked me to take it down. I told him the morse was German and he seemed satisfied.'

In the morning having shown Banner where the bridge was on the map the man gave him a cap and a satchel of food, for which Banner gave him the detachable tops of his flying boots. Walking all day, most of it in pouring rain, Banner passed a number of French people but, apart from a few curious glances, no one took the slightest bit of notice of him, and he saw no Germans. By the end of the day he had walked a good thirty-five kilometres and, with very sore feet, approached an isolated farmhouse (the recommended practice). He was again invited in by a woman and her husband. An English-speaking woman was summoned, who said that she would put him in touch with an organisation next day, 24 January. After spending the night at the farmhouse he was taken to the woman's house where he 'was visited by a middle-aged woman', who was a member of the organisation that took him down to Spain. From Spain he reached Gibraltar, and was flown back to England on the night of 20/21 March 1944.

Reain, LK739's pilot, found himself on 22 January being taken by some very poor French people to another man who spoke perfect English. He advised Reain to put on his RAF uniform (he had changed into civilian clothes earlier), go into Châlons-sur-Marne and give himself up to the Gestapo. Reain wisely left the man's house at once, learning later that the man had immediately contacted the Gestapo. In Châlons Reain was put in touch with the abbé Pierre Gillet, a member of the Resistance movement *Ceux De La Libération* (CDLL), who lived at 16, de la rue du Collège. Through CDLL Freddie Reain was moved south to Spain, and on the night of 4/5 May 1944 flown back to England from Gibraltar.

Frans Hals

In 1942 the German Abwehr, under Major Herman Giskes, captured several SOE agents and their wireless sets in Holland. Using these sets the Germans, in what they called "Der Englandspiel" (The England Game), fooled SOE's Dutch Section into sending over fifty agents to Holland, all of whom fell straight into the hands of waiting Abwehr agents, with SOE having no clue whatsoever of the catastrophe.[1044]

It was at this time that Comet, wishing to extend its reach into Holland, asked Airey Neave at MI9 to send someone over to assist them on the route between Amsterdam and The Hague. Neave therefore arranged with SOE's Dutch Section to parachute Beatrix "Trix" Terwindt, codename "Chicory", into Holland, and straight into the Abwehr's hands, on the night of 13/14 February 1943.[1045]

Another attempt to send an agent into Holland was made on the night of 22/23 June 1943, but not before Airey Neave had had considerable difficulty in persuading his superiors at the War Office to allow the operation. They, now appreciating that all contacts in Holland had been "blown", were concerned that no wireless operator would survive for long in view of the Germans' very effective wireless-detection units. Neave, however, was able to persuade them that the Dutch agent, Dick Kragt ("Frans Hals"), was a trained radio operator and could therefore take his own set with him. Neave did, however, promise Kragt 'that another operator would be parachuted to him later in the year.'[1046] Once a safe house had been found for Kragt, Neave decided to drop him "blind" into the open country of the Wesselse Veld to the west of Epe, fifteen kilometres north of Apeldoorn.

After three aborted flights (the aircraft crashing at RAF Tempsford on return after the third) Kragt was finally and erroneously dropped near Vaassen, seven kilometres north of Apeldoorn. Worse than the navigational error, though, was the loss of his wireless set, together with most of his money and extra clothing, which had landed in a tree in the garden of a Dutch Nazi-sympathiser, and were recovered by the wrong people later that day. Despite this major setback Kragt was able to pass messages to England 'through a secret intelligence agent who had landed safely with his set in the same month.' He was also able to fulfil the conditions of his operation, having made contact with Comet, by 'establishing a line to Brussels and sent through over 100 airmen'.[1047]

Despite initial fears over Kragt's future he was still active at the time of the Arnhem landings on 17 September 1944, following which he helped a number of British personnel to safety. He was also still going in December, when he was in contact with a 644 Squadron crew that had crashed in his area (see Chapter 14).

The Maca family

Another, very small, group doing what they could to assist evaders was made up of the Maca family, though linked to Comet. Several airmen were to benefit from the courage and generosity of the Macas in the autumn of 1943. Flight Sergeant J.E. Grout and Sergeant J. Bruce, shot down on an SOE operation to Belgium on the night of 18/19 October 1943, found themselves escorted to Brussels on 5 November. From a house on the outskirts of the city they were taken to a large house in the centre of Brussels, where they met Lili Dumon, and 'were told that she was suspected by the Gestapo'.[1048]

They were then moved to a third house, which was owned by Maria (aged nineteen) and by her brother Henri Maca. Though their parents lived in Avennes, some fifty kilometres from Brussels, Paul, their father, made frequent visits to the capital. He told Sergeant Grout 'that he had a large house in Avennes and has the inhabitants organised'. Furthermore, Paul Maca 'knew that there were sabotage organisations in Huy and Liège, but did not know how to make his own contacts.' Grout suggested that he should do this through his two children and the organisation (Comet) for which they were working.

Also in the Macas' Brussels house with Grout and Bruce were, briefly, Sergeant R.A.G. De Pape RCAF (Comet 194), Sergeant R.W. Cornelius (193), and two members of the USAAF, all of whom shared a flat at the back of the main house until they all left on 7 November. Two or three days later Grout and Bruce were sent on their way by Comet, arriving in Paris on 11 November. Resuming their journey to Spain on 21 November they met two more USAAF aircrew at Dax, Staff Sergeants Lloyd E. Frazer and Alfred R. Buinicky,[1049] and also "Franco" and a Frenchman. The airmen then split into pairs, and it was the throw of the dice that led Bruce and Buinicky to be picked up by two Germans in a motorcycle sidecar combination just outside Bayonne. Grout (Comet 204) and Frazer (205), who were only a hundred metres or so ahead on the road, safely reached Spain on 22 November 1943.

Luctor et Emergo/Fiat Libertas

This organisation is mentioned if only to show how precarious life could be for a clandestine group in the fiercely-policed Low Countries. It was founded some time in 1942 in the Dutch province of Limburg (south-east Holland) by, amongst others, Willem Marinus Kolff; R.D. Kloeg; J.C. Wannée and E. Vetermann. The organisation, whose name changed in April 1943 to *Fiat Libertas* (Freedom Will Come) had been badly penetrated by October 1943, due in the main to the treachery of Prospère Dezitter. All its founders were arrested. Sixty-year-old Kolff was caught in Brussels in the summer of 1942, and died on 25 January 1944 at Sonnenberg concentration camp. Kloeg, who had been trained for the priesthood before the war, was arrested in April 1943 and shot dead on 15 March 1944. Wannée and Vetermann, arrested on 29 September 1943 and 11 October 1943 respectively, were both condemned to death but survived because the orders for their executions came too late.

Fiat Libertas took many evaders and escapers from Holland to Brussels. One of its foremost *convoyeurs* was Karst Smit, who 'had already brought into Belgium some one hundred and fifty Dutch Jews, before he was posted as a member of the *maréchaussée* (constabulary) at Baarle-Nassau, in March 1943. From that time on and until November 1943, he brought to Brussels about thirty Dutch patriots and forty-three allied airmen'.[1050] Going into temporary hiding in The Hague, Smit returned to active duty after Comet had suffered many arrests in January 1944. Arrested himself by the SD in March 1944, he survived deportation to German concentration camps, and was liberated by the Russians on 5 May 1945.

CHAPTER 8

Boats, planes, more escape lines, France: 1942-1944

'Believe me, my young friend, there is nothing *– absolutely nothing – half so much worth doing as simply messing about in boats.'*

The Wind in the Willows,
Kenneth Grahame (1859-1932)

Following the fall of France the British secret services had no means of gaining access to that country, but when over a dozen French fishing boats were sailed across to England from Brittany in June and July 1940 they were gathered into what became known as the Helford Flotilla, simply because that was where they were based – on the Helford River in Cornwall – under the command of Lieutenant-Commander Gerald Holdsworth RNVR. The *Mutin*, a sixty-ton French yawl, became the flotilla's flagship in November 1940.

Another of the French fishing boats to sail from Brittany was the sixty-five-foot *Le-Dinan*, which went to Newhaven, where she was given the registration number N51 and served as an inshore patrol boat. She, and others, were to prove useful for the secret services running to and from Brittany, and a number of remarkable voyages would be made by these small boats with escapers and evaders aboard. One of the earliest involving British service personnel, however, occurred on 16 December 1940, when the sailing crabber *L'Émigrant*[1051] brought sixteen passengers over to England, among them soldiers Private C. Astley, 2nd Royal Warwicks and Driver Albert Craig RASC, who had been left behind following the evacuation in June.

As boats were a slow means of crossing to and from France, the idea of using light aircraft such as the Westland Lysander had been suggested, but it was not until 21 August 1940 that 419 (Special Duties) Flight RAF was formed,[1052] but would take some time to become operational. Colonel Stewart Menzies, head of British Intelligence's SIS, needing to produce Intelligence on French targets, meanwhile created two sections, under Commanders W.H. Dunderdale and Kenneth Cohen RN, for that purpose. At the same time he set up an Operations Section under Commander (later Captain) F.A. Slocum OBE, Assistant Chief Staff Officer, who in due course established the Inshore Patrol Flotilla, a cover name for its real undercover operations. Between 20 June and 12 October 1940 Slocum and his crews, using whatever fast surface craft they could get their hands on (mostly MTBs that had been built for the French), managed to infiltrate a number of agents into The Netherlands, Belgium and northern France.

Clandestine activity involving, mostly, Breton fishing boats continued throughout 1941 and 1942, but it was not until 5 February 1943, when established escape lines were experiencing serious difficulties moving evaders overland to Spain, that the next recorded sea crossings were made with airmen passengers. Sergeant R.G. Smith and two Americans, the first of that nation to be evacuated by sea but certainly not the last, came back on a small cutter, *L'Yvonne*, which escaped from Pont-de-la-Corde (Finistère), near Carantec, with eleven passengers on board, on what was the third of several operations to be organised by a local boat-builder, Ernest Sibiril.[1053]

Sergeant Reg Smith, shot down on the night of 20/21 November 1942 some thirty kilometres east of Paris and the only one of the five crew not to be captured, was passed on to Mademoiselle Ficke, headmistress of 'a girls' school, the Pension Severigne', on 22 November. Though he stayed in a disused room at the school for six weeks, he was not happy at the number of curious people who were allowed to call on him during his stay. Some of his visitors, mostly women, suggested ways and means of getting him out of the country, but he was unsure of their capabilities and, when one of them commanded him to leave with her at once because the Germans knew of his hiding place, he told her that he did not believe her. Flying into a temper, she called him a coward, and accused him of wanting to stay in France to avoid going back on operations.

In the end, tired of the squabbling, Reg decided to take a chance with Marguerite Laroux and her organisation, whatever it was, and on 11 January 1943 she escorted him to 19, rue des Ursins, Paris, the home of Paul Campinchi, a lawyer with the *Préfecture de la Seine*, and Thérèse his wife, a nurse. Reg stayed with them for the next three weeks, being 'provided with an identity card and other papers in the name of Roger Maes', which certified that he 'had been in an asylum from 1 July until 11 December 1942'.[1054] On 2 February 1943 Thérèse, wearing her nurse's uniform, took her "patient" by train to Quimper, on the Breton coast, where they were met by two agents, "Ronnie" and "Roger", who gave Reg a forged permit to enter the forbidden coastal area.

Two days later, after arrangements had been made for him to leave by boat for England that night, Reg was driven to Carantec on the north Breton coast, some eighty kilometres away. Driving through

Morlaix, which was full of German troops, Reg was amazed that they were not once stopped and asked for papers, nor questioned about the purpose of their journey. At Pont-de-la-Corde, a small village near the mouth of the River Penzé, he managed to get some sleep in a house near the beach while waiting for the other passengers to arrive – two American airmen (2nd Lieutenant Mark L. McDermott and Staff Sergeant Sebastian L. Vogel)[1055] and several members of the French Intelligence circuit Alliance.

At about 8 p.m. on 5 February, Reg reported, 'our party, numbering eleven in all, and including two French sailors, went on board a little boat about fifteen feet long.' As quietly as possible *L'Yvonne* was towed out to sea by a sailing boat and cast loose some ten kilometres off shore. The crew now tried to start *L'Yvonne*'s engine, but failed. This was not a good time to break down, for the wind was strengthening and the seas were growing rougher. Not surprisingly, as Reg said: 'We were all very sick.' Fortunately *L'Yvonne* was equipped with a sail, but no oars, and by early in the afternoon of 6 February, they reckoned that they were half way to England. Finally persuading the reluctant engine to start, good progress was made, and at around 10 p.m. a flashing beacon was spotted. Presuming that they were now somewhere off Cornwall, the engine was turned off and the anchor dropped.

The night was spent flashing "SOS" with a torch but to no avail, a worrying turn of events, for during the night the wind had changed, and by the morning of 7 February there was no land to be seen. Worse, the engine once again failed to start, and with a strong tide running slow progress was made under sail until, at around 11 a.m., land was sighted. Two hours later a Royal Navy patrol boat was spotted heading towards them. When it finally came alongside, Reg went on board to explain who they were. *L'Yvonne* was towed to Salcombe harbour, Devon, where the airmen, separated from the French, were received by Lieutenant Murch RNVR. Given a bath, a meal, and a day in which to recover they made their way to London on 9 February.

Reg returned to operations, on 218 Squadron, and on the night of 23/24 September 1943 was shot down over Germany. Fortune favoured him yet again for, though wounded, he was the only one of the seven crew to survive. This time there was to be no evasion, and after a year in prisoner-of-war camps, still not fully recovered from his injuries, he was repatriated to England early in 1945 in what would be the war's last prisoner-of-war exchange.[1056]

As a result of the successes of the German security forces against the major escape organisations in early 1943, particularly Comet and PAO, a large number of evading Allied airmen were effectively trapped in Brittany. Airey Neave and Jimmy Langley in Room 900 wondered about the possibility of bringing them out by boat in much the same way as Pat O'Leary had done from the south of France in the summer and autumn of 1942. They discussed ways and means of evacuating these airmen from the Brittany coast, though well aware that two earlier operations in conjunction with the Free French Forces had proved unsuccessful. On both occasions French naval officers had been 'sent over the Spanish frontier to Brittany to organise evacuation by ship. One was recognised and denounced by a former colleague, the other was shot by a German officer in a café brawl.'[1057]

Pat O'Leary, with his experience of sea evacuations, was asked to see what could be done for the airmen in Brittany. As Louis Nouveau, who was then in Paris, already had connections in Brittany he was deputed to explore possibilities. Louis made contact with François le Cornec, leader of a small Resistance group there, but with troubles of its own PAO was in no state to help shift the many airmen south to Spain. Neave and Langley were nevertheless determined to recover the airmen (it was, after all, a part of their remit to do so) and, despite the two earlier French fiascos, 'decided to have a third try, led by one of the few agents we had in training at the time of the Comet and PAO débâcles, a White Russian brought up in Paris called Vladimir Bouryschkine…' Langley 'gave him the code name of Valentine Williams, after the author of the famous Club Foot spy novels, always shortened to Val.'[1058] Operation Oaktree was about to begin.

With training completed in February 1943, Val Williams and his new French-Canadian radio operator, Raymond Labrosse, were taken to RAF Tempsford, Bedfordshire and handed over to 161 (Special Duties) Squadron for Operation Oaktree to start in earnest. During the last two weeks of February 1943, however, seven attempts were made to drop the two men and their equipment by parachute, but on each occasion Oaktree had to be aborted due to a failure to spot the reception committee on the ground. Obliged to wait for the next moon period two more abortive attempts were made on the nights of 12/13 and 14/15 March. On 20/21 March[1059] the crew of Halifax DJ996 were detailed to carry out Oaktree, yet again, together with operations Yolande and Dido.

Unable to get a pinpoint on the River Seine, or to see the ground due to low haze, Oaktree was abandoned, and the Halifax set course for the Dido drop zone.[1060] At 0210 hours on 21 March the main Paris-Châteauroux road was clearly identified, and the immediate decision was made to carry out a "blind" drop (that is, with no reception committee on the ground). Williams, Labrosse and a bicycle, to which his precious radio was attached, were dropped near a farm at les Etangs de Hollande (Yvelines), approximately forty kilometres west-south-west of Paris. The two agents landed successfully, unlike the bicycle. Its parachute failed to open properly thus causing irreparable damage to the radio.

Unable, therefore, to contact London directly Val Williams cycled to Paris. Contacting lawyer Paul Campinchi ("François"), 'one of our best agents',[1061] Williams asked him to go to Brittany to recruit helpers. There, armed with 'a large quantity of Players cigarettes', Campinchi discovered thirty-nine American and RAF airmen in hiding at the Château du Bourblanc, Plourivo, near Paimpol, the home of Comte Henri and Comtesse Roberta "Betty" de Mauduit,[1062] and a further fifty or so in hiding elsewhere. He reported back to Williams, who then went himself to the château on 10 April. Saying that he would be back to collect the airmen Williams departed, to arrange for their evacuation by sea.

Noted for his devil-may-care attitude, Williams disdained the strict rules taught to him in England, and 'in breach of all the normal security safeguards' made use of the radio facilities 'of other organisations in both Paris and Brittany'.[1063] His main contact was with the French Mithridate intelligence network run by the *Bureau Central de Renseignements et d'Action* (BCRA), which had been set up for the Gaullist Free French under Colonel Dewavrin ("Passy"). Intended to be run on parallel lines to SOE (though definitely not part of it), BCRA was manned entirely by Frenchmen, and it was one of Mithridate's wireless sets that was loaned to Raymond Labrosse. Aware of the unsatisfactory nature of the Oaktree/Mithridate wireless alliance Room 900, after much head scratching, arranged for Donald Darling to take a wireless set to Seville in Spain. Collected by Baron Jean-François Nothomb ("Franco"), he brought it over the Pyrenees to Bordeaux. It was then taken to St Jean-de-Luz railway station where, as arranged, Labrosse later picked it up.

The immediate problem for Williams, until such time as he could organise the sea evacuations from the Baie de St Brieuc area, was what to do with the evading airmen in Brittany, most of whom had been hidden by Oaktree in the St Quay-Portrieux (Côtes-d'Armor) area to the north of St Brieuc itself. With the sea route not at that moment an option, he had no choice but to shift the airmen overland, and over the Pyrenees, to Spain.

Among the first airmen to be helped by Oaktree were Sergeants E.R. Turenne RCAF, R. Martin and D.C. Young from the same 35 Squadron crew shot down in Halifax W7885 on 13/14 February 1943. Six of the seven crew baled out successfully.[1064] Landing within a few hundred metres of each other near Spézet in central Brittany, Turenne, Martin and Young soon found themselves together in a house in Châteauneuf-de-Faou. On 15 February Georges Jouanjean ("Geo", or "Joe" to the English-speakers) split them up, but they met up again on the evening of 17 February at Carhaix railway station when Georges and Jean Bach, a *passeur* of the PAO line, took them to Paris on the overnight train, being joined by their American pilot, Flying Officer J.C. Thomas RCAF, who had been staying with the Jouanjean family.

Sergeant Young, who had been suffering from a badly sprained ankle since his landing, went to stay with the Lévêcque family (father, mother, and daughter) at 19, rue d'Orléans, Paris.[1065] Their home, a PAO line safe house and headquarters, was, however, raided by the Gestapo on 3 March and, though Young made an escape via a back window, he was captured.[1066] Madame Lévêcque was also arrested, but her husband and daughter were out at the time, and were not caught.

Flying Officer Thomas was staying with Monsieur Lévêcque's sister when her house, too, was raided. He also made a run for it but, with so many members of the PAO organisation having been arrested, he was now effectively on his own. Nevertheless, helped by railwaymen from time to time, he succeeded in reaching Switzerland on the night of 12/13 March 1943. Here he remained for the next eighteen months when, with France all but free of the Germans, he returned to Allied lines, leaving behind his wife, whom he had married on 2 November 1943, and a young son, Peter, born on 28 August 1944.[1067]

Sergeant Martin was regularly moved from one Parisian address to another, finally staying with la Comtesse Hélène de Suzannet in the rue Greuze, but only for the night of 22/23 April. On the morning of 23 April he was taken to a café in Montparnasse, and reunited with Eddie Turenne. They left that same morning for St Brieuc, arriving at Étables-sur-Mer on the following day, and were taken to stay with the mayor, Monsieur Camard, whose son Jean was 'an active member of an organisation'.

Told that they would find more airmen at Brest, Turenne was taken there on 25 April by Jean Tromelin, only to discover that the airmen had already left. Tromelin therefore took Turenne to his house in St Pabu (some twenty kilometres north of Brest), when instructions were received to proceed to St Nic. Here, they were assured, they would find the elusive airmen. Drawing a blank yet again, they returned to M. Camard's house at Étables before, keeping well out of the way of frequent

Gestapo searches, going to M. Lévêcque's house at St Quay-Portrieux.[1068] They stayed there until 27 May, when Turenne was taken to the Château Bourg-Blanc, where he met his mid-upper gunner, Flight Sergeant J.N. Barry RCAF (see this chapter below). Together they travelled to Paris, and at Pau caught up with Squadron Leader P.W. Lefèvre DFC and his party.

Squadron Leader Lefèvre, shot down by flak on a Ramrod to Brest on 16 April 1943, had also been brought, on the evening of 29 April, to 'a house in the precincts of the Mairie belonging to M. Camard, the Mayor, who is a builder by profession'.[1069] Over the next few days several more evaders arrived, including Flight Lieutenant B.D. Barker; Sergeant R.W. Adams; and Staff Sergeant Allen H. Robinson USAAF.[1070]

Flight Lieutenant Barker, shot down in Belgium on 9/10 March 1943 half a dozen kilometres from the French border, soon found himself at a café in Valenciennes, France. Here he was assisted for a few days by Robert Armstrong, an Irish employee of the British War Graves Commission, then taken to the house of Madame Rosine Witton at 6, rue de Bapaume, Achicourt, on the southern outskirts of Arras. On 4 April Mme. Witton and a M. d'Allendre, chief engineer of the Arras section of the French railways, took him to Paris, where he met Robert Aylé and "Paul" (Frédéric de Jongh) at a café near the Gare du Nord. Aylé took Barker to stay with Jacques Ponty at 24, rue Ampère, until 27 April, when Val Williams took him to la Comtesse Hélène de Suzannet.

Williams then asked Barker to go to Château-Thierry to see whether a disused auxiliary aerodrome some three kilometres north of the American Monument would be suitable for a Hudson landing. The job done (the suitability of the site is not recorded), Barker returned to Paris. On 30 April, Williams and 'a French girl called Andrée' took him and a few other evaders, including 'an American, and two Englishmen, one of whom was Sgt. Cox', to St Brieuc.

On 3 May Squadron Leader Lefèvre was taken to Madame Cellarier's house at Lein-ar-lan, ten kilometres or so north of Plouha, where yet more evaders were being hidden, including Pilot Officer B.C. Dennison RCAF and Flight Sergeant G.L. Spencer RCAF (same crew); Sergeant D.M. Cox RCAF (same crew as Sergeant D.R. Howard); Flight Sergeant E.L. Bulman RCAF; Technical Sergeant Jack Luehrs USAAF; Sergeant Frank Greene USAAF;[1071] and Sergeant C.E. McDonald RCAF, an escaped prisoner of war.

McDonald, an American in the RCAF, was shot down on 21 August 1941 on a Circus to St Omer. Suffering burns to his face and hands as he baled out of his blazing Spitfire a farmer attended to them as best he could, and gave him a change of civilian clothing. Within a few hours, though, he had been taken prisoner of war. Appreciating that it was easier to escape from outside a prisoner-of-war camp, he volunteered to go on a working party at Gleiwitz, and on the night of 11/12 August 1942 escaped. With him went Sergeant K.B. Chisholm RAAF, Sergeant G.P. Hickman, and a Palestinian Jew known to them as Nick Carter, who was brought along because he could speak fluent Polish and German. Falling into the hands of the Polish Underground, it was not until 23 March 1943, however, that McDonald left Warsaw, where he had been hidden for the past six months or so.[1072] Five days later he was in Metz, in eastern France, and from there was brought to Brittany.

Sergeant R.W. Adams and four others of his crew – Flight Sergeant D.E. James RCAF; Sergeants W.G. Grove; J. Hall; and J.A. Smith – lost near Crèvecoeur-le-Grand (Oise), France on the night of 16/17 April 1943, had been helped by Oaktree to the St Quay-Portrieux area. While staying with Dr Pezé at Crèvecoeur-le-Grand they received a visit on 2 May from two of Oaktree's Paris-based members, Elizabeth Barbier and "Olga", who handed them their identity cards. On the morning of 3 May all took the train to Elizabeth's flat at 72, rue de Vanneau, Paris, where they met Val Williams. He took James and Grove to la Comtesse de Suzannet in the rue Greuze, while Hall and Smith went to a Madame Lescure, and Adams to a Monsieur Maillard (or Milliard). Four days later, Val Williams, Elizabeth Barbier, an unknown man and a man known to them only as Jacques escorted them to St Brieuc and Étables-sur-Mer, 'where they met a number of other evaders and stayed in various houses round about. Adams stayed at the Mairie in the town. On 10 May James, Grove, Smith and Hall were taken by the Comtesse de Mauduit to the Chateau de Bourg Blanc at Plourivo.'[1074]

Pilot Officer B.C. Dennison RCAF was another evader sent to Brittany in the expectation of being evacuated by boat. Shot down in north-eastern France on the night of 11/12 March 1943, he and his navigator, Flight Sergeant G.L. Spencer RCAF, were taken to Paris on 7 April by Stefan Brice in a group that included Sergeant D.R. Howard, Madame Fainot, 'and a woman friend of hers'. They were taken on arrival in Paris to Frédéric de Jongh's apartment, where they stayed for a month or so, meeting Flight Lieutenant M.A.J. Pierre, who was on his way to Spain with Comet. On 6 May Dennison, Spencer, Howard, Sergeant A.S. Kononenko (a Soviet Air Force escaper),[1075] and the American, Sergeant Frank Greene, were handed over to Oaktree, and left that day by train for St Brieuc. Their guide was a countess 'whose husband had been imprisoned by the Germans for helping evaders.'[1076] Taken to Étables-sur-Mer, from there 'one of Val's lieutenants took us to a farm near St

Quay [-Portrieux]', the home of Mme. Harvé. On 11 May they were moved again, to Mme. Cellarier's house at Lein-ar-lan, (though Spencer was adamant that her house was at Tréveneuc, a short way out of St Quay-Portrieux).

With no immediate prospect of a sea evacuation, it was now time for Williams and his team to move the ever-growing number of evaders and escapers to Paris. Spencer was asked to stay behind to help Val because he could speak French. Lefèvre, Dennison, James, Grove, Hall and Smith were among those who left on 12 May. A second group followed next day, including Barker, Adams and Martin. Entrusted by Val Williams to Pilot Officer Dennison was a collection of papers that 'dealt with various activities and projects of Val. They included some maps of airfields and full details and measurements of a lake just north west of Ploërmel (Étang-au-Duc).'[1077] Dennison carried these documents with him until they had reached Pau, when Squadron Leader Lefèvre ordered him to hand them over 'for transmission by some secret means to the British Embassy in Madrid'. Having no idea what was going to happen to *his* precious documents, Dennison reluctantly complied.

Those who had helped before in Paris, again helped to accommodate the evaders and escapers until, on 28 May, eleven airmen and five Frenchmen were assembled for the journey from the Gare d'Austerlitz. They travelled to Pau via Dax, where their identity cards withstood the scrutiny of a German control, arriving at around midnight on 28/29 May. At around 3 p.m. on 31 May the airmen – Lefèvre, Barker, Dennison, Adams, Cox, Barry, Turenne, Bulman, Howard, Martin, McDonald – and the five Frenchmen left by lorry, meeting their first Basque guide just outside the town. Squadron Leader Lefèvre, given to understand that Val Williams had paid the large sum of 20,000 francs per head for each "British" evader and 12,000 for each Frenchman, was not impressed by the organisation during this section of the journey: 'For example, we were told we need not take any food. In consequence all the food we had was what we could scrounge from some of the Frenchmen, who had been less trusting than we.'[1078]

Three more Basque guides joined the party and, though the going was tough, they crossed into Spain, near the Pic de la Coura, 'about two hours after daybreak on 3 June'. Burning all their remaining and incriminating papers as ordered, they were told to proceed to Isaba, and to the only hotel in the village: 'If questioned by the Spanish authorities all the Frenchmen were to give British names and to say that they were members of the RAF. We were also told that the Spanish civil guards in Isaba had been warned about our arrival, and would hand us over without demur to a representative of the British Consulate from San Sebastián.' Trusting this advice, they reported to the Guardia Civil who, knowing nothing of their arrival, 'promptly clapped us in gaol.' Dennison, outspoken as always, 'felt very strongly that the instructions to give ourselves up to the Spanish authorities at Isaba were wrong.' For him at least, it went against the grain to give himself up to anyone.

All was not lost, however, for a few hours later they received an unofficial visit from the commissioner of police, who handed over 150 pesetas to each man, which he in turn had received from the Uruguyan consul at Pamplona. The men were released and booked rooms at the hotel for the night. Next day, reporting to Pamplona prison, they were 'immediately placed in fetters though later these were removed'. Michael Cresswell and Mr Frost visited them before they were taken on 11 June, still under guard, to a hotel some fifteen kilometres out of Pamplona. On 22 June they were taken by car to Madrid, and four days later left by train for Gibraltar, arriving next day.

On 6 July the whole party was put aboard the troopship *Samaria*,[1079] which was still firmly anchored off Gibraltar a week later, causing Squadron Leader Lefèvre to note that there was 'much dissatisfaction among all on board the *Samaria* at the apparently inexplicable delay in sailing.' He and the others would not have known that their departure had been delayed due to the imminence of Operation Husky, the Allied invasion of Sicily, which began in earnest on 9 July. On 13 July Donald Darling managed to "rescue" Lefèvre, Barker, Barry, and Flight Sergeant O.W. Forland RCAF, shot down on 12/13 May 1943, and they were flown to England that same night, but it was another four days before *Samaria* sailed from Gibraltar for Liverpool with the remainder of Lefèvre's party and with other new arrivals.[1080]

After the Lèfevre and Barker parties had left for Paris from St Brieuc, Spencer, Kononenko, Sergeant H. Riley and Jack Luehrs remained at St Quay-Portrieux. Spencer, though, was moved to Andrée Charneau's house on the Allée du Martouret on 20 May, assured by Val Williams that if he stayed in St Quay he 'should eventually be taken to England by boat.' Val Williams, still using the Mithridate group and their wireless set, had been planning for the remaining Allied airmen evaders in Brittany to be evacuated by the Royal Navy from the beach at le Palus-Plage, three-and-a-half kilometres east of Plouha. Captain Frank Slocum, DDOD(I), was not, however, prepared to send the Royal Navy's slow "C-class" Fairmile motor gun boats (MGB) across the wide reaches of the Atlantic end of the Channel during the short May nights, and on 29 May 'the message "Denise est morte" was heard on the BBC indicating that the operation was cancelled.'[1081]

At this time, too, the Mithridate and Oaktree organisations, which had been penetrated by Frenchman Roger le Neveu, were about to come under serious threat from German security forces. Le Neveu ("Roger le Légionnaire") was the man who had been instrumental in the arrests of Louis Nouveau in February 1943 and of Pat O'Leary in March 1943. The result of le Neveu's double-dealings would be the collapse of Oaktree's "cells" in Brittany and the arrest of many of its personnel.

Unaware of the crisis, Lieutenant Claude Raoul-Duval FAF arrived in Brittany in the last week of May. Shot down in his Spitfire on 17 April 1943 in the Le Havre area, he spent a month on a farm near Rouen until a Madame Minou, 'who was working in Rouen with two men of the British Intelligence Service', got in touch with Elizabeth Barbier, who agreed to take care of Claude when he got to Paris. Arriving there on 22 or 23 May Claude immediately telephoned his father, who was living in the rue du Faubourg St Honoré, Paris. Explaining the situation to him, he mentioned Elizabeth: 'He said he knew her and that it was all right to entrust myself to her.'[1082]

Claude was also understandably keen to see his fiancée, Josette Devin, who was then living in Bordeaux, and asked her to come to Paris. She did, and they were married on 27 May. Any thoughts of a lengthy honeymoon, though, were cut short next day when Elizabeth Barbier introduced them to Val Williams who, on the day after that, sent the happy couple to Brittany to catch the boat to England. Unfortunately, this was the very day on which Captain Slocum had scrubbed the sea evacuations. Consequently, Claude and Josette went to St Quay-Portrieux to stay with Madame Charneau, who had looked after Claude when he was a child!

29 May was also the day on which USAAF B-17F Lady Godiva was shot down into the sea about a mile off St Brieuc. Three of its crew, 'F/Lt [*sic*] Petersen, T/Sgt Scott and an A/Engr. known as "Bill"',[1083] were rescued and brought to Madame Charneau's house, now getting rather full: 'At that time there were altogether twelve evaders living in Mme. Charneau's house – English, American, and one Russian.'[1084] Once the boat operation had been cancelled, however, 'this crowd was sent to Paris under Val's organisation' within the week. Off to Paris on 31 May went Spencer, Riley, Kononenko, Luehrs and Greene, who were dispersed from Elizabeth Barbier's flat to other safe houses. Claude and Josette, though, remained in St Quay, ever hopeful of being taken off by boat.

Although there were to be many arrests in Brittany as a result of Roger le Neveu's treachery, Val Williams was taken on 4 June while escorting two American and two Polish airmen[1085] by train to Orthez, near Pau. Details of their arrest on the train are sketchy. It seems, from the little that was told to Raoul-Duval, that Williams was not actually with the airmen when the Germans burst into their compartment, but that he had returned to it in an attempt to recover his case, which contained compromising documents and papers. It was likely, in Raoul-Duval's opinion, that Williams and the airmen had been caught 'due to Val's own carelessness. He should not have left the Poles alone in the train, and, once they had been caught he should not have gone into the compartment to try to recover his case.'[1086] All were taken under guard to Pau.

A week later, Elizabeth Barbier, her mother and at least three evading airmen were arrested in Paris, this time betrayed by another traitor, Jean-Jacques Desoubrie.[1087] Raoul-Duval was, again, led to believe that the arrests were the result of the incriminating papers that had been found on Williams. Raymond Labrosse also came close to being arrested when he went to Elizabeth's flat with a man known as "Joe". Labrosse stayed outside while Joe (Georges Jouanjeau) went in, and was immediately arrested. Apparently Joe had previously had a fight with Roger le Neveu, who had tried to shoot him. Oaktree's members in Paris were shaken by the arrests, 'much perturbed' in Spencer's words, and had no idea where to procure the necessary funds for identity cards for him or the other airmen, or for their journeys to Spain.

In the meantime, Spencer and Greene were taken to 25, rue Madrid, the home of Mesdames Couvé and Brouard, and introduced to Raymond Labrosse. On 8 July, they, and two more Americans, Staff Sergeants John H. Houghton and Lester Brown USAAF,[1088] met Georges Broussine, chief of the Burgundy line (see this chapter below), who sent them off to the Pyrenees with two Frenchmen as escorts. They crossed into Andorra on the night of 10/11 July, and walked into Spain as far as Manresa, where they arrived very early on the morning of 21 July. Catching the train to Barcelona, they reported to the British Consulate, leaving two days later for the British Embassy in Madrid, and for Gibraltar on 3 August. They were back in England within the week.

It is not clear when exactly Sergeant Kononenko made his way south, but he stayed in Paris for a further month and a half, 'when he left for Toulouse in a party consisting of one British airman, five Americans, and one Frenchman.'[1089] Having taken four days to cross the Pyrenees, he reached the British Consulate in Barcelona and the British Embassy in Madrid. With a Spanish passport and a Spanish guide he was taken by train to a place forty kilometres or so from the Portuguese border, where he was handed over to a second guide and taken across the frontier into Portugal. He spent another month and a half or so in a pension in the village of Paço de Arcos, a few kilometres west of Lisbon, before being flown to England, where he was interrogated by MI9 on 7 October.

The arrest of Val Williams also affected the crew of another B-17 shot down on 17 May and who were still in St Quay-Portrieux waiting to be moved on. Five of them[1090] were in hiding at the Château du Bourblanc, while five more were with Madame Cellerié in St Quay-Portrieux. Raoul-Duval, now effectively a courier for Oaktree, was asked to move the Americans from Madame Cellarié's house to the Château du Bourblanc. On 12 June, two days after he had done so, the Gestapo, acting on information received from Roger le Neveu, searched the château but failed to discover 'the Americans who were hidden under a floor'. They did, however, find some clothing belonging to the airmen, and arrested the countess, removing her to the prison in Rennes.[1091] The B-17 men later made their way barefoot and half-clothed back to the house of Madame Cellarié in St Quay-Portrieux but, as she still had one wounded airman with her, she thought it too dangerous for the others to stay there. Claude found them accommodation elsewhere, three going to Madame Charneau's house, where he and Josette were still staying. The five Americans did eventually reach Spain.

As for Val Williams, after further questioning at the hands of the Gestapo at Fresnes, he was moved to Rennes prison, and it was there, on 20 December 1943 during an air raid alarm, that he and a Russian prisoner, "Ivan" Bougaiev, escaped. Williams broke a leg jumping from the top of the prison's outer wall, but Bougaiev helped him to safety. Some time after Williams's leg had been set in plaster, contact was made with Paul Campinchi and, as "prisoners" of the gendarmerie, Williams and Bougaiev were taken to Paris. Williams then learnt that, in the months since his arrest, Labrosse had not only made his own way back to England but was now back in France again on a different mission.

In June 1943, following Williams's arrest, Labrosse had continued helping airmen from Brittany to Paris and Spain,[1092] with assistance from Raoul-Duval and his wife, Josette. She, however, returned to Paris on 28 June, Claude following on 1 July, to see if they could get themselves and the Americans in Brittany out of France. As none of the organisations in Paris could do anything for them, Claude contacted the *Bureau des Opérations Aériennes* (BOA) in London, but they, too, were unable to help. They did, though, ask Claude if he would stay on in Paris as their operative, and he agreed provided they could get formal clearance. At the same time, Claude's father said that 'there was a man in Paris who claimed he had been sent from London to arrange the repatriation of air crews.' Claude went to see this man, who 'turned out to be Jean Pierre, the head of the Burgundy organisation', otherwise Georges Broussine.

Claude then fell ill – he had an abscess in a wisdom tooth, which required attention and which confined him to bed for a fortnight – but Josette returned to St Quay-Portrieux, as did Labrosse, and between them they escorted the seven remaining American airmen to Paris on 15 July. There was a moment of panic at the station in Paris when a gendarme asked one of the Americans for his papers. Labrosse ran off, but the gendarme let the American go without questioning him. Josette found Labrosse again, who handed over the Americans to Georges Broussine, for whom he was now effectively working.

By the time that Claude had recovered later in July, he had still heard nothing about working for BOA, with whom he had lost contact anyway. On 1 August, he decided that it was time to get himself and his wife back to England. Turning to Broussine for help, Broussine told him that he was short of funds at that time and asked them to wait. On 24 August, at last, Broussine was able to send Claude and Josette, two French officers heading for North Africa, and four Americans by train with a guide to Toulouse and Foix.

Leaving Foix on 26 August, they made their way over the mountains to Auzat (Ariège) and, after a thirty-six-hour stay, crossed into Andorra, close to the Pic des Tri Stagnes (2,878 metres/9,350 feet). After a car had taken them some of the way to the town of Andorra, they continued on foot into Spain via the Pic de Monturull (2,752 metres/8,944 feet), and spent the night in Josa, in the Sierra del Cadi. For the next five days they walked for an average of eighteen hours per day until, at the town of Manresa,[1093] they caught the train to Barcelona, arriving on 6 September. On 3 October Claude Raoul-Duval sailed from Gibraltar, his ship berthing at Gourock a fortnight later.

Two more RAF evaders, Pilot Officer J.T. Hutchinson and Sergeant W.H. Marshall, were in hiding in Paris on 2 July 1943, when 'the chief of the "Burgundy" organisation – whose name we do not know – introduced us to a young Frenchman named Peter, who spoke perfect English.'[1094] Hutchinson and Marshall, from the same special duties crew shot down on 12/13 May 1943, were taken by Peter and another Frenchman called simply "Chief", but who had been in the French navy at Dakar, to catch the overnight train to Toulouse. It was very early on the morning of 3 July when the train was halted at the

Demarcation Line. Peter and Chief learnt that the Germans were making their way through the train and rounding up young Frenchmen for their labour service in Germany.

Seeing six young men being marched off under guard, twenty-two-year-old Hutchinson slipped unseen from the train and hid underneath another one on an adjacent track. But then he was faced with a problem, for heading his way was a "wheel-tapper", accompanied by a German guard, checking the carriages and peering underneath them. Drawing himself up Hutchinson managed to remain unseen and, just as the Toulouse train started to move off, he rapidly rejoined his companions. As it happened his departure was unnecessary, for the Germans never got as far as their carriage to test the false papers. Marshall, eleven years older than Hutchinson, might even have got through the control.

By late that same evening, Hutchinson and Marshall set out to cross the Pyrenees with their guides, but it was not until mid morning on 6 July that they arrived in Andorra. Resting until 11 July they set off across the Spanish border 'with two guides and a local tobacco smuggler'. Avoiding Spanish patrols they also walked to Manresa. It took them a week, but they finally arrived at the British Consulate in Barcelona on 18 July, where they 'were provided with clothes and accommodation'. Surprisingly, told to report to the Spanish police, Hutchinson was advised 'to say that he was nineteen, and Marshall that he was forty-two'. They were also told to say that they had escaped from a civil internment camp in France. Whether or not the police believed their stories, the two airmen were issued with ID cards and taken to a hotel, before leaving for Madrid on 22 July. They flew back to England from Gibraltar on 5/6 August 1943.

Leaving matters in Brittany in the hands of François le Cornec, Labrosse was himself helped to Spain by Georges Broussine, who had trained with him 'as a wireless operator in London'.[1095] With the departure of Labrosse, Oaktree was now in abeyance, if not totally finished.

Shelburne

On his return to London, Labrosse was able to convince Room 900[1096] that, though Oaktree had proved disappointing, they should make another attempt to evacuate the airmen by sea from Brittany. Labrosse himself was quite prepared to return as wireless operator to another leader. The man chosen to lead the second attempt was Lucien Dumais, who had been successfully evacuated by Pat O'Leary on 12 October 1942 in Operation Rosalind (see Chapter 5). This new operation would be codenamed Shelburne, and that would also be the name for the new network.[1097] As doubt remained in the minds of those in Room 900 as to Campinchi's loyalty – why had he not been arrested along with all the others in June 1943? Or, if he had been arrested and released from custody, could he now be working for the Germans? – Dumais and Labrosse were given a different contact in Paris, a Madame Georges, who ran a hairdressing salon at 6, rue des Capucines.

Operation Magdalen, the first attempt to fly in Dumais and Labrosse, on the night of 16/17 October 1943, was abandoned when the pilot of the special duties Lysander, Flying Officer Jimmy Bathgate RNZAF, was given a wrong back-bearing over the radio. A second attempt was made two nights later with Flying Officer J.A. McCairns DFC and Bar, MM[1098] at the controls, but again the mission had to be aborted, this time because there was no reception committee on the ground. The October "moon" period ended on the night of 21/22 October, and with flying only during the week either side of the full moon the next Lysander operation could not be mounted until 6/7 November.

The November moon period was to be a busy time for the RAF's special duties squadrons. Four American airmen were collected on the night of 7/8 November by McCairns in a Lysander from the field known as le Champ Sainte Marie, two kilometres south-west of Selens and a dozen kilometres or so north-west of Soissons. Four nights later Flight Lieutenant R.W.J. Hooper DFC brought Sergeant P.V. Matthews back, and six airmen were picked up on the night of 15/16 November in the double Lysander operation Water Pistol flown by Bathgate and Flying Officer J.McA. McBride.[1099] On the following night, 16/17 November, Dumais and Labrosse were flown to France in another double Lysander operation (Squadron Leader Hugh Verity and Flying Officer McCairns). There to welcome them at le Champ Sainte Marie were, among others, Capitaine D.E. Potier[1100] and Count Georges d'Oultremont, the latter having been parachuted into France during the night of 20/21 October 1943. The two Lysanders returned to England with Potier, Sergeant R.V.C. Johnson and another four USAAF aircrew evaders.[1101]

After their return to France on the night of 16/17 November Dumais and Labrosse made their way to Paris, some 120 kilometres to the south-west. Madame Georges temporarily lodged them with her assistant, Suzanne, who lived at Rueil-Malmaison in the western suburbs of Paris. Contact was also re-established with Paul Campinchi, who was found to be completely safe, and who agreed to work with Dumais in setting up Shelburne in Brittany. Within a few days of their arrival, however, Dumais and Labrosse learnt that both Madame Georges and Suzanne had been arrested. Perhaps because of this disaster, Labrosse worked his radio from the house of Monsieur Dorré, stationmaster at Gare la Chapelle.[1102]

It was not long before new agents were found in Brittany around the area of Plouha, where a possible beach, known locally as Sous-Kéruzeau, had been identified at Anse-Cochat for sea evacuations. Details of the site were sent back to England and approved by DDOD(I). The only potential drawback, from the evaders' point of view, was that there was no easy way to the beach from the cliffs, which rose to sixty metres (195 feet) in places. The only way down was to slide on one's backside – in the dark. François le Cornec was appointed beachmaster for Operation Bonaparte, also the name given to the beach below Anse-Cochat. According to Dumais the first operation was scheduled to take place during the night of 15/16 December 1943, but bad weather caused nine successive postponements.[1103] Historian Sir Brooks Richards, on the other hand, maintains that that date was too early, given that Dumais and Labrosse had not set foot in Brittany until 5 or 6 December. Furthermore, none of the boats of the Royal Navy's 15th MGB Flotilla (MGBs 502, 503 and 318), which had been earmarked for the operation, was operational, but Sir Brooks Richards concedes that MGB 503 might 'conceivably have been ready and available in the December no-moon period'.[1104]

In readiness for their evacuation by sea airmen were assembled in Brittany, but the first two sent by Campinchi were arrested when their papers did not show them to be residents authorised to live within the forbidden coastal zone, a mistake that was not repeated with a second batch of fifteen airmen. By late January 1944 all was ready for Operation Bonaparte I. Sixteen airmen (thirteen Americans, three RAF) and two Frenchmen, who were "burned", were assembled in one of the two rooms of the tiny house, which was to become known as la Maison d'Alphonse, in which Jean Gicquel lived 'with his wife and newborn baby',[1105] approximately one and a half kilometres from the cliffs.

The three RAF airmen were Flying Officer S.J.P. Blackwell and two from the same crew, Sergeant N.B. Cufley and Sergeant J. Harvey. Peter Blackwell, shot down in his Typhoon off the coast of France on 1 December 1943, had been captured, but had escaped near Lamballe (Côtes-d'Armor) from the train that was taking him to Germany, and made his way to the house of Monsieur Rohan, the village blacksmith, at Pléven (Côtes-d'Armor). Rohan was not himself involved in Resistance work but, by the time that Blackwell was obliged to leave, on 24 December, due to the house being requisitioned by the Germans, he had made contact with people who were engaged in resistance of some sort, and they took Blackwell to Guingamp. There word of his presence reached the ears of 'M. Branchoux, the local chief of the resistance movement', a potato merchant who 'distributes illicit literature, which he receives from Paris, and also hides arms.'[1106]

Mathurin Branchoux thereafter arranged shelter for Blackwell with M. and Mme. Georges Le Cun at Place du Centre, Guingamp. Hearing that Blackwell was being sheltered there, Captain Lucien Dumais, masquerading as Captain Hamilton, 'a British Intelligence Officer', went to visit the airman on 23 January 1944. As luck would have it, Blackwell was out for the day and could not be found, thus missing the opportunity 'to go on an operation which Captain Hamilton had planned for that night from Plouha.' The evacuation was, however, delayed by a storm.

On 24 January Dumais telephoned Branchoux and asked him to 'bring the sack of potatoes'. It was the 'very reliable' M. Le Cun, owner of a wireless business, who took Blackwell by car to Plouha and who gave him one half of a ten-franc note, saying 'that anyone wishing to get in touch with him should produce this as a means of identification. (Note: This note has been passed to Major Langley, IS9(X).)' Dumais, waiting for Blackwell in Plouha to check his *bona fides*, satisfied that he was genuine RAF, told him that the sea evacuation from Plouha had been delayed until the night of 28/29 January.

Blackwell, meanwhile, 'stayed with nine other British and American airmen at a house at Plouha rented by the organisation from a doctor, who visited us occasionally.' Two of the nine were Cufley and Harvey. Shot down on 18/19 November 1943 they had made their way over from north-eastern France, where their Halifax had crashed. Briefly with Etienne Dromas's organisation in Chauny (21-30 November), they left for Auneuil (Oise), where they stayed with a married couple, both retired schoolteachers. Also in Auneuil at the same time was Staff Sergeant John W. Lowther USAAF.[1107] A fourth evader, Sergeant R.E. Griffith, shot down on 19/20 November 1943, was brought to the schoolteachers' house on 8 December.

Five or six days later the four airmen left with Gilbert Thibault, 'a lawyer and insurance agent who had served in the French Army in Africa', driven to Paris in a van by a Belgian. There was a tense moment as they approached a bridge over the River Seine, which was controlled by Germans and French gendarmes. Though the gendarme must have suspected that the four occupants were not deaf and dumb as was claimed on their identity cards, he waved them through. 'In Paris we met in the street Thibault's cousin André and were taken to a church, where we met Mme. Colette or Madeleine, with whom we all went to the house of Mme. Schmidt in rue de Rochechouart, which seemed to be the clearing house for airmen arriving in Paris in the care of this organisation.'[1108] In the time that they were there several American airmen came and went, but it was not until 10 January 1944 that Griffith left with an American for Andorra. Cufley and Harvey were to have followed Griffith south, but a change of plan took them to Brittany instead.

On 28 January 1944 Dumais received a wireless message that Operation Bonaparte I was to go ahead that night. With the passengers now numbering nineteen – sixteen airmen (three RAF, thirteen USAAF) plus 'one Russian, one Frenchman, and a British Intelligence Officer' – the men filed out of the house in small groups, the first man clinging onto the coat tails of eighteen-year-old Marie-Thérèse le Calvez, the second man onto the first, the third onto the second, and so on. Ahead of Marie-Thérèse was Pierre Huet, a former French navy airman, and bringing up the rear was François le Cornec.

Half way down the cliff Joseph Mainguy, a merchant navy captain who, like Pierre Huet, 'had grown up in the area and knew it intimately',[1109] was busy signalling the letter "B" out to sea at one-minute intervals with a blue torch. Once at the foot of the cliff Marie-Thérèse, also with a blue torch, 'flashed it on and off continuously'. They couldn't be too careful, for though the nearest Germans were approximately 1,200 metres to the north and were unable to see the beach from their blockhouse, they could see directly out to sea, where the MGB would have to anchor during the evacuation, and they were equipped with a 76mm cannon, several heavy machine-guns and searchlights. There was also a radar station sixteen kilometres (ten miles) to the north, though a small, wooden MGB would have been hard to detect.

At long last, having waited on the beach from midnight to 2.30 a.m., four fourteen-foot surfboats appeared, launched from MGB 503 (Lieutenant R.M Marshall RNVR commanding), which had arrived unseen and unheard. Dumais called out the password "Dinan", and back came the correct response, "Saint Brieuc", from Room 900's Captain P.J.S. Windham-Wright MC.[1110] The nineteen men were loaded aboard the boats in twelve minutes and rowed out to the waiting MGB. 'Once they were alongside and passengers and boat crews had scaled the waiting scrambling-nets and reached the MGB's deck, the anchor was weighed and the homeward passage began on a silenced centre engine, towing the surfboats. When Marshall judged they were sufficiently far offshore, the engine was stopped and the boats were hauled back on board.'[1111] Course was resumed to the north-west, and a while later all three of the MGB's engines were opened up to full revolutions. Dartmouth was gained at approximately 9 a.m. on 29 January 1944.

Though the evacuation had proved hugely successful, there had been problems for Shelburne. The Gestapo had planted a Danish agent in Campinchi's network, but he was discovered; one of Shelburne's Frenchmen talked too much; and Val Williams had re-appeared in Paris with his broken leg and with his Russian friend, Bougaiev. To cap it all, relations between the regular soldier, Dumais, and the French communists with whom he was working were becoming strained.

Nevertheless, a second evacuation, Operation Bonaparte II, was planned for the night of 26/27 February. MGB 503 (Marshall) put in another appearance, bringing with it, in four surfboats, 'eight suitcases of equipment' including a large sum of money. After these had been landed, one RAF and sixteen American airmen and two more Frenchmen were taken aboard the MGB. Also returning to England were Val Williams, who had to be 'carried to the beach on an improvised stretcher', and Bougaiev. Bonaparte II went smoothly enough, despite the behaviour of Flight Sergeant L. J. G. Harmel, a Belgian in the RAF who had been shot down on 20 December 1943.

Harmel had made his way to Paris, where he was frequently drunk on liberal funds which had been provided by his father. At one point he and several young Frenchmen were rounded up by German soldiers for forced labour in Germany. At a given signal Harmel and six others pushed the guards over and ran off. Two months later he and an American evader were sent to Brittany but, failing to meet their contact at Guingamp station, decided to stay the night in the town: 'We went to one or two cafés and had several drinks, and I am afraid we got very drunk.'[1112] Despite such irresponsible behaviour they managed to make contact with Dumais who, furious at their indiscretion, nevertheless removed them to a safe house.

On the evening of 26 February 1944 Harmel and the American evaders were collected by four men, one of whom with a 'hooked nose' suddenly produced an automatic pistol and pointed it at Harmel while his hands were tied behind his back. As they left Harmel was then tied to 2nd Lieutenant Milton L. Church USAAF, who was told that Harmel was *his* prisoner.

Once back in England Williams was keen to return to France, but MI9 decided that he had done enough: 'Though enterprising and determined, he had risked his life too often and the extensive German dossier on him might lead them to others if he were caught again.' Colonel Claude Dansey, deputy head of MI6 operations, went so far as to have him temporarily locked up in Wormwood Scrubs prison.[1113] Bougaiev, after a spell in MI9's hands, was 'later handed over to the Soviet authorities and never heard of again.'[1114] Flight Sergeant Harmel 'shot down near Boulogne only five days previously',[1115] was brought to Brittany in time for this evacuation. Had he missed it, he would not have had to wait too long, for the third, fourth and fifth Bonaparte evacuations were scheduled for 16/17, 19/20 and 23/24 March 1944, before the end of the current moon period.

This gave Sergeant D. Brown plenty of time to reach Brittany for Operation Bonaparte III after his Lancaster had crashed on the way back from Berlin on the night of 27/28 January 1944 roughly halfway between Rouen and Beauvais, France. The pilot and rear gunner were both killed, and Brown, the only one of the five survivors to evade capture, made his way from Gournay-en-Bray (Seine-Maritime) to Paris with the help of a Monsieur Ballet, a tailor who had a flat there. Brown stayed with the Ballet family for a fortnight before being moved to 'a bootmaker's shop at 18 rue Dominil (phonetic spelling), Vincennes, Paris. The bootmaker was called Pierre and his wife Hannah, and I stayed with them for four weeks.'[1116] His next move was to the house of Monsieur M.J. Ch. Pradaf, at 44, rue Jeanne d'Arc, Paris, where he met Staff Sergeant Charles W. Cregger USAAF[1117] and spent the night of 13/14 March.

In the morning Brown and Cregger went by train to a station near St Brieuc. Told to look out for 'a man brushing his hair with his hand', they spotted him outside the station, and were taken 'to a small hotel where we had a meal. The owner of the hotel then took us in his lorry towards the coast. After we had gone some way we got out and walked for several miles to a farmhouse where we met fourteen members of the USAAF.' Cregger and Brown, however, spent the night at another farmhouse. In the morning they were joined by three more Americans, and six more that night. The following day, 16 March, they 'were told to be prepared to leave' by boat. At around 8 p.m. that evening Brown and Cregger were taken by their host 'to an unoccupied barn still nearer the coast where the other twenty-two Americans had already congregated.' The new arrivals were immediately questioned by 'a man who spoke good English… He took away all the French money in our possession.' Brown handed over 1,200 francs to the man – Dumais.

Dumais then led them off 'in single file by a circuitous route to the coast, just north of Plouha. After we had waited on the beach for about an hour and a half four rowing boats came into the shore' from MGB 502 (Lieutenant P. Williams RNVR). When 502 had earlier arrived off the French coast, it had been fired on by a German battery near Paimpol and had discreetly, but temporarily, withdrawn until things had quietened down. Communicating with Captain Patrick Windham-Wright aboard MGB 502 by use of an S-phone,[1118] Dumais had been able to direct the four surfboats to the right beach. There was, however, a very low tide and the outward-bound passengers[1119] had to cross 200–300 metres of exposed beach to get to the boats. They did so without being spotted by the Germans in their strongpoint atop the adjacent cliffs. Had the Germans done so, their heavy machine-guns would have exacted an awful toll.

Brown and six Americans got into one boat manned by two naval ratings and an 'officer who had a wireless transmitter'. They rowed out some four or five kilometres to the waiting MGB, and piled aboard. Having lost so much time, dawn was fast approaching before MGB 502 was able to get away, its powerful engines clearly audible from land. Though a long way out by first light, it was still visible from the cliffs, and the passengers were told that it was likely that they would run into German E-boats. None was encountered, but they did pass a German convoy, which fired star shells at them but nothing more, and Dartmouth was reached without further incident.

Wanting to cancel the next operation, Dumais despatched Labrosse to Paris to send an appropriate message to England. Confident that Labrosse would get the operation stopped in time, Dumais was away from Plouha on the night of 19/20 March, when Bonaparte IV nevertheless went ahead without him. MGB 503 (Marshall) made its third run to the beach, embarking twenty-five passengers (including sixteen American airmen, one French agent, and an Indian soldier) without a hitch.

The Indian soldier, Cook Buland Khan, 22 Animal Transport Company, Royal Indian Army Service Corps, had been captured by the Germans on 24 June 1940. From Stalag VIIIB (Lamsdorf) prisoner-of-war camp, he was moved, firstly, to Oflag 54(E) (Annaburg) in September 1941, and then to Rennes, France, in December 1942.

In February 1943 an Indian doctor, who had also been at Oflag 54(E), asked him to take on the duties of nursing orderly in the *École Première Supérieure*, a hospital for Moroccans, Senegalese, Indians and other Africans and Asians, which lay outside the camp. In March 1943 a French girl, Lise, said that she could help him to escape but would be unable to do anything for the next few months as she was away in Paris. When contact was re-established on 21 November 1943, Khan said that a friend of his, Sergeant Shahzaman, would also like to escape, and they arranged that she would be in the doorway of an orphanage opposite the hospital at 7 p.m. on 23 November. Khan had collected 8,000 francs and, on the evening in question, he and Sergeant Shahzaman 'managed to get through three lots of barbed wire which, being loose, we were able to separate.'[1120] Having easily overcome the last obstacle, a wall, Lise took the two escapers to her flat, where they changed into civilian clothes.

After two months they were taken to the boat *Le Jouet-des-Flots* (see below), but were forced to go ashore when it had to be beached near Plogoff on 3 February 1944. They were firstly sheltered in the area of Gourin (Morbihan), then Douarnenez, where Shahzaman was arrested when his papers, declaring him to be deaf and dumb, failed to satisfy the local gendarme. Khan's papers, on the other hand, did pass muster, but to be on the safe side he returned to Gourin. On 14 March he was taken to Guingamp, and was escorted to the coast on 19 March to join the Americans for Bonaparte IV.

MGB 503 (Marshall) was back yet again for Bonaparte V on 23/24 March, this time to evacuate thirty passengers,[1121] including twenty-six airmen (five RAF, twenty-one USAAF), and two young Frenchmen who were active members of the Plouha group, Jean Tréhiou and Le Bourhis. The five RAF airmen – Flying Officer G.C. Brickwood; Flying Officer R.E. Barnlund RCAF; Sergeant K.E. Lussier RCAF (same crew as Barnlund); Pilot Officer R.W. Daniel RAAF; and Flying Officer K.B. Woodhouse RCAF – had been brought with several of the Americans from Paris to Guingamp, some twenty kilometres from the Breton coast, within a day or two of each other in readiness for the evacuation. Early on the morning of 24 March they walked down to the beach, and to the four surf-boats from MGB 503. After a seven-hour crossing MGB 503 was back at Dartmouth. Woodhouse, shot down on the afternoon of 16 March 1944, had returned to England in only eight days.

Dumais wrote that in 'April [1944] we put on another operation from Plouha, our sixth. In the event, it was a routine affair, but beforehand, because of the firing on the previous occasion [i.e. Bonaparte III], London had objected that Plouha was burnt-out as a departure point. We had used it too much. I pointed out that I was on the spot and thus in a better position to judge than they were. They conceded the point, there was no trouble, and twenty-three fighting men were returned to their units. Among them was one "Leo the Belgian", a fighter pilot from the RAF who had come down north of Paris. He had the highest opinion of himself and was completely undisciplined.' Dumais goes on to say that Leo, drunk and unruly, 'was finally embarked bound hand and foot and gagged with adhesive tape.'[1122] Dumais's memory was at fault here for, as Sir Brook Richards notes, 'it was not until three months later that a sixth group of airmen was shipped out by Shelburne from Sous-Kéruzeau'.[1123]

Bonaparte V brought to an end, temporarily, the evacuation of airmen from the Sous-Kéruzeau beach at Anse-Cochat. Captain Slocum's records indicated that one hundred and eleven personnel (mostly airmen) had been brought out from under the Germans' noses by the MGBs in these five Bonaparte operations.[1124]

By the end of March 1944, with plans for the Allied landings on the Normandy coast of France well advanced, it was deemed inadvisable for clandestine MGB operations to the nearby Brittany beaches to be continued for the time being. In the interests of security, those at the sharp end of Shelburne's operations were told by Windham-Wright on Neave's instructions that the temporary closure of operations was due to the shortening nights.

Members of another Brittany group, SOE's Var organisation, which had been conducting evacuations from a beach at Beg-an-Fry (Finistère), eighteen kilometres northeast of Morlaix, were also told that operations would be suspended due to the shortening nights.[1125] Although the primary objective of the Var line was the infiltration and exfiltration of SOE agents, it also shipped back to England several airman evaders, including Typhoon pilots Flying Officer W.V. Mollett, a Rhodesian, and Flight Lieutenant G.G. Racine RCAF. Mollett, shot down on 15 February 1944, was helped, as Racine would be, by doctors le Janne and le Duc and by two sisters, Raymonde and Alice Jacob, before being picked up by MGB 502 (Williams) in Operation Easement II on the night of 26/27 February, with several SOE field agents.

Flight Lieutenant Racine, shot down near Morlaix on 31 March, was hidden by the Jégaden family (1–4 April) before being collected by Doctor le Janne, who took him to his house in Morlaix: 'He had scouts posted all along the road, who nodded as we approached to indicate that the coast was clear.'[1126] Another doctor, le Duc, came to see Racine that same afternoon, 4 April, but 'at first appeared suspicious, and asked me why I wanted a boat.' That evening le Duc took him on the pillion of his motor-bicycle to the Marzin family, but three days later, when firing was heard in the neighbourhood and it was feared that the Germans were making house-to-house searches, Racine was hurriedly returned to le Duc's house for the night of 7/8 April. It transpired, however, that the Germans had been fighting amongst themselves (three killed), and so Racine returned to the Marzins.

Early on the afternoon of 9 April, he followed the Marzins' daughter back to le Duc's house, where sisters Raymonde and Alice Jacob were waiting for him: 'They provided me with a bicycle and cycled ahead of me, past Morlaix aerodrome, right through German guards, to Guimaëc to their home, which was a grocer's store.'[1127] On 15 April he was told that he was to be evacuated by boat, and at about 11 p.m. that night was taken down to the beach at nearby Beg-an-Fry with two Americans. Coming to pick them up, having brought over a number of agents on the Var line's Operation Scarf, were MGB 502 (Williams) and MGB 718 (Lieutenant R. Seddon RNVR).[1128]

Leaving at about 2 a.m. on 16 April, they returned to Dartmouth with, among others, Suzanne Warenghem, Paul Cole's wife, and Var line's co-founder, Erwin Deman ("Paul Dent"), who was suffering from the nervous strain of having operated for so long in the field.[1129] Also departing, on MGB 718, was Blanche Charlet, another SOE agent who had been landed by felucca in the south of France early in the morning of 1 September 1942 but who had been arrested on 24 October 1942. Both Blanche and Suzanne had escaped from Castres prison in a mass breakout on 16 September 1943.

Scarf almost came to grief when the two boats were negotiating 'a narrow channel fringed by rocks and shoals whose only outlet was to the northward' and found their exit barred 'by three enemy patrol vessels waiting at the seaward entrance. By a judicious combination of speed and use of the special challenge and reply procedure provided by DDOD(I) for such emergencies, the enemy remained in doubt regarding [their] identity until they were abaft his beam. They then opened fire, but being still uncertain, ceased firing fifteen seconds later, with the result that the force escaped with the loss of one rating killed and superficial damage to both ships.'[1130]

Coincidentally, one of the Americans aboard MGB 502 on the night of 15/16 April 1944 was also a Williams. Leading an attack on 26 March 1944 on Châteaudun airfield in his P-47 Thunderbolt, First Lieutenant Ken Williams USAAF 'saw a light twin-engine bomber [Heinkel 111] being serviced by a refueling truck. One quick burst, and the plane and truck blew up, and Ken had the dubious distinction of shooting himself down in the process, crashing about two miles beyond the airfield.'[1131]

Crozier

Sea evacuations, under the codename Crozier, were resumed five weeks after the Normandy landings, but from a different beach. The first two operations (Crozier I and II) took place in July, and a third (Crozier III) in August 1944.

Crozier I was undertaken successfully from Sous-Kéruzeau to Dartmouth by MGB 503 (Marshall) on 12/13 July 1944, with eighteen personnel embarking.

One of them, Flight Lieutenant L.W.F. Stark DFC, had been shot down on 3 July 1944 flying on a Ramrod to a target near Mûr-de-Bretagne (Côtes-d'Armor). A shell from light flak hit the engine of his Typhoon, forcing him to bale out a kilometre or two south of the Bois de Coat-Mallouen. He gave his parachute, harness and Mae West to two farmers in a nearby field, but retained his revolver and fifty rounds of ammunition. The farmers told him 'that a number of patriots were in the wood about a mile north of where I had landed.'[1132] On his way to join up with the maquis ("patriots") he came across a farm, and was taken 'to a small outhouse near a château about half a mile distant'. On the morning of the following day he was taken to the maquis camp in the woods, and that evening they were joined by a 'French lieutenant paratrooper and about twenty men… They pitched two tents, and I spent that night in one of the tents with the lieutenant.'[1133]

The French paratroopers were members of 4th French Parachute Battalion, attached to the SAS, who had been dropped into Brittany on 6 June to hinder the movement of enemy forces towards the beaches in Normandy (see Chapter 11). A fierce battle with the enemy on 18 June had forced the paratroopers to disperse, but they were still very active and needed supplies to maintain their offensive. On 8 July Stark's group received a message that that night five aircraft would be arriving with supplies: 'That evening we went to the moor, and the expected five aircraft arrived at 0030 hours on 9 July. Each aircraft dropped approximately twenty-four parachute containers. The supplies were conveyed to the woods.'[1134]

This drop marked the end of Stark's association with these French soldiers, for later that morning a guide arrived to take him to the coast for evacuation by sea. They stopped at a house near St Fiacre (Côtes-d'Armor), half a dozen kilometres to the north, 'and met a French paratroop captain there. He was wearing civilian clothes. He told me that he was the commanding officer of all the paratroops in that area.'[1135] After lunch, handing over his revolver and ammunition, Stark and his partner were taken in stages to the headquarters of Lucien Dumais and Raymond Labrosse at a farm near Pléguien, arriving during the afternoon of 11 July. On the evening of 12 July, while the French captain was taken by a farmer's son by cart to la Maison d'Alphonse, Stark 'walked with a guide to a farmhouse about a mile from the beach near Kérégal. We met thirteen others who were to be included in our party to the UK.'

Five of the thirteen were airmen from a 28 OTU Wellington who had fallen victim to the subtle wiles of the Germans. They were on a leaflet-dropping exercise over France (Tours and Orléans) on the night of 20/21 April 1944 when they were fooled by German radio messages to fly off to Brittany, where their Wellington ran out of fuel. A sixth member of the 28 OTU crew, wireless operator Sergeant J. Kempson, died of injuries sustained on landing a few days after being shot down. Two of the Wellington survivors, Flying Officer H.J. Brennan RCAF (pilot) and Sergeant A. Elder RCAF (rear gunner), were fortunate not to perish when, sometime in the middle of June, the Germans attacked the village of Ste Fiacre 'and wiped out the patriots'. Brennan and Elder were forced to hide in the fields for two days, until they could be handed over to another maquis group. After a fortnight or so they were re-united with the other three of their crew, Pilot Officer A.J. Houston RCAF, Sergeant R.J. Dickson RCAF, and Sergeant E.J. Trottier RCAF.

In due course all moved closer to the coast in readiness for the evacuation, travelling from Plouagat to Plouha in 'a truck that the patriots had captured from the Germans… On the way we passed two carloads of Germans, but we were not stopped.'[1136] In Plouha they met François Le Cornec, 'the chief of the Resistance for that area', and also Lucien Dumais ("Léon") and Raymonde Labrosse ("Claude"). Dumais in turn passed on the airmen to Marie-Thérèse Le Calvez, 'who took us to a house near the shore in a neighbouring village. We stayed in a barn belonging to a man called Jean.' This was Jean Gicquel, owner of the Maison d'Alphonse, the cottage used by so many evaders and escapers over the past few months as the departure-point for the Bonaparte beach below.

On 26 June they met Sub-Lieutenant M.I.G. Hamilton,[1137] Leading Seaman A.H. Dellow, and Ordinary Seaman H.D. Rockwood, all RNVR, who had been left behind in error on Operation Reflexion (15 June) after landing French agents Jean Tréhiou (who had gone to England on Bonaparte V), Raoul Parent and Jean Hamon. The three RNVR men had been moved to Georges Roper's house, Camblac'h, Plouha, for the evacuation.

For three successive nights, 27-29 June, the operation was postponed until, on 30 June, it had to be postponed again until the start of the next moon period, on 11 July. This at least had given Dumais the opportunity during the past two weeks to bring in four USAAF officers, two of whom, Lieutenant Joe Lilly and 2nd Lieutenant Bill Hawkins,[1138] stayed with Brennan and his crew at Marie-Thérèse's house for one day. The total to be evacuated, therefore, was apparently fifteen (a total quoted in his report by Brennan) – presumably seven "RAF" (Stark and the five from Brennan's crew, plus one unnamed; four USAAF (confirmed by Hamilton); three RNVR (Hamilton, Dellow, and Rockwood); and the French paratroop captain. Hamilton mentions that, apart from the Brennan crew, Dumais also brought in 'a French parachutist, and two members of the RAF', while Stark confirms that he and the French Paratroop captain met 'thirteen others who were to be included in our party to the UK'.

At about 10 p.m. on the evening of 12 July Marie-Thérèse le Calvez escorted Brennan and his crew to la Maison d'Alphonse, where the others congregated. After they had been searched and had handed over all their French money they 'were then given instructions for the journey. We left the house in single file about 2330 hours. We were accompanied by about fifteen armed Frenchmen. We walked across the fields, and when we came to a mine-field, in which the mines had previously been marked with white cloths [by Joseph Mainguy], we all joined hands, still continuing in single file. We walked down the cliff and waited in a cove.'[1139]

They waited for an hour and a half or so, when two boats appeared on the high tide, having been signalled in by the French party higher up on the cliff at Anse-Cochat. The passengers were rowed out to the waiting MGB 503 (Marshall), and whisked over to Dartmouth, where they arrived at around 8 a.m. on 13 July.

Crozier II took place on 24/25 July, with MGB 502 (Williams) embarking six personnel, including two members of the SAS – Major Oswald Cary-Elwes and his batman Serjeant E. Mills – a "Major" Smith; and two airmen, Flight Sergeant T.P. Fargher and Major William A. Jones USAAF. Major Smith was Squadron Leader P.H. Smith, who had been parachuted into France on 10 June as liaison officer to the French SAS operation Samwest. Smith, who was not really suited to this tough, soldierly way of life, managed to lose his way in a wood on his way to take part in a parachute drop, and eventually attached himself to a Jedburgh team, Frederick, none of whose members had the slightest clue as to why he was there in the first place.[1140]

Robert Kehoe, Frederick's American wireless operator, described Smith as 'a tall, gaunt man in his forties who stood out in his bright blue RAF uniform… Clumsy and conspicuous, he was untrained in the ways of ground combat, let alone partisan warfare.'[1141] Despite the extraordinarily stupid decision to allow him to go to France, Smith somehow survived, to the great surprise of the

Jed men, who were greatly relieved to see him leave after only a few days.

Flight Sergeant Fargher, shot down on 11 July, had one of the quicker evasions, although he and the other would-be passengers for Crozier II had a very close call during the small hours of 23 July when a squad of drunken White Russians, in German uniforms, called at la Maison d'Alphonse. Their pretext for doing so was that the blackout curtain had not been fixed properly on one of the windows. Answering the door Jean Gicquel saw two "Germans" standing in the only doorway into the property. As he slammed it in their faces he yelled at the five evaders to hide in the loft as quickly as possible. The Russians, on the scrounge for alcohol, fired off their guns before bursting into the house. Seeing the last evader rushing into the loft, they shouted for those upstairs to come down and again let loose with their guns. Bullets ripped through the floorboards into the loft above, and it was only by sheer luck that no one was hit.

Downstairs, though, one of the Russians was hit in the backside by a mis-directed burst of "friendly" fire, and this, for the time being, put an end to their interest in those upstairs. Ordering Jean Gicquel to fetch a horse and cart, they put their wounded comrade into the cart before driving off into what was left of the night.

Fully expecting that the Russians would return once they had reported the incident, Jean Gicquel immediately evacuated the building. Sure enough, a strong force of Germans and Russians returned next day to eliminate the partisans but, finding no one and no weapons, razed the house to the ground. The evaders, meanwhile, who had been hiding in a nearby cornfield, were looked after by "Captain Harrison" (another alias for Lucien Dumais, but see Captain Hamilton page 168), who told them that they would be evacuated that night, 24/25 July.

In a repeat of Crozier I, the five evaders, and Jean Gicquel, now well and truly *brûlé*, made their way to the beach to await the incoming MGB 502 (Williams), whose surf boats appeared at 1.30 a.m. After the incoming goods had been off-loaded, the six passengers were rowed out to 502 and returned to Dartmouth, England.

A fortnight later, in a daylight operation on 9 August, Crozier III, MGB 718 (Seddon) embarked one member of the SAS and two French agents. This was Shelburne's last operation.

Although there is no consensus as to the number of airmen who were evacuated by MGBs of the Royal Navy's 15th Flotilla, the total for the five Bonaparte and for the Crozier I and II operations appears to be 111 – seventeen RAF and ninety-four USAAF. The number of airmen evacuated on Operation Envious IIB was eight, on Felicitate thirteen, on Easement II one, and on Scarf three, giving a grand total of 136 – twenty-one RAF and 115 USAAF.[1142]

Extraordinarily, not a single member of the Shelburne organisation was lost in the course of these operations.

Burgundy and Fan-Fan

Mention has been made earlier in this chapter of Georges Broussine (whom Airey Neave said 'was Jewish and enormously brave') and of the help that he gave to Labrosse to get him into Spain after the collapse of Oaktree in the summer of 1943. Over a year earlier Broussine had made his way to England via Spain with the help of the PAT line on 11 March 1942, to volunteer for the Free French Forces. Recruited by Airey Neave in London in the autumn of 1942 and trained as a wireless operator, he was to have been sent to assist Pat O'Leary in December 1942, but instead was given the chance to create the Bourgogne (Burgundy) line, one of several joint operations between MI9 and the BCRA (de Gaulle's Free French intelligence service) which were named after wines or liqueurs.

Having arrived in France on the night of 19/20 February 1943, not quite in the manner intended (see following chapter), Broussine proceeded to Lyon to make contact with the Brandy line operating in the Lyon area, with a view to establishing his own line from Paris to the port of Douarnenez (Finistère) on the Breton coast between Quimper and Brest. The Brandy line (set up by the appropriately named Christian Martell), which ran from 1 May 1942 to 23 June 1943, was responsible for the return to England of about seventy airmen. Maurice Montet became its chief on 14 July 1942, after taking over from his brother, Major Lucien Montet, formerly a pilot with the RAF. Other "wine" lines were Bordeaux (Jean-Claude Camors, see below this chapter); Pernod (Pierre Marie François Charles Guillot, "Gaspard"), which organised Lysander pick-ups from the Tours area, from November 1943 to April 1944, and which evacuated thirty Allied service personnel; and Patrick Hovelacque's Kumel. There was also Gerard van der Weerd (Wodka), who operated from Holland to Belgium in August and September 1944, and Yves le Hénaff's Curaçao, which lasted from May 1943 to February 1944.

Yves Henri-Léon le Hénaff was a French naval lieutenant who had been caught in Oran after the Allied landings in November 1942. Known to be strongly anti-Nazi, he was easily recruited for specialist training in England for sea evacuations and Lysander pick-ups. With aliases "Fan-Fan" or

"Alain Divanac'h" he was parachuted into Brittany on 14/15 June 1943 to establish escape organisation Dahlia (but known to MI9 as Zetland).[1143] No stranger to the Brittany area[1144] he had with him as his radio operator the French-Canadian soldier Robert Vanier ("Vincent", see Chapter 5).

Le Hénaff's first successful sea evacuation took place on 23 August 1943, though the operation itself was organised by Victor Salez and jointly financed by MI9 and the *Securité Militaire*, the Algiers-based arm of the French counter-espionage service. Le Hénaff and Salez combined again for their second venture, in the third week of September 1943, when twenty-five passengers (including four airmen – see below) were smuggled aboard the fifty-foot *Ar-Voualc'h* at Douarnenez.

On le Hénaff's third evacuation, on 2 October, Victor Salez was himself one of the twenty-two passengers on the thirty-foot cutter *La Pérouse*, along with two French navy commanders, two other naval officers and two American airmen. As *La Pérouse* approached the harbour control someone shouted to the two Germans on duty: 'We're off to England. There are still two places on board, if you'd like.' The guards laughed heartily and waved the boat through, wishing them a good trip! Two days later *La Pérouse* was in Penzance.

But then came a failure. In the last week of October 1943, ten Allied airmen had been brought to Quimper from Paris, including Flying Officer Watlington RCAF (see previous chapter) and Sergeant P.V. Matthews, the only survivor of a Lancaster that had crashed near Rugles (Eure) on the night of 15/16 August 1943. One of Sergeant Matthews's helpers, M. Fiquet, had brought him to Paris on 20 August, where he remained for several weeks in a number of safe houses. Eventually, he and two Americans were due to leave by train for Spain but, when no guide had turned up, 'we were taken, after an hour's delay, to a café in the district of Drancy (near Le Bourget aerodrome), where we met a man who was chief of the organisation in that district and known as Maurice.'[1145] Matthews and one American were then billetted on Madame Quenot in the rue Alcide Veillard, Bobigny (Seine-St-Denis).

After a month or so they were escorted to Quimper, where Matthews found himself with another American airman, Lieutenant Andrew Lindsay, at the house of Jacques Mourlet. They were told that they 'were to be evacuated by naval torpedo boat', the plan being for them to be taken to rendezvous with a Royal Navy MGB in a fishing boat yet to be purchased. The boat was duly purchased and arrangements were made for it to be looked after by the owner of a boatyard. The operation had to be cancelled, however, after the owner's wife persuaded him not to get involved and the 1 November deadline could no longer be met. Returning to Paris by train on 3 or 4 November Matthews 'stayed one night with the chief of the organisation who had been arranging the boat operation. He told me that he is known as FanFan.'

Another airman on his way back to Paris was Sergeant A.J.A. Reynolds, who had been on the run since 9/10 July 1943 when shot down over Holland. He was trapped in Brussels for three weeks in August as a result of the Gestapo arresting one of the organisation, but on 21 October, after several moves closer to France, he and Sergeant J.J. Dalinsky USAAF[1146] were escorted to Paris by Simone, ('a slimly-built girl aged about twenty-three-years, thin features, medium colouring'). A week later Simone took Reynolds and two other Americans, Bailey and Quinn, to Quimper. 'We joined a party of thirty evaders at a café. A man came in and took Sgt Fidler, Sgt Woolard [*sic*], three Americans and myself [Reynolds] to a house where we remained until 31 October, when FanFan took us to another house on the outskirts of town. The plan to evacuate us by boat miscarried, however, and we left for Paris about 5 November.'[1147]

Le Hénaff now temporarily left Brittany, moving to an area some fifty kilometres east of Poitiers (Vienne), where he planned a Lysander pick-up for the night of 9/10 November 1943. On his way through Paris, on 8 November, he collected Sergeant Matthews, and 'his wireless operator, and a British captain, who appeared to be in the Intelligence Service. We went by taxi to somewhere near Montmorillon. That evening the wireless operator and myself were taken by truck to a small town nearby. At about 2300 hours on 9 November we went to a rendez-vous at a landing field.'[1148] Coming to pick up their six passengers – le Hénaff, agents "Pointer" and "Tybalt", Matthews, an American airman and the Intelligence captain – in triple-Lysander Operation Oriel were Wing Commander Lewis Hodges DSO, DFC & Bar, Flight Lieutenant S.A. Hankey and Flight Lieutenant R.W.J. Hooper DFC. Failing to find the landing ground three-and-a-half kilometres from Haims (Vienne) due to the bad weather they returned to England with their outward-bound passengers.

Matthews, the American, and the Intelligence captain retired to a house in St Germain, half a dozen kilometres away, where they stayed until 11 November, when they returned to the landing ground for the second attempt to complete Operation Oriel. Flying the three Lysanders this time were Hooper, Flying Officer J.R.G. Bathgate and Flying Officer J.A. McCairns MM. Hooper landed first disembarking two agents but, finding the ground too muddy after all-day rain, cancelled the landings of the other two aircraft. After twenty-five minutes he managed to take off through the mud with two

French officers and Matthews aboard, and landed at Tangmere in the small hours of 12 November.

Le Hénaff was to have gone back on one of the Lysanders, as were Alfred Blondeel (Pointer) and Wendelen (Tybalt), two agents of la ligne Félix, to whom London had given permission to return on 1 November. Blondeel had already had a setback when he was due to have gone out in the cancelled sea operation at the end of October,[1150] and was, therefore, twice discouraged ('fut à nouveau découragé'). When another sea operation from Plougrescant on the north Breton coast was proposed for around 20 November Blondeel took himself off to the Prince Albert hotel in Paris to await events. Le Hénaff's plan was to seize a lighthouse-tender, *La-Horaine*, on her regular visit to the Roches-Douvres lighthouse and to use her to take the evacuees back to England. The German guards aboard *La-Horaine* were disposed of but, due to thick fog, the new crew were unable to find the twenty hopeful passengers, including the increasingly unfortunate Blondeel, and crossed to Dartmouth, England without them on the night of 22/23 November 1943.

Another attempt by le Hénaff to organise a Lysander pick-up around 6 December, to have included Blondeel, failed again on account of bad weather, although several Lysander landings were made in France at this time. Hearing of yet another proposed sea evacuation organised by le Hénaff for early February 1944, Blondeel decided not to go on it. He thought the plans to be too dangerous and, in the event, his fears were well justified. The operation began well enough with the thirty-one evacuees being assembled at a fisherman's cottage near the shore. A couple of hours later they 'went down to the beach through a German mine field, walking single file, one behind the other, following the fisherman.'[1151] The boat appeared in due course and the would-be passengers were ferried out to it.

The boat was a small sixty-foot coaster, *le Jouet-des-Flots* (the Plaything of the Waves), equipped with sails as well as an auxiliary engine. She sailed from Ile Tudy (Finistère) on the night of 2/3 February to rendezvous with an MGB off Ushant, despite having sprung a leak as it struck 'the bottom when entering Port-Tudy to pick up the passengers'.[1152] *Le Jouet-des-Flots* safely negotiated Pointe de Penmarc'h on its way north, but the leak worsened in bad weather as she approached the Pointe de Raz, at the tip of the long foreland that separates the bays of Audierne and Douarnenez. Attempts were made to pump out the sea water, but when the pump itself failed the skipper had no choice but to shut down the engine, make sail and run aground on the rocks at Feunten-an-Aod in the aptly named Baie des Trépassés (Bay of Lost Souls) near Plogoff.

It took a good half an hour for all the passengers to gain dry land by leaping onto the rocks every time the boat crashed into them, pounded by the heavy sea. The party became fragmented, and most, including an RAF airman, two American airmen, le Hénaff, Pierre Brossolette and Emile Bollaert, the last two having been trying for many weeks to get back to England by air, were captured. It was a disaster, not least because Brossolette and Bollaert were key members of the French Resistance. Brossolette was a deputy of the BCRA and Bollaert, a Prefect who had refused to serve Vichy, had been entrusted with a delegation to co-ordinate internal resistance in France.

For John Watlington this was his second failed boat evacuation. He and an American airman, "Mack" (probably Staff Sergeant Lee C. Gordon – see Appendix III) a gunner who had escaped from captivity in Germany, had a narrow escape when hailed by a German soldier but managed to run away without being caught. As Mack had lost his shoes, Watlington went off on his own and made his way to Paris once more. From there he was eventually taken south with the Dutch-Paris line and gained the safety of Spain.

Brossolette and Bollaert, however, now in German hands, spent the night in the prison at Place Mesgloaguen, Quimper, before being moved to the Jacques Cartier prison in Rennes on 5 February 1944. The Germans did not at first recognise Brossolette, who was using the name de Boutet, for the simple reason that he had dyed the distinctive white "flash" in his dark hair to match the rest. The dye, though, would not last forever.

London was soon alerted to the plight of these important men. Squadron Leader F.F.E. "Tommy" Yeo-Thomas MC, distraught at the news of the plight of his great friend and comrade, pleaded with his superiors to be allowed to go to France to rescue Brossolette. They agreed that he could go, though his primary undertaking would be to 'enquire into and report upon the state of the Resistance Movements in the Occupied Zone…'[1153] Parachuted into France on the night of 24/25 February 1944 Yeo-Thomas ("Asymptote"),[1154] despite spraining an ankle on landing, made his way to Rennes via Paris to see what could be done. One look at the prison was enough to convince him that a frontal attack on the place was out of the question, and he therefore retired to Paris to recruit help for his plan, which was to use disguise.

When notified that all was ready for the rescue attempt Yeo-Thomas decided to go back to Rennes on 21 March. First, though, he had to meet with one of his contacts at the Passy Métro station in Paris. When the other man was not there at the appointed hour Tommy went to see if he was elsewhere in the station, but was suddenly seized by five men in civilian clothes. As he was being led away in handcuffs he saw his intended contact also being bundled away by two men. Tommy was not to know that, two days earlier, Le Hénaff, Brossolette and Bollaert had been transferred to the SD headquarters at 84, Avenue Foch, Paris.[1155]

Yeo-Thomas was confined in the SD cells until 18 May 1944, when he was transferred to Fresnes prison. Evacuated to Buchenwald concentration camp in Germany during the second week of August he would survive the war,[1156] unlike his great friend Pierre Brossolette, whose identity had been revealed three days after the move to Paris. On 22 March, momentarily distracting his guard, Brossolette flung himself from a fifth-storey window.[1157] Grievously injured, he was taken to the Hôpital de la Pitié, but died later that same evening.

As for Lieutenant Yves le Hénaff, he died on 2 July 1944 in the hot and crowded cattle truck that was taking him from Paris to Dachau, credited with having helped some sixty persons to leave France. Blondeel was not one of them. Having had enough of trying to get to England by sea or by air, Blondeel decided to head for Spain, but even then misfortunes assailed him. Unable to find a *passeur* to guide him south, utterly defeated he made his way back to Belgium. Bollaert, also unrecognised by the Germans, was one of the many Fresnes inmates to be transported to Buchenwald concentration camp on 15 August 1944. Moved to Dora and, on 5 April 1945, to Bergen-Belsen, he was liberated by the British Army ten days later, and repatriated on 29 April.

According to Airey Neave 365 airmen 'owed their liberty to Shelburne',[1158] though several of these men were assisted by Georges Broussine's Burgundy line, which was itself ultimately responsible for sending 268 men to Spain.[1159]

Burgundy additionally helped a further ten American and four RAF airmen to be evacuated from Brittany towards the end of January 1944. The four RAF were Sergeant J.D.H. "Paddy" Carleton; Sergeant R. "Max" Fidler; Warrant Officer Russell A. Jones RCAF; and Sergeant Leslie C. Woollard. The last three, with 2nd Lieutenant James E. Armstrong USAAF and a second American (see Appendix III) had been taken by train from Paris by Robert Virmoux and a young woman as far south as Carcassone. Unable to find the appointed guide and continuing to Quillan they again were unable to find him. Returning to Paris next day, they met Carleton and the rest of the party at a church. Having been in the hands of the Bordeaux line until 24 December they – the four RAF and twelve Americans – were handed over to Burgundy and taken overnight to Quimper and Douarnenez, which they reached on Christmas Day. On that same night, half an hour before midnight, the whole party, now numbering some forty persons, including several Frenchmen, walked the short distance to Tréboul in their stockinged feet so as not to make a noise.

There was a major setback, though, when the crew of the boat that was due to take them suddenly announced that they were unable to go. 'These Frenchmen had the petrol for the journey locked up in another boat, and refused to give it up. The scheme accordingly had to be abandoned.'[1160] They all trooped back to Douarnenez, still in their stockinged feet, and all stayed in one house for the night. On 26 December they had to spend half the day in a wood because, apparently, the police were looking for them. Two days later the large group was split up. Fidler, Carleton, Woollard, First Lieutenant D.A. Fisher USAAF, and Technical Sergeant T.R. Moore USAAF went to stay with Madame Talec.

Almost four weeks later, on 21 January 1944, Georges Broussine told the group – fourteen airmen and sixteen Frenchmen – that they would be on their way that night. Once more they filed round to Tréboul harbour. Boarding the *Breizh-Izel*, which had been purchased for the sum of 300,000 francs after another boat had been rejected at 900,000 francs, skipper Gabriel Cloarec gave the order to cast off at 2.50 a.m. on 22 January 1944. As the boat silently passed the harbour mouth under sail the stillness of the night was shattered by a German guard shouting at them to halt. 'We heard a scream and were told afterwards that a German searchlight had been switched on and then went off suddenly, as a result of an attack on the Germans arranged by the organisation.'[1161] Once clear of the harbour, the engine was started, and after a rough, thirty-six-hour crossing the *Breizh-Izel* reached Falmouth, Cornwall at around 1 p.m. on 23 January.

Other Breton sea evacuations

Nineteen-year-old Englishman Flying Officer G.H.F. Carter RCAF,[1162] navigator of Halifax W7885 lost over Lorient on the evening of 13 February 1943 (see above this chapter), landed 'in a field about fifteen yards from a house, beside a group of about thirty people. I was taken into the house (at Kerlescoat) into which F/Sgt Barry was brought,'[1163] the home of the Lapous family. Carter's mid-upper gunner, Flight Sergeant J.N. Barry RCAF, was given civilian clothing, but Carter was already wearing "civvies" under his battle dress 'with the idea (my own) of facilitating evasion'. As both

Carter and Barry spoke fluent French they were able to decide with their helpers what should be done, and the decision was taken to move them that night to a farm at Gourin, a dozen kilometres south-east.

After a second night, at another farm, the two airmen walked to Guémené-sur-Scorff (some thirty kilometres east of Gourin) and waited for the bus to Pontivy. Though the bus was full when it arrived Carter 'told the conductor we were Canadians escaping, and he pushed us on. A man on the bus heard us talking to the conductor, and at Pontivy he took us to a café, where we stayed a night and two days. Here we got in touch with an organisation…'[1164] In the Grand Café (owned by Pierre Valy), Guy Lenfant, a London-based French agent, showed them an RAF button and compass and told them that their pilot, Flying Officer J.C. Thomas RCAF, was already in the hands of an organisation, in fact the long arm of the PAO line. Lenfant also introduced them to Guy Dubreuil 'who is in charge of an organisation receiving arms and ammunition by aircraft.'[1165]

Dubreuil took Carter and Barry to his house at St Méen-le-Grand (Morbihan), three or four kilometres south of Gourin, where they posed as refugees from Lorient, whilst helping Dubreuil move arms about by bicycle. The efficient Dubreuil had sent their details to England by wireless, but there was some delay in getting a reply which, when it came, asked for the original message to be repeated. The all-clear was eventually given and with it, on about 4 March, the news that they 'were to embark on a boat when the BBC passed a certain message', the boat in question being MGB 324 detailed to come over on the night of 9/10 March in Operation Mirfield.

Dubreuil immediately sent one of his men, known by the code R10, to make a reconnaissance of the proposed embarkation area, and on 8 March, Dubreuil, Carter, Barry, and Technical Sergeant Claiborne W. Wilson USAAF,[1166] whom the French called "Petit-Pierre" and who had been picked up by a farmer near Josselin, went by taxi to Plouégat. From there they walked the fifteen kilometres to Morlaix. Catching a train to St Pol-de-Léon, on the coast, they met R10, who said that everything was in order. The men booked in to the Hôtel des Voyageurs for the night.

They heard their special BBC message – "*La plume de ma tante est rouge*" – during the 7.30 p.m. broadcast of *Les Français Parlent aux Français* on 9 March, alerting them that the operation was on, and set out for the beach thirteen kilometres away. At one point they were stopped by two gendarmes but were allowed to carry on. Safely reaching the rendezvous, 600 metres north-west of the village of Bougourouan, they stayed on the beach until 3 a.m. on 10 March, but 'saw no sign of any boat, though we did see a green flash out to sea. We then left the beach and slept in some hay till 0430 hours. After this we returned to St Pol-de-Léon by road.' They were stopped again, at Sibiril, but the German customs officer was too sleepy to bother with them and let them continue. They then went to stay at a café in Cléder. After hearing nothing on the BBC for three days they returned to the Hôtel des Voyageurs at St Pol-de-Léon.

The reason for the failure to contact the MGB on 9/10 March then became clear – instead of going to the beach 600 metres *north-west* of Bougourouan, they should have gone 600 metres *north-east*. For the crew of MGB 324 it was a frustrating night, especially as they believed that it was *their* surfboat that had gone to the wrong spot.[1167]

Debreuil had meanwhile made contact with members of the PAO organisation that had been helping Flying Officer Thomas, and two of them – the Chief of Police in Pontivy, Henri Loch, and Henri Clements – took the airmen to the Trappist monastery at the Abbaye de Thymadeuc-en-Rohan (Morbihan).[1168] Joining them there was another American, 1st Lieutenant Robert E. Biggs USAAF.[1169] Three days later Georges "Géo" Jouanjean took them to Paris, collecting along the way a third American evader, possibly 2nd Lieutenant Robert E Kylius (shot down 16 Februrary 1943). In Paris, on 20 March 1943, they went to a café in the Place Denfret-Recheriaux, while Georges went to the PAO safe house at 19, rue d'Orléans. There he discovered the awful news that 'the Gestapo had arrested three members of the organisation a week previously. The place had been sealed by the Gestapo.'[1170] He learnt that the reserve headquarters had also been closed.

They left Paris that night, 20 March, with the idea of going to stay with la Comtesse Geneviève de Poulpiquet at Quéménéven (Finistère), who had already looked after five Americans for Georges Jouanjean, but instead they went to la Pie, half a dozen kilometres east of Carhaix-Plouguer. Unable to arrange for their onward journey in the immediate future, Georges sent the airmen to different safe houses, Biggs, the other two Americans, and Barry going to three separate houses in Carhaix, and Gordon Carter with Georges's brother-in-law, Raymond Cougard, at Gourin.

During his two weeks at Gourin, Carter frequently visited his friends in Carhaix posing as a university friend of Raymond, but one day went to Spézet 'and visited my original helpers, collecting souvenirs of the aircraft and my equipment.' He also learnt what happened to the survivors of his crew. Freeman he already knew had died, but the other four were safe in the hands of a section of the PAO line and had apparently gone off for Toulouse on 18 February.

In Carhaix, meanwhile, on 3 April Georges Jouanjean discussed a plan with Gordon Carter to steal a German MTB to get back to England rather than having to wait another two weeks for a boat. On 5 April, though, Georges 'arrived by car with two other Frenchmen' with the news that they would be leaving by private boat in a couple of days. Gordon asked him 'if he had brought Barry, and he said he had not and that Barry would probably come on a boat which a Frenchman was buying for 60,000 francs to send his son to Britain.'[1171] In fact, as seen, Napoleon Barry, with Eddie Turenne, headed south through France and Spain to Gibraltar, and was flown back to England on 13/14 July 1943.

Georges then drove Gordon and the two Frenchmen to a rendezvous at Douarnenez, where they stayed the night of 5/6 April at the house of Claude Hernandez. On the evening of 6 April they were picked up by Louis Marec, who was to be skipper of the boat, and after dark, having met up with fourteen other Frenchmen, 'went to the boat – a thirty-six foot motor pinnace with a thirty h.p. (French) motor which did an average of six-and-a-half knots.'[1172] Before sailing, however, there was the small matter of payment for one's passage – 4,000 francs per head. Gordon's fare was generously paid by the Abbé Cariou, who had also wished to go on the boat but had been forbidden to do so by his bishop. The abbé also paid the fare for two of the Frenchmen.

Once the financial business had been concluded, the fully-paid-up passengers slipped past the German guards on the quay and boarded the sardine smack *Dalc'h-Mad*, registered number DZ 3048. She cast off from Tréboul harbour at 8.45 a.m. on 7 April in broad daylight with nineteen aboard. Five of the party, dressed as fishermen, busied themselves about on deck while the others stayed below in the hold. As they passed the German customs office at Tréboul they signalled that they were going to Douarnenez, and were allowed to proceed. Again, when hailed by the Douarnenez customs officers, they signalled that they were going to get some fuel. Just in case, Claude Hernandez and Pierre Plouhinec, who had been briefed to create a diversion, suddenly distracted the officials, Hernandez by telling them that a sail had been stolen from his car. The Germans allowed the boat to continue.

The *Dalc'h-Mad* headed into Douarnenez Bay and, when out of view behind an island, went north along the shore of the bay. Some twenty minutes later they turned almost due west on a bearing of 280° true, and ran for 100 kilometres or so until, at around 7 p.m., a storm forced them to heave to. Once the storm had blown itself out at about 5 a.m. on 8 April they set course west-north-west. By the evening, when they were an estimated twenty-five kilometres west of the Scillies, having seen neither ship nor aircraft all day, they turned due east. A revolving white beacon was seen at about 2.30 a.m. on 9 April 'and a string of about thirty white lights like an aerodrome flarepath. A thick mist then fell on the sea, and though we heard a British aircraft three times, we did not see it.'[1173]

The boat had earlier sprung a leak and required constant bailing, but this did not prevent good progress being made. At 8.45 a.m., off Land's End, they saw their first aircraft and, continuing on an easterly course, the *Dalc'h-Mad* finally arrived at Coverack, Cornwall. Only Louis Marec and Gordon Carter were allowed ashore at first, with Gordon being taken by the police to Falmouth police station, where a telephone call to his station (RAF Graveley) and to his aunt Dot were sufficient to prove his identity. As for the other French passengers on the *Dalc'h-Mad* (which was temporarily taken over by the Royal Navy), they were removed to Penzance, and then, on 12 April, to the Royal Victoria Patriotic School in London for clearance by MI5. The BBC later broadcast the message "Sainte Anne a bien fait les choses", to notify those in Brittany that the *Dalc'h-Mad* had safely reached England.

The skipper, Louis Marec, joined the BCRA and continued his fight against the enemy, though he would later be arrested. Gordon Carter returned to operations but, now a squadron leader DFC and Bar, and a member of the highly experienced crew of Squadron Leader D.J. Sale DSO & Bar, DFC, was shot down again on the night of 19/20 February 1944. This time he became a prisoner of war, at Stalag Luft III (Sagan). When it was all over, he returned to France, to the love of his life whom he had had to leave behind, and married her. She was Janine Jouanjean, Georges's sister. It was a happy time, for Georges had also returned from the horrors of German concentration camps.

Two Lancashire lads from Wigan, Sergeants Syd Horton and D.R. "Bob" Parkinson, were wireless operator and rear gunner respectively of a Lancaster that lost a starboard engine on its way to Mannheim on the night of 5/6 September 1943. On the way home the other starboard engine gave up the ghost. The overworked port engines then caught fire, leaving the pilot, Warrant Officer R.G. Cant, with little choice but to order the crew to jump.

All seven landed safely on French soil. Cant, Flight Sergeant G. Dickson (flight engineer), and Sergeant W.R. Milburn (mid-upper gunner) reached Switzerland. The bomb aimer, Sergeant Denys Teare, was to evade capture for almost exactly one year before being liberated by US ground forces.[1174] Sergeant G.F. Thomas (navigator) made his own way south and west for the best part of 250 kilometres before he received any real help. He eventually 'joined a small multi-national group of civilians trying to escape occupied Europe.' During the last week of October 1943 a guide led them high into the Pyrenees, pointed them towards Spain, and then turned back, leaving the group to fend for themselves. Caught in a sudden blizzard, one of them died, the others surviving only by eating what little food they had and by scraping moss from the frozen rocks. Four days later, on 29 October, they were spotted by a German patrol and arrested.[1175]

Syd Horton and Bob Parkinson, meanwhile, also set off in a south-westerly direction: 'After walking for about two hours we heard someone shout and ducked into a hedge. Two German guards approached, found us, and took us to a house which appeared to be a sort of guardroom. We had not removed our tunics or chevrons. A German corporal who spoke quite good English took particulars from us… He then spoke on a telephone. He called out an escort of two men, youths of about seventeen or eighteen years of age,'[1176] and ordered the two prisoners to follow their escort. Noting that their guards somewhat casually kept their rifles slung over their shoulders, Bob Parkinson asked if they could have a cigarette, and please could the guards give them a light. Permission was granted. When they were close to the Germans 'Parkinson hit out at one … and Horton knocked the other one over.' Bundling the unconscious guards into a ditch, 'which was very swampy', the airmen ran off into the woods.

After being helped at Rupt-St Mihiel (Meuse) they walked to Villotte-sur-Aire, and at around 2 o'clock on the morning of 7 September climbed to the top of a haystack that was under cover: 'We slept all that night and through the following day, and the greater part of 8 September.' Leaving at around 9 p.m. they walked the twenty or so kilometres to Bar-le-Duc (Meuse) under cover of darkness, making their way to the station when it was light in the hope of catching a train to Paris. Spotting a German guard there, however, they decided to return to their hiding place. On the way back they persuaded a passing cyclist to buy them the tickets for the Paris train, giving him money from their escape boxes. He returned in an hour 'with the tickets and shaving kit, shaved us, and gave us fruit, wine etc. Later he returned in a car driven by a well-dressed man. In the car there were civilian shoes into which we changed.'

Driven to the station, Horton and Parkinson were 'introduced to the ticket collector, station master, and signalman as being English. As the train was not due until 0220 hours the following morning we were hidden in the control room of the signal box, where we slept until awakened at 0120 hours.' Arriving in Paris at 9 a.m. on 10 September their only plan was to head for the suburbs, as they had been taught to do in their escape and evasion lectures. They wandered about all day until, with evening drawing on, they saw a priest and decided to ask him for help. 'The priest took us to a sort of school and fetched another priest who could speak English, and who inspected our identity discs, etc. to make sure we were British.'

The second priest put them in touch with a woman 'who had to be persuaded of our real identity' and who took them to a block of flats about ten minutes' walk from a race course. After one night there, 10/11 September, a young couple took them off 'through an underground-railway passage to the house of the girl's father who as we learnt later was a French officer.' On 12 September they were moved to 57, Boulevard de Champigny, St Maur-des-Fossés, Paris, the home of Henri and Georgette Douley, where they stayed a further three nights. On the evening of 15 September Madame Douley took them to the Bastille station and handed them over to the French officer's daughter, Yvonne, who in turn 'introduced us to a girl who had tickets for us and travelled with us to Quimper, which we reached about midday on 16 September.'

Now in Fan-Fan's hands, on 18 September they 'were driven in a van to what appeared to be a shipping office. The man who drove the van said he had expected to see five RAF personnel… At 1900 hours the van came back with five French officers in plain clothes, and we were taken to Douarnenez, and stayed till about 2345 hours in a fish warehouse.'[1177] From there, actually a sardine factory, Horton, Parkinson and twenty-three others, including two American airmen, were smuggled aboard the *Ar-Voualc'h* at Rosmeur harbour (Douarnenez) at low tide. They stayed in the quarters aft until 5 a.m. when they 'were hidden in the ice box until the vessel had passed the inspection point'. They drifted about during 19 September pretending to be fishing, and in the night set course for England. On 20 September, still some sixty kilometres from the Cornish coast, a flight of Spitfires arrived, and at 1.30 p.m. *Ar-Voualc'h* and her passengers were brought ashore at Newlyn harbour, Cornwall.

Next to leave by fishing boat, on 2 October 1943, were two American airmen in *La Pérouse*. Then, on 23 October 1943, the lobster boat *Suzanne-Renée*[1178] departed from Camaret-sur-Mer with thirteen Americans and six RAF aboard – Squadron Leader J.M. Checketts DFC RNZAF; Flight

Sergeant T.S.F. Kearins RNZAF; Flight Sergeant T.J. Hedley; Flying Officer A.H. Riseley; Flying Officer D.F. McGourlick RCAF; and Second Lieutenant S.K. Liby RNorAF.

Squadron Leader Checketts and his squadron, 485 (RNZAF), were in their Spitfires on 6 September 1943 providing high cover for USAAF Marauders, 'which were attacking a concentration of ammunition [trucks] in a railway siding in Cambrai' marshalling yards, when a squadron of Fw190s headed for the bombers. Checketts led his squadron in to the attack and 'shot one down at ground level about forty miles inland… I broke off the attack and came out over the coast about five miles north of Le Tréport.'[1179] The 190s, however, were not finished with him, and though he hit one of them another went for him head on. Closing to within a few feet of each other, all guns blazing, the Spitfire's fuel tanks caught fire. Checketts, also on fire, baled out near Tours-en-Vimeu (Somme), south-west of Abbeville, 'narrowly missing a power cable on the way down'.

Rushing towards him as he landed in a field were about fifty French people who had been busy with the harvest. Yelling to a woman that he was English she called over a boy on a bicycle, who took the squadron leader on the back of his bicycle to a hiding place deep in a wood. 'I lay down here and lost consciousness within about ten minutes. I was badly burned on the face, arms and legs. Before I lost consciousness I could hear Germans searching in the wood.' When he recovered his senses he saw someone standing about ten paces away from him, and watched him for about a quarter of an hour, unsure as to whether he was German or French. Suddenly someone touched him on the back of the neck, and a voice whispered 'All right'. It was a young Frenchman, Marcel le Conte, who had crawled up to him: 'He told me that the man standing beside us was a German soldier. We crept away from the wood, dodging German soldiers and patrols.'[1180]

Marcel took the injured Checketts to his home in a village near Tours-en-Vimeu, where Pilot Officer E.A. Haddock, shot down in his Typhoon on 15 July attacking Poix airfield, was already being sheltered. Ted Haddock was later captured. Brutally tortured for six hours by the Gestapo at Tours (Indre-et-Loire) he was then threatened with the firing squad, and confined to nine weeks' solitary confinement, during the first week of which he was manacled. Following further appalling treatment he was sent to Stalag Luft III (Sagan) prisoner-of-war camp.

Checketts was nursed and fed by Madame Charlotte le Conte, she and her husband 'starving themselves that I might have plenty. I was unable to see for five days and could not walk on account of my burns.' After a fortnight's rest, most of which was spent in bed, he was well enough to be moved, on 23 September, to Auxi-le-Château (Pas-de-Calais), where he found another ten airmen being sheltered. On the following day he, Flight Sergeant Kearins, and two American airmen were driven to Amiens. Their driver, though, was no ordinary driver. He was Sergeant E.H.R. Merlin RAF, shot down on 16 August 1943, who had found his way into the company of a man by the name of Joseph Becker, who came from Alsace. Becker, who lived at the Café du Coin in Auxi-le-Château with his mistress, was a naturalised German, and owned and ran the Staubach Transport Enterprise, for which the Germans had given him permission to use a private car.

On about 17 September Merlin became the driver of Becker's private car and, between 18 September and 26 October, claimed to have helped some forty Allied airmen using this car. These included Checketts, Kearins and the two Americans and, also on 24 September, another group of airmen, including Flight Sergeant Hedley and Flying Officer Riseley, whom Merlin also took to Amiens.[1181]

Terry Kearins had been on the run since 15 July 1943. Shot down on a Ramrod to the Poix area flying as Number Two to Squadron Leader Checketts he, too, had suffered burns. At dusk on 17 July he approached one of two isolated farms near le Quesnoy-en-Artois (Pas-de-Calais), south-east of Hesdin, and asked an old woman, Madame Forgez, for help. As others had done, she suspected him of being a German: 'As I turned to leave her, I was so exhausted that I almost fell.' When she and her husband saw the extent of his burns they insisted on his staying: 'I was in bed here for the next six weeks. The local doctor was a German sympathiser, but the farmer got ointment from the chemist and treated me himself.'[1182] Kearins stayed with the Forgez at their farm until 24 September, when he was taken off to meet Checketts.

On his return to his squadron in England Kearins presented an amazing spectacle to his fellow squadron members: 'Terry had virtually turned into a Frenchman, and was still dressed in the clothing which he had worn for getting around in France. His black hair was long, thick and bushy, with a heavy moustache; and he was wearing a bright blue suit cut in the French style, with a bright red tie and great, thick shoes with rope soles.' Later awarded the French Croix de Guerre, Terry was reluctant to tell his squadron how he had come by it. Part of the story was, however, 'that when a particularly hazardous set-up had arisen, Terry had taken some hard-nosed action which had held the situation together.'[1183]

Flight Sergeant Hedley and Flying Officer "Rufus" Riseley were half the crew of a Boston that was hit by flak in the port engine over Albert on the way to the steel works/locomotive repair shop at Denain (Nord) on 16 August 1943. Without the mutual support of the rest of the squadron, the slow Boston became easy prey for German fighters. Hit in the starboard engine, it was forced down into a field east of Montorgueil, not far from le Quesnoy-en-Artois. All were hurt or injured to some extent. Though Riseley was only bruised, Hedley had a bullet in his leg and a doctor came just after midnight on 17 August to have a look at it. Able to remove a shell splinter from Hedley's knee he could not, however, shift the bullet in the bone itself. Flying Officer Langdon, the navigator, burnt by an explosion in the Boston, was captured on 17 August as he was being taken to meet Riseley. The gunner, Flight Sergeant Powell, was knocked about. Dropped off when Hedley was being moved, he was not seen again.

Hedley and Riseley were not to see each other again until 23 September at Auxi-le-Château. Hampered by the bullet in his leg, Hedley's evasion was relatively quiet, but Riseley had been far from idle. He 'heard that in one village that the local Gestapo chief had turned traitor. He met this man whose name, he learned, was Weiler [*sic*].'[1184] Using his position and authority, "Weiler", almost certainly Joseph Becker, whom Riseley says he first met on 3 September 1943, gave Riseley a guided tour of the Germans' local defences, of which he took due note. With the help of the Resistance and of a carrier pigeon, the information winged its way to England. Even more intriguing, however, was the news of secret German activity in a heavily-guarded wood near St Pol. Riseley was 'determined to discover what was afoot so, disguised as a French workman, he joined a lorry crew and was able to enter the site.'[1185] Needing more information, he went back to the site a second time. Drawing a picture of what he had seen, he hid it inside a loaf of stale bread. Although he knew not the significance of what he had seen, it was in fact a launch site for Hitler's V1 "flying bomb".[1186]

As to the other two RAF airmen on the *Suzanne-Renée*, Flying Officer McGourlick was in contact with "an organisation" within two days of his landing in France, on 7/8 August 1943. On 13 August he was reunited with two other members of his crew, Sergeant T.H. Adams and Sergeant H.L. Nielsen, and also met Lieutenant Lionel E. Drew USAAF. All four left together for Paris on 5 September with the chief of the organisation, "Raoul" (Jean-Claude Camors – see page xiii), staying in his apartment for two days before moving to the Grand Hôtel de France. They left Paris on 21 September for Nantes, remaining in the area until 5 October when they went on to Vannes (Morbihan). Drew, Adams and Nielsen left on 7 October (see Operation Felicitate below, this chapter), leaving McGourlick behind, until he was taken to a chapel in a small village on 15 October, where he met Riseley and Hedley and more of the party due to leave by the boat. On 18 October they were taken to Camaret-sur-Mer (Finistère), where the whole party was brought together – twenty-three British and American airmen.

Norwegian Flying Officer Sören Kjell Liby, shot down on 16 August 1943 and soon in friendly hands, found himself in Trouville on the evening of 21 August. His host was a garage mechanic, Henri Aubert,[1187] a saboteur who 'hides explosives etc. in his house. Whilst I was there a collaborator was blown up in his own garage by a mine which had been set by Aubert.' Following a Gestapo scare, Sören Liby was moved to Paris. In September he was called for by two men, 'Jean Claude and a French barrister',[1188] and taken to Joigny, where he 'stayed for one night at a house which was a German officers' mess or club.' After a few days 'at a farmhouse owned by Mme. Brun (an Englishwoman)' about twenty kilometres away, he returned to Joigny, and met up with Squadron Leader Checketts.[1189]

With the several dispersed airmen now all gathered together in the chapel at Sainte Marie du Menez-Hom,[1190] they walked a good twenty kilometres to Crozon and from there to Morgat, only a further three kilometres away. Six of the party, including Checketts, stayed 'in the house of the proprietor of the Hotel Sainte-Marie'. The airmen were then taken back through Crozon to Camaret-sur-Mer, a dozen kilometres north-west, and re-assembled in a bakery before boarding the *Suzanne-Renée*, which was 'lying about 20 yards off the promenade'. As the boat could take only nineteen airmen, four Americans were left behind – 2nd Lieutenants Bronner and Walter Hargrove and Staff Sergeants Lawhead and Wilson (see Appendix III, Operations Envious IIB and Felicitate).

For the fortunate nineteen it was their bad luck that, as a storm was blowing out in the Atlantic, for five days and four nights the boat remained in the harbour. Food was brought regularly by French helpers, but the men had to remain below deck during the hours of daylight, being allowed out only during the hours of darkness. Finally, on 23 October, the storm abated and it was time to leave. Hidden under a pile of lobster pots in the boat's hold the men waited anxiously as, at 11.30 a.m., the *Suzanne-Renée* and others of the local fleet made their way past the German control at the entrance to the harbour. Fortunately the control was not severe, a German sailor simply putting his head through the cabin door to check the fishing permit and failing to discover the airmen.

The *Suzanne-Renée* stayed with the rest of the fleet until the evening, when course was set by her crew (skipper Jean-Marie Balcon, aged fifty-five; Joseph Morvan, his brother-in-law; and Alain Marchand) for Penzance, England which was gained at 5.30 p.m. on 24 October.[1191] From there the airmen were taken to Falmouth. After a basic meal, it was off to an American camp (possibly the US Naval Base) for a bath and a new set of clothes to replace the disgusting rags that they had been obliged to wear for days. Under open arrest, they were escorted by train to London, for interrogation, and to continue their war.

Following the successful departure of the *Suzanne-Renée* from Camaret it had been planned to evacuate the airmen who had had to be left behind, Sergeant T.H. Adams and Sergeant H.L. Nielsen of McGourlick's crew for example, but so tight had the Germans' surveillance become that the boat that had been earmarked for the next trip, *L'Yvonne*, sailed from Camaret to Newlyn, Cornwall with her crew of four only. It was the Germans' usual practice, too, once they realised that a boat was missing, to close the boat's home port for anything from two to eight weeks.

Eight days after the *Suzanne-Renée* had departed, however, the *Requin* (Shark) sailed from Carantec on 30 October 1943 with Flight Sergeant G.A. Wood, shot down near Morlaix on 23 September. Found by a farmer up a tree, he was comfortably embedded in a haystack at Ploujean when visited on 24 September by Doctor Le Duc, from Morlaix, who returned later with a change of clothes. Driven off in the doctor's car, with a man called Loic Rault from Carantec, Wood was taken to Rault's house, and was visited that evening by Rault's sister, Madame Rothschild. Madame Le Duc was also there. Wood remained with the Raults until 4 October when, for safety reasons, he had to be moved to the home of Morlaix baker Lucien Marzin. The move was occasioned by Mesdames Le Duc and Rothschild having been 'summoned to the Gestapo in Brest in connection with an accusation of having helped some Americans to escape last October.'[1192] As the Gestapo could not prove the connection, the women were released.

While Wood was staying with Lucien Marzin, Doctor Le Duc bought a boat, on or about 20 October, but a combination of its old age and bad weather put an end to the venture. On 22 October, however, Wood was told that a boat was being built and that it would be ready to sail on about 30 October. Four days after he had received the news, Le Duc took him back to Carantec. The Germans, as was their wont, paid the boatyard (Ernest Sibiril's) a visit and noted the fact that there was a boat under construction. It was, apparently, only through Madame Le Duc's insistence that it was decided to go ahead with the scheme. All was ready by the evening of 30 October, when Wood and six other passengers and crew embarked on the *Requin* – Ernest Sibiril; his son Léon; Paul Daniel ("Charles", off to join de Gaulle); Fleurot (Christian name not known); a "colonial"; and "another Frenchman" – before slipping away in the darkness. Waiting until it was daylight and they were well out to sea before starting the engine, they came in sight of the Eddystone lighthouse at around 5 p.m. on 31 October. Shortly afterwards they were picked up by the minesweeper *Loch Park*[1193] and taken in tow. Transferred to a Royal Navy yacht they were landed at Plymouth, and handed over to security.

Quite apart from the Germans' presence, the winter months in Brittany in late 1943 were abnormally dangerous times, for working his rotten way through the Resistance organisations was Roger le Neveu ("Le Légionnaire"). Some of the RAF evaders who escaped on the *Suzanne-Renée* talked of two of their French helpers, Raoul and Pierre, who went missing, or disappeared, before they, the airmen, had gone to Camaret. Checketts, back in England, said that when he was in Camaret he 'heard that Raoul and Pierre and twenty-two pilots were missing between Lyons and Paris, although we could not ascertain definitely whether they were all together. The pilots were to have come to this country in another boat.' McGourlick also heard that Raoul and Pierre, 'who were coming from Paris with twenty Americans… had been arrested by the Gestapo.'

Riseley was more specific, saying that the departure of himself, Hedley, and an American from the home of Colonel Scheidhauer[1194] at 1, rue Neptune, Brest had been delayed because Raoul and Pierre had disappeared on either 11 or 12 October, 'probably with a party of British and American airmen on the way from Rennes. Pierre and Raoul were believed to have had four million francs with them.' Furthermore, said Riseley, Raoul had in his flat in Issy-les-Moulineaux, not far from the Bois de Boulogne in Paris, 'all the particulars and one photograph of all the members of the party' that eventually left Camaret. Luckily for the airmen these particulars were not found (if, indeed, they ever were) before their departure for England.

"Raoul" was otherwise Jean-Claude Camors, the same Jean Claude who had escorted Flying Officer Liby from Paris. He had begun his clandestine work as 'Bordeaux' in mid-April 1943, when he was parachuted into France near Loches to set up the *réseau* Bordeaux-Loupiac. Before the end of the month he was on his way back to England, escorting three RAF evaders to Spain. Flight Sergeant E. Durant, Sergeant W.J. Barber, and Sergeant J.W.E. Lawrence, all same crew, shot down on 16/17 April 1943 in eastern France, had been taken from Bar-le-Duc (Meuse) to Paris on 26 April by René Gerard and by Roger le Neveu. Placed in a flat in Montmartre 'occupied by an elderly hairdresser whose wife had been killed by German bombing earlier in the war,' they understood that they 'were now in the hands of the "Bordeaux" organisation'.[1195]

On the afternoon of 27 April Gerard and Le Neveu escorted them to Tours, and then to Gerard's house in Loches. Here they 'met Lieutenant Camors and a friend of his. Camors said that he was from the French HQ in London.' After staying for several days in the area of Loches everyone gathered again at Gerard's house on 10 May, when Camors told the airmen that arrangements had been made to take them to Spain. 'That night we were photographed and our identity cards were prepared. We were each given a special wallet containing about 1,500 francs and a number of letters, French stamps, and various small papers, purporting to be additional proof of our identity as Frenchmen.'[1196] On 11 May the three airmen and the three Frenchmen took the train to Châteauroux, where René Gerard and Roger le Neveu left them. Alone with the airmen Camors told them 'that Roger's loyalty was suspect, and that some day it might be necessary to kill him.'[1197] Camors and Le Neveu were to meet again.

Making their way to Toulouse after a night in a railway carriage – too dangerous to stay in a hotel – Durant, Barber and Lawrence reached Perpignan on the morning of 12 May, and 'were met by a very old woman, who took us to a hotel where we met two other members of the organisation. Later we moved to the Hotel Notre Dame, where we had a meal.' Rather than risk the night in the hotel, a friend of Camors found them shelter in a garage, and on 13 May they were rolled up in a large piece of canvas in the back of a lorry and driven off towards the Pyrenees. Waiting for nightfall in a vineyard, they began the crossing that night with their guide. Fording the River Tech near Céret at around 4.30 a.m. on 14 May, they 'stayed in a small farmhouse known to Camors. Here our guide was joined by another.'

Again waiting for the cover of darkness, they continued over the Pyrenees. Even though the two guides knew that the road from le Boulou to le Perthus (on the border) was patrolled by Germans, they decided to make use of it, and went on ahead to reconnoitre. While the others stayed hidden by the roadside, two German soldiers walked by heading in the same direction as the guides, who suddenly ran back and told them to disperse. When all was quiet again they resumed their walk along the road, in single file with the two guides out in front: 'Barber was leading the rest of the party and coming round a bend he saw the two guides talking to two German soldiers.' Unfortunately, the Germans saw the airmen and Camors, and shouted to them to halt: 'We immediately ran away from them, and they opened fire. We saw Durant fall heavily, and we think he may have been hit and captured. We saw no more of our guides.'[1198]

Camors, Barber and Lawrence made the decision to abandon the road, and with the help of an army-pattern compass that Camors had brought along crossed into Spain. Later that morning, 15 May, on the road from le Perthus to Figueras, they were stopped by members of the Guardia Civil. Taken to Figueras, all three claimed to be RAF, and were put in prison, where they met 'a Belgian flight lieutenant named Le Grand, Sgt [A.B.] Cox (USAAF) and an individual calling himself "Arthur George" who maintained that he was an Australian private soldier who had escaped from France.'[1199] On 26 May Camors and his two companions were transferred to Gerona, and three days later taken by a Spanish Air Force officer, via the Barcelona consulate, to Alhama de Aragon, where they arrived on 30 May. Wing Commander Vincent took them to the Madrid Embassy on 2 June, and twelve days later they were driven via Seville to Gibraltar, where they arrived on 16 June. Camors flew back to England on 20 June, two days before Barber and Lawrence, and was in London the next day.

It was not long before Camors returned to France. On 5 July he was once again dropped into France, near Lyon. Assuming the alias Raoul Caulaincourt he headed for Plomodiern (Finistère) to help re-establish the Paris-Brittany link for the pressing evacuation of airmen evaders from Paris. Having helped to move many of the evaders from Paris, as seen, he was in the Café de l'Époque on the rue du Pré Botté, Rennes on 11 October when he was spotted by Roger le Neveu, agent of the Gestapo and suspect member of the *réseau*.[1200] The café was run by Franz Nouët, himself an agent of the Intelligence organisation *Mouvement de Libération Nationale*, and at the back of the room, seated around a table with Camors, were Pierre Dumont, Rémy Roure (a writer on the newspaper *le Monde*), André Poirier (a French airmen who had been shot down and was hoping to get back to England), and Claude P. Depesme (a young Parisian *agent de liaison* known as "Jeannette").

At around 5 p.m. Roger le Neveu appeared. Spotting Camors, he drew a pistol and tried to arrest everybody at the table. In the confusion that followed, two shots were fired. This attracted the attention of a Luftwaffe sergeant outside in the street, who entered behind le Neveu. Roure managed to get outside, but was pursued by the German sergeant, who shot at and wounded him. Arrested and tortured, Roure said nothing. Camors and the other three, meanwhile, ran in the opposite direction to the rue du Maréchal Joffre, with Roger le Légionnaire in hot pursuit and firing away with his gun. The fugitives dived into a block of flats at 2, rue du Maréchal Joffre and made their way up to the attic with a view to escaping over the roofs. Not all of Roger le Légionnaire's bullets had missed their mark, however. Camors, too seriously wounded to continue his flight, stayed on a landing in the building to give the others the chance to get clear.[1201] With the help of one of the inhabitants of the building, Camors was able to destroy all incriminating documents, even eating some of them.

His body was found in the small hours of the following day. Persuaded that Camors had indeed eaten *all* the documents on his person, the Gestapo took away his body for an autopsy.[1202] It was never found, and is presumed to have been buried in the *carré militaire* in Rennes.

Thanks to Camors and to the other members of Bordeaux-Loupiac, it is estimated that some sixty Allied airmen were evacuated from Brittany to England between 23 October 1943 and 22 January 1944.

Probably the last airmen to return by French fishing boat were, as mentioned above, those on the *Breizh-Izel* on 21/22 January 1944.[1203] Before then, however, Sergeant T.H. Adams and Sergeant H.L. Nielsen, left behind in October (see above), had been spirited back to England in Operation Felicitate on 25/26 December 1943. Having left Flying Officer McGourlick behind in Vannes on 7 October 1943, they and the American Lieutenant Drew went to the village of St Nic (Finistère). 'While we were here we heard that Raoul had been killed at Reims [*sic* – Rennes] while in charge of a party of Americans. Jeanette and Pierre, also helpers, and a French aviator, had escaped. Raoul had intended bringing the party to St Nic for the boating expedition.'[1204] However inaccurate the story, the three airmen were stuck in St Nic until a Gestapo search forced them to move to Brest and, after two weeks, to Landerneau (Finistère).

Plans were now afoot for their rescue by boat, and three men were sent on behalf of the French Intelligence Service from the *réseau* Jade-Fitzroy to organise the evacuation. The leader of the three was Pierre Hentic ("Maho"), himself a Breton though now resident in Paris, who arrived with his deputy, Pierre Jeanson ("Sarol"), and with his wireless operator, Jean Bougier ("Jeannot").[1205]

Already involved in clandestine SOE landings, Hentic had been arrested when caught without papers after he had had to give them to Flight Lieutenant John Mott when his Lysander had got stuck in the mud bringing in Alex Nitelet on 28/29 May 1942 (see Chapter 5). Hentic (alias "Trellu" when not in Brittany) was one of those flown back to England on the night of 24/25 February 1943 on Operation Pampas in a Hudson flown by Wing Commander Percy Pickard after it, too, had had to be dug out by some fifty locals before it could take off, two hours or so behind schedule.[1206] The agent in charge of the operation was twenty-four-year-old Claude Lamirault ("Fitzroy"), founder of Jade-Fitzroy, who was also a passenger on the Hudson's return flight.[1207]

On 11/12 November 1943, after he had organised the sea evacuation from the Île Guennoc, Hentic returned to England in double-Lysander Operation Salvia, for which he himself was the organising agent (see *We Landed by Moonlight*, p. 203). Hentic was landed back in Brittany on 26 November 1943 in Operation Envious IIA (MGB 318), but was arrested on 6 January 1944. Deported in due course to Dachau, he survived to be liberated in 1945.

The place chosen for the evacuation, the Île Guennoc, lay just off the coast in the difficult waters on the north side of the Brest peninsula, more particularly between L'Aber Benoît and L'Aber Wrac'h estuaries. The mouths of these two estuaries, studded with small, rocky islands, convenient in favourable conditions for the Royal Navy's clandestine MGB operations, could become treacherous areas of water 'completely unprotected from the winds blowing in from the Atlantic, often reaching gale force in alarmingly short time.'[1208]

On 3 November 1943 Adams, Nielsen, Drew and others were taken to the Île Guennoc 'where we were supposed to contact a British boating party. We were a party of about twenty French and Americans. We remained on the island for five days without any form of shelter and food for one day only.'[1209] The wretched party was recovered to the mainland, and spent the night in Madame de la Marnierre's château at nearby Lannilis, dispersing on the following day. Drew, Adams and Nielsen returned to 17, rue Voltaire, Brest, which also belonged to Madame de la Marnierre.

The Royal Navy had tried its best to evacuate the airmen and others in Operation Envious on 3 November, but somehow the wires had got crossed and MGB 318 (Lieutenant Jan McQuoid Mason SANF(V)) had gone to the Île Rosservor, a short way to the south, when the relevant signal informing British Intelligence of the alteration to Guennoc had not been received in time. MGB 318 tried again on 26 November in Operation Envious IIA, but found neither reception committee nor evaders. The hardworked MGB 318, this time in the company of MGB 329,[1210] returned for a third attempt (Operation Envious IIB) on 30 November/1 December. 'At 2300 hours on 30 November 1943 the two MGBs anchored off the island of Guennoc. Three small boats were sent away to pick up a party of evaders on the island. The evaders were not contacted there, but a light was seen flashing from Tariec island, about 2 miles to the east. The boats made for the island and took aboard a party of about twenty-five evaders, and made to return to the MGBs.'

At this moment the weather worsened, a strong head wind and sea getting up, and only one of the three small surfboats managed to regain the MGBs, one each from MGBs 318 and 329 failing to do so. Sub-Lieutenant M.J. Pollard RNVR, in charge of 318's boat, made for the leeward side of Guennoc, where he landed at approximately 0500 hours on 1 December. Hurrying across the small island he tried to make contact with the MGBs, which were just getting under way, but his signals went unanswered, and all that the two MGBs had to show for their night's work was the collection of seven of the twenty-five evaders. Pollard then took his surfboat to Tariec, but it stuck fast on a sandbank to the east of the island, where it remained until 10 a.m. when local fishermen were contacted. The crew of the other surfboat[1212] had already been taken ashore by fishermen, as had most of the eighteen evaders, to a nearby farm. Adams, Nielsen and five of the Americans, however, were stuck on Guennoc. Left behind by Pollard, they were not taken ashore for two days, when they became guests once more of Madame de la Marnierre.

On about 10 December Pollard and Adams were taken to Paris by Pierre Hentic, who intended to have them flown back to England, but the weather was so bad that the attempt had to be abandoned.[1213] The two evaders therefore returned to Landerneau on 22 December in time for the evacuation – Operation Felicitate (MGB 318) – that had been laid on for the collection of the six Royal Navy personnel. Felicitate failed due to 'impossible weather conditions at pinpoint', Tariec, on 23/24 December. The six navy men had been taken to the pinpoint on the evening of 23 December and had made R/T contact with MGB 318, 'but the sea was too rough to take them off. The party returned to the mainland, were picked up by a lorry, and lodged at various houses in Lannillis for the night.'[1214].

The other evaders, now fifteen of them plus Nielsen, were brought back from Brest, where they had been hiding, on 25 December in a Red Cross van, accompanied by Madame Ghislaine Niox, youngest daughter of Colonel Michel Scheidhauer, and Madame Maguy ("Maggie" to the non-French). Joining Pollard and his party they walked across the sand to Tariec at 10.30 p.m., and waited for the return of an MGB. Pollard and his naval party, together with several airmen, Pierre Hentic and his two radio operators, Jeannot and "Pierrot" (Pierre Tissier), had been collected from Landerneau earlier in the day by Claude Tanguy in his lorry. They were dropped off 'at Bel-Air-en-Landéda, the point from which they were later to be led to Ile-Tariec by Guillaume Le Guen and his two nephews.'[1215] Also travelling with the evaders was a cartload of mail that had been accumulating throughout December.

Pounding her way over to France was MGB 318, which had cast off from Falmouth during the afternoon of Christmas Day. The seas were calmer than they had been two days previously, and the gunboat made good progress towards the gathering passengers. 'The expedition consisted of thirty-two people, twenty-eight of whom were due to be embarked. Apart from the six British naval personnel, they included Sarol [Pierre Jeanson], who was due to report to London, five other agents, two women and sixteen aircrew.'[1216]

It was fortunate that the sea was calmer, for MGB 318 had towed across the large SN6, a twenty-five-foot surfboat, which had been chosen on account of the large number of personnel waiting to be evacuated. John Garnett, an officer in the Royal Navy who had volunteered for special duties with SIS, was one of those on board the MGB and later described their arrival on the French coast: 'The navigating officer brought us right up on the buoy, unlit, at the entrance to the channel. We then threaded our way up the estuary, on silenced engines, anchored, and a boat's crew with Howard Rendle as coxswain and six SOE oarsmen went ashore to Ile-Tariec which lay eight hundred yards from the gunboat anchorage. They had to make two journeys and brought off thirty-two people.'[1217]

Five minutes after MGB 318 had dropped anchor Pollard had made contact with her crew, and the embarkation began soon afterwards. As well as the Allied military personnel some thirteen others, mostly French men and women who were *brûlé*, returned, among them Mesdames Niox and Maguy. Mme Niox brought with her plans of the German fortifications at Poulmic, while Merle Martin USAAF carried a rucksack full of information gathered by Colonel Scheidhauer and his daughter.

Eventually all those waiting to return to England were safely on board the gunboat, and the return journey began at around 2.30 a.m. on 26 December. Nobody really cared much that a while later all three of 318's engines spluttered into silence. Second Lieutenant Walter Hargrove USAAF was reassured by a sailor: 'Take it easy Yank. We just fouled the plugs.'[1218] Power was soon restored, the boat continuing on two engines, and three hours later she gained the mouth of the Helford river, where a rendezvous was made with RAF Boat No. 360, to whom the passengers were transferred for the final part of their journey.

In the days of peace RAF Boat No. 360 had been a seaplane tender but, with a shortage of suitable boats, she had been acquired by SOE early in the war as a possible means of infiltrating agents and materiel into France. Based on the Helford river, she proved too slow and too small for cross-Channel exploits, and so was replaced by a French yawl, the *Mutin* (Rebel). She and the *Mutin* were, nevertheless, fitted with an RAF W/T set, to be used only in emergencies.

The set operators, trained by the RAF, used RAF frequencies to fool the Germans into thinking that the transmissions were coming from the air and not the sea.

CHAPTER 9

Comet and PAT/PAO lines: 1942-1943

'In tragic life, God wot,
No villain need be! Passions spin the plot:
We are betrayed by what is false within.'
George Meredith (1828-1909), *Modern Love*

Heading 'straight into the moon at 17,000 feet' on the night of 28/29 August 1942 (Saarbrücken) Wellington Z1491 was attacked by an Me110.[1219] With severe damage to its tail Pilot Officer J. Tyszko (pilot) gave the order to bale out. The aircraft crashed near Rummen, half a dozen kilometres from St Trond, home to a formidable German night-fighter unit. Such was the way of things that the first three of the six crew to bale out were taken prisoner while the others – thirty-one-year-old Flying Officer Stanislaw Swida PAF (navigator, fourth out), Sergeant Antoni Wasiak (wireless operator, fifth), and Tyszko (last) – evaded capture.

Swida, whose left cheek had been grazed by a bullet, 'came down in an orchard beside a small farm'. Believing that he was too close to the scene of the crash he 'decided to get away at once'.[1220] Meeting a woman from the farm as he walked down a lane, she showed him the route to follow to avoid the Germans. Then a number of Belgians 'all advised me to go to the nearest village and give myself up to the police.' This was not what he wanted to hear, 'and after going along the road for a bit went across country again,' ignoring the earlier advice.

He was making his way through another orchard at around 4 a.m. (29 August) when a gamekeeper, alerted by his barking dogs, came out to investigate. As the gamekeeper could speak only Flemish, and neither could understand the other, Swida was taken to his employer, with whom he 'talked for about an hour in French'. This man, as the other Belgians had done earlier, suggested that, as two others of his crew had already been captured in the neighbourhood, he should also give himself up. Still not convinced as to the merits of such a course of action, Swida told the man that he would try to get away, and was shown a wood near the house where it would be safe for him to spend the rest of the day. He set off again in the evening and walked all night (29/30 August), 'getting bread, water and cigarettes from peasants in the small villages I passed.'

In the morning, having bought a jacket to put over his battledress, Stanislaw Swida caught a train to Brussels, some sixty kilometres to the south-west. Despite the jacket, he was obviously an airman, and one of his fellow passengers 'whispered to me to follow him when we arrived in Brussels, and took me to his house there.' Trying unsuccessfully to make contact with a "British organisation" during the day, his benefactor advised him to go to Dour and cross the frontier into France, only five kilometres or so away. Unable at first to find anyone to help, he got into conversation with a woman who appeared to be very anti-German. Swida took a chance and told her who he was: 'She arranged for her husband to take me to a village (no name) near the frontier, whence the husband and a friend took me across the frontier to another small village, where they found me shelter for the night.'

Early on the morning of 31 August his French host advised him to head for Switzerland 'rather than for Spain, in view of the difficulty in getting across the Line of Demarcation into Unoccupied France.' For once taking the advice offered, Swida walked to le Quesnoy 'intending to get the train to Nancy. I missed the only train of the day, and spent the night in an orchard.' On the train to Nancy on the following day two French plain-clothes detectives asked him for his papers, but 'when I said that I had no papers they began to search my pockets and found my RAF identity card. They taxed me with being English, and, when I agreed, warned me that there were many Germans in Nancy, wished me good luck, and went off.' Four Frenchmen who had witnessed this incident 'got very excited'. Questioning Swida as to his intentions, they confirmed that it was too dangerous for him to go to Nancy, as there were too many German troops stationed there, and decided that he should go with them to Pont-à-Mousson.

There, one of the four men took him to 'an officer of the gendarmerie, who gave me a French identity card, for which I supplied one of the two photographs of myself in civilian clothes which I had had taken privately in England.' After Swida had spent the night (1/2 September) at his home, the man took Swida to Nancy. Buying him a ticket for Belfort, the man advised him to go from there to Montbéliard and on by bus to the Swiss frontier. At Montbéliard, while waiting for the bus, Swida 'went into a café and got into conversation with the proprietor.' She advised him not to catch the bus as planned but to go to St Hippolyte (Doubs) (not to be confused with St Hippolyte-du-Fort), about twenty-five winding kilometres by road to the south, and walk to Chamesol, some three kilometres north of St Hippolyte, where he would find help at a certain café only three or four kilometres from the Swiss frontier.

Unable to find the woman who was supposed to have helped him in the café at Chamesol, he spent the night in the woods out of harm's way. Returning to the café next day (3 September), he failed yet again to meet the woman. Too dangerous to remain any longer in such a small place, he struck out on his own for the Swiss frontier, and crossed unhindered into Switzerland during the afternoon of 3 September having been 'directed through the forests by peasants'. Of German guards there was no sign, but no sooner had he crossed the border than he was arrested by the Swiss and taken to a frontier post for questioning. Having no identity card – he had left his RAF one at Pont-à-Mousson and had destroyed the French one while still in France – he was put in the prison at Porrentruy for seven days and then taken to Berne, where he saw the Polish consular authorities and the British air attaché.

Several weeks later, with the Swiss police believing him to be a spy, Swida was interned at Henniez (Canton Vaud) with a number of officers of the Polish Army's 2nd Infantry Fusiliers Division (2 Dywizja Strzelców Pieszych), who had crossed to Switzerland with their arms on 20-21 June 1940.[1221] In August 1943, long fed up with the attitude of the Swiss, he 'decided to try to get away alone. I had no money, having received none from the British authorities since my internment.'[1222] Even the Polish consulate in Berne, to whom he had gone for help, said that it was impossible for him to get away alone, and suggested he went back to Henniez to await a signal from them, which came at the end of September. Making his way to Geneva, on 1 October he 'met a Pole (Stanislaw Piela) who often crosses the frontier. I crossed the frontier the same day with Piela and another Pole (Perzanowski) who acts with him on Intelligence work for the Poles and possibly for the British. We walked across the frontier to St Didier-en-Chaulais, where we got a train for Aix-les-Bains.'

After three days in Aix he was sent to Toulouse to meet a Pole named Barzycki, who was organising a party to cross the mountains to Spain. It was fortunate for Swida that he failed to rendezvous with Barzycki, 'for the party which he sent off that day was seized by the Gestapo in Andorra and taken back to France.' Swida returned to Aix, and a fortnight or so later met Barzycki there. Meeting as arranged at Toulouse on 29 October they travelled together by train to Boussens (Haute-Garonne) and by bus to Salies-du-Salat, 'where there is a large Polish community living in a camp. In the camp there is an apartment reserved for men escaping to Spain.'

On 2 November Swida, nine other Poles and a guide took the bus to St Girons and to Massat (Ariège), where they were joined by two Frenchmen. Setting off next day, it took three days to get to Andorra. After one night in the town of Andorra, where Sergeant Raginis joined them (see Chapter 7), they crossed into Spain by bus, and went to Seo de Urgel. Swida and some of the party (not Raginis) were in Barcelona on 9 November. Spending the night at the Polish Red Cross, it was suggested that they should turn themselves in to the Spanish police next day, but Swida would have none of it, and reported instead to the British Consulate. Two days later, with two Americans and a Frenchman, he was at the British Embassy in Madrid. Eight days later he was on his way to Gibraltar, and flew back to England on the night of 23/24 November 1943.

Swida's pilot, Pilot Officer J. Tyszko, landed safely in a field. Cutting his parachute to pieces, but forgetting to remove his name from it, he made off in the bright moonlight. Not wishing to become involved with the people running towards him from a nearby village, he 'made a long detour round the village and encountered a lonely Flemish couple in an isolated farm, whom I asked for water. The couple entered the farmhouse and brought out about a dozen people, one of whom spoke French, showed me where I was on my map and indicated to me the direction of France.'[1223]

Though it was about 1 a.m. when he approached St Trond, his arrival was observed by four elderly men. As he got nearer, one of them suddenly yelled out 'Tommy!' 'I declared my identity and they gave me some brandy. One of them led me round St Trond to a quiet spot behind some houses. In fifteen minutes he brought me a civilian jacket, trousers and shoes, into which I changed immediately, giving him my flying clothes.' The man also advised him to take the train to Brussels, but he decided that as he was still too near the crash site he would walk the eighteen kilometres to Tirlemont (Tienen).

Arriving there around 9 a.m. an elderly lady, having asked if he were English, gave him directions to the station to catch a train to Brussels. From Brussels he made his way to Paris, arriving there on the evening of 30 August. Unable to find a distant relative, he went instead to a priest, 'who gave me lodging, changed my Belgian money into French, gave me bread coupons and 300 grammes of meat and butter. He also informed me about the trains from the Gare d'Austerlitz to Bordeaux.'

From Bordeaux (1 September) he took another train to Hendaye, 'where there were Germans controlling identity cards. In the dark I managed to scrape through unseen.' Hoping to cross the bridge over the Bidassoa that led into Spain he found that not only was it brightly lit but also that it was guarded by the Germans at one end and by Spaniards at the other. Finding no other bridge nearby he 'therefore decided to swim the river at about 0530 hours.'

Once across he made his way through Irún to San Sebastián (2 September), and as soon as possible went 'to the Bank of Biscaya to change my money, not realising that this is strictly forbidden.' No harm was done, however, and he was put in touch with the British vice-consulate, which opened at 10 o'clock. They arranged his journey on to Madrid and Gibraltar. One of the quickest wartime journeys by an evader from Belgium to Spain, it had taken him only five days, but it was not until 30 September that he sailed from Gibraltar, arriving at Gourock, Scotland, on 5 October.

Hard on Tyszko's heels was his wireless operator, Sergeant Antoni Wasiak PAF, who had been peppered by cannon-shell splinters from the Me110 that had brought about their demise. Parachuting down Wasiak 'saw the aircraft crash into a tram and destroyed by fire'.[1224] Landing 'in a field surrounded by woods, with a leg so badly hurt by shrapnel that I could hardly walk', near the village of Heure-le-Romain (about ten kilometres north-east of Liège), all he could do was hide his parachute and go to sleep. Making his way onto a road later on 29 August 1942, still in uniform, he met a number of Belgians, German soldiers and police: 'Often, when the Germans passed, civilian people would group round me, as if to cover me from observation.' Laying up in a wood overnight (29/30 August) he decided to make for the village of Wonck, only a couple of kilometres north of Heure-le-Romain. On the way, he was overtaken by a man on a bicycle who asked him if he were English: 'I declared my identity and he took me in.'

The man treated Wasiak's injuries and gave him food and drink: 'Before long a woman came to take me to another house. She gave me clothes and shelter for one night, and put me in touch with an organisation by means of which I was brought back to the UK.' The organisation was the Comet line, one of whose *convoyeurs*, Marguerite, took him 'for two nights to a fruit shop at 38, rue de la Vise, Liège. We went to Liège by tram, and on the way there I had the interesting experience of seeing my own aircraft lying on the road and surrounded by Germans, who were pointing it out with pride to the passers-by.'[1225] On 2 September "Edgar" (Wasiak was not sure of his name) took him straight to the Ministry of Justice in Brussels: 'Edgar took me to the concierge who was called Evrard.'[1226]

Taken to Paris a week later, he stayed with Captain and Madame Violette in Vincennes until, on 19 September 1942, Andrée de Jongh and Jeanine De Greef (on her third trip to Paris alone) took him, Sergeant J.E. Cope, Flying Officer R. van den Bok DFC, RCAF, and Flight Lieutenant E.A. Costello-Bowen to the Pyrenees. Andree remained with them as they crossed into Spain. The two officers were flown home on the night of 2/3 October, with Wasiak and Cope following three nights later.

Flight Lieutenant E.A. Costello-Bowen and his navigator, Warrant Officer T.J. Broom, had taken off in their Mosquito on the evening of 25 August 1942 to bomb an electricity station at Brauweiler, near Cologne, Germany: 'Early on the way out we hit an electric pylon, and had to fly at a fifty-foot level all the way, finally crashing into a wood near Westmalle some fifteen miles north-east of Antwerp.'[1227] Both were knocked out. Broom was the first to regain consciousness, and revived his pilot, who discovered that his 'leg was cut about and rather badly twisted, though I did not notice the latter trouble until I had walked some way.'[1228] It was still daylight when the two airmen moved off deeper into the wood, from where they were able to observe a crowd of curious Belgians gathering to look at the broken remains of their aircraft.

Leaving the wreck behind the airmen took a compass bearing and headed south-west. The going was difficult for Costello-Bowen, because of his twisted leg and also because he had lost his footwear in the crash. Stumbling upon some buildings a few hours later, discretion being the better part of valour, they remained in hiding until they saw a nurse emerge from one of the buildings. Broom quickly went over to her and explained their predicament. She told them that they were at the Lizzie Marsily sanatorium that the Germans had searched earlier that night. The tired and thirsty airmen were invited in, and Costello-Bowen's leg was given proper medical attention.

As the Germans were still searching the area, plans were made to move the airmen to Antwerp, but there was a setback on 28 August when they heard that the local mayor had been arrested. Furthermore, no civilian clothes were readily available for the two men, who were asked to leave the sanatorium immediately. They were only half a mile or so down the road when Doctor Etienne Debaudt caught up with them to say that clothes had now been found. On the following evening, now suitably dressed, the airmen were handed over to Comet. Albert Johnson ("B") escorted them to Paris and, separately, to the south-west of France, Broom, Fay, Price and Rowicki (see Chapter 5) crossing the Pyrenees with both Florentino Goïcoechea and Albert Johnson, eleven days ahead of Costello-Bowen, Wasiak, Cope and van den Bok.

Both van den Bok and Cope had been shot down on the same night as Wasiak and Tyszko, 28/29

August 1942. Van den Bok was the rear gunner of a 408 (RCAF) Squadron Hampden, which was being flown by Wing Commander J.D. Twigg RCAF (the first Canadian airman to command the squadron). Flying with him were the squadron's bombing leader (Flight Lieutenant G.C. Fisher RCAF, navigator), and Gunnery Leader (Flight Lieutenant I. Maitland DFC, rear gunner). All in all they were a highly experienced crew, but their experience counted for nothing when faced by Major Wilhelm Herget, one of the Luftwaffe's top-scoring night-fighter pilots. Both Twigg and Maitland lost their lives in the shattered Hampden, Maitland as a result of the German's guns. The body of one of the crew was buried near the place where the Hampden crashed. From the description van den Bok guessed that it was his pilot: 'The grave was piled high with flowers. I heard later that the Germans took the body for burial in the British Military Cemetery at Dinant.'[1229]

After he had landed in a field near Cerfontaine, twenty-five kilometres south of Charleroi, it took van den Bok little time to find friendly Belgians, though he was first received with caution due to the enemy's presence in the vicinity. Nevertheless, coming upon a farm, he waited until someone appeared: 'Finally I saw a farmer come out with an Alsatian dog. I whistled to the dog, which came and made friends with me.' As luck would have it, the farmer knew someone who could help, and van den Bok, too, found himself in Comet's capable hands.

Sergeant J.E. Cope was in a 115 Squadron Wellington on the night of 28/29 August 1942 when it was attacked by an enemy night-fighter: 'The rear gunner saw a fighter in pursuit, after we had received a long burst of incendiary bullets which set fire to part of our fuselage and hydraulic system. This burst was encountered from flak over Liège, and probably killed the rear gunner, but I saw two members of the crew fixing their parachutes.'[1230]

Landing in a turnip patch Cope, unable to bury his parachute as per instructions, covered it with turnip leaves, and started walking. Three hours or so later he rested in a haystack near the village of Folx-les-Caves, halfway between Namur and Tirlemont. Waking up at around 5 a.m. on 29 August he was seen by a farmer's wife, to whom he announced 'Je suis anglais'. After she had taken him in and fed him, he asked her where the nearest priest lived. Her reply was that 'he was not at home so I called at another farmhouse. This proved a wealthier household and I was given general refreshment, a complete set of civilian clothes and 1,500 Belgian francs.' Later that morning he was taken to Brussels by a member of the family, and put in touch with Comet.

One of the nine wing commanders to evade capture during the war over Western Europe was twenty-nine-year-old Wing Commander J.R.A. Embling, 77 Squadron's commanding officer. His moment came when he went on an operation 'to assess the performance of some new photographic equipment',[1231] classifying his duty that night as navigator. Joining a "scratch" 102 Squadron crew in Halifax DY-L, W7916, flown by Squadron Leader J.G.G. Walkington, they took off from RAF Pocklington at around 0130 hours on 3 December 1942. On their way back from the target at around 5,000 feet they passed too close to Crépy aerodrome, a dozen kilometres north-west of Laon (Aisne), and were hit by flak. Five of the eight men aboard managed to jump clear before W7916 exploded. Embling was later told that two of his crew were dead, but a third, having baled out too late, had been badly injured and was not expected to live, which indeed, sadly, came to pass.[1232] The real navigator, Flying Officer A.R. Haines RCAF, was the only one of the survivors to avoid capture.

Embling landed close to the wireless operator, Sergeant L.C. Fantini, who had himself landed rather heavily just outside the aerodrome. Embling helped him to a small wood, but, as they were trying to bury their parachutes, they were captured by a German patrol. Escorted to a nearby château, they were briefly interrogated and searched, before being taken to the Kommandantur in the village of Couvron (Aisne), where Sergeants R.C.A. Douglas (bomb aimer) and H. Johnson (mid-upper gunner) were already being held in separate rooms.

Not having eaten since before their capture at around 0630 hours Embling persuaded a German corporal to get them some food. In the afternoon the airmen were taken by lorry to Laon station and kept under guard by four Luftwaffe men in the porter's room. When an express train arrived they were bundled aboard and into the corridor of a second-class coach. The senior member of the guard, a warrant officer, 'then went along and turned the passengers out of one of the compartments.'[1233] There was a certain amount of confusion during this eviction and Embling found himself alone in the now vacated compartment with but the warrant officer for company. Sergeant Fantini was standing in the doorway. Seeing that the warrant officer was paying little attention as the train slowed down through Tergnier goods yard, Embling pulled down the window and, seizing the moment, climbed out. He had one leg out before the warrant officer grabbed the other, but Embling 'shook him off and got out. I ran across the goods yard under two or three stationary trains, and found a goods train which was moving off in the opposite direction to the express.'[1234]

Embling wasted no time climbing unseen into an open wagon filled with sugar beet. A few minutes later the goods train reversed into the goods yard and, though Embling could see many Germans looking for him, they failed to search the open wagons. Some two hours later, by which time it was cold and dark, Embling was suffering from cramp, and moved to a flat wagon piled high with bales of hay, and burrowed into them. The goods train, however, stayed put throughout the night and all of the next day, 4 December. Despairing of ever leaving, he waited until it was dark before setting off on foot in what he believed was the direction of Paris. In daylight on 5 December he approached a house occupied by an old woman, who gave him 'a drink, bread, and some baked apples', but she was frightened and asked him to leave as soon as he could, which he did in what he now knew to be the direction of Paris.

By early afternoon it began to rain and, seeking shelter in a farmhouse, he was given a drink. Again, the inhabitants were not keen for him to stay, but one of them suggested that he might find help at a certain house in the village of Faillouël (Aisne), half a dozen kilometres north-west of Tergnier. On his way, he met a Frenchman walking his dog. The Frenchman, who also lived at Faillouël and who worked in the nearby sugar beet factory, told him that the house to which he had been directed 'was unsafe and that the people who lived there had previously been responsible for getting someone caught.'[1235] Embling also learnt that the woods in the vicinity were heavily patrolled by the Germans, and that the old woman whom he had met earlier had told the Germans of his presence in the hope of securing the release of a friend of hers who was a prisoner in Germany.

Given 'an old coat and trousers, as well as some bread and meat and about 1½ lbs of sugar' by the Frenchman, Embling went on his way. Very tired, having had no proper rest for three nights, he looked for somewhere to sleep as soon as it got dark. All he could find was a woodcutter's shelter made of bundles of sticks, but with the cold wind howling through the many gaps he did not stay long. He then tried a half-finished building, but it was so cold that he decided to keep moving. Near the village of Beaugies-sous-Bois (Oise) he 'found a barn near an isolated farm. I got into the hay about 0300 hours (6 Dec) and went to sleep.' A few hours later he went to the farm. Having torn his trousers he 'asked the housewife for a needle and thread. She realised I was a British airman and took me in. I was sheltered in this house for three weeks.'[1236]

The farmer, Madame Legruson, was able to put him in touch with an organisation that had recently been started by Etienne Dromas in the nearby Chauny area.[1237] On 29 December Embling, Dromas's first airman escaper/evader (see Chapter 7), was taken back to Tergnier station by "Jean", chief of repatriation, and with another member of the organisation travelled to Paris, where they were met by Louis Nouveau. He took them 'to a flat at 6, rue Yvon Villarceau, which was being looked after by Mlle Paulette Gouber.'

During the following week, three other evaders joined Embling at the flat – Sergeant C. Penna; Flying Officer Prince Werner P.M.G. de Merode (see Hasler and Sparks, Chapter 7); and 2nd Lieutenant John Trost USAAF.[1238] De Merode had landed in the north of France: 'I knew of the existence of an organisation in Roubaix, and went straight to the florist's shop of M. Berrodier, 11 rue de la Gare, where I stayed for a few days.'[1239] After a few more days in Lille, he was taken to Paris on 19 December with Sergeant Cyril Penna (shot down on 28/29 November 1942).

On 7 January 1943 these four and eight others – "Jean"; three members of the PAO organisation under training as guides; a Belgian by the name of Louis Letory, another member of PAO, who was being evacuated; Sergeant J.G. Dawson; 2nd Lieutenant Grady Wayne Roper USAAF;[1240] and John Trost – left Paris by train for Dijon. From there they caught the bus to Chalon-sur-Saône. 'We were to have crossed the Line of Demarcation there on foot, but, as a German had been killed and a guide (not of the organisation) wounded the previous day, this plan was not carried out.'[1241]

Having spent the night in a hotel they crossed the Saône by boat on the evening of 8 January, '300 or 400 yards from a German post'. Walking some fifteen kilometres to Varennes-le-Grand, they stayed the night there, continuing to Lyon and Toulouse on 9 January. The British contingent stayed with Paul Ulmann at 39, rue Pierre Cazeneuve, but after two nights Embling and de Merode went to Bergerac. They were there for only one night, unable to proceed further due to the arrest of "Georges de Milleville" (Tom Groome), Pat O'Leary's radio operator, on 11 January (see below). The whole party was then taken to Marseille, and stayed with "Madame Thérèse Martin" (Maud Olga Andrée Baudot de Rouville) in her flat at 12, Boulevard Cassini, close to the Observatory Gardens.

Because of what Wing Commander Embling called 'a big clear out in the old port' – strong German police activity in le Vieux Port – it was deemed advisable for some of the party to return to Toulouse and for others, Penna and Dawson, to go in the opposite direction to Nice. After five days or so these two went to Toulouse, then to Bergerac (for one week), and back to Toulouse once more. At the end of January or early February a party of five – Embling; De Merode; Penna; Letory; and Nancy Fiocca, who had joined them from Marseille – was taken by Pat O'Leary to Perpignan to try to cross to Spain. Unfortunately, their guide had been arrested two days earlier by French police, as his papers were not in order, and the party had to retire to Toulouse. The same group tried again three days later, and failed again, this time the new guide saying that he could not make the journey.

Embling and de Merode then went to the port of Sète where they 'were to have been taken on a tramp steamer to Spain.' Once again their departure was thwarted, this time because the boat's owner had sent it elsewhere, and on 10 February they returned yet again to their base in Toulouse, the Hôtel de Paris. Two more evaders, Sergeants Canter and Robertson, had arrived from Ruffec on 6 February to swell the ranks (see Chapter 7). As they approached their room on the third floor of the hotel Robertson heard 'an unmistakable hum of conversation coming from behind one of the doors, and it was into this room our guide ushered us. The room was considerably larger than I expected, considering the size of the landing, and it too was very bare-looking. Against three of the walls were some double-tier bunks, with a various assortment of bedding. In the centre was a wooden table and three chairs.'[1242] The hum came from the several excited evaders, all anxious to be off to Spain.

On the evening of 10 February the party of ten (Embling; de Merode; Dawson; Penna; Canter; Robertson; Roper; Trost; Captain Richard D. Adams USAAF;[1243] and Letory), escorted by "Guy" and a Spaniard, left for Ussat-les-Bains (Ariège), chosen because the control on the train occurred further up the line at Ax-les-Thermes. The crossing into Andorra was to have been made that night but there was yet more trouble with the guides, and the party therefore had to stay the night, and all next day, in a deserted hotel. Their guide, who had left them to sort out the problems, returned with two other Spanish guides who would lead the party, now swollen to some twenty-five in number, over the Pyrenees. So it was that at last, on the night of 11/12 February 1943, they set off. They walked for an hour and a half to a barn, where they stopped for the night. The march next day began in bright sunshine, and the Spaniards set a cracking pace, but it was not long before Wayne Roper, who had been wounded when shot down, had to turn back. Jack Dawson was faring little better, and Wing Commander Embling decided that he should also turn back, though he was willing to carry on. Flying Officer de Merode, however, volunteered to go with them as their guide, and so these three departed whence they had come.

Having mercifully abandoned the crossing of the Pyrenees de Merode, Dawson and Roper returned to Ussat and Toulouse. While Dawson and Roper stayed with Paul Ulmann for a few days, de Merode went to "Madame Martin" at 12, Boulevard Cassini, Marseille, with Dawson and Roper following shortly. As seen (Chapter 7), de Merode and Dawson left on 1 March for Spain, with Hasler and Sparks, and successfully returned to England. Wayne Roper, on the other hand, fell in with the next group of evaders (see below).

The others, Embling and party, pressed on into the night. Soon conditions changed for the worse. Deep snow and a fearsome blizzard hindered their progress as they climbed ever higher. Sergeant Penna remembered 'that one of the Frenchmen, a boy of nineteen years named Louis was sure that he could see trains running along the crest of the ridge ahead.'[1244] Then the guides became confused, though convinced that there was another hut up ahead. Sergeant Penna took the lead with the guides, until at last they stumbled upon the hut. 'Built of wood on a low foundation of rocks, it was devoid of anything in the way of furniture, but round the inner walls was a rough kind of bench.'[1245] A fire of some sort was started and a modest meal handed out to the weary travellers.

In the morning the guides made them continue. Sergeant Penna already had frostbite. Having removed his shoes, he was now unable to put them on again. 'They were at best of times a size too small and with the extreme cold my feet had swollen until no attempt at persuasion would get my feet into the shoes. The guides were unimpressed and produced a knife, slit the front of the shoes from the toecap and in this way I was able to "wrap" the shoes round my feet. I tied them on using a scarf that I had had around my neck.'[1246]

They had to get over a certain pass during daylight, and once again the guides set a fierce pace. The snow was still deep, and somewhere along the trail 'Trost lost his shoes, but his feet were so numb that he did not notice it.' All, however, made it – just. Louis Letory had collapsed and had to be dragged up the steep slopes. Dick Adams, too, was weak, but somewhere near the Port de Siguer (2,378 metres/7,728 feet) they reached the top.[1247] It was too dangerous to continue in the dark and, when both guides admitted that never before had they experienced such appalling conditions, another night was spent in the mountains, this time under a snowy overhang.

Surviving an avalanche the frostbitten party slowly descended down the Valira del Norte to the isolated Andorran village of Lo Serrat (1,540 metres/5,053 feet), only to find that it was deserted because of the heavy snow. Pressing on, they arrived at a farmhouse at Llorts at about 3 a.m. on 14 February, and were taken in by the middle-aged couple, who evidently knew the guides. Letory, Adams, Trost and Penna had to be left at the farmhouse, all suffering from varying degrees of frostbite and exhaustion, while Embling, Canter, Robertson and the two guides went on to Escaldas on the morning of 16 February.

The guides returned to the farmhouse by car with a doctor to collect the other four, and took them to a small hotel in Escaldas. John Trost was, apparently, the worst affected of the four. Walking in bare feet for so long he had been oblivious to the severe lacerations caused by the sharp rocks. The freezing cold had stopped the blood from flowing, and his left foot had become infected. The doctor, Antonio de Barcia, who spoke no English, managed to converse with Penna in French, and provided some form of treatment for his patients, whose faith in him dwindled over time on account of his liking for the drink. When John Trost's foot became so severely infected with gangrene Dr de Barcia decided that he needed to cut away the infected flesh. One evening de Barcia came to the hotel with another man, apparently an anæsthetist, and with Penna's assistance as interpreter began the operation. Knocked out by ether, Trost's diseased flesh was cut away.

In the morning Cyril Penna, too, began to show signs of infection, and de Barcia considered that the immediate amputation of several toes on his left foot was necessary to save it from spreading. Having seen what the alcohol-loving doctor had done to Trost's foot, Penna was not keen on having him operate on his toes and demanded that he be taken to hospital, even if it meant being interned. This was done, and there a Professor Trias from Barcelona confirmed that there was no immediate need for any amputation, though it might be necessary eventually as one of his feet was in a bad way. It was only some weeks later, though, after more professional treatment from Professor Trias, that Penna was told that any amputation was no longer necessary but that some sort of surgery would be in the future.

Then, in a letter dated 4 March to Cyril Penna, John Trost confirmed that he was still in bad shape, that Louis Letory had been admitted to hospital and that Dick Adams still required treatment for his frostbite. It was apparent to Penna that urgent and proper medical attention was required for them all, but particularly for Trost and Letory, and so he asked Professor Trias for help. It was not long before a large American consular car arrived and, crossing into Spain, took the four patients to the British American hospital in Madrid, where they arrived on 11 March.

Embling, Canter, and Robertson left Escaldas by car on the morning of 17 February as far as Santa Juliá-de-Loría, and walked across the border into Spain with their guides. There was a minor problem when the guides discovered that the house for which they had been making was occupied by the Spanish police, but after two more nights in hiding, Mr Dorchy from the Barcelona consulate collected them in his car. On the morning of 21 February they were in Barcelona. Embling reached Gibraltar on 5 March, and flew back on 7/8 March,[1248] with Canter and Robertson following by ship on 8 March.

Delayed in Spain on account of his frostbite, Cyril Penna finally said goodbye to the staff at the British American hospital in Madrid on 15 April, when he and several others departed by bus for Gibraltar. At the checkpoint at La Linea on 16 April Spanish guards asked, routinely, to see all the passengers' papers. Only those of Sergeant Penna, the only one of British nationality aboard the bus, failed to satisfy the guards. Ordered off the vehicle he hobbled to a chair by the guardhouse, watching with mounting frustration as the bus proceeded to Gibraltar. A Canadian companion from the bus had gallantly elected to remain with Penna, and it was he who summoned the British Consul from Algéciras. Penna was allowed through, but not before words were exchanged with the guard commander.

After a further, short period of hospitalisation he boarded the troopship *Stirling Castle* late on 25 April, and reached Liverpool on 2 May. Admitted to the RAF hospital at West Mersey, his war was well and truly over. Despite all he had suffered, Penna was recommended for, and got, nothing for his evasion, except the subsequent disability pension from a grateful Air Ministry.

With German security forces slowly but surely gaining the upper hand, 1942 saw them cause grievous wounds to Comet and to the PAT/PAO line. Though Comet was always able to restore the line from Brussels to Paris and on to the Spanish border, Marseille had become too "hot" for Pat O'Leary and his clandestine activities, and at the end of November 1942 he was forced to move from Maud Baudot de Rouville's apartment (where based) to Toulouse (the Hôtel de Paris).

One place, however, where the long German arm could not reach, nor that of the *Organizzazione di Vigilanza Repressione dell'Antifascismo* (the OVRA, the Italian secret police), was the Vatican City, a neutral country within Italy, and the see of His Holiness the Pope. Not in their wildest dreams could two RAF Bomber Command airmen have imagined that at some time during the war they would not only get into the Vatican City itself but would also be granted an audience with the Pope himself.

Thirty-four-year-old Squadron Leader V.C. McAuley DFC, RCAF and Flight Sergeant F.K. Nightingale were navigator and mid-upper gunner respectively of Stirling bomber BF379 that failed to return from Turin on the evening of 11 December 1942. Due to haze over the target the pilot, Flight

Lieutenant W.T. Christie DFM, took BF379 down to 7,000 feet, where it was hit by flak and set on fire. Bombs and flares were jettisoned over Turin and course set for home to the south of the Alps. BF379 was losing height all the while until, over the Italian town of Cuneo some sixty-five kilometres short of the French border, Christie had no choice but to give the order to bale out.[1249]

McAuley's parachute failed to open properly, and he was knocked out as he hit the ground. Regaining consciousness in a ditch he discovered that he had dislocated his right shoulder: 'I had great difficulty in freeing myself from my parachute harness, and had not sufficient strength to conceal either my parachute or mae west… I could not get my tunic off, or remove my badges, but I managed to pull my trousers over my flying boots. In a short time I reached a canal about fifteen feet wide, with steep sides. I realised that in my condition I could not cross it. I threw my pistol into it, and sat down in a field close by.'[1250] Within an hour or so he was found by Italian soldiers, who took him away on a stretcher to a house, where an old woman gave him a glass of sherry. Thus fortified he was carried to a headquarters somewhere near Cuneo, and given 'some kind of anæsthetic' by a doctor.

During his interrogation he was told that the wireless operator, Flight Sergeant O. Falkingham DFM, had also been captured. Having met Falkingham in the morning, they had been sharing adjacent cells, though not permitted to converse, McAuley was again briefly interrogated, and informed that the Italians had now captured Flight Sergeant Nightingale and the bomb aimer, Flight Sergeant I.A. MacDonald. Taken to the military hospital at Fossano, thirty kilometres or so to the north, McAuley was X-rayed and his arm put in a cast. He was also told that Nightingale was in the same hospital.

Losing his flying boots as his parachute opened, Nightingale landed in a tree and broke his left ankle. Hobbling off with great difficulty in the direction of France he met MacDonald, who made a pair of crutches from some branches for his hapless comrade. After a few hours, though, Nightingale was too worn out to continue, and suggested that MacDonald should leave him, and take his escape aid box to supplement his own. MacDonald 'refused to leave me or to take my kit. We then lay up in some bushes.'[1251] Leaving in broad daylight on 12 December they were seen by some civilians, and an hour later captured by Italian soldiers. After a brief reunion with Falkingham and the flight engineer, Flight Sergeant J.G. Jeffrey, at an aerodrome, Nightingale was also taken to the Fossano hospital, where his leg was put in plaster.

On the evening of 22 December McAuley and Nightingale were taken by train from Fossano to Turin. While waiting at Turin station for an hour and a half for another train to Rome, 'some Italian soldiers came and shook their fists at us, and made various offensive remarks.' From Rome, the two injured airmen were taken to a 'decontamination and transit camp for RAF P/W' at Poggio Mirteto, some fifty kilometres north-east of Rome, which was administered by the Regia Aeronautica. Though segregated from the other prisoners of war, they nevertheless managed to catch a glimpse of their fellow crew before being transferred to the Regina Coeli prison's military hospital in Rome itself on 29 December 1942.[1252]

McAuley, who 'shared a room with a French major from Corsica named Boniface', discovered that it was possible to climb out of his window, information that was to prove more than useful when, on 20 March 1943, both he and Nightingale were warned that they were to be moved to a prisoner-of-war camp: 'We therefore began preparing to escape from the hospital to the Vatican City.'[1253]

The Italian guards kept a regular presence in the prisoners' rooms, but were getting slacker, and on 9 April all was ready for McAuley and Nightingale to escape. Going with them was a new arrival, thirty-six-year-old Company Quartermaster Sergeant William Cook, 1st Battalion, Parachute Regiment, who had been captured following a firefight with German Parachute men (*Fallschirmjäger*) on the road to Medjez-el-Bab, Tunisia, on 24 November 1942.

Cook was more than lucky to be alive. Confronted by the enemy his fighting patrol had been ordered by their commanding officer, Captain J.R.C. Stewart, to fight to the last man and to the last round. This they almost did. With ammunition practically exhausted and Captain Stewart among the dead,[1254] only Cook and four others were left standing, though Cook had taken a bullet through his body when the Germans mounted their final assault. The fight had not been one-sided, for Cook, a fluent German speaker, was informed that German casualties had been fifty-seven killed or wounded. Expecting to be shot out of hand, therefore, Cook asked a German lieutenant to 'hurry up with this unpleasant business.' The German officer 'seemed very upset, and actually burst into tears, saying "How could you think that I could do any such thing".'[1255]

In the event, the treatment of the British by their captors 'was very correct, and they dressed our wounds as soon as possible.' However, as Cook made his way to hospitals in Italy so his treatment deteriorated, but he was well enough to be taken to Campo 54 (Fara Sabina) on 31 December. He was well enough, too, to start a tunnel from the officers' latrines on about 14 February 1943, but it was discovered on 29 March before it could be used, and his punishment was thirty days' solitary confinement. His condition worsened so much, however, that within two days he was removed to the camp's hospital, and transferred to the Regina Coeli hospital on 4 April. There 'a Private Thomson of a Scottish regiment informed me of the presence of S/Ldr. McAuley and Sgt. Nightingale, and told me that McAuley was planning to escape.'[1256] Word of Cook's arrival was notified to McAuley by Leading Seaman F. Seaton,[1257] who also informed McAuley of Cook's resolve to join the escape.

Having collected boots and extra hospital clothes from other patients, a Lieutenant McKinnon sold them a shirt for eighty lire and a pair of old socks for six lire. McAuley had managed to hoard 200 lire, while Cook had 100, but Nightingale only eleven. McAuley 'also had a jack knife, which was bought from one of the guards'. On the night of Friday, 9 April the escapers' stores were hidden under McAuley's bed in readiness for the escape itself, which was scheduled to take place early on 10 April. The plan was to climb out of the window in McAuley's room, climb over the hospital wall, drop into the street on the other side and, with a good idea of how to get there, go to the Vatican City in the heart of Rome.[1258] McKinnon was to close the window after they had gone.

At about half past two on the morning of 10 April Cook and Nightingale 'made up their beds to look as if they were occupied and left the ward on the pretext of going to the lavatory. They then entered McAuley's room.' Donning their "civvies" they climbed out of the window that, as arranged, was then closed by another prisoner. Although they had to climb out of the window in what should have been full view of a guard, they reached the top of the hospital wall unseen. They had not, however, bargained for what they saw next – a drop to the road below of some twenty-five feet (seven-and-a-half metres). Deciding that Nightingale's ankle would be still too weak to take the impact of a landing from such a height, they reluctantly had to abandon the attempt, and regained their beds, again, without being spotted.

They determined to try again, this time using a home-made rope to get them down from the top of the high wall. The only "rope" available, however, was a hundred feet of string from Red Cross parcels, which was plaited by McKinnon. They also decided that their hob-nailed boots were too noisy and so, to extract the nails, "borrowed" the bayonet of a sleeping guard. As a further precaution bits of slipper were attached to the soles of their boots.

They were now ready for their second attempt, on 14 April. But when six new patients were brought in on 13 April it was feared that the guards would become more vigilant, and so it proved, for one of them noticed that a bar to McAuley's window was missing. Fortunately for the would-be escapers, though, the guard was on bad terms with his NCO, and as he could not be bothered to report the matter the escape went ahead as planned.

Safely over and down the outer wall the three men set off through the streets of Rome to the Vatican City. Failing to appreciate that it was on the other side of the River Tiber, Cook, in his best German accent, asked an Italian for directions, while the other two kept a discreet distance. In due course they reached their destination, and for ten minutes or so watched workers passing through the Porta Santa Anna into the Vatican buildings. Cook was volunteered to try his luck. Once through the Santa Anna gate he asked a Swiss guard, in French, if he were indeed Swiss. Receiving a reply in the affirmative, Cook told the guard who he was, and McAuley and Nightingale were called forward. A Vatican policeman was summoned, and took the men away to the police barracks.[1259]

They were fortunate to have reached the Vatican's sanctuary when they did for, even before Italy's capitulation in September 1943, Vatican authorities had 'sensed the danger of becoming a Mecca for escapers, and gave orders that all would-be internees should be forcibly expelled at the gates.'[1260] For the present, though, all was well, and after a visit from Mr Hugh Montgomery, First Secretary of the British Legation to the Holy See, they received fresh civilian clothes and shoes. On 25 April, His Holiness Pope Pius XII[1261] received them in audience and gave each his benediction (Cook was the only Roman Catholic), his good wishes and also a rosary. Papers for their repatriation were prepared, and on 7 June they were flown from Rome to Barcelona and Madrid, where they spent a night, before flying on to Lisbon on 8 June. Departing for England that night, they landed at Poole on the following morning.

By way of a footnote to this story, a so-called Rome Organisation had existed for some time with the purpose of helping escapers and evaders in the area of Rome itself and the surrounding countryside. By the time that Rome was liberated, on 4 June 1944, 'the Rome Organisation had on its books the names of 3,925 escapers and evaders, of whom 1,695 were British, 896 South African, 429 Russian, 425 Greek, 185 American, and the rest [295] from no fewer than twenty different countries. Fewer than 200 were billetted actually in Rome…'[1262]

The man most wanted by the Germans for his part in these activities was Monsignor Hugh O'Flaherty, an Irish priest who had been in Rome, on and off, since 1922.[1263] Ordained in December

1925, he had received the title of monsignor in 1934. It was, though, the Pope himself who, as war came to Europe, organised 'a chain of agents throughout Europe to gather news of prisoners of war, refugees, the unaccountable hordes of displaced and homeless',[1264] and it was he who appointed Monsignor O'Flaherty as his Papal Nuncio, or messenger, to the thousands of Allied prisoners of war in Italian camps in 1941.

By July 1943 there were some 74,000 known Allied prisoners of war in Italy. Following the Allied landings in Sicily and on the Italian mainland, many seized the opportunity to escape and to find their way to Rome. For Monsignor O'Flaherty it was the right and proper thing to do to help them, and many were smuggled by him past the Swiss Guards, the military guardians of the state, and into the Vatican City.[1265] Despite later orders from the Vatican Secretariat to the Swiss Guard to allow no one asking to be interned to enter the Vatican, and despite a constant watch by German secret police on the Vatican's several entrances, many an Allied escaper and evader, despite O'Flaherty's vehement dislike of the British, was to be grateful to the Irishman for his cunning and initiative in hiding them.

Somewhere in the dark sky over north-west France a Stirling bomber exploded on the evening of 23 January 1943. It was on its way back from Lorient at about 12,000 feet when a burst of flak shot away the controls of the port wing, and set the aircraft on fire. The pilot, Sergeant Robert Kidd RNZAF, gave the order to bale out just before the bomber disintegrated. He was the only survivor. 'I came down in a ploughed field about seven kilometres north-west of Morlaix. I must have been unconscious when I landed for, when I came to, I was lying face downwards in the centre of the field. I had broken my nose, but was otherwise uninjured.'[1266] Hearing voices speaking German nearby he looked up and saw eight or ten German soldiers about twenty-five metres away with their backs towards him. 'They were watching my aircraft burning about half a mile off, and were apparently billetted in an adjacent farm.'

Lying absolutely still for an hour or so, until the Germans had returned to the farm, he sat by a hedge for a further two hours before cautiously making off in a direction which he hoped was away from the heavily-defended coastal area. He was wise to be cautious for as he walked to Morlaix he twice passed German patrols, but was not seen. At daybreak on 24 January he spoke to a boy at an isolated farmhouse, who fetched his father. After managing to make himself understood to the farmer, a woman was summoned who could speak a little English, and he told her that he wanted to get to Nantes. She suggested that he should start walking along the railway running from Morlaix to Carhaix, as it was not guarded: 'About 2000 hours that night, 24 January, the farmer gave me a parcel of food and a bottle of brandy, and took me to the railway line. I walked along it all night, and about 0500 hours on 25 January I was near a village called Poullaouen.'[1267]

Now, very tired and with badly blistered feet, he called at another farmhouse. Unable to make himself understood, he was given only a glass of cider. He had more luck at a second farmhouse a kilometre or so down the road, where the farmer's daughter spoke 'fair English and told me that two of her brothers were prisoners of war in Germany. The farmer said that I could stay with him for as long as I wished. He gave me food, attended to my feet, and put me to bed.' They tried to get help for him, but were unsuccessful, though they were able to provide him with better civilian clothes than the ones he had been given earlier at Morlaix.

Early on the morning of 27 January another of the farmer's sons escorted him through Carhaix on the road to Pontivy. He had gone some ten kilometres from Carhaix when, near Quéhélen, 'an elderly man [M. Le Bec] touched me on the shoulder and said "RAF?" He then led me to the towpath of a canal and, pointing down it, said "Nantes". I walked along it, and in about half an hour a man on a bicycle overtook me, and made me understand that I was to go with him. He took me to his house near Quéhélen.' Again, his French hosts could not do enough for him, and offered to keep him there for the rest of the war, such was their generosity and courage. He remained with these people until 31 January, when a friend of the family, a tailor called "Joe", who had escaped from Poland, took him in Le Bec's car to Carhaix. Given a double-breasted suit in exchange for the RAF battledress that he had been wearing all this time, he was taken on 2 February to Gourin, 20 kilometres south of Carhaix.

Joining up with Technical Sergeant M.B. Jones USAAF,[1268] the local Resistance group had the two airmen in Paris on the morning of 4 February. They were off again next day to Tours with two more evaders, Technical Sergeant Arthur B. Cox USAAF (see previous chapter)[1269] and Flying Officer M.H.G. Wilson.[1270] Escorted over the Demarcation Line at Bléré (Indre-et-Loire), they caught the train to Toulouse. Arriving there at around 9 p.m. on 6 February, they were taken from the station to the Hôtel de Paris, and collected by Paul Ulmann, who took them to his house. While there they briefly met Sergeant Dawson and Flying Officer de Merode who were shortly to leave for Marseille. Pat O'Leary also paid them a visit.

On 19 February Guy [Berthet?] and Philippe Franc took Kidd and Jones by train to Perpignan, where they were met by Pat O'Leary and Nancy Fiocca. Also on the train were 'a Canadian of No.

7 Sqn, RAF, who had escaped from prison in Castres, and a number of Frenchmen.' Continuing towards Spain by train, it had been arranged that they would all jump off it just before it pulled in to Banyuls station. Most of them managed to do this, but someone saw them and raised the alarm. Challenges in German were followed by rifle shots as the party rapidly dispersed, but the Canadian and two of the Frenchmen[1271] were caught. Now thoroughly roused the Germans conducted a wide-spread search of the area, and apparently caught a further twenty-three evaders of various nationalities. Also caught next day, 20 February, was Guy.

Unable now to cross the Pyrenees, especially as their guide had failed to make the rendezvous, the remnants of the party retreated to Perpignan on 22 February, and were taken by Madame Lebreton to the Hôtel du Tennis at Canet-Plage (see Chapter 5). Kidd noted that Madame Lebreton 'was supposed to be collaborating with the Germans, and was therefore most unpopular locally. In reality she and her husband were helping Pat [O'Leary].'

Kidd, Jones, Cox, and Maurice Wilson left for Marseille on 25 February with Pat O'Leary, Nancy and Philippe Franc, arriving there on the following day. They were taken to Maud Baudot de Rouville's flat, but unfortunately were seen on the staircase by the manager of the apartment block, who lived on the sixth floor. He was fiercely anti-British and, worse, a member of the hated Milice.

With everyone keeping their heads down following the spate of arrests of members of the PAO line, it was not until 19 March, two weeks after Pat O'Leary's arrest, that it was decided to move the airmen again. Details of what happened to Cox hereafter are scarce, except that, as seen in the previous chapter, he had reached Spain safely by 15 May 1943.[1272] Maurice Wilson went to Nice for a week or so, before leaving on 10 March for Grenoble (one month) and thence to Toulouse. Leaving Toulouse on 10 June he spent two nights in Perpignan but was captured in a Gestapo ambush near le Boulou on the night of 12/13 June 1943 on the way to the Pyrenees (see this chapter below).

As for Kidd, Jones, Wayne Roper, Nancy Fiocca, and Danielle "Eddie" Reddé, they were escorted by Françoise Dissard's lieutenant, Bernard, by train from Marseille to Perpignan. After five days in the town the three airmen, plus Nancy, Philippe Franc, "Bernard",[1273] "Ronnie" (otherwise Renée Nouveau), "Eddie", and two Belgians 'left in a truck laden with charcoal for Ceret'.

Hiding in some bushes outside Céret until dark, they were joined by two guides and by a Spaniard named Juan who was, so Kidd understood, 'a prominent member of an organisation in this district'. Early on the morning of 25 March the party crossed the border into Spain. Juan left them at a house near the village of Tortellá, a dozen kilometres south of the French border and some forty west of Figueras, while he went on to Barcelona to inform the consulate of their arrival. Juan was back at Tortellá when, on 30 March, they were surrounded by civil guards. Bernard, Eddie, and one of the Belgians escaped, but the others were arrested. Handcuffed, the prisoners were made to walk the few kilometres to Besalú, 'where we were all confined in the same room under horrible conditions. Here the mayor, who had been in America, questioned us in English.' Having been advised by the guide to say that they were Americans who had escaped from German hands, Kidd, without answering any of the mayor's questions, maintained that he was 'a member of the USAAF'.

Nancy and Renée were allowed to go to a hotel, but on the following day, 2 April, handcuffed again, they were all put in a truck with an armed escort and driven to Gerona. Along the way, though, Kidd managed to work his 'handcuffs loose with a pin. Juan also managed to free himself. He then jumped off the truck and got clear away.' The others reached Gerona police station that afternoon, and were asked similar questions to those of the mayor of Besalú. It was not long before a representative from the American Consulate in Barcelona arrived and they were allowed, on parole, to go to a hotel. Nancy and Renée were taken to Barcelona on 6 April, but it was not until 14 April that a Spanish Air Force officer took Kidd and the two Americans by car to a hotel at Alhama de Aragon, where they stayed until 5 May. From Alhama they were driven to Madrid and to Gibraltar, which they reached on 7 May. After a wait of ten days, Kidd was flown back to England on 18 May 1943. Nancy Fiocca sailed from Gibraltar, reaching Gourock on 17 June 1943.[1274]

Embling's navigator, Flying Officer Alfred Roy Haines RCAF, landed near Guise (Aisne) at around 6 a.m. on the morning of 3 December 1942. Having spent the night in a wood, he ate some chocolate and Horlicks tablets (from his escape-aid box) in an isolated and unoccupied building, and then came face to face with an elderly Frenchman, the owner of the building, who told him 'that on the previous day two other RAF aviators had sheltered in the same buildings… He did not know where they had gone afterwards. He also told me that four members of their crew had been killed when the aircraft crashed.'[1275]

Given a little food by the Frenchman, Haines set off in the cold and the rain until, nearing midnight on 5/6 December, he saw a light in a house. When his knock was answered he declared himself to be RAF, and was admitted to the warmth of a Polish family's house. Given some more 'food, a civilian coat, and a beret' they told him that two of his crew had been captured and that the Germans 'were still looking for any possible survivors' from their aircraft. One of the family thereupon escorted him to the River Oise, with the warning that there might be a German sentry on the bridge over the canal at Tergnie. There was no sentry, and Haines crossed without alarm. He recrossed the Oise on 7 December at Compiègne, and saw a number of German troops there, this time with 'a sentry on the bridge, but he did not stop me.'

Deciding to walk to Paris, he was so tired and hungry that, next day, he called at the house of M. and Mme. Mailly for help, and was not refused. After dark he was taken to stay the night at another house, at la Chapelle-en-Serval, ten kilometres or so south of Senlis. In the morning his feet were so swollen that he was unable to put on his shoes, and so spent another night in the house. On 10 December M. Mailly drove him by car to Chantilly – 'full of Germans' – where he was given civilian clothing, and eventually helped on his way south by "an organisation". He left Paris on Christmas Day and, after several stops, had reached Lourdes on 29 December.

Here the American Red Cross still flourished, and a Mr Tuck and Colonel Scott gave Haines what help they could. On 6 January 1943, though, 'between thirty and forty Gestapo and Military police came to Lourdes'. Haines was told that they had come 'to suppress the traffic in evaders for which Lourdes had become notorious, and to investigate very closely the activities of the American Red Cross there.'[1276] Before coming under close surveillance, however, the Red Cross had managed to give Haines 3,000 francs, on top of the 2,000 francs that he had already been given by each of two Frenchmen, Lieutenant Pierre Brifaut and Guy Magnant. On 11 January M. Romain, of the Hôtel Londres et Gallia, warned Haines and his two French "financiers" that the Germans were about to check up on all people staying in the hotels in Lourdes. Brifaut, Magnant and Haines therefore caught the afternoon train for Pau, Oloron-Ste Marie and Tardets-Sorholus.

With their guides, they crossed into Spain near the Pic d'Orhy (2,017 metres/6,555 feet) on 22/23 January 1943 with an English girl, Miss Georgette Robinson, and two French pilots, Jules Joire and Guilleminot le Bel, but at the village of Irati they were arrested 'about 1530 hours by Spanish "carabineros", who confiscated our foreign money'. Taken on 24 January to Abaurrea Alta, they stayed the night in 'a primitive hotel'. Next day they went by bus to Aoiz and then by electric tram to Pamplona, where they were 'handed over to the civil police. Miss Robinson was sent to a hotel, but the rest of us were taken to the civil prison.'

Georgette Robinson managed to notify the British vice-consul at Barcelona of Haines's predicament, and on 30 January he was removed from the prison, 'with about twenty-five other internees', to a hotel at Betelu. A fortnight later he was on his way 'to Madrid in a Red Cross lorry, with fifteen Frenchmen', and on 16 February left by car for Seville, where he stayed with a Mr Cairns. Four days later he sailed on the SS *Saltwick*[1277] for Gibraltar, which he reached at about midnight on 20/21 February 1943. Four days later he landed at RAF Portreath in a B-17, together with Flight Sergeant W.W. Drechsler RCAF. Haines was detained in hospital at Portreath, while Drechsler was escorted to the London District Transit Camp[1278] at the Great Central Hotel, Marylebone Station, London.

After they had reached Bordeaux towards the end of April 1943 Sergeants D.L. Jones and J. Alderdice found themselves using one of the more unusual forms of transport – the canal barge. A fortnight earlier, on the night of 16/17 April 1943 attacking the Škoda works, Pilsen, their Halifax was hit twice by a night-fighter while still over northern France on the way out. Continuing until a few kilometres south of Mannheim, Germany, calculations showed that there was insufficient fuel left to get to the Czechoslovakian target and home. Dropping their bombs on a railway, they set course for England but, over northern France again, the fuel ran out. The skipper, Sergeant J.E. McCrea, ordered the crew to bale out.[1279]

Jones and Alderdice landed on the Luftwaffe's Laon-Athies airfield, Jones breaking two teeth in the process, while Alderdice banged his head on a brick which knocked him silly for a while, 'spending a considerable time in searching for locker keys and the exact sum of 3/4d. which had fallen from my trouser pocket.'[1280] He and Jones met up in the nearby village of Gizy (Aisne). The idea put to them by their French helpers that they should make for Switzerland appealed to neither of them, and so they asked the Frenchmen to buy them tickets for Paris, where they arrived on the evening of 19 April.

Catching the overnight train they were in Bordeaux, in the forbidden coastal zone, by 7.30 a.m. on the following day. Needing to cross the River Garonne to reach the Unoccupied Zone, and seeing that the bridges over the river were heavily guarded, they therefore planned to get a boat to Toulouse. Still wearing their RAF uniforms they approached a likely-looking boatman, who introduced them to Desiré Larose. Larose agreed to take them on his barge, the *Jane Henriette*, and they left on 22 April, but not before Alderdice's conspicuous red hair had been dyed to make him less obvious. The voyage was interrupted at Langon (Gironde) on 23 April, when German officers examined the boat's papers while the two airmen hid themselves among the merchandise. A few kilometres past Langon, at Castets-en-Dorthe, the barge left the river and proceeded along all 193 kilometres of the *Canal Latéral à la Garonne* to Toulouse, arriving there on or about 4 May.

Having been in the hands of an organisation since Bordeaux, they were well looked after for the next seven weeks. During this time they learnt 'that an RAF man named James Taylor… was in the hands of the French authorities in Castres prison', apparently being kept there to hide him from the Germans.[1281] Also coming across Private Ellis Phythian, 4th Cheshire Regiment, who had escaped from a prisoner-of-war camp in Poland, the three of them were taken by a removal van to Tarbes on 25 June, together with a young Frenchman from the north by the name of Charles Antoine d'Andleau. After they had been stopped by a gendarme and sent back to Tarbes, they tried again on the following day, and succeeded in reaching Pau without further incident. D'Andleau briefly left them.

The party was finally assembled at Luz-St Sauveur and taken to a rendezvous with a Basque guide. In the hills they met d'Andleau with a group of Frenchmen, and crossed into Spain to the east of Gavarnie on the morning of 2 July. Following the River Cinca along the Vallée de Pinède, having detached the French group, they were on their way to Espierba on the afternoon of 3 July when apprehended by a carabinero. The Spaniard took them to Bielsa, where Alderdice was able to post letters to both 'the British and American consuls in Madrid'. Two days later they were removed to the prison at Barbastro and, confined in appalling conditions, 'Jones, Phythian, and d'Andleau became very ill'. Another letter was delivered to the British ambassador in Madrid 'by means of a French Red Cross agent', but nothing came of this in the immediate future for, on 21 July, d'Andleau and Phythian were sent to Miranda de Ebro. What happened to d'Andleau is not known, but Ellis Phythian was back in England by the end of the second week of September 1943.

With wheels being set in motion on their behalf, however, the two airmen were visited at Barbastro on 27 July by a Captain Coborn, and on 6 August Group Captain Vincer drove them to Madrid. Five days later they took the train to Gibraltar, and were flown back to England in the middle of the month. Recommended for a Mention in Despatches, they were instead rewarded with the DFM, gazetted on 1 October 1943, with the modest citation: 'In air operations, these airmen have displayed great courage and fortitude setting an example of the highest order.'[1282]

With German security forces in France pulling tight the noose around the neck of escape lines, life for all helpers and evaders was becoming increasingly difficult. One airman who came close to being caught was Frenchman Capitaine (acting Squadron Leader) J.H. Schloesing FAF, shot down on Circus 262 on 13 February 1943 near Le Boisle with burns to his face. He was found by the Abbé Papillon, who passed him on to a Madame Tellier while the abbé's sister went to Paris. There she met Schloesing's sister, who provided the abbé with some of her brother's clothes. Schloesing's cousin, Jacques Bruston, who worked at a factory where he received a petrol allowance from the Germans, took Schloesing to stay with an uncle and aunt until 1 March. Both, however, as their nephew said, were 'very old and, while absolutely loyal to me and to the Allied cause, are not altogether discreet.'[1283]

Schloesing therefore went to see his sister in Paris, who had already contacted Robert Aylé, 'a prominent member of an organisation [Comet] working for the benefit of RAF evaders'. Aylé took Schloesing to stay with a Dr Tinel, who told him that 'he had just sheltered an American pilot passing by the name of "Second Lieutenant Aubert Simoniz" which I presumed to be his false name.' On 21 March, Robert Aylé produced an identity card for Schloesing, that enabled him now to 'walk about Paris openly. I met M. Aylé very often at his house in 67 rue de Babylon, and also some RAF pilots, whose names I do not remember. M. Aylé told me that his organisation had between seventy and eighty Englishmen still in hiding in France.'

One of these "Englishmen" was a PRU pilot, whose Spitfire had been shot down over Holland sometime in the middle of February. 'He had been staying with a Mme. Jeannot at 16 Avenue d'Eylau, Paris. Mme. Jeannot is a young woman whose husband is P/W in Germany.' Unfortunately for the PRU pilot he would be joining M. Jeannot as a prisoner of war in Germany before too long. On 12 April Schloesing and a Belgian guide, "William" (otherwise known as Jean-François Nothomb), who had the PRU pilot with him, went to the Gare d'Austerlitz and boarded the train for Bayonne. William and the Englishman sat in one compartment, Schloesing in another. 'The train was scheduled to leave at 2130 hours. It did not do so, and when we inquired the reason, we found that it was surrounded by German troops.' A French-speaking German boarded the train, and inspected Schloesing's cards and papers before moving into the next compartment. He approved William's papers, then turned to the English pilot and asked him if he spoke German. He replied in passable French that he could not speak German. The German asked him a second question, in English: 'Can you speak English?', to which he received no reply. A third question – 'Where is your comrade?' – elicited the response that he did not understand as he did not have a comrade with him. 'He was then taken out of the train and handed over to the German soldiers. Shortly afterwards the train left.'

Between Bordeaux and Bayonne there were two further controls, but each time Schloesing's papers passed muster. He and William arrived at Bayonne at 9.30 a.m. on 13 April, but if they thought that they were through with controls they were mistaken, for there were two more on the station platform. Surviving these, they left the station separately, though Schloesing followed Nothomb to a house that 'appeared to be occupied by a Mme. de Greef… a member of M. Aylé's organisation.' That evening Schloesing caught the train to St Jean-de-Luz, where he was met at the station by Nothomb, who had cycled there earlier.

After dark they walked to a house in Ciboure, where Schloesing stayed until the evening of 15 April, when he, Nothomb, and four French airmen set off for the Pyrenees with two guides, Florentino Goïcoechea and Pachi.[1284] They forded the River Bidassoa 'at about 0200 hours on 16 April. We saw no guards on the river banks. We then walked to Oyarzun. We arrived at Oyarzun at 0545 hours, which William said was a record for the trip… We then walked to Renteria.' Catching the tram to San Sebastián, they 'went to the house of a Spanish helper named Frederico', who alerted the British Consulate of their arrival.[1285]

Despite the glow of pride at the brilliant execution of Garrow's recovery (see Chapter 4), alarm bells started to ring in Room 900 when, not long after he had radioed to London that the Scotsman was on his way to Spain, Tom Groome failed to transmit at the pre-arranged time. A fortnight later, in Room 900, Jimmy Langley and Airey Neave discussed 'a decoded message requesting a parachute drop of arms and money to the Toulouse area'.[1286] It was marked 'Security check not given', and was purportedly from Groome. To the two MI9 officers, the deliberate omission of this vital check was the signal that all was not well, and could only mean that Groome was in German hands. They were right.

After Garrow's rescue, to keep one step ahead of the Germans and their radio detector vans, Groome had moved in with the Cheramy family at 13, rue de la Fraternité, Montauban, some fifty kilometres north of Toulouse. To keep in contact with Pat O'Leary Groome used 'a young French girl, a telephonist, named Reddé as a messenger to take decoded messages to room 202 in the Hotel de Paris at Toulouse, and return with O'Leary's reply for transmission to London.'[1287] According to Maud Baudot de Rouville, Groome was denounced by a Jew from Montauban for 20,000 francs[1288] but, true or not, German security forces caught Groome and Danielle "Edith" Reddé in the middle of a transmission to London at the Cheramy's house on 11 January 1943. With a pistol to his back Groome complied with the order to finish the message, but had the wit to leave out the vital security check. He, Reddé, Charles and Pat Cheramy were led away in handcuffs to the Gestapo headquarters in Toulouse. Their eighteen-month-old son Michel was taken, too, but the Germans allowed his paternal grandfather to come and take him away.[1289]

Groome was pushed into a room on the second floor of the building, where the interrogator's first words were to tell him that their detector vans had been listening to his transmissions for two months. With a desperate situation calling for desperate measures, Groome launched himself through the window to the street some ten metres below. Suffering nothing worse than a badly sprained ankle, he was able to put some distance between himself and his pursuers, until a passer-by gave him away to the Gestapo. Dragged back to their headquarters for further torture and interrogation, the Gestapo eventually sent him to Fresnes prison, Paris.

Forgotten in the furious pursuit of Groome was Edith Reddé who, left unguarded, simply walked out of the Gestapo headquarters. Making her way to the Hôtel de Paris, she reported the catastrophe to O'Leary, who told her to go to Françoise Dissard's apartment.

Then, in early February 1943, Louis Nouveau received a letter from O'Leary asking him to come to Toulouse at once. Louis had been persuaded by Pat to leave Marseille for Paris, while his wife, Renée, had gone to hide out with Françoise Dissard in Toulouse. Taking the opportunity to move five Americans from a B-17 bomber that had crashed in Brittany, Nouveau arranged to meet Roger le Neveu, Jean de la Olla and Norbert Fillerin at the Gare d'Austerlitz, Paris. Unable to get the necessary cards for admission to the railway station, le Neveu said that *he* could get them, and rushed off. He was soon back with the cards, and Nouveau and the five Americans were on their way. At St Pierre-des-Corps, outside Tours, they changed trains, and were waiting to leave when the carriage door suddenly opened. Nouveau felt a punch in the back followed by the command, in an unmistakeable German accent, to put up his hands.

Louis Nouveau, betrayed to the Germans by le Neveu (see previous chapter), had already discussed with Jean de la Olla and Norbert Fillerin a request by le Neveu to join PAO but, despite

Fillerin's strong doubts, le Neveu was given the benefit of the doubt and had been allowed to escort a number of airmen from Paris to Marseille. He was given a second group of airmen, Australians, to move south, but returned early with the story that the airmen had been arrested and that he had escaped by some trick or other. Louis Nouveau still had his doubts about the man, but these were allayed somewhat after he, le Neveu, had safely escorted four more airmen to the south of France.

News of Nouveau's arrest reached Pat O'Leary in Toulouse within twenty-four hours. That there was a rotten apple in the barrel was clear, and as to who it was he would soon find out, but not before Dr Georges Rodocanachi, too, had been arrested. It is not known why, at 6 o'clock on the morning of 26 February 1943, two Gestapo officers and six men burst into his Marseille flat,[1290] but it may simply have been because someone had reported him for his pro-British attitude. He was removed, firstly, to St Pierre prison in Marseille, and then, on 17 December 1943, to a prison at Compiègne. On 17 January 1944 he was taken to Buchenwald concentration camp, where he died early on the afternoon of 10 February.

Then Pat O'Leary was betrayed. Two evading airmen would get to hear of his arrest sooner than most. On the night of 19/20 February 1943 the eight crew of Halifax W1012, 138 (Special Duties) Squadron, were engaged on triple operation Burgundy/Director 24/ Buttercup 2. With low mist preventing the crew from being able to pinpoint one of the drop zones (a field several kilometres to the north of Bourg-en-Bresse, France) the pilot aborted the mission. Flying low on the return journey W1012 was shot down by light flak, and came to earth on the Plaine de Sorigny, between Sorigny and St Branchs (Indre-et-Loire) some twenty kilometres south-east of Tours.

Also on board W1012 was the French BCRA agent Burgundy, who was to have been parachuted into France on behalf of SOE/SIS. Having survived the crash-landing Burgundy took the airmen to unoccupied farm buildings belonging to Roger and Marcelle Bodineau, who had three sons, Raoul (aged sixteen), Daniel (fifteen) and Max (twenty-seven months), at Larçay (Indre-et-Loire), a couple of kilometres east of Tours. Leaving the airmen in good hands, Burgundy said that he would be back within forty-eight hours but, if not, they were to share out the 20,000 francs that he left with them and go to the Hôtel de Paris in Toulouse. With the forty-eight hours up and no sign of the French agent, the crew shared out the money and set off for Toulouse in pairs.

As for Burgundy, otherwise Lieutenant Georges Broussine (see previous chapter), he made his way to Paris on that night of 19/20 February 1943, coincidentally his twenty-fifth birthday. After two nights with friends and family, he set off to contact the Brandy organisation in Lyon, as instructed. Meeting up with its chief, Maurice Montet, they arranged between them to mount an operation to rescue the eight airmen at the Bodineaus' farm. Returning to Larçay with Hugues de Lestang-Parade of the Brandy line, Broussine was shocked to learn that the airmen had already left on their own initiative, and was even more shocked to learn later that all eight had been taken prisoner. Disappointed, he and de Lestang-Parade returned to Lyon. In due course Broussine made his way back to Paris and, with the help of his trusted friends, began to establish the *réseau d'Evasion Bourgogne* (Burgundy escape line), from Brittany through Andorra in the Pyrenees to Spain. Two months later, in April 1943, Burgundy guided its first three airmen to safety in Andorra, escorted by Claude Leclerc as far as Foix.

For Roger Bodineau, however, after Broussine's departure, there was the small matter of what to do with the eight airmen on his farm. Having enlisted the help of the teacher at Larçay and of the secretary of the town hall at Véretz, a short distance away, they were able to provide, albeit with some difficulty, shoes and clothes for the men. At around 3 a.m. on the intensely cold morning of 24 February 1943 (the temperature was reported to have been *minus* 15° Centigrade), Roger Bodineau led them across the Demarcation Line at Athée-sur-Cher, half a dozen kilometres away.

The pilot, Pilot Officer P. Kingsford-Smith RAAF, and second pilot, Flying Officer R.C. Hogg, travelled together. In the Forêt de Loches, to the east of Loches itself, at a château they met 'two French ladies who spoke English... They took all our particulars and we stayed there for five days… One of these ladies was in an organisation receiving stuff dropped from the air. Her son had been dropped from England some time before at that place.' After five days two escorts took them by bicycle to a little station to the south-east of Loches. Tickets were bought by the escorts and, after changing trains at Châteauroux, the four men arrived at Toulouse that evening, only to learn that the owner of the Hôtel de Paris had been arrested. Flying Officer Hogg reported:

> 'We spent the next two nights with a student and his girlfriend. I do not know their names. They were previous acquaintances of our companions but the meeting seemed to be unexpected. Next day we were handed over to a Frenchman married to an American woman "Jane". That night we stayed at their house, on a road near the canal. There we found an American airman, Second Lieutenant Dominic

> Lazzaro. At this house there were also several Frenchmen who had escaped from French concentration camps. Kingsford-Smith and I remained at home with this Frenchman and his wife that evening. A big party was being given elsewhere by or to these French escapees and the Americans.
>
> 'The next morning Paul left the house at about the time the revellers were returning. About midday a woman came to the house, very excited, and screamed that all the members of the organisation, including Paul and Pat, had been arrested at a café. I had heard talk of Pat being the man who would get us over the border.'[1291]

It was not to be, for Hogg and Kingsford-Smith were captured a few days later by French police and handed over to the Germans. They spent the rest of the war in prisoner-of-war camps in Germany, as did the other six of their crew, and 2nd Lieutenant Lazzaro USAAF.[1292]

On 1 March 1943 Pat O'Leary returned to Toulouse from Marseille, where he and Albert Leçuyras had been staying in Maud Baudot de Rouville's apartment. With a smile and a wave of the hand Pat said 'A Mardi, Albert' ('Until Tuesday, Albert'), and was gone. Urgently needing to speak with Françoise Dissard, even though it was three o'clock in the morning, he went to her home, in effect now the headquarters of the escape line. She brought Pat up to date with the news, and then advised him to get some sleep, not at her house, which was already full with Nancy Fiocca, Renée Nouveau and three airmen, but at the secret apartment at 18, rue des Puits Clos that she had rented for him at the end of January.

She also had in her care, or had recently had, 'ten men – American and Canadian servicemen, a big man from Nîmes called Gaston and one of the guards himself'[1293] who had been "sprung" from the prison at Castres. When Françoise learnt that one of the guards there, Raymond (or Robert), was sympathetic to their cause, and to General de Gaulle, she got him to drug some wine and to give it to the other guards on duty. When they were "under", Raymond released those to be rescued and escorted them to a waiting van.

At 9 a.m. on 2 March Paul Ulmann called on Françoise, and asked her to pass the message on to Pat that he had arranged three appointments for him later in the day, first at the Café de la Paix at noon for a meeting with the guides from Perpignan; then to the Super Bar at 12.30 p.m. to meet Roger le Neveu; and, finally, to the Café Glacier at 3 p.m. for a meeting with Géo de Loches. As arranged, Paul called again at Françoise's house at 11.30 a.m. to collect Pat, who told Françoise that he would be back at 1.30 p.m. to take Renée Nouveau and "Bernard" to lunch.

From the Café de la Paix the two men made their way to the small Super Bar on the rue d'Alsace-Lorraine. As they approached the bar Ulmann remarked that he didn't like the look of two men lurking about in the street. O'Leary 'saw nothing suspicious, remembered his gun strapped under his armpit and his eagerness to hear Roger's news and shrugged his shoulders: "I think it's all right."'[1294] Several other customers, and Roger le Neveu, were there. Straight to the point, O'Leary asked him who it was who was giving them away in Paris. No sooner had Roger replied that he knew the man perfectly well than O'Leary felt the cold, hard nose of a gun pressed into his neck. At the same moment the other "customers" revealed themselves as German agents. Counting six guns pointing in his direction, O'Leary was led away to the nearby Grand Hôtel et Tivollier on the rue de Metz, where his interrogation began.

Taken to St Pierre prison,[1295] Marseille, Pat O'Leary was seen by a *passeur*, Antoine, being marched along the Cannebière by four German officers. A soldier was following with a suitcase. From Marseille Pat was taken to Fresnes prison, where he caught up with Tom Groome who had been arrested two months earlier. The Gestapo got to work on Pat, for a fortnight, but neither he, nor Groome, would disclose any relevant information nor reveal the names of the other members of their organisation. Giving up, the Gestapo sent them to the extermination camp at Struthof-Natzweiler near Schirmeck (Alsace).[1296]

They were still there at the beginning of July 1944 when Pat saw the commandant's car arrive. That in itself was a rarity and cause for comment, but even more remarkable were the four women passengers who stepped out of the car. Women were rarely, if ever, seen in the camp, and when word got out that they were English, Pat, known for his Resistance work, was informed. He managed to call to the women who were in another block, and made the briefest of contact with one of them, establishing that they were English and French. Then they disappeared. On 6 July 1944 the four women – Andrée Borrel, Diana Rowden, Vera Leigh, and Sonia Olschanesky – who had been working in France for SOE, were cold-bloodedly killed 'by injection followed by cremation, in circumstances which gave rise to suspicions whether or not the victims were dead or even unconscious when they were put into the crematorium oven.'[1297]

As the Americans began to claw their way across France in August 1944, O'Leary and Groome were moved to Mauthausen and Dachau concentration camps, from which awful places both men would somehow return alive.

Aware of the probability that something had gone wrong when Pat O'Leary had not turned up as expected, Françoise Dissard told Bernard to try all three of Pat's venues to see if he could find him. Bernard was soon back with the news of the raid at the Super Bar and, when Imelda Ulmann telephoned Françoise to say that Paul had not returned either, Françoise realised that all three – Pat, Paul, and Roger le Neveu – had been arrested.

Albert Leçuyras, now *de facto* chief of the PAO line, arrived from Marseille during the night of 2/3 March and, fearing further raids by the Gestapo, agreed with Françoise to send Nancy Fiocca to another safe house, at 46, Route d'Espagne, Toulouse, and to take Renée Nouveau and some airmen to Bergerac. They left at 3 o'clock in the morning. Albert then made sure that Imelda Ulmann and her daughter, Rolande, were safe, before telling Bernard to take Nancy to Marseille and leaving himself for Paris to warn the organisation there.

Françoise remained in Bergerac until matters had quietened down, for member after member of the PAO organisation had or were being arrested, among them Jean de la Olla, Jacques Wattebled, Fabien de Cortes and the Martins with others in Marseille, and more elsewhere. Albert Leçuyras himself only escaped capture by the narrowest of margins. Returning to his lodgings at the Martins' house at Endoume, Marseille, he would have fallen into the arms of the waiting Gestapo had it not been for the Martin children shouting a warning to him. Just in time, he was able to escape to Spain.[1298]

The PAO line was not the only clandestine organisation operating in Toulouse at this time and which was to suffer losses, as Flight Lieutenant Allan M. Ogilvie DFC, RCAF (navigator) and Sergeant Ralph Henderson (flight engineer) were to discover a week or so after their Lancaster had been shot down on 11/12 March 1943. Meeting up in the village of Blaise-sous-Arzillières (Marne) in eastern France shortly after the Lancaster's demise – caused by an extraordinarily persistent Me109 which attacked the Lancaster some seven times[1299] – Ogilvie and Henderson were taken into the country to see 'a M. Collard, who had been an interpreter with the RAF in 1940. With him was his cousin [Jean] Verrier.'[1300] Collard gave them 'the name and address of Mme. Bardoux, Café Fregat, Toulouse, whom he said would help us.' From nearby Vitry-le-François the airmen were taken by Verrier to Paris by train. On 17 March they walked across the Demarcation Line (the River Cher at this point), from Marmagne to Chârost, and then by train to Toulouse.

Arriving there on the morning of 18 March they found their way to the Café Fregat, and met Madame Bardoux, an Englishwoman married to a Frenchman, with two children. To Allan Ogilvie's eyes she was a vision of loveliness, 'a beautiful woman, with a lovely figure; dark hair and perfect features – one of the best looking women I have ever seen.'[1301] Beautiful she may have been but she was also, as she herself told the two airmen, suspected by the Gestapo, adding 'that her café had already been searched several times by the Germans. For this reason she said it would not be safe for other evaders to avail themselves of her services.' She, therefore, arranged for them to stay with a Monsieur Collaine in his apartment at 14, rue Temponière, in the centre of the town.

Monsieur Collaine 'knew of an organisation working under a man known as "Eugene". This man was said to be a British agent.' Indeed he was, for Eugène, otherwise Maurice Pertschuk, had worked for the Political Warfare Executive (PWE) until taken over by SOE, who had sent him to Toulouse in April 1942 to organise the Prunus circuit. Though still only twenty when he arrived, he 'turned out to have qualities of imaginative audacity that made him a remarkable clandestine organiser.'[1302] A busy man, Pertschuk nevertheless found time to visit Ogilvie and Henderson, gave them each 1,000 francs, and arranged for them to be escorted well to the north of Toulouse for their own safety. 'On 29 March an unknown helper took us to a farmhouse owned by a man called Leven, at Lavilledieu [*sic*], about twenty kilometres west of Montauban.'[1303] Here, at la Ville-Dieu-du-Temple (Tarn-et-Garonne), Leven, clearly a member of the Prunus circuit, got in touch with London, who told him to send the airmen to an address in Pau. Before he could do so, however, Pertschuk appeared, early in April, to tell them that it was too dangerous to risk sending them.

Then Leven received a coded letter summoning him to Toulouse. When he returned, the two airmen could see from his face that something awful had happened. It transpired that Pertschuk and his wireless operator, Marcus Bloom, had been arrested, together with others of their circuit. Leven himself had narrowly escaped capture and now intended to lie low. In any event, he said, it was the end of Prunus. The exact date of these arrests is uncertain, but it was either 12 or 13 April 1943.

However dangerous life had now become in Toulouse, Leven took Ogilvie and Henderson back to the Collaines house on 21 April, and arranged for their passage across the Pyrenees. As the snow in the mountains was still too deep they had to wait at St Girons from 22 April until the night of 26/27 April when, with twelve others, they passed through Seix en route for the border: 'On the morning of 28 April we crossed the Spanish frontier.' Directing them to the village of Alos de Isil, the guides left them to their fate. Ogilvie and Henderson, with five companions, were arrested by carabineros on arrival. Telling their captors their true identity, but saying that they were escaped prisoners of war, the two airmen were well treated. After a night in a hotel, they were escorted to Esterri-de-Anéu and thence to Sort. Handed over to the Guardia Civil, they were then taken by bus to Lérida, and put in the civil prison.

Wheels were already in motion for their release, but it was not until 15 May that a Spanish Air Force officer took them by car to Alhama de Aragon. Next day Michael Creswell paid them a visit, and five days later they were in Gibraltar.

Henderson remustered as a pilot officer, and learnt to fly a Lancaster. On the night of 22/23 November 1943, he and all his crew were killed when Lancaster JB424 was shot down over Berlin. Nor did Lieutenant Maurice Pertschuk MBE survive. A victim of the Nazis, he was hanged at Buchenwald concentration camp on 29 March 1945. Lieutenant Marcus Bloom was also murdered, at Mauthausen on 6 September 1944. Allan Ogilvie, though, survived the war having been in the very first group of Newfoundlanders to enlist in the RAF in August 1940.

Françoise, meanwhile, appreciating that the organisation was for the moment all but finished, decided to continue running affairs and arranged for the last of the members and evaders to be gathered up from Bergerac, Marseille and Nice. She also helped the last party, including Albert Leçuyras and Georges Zarifi, to leave Marseille on 22 April 1943. Having crossed the Spanish frontier early on the morning of 28 April, they were immediately deserted by their guide. Arrested and imprisoned in the usual dirty and disgusting prisons and ending up at the Miranda de Ebro camp, they were released on 16 August 1943.

Around this time, Fabien de Cortes and Pat O'Leary were being moved to Paris from the St Pierre prison, Marseille. With Pat's help Fabien jumped off the train as it neared Paris, and managed to get to Lyon. From there he notified Françoise, who went to Lyon and took him with her to Switzerland to see "Uncle François", Victor Farrell,[1304] the British vice-consul, to give him all the information that Pat had passed on to him. It was also arranged, in agreement with London, that Françoise would rebuild Pat's organisation. Victor Farrell also assured her of regular, weekly payments.

It was now, during the second week of June 1943, that Françoise, financially assured, returned to Toulouse, and arranged for Fabien de Cortes, "Antoine", and Maurice Wilson to leave for Spain, but they were caught in the Gestapo ambush near le Boulou on 12/13 June.[1305] Their guide was arrested by the Gestapo a few days later. Once the dust had settled, Françoise went to Canet-Plage to settle all outstanding debts contracted by Pat O'Leary with Madame Lebreton ("Chouquette"), and then travelled the south of France paying off Pat's other loyal helpers.

Back in Toulouse she and Rolande Ulmann looked for another safe house, and on 15 July 1943 rented the Villa Pamplemousse (Grapefruit) at 27, Chemin Cazel [*sic*], installing there Rolande and "Thérèse Martin" (Maud Baudot de Rouville), who had been "evacuated" from Marseille earlier in the year. The two women failed to get along, however, and after a fortnight Rolande left. A week later, sometime in August 1943, she was arrested. The energetic Françoise then travelled to Bergerac, to pay off more debts, and there recruited Philippe Brégi, 'who was to become her right-hand man'. Together they slowly rebuilt the organisation, now effectively the Françoise line, which stretched from Annemasse, near the Swiss border, via Toulouse to Perpignan and the Pyrenees.

Squadron Leader Frank Griffiths, who encountered Françoise on his way from Switzerland to Toulouse, was surprised to find not 'a luscious blonde of some twenty summers' but a sixty-eight-year-old woman. 'She had two prominent top teeth and smoked incessantly. She carried a bag with her into which she was continually diving and producing things like a conjurer.'[1306]

It had been arranged that Griffiths would meet Françoise on the Toulouse train at Annemasse station. As several murders had been committed in Annemasse by French patriots the town was under martial law, and it was only through the courage of a uniformed French customs official, who at great risk to himself escorted Griffiths to his seat on the train, that he reached it without incident. There had also been a murder in Toulouse in Françoise's absence, this time of the chief of police himself, and there were strict controls at every station exit. All passengers were being searched and questioned by gendarmes and by German police. Sizing up the situation, Françoise, as Griffiths records, 'went up to a gendarme and created a minor disturbance – about what I do not know – which drew attention to herself while I walked out of the station.'[1307] She joined Griffiths outside the station a short while later, and took him in a horse-drawn *fiacre* (Hackney-carriage) to the Villa Pamplemousse, where he remained until 26 October 1943, meeting Thérèse, 'a friend of Françoise', and Staff Sergeant Joe Manos USAAF, a high-spirited, ill-disciplined, young American.

On 27 October the two airmen left the villa and went by train to Perpignan, Griffiths with Françoise, and Joe Manos with an English-speaking Frenchman whose name they did not know. There a Catalan, Antoine, and his uncle (no name) took the two airmen on foot through the Zone Interdite to the uncle's farm at Céret. They left for Spain on the night of 28/29 October via the Col de Perthus, to the north of Agullana (fifteen kilometres north-west of Figueras). Intending to catch a train to Barcelona, they walked on to Figueras but were arrested by a Spanish policeman as they waited for the train, and were locked up in the civil prison. They were released after a few days in the *Cellular Prisión de Figueras*, together with another American, Staff Sergeant Pete Seniawski, who had been shot down on the Schweinfurt raid and had reached Spain on his own in only eight days.[1308]

There was yet another setback for Françoise Dissard and her organisation when, on the night of 27 January 1944, a key member of the organisation, André, and his second-in-command, a new guide named "Sherry", were arrested in Perpignan. On their way there from Toulouse with two Frenchmen were Flight Sergeant J.H. McWilliams, Captain Raymond Sarrant, US Tank Corps, who had come (escaped?) from Germany, and two USAAF 2nd Lieutenants, William M. Foley and Larry E. Grauerholtz.[1309] They had spent the night at a hotel in Quillan and early on the morning of 28 January were driven to Perpignan. There they learnt that André, who had gone on ahead, 'had been arrested by the Gestapo. A Gestapo agent had approached him in the guise of an American officer escaper.'[1310] Suspicious of the "American", André proposed that Sarrant, then at Quillan, should interrogate the man, but he never got the chance, for the bogus "American" had shopped him and "Sherry". Worse, the Gestapo found a notebook on "Sherry" which contained several addresses, including that of the Villa Pamplemousse.

McWilliams and the Americans wasted no time, and set off for the Pyrenees that very night, finally reaching Spain on 31 January. Without being apprehended by the Spanish authorities, McWilliams boarded a ship at Huelva on 17 February, which sailed for Gibraltar two days later.

Forced to move from one hideout to another for a time Françoise finally returned to her apartment at 12, rue Paul Mériel in the centre of Toulouse, and not too far from Gestapo headquarters, reasoning that that would be the last place that the Gestapo would look for her. Now forced more than ever to rely on others she turned to Gabriel Nahas of the Dutch-Paris line (see Chapter 7), and gave him the funds to take "parcels" over the Pyrenees using his own guides of the railwaymen's Résistance Fer, the same organisation that had helped Brigadier Hargest to freedom.

Despite the several handicaps, Françoise's achievements were nonetheless impressive, helping almost 250 airmen return to England, 110 alone during her time on the run from the Gestapo. A measure of the flow of evaders (see Chapter 11) may be gathered from the many who were helped by her, Burgundy and Dutch-Paris during the second half of May 1944.

Flight Sergeant Fred Greenwell, and no doubt the others, left feeling immeasurably grateful to Françoise Dissard, this 'humorous, good-natured, chain-smoking indomitable woman with a huge adored cat', and whose 'fingers of her left hand were', he noticed, 'much mis-shapen due to an encounter with a window frame in the course of a dramatic escape from the Gestapo.'[1311]

Just as the PAO line had been decimated through betrayal, so too the Comet line was brought to its knees by the Gestapo and by the GFP. The arrests of Charles Morelle on 6 May 1942, and of Andrée Dumon and her family in August 1942, were bad enough, but there was worse to come.

Georges Maréchal had long been a member of Luc, the Belgian intelligence-gathering network,[1312] but it was not until March 1941, when his wife Elsie heard of an English soldier needing a hiding place, that they agreed to offer their home at 162, Avenue Voltaire, Brussels, as a safe house. In the event, the soldier was placed elsewhere, but it was not long, still sometime in 1941, before the Maréchals received a visit from a young woman known to them only as "D", but whom they later knew as Dédée (Andrée de Jongh). This time she needed help in sheltering a Belgian who had escaped from a clinic, and on her next visit brought two French escaped prisoners of war. All that is known of one of them was that his name was Henri Bridier and that he was 'small and dark' and was 'from the south of France'.[1313] The other was Charlie Morelle, who had featured significantly in Comet's operations until his own arrest early in May 1942.

All four of the Maréchal family – Georges, Elsie, young Elsie their daughter, and Robert their son – were involved in Comet work to some degree or other. Between 24 August 1942 and 1 November 1942 they sheltered or fed fourteen Allied airmen, including the two Russians Pinchuk and Stadnik (see Chapter 6), all of whom successfully reached Gibraltar and the United Kingdom.

18 November 1942 began as any other day in the Maréchal household. Georges left for work and sixteen-year-old Robert went to school. Young Elsie reported for duty at the Swedish Canteen. Ostensibly a charitable foundation run by Baron Jean Greindl ("Nemo") for the poor children of

Brussels it was in reality a front for Comet, for whom young Elsie ran errands, guided evaders and so on. On this November morning, however, she found the place deserted, but some hours after the post was normally delivered a letter arrived 'in an envelope of a common commercial type, made of green paper'.[1314] Wondering as to its contents she opened it and found a note saying that two *colis* ("parcels", evaders) would be arriving at 11.30 a.m. at the usual place, St Joseph's church, Place Orban. She was puzzled by this, as Comet's rule was that notice of the arrival of "parcels" should always be sent by postcard and at least two or three days in advance. Unable to get to St Joseph's church in time she went home and was discussing the strange business with her mother 'when the door bell rang and there was Nelly [Deceunynck] with the usual Namur guide and two men in civilian clothes.'[1315]

Finding no one at St Joseph's church the guide from Namur had taken his two "parcels" to the address to which he sent his postcards and the only one he knew in Brussels, namely the Deceunyncks's corner shop. All Nelly could do for her part was to take them to the only Comet address that *she* knew, namely the Maréchals' house, where she left the three men with Madame Elsie Maréchal. As it was lunchtime, they were invited to share the meal with young Elsie and her brother Robert back from school. The behaviour of the two "Americans" was not that expected of anxious evaders, however, and Elsie's suspicions were aroused when one of them announced in what seemed to be a non-American accent that he was from Jersey City. And one asked to go to the *Kabinett*, German for the toilet. Discussing these peculiarities the two Elsies decided to tell Greindl of their doubts as soon as the opportunity arose.

Robert had gone back to school and young Elsie had returned to her place of work when the doorbell rang. Madame Elsie immediately told the two "Americans" to hide upstairs while she went to answer the door but, instead of doing as they were bidden, one of them produced a gun, grabbed Elsie by the arm, and told her that the game was up. Meanwhile the other "American", both now revealed as GFP agents, opened the front door and admitted a third German. Madame Elsie was taken away.

Having returned to the Swedish Canteen young Elsie spoke to Jean Greindl and told him of their misgivings about the two "Americans". All he could do was to tell her to watch them closely and to let him know if things developed for the worse. She went home, with extra food for the new guests, and straight into the clutches of eight more GFP men. As he came back from school, so too Robert was arrested, and likewise their father, Georges, on his return from work.

Worried that he had heard nothing back from the Maréchals, Jean Greindl asked Victor Michiels, a twenty-six-year-old lawyer and Comet guide, to go to 162, Avenue Voltaire to see what was what, but on no account to enter the house. After watching the house for half an hour, and having seen nothing suspicious, Victor went up to the door and rang the bell. Immediately three German police sprang out of the darkness, their guns pointing at him. Ignoring the order to halt, Victor ran for it. Three shots rang out, and he fell down dead.

This was not the end of the affair, for the two "American airmen" had penetrated the Comet line 'from the Ardennes and Namur to the very centre of [the] organisation in Brussels. In two days, nearly one hundred people, all helpers of the line, were arrested. Some were guides, some shelterers, some innocent relatives thrown into prison as hostages.'[1316] Among them was Elvire Morelle, who had only returned to Brussels on the morning of 20 November from business elsewhere. As arranged, she went directly to the Maréchals' house, no one having been able to warn her of the danger, and she too was arrested. Also taken in the Germans' purge was Peggy van Lier, but she talked her way out of trouble and was released.

In the second week of January 1943, after the twenty-fourth and last of her journeys from Paris to Bilbao, during which she had escorted a total of one hundred and eighteen men over the Pyrenees, Dédée returned to Paris to see her father, Frédéric de Jongh, at the safe house in the rue Vaneau, to persuade him that it was time to leave the country. They left together on 13 January for Bayonne, with two other helpers and three RAF airmen – Flight Sergeant S.F. Hope; Sergeant W.G.J. Greaves; and Sergeant P.G.E. Ross.[1317] Elvire De Greef explained that conditions in the mountains were particularly bad and that it would be unwise for Frédéric to attempt the crossing. Leaving him and the other helpers behind, therefore, Dédée and the three airmen continued in a violent rainstorm to Francia Usandizaga's farmhouse at Bidegain Berri near Urrugne.

On 15 January 1943 a company of French police,[1318] tipped off by a farmhand called Donato, roared up to the farmhouse and arrested Dédée, the three airmen, and Frantxia Usandizaga, whose three young children would never see her again. After enduring twelve, brutal days at the Château Neuf prison in Bayonne and another twelve at the Fort du Hâ prison in Bordeaux,[1319] they returned to Bayonne before being taken to the Gestapo prison at Fresnes, Paris. It was there, states Greaves, that they lost contact with Andrée de Jongh ("Dédée"). Stan Hope was put into solitary confinement for the best part of four months, his solitary ordeal broken by visits to the Gestapo headquarters on the Avenue Foch, and it was there that the thugs finally broke him. Hoping that after so long anyone who had helped him would now be safe he gave them vague names. Unfortunately there was enough detail for those incriminated to be caught, and for some it was the end.[1320] Stan Hope was soon sent on to the Luftwaffe's famous interrogation centre, Dulag Luft, at Oberursel near Frankfurt-am-Main where he arrived on 24 May 1943, Greaves and Ross following in August.

As for Dédée, a plan was immediately hatched to rescue her while she was at the Château Neuf prison in Bayonne. Owners of the popular Bar Gachy, close to the prison, happened to be Comet members, and one of their regulars was a disgruntled warder from the jail. In return for his passage out of France he was willing to help get Dédée out, but before anything could be done for her she was moved to the Villa Chagrin in Bayonne, and then to the Fort du Hâ prison in Bordeaux. On discovering that she had returned to prison at Bayonne, plans were made to get her out, and on 20 January Jean-François Nothomb, Elvire De Greef, Albert Johnson, and Jean Dassié, another Comet helper, assembled at the Bar Gachy intent on her rescue. Scaling the outer wall but unable to get into the prison over the inner barrier, the attempt reluctantly had to be abandoned. Further plans were thwarted when Dédée was moved yet again, to Maison Blanche, a small prison in Biarritz, before being taken away in handcuffs to Fresnes prison, Paris.

At the same time as the southern end of the line was being dismembered, the noose was being tightened in Brussels. On 6 February 1943 the Gestapo called for Jean Greindl. They also collected his wife and another Comet man, Jean Naus. Jean Greindl's brother, Albert, was almost caught when he went to a safe house at the Place Blyckaert to remove incriminating papers, but left just before the Gestapo arrived. Eric de Menten de Horne, though, unaware that Albert had already been to the house, also tried to recover the papers, but found only the Gestapo waiting for him.

Albert Greindl made his way south at once, and crossed into Spain on 14 February with Jean-François Nothomb, Albert Johnson, 2nd Lieutenant John W. Spence USAAF, Technical Sergeant Sidney Devers USAAF,[1321] and Flight Sergeant J.B. Chaster RCAF. They were on their way by taxi to San Sebastián on 15 February when they were arrested by the Guardia Civil in the neighbourhood of Elizondo. Johnson and Greindl managed to escape, but the others were locked up in Elizondo jail: 'There we were without blankets or heating in a cell which had no windows. We got no food till noon.' On the following day they were removed to the prison at Pamplona 'which was horribly crowded and where the food was terrible.'[1322]

All was not lost, however, for far from deserting their four comrades Johnson and Albert Greindl had made their way to the British Consulate at San Sebastián and had notified the consul of their arrest. Within a few days the consul from Bilbao had paid them a visit, and on 26 February the military attaché from Madrid arrived to take them to a hotel for the night. The following day the three airmen were driven to Madrid while Nothomb made his way back to France to continue Comet's work, as did Johnson. Greindl meanwhile made his way to England, there to plead with Airey Neave to do all that he could to save his brother's life.

A while later, however, Albert Johnson and Elvire de Greef were removed from a train for questioning by the Germans. Though released, Johnson decided that it was best to return to Spain, and did so on 20 March. Nothomb, having also decided to make his way back to Spain, returned with a group of American airmen one week later.[1323]

Many of Comet's betrayals and arrests were occasioned by a man sometimes known as Captain Jackson, whose most profitable period appears to have been in the spring and summer of 1943. He was to do his treacherous job so well that, up to the time that the Allies had overrun Belgium in September 1944, it was estimated that he had betrayed around one thousand members of the Resistance, with perhaps five hundred airmen captured by the German secret police as a result of his information. In January 1943 Anne Brusselmans received a circular from Comet in Brussels 'warning us against a man who poses as an English captain. He calls himself Captain Jackson, but speaks English with an American accent. Full descriptions are given also of two women who work with him.'[1324] This man was Prospère Valère Dezitter,[1325] known to most of his aircrew victims as "the Captain" and noted for the gloves that he wore to hide the fact that two joints of the little finger on his right hand were missing.

The betrayal of the crew of a 77 Squadron Halifax, JD168, after it had been shot down on the night of 11/12 June 1943 was a good example of his technique. Arriving at the target just behind the Pathfinders, JD168 was picked up by three Me110 night-fighters: 'One fighter attacked from each side, while the third came from underneath, the sound of the shells entering the aeroplane sounding like "a wooden stick going along some railings". The mid-upper gunner had already shot down one plane, but by this time, there were holes all around, the port engine was on fire, and the rear gunner had been hit in the stomach. The pilot ordered them to get out.'[1326] Navigator Sergeant Reg Goodenough, who was next to the escape hatch, was the first to bale out, making his first, and last, parachute drop into an orchard close to a river not far from Liège, Belgium.

Floating down, Reg saw the mid-upper gunner, Sergeant D.E. Burrows, shoot down his second fighter, and later it was learnt that both the crew of one of the Me110s were killed, and the navigator of the second. At around 2 a.m. on 12 June JD168 crashed onto a house at 19, rue Sondeville, Oupeye, half a dozen kilometres north-east of Liège, killing three civilians.[1327]

Reg buried his parachute under a pile of hay, walked to the nearest village, and stayed in a wood until midday. When a couple of children came by he whistled "V for Victory" in morse code at them, and they came over to him. To show them that he was really English Reg produced a copy of the *Daily Mirror* that he just happened to have with him. They told him to wait there, and went off, returning four hours later with ten men, who gave him clothing, a jacket and trousers to hide his uniform. All left together, past two gendarmes who were in a nearby field. Reg was taken to Liège itself, where he was asked to identify some of his crew, with whom he was soon reunited. 'A well-dressed man visited a few times,' and Reg was taken for a ride in his car. He gave Reg details of potential targets, and wanted him 'to make notes such as "the real aerodrome is on the other side of the road, the other is a dummy".' Reg did not trust him, and threw away the notes as soon as possible. 'At another house in Liège, they were asked for, and gave away their escape aids; watches, special buttons, compass-shoes, etc. Unfortunately, they had fallen into the hands of an escape line infiltrated and run by Prosper Dezitter.'[1328]

Unaware that there was treachery afoot, a few days later a man whom they had already met, and who claimed to be from the Swiss Legation, took them by train to Paris. The evaders would have been unaware, too, that when they reached the French border it was most unusual for anyone to remain on the train as it passed through the border control. The man from the Swiss Legation told them to stay in the carriage. A railway official appeared and started talking in French to Reg, who replied 'oui' or 'non', the only words of French that he knew, while their escorts said nothing. The man in charge, Prospère Dezitter, 'called the official over, who went away after a small discussion and allowed them to continue on their way. Dezitter had been provided with a special pass by the Gestapo that allowed him to travel anywhere without question.'

When they got to Paris, they were handed over to a 'shifty-looking bastard', who took them 'to a very cheap hotel for the night. Next morning, they were taken to an open square, and left there to walk around for two hours. They were gathered together and walked past the Arc de Triomphe on the way to the railway station.' Sergeant L.S. "Danny" Blanchard and Reg Goodenough were on the opposite side of the road 'to the rest of the group to avoid suspicion. Just near a corner the guide stopped and, seeing them on the other side, called them over to join the rest. When they turned the corner, however, they were immediately surrounded by Germans.'[1329] Taken by car to Fresnes prison on 5 July 1943, they spent the next two years in captivity in Germany.

There was, however, an amusing incident on the civilian tram that was taking Reg and his comrades from Frankfurt to the Luftwaffe's interrogation camp, Dulag Luft, at Oberursel. They were loudly discussing what they would like to do to the sultry blonde woman sitting opposite them 'when she got up and said, "Excuse me, I have to get off now", causing much embarrassment.'[1330]

Despite the awful hole made in Comet's ranks by the arrests earlier in 1943, Jean-François Nothomb was still free. Tired but determined, he continued to help Allied airmen from Brussels, two of them possibly Sergeants S.J. Moore and D. Ferguson, from the same crew, who were taken from Brussels to Paris in April 1943 by a man named, they say, "Fernando", 'where we were handed over to M. Paul'. "Paul" (Frédéric de Jongh) then took them 'to the house of Mlle. de Bizien'. According to Moore, "Fernando" was 'apparently the head of the organisation' that was looking after them. 'He was aged about thirty, and could speak no English.'[1331] Whoever "Fernando" was, between July and October 1943 Nothomb and a compatriot, Max Roger, 'were bringing over as many as twelve men a month. Nothomb and Roger brought through two parties in July, four in August, and six in September. Nothomb himself made crossings on July 24th, August 13th, September 2nd and 28th, and October 6th.'[1332]

Having returned safely to England, Moore and Ferguson offered some advice on how, at that time, 'it was possible to enter Spain without difficulty, by the following route:- By train from Dax to Bérenx, (on the line to Orthez.) Thence by road to Aïnhoa. From here take the main road towards the International Bridge over the river Nivelle at Dancharia. Just before Dancharia there is a stone quarry on the east side of the road, and beyond it a hill with three crosses on the top. The best route is along the side of this hill and through some woods, towards the river. There are some stepping stones across the river, which here is usually forded also. Just opposite the stepping stones, on the Spanish side, there is a farmhouse, the owner of which is willing to help evaders.'

Moore and Ferguson added that in Aïnhoa there was 'a Belgian – the only mechanic in the village – who is willing to take evaders across the frontier for 3,000 francs per trip.' But, they cautioned, the village of Urdax, south of Dancharia and in Spain, was to be avoided as it was 'frequently visited by German troops on leave'. Avoiding Germans if one was engaged on clandestine work was sometimes difficult, all the more so if one had become too well-known to them to keep avoiding their clutches for ever. Though he knew that he was compromised in this way Jean-François Nothomb continued to do his duty as he saw it until, on 18 January 1944, his luck ran out and he was arrested along with the chief of Comet's Paris sector, Jacques Le Grelle.

Captain Airey Neave, at the War Office's Room 900, was deeply upset when news of the arrests reached him, as he had been trying his best for several months to persuade Nothomb 'to come out, but, like so many people of his type, he refused to do so because he did not think that he was really brûlé… Nevertheless, … he did magnificent work. His career was perhaps the most brilliant of all the Belgian agents employed by our service and we had intended giving him a DSO had he reached here safely. Unfortunately this was not to be and I am afraid that there is little we can do for him at present.'[1333] But Nothomb *did* survive, and he *was* awarded the DSO.

One of the small groups operating in Belgium and France and which also forged a link with the renascent Comet line was Possum/Martin. It was to play a brief but vital role in the lives of a few dozen airmen who had been shot down over Belgium, but its leader, as with so many others, would fall foul of the treachery of Desoubrie and, possibly, Dezitter. On the night of 15/16 July 1943 Captain Ed Potier[1334] and his radio operator Conrad Lafleur (see Chapter 5) landed by parachute close to a road running through the middle of Chiny forest in the Belgian Ardennes, not far from Florenville.

Captain Potier was a highly experienced pilot in the Belgian Air Force with over 1,100 flying hours by the time of the invasion of his country in May 1940. He was ordered on 25 May 1940 to deliver an important message to the Belgian army command that had been cut off in Flanders by the Germans' thrust to Abbeville to the south. Flying over the sea to avoid Luftwaffe fighters and German flak, his aircraft suffered an engine failure and he was forced to make 'un amerrissage' (sea landing) in the English Channel off Calais. He and his fellow crewman, Albert Colpaert, were picked up by Royal Navy destroyer and taken to Dover. The following day Potier was taken to Dunkirk, and the message safely delivered.

Rejoining his unit in France, Potier returned to Belgium on 20 August 1940, where he was recruited into the Belgian Resistance. Moving to Florenville he was given the task early in 1941 of forming a Resistance cell in the Belgian province of Luxembourg. On 13 November 1941, though, he was obliged to leave the country and made his own way into Spain on 14 February 1942. Five days later he was in Lisbon, and having been flown to England on 25/26 March enrolled in the Belgian armed forces. Sent to No. 5 (Pilot) Advanced Flying Unit at RAF Ternhill, Shropshire, on 4 April 1942 his experience was soon recognised, and he became a flying instructor, promoted to commander on 26 December 1942. Bored with his duties, he requested a return to operational flying, but this was turned down on the grounds that, at thirty-nine, he was too old.

Leaving No. 5 (P) AFU on 14 April 1943 he was seconded to MI9 on 1 June 1943, and was sent on a course to learn about operating behind enemy lines. Six weeks later, sent on their way by Airey Neave, Potier and Lafleur were flown to Belgium to organise an escape line for the evacuation of allied airmen. The area in which they were to operate extended from Belgium's Luxembourg province down to the Laon-Soissons-Reims triangle in northern France. The operation would be known as "Mission Martin" in Belgium and "Réseau Possum" in France.

Though spraining an ankle on landing Potier was able to reach Chiny with Lafleur, half a dozen kilometres through the forest, and contacted Emile Belva, a man whom he already knew and trusted. Madame Belva, his wife, summoned Doctor Dupont from Florenville to have a look at Potier's ankle. Told that it needed to be rested Potier (alias "Monsieur Labranche") and Lafleur ("Petit Pierre", "Charles Nicolas" or, simply, "the Canadian") stayed put in the area for the next few days, giving them the opportunity to make contact with a unit of the Belgian Resistance, the *Groupe Local des Corps Francs Ardennais*.[1335] Having also brought with him a large sum of money to finance operations, Potier entrusted it to a lawyer, M. Quinot, in Florenville, who became Possum/Martin's treasurer. Several safe houses were also arranged for the future use of airmen evaders and escapers.

On the recommendation of Joseph Godfrin, Potier appointed as his assistant Pierre Geelen ("Grand Pierre" in Belgium, "Amboise" in France). Geelen was, or had been, a member of SOE's collapsing circuit Prosper. Planning to go to France as soon as possible Potier, Geelen and Lafleur were taken to Muno, where they stayed for a fortnight with Godfrin while Arthur Dacremont, a member of Godfrin's group, obtained French identity papers, travel papers, ration cards and change of residence permits for their stay in France. Godfrin also introduced Potier to Jean-Pierre Lorgé, whom he agreed to employ as "protection" for Lafleur during clandestine radio transmissions, and also to take airmen picked up in the Florenville area to the "repatriation centre" in France.

During the second week of August 1943 Lafleur and Lorgé went to Paris, where Potier would later join them. Now assuming the name Jules Nollet, Potier arrived at the home of Raymond Gallet at 6, rue de la Huchette, Fismes (Marne) (thirty kilometres north-west of Reims) on 14 August. The purpose of his visit was to establish more safe houses in the area, and also to investigate possible sites for the evacuation of airmen by Lysander. Raymond Gallet was given the task of finding the accommodation,[1336] while both he and his brother, Maurice, were asked to look for suitable landing strips for the Lysanders. With the Possum/Martin route almost complete, holding points for airmen were established in Belgium at Chiny and Florenville. Crossing points into France were located at Muno and at Pussemange but, if crossing via Muno, airmen were taken to the French town of Carignan (Ardennes) or, if from Pussemange, to the French town of Charleville-Mézières (Ardennes), a dozen kilometres to the south-west. All roads led to Sedan (Ardennes), and thence to Reims and Fismes, 125 kilometres to the south-west, where further safe houses were established. With RAF and US Army Air Force operations to Germany becoming more frequent, it was anticipated that Possum/Martin would not be short of "customers".

Just before midnight on 9/10 August 1943, Lancaster W4236 "K for King of the Air", laden with a 4,000-lb "cookie" and other bombs, was on course from its 'base at Syerston near Newark, Nottinghamshire, to Beachy Head and climbing to 18,000 feet on its last flight. The all-sergeant crew, captained by pilot John Whitley... was on its fifth mission, a raid on Mannheim in Southern Germany.'[1337] Responding to the threat of over four hundred enemy aircraft picked up on its radar, the Luftwaffe ordered 'Leutnant Norbert Pietrek with his crew, Unteroffizieren (sergeants) Paul Gartig (wireless/radar operator) and Otto Scherer (engineer/gunner)... off from the German night-fighter base at Florennes, Southern Belgium. Their aircraft, a twin-engined Messerschmitt 110F-4 armed with four machine guns and two cannon, was directed by their ground controller, Leutnant Ernst Reith, to patrol an area called "Room 7B" around its base... At 00.32 hours they found a bomber which was identified as a Lancaster. Pietrek opened fire....', and within seconds the fuselage of Lancaster W4236 was ablaze. Sergeant E.F. "Fred" Gardiner, wireless operator, wasted no time in baling out: 'It took no courage to leave the inferno of "K for King" which roared away into the darkness. In a second or two it had gone. Completely disorientated I pulled the ripcord...'

W4236 crashed in the area of Marbehan, to the north of the valley of the River Semois, Belgium, killing three of its seven crew. Two of the four survivors – John Whitley and "Whiz" Walker – reached Switzerland on the night of 20/21 December 1943, after some four months in hiding in Etalle, barely half a dozen kilometres from the crash site. A third – Sergeant P.B. Smith (navigator) (see following chapter) – saw the wreck of W4236 'from a train on his travels to Brussels, before going on to Paris and the south of France on the famous "Comete" escape line. He eventually crossed the Pyrenees on foot [on 13 October 1943] and was imprisoned by the Spaniards. Later he was freed after representations by the British Consul and reached home via Gibraltar.'[1338]

First home, however, seven weeks before Peter Smith, was Fred Gardiner. Minus both flying boots, Fred landed in the Belgian darkness: 'There was nothing to do now except wait for daylight. Rolled up in the parachute I lay contemplating my good – or bad – fortune and wondering the fate of my crewmates. I felt a great feeling of thankfulness at still being alive. The gunfire had missed me. The big bomb had not exploded before it could be released. The aircraft had not blown up in the air. I had successfully jumped clear. The elderly parachute had opened. The ground was soft to land upon. Fate had been very kind to me, so far.' Fate would continue to smile upon him, as Belgian patriots sheltered him in Rulles, Marbehan, Villers-sur-Semois and Tintigny along the Semois valley.

On 13 August he was taken to meet gendarme Remi Goffin, with his motorcycle: 'I transferred to the pillion and we were off. I remember an exhilarating ride along the narrow Belgian roads, scattering chickens as we sped past little areas of habitation. The motorbike went well on what must have been at least a proportion of paraffin judging by the exhaust. After six or seven miles we approached a larger village and as we entered I noted the name Florenville.' Though Florenville is barely two kilometres from the French border, he was to spend two weeks at "La Sapinière", Avenue de la Gare, the home of Monsieur Charles Spruyt, his wife Geneviève (whom Fred was to call Madame Giny), and their eighteen-year-old daughter Charlotte, whose name was always shortened to Lolotte.

On 26 August 1943, after false papers had been prepared by Possum/Martin, it 'was time once more to move on. In the morning my new haversack was packed, Madame Giny making sure I had plenty of sandwiches. Then Charles and Lolotte pushing their bicycles accompanied me back to the village square where we took a road leading away in the opposite direction. Again there were few people and no traffic to be seen. Half a mile from the village we halted and rested on the grass verge. Two German military policemen cycled by but gave us no more than a glance. After a short wait a motorcyclist approached from the village. It was Dr Pierre who was to take me to my next destination. With farewells and good wishes from Charles and Lolotte and some regrets I was off again. Not a long journey, perhaps four or five miles and we arrived at Muno, another village in the chain.'[1339]

As the time was still not right for Fred to be taken to France, he spent another fortnight at a house called "Au Maqua", near Bouillon, where he was 'welcomed by the occupants. They were Monsieur and Madame [Denise] Pierret, a middle aged couple, typical workers of the land, and a somewhat younger woman whose name was Madame Simon. There was also an elderly lady, perhaps a parent of one of the others whose name I never knew.' On 10 September, it was time to head home and, after fond farewells had been exchanged, Fred was on his way to Bouillon – by taxi. Deposited at the Hôtel de Progress in Bouillon's main thoroughfare he was led inside for a meal, and 'was delighted to find that the youngest man present, apart from myself, was Flight Sergeant Herbert Pond of the Royal New Zealand Air Force.'

Flight Sergeant H.A. Pond RNZAF was flying Lancaster JA707 back from Nuremberg on 27/28 August 1943, when it was attacked by a night-fighter, which caused severe damage to the flying controls. It was not until JA707 was over Belgium, near Sibret (some fifty kilometres north-east of Florenville), that 'the aircraft literally flew into and along the ground, killing at least one crew member. The survivors spilled out from the wrecked aircraft and scattered in all directions fearing fire or an explosion. In the darkness they had become permanently separated. Herbert Pond had not seen any of his crew since then.'[1340]

After lunch at the Hôtel de Progress the two airmen and their guide, Monsieur Arnould, got into the waiting taxi: 'We were now to cross the border into France. At a convenient and quiet spot the taxi stopped and the three of us alighted. A young woman, who must have been awaiting our arrival, now appeared and escorted us into the thick woods bordering the road. The taxi driver would take his vehicle through the frontier barrier in the authorised manner while we were to cross unseen (we hoped) through the woods. After ten minutes or so of walking we arrived at a small building almost completely surrounded by the trees. Clambering down a slope, we entered via a back door which led into a tiny bar, almost English style. We were provided with drinks and although those present may have been aware of what was going on, Herbert and I stayed mute. We were now in France, at the Café aux Chapelle.'[1341]

Safely across the border and collecting his passengers once again the taxi driver, Paul Frerlet,[1342] took them to Sedan, where he left them to catch the train to Reims. Boarding the train separately Fred and Herbert were told that at their destination they would be met by a woman dressed in black wearing a floral buttonhole: 'We were to follow her, keeping at least ten metres apart.' Despite the train being crowded with German military personnel and Herbert spending the journey in the buffet car where someone had bought him a drink, they arrived at Reims within a couple of hours. After a night in a safe house[1343] they 'were visited by a suave, well-dressed Frenchman who spoke fluent English' and who, he told them, would be going with them on the next leg of their journey. Their guide, Jean-Pierre Lorgé (Lafleur's bodyguard), took them back to Reims station to make their way to Fismes.

Lorgé, a 'French (or Canadian) agent, … now had some remarkable and exciting news. It might be possible for Herbert and me to be flown out of France by an RAF 'plane which was expected to bring supplies in for the Resistance during darkness. This might be tomorrow, weather and moon permitting, but we would be kept informed. However, we were disappointed when, by the afternoon of the second day we learned that the operation was off.' But on the afternoon of 13 September hopes were rekindled when the two airmen 'were alerted for a possible rendezvous with the aircraft that night. As darkness fell, our small party – including three or four members of the Resistance – set off under a bright moon through the silent countryside in single file and with no talking allowed.'[1344] They were still some way short of 'the landing site when the aircraft arrived overhead, circled and flashed its identification light. We began to run whilst the 'plane made several circuits, occasionally going out of earshot.'

When those on the ground reached the landing field, one kilometre south-south-east of Dhuizel (Aisne), and about six or seven north-west of Fismes, they found 'that most of it had been ploughed, leaving only a strip of grass with a haystack at the end. Would such a restricted landing area be adequate? Torches attached to sticks were quickly set out as markers for the pilot, and it was [Fred Gardiner's] job to flash the letter "R" as a "safe to land" signal.'

'The aircraft came in over the haystack and landed with a considerable bounce a few yards in front of us, then quickly came to a stop and taxied back to our party.' It was also Fred's job to climb the fixed ladder to the rear cockpit on the port side and remove the two packages. Once done, he sat down on the floor of the cockpit, to be followed by Herbert Pond and Pierre Geelen ("Grand Pierre"), now wanted by the Germans: 'We flew back in bright moonlight at perhaps four or five thousand feet. There was no cloud and the ground could be seen clearly. At the coast, a few searchlights were evident but made no attempt to pick us up. Across the Channel and just off the English coast, I was able to identify Brighton and soon we were coming in to a smooth landing at Tangmere near Chichester. "Grand Pierre" was whisked away in a car while Herbert and myself were taken to the special quarters of 161 Squadron.' Operation Brasenose had been successfully completed, though the pilot, Squadron Leader Hugh Verity DSO, DFC, noted that he 'waited one hour for reception. Haystacks too close to lights.'[1345]

After intensive training in Scotland, and having been commissioned a lieutenant in the British Army, P.A.H. Geelen, formerly Grand Pierre but now Lieutenant Garde, was parachuted into the Creuse *département* of France on the night of 5/6 April 1944 with two French officers to form SOE's Labourer circuit. Their reception was arranged for them on the Chat field at Acre near Néret (Indre) by MURAS (United Movement of the Resistance Secret Army). But they were betrayed and arrested by the Germans on 27 April and taken to Fresnes prison. Removed on 5 August 1944 to Buchenwald in the company of other British agents the exact date of Geelen's execution, and of seventeen others, is a matter for debate. Possibly occurring on 9 September it is officially given as 14 September.[1346]

Gardiner and Pond were the first of Possum/Martin's airmen to be picked up by Lysander. Next to go, on the night of 7/8 November 1943, in Operation Magdalen (third attempt), were four Americans – Staff Sergeant T. Whalen; Technical Sergeant Herbert M. Browning; Technical Sergeant John M. Desrochers; and Staff Sergeant Ellis H. Klein.[1347] Flying the Lysander on this night was Flying Officer James McCairns, who brought with him to France MI9's Count Georges d'Oultremont. The four Americans were followed back to England on 16/17 November 1943 on the double Lysander operation Magdalen II by Sergeant R.V.C. Johnson RAF and by four more Americans – 2nd Lieutenants Charles Breuer and Stanley R. Chichester; and Technical Sergeants Fred L. Murray and Harold B. Maddox.[1348] Johnson, Maddox and Murray flew back with Squadron Leader Hugh Verity, the others with McCairns. Also returning with McCairns was Commandant Dominique Potier who had received a message on 13 November ("La pêche à la truite est difficile" – "Trout-fishing is difficult") calling him back to London. Georges d'Oultremont (alias "M. Gréville" or "Roméo") took charge in Potier's absence.[1349]

Bomb aimer Sergeant Johnson was one of a surprising number of operational bomber aircrew to survive the sudden explosion of their bomber in the dark night sky. He was aboard Stirling EH938 on the way back from the target on the night of 30/31 August 1943 when, he recalled, 'there was a violent explosion in the aircraft. I remember reaching for my parachute, but I do not know how I got out. The next thing I remember was that I was in the air and in a cloud. I had severe wounds in one arm, one leg, and my face.'[1350] Landing in a field somewhere, he thought near Weert in south-eastern Holland and close to the Belgian border, he managed despite his injuries to bury his 'parachute in a hedge and ran along the main road in a westerly direction. When it became light, I hid in a hedge in which I remained all day.'[1351] At dusk, with the help of his compass he continued in a westerly direction for about four hours, until his leg started to give him trouble. Spending the night in a bush in a field he set off on the morning of 1 September, still heading west. Seeing two Belgians at work in a wood, though, he went to ground again, and did not resume his journey until the following day.

Leaving the wood he made his way to Eksel, where he 'approached a cottage' and 'was beckoned in by a lad. I found a large family inside; the father told me, by signs, that he would fetch someone who could talk English. At about 1300 hours a girl turned up on a bicycle.' She proved to be English (her father was Alfred Woodis from Bradford, Yorkshire) and, telling him to stay where he was, went home to inform her mother. Later that afternoon the girl's mother arrived (Johnson could not recall her name) and asked him several questions. She said that 'she would see a man in an organisation'. Johnson managed a little sleep after she had gone, and at around 11 p.m. was awoken by two men, gendarmes in plain clothes, who, 'after stripping me of my badges and flying boots, took me by bicycle to another house quite near', at 66, Markt Street, Eksel, the home of Mr and Mrs Sols-Leskens and their six-year-old child.

Once a doctor had treated Johnson's knee and arm, which had turned septic, he was taken via Neerpelt (staying with Madame Spelters, who had six sons) to Antwerp, where he arrived on about 10 September. The next link in the chain was Monsieur Daelmans at whose house at 15, rue d'Orange, Antwerp, Johnson briefly stayed before being escorted by train to Brussels by Daelmans. Passed on quickly to Georges Hennaut, 'the local organist' at Virton, a town close to the French border in the south-east of Belgium, he was then taken to Florenville, where he stayed, again briefly, with a priest. Yet another family sheltered him, this time the Lemaires, at the village of Martue (two kilometres north of Florenville): 'A doctor who treated me here for my arm got me away by car on 30 September to Sedan, from where another man escorted me to Paris.'[1352]

In Paris he was met by "Captain Martin" (Commandant Ed Potier) and taken to the home of Madame Bastin on the rue de la Barre, Montmartre, where he found a further seven evading airmen – four Americans and three RAF, two from 218 Squadron and one from 7 Squadron. On 6 October "Captain Martin" appeared once more, and left with Johnson and three of the Americans for a farm near Quierzy, 100 kilometres north-east of Paris. The intention was to fly the four men back to England on one of SOE's clandestine flights but, after three days and no aircraft, they all went back to Paris, and from there to Reims. Johnson and one of the Americans were then taken by car by a girl to Sillery 'where we stayed, first in a hut in a wood, till 13 October, and then with M. Georgeton till 17 October.' When the Germans requisitioned one half of the house, they were obliged to move on yet again, to Monsieur Chandelot in Mailly-Champagne, who 'was a particularly staunch patriot'.

On 9 November Monsieur Chandelot hitched up his horse and cart and took the two airmen back to Reims. From there they caught the train to Fismes, where they stayed with Madame Lucienne Mulette and Mademoiselle Simone Ledru, dressmakers, in the rue des Conclusions. A 'girl took us by car on 13 November back to Reims, from there by train to Paris, and back to Mme. Bastin.' Their travelling was almost done, for on 15 November Commandant Potier reappeared and took Johnson and two of the Americans back to Quierzy.

The dream of a return flight to England became a reality on the following night, 16/17 November, when two Lysander aircraft (Verity and McCairns) arrived at le Champ Sainte Marie field. Dropping off their two "Joes" – the Canadians Raymond Labrosse and Lucien Dumais, who were on their way to set up the Shelburne operations in Brittany (see previous chapter) – the two Lysanders returned safely to England with their six passengers – Johnson, the four Americans, and Potier.

Apart from the eleven airmen who were flown home thanks to Possum, other airmen were helped with varying degrees of success, some not getting home until after the end of the war. It has been reliably suggested that the total number of airmen handled by Possum, including the eleven Lysander passengers, was thirty-eight (twenty-six Americans, twelve RAF), with Pierre Geelen making a grand total of thirty-nine. Seven of the Americans came back courtesy of the Royal Navy, and one reached Allied lines on 20 August 1944 after evading for ten months. One more had reached Gibraltar on 19 June 1944, and seven more were definitely arrested. The other two were possibly also arrested. Four of the RAF were definitely arrested, two more possibly, one had crossed into Switzerland on 9 July 1943 (Sergeant S.G. Holroyd), and two (Sergeants L. Marsh and H.N. Clarke) later reached Gibraltar.

Further attempts were made to revive the Lysander pick-up route following a report made by Georges d'Oultremont. As a consequence of the report, Commandant Potier returned to France by air on 20/21 December 1943 with Baron Jean de Blommaert and a Belgian wireless operator, Albert LeMaitre ("Louis London"), to assist in the restoration of an air escape route. Waiting for them was a reception committee of Raymond Gallet, Camille Rigault (a painter and decorator in Fismes), and a M. Litez. Three other packages were dropped by parachute containing 'several transmitters and arms'. All left for Paris that day,[1353] but Potier returned to Reims a week later, unaware of the disaster that was about to enfold him in its awful grip.

Conrad Lafleur had been pounding the keys on his transmitter arranging the drop with messages to and from London. But on 28 December 1943 'German radio detector vans, which had been listening in for some weeks,'[1354] caught him and his lookout, Raymonde Beure, in the act of transmitting from 161, rue Lesage, Reims, the home of Madame Fernande Mondet.[1355] It was around 5 o'clock in the evening when Raymonde mentioned that several vehicles had pulled-up outside the building. Realising immediately that this meant the Gestapo, Lafleur closed down the radio set, grabbed his gun, and fired at the enemy as they rushed up the stairs, wounding three or four of them before he jumped out of the window. Making good his escape, across backyards, walls and roofs, he reached Doctor Beaumont's house in Amiens. Two months later, Comet helped him to Spain, and so back to England.[1357]

Raymonde Beure, meanwhile, made her escape through the door to the house while the Gestapo were busy chasing Lafleur. Although the Gestapo failed to arrest her there and then, they found her *sac à main*, accidentally left behind in her flight. In the bag they found her photograph, identity card, papers, a hotel room key, and a notebook with the names and addresses of members of the Mission Martin organisation.

Raymonde Beure had taken two rooms at the hotel at 35, rue Jeanne d'Arc, Reims, one for herself and one for Commandant Potier on his return from England. Also making his way to Reims was Raymonde Beure's fiancé, Raymond Jeunet. Worried that he had not heard from her, he had gone to Reims to find her but, at Reims station at around 7.30 pm on 29 December, he was picked up by three

Gestapo agents and taken to their headquarters, also on the rue Jeanne d'Arc. They found on him a photograph of his fiancée, and when he in turn was presented with her photograph that they had found at Madame Mondet's house confessed that he knew her. The Gestapo did not yet know, however, which door in which hotel the key found in Raymonde Beure's hand-bag would open. Taking Jeunet with them, they tried several hotels until they came to the one on the rue Jeanne d'Arc. The hotel proprietress, Madame Herbillon, confirmed from the photograph of Raymonde shown to her that that person was known to her and, furthermore, that she had taken two rooms in her hotel.

It was the work of a moment for the Germans to discover that Raymonde Beure's room was empty (she had spent the night at St Brice, a short way to the west of Reims), but in the other room they found "M. Duchesne", Commandant Potier. Removed to their Reims headquarters, he was horribly and sadistically tortured for several days.[1358] At the limit of his endurance, he felt himself weakening, and made the decision to take his own life. On 8 January 1944, therefore, slipping out of the guards' care for a brief moment, he threw himself off the upper floor of the prison, and died three days later. Airey Neave was to describe Potier as 'one of the bravest of all the agents under my charge'.[1359]

On 31 December 1943, three days after they had found Raymond Beure's ID card, the Gestapo arrested some fifty-eight members of the Possum/Martin group, twenty-four alone in Fismes. Most were deported to Germany. Lucienne Mulette, who had sheltered Sergeant Johnson and one of the Americans, was among them, so, too, was M. Rigault, Camille's father, who was caught sheltering two evaders – Sergeants I.A. Robb and R. Harper. On that morning of 31 December, Ian Robb recalled that 'Harper and I were awakened by shouting and a general hullabaloo downstairs followed by the sound of heavy boots on the stairs. We were only half-dressed but in any event escape from the back bedroom was impossible as the only window opened onto a sheer drop into a high-walled courtyard with no exit. A Gestapo officer with a revolver burst into the room, followed by two army privates of the Feldgendarmerie with rifles.'[1360] Robb and Harper were sent to Reims and Fresnes prisons before being deported on 15 August 1944 to Buchenwald, where they spent several awful weeks before being released into the care of the Luftwaffe.

Madame Mulette's fellow dressmaker, Simone Ledru, was not arrested, but without any consideration for her own safety continued to hide two American airmen officers for several days before escorting them to a safe place. Jean Lorgé, on the other hand, was arrested on 31 December 1943 in a Paris hotel. After a brutal interrogation he was sent to Frontstalag 122 at Compiègne (Oise), and at the end of January 1944 was deported to Buchenwald. Put to work in the salt mines of Warsleben on 13 March 1944 he was liberated there by the Allies on 12 April 1945.[1361] Fourteen of the Fismes group, however, did not return from the Nazis' camps.

On 31 October 1944, with the Germans now gone from the area, a French military tribunal of the 6th Region, in Châlons-sur-Marne, sat in judgement upon five members of the Jeunet family – Camille (aged forty-eight), his wife Marie Jacques (forty), and three of their children, Raymond (twenty-one), André (twenty) and Colette (seventeen) – and upon Raymonde Beure (who was married to Raymond Jeunet on 13 June 1944) and Louise Jeunet, née Broie, wife of Roland Jeunet (himself on the run), who had been working for the Gestapo. After hearing damning evidence, the court ordered that all seven should be put to death. Madame Jeunet and two of her sons were executed, after their appeals had been rejected by a military tribunal of Cassation sitting in Paris. Roland, arrested some while later, was also executed, on 22 September 1945.

CHAPTER 10

Evasions: January–September 1943

'Do you remember our bridge party's here with Bob and Maarten. I miss that so when I hear the machines drone above our heads. I suppose you or Bob are with them and I bid for a happy landing.'
Mrs De Jong, October 1943, in a letter to Pilot Officer Al Hagan

On the night of 13/14 February 1943 RAF Bomber Command mounted its heaviest attack of the war to date on the Breton port of Lorient. Seven of the 466 bombers dropping over a thousand tons of bombs were lost, among them the Stirling flown by Sergeant R.A. Williams. Hit by flak over the target, and with fuel tanks ablaze, Williams gave the order to bale out. He and the rear gunner, Pilot Officer D. Harding-Smith RNZAF, were killed. Four of the five survivors became prisoners of war. The fifth, Sergeant Leonard Willis RCAF, evaded.

Soon after baling out over Plouay (Morbihan) Willis was found by a young Frenchman. Following him across marshy ground, in the course of which his flying boots were sucked off, Willis was taken to a house and provided with civilian clothes, a cap, and a pair of old boots. As it was too dangerous for him to stay indoors, he spent the next four nights in a wood, regularly provided with food by his helpers. Early on the afternoon of 17 February whilst talking to two of them Germans were heard close by. Willis immediately separated from the Frenchmen and hid for four hours or so before daring to look for them again: 'I then saw two men walking about near my former hiding place but as I could not recognise them I did not show myself.'[1362] Rather than risk going back to the house he set off 'heading due East by the stars'. Having covered fifty kilometres or so he spent the night of 18/19 February in a haystack near Josselin, and walked on to Ploërmel in the morning, 'where I saw many Germans. I therefore decided to continue eastwards.'

Turning south at Augan (Morbihan), and failing to buy food from a shop further on at St Laurent, he set off for St Congard, but 'was overtaken by a man on a bicycle who took me back to the shop I had left and gave me some food.' Given further help over the next few days, on the morning of 23 February a young Frenchman took him by bus to Rennes (Ille-et-Vilaine), paying for the tickets with Willis's escape money. At Rennes the Frenchman bought him a train ticket for Angoulême (Charente), a long way south towards Spain: 'I was supposed to change trains at Nantes and at Saintes. For some reason my train did not stop at Nantes but went straight through to Angers, where I arrived about 1600 hours.'

He then made the mistake of catching a local train which, he realised, was heading east. Getting off at a small station in the middle of nowhere he 'spoke to a woman railway official who brought me a timetable.' Approached by a Frenchman who 'spoke a few words of English' Willis was made to understand that he should go to Tours. Having personally taken him back to Angers the man 'spoke to a railwayman who took me to the correct platform for the Tours train.' Willis was put onto the train with six Frenchmen, all bound for Tours, and reached the town an hour or so before midnight. He then caught another train with one of the six Frenchmen at 1 a.m. on 24 February and arrived at Angoulême in the early hours of the morning, at no point having been asked to produce any papers. Abandoned by his French companion once they had arrived there Willis 'walked to the outskirts of the city and sat in a bush for a while.'

Setting off along the road to Ribérac (Dordogne), some fifty-five kilometres more or less south, he called that evening at an isolated farmhouse and asked for a drink: 'A man in the house invited me to come in. He could speak a little English, and had been in a German prisoner-of-war camp. He gave me food and shelter for three days.' On the morning of 27 February a friend of his host took Willis by car to Ribérac, where a second man drove him to Périgueux (Dordogne), where he stayed until 1 March: 'During this time I had my photograph taken and was provided with false identity papers.'

On the train to Pau Willis gave his escort 'what money I had left towards the cost of the ticket'. He stayed in a small hotel until 4 March, when another Frenchman took him by bus to Oloron-Ste Marie (Pyrénées-Atlantiques), where his papers passed inspection by the French police. From Oloron they caught the bus to Tardets-Sorholus: 'During this journey Germans twice boarded the bus and checked our identification papers. We arrived at Tardets about 1600 hours.' Willis was then taken to a house where a small party of six Frenchmen and two women were waiting for a guide to take them across the Pyrenees to Spain.[1363] An hour or so before midnight on 4/5 March the whole party set off with a Basque guide.

After six hours of climbing they had reached 'the high ground to the west of the River le Saison. Here we hid till midnight.' They could see lights in Larrau below them, which the guide said were Germans searching the place. Shortly after midnight on 5/6 March they continued behind their reliable guide up the valley of le Saison, keeping the Pic de Bizkarzé (1,656 metres/5,382 feet) on their right. Over the Spanish border and across the Rio Urchuria, they came to a farm in the middle of the afternoon, where they found some carabineros. One of the two Frenchwomen explained who they were, leaving the Spaniards in the belief that Willis, too, was a Frenchman. After staying the night at the farm the carabineros took them to Abaurrea Alta. Accommodated in various houses, the French generously payed for Willis's lodgings. Taken to Pamplona, some eighty kilometres to the west, they were handed over to the chief of police on 9 March.

Before the men only were imprisoned Willis managed to hand his ring and identity disc to one of the women who, Willis believed, contacted the British Consulate at Bilbao. As usual it was never a quick process extracting British personnel from prison, so it was not until 6 April that Willis was released. After a remarkable solo effort, covering some 700 kilometres from Brittany to the Pyrenees, he finally arrived at Gibraltar on 17 April, and was flown to RAF Hendon three nights later.

On the long, outward journey to Munich in southern Germany on the night of 9/10 March 1943 Stirling R9149 was attacked by a night-fighter near Sedan, France. With the aircraft on fire the pilot, Pilot Officer Frank Morton Tomlinson RCAF, ordered the rest of the crew to bale out. His decision to stay at the controls to give the other six of his crew the time to jump to safety was to cost him his life.[1364] The flight engineer, Sergeant Leonard Marsh, landed in a ploughed field about two kilometres from the village of Elan (Ardennes) and set off south-west 'carrying my parachute, mae west and harness, which I soon buried in a forest. I reached Elan, and not knowing where I was called at a house at about 0130 hours.'[1365] Despite the late hour Marsh was invited in and given a meal. Some four hours later he was shown the road to Reims.

On the way, 'a German patrol and then two [Fieseler] Storch observation planes' were enough to drive him back into the forest near Elan. Coming across a farmer, Len was taken to his house and given civilian clothes in exchange for his RAF uniform. However, the farmer 'could find no shoes for me, as my feet were too big. He also fetched a girl and her father, who said they knew of somebody who could help me. I went along with them and from this point my journey was arranged for me.'

His progress through France was very slow, however. Six months later he had progressed no further than the Reims area, barely seventy kilometres south-west of Elan. On 22 September, told by his helpers that there were some clothes for him in Ville-sur-Retourne, some forty kilometres away, he cycled over. He was on his way back on 24 September when he stopped for a drink at an estaminet at Heutrégiville. His thirst quenched, he 'went to the back yard of the estaminet seeking a lavatory. Here two German officers and a sergeant were supervising the distribution of meat, and one of the officers asked me who I was.' Not satisfied with his (false) identity card, the German demanded to see Len's labour card. Not having one, he was arrested. 'I then had no option but to admit that I was a member of the RAF. My rank, name and number were, however, not recorded.'

Removed under guard to Reims Len and his German escort were at the railway station on 25 September waiting for the train to Châlons-sur-Marne when Len was given permission to go to the lavatory. A sergeant remained outside the toilets with a corporal posted by the door. Once inside Len 'saw that it would be possible to climb into the women's lavatory next door. I did so and emerged on the other side on another platform.' Stealing a bicycle he pedalled off as fast as he could towards Châlons for some ten kilometres before leaving the bicycle and walking to the village of Beine-Nauroy.

Once again, the rest of his journey was arranged for him, and he was flown back from Gibraltar to the UK on the night of 5/6 February 1944.

The most senior RAF officer to evade capture in Western Europe was thirty-seven-year-old Group Captain J.R. Whitley AFC, station commander of RAF Linton-on-Ouse. On the night of 10/11 April 1943 he was flying as second pilot in a 76 Squadron Halifax when it was shot down near Hirson (Aisne) in north-eastern France close to the Belgian border. The local Resistance members, however, were unsure that Whitley was who he claimed to be, for two others of his crew, Sergeants M.B. Strange and M.A.T. Davies, who were being sheltered nearby, had mentioned that flying with them was a colonel with a large moustache. Here before them now was a clean-shaven "colonel". The matter was resolved to everyone's satisfaction when Whitley declared that he had shaved off his moustache before the operation and showed them his identity discs. Any lingering doubts were finally removed when he was driven to meet Strange and Davies.

Moved to a house in Aubenton (Aisne) on 4 May Whitley met Sergeant W.R. Laws, who had been shot down on 16/17 April some thirty kilometres to the north, near Montbliart in Belgium. They left that evening for Charleville to catch the train for Paris. Despite neither evader being in possession of an identity card they reached Paris without any problems. From the Gare de l'Est they caught the

Métro to Aimable Fouquerel's flat at 10, rue Oudinot, meeting Strange and Davies again, and two more evaders, Flight Sergeants D.R. Bradley and W.G. Allen, who had also been shot down on the Pilsen raid, and who were moved to another location that afternoon, after Frédéric de Jongh had paid them a visit. Due to the limited accommodation in Fouquerel's flat Whitley and Laws slept in the flat on the second floor of a woman whose name they did not know.

Having had their ID photographs taken at the Bon Marché on the previous day Whitley and Laws were taken to the Gare d'Austerlitz on the evening of 8 May, where they were joined by a guide called Jacques, and by flight engineer Sergeant G. Brownhill, reported erroneously by Whitley as 'Flt/Engineer Brown of 207 Sqn, RAF'.[1366] Taking the train via Nantes, they arrived at Bordeaux on the morning of 9 May. Elsewhere on the train were Pilot Officer B.H. Marion RCAF and Flight Sergeant D.A. Sibbald RNZAF, who were being escorted by "Madeleine". All met up at the station where, fortuitously, there was no control due to an air-raid exercise taking place. All walked out, singly, "François" giving each of them a new identity card and a special German *Permis de Circulation* for the St Jean-de-Luz area. Early that afternoon the whole party boarded the train for Dax, where they arrived at 4.30 p.m.

As Whitley and Laws spoke French they and Jacques spent the night at the Hôtel de Terminus, 81, rue Vincent-Depaul, Dax. Their papers described them respectively as a butcher, hairdresser and student, which seemed to the group captain to be 'a very ill-assorted trio'. François took the other three by bicycle to Bayonne. Catching the 8.05 a.m. train to Bayonne on 10 May Whitley, Laws, and Jacques rejoined Brownhill, Sibbald, and Marion at a flat there.[1367] Spending the night in the flat François cycled with Sibbald to St Jean-de-Luz in the morning, returning with the spare bicycle and taking Whitley and Marion to St Jean-de-Luz in the evening. Laws and Brownhill followed with Jacques half an hour later. Having dispersed to various cafés they all met again later except for Sibbald.

That evening they set off in pairs, walking along the main railway line south of Ciboure, where they met Sibbald and two "Spanish" guides, one of whom was Florentino Goïcoechea. At Francia Usandizaga's farm they took off their trousers and replaced them with overalls, at the same time putting on espadrilles for the journey over the Pyrenees. Carrying their own trousers and shoes, they departed at around midnight on 11/12 May.

The River Bidassoa was in flood, however, and this necessitated a lengthy detour to a footbridge, somewhere west of Mont Alecor, which they reached just before dawn on 12 May. The bridge was brilliantly lit up, but there was not a guard in sight and no sound of dogs as they filed across to Spain. When they were all over, or thought that all were across, it was discovered that Sergeant Brownhill was missing. How or why no one knew, but Florentino, François and Jacques went back to look for him. Brownhill, though, had vanished. The others carried on along the railway line towards Hendaye, and passing through a tunnel and over a small stream were, at last, safe. Comet "parcels", numbers ninety-six, ninety-seven, ninety-eight, and 100, had been delivered.

Brownhill (99) took a little longer. He lost his companions in the mountains, but carried on alone until he was arrested by a Spanish soldier seven kilometres from the frontier. He spent the next two days in jail, followed by two more in a hotel when he was sent to San Sebastián and allowed to see the British consul. After two more weeks in another hotel and two days in the Saragossa jail, he was sent to sample the delights of Miranda de Ebro for another two weeks or so. He finally sailed from Gibraltar on 23 June 1943, arriving at Liverpool, a month behind the others, on 29 June.

For some evaders, depending on their location and the state of the organisation into whose hands they fell, Switzerland had a certain magnetism. Squadron Leader F.V. Taylor RCAF was piloting a Wellington back from Stuttgart on the night of 14/15 April 1943 when it was shot down by a Ju88 near St Quentin (Aisne) in the north of France. Taylor, who had been on the squadron for only three days, was unfamiliar with his crew and, apparently with the name of his target, told MI9 that he had been to Karlsruhe! Two of the five crew were killed, while another, Sergeant H.N. McKinnon, was eventually taken prisoner of war (see Chapter 7). Taylor and Flying Officer G.C. Crowther DFC, RCAF were the only two to evade, Crowther (102) with Comet's help to Spain.

Surviving his parachute landing at Urvillers, just south of St Quentin, Taylor went in the opposite direction to Crowther and McKinnon, but not before witnessing the demise of a Halifax as it plunged into the ground a few kilometres away.[1368] Walking by night and resting by day Taylor made easterly progress, and had reached Soissons by 20 April. At Crouy farmer Maurice Dupuis gave him civilian clothing and a fake identity card. Another Frenchman, Léon Natier, took him to a railway station to catch the train to Dijon. With further assistance from the French, Fletcher Taylor crossed into Switzerland on 29 April.

As the senior officer, Squadron Leader Taylor 'was in charge of the RAF personnel at Arosa till the arrival of Wing Commander Bragg from Italy about the end of November 1943.'[1369] Five of those RAF personnel to come under his charge were the entire crew of a damaged 431 Squadron Wellington. Returning from the same raid as the one on which Taylor had been lost they had baled out over Switzerland, and had sought refuge there. They were, however, selected for an exchange of internees to take place in June 1943. While they would be returned to England, four German aircrew from two Fieseler Storch observation aircraft that had landed in Switzerland on 19 March 1943 would head for Germany. Departing on 18 June the five RAF airmen travelled across France and through Spain to Gibraltar. On 29 June they arrived at RAF Lyneham, Wiltshire.

The pilot of the 431 Squadron Wellington, Sergeant J.V. Avery, had a proposition to put to Squadron Leader Taylor before he left. It was made in all seriousness, and was, as many great schemes are, simplicity itself. Avery would, he said, come back with a Sunderland flying boat, land on Lake Geneva and pick up 'some of the escapers and evaders at present in Switzerland', all of whom were then 'living at the Hotel Angleterre, Vevey, on the edge of the Lake of Geneva'. Taylor said that he would be 'willing to arrange for a party to assemble on the lake in rowing boats, which can be easily procured… The boats are unguarded and generally have oars in them.'[1370] Avery had it all worked out. He had made a careful study of the lake and thought that if the Sunderland were to land 'near the middle of the lake, it would be difficult for the Swiss to decide whether it was on the Swiss or French side of the lake.'[1371] Taylor kept the scheme to himself, though Avery mentioned it to Donald Darling in Gibraltar and to Jimmy Langley on his return to England. It was never carried out.

On the morning of 31 December 1943 Taylor received a telephone call from Captain Pat Reid of the military attaché's office that he and Lieutenant Commander L.W. "Billie" Stephens RNVR were to report to the Legation in Berne.[1372] Plans were being made for their departure. Also going with them were Engine-room Artificer D. Lister RN; Sergeant R. Brown[1373] and Sergeant S.H. Eyre; Sergeant H. Colhoun (who, with Brown and Eyre, had been gainfully employed in the Legation's cipher office); Flight Lieutenant G.F. Lambert (also employed in the Legation, but on other duties); and two USAAF second lieutenants, Ralph Bruce and John M. Carah,[1374] who had passed his time in Switzerland as assistant air attaché and general aide-de-camp to Brigadier-General Barnwell Rhett Legge, the US military attaché.

The nine men, issued with new clothes for their journey, reported to Victor Farrell at the consulate in Geneva, who arranged for them to leave that night for the French frontier accompanied by a Swiss policeman. Billie Stephens, in charge of the party, decided that it was too late to make the crossing when they reached the frontier, and all returned to a hotel in Geneva for the night. On New Year's Day 1944 'Stephens reported to Mr Farrell that he had a leg injury, and Mr Farrell decided that he should not travel.'[1375]

On 8 January, each of the party, now with Squadron Leader Taylor in charge, was given 70,000 francs and a false French ID card, and was armed with automatic pistols.[1376] Escorted by the Swiss Intelligence Service to the frontier once again and, crossing into France from Soral, they walked the short distance to a house at Viry (Haute-Savoie). Put into a covered truck and driven the twenty kilometres to Frangy (Haute-Savoie), half the party stayed with Madame Marguérite Avons, while Lister, Eyre and the two Americans went some eight kilometres away in the mountains to the farmhouse called Aux Daines, which was, according to Taylor, owned by 'the local chief of the organisation, M. Blanc. (This is possibly an assumed name, as he was also known as Lambert. He was chief of the local Pétain Youth Movement).'[1377]

Charles Clément Blanc (his real name) and his wife, Laurence, were working for the British and for Richard Heslop ("Xavier") and his Marksman circuit (see Chapter 5). Heslop had been brought back to France by Hudson on the night of 18/19 October 1943 (Operation Helm) with his courier, Devereaux Rochester ("Elizabeth"), and wireless operator Captain Denis Johnson ("Paul"), both Americans. These last two were in the second of the two Hudsons which, being flown by Pilot Officer John Affleck, hit some trees as it was coming in to land not, as Rochester says, 'a church belfry'.[1378] A safe landing ensued.

According to Heslop Elizabeth 'was about twenty-seven, and looked as English as her name – but was American. She was tall, with a prominent nose, and she did not walk, she *strode*.'[1379] Born of American parents in New York in 1917 Devereaux, or Dev, had had a European education in England, France and Austria. At some point Dev's mother married Myron Reynolds, a wealthy businessman, and thus it is that this surname is sometimes ascribed to Dev. In 1942, when her mother and many other women were interned at Vittel, Dev made her way to Switzerland. With help from the British and from Swiss Intelligence she crossed back into France in February 1943, having been told to make her own way to Clément and Laurence Blanc's farmhouse. Clément later escorted her to Spain and, having reached England, she was recruited into the FANY, as were so many of SOE's female agents.

By 1944, though, her very "Britishness" was giving Richard Heslop problems: 'I felt that it would be wise to have her sent back to London, partly for her own sake and partly to relieve the minds of those she worked with... I took the coward's way out and asked London to recall her.'[1380] Arrangements were made for her to be picked up on 29 March 1944, and to this end she made her way to Paris. But as she was about to leave the city on 20 March on her way to a safe house she was arrested by the Gestapo. Sticking to her cover story that she was an American citizen who had only recently returned to France from Switzerland, she was nevertheless sent to Fresnes prison for three months, when she was released on condition that she, too, went to Vittel.

There was a delay to the evaders' departure from Frangy caused, so Taylor was told, by their two guides at Perpignan having been 'chased by the Gestapo and the whole organisation had been "blown up".' Clément Blanc in the meantime twice travelled to Perpignan and back to see what could be done to get the eight men across to Spain. On 2 February 1944, soon after his return to Frangy, the eight evaders and escapers left for Perpignan, accompanied by Clément and Laurence Blanc; Laurence's brother, Julien Viallet; Marguérite Avons, and her son, Serge, who was on the run from the French police; and Guy Lansy, or Lannacy, who had a false permit to carry weapons and to whom the evaders surrendered their arsenal before leaving. They caught the train to Lyon, Narbonne, and Perpignan, where they arrived on 3 February and were joined by another Frenchman from Frangy, 'who claimed to be a French Air Force pilot'.

The party now split up, some staying at the Hôtel du Centre, and others with Suzanne Dedieu, a teacher. While they remained for a day or two in Perpignan Joseph Marsal, a member of the Burgundy network, was busy 'organizing the provisions and guides necessary for the next stage of the journey.' This began on the afternoon of 5 February with Marsal leading the assembled company from the meeting place at St Martin's cemetery out of Perpignan. They rendezvoused at Al Peu de las Couloubres (Catalan for "the well of the grass-snakes") with Joseph Ferrusola, 'a Catalan native and Pyrenees guide, and together they trekked towards the Pyrenees Mountains.' The crossing of the Pyrenees was made on the night of 6/7 February, with some difficulty for the out-of-condition members of the party. Food, too, 'was quite scarce and at one point the group dined on roasted thrushes caught in traps previously placed by Ferrusola.'[1381]

Finally stopping about one kilometre into Spain they were joined by another guide, whom Serge Avons recognised from an earlier attempt of his to cross the Pyrenees 'with Lieutenant Millar's party when the crossing had been impossible because of the disappearance of the guide, who was reported drowned. After remaining three weeks in Perpignan on that occasion Serge had returned to Frangy.'[1382] This guide now 'had just brought a party of Spaniards from France. Serge did not tax the guide for fear of getting a knife in his back.'

The reported drowning of the guide was confirmed by Lieutenant G.R. "Josh" Millar,[1383] 1st Rifle Brigade, who had escaped with Lieutenant Wallace Binns (later re-captured) from *Arbeitskommando* 2903 in Munich, southern Germany, in the autumn of 1943. Millar had made his way to a house near Annecy on 2 November when he received a visit from Heslop, 'an officer known as Daniel or Xavier', who told Millar that on no account was he 'to go to Switzerland, as he was organising a service to Spain.'[1384]

At Frangy by the middle of November, Millar received a visit from Elizabeth on 17 November. She was going to take him away, but 'they were waiting for five RAF or American airmen (who could not speak French) and two Frenchmen.' Millar wrote that her 'appearance was intriguing. Mannishly impeccable. A superb tweed costume with a divided skirt, perfect shoes and stockings, expensive luggage... Her hair was reddish and her skin pale but healthy.'[1385] The idea was for Millar to go with the airmen by lorry to Perpignan but, when the airmen failed to arrive and Elizabeth discovered that there was talk in the town about Millar, she took him off on 22 November. Having hired a car 'from a man working for the Maquis' (his name was Angelloz, a garage owner), she drove Millar some twenty-five kilometres north-west to the village of Chaumont (Haute-Savoie). They then walked 'about four kilometres by lanes due west to a farm called Aux Daines, owned by Clément Blanc...'

Once again, plans were made to move Millar to Perpignan with the five airmen and two Frenchmen who were supposed to be arriving from Switzerland, but something went wrong. Apparently 'the five airmen had tried to cross the frontier with a guide but without any papers or other means of identification. They ran into Germans who opened fire. One pilot was killed and the rest got back unhurt into Switzerland.'[1386] It was now decided to move Millar to Spain with two Frenchmen, escorted by Madame Laurence Blanc, but in the event, on 15 December 1943, he left with only Serge Avons. At Perpignan Millar and Avons were accommodated in the Hôtel du Centre, where Laurence 'handed over 15,000 francs to Louis Brun, a Catalan, who said he would pass us over the frontier on 19 December. The 15,000 francs were from British funds supplied by Daniel [Heslop].'[1387]

On the evening of 19 December Millar and Avons, together with an elderly Belgian and five American evaders – Lieutenant D. Schrieber; Staff Sergeant William C. Howell; Technical Sergeant Otto F. Bruzewski; 2nd Lieutenant Eugene V. Mulholland; and Staff Sergeant Rosswell Miller[1388] – who had come from Paris on the Burgundy line were led out of Perpignan 'in a crocodile, escorted by men on bicycles'. Meeting their guide, 'a Spaniard or Catalan, who is a doctor in Barcelona', they were given espadrilles to replace their own footwear and food for two days, 'which would probably have been insufficient even in the best of circumstances'. At around 2 a.m. on 20 December they came to the River Tech at a point due south of Latour-bas-Elne. Germans regularly patrolled the southern bank of the river, which also marked the northern edge of the Zone Interdite. Normally placid enough, eight days of rain had turned the river into a flood. The elderly Belgian, already tired by this stage, handed his kit to others to carry for him. Taking off their trousers and coats, and holding hands, the group set out into the torrential river, which at this point was some eighty to 100 metres wide.

Just how dangerous the Tech could be was demonstrated when, over 16-18 October 1940, seventy-five centimetres (thirty inches) of rain fell in the hills several kilometres upstream of the Millar party's crossing point. The river, which descends between Amélie-les-Bains and La Preste at an average gradient of almost one in four, was flowing at a speed of some fifteen kph (ten mph). Such was the volume of rainwater that the river flooded to depths of ten metres or more, rising to twenty-five to thirty metres in some of the Tech tributaries. Massive landslides and severe flooding followed.

Also dangerous could be the River Bidassoa, at the other end of the Pyrenees, which claimed two victims on the night of 23/24 December 1943. From the house of Kattalin Aguirre in Ciboure ten men set off to cross the mountains to Spain. As Florentino Goïcoechea was suffering with the flu, Manuel and his friend Martin Erasquin acted as guides for Jean-François Nothomb, Comte Antoine d'Ursel, Albert Ancia, Roland Bru (alias "Richard", 'a Frenchman of unknown background'),[1389] and four Americans. As they were being led over the river 2nd Lieutenant J.F. Burch USAAF, already exhausted by the long journey and with a weak and wounded leg, stumbled in five feet of icy, rushing water, and was swept to his death, as was forty-seven-year-old Comte Antoine d'Ursel. Their bodies were recovered by the Germans, who put them on display in Biriatou as a warning to the inhabitants. When the Basques, far from being intimidated, bedecked the bodies with garlands of flowers, the Germans immediately removed them for secret burial.

After thirty-five minutes Millar and party were still ten metres or so short of the south bank, with the water up to their chests, when the Belgian collapsed, losing his leather coat, and one of the Americans lost his trousers with its US army belt. Serge Avons and the guide were swept away but were grabbed in time by the others, the guide then leading them back to the north bank after an hour in the water. When Millar spotted a German patrol, luckily on the southern bank, the guide quickly led the party a kilometre or so along the river and hid them in low scrub. Saying that he would return that evening, the guide slipped away and was never seen again. By then they 'were all frightfully cold, and the Belgian was practically delirious.' They waited in the scrub all night and all the next day, until they agreed to let Millar lead them back to Perpignan.

Managing to get lost at some point they were still four kilometres short of Perpignan by the curfew hour, 11 p.m. The Belgian, too tired to continue, was left behind with instructions to follow on as best he could, and to meet them at a café near the station in the morning. The rest spent the night in a vineyard a short way from the town, and set off again half an hour after the ending of curfew, 5 a.m., with the American who had lost his trousers in the river still wearing his "long johns". Three-quarters of an hour later they were in Perpignan, and Millar made contact with Louis Cartelet, the chief of the *Compagnons de France* in Perpignan, 'formerly a professor in the Institute Français in Barcelona, who works for our information side'. Millar had met him through Laurence Blanc, and 'knew that he was the go-between [for] the organisation which had sent me down and Brun's passeur organisation.'

It was from Louis Brun that Millar also learnt that the reason why the guide had failed to show up after the abortive river crossing was that he had been found drowned in the Tech, and the Germans were suspected of his drowning. As the documents that he had been carrying were still about his person, Millar firmly believed that the guide's death was accidental. Brun added that they would try the crossing again on Christmas Eve, when it was expected that all the Germans would be drunk, but it was not until 27 December 1943 that they left for the second attempt, the party now with two additional Frenchmen.

The guide led them off at great speed. After half an hour or so Millar noticed by the stars that they were heading north-east instead of south-east and told the guide, who flew into a temper. After three hours rambling around in the dark they discovered that they were back where they had started. 'The guide threw up his hands and said that he would put us across the frontier if I [Millar] took him and the party to the River Tech.' Getting only as far as the River Réart, still nine or ten kilometres short of the Tech, by about 3 a.m. on 28 December, the guide said that they would have to stay the night there. It was appallingly cold. The three Frenchmen had had enough and refused to go on anyway, and after an hour's arguing Millar once again led the party back to Perpignan, this time taking only two hours or so. Serge Avons and the other two Frenchmen went home.

During the next few days, with the Gestapo actively chasing Cartelet and the Brun organisation, it was not until the night of 3 January 1944 that Millar and the five American airmen left 'with a famous guide (no name) a man of fifty-five years of age who has been twenty-six years a smuggler. He was reputed to be wanted in both Spain and France and to have escaped from the Gestapo in the Citadelle in Perpignan.' They made good time, and crossed the Tech, now much lower and calmer, nearer the sea. Resting for much of 4 January, the guide led them on that night into the Pyrenees. After some three hours, 'all the Americans except one lieutenant, started passing out. They had been drinking stream water and eating snow, although we had told them not to do so. It was also by this time very cold. As we approached the final ridge two of the Americans – 2nd Lieutenant Eugene V. Mulholland and Staff-Sergeant Rosswell Miller – lay down. Mulholland refused to go on because his legs had "passed out". He asked for half an hour's rest.'[1390] With German patrols constantly passing the area, the guide could not agree to this, and so it was left to the others to drag him up to a clump of trees, where he adamantly refused to go any further. His pal, Miller, stayed with him.

The others carried on with the guide and crossed into Spain without being arrested, as, apparently, did Mulholland and Rosswell Miller, who managed to make the final part of the journey by themselves.

Resuming their journey in the dark the Taylor party got as far as Rabós, where Ferrusola had relatives. Here they were fed and watered before moving on to Figueras, a dozen kilometres south, and eventually reached Barcelona on 11 February, the British Consulate having been forewarned of their arrival.

All the servicemen reached Gibraltar in due course, the "British" returning to England on the night of 23/24 February 1944. As for the two Americans, Bruce had left for Miami on 22/23 February, and Carah, via Casablanca on 28 February, for New York, where he arrived on 2 March. Clément and Laurence Blanc returned to the Haute-Savoie, and came back with a second group of evaders and escapers. On arrival at Perpignan station, on 25 February, however, the Gestapo arrested them and the two American airmen in their charge. Clément was brutally tortured before being executed at Fort Montluc prison, Lyon on 7 April 1944. Laurence survived the horrors of Ravensbrück and Mauthausen camps before she was liberated on 20 April 1945.

Squadron Leader Wallace Ivor Lashbrook's great experience counted for little on the clear night of 16/17 April 1943 when Oberleutnant Rudolf Altendorf and his crew in their Me110 caught up with his Halifax over Belgium.[1391] Wally Lashbrook had already completed a tour of twenty-five operations by January 1941 (flying Whitleys on 51 Squadron), and his was one of eight crews (of 51 and 78 Squadrons) to be sent to Malta in February 1941 to carry out Operation Colossus (see Chapter 5). After that operation Wally Lashbrook landed back at Malta, but not long afterwards Italian bombs damaged his Whitley, and he was left on the island while the others flew home. He returned to England on 15 February, after his aircraft had been repaired using parts from other damaged aircraft, and was posted to 35 Squadron.

He and his crew had a "moment" on 15/16 April 1941 when their Halifax, damaged over the target, limped home and ran out of fuel on approach to base. In the inky blackness Wally "landed" the aircraft in a field with a large tree in it. Calling to his crew, all rallied to his side except for the rear gunner: 'His name was called and, in very strong language, a reply came from an area ten or so yards down the hedgerow. The gunner was trapped in his turret…'[1392] On 18 April 1941 Wally's DFM was gazetted. More operations and a period of training followed until, having risen to the rank of acting squadron leader, he was posted to 102 Squadron on 10 April 1943.

Six days later he and his crew went off in their Halifax on the Pilsen raid to meet their destiny at the hands of Altendorf and his crew in their Me110. On the way back, as the skies over the Low Countries began to clear, ideal conditions for enemy night-fighters, Wally warned the crew to 'watch out for the fighters. There's a Lanc going down on the port. Keep your eyes…' Before he could finish the warning a single, long burst of cannon fire raked the Halifax, killing the twenty-two-year-old rear gunner, Flying Officer G.G. Williams GM,[1393] and wounding the mid-upper gunner, Sergeant L. Neill.

The bomb aimer, navigator and wireless operator baled out through the forward hatch. The flight engineer, Flight Sergeant D.C. Knight, who had been an RAF apprentice at Halton with Wally way back in 1929 (they had consecutive service numbers), clipped on his pilot's parachute and then dived out himself. Wally, staying at the controls until everyone had got out, decided that at 3,000 feet it was time to make a move, but no sooner did he let go of the controls than the Halifax went into a spin. It was all he could do to leave: 'By pulling himself to the hatch and popping his parachute while leaning partially out of the aircraft, the parachute pulled him free like a champagne cork out of a bottle.'[1394] He estimated that he was only 500 feet from the ground at this point, and landed soon after the Halifax and barely 100 yards from it. So swift had his descent been that as he lay on the ground he saw Knight floating down a few hundred yards away. They would not see each other again until after the war, as Knight, and the wounded Neill, were both taken prisoner.

Wally made his way into France, and on 20 April was fortunate to come across an isolated cottage in which gamekeeper Henri Michel, his wife and baby daughter lived. Henri took him, by rail, to another gamekeeper, Albert, and between them the two Frenchmen got Wally safely to Reims. There Doctor and Madame Lechanteur gave him shelter, though for the six days and nights he spent hiding in the attic Wally was unaware that monsieur was a doctor and was carrying on his practice in the usual way in the house. On 26 April, advised that the Germans were carrying out a random search of houses in the area, Wally was driven by Christian Hecht, the local Resistance chief, by van to the house of Monsieur de Kegal, a butcher at Mailly-la-Champagne.

In 1944 de Kegal was to pay for his activities with his life, as were two more of Wally's helpers along the way, Georges Lundy and Joseph Berthet, neither of whom returned from Dachau concentration camp. Unaware of these impending tragedies Wally was taken to Paris by a young Comet guide, Madeleine Bouteloupt, and to the apartment of the Waeles family. Sometime in June Wally's evasion south continued when Madeleine escorted him to the Gare du Sud to catch their train to the south-west of France. There, to Wally's utter amazement, was his bomb aimer, Flying Officer Alfred Martin.

Alfred, or "Paddy" as the Ulsterman born in Belfast in 1920 was familiarly known, had also left his landing site as quickly as possible. Realising that he would make faster progress along the roads rather than across fields, he bumped into two gendarmes talking to a woman. One of them asked him for his papers, which he was unable produce. His impression of being dumb failed to convince the policemen, and they asked him to accompany them to the station. He was just about to make a run for it when one of the gendarmes asked him if he were 'Anglais'. 'Oui', replied the Irishman. Following a quick conference the two custodians of the law told Paddy to 'Allez vite'. Needing no second bidding he "went quickly" as ordered.

As lucky as his pilot in finding help, Alfred found himself in Comet's hands, at the Coolen family's farmhouse at Sains-du-Nord (Nord). His ginger hair was dyed black, as were his blue RAF trousers, before he was escorted by Madame Rosine Witton and a Monsieur Duclos to Lille and then to Arras, where he was joined by 2nd Lieutenant Douglas C. Hoehn USAAF, who had had the horrifying experience of watching his buddies being machine-gunned as they baled out of their stricken B-17 at 25,000 feet. Doug wisely decided to delay opening his parachute until he was only a few thousand feet from the ground.[1395]

After a couple of days in Arras Martin and Hoehn were moved to Paris, and spent a week there before Madeleine Bouteloupt took them to the Gare du Sud to meet Wally Lashbrook. The journey to Bordeaux was slow and uncomfortable. Also on the train, but at a discreet distance, were Jean-François Nothomb ("Franco", now head of the Comet line following Andrée de Jongh's arrest), and Rosine Witton. Leaving Madeleine and Rosine behind, their job done, Nothomb and the three evaders took the train to Dax. The next stage of their evasion was accomplished by bicycle, not without problems with tyres and chains, to Bayonne along minor roads, a distance of some sixty kilometres. Spending the night in Bayonne at a riverside café run by 'an incredibly fat and jovial Frenchman' who gave them an enormous meal with plenty of wine and coffee, they set off again on the following evening for St Jean-de-Luz, some twenty kilometres away.

An hour or two before midnight the four men were joined by a guide who supplied each of them with a pair of espadrilles and cotton trousers, the former to allow them to climb rocks more easily and the latter to replace their own trousers when crossing streams. The guide took them to Francia Usandizaga's farmhouse near Urrugne, where they were handed over to Florentino Goïcoechea, who 'looked astonishingly fit and agile'. Their impression of him was to prove only too accurate as he led the four men at a cracking pace up the rough mountain trail. At about 3.30 a.m. on 5 June they forded the Bidassoa. Comet had safely delivered "parcels" 110, 111, and 112 to Spain.

Finally reaching Sarobe farmhouse, the end of the line for Florentino, it was agreed to split up, and while Alfred Martin and Doug Hoehn rested, the tireless Nothomb and Wally Lashbrook pressed on to Irún and caught a tram to San Sebastián. Depositing Wally 'at a house near the sea front', where he received a warm welcome and enjoyed a hot bath, Nothomb returned in the evening to collect Alfred and Doug, and also brought them to the house near the sea front. Contact was made with the British Consulate in San Sebastián, and a car took them to Madrid, 475 kilometres (300 miles) distant, arriving at the British Embassy on the morning of 10 June. When papers were ready, they went to Gibraltar, by train. There Doug Hoehn very nearly came to grief. It was the practice for Spanish customs officials to ask everyone crossing to Gibraltar whether or not they were British. When Doug was asked by a Spanish official to state his place of birth he replied 'Canterbury'. To the next question, 'What county?', he replied 'Yorkshire', and was formally allowed to pass.

True to form, "red tape" caught up with Wally as soon as he crossed into Gibraltar. Having been shot down as an acting squadron leader, and having been paid accordingly, he was informed that that rate of pay had ended as soon as he was back on British soil. Once again a substantive flight lieutenant he received pay at the lower rate on the grounds that he was no longer 'filling a squadron leader vacancy'. He was restored to the higher rate, and to the rank of acting squadron leader, once he had returned to flying duties. There was some compensation, however, when he was awarded the DFC.[1396]

On 21 June Wally, Alfred and Doug, with Sergeants D. Ferguson, S.J. Moore (see previous chapter) and F.W. Pinkerton and Pilot Officer D.G. Ross (see Chapter 7), departed aboard a Dakota for Whitchurch airport, Bristol.

For his extraordinary evasion, which had begun on the night of 12/13 May 1943 after he had landed in a pine tree, Flight Lieutenant Douglas Julian Sale RCAF received the rare distinction of being admitted a Companion of the Distinguished Service Order. Shot down near Haaksbergen in the Dutch province of Gelderland, near the border with Germany, he made his way south by various means across some 1,300 to 1,400 kilometres of enemy-controlled territory with no help from any organisation, and reached the Prinicipality of Andorra on the night of 25/26 June.

Climbing down from the Dutch pine tree he set off west across country, minus one flying boot that had come off after he had baled out. A nervous Dutch farmer gave him a pair of clogs and some food, and pointed him in the direction of Arnhem. Sale and the clogs did not get on. Suffering badly from blisters, the clogs were rejected. After further help from a family near Linde, who gave him a change of clothes and a map, he decided to avoid Arnhem and head for Oosterbeek to the west. Hoping to find a bridge over the Nederrijn, he came across the Arnhem to Nijmegen railway bridge. Believing it to be unguarded he tried to cross in the failing evening light, but a sudden challenge in German, followed by the crack of a rifle shot, made him realise that it was not. Waiting until it was dark, he took off his clothes, tied them to a plank of wood, and pushed off to the other side.

By the afternoon of 22 May he had reached Belgium, on a bicycle kindly provided by some Dutch folk, when two Belgian policemen stopped him for not having the proper licence plate. They were friendly, however, and he was allowed to carry on after fashioning a plate from a cigarette box. Making excellent progress through Belgium he was shown the way across the border into France by a Belgian farmer in Grandrieu. It was now 23 May. Punctures were mended, and food provided by good French people, and pressing on through Laon (Aisne), Château-Thierry (Aisne) and Sens (Meuse), he reached Bourges (Vaucluse), and the Demarcation Line. A farmer helped him across an unguarded bridge a few kilometres south of Bourges, and by 1 June he was at Castres (Tarn). On the following day he was at Revel (Haute-Garonne), fifty kilometres north-east of Toulouse, but then rested at several farms in the area for the next three weeks.

During his stay he met a Frenchman who needed to leave the country, and they left together on 21 June, heading to Toulouse, with the intention of eventually crossing the Pyrenees. Catching a train to Carcassonne (Aude), a further ninety kilometres from Toulouse, they changed onto the local line for Quillan, fifty kilometres closer to the mountains. Here they caught a bus to Belcaire (Aude), ever closer to the Pyrenees, though Belcaire itself lies at an altitude of 1,000 metres. Joining a party of six others waiting to be guided over the mountains, they began their journey to the Pyrenees early on the morning of 24 June, though still some twenty-five kilometres distant.

Up in the mountains proper the guide became lost, and the group had to spend the night in the open, but by the afternoon of 25 June they were only three or four kilometres from Andorra. When the guide refused to go any further, Sale and his French companion headed off on their own through snowdrifts, even though it was early summer. Passing the high peaks of Pic Espaillat (2,263 metres/7,350 feet) and Pic de Ruille (2,783 metres/9,045 feet), they spent the night of 25/26 June in a hut. Arriving at Canillo in Andorra on 26 June a Spanish smuggler agreed to take them to the British Consulate in Barcelona. Although it was downhill most of the way, they had to walk a further, gruelling, 150 kilometres over the next ten days through Spain, until they reached the town of

Manresa. The smuggler went on to Barcelona alone and told the consul of the two men, who were collected by the consular car on 7 July.

It was not until 5 August that Flight Lieutenant Julian Sale sailed from Gibraltar.[1397] Sale returned to his squadron but, now a squadron leader DSO and Bar, DFC,[1398] he was shot down again, on the night of 19/20 February 1944, and was badly wounded. He died in captivity on 20 March 1944 aged thirty. It is said that this very brave man, no longer able to bear the awful pain, took his own life.

Many an evader was promised a return to England by air by optimistic helpers. For a lucky few, including Pilot Officer Robert Taylor, the dream became reality on the night of 23/24 June 1943. He had been navigating a Mosquito of 1409 (Meteorological) Flight on a Pampas operation (checking the weather on the continent prior to a bomber raid) on 14 June when it was shot down at 28,000 feet by two Fw190s. The pilot was killed, but Taylor baled out over Normandy and was taken in by a Madame Piegney and her son Guy who lived in the tiny village of Ginai (Orne). On the afternoon of 20 June, after contact had been made with 'the organisation', Taylor was picked up by car on a lonely road by two Frenchmen and taken to their house for the night. On the following day he was escorted 'to Paris by train with three Frenchmen. In Paris I was asked a set of questions to establish my identity, and at 1000 hours was taken to a flat, where I stayed the night.'[1399]

Then, on 22 June, he was taken to Amboise (Indre-et-Loire). The next night he was sitting in a Lysander aircraft and on his way back to England. He would be home within ten days, which was fast by any standards, on SOE's Operation Curator/Acolyte. He might have been back even sooner, for this operation was attempted by Squadron Leader Hugh Verity on the nights of 20/21 and 22/23 June. The landing field was one under the organisation of the double-agent Henri Déricourt, and was located near Pocé-sur-Cisse, just across the River Loire from Amboise. Also on his way back to England for a well-earned rest was SOE agent Richard Heslop, who said of Taylor that he 'was a fine man, but did not speak one word of French and looked as English as roast beef.' The two had met in Paris and travelled together to Amboise with "Claude" and "Auger", two of 'the men who were responsible for handling the reception of the Lysander'.[1400]

Verity had no difficulty locating the field near the river and, as it was a fine, starry night, he decided to land before the moon had risen by way of an experiment to see if such a landing were possible. In the event, unable to see whether there were any trees or not, he frightened himself so much that he vowed not to do it again.[1401] Heslop, mightily impressed by the timing and navigation of the lone airman, and Taylor were soon aboard, and on their way back. They encountered light flak at some point, and Verity took the Lysander down to only a few feet to avoid it, his skill giving Heslop even more cause to heap praise upon the pilot. Soon across the Channel Verity and his passengers landed at Tangmere, on the south coast of England.

It was rare enough for an RAF evader to be brought back by air, but even rarer was it for one to be brought back by sea from the German stronghold that was The Netherlands. So rare was it, in fact, that it happened to only three RAF airmen, one in May 1943 and two in July 1943.

First of the three was wireless operator Sergeant C.M.M. Mora RNZAF, shot down on 26/27 April 1943 after the incendiaries in his Stirling bomber had been set ablaze by a night-fighter. Landing at Breukelen, near Utrecht, he was the only one of the six survivors (one of the gunners was killed) to avoid capture, even though he crashed through the glass roof of a market-garden greenhouse. On 28 April he was in the hands of Anton "Tony" Schrader, head of the local resistance organisation and a senior official in the food control office of the Dutch Department of Agriculture. Tony took him in his German-approved car to The Hague, and told him that 'there was a boat leaving for England in two days'. He then 'explained that his duties take him round Holland and that he had Dutchmen working on various farms in his organisation. He said they were organised to inform him of the landing of any British airmen, although I was actually the first they had helped.'[1402]

Schrader left Mora with the Burgwal family at Populierstraat 19, The Hague, but on 29 April took him to see the boat that was to be used. It was some eighteen feet long, powered by an 85 h.p. Ford V8 engine, and was capable of a speed of 32-35 kph/20-22 mph.[1403] On 2 May Mora was one of a party of ten who made their way by truck to one of the islands to the south of Rotterdam to await the boat, which was to have been brought by barge from The Hague. Unfortunately, the boat failed to arrive, and the disappointed party headed back to The Hague. Time and the curfew were now against them, and they had to spend the night in the food control kitchen at Delft. News of the barge reached them next day – it had arrived barely ten minutes after they had left.

The second attempt to leave was made on 5 May. The same party assembled at the barge that evening, and waited until it was dark before loading their food and compass onto the motorboat, which was then lifted out of the barge's hold. As it was low water when they set off, they got stuck in the sand several times. About three-quarters of an hour after they had passed Hellevoetsluis, they got stuck again, and then ran into two German patrol vessels, possibly armed trawlers, lying in the estuary. When the Dutch boat was barely fifty metres to the port of them the Germans challenged them with a flashlight. Mora told the skipper to open up to full speed, but it took the German sailors five valuable seconds before they opened fire with cannons and machine guns. Underestimating the motorboat's speed, their shots fell well astern. Nevertheless, the Germans took up the pursuit, but the motorboat was too fast for them, and they were left well behind.

At around 3.45 a.m. on 6 May they passed four 'speed boats' (possibly E-boats), but were not seen. Some nine hours later, nearing the English east coast, they 'sighted aircraft and a convoy which appeared to be assembling'. Eventually making contact with a small cargo ship, they were taken on board, but the motorboat sank when attempts were made to tow it behind the ship. The Dutch party was dropped off at Harwich at 5.20 p.m. that evening.

It took the other two airmen – Pilot Officer (Lieutenant) J.B.M. Haye RNethAF and Pilot Officer Alfred Hagan – a little longer to get back from The Netherlands in July 1943. Bob Haye was brought down on the night of 13/14 May 1943, and Al Hagan on the night of 21/22 June 1943. Dutchman Haye, hidden with several people in The Hague, was also taken by Anton Schrader to the Burgwal family, on 30 May, where he assumed the identity of, and used the papers of, fellow Dutchman Rudolf Franz Burgwal, who had gone to England in 1941. While staying with the Burgwals, Haye frequently visited the de Jong family, a few doors away at Populierstraat 7, for a very good reason – 'one of their daughters is now my fiancée.'[1404]

Pilot Officer Al Hagan could not have known at the time just how fortunate he was to survive. His crew (Flight Sergeant E.A. Sims RAAF) were not posted for operations on the night of 21/22 June but, when another crew (Sergeant Gardner's) needed a replacement bomb aimer, Al Hagan "volunteered". It was to be Al's first bombing operation, and his last, just as it would be for Sims and the rest of his crew. On the very next night, 22/23 June, they and their replacement bomb aimer, Sergeant T.W.C. Luther, were lost over the North Sea. There were no survivors.

So it was that on the morning of 23 June Pilot Officer Al Hagan found himself on the outskirts of Esch, Rotterdam being helped by twenty-one-year-old Edward Reijnders, whose brother Bernard had coincidentally gone to England on the same boat as Mora. Passed on to a man known to him only as Gottfried, Al that night 'slept in a small tent hidden among some bushes in the garden of Gottfried's house. About midnight I heard rifle shots close by.' Gottfried came out to tell him to be prepared to leave immediately, and to make sure that he removed every trace of his ever having been there. Later Al 'heard some more shots, and finally a party of German troops, laughing and singing, marched towards the village of Esch.'[1405]

Early next morning, 24 June, Edward Reijnders took Al back to his house. That afternoon Tony Schrader arrived in a four-seater car with Dutch markings and with its windows painted over, driven by a man called Schneider. Al was taken away to Haarlem and transferred to 'a black closed van belonging to the food control office in The Hague'. Hidden beneath sacks of coke, fuel for the van, he was taken to the Burgwals' house, but had to go to Maarten Gutterling's house at Beeklaan 450 for a bath. Clean again,[1406] Al went back to the Burgwals, where he met Bob Haye, who that same day went off to stay at Maarten Gutterling's house. Al was sustained, meanwhile, on a prodigious diet of fruit, particularly strawberries, and by the news, on 14 July, that the next boat attempt to get to England was to be nine days later. As there was a continuing shortage of small, seaworthy vessels, Tony Schrader had had to commission yet another motorboat from boat-builder Meyer.

On 20 July 'a Dutch policeman called at the Burgwals' house. Apparently he had received an anonymous letter to say that Mme. Burgwal was receiving more food than that to which she was entitled… She denied the charge, and the policeman went away. He did not seem to take a very serious view of the matter.'[1407] Nevertheless, Tony Schrader was sufficiently worried to have to move Al to the de Jongs' house down the road.

It was not until the evening of 26 July, however, three days later than planned, that all was ready for the next boat crossing to England. Haye, Hagan and six Dutchmen were collected by Schrader and Schneider in an open truck carrying oil barrels. After a meal at Groot Hertogginlaan, 36 they drove through Rotterdam to Noord Beijerland. 'From here we went three miles along a canal, which we crossed near Goudswaard. On the south side of this canal we found a barge owned by a man named Kees.'[1408] Kees Kool's nephew, Willem Kool, was to join the group for England.

Concealed in the hold of the barge, loaded with potatoes, was the boat on which the crossing of the North Sea was to be made. At around 10.30 p.m. on 26 July Dolph Mantel, the skipper of the barge, ordered the boat to be lifted overboard. It was the same size as Mora's, some eighteen-twenty feet in length, and powered by a recently overhauled Ford V8 engine. It also had a smaller outboard engine, and was equipped with '400 litres of benzine, a supply of lubricant, a small quantity of fresh water, and four double loaves of bread' provided by Mrs Burgwal.

With the two airmen and nine Dutchmen ready to cast off from the mooring near the village of Goudswaard, close to the stretch of the Maas and Waal estuary known as the Haringvliet, Tony Schrader provided a rough course, which was calculated by Al Hagan. At 11.35 p.m. the little craft got under way, but at quarter speed to keep the noise down, past Hellevoetsluis and close to the south of the channel to avoid sandbanks and German patrol boats. At about 1.40 a.m. on 27 July, two German guard ships flashed the letter "B" at them. Ignoring it, the German vessels took no further action.

On 28 July the main engine broke down, the outboard gave only intermittent help and next day they were obliged to rig the sail and to use the four paddles that had been provided. Their course remained true, however, and just after 7 a.m. on 30 July, when they were some fifteen kilometres (ten miles) off the mouth of the Thames estuary they were picked up by the Royal Navy's HMS *Garth*, a modern "Hunt" class destroyer of 1,000 tons. The faithful Dutch boat, having served its purpose, was abandoned and sunk by *Garth*'s guns.

The passengers were landed at Sheerness at ten minutes past midday. As Hagan and Haye had arrived without proof of identity and in civilian clothes Captain Young, the Security Control Officer Chatham, needing to be satisfied as to their identity, telephoned their respective squadrons to check that the two men standing before him were indeed who they claimed to be. Al Hagan, he said, was: 'Height 5′ 3″. Weight 8 stone. Brown eyes and hair. Scar on right forefinger. Scar on left forehead.' And Haye, born in Pehalongon, Java, was described as: 'Height 5′ 9½″. Weight 10 st. 6 lbs. Brown hair and eyes, freckles.'[1409] 'After some difficulty their identity was established through contact with the squadrons to which they belonged, and they were sent on by car, to The London District Assembly Centre, Great Central Hotel, Marylebone'.

In October 1943 Al Hagan received a letter and some photographs from Elly de Jong's mother. They had been brought over by Tony Schrader, who had escaped from Holland on one of his own boats. Two earlier boats had had the misfortune to run into difficulties once at sea and had had to turn back, one of them after thirty-six hours in a storm. The occupants of the first were arrested on their return, but with each of the boats Mrs de Jong had sent a letter to Al Hagan. In what would prove to be her third letter, therefore, she asked: 'Do you remember our bridge party's here with Bob [Haye] and Maarten [Gutterling]. I miss that so when I hear the machines drone above our heads. I suppose you or Bob are with them and I bid for a happy landing.'[1410]

As for Tony Schrader, he had sent over eight boatloads of evaders and escapers before he himself had to escape on the last of them on 8 October 1943. He was too busy to meet up with Al Hagan, but did manage to write him a letter on 15 December 1943, enclosing one from Elly de Jong that he had had with him since leaving Holland in October: 'I had intended to meet you and hand over this letter to you, but the Dutch authorities need me now every day.'[1411] In her letter, Elly mentioned the failure of the first of the two boats, saying that Maarten Gutterling and fourteen other Dutch boys were on board, but 'are in German hands now. A pity. The second boat came back, and the five boys arrived here safely'. She, too, remembered 'the many bridge parties and ping-pong', and signed off with 'Happy new year, merry christmas, and so on. Cheerio, Elly.'[1412]

Tony Schrader later joined the American OSS. Parachuted into the Dutch province of Groningen on the night of 9/10 November 1944, he was arrested on 10 February 1945. Becoming a double agent, he continued to supply the OSS with much vital information, for which the Americans awarded him the Silver Star. From the Dutch he received the Verzetsherdenkingskruis (Resistance Commemorative Cross).[1413]

Edward Reijnders was also arrested, in July 1944, and sent to a concentration camp, not returning home until August 1945 in very poor health. He was still in hospital three months later, when his wife wrote to Al Hagan. At the end of the letter she asked if Al knew of a doctor who could send her penicillin for Edward.[1414]

The moving postscript to Bob Haye's story may be found in *Shot Down and on the Run*. Haye returned to The Hague after the war to see his fiancée, Elly de Jong, but 'was horrified to learn that she and other members of her Resistance group had been betrayed and arrested.'[1415] Sentenced to death, Elly was sent to Ravensbrück concentration camp and then Mauthausen, but was liberated before the sentence could be carried out. She became Mrs Haye soon after the war, and they were married for over fifty years.

Flying Officer H.T. Huston RCAF and Squadron Leader A. Lambert DFC, RCAF wandered off in what they hoped was a southerly direction after baling out of Halifax HR854, which had been shot down by a night-fighter on the night of 15/16 July 1943.[1416] They got as far as Châtelus Malvaleix

(Creuse), in the very heart of France, before coming to a halt for several weeks as they waited for the Resistance to provide them with false papers to allow them to continue their journey.

Eventually taken to Paris, some 300 kilometres north, they joined up with three American airmen and five Frenchmen, the latter hoping to get to North Africa. From Paris all went by train to Toulouse, continuing 'by a bus on a rail track to a mountain resort. Afterwards they travelled in a charcoal burning Peugeot car to a goatherd's hut on the slopes of the Pyrenees... They were the last group to be escorted over the mountains from France to Spain that year, crossing near the border of Andorra',[1417] though it was to be a gruelling five days and nights before they reached Spain, arriving at the British Consulate at Barcelona on 21 November 1943.

One of HR854's gunners, Flying Officer P.W. Simpson RCAF, managed to make his way to the Spanish frontier, where he was one of a party of thirteen to make the crossing of the Pyrenees. He and a fellow evader, Flight Sergeant R.F. Conroy RCAF, however, were worried: 'Being in such a large party to make the night crossing into Spain, we were making very slow progress. So Flying Officer Simpson and I thought the party was too large and broke away from it on August 15th. That day we walked to a town, which was probably Berga, and continued south. At the outskirts of a village we stopped a man and asked for cigarettes. We also asked for directions to Barcelona and enquired if there were police in the next village. The man went ahead of us and when we arrived at this next village the police were waiting for us. They took us to their police station and were quite friendly. After giving us lunch, a police escort took us to the Police HQ at Barcelona, where we remained in a cell until the 19th. We were then moved to a gaol at Barcelona, where the British Consul visited us.'[1418]

The two airmen were released on 8 September, and finally reached the United Kingdom on 2 October 1943.

Almost six weeks behind them was another airman shot down on the Montbéliard raid, Sergeant I.J. Sansum. Badly spraining an ankle on landing, he nevertheless managed to hobble to a haystack and get some sleep. He was found next morning by a boy, whose mother brought him some milk. She told him to move along, which he did with great difficulty, his badly swollen ankle still causing him great pain. He was resting in a field when a woman herded some cows into it, and told him to shut the gate when he left. Half an hour later a man appeared and told him that he had to be moved as there were a lot of Germans about: 'He then carried me across his shoulders into a nearby wood and later returned with some food and wine.'[1419] Sansum was well cared for as his ankle slowly recovered. Eventually it was time for him to leave, when contact had been made with 'an organisation in Paris, who arranged the rest of my journey for me. I finally reached Gibraltar on Wednesday, November 10th, 1943, and was flown back to the UK the following day.'[1420]

Luck ran out, though, for Sergeant B.A. Lee, in the same crew as Sansum. On the run for almost eleven months he met two soldiers of the Loyal Regiment – Gregory and Brierley – who had themselves been evading since Dunkirk. Lee and Brierley, in the hands of a group of ill-disciplined maquisards, were taken to a château somewhere, and joined by two RAF evaders and an American. When the Germans attacked early on the morning of 9 June the five evaders were forced to take to the woods. Soon rounded up they were taken by lorry to Romorantin. Sergeant Lee reported: 'We were beaten up with the rifle butts of the German guards. They also tried to smash our faces against a wall. Our wrists were tied up with wire and then we were all tied up to each other and knocked down and beaten with a whip. I was eventually cut loose and kicked into a room where I was interrogated by two German Army officers. I was beaten up so badly that I can hardly remember what I said to them.'

Ten months later, after he had returned home from Stalag Luft VII, Lee was informed that 'some of my helpers in France were put into concentration camps.' His capture was the result of the high spirits of the young Frenchmen with whom he had sought safety, and whose reckless behaviour probably led to the deaths of some of their compatriots, for few came back from those German camps.

A third member of the Sansum/Lee crew also failed to complete his evasion, not because of the ill discipline of his helpers but because of his own frailty. Sergeant P.D. Ablett had actually been guided to the heart of the Pyrenees near Andorra when his guide, having done his duty, left him to make his own way into Spain. No sooner was Ablett alone than he became ill and lost his way. He was captured in France on 29 August 1943, and after an unpleasant six weeks in Fresnes prison, Paris was also transferred to a prisoner-of-war camp in Germany.[1421]

Former engineering apprentice William Ronald Butterfield was a squadron leader with the DFC by the time he was twenty-three. It was touch and go, though, whether he would survive to see his twenty-fourth birthday when his Lancaster, on the way to bomb Milan on 12/13 August 1943, suffered severe engine trouble. Bombs were jettisoned and he turned for home. Clearly not going to get back to England and while still over France Butterfield gave the order to bale out when 'somewhere in the area of Issy-l'Evêque'. He came down in the Bois de Briffault (Nièvre), hurting his leg on landing. Heading more or less south he waded across the River Loire and found himself on a decent road that took him to Gannay-sur-Loire (Allier): 'I decided to skirt round Gannay and went across a field where ten men were threshing. They saw me and I hid myself. Three of them then came across and I told them who I was.'[1422]

They helped him find accommodation in a house several kilometres away and back across the Loire, where he remained until 17 September, 'prevented from continuing my journey owing to the lack of clothes and boots. I had been given a suit of old clothes which was much too small for me and my helpers had great difficulty in getting either shoes or a civilian suit for me, as I am very big.'[1423] All that could be found for him were a pair of carpet slippers, which were replaced after three weeks by a pair of jackboots, but these were too small and badly chafed his heels.

At some point joined by an American airman, F.D. Low, and after Butterfield had been given another pair of boots, they walked on 16 September to St Aubin-sur-Loire (Sâone-et-Loire) 'and there crossed the Loire by ferry'. They carried on through Dompierre-sur-Besbre to Saligny-sur-Roudon (Allier), a distance of some fifteen kilometres, 'where we arrived about midday. We had crossed the Demarcation Line by this time, but we had no trouble and saw no one there.'[1424] By the time that they had reached Varennes-sur-Allier on the evening of 18 September they 'were both very tired and hungry, and we therefore decided to take a train to Clermont-Ferrand. Although we had no identity cards we decided to risk a control, as we thought it would most probably be only on the old Line of Demarcation.' It was also a Saturday, and Low had found from experience that trains were invariably crowded at weekends and passengers were seldom asked for their papers. It was a good time to travel.

Proceeding with their plan they caught a train at about 6 p.m. and travelled third class to Clermont-Ferrand. Arriving there two hours later they then spent another two hours wandering aimlessly around the large town (population 87,000 in 1939) before asking for help at a house, but were turned away. They returned to the station just before midnight and tried to buy tickets for Brive-la-Gaillarde, some way to the south-west and well on the way to Spain, but were told that the train would not be leaving until 5 a.m. next morning and that they could not buy tickets until an hour before departure: 'We therefore went out of the station, and, passing three pairs of armed Germans with drill packs on their backs, we waited in some waste ground.'

Having had nothing but a cup of coffee to sustain them, they got to Brive during the afternoon of 19 September and walked half a dozen kilometres out of the town, stopping at a farm for food. Given only bread and wine, they plodded back to Brive station, and caught a train to Toulouse. Again, it was late when they got there, about an hour before midnight, and so they spent the night (19/20 September) in the station waiting room. When the first train came in they mingled with the passengers, handed their tickets over at the barrier, and walked out of the station.

Leaving Toulouse they headed for Foix: 'When we were about three kilometres from Auterive, we stopped at a farm and asked for food. This farmer gave us a meal and put us up for the night.' Fortunate to find such a good friend, their host cycled with them on the following day to another man who arranged for them, with the help of railway workers, 'to travel by passenger and goods train via Foix until we were near Puigcerdá. Here a helper who had travelled with us left us. He pointed out a stream to us and said if we followed it for about half a kilometre we would be in Spain.'[1425]

Puigcerdá is in Spain, at a height of 1,200 metres, so with little climbing to do the two evaders walked briskly across country and early on the afternoon of 23 September, four or five kilometres to the south of Puigcerdá, 'hit the main road. We walked past some Spanish policemen and set off along the main road to Barcelona. We had just passed through Talltorta when we were stopped by two members of the Spanish Civil Police.' The two airmen were searched and, back in Puigcerdá, put in the local prison, but next day were escorted to Gerona and interviewed by the civil governor. After another night in prison they were visited by 'the British Vice-Consul of Gerona and released'. Ten days later a Spanish Air Force officer escorted them to Barcelona, where they stayed the night, to Saragossa, for a second night, and then on to Alhama de Aragon by train. A week later Squadron Leader Taylor of the air attaché's staff took Butterfield to Madrid, where he spent yet another week before flying back to England from Gibraltar.[1426]

During the summer of 1943 the medium bombers of 2 Group, RAF were gainfully employed in the dangerous pursuit of the bombing of targets just across the English Channel. One such target, on 16 August, was the armament and steel works at Denain (Nord) in northern France. Though 88 Squadron lost four of its Bostons on the operation, there were several survivors, including Flight Lieutenant W.G. Brinn DFM, a member of Squadron Leader R.S. Gunning's crew.[1427] Brinn was looked after in the Bapaume area by several people, but spent eight days with Madame Eley, 'a Belgian whose husband, an employee of the War Graves Commission, is now in Germany… The mayor of Bapaume, M. Gidet, who won an M.M. in the last war, is the local chief of a De Gaulle intelligence organisation,' which had only a few days earlier sent three RAF sergeants on their way.[1428]

Living with the mayor since 14 February 1943, following his escape from Germany, was Soviet army tank crew member Lieutenant Vasily Ivanovitch Nekrasov, and together the mayor took them in his car on 26 August to Achiet-le-Grand to catch the train to Paris. Accompanying them was 'an elderly lady named Mme. Belitta, a member of an organisation' that was trying to get them away. In Paris, Brinn and Nekrasov followed Madame Belitta to a church, where a man asked them searching questions to establish their identities. They were then 'told to follow a lady with blonde hair and a red hat. She was Madame Germaine Badjpa [*sic*], whose husband, an Indian, is in India.'[1429]

On 29 August, Brinn and Nekrasov were escorted on the overnight train 'to Bordeaux by a Mrs. Wheaton, the French wife of an English employee of the War Graves Commission', and handed over to "Franco", Jean-François Nothomb. He then took them by train on his tried and trusted route to Dax, where they met Sergeant D.J. Webb RCAF and Sergeant R. Clarke, the only survivor of eight from a Stirling lost on 13/14 July. Webb and Clarke, who had been on the same train to Dax as Brinn and Nekrasov, had met each other for the first time in Brussels in the middle of August. Four days later they were in Paris, and four days after that caught the overnight express to Bordeaux.[1430] On the train to Dax, the officers travelled second class while the sergeants went by third.

From Dax the four men cycled to Bayonne and spent the night in a café just outside the town. On the following afternoon they cycled on to St Jean-de-Luz, and that night, 30/31 August, crossed the Pyrenees to a Spanish farm (probably Sarobe Farm, the usual first stopping place for Jean-François Nothomb) near San Sebastián in about ten and a half hours. By the evening of 31 August they had walked into San Sebastián.

Within a fortnight all three airmen and Nekrasov were back in England. Although interrogated by MI9 on 15 September, it was not until the Russian authorities had been consulted that it was discovered that Nekrasov was not a lieutenant in the Soviet army but a humble private. Captured by the Germans near Gomel, Smolensk, on 14 October 1942 in a tank battle, he had been taken to a camp near Duisburg, from which he had escaped on the night of 21 January 1943, during an RAF bombing raid.[1431] 'In this raid the building in which Nekrasov lived was demolished by blast, and many of his comrades and of the German guards were killed. In the resultant confusion he had no difficulty in getting out of the camp.'[1432] Walking from Duisburg to Holland, he was driven to Belgium on 2 February, where he was put in touch with an organisation, and with Monsieur Gidet on 14 February. Six months later he was on his way to England with Flight Lieutenant Brinn.

Gosnay power station, a couple of kilometres south-west of Béthune (Pas-de-Calais), was the target for six of 107 Squadron's Boston medium bombers on the evening of 27 August 1943. They went in at low-level: 'Two attacked before the third was hit by flak and collided with another and both of them crashed. On the way in and out Fw190s had attacked them destroying another Boston.'[1433] This last aircraft was Boston BZ237, which had been hit by flak in one of its two engines and, unable to keep up with the rest of the dwindling formation, was finished off by two Fw190s. The pilot, Flying Officer J.C. Allison, 'had to make a crash-landing about 1915 hours in a field about ten miles south of St Omer. None of us was injured and we all got out of the aircraft.'[1434] The crew were Allison, Flying Officer N.T. Fairfax (wireless operator/air gunner), Flight Sergeant R.J.A. Macleod (navigator), and Flying Officer G.W. "Skeets" Kelly, a camera operator and air gunner from 88 Squadron, who had already done twenty-four operations with his cameras.

Setting fire to the remains of their aircraft the four ran into a wood, where they stayed until it was dark. Agreeing that 'four was too many to be together', they tossed coins for partners, Allison leaving with Kelly. Fairfax and Macleod made good progress southwards, with considerable local help, and by the morning of 31 August had reached the area of Fillièvres, halfway between Hesdin and Frévent: 'We went to a farm in the evening. Among a crowd of people at the farm was a young Frenchman who took us to his home in Fillièvres and sheltered us for eight days (till 8 September).'[1435] They moved to another house for a week, during which time plans were being made to move them south. On 18 September they were collected by a guide and taken away, to be filtered down the Comet line.

Allison and Kelly decided to spend the night in a haystack but, when two French boys warned them that there was a German gun emplacement nearby, they waited until dusk before setting off. Avoiding the Germans, they then appeared 'to run into something, as we heard an alarm being raised and heard some German soldiers running. We lay flat on the ground for about half an hour and were not discovered.'[1436] It had been raining incessantly since they had been shot down and the two airmen were grateful to the farmer at Febvin-Palfart who took them in, dried their clothes, and replaced them with civilian ones. Refreshed after a night in the farmer's loft they headed for St Pol, having been told to avoid Heuchin 'because of the presence of Germans'. It was not long, however, before the two mutually agreed to part company 'as we had noticed that we caused a certain amount of interest in the villages through which we passed.'[1437] Kelly was taken prisoner soon afterwards, ending up at Stalag Luft III (Sagan).

Allison pressed on to St Pol with the intention of catching a goods train, but when he reached the small town he found that it was full of German airmen, and immediately gave up the idea of a train. Instead he spoke to a French lad and was given shelter for the night. At Frévent, while staying at a dentist's house, five men turned up. They spoke good English, and before cycling off with him removed from his person all traces of identification. One of the men, Jean Parsy, who claimed that he was a de Gaulle agent, was also a hairdresser and shaved off Allison's English-looking moustache. With further stops at Arras and Bapaume (where he spent a week 'in the house of a Belgian woman, known as Madeleine, whose husband was employed by the War Graves Commission'),[1438] he was taken to Paris on 16 September, and stayed a week there with a Dr Guyot at 50, rue de Rome. On 23/24 September, a woman escorted him on the overnight train to Bordeaux, together with Sergeant George Baker.

George Baker was flying a Halifax of "Shiny Ten" Squadron back from Nuremberg on the night of 27/28 August 1943 when it was attacked by a night-fighter at about 0230 hours on 28 August: 'All four engines stopped. My control column was completely out of action and the plane started to descend in a screaming dive. There was nothing for it but to bale out.'[1439] Baker, whose flying boots came off when his parachute snapped open, hurt his ankle when he landed in a field near the Belgian village of Harmignies. He managed to hobble only a few yards before deciding that enough was enough, and dozed off. He awoke to find a girl standing over him. Telling her in French who he was, she went back to her house and summoned her father, M. Frydryk: 'I hobbled to the house and was given food and a bed. I was told that when I was asleep three Germans had come to the village looking for airmen…'

He stayed with the Frydryk family until 5 September, when Madame Frydryk and her three daughters escorted him across the border into France, half a dozen kilometres away: 'We reached Villers-Sire-Nicole and went to a sort of inn. Whilst we were there one of the daughters told me she had heard of a man who had helped some escaped prisoners of war before. In an about an hour's time I was led to the home of a man, and from this point I was helped on my journey.'[1440]

On arriving in Bordeaux Allison and Baker were handed over to Jean-François Nothomb ("Franco"), who took them to Dax, and met Sergeant E.B. Dungey RCAF and Flight Sergeant A.T. Bowlby RCAF, pilot and rear gunner respectively of a Halifax that had been attacked by two Ju88s en route to Cologne on the night of 3/4 July 1943. After the bomb-bay was hit and caught fire, bombs were jettisoned and Dungey gave the order to bale out. Both he and Bowlby came down near Tessenderlo in north-east Belgium. Dungey crashed into a tree and was knocked unconscious. He was found a while later by a farmer, who recovered his parachute from the tree and took him home for a hot drink and food. Bowlby landed without a problem, and in due course emerged from a wood near Beringen to find a row of three cottages in front of him. Unable to decide which one he should call at, he tossed a coin and went to the middle one, where he was helped by a man and a woman.

On 6 July, taken by Inspector of Police Georges Glass to his home at Aarschot, he was joined by Dungey on 8 July. On about 13 July they were collected by 'three men of the "Brigade Blanche", an organisation of saboteurs', and taken to a policeman's house in Louvain, where they briefly met two more Canadian evaders, Flight Sergeant R.O. Williston RCAF and Warrant Officer J.D.H. Arseneaut RCAF (same 419 Squadron crew), who were subsequently taken prisoner of war.

Bowlby and Dungey were actually in the hands of Group EVA, a small "collecting" organisation, which moved them to two more houses in Louvain, firstly for twelve days to the house of Georges Gyssels, Park Straat 233, and secondly to François Lemaitre, Ryschool Straat 39. At Lemaitre's they were provided with 'plain clothes, which they had stolen from German officers'. The long wait in Louvain came to an end on 1 September when they were taken to Brussels and interviewed by Comet's Anne Brusselmans. After staying at separate addresses, the two men were taken to Paris on 16/17 September, and were moved by Lady Germaine Bajpai, again to two separate addresses, before being escorted to Bordeaux on 25/26 September. As with Allison and Baker, Jean-François Nothomb took them to Dax by train, and then cycled with them to Bayonne, where they were joined by a woman, who continued with them to St Jean-de-Luz. Here they met two more evaders, Sergeant G.W.H. Duffee and Sergeant E.A. Bridge RCAF.

Sergeant Bridge was manning the rear guns of a Halifax which ran into the balloon barrage over the target on the night of 13/14 July 1943. Flak then ignited the two starboard engines, leaving the pilot, Pilot Officer W.D.F. Ross RCAF with no choice but to order the crew to bale out. All did so but five, including Ross, were taken prisoner. Bridge and the flight engineer, Sergeant D.J. Webb RCAF (see above), both evaded.

On his way down Bridge lost his flying boots 'and I had only a pair of felt slippers that I wore inside my boots.'[1441] Despite this, he quickly made contact with the Comet organisation in Belgium and 'was taken to the house of an ex-Belgian soldier.' From this point his journey was also arranged for him.

There was little to worry twenty-year-old Sergeant Duffee after he had come down in Holland on the night of 22/23 June 1943 until the afternoon of 24 June when, hiding in some rushes in a large irrigation ditch near 's-Hertogenbosch, he saw a patrol of seven German soldiers disembark from a bus: 'They appeared to be searching the surrounding country, and I heard several shots. They returned to the bus about 2100 hours.'[1442] When all was quiet again he walked through the night heading for Berlicum (a couple of kilometres east of 's-Hertogenbosch) before going to sleep in a haystack in the early morning. A farmer found him and pointed him in the right direction. Deciding that he could risk travelling in broad daylight he walked into Berlicum with some children who were on their way to school, and was put in touch with Comet.

Prior to their crossing of the Pyrenees the six evaders assembled at a house near the French/Spanish border on the evening of 26 September. Led by Florentino Goïcoechea, and accompanied by Jean-François Nothomb, they crossed the Bidassoa and the mountains without any problem, reaching a Spanish village 'about seven kilometres outside San Sebastian' on 27 September. Before doing so, however, as they stood in the foothills in the dark of the early morning, the airmen had to dodge past the railway station below them, one at a time. All made it safely past, but Flight Sergeant Bowlby lost a shoe as he ran for cover, and cut his foot so badly on the sharp stones and wooden railway sleepers that he barely had any skin left by the time he rejoined the others.[1443] Taken to an isolated farmhouse, a meal was provided, and those who so wished got the chance to rest.

When Bowlby awoke from his sleep he discovered that Florentino had gone to San Sebastián with Dungey and one of the RAF evaders. At around midnight on 27/28 September the other four airmen were driven to the British Consulate in San Sebastián. Collecting Al Dungey and George Baker, they continued on to Madrid, suffering three punctures on the poor roads, and arriving at the British Embassy after a twelve-hour journey.

Allison, Dungey and Baker, after barely two hours rest at the embassy, were keen to press on, and went to Seville, on the River Guadalquivir.[1444] They stayed for four days at a house in Seville before being smuggled aboard a Norwegian ship, the *Sneland I*,[1445] on 3 October. The next five days were spent battened down in its hold. Food, bananas aplenty, was provided by the crew from time to time before sailing for Gibraltar on 8 October. The *Sneland I* was a collier, and the best part of a week living in and on a heap of coal does nothing for one's appearance. Hence, when they arrived at Gibraltar on the following day, they were considered the dirtiest evaders ever to have set foot on the Rock.

Art Bowlby stayed in Madrid for a week to allow his feet to heal before going to Gibraltar on 6 October. Possibly because of his feet, he was the first of the six to return, on 10 October. Allison and Dungey flew back on the following day, as did Bridge and Duffee. George Baker was the last of the six to leave, on 23/24 November, possibly due to his having been ill.

Some way behind the Allison group, Fairfax and Macleod were collected by a Comet guide on 18 September, and spent a further eighteen days at Bapaume, where they were wined and dined like lords. They were then moved to Paris, to the apartment of Madame Charmaine Hochepied, where they stayed for a further week before catching a train for the south on the evening of 11 October. En route to the station, after a meal, they were joined by Sergeant P.B. Smith (Comet 158) and Sergeant John F. Buise USAAF (159).[1446]

Smith had had a smooth evasion since being shot down on the night of 9/10 August 1943. He was the navigator aboard a Lancaster that was twice attacked by a night-fighter on its way to the target. Following the first attack the bombs had had to be jettisoned but, after the second, conditions in the bomber were so bad that the pilot, Sergeant J.C. Whitley, gave the order to bale out. Hiding for the rest of the day Peter Smith set out on 11 August to look for water, but near the village of Etalle, sixteen kilometres west of Arlon, he was 'observed by a woman who was leading some cows. I approached her and she immediately recognised me by my uniform… She then hid me behind a hedge, and shortly after brought me food and clothing.'[1447] He was in Comet's hands by the evening.

Leaving the train at Dax on the morning of 12 October the four airmen cycled to Bayonne, some fifty kilometres to the south, with Franco and his wife as their guides. They were joined along the way by two girls, and cycled in a group of eight until, beyond Bayonne, they stopped at the Café Pierre.[1448] They spent the night of 12/13 October there, and most of 13 October. Shortly before dusk, the eight of them cycled off to the foothills of the Pyrenees, and rendezvoused with two Basque guides in a field overlooking Biarritz. Franco and the three women now left the four airmen to the devices of their guides.

By 2 a.m. on the morning of 14 October 1943 they were in Spain. Their guides, professional smugglers, left them at a farmhouse but not before showing them the road to Elizondo, inland and well away from the usual route that led to San Sebastián. Nevertheless, they were arrested by the Guardia Civil, who threw them into a small, stinking room 'which contained a washbasin, a toilet and some terribly smelly blankets. That night we all curled up on the floor in our clothes as we were. The only food we got was a plate of beans and one potato. Next morning we left for Pamplona on the upper deck of a bus.'[1449]

Instead of being thrown into prison, they were interned in a hotel in Lecumberri, thirty-five kilometres north-west of Pamplona, from 16–24 October, when a civilian took them to Pamplona and handed them over to a Spanish Air Force officer. Their almost preferential treatment continued with this officer installing them, for a day and a half, in a hotel at Alhama de Aragón. Their next stop was Madrid, where Rod Macleod acquired an overcoat from the ambassador himself. A day or two later they left by lorry for Seville, and after a night there carried on to Gibraltar, which they reached on 29 October. They were back in England almost four weeks behind Jim Allison, but they crewed up again and completed a second tour together.

A month before Allison and party had left Seville, Flying Officer T.A.H. Slack, Sergeant K.D. Windsor RCAF, 2nd Lieutenant Tom J.E. Hunt USAAF, and Staff Sergeant William Aguiar USAAF had been and gone. Smuggled aboard another Norwegian ship, the *Borgholm*, they were 'hidden underneath the propeller shaft for a considerable time' until the ship sailed on 20 August 1943 for Gibraltar, where she arrived on the following day.[1450]

Before he had reached Paris on 21 July 1943, a month after he had been shot down, Sergeant Windsor had first met up with Flying Officer R.E. Barckley (shot down on 2 June) in the village of Wicquinghem (Pas-de-Calais) in northern France. Meeting again, at the house of Norbert Fillerin at Renty on 27 June, the two were taken to Paris together, where they separated. Windsor stayed with M. Routy, a fifty-five-year-old former pilot, and his 'niece Jeanne, aged thirty, who spoke perfect English,' until 1 August, when he stayed with a Dr Habrekorn.

Flying Officer Tom Slack, like Barckley a fighter pilot, had been shot down near le Quesne (Somme) on 18 July. One of two brothers named Angot, mechanics by trade, who had 'approached' him on 19 July cycled to the town of Hornoy 'and fetched a man named Joe Balfe. This man, aged forty-five, was Irish, had been an RSM in the Irish Guards in the last war, and had won the Military Medal. I think that his regimental number was 4512.'[1451] Intensely pro-British, Joe was keen to do what he could to help the Allied cause, not easy for the proprietor of the Café de France for some 300 Germans were garrisoned in Hornoy, and one of them was posted on guard outside his café.

Nevertheless, Balfe took Slack to the café for a few days. When the Angot brothers heard that Slack's presence in the community was common knowledge Joe and one of his two sons, also Joe, to be on the safe side took Slack to the house in Amiens of thirty-three-year-old old Jean Le Maitre, the hairdresser and self-styled terrorist. As Le Maitre did not, apparently, belong to any organisation Joe Balfe senior asked around until someone came to see Flying Officer Slack, and on 5 August 'a woman aged about thirty-five came from Paris, and met Balfe and myself [Slack] at a rendezvous in Amiens… She then took me by train to Paris.'

Having reached Paris on 5 August, Slack was taken to a metro station three days later, and on the platform met Jean-François Nothomb and Sergeant Windsor. That evening all three caught the overnight train to Bordeaux, and arrived there after a seven-hour journey, without any control either at the station or on the train itself. After a quick change of trains they went to Dax, and met up with Tom Hunt and Bill Aguiar, who had also been on the same train. Getting 'bicycles from a cloakroom at Dax station', they cycled 'to a café a little distance beyond Bayonne, where we arrived about 1800 hours. Here we spent the night.'[1452]

On 10 August they cycled to St Jean-de-Luz, arriving at around 7 p.m. that evening. Having left the bicycles at the station, there was then the small matter of walking to Ciboure across the nearby bridge over the River Nivelle, which 'was guarded by a German sentry on the North side. There was a good deal of traffic on the bridge, and he did not attempt to stop us.' Safely through Ciboure, they hid in some bushes and had some food while waiting for their guides to arrive. At around 10 p.m. they turned up – Florentino Goïcoechea, another Basque and a Frenchman. Nothomb remained in France while the airmen and their guides set off over the Pyrenees. Crossing the Spanish frontier between Biriatou and Irún at around 3 a.m. on 11 August, they spent a few days in San Sebastián and Madrid before being driven to Seville by the assistant consul from Seville, where they arrived mid morning on 19 August. Slack and Windsor, and no doubt the Americans too, were flown from Gibraltar to Whitchurch airport on 23/24 August.

The eighth member of George Baker's crew was "second dickey" Sergeant R.W. "Reg" Cornelius. He had already had an eventful war long before he enlisted in the RAF on 3 February 1941. Following in his father's footsteps he had joined the Merchant Navy, and was a deck hand on the 10,177-ton *Regent Tiger* when she was torpedoed by the *U-29* (Kapitänleutnant Otto Schuhart) on 8 September 1939 some 300 miles off the south-west coast of Ireland.[1453] Six months later, on 3 March 1940, his father, Able Seaman William Cornelius, was on the *Cato*, 710 tons, when she struck a mine in the mouth of the Bristol Channel, off the Welsh coast. There was only a handful of survivors, one of them sixty-year-old William Cornelius, but he died of exposure on the life raft before he could be rescued.[1454] In a grim coincidence the mine that *Cato* struck had been laid by the U-29.

Rather than return to sea, Reg enlisted in the RAF and, after training in Canada, was on his Halifax conversion course at 1663 HCU, RAF Marston Moor, when he was suddenly detailed for the Nuremberg operation with a 10 Squadron crew. As he later reported: 'On 27 August I was driven from my unit to a station that I have since been told was Melbourne.'[1455]

During his parachute descent Reg lost his flying boots, as did so many, and landed heavily in a Belgian field near the village of Harmignies (close to where George Baker had come down), knocking himself out. Regaining his senses he saw 'a house about 200 yards away. I went to the door and tried, unsuccessfully, to get help. I then knocked at a house nearby and was immediately taken in.' His benefactors were the Juste family, mother, father and daughter Eliane, with whom he stayed for five or six days before moving in with the Hervé family at 101, rue de Mons, Harmignies. Here Reg 'was visited by two members from the organisation in Mons. These two men, both electricians in the hospital at Mons, and one of whom was called Marcel Dubois… gave me overalls similar to theirs… They gave me one of their bicycles and we cycled into Mons. Here we were picked up by a civilian car and driven to the civilian hospital.'[1456]

It appeared to Reg that the matron at the hospital was the head of the local organisation and, as she could speak perfect English (her uncle, Mr J.W. Miller, lived at 14, Warwick Street, London W1), it was she who asked him searching questions about England and London because they were not satisfied with his answers to the usual questions about RAF squadrons: 'I could not tell them where we had taken off, who was my squadron commander or the names of the other members of my crew. The reason for this was that I had been driven to my station about an hour before taking off.'

At a house in Mons he met American airman Technical Sergeant Jarvis Allen USAAF, [1457]and the pair of them were escorted to Tournai, where they 'went to a house belonging to a man working for the British Intelligence.' Splitting up for three or four weeks, the two airmen were brought together again at the beginning of November for the journey to Brussels. Lili Dumon took them to her house in Brussels, 'where we had our photographs taken. Here we met Sergeant De Pape. Allen and I both left Lili's house that night; he, I was told, was going on ahead.'

Sergeant R.A.G. De Pape RCAF, who had also been flying as a "second dickey" on his first trip, had failed to return with a 431 Squadron crew on the night of 3/4 October 1943: 'About ten minutes off target on the way home we were warned of an approaching fighter. We took evasive action. After four successive blasts of flak the plane dived covered in smoke. The intercom was broken and the captain tapped me on the shoulder and indicated the escape hatch.'[1458] Ray De Pape, the only one of the eight of his crew to evade capture,[1459] came down somewhere in Germany: 'I am unable to locate the district where I fell. It was probably somewhere in between Prüm and Schleiden because the first town I reached after walking for four days in a south easterly direction was Laroche [*sic*].'[1460] This was La Roche-en-Ardenne, Belgium, almost sixty kilometres due west of Prüm, on the River Ourthe and at a point where five roads meet. It was 8 October when he got there, and found it full of German soldiers. He also found the town 'very difficult to skirt as it lay in a valley with steep banks all round.'

Late on the afternoon of 9 October, having walked a further twenty or twenty-five kilometres, he spoke to a farmer and asked for help. It was refused: 'By this time I was rather desperate and my feet were unbearably painful.' Being a fluent Flemish speaker (he was of Belgian extraction), Ray asked the farmer if anyone in the village (possibly Ambly) spoke Flemish. The man pointed to a certain house, which Ray cautiously circled before watching from behind a hedge. He was not well hidden, and after several Belgians had invited him to join them, he was taken to the very house identified by the farmer, and introduced to its occupants, Monsieur and Madame van der Haegen.

M. van der Haegen was not happy for Ray to stay with them and in the small hours, blindfolded for security reasons, Ray was led to another house in the village, where he was interrogated by members of an organisation. Over the next few days he was escorted in stages via Namur to Brussels, now in the safe hands of Comet. Lili Dumon ("Michou") took him to a large house: 'Twenty-two years old at the time, she dressed in a short skirt and her bobbed hair made her look like a fifteen-year-old schoolgirl. She spoke in a soft, child's voice. Her face was round and artless. When she sat in a tram, her feet barely touched the floor. Who would have supposed that she was one of the foremost couriers of the line?'[1461]

After Ray had had a new photograph taken of himself by Raymond Vignoble ('one of the photographers for the Comet Line in Brussels'), it was time to go to the far south. With Jarvis Allen long gone, about a fortnight later De Pape and Cornelius were taken to the railway station, where they met Lili again and two more Americans, Sergeant Robert Metlen and Sergeant Harold T. Sheets.[1462] They split up, separately taking the train to Mons, and then the tram to Rumes, a dozen kilometres south-west of Tournai (Doornik) and close to the French border. With the Americans elsewhere, Ray and Reg met up at around 5 p.m. one early November evening at the home of the Thomé family. Their daughter, Monique, was a courier for Comet, and next day she and the two airmen were spirited across the border, thanks to a doctor, his car, a pile of blankets and a patriotic Belgian border guard. They went to the doctor's house in Bavay (Nord), some way to the south-east, from where Monique, who had made her way independently into France, escorted the two airmen by train to Paris. There, a new guide took over.

On 12 November 1943, after four days in the French capital, having been joined by a Frenchman hoping to get to England to join the Free French, and by a Belgian who was posing as a wing commander, they left for the south-west. The guides changed at Bordeaux, where Robert Metlen also put in another appearance, and they cycled on to Bayonne. Met by Janine De Greef, she took them to a café on the other side of the town to spend the night.[1463] Continuing next evening to a safe house at Urrugne (Francia Usandizaga's farm was no longer viable following her arrest ten months earlier, in January), two new guides, one of them Florentino Goïcoechea, led them up through the foothills of the Pyrenees in pouring rain. Sheltering in a sheep barn for some of the night (15/16 November) they continued the climb, but the going that second night proved too hard for the Frenchman, and he was left behind. Reg Cornelius had also been finding it tough going and was on the point of collapse, but hard talking by his friends and the threat of a gun pointed at him by a guide got him under way once more.

After seven and a half hours, across the Bidassoa, the tired and hungry party stumbled down the mountains into the Spanish village of Santesteban. The British consul was notified, and after a few hours rest Cornelius, De Pape, Metlen, and the Belgian wing commander walked to the bus stop, but 'were picked up by two Spanish carabineri and taken to the police station.' Instead of being given a lengthy term of imprisonment, as would have been the case before the tide of war had turned against the Nazis, they were taken to Irún, briefly locked up, and interrogated before being released into "British" hands. In the case of the Cornelius/De Pape group after interrogation in Irún they were 'escorted to an inn, where the innkeeper was paid by the British Embassy for keeping them.'[1464]

Also there was Flight Sergeant Stan May RAAF (Comet 176), who had been brought over the Pyrenees at the end of October. He and Ray De Pape almost got into trouble with the Spanish authorities when they went to look at a company of 'the fascist Spanish Blue Division that had fought with the Germans in Russia', which was returning home to a hero's welcome.[1465] When a Spanish carabinero took a dim view of them not raising their arms in a fascist salute, they beat a hasty retreat to their quarters before anything nasty happened to them. A Spanish Air Force officer took them to a hotel at Alhama de Aragon for four pleasant days, before being escorted across the border into Gibraltar on 14 December 1943. Four days later Ray De Pape (Comet 194), Reg Cornelius (193), and Sergeant W. Todd (185), were flown back to England.

Reg Cornelius converted to Wellingtons, then to Mitchells at No. 13 OTU, RAF Finmere (Oxon). On 3 December 1944 he suffered injuries to his head when Mitchell FV966 hit some trees on approach to base. His commission as Pilot Officer Cornelius (186499) was notified in *The London Gazette* two days later, with effect from 14 October 1944. On 14 May 1945, now a flying officer (with effect from 14 April), he was home on leave at 19, St John's Crescent, Bedminster, Bristol when he went into the bathroom, and turned on the gas on the water heater taking his own life. He was buried, as his father had been five years earlier, in Bristol (Canford) Cemetery. He was one month short of his twenty-second birthday.

It was a long way in war-torn Europe from Berlin to Algiers via Switzerland, but one man to tread this long and dangerous path was Flight Engineer Sergeant Harry Simister. He and his crew had just dropped their bombs on Berlin on the night of 31 August/1 September 1943 when they were attacked by a night-fighter. With the two port engines of their Halifax on fire and with the main controls shot away the pilot, Sergeant K. Ward, had no hesitation in giving the order to bale out. Ward, though, and two others of the crew were to lose their lives, three more were taken prisoner, but Harry Simister landed in a field about ten kilometres south of Berlin. Hiding his parachute and mae west he laid up in a wood for the rest of the night. On the morning of 1 September, he removed his 'brevet and tapes… also cut off the pockets from my battledress and the tops off my flying boots.'[1466]

With the aid of his compass he headed north-west to Potsdam, deciding that he had no choice other than to walk right through the town – certain geographical obstacles (lakes etc) otherwise lay in his direct path – and did so without any difficulty. After another night in a wood, on the morning of 3 September he stole an unattended 'bicycle leaning against a house', and pedalled off, still heading north-west, to Schwerin (some 200 kilometres from Berlin). Carrying on to Lübeck on the Baltic coast, another fifty kilometres or so, he reached that port on the evening of 4 September.

It was remarkable enough that a man wearing RAF battledress, albeit without any obvious markings on it, could have brazenly made his way unchallenged over such a long distance, with a stolen bicycle, and that he was then able to enter the heavily-policed Lübeck docks, again without challenge, yet Harry was not finished. Wise to the temptation that ships sailing for Sweden provided for escapers and evaders, the Germans had posted a guard at the foot of every gangplank, to prevent these men sneaking aboard. This was no bar to Harry. Confronted by a guard, he simply walked past him up the gangplank of a Swedish ship 'and into the galley, where I found a party of about six Swedes. I showed them my cigarette case with the RAF wings embossed on it, and made them understand who I was.'[1467]

Asking if he could hide on their ship, he was told that it was not sailing until the morrow and that he should come back then and take his chances. Slipping off the vessel, Harry retrieved his bicycle and spent the night in a wood before returning to the docks, 'only to find that the ship had gone'. Hugely disappointed, he spent the rest of the day unsuccessfully looking for another neutral ship, and 'went back again to the woods for the night'. On 7 September he decided to try his luck at Rostock, 100 kilometres to the east along the Baltic coast. Having had to cycle through another town, Wismar, it was late in the evening when he reached Rostock. He went directly to the docks but, as it was getting dark, retired to the woods for the night. Returning to the docks in the morning his search revealed no neutral shipping, and so he cycled back to Lübeck on 9 September.

Wandering about the port he tried to buy some cigarettes, but was told that he needed coupons: 'I then went into a public house and asked for beer, displaying a 100-franc note and saying that I was Swedish. After some hesitation I was given some beer.'[1468] Until this point Harry had mainly survived on Horlicks tablets from his escape kit and apples stolen along the way. He was, consequently, exceedingly hungry and, spotting the proprietress of the bar in a corner of the room, asked her for some food. After a moment's hesitation she gave him 'a few pieces of black bread to eat'. Somewhat replenished he went back to the docks, where he saw a Swedish schooner. Again, walking straight past the German guard he boarded the ship. Finding that all the doors were locked and that the crew were ashore, he went to sleep in the wheelhouse.

Awakened by one of the crew, Harry once more produced his embossed cigarette case and asked if he could stow away on the ship. He was again disappointed to be told that it would not be sailing for eight days and, anyway, there was nowhere for him to hide. The crew gave him a meal before he made his way ashore, to spend the night in a bus shelter. Giving up hope of ever finding a neutral ship he decided to make for Holland, and on 10 September set off on his bicycle to Hamburg (fifty kilometres), Bremen (another 115), Osnabrück (115 again), until, after two days, he had reached Rheine (thirty-five), travelling the 315 kilometres or so still 'without incident' except for a puncture somewhere along the way. This was overcome by the simple expedient of exchanging his bicycle for another with two good tyres which he saw 'leaning against a café in a small village'.

At Rheine goods yards, still in Germany, unable to find any train marked for Holland, he 'retired to the outskirts of the town for the night'. The following day, 13 September, he cycled another 25 kilometres to the Dutch border near Hengelo, coming to an abrupt halt when he saw 'two guards examining the passes of the people crossing over'. Knowing that he would not get past the guards, he pushed his bicycle 'through a wood, across two fields and over the border into Holland' and carried on through Hengelo, spending the night in woods on the far side of the town.

Harry's next goal was Belgium. By 14 September he had reached 's-Hertogenbosch (150 kilometres), and was soon through Eindhoven (twenty-five kilometres), only a few kilometres from the Belgian border. Just before the border he stopped at a café near the villages of Borkel and Schaft, and asked the Steenbergen family for a drink: 'I declared myself to the proprietors, and was immediately taken round to the back of the house and invited inside.'[1469] Madame Steenbergen gave him a meal and civilian clothing, and told him that they would put him in touch with someone from an organisation. Dutchman Frank Spree then took him by bicycle across the border to Eksel on 16 September. The crossing was trouble-free, hardly surprising as Frank's brother was one of the border guards and the other guards were his friends.[1470]

After four days in Eksel a guide took him to Neerpelt, where he stayed for about a week, being joined by Sergeant R.V. Wallace. Shot down on the same raid as Harry, Wallace had also evaded from Germany, but from near Münster, rather than Berlin. At the end of September, supplied with false papers, a guide known to them only as Denise escorted them by train via Brussels to Virton, a couple of kilometres from the French border.[1471] Here they had to stay for two weeks as the line to Spain had been cut by German security forces.

The more usual route for evaders was south and west through France to Spain, but now Simister and Wallace were heading south and east towards Switzerland. On about 13 October they crossed into France, taking the train from the small town of Ecouviez to Nancy, where they stayed one night, to Belfort and then on to Montbéliard. On the evening of 14 October they walked the few kilometres to Audincourt, ever closer to the Swiss border, where they stayed the night. In the morning they joined a party of woodcutters, and went with them to the woods. In the evening, their work finished, one of the woodcutters took the two airmen to a guide, who led them into Switzerland. In the darkness they were climbing a wall at Fahy, just over the border, when a shout of "Halt!" in unmistakeable German and the sudden beam of a powerful torch stopped them in their tracks. Silhouetted by the light the two airmen saw the outline of two German helmets. With two rifles pointing at them, the game was up. The Germans had got them at last. It was all over.

Actually, it was not all over, for the riflemen were Swiss border guards, whose helmets were not too dissimilar in appearance to those of the Germans. Arrested for making an illegal entry into Switzerland Simister and Wallace spent two days in the cells at Porrentruy (discovering on the walls the names of other airmen who had preceded them), before being sent to the British Legation at Berne. The usual practice followed of keeping the men in a hotel, playing golf and, when the snows came, moving them to Arosa for skiing.

At the end of August 1944 Simister and Wallace decided to make their way back into France, now that the Americans were well and truly established in the south as well as the north, and spent some time giving maquisards a hand in driving the enemy out of their country. Once contact had been made with the Americans in the south, they were flown across to Italy and then, in what was becoming a well-beaten path for evaders, home via Tunis, Algiers, Oran and Casablanca courtesy of Coastal Command.

A number of evaders and escapers who succeeded in gaining Switzerland's neutrality were keen to press on, back to Britain to continue the fight, and headed off through France to Spain on their own initiative. Such impulsive behaviour, though, was frowned upon by the authorities, as Air Commodore Freddie West VC remarked: 'It could be awkward and sometimes lethally dangerous when amateur escapers trekked across France from Switzerland and got themselves unwittingly mixed up in Secret Service networks.'[1472] Not all Swiss arrivals were so irresponsible, as Brigadiers James Hargest and Reginald Miles, both New Zealanders, would demonstrate.

They arrived from Italy late on the evening of 31 March 1943, and were in no condition to go charging off anyway. They were two of the very senior army officers, prisoners of war of the Italians at Castello Vincigliata, Campo Concentramento 12, Florence, who had started an escape tunnel on or about 1 September 1942. Finished to within inches of the surface by mid-March 1943, they agreed to wait for as foul a night as possible to make the break, when they felt sure that the Italian guards would be sheltering in their boxes. Their chance came with the heavy rain on the night of 30/31 March 1943. Order of exit at 2130 hours, 30 March 1943, was Brigadier J. Combe, Brigadier Miles, Air Marshal O.T. Boyd, Brigadier Hargest, Major-General A. Carton de Wiart VC, and Lieutenant-General R.N. O'Connor. It was a brave effort but, for now, only Hargest and Miles avoided re-capture.[1473]

On 11 October 1943 Hargest and Miles were informed that the Dutch military attaché in Berne, General A.G. van Tricht, was prepared to assist them to get to England through France and Spain with the help of the Dutch escape line Dutch-Paris. Their guide to Spain would be the twenty-three-year-old Toulouse medical student, Gabriel Nahas (see end of Chapter 7). During the summer Hargest had suffered a problem with his hips, and had been obliged to rest for several weeks but Miles, after six months idleness, was anxious to press on to England and left Switzerland on 11 October 1943 with Nahas. Reaching Toulouse next morning, Miles rested there for three days before leaving for the Pyrenees, where he was handed over to members of the Résistance Fer escape organisation. Safely delivered to Spain, he apparently hanged himself on 20 October in a fit of depression in a hotel room in Figueras.[1474]

The sad news reached Hargest six days later when he was still in Switzerland waiting for Nahas to return. British Intelligence in Switzerland were concerned as to how and why Miles had committed suicide, but were keen for Nahas to take Hargest if all were well. After meeting with two of the top Dutch military officials, Baron J.G. van Niftrik and General van Tricht, Nahas spoke with Colonel Henry Cartwright MC, and with an American introduced to him as Colonel Alan Smith,[1475] and was persuaded to take Brigadier Hargest. Now recovered from his hip problem, Hargest left Berne on the evening of 30 October for Lausanne, and proceeded to Geneva by train on the morning of 31 October. There he met van Niftrik, who went with him to the Swiss police to obtain the necessary documents to enable him to proceed across France. Hargest met Gabriel Nahas in Geneva, and together they reached Toulouse on 1 November.

Hargest left on 5 November but, due to increased German activity in the Foix area, had to return to Toulouse on 9 November. With the help of the French railway staff, who formed the backbone of Résistance Fer, Hargest reached Porta, three stops short of the Spanish border, on the afternoon of the following day. Early on the morning of 11 November, after a crossing of barely two hours,[1476] he was in Spain. At Puigcerdà he gave himself up to the guardia civil, who did not detain him long, and on 28/29 November 1943 he was flown to Whitchurch airport, England.

Squadron Leader F.A.O. Gaze DFC was leading 64 and 133 Squadrons on an operation to Morlaix airfield on 26 September 1942 (see Pilot Officer R.S. "Bob" Smith, Chapter 5) when strong and unpredicted winds blowing from the wrong quarter caused the loss of eleven Spitfires of 133 Squadron and one of 64 Squadron.[1477] The blame for the tragedy, in which four pilots were killed, was heaped upon Gaze. Posted to 616 Squadron as a flight commander he continued to prove his worth, and by the time he was shot down on 4 September 1943 he was a flight commander on 66 Squadron with seven confirmed victories to his name and a Bar to his DFC.

On that morning of 4 September he and his squadron, in their Spitfire Vb's, were escorting Mitchell bombers back from the Amiens marshalling yards when they were attacked by a number of Fw190s. Shooting one down Gaze then found himself 'in the middle of the rest of the enemy aircraft with no other Spitfires near. After a dog fight, which lasted about ten minutes, I was hit in the radiator at about 500 feet, and crash landed at Baromesnil, about sixteen miles W.N.W. of Dieppe.'[1478] Though slightly wounded – the right side of his face and eye were cut and his knees grazed by fragments from 20mm cannon shells – he was able to avoid the searching German soldiers. A young Frenchman took him to the house of schoolmaster André Busson at Brunville, near Dieppe. Here he received a visit from the local representative of the organisation La Libération, a man calling himself Georges, 'who was in contact with an English agent in Rouen named Clement'.

On about 16 September, his facial injuries healed, Gaze was taken to Rouen, and then via Amiens to Arras, though a change of trains between those two places was necessary as the lines had been sabotaged. At Arras it was learnt that the Gestapo had arrested their contact, but when they tried to return to Rouen found that 'there were no trains running in any direction, because the lines from Arras were blocked by bombing.' There was nothing for it but to find what sleep they could in a field, before making their way back to Rouen. On 20 September Gaze was taken to 8, Place de Breteuil, Paris, the residence of British agent Gaby, a French-Canadian, who had somehow managed to escape from the Gestapo following his arrest by them and who was now waiting to leave France.

On 6 October, at the St Germain metro station, Gaze met Pilot Officer G.T. Graham RCAF, shot down on 16/17 September 1943, Sergeant B.C. Reeves, shot down on a "nickel" raid on 11/12 June 1943, and a Belgian guide called André. They caught the train to Laguépie (Tarn-et-Garonne), arriving around midday on 7 October. Picking up several more evaders along the way, including Flying Officer R. Isherwood, Sergeant A.F. Charman and two Americans, they went to Foix, and left in two parties for Andorra on the evening of 10 October. At the Andorran town of Ordino they stayed for three days at the Hotel Como before leaving by bus for the town of Andorra and crossing into Spain on foot near Sant-Julia. Before they left, some of the Americans, and Graham, wanted to send a telegram to Barcelona asking for a car to come and collect them, but Gaze told them not to send it, as it was bound to be "intercepted" by the Spanish authorities. One of the Americans, Steinmetz, told Gaze that they had not sent it.

The actual crossing took them six hours, and another four to reach their destination, a farm. That was as nothing to the long walk that lay ahead, seven days later, to Manresa (as Julian Sale and others had also done). They had to go there 'because two of the Americans in the party were exhausted, and had to be carried.' As they went to catch the train to Barcelona, in two groups, three of the first group – Isherwood, Reeves and one of the Americans – were detained at the station, 'but a kind-hearted policeman let them go'. Of the second group, Steinmetz and another American, "Shorty", were detected and taken off the train. Gaze was most indignant at the Americans' behaviour: 'On the journey the Americans would not stop talking, though told many times by the guides to keep quiet.' Despite the Americans' exuberance they all safely reached Barcelona, on 21 October, where Gaze discovered that Steinmetz had indeed sent the telegram. It apparently said that there were eight Americans in the party and would they send a car, but made no mention of the four RAF personnel in the party.

Four days later, after passing through Madrid, they reached Gibraltar, and a further two days later the RAF personnel were flown to England, no doubt with the lively Americans.

It was usually the Stirling bombers, with their lower ceiling, that tended to get in the way of bombs dropped by the higher-flying Halifaxes and Lancasters but, on the night of 15/16 September 1943, Halifax LK913 had just turned for home after bombing when it was hit by incendiaries dropped from a Stirling flying only fifteen metres (fifty feet) above. The incendiaries landed in the cockpit and on the starboard wing, destroying the flying instruments and setting the two engines on fire. Two of the crew, navigator Flight Lieutenant Edgar Bohun Mason RCAF and Pilot Officer R.O. Malins, baled out immediately, hearing only the last part of the order 'to stand by to abandon aircraft'. The pilot, Wing Commander D.W.M. Smith, flew on for as long as he could, until LK913, losing height all the while, crashed into a hillside to the south of the Forêt de Tronçais, near Cérilly (Allier). The aircraft caught fire immediately, and all personal equipment was thrown into the blaze, or so the crew thought. Frenchmen later recovered everything that had not been consumed by the fire, including the navigator's log, which had been blown out when the aircraft crashed.

Richard Malins landed in a field, buried his harness, wrapped himself in his parachute, and went to sleep. Thanks to the help of many French people he was able to get to Perpignan where, extraordinarily, he was able to witness the arrest of his pilot, Wing Commander Smith, and bomb aimer, Pilot Officer H. Dereniuk RCAF. Undeterred, Malins set off in the direction of the Pyrenees without waiting for a guide, and had walked barely twenty minutes or so south when he was stopped by two men: 'I turned to meet them – only to be faced with revolvers. The Gestapo had been tipped off!'[1479]

Dereniuk had been seen at Gelles (Puy-de-Dôme) by Sergeant D.A. Crome (pilot), Sergeant R.W. Paulin, Sergeant R.O. Hunter RCAF, and Sergeant T.J. Kanakos RCAF, some of the crew of a 161 (Special Duties) Squadron Halifax, DK119. They had taken off from RAF Tempsford just before midnight on 22/23 July 1943 to make three drops of desperately needed SOE supplies to the Resistance near Montluçon. The first two drops were made successfully, but at the drop zone for the third, St Sauvier, no signals were seen. In appalling weather – heavy rain and a thunderstorm – Crome took the Halifax round twice. On the third circuit, now at a necessarily low altitude, lights were spotted, and the last containers dropped. Suddenly one of DK119's four engines cut out, and Crome could do nothing to prevent it from crashing and killing the rear gunner, Pilot Officer L.M. Lavallee RCAF. The navigator, Sergeant S.F. Hathaway, and the despatcher, Sergeant E.A. Allen, were too badly injured to be moved any distance, and became prisoners of war.

Sergeant Crome and Sergeant D.G. Patterson (bomb aimer), who was himself slightly injured in the left arm and head, going to get help for the injured men, met two of the Frenchmen who had been helping to collect the vital supplies and who said they would arrange for a car to take the airmen away. The promised car took Crome, Paulin, Hunter, Patterson, and Kanakos to Montluçon, leaving Hathaway and Allen with the Resistance. Despite his injuries – wounds to the head, dislocated hip, and sundry aircraft parts embedded in his legs – Stan Hathaway was conscious enough to persuade the Resistance people to burn the wreckage of the Halifax, and also to recover the now empty containers that had been chucked into a nearby lake and which were floating on its surface for all the world to see. One of the Resistance women sat with Stan until a gendarme arrived to take him to Montluçon. He was transferred to a Luftwaffe hospital in Clermont-Ferrand, before departing to Germany and Poland for the rest of the war.[1480]

Once the other five had reached Montluçon, Patterson was dropped off. After a visit from a doctor, he was 'moved elsewhere'. The French Resistance had been quickly in contact with England however, and on the night of 23/24 August his squadron collected him in a Hudson crewed by Wing Commander Lewis Hodges DSO, DFC & Bar, Flight Lieutenant J.A. Broadley and Flight Lieutenant L.G.A. Reed, who had been carrying out Operation Trojan Horse.

Crome, Paulin, Hunter and Kanakos, meanwhile, had been taken from Montluçon to St Gervais-d'Auvergne (Puy-de-Dôme), some fifty kilometres to the south-east, and on about 22 August were taken to Gelles, where they met Dereniuk.

Sometime during the third week of September they went to a maquis camp, an abandoned house about two kilometres from Giat (Puy-de-Dôme), where eleven Frenchmen were avoiding deportation for forced labour in Germany. After about a week, they were joined by Flight Lieutenant Mason and by Sergeant Charles Heyworth[1481] and Warrant Officer J.M. Nelmes RCAF, two more of the crew of Halifax LK913. A fourth member of the same crew, Flight Lieutenant J.M. Forman RCAF, was brought to Giat on 8 October.

Mason, landing a few kilometres north-west of Montluçon, was walking south on 16 September when he met a Frenchman, who gave him food and clothing. Mason stayed in a wood until the following day, when the same Frenchman 'returned with more food and a member of the Resistance group, who took me to his home in Montluçon.'[1482] On 20 September, having spent three days with two brothers in the village of Billy (Allier), some eighty kilometres by road to the east, Mason was then moved to Giat, some 120 kilometres to the south-west.

Heyworth and Nelmes had had an uneventful journey to the camp near Giat. At Billy they were given food and shelter, and a change of clothing: 'After staying two days we were taken to Clermont-Ferrand and handed over to the chief of the parachute receptionists who drove us to a maquis camp in the woods near Giat.'[1483]

John Forman, badly shaken up by LK913's landing on the solid hillside, twisted a knee when he got out of the wreckage: 'A French doctor who examined me later thought it possible that I had broken two vertebræ in the spine.'[1484] Despite his condition he and the other five of his crew set off in the direction of Paris, but after only two or three kilometres they decided to split up, Forman leaving with Pilot Officer E.N. Bell RCAF, the second pilot. Continuing after a night in the forest to the south of St Bonnet-Tronçais (Allier), Forman was in such pain by the afternoon that he decided to seek help while Bell stayed behind in the forest.[1485] Forman got a lift through St Bonnet with a Frenchman carting a log, and was then put in touch with "an organisation", and brought to the "camp" near Giat on 8 October.

Two further evaders joined the camp at some point. Pilot Officer H.D. Rea RCAF, who was later taken prisoner, and Sergeant Peter Dmytruk RCAF had been lost in a 405 Squadron Halifax on 11/12 March 1943. Nothing is known of their activities prior to reaching the camp near Giat, but 405 Squadron received a message to the effect that Dmytruk 'was alive and in good health but he could not be expected to return to the UK for some time and this information was to be treated with the utmost secrecy.'[1486] On 9 December 1943, however, his luck ran out when he was killed in a German ambush as he and his French comrades tried to blow up a railway bridge with a train on it. According to Mason, he 'was shot by the Germans while driving in a Resistance car. His grave is at Auzat-sur-Allier, marked "Pierre".'[1487]

On 12 October Sergeant Crome was asked to inspect a possible landing-ground site near Toulouse. He was still absent two days later when Forman and the four 161 Squadron sergeants were driven to Clermont-Ferrand, 'where any deficiencies in our civilian clothes were made good'. A woman, Madame Marianne, and a man believed to be her husband, escorted the five airmen by train a long way west to Angoulême. 'As we crossed the Line of Demarcation by train there was an identity control by a German officer and a soldier.' The officer queried Forman's identity card which, issued in 1942, declared him to be deaf and dumb. Madame Marianne spoke to the German officer who, not apparently satisfied, nevertheless went on his way.

From Angoulême the airmen 'were taken by car to a large chateau, the home of Charles Franc, a wine-grower and cognac manufacturer, near Mallaville.' Two days after they had arrived Crome reappeared from his landing-ground expedition. He was in time for the two aircraft that were due to collect them on the night of 20/21 October, during the penultimate night of the current moon period. Flight Lieutenant R.W.J. Hooper DFC and Flying Officer J.R.G. Bathgate left Tangmere in double-Lysander Operation Water Pistol, but bad visibility in the pick-up area, one and a half kilometres south of Vibrac (fifteen kilometres west of Angoulême), forced them to abandon it. Those on the ground heard the two aircraft, but realised that it was impossible for them to land. There was nothing to do but wait for the next moon period in November. This was not welcome news for Charles Heyworth, who had contracted a severe lung infection.

Despite the considerable clandestine activity at Charles Franc's château near Mallaville, the Germans never went near it. Someone, though, did inform the gendarmes in Châteauneuf-sur-Charente (Charente) 'that if they went to Franc's house they would find something of interest to the Gestapo. The gendarmes, however, were friends of Franc's and knew what he was doing, and merely warned him to be careful.'[1488]

The next pick-up was scheduled for the night of 13/14 November and, as no message had been received by Franc to the effect that the operation was "off", the evaders were driven to the landing ground. The aircraft did not come that night, but all was set for the night of 15/16 November, when Forman, Hunter, Crome and Kanakos were driven from the château in two cars at 8.45 p.m to the landing ground, which Forman said was 'on an island in the river Charente, north of Chateaneuf'.[1489] The sick Heyworth was brought separately. They had to wait until 1.30 a.m. on 16 November before the two Lysanders landed, this time flown by Bathgate, again, and by Flying Officer J. McBride. Heyworth was loaded onto one of the Lysanders on a stretcher, and they were airborne barely five minutes later. Touching down at Tangmere at around 5 a.m. Heyworth was rushed to hospital, but it was all too late and he died on 25 November 1943.[1490]

Flight Lieutenant Hooper, who had been unable to complete Operation Water Pistol in October, was himself to become an evader. During the November moon period he had attempted Operation Scenery on 15/16 November 1943, but severe icing had forced him to abandon the flight. He tried again the following night but, as a result of one of the two on-board agents wrongly identifying the correct landing strip, one kilometre west-south-west of Périgné (Deux-Sèvres), Hooper's Lysander, V9548, became bogged down in a muddy field. A farmer living nearby was asked to bring his bullocks along to help drag the aircraft out, and he 'immediately did so, although this was the first he had heard of the operation. When interrogated next day by the Feldgendarmerie he stubbornly stuck to the story we had told him to tell, i.e. that he had been forced at the point of the revolver by three mysterious individuals, one of whom appeared to be a foreigner, to act as he did. This appeared to satisfy the Germans.'[1491] Hooper never discovered the farmer's real name, but he was known to them as "Adolphe". V9548, stuck fast in the mud, had to be destroyed by fire.

By the time Hooper had become grounded it was too late for any attempt to be made during the current moon period. For the rest of his time in France, therefore, he stayed with the same people (possibly M. and Mme. Bellot), some thirty kilometres from the scene of his landing. All the time in contact with London, it was arranged that he would be rescued during the next moon period. The first attempt, on the night of 15/16 December by Wing Commander Hodges with Squadron Leader J.C.W. Wagland DFC as his navigator, had to be aborted when the new GEE navigation system that was being tried out in the Lysander affected the compass so much that they found themselves well off track in foul weather over Normandy. All went well on the following night, however, and early on the foggy morning of 17 December 1943 Hodges, Wagland, and Hooper arrived safely at Tangmere.[1492]

Left behind at Giat, meanwhile, Mason and Nelmes were told that it was impossible to get them into the car with the others, but that they would be collected later: 'The car promised to return, but did not turn up; and we received word from the Resistance that an aircraft would arrive in November.'[1493] All that Mason and Nelmes could now do was to wait for something positive to happen. Little did, but the monotony was broken by the arrival of Warrant Officer G.P. "Chris" Columbus RCAF and Sergeant N.W. Lee, coincidentally from their own squadron.

Shot down on the German side of the border with Luxembourg on 4/5 October 1943, Columbus and Lee landed on the German side of the River Sûre, where it marks the border with Luxembourg, opposite the village of Dillingen. Here they were reunited and, after a brief stay, escorted to the town of Medernach,[1494] further into Luxembourg. Lodged in a bar-restaurant, they had been there for a week or so when they heard that the Gestapo were after them. After one night in a large house nearby, they went with two young ladies by train to the city of Luxembourg and then to Differdange, only two or three kilometres from the border with France. After a comfortable week staying with a bank manager and his wife the Resistance were ready to pass the two airmen into France.

Their escorts this time were two young Luxembourg lads, Adrian and Michel, who were fleeing their country to avoid being conscripted by the Germans, and the four of them made their way to Paris by train. After a night in a shabby pension they all took the train to Clermont-Ferrand, 380 kilometres to the south. Met by a member of a local maquis, the five of them walked out of the large town and into the countryside until, after several kilometres, they met a farmer who spoke no English. Lee and Columbus were told to go with him while Adrian and Michel departed with their first guide, the last that either pair saw of the other. The farmer took the airmen to his house, where they were given a great welcome.

The following afternoon a car drove up to the farmhouse, and out of it stepped an astonishing figure waving a Colt .45 automatic and adorned in a strange fusion of clothing: 'He looked like a mixture of soldier, mountaineer, gangster and Pyrenean smuggler…'[1495] He announced to the gawping airmen that he was "the Duke" and that he took care of everything in the area. His name was, apparently, Charbonelle and he was, reputedly, a millionaire. With a lot of roaring and noise the Duke drove off with Lee and Columbus, telling them that they were going to meet some more RAF boys and that in a few days they were to be flown back to England. Arriving unscathed at a dilapidated farmhouse down a rough track, which proved to be the maquis headquarters, the two airmen were delighted to be able to recognise among the welcoming party Ed and Johnny – Flight Lieutenant Edgar Mason and Warrant Officer John Nelmes.

The boredom and inactivity grew as the weeks passed, with promises of the mythical aircraft coming to pick them up broken time and again. Columbus was the worst affected, and he and Norman Lee, hitherto close friends, began to drift apart, even more so when yet two more evaders arrived, Sergeant G.H. Hirst and Sergeant E.W. Brearley, who had been shot down over Luxembourg on 27/28 August 1943.[1496]

As the months wore on, the occasional incident broke the daily routine, such as the time when an

RAF aircraft on a supply drop crashed into a hillside, killing six of the crew. Mason and Nelmes were out with the French maquisards for this operation, and Mason recalled that the supplies were dropped bang on target, but that the aircraft was far too low. He was in contact with the aircraft,[1497] and urged the pilot to climb, but to no avail. A horrible, smashing sound in the distance marked the end of the supply aircraft.[1498] The bodies of six airmen were recovered, and given a respectful burial, which was attended by some of the evaders: 'The most astonishing feature, however, was the guard of honour. This consisted of half a dozen or so young German soldiers, all very smart and very respectful, standing rigidly to attention under the supervision of a couple of gendarmes.'[1499] The Germans were not a danger, however, as they were prisoners of the maquisards. There was a further reminder of the brutality of war when a local farmer was shot dead by one of the maquisards for removing the wristwatch from the dead navigator of the supply aircraft. The watch was presented to Flight Lieutenant Nelmes, who was asked to return it to the dead airman's family when he got home.

With moves afoot to organise the several maquis groups into fewer, larger units, the airmen and their entourage, some fifty altogether, were brazenly moved south on 27 April 1944 to the Cantal department in a convoy of cars, lorries and vans. After a tip-off from a gendarme, another move followed to a camp east of St Flour (Cantal) on 7 May, which brought them into contact with 'some members of a British Intelligence mission'.[1500]

At this time, with preparations well under way for the long-awaited invasion of France, a number of secret missions were dropped into France to co-ordinate resistance by irregular forces. This one, codename Benjoin, was parachuted into the Auvergne by the RF section of the French BCRA on the night of 8/9 May 1944. Strictly speaking it was not "British", being made up of a British major, an American captain, and two French officers. Parachuted 'onto the Plongeon site, in the Margeride forest, during the night of May 8', only a dozen kilometres east of St Flour, the airmen were naturally excited by the news of their arrival: 'We were agog to meet these chaps – and were correspondingly crestfallen when we did, because they displayed no interest in us at all. Their business was to organise the maquis, and that was all they cared about.'[1501]

More airmen, British, Commonwealth and American, continued to arrive at the camp, among them Sergeant P. Wendt USAAF,[1502] Flight Sergeant J.E.G. Buchanan RAAF, shot down two months earlier, and Sergeant G.C. Fearman, shot down on 22/23 March 1944. According to Norman Lee, Buchanan 'was a cheery character and very good fun to be with. He spoke no French worth mentioning, but this never deterred him from enjoying life or making sure of getting what he wanted.'[1503] He had had an uneventful evasion up to this point, spending the two weeks prior to arriving at the camp helping the maquisards at Briffons collect supplies dropped by air. Moving into the woods near Eygurande, he was put in touch with the Mason group.

The leader of the Benjoin mission, Major Frederick Cardozo, South Lancashire Regiment, authorised his wireless operator to give details of the airmen to the authorities in England, but told the airmen to wait with him until a reply had been received. Whether or not one *was* received is not known, but the airmen thereafter 'worked for the mission', and on 1 June 1944 'moved to a cabin in the woods'.[1504] However uneventful their lives may have been up to this point, the evaders, and the maquisards, were soon to get all the excitement that they could handle.

So many Frenchmen were now gathering in the area that their presence could not be kept from the Germans, and Generalleutnant Fritz von Brodowski, chief of *Hauptverbindestab 588*[1505] at Clermont-Ferrand, having been informed of this on 1 June, demanded, and got, immediate action. The Germans' first attack on the French strongholds to the east of St Flour, on 2 June, was repulsed. Under the command of fifty-four-year-old Generalmajor Kurt Jesser, they tried again on the morning of 10 June. The fight lasted throughout the day but, at around 9 p.m., the French bowed under the onslaught and withdrew, leaving behind some seventy killed and thirty wounded, all of whom were later shot dead.[1506]

During the night a group of seventeen airmen moved to a wood north of Chazelles (some twenty-five kilometres east-north-east of St Flour), but with the break-up of the camp four of them decided to leave for Spain later that day. Another four, "Chris" Columbus and three of the Americans, followed next day, returning to the woods to try their luck there. On 2 July 1944, the maquisards with whom they had been fighting were attacked at Petit Parry by German forces. One of the Americans, Staff Sergeant Herbert A. Campbell USAAF, was killed, and Columbus was taken prisoner.[1507]

Five more, including Lee, Brearley and two of the Americans, headed for Switzerland. They decided to travel by day, the risk of losing one's way at night being too great. They made steady progress as far as the River Loire, to the west of St Étienne (Loire), when the prospect of having to cross a large bridge over the Loire loomed before them. Learning that the town had been bombed the day before and was full of Germans, Lee, Brearley and the two Americans took the bull by the horns and decided to cross the bridge anyway. By some miracle it was unguarded, and they reached St

Étienne without a problem. With help from its citizens the four men breezed through the town, and so confident did the two Americans become that they wanted to press on as fast as they could to Switzerland. Lee and Brearley were not of the same opinion, and by mutual consent they split up. It gave the two RAF boys no pleasure to hear that the Americans had been arrested by the Germans in the very next town.

Lee and Brearley plodded on in their own cautious, wet and weary way. As they walked through a forest in a downpour, not too far from Annecy (Haute-Savoie) and close to the Swiss frontier, they were intercepted by a group of maquisards, who took them to their camp in a small, mountain resort. A brief interrogation followed, conducted to their surprise by a young Canadian lieutenant-colonel and an older, British, captain by the name of Montgomery, who were there on military liaison with three others in their team – two Free French lieutenants and a sergeant wireless operator. The two airmen were more or less inducted into the maquis, but 'there wasn't a great deal for us to do. We were not army and we were not really maquis. We didn't mind helping Captain Montgomery or Ted, the sergeant wireless operator, with any jobs that needed doing, but we had no intention of being treated like dirt by the colonel and told him so on the only occasion he tried it.'[1508]

There was little to do but drink, until the Germans attacked, when they had to run for their drunken lives up the mountain in pursuit of the maquisards, who had already fled without them. With pressure mounting on the maquis in their mountain fastness, a further move was in order, and new headquarters were established in 'a big, rambling farmhouse next door to a church and about five miles outside the village of Vals, which was a mountain holiday resort quite similar to the one we had just left.'[1509] A few days later an American OSS team consisting of a 'couple of US Army captains and seven or eight master sergeants, all French-speaking, were parachuted in'.

To assist the Allied landings in the south of France on 15 August 1944, operations to harass the Germans were undertaken to the north, with Norman and Eric accompanying them, with varying amount of success, until the last of the Germans was gone. With Vals liberated it was time for them to make their way back to the bosom of the RAF and, rather than join in the celebrations, arrangements were made by Captain Montgomery for them to be driven south to Avignon by a maquisard. Beyond Avignon they found their first RAF unit, a mobile radio station under the command of a flight lieutenant, who directed them to an American airfield. On the following day they were flown to Naples, Italy, thence across the Mediterranean Sea to Casablanca, Morocco, and were actually sitting aboard a homeward-bound aircraft when they were ejected at the last minute in favour of two German prisoners of war. An RAF flight lieutenant very decently gave up his seat to Eric, but a squadron leader padré refused to do the same for Norman who, nevertheless, was back in England only a day after his friend.

Following the dispersal of the maquis camp at the beginning of June, Flight Lieutenant Mason, one of the four to stay behind, decided to return to the old maquis camp on 15 June, 'but on approaching the woods found that it was being searched by members of the Milice, so we detoured, and started south, with Spain as our objective.'[1510] They made contact with another Resistance group camped near Sarrus (Cantal) in the hills to the north of Aurillac, and 'met another British Intelligence Mission who advised us to stay with them and they would try to contact the first Mission to see if an answer had arrived to their message.'[1511] Whatever transpired, Mason and his companions were at the Sarrus camp on 20 June when the Germans attacked again, and yet again the airmen were obliged to beat a hasty retreat, this time to woods south-west of Cussac.[1512]

They stayed in the woods, fed by the Resistance, until 22 August when another member of the Resistance told them to go to Chaudes-Aigues (Cantal) and to stay there until he joined them. On 3 September they were sent to Aurillac (forty kilometres to the west), and met a major in British Intelligence. The major departed for Toulouse, but 'on his return he told us that he had made arrangements for us to leave France by air from Toulouse. On 7 September we left Aurillac, arriving in Toulouse the same day, and were flown over to Algiers in a Stirling bomber.'[1513] They finally left Algiers on 19 September, arriving in England on the following day. For both Mason and Nelmes, it had been a remarkable feat of patience and endurance.

CHAPTER 11

Evasions: October 1943–June 1944

'I needed to go to the toilet and opened the back door, only to find it blocked by a German soldier firing madly at an attacking aircraft. He paid no attention to me and I pushed past heading for safety in the toilet.'

Flying Officer J.E. "Jim" Mortimer RNZAF[1514]

Tired of the 'continuous loss of my flying mates without real contact with enemy aircraft', Pilot Officer J.E. "Jim" Mortimer RNZAF volunteered to go to the hottest spot of the war at the time, the besieged Mediterranean island of Malta. After his operational flying career had begun in April 1942, with a posting to 122 Squadron at RAF Hornchurch, his overseas posting came through on 8 July. He enjoyed a few days' leave before departing Britain's shores aboard one of the *Empire* cargo ships in a well-organised convoy bound for Gibraltar, where he transferred to the aircraft carrier HMS *Furious*. Together with thirty-seven other Spitfire fighter pilots on Operation Bellows, Jim flew off the carrier to Malta on 11 August 1942, joining hard-pressed 126 Squadron at Luqa.[1515]

Jim's flying career, and his life, nearly came to an end on 15 October 1942. Caught by "the Hun in the sun", he discovered that his Spitfire had suffered severe aileron damage and was unflyable below a speed of 160 mph or so. Making it back to the island he decided to land anyway: 'Managed the landing but owing to the [high] speed was unable to control the plane on the ground as the runways were not very long. I finally ground looped, finishing upside down. Was soaked by petrol and, the airfield being under massive attack, I was to put it mildly – worried.'[1516] Despite having their heads down in slit trenches on the edge of the airfield, a number of RAF groundcrew bravely rushed to his aid. At great risk to their own lives amid exploding bombs they lifted up the aircraft and released the pilot.

With little prospect of being relieved after one tour of operations, Jim completed two before finally leaving Malta on 17 February 1943 aboard a B-24 "Liberator". Arriving at Gibraltar via the Sahara Desert he sailed back to Britain on the *Johann van Oldervarnebilt*. Put on the strength of No. 1 Personnel Despatch Centre, West Kirby, Liverpool, he enjoyed a rest period until, on 10 September 1943, he was posted to 485 (RNZAF) Squadron at Biggin Hill, Kent.

On the morning of 3 October 1943 Jim flew with 485 Squadron to RAF Manston, Kent before supporting a flight of Martin Marauder medium bombers returning from a raid to the continent: 'We met them a long way into France and they were under sustained enemy attack. Our intervention enabled the bombers to fly on safely.' 485 Squadron was required for a further operation in the afternoon, this time in support of Douglas Boston bombers. As those who had flown on the morning operation were stood down, Jim went to retrieve his parachute from his Spitfire, MH490, just as the afternoon's operation was getting under way. When the pilot who was to have flown MH490 failed to show up on time, Jim was ordered to take his place.

485 Squadron found the Bostons over France under heavy attack from Fw190 fighters. A high-level and fierce dogfight ensued, in the course of which Jim pursued one of the 190s down to the ground, and destroyed it. Now at low-level he headed for home, but before reaching the coast he saw another 190 several hundred feet above him on an interception course. The pilot of the Fw190 spotted Jim as he was climbing to attack and, like knights of old, the two fighters charged towards each other with all guns blazing, each scoring hits on the other. In seconds they were miles apart and unable to resume combat, which was just as well for Jim as his Spitfire had been hit in the engine. Though oil was spewing all over his windscreen he nevertheless pressed on towards England.

He was over the Channel when the engine finally expired. A successful ditching followed, but MH490 began to sink even as Jim was trying to get out of the cockpit, and took him down with it: 'As the plane hit the bottom of the sea I was then able to struggle free because the water was no longer forcing me back into the cockpit. If I had not previously released my safety harness… I could never have managed to free myself under water. Now being free I started to struggle back to the surface…'[1517] This was quite a feat, for Jim was still wearing his parachute with its inflatable dinghy attached. His troubles were not yet over, though, for he still had to release his parachute and harness whilst holding on to his dinghy to prevent it from sinking. Eventually freeing himself from his waterlogged burden and opening the dinghy he tried to get into it. This was easier said than done, for the injuries to his head, which had only now become apparent, and his efforts to reach the surface had weakened him considerably. Nevertheless, he managed to climb into the dinghy, and passed out.

Regaining consciousness he saw in one direction the distant white cliffs of England and in the other, much nearer, the cliffs of France. Later identifying his position as off the mouth of the Somme estuary he drifted at the mercy of the tides. Late in the afternoon, he passed out for a second time. It was dark when he came-to again, and suddenly heard commands being given in German. He could see that he was passing a seaside town – 'which I later identified as Le Treport' – but then the tide changed and he drifted past it again before being pushed through a narrow gap with open lock gates, unseen by the guards on either side, who were too busy talking to each other to notice the prize slipping between them. Clearing the town it was not long before the tide that had been pushing him upstream began to turn, and he made what he called 'a one man invasion of France'.[1518]

Clinging to an overhanging branch he let go, dropping into a muddy inlet through which he waded to *terra firma*. Leaving the heavily-guarded coast he headed inland with help from French people along the way, but by the evening of the fourth day, hungry and thirsty, he approached some farm buildings in the hope of finding food and water. Seeing a box on the ground, and thinking that he could use it for collecting water, he picked it up. Swiftly and silently a large dog appeared from its kennel and sank its fangs into his knee: 'We stood there staring at each other but when I put the container down he let go and returned to his kennel still without a murmur.' Jim pressed on into the darkness, as hungry and thirsty as ever.

Weaker now on the morning of his fifth day ashore, he was making his way through a large wood when he came across a number of 'Catholic Brothers'. It was not until everyone else in the neighbourhood was asleep that they took Jim back to their school, in a château complete with fairy-tale turret. After a most welcome shower he was led up a very steep flight of steps to a bedroom in the turret, where food and drink were brought to him. On the following day, still in some pain from his head and back wounds, the good Brothers arranged for a doctor from Sailly-Flibeaucourt[1519] to have a look at him.

As the doctor was satisfied that time alone would heal the wounded airman, Jim stayed with the Brothers for several weeks. There was little to do, and the only time Jim was allowed to leave the château was when the Brothers, puzzled as to why a nearby wood had been extensively bombed, asked him if he 'would accompany them to the area and try and explain the reason for the attacks.' All Jim could suggest, having been told that there was nothing of importance in the wood, was that 'Resistance forces had advised that German troops and armour were hiding there.'

This may not have been such a bad guess on Jim's part, for it was at this time that reports were reaching England of a pilotless aircraft loaded with explosive being seen in northern France, later identified as the V1, Hitler's first "revenge weapon". At the end of October 1943, after eighty-eight V1 launch sites had been identified, with evidence of some fifty more, usually hidden in woods, orders were issued to 2 Group to attack them with its medium bombers. The first such attack was launched on 5 November 1943.

It was shortly after this bombing incident that Jim received a visit from an officer of the Resistance, 'who told me that he would take me away and put me in contact with others to help me escape back to England. This didn't happen overnight and the explanation given was that they had to check my ID first.' Once cleared, Jim was taken further inland, at some point being united with 'a fellow Brit pilot' (no name). They were told by the Resistance that they would be using the same route as that taken by Squadron Leader Checketts (see Chapter 8), but before they could follow in his footsteps the line was destroyed by the Germans, and the two airmen were immediately separated.

Jim was hidden in a farmhouse close to a railway line, though he could see German guards patrolling the station a few hundred metres away. Also sharing the sanctuary of the farmhouse was 'an Aussie pilot' (again, no name). The Australian became very ill after sunbathing on wet ground, apparently contracting pleurisy, and had to be treated by a doctor to reduce the lung inflammation using the "cupping" process. When it was time to move on again, the two airmen were, again, separated.

After staying at several safe houses, Christmas 1943 found Jim at a large house in 'a town called "Cinq Quent On"'.[1520] He was made thoroughly welcome by the family, and had a marvellous time, but then came the serious business of trying to get home. Members of the local Resistance persisted in the belief that he would be picked up by a Lysander, and Jim was moved into their hands in readiness for the aircraft when it came. With him was yet another pilot evader, and the two of them sat and waited day after day for a Lysander. The weather in January 1944 was too bad to allow any Lysander operations whatsoever, and it was not until February that the signal came over the air that the pick-up was on.

Jim and his companion were led off through the town, ignored by the several German patrols whom they passed on the way. It was later learnt that these Germans were on their way to the very house that Jim and the others had only recently vacated, and that the house and all those left inside it were utterly destroyed. More bad news followed when they heard that the Lysander that was coming to collect them had been shot down, and yet again Jim found himself 'being sheltered by a

Resistance Officer and his wife'. His host, a First World War veteran, belonged to an active Resistance group, and Jim spent some of his time making booby traps to hinder German motorised traffic. The pace of their activity increased as D-Day approached, and then came and went.

Jim was of some use one day when a group of men calling themselves American airmen were brought in. The French were suspicious of them because they had German-sounding names, but Jim was able to allay their fears that the men were Germans trying to infiltrate the Resistance.[1521] They were joined one day by another American pilot following a fierce dogfight over nearby marshalling yards. Baling out of his P-38 Lightning fighter-bomber, he landed in the very marshalling yard that he and his pals had just been bombing.[1522] It was, of course, broad daylight, and the airman was clearly visible as he slowly descended. Nevertheless, by the time that the Germans had rushed to the scene and demanded to know his whereabouts, there was no trace of him. With the French railway workers looking suitably blank, the Germans departed, failing to notice as they did so an odd-looking workman digging away with his shovel. Jim later met this American, who came from Hollywood and had worked in the film industry. Jim did note, though, that while the marshalling yards were relatively unscathed the town had been flattened.

The father of the family with which Jim was staying was a butcher, and a practical joker. The Frenchman was out one evening with his friend, the village mayor, and both were armed with pistols. 'A chance meeting with two Germans on a lonely stretch of road made them decide to attack, so drew their pistols to fire. One pistol jammed and before they could make much impression they were both hit in return. One German was killed and the other wounded. The mayor was also killed and the butcher slightly wounded.' Understandably, Jim thought it best if he left, but was still 'given a light machine gun in a sack, to defend myself… I was told to walk through the town to get to a new hideout but German patrols were everywhere making me uncomfortable, but I was not stopped or checked as I followed the guide some distance in front of me. We ended up at the local cemetery and into a disused morgue. I promptly rid myself of the gun as I could not see me threatening the German Army in any way as I only had five shells and the gun had doubtful capabilities.'[1523]

Jim was then moved to a house, the front door of which opened directly onto the road. The toilet was in the small back garden. Then it was time for the Germans to retreat and, looking through the curtains to the roadway a few feet away, Jim 'could see German columns retreating… They were being heavily attacked by strafing aircraft, and [German] foot soldiers were moving through house properties to gain shelter. I needed to go to the toilet and opened the back door, only to find it blocked by a German soldier firing madly at an attacking aircraft. He paid no attention to me and I pushed past heading for safety in the toilet.' Staying longer in the toilet than necessary, he nipped out during a lull in the firing and back into the house. The lull lasted longer and longer and 'it became strangely quiet, and lo and behold cautiously coming down the street was an American jeep all of 500 yards behind the last German patrol.'

Getting back to England in due course, Jim was questioned as to his experiences. When it was discovered that he had destroyed two aircraft in his final battle, he was recommended for the DFC. Now finding himself surplus to requirements, he was on the boat home to New Zealand when the war in Europe came to an end, and he was presented with his medal in New Zealand on 1 June 1945.

Pilot Officer Donald Wares and crew were on their first operation, 7/8 October 1943. As with so many "sprog" crews they were pleased to be "on ops" at last, and were delighted to be told by the squadron commander that they were to be flying a brand-new Lancaster. Things started to go wrong, though, when carrying out their pre-flight checks. The Lancaster developed engine trouble, and with the rest of the squadron on its way Wares and crew were hurriedly transferred to the squadron hack, Lancaster ED426, P-Peter, 'which had been used for many months by every Tom, Dick and Harry for practising "circuit and bumps" and was itself badly in need of new engines.'[1524]

With no hope of reaching the target in the safety of the main stream of bombers, Donald Wares nevertheless lifted the heavy bomber off RAF Fiskerton's runway. By the time that ED426 was over Holland the rest of Bomber Command was on its way home, as Sergeant Ray Barlow, wireless operator/air gunner, could testify: 'It was a moonless night and looking out of the port side window I could see the main stream of our other bombers returning safely from their mission homeward bound for England.'[1525]

Pressing on to Stuttgart alone, ED426 was easy prey for the night-fighters, which attacked the lonely Lancaster six or seven times. Temporarily repulsed by the guns of Sergeant Gilbert Attwood (mid-upper) and Flying Officer Archie Fitzgerald RAAF (rear), ED426 now received the full attention of the flak gunners: 'We seemed to be in the middle of a firework display. We were ringed all around and being the only one over the target area, we were given the full treatment and felt very vulnerable.'[1526] Somehow bombs were dropped on target, and with great relief Wares and crew turned towards home. Suddenly, cannon shells from a night-fighter thumped into ED426's starboard side. The outer engine caught fire, and had to be feathered, and Wares began the long journey home on three engines at 18,000 feet. Ten minutes later the fire had spread to the starboard inner engine and that, too, was feathered. Ray Barlow: 'We all knew how serious this was but nobody voiced their fears. We knew we had our work cut out to get back. With two engines gone we were facing disaster.'[1527]

Steadily losing height Don Wares struggled to keep control of the Lancaster, which was over eastern France and at a height of around only 2,000 feet, when it suddenly slammed into high ground near Bézimont in the Forêt de Commercy (Meuse), killing the flight engineer, bomb aimer and navigator. Ray Barlow regained consciousness inside the aircraft to the sound of exploding ammunition and oxygen bottles ignited by the fire that blazed from nose to tail. Unable to open the jammed escape door he staggered forward and found the unconscious pilot slumped in his seat: 'I shook him, called him, shouted at him and slapped his face and, after what seemed an age, he came round to be confronted by our broiling, noisy hot pot, and of course the instinctive urge to escape from it.' Finally managing to open the sliding window beside the pilot, the two jumped out into the burning undergrowth, fortunate not to be hit by their own exploding bullets as they fled the scene as quickly as possible.

German soldiers speeding past in their truck towards the crash site, failed to spot the two airmen, who walked through the chilly night until too exhausted to continue. Covering themselves with branches of fir, they 'slept back to back to keep warm. The following day we walked for a while; there was an autumn chill and we were feeling hungry and very thirsty. Hiding in a quarry about ten miles from the crash, we got rid of our flying gear, tearing off the lapels and badges from our uniforms. Using the knife, which had been hidden in them, we cut away the tops of our boots.'[1528]

The admirable inventor Clayton Hutton, who did so much for evaders by providing such things as the escape-aids box and silk maps ("eggs and bacon" was his codeword for the silk maps, "sausages" for the paper ones), also provided a new type of flying boot. He wrote that the factual reports of evaders of their clandestine travels 'helped us tremendously in the preparation of our pre-capture devices. Many a young flier frankly admitted that he would not have got very far without his map, compass and ration pack. Most of them had only one complaint to make – they were handicapped by their flying boots. In wet weather they became soggy and uncomfortable…'[1529] This was enough for the redoubtable Hutton, wartime scourge of the treasury and of red tape in general, who set about designing a new boot. He showed the finished article to Sir Arthur Harris, commander-in-chief of RAF Bomber Command, who was much impressed. The final mark of Hutton Boot contained a considerable array of escape aids – the heel could be opened to reveal a small cavity containing 'several silk maps, a compass and a small file'; the laces contained a Gigli flexible saw; and concealed in the cloth loop at the top of the boot was a small knife.

A toss of a coin decided that Don Wares and Ray Barlow would head for Switzerland, only 250 kilometres east, rather than Spain, some 1,100 kilometres south-west. Keeping away from towns and villages as much as possible they made steady progress, despite the cold and damp weather, surviving on stolen apples and river water, with occasional help from a farmer. They learnt from one of them that two of their crew were alive but, with broken arms and legs, they had inevitably been taken prisoner.[1530]

After several days, with Don's feet playing up and with both suffering from upset stomachs, help arrived from an unexpected quarter. They were near a wood when they saw a lorry stop nearby. A load of German soldiers jumped off it and ran into the woods leaving the vehicle unattended. For the two airmen this was too good an opportunity to miss: 'We managed to get the engine started and were feeling pretty good. We travelled all of ten yards when it stopped. We tried to start it but couldn't and then found out it was running on charcoal. It was the long walk for us again and we had to make a quick exit before the Germans came back for their lorry.'

Keeping to the fields they walked for most of the day, stealing apples as they went, but managing to buy some beer at a shop in a remote village. At dusk they came to another village 'where we asked for food and had a feast of bread, cheese and wine. We tried to sleep in a mangel pit at the side of the road but were kept awake by the howling of a mad dog. We made our way again, but it was a wet and very miserable day. We were spotted by a German patrol and after a harrowing time of hide and seek we managed to get away in the long grass. Exhausted we reached a farm at 5 p.m. and stopped to beg for food. We were invited in, and given food and warm hospitality.' They also had their first shave in ten days, before being offered the bliss of a soft warm bed.

After a wonderful breakfast their very generous hosts gave them each a coat, doubly welcome as it then rained continually for two days. Their sheepskin-lined boots became waterlogged, but they plodded on, eating carrots, apples and anything else edible to fend off their hunger, until finding shelter in the loft of a barn at Vanne (Haute-Saône). Leaving Vanne they gingerly crossed the ruins of the bridge over the River Saône at Soing: 'It was early dawn and we came across German patrol cars. We made a hasty dive into the ditch just in time and breathed with relief when they passed by without stopping. Walking all day we reached fields being tended by uniformed people so decided to hole up until dark. Under the cover of the night we reached a village called Neuvelle-lès-la-Charité, and got a bed for the night, next door to some German people!' It was now twelve days after the crash and, though their progress had been more southerly than easterly, they were now only some eighty kilometres from the Swiss border.

They were then taken to the château of Baron Henri Féron until the Resistance could be contacted: 'He was living in the basement because the Germans had stripped the chateau of all the furniture and paintings, and the walls had been used for target practice. The Baron gave us food and drink and provided us with money, which he was printing in the basement. These marvellous people made us very welcome and we spent the night in the chateau.' On the following day they met Claude, a member of the Resistance, at Velle-le-Châtel, a dozen kilometres up the road to Vesoul, 'and a celebration was held at the local butcher's – everybody invited to the party. That evening we slept at a friend's house in the village.'

For the next three days they hid in the village, getting plenty of rest and food but anxious to be on their way, especially as the Resistance was very active in the area and had blown up two bridges and killed three of the enemy. A French gendarme gave them false identity cards and papers, but something went wrong and they were taken to Vesoul. In due course a lorry was hired and, with their dirty uniforms hidden by civilian clothes, they were ready to travel to the Swiss border: 'The French had managed to forge German authorisation papers and we were given chemin-de-fer armbands. The lorry was slow but better than walking. On the way we passed many Germans but, thankfully, nobody took any notice of us.' At Montbéliard, where they saw a bombed-out factory, they stayed at the post office for the night to await the guides who were going to take them, and a French diplomat, over the border.

Somewhere along the way to the Swiss frontier they picked up Sergeant K.W. Thorpe, who had come down at Barisey-la-Côte (Meurthe-et-Moselle), to the south of Toul and a long way north of Monbéliard, after being shot down on 23/24 September. At 8 p.m. on 29 October 1943 the three 'walked over fields and crept through German frontier posts. A dog barking on the German side alerted the guards that there was something going on, so we had to run for our lives over the fields and in so doing lost our way. At last we regained the right path and stealthily crept on our hands and knees into Switzerland, where we offered up a prayer of thanks.'[1531] Ray Barlow was all for carrying on to the British Legation, but Don Wares was too exhausted and decided to give himself up. The police were contacted and they were put on a train for Porrentruy. Having rested and completed the formalities of interrogation Ray Barlow went to Berne, while Don Wares (and Ken Thorpe?) were interned with other escapers and evaders at Lugano.

Wares and Thorpe left Switzerland some time after 16 September 1944, but Ray was "employed" at the British Embassy, spending a few hours a day handing out clothes to newly-arrived personnel, until, on 4 October 1944, he left Lausanne for Geneva. Making his way from there to France he caught a train to Annecy, hoping for a flight back to England from the aerodrome, but when departures were delayed due to exceptionally heavy rain Ray was taken by the Maquis on 5 October to see seven 'Frenchmen shot for collaborating. They were buried on the spot in graves dug by Germans.' Then he was on his way home: '6th October, left Annecy at 10 a.m. Went to Lyon by lorry. Got a Dakota and arrived at Croydon 6 p.m. Arrived London 7.30. Arrived St. Albans at 11 p.m. I was over the moon. Peggy was waiting for me at the station. What a sight for sore eyes. I was home!'[1532]

It was sometimes the practice for units other than RAF bomber squadrons to take advantage of the mass of bombers heading for Germany so that they could carry out their duties while the German defences were occupied elsewhere. On the night of 3/4 November 1943 it was Düsseldorf's turn to suffer, and taking advantage of this was an all-Canadian crew from 24 Operational Training Unit (OTU) at RAF Honeybourne. They were to drop nothing more harmful than leaflets – in RAF jargon, a "bumph raid" – to gain experience for when they joined an operational bomber squadron.

The five-man crew of Whitley AD675 took off from 24 OTU's base on the evening of 3 November 1943 to drop their leaflets over Bourges, in the centre of France, but about five minutes before reaching the drop zone the Whitley developed engine trouble. In the spirit of RAF Bomber Command, they pressed on and successfully delivered the paper cargo. They were on their way home when sparks suddenly erupted from one of the two engines. Height was rapidly lost, and quick calculations by the navigator revealed that they would be unable to reach home. The pilot, Flight Lieutenant J.L. Kennedy RCAF, advised an immediate bale out.[1533]

Sergeant A.E. Spencer RCAF, rear gunner, landed in a wood and was knocked unconscious. Regaining his senses he found himself dangling from his parachute, which he had to leave high in the tree. Tearing off any obvious sign of his nationality and service, he walked and ran for several hours. Too tired to go on, he 'lay in some hay for about half an hour'.[1534] Continuing in the darkness he was somewhere near Busloup (Loir-et-Cher) when 'I was stopped by two men who shone a bright light in my face. Not being able to see who they were I said "Bonjour messieurs". They replied "Bonjour", and after saying a few words in German to each other they walked on.'[1535] As they did so Spencer saw, with a shock, that they were two German soldiers, complete with rifles and other nasty bits and pieces.

Continuing for another five kilometres, until it began getting light, he hid in a ditch until dark, when he went on his way. Reaching the main road (today the N157) from Busloup to St Calais (Sarthe), his feet were giving him such trouble – he was flat-footed – that he was forced to stop, and spent the night in a cemetery. Heavy rain at dawn obliged him to seek shelter elsewhere: 'I went on a little way until I reached a barn where I remained for three nights. During this time it rained nearly all the time. At intervals I went out and gathered up as many apples as I could carry. I lived on these apples, raw potatoes and the contents of my escape box.'[1536] Alone, cold, hungry and with both feet in a very poor state, he soldiered on – 'I think I probably passed through St Calais at midnight about 8 November' – reaching the outskirts of Bonnétable (Sarthe) two or three nights later, still sleeping in barns and living only off apples and raw potatoes. But then, walking past a house near Bonnétable, he heard an announcer on the radio say "Ici Londres". As it was "streng verboten" ("strictly prohibited") to listen to the BBC, Spencer thought that the people in the house would help him: 'As soon as I opened the garden gate the radio was turned off, and when I asked the woman who came to the door if she would give me some food she told me to go away.'

The woman's husband, however, dashed out and took Spencer back into the house, where he was given 'a good meal, a wash and a shave, and allowed to remain two days.' It was on or about 13 November that a refreshed airman set off once more, wearing a beret given to him by his host. For a further fifteen days of hard travel in the direction of the English Channel, he lived off a few handouts but 'chiefly on what food I could pick up from the fields and orchards.' On 28 November he reached the town of Gacé (Orne), half way between Rouen and Le Mans. There a young lad took him to meet Robert and Daniel Violet, who provided him with civilian clothing and false papers.

He was taken to Paris on about 6 January 1944, and met Sergeant H.W. Payne, who had been on the run since early November 1943. Payne, having himself only arrived in Paris on 3 January, had been brought from the Lisieux area to the French capital by Captain Gills, whom he called 'the chief of the organisation in Caen', and it was Captain Gills and two maquisards who, on 12 January 1944, took Payne and Spencer south-east to Ambérieu-en-Bugey (Ain) with a view to getting them through to Switzerland.

As seen, it was in the Ain that SOE's Richard Heslop ("Xavier"), head of the Resistance network Marksman, was highly active. The Germans were particularly keen to capture Xavier, a considerable thorn in their side,[1537] and it is likely that the disruption to be suffered by the airmen evaders was as a direct result of the very active Ain maquisards.[1538] Three days after the airmen had arrived at a maquis camp a few kilometres from Ambérieu the French captured a German. On the following day 'the camp was surrounded by the police. There was a certain amount of fighting, during which the maquis shot several policemen and took a large number of prisoners. Finally hostilities came to an end and the affair was settled by an exchange of prisoners.'[1539]

Too dangerous to remain in the area, the camp was struck and moved to a farm about ten kilometres from the town of Hauteville-Lompnes. Two weeks later the airmen met Xavier 'who was helping to organise the resistance movement'. Their troubles were far from over, however, for it was now that 'Vichy sent a force of about 4,500 miliciens and GMR into the departments [of Ain and Haute-Savoie], who stayed for two months and secured over a thousand arrests; but the maquisards were strong enough to drive them out'.[1540] As a result of this "drive", the airmen were forced to hide in the forests for five days: 'We had no shelter and were short of food, while the weather was bitterly cold with three feet of snow on the ground.'[1541] At the end of the five days, when the fighting had died down, the men returned to the farm, only to find that it had been burned down. With little to eat they stayed in a barn for a few days before moving to another farm.

It was to this farm that two more evaders were brought, Sergeants N.C.H. Pilgrim and D.E. Cadge, the two gunners of Stirling EF502 shot down by flak while on SOE duties on the night of 10/11 April 1944. EF502 crashed onto the roof of a farmhouse at St Jean-le-Vieux (Ain), killing the other five of the crew. Pilgrim, soon found by the local maquisards in the neighbourhood of St Jérôme, a few kilometres east of St Jean, was taken to 'a sort of shack', where he met Payne and Spencer. Barely had he had time to settle in on 11 April than the camp was attacked. He and Payne fled into the woods, returning a while later to find that in the meantime Sergeant Cadge had arrived.

Forced to move several times thereafter, to Montgriffon for four days, then Oncieu (to 6 May), and to Corlier for one night before coming to a halt at the maquis' HQ, yet another farmhouse, on 7 May. Two days later, 'having contracted tropical dysentery' Pilgrim was moved to a hospital at Nantua, where he rested until 23 May. The others also moved to Nantua, staying at a hotel opposite the gendarmerie for a fortnight before returning to the HQ. On 22 May they moved to the Hôtel de France at Oyonnax, where Pilgrim rejoined his comrades.

All the time that the airmen were with the maquisards 'all arrangements were made for us by Major Xavier (?), who was in command.' Heslop was in desperate need of heavy machine-guns and mortars with which to take on the enemy and made arrangements for an aircraft to land in the area. It would bring with it nine personnel and take eleven back. The operation, Mixer I, was undertaken by a C-47 Dakota aircraft from the USAAF's secret base at Harrington, Northamptonshire. The pilot was Colonel Clifford J. Heflin, and his crew Captain Wilmer Stapel (co-pilot), Major Edward C. Tresemer (navigator), Major Charles R. Teer (bombardier), and Technical Sergeant Albert L. Krasevac (radio). 'Their destination was an improvised Resistance airstrip at Izernore a few miles from Nantua'.[1542] A safe landing was made and the aircraft quickly camouflaged, as it would not be heading back to England for another day.

The new arrivals were bundled into two cars and driven to the maquisards' HQ 'at Château Wattern, which lay on a steep hillside overlooking the landing area'. The four evaders had been brought to the château while the Dakota was winging its way across on the night of 6/7 July, and they should have been flown back on the night of 7/8 July, but bad weather forced a further twenty-four-hour delay. Finally, the airmen were 'at 2315 hours on 8 July taken to a field (locality unknown) and taken off by air, accompanied by Major Xavier. We landed in the UK at 0425 hours 9 July.' Also aboard the Dakota were two American airmen – Jim Cater and French M. Russell – and two Indian soldiers who had been rescued from their German captors.

A few minutes after 1 p.m. on 3 November 1943 Henri Faure, sitting in the dining room of his flat on the outskirts of Valence (Drôme), turned on his radio in time to hear the BBC Overseas programme broadcast the morse dit-dit-dit-dah, V for Victory. As soon as he heard the phrase "Le sang est rouge" he switched off his set. This was the signal to him that the RAF was to make a drop that night at drop zone (DZ) "Fabert". This was a serious problem, however, for only the day before Noel, the man in charge of the Fabert reception committee, had been arrested. As he could not take the chance that Noel might not have talked under torture, Henri decided to cancel the Fabert site and to use another. But it was now too late for him to contact London so that alternative arrangements could be made.

Remembering that in his last drop he had received a battery-powered transmitter called a Eureka, he decided to test it out. He knew that Eureka had a range of some eighty kilometres and that with it he would be able to communicate with the aircraft that was to make the drop. All he had to do was to pick another DZ and talk the aircraft to that new location. The DZ chosen, codenamed "Temple", was situated on the Plâteau de Soulier, near Allex and Livron-sur-Drôme. Henri, or "Capitaine Albert" as he was known to his men, set the necessary wheels in motion, and when they once again heard the phrase "Le sang est rouge" on the 9 p.m. broadcast they knew that the drop was going ahead for that night.

All was set well in advance of the time for the drop, and Eureka was tested satisfactorily. There was nothing to do but wait. Tension heightened when, some fifteen kilometres to the north, the lights of Valence suddenly went out. Henri knew from experience that this meant that a hostile aircraft was in the vicinity, and all ears strained to hear the sound of the approaching aircraft. When none was heard, and the lights of Valence were switched on again, they all realised that there would be no drop for them that night. Then one of the men, who had been guarding the perimeter of the DZ, came up to Henri and told him that he had seen a brilliant flash away to the west, in the Ardèche, way across the River Rhône (at least fifty kilometres as the crow flies). Henri immediately thought that it *might* have been their aircraft, and a shiver ran down his spine.

It was not until the morning of 5 November that Henri learned that an aircraft had crashed on the Col des Quatre Vios, near the village of Marcols-les-Eaux (Ardèche), and that there had been one survivor. The Germans had been to the crash site and, as they had found seven bodies, the normal complement for a four-engined bomber, as the aircraft proved to be, they left the scene. Accordingly, Henri and two of his men, Longpierre and Marc, drove over to Marcols to see for themselves. When their contact there, Eli Combe, told them that the survivor was being hidden by Mademoiselle Giraud and her elderly parents in their farmhouse, Henri and his two companions went to find the airman. Mlle. Giraud, initially highly suspicious of the three men, took them to a back room, where they saw a young airman, in RAF blue battledress, clearly utterly bewildered and suffering from shock.

The airman had been found by a M. Croze on 4 November, but as he had a wife and seven children to think of, asked Mlle. Giraud for help. She went to the scene of the crash and saw the broken bodies and the wreckage, an awful sight, and agreed to take the airman. His name was John Brough, and he was the rear gunner of the Halifax of 138 Squadron that was to have dropped supplies to Henri Faure on Operation John 13. He told them that one of the crew was an American officer[1543] who had come along to gain experience, and that was why the Germans had found seven bodies. He explained that the Halifax was lost and as it descended through cloud to try to find the DZ its port wing had hit a rocky outcrop, and the whole aircraft burst into flames, but not before John's rear turret had been flung clear by the impact.

The three Frenchmen left with John for Valence, and a while later left by train for Lyon, where his false papers got him through the barrier at the station. He was driven away to a château near Lons-le-Saulnier, which was occupied by three women, and there he met Raymond Aubrac, a committee member of the *Conseil National de la Résistance*, his wife Lucie and their young son, Jean-Pierre, who was born in May 1941.[1544] Raymond Aubrac had already been arrested twice, in March 1943 and on 21 June 1943, the second time with the legendary Jean Moulin,[1545] and was keen to save himself and his family, especially as Lucie was pregnant again. They were all to have been flown to England in December, but the moon period was a bad one for 161 Squadron with bad weather and the tragic loss of two pilots on the foggy night of 16/17 December (which was also a very bad night for Bomber Command returning from a raid on Berlin).

An attempt to get them away, and John Brough, was made on 4/5 February 1944, but Operation Bludgeon failed due to more fog and to the reception committee being at the wrong landing strip. Flying Officer John Affleck DFC, DFM and crew in their Hudson tried again four nights later, and this time were successful, though coming very close to disaster. The field, "Orion", on which the heavy Hudson landed was thick with mud and as Affleck taxied to position the aircraft for take-off the port wheel stuck fast. Horses and oxen failed to pull it clear, and an army of diggers had to clear a path to firmer ground before the Hudson could move off. Even then it was touch and go, but go it was as the Hudson hit a bump when nearing the edge of the field and finally became airborne. With great skill Affleck coaxed the reluctant aircraft higher and faster, and home to England.

Dropping an anti-shipping mine at a particular point in the sea on a black winter's night was never easy, and many an aircraft was lost in the attempt. Obliged to fly low and usually over shipping lanes that hugged the coast a lone aircraft was fair game for alert gunners either ashore or, more likely, on a flak ship. Flying higher, it became prey for any lurking night-fighter. The crew of Stirling EF202 had dropped their mine in the Gironde estuary on the night of 25/26 November 1943 when they were found by a night-fighter and shot down in a vineyard near St Étienne-de-Montluc (Loire-Atlantique), twenty kilometres north-west of Nantes.

The first that mid-upper gunner Sergeant A.J. Rooney knew of their problems was when the Stirling went into a steep dive from 10,000 feet and he 'was thrown violently forward several times as the pilot tried to get it out of the dive.'[1546] All seven of the crew were severely shaken by the terrifying experience, but managed to get out of the aircraft before it caught fire. Rooney then went off with Sergeant E.C. Powell (navigator); Sergeant K.C. Richardson (pilot) with Sergeant K.B. Wootton (bomb aimer) and Sergeant S.W. Hitchman (flight engineer); and Sergeant J. O'Brien (rear gunner) with Sergeant W. Cross (wireless operator). Only the rear gunner and the wireless operator were taken prisoner, yet it was to be over nine months before the others were liberated.

The first contact that Rooney and Powell had with the French was with Emile Lemarie and his wife, who lived at Couëron, a few kilometres west of Nantes, on the north bank of the River Loire. They spent the day, 26 November, in various hiding places, but when it was dark Emile took them to his house. Two nights later Richardson, Wootton and Hitchman were brought in. They had been with a farmer, Alexandre Leray, at St Étienne-de-Montluc, eight or nine kilometres to the north-west of Couëron.[1547] On 29 November Emile took all five to the village of Le Temple-de-Bretagne, another six kilometres north-west of St Etienne, and handed them over 'to a party of five Resistance people. The group consisted of a schoolmaster named, I think, Giraffe – a stoutish fellow, aged about forty-five, clean shaven, height 5′ 9″… M. Lechat – plump face, wore spectacles, about 5′ 8″, wore clogs… Another member of the party was a young Frenchman aged around nineteen, a butcher by trade. His Christian name I think was Georges… The fourth member was the son of the Town Mayor and owned a café in Le Temple. A broad, well built-man about twenty-four, height around 5′ 8″, black haired and brushed back like Georges. The last member was small, of thin build, had a very narrow black moustache, black hair parted in the middle and brushed right back.'[1548]

That night they were again separated, Rooney and Wootton going to one barn, Powell, Richardson and Hitchman to another. The following night all five were moved, for ten more days, to a château in which 'a very sweet old lady', Madame Fonteneau, lived with her son, Pierre. On the evening of 12 December 1943, they were moved to a farmhouse near Le Temple, where Julien Riou and his wife lived with their son and daughter. They were to remain with the Rious for the next six months, as plans to fly them out or to get them through to the Pyrenees on foot failed to materialise.

Nothing happened until the Normandy landings had taken place when, on 15 June 1944, a gendarme[1549] appeared at Le Temple with a message to the effect that London required the five airmen to go to St Marcel. Obeying orders as it were, the five evaders were delivered the eighty or so kilometres from Le Temple by that same evening to find, according to Rooney, an estimated '3,000 patriots and 500 parachutists in camp, the former commanded by Commandant Barra and the latter by a French Lieutenant who had lost his left arm fighting in Sicily.' The French lieutenant, otherwise Commandant Pierre Bourgoin, was six feet three inches tall and weighed fourteen stone: 'Thickly built, broad-shouldered, and with a cold, hard face, he kept his good, left, hand in his pocket…'[1550]

Only those in high places would have been aware of another plan, this one, though, aimed at the Germans and definitely not at the five airmen of Stirling EF202. The plan was, in essence, to drop a number of French parachutists, and others, into Brittany on or soon after D-Day with orders to hinder the movement of German forces from western Brittany to Normandy, including cutting railway communications, and organising and arming the Resistance forces in the area. The bulk of the parachutists were to be provided by the 4th French Parachute Battalion attached to the British SAS under the command of the redoubtable, one-armed Commandant Bourgoin. A total of 328 troops were dropped into Brittany on 6 June 1944 and over the next few days on Operations Samwest, Dingson/Grog, and Cooney. The Samwest base was heavily attacked by the Germans on 12 June, and it was not long before the focal point for the separate operations became the Dingson/Grog base at St Marcel (Morbihan), two or three kilometres west of the small town of Malestroit.

One of the problems facing the French parachutists was the difficulty of keeping their presence in the region a secret from the Germans. Major A.W. Wise, who had been parachuted into the area on 9 June with Capitaine Bloch-Auroch and Sergeant R.R. Kehoe as the three-man Jedburgh team Frederick, wrote that two days after they had arrived 'the whole region knew where our base was and all the local Resistance chiefs came knocking to ask for weapons.'[1551]

Bourgoin himself 'described the atmosphere he dropped into as "like a fair"; shouting, fancy dress, crowds, exaltation, lights everywhere.'[1552] The number of drops by four-engined aircraft during successive nights following D-Day had put the German troops in the Morbihan area of Brittany on high alert, not least because of the amount of railway sabotage being committed by the French SAS (eighteen three-man teams engaged in Cooney). The Germans, however, had not yet discovered Bourgoin's HQ – a barn on Monsieur Pondard's farm La Nouette.

Within two weeks of D-Day Bourgoin and his staff had organised and trained the many willing Frenchmen in the area, and they 'could now boast that our own maquis was 4000 strong, while it was estimated that across Brittany there were upwards of twenty thousand maquisards waiting for the order to strike.'[1553] These were the men at St Marcel whom the Stirling crew were to meet when they arrived at the camp and who, on 18 June, would engage the Germans in a bloody, day-long battle for survival.

The battle began early in the morning when two German patrol cars ran into a French outpost. Both cars and all but one occupant were destroyed. The survivor unfortunately managed to escape and raise the alarm. At around 9 a.m. sounds of the approaching, and expected, German attack were heard, and the battle began. The Germans' set-piece attacks were repulsed with heavy losses to themselves, but after some four hours there was an unexpected lull probably, so the defenders thought, to allow the Germans to bring up reinforcements. This was more or less confirmed when a man arrived with the news that three German battalions, each 800 men strong, were massing to attack in the area of les Hardys-Béhélec, between St Marcel and La Nouette. The attack 'began at 1345 – precisely – with an immense barrage of rifle, automatic, and small-calibre mortar fire'.[1554]

Then the Germans brought up yet more reinforcements, an estimated two battalions, and some two hours later the pressure on the French had begun to tell. André Hue, an SOE officer attached to Bourgoin's mission, accordingly asked permission to call up air support. Taking the commander's lack of a response as a "yes", Hue fired a signal off to England. Three and a half hours later, with the situation worsening by the minute, the defenders heard above the noise of battle the glorious sound of many aircraft and then the magnificent sight of forty-eight American P-47 Thunderbolts. Able to talk directly to the formation leader (possibly by S-phone) Hue directed the massive fire power of the P-47s (each equipped with six 0.5 inch calibre machine-guns) against such enemy positions as he could identify.

In the temporary lull following this onslaught the defenders began their withdrawal, which was completed sometime after midnight in the direction of the woods around Trédion, a dozen kilometres to the west. Saint Marcel was burnt to the ground by the Germans, as were many other buildings and farms in the area. As for casualties, a monument close to La Nouette proclaims that though the French lost forty-two men in the fighting the enemy lost 560.

The point at which the five airmen withdrew from the scene of the battle is not known but, unharmed, they left with an American captain and two French officers, keeping to the woods until early on the morning of 19 June. Leaving the three officers behind, the airmen walked back to Le Temple to 'seek out our original hiding place'. Once again Madame and Pierre Fonteneau hid them in their château, but only for a few days. Somehow, probably after torturing Paul Lemarie, the Gestapo got hold of the addresses of the places where the airmen had been staying for the past six months, and paid them a visit. They took away Monsieur and Madame Lemarie, Julien and Madame Riou, and Messieurs Gerard and Bonnet (of Le Temple-de-Bretagne). The Gestapo also raided the Fonteneaus' château, but Pierre got away even 'as the Gestapo lorry drove up the drive'.

Now separated, Richardson, Hitchman and Rooney moved to a barn at the farm where Richardson had been hidden earlier, while Wootton and Powell went to Notre Dame-des-Landes before being taken to the home of Charles Mace at Fay-de-Bretagne. Contact was re-established with the Resistance, and four days later Wootton and Powell were taken to Pipy Island, in the River Loire, near Cordemais, living under canvas for a week until moved to the home of Monsieur Henri Clouet, Place de la Mairie, Savenay (half a dozen kilometres north of Pipy Island), being fed on stolen German provisions. Leaving on 3 September, they were guided through the German lines on the morning of 4 September to Couëron. With the Germans having been driven out of the area, Wootton and Powell cycled into Nantes on the following day. A Canadian captain, also a press censor, took the two to Rennes by car. Making their way to Paris, where they arrived on 10 September, they were interrogated by IS9 (WEA) and flown back to England on 11 September.

Being in the area for such a long time they had got to hear of some of the atrocities committed by the Gestapo, and of their methods. Wootton reported that during a raid on Nantes in May an American B-17 'was badly shot up. Four or five of the crew baled out, one of whom was shot on being captured by Heinrich Kaufmann (sergeant of Gestapo). Three went to the Maquis at Saffré, one being killed in action and the other two escaping. Rest of crew believed killed in crash of aircraft at Treillières.'[1555]

The fate of the murdered American airman was bad enough, though uncommon. What was all too common, on the other hand, was the arrest of French men, women and children who were suspected of having sheltered Allied airmen, as witnessed by the arrests of those who hid the Stirling crew. In his report, Wootton named those who had been caught:

- Emile Vincent: director of *Le Phare* (newspaper) at Nantes – tortured and believed to have been taken to a fortress in Austria.
- Willy Pelletier: Gendarmerie, Chantenay, Nantes – was taken and tortured by Gestapo. Died under torture (eight days). He said nothing.
- Jan Nieslierewiez: Taken by local chief of Gestapo (Sgt. Heinrich Kaufmann [Cologne]) 9 July 1944 at Couëron. Died 10 July by torture.
- Paul Lemarie: 10 Rue d'Enfert Rochereau, Couëron, Loire Infèrieure – forced by torture to give information of our hiding places. Last heard of with political prisoner at Belfort with family.
- Julien Riou: Tortured – also at Belfort with Madame Riou.

On 3 August, at Fougeray, where Richardson, Hitchman and Rooney were now staying, a Frenchman asked Rooney to accompany him in his car to contact the Americans: 'He drove a maroon coloured private saloon car. I gather he was the local chemist… I never learnt his name.'[1556] Contact was made with the Americans and, after Rooney had been questioned by an officer, he was put on a tank and taken to the Americans' HQ. Continuing to Avranches, on 7 August he was driven by the Americans to IS9 (WEA), 2nd Army, for interrogation, and made his way back to England, without seeing either Richardson or Hitchman again in France. These two, like Wootton and Powell, stayed behind until the Germans had gone, and returned to England on 11 September.

On the night of 2/3 December 1943 RAF Bomber Command flew to Berlin on what was the fifth raid against the German capital in the so-called "Battle of Berlin".[1557] One of the Mosquito aircraft supporting the heavy bombers all the way to Berlin was DZ479, 627 Squadron, with Flight Sergeant L.R. "Doggie" Simpson RAAF (pilot) and Sergeant P.W. Walker (navigator) on their first operation for their new squadron. Before crossing the English coast from their base at RAF Oakington they experienced navigational equipment failure, and Walker was thus forced to navigate by Dead Reckoning. All went well, however, despite the wind direction being the opposite of that forecast, until they were a hundred miles or so from Berlin flying at a height of 32,000 feet (9,850 metres), when, as Peter Walker later wrote, 'a predicted burst of flak took out the starboard engine. Doggie Simpson decided to carry on to the target on one engine.'[1558] Losing height all the while, they bombed their target, and were on their way back when they received numerous hits from further flak bursts: 'The aircraft was then at a very low altitude with a considerable number of pieces missing from the airframe.'[1559] Some fifty minutes later the Mosquito was abandoned over the Normandy countryside of France.

Peter Walker 'landed in a farmyard about five kilometres east of le Beny Bocage.'[1560] Actually, he had landed in a tree, but was able to climb down, after smoking a cigarette. Burying his parachute, he began walking: 'During the next hour I continually had to jump into the ditch to avoid German cars and motorcycles rushing to the scene of the burning aircraft.'[1561] At a small farmhouse he took a risk and knocked on the door.

The farmer and his wife took one look at the blood-stained airman and 'quickly ushered' him in. After some bread and cheese and a drink of cider, he was on his way once more: 'I had not walked far when I saw, in a lay-by, a large van. Without thinking, I jumped into the back and within minutes... I was asleep.'[1562] As he climbed out of the van before dawn he noticed on the side of it the German army insignia! Soon he found another farm, and stayed there in a barn until 9 December, when he 'was taken to Caen by a member of the FFI'.[1563] Another man in Caen took Walker to a house where he met Doggie Simpson, and two American airmen, Flight Officer Hubert E. Trent and 2nd Lieutenant Clarence Drew Willingham.[1564] On the next day, the four men were escorted, by train via Paris, to a house at Injoux-Génissiat (Ain), arriving there on 11 December. Five days later they were moved to a maquis camp at Brénod (Ain), where they met four more American airmen – 'Lt. Phillipi, USAAF, and two gunners of his crew; also a gunner of Lt. Trent's crew'.[1565]

On Boxing Day, the camp was visited by a man claiming to be a British captain, who stated that he had orders to assist evaders in that area: 'He ordered us to remain in the camp until we received instructions from him. He also said that if we left the camp without his orders we would be shot by the Maquis.'[1566] On 6 January 1944 an order was received from this captain that four of the airmen were to go with a maquis escort to Lyons, and First Lieutenant Phillippe, and the three gunners duly departed with a French lieutenant in charge. News was received on 10 January that the five men 'had been caught by the Gestapo at Perpignan and that the French lieutenant had been shot on the spot. We did not learn the fate of the other four.'[1567]

On the same day as the bad news was received the supposed British captain[1568] sent a second order that the four remaining airmen were also to proceed to Lyons under escort. This they did, accompanied by another French lieutenant, travelling by train third class. In Lyons the airmen split into pairs, the two Americans together, and Simpson with Walker. On 5 February, the four were re-united and taken to another maquis camp, near Arinthod (Jura), some 130 kilometres to the north-east. Here there was considerable German anti-partisan activity, which forced the camp to keep moving. After four days of this, the airmen decided to try to get to Switzerland. By this time the camp was near Moirans-en-Montagne (Jura), east of the Lac de Vouglans, and several kilometres nearer the Swiss border. Setting off on 14 February heading east, they were near St Claude (Jura) on the following day when they met two more French maquis lieutenants: 'They forced us to accompany them to their camp in the district. We were detained there until 21 February, when we were escorted by one of the lieutenants and a French smuggler to the Swiss frontier south-east of les Rousses.'[1569]

On 22 February they crossed into Switzerland without a guide, and gave themselves up to Swiss guards. After a night in custody they were taken to the British Consulate in Berne, and placed in quarantine until 16 March, when they were sent to Arosa. On 8 May they were moved to Montreux, where they languished, in some comfort admittedly, until 21 August, when Walker, Flying Officer F. Cunliffe, and Sergeant J.B. King 'went to Zurich on leave. We met a woman there and made plans to escape from Switzerland with her help. We returned to Montreux on 27 August.'[1570] Two days later, the three airmen took the train to Geneva, but King was arrested by the police at Geneva station and sent back to Montreux.

The day after his arrest, King left Montreux with Sergeant J.C. Whitley (see previous chapter) and travelled by train to Troistorrents, in the Val d'Illiez, where they met Flight Lieutenant G.M. Goodman (40 Squadron, another escaper from Italy) and Flight Lieutenant A.B. Simpson DFC RAAF. In the company of Private McCann (1st Cameronians), a New Zealand corporal and a South

: The greeting to many Allied airmen over Europe. remendous barrage through which many had to fly, l some failed.

Bottom: The Beginning. German soldiers passing Blenheim L9332, PZ-Z, abandoned by 53 Squadron in France, June 1940.

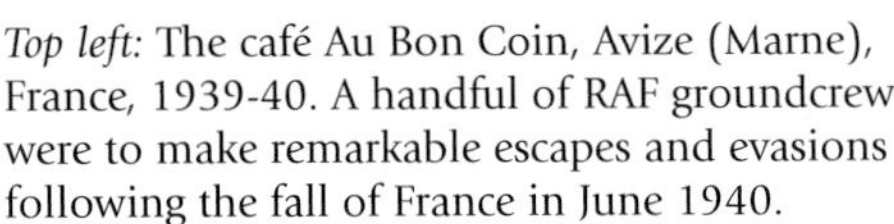

Top left: The café Au Bon Coin, Avize (Marne), France, 1939-40. A handful of RAF groundcrew were to make remarkable escapes and evasions following the fall of France in June 1940.

Top right: German guards on the Demarcation Line, France. Control points such as these were best avoided.

Right: Pau station, where Mary Lindell, Comtesse de Milleville, was arrested on 24 November 1943.

Below: 'Nach Frankreich. Hier einsteigen' – 'For France. Board here'. At the Belgium/France border, on the railway line from Brussels to Paris.

Top: Border post on the road from Cerbère to Spain, well-used in 1940.

Middle: St Jean-de-Luz, and the Pyrenees.

Bottom: The road from Luz-St Sauveur to Gavarnie in the Pyrenees. Evaders and escapers could only dream of such an easy route through the mountains.

Top left: Citroën truck winding its way through the Pyrenees.

Top right: Francia Usandizaga's farm, Bidegainberri, at Urrugne. Many evaders briefly stayed here before setting off across the Pyrenees. [*via John Clinch*]

Middle: La Toque Blanche, Ruffec, the café to which the Royal Marine survivors of Operation Frankton went after their escapade at Bordeaux, December 1942.

Bottom: Hôpital de la Pitié, Paris, where Pierre Brossolette die on 22 March 1944, and where a number of airmen were treat shortly before the Germans evacuated the city in August 1944

Top: Paris. A German wartime snapshot of Fort Mont Valérien (on the hill), where Frédéric de Jongh and so many other patriots were executed.

Middle: Camaret-sur-Mer. It was from here, on 23 October 1943, that the *Suzanne-Renée* sailed with 6 RAF and 13 American evaders aboard. Photograph taken by German soldier.

Bottom: German Navy *Schnellboot*. To be avoided by the Royal Navy's MGBs on clandestine operations to Brittany.

Top: German Kriegsmarine destroyers patrol the waters.

Above: "Het Jachthuis", Zevenhuizen, scene of a fierce gun-battle in April 1945. [*Historisch Genootschap Oud Soetermeer, via Annette Tison and B-24 website*]

Right: Sergeant (later Pilot Officer) W.J.Q. Magrath. Shot down and taken prisoner on 13 August 1940, he escaped from a repatriation camp in France in November 1941 (see page 47). Photo taken in 1943. [*Bill Magrath*]

Top left: Private Jim Cromar, Comet's first Allied serviceman. [*via John Clinch*]

Top centre: Sergeant H.E. Birk RAAF, Comet no. 7. Evaded September 1941-March 1942.

Top right: Sergeant A.D. Day RCAF. Comet no. 10. August 1941-March 1942. [*Al Day, via Diana Morgan*]

Middle left: Sergeant R. Ptáček, August-December 1941. [*Vítek Formánek*]

Middle centre: Flight Lieutenant A.L. Winskill, August-November 1941.

Middle right: At St. Hippolyte-du-Fort, November 1941. Standing, left to right: Porteous; Saxton; Pearman; McLarnon; Walsh. Sitting, left to right: Burrell; Hart; Dalphond; Hickton. [*Wing Commander L. Pearman MBE, MM, RAF Ret'd*]

Bottom: At St. Hippolyte-du-Fort, December 1941. Left to right: RAF Sergeants W.S.C. "Jack" Partridge, Harry Mossley, Alan W. Mills, Les Pearman. Partridge and Mossley, in the same crew as Mills, later went to Germany as prisoners of war. [*Wing Commander L. Pearman MBE, MM, RAF Ret'd*]

MARSEILLE ._Entrée du Vieux Port

Top: Detachment W, St. Hippolyte-du-Fort, December 1941. [*Wing Commander L. Pearman MBE, MM, RAF Ret'd*]

Middle: The entrance to le Vieux Port, Marseille, with Fort St Jean on the left. HMS *Tarana* was the first ship to pass the blockship after the city had been abandoned by the Germans in 1944. [*Editions Tardy, Marseille*]

Bottom: Fort de la Revère, France, "home" to many British internees, 1942.

Inset: Lieutenant-Commander Pat O'Leary.

› *left:* Gordon Mellor (left) and Michael Joyce RAF, •met nos. 69 and 70 respectively. At the Ritschdorff ters' house, Liège, October 1942.[*Gordon Mellor*]

› *right:* Sergeant A.E. Stadnik (left), Sergeant P.K. ıchuk (right). Soviet Air Force escaped prisoners of ı. Comet nos. 72 and 76.

ddle left: Flight Sergeant R.F. Conroy RCAF, ıe-October 1943. [*Alex Morrison*]

Middle centre: Sergeant R.W. Cornelius (centre), August-December 1943, with brother and sister. [*Paul Cornelius*]

Middle right: Sergeant J.E. Misseldine, June-August 1942. [*John "Jack" Misseldine, via Diana Morgan*]

Bottom left: Pilot Officer Al Hagan. The Hague, June-July 1943. [*Mrs Winifred Hagan*]

Bottom right: Pilot Officer J.B.M. "Dutchy" Haye with future wife Elly de Jong. The Hague, May-July 1943. [*Mrs Winifred Hagan*]

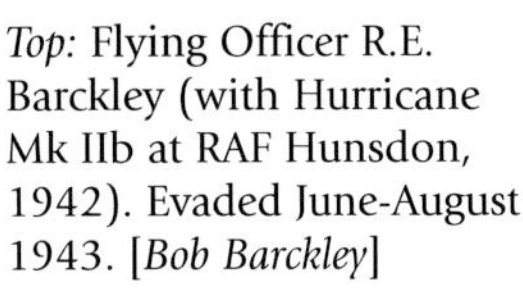

Top: Flying Officer R.E. Barckley (with Hurricane Mk IIb at RAF Hunsdon, 1942). Evaded June-August 1943. [*Bob Barckley*]

Middle from left to right 1: Sergeant D.J. Webb RCAF, July-September 1943. [*via Michael Moores LeBlanc*]

2: Sergeants S. Horton and D.R. Parkinson, September 1943. [*Denys Teare*]

3: Sergeant A.E. Spencer RCAF, November 1943-July 1944.

4: Flying Officer J.E. Mortimer RNZAF, October 1943-September 1944.

Bottom centre: Sergeant S. Munns, November 1943-January 1944. [*Stan Munns*]

Bottom right: Pilot Officer T.F. Bolter DFC, December 1943-June 1944. [*Terry Bolter, via Diana Morgan*]

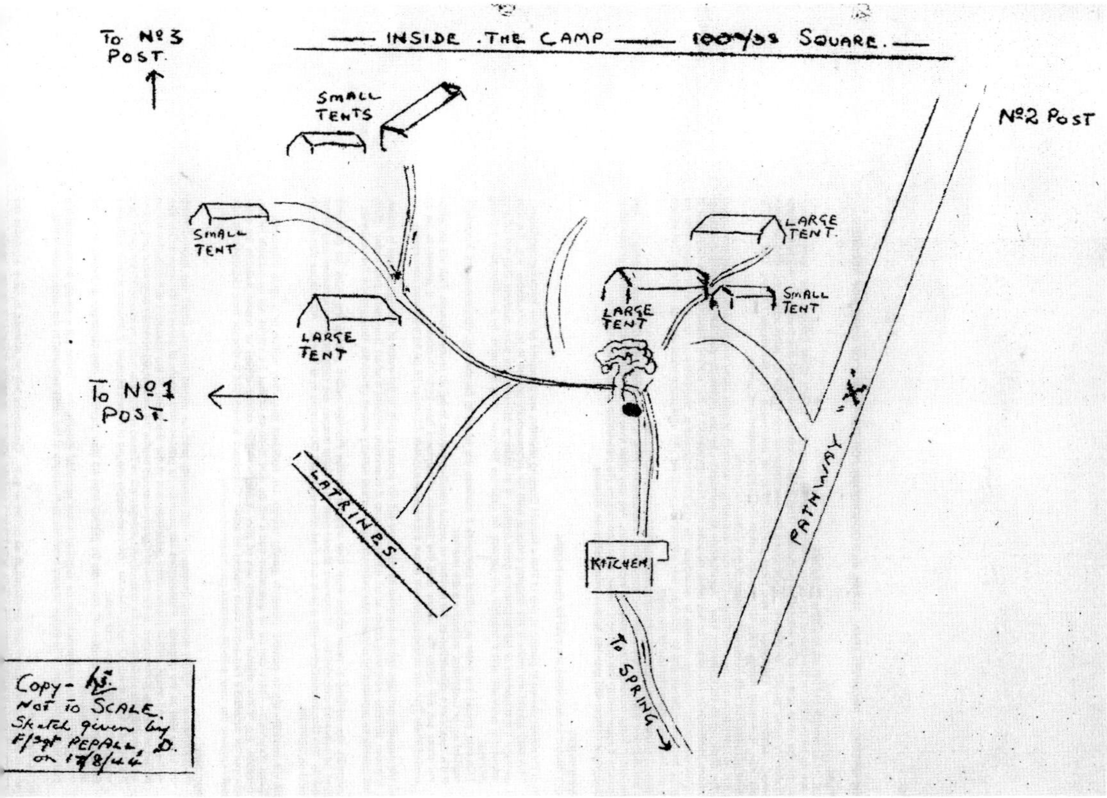

— INSIDE THE CAMP — SQUARE. —

To No 3 Post

No 2 Post

Small Tents

Small Tent

Large Tent.

Large Tent

Small Tent

Large Tent

To No 1 Post.

Latrines.

Pathway

"X"

Kitchen

To Spring

Copy –
Not to scale.
Sketch given by
F/Sgt Pepall, D.
on 17/8/44

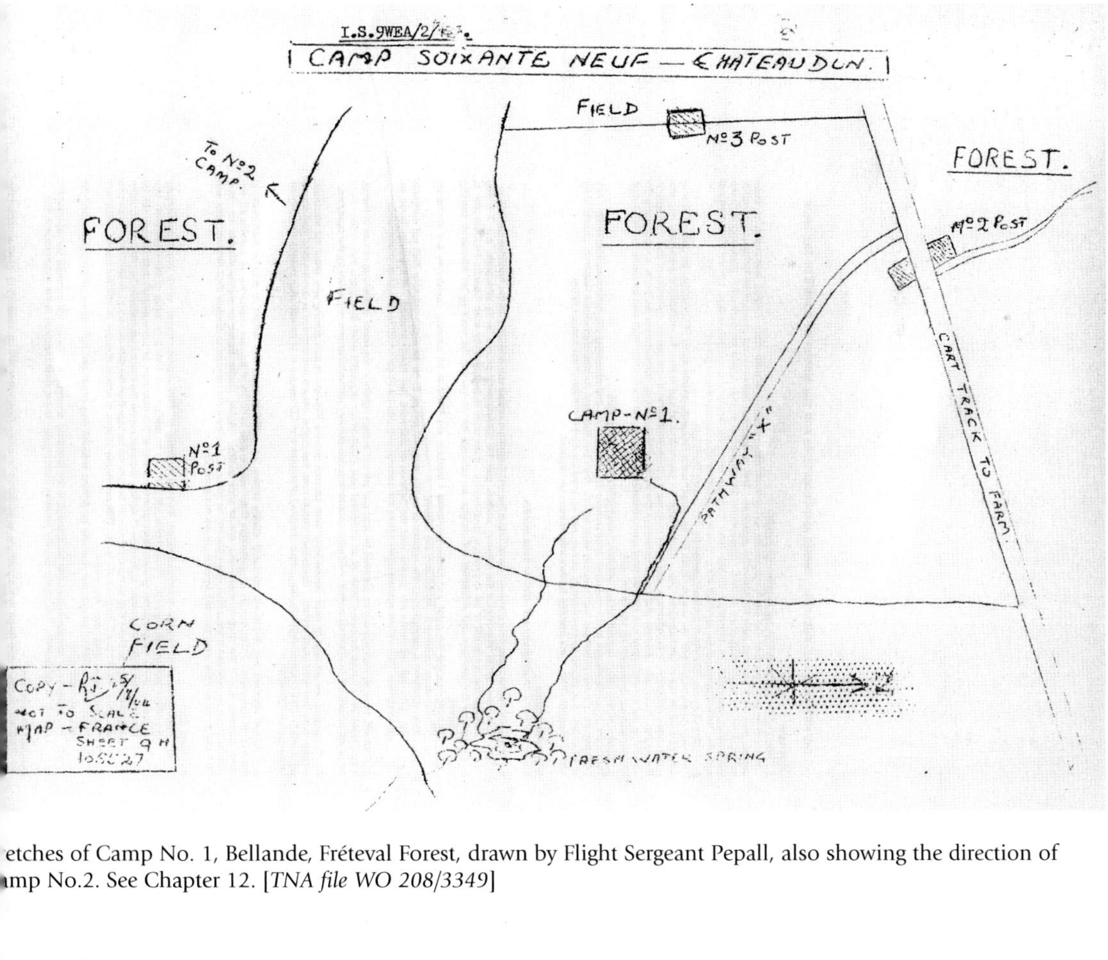

I.S.9WEA/2/

CAMP SOIXANTE NEUF — CHATEAUDUN.

Field

No 3 Post

Forest.

To No 2 Camp.

Forest.

Forest.

No 2 Post

Field

Cart track to farm.

Camp-No 1.

No 1 Post

Pathway "X"

Corn Field

Copy –
Not to scale
Map – France
Sheet 9 H
105527

Fresh water spring

etches of Camp No. 1, Bellande, Fréteval Forest, drawn by Flight Sergeant Pepall, also showing the direction of
mp No.2. See Chapter 12. [*TNA file WO 208/3349*]

Top left: Crew of Halifax LW275, NF-O "Orange", 138 Squadron, shot down on night of 7/8 February 1944. All evaded, February-May 1944. Left to right: Squadron Leader K.C.S. Cooke; Flying Officer L.J. Gornall; Flying Officer J.S. Reed; Flying Officer R.W. Lewis; Flying Officer A.B. Withecombe; Flying Officer E. Bell; Flying Officer R.L. Beattie. [*R.W. Lewis DFC*]

Top centre: Flight Sergeant D.R.R.J. Pepall, April-August 1944.

Top right: Warrant Officer II W.E.J. Brayley RCAF, April-August 1944.

Middle left: The Russian (left), whom some called "Cogi", with one of the South Africans (either Ebrihem Adams or Rudolph Hoover), Fréteval Forest, June-August 1944. [*Mrs Patricia Brayley, via Lorraine Vickerman*]

Middle centre: Jean De Blommaert.

Middle right: Pilot Officer P.J. Moloney, October-November 1944. [*Andrew Moloney, via Søren C. Flensted*]

Bottom: Sitting (left to right): Sergeant D.A. Lloyd; Flying Officer W.A. Robertson RCAF; Flight Sergeant J.H. Evans. Behind them stand five Russian escaped prisoners of war. At Vogelsanck, Belgium, 1944. [*John Evans, via Greg Lewis*]

Top left: Pilot Officer G.F. Pyle, June-August 1944. Photo taken 1943. [*George Pyle, via Diana Morgan*]

Top right: Sergeant T.H. Harvell, July-September 1944. [*Tom Harvell*]

Bottom left: Flight Sergeant Les Hood, June-August 1944. [*Les Hood, via Diana Morgan*]

Bottom right: Flight Sergeant H. Webb, August 1944. [*Reverend Harry Webb, via Diana Morgan*]

Top: Crew of Halifax LV790, 158 Squadron. Standing (left to right): Flight Sergeant J.J. Fernandez; Sergeant L.M. Byrne; Flight Sergeant H. Squires; Flying Officer C.W. Nuttall. Seated (left to right): Sergeant A.G. Thompson (replaced by Sergeant D.R. Arundel); Pilot Officer W.C. Reed; Flight Sergeant G. Titman.Fernandez and Nuttall were taken prisoner of war. The other five evaded, June-August 1944. [*via Pat MacGregor*]

Bottom left: Sergeant R.A. Hilborne (2nd f left), Sergeant Len Aitken, and their helpe Denis Esmard and his wife at the Ferme d Moslains, August 1944. [*Denis Esmard*]

Bottom right: Flight Sergeant G. Wood, September-October1944. [*Reverend Georg Wood, via Diana Morgan*]

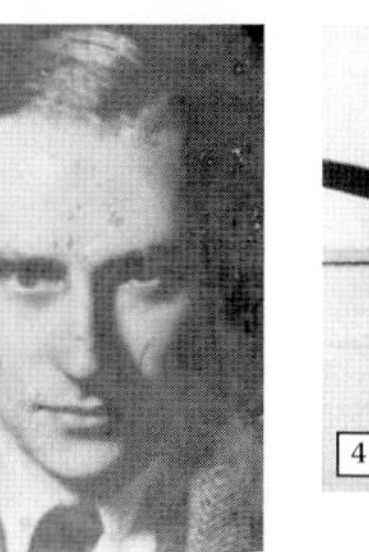

Top left: Flight Sergeant I.R.C. Innes RAAF (centre) with Madame and Monsieur Goustille at their house at 25 Rue St Jean, Mailly-le-Camp, July 1944. [*Bernard Bertin*]

Top right: Flying Officer F.H. Dell, October 1944-March 1945. [*Frank Dell, via Diana Morgan*]

Middle: The hated French Milice and German "friends".

Bottom 1: The remains of Pilot Officer P.J.W. Bell's Mustang KH860, shot down on 4 May 1945 over Denmark. Bell was wounded. [*Zone-Redningskorpset, via Finn Buch, from Søren C. Flensted's website www.flensted.eu.com*]

Bottom 2: Andrée, Frédéric, and Suzanne de Jongh. Photo taken before the war.

Bottom 3: Arnold Deppé.

Bottom 4: Wellington P9218, the first RAF aircraft to crash in Denmark during the Second World War. [*Wolfgang Falck, via Søren C. Flensted*]

Bottom 5: Nadine and Lili Dumon. [*Nadine Dumon, via John Clinch*]

Bottom 6: Albert Johnson, or "B". (The "B" stood for Bucket, an appellation from his childhood).

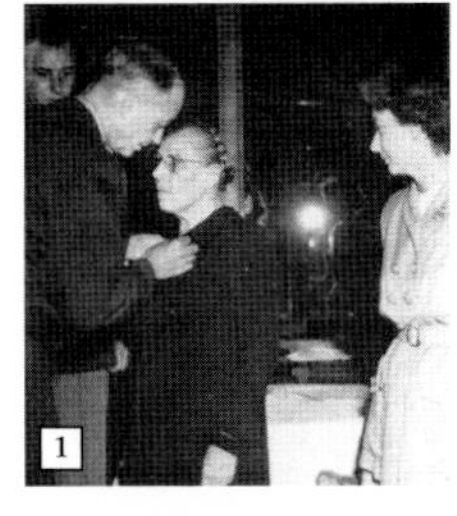
1

2

3

4

Top left: Renée Boulanger ("Nénette") and her partner, Ignace Sobiesuk. [*Phil Douglas, via John Clinch*]

Top right: Squadron Leader Lucien Boussa (2nd from right).

Middle: The De Greef family at St Jean-de-Luz, with Elvire in the centre. [*via Fred Greye*

Middle right 1: Françoise Dissard being presented by General Lewis with the American Medal of Freedom on 16 August 1946. Andrée de Jongh looks on.

2: Jean-François Nothomb.

3: Gaston Nègre. [*via Les Pearman*]

4: Nancy Fiocca.

Bottom: Journey's end. The Rock of Gibraltar.

African corporal whom they met near Troistorrents, the four airmen walked to Morgins, and crossed the frontier into France soon afterwards during the night of 30/31 August.

Walker and Cunliffe had, however, taken a taxi to Veyrier, a few kilometres south of Geneva and on the French border, but were caught by alert Swiss guards as they were climbing over the wire into France, and were returned to Geneva. Put in prison, they were released on 31 August, and also sent back to Montreux. They tried again on the very next day, and this time, in a different place, simply walked into France. They were led by a Frenchman of the FFI to a hotel where ten American airmen were also waiting to go home.

After a few days the escapers and evaders had been split into smaller groups and been directed to No. 2 Repatriation Depot at Ste Maxime (Var) on the south coast of France. While most of them were shipped across to No. 3 Base Personnel Depot, Naples (Italy), on 8 September, where they arrived five days later, Flight Lieutenants Goodman and Simpson managed to catch a flight to Naples. Goodman, now separated from Simpson, was flown home to the UK on 12 September, the other airmen being flown back over the next few days.[1571]

Flight Lieutenant F.O.J. Pearce (pilot) and Flying Officer F.H. Greenaway RNZAF (navigator) were on their way in their Mosquito to bomb a rocket installation near Abbeville on 4 January 1944 when, crossing the French coast, Pearce saw a flock of birds ahead. To avoid them he 'went two [*sic*] feet lower, with the result that the propeller[s] of the aircraft hit the sand in the middle of the Somme Estuary'. When both engines seized up Pearce was forced to land on the beach 'about fifteen yards from the edge of the water, after having jettisoned our bombs safely.' The crew destroyed the secret instruments and tried to destroy the aircraft, but this they could not do as they were under constant fire from the enemy, who soon took them prisoner. They were soon joined by a Typhoon flight sergeant[1572] and taken to a prison in Beauvais.

On 7 January the three originals plus a Spitfire pilot (possibly Flight Sergeant R.V. Smith RAAF) and 'an observer from a PRU Mosquito' were bundled into a van and driven towards Paris. En route one of the van's tyres burst, and the prisoners were transferred to a 'truck which had a canvas roof and a canvas back'. As this vehicle made its way to the Gare de l'Est in Paris Greenaway contemplated escaping. His moment came when the truck finally came to a halt and the four German guards, rifles slung over their shoulders, began unloading cases of goods from it. Greenaway waited until the last one was being off-loaded before vaulting over the side, using one of the guard's shoulders as a hand-rest in the process. Before anyone could react he was running off through the assembled crowd, and found help from a French couple, who gave him food, a suit of clothes, 100 francs and the chance to shave off his moustache. Thus equipped he made his way south, and was flown back to England on 9/10 April 1944 while his former co-prisoners were sent to captivity in Germany.

Many a Second World War airman would be grateful for Switzerland's neutrality. If nothing else, it allowed them the prospect of at least not being taken prisoner by the Germans, for the time being. Any attempt thereafter to regain Allied lines through German-occupied territory was another matter. One airman who was to sample Swiss hospitality was Sergeant Leo R. Fryer, an American in the RCAF. Obliged to bale out of his Halifax on the night of 20/21 January 1944 after it had been hit by flak, he parachuted down near Châlons-sur-Marne in eastern France. Walking south-east for two days he came to an isolated farmhouse 'where I was given first aid and something to eat.'[1573] The farmer had a cousin in Toul, some fifty kilometres south-east towards Switzerland, and suggested that Fryer should go and stay with him. After a week with the cousin, where he was provided with an identity card and civilian clothing, Fryer was put in touch with a woman who took him by train to Belfort: 'We took a taxi to within three miles of the Swiss frontier and walked from there. We avoided the guards at the frontier post and went straight to a farmhouse on the Swiss side.'

Fryer wasted no time in making himself known to the Swiss authorities and, after a night in custody, was sent to the British Legation at Berne. It was not until 20 August 1944 that he and three others – Sergeants J. Little, L.W. Canning and L. Newbold – made the crossing from Switzerland to the partially-liberated France: 'We approached the frontier from St Maurice and after climbing for eight hours we crossed the frontier and reached Châtel which was held by the maquis.' On their arrival at Châtel, on 27 August, they met Sergeant G.G. Arnold (from the same crew as Little) and Sergeant J.A. Hammond RCAF. All the airmen were then taken to Thonon-les-Bains, 'where we met another large party of evaders. We were then guided by the maquis to Grenoble, where we made contact with American troops.'[1574]

Among the "large party of evaders" at Thonon was Flight Sergeant J.F. Merchant DFM, who had also arrived there from Switzerland.[1575] He was an escaped prisoner of war from Italy, who had been shot down on the night of 15/16 July 1943 attacking a power station at Reggio nell' Emilia in the north of that country. On 3 October 1943, in the company of Sergeant G.E. Pearson, RASC, he managed to jump from the train that was taking him, and many other prisoners of war, to Germany, and they reached Switzerland on 13 October. Merchant finally left Switzerland on 20 August 1944.

Conveyed to Sisteron and then St Tropez, which they reached on 2 September, they were flown via Corsica to Naples (4 September). Still heading south, four days later their journey continued to Casablanca, and after two days they were flown back to England, arriving on 11 September.

SOE's Operation Jockey 5 was in the experienced hands of Squadron Leader T.C.S. Cooke DFC, AFC, DFM and crew until their Halifax aircraft, on the night of 7/8 February 1944, iced up as it was making its way to the south of France. With an engine on fire the entire crew of seven baled out over the Drôme department of France, halfway between Lyon and Marseille. Remarkable enough in that an entire bomber crew evaded, all seven were back in England by the first week of May. Four of them, however, were to receive assistance from an extraordinary warrior.

Flying Officer R.L. Beattie RCAF, Pilot Officer E. Bell, Flying Officers R.W. Lewis and J.S. Reed soon found themselves in the hands of a French organisation. Bell was told that he would be taken to see an "English Colonel" in the town of Valence. On 9 February a doctor drove up in his car, in which he already had Beattie, and took the two airmen to M. Chancel's chemist's shop in St Donat-sur-l'Herbasse, to which Reg Lewis had already been brought. At 10 o'clock that night the so-called English colonel arrived, bringing with him Flying Officer Reed.

The "English colonel" was actually Captain Peter Julien Ortiz of the US Marines. Born on 5 August 1913 in New York of a French father of Spanish ancestry and an American mother, he was educated at the University of Grenoble, France before enlisting in the French Foreign Legion in 1932 at the age of nineteen. Fighting against the Germans in 1940 he was wounded and captured when he went on a motorbike through a German camp to destroy a fuel dump that had been left intact in the general withdrawal. On the way back, a bullet caught him in the hip. As it exited his body it caught his spine, causing temporary paralysis. He spent the next fifteen months as a prisoner of war in Germany, Poland, and Austria before escaping in October 1941. He reached the United States by way of Lisbon on 8 December 1941.

Enlisting in the US Marine Corps he was commissioned (1 August 1942) and saw further active service as an assistant naval attaché at Tangier, Morocco. These were not his real duties, however, for he was severely wounded in the right hand when coming up against a German patrol on the Tunisian front. He returned to the United States in April 1943, and was flown back to England three months later and assigned to the shady world of the Office of Strategic Services (OSS). When plans were made to turn the Vercors region of France into a formidable maquis redoubt and centre of resistance against the Germans, a three-man Inter-Allied team, codenamed Union, was dropped into France on the night of 6/7 January 1944. The three were Captain H.H.A. Thackthwaite (British), of RF Section SOE, Ortiz (American), and C. "Monnier" (French), the radio operator, referred to in SOE's History as 'one of the bravest and most discreet wireless operators sent out to France'.

Late on 9 February, Ortiz drove the four airmen 'to a maquis camp in the mountains about eight kilometres south-east of Combovin. After we had been three days here the camp was moved to a small furniture factory on the plateau.'[1576] Ortiz radioed details of the airmen to London. When news was received on 1 March that the Germans planned to attack the camp, the airmen were taken to the home of an elderly retired French army doctor, Sambuc, and his wife in la Paillette where they remained, confined to one room, until 26 March. Ortiz had been instructed to go to an address in Aix-les-Bains, to the north-east, and to ask for a person by name giving the password "Saratoga". Ortiz found the man, with some difficulty, who was connected to a Polish organisation. The man said that if Ortiz could get his men to Carcassonne his organisation would pick them up there.

On 26 March Ortiz drove the airmen to Valence and then took them by train, none of them having ID cards, to Carcassonne on the following day. All went well, and the men were handed over to a guide and then taken by electric train to Quillan, where they 'were handed over to an organisation which seemed to deal mainly with Poles.' They left that evening in a taxi with six Poles, and started walking from Axat (Aude) with two Spanish guides. At a hut in the mountains they picked up six American airmen, among them Lieutenant Freeman and Sergeant McLaughlin.[1577] Before setting off over the mountains, at 10 p.m. on 28 March, a further ten Poles joined the party.

Crossing into Spain on the evening of 30 March they stayed in a sheep pen until early on 2 April, when 'a truck came and took us straight through to the Consulate-General in Barcelona.'

For Major Peter Ortiz, now that he had disposed of his charges, the war resumed. His promotion had come through earlier in a rather unusual way, his "pip" arriving by air in a scheduled supply drop from RAF Tempsford. The citation for the award to him of the US Navy Cross stated, inter alia: 'Repeatedly leading successful raids during the period of this assignment, Major Ortiz inflicted heavy casualties on enemy forces greatly superior in number, with small losses to his own forces.' The Union team withdrew to England in May 1944.[1578]

Ortiz returned on 1 August in an all-American mission to the Isère, with a mass drop of 864 containers for the French *Bulle Bataillon* and SOE's Francis Cammaerts. Things did not go so well this time, as part of the citation for his second Navy Cross testifies: 'After parachuting into a region where his activities had made him an object of intensive search by the Gestapo, Major Ortiz valiantly continued his work in coordinating and leading resistance groups in that section. When he and his team were attacked and surrounded during a special mission designed to immobilize enemy reinforcements stationed in that area, he disregarded the possibility of escape and, in an effort to spare villagers severe reprisals by the Gestapo, surrendered to this sadistic Geheim Staats Polizei. Subsequently imprisoned and subjected to numerous interrogations, he divulged nothing, and the story of this intrepid Marine Major and his team became a brilliant legend in that section of France where acts of bravery were considered commonplace.'

On 16 August 1944 Ortiz and his group had been surprised in the village of Centron (Savoie) on the banks of the Isère river by elements of the 157th Alpine Reserve Division. Fighting ensued, but the frightened villagers, fearing a massacre, pleaded with the American major to give himself up. This he selflessly did, as did the only two marines left with him, Sergeants John P. Bodnar and Jack R. Risler. Surprised not to have been shot out of hand, Ortiz was sent to the camp Marlag und Milag Nord for naval personnel at Westertimke, near Bremen, and tried on several occasions to escape. When it was made quite clear to him by the senior British officer, a Royal Navy captain, that such behaviour was not to be tolerated Ortiz solved the problem by declaring himself to be the senior American officer and announcing that he would make his own rules! Despite this, Ortiz was made a Member of the Order of the British Empire.

His last battle, a fight with cancer, ended on 16 May 1988.[1579]

Another crew grateful for Switzerland's neutrality was that of veteran Lancaster W4355, which was attacked by a night-fighter on the night of 15/16 March 1944 en route to Stuttgart. The pilot, Flight Lieutenant Walter Blott, who believed that a rocket projectile had been fired at them, was hit in an arm by a piece of metal. When the aircraft began to shake violently and he was unable to control it, all seven of the crew baled out successfully over Switzerland. Blott himself landed heavily on his back in a wood near Kallnach, halfway between Berne and the Bielersee. Making contact with a Swiss woman, he was given a bed in a nearby inn for the night.

After breakfast on the following morning he was visited by Swiss military police officers, who told him that they would be returning later in the day after they had collected others of his crew. Taken away in a car in which Sergeant G.D. Gill was already seated, they were driven to Aarberg hospital, where they met Sergeant D. Murphy and Flying Officer C. Nabarro, also of their crew. As Gill was not injured he left at once. Blott was left behind for his back and arm to be looked at and, after a visit from Wing Commander R.D. Jones, assistant air attaché at the British Legation, was taken to the Gürten-Kulm Hotel in Gurtendorf 'which was occupied principally by American airmen'.[1580] A few days later he was reunited with Gill and two more of his crew, Sergeant G.R. Mattock and Sergeant T.W. Forster. Also arriving at the hotel was 'Sgt Ruth, who was the sole survivor of another aircraft which had also crashed on 15 March'.[1581]

After some three weeks at the Gürten-Kulm hotel the RAF aircrew and the Americans were transferred to the internment camp at Adelboden where, Blott noted, there were some 600 army personnel and 500 Americans. The RAF were put in with the Americans. On 6 May Blott was taken to Berne, and given a passport and civilian clothes prior to being repatriated with the agreement of the Germans. In the small hours of 13 May he, six others from the same 100 Squadron crew, Gill and Pilot Officer R.G. Peter RAAF, were escorted to Basle by a Swiss courier and a Swiss military policeman. Travelling second class, the nine airmen and the courier left Switzerland by rail. As they crossed the frontier into Germany they 'were asked to pull the blinds down. At the first station after the frontier a German officer accompanied by an interpreter came into the carriage. He told us that we were being given safe passage and we were expected to behave well.'[1582]

Travelling through Freiburg they reached Baden Baden, and after a brief stop boarded the Vienna-Paris express late on 13 May, now travelling first class. In Paris they were met by a German officer and a civilian interpreter, Wolfgang, who told them that he had been at Cambridge University and that the previous day he had had lunch with the celebrated author P.G. Wodehouse.[1583] He also told the group, probably only to see what the effect would be, that they were not being returned to England but to Japan. Blott told him that that was of little matter, as they would eventually land up there anyway. The airmen were then treated to an excellent five-course lunch, which included a different wine with each course. Later that day, still with the Swiss courier, they boarded a train with a German captain and another interpreter and travelled, again first class, to Irún in Spain. From Irún they went to Madrid, and on 19 May to Gibraltar, being flown back by Dakota to Whitchurch airport, Bristol, five days later.

On its way back from Essen on the night of 26/27 March 1944 Halifax HX295 (Pilot Officer R.A. Simmons) was twice attacked by a German night-fighter. Mid-upper gunner Sergeant W.W. Farmer had a front seat in the action: 'It all happened so fast. The first burst of cannon missed us but the second burst hit us in the starboard wing and set it on fire. The pilot told us to bail out. Just as I got to the escape hatch, the wing came off and I reached for something to grab onto. It was the door handle. The door came open and I fell out of the aircraft. The next thing I knew I was on the ground in a forest.'[1584]

Hitting the tail of the Halifax on his way out Walter Farmer was knocked unconscious. Bruised and battered, his face badly cut and back and shoulders painful, he came round to discover that he had lost his boots when the parachute snapped open. And so, in the pitch dark of the night, wrapped up in his parachute, he went to sleep. In the morning, thinking that he was in Germany, he started walking west. People at a cottage gave him a worn but usable pair of boots, but refused admission. Continuing to the River Meuse, he was half way across the bridge at Hastière-Lavaux when he saw two German soldiers coming towards him. Quickly bending down he pretended to do up his boots, and the two soldiers walked past without a word. On through Blaimont, he was resting on a log by the side of the road when a young Belgian farmer, Louis Volbert,[1585] rode up on a horse. Establishing that Walter was an "aviateur" he took him to a field, and left him with two farmworkers while he rode off to fetch civilian clothing. The men gave Walter bread, cheese and cold coffee. Asking them where he was, Walter was surprised to discover that he was in Belgium, not far south of Dinant.

On his return Louis told Walter 'to hide in the woods and he would come back after it got dark. I was in rough shape so I had to trust him. True to his word, he came back later with a man from the Resistance.'[1586] On the following day Louis brought a doctor to see Walter, who was still in a lot of pain. The doctor did what he could, and left. Two days later another man arrived 'saying there was an airman in a nearby house. They were not certain if he were a German in disguise',[1587] so it was arranged that Walter should go and identify him. If he were a German, he would be shot. Happily the man proved to be Walter's rear gunner, Flight Sergeant R.C. Corby RCAF. Their mutual delight at seeing each other again was muted when they learnt that they were the only survivors: 'It was to my sorrow as they were a great bunch of men.'

On the following day, 1 April, Walter was taken to a lock-keeper's cottage at Blaimont, where he was once again reunited with Ross Corby. Before they left, on 6 April, a note was brought saying: 'We will do our best to get you back – you will be off in a week.' They were indeed off within a week, but only back across the Meuse to an inn, and then for a week with a farmer at Agimont. 'This farmer was a friend of M. Gegenne (café owner), who also helped with food etc.' Their next move, on 16 April, was by car across the very close French border to Foisches,[1588] where they met two Frenchmen, Marceau Devin and François, who hid them in a deserted house for a fortnight. François, an escaped prisoner of war from Germany, told them that the escape line to the south was broken: 'There had been a leak somewhere.'[1589] Then, on about 1 May, two more men, Boris Delaveau and Louis, took Walter and Ross to their house at Hargnies (Ardennes), which had been partially destroyed in the fighting in 1940, where they were looked after by Boris and his wife, who brought them two meals a day.

Village gossip, however, caused Walter and Ross to be moved on 14 May to a hut in the woods near Vireux-Molhain. Here they found two American airmen, Staff Sergeant Bob Augustus from Cleveland ('we called him Augie') and Staff Sergeant P.M. Clark,[1590] and on 7 June Marceau brought three more evaders to the camp – 2nd Lieutenant Carl I. Glassman USAAF; Flight Sergeant R.H.L. Potentier RCAF (a rear gunner on his first operation); and Sergeant D.S. Beckwith RAF.

Beckwith had been shot down by flak over the Dutch/German border on the night of 24/25 March 1944 and had landed five kilometres or so east of Haaksbergen, just south of Enschede in the Gelderland district of Holland. Slightly wounded, a farmer rendered him medical assistance before he was hidden in a house near Zutphen by the head of the local resistance group. On 15 April he was assisted to Heerlen and then, on 5 May, to Maastricht where he met Glassman and 2nd Lieutenant Myrle J. Stinnett USAAF (Glassman's pilot).[1591] They arrived in Liège on 13 May, and met Potentier.

Five or six days later the four airmen were escorted by eight armed men of *l'Armée Blanche* on the train to Hognoul, half a dozen kilometres north-west of Liège. After further moves to a farm at

Lowaige and to a house at Heusay near Liège it dawned on the four airmen that they would never get away. Indeed it was confirmed by one of their guides that they were expected to join hundreds of other airmen evaders 'and to fight the German advance against the invasion… Their duties were to include stopping Tiger tanks…' In view of this Beckwith, Stinnett and Potentier decided to head off on their own to Spain. This was easier said than done. Potentier recalled: 'We escaped through a hole in the back garden of the house to which we were taken… Lieutenant Glassman helped us but decided not to risk escape.'[1592] With a stolen map and compass they spent the first night in a disused limestone quarry at Esneux, on the River Ourthe.

Good progress was made over the next few days in the intended direction of south-west, and by 8 June they had reached Winenne, a stone's throw from the French border, 'where we were housed by a woman for five days 8-13 June. She contacted a man who guided us to the maquis near Vireux.' Beckwith recorded that, once in France, they went to 'a cabin in the forest between Vireux Wallarand and Hargnies. In this cabin we met the following evaders:- Flight Sergeant Ross Morly [*sic* – Corby] and Sergeant Farmer, RAF; three Americans and one Canadian, and Flight Lieutenant Whitehead, who was acting as Liaison Officer with the maquis.'[1593]

Impatient to be on the move, and perhaps sensing the danger that lay ahead, Potentier, Stinnett and Bob Augustus took off again on 17 June, ever hopeful of getting to Spain. But having met a number of poorly-armed and untrained Frenchmen in some woods they changed their minds and went back to Belgium. There they split up. Potentier stayed with a M. Bollen at Sart from 2 July until 11 September 1944, 'when the Americans came through'.

Flight Lieutenant George Whitehead, who had been brought to the camp near Vireux by Marceau Devin, was a member of an "Interallied" mission which had been sent into the field by air to bolster resistance after the collapse and destruction of so many intelligence networks in France. The first members of this particular mission, codename Citronelle, had arrived in the Ardennes on 12 April 1944. Initially, it was to have comprised Commandant Jacques Pâris de Bollardière (French); Captain D.E. Hubble, RA (English); First Lieutenant Victor J. Layton (a reserve officer in the US Army); and Flight Lieutenant Whitehead, but as it had proved impossible to locate and then to arrange a suitable drop zone in the Ardennes a three-man team – de Bollardière, Layton and Lieutenant Gérard Bréaux (wireless operator) – was sent in "blind" well to the south, parachuting onto the edge of the military training camp near Mourmelon, some twenty-five kilometres south-east of Reims (Marne). From there, the trio made their way north to 'an underground shelter near Laifour, where the Meuse forms an impressive loop under a 900-foot-high cliff',[1594] a section of the river known as les Dames de Meuse. They were now, as the crow flies, barely fifteen kilometres from Hargnies.

Reinforcements and fresh supplies were dropped to them on 5 June, when a B-24 from Harrington, Northamptonshire, the USAAF "Carpetbagger" air base in England,[1595] dropped five men and eight containers. The men were Captain Hubble, Captain Carrière, Flight Lieutenant Whitehead, and two sabotage instructors, Sous-Lieutenants Goetchebeur and Racine. According to Walter Farmer, one of the English officers had with him one hundred thousand francs in cash.

As the war turned more clearly in the Allies' favour after the D-Day landings hundreds of young Frenchmen – the *attentistes* (those who waited to see which way the wind blew) – flocked to join the irregular forces fighting the Germans, and the group now based on Citronelle received its fair share of these new recruits. There were some 230 of them but, unfortunately, one of them, who had gone home to see his wife, was captured by the Germans who, in their own horrible way, made the Frenchman reveal the location of the maquis camp. Oberst Grabowski, head of Feldkommandantur 684 in the Ardennes, mobilised his forces, some 300 German soldiers assisted by Ukrainian volunteers.[1596]

On the morning of 12 June 1944 First Lieutenant Layton and Captain Hubble had left the camp to reconnoitre a possible site for further airdrops some three kilometres to the north. They were on their way back during the early afternoon when a German soldier suddenly sprang out of the undergrowth. Pointing his gun at them he shouted: 'Halt. Hände Hoch!' Layton reacted quickly, and dived into the trees followed by a burst of automatic gunfire. Hubble, though, was wounded and captured. Dressed in civilian clothing, his only means of identification were his "dog tags", but they were not enough to save him. 'Twice on June 13th he was taken by car to Charleville to be brutally interrogated. A month later he was seen in the Saint-Quentin prison, walking with the condemned inmates, with a cross drawn in white chalk on his back.' Within a few weeks all trace of him in France was lost.[1597]

After Hubble's capture Layton rushed back to the camp to raise the alarm, but it was too late. The Germans had already surrounded it, and a fierce gunfight ensued. The retreating maquisards continued fighting until dark, when 'the Germans brought up their artillery and shelled us all night long'. The French took many casualties,[1598] and only four men – Whitehead, an American airman and two French partisans – managed to break through the German cordon that night.

Three days later Marceau Devin discovered the location of the rendezvous for the sixty surviving maquisards who had been scattered to the four winds by the brutal German attack, and Whitehead, Farmer and Beckwith went to join them. 'There we found these people who were really organised. The man in charge was a Free French major. Before the war, he was in the Foreign Legion, a real soldier. The second man in charge was an English captain of the SAS. There was also an American lieutenant.'[1599] The French commandant, Commandant de Bollardière, however, would have nothing to do with 'non-French-speaking evaders as it caused confusion in action'. Farmer and Beckwith therefore returned to the hut, where Ross Corby also re-appeared. He and Clark had made contact with the Maquis, and had met a further five American evaders. When Clark decided to go off with his fellow Americans, Corby went back to the hut.

Hearing that Germans were after them, Marceau took the three remaining airmen, Farmer, Corby and Beckwith, to the deserted house at Hargnies on 30 June. Though he had to provide for his family, Boris nevertheless brought them food every night, prepared by Boris's wife and by Marceau's mother. When the airmen learnt that the French were finding it hard to feed the extra mouths, they realised that they had to leave, especially as there appeared to be no organisation capable of taking them anywhere. With 2,000 francs donated by Flight Lieutenant Whitehead they set off on foot for Switzerland on 8 July.

Whitehead and company suffered a further attack, by a strong German force of some 1,000 men on 2 August. The maquis sustained only three casualties, but the Germans lost fifty-four men killed. Whitehead later 'assumed command of all operations', and the citation for his MC (gazetted on 8 March 1946) says that 'he proved himself to be a capable and fearless leader'.

After five days getting little to eat from cottagers and sleeping rough in barns Farmer, Corby and Beckwith meanwhile reached the village of Vienne-le-Château (Marne), still a long, long way short of their goal.[1600] Their progress had been slow, largely due to Walter's feet having become badly blistered thanks to his too-small wooden-soled boots. Discarding them, he then wore *chaussettes russe*, "Russian socks", strips of his parachute wound round the feet like bandages. They were thankful to come across another Maquis, and stayed with them in the woods for the best part of a week. With them were four other evaders, American paratroopers Privates 1st Class B. Rainwater and J. Sheeran, who had been taken prisoner just after D-Day but who had jumped off the train that was taking them to Germany, and Pilot Officer F.A. Smitton RCAF and Sergeant E.E. Thorn, pilot and flight engineer respectively of a Lancaster shot down on the night of 28/29 June 1944 (Metz).[1601]

The weather was pleasantly warm, and the accommodation comfortable enough – a log cabin in which bunks had been fitted – but food was always a problem, and Walter Farmer reckoned that he ate more than enough cherries to last him a lifetime. He was also given a new pair of boots to replace his Russian socks.

During their stay at the camp two Jews were brought in. They had escaped from a concentration camp, and were very, very thin. Farmer felt sorry for them, and 'talked quite a lot to the older of the two. He could speak very good English. He told me he was a Professor of Mathematics from a college in Paris. He could not tell me how he escaped. Every time he started to tell me, he would start crying…'[1602]

On 20 July, Beckwith, Corby and Farmer decided to move on. Near the village of Passavant-en-Argonne they were spotted by men in black uniforms, the hated Milice: 'They called on us to stop, so we started to run. They fired at us but we kept running faster, each one going in a different direction.'[1603] When Beckwith and Corby failed to make the agreed rendezvous Walter carried on alone for three days in a more or less southerly direction, but on the fourth day all three met up again. Having made up his mind that he travelled faster on his own, Walter parted company with Corby and Beckwith.

Corby and Beckwith stopped at Pierrefitte-sur-Aire for four days but two days later, at Delouze (Meuse), they joined, and fought with, a group of maquisards. On 26 August they somehow became separated. Corby made contact with the Americans, and was taken to Paris on 1 September. Four days later he was in England. Beckwith remained with the maquis until 1 September, when he made contact with the American 4th Armored Division (Major-General J.S. Wood)[1604] at Houdelaincourt, and he, too, was sent to Paris before making his way back to England.

Having parted from Beckwith and Corby, Walter Farmer came across a farmhouse after a couple of days, and took up the offer to stay the night. Declining the generous invitation to stay longer if he so wished, he ploughed his lonely, southward furrow on the morrow until, on a country road, he turned a corner and came face to face with a German soldier armed with a Schmeisser automatic sub-machine gun: 'I hoped he would walk right by but he did not. He stopped and asked me if there was a village nearby. I was really scared…' The German, noticing the fear in the Englishman's face, just laughed and carried on. Walter Farmer did likewise.

Coming upon an isolated farmhouse, he was struck by the poverty of the place. After he had spoken to the farmer and his wife, the Frenchman spoke to his young son, who suddenly disappeared. Asking the farmer where his boy was going, Walter was startled to hear that he had gone to fetch the Germans. It would be all right, the farmer explained, as the Germans would simply put him, Walter, in a prison camp. Anyway, he added, the war would soon be over. For this the farmer would receive 10,000 francs, which would be of great help to him and his family. Not wishing to be caught by the Germans, Walter regrettably hit the farmer over the head with a piece of wood, twice, and ran off as fast as he could.

Having now covered some 250 kilometres from Hargnies in five days with the help of many French people, he reached St Blin (Haute-Marne), some thirty kilometres north-east of Chaumont. A Frenchman, claiming to be in the Resistance, took Walter to his home and that night a number of Frenchmen asked him a few searching questions. On 7 August, satisfied that he was genuine, they took him to their hideout, a deserted farmhouse a couple of kilometres away in the Bois des Chaisaux. The group consisted only of the leader, known as "Gegoose", and seven other men, the eldest of whom was their cook. A fortnight or so later the small group moved to the woods north of Lafauche, where they joined other Frenchmen, now around a hundred all told. The leader of the group was Georges Lombert, whose home was at 34, rue de France, Neufchâteau (Vosges). Attached to this group were fifty or so Russians. Encamped nearby, they had their own leader, and more or less went about their own business.

Forced to steal to keep themselves alive, members of the maquis group raided a garage at Neufchâteau some sixteen or seventeen kilometres to the east and took a German car. They also relieved a known collaborator of a small van. Now mobile, the group could travel further afield and steal food and anything else they fancied from the homes of other collaborators. Weapons were obtained from a Stirling that had been shot down on its way to a drop somewhere. Bolder now that they were armed, the gang determined to eliminate a German officer who lived with his mistress in a house some ten kilometres away. Four of the Frenchmen, including Walter, got out of the van some way short of the house and walked up to it. While two went to the front, Walter and the fourth man walked round the back: 'Before we could get all the way to the back, some shots were fired. It was the German officer running out the back door firing. I fired at him, but he got away. Inside the house we found the woman, hysterical.'[1605] Having loaded the van with food and wine, there was room only for two of the men. Walter was one of the two who had to walk back.

On the next night another foray for food was made, this time in two trucks, to a farm which had been run by the Germans. When they got there they found that the Germans had gone, leaving behind several frightened Poles and a number of live animals. One of the trucks was loaded up with two big pigs and a few chickens, the other with two sheep and some cheese. Walter was in the latter truck when they ran into some Germans, who ordered the driver to stop, but he kept his foot hard on the accelerator pedal, and one of the Germans immediately opened fire with his machine pistol. The bullet that whizzed past Walter's head killed one of the sheep, covering him in its blood. Reaching their camp safely the surviving sheep jumped off the truck and ran away. It took the men a long time to catch it.

Though too small to do any serious damage to the enemy, the group were keen to help the Germans on their way home, and went so far as to attack a train of 'tank cars… There were two German guards on it and they started firing back at us… We didn't have much luck… I somehow have the feeling the tank cars were empty.'[1606] Another time they chanced upon three Germans – an officer and two men – whose car had broken down. Walter and the Frenchmen killed the officer and one of the men, but the survivor was very old and very scared, so they just took him prisoner.

It was on 5 September that the first American troops arrived – a reconnaissance party consisting of four jeeps and an armoured car. Walter spoke to the lieutenant in charge, who suggested that he went with them towards Neufchâteau. A major, angry because he was unable to get any proper information as to the disposition of the German forces in front of him, wanted to know what was going on in Neufchâteau. Walter, in civilian clothes, volunteered to go and find out.

He managed to contact the mayor of the town (population 4,000), who 'marked the German positions on a map and told me there were two hundred Germans in the town'. Passing this information back to the Americans, Walter went back again to Neufchâteau, believing that the Germans would pull out that night. In fact, they did the opposite. Instead of evacuating the town they brought in a further five hundred troops who were disposed in a ring around it. Walter was now trapped, but walking along the rue Victor Martin he met Frenchman Serge Louis, who proffered his help. When Serge offered to take Walter to his home, the prospect of sleeping in a real bed for the first time in months proved irresistible.

Walter was having a wash in the sink at the Louis' house in the morning when Madame, who was upstairs, saw two SS men coming out of the house across the road and head towards their house – and Walter. Then the bell rang. Picking up her three-year-old son, Madame Louis went to the door, telling her son to scream his head off before she let the Germans in. Serge, quickly appreciating the danger, had bundled Walter through the toilet window and out onto the roof, against the wall of the next house, but only just in time, for one of the SS men had run upstairs and was on his way to the attic. Serge showed the SS man the way, but got the fright of his life when he looked out of a dormer window and saw Walter's feet sticking out. Quickly standing in front of the window Serge blocked the German's view, and the danger, for the moment, had passed.

After a brief air-raid warning the Germans, loud-speakers blaring, ordered all Frenchmen to go to the Place Jeanne d'Arc in the centre of the town to have their papers checked. While Serge did as ordered Walter hid on the roof for the rest of the day. Madame Louis went to give Walter a pillow to make his stay more comfortable, but the hardened evader was sound asleep. As Madame said: 'I think he had known rougher times.' Walter was given a new identity – he was now Jean Vincent, the name borrowed from a young Frenchman who had died in a train bombed by the RAF.

The Americans made no effort to capture Neufchâteau for several days. General Patton was fast approaching with the US Third Army's XVth Corps (Lieutenant-General Wade H. Haislip),[1607] which had not been allowed to advance until the situation in the Pas de Calais area had been stabilised by General Montgomery. Once the order to advance had been given, the Americans entered Neufchâteau during the afternoon of 11 September. On the following day Walter made his farewells, and was about to leave Neufchâteau when he ran into a large convoy of the US 79th Infantry Regiment, XV Corps. Taken to a major and a brigadier, they asked him if there were any Germans still there: 'I said I heard the day before that there were about 600. He told me to get in a truck with one of his junior officers. I made my farewell to Mr Louis and left with the officer.' At Nancy, their destination away to the north-east, Walter was handed over to the military police.

Once cleared Walter was told to report to the Hôtel Meurice in Paris, and left on 14 September to do so. Hitching lifts it took him two days to get to the hotel, only to be told by a resident Frenchman that the RAF's Evaders Section had moved to another hotel. Unable to find it he bumped into a bunch of RCAF pilots of 443 Squadron, who said that he could stay at their hotel, the Excelsior, for the night. On 17 September they took him to their aerodrome eighty kilometres away at Illiers-l'Evêque, where the squadron Intelligence Officer was at a loss to know what to do with him. Group notified the IO that Walter should go with the squadron to Brussels: 'I went with the ground staff convoy as the whole squadron was moving to Brussels Airport.' Here at last, on 23 September, he was interrogated and *then* flown back to England – where he was interrogated again on 24 September.

It was his sad duty to hand over several photographs taken from two of the crew of a Lancaster that had been shot down on 13 July 1944 at Vignory (Haute-Marne), and also to report that Serge Louis had some photographs of the flower-bedecked graves of some of the crew of a Lancaster that had come down near Neufchâteau.[1608]

His job done, and on six weeks' leave, Walter headed for home: 'I was very happy to see my mother and father, sisters Gwen and Myra and my twin sister, Marge. My adventure had lasted for six months.'

Flying at 21,000 feet in poor visibility on its way to Nuremberg on the night of 30/31 March 1944 Halifax LV923, with its crew of eight, found itself well off to starboard of the main stream of bombers, so much so that the navigator calculated that a 60° turn to port was required. Aware of the dangers of such a manoeuvre, filtering back into the path of hundreds of other heavy bombers, the pilot of LV923, Squadron Leader G.J. "Turkey" Laird DFC, RCAF, ordered everyone to keep a sharp lookout. Fifteen minutes later the rear gunner, Flying Officer James Moffat RCAF, watched helplessly as Lancaster ND767[1609] hit them very close to his turret: 'The starboard rudder was torn off in the collision and a large hole made in the top of the fuselage near the tail turret. I had great difficulty in getting my parachute as it was tangled with the tail control wires, which were all broken. The aircraft went into a spin immediately after collision and I baled out at Halanzy at 0400 hours 1 April [*sic*] 1944.'[1610] Lady Luck was certainly smiling on him that night, not only because he would normally have been occupying the mid-upper turret, which was crushed by the Lancaster, but also because he had baled out at the very low height of 1,000 feet or so.

There were five bodies for the Germans to find in the wreckage of LV923. They found another member of the crew, flight engineer Flying Officer John Morrison DFC, in a tree. He was still alive, but was to succumb to his awful injuries three weeks later at Arlon hospital, the Germans burying him with full military honours in Arlon (Aarlen) Communal Cemetery. James Moffat heard that four of ND767's crew had baled out but one of them had hit a tree and had been instantly killed. The bodies of the other three were found near the wreckage of their aircraft, their parachutes unopened.[1611] Of the fifteen airmen involved in the collision Jim Moffat was to be the only survivor.

Wrapped up in his parachute Jim slept in a wood until woken by church bells at around 9 o'clock next morning. Unsure of his whereabouts, he approached three men chopping wood, but they ignored him. Making his way to some houses he asked a curious youngster if he were in France. 'Nein, nein' replied the youth. German! Moving swiftly away Jim came to a signpost that said "Halanzy", which he thought was neither French nor German. He was not to know it just then, but he had landed near Battincourt at a point in Belgium where the borders of both France and of the Grand Duchy of Luxembourg are barely five kilometres away.

As he walked along the road a man wearing some sort of uniform cycled past him. Then four more men, also on bicycles, appeared and stopped, blocking the road as they did so. Fearing that he was now a prisoner of the Germans, Jim was greatly relieved when one of them, who said that he came from Birmingham, told him to get a move on – the Boches were coming! The cyclists pedalled off, leaving Jim hiding behind a hedge. In the evening he was taken to a bakery, that also sold beer and wine, where he was fed and given civilian clothing before being returned to the woods.

Some time later he heard a man calling. Hoping that the man was looking for him, Jim stepped out into the open. The man, Vital Paul, ran over to him, but continued to loudly call out 'Albert'. Jim realised that there was someone else in the woods, and soon two gendarmes appeared, one of whom it transpired was Albert Paul, Vital's younger brother.[1612] They took Jim to Vital Paul's home at Halanzy, where he met Marie-Claire, Vital's wife, and their two children, aged eight and seven. In the morning the two gendarmes re-appeared, with a car. As he climbed into the back of the car Jim was surprised to find a woman with a baby on her knee and another man already seated. The woman was Cécile Paul, Albert's wife, and the man Sergeant William Jones, another survivor of the Nuremberg massacre.[1613] After a drive of some twenty kilometres to the north-west the car pulled up at Albert and Cécile Paul's house in Etalle. It was 1 April.

Though Albert was an officer of the law, and had been since 1939, he had for the wrong reasons come to the notice of the Gestapo. He was also a member of the *Armée Secrète Ardennes*. On duty early on the morning of 17 May 1944 in Buzenol, some four kilometres south of Etalle, a convoy of vehicles suddenly drove up, and Albert was bundled into one of the cars. The Germans, an estimated eighty of them, then sped over to his house. Taken completely by surprise Jim Moffat, without his boots, and Bill Jones jumped from their bedroom window and started running. The Germans opened-up on the fleeing men with "Tommy guns" and rifles. Bill Jones was hit in the leg, and captured.[1614] He was taken to the front of the house, where Albert Paul was being closely guarded, and the two men were tied together. A German began asking Bill questions. When Bill told him that he was an airman, the German called him English piss and knocked him to the ground. Bill was about to retaliate when a sharp tug from Albert brought him to his senses.

Taken to Arlon for questioning, Bill and Albert were separated, and though Bill never saw Albert again he was convinced that Albert saved his life by insisting to the interrogators that he was an airman and not a spy. Bill, however, suffered further brutal torture in an attempt to extract names and places from him, and even though he was given no food for a week he managed to say nothing. Beaten to within an inch of his life he was moved to further jails in Belgium, suffering similar treatment at each of them, before being one of the first airmen to be sent to the newly-opened Luftwaffe airmen's prisoner-of-war camp at Stalag Luft VII (Bankau).[1615] As for Albert Paul, he was condemned to death on 27 June and shot by the Germans in La Citadelle Saint Walburg, Liège, on 14 August.

Leaving behind his false Belgian identity card and his RCAF tags as he fled, Jim Moffat managed to hide in a thicket, and though searching Germans passed literally within inches of his trembling body he remained undetected. Naked as a jaybird from the waist down, Jim spent two cold and hungry nights in hiding before daring to seek help, which he found in the form of a woodcutter, who fetched him 'a pair of slippers, *pantoufle*, a dirty, old pair of pants, and most important of all black bread smeared with bacon grease'[1616] before taking him home. Now better equipped to take on the Germans, Jim left the woodcutter and his wife, who had given him a big bowl of cabbage soup to drink, and headed towards Switzerland, walking only at night 'because I was scared the Germans would shoot me if I were caught.'[1617]

Spraining an ankle when he fell down an embankment, Jim crawled to a field, where he saw a young shepherd. The man said that he could get some rest in a large nearby haystack, but was not to go to the shepherd's house. Jim was awoken in the morning by the shepherd shouting to him that he had a friend. The "friend" proved to be Desiré Paul, cousin to Vital and Albert, and was himself a forester. He had been told to keep an eye open for Jim, though Jim never discovered how he had come to be there that sunny May morning. Nevertheless, he led Jim to his house at Torgny, a stone's throw from the French border.

For the next few weeks, having been told that it was impossible for him to get to Switzerland, Jim was hidden in a church. Desiré provided him with food, but when he became ill from scabies, took him back to his house. Jim was in such a bad state that he was taken next day the half a dozen kilometres or so to the house of the mayor of Dampicourt, a Monsieur Adam, whose wife, Jim was delighted to discover, was an Englishwoman from Pontefract who had been a nurse in the First World War and had stayed behind afterwards. By coincidence, Jim's mother also came from Pontefract. Next day Jim was taken away in an old charcoal-burning truck to the forest, and to a section of the Belgian Resistance, the Armée Blanche, with whom he stayed until 1 August. It was about a week after his arrival in the woods that a doctor arrived and, assessing Jim as suffering from scabies and severe malnutrition, stabbed him in the arm with a large syringe. Jim passed out, crumpling to the ground. Two days later he was taken to Couvreux, two kilometres from Dampicourt, and to the home of Madame Germaine Autphene, whose job it was to fatten up members of the Resistance who had fallen ill.

Her job done, Jim returned to the woods, to the Resistance, who were hiding in the Bois de Lahage, ten kilometres north of Dampicourt. Unhappy at the way of life, Jim wanted to move on: 'The White Army did no sabotage whatever, and I began to get scared that they were bandits, so with two Russians and two Algerians, I started for France to try to get to Switzerland.' Their departure, however, needed careful planning, for Jim was sure that the *Résistants* would do what they could to stop them. One day, the conspirators met deep in the woods and ran for it, for three days without food. Somewhere, now well into France, they came across an elderly Italian farmer, who put them in touch with Louis Paul (no relation). The Algerians disappeared, and Louis took the two Russians to a Polish camp, and then showed Jim his maquis unit in the Bois de Chênois, a short distance from the village of Baâlon (Meuse).

Jim went on with Louis to his house at Baâlon but, before he had even had time to eat the meal being prepared by Louis's wife, the Germans arrived. On the run once again Jim escaped to the woods. It was night time when he decided to head back in the moonlight to the maquisards in the Bois de Chênois. Puzzled by the absence of sentries when he got there he could nevertheless see the men asleep. Calling out, he got no reply. The reason then became clear. They were all dead. They had been shot. 'All twenty of them… Most of them had had their heads caved in.'[1618] In a state of deep shock Jim just ran and ran and ran until he fell exhausted into some bushes by the side of the road.

He was now in le Bois d'Iré-le-Sec, in the Forêt de Wœvre, home to a small group of eighteen maquisards. Very suspicious, they kept a close guard on him for the first three days. On the third day a man who was clearly the chief in the area turned up and asked Jim the usual searching questions about his air force background. No doubt this man already had the answers, for he duly proclaimed Jim to be a genuine member of the RCAF. The seal of approval came when the leader of the maquisards, Lucien Sibénaler, issued him with a French carbine. From then on Jim took part in a number of raids against the enemy, mostly robberies, stealing food and such like. Jim was still not in the best of health when the camp was moved to the Bois de Juvigny, barely three kilometres south of Montmédy.

In his report Jim briefly stated: 'Being a gunner I helped with a machine gun that the FFI had and shot a few Germans. On 3 September 1944 we attacked the village of Quinzy. Two of the FFI were wounded and the Germans hanged them in the village.'[1619] Before then, however, a new leader was appointed late in August, former soldier Lieutenant Emile Randolet. With the Germans now in retreat the action took on a grimmer slant. Randolet, on Jim's advice, decided to cut the powerline to a nearby German radar station. The Germans repaired the line, then the maquisards cut it again, and waited for the Germans to come and repair it. Two did so, and both were shot dead. One of them was wounded, and cried out for mercy, but the maquisards shot him anyway.

Discretion being the better part of valour, Jim and his comrades moved camp again, but the brutality continued. One of the maquisards, James Grunenwald, went to visit his mother in nearby Longuyon on 24 August. A woman spotted James and, recognising him as a maquisard, called out to the Germans that there was a terrorist next door. As he pedalled furiously away on his bicycle James was shot dead by the pursuing Germans. Randolet, on being informed of this, asked for a volunteer to exact revenge on the woman collaborator. Maquisard Jean Martin volunteered to deal with her. Going straight to her house he said to the woman: 'Madame, you know what you have done', and shot her in the head.[1620]

Then, on 3 September (as Jim reported), came the news that ten to fifteen Germans were in Quincy-Landzécourt. Eighteen maquisards under Randolet, including Jim, set off to capture them. Nearing the village, a man told them where the Germans were disposed, with machine-guns in several places and a mortar, but rather than ten or fifteen there were some two hundred of them. Too late to warn half the maquisards who had gone on ahead, the Germans opened up with all they had got. Most of the maquisards survived, but one man was killed and two were captured – René Warion and Joseph Pawlak. They were hanged in the village square in front of the assembled villagers.

Five days later the Americans arrived. After a couple of days with a flak-happy reconnaissance unit, during which they charged a German gun across a bridge without getting hit, Jim was deposited at Montmédy, and thought he would be heading home. The Americans had other ideas – he was too useful – and took him on to Bastogne. There, however, the Americans had rounded-up thirty other evaders – three Canadian, five British, and twenty-two American airmen – and all were taken to the Hôtel Metropole in Brussels. A day or two later, on 15 September, they were flown to an American airbase in a C-47 Skytrain. Jim was still suffering from his earlier deprivations, and was removed to a hospital at Watford for three weeks. Shipped to New York aboard the *Queen Mary*, he finally arrived at Rockliffe RCAF airbase, Ottawa, on 22 October 1944.

Taking advantage of the main Bomber Command raid to Nuremberg on the night of 30/31 March 1944, SOE laid on Operation Osric 27. Given the responsibility for this operation, the dropping of two "secret agents" near Antwerp, were the eight crew of Halifax LL287, 138 (Special Duties) Squadron. Before they could make the drop, however, LL287 was hit by flak over the Westerschelde and crashed into the River Scheldt (Schelde). Both agents, Lieutenants R. Deprez ("Lucullus") and A. Giroulle ("Troilus"), and three of the crew failed to survive, but the rest were able to paddle ashore in the aircraft's dinghy. Splitting into two groups, they set off in different directions.

Warrant Officer 2nd Class S.E. Godfrey RCAF, Warrant Officer J. Weir RAAF, and Flight Sergeant G.W. Kimpton were taken prisoner at s'Gravenpolder, Zuid Beveland, Holland. The other two, pilot and second pilot, Flight Lieutenants Brian Mill and Dennis Beale, were more fortunate, at least for a while. They met members of the Dutch Resistance at a farm near Biezelinge, and in due course were taken across the Scheldt Estuary to Breskens, a dozen kilometres north of the Belgian border. Early in May 1944 they were brought to the Belgian town of Zelzate, where they were put with the Pierets and De Colvenaer families, 'who were already hiding forty-seven other Allied airmen'.[1621]

Some while later they were joined by a Dutch lieutenant, Gilbert Beleir, and by an American airman, H. Lang (or Langh). The weeks rolled slowly by until, on 7 September 1944, the alarm was raised when a German patrol was learnt to be on its way to raid the house of Albert de Colvenaer, in which the four evaders were living. Mill, Lang and Beleir managed to get out over the roof, and disappeared into the woods.

Dennis Beale, for some reason, decided to hide in a bedroom, but was discovered, and spent the rest of the war as a prisoner of war.[1622] There was to be no happy ending to this small drama played out on the sandy margins of the Dutch and Belgian coasts. Dennis Beale was taken along with Albert De Colvenaer, his seventeen-year-old son Yvan, and André Pierets to the German Feldgendarmerie at Zelzate, where they were interrogated by a Leutnant Hoffmann. De Colvenaer father and son were taken to Vlissingen (Flushing) and, after trial by a German military tribunal under Oberst Reinhardt, were condemned to death. At 8 o'clock on the morning of 11 September 1944, together with two other so-called "convicts", M. Dieleman and Wim Niesthoven, they were taken to the dunes of Koudekerke and shot.[1623]

Just as the crew of Halifax LL287 had discovered that flying low and slow over enemy territory, even in the dark of night, was not a safe way of waging war, so too did that of a 620 Squadron Stirling on the night of 11/12 April 1944. They, too, were engaged on a supply drop for SOE when the aircraft was hit by machine-gun fire at about 1.20 a.m. on 12 April, and force-landed near Anzex (Lot-et-Garonne) in the south-west of France. Two of the crew, Pilot Officer C.G. Griffin and Flight Sergeant L.J.S. Brown RNZAF, 'managed to evade capture and remain in hiding until 14 May. On that date we reached Larroqe [Larroque-Engalin] near Condom. Here we met the chief British Intelligence Officer for the S.W. of France, who was known as "Hilaire".' [1624]

"Hilaire" was the codename for George Starr MC, chief of SOE's Wheelwright circuit. Starr's cover, that he was 'a retired Belgian mining engineer who had made his pile in the Congo'[1625], was so effective that he had been made deputy mayor of Castelnau-sous-l'Auvignon (Gers). Quite apart from arming the local resistance, Starr helped numerous evaders and escapers on their way to the Pyrenees, including Griffin and Brown, but first, on 6 June, they had to move to Starr's headquarters at Castelnau-sous-l'Auvignon. With the Normandy landings under way, the word had gone out to all Resistance people, SOE, maquis, or whatever, to harass the Germans. Starr's unit went out that very night, 6/7 June, to cut the main railway line from Auch to Agen near Lectoure (Gers).

On the way, however, they were ambushed by the Milice, and Griffin was captured. He was later reported to be held in Lectoure, by the Milice, but all attempts to arrange for an exchange failed.[1626] Now fully aware of the presence of a maquis at Castelnau-sous-l'Auvignon, the Germans attacked it in force on 14 June. The village had to be evacuated, but a running fight was maintained by the evacuees 'with the Germans, inflicting considerable casualties, first at Condom, then at Lanne Maignan.'[1627]

Here Brown stayed for ten days, meeting Sergeant Ralph J. Workman USAAF and Staff Sergeant Howard C. Brooks USAAF.[1628] After meandering about the region for a few days, the two Americans set off on their own to Spain, and reached it. At Hontanx (Landes) Brown met three more of the Workman/Brooks crew – 2nd Lieutenant Robert C. Disbrow (co-pilot); Flight Officer Frank A. Champ (navigator); and Sergeant Alfred M. Campbell (right waist gunner). Together with a few others collected along the way, the four airmen were near Malvezie (Haute-Garonne), a few kilometres from the Pyrenees, on 29 July, and with two French guides arrived at Caneja in Spain on 4 August, Spanish authorities taking them to Les and Bosost for interrogation. Brown was flown back from Gibraltar on 5 September.

Another Halifax, LW591 of 425 RCAF 'Alouette' Squadron, was shot down on the night of 24/25 April 1944. Sergeants A. Best, J.A.E. Michand RCAF, and W.B.P. Whalen RCAF, evaded capture. The other four, including Pilot Officer H.E. Dubé RCAF, were taken prisoner. Dubé managed to escape from a train and hide near the village of Chenet, some fifteen kilometres south-west of Bastogne, in the Belgian province of Luxembourg. Three months later, having decided to join the Resistance forces in France, he and fellow evader First Lieutenant Richard Noble USAAF were captured by German forces early on the morning of 8 August 1944 in a wood near Olizy (Ardennes). Tied to a drainpipe of the local church, they were left out in the hot sun with no water for much of the day. Towards evening they were untied and made to dig their graves with their bare hands. Once they had finished, they were shot in the back of the head and buried.[1629]

The spring of 1944 was a busy period for escape lines, especially for Bourgogne (Burgundy line) and Dutch-Paris, with large numbers of Allied evaders and other refugees being funnelled through Paris and Toulouse on their way to the Pyrenees and Spain.

On 11 May Flight Sergeant F.A. Greenwell and Lieutenant West USAAF arrived in Toulouse from Paris, and stayed the night with Françoise Dissard – who told them that she was the chief of the organisation. They stayed at another house in Toulouse until 14 May when, with four more American airmen – Lieutenant-Colonel Robert F. Montgomery,[1630] First Lieutenant Harry E. Bisher, 2nd Lieutenant Walter A. Meldrich, and Flight Officer Ramsay – they took the train (third class) south to Montréjeau (Haute-Garonne). They were joined by a Jewish family of four and by Daniel Héricault, a French schoolteacher.[1631] Abandoned by their guides as they crossed the Pyrenees, they finally reached Spain on 17 May, and were arrested at Les. After reaching Alhama (7 June) the Americans left three days later, while Greenwell made his way to Madrid four days after that. He was flown to England on 23/24 June.

Flight Sergeant A.V. Jackson, whose journey south from Belgium had been interrupted for several weeks in Paris, was finally escorted to Toulouse on 19/20 May 1944. At Françoise Dissard's house he 'met about thirteen Americans, including Major [Roderick L.] Francis, Captain [Arthur T.] Cavanaugh, First Lieutenant [Monroe J.] Hotaling, First Lieutenant [William O.] Ross and First Lieutenant [Earl E.] Woodard.'[1632] Françoise told them that they would be leaving in two parties, one of eight and one of six. Jackson went in the first group, the second one hopefully meeting up with them for the crossing of the Pyrenees. Unfortunately, the guide of the second group was arrested in Toulouse and the meeting of all fourteen was delayed until 23 May.

Two days later two more USAAF airmen arrived – First Lieutenant Ivan E. Glaze and Staff Sergeant Warren W. Cole.[1633] On 26 May they 'were taken in two carloads to the foothills. Just before our party arrived at its destination a car standing on the road fired two shots at our tyres. They missed, and chased us.'[1634] Stopping the car a couple of hundred metres up the road the airmen scattered into the hills. Whoever was in the enemy car did not pursue the matter, and the airmen met up at the agreed rendezvous. Also there were two other RAF evaders – Flying Officer J.A. Smith RAAF and Pilot Officer R.G. Hoare.

These two, with a Flight Lieutenant Foster, Pilot Officer D.R. Murphy, and First Lieutenant Donald E. Swanson USAAF, had been hoping to catch a train from Toulouse to Tarbes. Having missed the connection they 'climbed over a wall and slept in a wood. At dawn we started to walk along a path by a railway track and ran into a German patrol of two men.' They had unwittingly walked into an ammunition works, but with the help of the French nightwatchman were able to convince the Germans that they were French workers. They reached Tarbes in due course, but found that the address that they had been given was non-existent. Deciding that it was too dangerous to continue together, they split up. Smith and Hoare did not see the other three again.[1635]

They tried to cross the Pyrenees by themselves, but failed and found themselves back at Bagnères-de-Bigorre on 15 May. Soon after, First Lieutenant Jesse M. Hamby USAAF[1636] appeared. They were on their way over the mountains with a guide and four maquisards when they bumped into Jackson and his Americans. They all reached Caneja in Spain on 29 May and were taken into custody by Spanish police, who took them to Les next day, and then to Viella, and to Sort (6 June). After several more stops they left Madrid on 23 June for Gibraltar.

On 23 May several evading airmen were brought together at a hospital near the Gare d'Austerlitz. That night they boarded the 2000 hours overnight train for Toulouse. Sergeant C.G. Virgo, Flight Sergeants D.J. Hoad and J.R. Wallace RAAF arrived with another seven Americans, among them Sergeants John Katsaros and Jack W. Stead, Lieutenant Bud Thacker, First Lieutenants Raymond K. Holz and Charles J. McLain, and Captain Merlin K. Burgess.[1637] The journey was without incident and, after spending the day in Toulouse, they caught the train for Pau, but alighting at Labarthe-Rivière, a stop or two past St Gaudens and a good many kilometres short of the Pyrenees. It was not until late on 25 May that their guide, bringing with him ten Frenchmen, led them off across the mountains. 'During the next three days we did not change our guides and never stopped to sleep for more than three hours at a stretch.'[1638] Crossing the border during the night of 29/30 May, the guides having shown them the way, the first town they reached was Les, where they gave themselves up to the carabineros.

Hot on the heels of this group, yet more evaders in Paris were assembled on the top floor of a clinic (the same place as "the hospital near the gare d'Austerlitz" perhaps) on 24 May. Sergeant John McKenzie Alexander arrived in Paris in April 1944, and was staying at the house of a Mme. Crabbe when she 'got in touch with a resistance organisation through a friend of her husband'. On the evening of 26 April Alexander was collected by policeman Georges Prévot (see also p. 270) and taken to his home at 20, Boulevard de Sébastopol, to which Flight Sergeant Wallace and Captain Burgess would later be brought and, on 22 May, Pilot Officer H.H.J. Fisher. The following day Alexander joined Fisher, Flight Sergeant H. Bossick (Fisher's flight engineer) and Pilot Officer D.H. Courtenay, and all were taken to a clinic where they 'picked up five more British and American evaders, who included Sgt. Daugherty (E & E 774).'[1639] Also in the party were Warrant Officer II A.J. McPhee RCAF (same crew as Fisher and Bossick) and Staff Sergeant George R. Miller USAAF.[1640]

McPhee, Fisher, and Bossick, all from Stirling EH942, were shot down by a night-fighter on the night of 22/23 April 1944. McPhee, bomb aimer, remembered nothing after hearing that the port-outer engine was on fire. He regained consciousness around midday on 23 April to find himself suspended by his parachute in a tree with his feet about four feet off the ground. Managing to disentangle himself, but leaving his parachute in the branches, he discovered that two of his teeth were broken 'and my lip, eye and hand were cut. I staggered into a nearby farm somewhere just north-east of Vic-sur-Aisne. The farmer removed my mae west and asked me where I had left my parachute. I walked out of the farm with him and pointed to where I thought it was. I then fainted.'[1641] A doctor was summoned, and when McPhee came round it was to find the doctor sewing up his lip: 'I was then given a draught and I slept for the next two days.'

Either that night or on the following day Fisher was brought to the farm, and the two airmen were moved to a large cave, where they stayed for the next eight days.[1642] Food was brought to them every day, and every second night they returned to the farm for a bath, a shave and a meal. On 3 May they were taken by cart to the house of the local Resistance chief in Vic-sur-Aisne, and the following day by motorbike to a farm near Morsain, where they stayed for a further five days. In Paris, on 8 May, Fisher and McPhee met EH942's flight engineer, Harry Bossick, who had been taken there on 23 May.

Pilot Officer Courtenay, pilot of Lancaster ND508, also lost on the Laon raid of 22/23 April, had been very fortunate, for when ND508 was hit by a night-fighter it exploded before anyone had had the chance to bale out.[1643] Blown into the dark night sky he was able to open his parachute before making a heavy landing near Vic-sur-Aisne. Unable to move, he was found by a farm labourer, and on 24 April taken by train to Paris, where he received medical attention.

Alexander and the others were provided with false papers and escorted by train – third class – by two women guides (five to each guide) to Toulouse and then to Pau, where they arrived late on 26 May. Sent to various houses, the airmen met up again on the following evening ready for the move to the Pyrenees. It was decided that only eight could go and so the two youngest, Alexander and Daugherty, stayed behind and were taken by their guide, Rosemarie, to a hotel. They were joined on 30 May by another ten evaders, including Squadron Leader E.N.M. Sparks, Flying Officers A.W. Alliston and M.S. Steel (from the same 10 Squadron crew), Flight Sergeant J. Pittwood, and Sergeants W.A.

Greene RCAF and J.G. Pearce. Three of the other four were Captain Maurice S. Thomas, First Lieutenant Charles R. Clonts Jr. and Technical Sergeant Kenneth H. Nice, all USAAF.

They had to wait for a further four days before setting off for the Pyrenees. Along the way their ranks were swollen by 'a party of civilian Jewish refugees consisting of about twelve men, twelve women and several small children. These people were guided by four young Frenchmen carrying Sten guns.'[1644] Also added to the party was Staff Sergeant Lester W. Knopp USAAF.[1645] The large, mixed group set off for the Pyrenees shortly after midnight on 31 May. The Jewish refugees were in poor condition and struggled to keep up with the pace, forcing the party to stop at a shepherd's hut four hours later for the rest of the day, as McPhee explained: 'We tried to help them at first by carrying their luggage and children but eventually we became so weak through lack of food and the difficult country we were crossing that we could scarcely walk ourselves.'

With new guides they continued later that evening (1 June) but once again, this time after barely an hour and a half, the guides stopped at another hut, realising that at such a slow pace they could not reach the next scheduled stopping-place before daybreak. Those who were strong enough carried on at around 8 p.m. that evening and walked for nine and a half hours until they came to a hut near Ste Engrâce (Pyrénées-Atlantiques), barely half a dozen kilometres from the Spanish border (2 June). At around 4 p.m. that afternoon another guide took them to a forest, where they were fed. An hour or so later the march continued, and it was not until 6 a.m. on 3 June that the remnant of the large group crossed the border into Spain.

Having been provided with little in the way of food and drink, most of the party were exhausted, and only seventeen or eighteen of the party, mostly the airmen and the four Frenchmen, had in fact been able to continue. At some point George Miller, as a result of a wounded arm, said that he could not go on. McPhee was also 'very fatigued' and decided to stay with Miller. While the rest of the party continued, Miller and McPhee stayed behind in the shepherd's hut. They were sufficiently recovered by morning to carry on, but after a while they 'heard a shout and we saw the four Frenchmen, three or four of the Americans, Courtenay, Fisher and Bossick coming towards us.'[1646] They were lost, and had been wandering around all night. They set off once more, on 5 June, leaving Miller and McPhee behind yet again.

Shortly afterwards, as they were heading across the hills for Isaba at their own pace, Miller and McPhee heard a rifle shot coming from the direction in which the others had been walking. Unaware of the shot's significance they continued to a farmhouse, where they were given food and wine. Later that day the farmer took them in his cart to Isaba and handed them over to the carabineros. After a few days at Miranda de Ebro, McPhee was admitted to hospital at Vitoria until 1 July. He was flown back to England from Gibraltar on 10 July.

As for the Courtenay, Fisher and Bossick group, they were some two kilometres from Isaba, well inside Spanish territory, when they were confronted by two German soldiers who had also illegally crossed the frontier. While the Frenchmen managed to escape, Bossick, Fisher, Courtenay and Knopp were captured and escorted back to France. Searched and given a perfunctory interrogation, they spent the night in a cell in a private house before being taken to Pau on 6 June, and then to St Michel prison, Toulouse. Here they joined nineteen other Allied airmen, one of whom was Flight Sergeant H.T. Jeffrey.

Jeffrey had been shot down on the night of 10/11 April 1944 when his Halifax, returning from the target (Tergnier) in north-eastern France, was hit by flak and immediately burst into flames. Jeffrey was quickly picked up by the maquis and taken to Paris, where he stayed for approximately one month until taken to Toulouse with Pilot Officer David Thompson RCAF and 2nd Lieutenant Richard M. Miller USAAF.[1647] On 13 May, after five days in Toulouse, they left by train for the Pyrenees with four Belgian evaders and two Spanish guides. Disembarking at Sarrancolin, in the Vallée d'Aure, which they had been told was not occupied by German troops, they set off in single file for the nearby Pyrenees.

Unfortunately, their information about the town being unoccupied proved to be false, and they were spotted leaving the platform by two German frontier guards. The men were captured and taken to the town of Arrien, where they stayed overnight: 'During the night we were badly beaten up by the German Gestapo there. We had to strip and were put against a wall and beaten with canes and with fists.'[1648] Jeffrey suffered almost an hour of this torture, but on the morrow he and the others were taken by Waffen SS troops to Tarbes, and on 16 May to St Michel prison, where they 'met about twenty more Allied aviators. Amongst them were:- Captain Henry Aldridge, USAAF; T/Sergeant. Henry, USAAF; Flight Lieutenant William Forster, RCAF; Pilot Officer Murphy, RAF; and 2nd Lieutenants Bangos, Hart and Campbell, USAAF.'[1649]

On 15 June eighteen of the airmen were sent to Germany, leaving behind the four captured in Spain plus Flying Officer D.A. Lennie RCAF, one of the original nineteen, who had been lost on 8/9

May flying an SOE operation to the Haute-Vienne department of France.[1650] The eighteen were taken to the Wehrmacht *Gefängnis* (prison) at Fresnes, to the south of Paris, where they were put four to a cell: 'The food was poor, and we only got fifteen minutes exercise per week and one shower in three weeks, with no soap or towels. On 1 August sixty of us were evacuated and placed under Gestapo guard on a train bound for Frankfurt, Germany. We were handcuffed in pairs.' Jeffrey was manacled to one of the Belgians whom he had met in Toulouse and who had declared himself to the Germans to be Sergeant Dubois RAF.[1651]

During the night of 2 August Jeffrey was able to undo his handcuffs thanks to 'a small penknife which I was able to smuggle out of the suitcase which I had to carry.' Pulling one of the oldest tricks known to prisoners on a train, Jeffrey and Dubois pretended that they wanted to go to the lavatory. Whipping off the handcuffs they 'left the train by the window', but Jeffrey hurt his leg and shoulder when he hit the ground and, rather than slow down the uninjured Dubois, told him to go on without him. Despite his injuries Jeffrey was able to find his way to a farm at Waville (to the west of the Moselle river and, more importantly, in France), and a doctor was brought to attend to his injuries.

Fit enough to leave on 4 August Jeffrey walked all day in a westerly direction to the village of Dommartin-la-Chaussée, staying for a week at another farm there. On 11 August he was put in touch with a local maquis, and stayed at their camp near Viéville-en-Haye until 16 August, when it was attacked by German forces. Jeffrey did his bit in the fighting, which saw some thirty-six Germans killed, but the camp was broken up and he fled to Hattonchâtel, where he was reunited with Dubois. After several moves in the locality they ended up at Toul 'with three Canadians' on 21 August, staying with 'a Count, who seemed to be some sort of leader in the FFI, because he told us a lot about the organisation.'[1652] When Toul was liberated by the Americans on 2 September Dubois revealed his true identity and went off with a US reconnaissance unit as a liaison officer/interpreter. Jeffrey reported to a US major and was sent back through channels to England, where he arrived on 10 September.

The five airmen who had been left behind at St Michel prison were still there when the Germans evacuated Toulouse on 19 August, and were liberated by French irregular forces. They remained in Toulouse until arrangements were made for their return by air from Garlin (thirty kilometres north of Pau) on 6 and 7 September 1944, two months behind McPhee, who was back in England on 11 July.

11 July 1944 was also the date on which Flying Officer A.A.H.J.N.A. Duchesnay RCAF was interrogated by MI9 following his evasion. He had come down in Holland towards the end of April 1944, and had been hidden by the Dutch Resistance in a hut in some woods together with Sergeants A.J. Keveren, J.W. Firth, and M.F. Williams. When the hut burnt down they moved on, until Duchesnay parted from them on 24 May and made his own way down to Toulouse and into the hands of Françoise Dissard's organisation on 1 June. A fluent French-speaker he was regarded with much suspicion by Françoise, and had to be given the all-clear by Lieutenant Commander W.L. "Billie" Stephens (see previous chapter), who had escaped from Switzerland to France on 5 June 1944 and had arrived in Toulouse a few days after Duchesnay.

The details of the RAF Bomber Command attack on the German depot at Mailly-le-Camp on the night of 3/4 May 1944 are well documented,[1653] but suffice it to say that, as they orbited the target in bright moonlight awaiting the order from the "Master of Ceremonies" to go in and bomb, the bombers were savaged by skilled German night-fighter crews. Forty-two Lancasters of the main force were shot down, as were two "supporters", a Mosquito and a Halifax, of 100 Group. Only fifty-eight of the 315 men lost in these forty-four aircraft survived, twenty-four were taken prisoner of war and thirty-four evaded.

One Lancaster that just managed to stay aloft was ND733. It was on the homeward leg, just south of Paris, when it was attacked by a night-fighter. With the trimming tabs shot away the pilot, Flight Sergeant T.A. Lloyd, struggled to keep control of the aircraft 'but managed to shake off the enemy fighter. Five minutes later a second attack set fire to the aircraft's bomb bay and fuselage.'[1654] The order to bale out was obeyed by the mid-upper gunner, rear gunner and bomb aimer. Bomb aimer Flying Officer E. Yaternick RCAF and rear gunner Sergeant A.C. Crilly were captured, but mid-upper gunner thirty-year-old Sergeant J.G. Pearce managed to evade, despite his parachute catching in some telegraph wires. That proved to be his only worry, for by late evening on 4 May he was in the hands of the Resistance and, helped on his way to Gibraltar, was flown back to the UK on 23 June.

Before anyone else had the chance to bale out of ND733 it went into a dive, which helped to extinguish the fires, and Lloyd managed to put the stricken bomber down at RAF Ford, on the south coast of England. Though aircraft and crew were badly shaken, all returned to fly again.

Also shot down on the Mailly-le-Camp raid was a Lancaster flown by Squadron Leader R.W.H. Gray. Crashing at St Agnan (Yonne), some twenty-five kilometres south-east of the Forest of Fontainebleau, only Gray, who was taken prisoner, and Sergeant P.J. Evans, the wireless operator, survived. Evans landed safely near Villethierry, five kilometres south of St Agnan. Helped at first by the baker and his wife and by the local schoolteacher, he then asked to be put in touch with the local priest, as he had been instructed to do during his escape and evasion lecture in England. This bore fruit, and he was taken away to Nevers (Nièvre) some distance to the south. After four days there a young woman escorted him north to Paris by train, where he was hidden in two safe houses, firstly in the home of two women doctors and, next, with Monsieur and Madame Olga Christol (who would shelter a total of thirty-nine airmen in their house).

It was while Evans was at the Christol's that Sergeant J. McK. Alexander, flight engineer of a 101 Squadron Lancaster shot down on 10/11 April 1944 and one of only four survivors, all evaders, was brought to the house. Landing near Willencourt (Pas-de-Calais) in northern France, his evasion was routine until the morning of 15 April, when he arrived at Flesselles (Somme), a short way north of Amiens. There were 'a good many German troops about here', and he had to walk past an HQ, with a sentry at the door. 'After I had gone about fifty yards past the sentry I realised that a party of Germans was following me. I continued ahead of them till we reached a fork in the road. Here I continued straight on, while the Germans took the right fork.'[1655]

By the time he had reached the outskirts of Amiens his feet were giving him trouble, and when a storm broke over him he took shelter in a barn full of straw. There he was found by three boys, who reported him to a man, a railway worker, who took Alexander back to his house in Amiens. Trying to get help from two priests, both of whom refused it, Alexander was taken to the railway yard and allowed to sleep in an office there. In the morning, 16 April, the workers gave him a white armband, to denote his status as a railway worker, and put him on the train for Paris, which was also being boarded by several Germans. Alexander was more than concerned when his French helper persisted in giving the "V for Victory" sign, but all was well, and he duly reached Paris later that morning.

Wandering about the city, his feet now quite raw, he tried to get help, but everyone he approached was too scared to do more than give him a glass of wine. Even the priests he asked would do nothing for him. When he 'felt like giving the whole thing up', he went to a police station near Notre Dame, and after some time was able to get policeman Georges Prévot to escort him to an address elsewhere in the city, the Christol's house.

It was usual for civilian aircraft flying from Lisbon airport to England to land at Whitchurch airport, near Bristol, and routine for all passengers disembarking to be checked to ensure that they were not enemy agents trying to enter the country. One man who arrived from Lisbon on 15 July 1944 did so 'with a bogus British Emergency Certificate and claimed to be a member of the RAF'.[1656] This was the story that that man, Nicholas John Stockford, told.

He was the flight engineer aboard a 207 Squadron Lancaster (Warrant Officer L.H. Lissette RNZAF) which was so badly damaged on the Mailly-le-Camp raid that at '00.30 hours on 4.5.44 the state of the aircraft necessitated a baling-out operation. He [Stockford] landed near the village of Ferrières, sixteen miles north of Montargis and hid in a wood.'[1657] Believing that he was heading due south Stockford was in fact walking north-west. He continued west and then south-west for the next four days. On 8 May a man whom he met in the village of Boiscommun contacted the abbé of St Loup-des-Vignes. The abbé in turn contacted the schoolteacher in the village, Yvette Jublot, and on 10 May she hid him above the school.

Having found him a set of civilian clothes, he was escorted by "Jean" to Paris at the end of May. On 13 June he was taken to Lyon and, after an evening meal, moved on to Toulouse and to Bordeaux, where he was again hidden. Two days later a guide called Benito arrived, and Stockford 'was fixed up with Organisation Todt papers to state that he was going on leave.' Making their way to St Jean-de-Luz, each with a bicycle, they pushed on to the Spanish border on 21 June until they were within four kilometres of Hendaye. From there 'they went on to a farm-house 200 yards from the Franco-Spanish frontier. They went down to the [River] Bidassoa and Benito forded Stockford over on his back, the former being conversant with the various conformations of the river-bed.'[1658]

Once in Spain, they went to Irún and San Sebastián, where they stayed the night. Continuing on to Bilbao, Stockford stayed there for a week while papers were prepared in the name of John White, a civilian escaper from the internment camp at Vittel, France. On about 2 July, having been provided with a safe-conduct pass and an identity card, he was taken to León. There a Spanish guide took him to the Portuguese border, and handed him over to two Portuguese guides, one called Manuel, who took him to Murça, 100 kilometres or so down the road to Oporto. On 7 July 'he was contacted by a Frenchman named Guerché and a Portuguese named Mirandella, who told him that the line had been broken owing to the arrest of an organisation member in Oporto.' Nevertheless, Stockford was taken to Oporto on 12 July, and after dinner with the assistant British Consul there, Mr Connolly, 'took the Lisbon train with no identity papers'.

In Lisbon, 'he went to the embassy and was seen by a man named "Terry" aged about twenty-one, who took him to 37c, Rua de Buenos Aires.' Issued on 13 July with emergency certificate number 1398, "John White" was given a place on an aircraft returning to Bristol (Whitchurch) Airport, England, on the night of 14/15 July, where his true identity was soon established to the satisfaction of the security control officer.

The railway yards at Hasselt in Belgium were the target for the crew of a 158 Squadron Halifax on the night of 12/13 May 1944. On the way out a faulty starboard-inner engine began overheating and slowed down their progress, but the skipper, Flight Sergeant J.H. Evans, and flight engineer Sergeant Leslie Board decided to press on to avoid being labelled LMF (Lack of Moral Fibre) – the awful RAF phrase used where cowardice was suspected. Despite the handicap of the sick engine Evans got the Halifax to the target on time, and bombs were dropped. They were, however, destined not to get home, for a flak shell took out the starboard-inner and set the wing alight.

In all the confusion everyone baled out except for Leslie Board who was trying to get extinguishers to put out the raging fire. A while later he realised that he was alone in a steeply-diving aircraft, and managed to don his parachute pack, the corner of which was already beginning to burn. Lucky not to be hit by bullets pouring into the fuselage from a night-fighter that had latched on to the stricken bomber, Leslie made it to the nose escape hatch. Due to the angle of descent and pressure forcing him in all the wrong directions he had great difficulty in jumping out head first. Then alarmingly his legs were trapped by the hatch door as it closed, and his head was repeatedly slammed against the fuselage. But luck stayed with him, and he managed to wriggle free of his old-type flying boots, which were left in the hatch, and open his parachute.

He and four others evaded, but both gunners were taken prisoner.

The Normandy landings were the signal for the French Forces of the Interior (FFI) to take the offensive and smight the enemy wherever he might be found. It was with the scent of victory in the air, therefore, that one of the FFI units near Moncontour (Côtes-d'Armor) in Brittany, took Warrant Officer R. Ossendorf, Czech Air Force, under their wing. Shot down by flak near le Havre in his Spitfire on 21 May 1944, Ossendorf had obeyed instructions to stay put, and was quite content to sit it out until such time as he might be liberated.

The Frenchmen, however, took offence at his inactivity, especially as they themselves were engaged in various highly dangerous activities. They therefore suggested that he might like to assist them in their struggle against the Germans. As Ossendorf felt that they had looked after him well, he took the hint and with one of the FFI, Jean, obtained permission from the chief of the FFI in that region, Commandant Pierre, 'to do an unspecified job of sabotage. I obtained a pistol and two hand-grenades. Jean had a Sten gun.'[1659] Thus equipped, he and Jean set off on the evening of 24 June down the road to Collinée, Jean with his Sten gun slung by its strap over his shoulder, but under his coat.

At about 8.30 p.m. they bumped into a squad of six or eight German soldiers 'who were gathered round a field telephone, or wireless apparatus, close to the roadside'. An NCO demanded to see their non-existent papers. Appreciating that it was the Germans' practice in such a situation to search people whom they had stopped Ossendorf, hands in pockets and gripping his pistol, said that he would return with them in ten minutes as they had forgotten to bring them. The NCO, already suspicious, opened Jean's coat, and saw the Sten gun. 'O la la' exclaimed the German, putting his hands in the air. A second German, standing two or three metres away, tried to get his handgun out of its holster, but he was too slow. Ossendorf shot him in the stomach, and then shot the NCO in the chest.

Jean, who could do nothing because his Sten gun was still trapped under his coat, ran off, but Ossendorf had noticed a third German leaving the group, 'and I fired three shots at him at a range of about fifteen or twenty metres, but I did not see him fall. I then began to run in the same direction as Jean had gone, and I jumped into some bushes just off the road.' He was still close enough to throw one of his hand-grenades at the Germans, but it failed to explode. The rest of the Germans were by this time firing at him with rifles and machine-guns, and a bullet hit him in the right hip. Deeming it wise to withdraw, Ossendorf ran off as fast as he could, using the available cover. A few minutes later he chanced upon Jean, and the two of them hid in a field until it was dark.

When they came to leave the field Ossendorf found that his wounded leg was numb and saw that his trousers were saturated with blood. Feeling very weak and giddy, he tried to walk, but so great was the pain that he fainted. Jean carried him towards a nearby farmhouse. Regaining his senses early in the morning of 25 June, Ossendorf felt strong enough to walk to Montcontour, where his wound was dressed. Later that morning he walked eight kilometres 'to an uninhabited district, where I stayed in the bushes for four days. The patriots supplied me with food all this time.'[1660] He was then taken to a château near Pommeret, to the north, where he had an operation to remove the bullet from his hip.

A day or two later Commandant Pierre put in an appearance, proudly announcing that he, Ossendorf, was to be awarded a medal, as he was the first foreigner to fight with the FFI in his area. On his return to England Ossendorf was, ordered Commandant Pierre, to report the full details of the fight to the French authorities in London and a medal would then be given to him.

Ossendorf did not report to the French in London, only to his MI9 interviewer on 31 July, eighteen days after he had made his first report on his safe return to Allied lines.

For the crew of Lancaster NE134 the trip out to Germany on the night of 22/23 May 1944 was routine, until Pilot D.C.H. Maxwell turned for home at a height of well over 20,000 feet. Suddenly, the aircraft was coned by thirty or forty searchlights. Maxwell did what he could to shake them off by taking violent evasive action, but after being held in the fierce glare for some three minutes the Lancaster was down to around 12,000 feet. Now within range of light flak, a burst hit the port-inner engine. The flight engineer, Flight Sergeant P.J. Hyland, was ordered to feather it, and pressed the Graviner fire extinguisher. By now, though, the port wing was well alight and, anticipating the inevitable, the crew put on their parachutes. Maxwell, who was otherwise occupied in holding the aircraft straight and level, had to be helped with his by Hyland. Three minutes later, with dense smoke pouring through the fuselage, Maxwell ordered the crew to jump. The bomb aimer went out first, followed by Hyland, who pulled his ripcord after counting to six. The Lancaster, which had been heading north-west, crashed on German soil a few kilometres west of the Rhine, killing both pilot and rear gunner.

Hyland was the only one of the five survivors to evade capture. Floating down, he saw that the 'sky was lit by a great fire, which I presumed was the target burning. After dropping through cloud I saw on the south a bend in the Rhine, so I blew up my mae west. In actual fact I landed easily on soft ground two fields west of the river… My hands were numb and swollen but a few minutes later I obeyed my briefing orders and buried my chute, harness and mae west and helmet complete in a hole at the edge of the field.'[1661] Clearly well versed in evasion techniques, Hyland made his way 'towards Emmerich and Anholt an area which we had been told at briefing was suitable for crossing the Dutch border.' This area lay to the north-west and, with the starry Plough to guide him, he set off, having first cut off his 'badges and the tops of my flying boots'.

Avoiding all houses wherever possible he made steady progress, laying up by day and travelling by night. On 24 May, however, he had a close shave when three German soldiers who were searching the area failed to find him. That night he saw Luftwaffe night-fighters taking off to deal with the bombers passing overhead (probably on their way to Aachen). The following night he had reached the Rhine near Emmerich, still in Germany, where he 'got caught up in barbed wire and electrified wire. This wire is easily seen as it is white compared to the ordinary barbed wire which is rusty and brown. I was lucky in that I was moving during a moon period.' Though it had rained during the night of 26/27 May, he was washing himself in the Rhine in the morning when a number of civilians saw him, but took no notice of him.

By now Hyland must have been to the north of Kleve, for he soon came to the Alter Rhine, which flows into the Rhine itself a few kilometres further on. Beyond it, though, lay Holland, and he set off in daylight 'in order to find a means of crossing the Alter Rhine'. Luckily, he found a boat and was making his way across when he was seen by a girl. She called out to him, but too late, for he was already on the other side. With night having fallen he continued 'over soft sandy soil and a countryside which was riddled with small dykes, through which I had to wade.' When dawn came on 28 May he realised that he had no idea where he was: 'I remember seeing a large bridge W.S.W. and now realise it was the one at Nijmegen.'[1662]

He turned south to avoid the town but, though there were many people about, they also took no notice of him. It was a very hot day, and he had taken off his white aircrew sweater when he reached a small bridge on which three or four men were standing. One of them tapped him on the shoulder and, pointing in the direction in which Hyland was going, shook his finger. Despite the language barrier and with the help of his phrase card Hyland was able to understand that he was no longer in Germany but in The Netherlands. The man told him to get on the back of his bicycle, and thus was he transported to the small village of Ooij to the north-east of Nijmegen.

From this point on Hyland's journey was arranged for him.[1663]

CHAPTER 12

Operation Marathon: 1944

'Do any of you bastards speak English?'
US Army motorcycle outrider, Fréteval Forest, August 1944

As early as the autumn of 1943 Airey Neave and his colleagues in Room 900, though not privy to its finer details, had been given the task of 'planning underground escape operations before and after the landing [in Normandy] had taken place.'[1664] The concern was for the safety of any Allied personnel, particularly shot-down airmen, who would almost certainly be trapped behind German lines once the "big show" had started. If it were too dangerous for evaders and escapers to attempt to break through a battle line or 'impossible to get them over a neutral frontier', Neave reasoned, then 'the safest plan was to evacuate the men, especially from Paris and Brussels, and hide them as far away as possible from German troop concentrations.'[1665] With 'the help therefore of the Belgian Sûreté and the BCRA, I secured a magnificent group of agents to organise concentrations of airmen away from the battle zone. The whole scheme, known as Operation Marathon, covered Holland, Belgium and France.'[1666]

Marathon camps were to have been established in three areas – two in France, near Rennes (Ille-et-Vilaine, Brittany) and near Châteaudun (Eure-et-Loir), and the third in Belgium in the vast Ardennes forest – but when he had crossed to France in August 1944 Neave found that at 'Rennes, to my mortification, the camp of evaders had already dispersed.'[1667] It had been the intention that those evaders who had not been taken off on Shelburne operations (see Chapter 8) should be gathered at the Rennes camp, but they had mostly been delivered to the south by networks such as Burgundy. All the energy in the French part of Marathon, therefore, was concentrated on what Neave would call Sherwood, the camp in the woods near Châteaudun.

Having 'spent much time pondering how large groups of men could be sheltered and supplied by air', Neave sent Baron Jean de Blommaert de Soye ("Rutland") and a fellow Belgian, Albert Ancia ("Daniel Mouton"), to France to prepare the groundwork for Marathon. The operation got off to a shaky start on the night of 9/10 April 1944 when, dropped into France, Jean de Blommaert's parachute caught in overhead power lines and had to be abandoned for all the world to see. Nevertheless, he and Ancia reached Paris safely, together with the two million francs for Comet's use entrusted to them by Airey Neave. On arrival in Paris they were chastened to learn that the only part of the Comet line that had not been seriously affected by German security forces was the southern section run by Elvire De Greef ("Tante Go"). The section from Brussels to Paris had been seriously disrupted, mainly due to Prosper Dezitter ("l'homme au doigt coupé") and Jean-Jacques Desoubrie, two men who, between them, betrayed hundreds of their own countrymen and scores of evading airmen.

It was Lili Dumon, though, who recognised a man she knew as Pierre Boulain at a rendezvous in Paris on 24 February 1944. Lili was there with a friend, Martine Noel, who provided safe houses for evaders in Paris, and noticed Boulain's polka-dot tie. Something rang a bell, and she realised that such a tie spelt danger, though she could not put her finger on why. Weeks later, after her delayed return from Spain, Lili went to Paris, and tried to contact Martine by telephone. When an unknown voice answered, Lili knew that Martine had been caught.

After going to Bayonne to think things over Lili went to Fresnes prison on 13 March 1944 to try to discover what had happened to her friend. Although she was herself imprisoned for a few days, Lili managed to make contact with Martine, who told her that she had been betrayed by Pierre Boulain. Now Lili understood why she had been concerned about that polka-dot tie – it was a Gestapo trade-mark, and the man whom she had met at the rendezvous in Paris she had known before as Jean Masson. Boulain and Masson were one and the same – Desoubrie.

She managed to meet up with de Blommaert and Ancia, and gave them the news about Desoubrie. The two were stunned by the accusation, after all Boulain/Masson had done great work for the organisation. They needed more proof before being convinced and on 7 May, as arranged, Ancia met with Desoubrie. Lili watched discreetly to make sure he was the right man, but as the two men left Desoubrie spotted Lili, and he knew that the game was up unless he got to her first. Lili managed to give him the slip by running into the Concorde Métro station, but she was now the hunted, and so made her way down to Bayonne again to see Tante Go, who advised her to lie low for a while. Crossing on her own to Spain on 11 May she was persuaded by Michael Creswell to stay in Madrid for the time being.[1668]

Back in Paris, Ancia and de Blommaert were now convinced, following the incident at the Place de la Concorde, that Desoubrie was indeed a traitor and a great danger to Comet. They decided that he should be eliminated, and asked for a member of the FFI to bump him off. They met Desoubrie in Paris on 16 May 1944, and he 'offered to turn double agent. Ancia, accompanied by a Free French "executioner", asked him to take 500,000 francs to Comet in Brussels, the money to be handed over next day.'[1669] The Free French received permission for Desoubrie to be liquidated by their special assassination squad, and on 22 May this was apparently done. Unfortunately, a week later Desoubrie was seen alive. The wrong man – whoever he was – had been liquidated.

Before this dismal event had taken place, however, Ancia and de Blommaert had already parted, Jean de Blommaert heading off to the Châteaudun area, Ancia to the Belgian Ardennes to organise Marathon evaders there. De Blommaert was on his way to meet another Belgian, Squadron Leader Lucien Boussa DFC ("Belgrave"), whom Airey Neave had also sent into the field to help set up Sherwood. Because of a dislike of parachuting Squadron Leader Boussa and his wireless operator, François Toussaint ("Taylor"), were put ashore on 24 April 1944 near Huelva, to the west of Seville on the southern coast of Spain. From Madrid, where the British Embassy supplied them with money and false papers, Boussa and Toussaint made their way to San Sebastián, arriving on 7 May. Crossing the Pyrenees into France with the help of two Spanish guides, they were in St Jean-de-Luz by the morning of 8 May, and stayed with Elvire De Greef and family.

Leaving their radio set behind, they got to Paris on 13 May, and made contact with Maurice Clavel ("Sinclair"), commander of the FFI in Eure-et-Loir. Clavel, accompanied by Sylvia Montfort, went to Paris to fetch Boussa and Toussaint, bringing them back to Châteaudun station on 18 May. Thanks to the bombing of the railway line in preparation for the Normandy landings, though, the train was over three hours late but, in the early afternoon, the reception committee of Omer Jubault,[1670] Maurice Serein, Lucien Bezault and Roger Poupard escorted Boussa and Toussaint by bicycle to the home of M. and Mme. Hallouin.

Gamekeeper to the Marquis de Levis de Mirepoix, Monsieur Hallouin and his wife lived in an isolated lodge at Bellande on the western edge of the Bois du Verger, a couple of hundred metres from Fréteval Forest, and three or four kilometres south-west of the small town of Cloyes-sur-le-Loir, itself a dozen kilometres south of Châteaudun.[1671] Ideally situated in the woods, Boussa decided to make it his headquarters. In the interests of security, though, Omer Jubault took Toussaint, still without radio equipment, to Doctor Chaveau's house at Moulineuf, near Romilly-sur-Aigre, some ten kilometres to the east. Communications between the two places were maintained by Jubault's wife and by their daughter Ginette, aged sixteen, and son Jean.

The days that followed were spent organising food supplies and lodging for the evaders and escapers who were, in accordance with instructions from England, already being filtered through to Paris. During the week after Boussa's arrival at Bellande, thirty-five Allied personnel had already been collected in Paris but, as food was generally in short supply in the capital, it was decided to move the extra mouths as soon as possible to lodgings in the Cloyes area. With the railway line from Paris operational for once, they were able to stay on the train all the way to Châteaudun. From there they were taken to a small grocery store run by M. and Mme. Coeuret, and then by one of many willing helpers along back roads to the Cloyes area.[1672]

Not long afterwards, however, the Paris–Châteaudun line was again bombed and so the journey from Paris for further evaders ended at Dourdan, fifty-five kilometres from Paris and still some seventy-five kilometres from Châteaudun. From Dourdan, it was a further forty-five kilometres to Monsieur Leroy's farm at Sazeray, from whence the evaders were collected by Gaston Duneau. Carrying various agricultural implements to make them look like farm workers, the men would be led in small groups across the fields to Duneau's home at Montboissier (Eure-et-Loir), still thirty kilometres shy of their destination. Pierre Dauphin and Marcel Huard then took the airmen on to the next refuge, M. Fougereux's house in the small village of Chênelong, another ten kilometres nearer the forest.

Of these first thirty-five airmen to reach the Cloyes area, five were placed with Pierre van Bever and Madame Tessier at le Rouilly, St Hilaire-sur-Yerre. Another five went to M. Doubouchage at le Rameau, and two to M. Chesneau at Chanteloup. Sergeants R.H. Banks RCAF and Gordon Hand stayed with René Jacques at the house at level crossing number 103 before moving to the camp on 9 June. Two more (one of them Sergeant R.H. Hortie RCAF) went to Mme. Jeanne Demoulière, whose husband was stationmaster at St Jean-Froidmentel (Hortie called it St Jean de la Forêt); a further nine to three homes in Corbonnière, near Morée; and another five to M. Fouchard at Bellande, near Lucien Boussa's HQ.

These last five had met on 3 June 1944 at an apartment in Paris before being taken to stay with Armand Guet near Cloyes. They were Sergeant Tom Yankus and Lieutenant Jonathan Pearson, both USAAF and from the same crew;[1673] Flight Sergeant D.R.R.J. "Denny" Pepall; Warrant Officer W.E.J. "Bill" Brayley RCAF; and Flight Lieutenant L.F. "Peter" Berry. Navigator "Bill" Brayley had been shot down on 10/11 April 1944. Homeward bound at around 12,000 feet and some thirty kilometres from the French coast he suddenly 'heard the sound of cannon shells and smelt cordite. I noticed a hole above my navigation table. I got on the intercom to the pilot. He answered in a strained voice "Get out. Get out". I folded up my table, threw off my helmet and tried to get up to the pilot when somebody pushed me back.'[1674] Quickly clipping on his parachute he jumped out after the bomb aimer and wireless operator. They were the only survivors.

With help from a farmer Bill Brayley made his way by train from Montdidier to Amiens, having been told to go to the store of Dufred Frères situated on the corner of the rue de Noyon and rue Robert de Luzarches, in the centre of the town. Waiting for the store to open Bill told the manager who he was. The manager replied that he was unable to help further as the store's owner was in prison for helping other Allied personnel but suggested that Brayley should contact a doctor in St Sauflieu, some fifteen kilometres south of Amiens, whom he thought could help. This Brayley did, and the doctor (apparently a Rumanian Jew) drove him to the house of Georges Haas, the local Peugeot agent. For the next few weeks he stayed in several houses until on 3 June he was taken by bicycle to the house of the town clerk of Clermont (Oise), who was also the local Resistance chief. Here he would meet Flight Sergeant D.R.R.J. Pepall.

Denny Pepall was rear gunner of a Stirling lost on the attack on Chambly (Oise) railway depot on 20/21 April 1944. Great secrecy surrounded the flight of the Stirling, for, in the words of Denny Pepall, this 'was the first time we had been on the new radio bombing and only the pilot and navigator knew the target. We flew on a straight beam, dropped our bombs and hit the target about midnight.'[1675] A few seconds later, there was a terrific explosion in the aircraft. In the absence of flak and fighters the crew concluded that their photoflash had exploded prematurely. Their immediate problem, though, was to do something about the fire now blazing from mid-upper to rear turret. The wireless operator and flight engineer did what they could, but the flames were too strong and, reluctantly, the pilot, Flight Lieutenant G. McG. Doolan RAAF, 'gave orders to blow up the secret equipment and to bale out… He was very calm and there was no panic.'[1676]

Pepall might have been tempted to panic when his turret doors failed to open but with the help of the mid-upper gunner, Sergeant C. Robinson (the only one of the five survivors to be taken prisoner), he wrenched them open and baled out through the fuselage door. After walking for two days Pepall got help from a Czechoslovakian couple at Belloy-en-France (Val d'Oise) but just as he was leaving them someone whistled at him. Putting his hand in his coat pocket, as if he had a gun, he turned to face the whistler. A smartly dressed Frenchman approached and asked: 'Parachutiste anglais?' Receiving an affirmative reply the Frenchman, André by name, took Pepall to a one-room flat in St Martin, gave him a change of clothes and said he would find someone who could speak English. He was back within the hour with another man, and Pepall was taken to a working farm, where he spent the next twelve days. On 5 May he was taken into Paris, and stayed with a French naval officer, Boubony, and his wife at 28, rue de Montmartre.[1677]

Boubony took him to see an English lady who 'looked after the English church in Paris', and 'she offered to contact another organisation, who worked with an Irishman and had got 170 escapers and evaders through Spain, if the one I was with failed.'[1678] Pepall's organisation, in fact Comet, did not let him down, and moved him from one place to another over the next few days until he was taken on 2 June to the town clerk at Clermont, where he was joined by Bill Brayley and, on 3 June, by Flight Lieutenant Berry.

Thirty-five-year-old Peter Berry was the rear gunner of a Lancaster shot down on its way to the target on the night of 31 May/1 June 1944. Berry had spotted their attacker, a Ju88, when they were some fifty kilometres north of Beauvais, and reported his sighting to the pilot, Flight Lieutenant F.R. Randall, 'who took our aircraft starboard quarter down. At 500 yards I gave the Ju a short burst and he closed in and went starboard beam up of us. Our rear guns could not bear on him and I told the pilot to corkscrew to starboard. The Ju passed underneath and appeared on our port beam up, flew level for a minute, attacked and passed underneath and appeared on our starboard beam up. He repeated these tactics and attacked us five times, and in spite of our evasive action I could not get the rear guns to bear on him and could not touch him.'[1679]

All this time the mid-upper guns remained silent, probably because the gunner, Flight Sergeant E.G. Small, had been killed during the first attack, which had also set the starboard-inner engine ablaze. Flight Lieutenant Randall remained calm to the last, and ordered the crew to bale out. Berry made his way into the fuselage (the 'aircraft was blazing furiously inside') and baled out via the Lancaster's rear door. Temporarily knocked out when his parachute opened, he saw in the clear moonlight 'the aircraft blazing on the ground about ten miles north. I looked round for other parachutes but could not see any.' He was told later 'by a Frenchman, who records the graves of English airmen and was present at the funeral, that my crew were buried together nearby and were recorded as five bodies'. Berry was sure, however, that all six had perished, and sadly this was proved to be correct.

It was with this recorder of graves that Berry found help. The man, name unknown, was apparently 'a lawyer and held a liaison position between the French and Germans relating to the proper funeral of Allied airmen.' The lawyer took Berry 'in a large black Citroen car to a house, where I stayed with the local schoolmaster'. The man reappeared on 3 June with his car: 'We went straight through Beauvais, and picked up an armed gendarme who sat in front. At Clermont the car stopped at a house where the local Resistance chief lived.' Bill Brayley and Denny Pepall were brought out of the house and joined Peter Berry in the car.

In Montataire (Oise), transferred to a dairy van, they were joined by Madame Dorez, the owner of a dairy shop and of the van, and by her daughter. Still with the escorting gendarme sitting in front, they were driven to a butcher's shop in Chantilly. A woman guide took them to Chantilly station, gave them a ticket each, and went with them on the train to Paris. At the Gare du Nord they caught the metro, but it was their bad luck to be in a carriage full of German SS troops when the air raid siren went off, and an uncomfortable hour or more was spent in their midst pretending to be half asleep. Surviving that ordeal they changed trains twice more, eventually arriving at a florist's shop, where their guide from Chantilly left them.[1680] Yet another guide,[1681] Germaine Mellisson (alias "Anne" or "Annie" who, according to Berry, was aged about thirty-two and 'worked in the coupon office in Paris'), led them to an apartment on the first floor of a large block of flats ten minutes' walk away, at 1 bis, rue Vaneau. Here they were introduced to Paul and Virginia le Blanc, and were to meet Tom Yankus and Jonathan Pearson, who had been brought to the apartment from Senlis by a man known to them as "Petit Pierre" (Conrad Lafleur?).

Paul and Virginia le Blanc were otherwise Philippe d'Albert-Lake and his American-born wife Virginia.[1682] As well as having the use of the Paris apartment,[1683] Philippe and Virginia had a house at Nesles-la-Vallée (Val d'Oise), some thirty-five kilometres north-west of Paris, and it was there that they had been introduced to the dangerous world of evasion. The local baker, Marcel Renaud, knowing that they spoke English, asked them to "screen" three USAAF airmen who were hiding in his bakery – 2nd Lieutenant Robert Stoner, co-pilot; 2nd Lieutenant Wilbert K. Yee, bombardier; and Sergeant Bruno Edman, top turret gunner.[1684] The airmen were taken south from Paris after several weeks, but at Pau station the Gestapo boarded the train and, when their papers were found not to be in order, they were arrested.[1685] After three days' interrogation at Biarritz they were handcuffed and, with five other prisoners and twelve guards, taken to Fresnes prison, and from there removed to Germany for the duration.

The chance for Philippe and Virginia to do something more came late in December 1943, when Philippe's cousin, Michel de Gourlet, asked him if he would be prepared to meet a certain Jean Leduque. Philippe agreed, and a meeting at rue Vaneau was duly arranged. Jean Leduque proved to be Jean de Blommaert, who had returned to France on 20 December to work with Commandant Potier and his "Possum" line (see Chapter 9). De Blommaert asked Philippe to carry on Comet's work in Paris, adding that he would be contacted by a certain Lili du Chaila, then living at 36, rue d'Artois, Paris, who had had to leave Brussels with the Gestapo hot on her trail.

A few days after de Blommaert had gone back to England, Philippe was indeed contacted by Lili, otherwise Micheline Dumon ('Michou'), who explained that, following numerous arrests, she was the only one remaining who knew Comet helpers in both Paris and Brussels. With other Paris Comet workers "Max" and "Daniel" temporarily in London, she asked Philippe to take care of Comet's Paris link until they returned. He agreed to do so, but when Jean de Blommaert, Max and Daniel were back in Paris by April 1944, Philippe continued to work for Comet as de Blommaert's deputy.[1686]

This was, therefore, the position when, the day after Berry, Pepall, Brayley and the two Americans had been gathered in his flat, Philippe told them that the line to Spain was broken. Berry, with his knowledge of machine guns, suggested joining a sabotage group somewhere, but Philippe replied that they would get enough excitement before too long. The two Americans then went off, on 4 June, with Virginia to another apartment, while the other three went to Germaine's flat at 8, Rue de Monttessuy, near the Eiffel Tower.

On 5 June, early in the morning, Germaine took them to the Gare d'Austerlitz to catch the train to Châteaudun. They had gone only as far as Choisy-le-Roi, still in the Paris suburbs, when the train came to a halt. The line had been bombed, and all passengers were ordered off the train. They then had to walk to Juvisy-sur-Orge along the line near the River Seine for some fourteen kilometres. 'At Juvisy we boarded a train and there met the two American airmen guided by Anne-Marie. We all travelled together to Châteaudun.'[1687] It was early afternoon when they arrived, but it was some while before Germaine finally found their guide, Omer Jubault, who cycled 'ahead and then stopped to pump his tyre so we could catch up.' It was a long walk for the men, particularly for Peter Berry, whose feet were hurting so much that he had had to remove his shoes and walk in his stockinged feet. By the time that they had covered the twenty or thirty kilometres to their destination, a farm near Cloyes, their feet were covered in blisters: 'From there we were taken by Gilbert to a farm belonging to M. Guet', and stayed until 10 June.

Boussa and de Blommaert had already been discussing with Omer Jubault and M. Hallouin the possibilities of setting up the camp for the evaders and escapers at a spot some 800 metres from Hallouin's lodge at Bellande, in the Forêt de Fréteval. Hallouin and his wife[1688] already had in their grounds two tents supplied by de Blommaert, in which Americans Sergeant Marion Knight, Staff Sergeant Donald F. Hoilman, Technical Sergeant George Solomon, and "Lucky" were living.[1689]

Peter Berry learnt that a camp was being formed in the district for escapers and evaders when news of the invasion on 6 June was brought to M. Guet's house by Jean de Blommaert, who told Berry that he 'was to be camp commander in charge of the internal working of the camp. He and Lucien would be our outside contact; they would organise and supply the food for the camp, and bring in the Es. and Es. to hand over to me inside the camp.'[1690] Returning on 7 June with a pair of shoes for Berry, de Blommaert took him to the site of the proposed camp. Berry slept there alone until the four American sergeants from the Hallouins' tents, and Pepall and Brayley moved in on 10 June.

De Blommaert, Boussa and Philippe d'Albert-Lake 'provided tents, food, blankets, pots and pans etc. to start with as required. A communal site was selected for men to sit and rest. This was called "Piccadilly Circus". The kitchen site was nearby, the entrance to which was called "Haymarket". The kitchen was built of corrugated iron to kill and spread smoke and protect the sight of fire.' Sawn logs were used for fires until such time as charcoal, smokeless and with no smell, had been made by Henri Lefevre of l'Estriverds, and brought to the camp (Camp No. 1) by his wife. Sergeant Tom Yankus USAAF, became chief cook 'as he had been connected with restaurants'. Technical Sergeant Joseph I. Gorrano USAAF[1691] was second cook, and Marion Knight, formerly a cattle rancher, was appointed butcher and slaughterer. He 'also used to go out and kill a sheep, or pigs or rabbits and then cut them up – by arrangement with both "Boulanger" and Hallouin, who also supplied milk, butter and eggs.'[1692] To vary the diet, night-time fishing trips to the River Loir were later organised by André Saillard and Eugene Legeay.

Water was collected from a spring in a nearby paddock, well hidden from prying eyes. Food for the men was provided from far and wide by farmers, meat merchants, bakers and others. Bread made by Théophile Trecul at Fontaine-Raoul, four kilometres away, was brought to the camp by young Micheleine Fouchard on her horse and cart. Brave girl, she was once strafed by Allied aircraft as she went about her business. To pay for all the goods when the camp opened Boussa had been given five million francs, and it was estimated that each week he was paying out some 20,000 to 24,000 francs.

Soon after 10 June all the Allied personnel who were being sheltered in the Cloyes area had been brought to the Bellande camp. Berry noted that as more men arrived Armand Guet 'gave us a truck cover and Belgian Army ground sheets and capes for further tents, the ends of which were made of sacks. We also obtained some tarpaulin covers, lorry sheets and finally had ten tents in all, three of which held sixteen men apiece.'[1693] When Sergeant C.F. Weir arrived he noted that 'there was some sort of shelter formed by draping a tarpaulin sheet over two or three strong crosspoles affixed to suitable trees. The sides had been pegged to the floor so I supposed it could be rightly called a tent.'

Conditions were basic, if not primitive. Latrines were dug, but were no more than ten-foot long holes with a bench made out of a tree trunk on which the men sat to go about their business. At first, each man was given a blanket and two sacks for his bedding, and a knife, fork, spoon and cup for his meals. Later, when numbers had risen dramatically, new arrivals had the choice of either one blanket or two sacks, and the cutlery was 'pooled to prevent confusion in washing up'. Three men were detailed each day for kitchen fatigues, and this was apparently known as "Their Day" when, as a reward for their labours, 'they could cook [for] themselves and eat whatever they wished during that day.' According to Peter Berry, it 'was also understood in the camp that any man who felt genuinely hungry could ask for a meal at any time apart from regular meal times.'[1695]

Boussa always interrogated new arrivals outside the camp. Once cleared, they would be permitted to enter it and be taken to Flight Lieutenant Berry, the senior Allied officer. If Boussa were not available, vetting duties fell to Berry, who usually took Pilot Officer J.L.J. Croquet[1696] with him as interpreter. To guard the camp, six sentries were posted at three points around it, on four-hour shifts, twenty-four hours a day. The sentries were in pairs, one to keep watching and the other to act as a runner should anything suspicious be seen. The runner would report the incident to Flight Lieutenant Berry, who would immediately investigate.

For everyone except Peter Berry, the senior officer, 'all rank and seniority was washed out' and, in what was intended to be a democracy, all men 'had the same food, duties and fatigues and were controlled by the same laws. Every man was informed on entering camp what this law was, and his rights and privileges.' Any transgressions 'were enforced by such punishments as stoppage of cigarettes or camp fatigues'. Every man, however, had the right to 'call a camp meeting on any point whatever. This was known as a "Bitch Session". He could state his case, complaint or criticism without future prejudice whether it was against an officer or not,'[1697] including the senior officer. A vote would be held at the end of the session on whether or not to make a new camp order, though Peter Berry retained the right to refuse to sanction a new order if, in his opinion, it would have been prejudicial to the wellbeing or safety of the camp as a whole.

Though there was a small German garrison at Cloyes, a few kilometres away, there was no trouble from the Germans by and large, and the view was taken that for everyone's safety no resistance should be offered were the Germans to attack the camp. Just in case, there was one revolver, buried, inside the confines of the camp, with five more and a Sten Gun outside it in the hands of Squadron Leader Boussa. One night, however, about a week after Berry's arrival at the camp, a small party which included airmen and members of the French Resistance raided a German arms dump seven kilometres away in the forest. It was 'guarded by thirteen elderly Germans, the only ones in the neighbourhood', who failed to stop the seizure of forty-eight British hand grenades (five-second fuse). Before any further raids could be mounted, 'the Germans moved and took all the dump with them.'[1698]

Also in the camp with all the airmen were two South Africans, Privates Ebrihem Adams and Rudolph Hoover, escaped prisoners of war. Flight Lieutenant Berry thought highly of Adams: 'His morale, spirit and discipline were very fine the whole time. He never complained, and would immediately stop anyone else he heard complaining. He showed up many white men by his cheerfulness and fine example.'[1699] Sergeant Cliff Hallett, who shared a tent with Adams and Hoover and others, remembers that Adams was a superb tracker, whose talents in that field were to prove of great value one night when a number of Germans, on their way to the Normandy front, spent a night laagered about 400 metres from the camp. 'We could hear them singing and talking, and we kept special guard, but they did not find us.'[1700] It was Adams who located the Germans and reported back with the details. Orders were immediately given that no fires were to be lit and that everyone was to remain absolutely silent.

Adams and Hoover had come a long, long way to be in hiding in a forest in the middle of France, and were there, certainly in Adams's case, due to some luck. Twenty-five-year-old Adams had been attached to 1st Field Company, SAEC, South African Malay Corps, and was captured at Sidi Rezegh in the desert when German tanks broke through on 23 November 1941. A month or so later he and other prisoners of war were on their way to Italy by ship when it was torpedoed near the Greek coast. The Italian master and most of his officers immediately abandoned ship, being 'fired upon by a German officer who took charge and beached the ship. There were heavy casualties caused by the explosion of the torpedo and later when prisoners of war attempted to swim ashore and were drowned.'[1701] Adams was one of the survivors to arrive at a camp at Tuturano in January 1942. He survived the bombing of the airfield at San Pancrazio in July 1943 when one prisoner of war was killed and nine others wounded. In August 1943 he was sent back to Tuturano, where he met Private Rudolph Hoover, 101 South African Reserve Motor Transport, South African Indian Malay Corps.

Hoover, then aged twenty-one, had been captured at Mersa Matruh in the desert on 28 June 1942 helping to evacuate troops from the battle at Halfaya Pass ("Hellfire Pass" to those who were there). As with Adams, he was caught when Afrika Korps tanks rumbled into the town. He was quickly put to work on the Mersa docks off-loading fuel and ammunition, and survived an RAF bombing raid. Five days later, suffering with dysentery, he was moved away, receiving treatment from captured medical staff.

The NCO in charge of the Italian camp for non-Europeans in Benghazi in which Hoover was then held was a certain Sergeant-Major Gibson of the British Army. This NCO's 'treatment was very harsh and he forced the men to work, withholding their rations if they did not do so… He appeared to be on friendly terms with the Italians and was free to go outside the wire.'[1702] Furthermore, when two non-Europeans were shot at and wounded in the camp after they had refused to go to work Gibson took no action. A formal complaint was made against him to a South African medical officer.

Hoover was shipped from the Benghazi camp to Naples, Italy in November 1942, and was eventually transferred to Tuturano on 15 August 1943. A week later the whole camp was moved to Lucca, but he, Adams and the others had to march over 100 kilometres owing to bomb damage to the railways. A fortnight later the Anglo-Italian armistice came into effect, but this was one of the camps where the Italian guards remained at their posts. On 11 September 'three truck loads of German troops took over the camp, shot the Italian commandant and imprisoned the Italian guards.' Most of the over 1,800 black prisoners of war at Lucca were then transported to a stalag at Jacobsthal,

Germany, a transit camp for Soviet prisoners of war. Adams and Hoover were there for a fortnight before they were moved to Orléans, France, and then on to Beauvais.

The camp there was simply a disused factory in the centre of the town, and the 350 non-European prisoners of war were put to work 'on repairing bomb-holes at the Tille aerodrome and construction of gun-pits for A.A. guns on the aerodromes and near the town of Beauvais itself.' After many months there, the German commandant, Oberfeldwebel Visser, informed the men on 5 May 1944 that in four days' time the whole camp was to be moved to Germany. Several managed to escape at once, causing the guard to be reinforced on 6 May. With only one entrance, the camp was surrounded by an eight-foot high wall surmounted by an electrified wire. All around the base of the wall were coils of barbed wire. Nevertheless, Adams and Hoover, and a man called Luiters, Cape Corps, decided to escape, and at around 10 p.m. on the night of 7 May 'they separately climbed up the barbed wire and crawling through under the electrified wire, jumped over the wall. A German sentry patrolling inside the grounds did not see them.'

Still wearing battledress they made their way to some woods. Hoover had 2,000 francs which he had managed to save, but had neither food nor maps nor papers. Leaving before dawn they by-passed Auneuil (Oise), and spent a further three days in woods beyond it. Luiters left on the second day to make his own way, and was re-captured. Adams and Hoover, though, were befriended by farmer Roger Lecomte, who gave them food and blankets and looked after them. On 26 May Roger gave them the address of his parents and train tickets for St Gratien (Val-d'Oise), on the north-western outskirts of Paris. Roger saw them off, and a few hours later Adams and Hoover arrived at St Gratien station, where his father was waiting to meet them and took them to his home at 5, Avenue des Belles Feuilles. On 4 June they were taken by truck to a house in Paris. Given fresh clothes they then went to a bicycle shop 'where they met a man called Phillip' [Philippe d'Albert-Lake], who took further details from them and then sent them to a flower shop in the city where they stayed for two days.'[1703] On 7 June they were on their way to the camp in Fréteval Forest.

As the safety of the camp was paramount the rule about not leaving it without permission was taken very seriously. Should one of the men have a strong desire to regain Allied lines the risk of his being captured and being made to talk by the Gestapo was considered too great, and everyone was warned that the local Resistance had instructions to shoot, dead if necessary, anyone who transgressed in this way. Anyone who survived a "break out" but was returned to camp would be reported to the appropriate authority for a court-martial once liberated. 'Only one man broke this rule for some weeks to go to a local farm, for which he was completely confined to camp for three weeks.' Up to the time that news of their immediate liberation had reached them only two men, both Americans, broke this order. George Solomon and 2nd Lieutenant Abraham Wiseman stole the camp's bicycle and one belonging to Monsieur Hallouin to make their getaway. Peter Berry 'never heard of them again'.[1704]

Sergeant N.J. McCarthy reported that there was a feeling among some of the men 'that the order they must NOT leave camp to reach our lines, even if they wanted to, was contrary to evasion training which teaches an evader he should leave any organisation and reach our lines on his own if he feels the organisation is not doing sufficient for him in respect of getting home.'[1705]

The numbers of Allied personnel being brought to the Bellande camp continued to increase rapidly throughout June, and sleeping space within the tents had become much restricted. On 15 June, therefore, it was decided to adopt the name *Escadrille Soixante-Neuf*, the sexual connotation being quite deliberate. It was clear, however, that the over-crowding was becoming untenable – over seventy men, in twenty-five tents – and following consultation between Boussa, de Blommaert and Philippe d'Albert-Lake the decision was made to open a second camp. It was Omer Jubault, with his local knowledge, who suggested siting it at Richeray, three kilometres north of Busloup, on the southern edge of Fréteval forest and seven kilometres from Bellande. Jubault knew it well, for it was a place that he had previously chosen for his own headquarters. Near a stream running into a small lake[1706] and a forester's lodge it was satisfactory for their purposes.

Camp No. 2 (Richeray) was opened on 25 June. First Lieutenant Geno Dibetta USAAF,[1707] who had been Berry's second-in-command at the Bellande camp (which now became Camp No. 1), was appointed senior officer, and he and ten fellow "Americans" were the first to occupy it. Taking charge of the new camp was Jean de Blommaert, who organised outside supplies. One of those transferring on 25 June was Bill Brayley, who 'found that morale was far better in No. 2 Camp than in No. 1 … The commander of No. 2 Camp was … very popular and put up a good show.' Brayley also reported that 'they were visited by two local civilians M. Rideau, game warden, and René, who lived in Busloup. They were the only civilians in the area to come into the camp and who knew who we were. They worked extremely hard for us. With "Gilbert" they were responsible for all our food supplies.

On approximately 15 July a M. Louis René Desforges (?) came to give a hand to Jean for the running of the camp.'[1708]

Another Canadian to go to Camp No. 2, on about 28 June, was Flight Sergeant D.B. Hyde RCAF. Shot down on the night of 15/16 March 1944, he landed safely near Formerie, 35 kilometres north-west of Beauvais in northern France. Having bombed the target his Lancaster was on its way home when flak holed the port fuel tanks: 'The outer tank emptied in three minutes and the gauges failed on port tanks. The motors were OK so we set course for Base. The second port tank ran out, and within twenty-five miles of Paris we knew we could not reach England.'[1709] By 19 March he was in the hands of "an organisation", and by the first week of April he was at Pontoise, a few kilometres to the north-west of Paris, where he met Flying Officer R.B. Gordon, 2nd Lieutenant Theodore J. "Ted" Krol USAAF, 'and seven others'.[1710]

Gordon was the navigator/observer of a Mosquito that came to grief in a most unfortunate manner. On the morning of 8 February 1944 his pilot, Flying Officer W.F. Bender RCAF, put the aircraft into a shallow dive to drop their bombs on the Noball target (V1 launch site) north of Tôtes (Seine-Maritime), France: 'At the bottom of the dive, the bombs of our own or preceding aircraft exploded beneath us and lifted our aircraft, and destroyed the starboard wing outboard of the motor. Both motors were hit but the port one was feathered and a crash landing was made on the starboard motor, which had actually caught fire.' Bender performed a minor miracle as he steered the doomed Mosquito 'under some telegraph wires and the landing was actually made uphill at 180 m.p.h.'[1711]

As there was 'imminent danger of the remnants of the aircraft exploding', the two Canadians, more or less unharmed, fled at an understandably high rate of knots into the countryside. Early on the morning of 9 February they were just about to enter a farmhouse when they heard German voices. Again running off, they 'walked straight into a German soldier holding a horse. After staring at each other for a few moments he moved off with the horse.' They had no further alarms at the next farm they tried. There they met 2nd Lieutenant Alfred Louis Wickman USAAF[1712] and, at another house, fellow American Lincoln Teitel. Leaving Teitel and Bender behind (though Bender was to be re-united with his navigator two days later), Gordon and Wickman continued their journey, meeting David Hyde at Pontoise on 5 April, and eventually falling into the hands of Philippe and Virginia d'Albert-Lake.

On 10 June, Philippe told the assembled company that, as the route to Spain was no longer open, they could choose either to remain in Paris or go to a camp near Châteaudun 'to await the arrival of the Allies. We chose the latter course and at 0600 hours on 10 June we left by train for Dourdan.'[1713] In the party of ten, escorted by Michelle, Anne-Marie and "Annie" (Germaine Mellisson) were four members of the RCAF (Bender, Gordon, Hyde, and Flying Officer S.D. Taylor), three of the USAAF (Blair, Johnson, Krol), Sergeant E.W. Wright RAF, and the two 'coloured troops', Ebrehim Adams and Rudolph Hoover. Wickman had left Paris by bicycle with Philippe and Virginia to rendezvous with the larger party later that day.

The ten airmen and their three guides left the train at Dourdan, and headed off for the planned rendezvous in the forest of Ouye, some fifty or sixty kilometres from the centre of Paris. It was only a short walk from Dourdan station to the forest, and the two groups met successfully at around 4 p.m. that afternoon. All then walked to Denonville (twenty kilometres or so), and spent the night in a barn, with the farmer's permission. Next morning, 11 June, the party split up.

Bender, Gordon and Annie went off on their own, their destination being the village of Villentière, a few kilometres east of Châteaudun, but some seventy kilometres away. Proving too great a distance to cover in a day they spent the night in the open, and arrived at the village at around 11 a.m. on 12 June. They stayed with Madame Leroux until the next day when they hoped to hear from Philippe. Early on the afternoon of 13 June Bender and Gordon were taken by cart (the driver of which was a gymnastics instructor from Châteaudun) to another rendezvous near Villebout, on the northern edge of Fréteval Forest, and arrived at the Bellande camp (Camp No. 1) at around midnight.

All had not gone well, however, for others of the party. After the separation at Denonville on the morning of 11 June, Hyde, Taylor and the other four Americans went off with Virginia and Michelle, while Philippe took the two South Africans. At a farm near Civry-St Cloud (Eure-et-Loir) one of the airmen in Hyde's group, worn out, had to be left behind.

On 12 June, Hyde and the others were collected in a covered cart driven by Jean Meret, with Robert Poupard and Michelle sitting beside him. In the lead was Daniel Cogneau on a bicycle, with Virginia and Al Wickman riding on their bicycles in front of the cart, some fifty metres behind Daniel. A stranger, also on his bicycle, joined them from a side road. Then, at a junction in the road as the convoy neared le Plessis, five kilometres north of Châteaudun, a black car appeared, with three Feldgendarme in it. The car stopped, and an officer, the senior of the policemen, ordered Virginia, Al Wickman and the stranger to dismount. In perfect French he asked them for their identity papers. Virginia handed hers over to the officer, who, noting that she came from Paris, asked her what she was doing in the area. As soon as Virginia told him, untruthfully, that she was looking for fruit and eggs, he detected her pronounced American accent. That in itself would not have been a problem, as she explained that she was now French, married to a Frenchman, but after the stranger had been sent on his way the officer turned to Al, who was unable to speak French at all. The game was now well and truly up.

Realising that Virginia and Al were not the innocents they were pretending to be, the officer opened Virginia's bag: 'He saw the map, food tickets, an envelope with paper money, my fountain pen, compact, nail file, and the piece of note-book paper on which were written the addresses.'[1714] Having explained to the officer that she and her friend were trying to reach the Spanish border, and that this accounted for the 127,000 francs in the envelope and the pencil sketch of the route to the camp, the German, amazingly, handed the bag back to Virginia with all its contents. The map, with directions of how to get to the forest camp, should in itself have provoked further interest, as should the list of addresses of members of the local Resistance which Philippe had given her the previous day. With the officer's attention turned once again to Al, Virginia managed to put her hand into her bag and to extract a piece of paper, hopefully the list of addresses, and put it into her jacket pocket.

Once the officer had finished with Al, Virginia was ordered to get into the front of the car, between two of the Germans, while Al was ordered to sit in the back with the third, and so they were driven to the Feldgendarmerie offices in Châteaudun. Waiting to be interrogated by the Gestapo, Virginia managed to extract the incriminating piece of paper from her jacket pocket, tear it into small pieces and, with some difficulty, swallow all of the evidence except for one tiny scrap. When this was later found on the floor it dawned on the Germans that she had eaten the evidence.

That night she and Al Wickman were taken to Chartres prison, and on the following day to the rue des Saussaies, Paris, for further interrogation. While Wickman was sent to Stalag Luft I (Barth) prisoner-of-war camp, Virginia was removed to Fresnes prison, and thence to Romainville on 1 August. On 15 August, as the American forces closed in on Paris, the Germans began the final evacuation of their civilian and military prisoners, and Virginia and hundreds of other men and women were forced, eighty or more at a time, into the too few railway wagons. Most of the women, including Virginia, went to Ravensbrück concentration camp, after a nightmare journey that lasted twelve days. Surviving the horrors of this camp and also of Torgau and Königsberg, she was moved from Ravensbrück to the Red Cross camp at Liebenau on 28 February 1945, a journey of 650 kilometres that took six days. The camp was liberated by French forces on 21 April 1945, by which time Virginia weighed seventy-six pounds, fifty less than her normal weight.

Back at the chance meeting with the convoy of evaders on 12 June 1944 the Germans had not seen Daniel Cogneau rush off to raise the alarm, and were too busy arresting Virginia and Al Wickman to notice the airmen also rushing from the cart into a wheatfield near a farm and dispersing in all directions. Meret, Michelle and Poupard, however, in the now empty cart, were questioned but allowed to proceed. Maurice Serein, Lucien Bezault and Robert Poupard found two of the scattered airmen the same day, and a third was found by chance by M. Prieur in the market place at Bonneval, fifteen kilometres away to the north. The last two, one of whom was Flight Sergeant Hyde, were discovered at a nearby farmhouse, where the farmer told them that Virginia and Wickman had been arrested. They asked the farmer 'to contact the Resistance at Châteaudun, and slept in his barn that night. Next day these Frenchmen came over on bicycles and hid us in a bush. On 13 June a truck picked us up and drove us through Cloyes to Camp No. 1.'[1715]

The recovery of the airmen from the farm had not been immediate, however, for it was thought, erroneously as events were to prove, that the farmer and his wife were collaborators, and none dared approach the farmhouse for fear that it was being watched by the enemy. The postman, with legitimate business there, said that he would go. All was well, for the good people were not collaborators as feared, and once the five airmen had been gathered together at the home of Abel Meret, they were driven off in Lucien Thibault's car. Unfortunately, under the extra weight the springs yielded and Thibault had to go back to his garage for another vehicle, which successfully completed the journey to Bellande.

Another evader to reach Bellande at this time was bomb aimer Sergeant C.H.T. Martin. On the night of 18/19 April 1944, just two seconds after bombing the target at 7,000 feet, there was a blinding flash beneath Lancaster LM361.[1716] In no time two engines and both wings of the Lancaster were on fire and the aircraft filled with smoke: 'The pilot asked if we were all O.K. but the rear gunner did not answer. I checked all my bombs had gone, the engineer tried to feather the engines, but the pilot gave the order to prepare to abandon aircraft and I put on my parachute.'[1717] When the third engine caught fire and LM361 began losing height rapidly the pilot, Flying Officer J.A. Smith RAAF, ordered the crew to bale out quickly. Martin wasted no time opening the escape hatch, and jumped from 4,000 feet. Ten seconds later, before he had even landed on French soil, the Lancaster hit the ground: 'I doubt if they all got out.' He was right. Four of his crew perished, but Flying Officer Smith evaded capture, and the mid-upper gunner, Flying Officer K.W. Light RAAF DFM, was taken prisoner.[1718]

By 20 April Martin was in contact with the Resistance, and spent the next five and a half weeks at 29, Route de Longpont, Sainte Geneviève des Bois, on the southern outskirts of Paris and barely a handful of kilometres from the target at Juvisy. His host, Gaston le Boutet, worked in the pensions office for war wounded in Paris, and was chief of the local Resistance group. Though he claimed to have taken many people across into Unoccupied France, Martin was his first airman. Some time later Gaston told Martin that he had spoken to his chief in Paris and that an air passage back to England had been arranged for him on 20 May. The green light for the airlift was given when the BBC broadcast the message 'Raoul expédier son colis' ('Raoul is to send his parcel') but, on the day, the guide failed to arrive and Martin had to remain at Sainte Geneviève des Bois. The reason given, so Martin was later informed, was that the invasion was imminent.

On 29 May he was moved to Paris in the hands of patriotic policemen. On 10 June he was taken to a block of flats, and met Flying Officer Croquet and Flight Sergeant L.N. Clay, who had been shot down on 22/23 April. The following morning the three airmen were taken to the Gare d'Austerlitz, Paris, where two more American airmen, Flight Officer Stuart K. Barr and Staff Sergeant Robert E. Sidders, joined the party: 'We picked up two guides, Pierre and Robert, who told us that we were going to Châteaudun. We travelled by train to Dourdan and walked the rest of the way to the camp, where we arrived on 14 June.'[1719]

Berry was already having difficulty running the camp, and believed that he was not being helped by Lucien Boussa. Boussa, who did not live in the camp, 'was excellent in all he did for the camp on the outside' but was 'less successful when he interfered within the camp. He did not understand British mentality, and his excitable way upset the men.'[1720] Boussa was respected by the men for his efforts on their behalf, but when he told them that they would be liberated by 15 July, and days passed without their being liberated, his stock fell. Sergeant McCarthy thought that it would have been better had Boussa 'made his HQ in the camp and seen the conditions and requirements at first hand instead of delegating this to a camp commander, who was an evader.' He added that this 'resulted in a lack of understanding of the mental attitude of the men in the camp and resulted in a misunderstanding towards Lucien.'[1721] Flying Officer Greenburgh DFC, on the other hand, observed that 'the camp was run rather autocratically, and that Lucien was blamed unduly when anything did not go right.' Greenburgh also believed that 'Lucien had control of the camp and did a difficult and excellent job.'

Low morale was not improved when, after de Blommaert had organised a supply drop (the BBC message 'Don't wait on the stairs' alerting them that it would be 'on' for the following night), Flight Lieutenant Berry noted that the camp received 'one packet of twenty-four hour rations, 200 packets of cigarettes, razors but no blades, [and] delousing powder which was not necessary'. Following another drop, intended for the Resistance in the nearby area of St Hilaire-la-Gravelle (Loir-et-Cher), there was a scare when, on 22 July, Maxime Plateau, one of the main food suppliers to the camp, was arrested by the Germans. Revealing nothing under torture, he was sent to a concentration camp.[1722]

A few days earlier the evaders had made their own arrest when one of the sentries spotted a man strolling near Camp No. 1. Quickly brought into the camp, Berry discovered that he was 'a Russian Godfr Chichldse from Georgia'. Sergeant J.R.W. Worrall recalls that they called him "Cogi", for want of any other name, and gave him all the unpleasant and dirty jobs to do: 'However we dare not let him go as he might have been picked up by the Germans, or unfriendly French.'[1723] He was kept as a prisoner until he could be handed over after the liberation at Le Mans, 'where he was put into a civilian concentration camp'.[1724]

With so much traffic to and from the camp the possibility of detection by the Germans had long been appreciated, and Omer Jubault advised Lucien Boussa to move his HQ to St Jean-Froidmentel, some four or five kilometres to the east. Though to the east side of the Châteaudun-Vendôme main road, the camps being to the west, it was still uncomfortably close to the Château de Rougement which was occupied by the Germans and was itself barely a kilometre from St Jean-Froidmentel. Again for security reasons François Toussaint also moved, from Dr Chaveau's house to that of Robert Guérineau, a baker at Romilly-sur-Aigre. His daughter, Roberte, became the runner for messages between Toussaint and Boussa. Toussaint kept on the move, one of the other people to take him in being M. Dauvilliers, an electrician capable of repairing Toussaint's radio as and when required. According to Berry, however, all was not sweetness and light between Boussa and Toussaint. Messages from London, prefixed "Pour Lucien", were passed on by Toussaint to Boussa, and on to the camp, but they 'were few and far between as he [Boussa] had trouble with his wireless operator whom he distrusted. Unfortunately he [Boussa] told this to the camp which affected morale and caused uneasiness.'[1725]

It is unclear as to when precisely Toussaint received a new radio set, probably not until early July, for attempts to recover the set that he had left behind on arrival in the south-west of France appear to have been abandoned, and Philippe d'Albert-Lake, who had also been obliged to leave France on account of Gestapo interest, was asked by Jean de Blommaert to speak with Michael Creswell on his arrival in Spain to 'try to obtain an immediate parachute operation for the camp, sending them a radio set (they still remained without contact with London), cash and various supplies'.[1726] It took Philippe from 25 June to 1 July 1944 to get from Paris to Bordeaux, but he reached Spain without incident and did speak with Michael Creswell, who immediately requested the airdrop. Philippe was informed on his subsequent arrival in London that it had been successful.

New escapers and evaders were arriving all the time at the camps, some a little the worse for wear as a result of their experiences while being shot down. On 30 June 1944, for example, 2nd Lieutenant Warren E. "Bud" Loring was flying as wingman to Captain Robert L. Buttke, in their twin-boom, twin-engined P-38 Lightnings, when Loring's aircraft was hit by anti-aircraft fire over the airfield at Nevers, France. A fire started in the starboard engine which, together with the starboard wing and part of the tail-boom, fell off the aircraft. Loring received severe burns to his upper body, face and arms as he baled out. Picked up by French farmers he was brought to Fréteval Forest where, to his surprise, he met the man whom he had replaced as Captain Buttke's wingman, First Lieutenant Rex P. Hjelm, who had been shot down on 11 June.

Born in Brockton, Massachusetts, USA on 19 July 1923, Bud Loring "celebrated" his twenty-first birthday whilst on the run, and he may well have been one of the injured who were tended to by Doctor Teyssier and his son Louis, who regularly made visits to the camp from their practice in Cloyes. When the doctor was not there, patients, who were kept in separate "hospital" tents, were looked after by fellow evaders who had some idea of medical treatment, but it is believed that some of the worst cases were clandestinely removed to a proper hospital bed.

Following RAF Bomber Command's three raids on Stuttgart during the last week of July 1944, several more RAF aircrew arrived. All airmen who survived to evade were lucky to some degree or other. Sergeant John Sandulak RCAF, though, had more than his fair share of it, but would not have known how lucky he had been until after the war. He was manning the rear turret of a Lancaster on the first of the three Stuttgart raids, 24/25 July, when his Lancaster collided with another aircraft. The starboard engines of his Lancaster were wrecked, and the petrol tanks in the same wing burst into flames. The pilot, Flight Sergeant Cecil M. Corbet RCAF, decided that a bale-out was in order. With flames streaming past his turret, Sandulak needed no second bidding. Grabbing a parachute from its stowage in the fuselage and buckling it on, he was gone – too soon to hear the pilot say that there was a chance that the fire would go out and that he was cancelling the order to bale out.

As John Sandulak floated down, minus one flying boot, the crew of his Lancaster assessed the damage and reckoned that if they were to jettison the bomb load they could make it to the emergency landing strip at RAF Woodbridge, Suffolk, which, with its extra long and wide runway, gave lame ducks a chance of surviving a dicey landing without brakes.[1727] Corbet succeeded in flying his particular lame duck back to Woodbridge, and made a wheels-up landing with no harm to any of the crew. Meanwhile, a check had been made on the rear gunner. When he was found to be missing and his parachute was still aboard, the rest of his crew feared the worst.

For over a year they believed that Sandulak had perished, not realising that somehow an extra parachute had been placed in the aircraft. Their war, though, was far from done, for less than a month later Corbet, now a pilot officer, and his crew were shot down on 18/19 August. This time, all survived as prisoners of war, except for the replacement rear gunner, twenty-year-old Pilot Officer R.E. Good RCAF, who was killed in his turret. It was not until Corbet's original crew (minus the English flight engineer) had met up again in Canada in August 1945 that they heard of Sandulak's great fortune, which continued after he had been found on the ground: 'For a couple of days I stayed with a French family, wearing old clothes, and even hoeing sugar beets. Then the underground arrived. I was interrogated, cleared and taken to the Forest of Freteval.'

After he was shot down on the second Stuttgart raid, 25/26 July, Pilot Officer Harry Chamberlain stayed at the house of a road-mender near Villamblain, not far from where his Halifax had crashed – the 'house was on the flare path from Bessay aerodrome to Orléans' – before arriving at Bellande with six other evaders, two from his own crew – bomb aimer Flying Officer M.F.C. Grimsey RCAF, and navigator Flight Lieutenant H.J.S. Kemley (see Wing Commander MacDonald's story in the following chapter) – and four from a 514 Squadron crew shot down on the third Stuttgart raid, 28/29 July – Flight Lieutenant E.A. Campbell RCAF; Sergeant A.R. Lyons; Sergeant W.A. Donaldson; and Sergeant E.R. Jones RCAF. When he reached Camp No. 1 on 31 July Chamberlain noted that 'there were approximately sixty-eight other men there, some British 8th Army P/W's, British 1st Army, RAF – Belgian, RCAF, USAAF, and US Airborne personnel'.[1729] Four or five days later he and

Sergeant Lyons were told that they were moving to Camp No. 2, where they found 'about fifty people, mostly RAF and USAAF'.

Meanwhile, it had become only too clear that Flight Lieutenant Berry, suddenly thrust into the unenviable position of camp leader after his traumatic experience in the air, was not the right man for the job. His running of a camp full of boisterous and headstrong young airmen, all straining at the leash to get home, had not met with universal approval, as one of them was moved to report: 'He had little idea of organisation of such a camp or of handling the men, especially under those conditions.' This same person thought that Berry was too lax, particularly in enforcing the few laws that did exist within the camp: 'Stricter control was necessary. He aired his personal views, and having no family ties himself he had no understanding for those who had and were worrying… and he gave me the impression of having little interest in the camp or personnel. I believe that as a result the majority had no confidence in him, or any feeling of approach.' Berry, whose thirty-sixth birthday was to fall on 20 July 1944, was clearly disliked by the rank and file. He was mistrusted, too, for few could appreciate how it was that a flight lieutenant could be a rear gunner. How, too, they reasoned, was it that he was the sole survivor of his Lancaster? And why, for good measure, was his private address c/o Cox & Kings, bankers, Pall Mall, London?[1730]

Matters came to a head after "an incident" when he had had to leave the camp for a short while: 'He put F/O Gordon in charge during his absence. From that time Gordon assumed an authority which he tried to enforce and at a Bitch meeting he suggested corporal punishment should be introduced.' Not surprisingly this suggestion was rejected, but when Flying Officer Gordon asked the duty chef, Flight Sergeant B.E. Brakes, for some extra food, and Brakes declined to give it to him, Gordon tried to strike him. Gordon makes no mention of this incident in his report, but does say, however, that he left Camp No. 1 because he 'was dissatisfied, from the disciplinary and security angles, with the way it was run.'[1731] The unpleasantness ended when Gordon was replaced by Flying Officer N.S. Eliot RAAF, and was moved with Flying Officer Bender and Marion Knight to Camp No. 2 on 30 July. Sergeant Weir, a member of Eliot's crew, recalled that Eliot 'wasn't a particularly forceful man but he had a way about him which defied non-cooperation; the "right man for the job" as one of the Americans put it.'[1732]

A late arrival, on 8 August, and extremely fortunate to be there, was Flight Sergeant C.W. Schwilk RAAF. He was the navigator of a Lancaster that was shot down en route to its target by a night-fighter on the night of 22/23 June 1944 (Reims railway facilities). The aircraft 'quickly burst into flames from mid-upper to tail', and no sooner had the pilot given the order to abandon it than he gave the order to jump. The aircraft was already low, at an estimated 6,000 feet, when it went into a dive and Schwilk 'was more or less thrown out'. This violent action also caused the shoulder straps of his parachute harness to break, and as a result the parachute bag was hanging down below his knees: 'What appeared to be a flare from the aircraft suddenly lit up the sky and I then saw my parachute and pulled the release.'[1733]

As he floated down he saw his Lancaster blazing on the ground, not too far away, to the north of Buy (Oise) and a dozen kilometres to the south-east of Compiègne. Then the bomber exploded, and though bits of flying metal ripped through his parachute he landed safely in the same cornfield as the Lancaster. But then, in a tree close by, he saw 'someone who I took to be the mid-upper trying to disentangle himself, but as some more bombs were exploding in the aircraft I lay down flat.' When Schwilk next looked up the body in the tree was motionless. Only he and the bomb aimer, fellow Australian Flight Sergeant W.J. Flynn, survived the exploding bombs.

Schwilk buried his equipment before crawling through the cornfield, but no sooner had he reached a sunken road than he came face to face with two 'oldish' Germans, who took him away on their motorcycle and sidecar. Locking him up in the loft of an old stone barn one of the Germans kept guard while the other went to fetch help. Noticing several heavy, wooden boxes in the loft Schwilk formed a cunning plan. Putting one of the boxes on a beam above the trap door into the loft he called out a number of German phrases in the hope that the remaining guard would come up to see what was going on. Schwilk stood by with a pole ready to knock the box off the beam when the German put his head through. The plan worked perfectly, and the German fell back down the stairs. Schwilk had no time to see whether he was dead or unconscious for, as he clambered down from the loft, the other German came back with several others. Hiding behind a couple of barrels Schwilk was not seen, even though a torch was flashed around. Eventually the Germans left, and so did Schwilk.

He was put in touch with the Resistance, and taken to a hideout in the Fôret de Compiègne, which 'was organised by Georges Ardenois, who seemed to be the local *chef de Résistance*.' Here he met Flying Officer P.G. Agur RCAF, who had also come down in the forest to the south-east of Compiègne on the night of 28/29 June. He, too, had had a lucky escape after a night-fighter had attacked the Halifax that he was piloting and had set the starboard-inner engine on fire. Ordering his crew to 'Put on parachutes', no sooner had he done so than the aircraft was attacked again. This time the aileron controls were destroyed and, without hesitation as they were now down to 10,000 feet, Agur ordered 'Jump! Jump!' The navigator, bomb aimer and wireless operator were soon out of the forward escape hatch, with Agur right behind them: 'The leg straps of my harness broke when the parachute opened, and I had to grasp the harness above my head. On landing, I fell into some trees and was partially knocked unconscious. I went right through the trees and lay on the ground for some time.'[1734] He, too, made contact with the Resistance, and was brought to their forest hideout on 30 June.

Already there were two Americans – 2nd Lieutenant John E. Hurley USAAF and Sergeant Leo Williams USAAF – and later that day they were joined by Sergeant J.C. Watkins, Technical Sergeant Harry G. Pace Jr USAAF, and by Schwilk. Four days later 2nd Lieutenant Peter D. MacVean USAAF was brought in.[1735] After a few days all were taken to Parmain (Val-d'Oise), a village next to Nesles-la-Vallée, 'where we stayed for ten days during which time we were joined by F/Sgt Fisher and an American airman, Orion Chumley.'[1736] The evaders were now in Philippe d'Albert-Lake's sphere of operations, and were being prepared for the journey to Fréteval. On 31 July, however, the group split up after they had been taken to a disused hospital at Argenteuil in the north-west of Paris.

Agur and Fisher went to stay with a Madame Diximier, as did Schwilk and Watkins two days later, but Agur was already on his way. That morning, Mme Diximier took him 'to the station where we met two more evaders, Sgt W. Brown RAF and Sgt F. Gleason USAAF. There was also an English girl called Anne and a French youth named Raoul.'[1737] Anne and Raoul escorted the three evaders by train to Étampes (Essonne) and then along secondary roads to Angerville, some twenty kilometres away. Staying there for the night of 3/4 August they left on the following morning to a farmhouse one kilometre south of Voves (Eure-et-Loire). Their sleep that night was interrupted by a German convoy that was heading south from midnight to 8.30 a.m. The French insisted that it should have been going north, towards the Normandy front, but the Resistance had switched the road signs!

They then left 'with a short fair young man as guide' to Montboissier, where three more evaders were waiting for them – 2nd Lieutenant Heyward C. Spinks USAAF; Technical Sergeant Joshua D. Lane Jr USAAF; and an unidentified RAF pilot.[1738] They stayed until 6 August on a farm about three kilometres west, which was owned by a man named Marcel, who 'was an agricultural mechanic. His wife and brother also lived here and all of them had arms.' Their walking days over, they were taken by car to the camp in Fréteval Forest.

Meanwhile, on 4 August Schwilk 'was taken alone to the station by Mme. Diximier', where he met Flying Officer J.F. Kennedy RCAF (of Agur's crew), 'and also two girls, one of whose names was Janine Carré'. They also went to Étampes and Angerville, and then on to the farmhouse near Voves. Their guide, who had also escorted Agur and party, was 'a Basque, tall, swarthy with silver teeth. He had been a gunner in the French A.F. and came from Tunisia.' On 7 August a 'very old man and a youth' took them to Montboissier, and next day two men took them 'in a small covered telephone truck', which was followed as escort by a larger truck with several armed men aboard, to the big camp at Fréteval.

Schwilk's partner, John Watkins, was taken with five others (one RAF, one Canadian, and three of the Americans) to the Gare d'Austerlitz in Paris to catch the train to Étampes, but they got caught up in the aftermath of a battle between the Resistance and the Germans. Following the fight all French males between the ages of eight and eighty were rounded-up, including the six airmen, who were sent into captivity for the rest of the war.[1739]

No sooner had Agur, Schwilk and company arrived at the Fréteval camp than the distant sound of battle could be heard, as the US Third Army (General George S. Patton, Jr) fought its way south from the Normandy beachhead. Before striking east and south Patton's forces had first to turn west to quell German opposition in Brittany, and so their forward units had reached no further than Avranches by 1 August, still some 250 kilometres north-west of Châteaudun. It was not until 9 August that XV Corps, US Third Army, was able to launch an attack on Le Mans, barely eighty-five kilometres to the west of Châteaudun.

In Fréteval Forest some of the men 'were getting very restless and feared that if we stayed we would be discovered by the Germans anyway and we would be sitting ducks.'[1740] Aware of both the men's feelings, and of the Americans' arrival at Le Mans thanks to Toussaint's radio, Boussa made it quite clear to the men – by the end, there were 152 of them – that to leave the camp and to try to get through to the advancing Americans would be courting disaster. They would just have to sit it out. Boussa, though, decided to go to Le Mans to try to get the Americans to speed up the liberation of the two camps. Taken by Etienne Viron in his baker's van he reached the Americans' lines.

Also heading to Le Mans was Airey Neave, anxious to know how Operation Sherwood had fared. Having left Room 900 in the hands of Donald Darling (now transferred from Gibraltar), he had made his way by MTB to Arromanches, but had had to wait to go to Fréteval until the Americans had broken through. No sooner had they done so than he packed his jeep and arrived in Le Mans on 10 August, 'confidently assuming that [the] American Third Army would attack towards Chartres and Vendôme.'[1741] This was not to be, however, for now Patton was about to swing north and east to spring the trap on the Germans caught in the Falaise pocket.

This put Neave in a difficult position for, with only six jeeps and a few automatic weapons to see him through the last few miles to Fréteval he had counted on American armour to take care of the German units that were reportedly in the way. Having established himself in the Hôtel Moderne[1742] in Le Mans Neave tried to persuade headquarters XV Corps (Lieutenant General Wade H. Haislip) to help in the rescue mission. They, however, were about to take part in the thrust northwards towards Alençon, and so it was a case of "no can do". Empty-handed and disappointed Neave returned to Le Mans, but was delighted to discover that in his absence an SAS squadron had arrived in the form of Captain A. Greville-Bell DSO and five officers and thirty-four men to undertake Operation Dunhill.[1743] Then, adding to Neave's joy, twenty-three men of the Belgian Parachute Company, under Lieutenants Debefre and Limbosen, arrived following the completion of Operation Shakespeare (harassing the enemy north of the River Loire and to the west of Paris).

So it was on the morning of 11 August that an agitated Boussa appeared at Neave's hotel. Explaining to his boss the urgency of the situation in Fréteval Forest, he suggested that they had to go and fetch the men at once, adding that there were no Germans in the vicinity, all having withdrawn towards Chartres. Neave, however, was reluctant to go charging off despite the apparent lack of Germans, and decided to send Captain Peter Baker of IS9 (WEA) with an escort of five SAS troops to the forest to explain to the men that help was on its way. Despite being shot at by Germans en route (one man was slightly wounded) Captain Baker arrived at the Fouchards' farm at Bellande, according to Flight Lieutenant Berry, during the afternoon of 11 August 'and the men who were fetching milk from there brought them to the camp… Boussa, who had returned with Captain Baker, appeared a while later, and all three [Baker, his driver, and Boussa] stayed the night in the camp.'[1744]

There is some confusion as to the exact sequence of events hereafter, but Sergeant Cliff Hallett was somewhere in the forest with Sergeant Charlie Martin when they saw Boussa returning from Le Mans, alone, in a car. Boussa drove rapidly past them and disappeared round a bend, followed by a loud banging and rattling. Running in the direction of the noise the two airmen found Boussa and his car upside down. Putting the car back on its wheels, Boussa told Hallett and Martin to alert the camp that a rescue party from Le Mans would be arriving to collect them at 10 a.m. the following morning, and drove off.

Captain Baker left for Paris on the following day, 12 August, having told them that the Americans would be coming to liberate the camps on the next day, and obligingly left his Jeep behind. When 13 August dawned, and still no sign of either the Americans or of liberation, Flight Lieutenant Berry announced, according to Charlie Martin, that Lucien Boussa 'ordered the camp to break up. We packed and returned all the gear to Hallouin's farm in Captain Baker's Jeep which he had left that day when he changed to go on to Paris. As no one arrived Lucien told us to disperse to farms and get our own meals. He had given us 1,000 francs each on arrival.'[1745] Berry also apparently 'said anyone who wished to make their own way to our lines could do so, provided they told him first.'

On this same day, as Neave was preparing to send a second officer to Fréteval, Jean de Blommaert arrived, having also been driven to Le Mans by Viron. De Blommaert's news was not encouraging. Some of the men, he said, had already left the camps and were settling in nearby villages, which were already *en fête* at the prospect of liberation. The villagers of Busloup and St Jean-Froidmentel had been astonished to see so many English-speaking young men in their presence, and had put up the flags in celebration. This was particularly worrying to those back in the forest when news was received at midday on 13 August that the Gestapo had arrived in Cloyes-sur-le-Loir, already lightly garrisoned by the Germans. Berry, with Pilot Officer Croquet, immediately left to investigate, telling Staff Sergeant Norman Wright USAAF[1746] 'that if I did not return by 1600 hours something serious had happened.' Nothing serious did happen, however, for Berry discovered that the "Gestapo" were nothing more than two truckloads of men of the TODT organisation – civilians engaged on military construction work – evacuating through Cloyes.

Sergeant Martin was taking no chances, and on 13 August he left with 2nd Lieutenant Boggan USAAF, and Sergeant McCarthy 'to find our own way to our lines. In the afternoon we stopped at a farm near Chauvigny, where the farmer gave us food and a map. We continued on to St Marc du Cor which the FFI had taken over. The chief organised a car to Mondoubleau where we contacted Americans and stayed the night. Next day, they sent us in a jeep to General Irwin's HQ where we gave what information we could.'[1747] The Americans were surprisingly close, for Mondoubleau lies but twenty kilometres west of Fréteval and considerably closer to the camps than Le Mans.

The Gestapo scare also made up the minds of the six survivors of a 44 Squadron Lancaster to leave together. They went to 'a village shop where we were given red wine and although there was no food there was a girl who could speak a little English. She went and got some eggs and made omelettes which we ate washing them down with red wine.' After more wine, yet more eggs and yet more wine, they spent the night in a farmer's barn before making their way back to the forest on 14 August. As they did so they heard a motorcycle approaching fast from behind. All thought that they were about to be re-captured, until they heard the rider say: 'Do any of you bastards speak English?' The American then gave them the good news that an armoured convoy was on its way to the forest.

Sure enough the convoy arrived, and most of the evading personnel, including the 44 Squadron boys, jumped aboard the trucks. As the convoy departed gunfire broke out, and the American drivers and their mates grabbed their rifles and started firing. Sergeant Raymond Worrall thought that they were all going to be killed, but after a while the firing died down and the convoy moved off towards Cloyes. As it did so, it passed a convoy of 'buses all decked out with the Free French insignia and French flags'[1748] heading in the opposite direction for the forest.

It had taken Neave some time to assemble several old charcoal-burning buses in Le Mans, but at 8 a.m. on 14 August a number of soldiers in uniform and Frenchmen wearing their FFI armbands joined the convoy outside the Hôtel Moderne: 'It was a fine, hot morning and in high spirits we set off along the road to Vendôme with a patrol of SAS ahead of us. I had given orders to travel as fast as possible. Within three-quarters of an hour, despite much spluttering from the "buses" we turned off through gay villages towards Cloyes and up the road through the forest to the rendezvous,'[1749] passing as it did so the American convoy. Neave rounded up those of the men who were left, only some twenty-five all told, and followed the American convoy back to Le Mans. According to Neave the two convoys had 132 evaders between them, but at 2000 hours that evening Captain Greville-Bell signalled this brief message to his HQ: 'Dunhill 14/8/44 2000 ref Neave operation. Received 137 Allied airmen. OK.'[1750]

Sergeant Charlie Martin and his two companions, Boggan and McCarthy, were just three of the fifteen or twenty men who had not been bussed back to Le Mans. Having made contact with the Americans on 14 August, they were billeted under guard with XX Corps (Lieutenant General Walton H. Walker), US Third Army. Next day they were sent to a prisoner-of-war cage at Le Mans for the night, but on 16 August an American colonel said that he could 'truck' the men anywhere they wished – except England. He suggested that they went to an airfield near Avranches and hitched a flight back across the Channel. Having no success at that airfield, it was suggested that they try the airfield at St Jacques near Rennes. This proved more promising when a major offered to try to organise an airlift back to England, but it was not until 18 August that they were flown to airfield A.20, and on to IS9 (WEA) for interrogation on 19 August.

After the majority of the evaders and escapers had been re-united at Le Mans, they piled aboard American trucks, and were taken to Laval on 15 August. When the inhabitants of Laval, celebrating their newfound freedom, spotted the scruffy-looking individuals aboard the American trucks they assumed that they were German prisoners of war and started to "get nasty", until someone produced his RAF insignia and everyone shouted 'RAF', and celebrations resumed. The convoy of six trucks moved off to Bayeux at high speed along narrow, winding roads when they suddenly came to a bend that was sharper than it looked. The first two trucks negotiated it without difficulty. The third and fourth swerved and swayed round it. The fifth, however, lost control, hit the bank, and overturned, flinging its passengers everywhere and trapping two of the Americans. Those in the last truck, which thankfully had managed to stop in time, got out to render assistance.

Among those injured were Sergeant W. Brown (sprained left wrist, damaged fingers on right hand) and Flight Sergeant K.J. Lynch RAAF, both of whom required hospitalisation on return to Britain.

One of those to help the casualties was Cliff Hallett, who would have been on the fifth truck but for an anti-English American. As Cliff had tried to board the truck at Le Mans he got a boot in the face, the owner of the footwear telling him at the same moment that they didn't 'want any Goddam Limey on here'. Cliff thanked him very much and jumped onto the next one.

Seeing the two Americans trapped under the overturned lorry and lying in a pool of oil and fuel, Cliff and several others found a hefty branch, and levered the lorry off the two Americans. Before the two were freed Cliff had noticed Flight Lieutenant Berry standing at the scene, pointing his loaded gun at them. Once the Americans were safely released Cliff and the others asked Berry what the hell he was doing. He replied: 'I couldn't let them burn if the oil had caught fire.'[1751] When the injured had been taken away by American army ambulance the rest squeezed into the five remaining trucks and proceeded to Bayeux. As it was dark before they could reach the town, they stopped at a camp of German prisoners of war. Food was available but, as there was no accommodation for the men from the convoy, they had to pass the night in the open and close to the barbed wire behind which the German prisoners were penned. Just in case, each man was given a loaded rifle.

One sour note to this tiny episode of the tragedy of war was the removal by the Americans of the Russian "Cogi", or whatever his name was, who had been in the forest with the men, and who had uncomplainingly done much of the dirty work. Despite strong protests from his fellow evaders he was put in with the Germans, and was never heard of again. The rest reached Bayeux safely, the RAF aircrew being handed over to RAF Intelligence. Seats on flights home were at a premium, and it was to be several days before all were returned to England. Some of the Commonwealth aircrew thereafter returned to their mother country, but not a few went back on operations. According to Airey Neave, 'thirty-eight of them were killed in action before the end of the war.'[1752]

For his part in Operation Sherwood Jean de Blommaert was awarded the DSO, and Squadron Leader Lucien Boussa the MC. Both also received the French and Belgian Croix de Guerre. Omer Jubault was also decorated.

The Marathon camps in the Belgian Ardennes

Back in May 1944, following the Desoubrie incident in Paris, Albert Ancia set off for the Ardennes but, according to Airey Neave, 'experienced great difficulties with the Comet organisation. They were unenthusiastic about the Marathon plan and reluctant to establish a camp in the Belgian Ardennes. Moreover they were suspicious of Ancia's identity, with the result that he was unable to do much useful work.'[1753] According to "Rémy", however, who had been involved in running the organisation *Confrérie Notre-Dame*, which operated throughout the whole of Occupied France and Belgium, it was at the beginning of April 1944 that he was told by Yvon Michiels ("Jean Serment"), one of Comet's leaders in Brussels,[1754] that as the route to Spain was becoming more and more precarious – due to both increased Gestapo controls on the trains and to heavy Allied bombing of the railways themselves – they should think about forming a number of camps in the Ardennes in which the airmen could be gathered ('… nous allions avoir à former des camps dans les forêts ardennaises pour y rassembler les aviateurs…').

In the event, some half a dozen camps were formed in the Ardennes – at Beffe, Bellevaux (la Cornette), Acremont (Forêt de Luchy), Porcheresse,[1755] Villance, and Bohan-sur-Semois – and over one hundred Allied airmen (see list in Appendix IV) would be brought to them from time to time during the summer of 1944. According to Rémy the Belgian helpers kept the evaders on the move from camp to camp at regular intervals to keep their minds off wandering into German hands.[1756]

Michiels also told "Rémy" that a number of Comet helpers had already been sent to the Ardennes to prepare the ground, some of whom were "Paul-Antoine" (la comtesse Paul d'Oultremont); "Madame François" (Madame Dumon, mother of "Nadine" and "Michou"); "Parrain" (le Père van Oostayen); "Henri" (Henri Nys, a foremost *convoyeur* in Belgium); "Albert le Pâtissier" (Georges Arnould); "Emile le Plombier" (Emile Roiseux);[1757] "Guy"; and Henri Maca. Michiels had also asked Madame Yvonne Bienfait, who worked at a hospital in Schaerbeek in Brussels, to be his right arm in the search and reception of airmen. Typical of so many, without hesitation she agreed. Another young woman to be involved was Mademoiselle Clair De Veuster, one of Comet's principal "lodgers", but José Grimar ("Marc"), another key Comet member who would have been the replacement for Yvon Michiels and who would have been involved in helping with the camps, was arrested at his home on 12 May 1944, two days before Michiels did in fact have to leave Brussels due to Gestapo pressure.

Comet's problems in Brussels had repercussions for Flying Officer R.F. Brailsford, who had been shot down during the Louvain raid on 11/12 May 1944. Three days after baling out he was moved into the centre of Brussels. The reason for his move 'was that one of the chiefs of the underground movement had been denounced and arrested by the Gestapo.' On 9 July Brailsford was visited by the man with whom he had first stayed, ostensibly calling to make sure that he was being well looked after. Despite the several weeks of his enforced stay in Brussels Brailsford was still very much on the alert: 'I had been suspicious of his actions for some time, so therefore asked the woman with whom I was staying to report his visit. She did so. The organisation had him followed and found him dealing with the Gestapo. They dealt with him in the customary manner and left him for dead. I understand that he is still alive but will either die very shortly or go insane if he lives. The name by which I knew him was Raymond Chorlet, but he appears to have had many names.'[1758]

While Brailsford remained stuck in Brussels, Comet moved their last group of "parcels" over the Pyrenees on 4 June 1944 – Lieutenant-Colonel Thomas H. Hubbard, Major Donald K. Willis, 2nd Lieutenant Jack D. Cornett, all USAAF, and Pilot Officer L.A. Barnes and Sergeant R.T. Emeny.

Pilot Officer Barnes, shot down in the middle of March 1944, had been so long in hiding with Léon Coigne and family that he 'had practically given up hope of getting back'. It was by chance that he was seen by a Madame Peanneau from Paris. Learning of Barnes's predicament she said that she knew someone in Paris who could help him. Nothing happened, though, and when he learnt of another airman evading at a château nearby, he went over to see him, on 6 May. The other man, Flying Officer W.A. Jacks, was about to be taken to Paris by a girl called Odile, who said that she would take Barnes too. A week later, in Paris, they stayed at the flat of Madame Lesguillier, who also owned the château in which Jacks had been hiding.

A few days later Odile brought an ID card for Jacks (Comet 282), who was then sent down the line. On 29 May Barnes was moved to another house, in the Boulogne district of Paris, and two days later to Philippe d'Albert-Lake's apartment, where he met Emeny, Hubbard, Cornett, and Sergeants R.H. Banks RCAF and G. Hand, these last two being taken to the camps at Fréteval. The rest of the party took the train to Bordeaux on 1 June with one guide: 'We arrived at 1830 hours and walked round the park till midnight, when we caught the midnight train for Bayonne. We left the train at Boucau and walked through Bayonne to the further outskirts of the town, when we reached a small café.'[1759]

Shortly before midnight the café owner took them to meet their guide, who led them up into the mountains. At around 2.30 a.m. on 4 June Comet's last Allied airmen "parcels" were safely delivered over the border into Spain. Their arrest by the Spanish police was a mere formality, and on 23 June they were in Gibraltar.

On 6 June 1944 the Normandy landings rendered further journeys to Spain obsolete, even more so in the light of the proposed Marathon camps. In Paris, Henri Nys confirmed to Gilbert Renault (Rémy) that it was useless to attempt another Pyrennean crossing, and mentioned that Albert Ancia was on his way to Brussels to help set-up the camps in Belgium.

One thing that was certain, given the vast aerial armadas continuing to fly day and night over Belgium, was that there would be no shortage of *colis* (parcels) for the Comet helpers on the ground. The ball was set rolling after the burgomaster of Wavre, Monsieur Bosch, announced that a good number of airmen were currently in hiding in his town and in the surrounding area. Plans were therefore made to move the airmen to Beffe. After a stop at Malonnes, near Namur, where a boat would be required to get the men across the Meuse (its bridges were heavily guarded by Germans), the airmen would travel by local train to Hotton, the nearest station to Beffe.

RAF Bomber Command's attack on Wesseling on the night of 20/21 June 1944 proved to be one of those disastrous occasions when several squadrons each lost a high percentage of its aircraft. Six of 5 Group's squadrons between them lost thirty-four Lancaster bombers.[1760]

From one of these Lancasters, LL973, four men would survive, two as prisoners of war and two, Sergeants A.E.J. Barton and F.R. Haslam, as evaders. They were on their way to the target when a night-fighter attacked and set both of LL973's port engines on fire. The pilot, Pilot Officer C.J. "Mike" Solly, gave the order to bale out. Sergeant Frank Haslam knocked his head against the tailplane as he jumped from the rear door of the aircraft. Given treatment by the Dexter family, he decided against staying with them when he found that there were eight children in the house, too much of a risk for all concerned, and so went on his way: 'It was mid afternoon on 22nd June 1944 that, in accordance with our training, I was observing an isolated house on the outskirts of the village of Wiemismeer near Genk from a nearby coppice. There was a man tilling some land and occasionally a young woman came out to hang out washing, accompanied by a little brown dog. I crawled into the wheat field behind the coppice and fell asleep. At dusk I continued my observation of the house. The man was still working the land. I walked round the side of the house out of his sight and found the woman working in a bakehouse at the back, chopping wood.'

'I had to knock loudly at the bakehouse door before she looked up, startled. I told her I was "English airman". She showed me into the house from where I could see the man working. She called him in and told him I was an "Engelsch fliegeren". He pounced on me and hugged and kissed me on the cheeks, time after time crying "Engelsch! Engelsch!" This was Gerard. Helena stood by with a big smile. And there was me, one dishevelled and very embarrassed airman, not used to all this enthusiasm. This was my introduction to my saviours, the Delsaer family.'[1761]

Interviewed by a couple of members of the local underground to whom he gave his name, rank and number, they said that London would be informed of his survival, and from time to time was told that he would be put on a barge on the Albert Canal to go to the coast, or that he would be picked up by Lysander. 'I doubted this – I was just an ordinary airman. In the end I was told to stay put as the approach of the Allied forces meant it would be too dangerous to be taken into the rear of the German lines.'[1762]

The weeks rolled monotonously by until, one afternoon early in September, Frank had a very close shave. When a German officer appeared unannounced at the Delsaer home, Gerard told Frank to hide in the bakehouse: 'Panic stations – where could I go? Only one place and that was into the oven. There was no door, just an aperture in the front wall of the oven.' The officer wanted to see the bakehouse, and he went close enough to the oven for Frank to be able to read the initials on his signet ring. Had he bent down, he could not have missed seeing the trembling airman, but he left without spotting him. After the German officer had left Gerard explained that the Germans were going to use the bakehouse, with its views over the nearby heath, as an R/T control office for the aircraft that they were planning to fly from the heath.

The Germans were soon back, and installed their equipment in the bakehouse, with Frank now effectively trapped in the house. He was seen one day by one of the Germans, who failed to regard him as anything other than one of the family. Over the next few days the Germans moved out, and the fighter aircraft that had been using the heath airfield left at first light one morning. Although the immediate locality was clear of Germans, care still had to be taken over those who were retreating, but at the end there was as much danger from the advancing Americans as there had been from the Germans. When the village was liberated Frank was playing with the Delsaer children when an American tank approached and traversed its gun towards him because, as the crew said afterwards, his RAF uniform looked suspiciously like the German field grey. The Americans, though, could do nothing for him and suggested that he should try to get through to the British forces pushing forwards. Contact was made with British soldiers picking mushrooms and, after he had been taken to their HQ, Frank was immediately driven to Brussels.

Sergeant Arthur Barton, the flight engineer of "Mike" Solly's crew, rolled himself up into a ball to bale out of LL973 but got himself jammed in the front escape hatch. Managing to climb back in he dived out successfully, landing in the north-east of Belgium. Having received help from Leonard and Hubertine Martens, he was escorted by a Mr Van Oppen to the nearby town of Genk, and interrogated at gunpoint by members of an organisation: 'They threatened to shoot him if he did not give more than his name, rank and number.'[1763] Arthur gave them the name of a new arrival on his squadron, and when this was confirmed by London, the tense situation was defused. 'Did we frighten you?' they joked, moving him to the home of Mr and Mrs Gebeelen in Genk, where his hiding place was a space under the dining room floorboards. Though the headroom was only eighteen inches (forty-five centimetres) the space did have electric light, a mattress and blankets.

But when Monsieur Gebeelen got a little drunk at a wedding and boasted that he knew where an Englishman was hiding, it was time for Arthur to move on. With Van Oppen again providing the lead on his bicycle, Arthur, over six feet tall, would follow on a tandem with Mr and Mrs Gebeelen's daughter, Betty: 'He was just beginning to master riding the small tandem when a patrol of six Germans came round the next corner. One, pointing at the tandem, made a remark to his colleagues, who burst out laughing. There was a bit of banter and wolf whistling as the frightened pair cycled unsteadily past them.'[1764]

After further journeying with Van Oppen they arrived at Momalle, a dozen kilometres north-west of Liège, where Arthur stayed with a couple who 'were very poor and the accommodation was extremely basic with no proper sanitation.' He also discovered two other RAF lads in hiding in the village – Flight Sergeant Ron Dawson and Sergeant F.W.C. "Bill" Robertson.[1765] On the move again, ever southwards, with the faithful Van Oppen the three airmen found themselves at Hotton, in the middle of the Belgian Ardennes and the nearest station to the small village of Beffe, half a dozen kilometres away, to which they were taken by Van Oppen and where, as Arthur Barton wrote, he 'left us standing beside the church telling us to keep out of sight. How we were supposed to do this I do not know; there was nowhere to hide. We huddled together alongside one of the pillars of the church wall, probably looking more suspicious than if we had stood in the open. Although there were houses around there was no sign of human habitation, but I have no doubt that there was someone behind at least one of the curtained off windows watching us.'

'Our guide came back with a young man dressed in shorts looking for all the world like a boy scout, and we were taken to a building near to the church which turned out to be the school house. Climbing the stairs, I could see through the open doors that the various rooms were fitted out with bunk beds, some six or eight to a room. A buzz of conversation was heard as we climbed the final set of stairs which revealed an attic virtually full of men.'[1766] There were, according to Rémy, twenty-nine airmen in residence, the majority Americans.

One truckload of ten evaders was brought from Liège on 4 July 1944, eight Americans and two RAF – pilot Flight Sergeant J.H. Evans and wireless operator Sergeant D.A. Lloyd, both from a Halifax that had been shot down on 12/13 May 1944 over Belgium, half a dozen kilometres north-east of their target (Hasselt). For several weeks they had been in hiding in the village of la Préalle with two Americans, Ken Griesel and Alvis D. Roberts, but, when the Germans began looking for young men who were trying to avoid forced labour in Germany, the four airmen were escorted to a garage in nearby Herstal, half a dozen kilometres north-east of Liège, and there met a further six American airmen.

After a three-hour journey the ten airmen reached the Wuyts-Denis' house in Beffe. Looking after all the evaders were Vincent and Ghislaine Wuyts-Denis. Vincent, on the run to avoid STO (forced labour for the Germans), and Ghislaine had been asked by "Guy" to organise the camp in Beffe, with Ghislaine doing the cooking for the many airmen. Only a handful of locals were aware of the existence of the safe house, among them 'the Burgomaster of Beffe, the local forester and an English lady married to a Belgian farmer who lived a few miles away.'[1767] The Englishwoman baked the bread for the hungry mouths, which Vincent would go and collect, while other food had to be brought to the house in small quantities to avoid suspicion.

When life within the four walls became a strain for the evaders Vincent would take them for a walk through the woods or for a bathe in the river to keep them occupied. One airman, though, who could take it no longer decided to leave. He was 'a rear gunner and came from North Wales', and took with him a compass, a map, a loaf of bread and some tobacco. John Evans never heard what happened to his fellow Welshman, but to leave like that was a dangerous thing to have done for, had he been caught and been made to talk, it would have gone ill for those who remained in Beffe. Life, however, continued pleasantly enough for the rest until one day towards the end of July. Almost certainly after a tip-off from an informer a truck full of Germans suddenly raided the village.

It was barely 4 o'clock in the morning when, so Vincent was told by the Burgomaster, the Germans went straight to the house in which four members of the Armée Blanche were resident. As the enemy broke down the door one of the Belgians inside shot and wounded a German officer. The Belgian and one of his comrades were promptly gunned-down. A third was shot as he ran off across the fields but the fourth, hiding in the cellar, remained undiscovered. In any case, the Germans burnt down the house, and warned the Burgomaster that if there was any more trouble they would put a torch to the whole village. There was another story, that the Germans had gone to Beffe with no hostile intentions but simply to procure some food.[1768]

The alarm, meanwhile, had been quickly raised in the Wuyts-Denis' house: 'Our few belongings were hastily collected and we left by the back door, climbed the high wall at the end of the yard, and into the woods.'[1769] Most of the party stayed in the woods for four days and nights before being moved on to another camp, but on the last night, 28/29 July, a 'tremendous thunderstorm broke at about 12.30 am and so heavy was the downpour that it was impossible to find any shelter anywhere. We were all soaked through to the skin. Our clothes, blankets and palliasses were all wet through and, worst of all, our tobacco and cigarettes were completely destroyed.'[1770]

The soaking was too much for Vincent, Arthur Barton, Bill Robertson and two others, who decided to risk going back to the schoolhouse just to get dry and to get a good night's sleep. They were in for a second rude awakening. In the early hours of the morning, Vincent roughly woke Arthur to tell him in a hoarse whisper that German troops were outside: 'A quick peek out of the front window revealed a lorry unloading troops in the square. By now the others were alerted and we were all trying to scramble into still wet clothes. One clot without thinking of the implications actually switched on the light.'[1771] For the second time, flight was made from the rear of the house.

Weathering the storm, the evaders were greeted by the sight of Abbé Arnould 'in full clerical garb', who 'arrived with the news that six bicycles had been brought to a nearby village'.[1772] Lots were drawn to see who the lucky six would be, and John Evans was one of them. They set off in pairs with strict instructions to keep a large gap between each pair, and made their way through la Roche-en-Ardenne, until they came to St Hubert having cycled a good thirty-five kilometres. It was late in the evening when the exhausted cyclists stopped at a café run by one of Comet's men. Two bottles of beer for each man were produced but they did more harm than good, and Alvis Roberts 'collapsed on the table and was unable to continue any further.' He was left behind, to follow a couple of days later. Arnould left the men there and returned to Beffe. His place as guide was taken by Louis Vanlierde.

Louis stressed that they had to be through the small town of Paliseul a quarter of an hour before curfew (10.30 pm), but the target became unattainable as the weary men struggled on. Two of the five, Americans Ken Griesel and Hank Gladys, were in the worst state and, having reached the top of a hill, Griesel fell flat on his face on the side of the road. Too late now to reach Paliseul by the curfew the men bedded down in a dilapidated shed. Continuing through Paliseul next day Louis led them to a farm where another member of the organisation provided them with a meal, after which they had a sleep in a barn.

Louis also returned to Beffe, and his place was in turn taken by another guide, Albert [Albert

Louis?], who took them on a two-hour walk to a cabin in the woods between the villages of Daverdisse and Porcheresse. Here they found already in residence Mosquito pilot Flight Lieutenant G.R. Morgan RCAF and two Americans, First Lieutenant S.G. Schleichkorn and Flight Officer H.P. Maupin.[1773]

Morgan had been shot down in his Mosquito on the night of 20/21 April 1944 supporting the Bomber Command raid on Cologne. After five days with a farmer, Auguste Santrone, during which time contact was made with l'Armée Blanche, he was moved to various safe houses in the Gembloux area. He then went to the home of René Denis, charcoal maker, at Malonne a couple of kilometres east of Floreffe 'who kept me for ten days and gave me a bicycle to continue my journey to the Forest de Luchy, where our guide of the organisation kept us supplied with food for nine days.' The busy Abbé Arnould then led Morgan and the others 'to another camp between Porcheresse and Daverdisse, where our guide fed us for twenty-eight days.' The priest 'then conducted us to another camp on the frontier near Bohan, where we were kept by the organisation for seven days.'[1774]

Back at Beffe the main body of airmen in the woods were led away from the danger area by the Abbé Arnould and Louis Vanlierde: 'After many hours of stumbling along in the dark, at the first light of day we were offered a rudimentary shelter in a cowshed in a field. The building itself was badly neglected and offered little in the way of protection from the rain, most of the roof was missing but the walls were reasonably intact and did offer some guard from prying eyes of anyone who might pass along the nearby road. The biggest problem was trying to find sufficient clean ground between the cowpats to sit down… Tired though we were, sleep proved impossible for most of us. After an hour or so without any, most of us were stamping about trying to keep warm. We were all wet and for the most part feeling pretty miserable. The arrival of hot soup improved our morale and cheered us up no end. Feeding such a large number of hungry men must at times have been very difficult for the helpers to resolve. Such was the case with transport for us. Yet, somehow, right out in the middle of nowhere, the resistance conjured up some thirty bicycles.'[1775]

Mounting their steeds the long column wound its way along side roads, keeping out of harm's way, but Arthur Barton remembered 'riding past an armed German sentry standing in front of a large pair of wrought iron gates.' Fortunately for the cyclists, the guard did absolutely nothing, though he must have been curious as to why so many had ridden past him. One of the cyclists' escorts was Rémy, who mentions that he led a contingent of cyclists from Beffe and made a stop at the Château de Sainte Ode, some five kilometres south-east of the Barrière de Champlon, a place where two significant roads crossed.[1776]

Arthur Barton remembered that they spent the night 'in a large deserted mansion. We did not see much of the outside as it was getting dark, but from what we did see it was quite a substantial building and partly in ruins. Clearly our arrival was expected. In one of the more habitable rooms, straw had been laid out to form makeshift beds. Alongside each bed was a packet of biscuits and something that none of us had seen for some time – a packet of twenty Players cigarettes.' This large house was the property of a Monsieur Fabry, who entertained them magnificently with several bottles of wine as well.

Somewhat refreshed, Rémy led his cyclists off through Villance, Lavacherie, east of the Forêt de Freyr, St Hubert, Poix-St Hubert and Libin, a distance all told of some thirty kilometres. The airmen were warned that some recently-cut pit props needed loading onto railway wagons in a railway siding near Poix and that, were a train due, it was certain that the Germans would round-up everyone in sight to assist with the loading. Inevitably, a train whistle was heard in the distance as the fateful spot was approached: 'The general pace of the pedalling became more urgent and what up to then had been an orderly procession now began to fray at the edges. The train whistles getting ever closer urged everyone to greater efforts and the stronger cyclists were catching up with the weaker ones. It was just as well that there were none of the enemy at the siding because, by the time we reached it, discipline had deserted some of the men and the whole ride had degenerated into a shambles. To the few people gathered at the siding, seeing some thirty odd cyclists, all young men, racing along, it must have been painfully obvious that something was amiss. Once again good fortune was on our side. We moved on to a side road a little after passing the siding and before the train arrived.'[1777]

On reaching Villance Rémy decided, a little unwisely in his own admission, to let the airmen recover in the local hotel while he went off in search of a lorry. In his absence the men 'enjoyed a magnificent meal of grilled trout'. After they had been fed and watered the twenty-nine men split into two groups, one going to Porcheresse, a dozen kilometres west of Villance, in the lorry that Rémy had succeeded in finding, and the other cycling on into the Ardennes forest to spend the night at a children's home run by some nuns at la Maison Blanche.

The cyclists, including Arthur Barton and friends, were met by "Albert le Pâtissier" (Georges Arnould):

> 'Who took us to a spot deep in the forest where we set up camp. With few tools and Albert's guidance

we set about building shelters. Trees with about a four to six inch diameter were cut down and stripped of branches and foliage. Selecting two trees standing about eight to ten feet apart, Albert fixed a pole horizontally between them about seven feet from the ground. Two more poles were stood upright a suitable distance from the first two to form two corners of what was to be our hut. These were now fixed to the first two with sloping poles to form the roof. Around this basic rectangular framework we built our shelter.

'Three of the sides and roof were covered with thinner poles, twigs and foliage. A large communal bed or sleeping platform was constructed. This consisted of a strong framework raised about two feet from the ground. Saplings of about two inches in diameter were now laid close together on this framework but fixed at one end only. This permitted the other end to slide on the frame and when covered with a thick layer of foliage made a very effective spring bed. A second hut similar to the first was made and a latrine dug. The latter however did not enjoy any privacy, it was just a trench in the ground over which was slung a pole between two trees. We soon discovered that it was not wise if sitting on the pole to be near the middle. The pole itself was quite flexible and springy and if anyone vacated a seat near you it was necessary to hang on for dear life to prevent being bounced into the trench.

'Food was very scarce as it all had to be transported on foot into the camp. Our rations consisted of a small bowl of rice in the morning and a similar amount of mashed potatoes in the evening. I can recall only one occasion when we had meat. It was very suspect. Our endeavour to make it last an extra day or so was a mistake, it soon became fly blown and maggoty. However, this did not deter us, the maggots were cleaned out and the meat eaten. We were all very hungry and glad of any sort of food.'[1778]

Although neither Arthur Barton nor Rémy name the camp, it was probably the one near Acremont in the Forêt de Luchy, a couple of kilometres from Jehonville and ten or so *south* of Villance. It was also some fifteen kilometres south-east of the Daverdisse/Porcheresse camp. Rémy does mention, however, that work on the construction of the camp at Acremont began on Saturday, 10 June 1944, when Georges Arnould (Rémy's cousin), Eugène Guérard and René Soroge began erecting a cabin in the Forêt de Luchy, and that it was finished on 12 June.[1779]

A frequent and welcome visitor to the camp was Gaston Matthys, 'a short dapper little man with a huge mop of curly hair', who would bring news of the war on the western front. He would never enter the camp, though, until he was sure that it was safe to do so, and would first whistle the first few bars of *It's a Long Way to Tipperary*. On hearing someone in the camp whistling the next few bars he knew that it was safe to approach. Formerly a policeman in Brussels he was a cautious man, not least because, as head of Comet in Brussels following Yvon Michiels's departure, he was much sought after by the Germans. And, as did many others, he used several aliases – "Christian", "Roland" or "Vanesse" – to confuse people.

After a fortnight at Acremont it was time for Barton and company to move to another camp, possibly that at la Cornette:

'We set off across country moving down toward the French border. At one stage we had to cross a stream, about five feet from bank to bank. We all managed to jump it successfully except Bill [Robertson], who got very wet in the process as it was quite deep… What we did not know at this time was that Bill was suffering from an onset of a problem that was soon to paralyse his legs.

'Our new camp was again deep in the forest, this time near the summit of a steep hill. We once again set about building shelter for ourselves but lacked the initial enthusiasm. Our cooking facilities were more basic than before and food was even in shorter supply. The only receptacle we had of any sort was an old dustbin. This was cleaned out in the nearby stream and lived permanently on the fire as a giant cooking pot. Into this stew pot went everything that we could lay our hands on that resembled food. On one occasion a sack of dried peas was brought to us some of which went into the bin but after days of cooking they failed to soften. The remainder were left in the sack and thrown in the stream to soak, to no avail. They remained as hard as stones.'

The monotony of camp life was relieved one day when Gaston Matthys brought in a man, dressed in khaki uniform, claiming to be a British soldier who had escaped from a prisoner-of-war camp in Germany. Hard questioning revealed, however, 'that he was an Arab in one of the labour battalions of the British Army. Mohammed turned out to be a tower of strength. Whereas we were all in a weakened state from lack of the right food, he on the other hand seemed to thrive on our meagre rations. He proved to be immensely strong and spent hours felling trees for wood for our fire.'[1780]

So life went on, the sound of battle getting ever closer until it seemed to be all around them. Fearing for their own safety tension among the evaders heightened when someone rushed into the camp yelling that Germans were heading their way but, just before panic could set in, the familiar whistling of "Tipperary" was heard, followed by Gaston and by *American* soldiers! Having made his way through the front line Gaston contacted the Americans and requested that they should go to the camp to rescue the evaders. The Americans were understandably wary that it might be a trap, and it was their helmets that had been seen making their way to the camp when the alarm was raised. On 8 September, therefore, the airmen gathered together their meagre possessions, doused the fire, and 'departed, hopefully, towards liberation'.

Wireless operator Sergeant J.W. Stone, relieved to have survived the loss of his Lancaster after it had been shot down by a Ju88 on the night of 11/12 May 1944, was enjoying his descent until his parachute canopy caught on the chimney of a tall house near Rixensart (twenty kilometres south-east of Brussels) and slammed him against the wall. Freeing himself he made off as fast as he could, until he thought he saw his mid-upper gunner, Sergeant F.W. Brown. The man was in fact a very frightened off-duty Belgian gendarme, who recovered sufficiently to take John Stone to his home and very quickly burnt his uniform – after John had exchanged it for some old clothes. When it was light the gendarme escorted John to the road to Brussels and left without saying a word, leaving a bemused John to find his own way.

It was a very hot and sunny day when John, passing through Waterloo, chanced upon 'a German army camp in the woods. Motorcycles with sidecars were scouting the roads presumably looking for shot down aircrew… The patrols, which included dogs in the sidecars, took no notice of John.'[1781] In due course he reached Brussels, but again came into contact with a German soldier when he was turned back from a "no go" area near the Palais de Justice. After a quick beer at a bar full of German soldiers, who again ignored him, he had to wait until 5 o'clock next morning before leaving Brussels on foot in the vague direction of France. At 8 p.m. that evening he reached Halle, where people were sitting out in the late evening sunshine. Spotting a man playing with a frog and therefore likely to be trustworthy, John spoke to him. The man, as the gendarme had been, was very frightened, but nevertheless took John into his house and put him to bed. John knew this brave Belgian only as Marcel.

A couple of hours later John was woken up and 'interrogated by a man who spoke perfect English. This man, Fred, had been raised in Spalding, Lincolnshire. Fred and his wife, Molly, had been evacuated to England during the first war.'[1782] Fred was satisfied that John was what he claimed to be, and agreed to take John into his home in the morning. Actually, his home was a brewery, and Fred was the local brewer, and it was there that John was to spend the next five weeks. Halle was also a German infantry-training centre, and from the roof of the brewery there was a fine view of the Germans on manoeuvre.

When it was learnt one evening that the Gestapo would be searching the area for evading airmen, John was hidden in a disused drain in the basement. Though he could hear the Gestapo carrying out their search he remained undetected, but two boys living next door to the brewery were taken away, never to be heard of again.

After five weeks, John was taken to Brussels on 23 June, staying at Clair de Veuster's flat before leaving on 30 June with two Americans, 2nd Lieutenant James M. Cochran USAAF and Technical Sergeant Raymond Koch USAAF, who had managed to escape from the Gestapo's clutches as they were being escorted through a park in Aalst. Not so fortunate was their navigator, Lieutenant Michael N. Stanko USAAF, who was captured.[1783]

Handed over by Madame Yvonne Bienfait to another member of Comet, John and the two Americans were driven in a baker's van across Brussels to Namur without incident. Transferred to a lorry they were driven the thirty kilometres to Dinant, picking up along the way several hitch-hikers from another lorry that had broken down. Towing the broken-down vehicle the hitch-hikers, minus their lorry, were dropped off at Dinant, where it was necessary to cross the River Meuse. As usual, there were German soldiers posted on it carrying out identity checks, and the lorries and their passengers were forced to stop. It was a nerve-tingling moment before they were allowed to proceed but then, as the two lorries crossed the bridge, the tow-rope parted, bringing yet more unwanted attention upon them. Suffering considerable German wrath from both sides of the bridge, the rope was mended and the crossing made without further problems.

Eventually leaving the lorry, the airmen made their way across another river with the help of the ferryman, and climbed the cliffs alongside the river in pouring rain. In a forest near Porcheresse they found an agent who, despite the rain and a complete lack of shelter, had a fire going. "Robinson", the agent, obligingly brewed some coffee: 'Worn out, they fell asleep on sodden ground.'[1784]

The camp that sprang up in due course was very basic, the only shelter at first being branches, but when a disused hut was found bunks were built with the help of tools provided by Belgians, and food was occasionally provided by the local priest and by his sister. The camp was established by Emile Roiseux ("the plumber"), assisted by several other Belgians, especially Albert Louis (forester), Béatrice Davreux, Léona Lecuit, Jacques Bresmal, and Emile and Joseph Hernandez. John Evans remembers, however, that Emile Roiseux was assisted by a man named Raymond and that both of them lived in Porcheresse. Funds were made available by Comet for Emile to buy food for the airmen, who would go and 'collect it in sacks. Each night after dark three or four of us would go through the woods into the village to the house where Emile lived… There were always plenty of volunteers for this job as it meant that we could listen to the news in English.'[1785]

John Evans and six others had arrived at Porcheresse on 4 August, and for the rest of the month the weather was gloriously sunny. There was a river [possibly the Our or the Lesse] not far from the camp where the men could enjoy a refreshing bathe. Otherwise the days could be spent sunbathing, playing cards or making model aeroplanes, but when 'it became dark we would light a log fire, gather our chairs around it and just talk. Sometimes there would be a little community singing – very softly, of course.'[1786]

The days passed pleasantly, but towards the end of August one of the Belgian helpers, a man called Jean, suddenly came across five German soldiers in the middle of a clearing. They shouted to Jean to halt, but the Belgian ran off into the trees. He wasn't quick enough, though, for a bullet grazed his head. A few hundred metres away the men in the camp were alerted by the sound of the gunfire and, when Jean appeared with blood streaming from his head, made off rapidly to another place of shelter. The Germans were not seen again, and an hour or two later the all-clear was given.

On 28 August the camp was effectively struck and, saying a fond farewell to Emile Roiseux, the airmen were led away to a new camp nearer to the front line. Their destination was the woods near Bohan-sur-Semois, very close to the French border. The camp, says John Evans, was very basic: 'There was nowhere to sleep except above ground with whatever shelter one was able to improvise from trees and bushes. Food was a problem especially as we were now such a large contingent but a few villagers including Alexis Henry who was a Belgian customs officer brought us what they could.'[1787] It was fortunate that the Germans were now retreating steadily towards their Fatherland, for after only a few days at Bohan the Americans arrived. Breaking out their "K" rations for the joyous airmen the Americans efficiently trucked them back to Paris, to the 200-bedroom Hôtel Meurice in the Rue de Rivoli.[1788] The men enjoyed a few more days of comparative luxury before arrangements were made for their return to England or, in the case of the Americans, "to ship them Stateside".

Pilot Officer Donald Harrison RCAF eventually arrived at la Cornette/Bellevaux camp, some twenty kilometres south of Porcheresse and half a dozen north of Bouillon, also close to the border with France, at the beginning of August 1944. Shot down on the night of 27/28 April 1944, it was a bad night for his squadron, No. 431 (RCAF), which lost four of its Halifax aircraft.[1789]

Wounded in the arm, Harrison baled out north of Diest at around 1 a.m. on 28 April. Having landed safely, he saw a light coming from a house a 'short distance away… and a man was standing at the side. He took me in and bandaged my arm and gave me something to eat. He gave me a suit, coat and cap and motioned for me to leave. He pointed out a road to take.'[1790] Walking through the night he reached Diest at about 6.30 a.m. To the citizens of that town his identity was obvious, and on the road south to Tirlemont (Tienen) he 'was picked up by a member of the Resistance group'. He spent the night in Tirlemont and the next three days in three different houses there.

For the following ten weeks he stayed in four villages, all close together, halfway between Tirlemont and Diest – Glabbeek (six days), Meensel (ten days), Attenrode (six weeks) and, finally, Wever (two weeks). It was well into July when, wearing the uniform of a gendarme, he was driven by four other gendarmes to Brussels, some forty kilometres to the west. At the end of the month, together with 'a member of the RAF, Richard Irwin',[1791] and Woodrow Tarleton USAAF, Harrison was taken by car to 'a place just outside Namur. After two nights we were given bicycles and a guide, and after two days we reached a camp in the Ardennes Forest.'[1792] Along the way they picked up a second American, Sergeant Charles S. Bowman.

Sergeant R.P. Irwin's Halifax was shot down by a combination of fighter and flak on the night of 12/13 June 1944 on its way back from a raid on Cambrai. He came down near Furnes (Veurne in French), just in Belgium and barely five kilometres from the French border. His initial contact fed him and gave him civilian clothes before taking him to a café in the market square in Furnes. A British agent (name not known) was then contacted, and took him to the "American garage". The owner of the garage drove him to a disused farmhouse, where he stayed for three weeks, being fed by the Burgomaster of Bulskamp, a village two or three kilometres from Furnes. After returning to the American garage for two days, he moved to Dixmude with the British agent, who also took him to Brussels. 'I stayed in a butcher's shop for two days. The woman had a deformity of the right elbow.

From there I went to a blonde woman's flat, where I stayed for two days. Then to a Mr Gaston Scheff's, 25, Victor Aagart Street, where I stayed for ten to fifteen days. Then I was taken by Gaston Matthys… to a camp in the Ardennes Forest.'[1793]

Airmen came and went, but by the end of August 'there were twenty of us at this camp. Twenty more came in on 29 August, so we were moved by a priest to another camp near Bellevaux'. The camp was overrun by US ground forces on 8 September, and four days later Donald Harrison was flown back to England. Among the others who were at the camp at one time or another were Sergeant A.F. Gunnell; Sergeant R.P. Irwin; Flight Sergeant R. Dawson; Sergeant W.C.L. Western; Flight Lieutenant E.L. Mallet RCAF; and Warrant Officer 2nd Class K.C. Sweatman RCAF.[1794]

Mallet and Sweatman were separated after baling out from their Halifax on the night of 27/28 May 1944, but met up again in the village of Balen (Neet) on the evening of 28 May: 'We stayed nine days in the woods nearby and food and civilian clothing were brought to us.'[1795] They stayed for the following eight weeks with a Miss de Nies at Geel,[1796] before being taken by bicycle by two members of the Athos group, Juul Gendens and G. Renaerts, to Madame Verstraeten at 80, Kwalemstraat, Turnhout. On 4 August, in the hands of the Comet line, they were moved to 78, Joseph Brand Street, Brussels, the home of Monsieur Fernand Jacquet, where they stayed for a further week before going on 'to the Ardennes Forest where there was a camp which was run by a Mr Gaston Matthys, who is chief of the organisation in Brussels. At this camp we were also assisted by a Mr De Buis of Vellance. We stayed at this camp until 8 September, when an advance army patrol picked us up.'[1797] "Mr De Buis" was Monsieur Durbuy, and it was he who brought Mallet and Sweatman from Jacquet's house to the Hôtel du Vieux Jambon at Villance (not Vellance), a village just over twenty kilometres to the north and east of Bellevaux.

Airey Neave, having finished his business in France, made his way to Belgium, reaching Brussels on 3 September 1944, the day on which it was liberated by the Guards Armoured Division. Here he met up with Albert Ancia, and learnt of Comet's initial reticence to help with the setting-up of camps for evading airmen. Marathon was now over, but in the great rejoicing in the Belgian capital there was only little time to enjoy it, for the fighting continued. The Netherlands, Belgium's neighbour, was still in German hands, and the work of helpers there was as dangerous as ever.

CHAPTER 13

Evasions: June 1944–May 1945

'Evaders in uniform should be told that there is a curfew in most parts of France especially near the battle area, also in Brittany. Therefore all roads must be avoided. In Brittany, also, it is dangerous to ride a bicycle as the Germans are collecting them and may stop anyone riding a bicycle in order to confiscate it.'[1798]

Instructions issued to aircrew by the RAF on the advice of MI9

When Flight Lieutenant G.H. Thring RCAF and his 620 Squadron crew took off from RAF Fairford in their Stirling just after 10 a.m. on 6 June, the Normandy landings had been under way for only a few hours. They had just completed their 'special mission to France', dropping supplies, when the Stirling was hit by machine-gun fire from the ground. Owing 'to the fact that the dinghy was on fire and the sea near the coast was crowded with shipping, I considered that it was inadvisable to "ditch". I crash-landed near Périers-sur-le-Dan, about six miles north of Caen.'[1799] Périers-sur-le-Dan, barely five kilometres from Sword Beach, was being bitterly contested at the time by British troops of the 3rd Division.

Somehow Thring and his five crew managed to hide in a field behind enemy lines until it was dark when, walking openly towards the coast in the darkness, they were spotted by two German soldiers on bicycles and taken prisoner: 'We were escorted to a dug-out where we were searched. We were then taken under armed guard to near Caen, but a short distance from the town we turned North to Mathieu… arriving at a chateau there at dawn on 7 June.'[1800] They were fed and put in a barn but, as Thring noted, 'were aware of Allied activity in the area'.

Whereas some German officers in such a situation would not have hesitated to have done away with the prisoners, the German colonel under whose control they had come had a use for them alive. Most concerned for their welfare, they spent about four hours that evening at his suggestion in a trench with their captors. It was as well that they were no longer at the château, for it was even then being attacked. The Germans now wished to surrender, and Thring's flight engineer, Sergeant Buchan, was asked to approach the attackers with his hands in the air. Thring, however, was not prepared to allow him to take such a risk.

Fighting around the château had ceased by dusk, and shortly before midnight on 7/8 June a German captain asked the airmen to go into the cellar, where they were joined by the rest of the German soldiers who had been defending the building. The captain then announced that he intended to surrender at dawn but, when day broke, the captain and his colonel were nowhere to be found, and it was left to a lieutenant to order his men to lay down their arms. At around 10.30 a.m., when two British soldiers appeared, the German lieutenant and his men surrendered. Picking up the discarded weapons the airmen marched their German prisoners, all sixty-one of them, outside. Handing over their charges at a local headquarters, the airmen were sent to the beachhead and 'despatched by boat' to Gosport.

With all the hustle and bustle surrounding the greatest sea-borne invasion of all time, it was not surprising, perhaps, that the correct procedure was not followed when the Thring crew arrived at Gosport. Delivered 'in a small assault craft from a larger craft at a point between G.3 and G.4 Hards'[1801] they were received by Flying Officer Bugg, the embarkation officer on duty at G.3 Hard. As the airmen were wet through, Bugg 'wanted to get them away as quickly as possible, and he himself phoned RAF Gosport [Gosport 8174]. He said that he asked RAF Gosport to lay on the necessary drill as the men had been in enemy hands, but he did not inform security personnel.'

This he should have done of course, and it was no defence, in the eyes of Captain B. Gordon-Stables, security control officer, Portsmouth, that Bugg had 'contacted RAF Section, Portsmouth Sector, movement control' nor that they had 'approved his action in sending the men to the nearest RAF station.' The question of Bugg not contacting the SCO 'regarding these arrivals, in accordance with para 2a. of W.O. Circular 24/Gen/2278 (A.G. 1B) dated 10 Dec 43, has been taken up with the Embarkation Commandant.'

While Gordon-Stables attended to his efforts to help win the war, Thring and crew returned to their unit, and the bloody conflict on the near Continent raged on.

Flying Officer E.Q. Semple RCAF was the second pilot of a Dakota on 6/7 June 1944 on a supply-drop mission, Operation Rob Roy I, to the east of the River Orne for 6th Airborne Division. Hit by flak whilst over the sea, and when crossing the coast, the Dakota was set on fire. The pilot, Squadron Leader C. Wright AFC, landed in a hay field bristling with anti-glider obstacles near Giberville, half a dozen kilometres to the east of Caen. Semple received a deep head wound, and others of the crew were badly shaken up, one receiving a couple of cracked ribs. On instructions from Squadron Leader Wright, the party split into two sections. Semple, despite his wound, took charge of one section consisting of Flying Officer C.J. Williams and three of the four Royal Army Service Corps despatchers (the fourth having broken his arm):

> 'Semple's group presently found an abandoned house on the edge of Giberville, where its members proceeded to establish themselves as well as possible. The first person to challenge them was a Frenchwoman, who shouted the traditional "Qui va la?" Learning the evaders' identity she soundly kissed Semple and one of his companions again and again. (This was but another of the hazards of evasion.) She directed them to another house, where they were given food and shelter by the owner, and had their wounds dressed by the village curé. They were also outfitted with civilian clothing.
>
> 'Soon moving to the nearby village of Tilly-la-Campagne, they there occupied a fully furnished house, which they had all to themselves, having been given the key by the owner who was temporarily living elsewhere. There was considerable German activity in the village both by day and by night, but especially by night when motorized columns were passing through. Nevertheless, the evaders were undetected. They were even bold enough to venture forth and reconnoitre Giberville in an attempt to learn the whereabouts of the British forward troops. En route thereto they were stopped by German guards to whom they pleaded that they were on their way to bury a dead friend who had been left in the town. (This was true. One of their French assistants had been killed during a shelling of the town two days before, and they later buried him.) After considerable arguing they were allowed to pass, but were warned that any civilians found in Giberville were liable to be shot. Despite the warning they settled down more or less permanently in an empty house in the village, having decided to hide out in Giberville to await the arrival of British troops. During this resettlement period Semple was again the recipient of a kiss, this time by an attractive mademoiselle who had vowed thus to favour the first Allied soldier she met.
>
> 'His closest call came during one of his frequent forays for food. On his way out of a deserted farmhouse he found himself face-to-face with two grey-clad members of the Wehrmacht. Maintaining his composure, he smiled broadly and greeted them with "Bon jour". When they inquired in French what he was doing there, he replied that the house belonged to his family, who had been evacuated, and that he had returned for a fresh pair of socks, his old ones being worn out. (He had snatched a pair during his foraging, and these he now held up for display). The Germans fell for the line, remarking, "C'est la guerre", to which he replied "Oui, certainement – c'est la guerre".
>
> 'Shortly after he returned to the hide-out, deserted Giberville was "zeroed in" by British artillery, and the evasion team had to take shelter in a slit trench for thirty minutes. That was exactly three weeks after D-Day.
>
> 'The following day they learned from an itinerant Italo-Frenchman that British troops were in Longueval, but a short distance away. Next morning, at 0315 hours, they set out for that town. The rest of their adventures, as described in Semple's words, went like this:
>
> "… I split the group into two sections. The first was made up of F/O Williams, a French boy who knew the district well, and me; another section of six followed some distance behind. I gave explicit orders that the rear section should do exactly as we did, that is, stop when we stopped, and move when we moved, keeping their distance. I also said that in the event of a definite risk of capture, every man should fend for himself.
>
> "We cut across the fields, avoiding enemy positions about which the Italian had warned us. At 0400 hours, while we were passing a wood, snipers opened up with tracer fire, and we had to throw ourselves flat on the ground. They were so near that we could hear them working their rifle bolts. It was still dark, but the light of dawn was beginning to show on the horizon and luckily was in the sniper's eyes. After a few minutes the firing stopped and we went forward on our hands and knees. Having moved on about fifteen or twenty yards, I stopped to check on the rear party. As it was nowhere in sight I crawled back to the area where we had last stopped and continued for perhaps fifty yards beyond. There was still no sign of any of the party. I even called out its members' names, but the only result was a few more shots that arrived in my vicinity. I returned to my section and we waited ten minutes for the others to turn up, all the while crouched in a cornfield. As it was now getting too light for comfort, we decided to go on without them. We suddenly reached the end of the cornfield and made a mad scramble on our hands and knees across 200 yards of open country with no reaction from the enemy. We would proceed in this fashion until reaching another cornfield and then, upon hitting Longueval, we stumbled upon a

minefield. Luckily several mines were wired together and were clearly visible. While retracing our steps we were overjoyed to hear the typical English exclamation, 'Oy!' We had reached our objective; we were in the hands of the British 51st Division."'[1802]

Both Semple and Williams had returned to their squadron on 3 July, flying back in an aircraft of 271 Squadron. On 9 March 1945 Semple was admitted a Member of the Order of the British Empire for his leadership of the evaders, the citation for which reads as follows:

'During this time other evaders joined the party under Flying Officer Semple's leadership. Finally it became necessary to split the party into two sections and Flying Officer Semple successfully led his section through the firing line into the British lines. At all times Flying Officer Semple showed a singleness of purpose and consideration both for the French civilians who helped him and for the other members of his party.

'Since this officer's return to duty he has carried out two resupply missions over Arnhem as a pilot with No. 437 (RCAF) Squadron.'[1803]

When Flight Sergeant J.E. Parkinson enlisted in the RAF at twenty-nine years of age, leaving behind his poultry farm business at Appley Bridge near Wigan in Lancashire, he could never have known that after being shot down into a French potato field early on the morning of 8 June 1944 a broken bone would save his life.

He was the navigator of a Lancaster that was attacked by a night-fighter on the night of 7/8 June 1944 as it made its way to bomb "communications" at Chevreuse, a small town barely twenty-five kilometres from the centre of Paris. Having buried his equipment in the potato field, despite a badly cracked ankle he had hobbled barely two kilometres towards Paris when he was accosted by two members of the French Resistance. Five minutes later they met Parkinson's bomb aimer, Flight Sergeant G. Washbourne RAAF. The two airmen were taken to Châtenay-Malabry on the south-west outskirts of Paris, where Parkinson's ankle was bandaged. While he rested Gordon Washbourne 'went into Paris the following morning in civilian clothes along with armed Resistance members where they were captured.' Details of what happened to Washbourne thereafter are not known, except that he was not to survive.[1804]

On the night of 9/10 June Parkinson was moved to another house in Châtenay-Malabry, where he stayed for approximately four days before going 'to the barracks of a guard and from there to a warehouse of another member' in Paris. With his ankle mending well, he enquired as to how he might regain the Allied lines, but was told that that was quite impossible. On 5 July he went to Feucherolles planning to escape from his benefactors, and was joined by his flight engineer, Sergeant W. Russell, and by his mid-upper gunner, Sergeant P. Murphy. On 6 July they contacted another Resistance group at Poissy, across the River Seine to the west of Paris but, still unable to get away, went to Evancourt three days later 'to await the arrival of an intelligence agent (maquis) to journey to the lines in Normandy.'

After waiting for a further ten days they were informed that the agent had been killed at St Lô 'owing to having German agents amongst the aviators'. Accordingly, on 19 July they were passed on to another organisation, at Gournay-en-Bray, where they learnt that the heads of the Resistance had been arrested two months previously. Growing ever impatient they were given an address in Puys, a couple of kilometres north of Dieppe, where they understood that they would be able to get away by fishing boat. They left on 21 July but, with no boat, transport was arranged some days later to take them back to Paris. Before they could leave, however, it was discovered that Paris was now a "closed" city. Russell and Murphy left anyway on 17 August in the hope of getting through to the Allied lines. Parkinson stayed behind and, after a close encounter with some German soldiers who appropriated a couple of bicycles and demanded food and drink, was liberated on 20 August barely three hours after Russell and Murphy.

Pilot Officer D.E. Melcombe RCAF was in hiding at Châteauroux after being shot down on the night of 11/12 June 1944. Another member of his crew, Flying Officer James Clement RCAF, had been found by a friend of Roger Bodineau and family (see Chapter 9) and had been taken to their farm, la Salle Girault, at Larçay, where he was to spend the next five weeks.

Having learnt of Melcombe's whereabouts Clement decided on 20 July, against the advice of Roger Bodineau, to send him a note, which was duly collected by the "postman" used by the *Réseau* "Marco Polo". The French Milice and the Gestapo had been looking for this postman, and at around 11 p.m. on 23 July 1944 tracked him down to the Hôtel Leminor, Places des Halles, Tours. Chasing him onto the hotel roof they shot him dead, and on his body found forty-three letters, among them the note from Clement.

The investigations of the Milice and Gestapo into the origins of this letter led them to pay a visit to the Larçay post office on the afternoon of 24 July, where postman Raymond Cras was forced to show them the way to la Salle Girault. The Bodineaus were at work in their vineyard when the eldest son, Raoul, saw several cars and a lorry heading rapidly in their direction. As this could mean only one thing he immediately warned his father, who told Raoul to go to la Giraudière farm at Véretz to raise the alarm. Slipping away before the Milice and Gestapo had surrounded la Salle Girault, Raoul did not see them beat young Daniel with a bull-whip for the best part of an hour. They beat him until he told them where the airman was hiding. No mention was made of the radio transmitter/receiver hidden on the farm, but Roger and Marcelle Bodineau, Raymond Cras, Maxime Piette (the radio operator), and James Clement were taken away. The farm and all its contents were either wrecked or looted. Left behind, all alone, were Daniel and Max.

Roger Bodineau and James Clement were locked-up in the prison at Tours until 9 August. On that day, they and twenty-four others were driven from the prison in three lorries to Parçay-Meslay airfield near St Symphorien, north-east of Tours, and murdered. Marcelle Bodineau survived the horrors of Ravensbrück concentration camp weighing 29 kilograms ($4^1/_2$ stones). Though extremely ill, Maxime Piette also survived. Raymond Cras, however, died at Bergen-Belsen concentration camp on the very day on which it was liberated. *'Voici le lourd tribut payé par une famille de résistant qui a toujours refusé de se coucher devant le nazisme et le pétainisme.'*[1805]

Probably not many aircrew could claim that they had been hospitalised due to the prop wash from their own Halifax bomber blowing them down the runway with such force as to cause bodily harm. But that is what happened to the mid-upper gunner of Pilot Officer W.C. Reed's crew one night in June 1944. As a result, when Bill Reed and crew were slated for operations on the night of 12/13 June (the Amiens marshalling yards), they were short of a gunner. Sergeant D.R. Arundel, 158 Squadron, 'was the only spare gunner that night and for some reason I did not feel comfortable with it. It was as if I had a premonition. I just felt that things were going to go wrong and I took my razor with me for the first time.'[1806]

All went well until they were leaving the target when the rear gunner suddenly shouted 'Corkscrew port!' At that moment Dave Arundel in the mid-upper turret saw tracer bullets and cannon fire heading in his direction. Hit in the right eye and neck and briefly falling unconscious he came round in time to see another member of the crew signalling that it was time to bale out. The Halifax was already on its way down when Dave jumped. Landing a good way from the wreckage, but in considerable pain from his wounds and bleeding very heavily, he crawled into a ditch at the edge of the field in which he had landed. Surviving a close call with a herd of cows – he thought the sound of their hooves were Germans coming to get him – he discovered a cherry tree close by, laden with fruit. Ravenously hungry, he 'had a good feed. By this time my eye was very swollen and was beginning to fester, as there was yellow puss on my hand when I tried to rub it.'[1807]

Appreciating that he needed medical attention he made his way to a farmhouse which, he noted, had no telephone wires leading to it. The farmer, Julien Genty, answered Dave's knock on the door, greeting him with 'Camarade!' Thinking that this meant that he was to give himself up, Dave turned and was about to run off when Julien made him understand that a comrade was also being hidden on the farm, near Haussez (Seine-Inférieure). Taking Dave to a hayloft he met his wireless operator, Flight Sergeant Harold Squires: 'When Squires saw my eye he passed out. He later told me it was in a right mess.' Madame Genty did what she could for the damaged eye, bathing it with disinfectant, 'but it was still badly swollen and would not open.' She was, though, concerned that the Germans would come and find the two airmen on their property. Accordingly, Dave Arundel and "Darky" Squires decided to move on.

In view of the curfew, Julien Genty said that he would fetch help, and returned with the gamekeeper of the estate of the Duc de Polignac, who lived at the Château de Mercastel. Squires went off to the château, while Dave Arundel went to the home of Monsieur le Rousset, curé of Villers-Vermont a kilometre or two away. In a bar 'about three big gardens away from the priest's house… was Tom from Texas who was a first lieutenant and second pilot in a Flying Fortress.'[1808] When news of the Normandy landings were gleaned from the curé's secret radio, and the Allies seemed to be making no headway, Dave Arundel and Harold Squires decided to steal 'a wood burning van and set off for Paris. We were stopped two or three times but we were waved through. We got quite confident and arrived in Paris only to be asked for our papers. That was it. We had no papers for the van so we were handcuffed with our hands behind our backs.'[1809]

It was not long before a large Mercedes car drove up, and out got members of the SD, resplendent in their black uniforms, with the Death's Head cap badge and SS "lightning flashes" on their collars. Squashed between two guards they were driven off to the SD's headquarters at 82–86 Avenue Foch (known to Parisians as "Avenue Bosches"). The usual interrogation followed, accompanied by beatings and threats of being shot as spies as they had been caught in civilian clothes. In their defence the two airmen showed their RAF dog-tags, but were told in no uncertain terms that they could have got them from anywhere. Squires was then hit very hard, and the pair of them, handcuffed together, fell to the floor. 'We were dragged to our feet and isolated in small dark cubicles with no room to sit or lie down. We were also forbidden to speak and though we had no watches we knew we were there for a long, long time.'[1810]

When the SD had finished with the two airmen they were removed to Fresnes prison to await their deportation to Germany. For some reason they were not put in the cells with all the other captured airmen who were sent to the hell of Buchenwald on 15 August 1944. Instead, on the night of 20 August French warder Louis Bossarrie opened their cell doors, saying: 'Partir. Ici. Vite' ('Leave. Here. Quickly'). They followed him and other warders out through their quarters at the back of the prison and into the street. 'Once outside they pointed in the direction from which the Allies would come. We kept walking until daylight, then hid until the Free French passed.'[1811]

After celebrating the liberation of Paris they decided to enjoy a quick tour of the various battle fronts before handing themselves over to the authorities. They were taken to an army camp near Caen, and told that they could be back in England in eight hours. As this was too long to have to wait they made their way to the nearest airstrip and hitched a flight home in an RAF Dakota to RAF Northolt. Harold Squires was sent on his way after the required debriefing, but Dave Arundel needed further treatment to his eye and was driven by staff car to the hospital at RAF Halton.

After a few days observation he was sent to Harley Street, London so that specialists could have a look at his eye. He was not so ill, however, that he wasn't able to have a beer or two. The only snag was that he was dressed in hospital blues – a blue suit with a red tie – which alerted pub landlords to the fact that he was under medication and therefore should not be served alcohol! The answer to this was quite simple: 'I used to wait outside the pub and get a pal to bring one out to me.' The news about his eye was not so good, though. A specialist told him that there were still three splinters in it and that he would not regain his sight.

Back in hospital for a further three weeks, he was cheered one day when Matron brought him a bottle of Guinness and asked him if he had seen the *London Gazette*? No, he hadn't, and in it, 14 July 1944, was the notice that in a joint citation with three of his former crew (Tansley, Bancroft and Fripp, each of whom received the DFC) he had been awarded the DFM for struggling out of his damaged turret and helping to extinguish the several fires in their aircraft which had been started by an enemy fighter on the night of 2/3 June.[1812] His proudest moment came on 31 August 1945 when he went to Buckingham Palace to receive his well-earned medal from His Majesty King George VI.

The Normandy landings were already twelve days old when Flight Lieutenant R.G. Brown RCAF and his No. 2 were ordered off from RAF Gatwick in their Mustangs to carry out a late-evening reconnaissance of the railway line running west-south-west between Paris and Laval. Crossing the French coast over Dieppe they ran into low cloud, which forced them to fly below 200 feet.[1813] They were over Paris at around 10.30 p.m. when they ran into light flak and headed into the low cloud. Losing contact with each other Brown radioed his No. 2 to return to base, and told him that when he was over Dieppe he was to climb to 1,000 feet and ask for a "homing". The two pilots thereafter kept in touch with each other until Brown heard the homing signal being given from England.

Continuing above cloud on a compass course the more experienced Brown let down through the overcast, and found himself slap bang over a marshalling yard, but with no idea which one it was. He also found himself at the centre of an intense barrage of light flak. His Mustang received numerous hits before he was able to pull up into the cloud and so, with his compass wildly gyrating through ninety degrees, he set course for what he hoped was the Normandy beachhead. Climbing to 13,000 feet he also radioed for a 'homing', but pressing all the buttons produced nothing but silence. Now forced to drop much lower in the gathering dark so that he could get some idea of his location, he was flying at an estimated 3,500 feet, straight and level, when he was once again hit by flak, this time in the engine 'which lost power and the aircraft went into a steep glide and caught fire. I could not see the ground, and after jettisoning everything I baled out at 2,500 feet at 2345 hours.'[1814]

Despite the dark he made a good landing a few kilometres north-east of Brest and to the west of the River Elorn. Laying-up in a copse near Landerneau (Finistère) for the rest of the night and day (19 June) he decided to make for the beachhead. In pouring rain he came across a small cluster of farmhouses. Asking one of the farmers if he could sleep in his barn the man agreed, and said that he could supply civilian clothing for 250 francs. Brown took him up on the offer, and chucked his service clothes, less his RCAF badges, down a well. After breakfast on 20 June he walked for several hours, covering some thirty kilometres, until he reached the village of Pleyber-Christ (Finistère), half a dozen kilometres south of Morlaix. His feet being considerably the worse for wear he was glad when he 'found friends, with whom I stayed until I made contact with the American forces on 6 August 44.'

Nothing remarkable about that, one might say, nor about his arrival at Pleyber-Christ even when he 'came upon a communal laundry centre at which were working a number of women'. Feeling in need of a shave and a good wash he asked one of the women if she could get hold of a razor. Neither she nor the others were prepared to take a chance on his being friendly until he had proved his identity, which he did by producing his RCAF insignia. Immediately made welcome he was told to hide himself near the boilers while a razor and food were fetched. After his meal and a shave he set off again, but with the warning to be careful as the area was swarming with Germans. He had not gone far when two women came running after him. One of them, a schoolmistress from Morlaix, told Brown to contact the maquis. He was to go south to the village of le Releg and 'try an indirect approach to the local curé'. If he failed with the priest, then he was to go on to Trédudon, three or four kilometres south of le Releg, 'which was a centre of patriotic activity'.

At le Releg Robert Brown, showing his insignia to another French farmer, was allowed to use his barn. The man gave him some food, but as he was clearly not going to help him further Brown decided to push on to Trédudon. Forced to keep to the roads because the 'tops of the hills and moors were fenced off with "mine" notices and were full of anti-glider stakes' he reached Trédudon on 21 June, and fell in with patriotic French people. Once satisfied as to his genuineness they were prepared to help him, but as there were too many Germans passing through the village it was decided to take him by bicycle to Grinec, a hamlet well out of the way in the hills to the south-east of Pleyber-Christ: 'Here I was introduced to Pierre le Cheur and invited to stay with him and his family. They had a secret room over the stables and I slept there.'

Anxious to get back to England, Brown asked his host what could be done about it. Pierre said that he would make enquiries at Callac (Côtes-du-Nord), a small town of some 1,650 inhabitants about thirty kilometres south-east of Grinec, 'where a great number of French parachutists had been dropped from England, and in which locality the patriots were holding in force.'[1815] These 'parachutists' were from the 4th French Parachute Battalion attached to the British SAS. Having been dropped in Brittany on 6 June 1944 on Operation Samwest (see Chapter 11) they were engaged in a fierce battle with German troops at St Marcel (Morbihan) on 18 June. The many French survivors, SAS and maquisards, retreated north-westwards to Callac.

Having learnt that it was the intention to construct an airstrip at Callac to receive Lysander aircraft from England, Pierre le Cheur sent a girl, Emma, to see if it would be possible for Brown to return on one of them. It was a fortnight before she had returned from her mission, for while on her way to Callac her bicycle was appropriated by the Germans, and she had then fallen into the hands of the Gestapo. Happily none the worse for her ordeal, she was released and brought back news of the pitched battle on 18 June between the Germans and the French parachutists who had, temporarily, dispersed.

With no immediate prospect, therefore, of a swift return to England, Robert Brown made himself useful on Pierre's farm until 13 July, when the head of the local Resistance came to see him. About fifty years of age and 'known to all as "Madame"' she lived in Trédudon. She brought with her an identity card using a "mug shot" photograph that Robert had previously handed over. Included in his papers was a *laissez passer* for the German coastal zone and also a pass to allow him to get to and from his "work". 'There was some sort of plan to get me away dressed as a German officer for which I was to go to Laz.' Brown cycled with Pierre to Trédudon on 14 July intending to go on to Laz (Finistère) on the following day. At Trédudon, though, they were told that the Germans were threatening to arrest a hundred Frenchmen from several villages in the area and to shoot them as a reprisal for the shooting of five German soldiers. It was therefore deemed inadvisable to go anywhere for the time being.

All was clear on 15 July when Brown joined some maquisards to help with an arms-supply drop some ten kilometres away. In the event the drop was not made, although the aircraft was heard circling overhead. No fires were lit to help the airmen spot the DZ, and Brown doubted that their torches could have been seen anyway. Present at the DZ was a French officer, Captain P. Lebel, to whom Brown submitted his case to be sent home. Lebel suggested that he should go with him to Laz 'and there would see what could be done'. On 16 July Brown was introduced to Captain B.M.W. Knox ("Kentucky"), the leader of the three-man Jedburgh ("Jed") team Giles that had been dropped nearby on 9 July. Captain Lebel ("Loire", real name Grall), was also one of the Giles team, whose third member was a British soldier, Sergeant Gordon H. Tack ("Tickle").

Knox said that he would radio London to ask for instructions as to what could be done for Brown, but that in the meantime he, Brown, 'could be very useful to him'. Brown effectively became a member of Giles, taking over the coding and decoding of signals and helping 'to recce proposed landing strips and dropping sites'. There was a problem, though, with the signals, which neither Knox nor Lebel could interpret. As they were apparently being sent from England by a Frenchman, Knox asked for them to be sent in English, to give them all a chance of deciphering them. Matters improved somewhat thereafter, though it was clear that the French operator in London was having his own problems translating the French text into English for transmission.

This was only an irritation, but much worse was the night of an arms drop when, with lights and fires ablaze to welcome the RAF transport aircraft, a Ju88 appeared instead and gave the reception area a good going-over with cannon and machine-gun. No-one was injured, but all were surprised that the local Gestapo did not follow-up on the ground. The only explanation that the Giles team could come up with was that the Ju88 pilot had probably not got an accurate fix on the site.

The Gestapo were, however, busy elsewhere. Together with other German troops, including men of the 2nd Parachute Division and submarine crews on rest at a château near Châteauneuf, they were doing their utmost to eradicate the local opposition. This particular château, an important rest centre for the Kriegsmarine, was a great thorn in the side of both the Resistance and of the Jeds, for it 'held a completely dominating view of the countryside for miles around, and was used by the Germans as an observation tower'.[1816] One day, when the Germans had almost succeeded in surrounding Brown and his companions, he suggested that an air strike be requested to demolish the place. Two days after the signal was sent the château was bombed and strafed: 'The maquis sent a recce in force to check the result. Two wings of the chateau had been flattened. One wing still remained and was occupied by the Germans. The recce force attacked, killed seventeen and brought back some prisoners of war.'[1817]

A second signal was sent to London not only thanking them for the strike but requesting a second attack to finish off the place. A lone Spitfire came over on the following day and gave the remaining wing and surrounding area another pasting. That night three companies of maquisards, 'each led by a French officer dropped from London, went in and cleaned up and occupied the place.' German casualties were heavy. Even so, the "Germans", many of whom were White Russians, were far from finished in the area and two maquisards 'on the administrative staff' were captured. Their bodies were found in a house two days later, almost unrecognisable after they had been horribly tortured before being shot.

When one of the German prisoners managed to escape, the gloves came off, and the order was given that any more prisoners, once their interrogation had been completed, were to be 'speedily dealt with'. Captain Knox recalled that the prisoners 'were mostly very young. We found jewelry, money, [and] civilian ID cards in their pockets. They refused to tell us where these things came from, but they did admit to having participated in extorsions [*sic*]. They were later shot by the FFI.'[1818]

Clashes between the Germans and the Allies were constant in Brittany, and Major C.M. Ogden-Smith RA, leader of Francis, another Jed that had been parachuted into Finistère on 10 July,[1819] was killed on 29 July in one such scrap. While resting at an isolated farm Francis had been surrounded by six hundred Feldgendarmes. Ogden-Smith, wounded in the stomach, was captured and finished off by the enemy, as was Moydon, a member of the SAS who had teamed up with Francis after he had become detached from his own party.[1820] Moydon had suffered a broken leg as a result of a hand-grenade explosion and, having run out of ammunition, was cut down by a burst from a sub-machine gun. Both he and Ogden-Smith were in uniform and wearing the badges of their rank. Not content with their victory, the Germans then burnt down the farm, slaughtered all the animals and shot the farmer for good measure.[1821]

In such turmoil little could be done for Robert Brown, whose chance to leave the safety of Captain Knox's party came on 5 August with news of an American breakthrough. On 31 July 1944, when units of the 4th Armored Division (US Third Army) had reached the River Sélune in the area of Pontaubault (Manche), General George S. Patton Jr, commanding the Third Army, 'told Middleton[1822] to head for Brest and Rennes, with the 6th Armored Division and the 79th Infantry Division on Brest, and the 8th Infantry Division and 4th Armored Division on Rennes…'[1823]

When, therefore, a message was to be delivered on 6 August to the commander of the 6th Armored Division (Major-General R.W. Grow) by "Squadron Leader Smith" (*nom de guerre* of Frenchman Captain le Blond, and not to be confused with the squadron leader of the same name in Chapter 8), Brown 'was invited to join him'. They departed from their base in Finistère in an ambulance driven by Mademoiselle G. Willmann. Brown noted that she 'was amazingly brave and later displayed a complete disregard to shellfire and snipers' bullets.' Having no real idea as to the location of the nearest Americans when they set off, their 'plan was to drive to a village as near the German forward positions as possible' and for le Blond and Brown to then get through on foot. Reaching the vicinity of Plabennec, barely ten kilometres north of Brest, on the evening of 6 August they found that the

Americans were not as far forward as they had thought, though the 6th Armored Division, having punched its way over 200 kilometres south-west from Avranches in almost a week, was not far away.

Sometime during the night of 6/7 August near Plabennec Brown and his companions found an American convoy heading towards Brest, but had to leave it when one of the ambulance's tyres punctured. While le Blond left to fulfil his mission to deliver the "sit rep" to General Grow, Mlle. Willmann drove the ambulance on the rim of the punctured tyre to a barn in a village three or four kilometres south-west of Plabennec, where she and Brown ran into an American armoured reconnaissance patrol under Lieutenant Rochester. Telling them that the Germans were making a counter-attack he suggested that they 'should get into his armoured car and go forward' with him. This they did, until they encountered another American unit under the command of a colonel, 'who confirmed that the Germans had cut his lines of communication.'

They stayed at the colonel's HQ until the night of 7/8 August, when they 'were given seats in a very heavily escorted column of empty trucks, and some others with 700 German prisoners of war.' They drove all night, but when Brown's driver was so sleepy that the ten-ton truck was swaying 'all over the place' Brown took the steering wheel. He had never before driven such a large vehicle but, understandably, 'felt happier' when he was driving. Heading north they dropped off Mlle. Willmann at St Brieuc, and Brown continued with the American convoy before hitch-hiking his way to the Allied Expeditionary Air Force on the night of 9/10 August. After a brief stop at 2nd Tactical Air Force HQ he was passed on to IS9 (WEA) for a full interrogation on 15 August.

Towards the end of the war Warrant Officer W. J. "Jim" Kelly RCAF, was enjoying a beer in an English pub when in came another airman whom he knew very well. 'My god! You're dead', said Kelly. 'Yeah. Dead thirsty', replied Flying Officer G.P. Brophy RCAF.

Kelly had every reason to believe that Brophy was dead, for they had last seen each other aboard a blazing Lancaster, KB726, 419 Squadron, en route to the Cambrai railway yards on the night of 12/13 June 1944. A Ju88 had attacked KB726 and had set the two port engines and the rear of the fuselage on fire. The pilot – Flying Officer Arthur de Breyne RCAF – had no hesitation in ordering the crew to bale out. Obeying his skipper's instructions the mid-upper gunner, Warrant Officer II Andrew Charles Mynarski RCAF, left his post and made his way to the rear door before baling out. Pausing briefly he could see that the rear turret, which had been jammed by the Ju88's shells, was engulfed in flames and trapped inside it was his friend and fellow gunner, George Brophy. With no thought for his own safety Mynarski's first thought was to get his pal out.

Through the flames, Brophy could see Mynarski trying to open the doors of his turret with his bare hands, then watched in horror as Mynarski's clothing caught fire. Knowing that Mynarski had not a snowball in hell's chance of opening the doors Brophy signalled to him to jump. Saluting his comrade in a gesture of farewell Mynarski jumped from the doomed aircraft, but the same flames that had been licking at his clothing had also burnt into his parachute, and he crashed heavily to the ground. Though found alive by a Frenchman, he soon succumbed to his injuries.[1824]

By extreme good fortune George Brophy was to survive the crash of KB726, thrown clear of the wreckage, as were the others of the crew. "Art" de Breyne, Flying Officer Robert Body RCAF, (navigator), Jim Kelly and George Brophy all evaded capture, but Sergeant R.E. Vigars (flight engineer) and Sergeant J.W. Friday RCAF (bomb aimer) became prisoners of war. Jack Friday, knocked unconscious as he opened the front escape hatch, was bundled through the hatch by others of his crew as one of them pulled the ripcord of his parachute.

It was while they were in hiding together that Kelly and Body learnt of the death of Mynarski and, incorrectly as he was later to prove, that of George Brophy.

These were hard times for the boys of 419 Squadron RCAF, which lost three Lancasters on the Cambrai raid and two more on the night of 16/17 June with only two survivors. The squadron lost no more Lancasters until the attack on the marshalling yards at Villeneuve-St Georges on the southern outskirts of Paris on the night of 4/5 July 1944. It should have been a low-risk attack, but Luftwaffe night-fighters shot down six Lancasters and five Halifax bombers. Three of the six Lancasters – KB718, KB723, KB727 – each with a crew of seven were from 419 Squadron.[1825]

The pilot of KB718, Flying Officer L.W.A. Frame RCAF, was on his thirteenth operation when the Lancaster was hit by flak and attacked by a German night-fighter shortly after bombing the target. With the two engines and main fuel tank on the port side on fire, and with the aircraft becoming more and more uncontrollable, Frame ordered the crew to bale out. All did so, three being taken prisoner and four evading capture. Frame himself landed uninjured on the edge of Fontainebleau Forest,[1826] some fifty kilometres south of Paris. After walking all night he slept for two or three hours in the woods near Barbizon (Seine-et-Marne) on the north-west edge of Fontainebleau Forest, before being woken up by people at work in adjoining fields. An elderly man checking his rabbit snares offered to fetch someone who could speak English, and returned with Kay Devigne, a twenty-six-year-old Yorkshirewoman, mother of two children, who had married Frenchman Robert Devigne before the war. She took Frame to the Villa L'Écureuil (the Villa Squirrel) in Barbizon, the home of Madame Drue Tartière, an American married to a Frenchman.

Drue, a former film actress,[1827] met French actor Jacques Tartière (stage name Jacques Terrane) in New York in 1937. They married in England in September 1938, before moving to France in 1939. When war was declared Jacques tried to join the French army, but a pulmonary complaint precluded him from too active a service. Instead, a fluent English-speaker, he served as a liaison officer with the British army, and managed to wangle himself a berth as an interpreter onto the Norwegian expedition in April 1940 – without being able to speak one word of Norwegian. In England when the Franco-German armistice was signed in June 1940 he enlisted in the Gaullist Free French forces, and was in Syria on 18 June 1941 when he and two fellow French officers were sent under the white flag to demand the surrender of General Henri Dentz's Vichy French troops in Damascus. As they returned to their lines the three officers were shot in the back. Jacques died in hospital on 20 June. On the following day Free French forces under General Catroux entered Damascus.

With her husband away on active service Drue worked in Paris at the French government's short-wave radio station Paris Mondiale. It ceased transmitting from Paris on 17 June 1940 and moved to Bordeaux to avoid the Germans. Drue went with it, and was there when Pétain made his speech to the French nation on 20 June 1940 (see Introduction). The president of Paris Mondiale, Jean Fraysse, was himself to become heavily involved with the nascent Resistance, and it was through him that Drue became caught up in underground activities

Now a widow and having given up her radio work, she moved into the Villa L'Écureuil at Barbizon, where Jean Fraysse was a frequent visitor, and it was while out walking on the nearby plain together that he and Drue noticed a small farm tucked out of the way. Jean thought that it would be ideal as a repository for arms for the Resistance. With food already in short supply, Drue appreciated that the few acres that went with the farm would also be ideal for raising crops and animals, and by the end of March 1942 had struck a deal with the farm's owner, Madame Fontaine of Barbizon. The farm, given the name Bel Ébat ("fine frolic"), became the centre for Resistance men from the nearby towns of Melun and Milly-la-Forêt.

During 1942, as a reprisal for the alleged similar treatment of German women in the United States, the Germans began rounding-up all American women up to the age of sixty-five, taking them away for internment at Vittel (Vosges). On 22 September 1942 Drue and another American inhabitant of Barbizon, sixty-four-year-old and somewhat deaf Miss Marion Greenough who had been resident in France since before the First World War, were collected by a large German feldgendarme and bundled off to Paris. As she was only days short of her sixty-fifth birthday Marion Greenough was soon released, but Drue and many others were despatched from the Pantin freight yards in Paris to the 225-room Grand Hôtel in Vittel, where they joined many English internees, some of whom had been there since 1940.

To accommodate all these internees the Germans had appropriated several hotels in France. Those in Vittel, which had been in use since 1940 and were commanded by SS Hauptmann Otto Landhauser, housed about two thousand internees, mostly Americans and British, but with some Russians and Jews from Poland and Austria who had falsified British and American passports.[1828] The low morale of all internees was given a tremendous boost on the night of 22/23 November 1942 when over two hundred RAF bombers flew right over Vittel on their way to Stuttgart. The internees went wild for an hour or so, but paid for their joyous excesses when their captors cut food rations and the electricity to their rooms.

On 11 December Drue was on her way home. She had managed to bring with her a medical certificate stating, falsely, that she was suffering from cancer of the womb, and with the help of several doctors in Vittel was released from internment so that she could go to Paris for a course of X-ray treatment. One of the conditions of her release, though, was that on her return to Paris she had to report to the Gestapo headquarters on Avenue Foch. This she did, and persuaded 'Hutterman, a polite Austrian, [who] was head of this office'[1829] to give her a *laisser-passer* for the journey from her home at Barbizon to Paris. Importantly, this pass had no expiry date, thus giving her the opportunity to come and go as she pleased between her home and the capital.

After her interview with Hutterman Drue returned to Barbizon, and became more and more embroiled in Resistance affairs. At first she helped Frenchmen escape to Unoccupied France to avoid the STO, but then in September 1943, on a visit to friends in Paris, she was told that there were a number of airmen being sheltered in the area. It was made clear to her that there was a great shortage of food and clothing in the capital, and her friend Dr Lamour asked if she would help. Drue agreed, and at the Paris home of Madame Heraux on the Avenue d'Orléans she met three American airmen

– Bob Giles, Carroll Haarup and Tom Mezynski.[1830] Seeing them, she decided that she could do nothing more useful in the war than to provide food and clothing for evading airmen, and this she was to do for the next eighteen months or so.

After the three Americans she assisted five unidentified Polish airmen who had apparently escaped from a prisoner-of-war camp in Germany and were being looked after by Madame Heraux and another stalwart, Olga Christol.[1831] Then Drue met two members of a 90 Squadron Stirling shot down on an SOE drop on the night of 4/5 March 1944, who had been brought to Olga Christol's house – Flying Officer H.C. Yarwood and Flight Sergeant S.T. Bulmer. However, the first RAF evader to be cared for by Drue at Barbizon was Lorne Frame.[1832]

Next to arrive following the Villeneuve raid were the pilot and navigator of Lancaster KB723, Flying Officer C.A.D. Steepe RCAF and Flying Officer D.G. Murphy RCAF, who had been found in the forest. Don Steepe had 'a big gash in the back of his head'. He also had 'an open cut on his forehead, all the hair was burned from the back of his head, and his upper lip was hanging down'. Dannie Murphy, too, was in poor shape. His 'left leg was broken, and it had swollen to twice its normal size. He had third degree burns on his legs, and his right hand was burned through. In addition he had cuts in various places.'[1833] With the help of two Frenchmen the Canadians were moved to a cottage, where Drue put four stitches into Don Steepe's lip. Dannie Murphy was made as comfortable as possible in the circumstances.

Information had meanwhile been brought of another airman who had been found in a haystack, and this proved to be Lorne Frame's navigator, Flying Officer W.C. "Bill" Watson RCAF. Sheltering at the home of Madame Marie Rode, Drue took him back to the Villa L'Écureuil. With the help of another Frenchman and his lorry, Don Steepe and Dannie Murphy were then collected and driven to May de Gesnes' house in Barbizon, though the journey had not been without considerable tension due to German patrols and road blocks in the area.

Doctor Philardeau agreed to come over from Fontainebleau to do what he could for Dannie Murphy's painful and swollen leg. With the four airmen now safely housed, Drue thought she could relax, but when two Resistance men arrived from Melun on Sunday morning with news of yet another airman, she told them to bring him to her house. 'An hour later in walked "Shorty", a sawed-off young Englishman from Croydon, outside London. He was dressed in reddish pants, raggedy, and much too big for him. He wore a ragged shirt and his own sleeveless sweater, full of holes, which he called his lucky sweater and wore on every mission.' The two Canadians were so delighted to see Sergeant P.P. "Shorty" Barclay, KB718's flight engineer, that 'they picked him up bodily and tossed him to one another.'[1834]

Phil Barclay's report was short, but to the point:

> 'An American, Mme. Dorothy Tartiere, whose husband was killed in Syria and whose brother is still in some form of espionage for the French, has been helping to hide Allied airmen for the past two years. I was number 197. She had at one time been in a German concentration camp, but managed to escape through feigning illness, and has since been fooling the Gestapo day after day. She was aided in her work by a Miss Greenough from Boston, and by a Miss Kaye de Vigne. It is impossible to thank or to praise any one of these ladies too much.'[1835]

Having jumped out of the blazing bomber Phil Barclay wondered as he drifted down in the quiet, moonlit night what would happen when he landed. He soon found out. Crashing through some trees he released his parachute and dropped to the ground. Walking by the aid of his compass for a while he came across a number of French people watching an aircraft burning in the adjacent field (presumably his, he thought). They saw him, and beckoned him over. He 'was given a coat to cover my uniform' and told to follow two young ladies to what proved to be a summer school for young children evacuated from Paris. Moving on to the village of Chailly-en-Bière, on the edge of Fontainebleau Forest, he was told to hide in the church porch until his guides reappeared, which they did some while later but having been unable to find the contact. Going back to the summer school, Phil made himself comfortable in the boiler house.

Another "summer school" was run by Marie-Madeleine Davy at the Château de la Fortelle, Rosay-en-Brie, north of Paris. She was known to evading airmen as Mademoiselle Bourgeois. Little teaching went on at the château, except perhaps the giving of instructions to the evaders. Marie-Madeleine had been a professor at the French Institute of Berlin, but on the declaration of war had returned to Paris to teach philosophy at the Sorbonne. Although running an independent organisation she helped several airmen to be passed on to other lines, providing false papers, clothing and lodging for Comet evaders in Paris, and feeding airmen into the Burgundy line.[1836]

One of the airmen to pass through her hands was bomb aimer Flying Officer Pierre Bauset RCAF, shot down on the way back from Frankfurt on the night of 25/26 November 1943. Having reached Paris by train a member of the Red Cross took him to Comet's Father Michel Riquet, who in turn passed him over to Marie Madeleine.[1837] Unable to move him down the line because of the numerous arrests within the organisation Pierre Bauset was handed over to the Marcus family, with whom he lived until a guide could be found to take him to Switzerland in January 1944. He travelled by bus to Annecy, and was then taken by a guide to Collonges-sous-Salève (Haute-Savoie) (where Johann Weidner of Dutch-Paris had lived) and then to Bossey. Giving the correct password to a grocer, Vuaillat, he was handed on to a *passeur*, who led him across the Swiss frontier. At 10 p.m. on the night of 18 January 1944 Corporal Chaperon of the Swiss frontier guard arrested him.

On the morning of 1 September 1944 Bauset crossed back into the Haute-Savoie region, and made his way to Marseille. With no official help to be found, he went to Paris, and on 19 September was back in England.

Two days after he had returned to the summer school, and having been moved to several other hiding places in the area, two men took Phil Barclay by van to Barbizon. Phil got out 'and followed one of the men at a distance. We made our way to the main street and he walked up to a small house with high gates and rang the bell. As the gate opened he turned and beckoned me to cross the road and enter the house. I had arrived at the Villa L'Écureuil, home of Drue Tartière… I was greeted by a charming, blonde, American lady and right behind her Lorne Frame and Bill Watson.'[1838]

In a few days time, when they were well enough to be moved, Don Steepe and Dannie Murphy were also taken to the Villa L'Écureuil. It was a bit of a squash, and food was not overly plentiful, but they survived. On 18 August the household was awoken by the longed-for sound of the German Army on the retreat, which would mark the beginning of the end of the airmen's evasion. Barbizon, though, was still in the fighting zone. Artillery shells spasmodically flew overhead for several days, until the shelling became even heavier on 21 August, heralding the arrival, at six o'clock that evening, of the Americans in the village of Villiers-en-Bière, half a dozen kilometres to the north. But it was not until mid morning on 23 August that the Americans arrived in Barbizon – two soldiers in a jeep, First Lieutenant Charles Whipple and his driver, Bob Close.

The five airmen remained with Drue until 26 August, when a Lieutenant Preston came for them in his jeep from Fontainebleau. It was a sad parting for the five "boys" as they said their goodbyes to Drue, whom they affectionately called "Mom". In due course they were taken to B.14 airstrip, Banville, on the Normandy coast, for the short flight to Northolt with many other evaders, in an American DC-3 Dakota. On arrival at the interrogation centre at Baker Street, London, Phil 'said goodbye to the others as they went for immediate repatriation to Canada.'

Wing Commander D.R. Donaldson and crew in Lancaster LM597 were a little early over target, the V1 site at Prouville in northern France, on 24/25 June 1944, so he decided to go round again. This was never a recommended course of action over heavily-defended targets but, as many French ones were considered to be not too dangerous, a second orbit might not have been too risky. As events were to prove, Prouville was well defended, and Donaldson's second circuit, at only 12,000 feet, allowed German flak gunners to get the range. A burst of heavy flak exploded beneath LM597's port inner engine, and set it on fire. 'In feathering the port inner, the engineer feathered the port outer as well and owing to a failure of our accumulators we were unable to un-feather the port outer.'[1839] With the port inner still ablaze and the rudder controls shot away – Donaldson had no control over the Lancaster's swing – he gave the order to jettison the bombs and to bale out.

As Donaldson left the cockpit to bale out through the forward hatch he noticed all four rev counters reading "nil". He also noticed as he was hanging beneath his parachute 'three members of the crew being engaged by searchlights and light flak.' Searchlights wavered on him, too, and light flak was also flying around in his direction, but without hitting him. 'As I neared the ground I heard voices, and rifle bullets seemed to come very close to me.' Despite the uneven contest, none of the crew was hurt. Donaldson was one of the four to evade capture, while the other three were taken prisoner of war.

The wing commander, landing near St Pol, headed for a nearby wood, which happened to contain another V1 site and which was then bombed by other RAF aircraft.[1840] That they missed their target, and Donaldson was clear when he saw a V1 being launched shortly afterwards. Needing to remove himself from the scene, he found the area to be crawling with Germans, and had several close shaves over the next four days as he made his way 'towards Amiens, meantime receiving food, [and] civilian clothes from people who would not give any further assistance.' Keeping to main roads and walking by day was not the practice recommended in the evasion manual, but he reached Amiens, via St Pol and Doullens, without any problems. There, however, he noticed that 'the bomb damage was severe, and the population seemed very upset.' Discretion being the better part of valour, therefore, he decided to leave quickly, and took himself off to the next village. Contacting the curé he was sent to see a Frenchman 'who could speak English, and with whom an R.V. [rendezvous] was made for the following day, in Amiens.'

Donaldson's bold middle-of-the-road walking might have gone unnoticed by the Germans, but it had certainly been noted by the French Resistance, who regarded such behaviour as distinctly suspicious. Accordingly other RAF evaders in Amiens were asked to question him very carefully to prove his bona fides, but the matter was only resolved when a confirmatory reply to a radio message had been received from London. This was a frustrating time for the airmen "trapped" in Amiens, the Caen bridgehead seemingly so static, and all wanted either to get to Spain or to try to break through the frontline. The organisation in whose hands they found themselves, however, refused to let them go – far too dangerous – and so they had to wait until 31 August to be liberated.

Sergeant L. Boness, LM597's flight engineer (and the only Englishmen among six Australians) was hidden in the villages of Boubers-sur-Canche, Fillièvres, and Monchel-sur-Canche (both Pas-de-Calais). He believed that the flak burst that had hit LM597 had set No. 1 starboard fuel tank on fire. Overcome by fumes as he left the aircraft he came to his senses as he floated to earth coned by two searchlights, but was not aware of anyone shooting at him. After walking as far as he could that night, he 'went into hiding for forty-eight hours'. He 'then went to a farm house at the village of Boubers where they gave me food and clothes. I eventually met a schoolmistress who put me into the hands of the French Army of Resistance at the village of Fillevres [*sic*], but I was later moved to the village of Monchel.'[1841] Here he was looked after by Mesdames Ernestine Sainsolieux and Hermance Turpin, and by Camille and Raymonde Soualle, until liberated by British forces on 4 September.

Another airman to come across a Jedburgh team was Sergeant H.D. Davies, shot down on 27/28 June 1944. He headed a long way south-west, reaching the area of St Benoît-du-Sault (Indre) on about 7 July. Staying with a photographer for the night the Frenchman instructed him to cycle 'to the house of Mme. Troubelet, Bélâbre. After three hours a French captain, who called himself "Captain Frank", came and took me to a hunting lodge called "Monjoie" near Prissac. Here I met an English captain, who called himself "Captain Crown".'[1842]

"Captain Franc" (not Frank) was the codename of Captain L. l'Helgouach, who was himself one-third of the Jed team Hugh, led by a British officer, Captain W.R. Crawshay ("Crown"). The third member of the party was another Frenchman, Lieutenant R. Meyer ("Yonne"). Flown from RAF Tempsford with two officers of 1 SAS engaged on Operation Bulbasket,[1843] they had been dropped "blind" into the Indre department of France on the morning of 6 June, where they and the SAS went their separate ways.

Word of Hugh's base at the hunting lodge must have reached the ears of the Germans, for four days after Davies's arrival the Germans attacked, but, as he understates, 'we managed to escape. We went to a farm about twelve kilometres away… We moved every few days, but the only place I can pin-point was Chaillac, where the people were very patriotic.' After a fortnight, a pick-up was arranged, and Davies and an American who had joined the party were taken to a nearby airfield and flown back to England (location unknown), arriving at 4.45 a.m. on 28 July.

Getting a bit too close to a column of tanks on the afternoon of 27 July 1944 Flight Lieutenant H.J. Nixon RCAF was shot down near Grainville (Eure), some twenty kilometres east of Rouen. A woodman, Marcel Dalaisment, and his son-in-law, Louis Lemire, took him to Fleury-la-Forêt (Eure), handing him over to Lieutenant André 'chief of the Armed Resistance in the district'. Told that he would be flown home in a day or two he was passed on to Monsieur Touraine 'who was the head of the Unarmed Resistance. He is a notary and a very fine gentleman.'[1844] Nixon would be company for 2nd Lieutenant Theodore R. Baskette USAAF, who had been with M. Touraine for the best part of six weeks since parting company from his B-17 on 14 June.[1845]

A week later, and no sign of an aircraft to take them home, the two airmen were moved from M. Touraine's house when it was learnt that the Gestapo had his name. They now stayed with Madame Huguette Verhague at the Abbé de Mortemer near Lisors, on the south side of the Forêt de Lyons. Fitted out with civilian clothes they agreed to join the Armed Resistance, and that very night they were sent out to attack a German patrol to get more weapons. Six men with four Sten guns between them set out to take on the Wehrmacht, as Nixon recalls: 'We laid in ambush at dusk and I was to fire first. Some very tired Jerries came along, and I loaded the Sten four times, but it misfired each time. The Boches were too tired to hear the click and walked away, passing within four yards of where I stood.'

On the following day, 23 August, by which time the Resistance had procured more arms from somewhere, they were ordered to attack two Germans near the village, where some fifty German troops were encamped. Against Nixon's advice the French went ahead anyway: 'The chief's Sten only fired one shot, wounding one man. He ran back for help, while the other defended himself with a sub-machine gun. Within a few minutes the Germans were searching the wood and in half an hour 250 SS had encircled the district and were shooting up everyone in the forest.' Nixon and Baskette took refuge in the loft of a cottage. Pulling up the ladder after them and firmly securing the hatch, just in case, they made a hole in the wall and had a length of rope handy. Twice the Germans searched the cottage but both times Mme. Verhague managed to persuade them not to search the loft.

These were nerve-wracking times, for the Germans had been well and truly stirred up and had arrested nine men of the Resistance, including the brave but foolhardy chief. Then, on 26 August, Nixon was told that the mayor of Lisors had been betrayed. He just happened to be the man who was feeding the airmen evaders and as 'thirteen people in Lisors knew that Mme. Verhague had looked after five airmen she was afraid of gossip getting to the ears of the Gestapo.' It was time for Nixon and Baskette to disappear. It was a dark and foggy night when 'we got out through the hole and took cover in a cave in the forest about 400 yards away.' Madame Verhague, who had earlier shown them the cave for this very purpose, kept them supplied with food until the evening of 27 August, when the Germans pulled out.

Three days later Mme. Verhague came running from the village to say that the Tommies had arrived, a Welsh division, and on the last day of August Nixon and Baskette were reporting their adventures to IS9 (WEA) at Bayeux. Their saviour, Madame Verhague, was clearly a remarkable woman. Quite apart from helping Allied airmen she did her bit by talking with the German troops – she could speak good German – and doing her best to lower their morale. She did, however, keep on their good side as cover for her clandestine activities, but her greatest triumph, in Nixon's eyes, was when she saved the lives of two young Resistance boys, one of whom she rescued by walking through the German lines while pretending to be his lover. As Nixon said: 'I have never met a woman of such sublime courage and daring.'

On three heavy raids to the industrial area of Stuttgart on the nights of 24/25, 25/26, and 28/29 July 1944, RAF Bomber Command lost sixty-four Lancasters and eight Halifaxes. Flying one of the five Halifaxes lost on the second raid was the experienced Wing Commander John Kennedy Francis MacDonald RCAF commanding 432 (RCAF) Squadron,[1846] assisted by a "scratch" crew of one flight lieutenant, four flying officers and a flight sergeant. Despite all their experience the first thing that the crew knew about the attack was when they heard the flight engineer call up the pilot and say 'I think we had better bale out, skipper,' immediately followed by MacDonald's terse 'Bale out, boys.'[1847]

With the Halifax on fire and its flying controls badly damaged, it was all that Wing Commander MacDonald could do to keep the aircraft flying straight and level while his crew took to their parachutes. All managed to land safely in an area near Villampuy (Eure-et-Loir) some fifteen kilometres south-east of Châteaudun, except for Flying Officer S.P. Wright, the rear gunner, whose broken body and unopened parachute pack were found nearby. Three of the six survivors, Grimsey, Kemley and Chamberlain, were taken to the nearby Marathon camp in Fréteval Forest (see previous chapter), while the other three – MacDonald, Flying Officer William "Jock" Calderwood (wireless operator) and Flight Sergeant B.R. Justason RCAF (mid-upper gunner) – went in the opposite direction.

Jock Calderwood landed in a field some five kilometres from Villamblain (Loiret) and started walking away from the aircraft and towards the village. Seeing a light on in a house he knocked on the door and was allowed to stay, but only for as long as it took him to have something to eat and to drink some wine. The occupants advised him 'to go to the woods, owing to the proximity of the Germans'. Losing his way in the woods he found himself once more back at Villamblain, where this time his approach to a house yielded a set of civilian clothing and more food. Heading off he was overtaken by a boy on a bicycle, who then procured similar transport for him and escorted him to a château near la Chapelle-Onzerain. The son of the château's owner took him to the home of M. and Mme. de Laubert at Orgères-en-Beauce.

Justason received help from a farmer who took him by cart to Villamblain, where he met his skipper, MacDonald, who had badly strained his back when he landed in a ploughed field, and had been unable to move for three hours or so. Crawling to the edge of the field as daylight approached MacDonald lay there until midday, when he hailed a farmer working nearby. The man told him to hide in the woods and that he would return later to help him, which he did. Taken to the man's farm by cart MacDonald was able to get some rest before, at around 3.30 a.m. on 27 July and with the pain in his back easing, he cycled to Villamblain with the farmer. Given something to eat at the grocery store the grocer took him 'to a miller at about 0800 hours who lived just across the street from the church'.

About an hour later Justason was brought in, and a couple of hours after that a young man aged about twenty arrived with instructions for them to accompany him by bicycle to Orgères. There, at the de Lauberts' house, they found Jock Calderwood, who had arrived the day before. While Jock stayed put, MacDonald and Justason were moved to the house of Madame Clare Malaure: 'These people were butchers and her brother Edouard Pinsard was running the business.'[1848]

The three airmen, in the village for eleven days, were joined on 3 August by Sergeant Alexander Balfour, who had been shot down near St Denis-en-Val (Loiret) on the Stuttgart raid of 24/25 July. On 2 August he was taken by one of his French helpers to the maquis headquarters in Orléans, given a railway worker's armband, and brought to the butcher's shop in Orgères on the following day.

One of the main organisers of assistance to airmen in this small corner of France was Raymond Alfred Edouard Picourt. Born on 21 October 1900 at le Tréport, an ex-French Army officer and chemist in Chartres since 1934, he had already helped over forty airmen (mostly Americans).[1849] Hearing that four airmen had baled out near Orgères Picourt cycled over from his hiding place at Villebon, some seventy-five kilometres away, to see what he could do for them. He told MacDonald that 'he belonged to the French Intelligence and since 1940 had been instructed in passing information of value to Allied Intelligence by means of radio.' These were doubly dangerous times for Picourt and his *réseau*, for not only was he wanted by the Gestapo but Jean-Jacques Desoubrie was also now operating in the Chartres area, assisted in his treachery by 'an unpleasant-looking woman with copper-coloured hair and spectacles'.[1850] This was Madame Orsini, the wife of the manager of the buffet at Chartres railway station. She also had an apartment at 7, rue des Batignolles, Paris.[1851]

On 9 August Picourt said that he would take the airmen to Paris as he was off to take an active part in the organisation of the maquis in the Chartres area. When Picourt heard that the contact in Paris 'had not materialised', he decided to take the airmen by bicycle to Chartres, and to get them as close as possible to Mortagne-au-Perche (Orne) some seventy kilometres to the north-west of Chartres. Though Desoubrie was to trap many airmen and was to dupe Picourt himself, with the help of François de Laubert (son of the de Lauberts at Orgères-en-Beauce) and of Picourt and his wife and two sons, the four evaders in a couple of days had safely reached the house in Villebon of a man by the name of Chateau, an ex-French Army officer with the Croix de Guerre. Although little is known of their time there, in his report made in Paris on 15 May 1945 Picourt wrote that one of the airmen 'found a bicycle thinking he could reach the Spanish border all by himself. I hope that he succeeded in his attempt. On the following day our go-between was found out, so I led the two fellows of his team to Orléans on bicycles.'[1852]

On the evening of 14 August, the airmen were picked up by an American Army reconnaissance patrol and taken north to the St James (Manche) fighter airstrip, approximately twenty kilometres south of Avranches. Nobody claimed these evaders, however, and on the advice of the local Intelligence Officer, the operations officer forwarded the strays to A.22 airstrip at Rennes. Justason scrounged a flight to England on 15 August, Jock Calderwood and Balfour doing likewise two days later, but Wing Commander MacDonald 'spent two nights at Rennes making enquiries as to where to report. I imagined the interrogation centre would be in London, and I was looking for transport to get me there. Eventually I was taken to T 2 airfield north-east of Bayeux where we were directed to IS9 (WEA) after having spent four days searching for it.' No marks for initiative, but he was interviewed on 19 August and finally made it back to England next day.

Another airman evader to have a close association with the town of Neufchâteau (see Walter Farmer, Chapter 11), was Sergeant T.H. Harvell, flight engineer of a Lancaster that was shot down on 28/29 July 1944 by Hauptmann Heinz Rökker and crew of 1./NJG2 in their Ju88 night-fighter. Twenty-three-year-old Rökker, who had volunteered for the Luftwaffe in 1939, now used all his experience to bring his Ju88 with its upward-firing cannons (*Schräge Musik*, "Slanting music") underneath the lone bomber without being spotted. Rökker's cannon shells blasted into the port wing of the Lancaster and knocked out one of the engines.[1853]

The Lancaster's pilot, Flying Officer R. Jones, for some unknown reason, continued to fly straight and level. This at least gave Tom Harvell the opportunity to throw bundles of Window out of the Lancaster in an attempt to confuse the enemy's radar, but Rökker, keeping the bomber in sight, had swung over to the starboard side and raked it yet again with his cannons. This time the fuel tanks caught fire. The Lancaster started to plunge earthwards, then exploded. Tom was blown out and knocked unconscious on a piece of the aircraft. Regaining his senses only at the last minute he managed to deploy his parachute shortly before hitting the ground. Landing heavily he injured his leg in the process. At least he, and the navigator, Sergeant George Robinson, were still alive, unlike the other five of their crew who perished in the explosion.

Found by a member of the FFI Tom's injuries were treated by a Doctor Cornu, who practised in Neufchâteau. Several attempts were made thereafter to get Tom back to England but, as it was too dangerous, he stayed in the area with the FFI for the next six weeks. After the last, failed, attempt Tom was given a bicycle and a false identity card and heading south-east towards Switzerland made contact, as instructed, with the commander of the Doubs FFI, Jean Lapprand, somewhere east of Besançon. Also making contact with him were some 450 Ukrainians who had been ordered by their German SS officers to destroy Jean Lapprand and his band. These Ukrainians, White Russians to distinguish them from the Reds so hated by the Nazis, instead deserted to the French en masse, but not before killing their SS officers.[1854]

Together, the French, the Ukrainians, and Tom Harvell helped to liberate the town of Pierrefontaine-les-Varans (Doubs), strategically situated at the junction of five roads. All this was to help with the advance of the US 7th Army which had landed in southern France in August. Tom and another evader, Sergeant Paul Bell RCAF, made contact with the Americans and got a lift some of the way home in the personal Dakota aircraft of the US 7th Army's commander, Lieutenant-General Alexander Patch.

Paul Bell had used up all his luck early on the morning of 23 July 1944 when Stirling LJ882 with six crew and nine SAS soldiers aboard hit high ground near Graffigny (Haute-Marne). The only other survivor, Parachutist R. Boreham SAS, was captured. The SAS were to have been reinforcements for "G" Squadron, 2 SAS, which was currently engaged on Operation Rupert, the harassment of enemy communications in an area to the east of the River Marne.[1855]

A week or so after the Normandy landings "D" Squadron, 1 SAS, was given the job of harassing the enemy in the area to the south of Paris known as the Orléans Gap, between the Forêt de Fontainebleau and the River Loire. The whole operation, codenamed Gain, was under the command of Major Ian Fenwick. With him were some ten officers and fifty men.

In the hectic way of things in that part of France in July 1944, three evaders were taken to a maquis camp in a wood near Chambon-la-Forêt (Loiret). 'We stayed with the maquis one night and then joined Major Fenwick's Paratroop Unit, 1st SAS, "D" Squadron in the same wood on 17 July.'[1856] "We" were Pilot Officer F.H. O'Neill RAAF, Flying Officer A.E. Vidler (of the same crew as O'Neill), and Technical Sergeant Frank E. Hines USAAF.[1857] A week later a fourth evader, Sergeant Philip King, was brought to the camp. O'Neill and Vidler by this time had been on the run for over three months, Sergeant King for a fortnight less. The airmen left the SAS on 4 August but were back on the following day, rejoining them in a small wood a kilometre south-east of Nancray-sur-Rimarde.

On 6 August Major Fenwick took a party of five in a jeep to collect supplies from the main camp south-west of Chambon. They were on their way back when they ran into some 600 Germans at Chambon. Major Fenwick, Lance-Corporal Menginou (known to the airmen as "Maginot"), and a sergeant in the FFI were killed in the ensuing skirmish. Corporal Bill Duffy was wounded and taken as a prisoner to a hospital, from which he later escaped. Sergeant F.W. Dunkley, also taken prisoner, was never seen again.[1858]

While Vidler and King went off together and to eventual liberation, O'Neill, Hines, and three SAS (Corporal Curran and Troopers Hunt and Phillips) went to a barn on the outskirts of Nancray. After the SAS left a couple of days later to rejoin their unit, the two airmen stayed put until liberation on 22 August.

General Lewis H. Brereton noted the war situation in France in his diary on 12 August 1944: 'Our forces have a ring of armor around Le Mans. General Bradley has turned north towards Argentan with two armored and two infantry divisions... One division was told to take a position west of Paris and wait for its tail to catch up with it. Our air superiority has prevented the enemy from bringing up his forces in any order.'[1859] Up to this date Allied ground forces, particularly the British and the Canadians, had been unable to make much headway against formidable German opposition around Caen, but all would change during the second week of August when a pincer movement trapped large German forces in the Mortain-Argentan-Falaise pocket.

Adding their weight to the battering of the Germans on the ground were, among others, the Typhoons of the RAF's 2nd Tactical Air Force. Whether a "Rockphoon" (Typhoon armed with rockets) or a "Bombphoon" (bombs) all had to go down low to do their job, and in so doing came well within range of the Germans' lethal light flak. Heavy losses were suffered among the Typhoon squadrons throughout the campaign, and right up to the end of hostilities.

One Typhoon pilot to fall foul of German flak was Rhodesian Flight Sergeant P.C.N. Green, hit while strafing German transport on the afternoon of 9 August near Falaise (Calvados). Baling out he managed to make contact with the head of the local Resistance movement in the village of le Marais la Chapelle. Taken to a disused farm about three kilometres north of Trun on 12 August he joined four more airmen – Flight Sergeant H.P. Pergantes RCAF; Sergeant P.A. Reeve RCAF; and Sergeant A.R. Hutchinson RCAF, all from the same bomber crew shot down on 4/5 July; and by Pilot Officer L.W.C. Lewis, who had been shot down on 7/8 June. Two days later an SS soldier appeared and asked them who they were. His French was not good, and he left satisfied with the answer from Pergantes that they were refugees.

Next day, 15 August, they 'were discovered by a patrol of a Luftwaffe AA unit. They had also found Fernand and a Free French Spitfire pilot. The latter said that he would probably be shot by the Germans and so we gave him a fictitious name "Jean Barclay from Montreal", also a number which we now believe was R.154217.'[1860] It was believed that they had been betrayed by the mayor of Montreuil-la-Cambe. Fernand, who lived nearby and had been providing the airmen with three meals a day, 'appeared with his face badly beaten up'[1861] as he had refused to talk when asked to give the names of others in his organisation.

The five airmen, Fernand and "Jean Barclay" were taken off in trucks. The Luftwaffe treated them well, and even went to some lengths to ensure that they did not fall into the hands of the SS, passing them on to another unit which, on 16 August, locked them up in the jail at Bernay 'to safeguard us from the SS'. They were kept there until 20 August, where they were joined by Major Nathan Feld USAAF ('a Thunderbolt pilot believed shot down on 15 August'), Captain Howard, US Army, and by a Free French lieutenant (not the pilot) named Pierre. Howard and Pierre, both supposedly captured near Alençon, were regarded by the others with some suspicion. 'These two may have been stool-pigeons, but we have no evidence.' They did, however, discover some sort of recording apparatus in the prison.

On 19 August another American prisoner of war arrived, 'a US soldier from Mississippi named Kelly', and he and the rest were moved off in a convoy of trucks next day. At around 6 p.m. when some fifty kilometres to the north-east, in an area 'packed with troops and material', two USAAF Lightning fighter-bombers caught them on the edge of the Forêt de la Londe and almost within sight of Rouen. Green dived into a ditch and escaped injury but Major Feld, severely wounded in the head and groin, died at 8.30 a.m. on the following morning having received no medical attention from the Germans.[1862]

Kelly was hit in the leg, Pergantes was seriously wounded in the chest and shoulder, and Lewis in the left leg, the latter two being taken to Rouen by the Germans for treatment. Lewis's fate is not clear, but Pergantes was then sent to Amiens (one day) and Tournai, where he remained until 2 September, the day on which the Germans evacuated their own wounded and left Pergantes behind to be liberated by the Americans on the following day.[1863] Green last saw Hutchinson and Reeve in the woods, and thought that they might have been killed.

Happily that was not the case, though Reeve had received a slight wound to the foot. Both had made good their escape in the general stampede into the safety of the woods and had found shelter with some Polish refugees at a farm. Liberation came on 27 August with the appearance of Canadians of the 8th Reconnaisance Unit. The two Canadian airmen were back in England on 30 August.

The five other survivors – the three Frenchmen, Captain Howard, and Green, all relatively unscathed – were taken to Rouen, where they arrived at 2 a.m. on 20 August. Fernand was taken away and shot. The following day Green, Howard and the two Free Frenchmen were taken to Amiens and from there, after two days of solitary confinement and interrogation, by truck to Châlons-sur-Marne. En route Captain Howard cut a hole in the roof of the truck and slipped out. Green reported: 'We were going to follow, but had not time before reaching the town. Here we were put in the French barracks, and left without food or amenities of any kind.' On 25 August their journey east continued, this time in railway cattle trucks, to Nancy: 'The journey took four days. There were forty men in each truck, including some wounded and some men with dysentery. The doors were opened once a day and at dusk. We were given one drink of water per day and one loaf and a Red Cross parcel to last for the whole journey.'[1864]

Near Vitry-le-François the train was strafed. An American paratrooper sergeant, who was on parole and on the outside of the wagon, refused to open the doors for the prisoners.[1865] No damage was done by the strafing, and when they had safely reached Nancy the prisoners were 'put into the old French barracks with a lot of native troops'. The following day Green got to hear that the RAF prisoners were to be moved out of the barracks and so hid in a straw palliasse in the sleeping quarters. Even though rooms were searched and his palliasse kicked by a guard he remained undiscovered, surfacing later to mingle with the native troops with whom he was able to converse in an African dialect.

On 1 September it was the turn of the native troops to be moved. Again hiding, Green waited for four hours before daring to surface: 'I came out and finding no signs of guards I walked over to the sick quarters. I expected the Americans would arrive shortly and so remained in the camp.' His expectations were dashed however, for on 6 September the Germans returned and he was a prisoner once more. As he and the walking wounded were being marched to Nancy railway station on 7 September, he seized the opportunity 'to slip down a side street and continued running until a Frenchman pulled me into a house. I was given civilian clothes and remained in hiding until the Americans arrived on 14 September.'

Sent to Paris for a friendlier interrogation at the hands of IS9, he was then able to rejoin his own squadron, 266 'Rhodesia' Squadron, near Lille for a few days before being flown back to England from Ypres on 24 September.

The danger of untrained men taking on the well-trained enemy was never more clearly demonstrated than in an incident that took place in Belgium on 21 August 1944. Four evaders from a Halifax that was lost over Belgium on the night of 12/13 August – Sergeant W.A. Ezra; Sergeant A. Goddard; Flight Sergeant B.F. Harkin RAAF and Flight Sergeant K.W. Trueman – had been joined by Australian Warrant Officer Alwyn Terence Till RAAF at a maquis camp near Laloux, twenty kilometres east-south-east of Dinant. Till had been shot down in the same raid as the Halifax crew.[1868]

On 21 August the leader of the Belgian group, "Monsieur Tom", 'organised an ambush party. Two carts were placed across the road. Unfortunately for us, two lorry loads of Germans drove up to the barricade. They opened fire on us and we retreated back into the woods in rather a disorganised rabble.'[1867] The saddest part of the whole, unnecessary business was that Till was killed even though as Ezra and company pointed out in their report the 'raid was a purely voluntary affair. Each person went of his own free will.'[1868]

On 26 August the rabble moved on to Maissin, some twenty-five kilometres south of Laloux, and eight to the east of Porcheresse, 'and waited in a barn. Whilst we were there, someone must have warned the Germans we were in the vicinity. We were attacked but no one was hurt.' Fortunately for the surviving airmen the US army was pushing ever closer, and two Belgian boys went off to locate it: 'They returned shortly with two jeeps. We were taken back to Paris, arriving on 9 September 1944.'

In the early afternoon of 26 August thirty-year-old Frenchman Sous Lieutenant P. Parent, 341 Squadron, was busy strafing German vehicles east of Rouen in his Spitfire when both he and his aircraft were hit by Fw190s. Despite being wounded in his left arm he landed the Spitfire to the south-east of Forges-les-Eaux (Seine-Maritime) and made for the nearby Forêt de Bray. He met a fellow countryman, a chemist by profession, who bound up his profusely bleeding arm, before leaving with all Parent's papers, which were to be destroyed, and saying 'that he would return with something to quench my thirst.'[1870] In the meantime, Parent was provided with civilian clothing by a woman.

When the chemist returned after three hours, however, he was not alone. With him were a German officer and men. It transpired that the chemist had been picked up by the Germans who, finding Parent's papers about his person, had forced him to divulge the airman's whereabouts. The German officer asked Parent what he was. Parent told him that he was a French pilot, to which the officer replied: 'You make war on women and children. Anyway, you are in civilian clothes and you will be shot.' Parent was taken to a prison at Forges-les-Eaux, where his arm was dressed and he was given a little food. At 4 a.m. on 29 August, after two days by himself in a cell, two fully-armed German soldiers took him to Aumale, some twenty kilometres to the north-east. Parent believed that he was going to be shot. En route his arm was once again dressed, by a French doctor, and he was put in a stable. On the evening of 30 August, one step ahead of the advancing British army, he was taken to Amiens and 'put into the citadel north of the town. The Germans appeared to be leaving Amiens, but the citadel held out until 1600 hours [31 August], when the FFI burst into my cell and liberated me.'[1871] Taken to a hospital, a French doctor immediately operated on Parent's arm: 'The following day I was passed back to the main British forces.'

"The Ghost Train"

During their four years of occupation of France the Germans had collected thousands of prisoners whom they kept in French prisons. Following the Normandy landings in June 1944 the Germans began to move these prisoners by train to Germany to prevent them falling into Allied hands. One such train left Toulouse on 3 July 1944, many of the 610 prisoners on board coming from the brutal French internment camp at Le Vernet in the foothills of the Pyrenees. The train, *le Train Fantôme* as it was called, eventually reached Dachau concentration camp, Germany, on 27 August, having taken fifty-five days to reach the German border. Only 543 of the prisoners were delivered alive to Dachau. Some had been killed by strafing P-38 Lightning aircraft on 4 July, others crushed to death by the train's wheels as they escaped through the floor of their wagon.[1872]

As the Americans fought their way ever closer to Paris another trainload of prisoners, including 168 Allied airmen, left that city on 15 August 1944, its human cargo bound either for Buchenwald (men) or for Ravensbrück (women). It took only five days to reach its destination. Then the time came for the Germans in Belgium to move their prisoners away from the advancing Allied ground forces, and the sound of the guns to the west early on the morning of Saturday, 2 September 1944, meant only one thing to the citizens of Brussels – liberation.

For the 1,538 political prisoners and forty-two Allied airmen incarcerated at St Gilles prison, however, a large question mark hung over their freedom. Aware of the impending liberation of Belgium the International Red Cross, with the Swedish Consulate in Brussels, held a meeting on 25 August 1944 to see how they could prevent the Germans from deporting their Belgian prisoners to Germany. Four days later, after further discussions on the previous day, the request to release the prisoners was passed to the German ambassador. They soon got their answer.

It was at around 4 a.m. on that Saturday, 2 September, that in furtherance of orders from thirty-eight-year-old SS Gruppenführer[1873] Richard Jungclaus to remove the prisoners to Neuengamme concentration camp in Germany shouts of 'Fertig machen' ('Get ready') echoed through the prison corridors. Urged on by their SS guards the prisoners were assembled in the courtyard, where each received a generous allowance of two Red Cross parcels. Some two hours later they were loaded onto covered lorries and taken to Brussels South railway station. At around 8 a.m. they were ordered off the lorries and marched in rows of four into the station. Separating the men from the women, the guards forced them into the thirty-two waiting railway trucks, seventy or eighty at a time, packing them in so tightly that it was impossible to sit down. As usual there were no sanitary facilities. Time for departure was scheduled for around 8.30 a.m.

The Germans of course needed a locomotive to pull the train, designated FAHR 1682-508,[1874] and one was found by the obliging Belgian railway staff. In the knowledge that another trainload of some 1,500 prisoners had made its way to Germany on 31 August 1944 the railwaymen were determined that this second train should not reach its intended destination, and a railwayman by the name of Roelands bravely damaged the oil pipes. A second engine was then found, and closely guarded by the anxious Germans. Somehow this locomotive – number HI 1202 – also developed a defective waterpump and also, as the Belgian railwaymen knew only too well, it was not built for pulling a heavy train of wagons. For some obscure reason repairs to 1202's pump took an inordinately long time to complete, and the departure was further delayed when the first engine driver allocated to 1202, Georges, suddenly felt unwell and had to be replaced. Georges's replacement, Vanderveken, then had a fall that fooled the Germans so well that he was carried off to hospital.

As the sun rose higher so too did the temperature until conditions within the trucks became unbearable, but there was some relief for the prisoners in the early afternoon when the Belgian Red Cross brought them soup. On the platform armed SS guards watched and waited.

At 2 p.m. the railwaymen's shifts changed, and engine driver Louis Verheggen and stoker Ponchet "clocked on". It was not until 3.45 p.m., however, that they were assigned to 1202, and prepared it for departure. At 4 p.m. the doors of the wagons were closed and they and the windows were secured with barbed wire. Fifty minutes later, after more delaying tactics by Louis Verheggen, the train finally but slowly nudged its way out of Brussels. On the footplate of 1202 with Verheggen and Ponchet were three, armed German soldiers. Despite their presence Verheggen did what he could to hold up the train, frequently testing the brakes, in the hope, vain as it proved, that by violently stopping and starting he could break the couplings.

The train was allocated a slow track through Ruisbroek, south-west of Brussels, but by a surreptitious switching of points Verheggen managed to take the train up a dead-end track. He got into a heated discussion with the chief station master, for the Germans' benefit of course, but before the train could reverse to the through line another one arrived from Halle, and blocked the line. This was one incident at least with which the Belgians had had nothing to do, for the engine driver of the "blocking" train proved to be a German who was fed-up with the war, and who refused to go any further. Even at gunpoint he remained obstinate and had to be carted off by German guards. Eventually a German engineer who was on the prisoners' train had the blocking carriages shunted off allowing Verheggen to pass, but not without Verheggen asking permission for another brake test!

The train now headed back towards the south-western outskirts of Brussels, to pick up a flak carriage at Vorst, where Verheggen took the opportunity of refuelling 1202 and filling it up with water. It was now 5.45 p.m. The station master at Vorst, seizing his moment, told Verheggen that the Resistance knew of this train but had too few men to undertake a full-scale confrontation with the heavily-armed Germans. From Vorst the train, with the flak carriage now attached to the rear, headed west and then north arriving in Schaerbeek, on the north side of Brussels, at about 7.35 p.m.

Unfortunately, the track ahead was clear, and 1202 was given the green light to proceed. Thinking quickly Verheggen stopped the train and tried to abandon his post, but was prevented from so doing by the guards, who grabbed his collar and dragged him back onto the footplate. They also warned him that if he tried it again they would shoot the prisoners.

Slight progress was then made as far as Vilvoorde, barely a dozen kilometres from the heart of Brussels, when Verheggen was confronted with a red signal. It remained on red for a very long time. Eventually the Germans realised that something was afoot and ordered Verheggen to proceed. He 'tried to argue with them that this was a very dangerous thing to do but they would not hear of it. They ordered me to ignore the red sign and I had to go on. A bit further at Eppegem the same story. Another red signal was ignored. So at about 23.00 hours we arrived in Mechelen.'[1875] Eppegem was five kilometres or so from Vilvoorde, and Mechelen (Malines in French) another half dozen beyond that.

Verheggen was pleased to see that the signals at Mechelen were out of order, and so had to ask German permission to go to the phone to get the all-clear to move on down the track. The Germans agreed, but a guard went to the phone-box with him all the same. Verheggen 'got permission by phone to go further. I took the opportunity to ask for water again. Although I had enough water to reach Antwerp I used this to hold up the proceedings again.'[1876] Arriving at Muizen at a quarter past midnight on Sunday, 3 September shots were heard in the distance. Verheggen brought the train to a halt.

Meanwhile, the fate of the prisoners aboard what was now being referred to as the "Ghost Train" was being urgently discussed by Red Cross representatives with General Jungclaus. Also putting pressure on Jungclaus to order the prisoners' release was General Werner Wachsmuth,[1877] German commander of the Brussels Military Hospital and of all sick and wounded in Brussels. With the Allies drawing nearer he had been ordered to evacuate the city and to leave all non-walking wounded behind, but this he was not prepared to do. In the prevailing circumstances Jungclaus agreed to give the order for the train to return to Brussels for the release of all political prisoners into custody of the Belgian authorities.

It was not until about 5.30 a.m., Verheggen recalled, that 'a German came on the locomotive and said: "Zurück nach Mechelen" ["Go back to Mechelen"]. At the entrance of the station at Mechelen the wheels of the locomotive slipped in a turn and we broke down. I now had to ask for a new locomotive to pull us further.' By chance another locomotive of the same class as 1202 was passing on track to Brussels. It was halted by the Germans and ordered to back onto the flak carriage. The German gunners, however, were not comfortable at being so close to the locomotive (the first target for marauding Allied fighter pilots) and demanded that the flak wagon be put to the back of the train. In all the confusion Verheggen told Gérardy, the driver of the Brussels-bound locomotive, what was going on and between them a plan was hatched. Verheggen told the German train commander that the proposed shunting could be done only further down the line where there were suitable sidings. And so, between them, Verheggen and Gérardy managed to leave the flak wagon on one of the sidings. As for the German guards on the prisoners' train, they were blissfully unaware that their gunners had been left behind.

On the way back to Brussels the train was subjected to small-arms fire by the Belgian Resistance. Through the cracks and small windows in their wagon, seeing Verey lights being ignited all around, the airmen kept their heads well down. Sporadic firing continued as the gallant Verheggen brought the train back to Klein Eiland (Petite-Ile, "Little Island") station in Brussels. 'Once there I managed to get my locomotive disconnected from the train and was able to drive it to a dead-end track. (My guards who were with me had disappeared when we arrived). I saw some Germans in the distance messing around with the working of the points in the signal box. I decided the time had come to get out. I descended from my locomotive and at first walked around it as if I was taking care of the mechanical problems. I saw a German observing me and expected to be called over. He did not say anything, however, and I distanced myself further and further from my locomotive.'[1878] Walking away as casually as possible until the German was out of view, Verheggen then started running. He went home and 'waited there until Brussels was well and truly liberated.'

As the Ghost Train had been expected at Brussels South station, it was not until around 9 a.m. on 3 September that the order to release the Belgian prisoners reached the German guards at the Klein Eiland shunting yards. The last of the SS guards released the Belgian prisoners from the front wagons, before they themselves disappeared. The forty-two airmen seem to have been overlooked, for it was not until dark that they managed to get the door open and, more or less in groups of four, stole away into the darkness.

Sergeant R.C. "Roy" Brown RCAF (shot down on 8/9 May 1944); Flying Officer W. Cunningham RCAF; Sergeant W. Mason; and Flight Sergeant J.W. Murphy RNZAF made up one of the groups, the last three having baled out of a Lancaster after it had been attacked and seriously damaged by a fighter on its way back from the target on the night of 18/19 July 1944. Cunningham came down in a tree and had to leave his parachute hanging from it. Mason missed the trees in a wood south of Mons, but Murphy scored a bulls-eye on a barbed-wire fence near the village of Hyon. None of them was hurt, however.

Cunningham and Murphy were separately put in the hands of "an organisation" and taken to Brussels, where they met up at the same safe house. Mason, on the other hand, was found by a farmer and put in touch with a schoolteacher, 'who gave me civilian clothes and kept me for a month.'[1879] He was then taken with two American airmen by car to Brussels, staying at one house for four days before 'being transferred to another house in the town where several men asked us many questions about the effects of V1, and gave us a form to fill in which had several military questions on it. As most people thought the form was all right, I did fill in most of the questions, including the Squadron number.'[1880]

Perhaps Mason had not understood that he was then well and truly in the grasp of the German secret police, and that he had been betrayed somewhere along the line. He was removed to the St Gilles prison where, on 31 August, he was interrogated by one of the men who had been asking him questions in the house in Brussels.

Cunningham and Murphy, having been well treated, were on the move again on 25 July, 'when we were turned over to our would-be guides and given a long form to fill in. The details required were:- name, rank, number, home address, religion, squadron number, base, target, etc. I refused to fill in these details, as I was suspicious. We then discovered that we were in the hands of the Luftwaffe police, and that we had been tricked.'[1881] Their next move was also to St Gilles.

There seems to be little doubt that they had been betrayed by René van Muylem, one of the most notorious traitors to be operating in this area at this stage of the war. If it were indeed he, then he had further success shortly after Cunningham and Murphy had been "bagged", when five more airmen were arrested in Brussels on 1 August – Roy Brown; Flying Officer L. Panzer RCAF, who had also been shot down on the Haine-St Pierre raid; 2nd Lieutenant Levy USAAF; and two more unnamed American airmen.

Roy Brown, whose false identity card provided by the Belgian Resistance proclaimed him to be Turkish, was being sheltered in a small house with Levy when a man called for them on 1 August. Together with Panzer and the other two Americans they were driven to a house in Brussels. At the end of May 1944 a 'Catholic priest, connected with the Resistance movement, took charge' of Flying Officer Panzer and moved him to the village of Templeuve, a stone's throw from the French border. 'Here I went to the house of the brother of the convent's Sister Superior. I stayed here till 1 August, when plans were made for my repatriation to England via Switzerland.'[1882]

Unaware at that point that they also had been betrayed Leon Panzer, Roy Brown, Levy and two other Americans were kept for two days in the first house before being moved by car to a larger house. To keep them interested, they were told that they were going to Switzerland and given the long form to fill in by three men who said that they were 'members of a Resistance movement'. Dutifully completing the form, the airmen were taken by a lorry to another house 'and were met by two German guards. They got into our truck and took us to some HQ in Brussels.'[1883] After being searched they were taken to St Gilles on 3 August.

Now having escaped from the Ghost Train, Brown, Cunningham, Mason and Murphy made their way on the afternoon of 3 September to a house near the station. Asking if they could stay they were given accommodation overnight in a shed. On the following day a Roman Catholic priest took them to a British major. From Brussels they were sent to Amiens, and flown back to RAF Northolt on 6 September.

Flying Officer Panzer and others waited until the morning of 4 September before going into Brussels itself, 'afraid that the numerous objects scattered about the tracks might be booby traps or mines'. Leon Panzer met an officer of the RAF Regiment, who took him to an airfield at Douai. 'The next day (5 September) I asked his permission to return to Templeuve to see if the people who had hidden me were all right. Having visited them, I returned to Douai on 7 September. I was flown back to England, and arrived at Northolt on 8 September.'[1884]

Two other airmen on the Ghost Train were Flying Officer W.J. Elliott RCAF and Sergeant M. Muir from the same 424 Squadron Halifax lost on the night of 27/28 May 1944. They were brought together on 30 May but their betrayal, as with the others, was not long in coming. On 22 June, cycling to the outskirts of Veerle, they were met by two men in a car and taken to 19, rue Forestière, Brussels, barely half a kilometre from the St Gilles prison. They stayed at this house until 3 July when they were taken by car to another house. Sergeant Muir: 'On arrival there we met five men and we were told that we were to have our photographs taken. Four of the men escorted us to a car outside the house. As I was getting into the car a German soldier appeared. At that moment the four men produced revolvers and we were instructed to get into the car. The German soldier was the car driver.

We were taken to the secret Luftwaffe Police Headquarters on the Avenue Louise, Brussels, where we were searched and then taken to St. Gilles prison, Brussels.'[1885]

In the prison Muir and Elliott were put into different cells. Elliott 'learned about the German treatment from Sgt. Dykes (USAAF), Sgt. Elsliger, J.H. (RCAF) and P/O K. McSweeney, RAAF who were in my cell. Elsliger left shortly afterwards. 2nd Lieutenant F. Babcock joined us shortly and also a Polish boy called Ziegfried Chmieleski.'[1886] 2nd Lieutenant F.W. Babcock USAAF had been arrested with Flying Officer J.J. Thurmeier RCAF (see below).

One of the guards at St Gilles was a very unpleasant character whom the prisoners called "Polak", as he was apparently half German and half Polish. About three weeks after Elliott's arrival at St Gilles Polak appeared at the peephole of the cell door and screamed something at him which he did not understand. Incensed, Polak opened the door, grabbed Elliott and put him in a cell with 'nine Belgian, French and other nationalities where we stayed for an hour or so and nearly suffocated.' The same thing happened to Elliott again, this time for three hours after apparently disobeying some regulation of which he was completely ignorant. One of the prisoners collapsed before they were let out. Though this particular treatment in a stuffy, overcrowded cell was bad enough the "black", or "dark", cell treatment was worse. Both Elliott and the American Dykes were given a taste of this cell after they had been further interrogated on 1 August. They 'were both put in a small black cell to spend the night in which it was impossible to lie down or move around with any freedom of body.' Released in the morning from this purgatory Elliott, who dreaded the thought of going back to it, 'because I was getting sick in the stomach', knew of some prisoners who had had to endure this form of torture for a month.[1887]

Released for further interrogation on 1 September, when he was told precisely when he had been shot down and where, Elliott was reunited with Muir on the Ghost Train. Leaving it together, and at the same time as the others, roughly 4.30 a.m. on 3 September, they walked into Brussels, and found someone to keep them until 9 September, when they went to the Hotel Metropole. After being interviewed by an army captain, they were flown to Paris on 10 September, interrogated again, this time by IS9 (WEA), and were flown to RAF Heston on 12 September.

There was a sad postscript to Flight Sergeant Murphy's story. While imprisoned at St Gilles he met several other airmen, among them Flight Lieutenant S.M. McGregor RNZAF, a Typhoon pilot, 'a Halifax pilot, Sgt. Ormerod, RAF, of Surrey, England (who had been five months in prison); and a Canadian, S/Ldr. Blenkinsop.'[1888] Squadron Leader E.W. Blenkinsop DFC, RCAF, who had been shot down at the end of April 1944, told Murphy 'that while evading capture in Belgium he was helping the White Army. One day he was with a group of them on the way to blow up a house occupied by the Germans, when they ran into 200 Gestapo men armed with machine guns. He fled into a wood, being unarmed, and was captured by the Germans. He had not done any sabotage. He was threatened with torture, but refused to speak. Three of the Belgians, after torture, did reveal their plans and said Blenkinsop had been implicated. On this evidence the Germans said they would shoot him.' Murphy adds: 'At the time of our meeting S/Ldr. Blenkinsop asked me to relate this part of his story to our Intelligence if I got back safely to the UK.'

This account is roughly accurate. The sad truth was that Blenkinsop was being kept the virtual prisoner of a small-minded Belgian who wanted the *kudos* of being able to produce his "prize" to the British when they liberated his village. Prevented, therefore, from being escorted down the line, the squadron leader was still in the area of the villages of Meensel and Kiezegem on 11 August 1944 when they were surrounded by Belgian fascists acting under German orders. Blenkinsop was caught in the raid and, with seventy-two other men and three women, was taken to Gestapo HQ at the Vital Decosterstraat, Louvain (Leuven) and then to the Central prison there. A few days later he arrived at the prison at St Gilles, Brussels.[1889]

Squadron Leader Blenkinsop was fated not to leave on the Ghost Train. Instead he was taken with others to Germany, ending up at Neuengamme concentration camp, some twenty kilometres east of Hamburg. Put to work with little or no food and in appalling conditions, not least the shockingly cold weather, he developed tuberculosis. With no one in authority caring a fig for him, the twenty-four-year-old Canadian died, officially, on 23 January 1945 at Neuengamme concentration camp, but by this time he was at Bergen-Belsen and died sometime between 28 January and 3 February 1945.[1890]

Flying Officer J.J. Thurmeier RCAF had been on the run since the night of 25/26 November 1943, when Halifax LK995, of which he was the navigator, was shot down by a night-fighter. After a fire had developed in the bomb bay LK995 blew up in mid air, by which time all except for the rear gunner, who was killed, had baled out. Thurmeier was soon in the hands of the Belgian secret army, the so-called White Army, and spent several months in Antwerp and Brussels. He came into the care of Anne Brusselmans of the Comet line after she had received a call that one of her agents had an airman on his hands and did not know what to do with him. She 'decided to go and get him'. When she first saw Thurmeier he looked 'a bit dazed and it appears that he has been constantly taken from one place to another – always having to leave at a moment's notice – and his nerves are at the moment a little the worse for wear. He has also a hunted look in his face.'[1891] Anne arranged for him to go to a house in Schaerbeek near her flat in Brussels.

He was in Schaerbeek with the American Babcock when their helper was arrested by the Gestapo and they had to leave in a hurry. Two weeks later, in the middle of June 1944, with Comet helpers Gilbert Tedesco and his wife they were caught by the Gestapo and, after interrogation, taken to St Gilles prison. Thurmeier received 'three days dark cell for sending morse on a heating pipe.' He also noted that the 'sergeant in charge and the Polish guard used brutal means with other P/W.'[1892]

Five of the American airmen aboard the Ghost Train were Lieutenants H.W. Wolcott, R.F. Auda, W.G. Ryckman, W.O. Cozzens, and Technical Sergeant D.S. Loucks, all members of a B-24 based at Harrington, home of the "Carpetbaggers".[1893] They belonged to an experienced crew that had already flown eighteen supply missions when, on the night of 28/29 May 1944, they were flying Operation Osric 53 to Belgium. Failing to get any sign from the ground at the drop zone they turned for home. Suddenly, a night-fighter fired three damaging bursts into the B-24, and though the pilot, Henry Wolcott, managed to lose it for a while, another burst of shells 'ripped through the right wing tanks, [and] through the navigator's compartment. Violent fires broke out, and since the pilot could no longer maintain control of the airplane he pushed the bail out alarm.'[1894]

The B-24 crashed near Aaigem, thirty kilometres west of Brussels. The only fatality was tail gunner Staff Sergeant Richard G. Hawkins. After receiving help from many Belgians, some of whom paid for this with their lives when betrayed to the Germans, Henry Wolcott was taken to an apartment in Brussels which later became known to the Americans as "the dog house". It was from this place that so many of Prosper Dezitter's victims were handed over to the Gestapo. Henry was in "the dog house"[1895] for three days, well treated, before he was taken to a second house and arrested by the Gestapo. Next day he was a prisoner in St Gilles.

William Ryckman and Wallis Cozzens were brought together at the Château du Parc, Herzele, a couple of kilometres from the crash site, before being taken to Brussels on 17 June. They, too, were eventually taken to the dog house, and on 18 July were handed over to the Gestapo. Their treatment at St Gilles, which they, and others, had to endure for nearly six weeks, was deplorable. Their food was usually 'coffee, carrots, potatoes and sour bread', and four times a week 'they were treated to watery, tasteless soup'. As to their accommodation, four or five men to a cell, they had to sleep on the floor, on straw sacks crawling with lice. Once a week they were permitted a bath of strictly five minutes only.

After Ryckman and Cozzens had been interrogated on 26 August, and had refused to co-operate, they were sentenced to the dark cell, even worse than the one in which they had already been confined. Their new cell measured six feet by four feet, and the only ventilation was three small holes in the door. They had to sleep on a bare concrete floor with no blankets and for sanitary purposes only a bucket in the corner was available. They were given no water for the entire five days they spent in the dark cell. The end to this little piece of hell came on the evening of 1 September when they were removed for further interrogation and returned to the "normal" cells.

The rest of the B-24 crew – Loucks, Technical Sergeant D.D. Deihl, Lieutenant C.T. Vozzella and Staff Sergeant F.A. Tuttle – were found by a local Resistance group in a wood near Herzele, and taken to the home of English-speaking Roger Schollaert at St Lievens-Esse. It was decided to move the men separately to Brussels, but what happened thereafter to Deihl and Vozzella is not known. Tuttle was hidden in a Brussels fishmarket for a month before being taken to Camp "Acremont" in a forest near the French border (see previous chapter), and had reached Paris on about 2 September. Dale Loucks, on the other hand, was hiding with M. and Mme. Gaston Waroquier in an upstairs bedroom of their house in Brussels when, on his second night there, the house was raided by the Gestapo and he was carted off to St Gilles. It was not until he was on the Ghost Train that he knew that the other four – Wolcott, Auda, Ryckman and Cozzens – were also on the train. They could hear each other but could not get together because of the crush of bodies.

Wolcott, Auda, Ryckman and Cozzens went out together in the mass exodus after the guards, 'completely frightened and demoralized, abandoned the train.'[1896] They walked down a road next to a canal until they came to a large warehouse with a fence around it. Suddenly the beam of a torch pierced the dark. Desperately looking for a means of escape, the warehouse fence being too high, they ran to the canal. Luckily, right in front of them was a barge, and not a second was wasted in jumping into it. Not a moment too soon, either, for no sooner had they done so than a squad of twelve German soldiers walked past them at barely arm's length.

Some time later the Dutch owner of the barge discovered the four airmen. Warning them that there was open fighting in the streets of Brussels he allowed them to stay there for the night. On the following morning, the bargee's son came rushing in shouting 'Tommy! Tommy! Tommy!' The British army was in town. Safe to leave, the four Americans went into the centre of the city and made contact with a British officer. After a night in a hotel they made their way on a British army truck to Amiens, and from there back to England aboard a C-47 Dakota, on 6 September.[1897]

As well as moving their fit prisoners to Germany on the Ghost Train, the Germans were also evacuating the injured by road from Brussels, among them wireless operator Sergeant E.G. Durland, shot down some thirty kilometres south of Brussels on 12/13 August 1944 in Lancaster LM180. Breaking an ankle on landing he waited until dawn before crawling to a nearby farmhouse. A doctor was brought to examine him, and pronounced that it would be three or four weeks before he would be able to walk again. When the farmer and his family said that they were not prepared to keep him for that length of time Durland, at his own request, was handed over to the Germans.

That he had lived at all was due to the supreme sacrifice made by his pilot, Pilot Officer John Lawrie RNZAF.[1898] He was bringing LM180 back from the target when the rear gunner, Flight Sergeant R.C. Chester-Master RAAF, spotted a Ju88 night-fighter and called for a "corkscrew". Though too late to prevent cannon shells from hitting the Lancaster the damage was not one-sided. As the pilot of the Ju88 broke away from his attack the night-fighter's underside was exposed to Chester-Master's four guns, and he shot it down in flames. The Lancaster was now steadily losing height, and John Lawrie struggled to keep it straight and level long enough for his crew to bale out. Sergeant Tom Young, flight engineer, offered to help his skipper into his parachute, but Lawrie could not let go of the control column for one second for fear of the Lancaster plunging out of control into the ground.

He was on his own.

One hundred metres or so from the back fence of shoemaker Nestor van Heyden's home in the village of Bavegem, Belgium, LM180 crashed into the unyielding Belgian soil: 'A parachute was tangled in the fence, so the shoemaker guessed at least one crew member had not been able to get out. He waited for the wreckage to cool and retrieved John Lawrie's remains. In a makeshift coffin, he buried the pilot in his own yard so the Germans would not find Lawrie and take him away. After the war, he advised the authorities. John Lawrie's remains were reburied, with full military honours, in Antwerp's military cemetery.'[1899]

George Durland was taken to the military hospital at St Gilles prison, where his ankle was set in plaster of Paris. On 15 August he and a fellow patient, Lieutenant Hewitt USAAF, planned to escape. After five days of filing through the iron bars of the window in their room Durland requested that his plaster cast be removed, and the German doctor duly obliged. The following day, however, they 'were told that if Brussels were evacuated we should be left there to be picked up by the Allied forces. We then abandoned our idea of escaping.'[1900] In the event they were not left behind, for on 3 September the hospital was evacuated and Durland, Hewitt, Lieutenant Stein USAAF, and two more wounded prisoners of war were driven off in a truck marked with a Red Cross.

Durland and his companions were to discover for themselves that the sign of the Red Cross was no guarantee of their safety. Driving through the town of Assent the convoy was spotted by USAAF P-47 Thunderbolts, which attacked. In the confusion the five Allied servicemen escaped, but only Durland, Hewitt and Stein reached the safety of a farmhouse a little over a kilometre away, Durland having had to crawl most of the way as his ankle had still not fully mended. They did not have long to wait before liberation, which came on 6 September. Durland left for England the next day, and landed at 'Newbury' (probably the American airbase at Greenham Common).

Although Durland and his companions had been legitimately placed under the sign of the Red Cross, Germans in Normandy, and later on the Belgian battlefields, had had to resort to abusing it because of Allied aerial supremacy. This was one of the few ways in which men and materiel could be moved to and from the frontline in daylight. To pilots of the AEAF swarming virtually unchallenged across the skies of northern France the evidence was there for all to see. They knew that German vehicles and trains, though prominently displaying the Red Cross, were engaged in warlike pursuits. This was frustrating for them, as they were under strict orders not to attack any form of transport bearing the Red Cross. The problem was eventually kicked upstairs, and matters came to a head when a photograph, reputedly showing fuel and ammunition being unloaded from an ambulance in Normandy, somehow slipped past the censors and appeared in the *Daily Mirror*.

Other evidence came from pilots of the USAAF's 78th Fighter Group, who saw about twenty large ten-wheeled vehicles at Vernon, and attacked. An explosion and a large fire ensued 'as if vehicles contained fuel. Pilots then noticed the Red Cross painted on tops and broke off attack.' Pilots of the 353rd Group also observed approximately two hundred Red Cross ambulances heading west at

Mantes-Gassicourt (fifty-five kilometres east of Paris). Enough was enough, and on 13 August 1944 Air Chief Marshal Sir Arthur Tedder, deputy to Supreme Commander General Eisenhower, 'authorised attacks on vehicles bearing the Red Cross under the following conditions:

1. Vehicles must be moving West or definitely identified as moving toward the battle.
2. It is left to the pilot's judgement to decide whether the character of the vehicle or the convoy justifies the attack. He is to make such reconnaissance as circumstances permit.
3. On no account are vehicles bearing the Red Cross moving East or away from the battle area to be attacked unless they open fire first.
4. Pilot is justified in attacking any vehicle marked with a Red Cross if the vehicle opens fire on him first.'

Eisenhower, however, thought otherwise, and the following day countermanded his deputy's order: 'The supreme commander has decided that despite the clear evidence that the enemy is misusing the Red Cross symbol, no attacks should be made on vehicles so marked. This does not affect a pilot's right to defend himself if fired upon by vehicles marked with the Red Cross.'[1901]

Sergeant Denys Teare, evading in Revigny in eastern France, also saw evidence of the abuse: 'Another thing we noticed was that lots of Red Cross trains loaded with wounded were passing along the railway lines coming back from the Normandy front. Our Allied pilots had deep respect for these trains, with their huge red crosses painted on roofs and sides; it is a pity they did not know, as we did, that these same coaches were being used to take hundreds of fully armed unwounded men to the front on their return journeys.'[1902]

It was late on the afternoon of 6 September 1944 when a number of German army lorries squealed to a halt in a street in Liège, Belgium. Armed German soldiers poured out, and in no time had collected forty hostages from the nearby houses as a reprisal for the killing of two German soldiers that morning. Carting them over the River Meuse and locking them in a barn for the night the hostages were told, as the barn door was being shut, that they were to be shot on the morrow.

Early next morning German guards ordered the men out of the barn, gave them spades, and told them to dig their own graves. A few hours later their gruesome task was done. Two of the forty, who had already been beaten-up by the Germans, were the first to be called forward to face the firing squad. Standing in front of their graves, a German officer gave the order to fire. As the sound of the volley echoed through the morning stillness the two Belgians fell dead into their graves. The officer then turned towards the remaining thirty-eight hostages, all wondering who would be next, when, unbelievably, he told them that they were all free to go. What the Germans never knew was that one of the thirty-eight to be freed was Canadian airman Flying Officer Jack Gouinlock RCAF.

Jack had already heard that the two gunners from his Halifax, LK811, 'had been executed by the SS for trying to escape'[1903] and so, as he stood before the German officer, held out little hope. He had been shot down on the night of 27/28 May 1944, when LK811, "N for Natch", on its way back from the target in north-east Belgium was attacked by a German night-fighter from behind and below. With both port engines ablaze the skipper, Pilot Officer H.J. Menzies RCAF, ordered the crew to bale out.

Jack Gouinlock landed in a ploughed field and after managing to avoid falling into the blazing remains of LK811 discovered from the farmer and his wife to whom he had gone for help that he was in Holland. Unable to do any more for Jack the farmer waited until nightfall before pointing the way south to the Belgian border, which was marked at that point by a canal, the Zuid-Willems Vaart. Warned that the crossing over this canal would be guarded, Jack spotted the sentry box. Deciding to wait for the moon to set, he fell asleep in a bush.

Awaking with a start at around 2 a.m. he crept onto the bridge, and found the sentry snoring his head off. Taking off his shoes Jack crawled on hands and knees to Belgium. After walking a considerable distance he was enthusiastically welcomed by a family at an isolated farmhouse to which he had gone for help. The children were quickly despatched and returned with 'two attractive young women… Mary and Golly Smets… no novices at the dangerous business of separating air force sheep from Gestapo goats.'[1904] They left when they were satisfied that Jack was indeed a Canadian airman, but returned after curfew to take him to their own home in the village of Eksel, two or three kilometres north-east of Hechtel. Here he endured further questioning from the girls' English mother and learnt that he was the seventh airman to have been helped by the Smets. Due to the proximity of the local Gestapo office, however, he was moved to Wijchmaal, a couple of kilometres to the south-east. Here he remained with the Van der Hoedonck family for two months, living a precarious existence in a small bedroom of their farmhouse, for also billetted on them was a young German evacuee, a 'schoolboy orphaned by Allied air raids'.

With the Normandy landings, it was agreed that the safest course of action would be to keep Jack at Wijchmaal until such time as the Allies liberated the village. The days rolled monotonously by until 24 July, when a USAAF B-17 was shot down nearby: ‘The entire crew baled out and all of them, with the exception of the pilot who broke his ankle on landing, avoided capture.’[1905] With so many airmen now in the vicinity the strain of feeding them proved too great, and they were moved to pastures new. With the two Smets girls and young Belgian Freddie Ceyssens as company Jack cycled to Bourg-Léopold, noting with satisfaction the damage done to the German camp by the American bombs. Moved to Liège with one of the Americans from the B-17 they stayed at several homes in the area, and were still in Liège when the two German soldiers mysteriously disappeared on 6 September.

In the time that it took Jack and the other thirty-seven hostages to return to Liège from the barn on 7 September, the American army had arrived. Everyone poured out of their houses to greet the liberators, and Jack was amazed to see amid the wildly celebrating citizens how many more airmen had been hiding in the town. His astonishment rose even higher when, having reported to the American command centre, he was greeted by his bomb aimer, Flying Officer D.E. Rutherford RCAF, who had been in the hands of the same organisation as Jack's since May!

Halifax MZ763 was on its way back from Neuss on 23/24 September 1944 when the rear gunner, Flying Officer W.T. Grew, spotted an Fw190. The pilot, Flying Officer J.S.R. Swanson, took evasive action, but too late. After bomb aimer Sergeant L. Robert[1906] had informed the skipper that the starboard inner engine was on fire several minutes were spent vainly trying to extinguish the blaze. In the end Swanson gave the order to bale out. Everyone responded except Grew. For some reason the wireless operator's parachute failed to open and he was killed, as was the flight engineer who was the first of the crew to bale out.

MZ763 crashed near Weert, Holland, half a dozen kilometres north of the Belgian border. As it spiralled down in flames civilians watched the victorious Fw190 follow it down and shoot it up after it had crashed. In the wreckage they found the bodies of the pilot and rear gunner. Robert was later led to believe that ‘the pilot remained with the aircraft instead of baling out, and tried to crash-land, because he knew the rear gunner had not baled out or spoken after his first warning, and therefore the pilot thought he might be wounded and alive. They were both found dead in the aircraft, the rear gunner with broken legs but dead, and the pilot badly smashed.’[1907]

Robert was knocked out as he pulled the ripcord of his parachute. Regaining his senses in a field near Swartbroek, a couple of kilometres south-east of Weert, he hid for the rest of the night in a pile of brushwood. Coming out of his hideout at daybreak he heard people talking in a language that he thought was German. Retreating to his cover, he watched several people, ‘including one with a brassard with three stripes, Blue-Orange-Blue, which I later discovered was Dutch resistance movement and friendly.’ He was then spotted by a small boy, who ran off but who later returned with his parents. They took Robert back to their house, and fed him. The Resistance leader was summoned, and took Robert to Weert town hall to identify the bodies of the pilot, wireless operator and rear gunner.

Robert was to discover that he had been hiding unnecessarily, for Weert was now in British hands, and British army chaplains were already preparing the bodies of his dead comrades for burial.

Flying Officer W.A. Rupert RCAF and Flight Sergeant P.L. Whittaker DFM, bomb aimer and mid-upper gunner respectively of Lancaster NF923, 617 Squadron, were also shot down on the night of 23/24 September 1944 (Dortmund-Ems Canal) when ‘tooling around for about five minutes’ over the target with a single 12,000-lb. “Tallboy” bomb aboard. The “Master of Ceremonies”, Wing Commander W.B. Tait DSO, DFC, told them to make individual runs and to drop their precious bomb only if they could clearly see the target.

Unable to do so the pilot, Flight Lieutenant G.S. Stout DFC, turned for home, but somewhere over Holland the Lancaster was blasted by cannon shells and all except Stout baled out. The grievously wounded navigator, Flying Officer C.E.M. Graham MiD, was pushed out of the forward hatch after a parachute had been attached to him. Whittaker was told that Graham was found by the Dutch ‘beneath a tree, through which he had apparently fallen, as his ’chute was still entangled in it, but the lanyard was slack, and he must have hit the ground very heavily.’[1908] The Dutch also told him that the Germans had given a military funeral to the navigator and to the flight engineer, Pilot Officer A.W. Benting, who had died in hospital on 25 September.

Whittaker himself had been hit by splinters in his right elbow (‘I could not bend my arm’) and also in the head. But he could still walk, and after an hour or so heading south-west from near Markelo towards Arnhem he came to a farm: ‘It was 2300 hours by my watch. The door was opened by a young girl. My reception seemed a bit odd, but I was invited to come into the living room where there were some people. I was in my battle dress (blue) and A.G. insignia was clearly visible; also I said

"Englander". Whilst I was applying my field dressing to my elbow, I noticed one of the men leave the room. It seemed to me that he might be off to fetch the Germans and I got up to leave too. The other man in the room got between me and the door and held me up with a pistol. I got him to look over his shoulder and at that moment kicked him hard in the stomach. Whilst he was on the ground I grabbed his pistol and bolted.'

As he made a run for it Whittaker saw a car heading towards the farm. He was later told that the farm was owned by pro-Nazis, and that the car he had seen had probably contained Germans. He understood that 'the family were "taken care of" by the Underground Movement'. At the next farm he was fed and his wounds were dressed. A doctor put his elbow back into joint and took a metal splinter from his head. On the eighth day he cycled over to where Bill Rupert was in hiding, a large farm which was a centre for the Dutch Underground. Peter Whittaker remembers that whilst they were there 'a successful drop of arms was made from about 500 feet' from a Stirling.

They were shortly to be joined by Lieutenant E.A. James MC and Lieutenant D.R. Guthrie (both 1st Parachute Division), Sergeant J.L.N. Warren RCAF, Sergeant P.S.C. Thorne, and Private J. Granat (10th [Polish] Dragoons, 1st Polish Tank Division).[1909] On 17 October bicycles were brought, and the Allied evaders, plus some eighty or ninety Dutchmen all on the run from the Germans, cycled off 'to a marsh in the middle of which was a little island where some sort of camp had been prepared... This camp was a kind of arsenal to which supplies were brought daily.'

Then Peter Whittaker began to run a high temperature and had to cycle to Laren for medical attention. Word was received that the Gestapo were in the vicinity, and he was moved to yet another farm where he rejoined Thorne and Granat. To be on the safe side, though, they slept in a chicken shed in the nearby woods. For three weeks all was relatively peaceful until, at about 4 a.m. on 1 November 1944, they learnt that the Landwacht were coming. Whittaker hurriedly buried an army wireless transmitter and a set of number plates from a Gestapo car that had been blown up by the Resistance, but he, Warren, Thorne and Granat were captured. Just as they were about to be searched Whittaker dropped the pistol he was holding, and Thorne trod it into the ground.

From Laren a car took them to the SD prison at the Landwacht HQ in Deventer ('on the road Deventer-Zwolle and south of the old Dutch barracks'). Whittaker recognised a number of the Dutchmen who had been with them earlier, including one of the farmers who had given them shelter. For a week, twenty-four men were kept in a cell measuring eighteen feet by eight and a half feet. Exercise was non-existent, and food scarce, though Landwacht Rottenführer Kuehne did what he could for the prisoners by slipping them extra rations. Their awful treatment continued[1910] until, on 1 February 1945, the prisoners were told that they were to be moved by rail to Hamburg, Germany. The journey was to take six days, and their rations were one loaf of bread each. Ninety-four prisoners were crammed into two 'box cars'. Realising that their last, realistic chance of escaping would be on the train journey most ate their full rations immediately, and set to work prying open a small window: 'We got the window open and in the night five of us dropped off the train...'

They were, however, seen by the guards, who opened fire as everybody ran for it. Warren understood later that somehow Thorne had been wounded and had been taken back to Doetinchem, while Bill Rupert heard that 'he was believed to have died of injuries sustained in jumping from the train'.[1911] Peter Whittaker, preferring to travel alone, was sheltered by two Dutch farmers in the Varsseveld area. On 31 March 1945 he headed off in the direction of an approaching battle, and on 2 April was safely in British hands. Warren was himself liberated a fortnight later and in due course received the award of the British Empire Medal (Military Division) for an outstanding escape. Granat was also liberated, being interviewed on 17 April.

As for Bill Rupert and Lieutenants James and Guthrie they avoided the Landwacht raid on 1 November 1944, but five days later James went off on his own and remained in hiding in Holland until liberated on 31 March 1945. Rupert and Guthrie, however, were staying at a house in Eibergen when it was raided by some twenty-five men on the night of 6/7 November. Hidden in the roof the two men escaped detection, but the members of the family who had been sheltering them were taken away. Rupert and Guthrie found shelter elsewhere until liberated by the Guards Armoured Division, also on 31 March 1945.

Intriguingly, Rupert mentioned in his report that two or three kilometres away from one of the houses in which he was staying there was another house, 'owned by a man known as "Toyo" of Eibergen, head of the local Underground movement. This man, together with his second in command known as "Leo", is reported to have broken into a bank in Hengelo and taken the Queen's jewels and three million guilders.'[1912]

Pilot Officer John Carey was soon found by the Dutch Resistance after his Stirling aircraft was lost on a supply mission to Arnhem (Operation Market Garden) on 21 September 1944. From his hiding place, a boat either on or near the Rhine, he was taken to a house which, judging by the number of people there, appeared to be the local Resistance HQ. On the following day he was joined by three more of his crew – Flying Officer C.C. King, Flying Officer R. Newton RCAF, and Sergeant T. Haig. All four were then 'hidden in a tent in the undergrowth until 23 September, and were about to cross the river in a boat when a German recce patrol arrived and we had to make a dash for cover. After an hour our friends produced bicycles and we split into two parties and rode into Wageningen. Later the coast was reported clear and we crossed the river without incident.'[1913]

Making contact with a unit of the British Army, with which they spent the night, the four airmen reported to Division HQ and to 30 Corps HQ on 24 September. They were most fortunate to have been ferried across the river so swiftly, for many of those who were trying to get back after the failure of Market Garden – the very gallant attempt by the airborne forces to hold the bridges over the River Rhine – had to wait a month longer to return. Major Airey Neave, concerned that there were several hundred evaders and escapers left on the wrong side of the Rhine as a result of the Arnhem failure, made his way to Eindhoven and established himself at the Royal Hotel.

Brought to him there on 6 October was Flight Sergeant G. Wood, another to have been shot down while dropping supplies to the troops at Arnhem, on 18 September. With local Dutch assistance he had made his way across the Rhine 'in a dinghy at 1500 hours in full view of two German soldiers who were watching'. Interrogated when first across the river at the Guards Armoured Division's HQ at Nijmegen, Wood was sent back to 30 Corps HQ and then by jeep to Eindhoven for further interrogation by a number of officers, including Airey Neave, at the Royal Hotel. As well as 'a roll of film showing the depths of the waterways of Rotterdam' that he had brought back with him wrapped round one of his ankles, Wood also had important 'information relating to the localities of evaders in hiding West and North of Arnhem'. Major Neave immediately took him back to Nijmegen, where he told the SAS all he knew.

No doubt in part as a result of Wood's information a rescue Operation, Pegasus I, was launched, literally, for many of the soldiers were brought across the Rhine near Randwijk, between Wageningen and Renkum, a dozen kilometres west of Arnhem itself, in assault boats provided by a company of Royal Canadian Engineers. 'A party of as many as 138 evaders were ferried across on the night of 22/23 October, headed by (Sir) Gerald Lathbury, one of the Arnhem brigadiers.'[1914]

One of those to be taken across was Sergeant P.J. Mahoney, "F" Squadron, 2 Wing, The Glider Pilot Regiment, who, with Major John Coke (see following chapter) and a Sergeant Freeman, was being cared for at Glinden, near Barneveld, on 20 October when he was told that 'the Germans had cut the escape route across the Rhine, burned the boats, and arrested twenty-one men of the Underground movement.'[1915] Better news arrived on the evening of 21 October when he was told that there was a chance that they could fight their way to the river. Major Coke, due to a nasty boil on his shin, was not fit enough to travel, but Mahoney and Freeman were given bicycles and rode off in daylight to Lunteren.

On the morning of 22 October two guides took them to a rendezvous in a wood near Renkum. On their way through Ede 'we rode down a narrow lane filled with German cycle troops lined up waiting to move. One man greeted me, but I did not reply.'[1916] From the first wood, they were taken to another where they joined about ninety other British troops. That evening two ambulances drove up, 'and another forty British and Dutch joined us'. Two hours later the large group made its way to the Rhine, meeting along the way a four-man German patrol, who fired before running off. A Bofors gun on the south side of the river fired red tracer to indicate the position of the boats. 'Then we met a Canadian who led us to the boats. American patrols had landed and covered both our flanks.' The operation was successfully completed in the small hours of 23 October.

From information provided by those who had made the crossing it was clear that there were plenty more where they came from, and a second operation, Pegasus II, was therefore planned for a month's time. Unfortunately, an article describing Pegasus I was published in a London newspaper. Had it been brought to the eyes of German Intelligence it may have been one reason why Pegasus II was to prove such a disaster (see following chapter).

Flying to Potsdam, Germany, on the night of 14/15 April 1945, on the last of RAF Bomber Command's mainforce raids of the war, one of Lancaster PB377's engines caught fire. Ordering the crew to bale out, the pilot, Flying Officer U.B. Bowen-Morris, waited until the other six of his crew had jumped, and was preparing to go himself when he regained control of the bomber. He managed to fly it back, alone, to friendly territory over Holland before taking to his parachute. Of the six who had baled out near Potsdam, south-west of Berlin, four were captured, one was killed and one, Flight Sergeant J.W. Tovey, evaded capture. After two days of walking westwards on his own Tovey ran into a party of French prisoners of war. Disclosing his identity to one of the Frenchmen, he was taken 'to the British Man of Confidence at a camp at Schiameirtz'.

Changing into army battledress he stayed in the camp for four days: 'The Germans did not notice me, as there was no organisation in the camp. After four days I walked out with two soldiers and continued south until we joined up with the American First Army at Grimma five or six days later.'[1917] Grimma, not far to the north-west of Colditz, was well over 100 kilometres from Schiameirtz, and it was some feat to walk such a long way in an area infested with German troops. Perhaps Tovey deserved to get away with it, after all not many free men voluntarily admitted themselves to a prisoner-of-war camp.

CHAPTER 14

To The Bitter End

'On 6 Sep Marthe, who was a registered French nurse, was returning in an ambulance from Turcoing when she was attacked by Germans with hand grenades and machine guns. She was left lying in the street for several hours severely wounded. The Germans refused all efforts of civilians to render first aid. After some time a German officer shot her through both eyes.'[1918]

Shortly before 10 p.m. on 21 April 1940, on a bombing raid to Aalborg West airfield, Wellington P9218, 149 Squadron, was hit in an engine by flak from 5./Res. Flak Abteilung 603. Ditching in the Limfjorden, 500 metres east of the Aggersund bridge, the pilot, Flying Officer F.T. Knight, and the other five of his crew became prisoners of war. P9218 was the first RAF aircraft to crash in Denmark during the Second World War. By the end of the war, of the total of 665 airmen who had survived being shot down either on Danish soil or in the sea around the Danish islands, only ninety-eight had managed to evade capture.[1919]

The first of them was Sergeant Donald V. Smith RCAF, flight engineer and only survivor of Stirling R9261, shot down on the night of 20/21 April 1943. Hit in one of its four engines over the target R9261 left the area at a height of 2,000 feet on a north-westerly course across the island of Falster and The Great Belt, turning to starboard to avoid a ship, in case it were a flak ship. As the pilot, Flight Lieutenant Charles W. Parish, flew the Stirling towards the island of Sjælland (Zealand) Donald Smith suddenly saw an Me110 night-fighter on their port side, and shouted a warning over the intercom. It was too late, for no sooner had he done so than the Stirling came under fire from the Me110.[1920]

With R9261 out of control, Parish gave the order to bale out. Crawling towards the rear emergency exit Smith found the wireless operator, Flight Sergeant Louis J. Krulicki RCAF, crouching next to the half-opened door unable to bale out. So it was Smith who had to fully open the door, and as he did so was sucked out. In the short time that it took him to land safely on Danish soil R9261 had exploded in a ball of fire, killing all seven left on board.[1921]

For the next three days Don Smith headed north, making full use of the mirror, compass, comb and shaving kit that he found in his escape kit, though the French francs and the map of Middle Europe proved of little value. He did, however, meet with much kindness and help from local people along the way. A farm hand at Regnemark provided him with civilian clothing, while a schoolteacher from Taastrup, buying the train tickets, escorted him all the way to Helsingør, on the north-east corner of the island.

As Helsingør was only five kilometres from the Swedish port of Hälsingborg across the Öresund (The Sound), Don decided to get away in a small boat but, finding them all guarded or chained to piers, he decided to get help. On 26 April he knocked on the door of Strandvejen 206 in Aalsgaarde. Mr and Mrs Dalsborg, who spoke English, asked him in, and gave him a big meal and a shower. Mr Dalsborg then went out, and came back with sixty krøner that he had collected from friends, but told Don that, as they had small children, he was to stay the night two doors away with Einar Knudsen, an engineer at the Diesel factory in Copenhagen. The following afternoon, wheels having been put in motion, Don was visited by a Mr Barson, a banker in Copenhagen and married to an Englishwoman, who took him back to his house in Hellerup, a northern suburb of Copenhagen. Mr Barson introduced Don to a Mr Muller, 'a Dane, who is in charge of the organisation', who took down Don's details, and contacted London.

Don enjoyed life with sight-seeing trips to Copenhagen and cocktail parties, until the night of 29 April, when Ejnar and Sylvia Tjørn, who were involved in underground activities, took him to Skodsborg, a few kilometres up the coast from Hellerup. There they 'met some Danish policemen, a Danish army officer, and an ex-officer of the Danish army, Lieutenant Lars Troen, who was to travel with me by kayak (eskimo canoe) to Sweden.'[1922] As they were unable to steal the kayak from the Germans and assemble it in time for them to leave that night, Don stayed with Gert Baumgarten, one of the policemen.

The kayak was assembled on the following day, and after arrangements had been made with the Danish police on land and with the Danish patrol boats in the Öresund to keep out of the way, Troen and Don Smith made their way to the shore an hour or so before midnight. Just after midnight on 1 May they set off across the narrow stretch of the Öresund, and in a little under two hours had reached the Swedish island of Hven (Ven), half way across. Dodging two Swedish patrol boats they paddled on towards the mainland. Negotiating barbed-wire entanglements stretching 600 or 700 metres out to sea, they came ashore just after 3 a.m. somewhere near Rydebäck, a small town to the south of Helsingborg. Sinking the canoe, they walked to Helsingborg and contacted the British Consul, 'who made arrangements for us to be taken to the police station.'

There was no doubting which side the police were supporting, for hanging on the walls of the police station were a Union Jack and a portrait of Winston Churchill. It was, therefore, only a matter of days before the formalities were completed. With a police escort Don was taken to Stockholm, and flown back from Bromma airport to Leuchars, Scotland on 12/13 May 1943 aboard BOAC's civil-registered Dakota G-AGGA.[1923] Don Smith died in Ontario, Canada on 10 October 1998, his last wishes being that he be laid to rest with his crew. On 4 May 1999 an urn containing his ashes was buried next to the graves of his fallen comrades in Svinø cemetery.

On 17 May 1944, 65 Squadron sent some of its Mustang III aircraft over to Denmark on a "Ranger" mission. Looking for trouble they found it near Aalborg in the north of the country when both Flight Lieutenant Richard Barrett RNZAF and Flight Sergeant R.T. "Rowly" Williams were shot down. Barrett was killed, but Rowly Williams, his aircraft hit at fifty feet, somehow survived, but not before he had shot down two training aircraft, believed to be Ju34s, plus a probable third, and two Heinkel 177s, one of which he shared. Hit by return fire from one of the Heinkels, he crashed at Stagsted, smashing through high-tension wires as he did so.

Dazed by the crash, Rowly regained his senses, only to see a group of people heading towards him whom he feared might be Germans. Running away from his wrecked Mustang, despite considerable pain from an injured shoulder, he found help from Danish farmers before heading for Frederikshavn on 19 May. It was his intention somehow to catch a boat to Sweden, but when he saw how many Germans were in the town, and as he was still in RAF uniform, he gave up the idea, even though a little later a farmer gave him a smock in exchange for his battledress blouse. While having some food at a farm at Elleshoj the farmer told him that the Germans knew of his presence and were coming to get him. Understandably, he 'left the house in a hurry and ran for several kilometres'.[1924]

Twice refused help by local farmers he was obliged to spend the night in the hills between Estrup and Sörup. Still very tired, and with the sores on his feet turning septic, he tried another farm, on 20 May. This time his prayers were answered, and a Resistance organisation arranged for his passage by boat to Sweden. He was flown home to RAF Leuchars on the night of 18/19 June, ten days after his twenty-first birthday.

An unusual pairing of a New Zealand pilot and a Dutch navigator took off in their Mosquito from RAF Upwood on the night of 7/8 July 1944 to bomb Berlin. Some three and a half hours later, engine failure forced Flight Lieutenant J.D. Robins RNZAF to land the Mosquito at Kalmar aerodrome in Sweden. Interrogated at the airfield by a Swedish colonel, Robins and his navigator, Sub-Lieutenant Benjamin Marius Vlielander Hein RNethAS, were taken to Falun internment camp, and a few days later 'to the air attaché's office in Stockholm for further interrogation'. They told their interrogators that they had force-landed while on a training flight, but both sides knew that that was not true. Asked again, they told the Swedes 'exactly what had happened'.[1925]

Fearing that his internment might be lengthy, Vlielander Hein, before he was returned to Falun, made contact with Lieutenant C. Knulst of the Dutch Legation in Stockholm, who said that he could provide him with civilian clothing and get him to Norway where he would be able to contact an escape organisation. On the morning of 21 July, therefore, Vlielander Hein slipped out of the Falun camp and met a Norwegian guide, who took him on the long journey north and west to Karlstad, by train. Arriving there at around 7 p.m. Vlielander Hein was supplied with Norwegian clothes and ski boots. Taken by car towards the Norwegian border – no more than a trench running through a wood – he crossed over it at about 6 a.m. on 22 July with instructions to make for Hamar. Five hours later he was arrested by a German patrol and taken to a small hut in a forest, where he was asked a few questions: 'Although I speak fluent German, I pretended not to understand. My RAF watch and cuff links were taken from me and I was then locked in and left alone.'[1926]

Being somewhat more alert than his guards he pushed his way out through a loose window, and set off for an address that he had been given by his friends in Sweden. After several hours, now completely lost, he decided to head back to Sweden, but, as there was nothing to distinguish one country from the other, he was unaware that he was in Sweden until he called at a farm early on the morning of 23 July. Contacting the Swedish police himself, he was taken away for questioning. He made up a story that he was a refugee from Holland, but the police were highly dubious of his nationality, as 'there was a constant trickle of Germans crossing the frontier under assumed nationality.' Taken to Karlstad, he was imprisoned and again interrogated. Sticking to his fanciful story of his life in Holland, he was told that the details would be forwarded to the Utlands department (security authorities) in Stockholm. During the fortnight that he was in prison, he managed to get a letter to his friends in Stockholm, and one of them came to Karlstad to identify him.

On 7 August he was taken under escort to the Utlands department, where he was given a visa. Reporting to the Dutch legation, he was registered as a civilian refugee from Holland. But, to clear up his identity finally, the Legation were told that he was the same person who had escaped from Falun, and he was now required to report to the Falun camp himself. There, on 9 August, he was sent to see Count Folke Bernadotte,[1927] who held an official position in the camp, and was also identified by Flight Lieutenant Modelin from the air attaché's office. He was now confirmed as 'an Allied officer who had escaped from enemy hands', and locked up for another four days. Released by the Swedish army on 12 August, he stayed in Stockholm until he was finally given a Swedish and a British passport and was flown back to Britain on 6 September, nineteen days before Flight Lieutenant Robins who, wisely, had remained in internment.

Confined to a hospital in Rennes three wounded airmen would have been unaware that on 28 July 1944 General George S. Patton jnr was appointed to command the US Third Army in Normandy (VIII Corps on the right, XV Corps on the left facing south down the Cotentin peninsula). Although the Third Army did not become officially operational until noon on 1 August, its units were ready to roll, and when reports reached Patton that the 4th Armored Division had captured some dams over the River Sélune near Pontaubault he 'told [Major-General Troy H.] Middleton to head for Brest and Rennes, with the 6th Armored Division and the 79th Infantry Division on Brest, and the 8th Infantry Division and 4th Armored Division on Rennes'.[1928] On 1 August the divisions advanced, and punched their way out of Normandy.

Unaware of this, too, were the three airmen – Flight Sergeant P.C. Boon DFM (broken jaw, shoulder and head injuries); Flight Lieutenant P.D.L. Roper (bullet in leg), both shot down over Brittany; and Sergeant P.C. Heal (broken leg and burns) shot down in Stirling LJ621 on 5/6 June 1944. LJ621 was on its way to drop supplies to the FFI some fifty kilometres west of Aunay-sur-Odon (Calvados) when, flying at only 150 metres (500 feet), it was brought down in flames by a burst of flak, too low for anyone to bale out. Peter Heal, a last-minute replacement despatcher, who knew none of the other eight crew, was one of only three to survive the resulting and inevitable crash, in which he suffered a broken leg. Burning his hands as he clawed his way out through the wreckage he was found two hours or so later by men of the flak battery who had shot him down. Receiving no medical treatment for the next twelve hours he was moved in stages until he arrived at the hospital in Rennes on 19 June, and was still there, with Peter Boon and Peter Roper, when the 8th Infantry and 4th Armored Divisions captured the town on 4 August 1944.

Always keen to blow his own trumpet, and with some justification, General Patton wrote that as of 14 August 'the Third Army had advanced farther and faster than any army in history.'[1929] With Brittany now more or less secure, apart from the odd pocket of stiff resistance, the Third Army now with XX Corps added to its ranks was ordered to head east and south of Paris and to advance on the line Metz-Strasbourg, though Patton was convinced that if he had been allowed to get through the Nancy Gap he could have been in Germany within ten days. By 27 August XX Corps had taken Nogent-sur-Seine and was closing in on Reims to the north, while the recently-formed XII Corps (5th Infantry and 4th Armored Divisions) went for Châlons-sur-Marne and Vitry-le-François.

The Americans' eastward sweep liberated several more airmen, among them wireless operator Flight Sergeant R.I. Hunter RAAF, who had been injured when his Lancaster had been shot down on the way back from Mailly-le-Camp on 3/4 May 1944. Having tried to bale out via the forward escape hatch he was forced to go back to the rear door with the aircraft well ablaze. Robert Hunter then fell through the floor 'but was suspended by my parachute on my back, completely surrounded by flames. After considerable effort I was able to open the door in the rear and jump. By this time I was badly burned on my hands and face and different parts of my body.'[1930]

Nevertheless, he managed to land without further injury, though nearly unconscious, and was unable to remember much of what happened thereafter. He made his way to les Grandes-Chapelles (Aube), a base for aircraft of the AASF in 1940, and asked for help. Most people were too frightened and turned him away, but one brave woman took him in. Despite his burns and his dizzy state a 'member of the FFI arrived and took me to their camp about two hours away', where he briefly met another evader, Flying Officer N.E.S. Mutter.[1931] Moved to Troyes later that day, 4 May, Robert received the first medical treatment for his burns. The pessimistic French doctor who attended him said that he would have to go to a hospital to have his hands amputated as gangrene had set in and the blood had practically stopped circulating. A Frenchman and his wife took him to 'the Hôpital de Dieu' [l'hôtel-Dieu Saint-Nicolas] that evening, and the Germans were notified.

Operated on on 5 May, Robert Hunter remained unconscious for the next two weeks, but the good news was that doctors had been able to save his hands. 'After I had regained consciousness the Gestapo tried to take me away, but the doctor did not grant permission.' The Gestapo tried to get him to talk but, using his burnt and badly swollen lips as an excuse, pretended that he was unable to do so. When the time came to evacuate the hospital on 22 August the Australian patient was ignored. Just in case, a French doctor gave him an injection to raise his temperature. Sent 'to an isolation hospital as a scarlet fever case' he remained there until the US Third Army arrived on the night of 27/28 August.

Another victim of the Mailly raid was nineteen-year-old Sergeant Jack Marsden, whose 166 Squadron Lancaster was one of those hacked down by rampaging German night-fighters on the way home. Having extricated himself from the tree in the Forêt d'Othe in which his parachute had caught, Jack was soon found and sheltered by several people before being taken to a maquis camp near Dixmont (Yonne), a dozen kilometres south-east of Sens. Shortly after arriving there a motorbike roared up, and to their mutual delight Jack was re-united with his pilot, Pilot Officer G.T. Harrison RAAF.

Their time together at the camp was cut short on 15 May when the Germans arrived, with all guns blazing. Three of their bullets struck Jack, two of them grazing his forehead and chin. It was the third, though, that did the damage, smashing its way into the left side of his skull. Ten days later he regained consciousness in Sens hospital, whither taken by his captors, but it was to discover that his right side was now partially paralysed, and that he was unable to speak.

He was cared for by the French hospital surgeons and staff, who falsified his records to show that his recovery rate was poor, as it was feared following an inspection by a German doctor on 14 June that he was to be moved to Germany. Wasting no time Jack, though still very weak and unable to speak, was removed from the hospital on the next day by six members of the Resistance. Though over the ensuing weeks he was moved from one house to another, doctors and nurses from Sens hospital continued to care for him, providing such medication and care as he required.

It could all have been a wasted effort, though, when he was caught in an allied air raid whilst being ferried by cart to another safe house. When a nearby oil depot and railway station were bombed everyone ran for cover, everyone that is except for Jack who was in no condition to go anywhere. Happily unscathed he was taken to the house of a blacksmith in Chaumont, where he stayed for three weeks until liberated by the Americans on 22 August.

His ordeal was far from over, for he could not yet speak and the Germans had long ago removed his dog tags. Suspicious Americans, believing him to be a German, put him in a prisoner-of-war cage with genuine Germans, but there he was spotted by a comrade from the Resistance and was soon released. A day or so later he was flown back to England, and spent the next four years in Wharncliffe hospital, Wakefield. He was discharged in 1948 with a one hundred per cent disability pension, and records that as 'time went by, I began to remember more details of the time I had spent in France… I also had great difficulty in remembering names and places. Despite this, I never lost the feeling of gratitude for the many brave people who had risked their lives to help me, a severely wounded airman.'[1932]

As a rule, when the Germans were obliged to withdraw in the face of the Allies' advance, they took with them all fit prisoners of war and the "walking wounded". The more seriously wounded were, on the other hand, too much trouble to move and were abandoned where they lay. Flying Officer E.L. Hogg, for example, who had sprained an ankle and broken an arm on landing, was put in the hospital at Stalag 221, Rennes, on 21 June 1944 and abandoned there on 4 August when the Germans left. Several other wounded and injured aircrew found themselves in hospitals in Paris when the city was abandoned by the enemy.

Flight Sergeant Cyril Rattner, badly injured in the left shoulder, was one of several airmen who had been brought to the Luftwaffe's Beaujon hospital in Clichy, Paris. Others were at the Hôpital de la Pitié, also in Paris, among them Squadron Leader G.B. Philbin RCAF; Flying Officer James Archibald RNZAF; Flight Sergeant N.M. Davidson RAAF; Flight Lieutenant M.P. Stronach RCAF; Flying Officer W.W. Robinson RCAF; Flight Lieutenant J.A. Levi RCAF; and Flight Sergeant W.G. Hammond.[1933] Philbin had had a near miraculous escape from his Halifax after it had been hit by flak on 5 August 1944: 'I believe that the machine exploded in the air, as I was wounded in the face and broke two ribs; also my legs were black and blue as if having been knocked against something very hard.'[1934] He was immediately captured and taken to the Beaujon hospital in Paris. Moved to the Hôpital de la Pitié on 18 August he was still there when the Allies arrived on 26 August.

Rattner was still in the Beaujon hospital on 17 August when the Germans began moving patients from Paris to Germany. French irregular forces, however, had other ideas, and prevented the lorries and ambulances onto which non-German patients were being loaded from reaching the Parisian railway stations. The French 2ème Division Blindée (2nd Armoured Division) and the US 4th Infantry Division (Major General R.O. Barton) reached the outskirts of Paris on 23 August, but came up against stiff opposition, the French especially as Major-General Leclerc[1935] had disobeyed orders and had advanced on a different heading from that agreed. Nevertheless, by 10.30 p.m. on 24 August a small French unit had entered the city. On the following day the German commander of Paris, General Dietrich von Choltitz, surrendered despite having been ordered by Hitler not to let the city be taken except as a heap of ruins.[1936] It was two or three days before the Allies had located all sick airmen in Paris.

Others to the north and east of the capital, well away from the fighting in Normandy, experienced a similar pattern of being centralised to larger hospitals, the American Memorial Hospital at Reims being well used, as was the hospital attached to the prisoner-of-war camp at Châlons-sur-Marne. It was just a few kilometres to the east of Reims that Flying Officer Eric Brown RCAF, pilot of a Halifax on its way to bomb Metz on 28/29 June, suffered a dreadful injury. Attacked by a night-fighter the bomber was set on fire. Coming in a second time a shell from the fighter blew off Brown's right foot: 'I lost consciousness for a few seconds. When I came to I managed to put a tourniquet on my right leg and bale out. I landed in a field outside Cernay-les-Reims and started crawling towards a farmhouse, but I was in such pain that I had to blow my whistle to attract attention.'[1937] A doctor was summoned, bandaged the injured leg as best he could and gave him morphia before handing him over to the Germans. Taken to a prison in Reims he lay for two days with no further medical attention: 'By this time I was delirious.' On the third night he was taken to a hospital, and awoke next morning to discover that his right leg had been amputated.

In the same room with him were two Canadian NCOs, whose names he was unable to remember, and Sergeant H. Middleton, who was later apparently taken to Germany. They were to lie in this room for sixteen days without further medical attention. 'After that the doctor used to come and see us about every fifth or sixth day until about 15 August, when he started to come more often, and the treatment was a lot better.' A fortnight later the Americans arrived, and Brown was flown back to England.

Flight Sergeant Gordon Lusk RAAF had reached Antwerp before his evacuation to Germany was terminated on 1 September 1944. Lusk, too, had been lucky. He baled out of the rear door of his Halifax after flak had set it on fire: 'I think I must have hit the tail of the aircraft, as I cannot remember anything until I regained consciousness in a military hospital in Amiens.'[1938] Shot down on 9 August, it was five days before he was moved, to Arras and then to Lille (16 August). At the end of the month he and other wounded prisoners of war were put on a train and sent towards Germany. At Antwerp he and a US Army officer by the name of Bell, possibly a lieutenant, 'were taken off the train and placed in a Belgian Red Cross ambulance. After about two hours we arrived at a house, where we remained until 3 September. We were then taken by members of the Resistance Movement in a car through the enemy lines to a hospital in Antwerp.'

Antwerp was officially liberated, by the British 11th Armoured Division, on 4 September, though its vital port was not usable for a few days thereafter, once the Breskens pocket had been cleared by the First Canadian Army. In France, however, the ports of Cherbourg and St Malo had been captured by the Americans on 27 June and 8 August 1944 respectively, though several key ports garrisoned by German troops were by-passed as part of the Allies' overall plan to drive the enemy back to his homeland.[1939] Among these were Bordeaux (liberated on 24 August), Le Havre (12 September), Brest (19 September), and Calais (30 September). La Rochelle, Lorient, St Nazaire, and Dunkirk, however, were to remain in German hands to the end of the war.

So it was that early in September 1944 six airmen found themselves in the Fort de Tourneville, a prison fort on a hill near Le Havre, still in German hands. Flying Officer A.G. De Beer, shot down in the daylight raid on enemy positions at Le Havre on 8 September, was captured and brought to the fort where he was to meet Pilot Officer G. Mackenzie, Warrant Officer Waclas Kubiak RCAF, Sergeant K.J. Feary, Sergeant Alexander Walls and Sergeant Edmund Backhouse, the last three from the same crew. Their liberation by the British 49th Division was only four days away.

Further along the coast such was the determined resistance at Calais that RAF Bomber Command was summoned to end it, attacking on 20, 24, 25, 26, 27, and 28 September 1944. On 24 September nine bombers were lost. One of them, Lancaster NF914, was shot down by flak into the sea about half a mile off shore. Only Flight Sergeants H.S. Rosher, D. Gordon, and P. Cook baled out, Rosher and Gordon managing to do so over land. Horace Rosher suffered a broken leg on landing and was easily captured. As Duncan Gordon floated down onto the beach German soldiers fired at him and he was hit in the right leg ('a flesh wound'). He, too, was captured, and he and Rosher were taken by ambulance to the Germans' main hospital in Calais.

They were joined on the following day by Cook, 'who was badly burned on his face and arms'.[1940] Twenty-one-year-old Phillip Cook, the third to bale out, was temporarily blinded by the burns to his face. Landing in the sea, the wind caught his parachute and blew him back onto the shore where he was immediately seized by a German gun crew. After interrogation he was also taken to the hospital in Calais, and met Gordon and Rosher.

They were still in the hospital on 27 September when Bomber Command mounted the fifth attack on the Calais garrison. The bomb blast from a near miss shook the hospital and blew the three RAF patients out of their beds. Duncan Gordon was knocked out for a short time, but came round to see 'that part of the ceiling was down and that the windows were out. There was a lot of commotion throughout the whole hospital.' Rosher and Cook were 'in the room next door. I saw that I was unable to do very much for my two friends. I went through the window, slid down a drain pipe about thirty feet, and made my way to the gate of the hospital.' A French policeman took him to a café, where he was given civilian clothing, and asked if there were any more Allied personnel in the hospital. Gordon told them that there were two more, whereupon the policeman returned to the shattered hospital and came back with Phillip Cook. The Germans, however, were not far behind, and while Gordon made his escape through the back window Cook was taken back to the hospital.

Rosher must have been further injured by the bombing, for Cook heard him 'shouting after the bombing, and think he was badly hurt. I never found out what happened to him.' He would have been saddened to have learnt that Horace Sydney Rosher succumbed to his further injuries. Two days later Calais and Gordon and Cook were in Canadian hands.

Also landing in the sea, but on the Atlantic side of France, was Warrant Officer John Hill. Late on the evening of 29 August, having departed RAF St Davids, Cornwall on an anti-shipping patrol down the west coast of France, the crew of a Coastal Command Halifax (pilot Flight Lieutenant G.B. Eccles) spotted an enemy minesweeper off the mouth of the Loire and moved in to the attack. Shortly after midnight the Halifax crashed into the sea. Shot down by its intended victim, it took down with it eight of the nine crew, including an extra pilot and wireless operator. Warrant Officer John Hill found himself floating in the sea having suffered nothing worse than a dislocated shoulder. Rescued by the crew of the minesweeper he was taken to St Nazaire and, after a short interrogation, removed to a military hospital at La Baule, a dozen kilometres away, where he received attention to his shoulder.

On 5 September he was transferred to a make-do prisoner-of-war camp located in the Arado Werke (aircraft factory) on the outskirts of St Nazaire. Hill was in no fit state to do much when, a day after his arrival, two other prisoners, Captain M.R.D. Foot SAS, and Captain Goss RE, escaped. Foot was caught within hours (and received ten days' solitary confinement by way of a punishment), but Goss got clean away.

Two months later, determined to mark Remembrance Day in a fitting manner, Captain Foot organised a parade of all prisoners, but without the Germans' permission. His captors took a dim view of this, and he was given a further five days in the cells.

Undaunted, Captain Foot escaped again, on 19/20 November, this time with Frenchman Lieutenant Leo Rollin of the FFI, who had arrived at the camp on 10 October. Two Americans, First Lieutenant Keller and Flight Officer Norelius,[1941] also made their getaway and reached Allied lines, but Foot and Rollin, exhausted by their exertions, decided to make use of an isolated and apparently deserted farmhouse. Receiving no response to their calls, they broke a window and climbed in. To their surprise they discovered that there were several people inside, who did not believe the escapers' story. Fifteen minutes later Michael Foot found himself 'fending off pitchfork blows',[1942] and remembered nothing more until regaining consciousness in a German hospital on the evening of 20 November. When Foot had left the farmhouse he fell 'across the doorsteps' and Rollin, who had also received a cut over an eye, had then carried him to a haystack before fetching the Germans.

On 29 November, as a result of efforts made by Andrew Hodges of the American Red Cross, Captain Foot, Warrant Officer John Hill and others were released into Allied control as part of an exchange.

Further down the Atlantic coast of France Lancaster PD237 was shot down by flak on a daylight attack on an oil depot at Bordeaux on 13 August 1944. The bomb aimer, Sergeant W.J. Gray, 'landed on the North bank of the River Gironde amidst a German coastal battery and was immediately taken prisoner.'[1943] He was lucky to be alive as the Germans had been shooting at him as he floated down. Taken to the garrison guard room he was searched and put into a cell. Three others of his crew were also shot at as they came down, but neither Sergeant F.R. Stearn nor Sergeant Peter Antwis was badly hit, though the latter's leg was grazed by an incendiary bullet. Sergeant T.F. Hart, whose parachute was riddled with machine-gun bullets, landed heavily as a result and sprained both ankles. He was captured within twenty minutes. Sergeant J.W. Sanderson and Sergeant G.A. Sandvik, two more of PD237's crew, both reported being shot at but without injury. Sandvik was captured after walking a short distance, while Sanderson 'landed right in the centre of a German camp. I was taken to the Commandant and made to hand over all my possessions.'[1944]

By the morning of 14 August all six had been gathered together in one cell, when they were given the sad news that their pilot, Flight Sergeant P.D.A. Lorimer RAAF, had been killed. Desperately trying to keep the crippled bomber on an even keel Lorimer, very much alive, was unable to bale out until he was barely 1,000 feet from the ground. As he had not been seen to do so by the angry Germans who had assumed that he had perished in the crash, he was able to hide until they had left the area.

As for the rest of his crew the Luftwaffe removed all their remaining possessions and valuables, including identification tags, before taking them 'to the Municipal prison at Cognac, where the six of us were confined in a large cell and were given very little food.' On the following afternoon (15 August) they 'were removed to the Luftwaffe and Military prison at Bordeaux', and after a brief interrogation by a German army officer next day (16 August) they 'were put in a small chapel with twelve American and British airmen.'

Following the Allied landings in the south of France on 15 August the Germans were now preparing to evacuate the Bordeaux area,[1945] and on 17 August the airmen in their chapel prison were told to get ready to leave for Germany. Defiantly they refused to go without having their identification tags returned to them. Returned to their cells they were joined by two more American airmen and on the morning of 19 August were told that they were to be transported to Germany. Once again the Luftwaffe intervened and they were driven by lorry to the airfield at Mérignac, which the Germans were in the course of systematically destroying. The prisoners were put into a room in the one remaining building while over the next two days the Germans continued to blow up the airfield. On 21 August the prisoners were moved for their own safety to the cellar of the hospital block while the runways and hangars were destroyed.

The Germans' final evacuation from Mérignac began on 22 August – 'we noticed many vehicles and personnel leaving the aerodrome' – and that evening twenty-two prisoners and six guards were 'put in a small open lorry which was one of a large convoy.' They 'spent two days and nights in this lorry sitting on boxes of hand grenades and sticks of TNT. It was raining most of the time and we had no means of shelter. We made several attempts to escape, but unsuccessfully, as the convoy was very heavily guarded.'[1946] On 23 August the convoy stopped for the night at a small farm near Châteauneuf-sur-Charente, but it was not until the morning that the prisoners were put into a filthy barn and given straw for bedding. By this time most were ill from a lack of food, and several were suffering badly from dysentery.

That evening a local group of maquisards attacked the convoy at the farm, but the attack was beaten off in about twenty minutes. This did not, however, interfere with four of the prisoners being sent to hospital at Angoulême, a dozen kilometres away, while the rest were given half a bottle of Cognac each as medicine. Proper rations were still short when, on 26 August, a further eight men were sent to the Angoulême hospital, as were the remaining prisoners two days later. Three days later, early on the morning of 1 September, the maquis drove the Germans from Angoulême and liberated the Allied prisoners.

Very early on the morning of 26 September 1944 Coastal Command sent a Mark XIV Wellington aircraft of 407 (RCAF) Squadron on a routine patrol to Norway. At around 12.45 a.m. the Wellington lifted off from RAF Wick, Scotland with its all-RCAF crew – Flying Officer G.A. Biddle (pilot); Flight Lieutenant M.M. Neil; Flying Officer G.F. Death; Pilot Officer K.W. Graham; Warrant Officer G.E. Grandy; and Flight Sergeant E.H. Firestone. During the patrol one of the Wellington's two Hercules engines failed. In an attempt to get back to dry land fuel was jettisoned to lighten the aircraft but, unfortunately, the fuel cock jammed open. With fuel pouring out George Biddle had no option but to head for Norway. At around 6 a.m. a small enemy convoy in a Norwegian fjord opened fire on the doomed aircraft, but Biddle was already looking for somewhere to land. He managed to put the aircraft down at Haugland, on the Björne fjord, some ten kilometres south-west of Os (Osöyra) and twenty-five or so south of Bergen. Having thrown all their 'parachutes, harnesses and bags into the sea'[1947] they 'set fire to the aircraft, and then talked to one of the Norwegians who had gathered around the crash. He informed us that there was a German garrison at Os and another at Bergen.'[1948]

The Norwegian, Magnus Askvik, advised the six Canadian airmen to cross a neighbouring mountain to the settlement at Björnen. Cautiously, Neil approached one of a group of four houses while the rest of his crew watched from a safe vantage point. They saw Neil being greeted by a Norwegian who then pointed him to another house. There the lady of the house, Ingeborg Bjornen, already knew of the crash. Getting her cousin to hide the men on the mountain she went off to see what could be done about getting them back to Britain by fishing boat. She was back at noon with some milk and with the news that her father would be making further enquiries that night. She returned at around 8 p.m., this time with Einar Evensen, who took them to a small cove where two Norwegians were waiting for them in a rowing boat. They thereupon rowed the airmen to a small island, where three more Norwegians were waiting in a second boat. Three to a boat, the airmen were rowed to the small island of Ströno, 'almost due west of where we crashed.'

The airmen spent the night of 26/27 September in the upper storey of a boat-house, but were off before dawn to the hills. The Norwegians brought food and civilian clothing and told them to shave off their moustaches. At around 10 a.m on the morning of 1 October they were picked up by a motorboat and taken to another boat-house some five kilometres north of Hattvik, where there was a German U-boat training base from which the airmen saw 'three submarines operating'. Avoiding the Germans the Canadians were taken to a nearby farmhouse where they met the head of the local underground movement and were fed and given dry clothing: 'At the farmhouse there were eight other members of the underground movement. The chief sent a message to the UK saying we were safe.'

Before dawn on 2 October the airmen were off once more, this time to a small cabin hidden away in the mountains, 'where we stayed with a Norwegian who cooked for us and looked after us until 8 October.' Though there were plenty of weapons to be had – three Sten guns and pistols (one a Colt, another a German Lüger) – the airmen never had the opportunity to use them. On 8 October the Resistance leader took them to another farmhouse, from which, at 3 a.m. on 9 October, they stealthily made their way to a boat-house barely one and a half kilometres north of Hattvik, 'where we transferred to another fishing boat'. This boat took them to a small island almost due west of Austervoll and north of Selbjörn fjord, where they stayed, in a fisherman's hut, with a Norwegian merchant seaman. On the night of 11 October, they were 'picked up in a motor launch and taken to a waiting Norwegian naval vessel.' On 12 October the six airmen and the Norwegian sailor were landed at Scalloway in the Shetland Islands, a distance as the seagull flies of some 350 kilometres (220 miles).

The remarkable recovery of the Canadians had taken just seventeen days. The Norwegian naval vessel mentioned by them in their report was, however, no ordinary naval vessel. They had been picked up by one of the three former US Navy submarine chasers that had been made available in August 1943 to the Royal Norwegian Navy, and which were then based at Scalloway. These boats, named *Hitra*, *Hessa* and *Vigra* after islands off the west coast of Norway, 'were 100 feet long and powered by two 1,200 hp General Motors engines, which gave them a cruising speed of 17 knots and a top speed of 22 knots. They were so well armed that German aircraft kept their distance and their speed was sufficient to get them quickly out of trouble.'[1949] Each boat had a crew of twenty-six men, three of whom were officers, and were skippered by Petter Saelen, Ingvald Eidsheim and Leif Larsen. As a measure of the speed and seaworthiness of these boats the record crossing to the Norwegian coast and back by Ingvald Eidsheim on the *Hitra* took just twenty-five hours.

Their crews were Norwegians, most of whom had been keen to carry on the struggle against the German invaders following their country's surrender on 10 June 1940. Some forty boats, mostly small fishing cutters, ploughed the long and dangerous furrow across the North Sea to Britain with around 600 Norwegians on board, but left behind thousands of Norwegian servicemen in hiding, who needed arms and wireless sets if they were to become an effective resistance movement. In the summer of 1941, therefore, a secret base was set up at Lunna, on the north-east coast of the Shetland mainland and the nearest point in the United Kingdom to Norway. Off the main road and away from the main shipping area Lunna was ideally situated for clandestine operations, and during the following winter many successful missions to Norway were carried out.

Using the very boats that had carried refugees to Shetland, agents, radio sets, arms and ammunition were landed, and they returned with yet more refugees. In the foreword to his book *The Shetland Bus* David Howarth wrote: 'During the German occupation of Norway, from 1940 to 1945, every Norwegian knew that small boats were constantly sailing from the Shetland Isles to Norway to land weapons and supplies and to rescue refugees. The Norwegians who stayed in Norway and struggled there against the invaders were fortified by this knowledge, and gave the small boats the familiar name which is used for the title of this book: "to take the Shetland bus" became a synonym in Norway for escape when danger was overwhelming.'[1950]

Unfortunately, Lunna had proved 'so remote that it was difficult to supply in winter'[1951] and it also lacked adequate repair facilities. Accordingly, in 1942, the Norwegians decided to move across to the "wrong" side of the island, to Scalloway, where Jack Moore, of the local firm of William Moore and Sons, with forty years of engineering skills behind it, enabled them to remain independent of outside help. A slipway was built at Scalloway to service and repair the fishing boats, and Crown Prince Olaf of Norway, having agreed that the base could be given his name, visited it in October 1942.

There had been losses of men and boats in that first winter at Lunna, and these steadily increased after operations had begun from Scalloway until the call for a superior vessel was answered by the supply of the three US submarine chasers. It is worth noting that from November 1943 until the end of the war they carried out 114 missions to Norway on the same kind of operations as the fishing boats. Apart from one incident when a Canadian aircraft opened fire by mistake on the *Hessa*, these trips were uneventful and there were no casualties.

The Biddle crew in October 1944 could at least testify to the efficiency and seeming impunity of the Shetland Bus as they were ferried back aboard the *Vigra*, captained by the highly-decorated Leif Larsen DSC, CGM, DSM & Bar, which had departed Scalloway only the day before.[1952]

Whereas the waters of the North Sea were a natural environment for the boats of the Shetland Bus the watery maze that was Holland was an unwanted hazard to the Twenty-First Army Group[1953] advancing towards Germany. In the way of the main seawards thrust into Germany were the Maas and Waal rivers some forty or fifty kilometres from the Belgian border, and beyond them the mighty River Rhine. Once Belgium had been freed the outline plan was for the British 2nd Army to advance approximately 110 kilometres (seventy miles) 'to seize the Grave-Nijmegen-Arnhem area and then penetrate still farther northwards to the Zuider Zee in order to cut off all the enemy forces in the Low Countries from those in Germany.'[1954] To achieve this they needed to capture the bridges over the Rhine at the Dutch town of Arnhem, and so the airborne Operation Market Garden was launched on 17 September 1944 to accomplish this. Eight days later, after extraordinary courage and durability had been shown by the British and Polish forces involved, the battle for Arnhem was over.

Market Garden had failed at a considerable cost in lives not only of those on the ground but also of Transport Command's extraordinarily brave aircrew and RASC despatchers who were called upon to bring in badly-needed supplies and reinforcements for the men trapped on the ground. Coming in slowly and at suicidally low levels in their large transport aircraft in broad daylight they were easy targets for waiting German flak crews.

One man who went to see for himself, on the fourth day of the operation, was a reporter from the *Daily Telegraph*, Mr Edmund Townshend, who flew in with a crew of 190 Squadron in Stirling LJ982 flown by Flying Officer J.D. Le Bouvier. The aircraft was hit by flak in the port wing before it had reached the drop zone. The cargo was immediately dropped, and the crew ordered to bale out. Suspended beneath his parachute Mr Townshend, who was on his first ever flight, watched breathlessly as LJ982 roared away in flames while he came to earth in a ploughed field to the south of the Rhine, and into the waiting arms of the Dutch Resistance. Together with four of LJ982's crew – Le Bouvier, Flying Officer T. Oliver, Flight Sergeant S.F. Saunders, and Sergeant C. Ryan – he safely returned to Allied lines four days later.

The day on which LJ982 was lost, 21 September, was an awful day for the Stirlings of Transport Command, twelve of them failing to return. 190 Squadron alone lost six, with two more having to be written off on return due to battle damage. 196 Squadron lost three, with 295, 299 and 570 Squadrons each losing one. Over the week 17-23 September, thirty-six Stirlings were lost, including the two battle damaged. Flight Lieutenant J.K.O. Edwards wrote that, flying supplies to Arnhem in Dakota KG444 on 21 September, luck was on his side 'because the Huns chose to fire at the Stirlings which were mixed up with us, because they were twice our size and made much easier shooting. In the few minutes that I was over the target I saw several Stirlings brought down.'[1955]

Actually, luck was not on his side for climbing *up* to 7,000 feet and still short of Allied lines KG444 was spotted by an enemy fighter. At first Jimmy Edwards thought that the damage being inflicted on his aircraft was the result of flak bursts and 'took suitable evasive action. After a moment, however, I saw, out of the corner of my eye, what was unmistakeably a Fw190 commencing an attack from the port side. His cannon fire was passing across ahead of the aircraft so I pulled back the stick and kicked hard on left rudder.'[1956] Edwards managed to reach what little cloud there was without further attack, but as KG444 dodged from one cloud to the next so it was subjected to a further five attacks.

Taking considerable punishment from the Fw190, Edwards lost aileron control during the sixth, and final, attack 'and so gave the order to bale out. The co-pilot and navigator jumped[1957] and at that time I was under the impression that the rest of the crew and despatchers had also gone… After barely a minute I looked round and saw three despatchers sitting by the cabin door and asked why they hadn't jumped and one of them said they could not.' Realising that they must be wounded Edwards decided to stay in the Dakota and crash-land, 'but almost immediately both propellers went into "fully fine" and I throttled back in preparation for crashing.' From a height of approximately 6,000 feet KG444 suddenly went into a steep dive. As it neared the ground Edwards regained some aileron control and when barely 100 feet up 'held off to reduce speed. We were passing over a village with numerous haystacks… I selected "flaps down" but whether I got any flap I shall never know. I remember frantically trying to strap myself in with one hand but found this impossible. At about fifty feet up I opened the pilots' escape hatch and the draught caused a great rush of flame from the back of [the] cabin. A despatcher came lurching forward crying "Christ. The flame is coming right in." This was the first idea I had that the aircraft was on fire.'

KG444 was already well alight, and the only way for Edwards to see ahead was to stick his head through the escape hatch whilst keeping one hand on the control column. Looking along the port wing he was in time to see it smash through a clump of small trees before hitting the ground. Half thrown out by the impact and surrounded by flames he hung on grimly for fear of being thrown into the path of his own aircraft as it careered along. 'Suddenly the nose dipped down and the tail came up almost vertical and as it fell back again I was flung out backwards onto the top of the aircraft whence I fell to the ground in front of the starboard engine.' Looking up Edwards saw the victorious Fw190 doing a steep turn at barely 100 feet and shouted a warning to the only two personnel he could see, Flight Sergeant Bill Randall and the RASC corporal despatcher (the only one of the four despatchers on board to survive). Sure enough, as they dived for cover, the Fw190 'commenced to strafe us.' Edwards heard only three shells and 'assumed that the enemy had run out of ammunition, which was a good thing as I was still wearing my mae west.' Randall was unhurt though the corporal 'was suffering from flesh wounds but could easily walk.' Edwards himself 'was burned in face and arm but otherwise felt fit enough for travel.'

No sooner had they decided to head off in a southerly direction than they heard voices, and through the trees saw a man and a woman. Edwards's 'attempts at friendly relations were nearly doomed to failure. I asked where the Bosche were and the woman, apparently thinking I meant who was the "Boss", waved towards the man and said "the Bosche", with the result that I was about to let him have it from my pistol.'[1958] The Dutchman and his wife ignored the pistol and took Edwards and his two companions off through the woods 'stiff with Germans', where they temporarily left them. That evening they were led away to a house at St Anthonis (twenty kilometres due south of Nijmegen) where a doctor who had attended to them earlier in the day re-dressed their wounds. The nearest Allied troops, British, were apparently at Grave, some fifteen kilometres north-west, and a horse and cart were laid on for the first part of the journey there. All 'along the route there were men at intervals of about a mile who would suddenly loom up out of the darkness and tell us that the next stretch was clear. We were most impressed by the efficiency with which the whole affair was handled.'

At a farmhouse the travellers rested in the kitchen, and when Bill Randall fell asleep they were put to bed, not waking until 6 o'clock next morning. Two hours later a large, ancient gas-powered saloon car drove up 'and we all got in… We went into Grave with two men on the front mudguard and one on each step, quite a triumphal procession, and were taken to a dressing station.' Once they had been attended to they were taken to Driest. Edwards remained there for three days before being taken to Brussels, where he spent a further two days being treated for his burns. On 27 September he cadged a lift back to his squadron's base at RAF Down Ampney in a Dakota of 48 Squadron, Down Ampney's other resident squadron.[1959]

Though the Arnhem attempt was over supplies were still required beyond the Rhine, deeper into Holland, and the drop zone (DZ) for the crew of a Halifax of 644 Squadron on the night of 5/6 October was some fifty kilometres north-west of Arnhem. Flight Lieutenant R.B. Baird was circling the DZ between Nijkerk and Putten when there was a sudden shout from the bomb aimer of 'Fighter flares!' At the same moment wireless operator Flying Officer J.A. Goggin noticed that they were steadily losing height and urgently called the pilot to pull up. Too late, the Halifax's port wing hit a tree. The aircraft staggered through the air for a further ten seconds, long enough for the crew to take up their crash positions before hitting the ground. Everyone escaped injury except Goggin, who sustained three cuts to his left hand and one to his right knee.

Aware that there was to be a supply drop by another aircraft only a couple of miles away the crew headed towards the DZ. Approached by a non-uniformed man clutching a Sten gun they rightly deduced that he was a member of the other DZ's reception committee, and he took them to the farmhouse of Herr Kemphuis at Voorthuizen, where they remained until 14 October. Two months later they were told by agent Frans Hals (see end of Chapter 7) that members of the *Nationaal Socialistische Beweging* (NSB – National Socialist Movement)[1960] had raided the Kemphuis farm. Albert Kemphuis, the son of Herr Kemphuis, and several companions shot their way out but Albert's father did not and was killed. Albert and his eight comrades had earlier suggested that the airmen might like to go with them to shoot-up German patrols. The matter was referred to a Captain King who said 'that on no account were we to participate in their activities'.[1961]

Two of the 644 Squadron crew, twenty-six-year-old former Leicestershire farmer Flight Lieutenant R.D. Ward DFC and Warrant Officer W.G. McGeachin were moved to another hide-out while the others went to the nearby home of the Klooster family at Amersfoortstraat 71, Barneveld.

Herr Klooster worked at the post office and supplied the Resistance with any information he could glean, while his daughter, Jo, worked for a railway company and supplied the Resistance with information on train movements. As John Goggin noted: 'A thoroughly pro-English household.'

Having been sheltered on two farms David Ward and McGeachin were taken on 25 October to an address in Achterveld, east of Amersfoort, and given civilian clothing. On 1 November they were sheltered at a third farm where they remained until they 'received orders to join operation "Pegasus", which unfortunately was a failure.'[1962]

Joining the operation were the others of their crew who had left the Kloosters on the evening of 16 November and who had been moved to a rendezvous to meet Major Hugh Maguire, Frans Hals and 'a large party of evaders, mostly Airborne personnel. Around 2100 hours the whole party moved off to another RV, two sheds in a field, containing food, uniforms, arms and ammunition. People in civvies were given uniforms, sten guns were cleaned, magazines loaded and all preparations made for the next leg of the journey.'[1963] Major Hugh Maguire, Intelligence staff officer of the Airborne Division, was in charge of Operation Pegasus II, the object of which was to return as many Allied evaders as possible to the other side of the Rhine.

Timing was very much of the essence for this second operation, for the Rhine was filling rapidly and at the chosen point, near Heteren, it was expected to be flowing at around five knots by the middle of November. In view of the strong current boats fitted with outboard motors would have to be used and to cover the noise of these motors a vigorous and noisy fire would be maintained for the duration. As bad weather was expected the date chosen by the staff of IS9 (WEA), prompted by Airey Neave, would have to be flexible, and so a period of three nights from midnight on 22 November was selected. Communications from one side of the river to the other, though, were very rapid thanks to a direct telephone line across the Rhine to Ede power station of which the Germans appeared to be ignorant.

When the bad weather showed signs of calming down Operation Pegasus II was given the go-ahead for the night of 23/24 November. David Ward, however, would not be present at the fiasco that was to follow. He and 130 or so companions – aircrew, airborne and army personnel – were on their way from the large shed to the intended crossing point at Heteren, but 'the noise the Americans and the RAF pilots made had to be heard to be believed.'[1964] Then, still some five or six miles from their goal, they stumbled in the rain and darkness upon a German patrol, which ordered them to halt. Most of the large party of evaders scattered in all directions. David Ward and a Scots major were confronted by a German who had stepped out from behind a tree. Ward dropped to the ground, but the major was killed by the German who then turned his gun on Ward hitting him in the back and left heel, a bullet in each.[1965]

Evacuated by the Germans to a makeshift hospital at Hoenderloo, between Arnhem and Apeldoorn, Ward was transferred to St Joseph's hospital, Apeldoorn early in December. There, too, were Major Gordon Sherriff, 1st Airborne Division, and Sergeant de Lange USAAF. Before his transfer to St Joseph's Major Sherriff had been hospitalised at Wapenveld, ten kilometres south of Zwolle where he had made a friendly contact. The three patients decided to escape and to find this contact at Wapenveld, and at around 10.30 p.m. on 18 January 1945 they climbed out of a window, and legged it. After five and a half hours, having covered barely two-thirds of the twenty-five kilometres to Wapenveld, they hid in a haystack. Five hours later they were so cold that they decided to ask a farmer for help, which was given, and stayed with him until it was dark. In Wapenveld, after some difficulty, they found the contact, who hid them until 23 January. They were then passed to another place at Hattem, where they stayed until 23 March, and to their final hideout at Nijkerk. On 18 April 'some SAS troops attached to 1st Canadian Army who had been informed of our whereabouts by a Dutch Underground member called "Dick" came and liberated us.'

Back at the Rhine on the wet and dark night of 23/24 November 1944 chaos prevailed, and it is thought that only seven Allied personnel had got across. Airey Neave records that three of them appeared on the far bank of the river at 3 o'clock in the morning of 24 November. One was 'an RAF sergeant, with a strong Irish accent named O'Casey, and two Dutchmen'.[1966] The other four were an American major, a Pole, and two guides. The rest were indeed scattered to the four winds, and many were picked up by the very active Gestapo over the ensuing days and weeks. "Frans Hals" for his part was doing all he could to prevent evaders from being arrested, and on 29 December 1944 paid a visit to a farm at Hoogland near Amersfoort, called "The Falkenhoff", but more particularly to a chicken-run in which several evaders were living.

Two days later, when Flying Officer Jack Craven DFC and Flying Officer Ross A. Stoner RAAF arrived at the farm, they found Pilot Officer Brock Christie, Flight Sergeant Frank Fuller, and paratrooper Lieutenant Brian Carr already in residence. A week or so later two more Americans, First Lieutenant C.A. Stearns USAAF (a P-51 Mustang pilot) and Staff Sergeant T.P. Reilly USAAF (B-

17 tail gunner), came in. Carr left them on 9 February 1945, going to a very well camouflaged hut near Doorn, where he met Pilot Officer F.W. Batterbury and Flying Officer A.G. Davies. In due course the three of them were smuggled across the numerous rivers to safety, while Craven and Stoner, having briefly separated, met up again on 12 March and also managed to reach Allied lines safely within the week.

Returning from a highly accurate raid on the afternoon of 22 December 1944 (Bingen railway marshalling yards) a Halifax bomber was flying at 17,000 feet above Berncastel, Germany when a German fighter attacked head on and set the port wing near the fuel tanks on fire. Without hesitation the pilot, Flying Officer G.S. Watson, ordered the crew to bale out. The bomb aimer, Pilot Officer Neville E. Donmall, landed in a ploughed field but in so doing his knees hit his chin and knocked him out. 'When I got up, I was so groggy I almost walked into a Tiger tank. I heard men speaking German a short distance away.'[1967] Heading for the Allied lines in Luxembourg he bedded down in some bushes for the night and remained there until dusk on the following day, when he set off along a main road towards Trier. Having covered some forty kilometres he arrived at Trier at 5 a.m. on 24 December and tried to sleep under a bush. It was too cold, though, and five hours later he watched P-38s bombing Trier: 'One of them was shot down. The pilot didn't bale out.'

Making his way into Trier that evening he found that German military traffic through the town was heavy. 'A German soldier jumped down out of a lorry and asked me directions. I played my deaf-mute role, and he left me. Ten minutes later another soldier asked me the same question, with the same results. Shortly afterwards a German officer with a girl made me repeat the performance.' Anxious to leave the town he continued westwards for ten kilometres or so until he came to the River Sauer. Unable to find any bridges he went to sleep in a shed but awoke on Christmas Day to find that he was close to a German pillbox with a machine-gun sticking out of it.[1968] Quickly making his way to another barn he made a raft from several planks and launched it on the Sauer. He had gone only ten yards or so when it sank, leaving him with no choice but to swim the rest of the way across. By the time that he had walked to the village of Moersdorf and had found a deserted but fully-furnished house he was extremely cold 'and my hands and my feet were frostbitten'. Taking off his wet clothes he wrapped himself in an eiderdown 'and went to sleep in a soft bed'.

In the morning he lit a fire, dried off his battledress, had a shave in hot water and ate two potatoes that he had baked in the stove. Early that afternoon he walked off up a hill in sight of several pillboxes and turned west away from them. Coming out of an orchard he spotted four men behind some bushes but waited until dusk before trying to get round them. He was, however, seen and a shot whistled over his head. The men waved him towards them. Slipping his RAF tabs back onto his shoulders he raised his hands and went over. 'I saw that one of them was wearing the "T/5" of an American corporal. They were American artillery observers.' Neville Donmall had found elements of the US Third Army, and safety.[1969]

There is no question that as the frontline moved ever closer to western Germany the ruthless efficiency of its civilian and quasi-military policing bodies began to crumble. A number of shot down airmen took advantage of this, not least Donmall, and Frenchman Sergeant R.D. Renet,[1970] whose Halifax bomber had been shot down by a night-fighter some twenty-five minutes into its return journey on the night of 16/17 January 1945. Landing a kilometre or so from Diekholzen, a short way to the south-west of Hildesheim, he made good progress west, and managed to keep out of German hands until 22 January when, at Herford station, he was caught in a check on a train that had halted due to an air raid. The police sergeant who arrested him punched him in the face for good measure.

Then the fighters arrived and strafed the station. Renet's guards scrambled for shelter, allowing their prisoner to make good his escape. Again he travelled a good distance, through Bielefeld and Dortmund to Mühlheim, having hitched a ride with Belgian soldiers of the SS Wallonien Division, to whom he declared that he was a French worker. He then met a group of Polish and French workers and had got as far as the village of Steinstrass, west of Cologne, when he was stopped by German soldiers as the area was under fire. Rather than arrest him Renet was given the job of driver to the chief of the Arbeitsamt (office of works) for the Cologne area, but it was not until early on the morning of 1 March 1945 that he seized the opportunity to cross the Allied lines to safety.

Another airman to walk out of Germany was Welshman Sergeant H.T.S. Jones who crossed to the American lines on the Luxembourg/German border in a week, following more or less the same route as that taken by Neville Donmall. On the way back on 21/22 February 1945, flying at around 16,000 feet in bright moonlight north of Kaiserslautern, a night-fighter shot down him and his crew in the classic "below and behind" attack. All seven baled out, but not before Jones had burnt his right hand 'extinguishing a curtain which was alight'.[1971] Landing somewhere east of the winding Mosel he reached it on 23 February. Wondering how to cross the river he spotted a large bridge somewhere near Schweich, which he decided to cross during the hours of darkness. Making his way towards it he found himself in a village full of German soldiers. 'They saw me, but took no notice of me. I crossed a railway line and [reconnoitred] the bridge for possible sentries. I could see none, however, and so walked over a three span bridge, turned left, passed some empty sentry boxes, and up into a vineyard.' It was that easy.

Moving on, and noting a crashed Halifax on the way, he 'came across some parked carts along the side of a road. They were covered with tarpaulins.' Unable to resist the temptation to look inside he found that the carts were loaded with rolled blankets, but just as he was about to appropriate one he was surprised by a German sentry: 'I put my hands up – he talked a lot of German and moved me on. As I was still in his sight, I was forced to continue on the road, and passed several German soldiers who did not take any notice of me.' A little further on, near Welschbillig (between Trier and Bitburg), he had no sooner settled down in a haystack than he heard a cart draw up. Suddenly the Americans began shelling the field and the cart was driven away. The shelling went on for a good two hours, and a splinter hit Jones in his right shoulder blade. It was only a flesh wound, and not painful.

In the morning (25 February) he walked across the field, which 'was potted with shell holes', until he came to the main Trier-Bitburg road. Hearing gunfire to the west he headed north towards Bitburg. Passing through the village of Helenenberg he was joined by a German soldier who 'seemed interested in my clothes, and said something about my being French. I replied "Ja" which seemed to satisfy him.' Jones managed to shake him off when six USAAF Thunderbolts roared over. Turning off the main road he was near the village of Ober Stedem when more Thunderbolts attacked: 'I took cover in a barn together with a lot of German soldiers. The Germans seemed too scared to bother about asking me any questions.' Once they had gone Jones set off again. Encountering more shelling he hid in an empty concrete shelter, only to be joined by four more German soldiers, one of whom offered him a cigarette. The Germans left when the shelling stopped but Jones decided to stay for much of the night in the safety of the shelter.

Leaving at around 3 a.m. on 26 February – his way being lit by the Americans shining searchlights onto the clouds – he reached the village of Wettlingen on the east bank of the River Prüm. Seeing a truck bearing USA markings he was unsure whether or not it had been captured until he saw more trucks similarly marked and heard American voices. Running up to the Americans and telling them who he was he 'was promptly seized, questioned and taken to the CO.' Eventually handed over to a mobile RAF radar unit his wounds were dressed by a medical orderly, but on the night of 27 February his temperature had risen to 104 degrees. His wounds had turned septic. Sent to the US hospital at Luxembourg he was given penicillin for thirty-six hours, and after six days was well enough to be moved to Brussels, and into the hands of IS9 (WEA).[1972]

Rather than waste too much time and energy trying to flush out the Germans from the area of Holland from the Scheldt estuary northwards, the Allies made the decision to press on for the industrial heart of Germany to the east. The area south of the Scheldt was cleared by 31 October, but the Rhine itself, allowing access to the rest of Holland and to Germany, was not crossed until 24 March 1945 when Operation Varsity, 'the biggest and most successful airborne operation in history',[1973] was launched.

In support of Varsity were fighters flying from continental air bases, among them Wing Commander C.D. North-Lewis DSO, DFC who, half an hour after taking off in his Typhoon from airfield B.86, was shot down near Wesel, thirty kilometres or so inside Germany. Leading 137 Squadron in an attack on the fortified village of Krudenburg to the east of Wesel he was pulling out of his dive at 500 feet when flak hit his engine: 'I decided to try and reach my own lines which were approximately six miles to the west. When over Wesel, however, my engine stopped; I glided until I was out in the open, put my flaps down and crash-landed on the only bit of flat ground I could see... I made a very smooth landing, not hurting myself at all.'[1974]

Setting off, he found a line of white tapes, which he took to have been laid down by commandos on the previous night, and followed them in the direction of heavy gunfire towards Wesel, on the east bank of the Rhine. He had gone barely 200 metres, though, when he was challenged by enemy parachutists in a slit trench. 'I walked over to them and found myself to be in the main Rhine defensive trench system of that area. I was warmly shaken by the hand by the first four Germans that I saw and told to get into a small dug-out.' They were not Germans but Austrians, and 'wanted to know if they would be well-treated if they surrendered; their main fear being that we would cut their throats.' They even produced a safe-conduct pass signed by General Eisenhower and wanted to know if *that* would be honoured. North-Lewis was able to assure and to re-assure them on all counts.

With them for much of the day, he watched Varsity's mighty airborne assault pass over their heads.[1975] Taken away for interrogation he met a very laid-back lieutenant, who was not in the least bit bothered by the aerial armada, nor even by a squadron or two of Liberators that roared overhead at zero feet. At about 8 p.m., the lieutenant sent him off to the rear with an escort, but immediately changed his mind when he realised that they were now cut-off, and told his prisoner that he was prepared to surrender.

Later in the evening another lieutenant appeared, altogether of a more warlike disposition, with duelling scars on his cheeks and festooned with weapons and hand grenades. After the newcomer had gone, everyone went to sleep. On the following morning, 25 March, North-Lewis attempted to effect a surrender, but failed to contact a passing Auster aircraft which was spotting in the area. Tearing up white towels he spelt out the message "RAF HAVE HUN PoW. GIVE ORDERS" and, waving the lieutenant's vest, managed to attract the attention of the pilot of an American Piper Cub. 'He read my message but instead of dropping written instructions tried to yell them out of the cockpit.' Needless to say, North-Lewis could not hear a word.

Walking along the trench system he spotted four friendly tanks on the far side of the Rhine and shouted an explanation of his situation to their crews, who said they would send a boat. When after an hour the boat had not appeared North-Lewis found a canvas canoe and paddled across the river to the British lines. Taken to Brigade HQ he told the brigadier that the enemy opposite wished to surrender. His job done, the wing commander went back to his unit, the enemy surrendered, and the war moved on.

German ground fire also accounted for Norwegian fighter pilot Second Lieutenant Hans Wichmann Rohde. He was on patrol in his Spitfire on 2 April 1945 when small-arms fire hit his engine, which seized up after all the glycol coolant had drained out. He thought he had landed in Holland but was not sure until he asked a farmer where he was. The man confirmed that he was indeed on German soil, some three kilometres south of Uelsen almost on the Dutch border. The farmer probably alerted the authorities, for in no time Rohde was surrounded by a dozen members of the Volkssturm, who removed his watch and revolver and tied his hands behind his back. Discovering that he was Norwegian he 'was very brutally treated' before being handed over to the Wehrmacht, who handed him over to the police at De Wijk in Holland. After a couple of hours in a prison at Meppel he was put in the hands of the Luftwaffe 'who took me to Havelte, and there put me in a prison cell on my own.'[1976] On the morning of 5 April after interrogation he was taken back to another cell, where he discovered Warrant Officer Johannes ("Hans") Cornelis van Roosendaal, who had been shot down three kilometres east of Deventer, Holland on 2 April.

Hans van Roosendaal and his family had been living in Kapellen near Antwerp, Belgium when the Germans attacked on 10 May 1940 and moved to Paris. By 28 May Hans was driving an ambulance for the French. Having saved two wounded Frenchmen just as the Germans were attacking he was awarded the Croix de Guerre. Early in 1941 he led some Dutch students over the Pyrenees and into Spain and Portugal, where he and one of the students, L.D. "Bert" Wolters, caught a KLM DC3 to England. After two years flying training both Hans and Bert joined 322 (Dutch) Squadron.[1977]

Barely twenty minutes after landing Hans was caught by feldgendarmes who took him to a medical officer to see to the gash on his forehead (probably caused by hitting his head on the gunsight of his Spitfire XVI). When the doctor refused to treat him he was taken to a prison in Deventer and put in a cell that 'had no windows and a big metal door which closed with a big lock on the outside'.[1978] There was in the door, however, a small, round hole with glass in it to enable guards to see what the prisoner was up to. In the night he broke the glass, unlocked the door and made his way out of the prison. Knowing that all roads were guarded he decided to contact a civilian. 'Unfortunately the first house I went to was occupied by German soldiers who took me in again and brought me to the same cell from which I had escaped.'

Next evening, in a wagon with thirty-five paratroops and accompanied by four guards, Hans was moved by train to Zwolle, leaving only when it was fully dark to avoid attack from the air by roving Allied fighters. Consequently, when they arrived at Zwolle in the pitch dark and he was ordered to get out, he made a run for it out of another exit and was able to get out of the town without being seen. Coming to a bridge over a large canal or river he was caught by a guard who was *under* the bridge and taken back to Zwolle station where the paratroopers kicked lumps out of his shins until they 'were bleeding freely'. Next day, 4 April, he was driven to Meppel and after a couple of hours in the civil jail was driven by the Luftwaffe to Havelte. On the morning of 5 April Rohde and an American pilot, 2nd Lieutenant Kenneth E. Foster USAAF, were brought in.[1979]

It was fortunate for the other two that Foster was there for he had been given a hacksaw blade by the Dutch Resistance before capture, and he still had it with him. They spent all day sawing through two iron bars in the window, but just as it grew dark one of the guards closed the shutter across the window. Dismantling a bed, however, they used bits of it to open the shutter and at around 10.30 p.m. that night slipped away into the darkness. They had a close shave in a wood full of German tanks when a soldier relieved himself only feet from Rohde, but they were not seen, and at Nijeveen, half way between Havelte and Meppel, they were able to find shelter first at the Buitenhaus house, then with Mijnheer G. Wildeboer for five days, until liberated by Allied troops on 13 April.[1980]

Just after midnight on the night of 11/12 April 1945, in the skies over Holland, Luftwaffe night-fighters shot down a Stirling aircraft engaged on a supply drop for SOE. A few kilometres to the north of Rotterdam, the six crew, battered and bruised, made their way severally to the home of farmer A.G. Kok and his wife at 2de Tachtweg 41, Nieuwerkerk am der Ijssel. Flying Officer D.W. Anderson was grateful to them for dressing 'the wounds of my face, legs, and arms' and for the precious milk and food that he received. Flight Sergeant B. D. Rowland's wounds – a broken jaw and splinters in his left leg – were also washed and dressed, but Flight Sergeant W.H. Bell was in such a state that he was confined to bed for five days. Flight Sergeant G.D. Hollick was found by his skipper, Flight Lieutenant G.E. Sharp, 'just recovering consciousness under the starboard wing of the aircraft', both having been knocked about in the crash. The sixth man was the flight engineer, Sergeant Johnstone.

Farmer Kok, himself a member of the Dutch Resistance, contacted the Zoetermeer section of the *Nederlandse Binnenlandse Strijdkrachten* (Netherlands Interior Forces – NBS) under the command of Dr Joop Kentgens[1981] and his deputy, Jacob Leendert van Rij, a thirty-eight-year-old police sergeant. Most of the airmen were moved by bicycle to the Zoetermeer NBS headquarters, which were located at a remote hunting lodge, "Het Jachthuis", on the banks of the River Rotte at Zevenhuizen.[1982] Basil Rowland, however, was conveyed thither in a wheelbarrow.[1983] Anderson was kept in bed for eight days while Dr Kentgens 'dressed my wounds twice every day, fed and clothed me, and supplied me with books and cigarettes.'[1984] The only other house nearby was occupied by Jan and Pie de Koster and their two small children. She knew that the hunting lodge was being used by the Resistance and helped them when she could.[1985] Already at the hunting lodge was Staff Sergeant John E. McCormick USAAF who had been there for some seven weeks, more or less since he had been shot down.[1986]

Four days after McCormick's bomber had crash-landed at a farm at Zoeterwoude an RAF photo-reconnaissance Spitfire of 542 Squadron flew over it with its camera running. The developed photographs duly revealed the wreckage. Following the usual practice completely to destroy a crashed aircraft to prevent any secret technology from falling into enemy hands three fighters were sent to finish off the B-24, but long after the Germans had removed what they wanted. The fighters plastered the area, and though German soldiers guarding the bomber ordered everyone to take cover – there were several sightseers around – two little boys were badly wounded in the stomach before their mother could get them to safety in the farm's cellar.

Others in the open were also wounded, but a German guard and four of the Dutch sightseers were killed. 'Fifteen-year-old Jopie van Bemmelen – sister of the two wounded boys in the cheese cellar – had tried to protect her four-year-old brother Gerrie by hiding him under her dress. Jopie's body was so badly mangled by the bullets that she could hardly be recognized. Gerrie was hit in his abdomen by one bullet. He was bandaged up by Dr Kortmann, the local doctor, who used a first aid kit from the [B-24] which he had retrieved on the day it crashed. Young Gerrie died on the way to a hospital in Leiden. Also killed were Martinus Janson, the sixty-two-year-old owner of the farm where 241 crashed and Maria den Elsen-Zonderop, a thirty-six-year-old mother of five.'[1987]

Dr Kentgens, who spoke good English, gave John McCormick a choice – either surrender to the Germans, become a prisoner of war and most likely survive, or join the Resistance. John chose the latter, and during the following weeks led them in physical training, helped them make fake passports and false identification cards, and stole food ration cards that were then used to provide food for the Resistance and for those in hiding. Furthermore, when the Zoetermeer NBS went out on a raid, John went with them, armed as they were armed, on one of these raids robbing three Germans of their guns, ammunition, jewellery, money, and ration cards.[1988]

Though the hunting lodge became known to the Stirling crew as "The Jolly Duck"[1989] what was to happen there a few days after their arrival was far from jolly. Present at the lodge on the afternoon of Sunday, 29 April were Dr Joop Kentgens, Wachmeester Jacob van Rij, his wife Ali and their ten-year-old son Jaap, John McCormick, the six Stirling crewmen, several other members of the Zoetermeer NBS and their children, Mance and Richard van Romunde, Joop Havenaar, Jonker de Milly van Heijde Reynestein, and W. Vernooter, a Dutch nazi from Rotterdam who was being held prisoner.[1990] Dr Kentgens' wife, who had been visiting her husband, had already left when, at approximately 6.30 p.m., twenty-five heavily-armed troops of Feldpost 23285 from the village of Bleiswijk attacked the hunting lodge under the command of Hauptmann Ludwig Schmidt. Schmidt had earlier been fired upon when he and another soldier, Karl Silbemagel, were making their way across flooded land close to the lodge.

The action began when, on Schmidt's order 'Raus! Sofort raus!', some of the Germans rushed up to the house and threw in four hand grenades. Ordering everyone to fight back Dr Kentgens set a fine example when one of the Germans managed to get into the house through the front door and 'kicked down the door leading to the dining room. He was fired at by the doctor, but the German returned fire and the doctor was seriously wounded and later left for dead.'[1991] Flying Officer Anderson, who was positioned on the stairs, killed the German as he ran back outside.

After some twenty minutes of fighting so desperate had the situation become for those inside that Jacob van Rij gave the order for everyone to fight their way out. Leading the way himself he charged at two Germans who were guarding the escape route. Blazing away with his Sten gun he killed them both but was then hit twice himself. Losing consciousness he fell into the river and drowned. Another casualty was John McCormick. Shot through the back of the head he died shortly afterwards. Ali van Rij was hit on the knee and lost a kneecap.[1992] As for the Germans it was believed that ten of them were killed, but there were enough left to capture Flight Sergeant Johnstone.

The survivors from The Jolly Duck made their getaway during van Rij's gallant breakout, and though the Germans continued to shoot at them as they fled there were no more casualties. The survivors – Sharp, Anderson, Hollick, Bell, Rowland, "Lewis" of The Hague NBS, "Joe", and Mance van Romunde – successfully reached a farmhouse at Moerkapelle three or four kilometres away. On 30 April, after the new commander of the Zoetermeer NBS, Piet van Dreel, had made arrangements for the airmen to be hidden in several homes in Moerkapelle, Sharp and Anderson were billeted with a baker, Jan de Graafe, a member of the Moerkapelle NBS, and his wife at Dorpstraat 69. Bell and Hollick were taken to the home of Mr G. Bergshoof at Horenweg 29, while Rowland went to the home of Mr G. Jonker, commander of the Moerkapelle NBS, at Rooseboom, Heerennes 38. Jonker was able to supply Rowland with 'clothing and food plus a few comforts', as were the others of his crew by their generous hosts.

When the dust had settled, Pie de Koster was questioned by the Germans as to the identity of John McCormick. Terrified that she would be shot if she said he was an American airman, she replied that he was a stranger from The Hague. The 'Germans removed their own casualties and on 2 May gave the people of Zevenhuizen permission to search for Dutch casualties. John McCormick's body was found some twenty metres from the Jachthuis next to a barn. Jacob van Rij was found in a small creek, still holding his Sten gun.'[1993] The two men were buried next to each other in Zevenhuizen on Friday evening, 4 May 1945, their funeral being attended by Flying Officer Anderson. On 31 October 1945 John McCormick's remains were reburied at the Dutch Reformed Church in Zoetermeer, this time with full military honours. Interred next to him were Jacob van Rij and two other Dutchmen, members of the Resistance, Cornelis van Eerden and Jan Hoorn.[1994]

With the fighting in this small part of Holland all but over the German High Command in Holland had earlier on 4 May surrendered all their forces in that country in a "truce of God" that was intended to avoid further bloodshed in the region. Fighting was to cease by 8 a.m. on 5 May, when members of the Resistance were told that they could come out of hiding. So it was that on that morning many were gathered at a schoolyard in Zoetermeer, some of them wearing their "uniform" of blue overalls with a red, white, and blue armband. A truckload of Germans drove by and opened fire, killing Cornelis van Eerden and Jan Hoorn.[1995]

Liberation in this part of Holland finally came on 9 May, a day after the official end of the war. On that day Max Kadicks, like de Graafe an officer of the Moerkapelle NBS, took Flight Lieutenant Sharp on his motorbike to Rotterdam. Reporting to the headquarters of the First Canadian Army arrangements were made for Sharp and his crew to be transported by jeep to Rotterdam. On 10 May they were taken to the transit camp for returning prisoners of war at Nijmegen, and were interviewed on the following day.

The war had been over for two months when Flight Lieutenant J.S. Robertson, signals officer of "B" Squadron, 8701 Wing, RAF, was sent to investigate a report that a German transmitter had been hidden in the hunting lodge. On his arrival at Zevenhuizen on 7 July 1945 he contacted Mynheer L. Knott, now commander of the local NBS section, who detailed one of his men to accompany Robertson to The Jolly Duck, which had been under NBS guard since the liberation. Robertson was then told of the gunfight on 29 April and also that the six British airmen 'had with them a Dinghy transmitter, which they rigged up in the attic and attempted to get into communication with Allied Authorities.' No trace of the transmitter could now be found, 'only a length of the aerial wire', but

Robertson was satisfied from the description of it 'that it was in fact an RAF type Dinghy transmitter'.

Before he left Robertson paid his respects to the dead American airman, John E. McCormick, and collected his personal effects from Mynheer Knott.

In another part of Holland, at Aalsmeer, a few kilometres south of Amsterdam, liberation might have come on 5 May 1945, when two scruffy-looking individuals, one of them wearing a raincoat on top of his uniform, cycled into the Aalsmeer garrison hoping to hoodwink the German commander into surrendering: 'After a bit of trouble at one headquarters, we were taken to the commander, a captain… Our terms were that all German troops were to disarm, but that officers would be allowed to keep revolvers and take charge of their troops.' The man in uniform claimed that he had been dropped from a Flying Fortress earlier that day to negotiate the Germans' surrender, but the hauptmann was not to be fooled. He was sure that German forces in Holland would never capitulate. The man in uniform was, to his surprise, thereupon allowed to leave.

One of the two scruffy individuals was the local Resistance chief, and the man in uniform was Flying Officer Donald Lowry Boyd RAAF. Shot down in his 274 Squadron Tempest on 28 March 1945 Boyd had been captured south of Arnhem. After two weeks in custody at Amersford he was transferred to Aalsmeer and imprisoned in a convent that was attached to a church by a flat-roofed building. It took Boyd but little time in which to appreciate that he could get out of the room in which he was locked, onto the flat roof which was covered in loose gravel, and into the church itself. On 19 April he and two other prisoners, Lieutenant Robinette USAAF and Sergeant Norm USAAF, decided to escape.

First, though, they had to get past a guard who was blocking the way from their room to the one across the passageway from which they hoped to escape. Two other prisoners distracted the guard by asking him for a cigarette paper, and then lit a match in front of his eyes. The three escapers made it safely into the room. Alarmed to discover that the flat roof was bathed in the light of a bright moon they waited until it was hidden before lowering themselves onto the roof, making 'a frightful noise' as they walked on the gravel. Robinette wanted to climb down a drainpipe, but that plan was discarded when they spotted a guard patrolling below, and so they decided to continue with the original plan, to get through the church window.

The window in question was of the traditional leaded-glass type, but it took them about three hours to remove enough of the lead and glass to allow them to get through. Then Sergeant Norm coughed loudly, and a piece of glass fell into the church. As they could not be certain that the guards had not been alerted by the racket, they waited for a quarter of an hour, sitting absolutely still, before climbing down a rope that they had fabricated from the window cord. But, as Robinette was making his way down, the rope broke, and he fell four or five metres to the floor. Norm then made the drop followed by Boyd, who fell onto 'the other two which softened the fall a little'.[1997] It was all in danger of becoming slapstick, however, when Norm found the church's main door in the pitch darkness and fell down the steps. The German guard stationed at the corner of the church and who was enjoying a crafty smoke heard nothing.

Safely away, the three airmen were passing a house at around 5 a.m. on 20 April when they were hailed by a woman. Making her understand that they were British and American airmen she took them inside and after breakfast contacted the local Resistance. Provided with a suit of overalls each they were split up in separate houses, where they remained until liberated by Canadian forces on 8 May.

Though everyone knew that the war was as good as over, the RAF continued to fly supplies to the Danish Resistance throughout April 1945, and on the night of 2/3 April the crews of three Stirlings were given the task of dropping supplies to the island of Orø in Issefjorden. Bad weather forced two of the Stirlings to return to base. As newly-promoted Pilot Officer C.T. Dillon and his crew in the third Stirling, LJ942, had had difficulty pinpointing their position Dillon flew over Sjælland (Zealand, Denmark's largest island) from the west before circling over the town of Hundested. An easy target for German flak gunners at Melby LJ942 was hit in the tail.

Flying low over Roskilde fjord inlet Dillon then turned south, but when the elevators failed to respond properly LJ942 hit the water at high speed, approximately 600 metres to the north of Stenø and 100 metres from the beach, at around 2 a.m. on 3 April. The bomb aimer, Pilot Officer Thomas A. McBeath RCAF, also newly promoted, was killed on impact.[1998]

The flight engineer, Flight Sergeant Harold J. Farmer, was knocked unconscious, and concussed. Wireless operator Flight Sergeant Cyril V. Laing broke a leg and a finger. Navigator Warrant Officer H.J. Hart RAAF, unharmed, helped his comrades out onto the wing, and released the dinghy. Escaping from the rear turret, which had broken off from the rest of the fuselage and was lying some

200 metres from the forward part of the aircraft, rear gunner Warrant Officer R.A. Hills made his way through three-foot deep water to help. Unable to wade through the water because of their injuries Dillon, Laing and Farmer were pushed ashore in the dinghy by Hills and Hart.

Once on dry land Hart slashed the dinghy and threw the pieces into the water. Dillon, Laing and Farmer (who needed urgent attention) were taken to a nearby cottage while Hills and Hart took cover in nearby bushes. The man who lived in the cottage, fisherman Alfred Olsen, came out and invited them in too. His advice was to make for the town of Helsingör on the east coast of Sjælland but, as only Hills and Hart were fit enough to make the journey, Olsen said that he would fetch a doctor to look after the other three. He could not, however, 'guarantee the doctor's good faith'. The doctor, indeed a loyal patriot, arranged for an ambulance to take the three injured men to the hospital in Frederikssund, where Chief Physician Gejlager decided that it would be safe to move Dillon.

At 11 a.m. he was picked up by two armed men and removed to Over-Draaby. On 10 April he was on his way to Sweden. Farmer and Laing, however, were not so fortunate. Captured by the Germans they were moved to the Lazarett at Værløse. Farmer was later transferred to Lübeck, Germany where he was liberated by the British, but Laing stayed in Værløse until the liberation.[1999]

Leaving their three comrades with the fisherman Hills and Hart cut off their badges, left their mae wests in a pond and, barely an hour after their sudden arrival in Denmark, walked off along a road until daylight approached. Deciding to hide, the only shelter that they could see was 'a small stunted tree on a hill about half a mile from the road'. It was better than nothing, but at midday they 'were discovered by a dog and shortly afterwards a farmer came out from his farm and looked at us but went away again without addressing us.'[2000] Towards dusk, not having moved from their tree, the farmer returned, and took the two airmen back to his farm, where they were fed and given fresh socks. Contact was made with another farmer who had connections with the Danish Resistance at Hilleröd. He took them to his farm, and exchanged their battledress for civilian clothes. Two members of the Resistance arrived, took their measurements and returned in due course with a new suit for each of them.

On the evening of 4 April they left by bicycle with the two Resistance men, and stayed at Hilleröd, half a dozen kilometres away, for the next two days. On 7 April two guides took them by train to Köbenhavn (Copenhagen) where they remained for a further eight days. 'At 2130 hours on 15 April we were taken down to the docks and, after evading the control, we joined a small party which was extremely well armed. We went with them to the sea front, crawling spasmodically, and stayed in a little shack waiting for the outboard motor launch.'[2001] The boat arrived in the small hours of 16 April and took them across the water, past Saltholm Island, to Malmö, Sweden, successfully dodging the German patrol boats. The British Consul sent them to Stockholm, where they stayed for the best part of a month before being flown back to the UK on 11 May.

Shortly before take-off on the evening of 27 April 1945, Flight Sergeant Thomas Jones, navigator of Stirling LK567, coded 8Z-L, 295 Squadron, was called to the operations room and told that the original drop zone, "Arthur", had been compromised. The new DZ for their SOE operation was now at "Holsteinshus", near Faaborg on the Danish island of Fyn. At 9.12 p.m. LK567 took off from Rivenhall, Essex and set course for the new location.

Flying at low level over the North Sea and Jylland the Stirling with its six-man crew turned to the south of Fyn to approach the DZ from the south. When they thought that they were there the crew saw no signal lights. The reason was simple enough – the Danish reception committee had not been told of the change in DZ and had been waiting at "Arthur" until four o'clock in the morning, when they left without having heard an aircraft.

Having circled a couple of times over the unmanned DZ "Holsteinshus" the pilot, Warrant Officer Edward (Ted) A. Dax, turned the Stirling onto a course back to base while unwittingly flying at only fifty or sixty metres over Fliegerhorst Vejle (Luftwaffe airbase), and wide-awake German flak gunners set the port-inner engine ablaze. The Stirling crew tried unsuccessfully to extinguish it, but when fire then broke out in the starboard-inner engine Ted Dax ordered the crew to bale out. A quick look at the altimeter, though, told him that they were too low and, cancelling his first order, told the crew to prepare to crash land.

At 0100 hours on 28 April the Stirling hit the ground at Plougslund moor to the west of Fliegerhorst Vandel. As soon as the Stirling came to a halt Dax, Jones and Flight Sergeant Frank Fuller, the wireless operator, jumped out of the front exit to the ground ten feet below, landing in mud and water up to their knees. They called out to the rest of the crew – rear gunner Flight Sergeant Edward Tate, flight engineer Flight Sergeant Ronald S. Day, and bomb aimer Flight Sergeant John Ayers – but got no reply. Ditching their parachute harnesses and mae wests Dax, Jones and Fuller started to walk away from the aircraft. All three were carrying pistols but decided that it would do them no good if they were captured and the weapons were found on them, so left them in a sandy spot on the moor.

Walking all night to put as much distance between them and the Stirling as possible, they hid in a wood for the day. It started to rain and soon they were soaking wet and cold. Managing to sleep for only a few minutes at a time they gave up and left the wood. After a while they came across a farmhouse which they watched for about three hours to make sure that there were no Germans in it. Hungrily they watched a farmer feeding his pigs. No sooner was the farmer's back turned than Tom Jones was off. Running into the pigsty he punched a pig on the nose and ate some of its feed. Whatever it was it did him no good, and it took a couple of days for his stomach to recover.

Late in the afternoon they knocked on the door of the farm, which was opened by a small girl. Unable to make themselves understood, she closed it. Not wishing to frighten her they made their way to the stables, and in the hayloft ate some turnips that they had found, and went to sleep.

The next morning, 29 April, the farmer and his wife gave them a proper meal. Informed that the Germans were searching the area for them the three airmen left the farm before midday and headed for a large wood some way to the south, where their hosts had advised them to hide for a few days. They got there late in the afternoon and tried to get some sleep, but at about 4 o'clock in the morning of 30 April it was so cold that they decided to leave. Making their way to a farm at dawn they got no reply to their knock, but at another farm the door was opened by a young woman with a small baby in her arms. She invited them in and gave them food. When Dax, Jones and Fuller were ready to leave she insisted that they take some hard-boiled eggs with them.

They headed south with the aid of the small compass from their escape kit, but after about an hour walked into what seemed to be a German rifle range. They crawled on their stomachs until clear of the range and followed a road going south-east. They spent the night in another hayloft, but at midday were woken up by three children playing in the barn. The oldest, a girl of about eleven, came to the loft and almost tripped over the airmen before seeing them. They tried to explain to her that they were English, and she told them that her name was Karen. The other two children, one a boy aged six and the other a girl aged five, climbed into the hayloft. Making them understand that they were hungry the boy went to the house and returned with his mother. After some talking between Karen and her mother the airmen were taken to the house and given a meal. An English-speaking woman arrived and in broken English tried to explain where the Germans were camping in the area.

When the airmen left the mother led them to the road that she had advised that they should follow. They walked all night and when dawn broke found a barn and climbed to the hayloft and went to sleep. They were woken at around 7 a.m. when a farmer started moving around in the barn. Then a hen came into the loft and laid an egg. After a little more searching they found two more eggs. Eggs for breakfast.

When it was dark the airmen went to the house but left when they heard the farmer say something that sounded like "go away". Filling their water bottles with milk from some churns they carried on. At a house near the road they were given a sandwich and something to drink before walking through the night again. Crossing streams and bogs and marshes they fought their way through some small woods. Ever hungry they spent the rest of the day in yet another hayloft. Any thoughts of sleep were interrupted by a dog that stood barking in the barn for half an hour before someone called it into the house. The dog was back late in the evening, once again barking for a long time. After a while a boy came to fetch it, and saw the airmen. Returning to the house he came back with his father, Lars P. Jensen. When the airmen stood up, covered with mud and straw, father and son burst out laughing.

Taken to the house a kettle was put on the stove, and soon the airmen were enjoying the luxury of their first wash and shave in warm water since their arrival in Denmark. After a meal prepared by his wife, Lars told them where the German camps in the area were located, and that by heading east for a couple of miles and then south they would get round the largest of them. They followed the road for a while and then left it to be able to travel east. Suddenly they head a shout followed by three shots. They froze in their tracks. As nothing happened for several minutes they headed for Vorbasse. After a while they turned south until confronted by marshy ground. They tried to cross it, but had to give up and find another way around it.

It was now morning, and near Bække they found some milk churns. As they were drinking a door opened at a nearby house and a man came out. He stood looking at them, smiling. By signs they asked him if they could sleep in his hayloft, and he agreed. They awoke at five in the afternoon when the man and a girl, another Karen, came to the barn with trays of food, three beers and milk. The farmer then returned to the house to listen to the radio while Karen stayed with the airmen until they had finished eating. Later that evening the farmer, with an older man and Karen, returned to the barn. They were all laughing. The war in Europe was over.

Following the farmer to the house Dax, Jones and Fuller listened to the news on the BBC. A bottle of wine saved for the liberation of Denmark was opened and a toast proposed. Farmer Hans, his wife Mor, son Lauge, and daughter Karen invited the airmen to stay at "Grandal" until the British army arrived, but they were collected by members of the Danish Resistance and taken to Kolding. Here they received the news that Ronald Day and Edward Tate were in Vejle and went there to meet them at "Store Grundet".

They heard that Tate and Day had managed to get out of the Stirling's rear exit, bringing the severely injured John Ayers out as well. They did what they could for him before leaving him a short distance from the aircraft and walking away. After a couple of days, when they were on the road to Vorbasse, a passing Dane, Søren Ohlenschlaeger, tried to buy cigarettes from them. Realising that they were RAF airmen he took them to his house at Frederiksnaade and contacted Doctor O. Clausen at Vorbasse, who arranged for them to be hidden in a smallholding just outside Hovborg belonging to Jeppe Nikolajsen and his wife Mia. The doctor picked up Day and Tate in his car and took them to the Nikolajsens, with whom they stayed until the liberation of Denmark, and at "Store Grundet" near Vejle met Dax, Jones and Fuller. All five stayed there for a few days enjoying the victory celebrations in Vejle.

They then returned to their wrecked Stirling to look for the buried pistols. With the help of local peat cutters they formed a line abreast and walked across the moor, but found nothing. They also met some other people, who told them that the Germans had found the injured Ayers and had taken him to a Lazarett in Fredericia, but he died on 30 April. On 4 May he was buried in a common grave with twenty-four Germans, but on the last day of the month his body was exhumed and re-interred in the Nordre cemetery in Fredericia with a proper Christian funeral. Six members of the Resistance carried the coffin and Reverend Erik Christensen officiated at the graveside ceremony that was attended by numerous Danish citizens as well as a guard of honour of British soldiers.

Tate and Day found time to revisit Mia and Jeppe Nikolajsen, before the Stirling's crew were driven to København on 12 May. They spent a week sightseeing and celebrating before being flown back to England.

Fifty years later, on 27 April 1995, a memorial was erected near the crash site. On 27 April 2005, a propeller from the Stirling was added to the memorial. Both Fuller and Jones were present at the ceremony.

Though Flight Sergeant P.W.W. Millard, whose Typhoon aircraft came down in Germany on 3 May 1945, can claim to have been the last of over two thousand RAF aircrew to have evaded capture in Western Europe, Warrant Officers Philip Brett (pilot) and William Boorer (navigator) have another claim in that they were the only airmen to have been shot down *during* the war and to have landed, in Denmark, after the war. On 3 May 1945, just before five o'clock in the afternoon, Brett and Boorer took off in their 144 (Coastal Command) Squadron Beaufighter, NE955, from RAF Thornaby-on-Tees on an anti-shipping operation to Kiel Bay.

Though the war was all but over in Western Europe, RAF Intelligence had been alarmed by the presence in north German ports of a number of large ships which, it was believed, could be used to transport German troops to Norway, from where they could continue the fight. In Lübeck Bay there were three large targets – the *Cap Arcona* (27,571 tons), formerly known as the Queen of the South Atlantic; *Thielbek* (2,815 tons); and *Athen* (1,936 tons). Also in the vicinity was the former liner *Deutschland* (21,046 tons), now being used as a hospital ship.

What the RAF did not know when they ordered four squadrons of Typhoons to sink these ships on 3 May was that they were full of prisoners from the concentration camps of Neuengamme, Stutthof, and Dora-Mittelbau. On the *Cap Arcona* there were 4,500 prisoners, on the *Thielbek* 2,800, and on the *Athen* 1,998. Altogether some 7,500 prisoners of war of many nationalities were killed as a result of these attacks, some by the bombs and rockets and cannons of the Typhoons but most drowned because the SS guards refused to let them off the sinking ships. A few survivors who had managed to escape from the ruins of their ships and had reached the shore were gunned to death by the waiting SS guards. After these three ships had been sunk it was the *Deutschland*'s turn to face an attack by three squadrons of Typhoons. As luck would have it, there were no casualties from these attacks, though the *Deutschland* was sunk.

Oblivious to this awful episode Philip Brett was forced to ditch NE955 after it had been hit by flak in one of its engines. Coming down 100 kilometres west of Jylland he and Boorer climbed into the aircraft's dinghy and drifted for four days. On the afternoon of 7 May, fifty-five kilometres west of Esbjerg, they were rescued by the crew of a Danish fishing boat, E 428 *Ella* of Esbjerg. After the *Ella* had reached her home port on the morning of 8 May the two airmen were taken to the Centralsygehuset hospital in Esbjerg. They were in a poor condition but it became clear that, apart from the frostbite to their feet, they would be all right after a rest.[2002]

A happy ending to five years of unremitting, global slaughter.

Postscript

When Tom Groome was flown to Gibraltar from England in 1942 he left his flying suit with Donald Darling. The two met again in Paris in 1945, after Groome had returned from the German concentration camps to which he had been sent two years earlier. Darling remembered: 'I had the Union Jack flying from the balcony of my office. Groome looked hard at it and then suddenly knelt down, weeping and kissed the corner of it. There was no need for anybody to speak.'

APPENDIX I

List of RAF evaders: 1940–1945

A list of the names and brief details of 2,198 RAF evaders who flew from the United Kingdom on operations over Western Europe, 1940-1945.

The seventeen columns in the list below are as follows:

1. Name — Surname.
2. Init — Initials.
3. Rank — Rank held at time of evasion.
4. Nat — Nationality. If blank, evader was RAF – British.

Otherwise:

AUS – Australian; BEL – Belgian; CAN – Canadian; CZ – Czechoslovakian; EIR – Irish (not Northern Ireland); FRA – French; HOL – Dutch; NOR – Norwegian; NZ – New Zealander; POL – Polish; RHO – South Rhodesian; RUS – Russian; SAF – South African; SEY – Seychellois; USA – American.

5. No — Evader's service number.
6. Sq — The squadron on which evader was serving when shot down.
7. A/C — Serial number of aircraft in which shot down.
8. Type — Type of aircraft in which shot down:
   ALB – Albemarle; BA – Battle; BFR – Beaufighter; BFT – Beaufort; BL – Blenheim; BOS – Boston; DAK – Dakota; DF – Defiant; FT– Flying Fortress; HAL – Halifax; HN – Hampden; HUD – Hudson; HUR – Hurricane; LA – Lancaster; LIB – Liberator; LYS – Lysander; MAN – Manchester; MCL – Mitchell; MOS – Mosquito; MU – Mustang; SP – Spitfire; ST – Stirling; TEM – Tempest; TY – Typhoon; WE – Wellington; WH – Whitley; WW–Whirlwind.
9. Date — Date on which shot down. First day only shown if operation continued past midnight into the following day.
10. Duty/target — Operational duty/target when shot down. Note: A/S – anti-submarine. NK – not known. M/Y– marshalling yards.
11. Where — The country in which the evader first landed when shot down.
12. To — Other countries to which the evader went or passed through, where known:
   And – Andorra; Bel – Belgium; Dk – Denmark; Fr – France; Ger – Germany; Gib – Gibraltar; Hol – Holland; Nor – Norway; Por – Portugal; Rus – Russia; Sp – Spain; Swe – Sweden; Sz – Switzerland.
13. Left for UK — Date on which evader left for the United Kingdom.
14. UK — Date on which evader arrived in the United Kingdom.
15. Where in UK — Place where evader landed back in the United Kingdom. It is probable that the three destinations "Greenock", "Gourock", and "Glasgow" were the one and the same place, in effect the port of Gourock.
   the place is not always given, it is sometimes possible to make an educated guess where, for example, several evaders returned to the UK on the same date and by the same method.
16. WO 208 — Number of evader's report in The National Archives file series WO 208, e.g. 3310 863 is (MI9) report number 863 in file WO 208/3310.
   "NF" indicates no report found. In some of the early evasions, during the "Battle for France", it is highly unlikely that a report would have been made.
17. Comments — (a) The two letters "ss" followed by a number, e.g. ss7, indicate that that evader was the sole survivor of a crew of seven.
   (b) References to "Comet", e.g. Comet 77, should be read in conjunction with Appendix II.
   (c) For Sherwood or Marathon see Appendix IV.
   (d) Awards, e.g. DSO, DFC, MiD, etc are given where known. Dates in brackets after awards are those of publication of the award in *The London Gazette*.
   (e) References to books ("See…") may indicate either a passing mention of the evader in question or a fuller account of the evasion.
   (f) In some cases the full number of the evader's report is given, e.g. IS9/WEA/2/166/2319 (Kaminek) where, in column 16, only 3351 2319 is shown.

Other Notes:

(a) A question mark in any of the seventeen columns signifies that the information to which it relates is questionable.
(b) Twelve airmen evaded twice, but each evasion is counted separately.
(c) Awards to Polish aircrew were not published in *The London Gazette*, for to have done so might have compromised relatives in their homeland. It is, therefore, difficult to give any relevant date of an award, but such date as is given is that of its approval by His Majesty King George VI, to whom the recommendation was presented through appropriate channels for approval. The date of his signature of approval was deemed to be the date of the award.

Name	Init	Rank	Nat	No	Sq	A/C	Type	Date	Duty/target	Where	To	Left for UK	UK	Where in	WO 208	Comments
Aasberg	BS	SGT	NOR	F.P.5908	332	NH425	SP	16/4/45	Armed recce	Holland	Hol			NK	3352 3043	Interviewed 2 May 1945. Report IS9/WEA/1/404/3043
Abbott	LC	F/O	AUS	155130	466	MZ313	HAL	18/7/44	Vaires	France	Fr	7/9/44	7/9/44	NK	3323 2421	Left for UK from Bayeux - B.14 airstrip, Banville
A'Court	HG	F/L		149875	109	ML985	MOS	31/8/44	Leverkusen		Por			NK	NF	DFC (5/10/43) & Bar (21/9/45, squadron leader). MiD (14/1/44)
Adams	RW	SGT		1380224	214	BK653	ST	16/4/43	Mannheim	France	And, Sp, Gib	17/7/43	24/7/43	Liverpool	3314 1321	Oaktree. Back to UK on SS *Monarch of Bermuda*?
Adams	S	F/S	AUS	A.426290	467	LM219	LA	7/7/44	St Leu d'Esserent	France	Fr		5/9/44	NK	NF	
Adams	TH	SGT		908221	106	DV196	LA	7/8/43	Milan	France	Fr	26/12/43	26/12/43	Helford	3317 1650	Sprained ankle. Back via Bordeaux line on Operation Felicitate, MGB 318. See Sergeant H.L. Nielsen
Adams	W	FT/O	USA		630	PA992	LA	24/7/44	Stuttgart	France	Fr			NK	NF	Note: he was a USAAF flight officer
Adcock	RS	P/O			3	EJ812	TEM	14/2/45	Armed recce	Germany	Ger			NK	NF	Baled out after being hit by flak over Quackenbrück airfield
Agur	PG	F/O	CAN	J.24984	429	MZ302	HAL	28/6/44	Metz	France	Fr			NK	3348 316	Sherwood. Interviewed 17 August 1944. Report IS9/WEA/2/83/316
Ainger	SRJ	SGT		1256129	49	AT156	HN	5/4/42	Cologne	Belgium	Fr, Sp, Gib	27/9/42	28/9/42	Mount Batten	3310 863	Burns to the head. See *The Evaders* (Cosgrove), p. 101. Commissioned (181437) wef 5 August 1944
Aitken	L	F/S		1219321	207	ME814	LA	18/7/44	Revigny-sur-Ornain	France	Fr	7/9/44	7/9/44	NK	3322 2269	ss7. See *Massacre over the Marne*
Alderdice	J	SGT		1095982	51	DT690	HAL	16/4/43	Pilsen	France	Sp, Gib	15/8/43	16/8/43	Holme (Yorks)	3314 1358	Recommended for MiD but awarded DFM (1/10/43)
Alderton	M	F/O		172753	207	ME805	LA	7/7/44	St Leu d'Esserent	France	Fr			NK	NF	
Alexander	JMcK	SGT		1571750	101	DV288	LA	10/4/44	Aulnoye	France	Sp, Gib	23/6/44	24/6/44	Lyneham	3320 1987	Burgundy line with Sergeant P.J. Evans. Report states landed UK at "Swindon"
Allen	FEP	SGT		1585144	78	JN974	HAL	20/12/43	Frankfurt	Holland	Bel	9/9/44	9/9/44	NK	3325 2874	Back to UK from France. Interviewed 9 September 1944. Report IS9/WEA/MB/1116 also in WO 208/3350
Allen	PF	P/O		102973	101	R1699	WE	10/9/41	Turin	France	Sp, Gib	22/11/41	23/11/41	Pembroke Dock	3307 599	Crossed Pyrenees with Christensen and Zulikowski. DFC (13/3/42)
Allen	WG	F/S		903697	35	W7873	HAL	16/4/43	Pilsen	France	Sp, And, Gib	21/6/43	22/6/43	Hendon	3313 1251	DFM (7/9/43). Killed in action 31 March 1944. See *We Act With One Accord*, p.118
Allison	JC	F/O	SAF	124217	107	BZ237	BOS	27/8/43	Gosnay power station	France	Sp, Gib	11/10/43	12/10/43	Lyneham	3315 1461	Comet 147. MiD (8/6/44). DFC (29/6/45, squadron leader, 88 Squadron)
Alliston	AW	F/O		161623	10	LV858	HAL	10/4/44	Tergnier	France	Sp, Gib	21/6/44	22/6/44	Whitchurch	3320 1981	Burgundy line. DFC (23/3/45). See *Free to Fight Again*, pp. 84-8; *The Easy Trip*, pp.77-8.
Anaka	P	F/O	CAN	J.25832	115	HK550	LA	15/6/44	Valenciennes	France	Fr	6/9/44	6/9/44	Croydon	3350 1276	Flown back in USAAF C-47. Interviewed 5 September 1944. Report IS9/WEA/7/184/1276. His story written in *The One Hundredth Airman*
Anderson	AP	W/O			48	KG428	DAK	19/9/44	Arnhem supply drop	Holland	Hol			NK	NF	Name given as Henderson in report IS9/WEA/1/286/2378 of Lieutenant B.D. Carr, 1st Airborne Division
Anderson	CE	F/O	CAN	J.13450	298	LL407	HAL	6/6/44	Dropping troops	France	Fr	7/6/44	8/6/44	Newhaven	3320 1958	Dropping parachutists in support of the D-Day landings. Killed on operations 5/6 August 1944
Anderson	DW	F/O		153231	570	LJ638	ST	12/4/45	SOE supply drop	Holland	Hol			NK	3348 197	In a house when attacked by Germans on 29 April 1945. Interviewed 11 May 1945. Report IS9/WEA/PLM/197
Anderson	EJ	SGT	AUS	A.423579	27 OTU	X3966	WE	23/9/43	Nickel	France	Sp, Gib	5/12/43	6/12/43	London	3317 1605	Killed on operations 18/19 August 1944 (Sterkrade) on 51 Squadron
Andrews	KG	SGT	AUS	1723201	44	ME694	LA	25/7/44	Stuttgart	France	Fr			NK	3348 295	Sherwood. Interviewed 27 August 1944. Report IS9/WEA/2/97/295
Angers	JAAAB	SGT	CAN	R.78161	419	X3359	WE	16/6/42	Essen	Belgium	Fr, Sp, Gib	18/8/42	19/8/42	Whitchurch	3310 810	Comet 30. MiD (1/1/43)
Annat	DJ	F/S	AUS	A.426279	460	ND654	LA	20/7/44	Courtrai	Belgium	Fr			NK	3322 2320	Liberated 2 September 1944. Back in UK by 9 September 1944
Annon	E	SGT		1685669	298	LL407	HAL	6/6/44	Dropping troops	France	Fr	11/6/44	12/6/44	Port of London	3320 1966	Dropping parachutists in support of the D-Day landings. Commissioned wef 21 May 1944 (18/8/44)
Annon	E	F/O		178837	298	LL334	HAL	5/8/44	SOE	France	Fr	13/9/44	13/9/44	NK	3324 2545	See *Massacre over the Marne*, p.126 and photo p.107
Antwis	PWN	SGT		1665338	50	PD237	LA	13/8/44	Bordeaux	France	Fr			NK	3345 645	Captured. Liberated from hospital in Angoulême 1 September 1944. Interviewed 3 September 1944. Report MI9/S/PG/MISC/INT/645. See *D-Day Bombers...*, pp. 241-5
Archibald	J	F/O	NZ	NZ.42786	576	PB253	LA	28/7/44	Stuttgart	France	Fr			NK	3345 748	Wounded. Captured 29 July 1944. Liberated in hospital in Paris on 27 August 1944. Not interviewed (compiled from questionnaire). Report MISC/INT/748
Arderne	PV	P/O		40658	110	R3670	BL	8/6/40	Amiens	France	Fr			NK	NF	Possibly not an evader. DFC (13/9/40)
Armstrong	JB	F/O	CAN	J.23723	582	ND910	LA	3/5/44	Montdidier	France	Fr			NK	3349	ss7. Burned in the face. Liberated September 1944 after almost four months at Canny-sur-Matz. Service number?
Arnold	GG	SGT		1417057	158	HR752	HAL	15/7/43	Montbéliard	France	Sz, Fr	11/9/44	11/9/44	NK	3322 2293	Left Switzerland on 25 August 1944 with Sergeant J.A. Hammond RCAF. Back to UK from Casablanca

Arnold	PE	F/O		151369	9	JA690	LA	7/7/44	St Leu d'Esserent	France	Fr			NK	NF	See *Bombers First and Last*, pp. 246-52, 271 etc
Arnold	RS	F/O	CAN	J.25365	44	LM638	LA	12/7/44	Culmont-Chalindrey	France	Fr	8/9/44	8/9/44	NK	3322 2268	Liberated in France. See *Massacre over the Marne*, pp.124-6 and photo p. 104
Arscott	JEJ	F/O		131776	434	LL243	HAL	27/4/44	Montzen	Belgium				NK	NF	
Arundel	DR	SGT		1567566	158	LV790	HAL	12/6/44	Amiens	France	Fr			Northolt	NF	Severe wound to one eye, causing blindness. Captured. Released from Fresnes prison 20 August 1944. Back by RAF Dakota. DFM (14/7/44)
Asker	HA	SGT		580505	226		BA	13/6/40	German tanks	France				NK	NF	Rejoined squadron. See Leading Aircraftman Kirk. DFM (23/12/41). Commissioned (47171) wef 8 November 1941 (19/12/41). DFC (18/9/42, and also on 2/10/42) for the Dieppe raid
Atkinson	RB	F/O	CAN	J.25128	9	JA690	LA	7/7/44	St Leu d'Esserent	France	Fr			NK	NF	With Pilot Officer Gradwell. Liberated by British troops. See *Bombers First and Last*, pp. 246-52, 271 etc
Avery	AN	SGT		2226416	61	ND987	LA	24/6/44	Prouville	France	Fr	5/9/44	5/9/44	NK	3322 2312	ss7. Back to UK from Beauvais. Service number?
Avery	JV	SGT		1041098	431	HE374	WE	14/4/43	Stuttgart	Switzerland	Fr	28/6/43	29/6/43	Lyneham	3313 1274	Repatriated in exchange with Germans. Interviewed 29 June 1943. Killed as flight sergeant at 15 OTU on 1/2 March 1944
Backhouse	E	SGT		1464745	115	HK579	LA	8/9/44	Le Havre	France	Fr	13/9/44	13/9/44	NK	3345 678	Captured. Liberated when Fort Tourneville, Le Havre surrendered 12 September 1944. Interviewed 14 September 1944. Report MISC/INT/678
Bailey	FC	SGT		1817259	405	ND344	LA	11/6/44	Tours	France	Fr			NK	3349 374	With Sergeant H. Braithwaite. Liberated 17/18 August 1944 by US troops. Interviewed 27 August 1944. Report IS9/WEA/2/198/374
Bailey	HW	SGT		1624948	101	DV308	LA	1/1/44	Berlin	Belgium	Fr, Sp, Gib	9/2/44	10/2/44	Lyneham	3318 1753	
Bailey	WG	SGT	CAN	1392374	429	HZ355	WE	11/6/43	Düsseldorf	Belgium	Fr, Sp, Gib	5/11/43	6/11/43	Portreath	3316 1541	Comet 141
Bain	GEJ	F/O	CAN	J.24122	576	ME811	LA	6/6/44	Vire	France	Fr			NK	3349 346	Broke right leg above ankle. Liberated 17 August 1944. Interviewed 19 August 1944. Report IS9/WEA/2/156/346
Baird	RB	F/L		133622	644	LL403	HAL	5/10/44	Supply drop, Dodex III	Holland	Hol			NK	NF	With "SAS" in Holland
Baker	AS	F/L		89788	34 Wing	AG519	MU	23/6/44	Photo recce	France	Fr	22/8/44	22/8/44	NK	3321 2137	Target area was Sens-Montdidier. 34 Wing, 2nd Tactical Air Force. Reached Allied lines 18 August 1944. Interviewed 23 August 1944. DFC (10/4/45). MiD (14/6/45)
Baker	DA	SGT		1193117	149	W7572	ST	24/8/42	Frankfurt	Belgium	Fr, Gib	18/10/42	19/10/42	Poole	3311 919	Evacuated by *Seawolf* 12 October 1942. See *Jump For It!*, pp. 128-131
Baker	G	SGT		1392511	10	JD368	HAL	27/8/43	Nuremberg	Belgium	Fr, Sp, Gib	23/11/43	24/11/43	Whitchurch	3316 1586	Comet 148. Killed in action as flying officer (157833) on 101 Squadron, 3/4 May 1944 (Mailly-le-Camp). Whitchurch?
Baker	KN	F/O	AUS	A.410205	453	MK260	SP	6/7/44	Sweep	France	Fr			NK	3348 314	Liberated 18 August 1944. Interviewed 21 August 1944. Report IS9/WEA/2/181/314
Balcombe	G	F/L		128967	91	MK635	SP	1/9/44	Transport	France	Fr	8/9/44	8/9/44	NK	3323 2474	Back to UK from Vitry. MiD (1/1/46)
Balfour	A	SGT		1021030	576	PB265	LA	24/7/44	Stuttgart	France	Fr	17/8/44	17/8/44	Northolt	3321 2093	Left for UK from A22 airstrip near Rennes. Northolt?
Ballance	HC	F/O		80450	266	MN297	TY	8/6/44	NK	France	Fr			NK	NF	DFC (5/9/44)
Balmer	DP	F/S		1504649	35	ND759	LA	27/4/44	Friedrichshafen	Boden See	Sz, Fr	31/12/44	31/12/44	Lyneham	3325 2822	The Swiss-German border runs through the Boden See (Lake Constance)
Banks	RH	SGT	CAN	R.190579	432	LW594	HAL	8/5/44	Haine-St Pierre	Belgium	Fr	18/8/44	18/8/44	Northolt	3321 2136	Sherwood
Banner	WT	SGT		1336395	428	LK739	HAL	20/1/44	Berlin	France	Sp, Gib	20/3/44	21/3/44	Whitchurch	3319 1851	Crossed Pyrenees with a large party of USAAF and Sergeant J.H. Upton RCAF
Banville	RT	F/O	CAN	J.24778	166	LL896	LA	12/7/44	Revigny-sur-Ornain	France	Fr	5/9/44	5/9/44	NK	3323 2380	See *Massacre over the Marne*
Barber	VE	W/O	CAN		402	RM875	SP	20/4/45	Armed recce	Germany				NK	NF	Germany? Shot down attacking train near Kiel. Apparently second evasion - see *Fighter Command Losses of the Second World War, Volume 3*
Barber	WJ	SGT		1319207	158	HR779	HAL	16/4/43	Mannheim	France	Sp, Gib	22/6/43	29/6/43	Liverpool	3313 1279	With Sergeant J.W.E. Lawrence. Helped by Roger le Légionnaire and by Jean-Claude Camors. DFM (10/8/43)
Barbrooke	DJ	CPL		551271	142	P2246	BA	14/5/40	Sedan	Belgium	Fr			NK	NF	Belgium? DFM (31/5/40). See *The Colours of the Day* pp. 242-3
Barckley	RE	F/O		138650	3	EK227	TY	2/6/43	Rhubarb, Belgium	Belgium	Fr, Sp, Gib	16/8/43	17/8/43	Hendon	3314 1361	Shot down attacking transport. Comet 117. Sailed on the *Esneh* from Seville to Gibraltar 11-13 August 1943 with Sergeants J.R. Milne and H. Riley. MiD (8/6/44); DFC (3/11/44)
Barclay	PP	SGT		1386435	419	KB718	LA	4/7/44	Villeneuve-St Georges	France	Fr	25/8/44	25/8/44	Northolt	NF	Hidden by Drue Tartière. To UK by US Dakota. Date back based on interview date, 26 August 1944. Report IS9(WEA)/8/162/381
Barclay	RGA	F/L		74661	611	W3816	SP	20/9/41	Circus 100B	France	Sp, Gib	9/12/41	10/12/41	Stranraer	3307 606	DFC (26/11/40, 249 Squadron). Back by Catalina. MiD (1/1/43). Killed in action 17 July 1942 in Desert. Wrote a diary which was published as *Fighter*

																Pilot. A Self-Portrait.
Barker	BD	F/L		129452	77	DT734	HAL	9/3/43	Munich	Belgium	Fr, Sp, Gib	13/7/43	14/7/43	Whitchurch	3314 1298	DFC (17/8/43). Oaktree. Flown back after a week aboard *Samaria* in Gibraltar harbour. MiD (14/6/45)
Barker	FA	SGT		1377581	102	R9528	HAL	27/4/42	Dunkirk	France	Sz, Fr, Sp	13/9/42	14/9/42	Whitchurch	3310 856	DFM (20/10/42). Helped by Francisco Ponzán network. See *Safe Houses…*, p. 208; *The Evaders* (Cosgrove), p. 99; It's Suicide..., pp. 64-7
Barker	RRC	F/O		137533	106	ND680	LA	6/6/44	Coutances	France	Fr			NK	3348 7	Report IS9/WEA/2/7/7
Barlow	JR	SGT		1330226	49	ED426	LA	7/10/43	Stuttgart	France	Sz	6/10/44	6/10/44	Croydon	NF	Reached Switzerland on 30 October 1943 with Pilot Officer Donald Wares. Back to France 4 October 1944. Published booklet *They Died – That Freedom Might Live* (1993)
Barnard	DB	S/L		40352	142	DF550	WE	16/9/42	Essen	France	Sp, Gib	20/1/43	26/1/43	Gourock	3312 1040	With Glensor and Pilot Officer R.S. Smith. DFC (22/9/42). Dismissed RAF by sentence of General Court-Martial 17 January 1946. See *Safe Houses Are Dangerous*, p.211
Barnes	FA	F/S		1323587	298	LL333	HAL	20/9/44	Supplies to Germany	France	Fr		28/10/44	NK	3324 2735	Hospital. Flown back from Naples
Barnes	LA	P/O		168998	630	ND530	LA	15/3/44	Stuttgart	France	Sp, Gib	24/6/44	25/6/44	Whitchurch	3320 2000	Comet 287
Barnes	R	F/S		1046311	158	HX320	HAL	24/5/44	Aachen	Holland	Bel			NK	NF	With Dutch family for three months before joining Belgian Resistance. Liberated by advancing Allies. DFM (13/4/45)
Barnett	MG	F/L	NZ	NZ.391338	485	BL699	SP	31/5/42	Roadstead	France	Gib	30/9/42	5/10/42	Greenock	3310 887	Escaped from Fort de la Revère 23 August 1942. Back on HMS *Malaya*. DFC (3/10/44)
Barnlund	RE	F/O	CAN	J.27284	408	DS845	LA	25/2/44	Augsburg	France	Fr	24/3/44	24/3/44	Dartmouth	3319 1859	Evacuated from Brittany by MGB503 in Operation Bonaparte V. MiD (14/6/45). See *The Evaders* (Lavender/Sheffe), Chapter 11
Baroni	RB	F/L	CAN	J.19400	405	PA970	LA	8/9/44	Le Havre	France	Fr			NK	NF	DFC (13/10/44) & Bar (16/1/45)
Barrett	FO	F/L		40355	226		BA	13/6/40	German tanks	France	Fr	16/6/40	16/6/40	Southampton	3298 14	Wounded in right arm. DFC (1/6/45, squadron leader, 305 [Polish] Squadron)
Barry	JN	F/S	CAN	R.135217	35	W7885	HAL	13/2/43	Lorient	France	Sp, Gib	13/7/43	14/7/43	Whitchurch	3314 1299	Oaktree. With Flying Officer G.H.F. Carter in March 1943, and with Flight Sergeant E.R. Turenne in May 1943. On *Samaria* in Gibraltar harbour. MiD?
Bartkowiak	Z	F/S	POL	781307	303	EN836	SP	22/5/44	Ramrod 909	France	Fr	4/9/44	4/9/44	Hendon	3324 2597	
Bartle	MT	F/S	AUS	A.415653	35	ND759	LA	27/4/44	Friedrichshafen	Boden Zee	Sw, Fr			NK	3325 2834	The Swiss-German border runs through the Boden See (Lake Constance)
Bartlett	EW	F/O		139599	44	ND520	LA	25/2/44	Augsburg	France	Sz	19/9/44	19/9/44	Heston	3323 2513	In Switzerland 14 March 1944. Left 22 August 1944. Back to UK from Annecy. AFC (12/6/47, flight lieutenant)
Bartlett	FR	F/O	CAN	J.23044	414	MJ732	SP	5/1/45	Tac/R	Holland				NK	NF	DFC (1/6/45)
Bartley	G	SGT		1499890	9	ED480	LA	9/7/43	Gelsenkirchen	France	Sp, And, Gib	1/9/43	2/9/43	Whitchurch	3314 1386	
Bartley	JE	AC1			21	L8738	BL	14/5/40	Enemy troops	Belgium	Fr			NK	NF	Wounded
Barton	AEJ	SGT		1605577	207	LL973	LA	21/6/44	Wesseling	Belgium	Bel			NK	3350 1326	Comet line to Marathon holding-camp in Ardennes. Interviewed 11 September 1944. Report IS9/WEA/MB/1326. Author of *In Pursuit of Freedom*
Bartter	AC	F/L		110875	138	BB378	HAL	10/12/43	SOE	Denmark	Swe	5/1/44	5/1/44	Leuchars	3317 1670	See *Making for Sweden*, pp. 95-8
Barzeele	CS	WO2	CAN	R.128361	431	MZ629	HAL	12/5/44	Louvain	Belgium	Bel			NK	3350 1117	ss7. Marathon. Interviewed 9 September 1944. Report IS9/WEA/MB/1117.
Bastian	H	SGT	FRA	F.2576	347	LL557	HAL	5/1/45	Hanover	Germany	Hol			NK	3352 2444	Interviewed 7 April 1945. Report IS9/WEA/1/332/2444
Bastick	TW	F/S	AUS	A.408416	102	NA502	HAL	28/6/44	Blainville	France	Fr	1/9/44	1/9/44	NK	3324 2563	
Bastow	GH	F/L	CAN	124697	16	PL834	SP	20/9/44	Arnhem supply drop	Holland	Hol	24/9/44	24/9/44	Barkston Heath	3324 2681	DFC (26/1/45). Canadian in RAF. See *Canadians in the Royal Air Force*, p. 106
Batey	AC	SGT		1565790	298	LL332	HAL	10/9/44	Special mission	France	Fr	27/9/44	27/9/44	Heston	3324 2625	Back to UK from Cherbourg
Batterbury	FW	P/O		174956	107	HR193	MOS	5/10/44	Intruder, Holland	Holland	Hol			NK	3352 2377	Met Flying Officer A.G. Davies. Was rowed to freedom 16 February 1945. See *Shot Down and on the Run*, pp.110-118. Report IS9/WEA/1/285/2377
Batty	JJC	SGT		525889	12	L5396	BA	14/6/40	Evreux	France	Fr			NK	NF	His pilot was killed on ground by tank fire. Batty was killed on 8 February 1941 when Wellington W5365 crashed landing at Tollerton
Bauset	JCP	F/O	CAN	J.23639	431	LK967	HAL	25/11/43	Frankfurt	France	Sz, Fr	19/9/44	19/9/44	NK	3323 2517	To Switzerland on 18 January 1944. Left 1 September 1944. MiD (14/6/45). See *Women in the Resistance*, p.46 & *Aviateurs Piétons…*, pp. 167-8
Baveystock	LH	SGT		1376820	50	L7301	MAN	30/5/42	Cologne	Belgium	Fr, Sp, Gib	6/7/42	12/7/42	Gourock	3309 772	Comet 20. Back on the *Narkunda*. DFM (6/10/42). Later DSO (13/10/44), DFC (25/1/44), Bar to DFC (25/8/44) (no. 139324). Author *Wavetops at my Wingtips*, and see *Free To Fight Again*, pp. 140-64
Bawden	JD	F/S	CAN	R.136138	103	LM343	LA	5/9/43	Mannheim	France	Sp, Gib	23/12/43	23/12/43	Portreath	3317 1641	Crossed Pyrenees with Flight Sergeants W. Booth and T.B. Hannam
Baxter	DW	W/O	AUS	A.416083	460	ND394	LA	24/2/44	Schweinfurt	France	Sz			NK	NF	Left Switzerland on 4 September 1944

Bazin	JM	F/O		90281	607		HUR	15/5/40	Patrol	France	Fr			NK	NF	Commandeered a car and managed to rejoin his squadron. DFC (25/10/40). MiD (1/1/43, wing commander). Transferred to Bomber Command. CO of IX Squadron. DSO (21/9/45)
Beard	AW	SGT		1159543	77	JD371	HAL	27/8/43	Nuremberg	Belgium	Fr, Sp, Gib	6/11/43	7/11/43	Whitchurch	3316 1539	Escaped from a Resistance camp in Ardennes attacked by Germans on 19 September 1943. Comet 163. DFM (7/1/44)
Beaton	JJ	F/O	CAN	J.22490	426	DS689	LA	7/10/43	Stuttgart	France	Sz, Fr			NK	NF	See *Aviateurs Piétons Vers la Suisse*, pp.98-100
Beattie	CM	F/S	AUS	A.428899	626	LM633	LA	20/7/44	Courtrai	Belgium				NK	3350 1478	Liberated by Canadians 13 September 1944. Interviewed 14 September 1944. Report IS9(WEA)/1/212/1478
Beattie	RL	F/O	CAN	J.17090	138	LW275	HAL	7/2/44	SOE	France	Sp, Gib	11/4/44	12/4/44	Lyneham	3319 1879	DFC (3/10/44). See *Free to Fight Again*, pp. 77-81
Beauchesne	NE	SGT	CAN	R.200224	432	LW582	HAL	7/6/44	Achères	France	Fr	18/8/44	18/8/44	Northolt	3321 2096	Sherwood. Northolt?
Beber	AA	SGT		1282540	158	W7750	HAL	6/8/42	Duisburg	Belgium	Fr, Sp, Gib	30/9/42	5/10/42	Greenock	3310 900	Comet 45. Escorted from Paris by Elvire Morelle and Jeanine De Greef. Back on HMS *Malaya*. DFM (5/2/43) & Bar (16/2/45, 571 Squadron)
Beckwith	DS	SGT		1481231	625	ME684	LA	24/3/44	Berlin	Holland	Bel, Fr			NK	3322 2279	With Flight Sergeant R.H.L. Potentier RCAF. Contacted US troops on 1 September 1944. In UK by 7 September 1944
Beeby	AS	SGT		629952	82	P6925	BL	13/6/40	Tanks, Forêt de Gault	France	Fr			NK	NF	Possibly not an evader. Killed in action 13 August 1940. DFM (13/9/40)
Beecroft	J	SGT		1104336	101	X3472	WE	19/5/42	Mannheim	France	Sz, Fr, Gib	24/7/42	30/7/42	Greenock	3309 795	Evacuated by HMS *Tarana* 14 July 1942. To UK on *Llanstephan Castle*. DFM (18/9/42). See *Shot Down and On the Run*, pp.50-4
Beeley	K	P/O		173165	426	LW198	HAL	28/6/44	Metz	France	Fr			NK	3324 2565	Joined an American convoy on 3 September 1944
Beevers	GA	SGT		1624154	100	ND595	LA	25/2/44	Augsburg	Switzerland	Ger, Fr, Sp, Gib	24/5/44	25/5/44	Whitchurch	3319 1936	Repatriated with German agreement. Back on BOAC Dakota
Bell	DS	F/O		132618	161	V9605	LYS	3/3/44	SOE	France	Fr	14/3/44	15/3/44	Tangmere	3319 1841	DFC (9/11/43). His two passengers also evaded. Back by SOE Lysander. Tangmere?
Bell	E	P/O		142874	138	LW275	HAL	7/2/44	SOE	France	Sp, Gib	11/4/44	12/4/44	Lyneham	3319 1878	DFC (16/1/45). See *Free to Fight Again*, pp. 77-81
Bell	H	SGT		1084611	460	W4988	LA	3/9/43	Berlin	Denmark (sea)	Swe	30/9/43	1/10/43	Leuchars	3315 1428	Picked up, with Flying Officer F.A. Randall, by small coaster taking concrete to Swedish island of Hven
Bell	P	SGT	CAN		190	LJ882	ST	22/7/44	SAS supply drop	France	Fr			NK	NF	ss6. Met Sergeant T.H. Harvell. Rank?
Bell	PH	SGT		915544	602	AB780	SP	21/9/41	Circus	France	Sp, Gib	30/12/41	5/1/42	Gourock	3307 628	To UK on Polish ship *Batory*. Commissioned (120021). MiD (1/1/43, pilot officer). Killed 9 July 1943 (flight lieutenant, 19 Squadron). See *Fighter Pilot*, pp.167 & 174
Bell	PJW	P/O		184700	234	KH860	MU	4/5/45	Shipping, Kattegat	Denmark	Den	15/5/45	15/5/45	NK	NF	Wounded. In hospital at Løgstør until repatriated
Bell	WH	F/S		1595202	570	LJ638	ST	12/4/45	SOE supply drop	Holland	Hol			NK	3348	In a house attacked by Germans on 29 April 1945. Interviewed 11 May 1945. Report IS9/WEA/...
Bemrose	M	F/S		1505087	426	NA510	HAL	12/6/44	Cambrai	France	Fr	11/9/44	11/9/44	NK	3322 2306	
Benabo	R	F/S	CAN	R.191174	405	PA970	LA	8/9/44	Le Havre	France				NK	NF	
Bender	WF	F/O	CAN	J.11766	21	LR404	MOS	8/2/44	Noball site	France	Fr	18/8/44	18/8/44	Northolt	3321 2116	Sherwood. Left for UK from Bayeux - B.14 airstrip, Banville. MOS?
Bennett	AW	W/O		1379973	35	LV861	HAL	15/2/44	Berlin	Holland	Bel, Fr, Sz, Fr			NK	3322 2326	DFC (10/12/43). Left Switzerland 27 August 1944 with Sergeant H. Simister and Flight Sergeant J. Quinn. Back in UK by 11 September 1944 - see *We Act With One Accord*, p.167
Bennett	DCT	W/C	AUS	32065	10	W1041	HAL	27/4/42	*Tirpitz*, Norway	Norway	Swe	24/5/42	24/5/42	Leuchars	3309 741	Commanding Officer 8 (PFF) Group, air vice-marshal CB (8/6/44), CBE (1943), DSO (16/6/42). MP for Middlesbrough, 1945
Bennett	JS	SGT		553903	78	MZ763	HAL	23/9/44	Neuss	Holland		4/10/44	4/10/44	NK	NF	Date back given on aircraft loss card
Bennett	JT	SGT		928104	35	W1147	HAL	25/7/42	Duisburg	Holland	Bel, Fr, Sp, Gib	13/9/42	14/9/42	Whitchurch	3310 854	ss7. Injured leg and captured. Escaped from toilet by smashing window. Comet 41. DFM (20/10/42)
Bennett	RHM	P/O	CAN	41656	107	R3685	BL	9/6/40	Enemy columns, Poix	France	Fr			NK	NF	Canadian in RAF. Possibly not an evader. Killed in action 30 June 1940. MiD (1/1/41)
Bennett	WG	SGT		2221150	76	MZ539	HAL	28/6/44	Blainville	France	Fr			NK	3350 1266	Liberated by US forces 29 August 1944. Interviewed 1 September 1944. Report IS9/WEA/7/124/1266
Berry	H	SGT		514724	150	L5524	BA	13/6/40	Vernon-Poix	France	Sp, Gib	1/6/41	2/6/41	Mount Batten	3303 296	Passed unfit by medical board. Left France 19 May 1941. MiD (11/6/42). See AIR 2/5684
Berry	LF	F/L		77960	622	ND926	LA	31/5/44	Trappes	France	Fr			NK	3348 145	ss7. DFC (6/6/44). Sherwood. Interviewed by WEA 16 August 1944. Report IS9/WEA/2/79/145
Berry	W	F/S		1080826	426	LK883	HAL	12/5/44	Louvain	Belgium	Bel			NK	3350 1120	DFM (16/11/43, 76 Squadron). Helped by Anne Brusselmans. See photos

																Belgium Rendez-Vous 127, p. 94. Interviewed 9 September 1944. Report IS9/WEA/MB/1120
Bertera	DF	F/O		118065	158	HR779	HAL	16/4/43	Mannheim	France	Sz			NK	NF	To Switzerland 12 May 1943. Report Switzerland/5
Berthelsen	FJ	SGT	NZ	NZ.41530	149	W7572	ST	24/8/42	Frankfurt	Belgium	Fr, Gib	18/10/42	19/10/42	Poole	3311 917	Evacuated by *Seawolf* 12 October 1942
Bertie	MH	P/O	AUS	A.433499	103	ME449	LA	12/3/45	Mining	Denmark	Swe		16/4/45	NK	3327 3093	With Flying Officer H.A.S. Mitchell. Crossed to Sweden by boat on 3 April 1945. Flown to UK by BOAC
Best	A	SGT		2207320	425	LW591	HAL	24/4/44	Karlsruhe	Luxembourg	Fr, Bel			NK	3350 1355	Marathon. Interviewed 10 September 1944 with Sergeant Michaud. Report IS9/WEA/MB/1355
Best	WF	F/S	CAN	R.206403	9	JA690	LA	7/7/44	St Leu d'Esserent	France	Fr			NK	NF	See *Bombers First and Last*, pp. 246-52, 271 etc
Bester	JF	F/O	CAN	J.35747	427	LW166	HAL	4/7/44	Villeneuve-St Georges	France	Fr	18/8/44	18/8/44	Northolt	3321 2122	Slightly injured. Sherwood. Left for UK from B.14 airstrip, Banville
Bettesworth	CJ	SGT			426	DS689	LA	7/10/43	Stuttgart	France				NK	NF	Evaded over Pyrenees
Bickley	LF	F/O		137189	109	LR499	MOS	2/12/43	Bochum	Holland				NK	NF	
Biddle	G	F/O	CAN	J.19606	407		WE	26/9/44	A/S patrol off Norway	Norway	Nor	11/10/44	12/10/44	Scalloway	3324 2657	Came back on the Shetland Bus service. See *Shot Down and on the Run*, pp. 141-8
Billing	GD	F/O	CAN	J.18371	401	ML135	SP	1/7/44	Patrol	France	Fr			NK	3348 29	Liberated by US soldiers on 31 July 1944. Report IS9/WEA/7/16/29
Billows	CJ	F/S		1530086	97	JB367	LA	18/11/43	Berlin	Belgium	Fr, Sp, Gib	16/1/44	17/1/44	NK	3318 1711	On 29th op. when shot down. Comet 252. Left Seville by ship 8 January 1944 to Gibraltar on 9 January 1944
Bilton	WHB	SGT		1215114	10	HR920	HAL	15/9/43	Montluçon	France	Sp, Gib	15/2/44	16/2/44	Prestwick	3318 1773	Hidden by the Malard family at St Aubin, Morbihan, while his injured foot mended
Binnie	N	SGT	CAN	R.66854	420	LW674	HAL	10/6/44	Versailles	France	Fr	20/8/44	20/8/44	NK	3321 2145	Sherwood. Interviewed 19 August 1944
Birk	HE	SGT	AUS	A.402634	99	X9761	WE	28/9/41	Frankfurt	Belgium	Fr, Sp, Gib	4/3/42	10/3/42	Gourock	3308 695	Comet 7. MiD (1/1/43). Killed on active service in N. Africa 15 July 1942
Bishop	EG	SGT		1474540	44	LM631	LA	7/7/44	St Leu d'Esserent	France	Fr	8/9/44	8/9/44	NK	3322 2341	
Bjarnason	SA	F/O	CAN	J.27581	106	LM641	LA	7/8/44	Secqueville	France	Fr	27/8/44	27/8/44	Northolt	3322 2221	Left for UK from 'Allied beachhead'
Bjornstad	HE	SGT	NOR		332	NH172	SP	8/6/44	NK	France				NK	NF	
Black	JBR	SGT		1251740	24 OTU	BD347	WH	31/7/42	Düsseldorf	Belgium	Fr, Sp, Gib	13/9/42	14/9/42	Whitchurch	3310 855	Comet 43. MID (1/1/43)
Blackett	H	SGT		1523770	161	LL183	HAL	9/5/44	SOE	France	Fr	9/9/44	9/9/44	Tempsford	3323 2415	
Blackwell	SJP	F/O		80453	266	JP906	TY	1/12/43	Roadstead	France	Fr	29/1/44	29/1/44	Dartmouth	3318 1727	Came down off coast of France. Captured. Escaped from train. Back to UK by MGB from Brittany in Bonaparte I. DFC (24/3/44)
Blair	D	P/O		190913	349	TA837	SP	6/2/45	Armed recce	Holland	Hol	20/4/45	20/4/45	NK	3327 3058	Belgian squadron
Blake	LAE	W/O	AUS	A.414752	451	SM465	SP	9/3/45	Armed recce	Holland	Hol			NK	3348 203	Interviewed 11 May 1945. Report IS9/WEA/PLM/203
Blakemore	EJ	P/O		169156	50	LL840	LA	21/6/44	Scholven/Buer	Holland	Hol			NK	3352 2389	DFM (23/12/41 - 9 Sq). Hidden at 5 Frieslaan, Apeldoorn (see WO 309/44). Liberated 10 March 1945. Report IS9/WEA/1/299/2389
Blakey	J	SGT		1582692	625	PB126	LA	30/6/44	Vierzon	France	Fr	18/8/44	18/8/44	Northolt	3321 2125	Sherwood. Left for UK from Bayeux - B.14 airstrip, Banville
Blanchet	JPG	SGT	CAN	R.56057	35	W1048	HAL	27/4/42	*Tirpitz*, Norway	Norway	Swe	8/4/43	9/4/43	Leuchars	3312 1153	DFM (25/5/43). *See Making for Sweden*, pp. 33-35
Blandford	JG	P/O		158898	101	DV285	LA	26/11/43	Berlin	Belgium				NK	NF	In UK October 1944
Blaydon	RW	SGT		755395	9	R1244	WE	11/1/41	Turin	France	Sp, Gib	5/6/41	14/6/41	Greenock	3308 714	To UK on HMS *Argus*. Not interviewed until 29 April 1942. DFM (11/8/42). KIA as flying officer on 7/8 August 1944 on 582 Squadron. See *Bombers First and Last*, pp. 41 etc
Blott	W	F/L		115303	15	W4355	LA	15/3/44	Stuttgart	Switzerland	Ger, Fr, Sp, Gib	22/5/44	23/5/44	Whitchurch	3319 1930	Repatriated with German agreement. Back on BOAC Dakota. MiD (1/1/45)
Blumer	RAB	W/O	AUS	A.411845	91	EN626	SP	6/11/43	Rhubarb	France	Sz, Fr, Sp, Gib	5/6/44	6/6/44	Whitchurch	3320 1950	In Switzerland 13 March 1944. Left 13 September 1944. See *Aviateurs Piétons vers la Suisse*, p. 165. Killed in take-off accident on 26 June 1944 in Spitfire RM617
Blyth	CA	SGT		1077501	161	Z9131	WH	24/9/42	SOE	France	Gib	18/10/42	19/10/42	Poole	3311 925	Evacuated by *Seawolf* 12 October 1942
Board	KB	SGT		3030159	75	HK567	LA	7/8/44	Mare de Magne	France	Fr	28/8/44	28/8/44	NK	3321 2192	
Board	LE	SGT		1604551	158	HX334	HAL	12/5/44	Hasselt	Belgium	Bel			NK	NF	With Belgian Resistance until liberated by Allied forces
Boddington	RA	F/L		104534	635	ND965	LA	11/6/44	Nantes	France	Fr			NK	3348 78	DFC (31/7/42). Aircraft returned to base. With Sergeant J. Harrowing. Interviewed 9 August 1944. Report IS9/2/17/78. Bar to DFC (12/2/46, squadron leader)
Boddy	TI	SGT		544755	7	R9262	ST	21/12/42	Munich	France	Sp, Gib	28/3/43	5/4/43	Liverpool	3312 1141	DFM (4/6/43)
Boddy	W	SGT		1577663	431	HE374	WE	14/4/43	Stuttgart	Switzerland	Fr	28/6/43	29/6/43	Lyneham	3313 1277	Repatriated 29 June 1943 in exchange with Germans
Bodey	LR	F/S	AUS	A.434213	578	LW383	HAL	12/8/44	Rüsselsheim	Belgium	Bel	7/9/44	7/9/44	NK	3323 2361	Captured 29 August 1944 by Gestapo. St Gilles prison, Brussels. "Ghost

																Train" 3 September 1944. Flown back from Brussels
Bodie	AR	F/O	CAN	J.26292	419	KB726	LA	12/6/44	Cambrai	France	Fr	6/9/44	6/9/44	NK	3323 2396	In same crew as Mynarski VC
Bolter	TF	P/O		156606	77	LL125	HAL	20/12/43	Frankfurt	Belgium	Fr, Sp, Gib	24/6/44	25/6/44	Whitchurch	3320 1994	DFC (14/11/44). Wrote Escape from Enemy-Occupied Europe (unpublished)
Bolton	JH	F/O		175108	630	LM269	LA	18/8/44	Bordeaux	France	Fr			NK	3350 1334	Interviewed 10 September 1944. Report IS9/WEA/MB/1334
Bolton	KJ	F/O		45525	102	HR663	HAL	16/4/43	Pilsen	Belgium	Fr, Sp, Gib	1/6/43	2/6/43	Hendon	3313 1231	Comet 101. DFC (6/7/43). See also entry for Squadron Leader K.J. Bolton
Bolton	KJ	S/L		45525	295	LK171	ST	2/11/44	SOE supply drop	Norway	Swe		2/1/45	NK	3325 2844	DFC (6/7/43). To Sweden on boat *Augusta* - see *Shot Down and on the Run*, pp. 133-41. MiD (1/1/45). See entry for Flying Officer K.J. Bolton
Boness	LF	SGT		1649548	463	LM597	LA	24/6/44	Prouville	France	Fr			NK	3350 1346	Liberated 4 September 1944. Interviewed 12 September 1944. Report IS9/WEA/MB/1346
Booker	EJ	SGT		571343	120	AM924	LIB	28/5/42	*Tirpitz* recce	Norway	Swe	31/8/42	1/9/42	Leuchars	3310 832	Came down in the sea sixty miles off Lofoten Islands. Reached Sweden on 30 June 1942. MM (1/12/42). See *Making for Sweden*, pp. 35-8 & *Shot Down and on the Run*, pp. 127-33. Pilot officer (51689) wef 5 April 1943
Boon	PC	F/S		1311816	65	FB173	MU	27/6/44	Vehicles	France	Fr			NK	3345 746	Wounded. Multiple head injuries. Liberated 4 August 1944 in a hospital at Rennes. Interviewed 11 September 1944. Report MISC/INT/746. DFM (11/8/44)
Boorer	WG	W/O			144	NE955	BFR	3/5/45	Anti-shipping Kiel Bay	North Sea	Dk			NK	NF	With Warrant Officer Brett was rescued from dinghy on 7 May 1945 by fishing boat *Ella*. After arrival in Esbjerg harbour on 8 May they were taken to the Centralsygehuset hospital in Esbjerg
Booth	M	F/O		176708	190		ST	21/9/44	Arnhem supply drop	Holland	Bel	25/9/44	25/9/44	NK	3325 2877	Back to UK from Brussels
Booth	W	F/S		1148674	10	JD315	HAL	16/9/43	Modane	France	Sp, Gib	11/12/43	12/12/43	Lyneham	3317 1612	Baled out as ordered - aircraft returned to UK. Crossed Pyrenees with Flight Sergeants J.D. Bawden RCAF and T.B. Hannam. Shot down again 22/23 April 1944 (pilot officer, 76 Squadron) and taken POW
Boothby	CD	P/O		126120	161	Z9131	WH	24/9/42	SOE	France	Gib	18/10/42	19/10/42	Poole	3311 923	DFM (22/11/40). Evacuated by *Seawolf* 12 October 1942. DFC (8/12/42). Killed in action 10 September 1943 as flight lieutenant on 624 Squadron. Commemorated on the Malta Memorial
Boots	RF	F/S		1385979	582	ND502	LA	15/6/44	Lens	France	Fr	11/9/44	11/9/44	NK	3322 2291	ss7. Bordeaux-Loupiac line
Bossick	H	F/S		1803126	218	EH942	ST	22/4/44	Laon	France	Fr	7/9/44	7/9/44	NK	3323 2394	Flown back to UK 'in a supply aircraft' with Staff Sergeant L.W. Knopp USAAF
Bostock	D	F/S		1313365	122	MA764	SP	25/11/43	Sweep, French coast	France	Sp, Gib	16/1/44	17/1/44	NK	3318 1713	Recommended for MiD. Not given?
Bostridge	IW	SGT		1322582	90	EF294	ST	2/6/44	SOE	France	Fr			NK	3350 1004	Interviewed 4 September 1944. Report IS9/WEA/2/359/1004
Boucher	EG	F/S		1332744	174	JP547	TY	5/10/43	Rhubarb	France	Sp, Gib	29/11/43	30/11/43	Whitchurch	3316 1595	In party of thirty-four. Killed in action 5 August 1944 as pilot officer (174408), still on 174 Squadron (Typhoons)
Bourner	GGE	SGT		1399372	630	ME739	LA	10/4/45	Leipzig	Germany	Ger		30/4/45	NK	3327 3070	'Hid' in British army work camp. Liberated by US army 19 April 1945. See also Flight Sergeants G. Gould and J.W. Tovey
Bowers	D	SGT	EIR	1796269	295	LJ618	ST	20/9/44	Arnhem supply drop	Holland	Hol	22/9/44	22/9/44	Harwell	NF	Operation Market IV. Returned to base within 50 hours
Bowlby	AT	F/S	CAN	R.124853	408	JB913	HAL	3/7/43	Cologne	Belgium	Fr, Sp, Gib	10/10/43	11/10/43	Chivenor	3315 1459	DFM (19/11/43). Helped by "Service EVA" until 8 September 1943. Helped by Anne Brusselmans. Comet 146. With Sergeant E.B. Dungey as far as Madrid
Bowman	PV	SGT	CAN	R.265181	419	KB814	LA	15/3/45	Hagen	Germany				NK	NF	Prisoner of war?
Boyd	DL	P/O	AUS	A.404982	274	EJ887	TEM	28/3/45	Offensive operations	Holland	Hol			NK	3327 3076	Captured 28 March 1945. Liberated by Canadian troops on 8 May 1945
Boyle	AN	SGT	CAN	R.212438	434	LW436	HAL	4/8/44	Bois de Cassan	France				NK	NF	
Braathen	H	F/O	CAN	J.23990	620	LJ849	ST	6/6/44	Supplies to Normandy	France	Fr	8/6/44	9/6/44	Gosport	3324 2744	Left Normandy from Allied beachhead. LJ849?
Bradbury	K	F/S		1213065	143	LZ406	BFR	6/9/44	NK	Belgium	Bel			NK	3350 1456	Liberated by Canadians 8 September 1944. Interviewed 9 September 1944. Report IS9/WEA/1/188/1456 jointly with Flight Sergeant C. Cash
Bradley	DR	F/S		1377851	35	W7873	HAL	16/4/43	Pilsen	France	Sp, And, Gib	21/6/43	22/6/43	Hendon	3313 1252	DFM (7/9/43). See *We Act With One Accord*, p.118
Bradley	S	SGT		990430	101	X3472	WE	19/5/42	Mannheim	France	Sz			NK	None	Drowned 16 June 1942 swimming the River Doubs - see *Shot Down and On the Run*, pp.50-4
Bradshaw	E	SGT		944855	49	R5763	LA	2/9/42	Karlsruhe	Belgium	Fr, Sp, Gib	24/10/42	25/10/42	Portreath	3311 940	Comet 59. Killed in action on 17 August 1944 (warrant officer, 31 Squadron)
Bradshaw	W	SGT			21	L8743	BL	11/6/40	La Mare	France	Fr			NK	NF	Possibly not an evader
Brailsford	RF	F/O		144333	514	LL739	LA	11/5/44	Louvain	Belgium	Bel			NK	3350 1306	Helped by Anne Brusselmans. Liberated in Brussels. Interviewed 14 September 1944. Report IS9/WEA/MB/1306. See *Rendez-Vous 127 Revisited*,

																p. 148
Braithwaite	H	SGT		1685138	405	ND344	LA	11/6/44	Tours	France	Fr			NK	3349 421	With Sergeant F.C. Bailey. Liberated 17/18 August 1944 by US troops. Interviewed 27 August 1944. Report IS9/WEA/2/197/421
Brakes	BE	F/S		961438	420	LW674	HAL	10/6/44	Versailles	France	Fr	18/8/44	18/8/44	Northolt	3321 2117	Sherwood. Left for UK from Bayeux - B.14 airstrip, Banville
Brandt	J	S/L		39849	137	MN474	TY	23/5/44	Rhubarb	France	Fr			NK	3350 1261	DFC (10/11/42). Interviewed 30 August 1944. Report IS9/WEA/7/91/1261
Bratley	HW	SGT		755503	9	R1244	WE	11/1/41	Turin	France	Sp, Gib	9/5/41	16/5/41	Liverpool	3304 351	To UK on *Monarch of Bermuda*. MiD. See AIR 2/5684. Commissioned (145716) wef 7 April 1943; flying officer 7 October 1943. See *Bombers First and Last*, pp. 41 etc
Bray	J	SGT	CAN	R.216277	44	LM638	LA	12/7/44	Culmont-Chalindrey	France	Sp	13/9/44	13/9/44	NK	3323 2491	To Hendaye, SW France, on 8 September 1944. See *Massacre over the Marne*, p.124
Brayley	WEJ	WO2	CAN	R.108037	158	LW723	HAL	10/4/44	Tergnier	France	Fr			NK	3348 188	Sherwood. Liberated 13 August 1944. Interviewed 18 August 1944. Report IS9/WEA/2/148/188
Brazill	W	SGT		1384539	150	BJ877	WE	16/9/42	Essen	Belgium	Fr, Sp, Gib	3/1/43	3/1/43	Hendon	3311 1014	Comet 79. DFM (2/4/43)
Brearley	EW	SGT		1035032	158	JD298	HAL	27/8/43	Nuremberg	Luxembourg	Fr, Sp, Gib			NK	NF	With Sergeant G.H. Hirst and Sergeant N.W. Lee. UK September 1944. Report CSDIC/CMF/SKP/3632. See *In Brave Company* pp. 96-8
Brennan	HJ	F/O	CAN	J.23877	28 OTU	LN896	WE	20/4/44	Nickel	France	Fr	12/7/44	13/7/44	Dartmouth	3320 2025	Aircraft ran out of fuel when directed by German radio to Brittany. Back by MGB 503. See *Silent Heroes*, p. 35
Brett	P	W/O			144	NE955	BFR	3/5/45	Anti-shipping Kiel Bay	North Sea	Dk			NK	NF	With Warrant Officer Boorer was rescued from dinghy on 7 May 1945 by fishing boat *Ella*. After arrival in Esbjerg harbour on 8 May they were taken to the Centralsygehuset hospital in Esbjerg
Brickwood	GC	F/O		55021	2	AM188	MU	29/1/44	Photo recce	France	Fr	24/3/44	24/3/44	Dartmouth	3319 1854	Evacuated from Brittany by MGB503 in Operation Bonaparte V
Bridge	EA	SGT	CAN	R.130220	428	ED209	HAL	13/7/43	Aachen	Belgium	Fr, Sp, Gib	11/10/43	12/10/43	Valley	3315 1462	Comet 144
Bridges	MC	F/L		132001	7	JA682	LA	12/8/43	Milan	France	Sz			NK	NF	
Bridges	RK	SGT		652549	101	LL750	LA	27/4/44	Friedrichshafen	Switzerland	Fr	6/10/44	6/10/44	Hendon	3324 2635	Blown out of aircraft. Injured. Escaped to France with group of repatriates on 4 October 1944
Bright	TJ	F/S		1270593	419	LW240	HAL	16/9/43	Modane	France	Sp, Gib	17/3/44	17/3/44	Lyneham	3319 1840	Evaded over Pyrenees. DFM (7/7/44)
Brinkhurst	D	SGT		647699	101	DV264	LA	30/3/44	Nuremberg	Germany	Sz, Fr			NK	NF	Rejoined squadron and flew further twenty operations
Brinn	WG	F/L		46463	88	BZ242	BOS	16/8/43	Denain	France	Sp, Gib	14/9/43	15/9/43	Whitchurch	3315 1404	DFM (17/5/40, 107 Squadron). Comet 130. To Spain with Private V.I. Nekrasov, Soviet Army - see Chapter 11. DFC (26/10/43). MiD (1/1/46)
Bristow	TJ	SGT	CAN	R.292668	419	KB814	LA	15/3/45	Hagen	Germany				NK	NF	Prisoner of war?
Brittain	BW	F/O	AUS	A.414756	630	LM117	LA	18/7/44	Revigny-sur-Ornain	France	Fr	4/9/44	4/9/44	NK	3325 2872	See *Massacre over the Marne*
Broad	SP	F/O		152211	166	JB644	LA	12/7/44	Revigny-sur-Ornain	France	Fr	28/8/44	28/8/44	Lyneham	3322 2211	Back on RAF Dakota to UK from Orléans. See *Massacre over the Marne*
Broadhead	D	SGT		3041042	463	NX584	LA	8/4/45	Lützkendorf	Germany	Ger			NK	3326 2949	ss7. Liberated by US troops 10 April 1945
Broadland	E	SGT			21	L8738	BL	14/5/40	Enemy troops	Belgium	Fr			NK	NF	
Broadley	J	F/O		147712	109	ML932	MOS	31/8/44	Cologne	Belgium	Fr	15/9/44	15/9/44	Hendon	3324 2562	
Bromwell	AV	LAC		250433	None	None	None	14/6/40	None	France	Sp, Gib	10/5/43	11/5/43	Hendon	3313 1193	RAF groundcrew, No.1 Servicing & Repair Flight, AASF. Wounded. Escaped from Frontstalag 203 (Mulsanne)
Brook	DA	P/O		175858	297	P1400	ALB	27/7/44	SOE 'Harry 41'	France	Fr	2/8/44	4/8/44	Southampton	3321 2064	Returned aboard an LST from the Allied beachhead
Brookes	J	SGT		560537	142	L5238	BA	10/5/40	Enemy troops	France	Fr			None	NF	MiD (23/7/37, corporal) for distinguished services in Palestine, 1936. KIA 14 May 1940, aged twenty-nine
Brookes	R	F/S		1577901	100	LL887	LA	22/4/44	Düsseldorf	Belgium	Bel			NK	3350 1494	Interviewed 14 September 1944
Brooks	HL	SGT	CAN	R.168211	44	LM638	LA	12/7/44	Culmont-Chalindrey	France	Fr	8/9/44	8/9/44	Middle Wallop	3323 2365	See *Massacre over the Marne*, pp.124-7 and photo p. 104
Brooks	RJ	SGT		1867783	115	LM166	LA	8/8/44	Lucheux	France	Fr	6/9/44	6/9/44	Northolt	3322 2288	Back to UK from Amiens
Broom	TJ	W/O		515779	105	DK297	MOS	25/8/42	Brauweiler	Belgium	Fr, Sp, Gib	30/9/42	5/10/42	Greenock	3310 897	Landed 15 miles NE of Antwerp. Comet 51. Back on HMS *Malaya*. DFC (3/10/44, 571 Squadron) & Bar (27/2/45, 128 Squadron) & 2nd Bar (26/10/45, 163 Squadron). Squadron leader (51227)
Brophy	GP	F/O	CAN	J.35142	419	KB726	LA	12/6/44	Cambrai	France	Fr	4/9/44	4/9/44	Hendon	3324 2598	In same crew as Mynarski VC
Brough	JFQ	SGT		1481301	138	DT726	HAL	3/11/43	SOE	France	Fr	8/2/44	9/2/44	Tempsford	3318 1752	ss8. Back by SOE Hudson on Operation Bludgeon. See *Flight Most Secret*, pp.169-172, and *Free to Fight Again*, pp. 73-7. Commissioned 23 November 1943 (158900) wef 12 September 1943
Brown	D	SGT		1604293	625	ND461	LA	27/1/44	Berlin	France	Fr	16/3/44	17/3/44	Dartmouth	3319 1848	Back from Brittany by MGB 502

Brown	E	F/O	CAN	J.24772	424	LV910	HAL	28/6/44	Metz	France	Fr	2/9/44	2/9/44	NK	3345 752	Right leg amputated, Liberated Reims hospital 29 August 1944. Interviewed 2 October 1944. Report MISC/INT/752
Brown	GA	F/O		39851	66	N3027	SP	13/5/40	Escort	Belgium				NK	NF	See *Twelve Days in May*, p. 100, (Cull, Lander & Weiss). DFC (26/12/41, squadron leader, 71 "Eagle" Squadron)
Brown	H	SGT		1822921	424	LV910	HAL	28/6/44	Metz	France	Fr	5/9/44	5/9/44	NK	3322 2283	
Brown	HT	F/S		1262465	9	ED480	LA	9/7/43	Gelsenkirchen	France	Sp, Gib	25/9/43	26/9/43	Whitchurch	3315 1423	His report states he landed at Bristol
Brown	JT	SGT		1397192	467	PB234	LA	18/7/44	Revigny-sur-Ornain	France	Fr	9/9/44	9/9/44	NK	3325 2890	See *Massacre over the Marne*
Brown	LC	P/O	NZ	147136	88	BZ296	BOS	8/8/43	Rennes	France	Sp, Gib	6/11/43	7/11/43	Whitchurch	3316 1535	ss3. NZ?
Brown	LJS	F/S	NZ	NZ.421014	620	LJ867	ST	11/4/44	SOE	France	Sp, Gib	5/9/44	5/9/44	Hendon	3322 2285	MM (12/6/45). Aircraft number from *The Stirling Bomber*, p. 214, M.J.F. Bowyer
Brown	R	SGT		1046183	207	W4172	LA	9/3/43	Munich	France	Sz, Fr, Sp, Gib	23/2/44	24/2/44	Whitchurch	3318 1782	Into Switzerland on 18/19 March 1943. Left on 8 January 1944 with Squadron Leader F.V. Taylor's party
Brown	R	SGT		952445	78	W7782	HAL	8/9/42	Frankfurt	Belgium	Fr, Sp, Gib	18/10/42	19/10/42	Poole	3311 926	Comet 58. DFM (5/2/43)
Brown	RC	SGT	CAN	R.185580	425	LK798	HAL	8/5/44	Haine St Pierre	Belgium	Bel	6/9/44	6/9/44	Northolt	3322 2286	Betrayed to Germans. St Gilles prison, Brussels. Escaped from "The Ghost Train" 3 September 1944. Back to UK from Amiens
Brown	RG	F/L	CAN	J.9451	268	FD447	MU	18/6/44	Sweep	France	Fr			NK	3348 268	Liberated by US troops 6 August 1944. Interviewed 15 August 1944. Report IS9/WEA/2/73/268
Brown	WC	SGT		1826198	78	LK840	HAL	22/6/44	Laon	France	Fr	15/8/44	15/8/44	NK	3321 2196	Sherwood. Arrived at camp on 30 July 1944. Injured when lorry overturned after liberation. To Hospital at RAF St Athan
Brown	WRM	F/S		1322443	207	ND567	LA	7/7/44	St Leu d'Esserent	France	Fr			NK	3350 1018	Interviewed 2 September 1944. Report IS9/WEA/2/320/1018
Browne	SF	SGT	NZ	NZ.411853	485	BM383	SP	31/5/42	Roadstead	France	Gib	30/9/42	5/10/42	Greenock	3310 890	Evacuated by *Seawolf* 5 September 1942. Back on HMS *Malaya*. DFC (28/9/43, flying officer, 93 Squadron) & Bar (14/9/45, CO of 485 Squadron). See AIR 40/1533
Brownhill	GI	SGT		649093	207	W4172	LA	9/3/43	Munich	France	Sp, Gib	23/6/43	29/6/43	Liverpool	3314 1295	Comet 99. Lost his companions when he crossed into Spain on 10 May 1943. Spent several weeks in Spanish jails. His home was in Hamilton, Canada
Brunton	GA	F/O		150278	75	HK567	LA	7/8/44	Mare de Magne	France	Fr	28/8/44	28/8/44	Northolt	3321 2154	Left for UK from Bayeux - B.14 airstrip, Banville
Bryan	AJ	F/O	CAN	J.21120	403	MJ645	SP	21/5/44	Ramrod 905	France	Fr	7/9/44	7/9/44	NK	3323 2498	DFC (31/7/45)
Bryant	AG	F/S		1601736	156	NE143	LA	31/5/44	Tergnier	France	Fr		8/9/44	NK	NF	Joined the Resistance
Bryant	SW	F/L		110866	512		DAK	18/9/44	Supply drop	Holland	Bel	28/9/44	28/9/44	NK	3324 2607	MBE (8/6/44)
Buchan	W	SGT			620	LJ849	ST	6/6/44	Supplies to Normandy	France	Fr	8/6/44	9/6/44	Gosport	NF	Left Normandy from Allied beachhead. No MI9/IS9 report listed. LJ849?
Buchanan	JEG	F/S	AUS	A.426954	90	EH906	ST	4/3/44	SOE	France	Fr	19/9/44	20/9/44	NK	3323 2493	Back to UK from Algiers
Buckley	K	SGT		1534134	462	LL604	HAL	9/10/44	Bochum	Holland			10/5/45	NK	3327 3084	Landed near Rheden
Budd	ACD	SGT	CAN	R.215226	405	PA988	LA	16/8/44	Stettin	Denmark	Swe	8/9/44	9/9/44	Leuchars	3323 2392	Evaded from Copenhagen to Malmo, Sweden, on a coal boat with Flying Officer Walter & Warrant Officer Rafter of his crew
Budzik	K	F/L	POL	P.0800	308	NH339	SP	6/11/44	Bombing	Holland			7/11/44	NK	NF	
Budzynski	J	SGT	POL	783405	300	R1705	WE	7/11/41	Mannheim	France	Sp, Gib	4/3/42	10/3/42	Gourock	3308 686	MiD (11/6/42). See AIR 2/5684
Bufton	HE	S/L		33223	9	W5703	WE	26/8/41	Cologne	France	Sp, Gib	19/12/41	20/12/41	Milford Haven	3307 610	With Crampton and Read of his crew. Back aboard HMS *Manxman*. See *Bombers First and Last*, pp. 58-9, and *Fighter Pilot*, pp.167-75. DSO (5/5/44). DFC (29/1/43). AFC (29/1/43). MiD (1/1/43)
Bullivant	B	F/L		115673	297	P1400	ALB	27/7/44	SOE 'Harry 41'	France	Fr	2/8/44	2/8/44	Calshot	3321 2063	Returned by RAF Air/Sea Rescue launch from Cherbourg
Bulman	EL	F/S	CAN	R.72937	405	BB250	HAL	11/3/43	Stuttgart	France	Sp, Gib	17/7/43	24/7/43	Liverpool	3314 1326	Oaktree. Back to UK on SS *Monarch of Bermuda*? Recommended for MM but MiD (8/6/44). Later, pilot officer (J.18603)
Bulmer	ST	F/S		1476187	90	EH906	ST	4/3/44	SOE	France	Sp, Gib	22/5/44	23/5/44	Whitchurch	3319 1927	Burgundy line
Bulow	KG	SGT		3005157	427	LW135	HAL	12/6/44	Arras	France	Fr	5/9/44	5/9/44	NK	3323 2430	Left for UK from Beauvais
Burchell	EJ	P/O	CAN	J.25038	101	DV288	LA	10/4/44	Aulnoye	France	Fr	4/9/44	4/9/44	Hendon	3324 2596	
Burchill	JG	F/L	CAN	J.26989	412	MJ660	SP	26/3/45	Offensive operations	Germany				NK	NF	Baled out ten kilometres north-west of Dorsten
Burford	LR	F/S	AUS	A.437391	514	LM180	LA	12/8/44	Rüsselsheim	Belgium				NK	NF	
Burgess	RWA	F/S			620	LJ849	ST	6/6/44	Supplies to Normandy	France	Fr	8/6/44	9/6/44	Gosport	NF	Left Normandy from Allied beachhead. No MI9/IS9 report listed. LJ849?
Burnham	RC	SGT		1868422	44	ME634	LA	7/7/44	St Leu d'Esserent	France	Fr	3/9/44	3/9/44	NK	3325 2879	
Burns	SG	F/S	AUS	A.429919	467	DV171	LA	24/9/44	Calais	France	Fr			NK	NF	
Burridge	J	SGT		553501	220	P5146	HUD	2/4/41	Crossover patrol	France	Sp, Gib	1/10/41	6/10/41	Gourock	3306 562	Interned at St Hippolyte. Escaped on 21 August 1941 with Sergeant A.C.

																Roberts. Report says landed at "Greenock"
Burrows	G	SGT		1226439	626	LL839	LA	26/3/44	Essen	France	Fr			NK	3350 1265	Helped by Comet line. Interviewed 30 August 1944. Report IS9/WEA/7/123/1265
Burrows	GA	F/O		113064	21	NS831	MOS	1/8/44	Barracks, Poitiers	France	Fr	16/9/44	16/9/44	Tempsford	3323 2438	Back to UK from Limoges
Burton	JTH	SGT		1551443	10	HX347	HAL	1/5/44	Mechelen	Belgium	Bel	10/9/44	10/9/44	NK	3325 2873	ss8. Marathon
Butcher	RD	SGT		1592108	166	NE112	LA	31/8/44	Agenville	France	Bel	10/9/44	10/9/44	NK	3323 2475	Captured on landing. Driven by van to Belgium. On 4 September 1944 his guards let him go free having been ordered to shoot him
Butler	KG	SGT		1106021	460	ND654	LA	20/7/44	Courtrai	Belgium	Fr	12/9/44	12/9/44	NK	3325 2880	With Pilot Officer R.H. Jopling RAAF. Liberated 7 September 1944 in Halluin. Went to Lille with Jopling on 10 September 1944
Butterfield	WR	S/L		67056	7	JA682	LA	12/8/43	Milan	France	Sp, Gib	5/11/43	6/11/43	Portreath	3316 1542	DFC (22/9/42). With F.D. Low USAAF in France. MiD (8/6/44). Killed in action on 5/6 June 1944 (bomber support) on 515 Squadron, Mosquito PZ189
Byrne	LM	SGT		1833328	158	LV790	HAL	12/6/44	Amiens	France	Fr	2/9/44	2/9/44	NK	NF	Liberated by London Rifles on 29 August 1944. To UK by Dakota
Cadge	DE	SGT		1865798	149	EF502	ST	10/4/44	SOE	France	Fr	8/7/44	9/7/44	Tangmere	3320 2011	With Flight Sergeant N.C.H. Pilgrim. Flown back on Operation Mixer I in a USAAF Dakota from a field near Nantua (Ain) with "Major Xavier" (Richard Heslop)
Cairns	GM	F/O	CAN	J.27280	196	LK556	ST	20/9/44	Supply drop	Holland	Bel	4/10/44	4/10/44	Ramsbury	3324 2639	Back to UK from Brussels
Calderbank	JR	F/O	CAN	J.27605	429	LV973	HAL	10/6/44	Versailles	France	Fr	18/8/44	18/8/44	Northolt	3321 2107	Sherwood. DFC (3/11/44)
Calderwood	W	F/O		162625	432	NP687	HAL	25/7/44	Stuttgart	France	Fr	17/8/44	18/8/44	NK	3321 2100	Left for UK from A22 airstrip near Rennes
Callard	AE	F/L		126495	515	NS993	MOS	30/9/44	Day Ranger	Switzerland	Fr	18/10/44	18/10/44	NK	3324 2670	Forced down by Swiss fighter. To Lyon, France, 18 October 1944. DFC (19/12/44). See *Confounding the Reich*, pp. 79-81; *Infringing Neutrality...*, pp.155-64
Cameron	D	F/O		146616	635	ND811	LA	4/8/44	Trossy-St Maximin	France	Fr			NK	3350 1062	DFM (12/2/43, 149 Sq). Interviewed 2 September 1944. Report IS9/WEA/2/318/1062. MiD (8/6/44)
Cameron	LM	S/L	CAN	J.15378	401	MJ131	SP	3/7/44	Armed recce	France	Fr			NK	NF	DFC (4/4/44). Safe in UK by 3 September 1944
Cammish	HS	SGT		1624536	50	LL791	LA	25/2/44	Augsburg	France	Sp, Gib	5/6/44	6/6/44	Whitchurch	3320 1944	
Camp	AJ	SGT		956353	466	LV956	HAL	18/4/44	Tergnier	France	Fr			NK	3350 1281	Interviewed 19 August 1944. Report IS9/WEA/8/516/1281
Campbell	CA	F/S	AUS	A.426306	467	LM376	LA	30/3/44	Nuremberg	Belgium	Fr, Sz, Fr	4/9/44	4/9/44	NK	3323 2507	Reached Switzerland on 1 May 1944. Left on 12 August 1944 with Flight Lieutenant L.A. Miller
Campbell	EA	F/L	CAN	J.25414	514	LL692	LA	28/7/44	Stuttgart	France	Fr		17/8/44	NK	3348 103	Sherwood. Interviewed 15 August 1944. Report IS9/WEA/8/70/103. DFC (3/11/44)
Campbell	G	SGT		974095	101	R1699	WE	10/9/41	Turin	France	Sp, Gib	30/12/41	5/1/42	Gourock	3307 634	Crossed Pyrenees with Lieutenant R.E.H. Parkinson and Sergeant Worby. To UK on Polish ship *Batory*. MiD (1/1/43)
Campbell	J	SGT		1897044	298	LL293	HAL	14/10/44	Supply drop	Zuider Zee	Hol	25/4/45	25/4/45	NK	3327 3030	
Campbell	JL	F/L	CAN	J.9429	416	MJ141	SP	12/7/44	Escort	France	Fr			NK	3349 372	Shot at when parachuting. Captured. Escaped. Interviewed 24 August 1944. Report IS9/WEA/2/191/372
Campbell	JM	SGT	CAN	R.108160	431	KB817	HAL	1/11/44	Oberhausen	Holland				NK	3348 2302	Report IS9/WEA/2/1092/2302
Cann	RJB	F/O		172869	166	JB649	LA	25/7/44	Stuttgart	France	Fr	8/9/44	8/9/44	Middle Wallop	3323 2445	DFC. Back from Orléans with 1 SAS
Canning	LW	SGT		1160100	218	BF514	ST	16/4/43	Mannheim	France	Sz, Fr	11/9/44	11/9/44	NK	3322 2297	In Switzerland 28 April 1943. Left 26 August 1944. See *Strike Hard*, pp 98-9 (JB Hilling)
Cant	RG	W/O		1433098	103	ED751	LA	5/9/43	Mannheim	France	Sz			NK	NF	In Switzerland 18 September 1943
Canter	HJB	SGT		1319407	76	BB242	HAL	6/12/42	Mannheim	France	And, Sp, Gib	8/3/43	15/3/43	Liverpool	3312 1127	DFM (11/5/43). See *Dangerous Landing*
Canter	WL	SGT	CAN	R.127907	408	JB909	HAL	14/4/43	Stuttgart	France	Sp, Gib	23/6/43	29/6/43	Liverpool	3314 1294	Broken leg treated in Paris. With Flying Officer G.C. Crowther. Comet 106. DFM (27/8/43)
Capusten	A	F/S	CAN	R.176117	429	LW128	HAL	7/6/44	Achères	France	Fr	9/9/44	9/9/44	NK	3323 2488	Left for UK from B.14 airstrip, Banville
Carbutt	D	SGT		565881	82	P6925	BL	13/6/40	Tanks, Forêt de Gault	France	Fr			NK	NF	Possibly not an evader
Carey	JCL	P/O		172120	620	LJ830	ST	21/9/44	Arnhem supply drop	Holland	Hol			NK	3350 1424	Liberated 23 September 1944. Interviewed 25 September 1944. Report IS9/WEA/2/550/1424. Aircraft and date are a guess
Carey	JWD	SGT		967050	467	LM450	LA	24/6/44	Prouville	France	Fr			NK	3322 2310	Back in UK by 10 September 1944
Carleton	JDH	SGT		612564	620	EE905	ST	30/7/43	Remscheid	Belgium	Fr	22/1/44	23/1/44	Falmouth	3318 1720	With both Bordeaux and Burgundy lines. Back to UK from Brittany on the *Breizh-Izel*. Interviewed 24 January 1944
Carmichael	JD	W/O	AUS	A.414991	453	SM255	SP	21/2/45	V2 site, The Hague	Holland	Hol			NK	3327 3050	Liberated by Canadians 11 May 1945. Report IS9/WEA/PLM/196 also in WO

																208/3348
Carpenter	CC	SGT		1320995	10	LV870	HAL	28/6/44	Blainville	France				NK	NF	
Carpenter	JO	F/L		113856	132	MH972	SP	21/5/44	Rhubarb	France	Fr	3/9/44	3/9/44	NK	3322 2266	
Carr	LW	F/S		1250644	102	W7653	HAL	27/4/42	Cologne	Belgium	Fr, Sp, Gib	18/6/42	23/6/42	Gourock	3309 749	Comet 17. MiD (1/1/43). See AIR 2/5684. See *Shot Down and On the Run*, pp.60-4, & *It's Suicide...*, p.67
Carr	RB	F/S		1577052	100	ND595	LA	25/2/44	Augsburg	Switzerland	Ger, Fr, Sp, Gib	24/5/44	25/5/44	Whitchurch	3319 1938	Repatriated with German agreement. Back on BOAC Dakota
Carroll	HB	P/O		68806	207	L7321	MAN	13/10/41	Cologne	Belgium	Fr, Sp, Gib	20/1/42	21/1/42	Plymouth	3307 666	Comet 8. Reached Spain 10 December 1941. MiD (1/1/43). Killed in an accident 19 November 1945
Carson	RA	F/O		144937	222	MK774	SP	28/9/44	Enemy transport	Holland	Hol			NK	3351 2256	Interviewed 6 November 1944. Report IS9/WEA/2/766/2256. MC (13/7/45)
Carter	GHF	F/O	CAN	J.11213	35	W7885	HAL	13/2/43	Lorient	France	Fr	6/4/43	9/4/43	Coverack	3312 1155	Back on French boat *Dalc'h-Mad*. DFC (6/7/43) & Bar (18/1/44). Shot down again on 19/20 February 1944. Prisoner of war
Carter	MJ	SGT		1811354	514	LM180	LA	12/8/44	Rüsselsheim	Belgium				NK	NF	
Carter	YK	F/O	CAN	C.88282	433	LV839	HAL	28/6/44	Metz	France	Fr		4/9/44	NK	3326 2969	Baled out. Aircraft returned to UK. Liberated in Paris 31 August 1944. DFC (21/9/45)
Cartwright	NE	F/S		636772	90	EF147	ST	5/3/44	SOE	France	Fr	11/9/44	11/9/44	NK	3322 2324	
Casey	AM	WO2	CAN	R.115376	431	MZ521	HAL	8/5/44	Haine St Pierre	Belgium	Fr	10/9/44	10/9/44	Hendon	3324 2604	
Cash	C	F/S		1318226	143	LZ406	BFR	6/9/44	NK	Belgium	Bel			NK	3350 1456	Liberated by Canadians 8 September 1944. Interviewed 9 September 1944. Report IS9/WEA/1/188/1456 jointly with Flight Sergeant K. Bradbury
Cash	JC	SGT		1078263	431	HE374	WE	14/4/43	Stuttgart	Switzerland	Fr	28/6/43	29/6/43	Lyneham	3313 1278	Repatriated 29 June 1943 in exchange with Germans
Casselman	DE	SGT	CAN	R.183978	50	JA899	LA	24/6/44	Prouville	France	Fr	11/9/44	11/9/44	Northolt	3323 2411	Back to UK from Amiens
Catley	WF	SGT		1330807	77	JD371	HAL	27/8/43	Nuremberg	Belgium	Fr, Sp, Gib	2/12/43	3/12/43	St Mawgan	3316 1598	Comet 168. With Pilot Officer R.G.T. Kellow
Cawley	JG	SGT	CAN	R.68667	460	ND654	LA	20/7/44	Courtrai	Belgium	Fr			NK	3322 2318	Liberated 5 September 1944. Back in UK by 6 September 1944
Cawthorne	CA	P/O		54753	61	LM718	LA	23/9/44	Ladbergen	Holland				NK	3350 1429	DFM (19/10/43, 467 Squadron). Interviewed 27 September 1944. Report IS9/WEA/2/657/1429. See article in *Daily Telegraph* 28 April 1997
Chadwick	J	F/S		857452	61	ME385	LA	8/4/45	Lützkendorf	Germany	Ger		17/4/45	NK	3326 2952	Liberated by US 9th Armored Division 12 April 1945
Chamberlain	H	P/O		172208	432	NP687	HAL	25/7/44	Stuttgart	France	Fr			NK	3348 36	Sherwood. Liberated by Americans 2 August 1944. Report IS9/WEA/8/47/36
Chapin	RL	P/O		179237	295	LK171	ST	2/11/44	SOE supply drop	Norway	Swe		2/1/45	NK	3325 2845	To Sweden by boat *Augusta*
Chapman	JE	F/O	CAN	J.29670	514	LL692	LA	28/7/44	Stuttgart	France	Fr	17/8/44	17/8/44	NK	3326 2935	Sherwood. Report compiled from questionnaire in April 1945
Chapman	K	SGT		1581545	61	LM518	LA	24/6/44	Prouville	France				NK	NF	ss7. Prisoner of war?
Chapman	TB	SGT	USA	R.174900	429	LV973	HAL	10/6/44	Versailles	France	Fr	18/8/44	18/8/44	Northolt	3321 2101	Sherwood. In RCAF
Chappell	GE	SGT		1589541	640	LW464	HAL	24/7/44	Stuttgart	France	Fr			NK	3349	Interviewed 23 August 1944. Report IS9/WEA/8/535/*
Chappell	HS	SGT		1819696	9	LL787	LA	3/5/44	Mailly-le-Camp	France	Fr			NK	3349 481	Report IS9/WEA/MB/481
Chapple	DA	P/O	AUS	A.420451	90	EF509	ST	9/5/44	SOE	France	Fr	18/8/44	18/8/44	Northolt	3321 2085	See *Agents for Escape...*, Chapter 14. See *Silent Heroes*, p.39
Chapple	JK	SGT		1800731	207	PD210	LA	18/7/44	Revigny-sur-Ornain	France	Fr			NK	3350 1333	ss7. Back in UK early September 1944. See *Massacre over the Marne*
Chard	EG	SGT	CAN	R.126321	158	HR791	HAL	11/11/43	Cannes	France	Sz			NK	NF	Report Switzerland/114
Charman	AF	SGT		1812709	78	LW273	HAL	23/9/43	Mannheim	France	And, Sp, Gib	5/11/43	6/11/43	Whitchurch	3316 1531	With Flying Officer Isherwood at some point during evasion
Charman	ER	SGT	AUS	A.400859	174	BP768	HUR	30/7/42	Ramrod	France	Gib	30/9/42	5/10/42	Greenock	3310 892	Evacuated by *Seawolf* 21 September 1942. Back on HMS *Malaya*
Charnock	W	SGT		1594840	576	ME811	LA	6/6/44	Vire	France	Fr			NK	NF	Briefly met P/O G.F. Pyle while evading. Service number?
Charteris	WD	SGT		1565842	57	ME868	LA	7/7/44	St Leu d'Esserent	France	Fr	28/8/44	28/8/44	Northolt	3322 2218	
Charters	RB	P/O	CAN	J.18469	199	EE957	ST	3/3/44	SOE	France	Sp, Gib	1/5/44	2/5/44	Whitchurch	3319 1894	Burgundy line. DFM (16/4/43)
Chaster	JB	F/S	CAN	R.92063	207	W4134	LA	3/1/43	Essen	Holland	Bel, Fr, Sp, Gib	8/3/43	15/3/43	Liverpool	3312 1125	Comet 89. See *We Flew, We Fell, We Lived* pp. 343-7
Checketts	JM	S/L	NZ	NZ.403602	485	EN572	SP	6/9/43	Ramrod	France	Fr	24/10/43	25/10/43	Penzance	3315 1495	DFC (17/8/43). Burned and wounded. To UK by fishing boat & Royal Navy launch. DSO (3/12/43). Silver Star (USA) (17/4/45). Died 21 April 2006 aged 94
Cheeseman	WG	F/S		1895497	207	NN724	LA	7/2/45	Ladbergen	Holland				NK	NF	Evaded with Flight Sergeant S.E. Hanson
Cheney	DN	F/O	CAN	J.18295	617	JB139	LA	5/8/44	Brest	France	Fr	29/8/44	29/8/44	Northolt	3322 2215	In the sea for several hours - see *Silent Heroes*, pp. 56-7
Chester-Master	RC	F/S	AUS	A.434592	514	LM180	LA	12/8/44	Rüsselsheim	Belgium	Bel	10/9/44	10/9/44	NK	3323 2473	Back to UK from Brussels. See Orth's report & *Free to Fight Again*,-pp. 17478
Chew	F	F/S		810195	235		MOS	12/8/44	Bordeaux area	France (sea)	Fr			NK	3345 637	Shot down in sea. Rescued by German trawler.
Chisholm	WA	P/O		172980	19	FX990	MU	22/4/44	Sweep	France	Fr			NK	3350 1019	Interviewed 2 September 1944. Report IS9/WEA/2/321/1019
Chowne	HW	SGT		1585682	158	LK877	HAL	1/6/44	Trappes	France	Fr			NK	3348 100	Liberated by US troops on 13 August 1944. Interviewed by WEA 14 August

																1944. Report IS9/WEA 7/39/100
Christensen	JRW	SGT	AUS	A.402224	101	R1699	WE	10/9/41	Turin	France	Sp, Gib	30/12/41	5/1/42	Gourock	3307 635	To UK on Polish ship *Batory*. MiD (1/1/43, pilot officer). AFC (1/9/44, flying officer)
Christian	HJ	W/O	NZ		644	NA672	HAL	26/4/45	SOE Tablejam 353	Denmark	Dk	19/5/45	19/5/45	NK	NF	Flown back to UK over Hamburg by DC-3 Dakota
Christie	VB	P/O	CAN	J.87853	48	KG428	DAK	19/9/44	Arnhem supply drop	Holland	Hol			NK	3352 2405	Interviewed? Liberated April 1945. See Flight Sergeant F.E. Fuller. See *Free to Fight Again*, pp. 201-205
Christoff	C	SGT	CAN	R.200321	432	LW616	HAL	12/6/44	Cambrai	France	Fr	4/9/44	4/9/44	Northolt	3323 2385	Left for UK from Bayeux - B.14 airstrip, Banville
Chudleigh	RN	S/L		39712	151		MOS	4/8/44	Railways, Bordeaux	France	Fr	2/9/44	2/9/44	NK	3322 2256	Left for UK from Normandy. DFC (3/10/44)
Ciula	T	W/O	POL	793977	305	LR313	MOS	22/4/44	Leeuwarden airfield	France	Sp, Gib	21/6/44	22/6/44	Whitchurch	3320 1985	Crossed to Spain with Pilot Officer W.F. Dobson, Flying Officer Rosinski and Sergeant D. Shepherd
Clapin	BPW	F/L		43541	65	FX944	MU	24/6/44	Armed recce	France	Fr	27/8/44	27/8/44	Northolt	3322 2237	DFC (26/2/43). Left for UK from Bayeux - B.14 airstrip, Banville. Was 2nd lieutenant in RE before RAF commission. Rejoined RE as lieutenant w.e.f. 12/6/46
Clare	VH	SGT		1605068	77	LK710	HAL	22/4/44	Laon	France	Sz			NK	NF	DFM (19/12/44). Report Switzerland/30. Killed in flying accident on 8 June 1945
Clark	WA	SGT		1571071	619	ME745	LA	7/7/44	St Leu d'Esserent	France				NK	3349	
Clarke	HN	SGT		1392903	149	BF477	ST	5/9/43	Mannheim	France	Sp, Gib	5/2/44	6/2/44	Whitchurch	3318 1756	Possum line
Clarke	R	SGT		1002829	90	EE873	ST	13/7/43	Aachen	Holland	Bel, Fr,Sp, Gib	10/9/43	10/9/43	Whitchurch	3314 1401	ss8. Comet 128. Interviewed on 12 September 1943. MiD (8/6/44, flight sergeant)
Clarke	RC	F/S	AUS	A.418252	626	LM633	LA	20/7/44	Courtrai	Belgium				NK	NF	
Clary	JT	2LT	USA	O-885969	434	DK259	HAL	29/9/43	Bochum	Holland	Bel, Fr, Sp, Gib	29/11/43	30/11/43	Whitchurch	3316 1594	Comet 179. With Sergeant J.H.J. Dix & two USAAF airmen
Clay	LN	F/S		1575438	218	EH942	ST	22/4/44	Laon	France	Fr			NK	3348 272	Sherwood. Interviewed 19 August 1944. Report IS9/WEA/2/152/272
Clayton	AD	W/O		1869599	635	PB564	LA	5/1/45	Hanover	Holland	Hol		26/4/45	NK	3327 3104	Shot down near Groningen. Liberated 15 April 1945 by Polish tank crews. Interviewed 20 April 1945. Report IS9/WEA/1/514. DFC (18/9/45) wef 4 January 1945
Clayton	HK	SGT		939118	None	None	None	22/5/40	None	France	Sp, Gib	4/3/42	10/3/42	Gourock	3308 701	Acting interpreter. Captured by Germans 22 May 1940. Escaped 1 June 1940. Worked for escape organisation in Lille and Marseille
Cleaver	RFW	F/L		124411	644	LL228	HAL	5/4/44	SOE	France	Sp, Gib	16/6/44	17/6/44	Whitchurch	3320 1967	DSO (29/10/43), DFC (3/10/44). Died in flying accident in 1953. See his story in *Home Run* (Bickers) Chapter 11. Aircraft number is a guess
Cleland	MJ	F/O		152044	619	ME866	LA	9/8/44	Châtellerault	France				NK	NF	ss7
Clements	RS	F/O	CAN	J.6645	57	W4822	LA	3/11/43	Düsseldorf	Belgium	Fr, Sp, Gib	28/12/43	29/12/43	Whitchurch	3317 1657	Comet 217. Left Seville on the *Tudor Prince* c. 21 December 1943 with Flight Lieutenant J.L. Kennedy and Sergeant R.C. Morley
Clenard	AB	WO2	CAN		403	MK570	SP	17/6/44	Scramble	France			18/6/44	NK	NF	
Clifford	R	AC2		617217	13	None	LYS	26/5/40	None	France	Sp, Por	25/8/40	26/8/40	NK	3299 58	Groundcrew on 13 (Army Co-op) Squadron. Left behind on ground. Flown home from Lisbon
Clinton	JF	SGT		2211527	90	NE177	LA	10/6/44	Dreux	France	Fr	28/8/44	28/8/44	NK	3322 2233	Left for UK from Bayeux - B.14 airstrip, Banville
Clissold	GA	F/O			245	EJ971	TY	25/3/45	Offensive operations	Germany				NK	NF	Baled out east of Dingden. Possibly briefly prisoner
Clowes	WA	F/O		151742	207	ME805	LA	7/7/44	St Leu d'Esserent	France	Fr	2/9/44	2/9/44	NK	3322 2255	Left for UK from Normandy
Clulow	P	LT	SAF	328375v	245	MN915	TY	18/8/44	Vehicles, Falaise	France	Fr	26/8/44	26/8/44	NK	3345 816	Shot down by Flak. Wounded. Captured. Liberated 19 August 1944 by FFI. Interviewed 17 January 1945. Report MISC/INT/816
Coates	EA	SGT	AUS	A.403798	115	BJ842	WE	22/11/42	Stuttgart	France	Sp, Gib	8/2/43	17/2/43	Gourock	3312 1089	Solo to Spain in 55 days. Author of *Lone Evader*
Coates	GS	SGT		653299	44	LM455	LA	6/8/44	Bois de Cassan	France	Fr	7/9/44	8/9/44	NK	3323 2497	Mid-under gunner. Baled out after aircraft damaged by flak. Back to UK by sea
Cockrean	MA	F/O		145384	619	ME745	LA	7/7/44	St Leu d'Esserent	France	Fr			NK	3350 1075	Interviewed 5 September 1944. Report IS9/WEA/2/427/1075
Coen	OH	P/O	USA	62244	71	AB827	SP	20/10/41	Rhubarb	France	Sp, Gib	25/12/41	25/12/41	Plymouth	3307 612	DFC (4/8/42). MiD (1/1/43, flight lieutenant). See *Fighter Pilot*, p.160-75, and *Aircraft Down!*, pp. 9-51
Cogman	WCG	F/O		39274	102	N1417	WH	19/5/40	Gelsenkirchen	Holland		28/5/40		None	NF	Possibly drowned in sinking of SS *Abukir*, 28/29 May 1940 (official date of death 27 May 1940). No known grave
Coldridge	AS	F/O	CAN	J.26625	161	LL183	HAL	9/5/44	SOE	France	Sp, Gib	5/9/44	6/9/44	NK	3323 2387	Sprained both ankles. With Flying Officer Medland. Left Paris 18 July 1944. Arrested in Spain. MiD (14/6/45)
Coleson	PJ	P/O		42695	53	T1816	BL	11/8/40	"Dundee 2"	France				NK	NF	Squadron records state that he was a prisoner of war

Colgan	T	F/S		532713	10	W1041	HAL	27/4/42	*Tirpitz*	Norway	Swe	23/9/42	24/9/42	Leuchars	3310 862	Left from Stockholm. Shot down again on 23 August 1943 on 35 Squadron. Prisoner of war
Colhoun	H	SGT		1028525	101	X3391	WE	28/8/42	Nuremberg	Germany	Sz, Fr, Sp, Gib	23/2/44	24/2/44	Whitchurch	3318 1786	Left Switzerland 8 January 1944 with seven other internees. Flown back in a Dakota. Author of *One of a Few*
Coller	JH	F/L		115590	10	LV858	HAL	10/4/44	Tergnier	France	Fr	31/8/44	31/8/44	NK	3322 2230	DFC (9/2/43). Liberated Paris, August 1944 Left for UK from 'Bayeux' - B.14 airstrip, Banville. MiD (8/6/44). DSO (5/12/44, squadron leader). See *Free to Fight Again*, pp. 85-8; *The Easy Trip*, pp.77-8
Collins	GA	WO2	CAN	R.160042	106	ND850	LA	26/4/44	Schweinfurt	France	Sz		5/9/44	NK	3323 2472	Crossed into Switzerland on 13 May 1944 with Flying Officer Fraser and Sergeant McKenzie of own crew. Left c. 12 August 1944
Collins	MA	SGT		1258829	226	AL743	BOS	22/9/42	Chocques power stn	France	Sp, Gib	28/3/43	5/4/43	Liverpool	3312 1145	DFM (15/6/43). Commissioned (179327). DFC (29/6/45, flying officer). See *The Reich Intruders*, p. 86
Collins	OR	P/O	CAN	J.36710	425	LW715	HAL	15/6/44	Boulogne	France				NK	NF	Service number?
Collins	RJ	SGT	AUS	A.404035	15 OTU	W5586	WE	30/5/42	Cologne	Belgium	Fr, Sp, Gib	21/7/42	30/7/42	Gourock	3309 792	Comet 26. MiD (1/1/43)
Comley	JH	SGT		2206002	166	NE170	LA	29/8/44	Agenville	France	Fr			NK	3345 658	Captured on landing. Handed over to gendarme 2 September 1944. Liberated 4 September 1944. Interviewed 10 September 1944. Report MISC/INT/658
Compton	B	SGT		1850671	76	LL116	HAL	20/1/44	Berlin	France				NK	NF	
Conde	R	SGT		1621820	10	LV870	HAL	28/6/44	Blainville	France				NK	NF	
Congreve	GH	P/O	CAN	174045	426	MZ598	HAL	8/5/44	Haine St Pierre	Belgium	Bel			NK	NF	ss8. Marathon
Conrad	WAG	F/L	CAN	J.5023	403	LZ997	SP	17/8/43	Ramrod 206	France	Sp, Gib	9/10/43	10/10/43	NK	3315 1458	DFC (22/1/43) & Bar (11/8/44, 421 Squadron). Collided with another Spitfire. Later, wing commander
Conroy	RF	F/S	CAN	R.55965	429	HE593	WE	11/6/43	Düsseldorf	Holland	Bel, Fr, Sp, Gib	1/10/43	2/10/43	Whitchurch	3315 1429	ss5. Burgundy line. See Flying Officer T.W. Simpson. J.17939 Flying Officer Conroy was killed on 24/25 March 1944 (Berlin) when he stayed at the controls while crew baled out
Conway	J	SGT		1569273	576	ME811	LA	6/6/44	Vire	France	Fr			NK	3348 294	Liberated by US troops 14 August 1944. Interviewed 18 August 1944. Report IS9/WEA/2/146/294
Cook	O	F/O	CAN	J.37165	426	NP800	HAL	4/11/44	Bochum	Germany	Ger	11/11/44	11/11/44	NK	3326 2936	Evaded near Gladbach. Flown back to UK from France
Cook	PE	F/S		1318386	61	NF914	LA	24/9/44	Calais	France	Fr	1/10/44	1/10/44	NK	3345 804	Burns to face. Blinded. Captured on landing. Liberated 30 September 1944. Interviewed 17 November 1944. Report MISC/INT/804
Cook	WF	F/O	CAN	J.16201	421	BS532	SP	3/10/43	Ramrod 259	France	Sp, Gib	15/11/43	16/11/43	Lyneham	3316 1577	Comet 182. Flew with 421 Squadron again. DFC (29/12/44). Lyneham?
Cooke	TCS	S/L		103506	138	LW275	HAL	7/2/44	SOE	France	Sp, Gib	4/5/44	5/5/44	Whitchurch	3319 1899	DFM (23/9/41, 104 Squadron). AFC (1/1/43). DFC (11/6/43, 214 Squadron). On his 63rd operation. See *Free to Fight Again*, pp. 77-81
Coombs	RJ	F/L		60324	487	HP933	MOS	6/8/44	Intruder	France				NK	NF	Take-off was at 0330 hours. DFC (29/6/45). Mosquito HP933 or NT125? - see Flight Lieutenant Judson RNZAF
Cooper	D	SGT		1595345	578	LL584	HAL	11/9/44	Gelsenkirchen	Belgium	Bel			NK	3350 1412	Interviewed 26 September 1944. Report IS9/WEA/2/551/1412
Cooper	MHF	F/O		133025	616	BR987	SP	16/8/43	Ramrod	France	Sp, Gib	20/12/43	21/12/43	Whitchurch	3317 1635	Born in Kenya, 7 March 1922. Helped by Marie-Claire line. See Flying Officer H.F.E. Smith RCAF. MiD (1/1/45). Author of *One of The Many*
Cope	JE	SGT		1377332	115	X3675	WE	28/8/42	Nuremberg	Belgium	Fr, Sp, Gib	5/10/42	6/10/42	Hendon	3310 869	Comet 54. Escorted from Paris by Andrée de Jongh and Jeanine De Greef. DFM (18/5/43)
Copley	EH	SGT		1880030	207	NN724	LA	7/2/45	Ladbergen	Holland				NK	NF	
Corby	RC	F/S	CAN	R.184869	10	HX295	HAL	26/3/44	Essen	Belgium	Fr	5/9/44	5/9/44	NK	3323 2465	False papers prepared by Ann Brusselmans. With Sergeant W.W. Farmer. Back to UK from Paris
Corcoran	J	F/S	NZ	NZ.422089	295	LJ618	ST	20/9/44	Arnhem supply drop	Holland	Hol	22/9/44	22/9/44	Harwell	NF	Operation Market IV. Returned to base within fifty hours
Corkran	TJ	P/O	AUS	A.404078	120	AM924	LIB	28/5/42	*Tirpitz* recce	Norway	Swe	31/8/42	1/9/42	Leuchars	3310 831	Came down in the sea sixty miles off Lofoten Islands. Reached Sweden 30 June 1942. MC (1/12/42). See *Making for Sweden*, pp. 35-8 & *Shot Down and on the Run*, pp. 127-33
Cornelius	RW	SGT		1314549	10	JD368	HAL	27/8/43	Nuremberg	Belgium	Fr, Sp, Gib	19/12/43	20/12/43	Lyneham	3317 1632	On detachment from 1663 HCU. Comet 193. With Sergeant DePape. Injured as flying officer in Liberator accident on 3 December 1944. Took own life 14 May 1945
Cornier	AA	WO2	CAN	R.121517	425	LK798	HAL	8/5/44	Haine St Pierre	Belgium	Bel	23/9/44	23/9/44	Northolt	3324 2556	
Corrigan	GL	F/S	CAN	R.218547	49	RF153	LA	14/3/45	Lützkendorf	Germany				NK	NF	ss7
Costello-Bowen	EA	F/L		46332	105	DK297	MOS	25/8/42	Brauweiler	Belgium	Fr, Sp, Gib	2/10/42	3/10/42	Mount Batten	3310 868	Landed fifteen miles NE of Antwerp. Comet 56. Escorted from Paris by

																Andrée de Jongh and Jeanine De Greef. MiD (2/6/43). Killed (squadron leader) on 9 August 1943 air testing Ventura AJ454, 487 Squadron. AFC (1/1/44)
Côté	MJA	F/O	CAN	J.14529	439	MN375	TY	28/9/44	Patrol	Luxembourg			1/10/44	NK	NF	See 14 January 1945
Côté	MJA	F/L	CAN	J.14529	439	RB204	TY	14/1/45	Road bridges etc	Holland	Hol	4/4/45	4/4/45	NK	3326 2939	See 28 September 1944
Cotter	DW	F/O	AUS	A.426546	619	ME745	LA	7/7/44	St Leu d'Esserent	France				NK	3349	
Cottrell	L	SGT		2206047	158	LV792	HAL	1/6/44	Trappes	France	Fr	28/8/44	28/8/44	Northolt	3321 2204	Left for UK from Bayeux - B.14 airstrip, Banville
Couchman	E	F/S		1253653	630	LM117	LA	18/7/44	Revigny-sur-Ornain	France	Fr		1/9/44	NK	3349 423	Interviewed 31 August 1944. Report IS9/WEA/8/253/423. See *Massacre over the Marne*
Courtenay	DH	P/O		158785	635	ND508	LA	22/4/44	Laon	France	Fr	6/9/44	6/9/44	Tempsford	3322 2282	Blown out of aircraft. Injured. Captured in Spain by Germans. Freed by French from Toulouse prison on 19 August 1944. Back by Hudson. Tempsford? DFC (21/9/45)
Couttie	S	F/S		1345942	235		MOS	12/8/44	Bordeaux area	France (sea)	Fr			NK	3345 638	Shot down in sea. Rescued by German trawler.
Covington	WI	F/L		119537	97	JA716	LA	10/8/43	Nuremberg	Belgium	Fr, Sp, Gib	17/1/44	17/1/44	Portreath	3318 1707	DFC (9/7/43), MiD (8/6/44)
Cowan	RE	SGT	CAN	R.214409	429	MZ362	HAL	25/7/44	Stuttgart	France	Fr	18/8/44	18/8/44	Northolt	3321 2121	Sherwood. Left for UK from B.14 airstrip, Banville
Cowell	DWG	SGT		1315850	78	JD108	HAL	13/7/43	Aachen	Belgium	Fr, Sp, Gib	3/11/43	4/11/43	NK	3316 1553	In Spanish jail with Sergeant R. Falcus
Cox	DM	SGT	CAN	R.104339	7	R9149	ST	9/3/43	Munich	France	Sp, Gib	17/7/43	24/7/43	Liverpool	3314 1328	Oaktree. Back to UK on SS *Monarch of Bermuda?*
Cox	GT	SGT		1251523	207	L7321	MAN	13/10/41	Cologne	Belgium	Fr, Sp, Gib	4/3/42	10/3/42	Gourock	3308 694	Comet 11. MiD (1/1/43)
Cox	WE	LAC			264	L6965	DF	13/5/40	EA, The Hague beach	Holland	Bel		17/5/40	Folkestone	NF	Returned by destroyer from Antwerp
Crabtree	DB	SGT		740434	616	P7980	SP	3/7/41	Sweep	France	Sp, Gib	26/8/41	26/8/41	Calshot	3305 490	Flown back by Sunderland. MiD (11/6/42). See also Falcon-Scott & Robillard
Crabtree	M	SGT		1206747	77	DT734	HAL	9/3/43	Munich	Belgium	Sz, Fr		6/10/44	NK	NF	Back by C-47 from France - see *Aviateurs-Piétons...*, p. 252. Report Switzerland/38
Crampton	WF	SGT		988785	9	W5703	WE	26/8/41	Cologne	France	Sp, Gib	8/1/42	9/1/42	Pembroke Dock	3307 627	With Bufton and Read of his crew. MiD (1/1/43). See *Bombers First and Last*, pp. 58-9, and *Fighter Pilot*, pp. 167-75
Crane	KN	P/O		195135	199	RG373	HAL	2/5/45	Bomber support	Germany		9/5/45	9/5/45	NK	3327 3082	ss8. Last Bomber Command evader of the War
Craven	J	F/O		127012	50	LL840	LA	21/6/44	Scholven/Buer	Holland	Hol			NK	3352 2402	DFC (10/9/43, 61 Squadron). Hidden at Frieslaan 5, Apeldoorn. See WO 309/44. Interviewed 18 March 1945. Report IS9/WEA/1/308/2402
Crayden	B	SGT		1331987	102	MZ644	HAL	28/6/44	Blainville	France	Fr	28/8/44	28/8/44	Lyneham	3321 2189	Back on RAF Dakota to UK from Orléans. See *Massacre over the Marne*, pp. 134-42
Crighton	J	SGT		1124472	12	LM514	LA	3/5/44	Mailly-le-Camp	France				NK	NF	See *Shot Down and on the Run*, p. 92
Croad	IAH	F/S		1801318	158	NR251	HAL	5/1/45	Hanover	Holland	Hol			NK	3352 2487	Interviewed 11 April 1945. Report IS9/WEA/1/349/2487
Crome	DA	SGT		1318539	161	DK119	HAL	22/7/43	SOE	France	Fr	15/11/43	16/11/43	Tangmere	3316 1572	DFC. Back by Lysander in Operation Water Pistol
Croquet	JLJG	P/O	BEL	159234	349	AB175	SP	11/2/44	Ramrod 545	France	Fr			NK	3349 363	Sherwood. Interviewed 16 August 1944. Report IS9/WEA/2/84/363
Crosby	RG	F/O	CAN	C.22655	56	JP446	TY	3/1/44	Rhubarb	France	Sp, Gib	5/5/44	6/5/44	Whitchurch	3319 1908	Joined up with Flight Lieutenant D. Goldberg in Paris. MiD (1/1/45). Evaded again in 1945
Crosby	RG	S/L	CAN	C.22655	439	MP134	TY	22/1/45	Armed patrol	Germany				NK	NF	Shot down at Uetterath. Also evaded in 1944. DFC (3/4/45)
Crowley	HE	F/S		1422158	61	EE186	LA	4/7/44	St Leu d'Esserent	France	Fr	29/8/44	29/8/44	NK	3322 2234	Left for UK from Bayeux - B.14 airstrip, Banville
Crowley-Milling	D	F/L		78274	610	W3455	SP	21/8/41	Circus to Lille	France	Sp, Gib	1/12/41	2/12/41	Plymouth	3307 604	DFC (11/4/41). See *Free to Fight Again*, pp.43-6. With Sergeant Ptácek. Bar to DFC (29/9/42), DSO (24/12/43). Died 1 December 1996 as air marshal KBE DSO DFC & Bar
Crowther	GC	F/O	CAN	J.12975	420	HE550	WE	14/4/43	Stuttgart	France	Sp, Gib	1/6/43	2/6/43	Hendon	3313 1230	With a commando, Corporal M. César, and Flying Officer K.J. Bolton. All helped by Aimable Fouquerel in Paris. Comet 102. DFC (27/7/43)
Cruickshank	DJ	F/S	NZ	NZ.421336	50	NF984	LA	1/1/45	Mittelland Canal	Holland	Hol	8/1/45	8/1/45	NK	NF	The only one of the crew to bale out. Landed behind enemy lines but soon made his way to the American lines. See *Night After Night*, pp.481-2
Cufley	NB	SGT		1386671	77	JD247	HAL	18/11/43	Mannheim	France	Fr	29/1/44	29/1/44	Dartmouth	3318 1728	Chauny. Back to UK by MGB from Brittany on Bonaparte I
Cullen	R	F/O			190		ST	19/9/44	Arnhem supply drop	Holland	Bel			NK	NF	Shown in squadron records as having evaded with Flying Officer R. Lawton
Cullen	WC	F/O	CAN	J.21360	428	KB756	LA	4/7/44	Villeneuve-St Georges	France				NK	NF	
Cullity	JA	F/O	AUS	A.427302	463	LM597	LA	24/6/44	Prouville	France	Fr	9/9/44	9/9/44	NK	3322 2337	
Cunliffe	F	F/S		1072609	466	HX341	HAL	15/3/44	Stuttgart	France	Sz	17/9/44	19/9/44	Newquay	3323 2518	Into Switzerland on 22 March 1944. Back into France on 1 September 1944 with Sergeant P.W. Walker. Later, pilot officer 173301
Cunningham	W	F/O	CAN	J.28238	75	LL921	LA	18/7/44	Aulnoye	Belgium	Bel	6/9/44	6/9/44	Northolt	3324 2621	Betrayed to Germans on 25 July 1944. St Gilles prison, Brussels. "Ghost

																Train" 3 September 1944
Curl	CP	SGT		1628364	467	LM376	LA	30/3/44	Nuremberg	Belgium	Bel	9/9/44	9/9/44	NK	3325 2895	Liberated by Americans on 8 September 1944
Currie	XX	SGT			40	R3693	BL	14/6/40	Merville airfield	France	Fr			NK	NF	Possibly not an evader
Curry	JH	SGT		1335808	165	BM518	SP	9/2/43	Rhubarb	France	Sp, Gib	21/5/43	22/5/43	Hendon	3313 1210	Comet 93. Killed in action 25 July 1943, still on 165 Squadron
Curtis	A	F/S		1579599	617	JB139	LA	5/8/44	Brest	France	Fr			NK	3345 689	Captured. Liberated from camp at Rostellec on 18 September 1944. Interviewed 23 September 1944. Report MISC/INT/689
Cuthbertson	FW	W/O		1090342	182	PD477	TY	12/10/44	Strafing	Holland				NK	3348 2307	Interviewed 23 November 1944. Shot down again on 28 February 1945, but murdered - see files WO 235/61 & WO 309/544
Czekalski	W	SGT	POL	784143	305	Z8599	WE	5/5/42	Stuttgart	Belgium	Fr, Sp, Gib	21/7/42	30/7/42	Gourock	3309 794	With the Brusselmans in Brussels. See *Belgium Rendez-Vous 127* pp. 39-40. Comet 28. Killed on operations 10 April 1944
Czerwinski	A	P/O	POL	P.2232	308	AA935	SP	23/9/43	Ramrod	France	Sp, Gib	15/11/43	15/11/43	Lyneham	3316 1578	Comet 184. Killed on operations 7 December 1944. Lyneham?
Daft	G	SGT		1153359	35	W7658	HAL	19/5/42	Mannheim	France	Gib	18/10/42	19/10/42	Poole	3311 922	Evacuated by *Seawolf* 12 October 1942. DFM (5/2/43). See *Airmen on the Run*, pp. 54-72
D'Albenas	PW	F/O	CAN	J.86333	183	MN452	TY	24/1/45	Armed recce	Holland	Hol			NK	3352 2394	Interviewed 13 March 1945. Report IS9/WEA/1/302/2394
Dalphond	MHJ	SGT	CAN	R.60726	405	W5551	WE	24/7/41	Brest	France	Gib	30/9/42	5/10/42	Greenock	3311 907	Evacuated by *Seawolf* 21 September 1942. Back on HMS *Malaya*. DFM (5/2/43)
Dalton	R	W/O		1074412	295	LK171	ST	2/11/44	SOE supply drop	Norway	Swe		2/1/45	NK	3325 2846	To Sweden by boat *Augusta*. See AIR 14/464. Air Medal (US) 27 April 1945
D'Andrea	DA	F/O	CAN	J.28953	432	LW583	HAL	8/5/44	Haine St Pierre	Belgium	Fr	8/9/44	8/9/44	NK	3323 2468	Back to UK from Paris
Daniel	RW	P/O	AUS	A.413833	35	HR985	HAL	11/11/43	Cannes	France	Fr	24/3/44	24/3/44	Dartmouth	3319 1855	ss8. Evacuated from Brittany by MGB503 in Operation Bonaparte V. See *We Act With One Accord*, pp.150-1
Daniels	JB	F/O		136357	158	HX334	HAL	12/5/44	Hasselt	Belgium				NK	NF	
D'Arcey	A	F/O	AUS	A.422445	460	ND394	LA	24/2/44	Schweinfurt	France	Sz			NK	NF	Escaped from German guard. To Switzerland 1 March 1944. Left 4 September 1944
Darcy	GJ	WO2	CAN	R.154763	405	PA970	LA	8/9/44	Le Havre	France				NK	NF	
D'Arcy	G	P/O		169392	426	NP683	HAL	28/6/44	Metz	France	Fr	27/8/44	27/8/44	Northolt	3322 2236	Left for UK from Bayeux - B.14 airstrip, Banville. Canadian?
Davenport	RM	F/O	USA	J.18048	401	MH827	SP	9/1/44	Rhubarb	France	Sp, Gib	9/4/44	10/4/44	Lyneham	3319 1869	American in RCAF. Helped by Dutch-Paris. To UK May 1944. DFC (31/10/44). MiD (1/1/45)
David	JAAM	P/O		125991	76	JB871	HAL	10/4/43	Frankfurt	France	Sp, Gib	5/8/43	6/8/43	Portreath	3314 1336	Comet 113. DFC (14/9/43)
Davidson	J	SGT		1003978	12	LM514	LA	3/5/44	Mailly-le-Camp	France	Fr			NK	None	Wounded in firearms accident 26 May 1944. Died 30 June 1944 – but see *Shot Down and on the Run*, p. 92
Davidson	NM	SGT	AUS	A.426794	463	LM589	LA	24/7/44	St Cyr	France	Fr	29/8/44	29/8/44	NK	3345 786	Wounded in left leg. Liberated in Paris hospital 24 August 1944. Interviewed 1 November 1944. Report MISC/INT/786
Davidson	R	F/S		1365234	622	LL782	LA	31/5/44	Trappes	France	Fr	4/9/44	4/9/44	Hendon	3323 2459	Back to UK from Paris
Davidson	RG	SGT	CAN	R.144478	408	HR656	HAL	11/3/43	Stuttgart	France	Sz			NK	NF	In Switzerland 18 March 1943
Davidson	RTP	W/C	CAN	39968	438	MM957	TY	8/5/44	Douai m/y	France	Fr	5/9/44	5/9/44	NK	3322 2345	Canadian in RAF. DFC (1/10/43, 182 Squadron). 143 (RCAF) Wing Leader (438/439/440 Squadrons). Liberated by US troops September 1944. Later, group captain. Transferred to RCAF
Davies	AG	F/O		88131	263	PD506	TY	7/11/44	Railway near Zwolle	Holland	Hol		17/2/45	NK	3352 2375	Met Pilot Officer F. Batterbury. Was rowed to freedom 16 February 1945. Interviewed 17 February 1945. See *Shot Down and on the Run*, pp.115-16
Davies	ER	P/O		173285	19	FB168	MU	11/8/44	Armed recce	France	Fr			NK	3350 1038	Interviewed 30 August 1944. Report IS9/WEA/2/277/1038. Aircraft FB168?. MiD (14/6/45). Chevalier of the Order of Leopold II (Bel) (27/6/47, flight lieutenant)
Davies	HD	SGT		1836026	12	ND424	LA	27/6/44	Vaires	France	Fr	28/7/44	28/7/44	NK	3320 2059	Back by aircraft (with unknown USAAF evader) on night of 27/28 July 1944 from somewhere near Chaillac (Indre), France
Davies	IH	F/O	AUS	A.400528	158	W7750	HAL	6/8/42	Duisburg	Belgium	Fr, Sp, Gib	30/9/42	5/10/42	Greenock	3310 896	Comet 47. Escorted from Paris by Elvire Morelle and Jeanine De Greef. Back on HMS *Malaya*. DFC (5/2/43). See *A Quiet Woman's War*, p.28
Davies	MAI	SGT		1072959	76	JB871	HAL	10/4/43	Frankfurt	France	Sp, Gib	6/6/43	7/6/43	Hendon	3313 1235	Comet 104. DFM (6/7/43). Commissioned (143992) wef 25 March 1943 (gazetted 1/6/43)
Davies	VW	SGT		1580346	10	JD368	HAL	27/8/43	Nuremberg	Belgium	Fr, Sp, Gib	1/1/44	2/1/44	Whitchurch	3317 1664	Comet 231. Commissioned (no. 161692) and flew further operations in Mosquitoes on 627 Squadron. DFC (21/9/45)
Davis	BH	W/O	AUS	A.416563	103	ME722	LA	21/5/44	Duisburg	Holland				NK	NF	

Davis	J	SGT			600	L6616	BL	10/5/40	Waalhaven airfield	Holland	Hol	12/5/40	13/5/40	Harwich	NF	ss3. Probably back aboard HMS *Hereward*. See photo in *The Bristol Blenheim. A Complete History*, p. 189
Davis	NCW	P/O	AUS	A.413835	35	ND759	LA	27/4/44	Friedrichshafen	Switzerland	Fr	8/10/44	8/10/44	Northolt	3324 2640	Came down in Lake Constance. Rowed to Swiss side. Escaped to France with group of repatriates on 4 October 1944. Northolt?
Dawson	CM	SGT		1895949	466	LW116	HAL	22/6/44	Siracourt	France				NK	NF	
Dawson	JG	SGT		1097962	199	BK514	WE	11/12/42	Turin	France	And, Sp, Gib	4/4/43	11/4/43	Liverpool	3312 1160	Crossed to Spain with Major Hasler & Marine Sparks (Operation Frankton). Gave talk about his evasion to 12 Squadron on 6 July 1943
Dawson	R	F/S		1884989	429	LK800	HAL	30/3/44	Nuremberg	Luxembourg	Bel			NK	NF	Marathon. Liberated by US forces on 8 September 1944
Dax	EA	W/O		1338874	295	LK567	ST	26/4/45	SOE supply drop	Denmark	Dk	16/5/45	16/5/45	NK	3327 3041	On supply drop for Danish underground. DFC (14/9/45)
Day	AD	SGT	CAN	R.10263 A	77	Z6826	WH	5/8/41	Frankfurt	Belgium	Fr, Sp, Gib	4/3/42	10/3/42	Gourock	3308 693	Comet 10. Reached Spain 26 December 1941. MiD (11/6/42)
Day	RF	W/O		1890829	295	LK567	ST	26/4/45	SOE supply drop	Denmark	Dk	16/5/45	16/5/45	NK	3327 3052	On supply drop for Danish underground
De Beer	AG	F/O	RHO	131590	582	PB123	LA	8/9/44	Le Havre	France	Fr	13/9/44	13/9/44	NK	3345 675	Captured. Liberated when Fort Tourneville, Le Havre surrendered 12 September 1944. Interviewed 14 September 1944. Report MISC/INT/675. DFC (12/2/46)
De Bruin	AE	SGT		1880577	630	ME796	LA	18/7/44	Revigny-sur-Ornain	France	Fr	9/9/44	9/9/44	NK	3323 2390	See *Massacre over the Marne*
De Larminat	BNM	LT	FRA	F.39453	341	TB497	SP	1/4/45	Armed recce	Holland	Hol			NK	3352 2446	Interviewed 8 April 1945. Report IS9/WEA/1/339/2446
De Merode	WPMG	F/O	BEL	116473	350	AD550	SP	12/12/42	Circus 242	France	And, Sp, Gib	27/3/43	28/3/43	Portreath	3312 1131	Belgian in RAF. Helped by Ponzán network. See *Saturday at M.I.9*, p.203, and *Cockleshell Heroes*, p.217. Died Brussels 22 December 1995
De Mone	HE	SGT	CAN	R.88360	16 OTU	DV763	WE	1/6/42	Essen	Belgium	Fr, Sp, Gib	6/7/42	12/7/42	Gourock	3309 778	Back on the *Narkunda*. Comet 19. DFM (1/9/42). See *Wavetops at my Wingtips*
Denison	HT	SGT		552584	107	R3685	BL	9/6/40	Enemy columns, Poix	France	Fr			NK	NF	Possibly not an evader. Killed in action 30 June 1940
DePape	RAG	SGT	CAN	R.152875	431	LK925	HAL	3/10/43	Kassel	Belgium	Fr, Sp, Gib	19/12/43	20/12/43	Lyneham	3317 1633	Comet 194. With Sergeant Cornelius. Both escorted to Pyrenees by Janine de Greef. MiD (8/6/44). See *The Evaders*, pp. 57-71 - Lavender/Sheffe
De Vetter	L	SGT		1814893	640	LK866	HAL	7/6/44	Versailles	France	Fr			NK	3348 171	Sherwood. Helped by Raymond Picourt. Interviewed 16 August 1944. Report IS9/WEA 20/80/171
Deacon	RMcL	F/O	CAN	J.86384	49	JB473	LA	18/7/44	Revigny-sur-Ornain	France	Fr			NK	3345 634	Wounded. Captured 20 July 1944. Liberated by US troops in Châlons-sur-Marne hospital. Interviewed 2 September 1944. MISC/INT/634
Deakin	AG	SGT		1818772	405	ND344	LA	11/6/44	Tours	France	Fr			NK	3348 32	Liberated by Americans south of Le Mans 9 August 1944. Interviewed 11 August 1944. Report IS9/WEA 8/47/32
Deas	GCT	F/O		150032	164	PD515	TY	13/9/44	NK	Holland				NK	NF	MiD (14/6/45)
Death	GF	F/O	CAN	J.26374	407		WE	26/9/44	A/S patrol off Norway	Norway	Nor	11/10/44	12/10/44	Scalloway	3324 2656	Came back on the "Shetland Bus" service. See *Shot Down and on the Run*, pp. 141-8
Debreyne	A	F/O	CAN	J.24319	419	KB726	LA	12/6/44	Cambrai	France				NK	NF	Same crew as Mynarski VC
Dell	FH	F/O		131049	692	MM184	MOS	14/10/44	Berlin	Germany	Hol	29/3/45	29/3/45	Northolt	3352 2417	Shot down at 29,000 feet. In Holland with Warrant Officer 1 C.O. Huntley and Flying Officer J.A. Strickland. Interviewed 31 March 1945. Report IS9/WEA/1/323/2417
Delorie	FBG	SGT	SEY	1384517	101	W4275	LA	8/7/43	Cologne	France	Sp, Gib	20/12/43	21/12/43	Whitchurch	3317 1637	Burgundy line?
Dench	RLH	F/S		1270915	182	JP552	TY	19/8/43	Ramrod	France	Sp, Gib	15/11/43	16/11/43	Lyneham	3316 1576	Comet 181
Dennehy	FW	F/S			514	LL716	LA	3/8/44	Bois de Cassan	France				NK	NF	Mid-under gunner. Aircraft hit by bombs at 15,000 feet
Dennison	BC	P/O	CAN	J.16008	405	BB250	HAL	11/3/43	Stuttgart	France	Sp, Gib	17/7/43	24/7/43	Liverpool	3314 1325	Oaktree/Burgundy from Brittany to Spain. To UK on SS *Monarch of Bermuda?* Recommended for MiD but awarded DFC (2/11/43, pilot officer J.16008)
Dennstedt	WG	WO2	CAN	R.86155	433	LV840	HAL	22/4/44	Düsseldorf	Holland	Bel			NK	3323 2404	Back in UK by 10 September 1944. Evaded with Warrant Officer A.T. Till RAAF (killed in gunfight with Germans on 21 August 1944)
Dent	AN	SGT		1299327	138	BB340	HAL	12/4/43	SOE	France	Sp, Gib	1/6/43	2/6/43	Hendon	3313 1233	
Derham	J	F/S		1436805	625	LM139	LA	10/6/44	Achères	France				NK	NF	
Desautels	RV	F/O	CAN	J.26303	50	DV312	LA	18/7/44	Revigny-sur-Ornain	France	Fr	28/8/44	28/8/44	Lyneham	3321 2184	ss7. Back on RAF Dakota to UK from Orléans. See *Massacre over the Marne*
Desmond	HWM	F/S		1318659	181	MN819	TY	1/4/45	Offensive operations	Germany				NK	NF	Came down east of Nordhorn. Report IS9/WEA/2/1055/2464
Dickens	JD	SGT		1177399	466	LV943	HAL	6/5/44	Mantes-la-Jolie	France	Fr	18/8/44	18/8/44	Northolt	3321 2082	Sherwood. Left for UK from B.14 airstrip, Banville
Dickerson	RG	SGT		1436082	578	LL584	HAL	11/9/44	Gelsenkirchen	Belgium	Bel	28/9/44	28/9/44	NK	3324 2586	Back to UK from Brussels
Dickie	KJA	F/O		156303	245	MN377	TY	7/6/44	NK	France	Fr	20/8/44	20/8/44	Northolt	3321 2113	Sherwood? Left for UK from Bayeux - B.14 airstrip, Banville. Northolt?

Dicks	JB	SGT	CAN	R.65466	99	X9761	WE	28/9/41	Frankfurt	Belgium	Fr, Sp, Gib	4/3/42	10/3/42	Gourock	3308 696	Solo to Spain. MiD (11/6/42)
Dickson	ED	F/S		572272	103	ED751	LA	5/9/43	Mannheim	France	Sz			NK	NF	In Switzerland 18 September 1943
Dickson	GR	P/O	NZ	NZ.405261	129	MA596	SP	14/7/43	Ramrod	France	Sp, Gib	17/9/43	18/9/43	Lyneham	3315 1408	One of those to fly off aircraft carrier USS *Wasp* to Malta in April 1942. His report states he landed at "Swindon". MiD (14/6/45)
Dickson	RH	F/S		994641	158	NR251	HAL	5/1/45	Hanover	Holland	Hol			NK	3352 2482	With Flight Sergeant P.D. Watson. Liberated by Canadians on 9 April 1945. Interviewed 12 April 1945. Report IS9/WEA/367/2482
Dickson	RJ	SGT	CAN	R.215103	28 OTU	LN896	WE	20/4/44	Nickel	France	Fr	12/7/44	13/7/44	NK	3320 2028	Aircraft ran out of fuel when directed by German radio to Brittany. Back on MGB 503
Diley	JA	SGT		1121583	49	JB473	LA	18/7/44	Revigny-sur-Ornain	France	Fr	3/9/44	3/9/44	NK	3322 2267	See *Massacre over the Marne*
Dillon	CT	P/O		190476	299	LJ942	ST	2/4/45	SOE Tablejam 283	Denmark	Swe	17/4/45	17/4/45	Leuchars	3327 3075	To Sweden on 10 April 1945
Dilworth	AA	F/O	CAN	J.21747	106	LM641	LA	7/8/44	Secqueville	France	Fr			NK	3326 2999	Reached British lines 27 August 1944. Evaded with Sergeant Robert Reiner USAAF. See also AIR 14/2073
Dineen	WW	SGT	CAN	R.251731	44	LM631	LA	7/7/44	St Leu d'Esserent	France	Fr			NK	3323 2359	Liberated 1 September 1944. Back in UK by 6 September 1944
Dinney	W	F/O	CAN	J.22061	550	NE164	LA	28/7/44	Stuttgart	France				NK	NF	
Diver	RA	SGT		1600611	158	LK863	HAL	7/6/44	Versailles	France	Fr			NK	3352 2363	Hidden in Paris with Sergeant A. Herd until its liberation. Interviewed 28 August 1944
Divers	JG	SGT		1126537	158	LW635	HAL	1/6/44	Trappes	France	Fr	27/8/44	27/8/44	Northolt	3321 2202	Met Flying Officer R.H. Riding during evasion. Left for UK from Bayeux - B.14 airstrip, Banville
Dix	JHJ	SGT		1320215	158	JD298	HAL	27/8/43	Nuremberg	Luxembourg	Bel, Fr, Sp, Gib	6/12/43	6/12/43	Portreath	3317 1600	Comet 178. Crossed with two USAAF and 2/Lt J.T. Clary, an American in RAF. Back on a Liberator with no oxygen nor heating. See In *Brave Company* pp. 96-8. Commissioned (155581) wef 29 July 1943 (LG 24/9/43)
Dixon	RK	W/O	AUS	A.421256	463	LM548	LA	21/2/45	Gravenhorst	Holland				NK	NF	
Dmytruk	P	SGT	CAN	R.114740	405	DT745	HAL	11/3/43	Stuttgart	France				NK	None	Killed by Germans 9 December 1943 helping French Maquis blow up a train
Dobson	WE	SGT		1255769	432	LW582	HAL	7/6/44	Achères	France				NK	NF	
Dobson	WF	P/O		170956	50	ND953	LA	3/5/44	Mailly-le-Camp	France	Sp, Gib	21/6/44	22/6/44	Whitchurch	3320 1982	Crossed to Spain with Warrant Officer Ciula, Flying Officer Rosinski and Sergeant D. Shepherd
Dodds	R	SGT	CAN	R.204941	76	MZ531	HAL	7/6/44	Juvisy	France	Fr	31/8/44	31/8/44	Beaulieu	3322 2247	Flown back to Hampshire by USAAF from Étampes
Dodgson	WK	F/L		48777	168	AG477	MU	22/6/44	Sweep	France	Fr			NK	3348 286	Liberated 16 August 1944. Interviewed 27 August 1944. Report IS9/WEA/2/78/286
Dodrill	KS	SGT		581086	8882	R3754	BL	8/6/40	Abbeville	France	Fr			NK	NF	Possibly not an evader. DFC (26/6/42, 107 Sq) as warrant officer. Commissioned 49027 (10/7/42, wef 1/5/42)
Doidge	RW	F/O	CAN		440	MN257	TY	7/6/44	Ramrod	France				NK	NF	
Donaldson	DR	W/C	AUS	A.400631	463	LM597	LA	24/6/44	Prouville	France	Fr			NK	3350 1023	Interviewed 2 September 1944. Report IS9/WEA/2/327/1023. AFC (1/1/46)
Donaldson	LG	SGT		1280330	78	JD108	HAL	13/7/43	Aachen	Belgium	Fr, Sp, Gib	4/9/43	5/9/43	Whitchurch	3314 1390	Comet 125
Donaldson	WA	SGT		1821127	514	LL692	LA	28/7/44	Stuttgart	France	Fr		17/8/44	NK	3321 2110	Sherwood. DFM (3/11/44)
Donmall	NE	P/O		187082	578	NA501	HAL	22/12/44	Bingen	Germany	Ger			NK	3352 2599	Walked into forward US positions 26 December 1945
Donnan	M	SGT	CAN	R.171503	427	LV987	HAL	7/6/44	Achères	France	Fr			NK	3350 1271	Interviewed 1 September 1944. Report IS9/WEA/7/143/1271
Donne	EH	SGT		778976	266	DN562	TY	6/6/44	Recce for tanks	France	Fr	8/6/44	8/6/44	Southampton	3320 1979	
Donnell	AC	P/O	CAN	J.85144	431	MZ522	HAL	27/4/44	Montzen	Belgium	Bel		15/9/44	NK	NF	Liberated by US forces 8 September 1944
Donovan	GH	SGT	CAN	R.190192	434	LW436	HAL	4/8/44	Bois de Cassan	France	Fr	3/9/44	3/9/44	NK	3323 2358	
Doorly	E	F/O	USA	101458	133	BS276	SP	6/9/42	Circus	France	Sp, Gib	27/3/43	27/3/43	Hendon	3312 1129	With Pilot Officer R.S. Smith. See *Aircraft Down!*, pp. 52-105 (Chapter 3)
Doubt	RH	F/O	CAN	J.26935	426	LK883	HAL	12/5/44	Louvain	Belgium	Bel	8/9/44	8/9/44	NK	3323 2378	
Douglas	WM	F/L		151153	635	PB564	LA	5/1/45	Hanover	Holland	Hol			NK	3327 3011	DFC (16/1/45). Liberated circa 15 April 1945
Dowd	AHA	F/O		144347	77	MZ748	HAL	28/6/44	Blainville	France	Fr	30/8/44	30/8/44	NK	3321 2194	DFC (16/1/45)
Dowling	GL	F/S	AUS	A.412500	27 OTU	X3966	WE	23/9/43	Nickel	France	Sp, Gib	6/11/43	7/11/43	Whitchurch	3316 1548	Imprisoned at Barbastro, Spain 11 days. Joined 76 Squadron
Down	JWB	F/S	AUS	A.418086	467	LM450	LA	24/6/44	Prouville	France	Fr	6/9/44	6/9/44	NK	3324 2543	
Downe	EH	SGT			266	DN562	TY	6/6/44	NK	France				NK	NF	
Downie	JA	SGT		1367061	100	LM658	LA	12/8/44	Brunswick	Holland	Hol			NK	3352 2456	Interviewed 8 April 1945. Report IS9/WEA/2/1050
Doyle	KJ	F/S	CAN	R.157883	432	LW592	HAL	27/4/44	Montzen	Belgium	Bel	6/9/44	6/9/44	NK	3322 2316	Marathon. Back to UK from France
Doyle	WA	F/O	CAN	J.22160	132	NH575	SP	20/8/44	Vehicles	France	Fr	27/8/44	27/8/44	NK	3345 806	Shot in jaw. In hospital treated by nuns. No Germans about. Liberated 25 August 1944. Flown back to Basingstoke hospital. Interviewed 27 November

																1944. Report MISC/INT/806
Drage	AW	F/O		135745	103	JB732	LA	10/4/44	Aulnoye	France				NK	NF	
Draper	PG	SGT	CAN		425	MZ573	HAL	24/4/44	Karlsruhe	Holland				NK	NF	
Drechsler	WW	F/S	CAN	R.75287	150	BJ877	WE	16/9/42	Essen	Belgium	Fr, Sp, Gib	24/2/43	24/2/43	Portreath	3312 1093	Walked for twenty-five days from Belgium before reaching Unoccupied France. Back to UK by B-17 with Flying Officer A.R. Haines. DFM (14/5/43)
Dromlewicz	A	P/O	POL	P.2857	308	MJ787	SP	15/3/45	Enemy positions	Holland	Hol			NK	3348 192	Interviewed 11 May 1945. Report IS9/WEA/PLM/192
Drongeson	RS	SGT		1833280	166	JB649	LA	25/7/44	Stuttgart	France	Fr	8/9/44	8/9/44	Middle Wallop	3323 2450	Back from Orléans with 1 SAS
Drover	JE	SGT	CAN	R.191697	50	W4824	LA	6/8/44	Bois de Cassan	France				NK	NF	
Druett	EJ	SGT		575323	434	LK801	HAL	16/6/44	Sterkrade	Holland				NK	NF	
Drummond	MKP	F/S	NZ	NZ.425389	75	NE148	LA	28/7/44	Stuttgart	France	Fr			NK	3348 315	Broke leg on landing. Liberated 14 August 1944. Interviewed 17 August 1944. Report IS9/WEA/2/200/315. See *Night After Night*, pp.353-4
Dryland	R	F/O		162837	3	EJ747	TEM	24/12/44	Patrol	Belgium				NK	NF	DFC (27/10/44) for having destroyed a total of eighteen flying-bombs, five of them on one day
Drylie	J	F/O		140868	106	NE150	LA	6/6/44	Coutances	France	Fr		11/8/44	NK	3348 13	Liberated by US troops 17 July 1944. Report IS9/WEA 7/3/13. See also AIR 14/464
Dubé	HE	P/O	CAN	R.96579	425	LW591	HAL	24/4/44	Karlsruhe	France				NK	None	Killed by Germans 8 August 1944. Officially presumed dead 6 November 1944
Duchesnay	AAHJNA	F/O	CAN	J.11502	10	LV867	HAL	22/4/44	Düsseldorf	Holland	Bel, Fr, Sp, Gib	10/7/44	11/7/44	Whitchurch	3320 2020	In Toulouse 1 June 1944. Helped by Françoise Dissard. Identified at her house by Lieutenant Commander "Billie" Stephens. DFC (22/9/44)
Duffee	GWH	SGT		1384785	78	JB855	HAL	22/6/43	Mülheim	Holland	Bel, Fr, Sp, Gib	11/10/43	12/10/43	Valley	3315 1465	Comet 143. (Lyneham or Valley? - see Flying Officer J.C. Allison and Sergeant E.A. Bridge RCAF). DFC (17/7/45) (as flying officer 175105)
Dumbrell	AG	P/O		159001	408	DS704	LA	20/12/43	Frankfurt	Belgium	Bel			NK	3350 1233	Marathon. Interviewed 13 September 1944. Report IS9/WEA/2/440/1233.
Dumont	FJ	W/O	FRA	F.39972	342	BZ390	BOS	4/8/44	MT in Falaise area	France	Fr			NK	3349 353	Took off at 0230 hours, 5 August. Liberated by US troops 17 August 1944. Interviewed 21 August 1944. Report IS9/WEA/2/177/353
Dumsday	WJ	P/O	CAN	J.17761	180	FL190	MCL	30/8/43	V1 site, Watten	France	Sp, Gib	29/11/43	30/11/43	Whitchurch	3316 1593	Burgundy line
Duncan	JD	SGT	CAN	R.119731	9	ED480	LA	9/7/43	Gelsenkirchen	France	Sp, And, Gib	1/9/43	2/9/43	Whitchurch	3314 1388	
Duncliffe	DA	P/O		174413	514	DS818	LA	12/6/44	Gelsenkirchen	Holland	Hol			NK	3327 3016	Flown back from Brussels end of April 1945
Dungey	EB	SGT	CAN	R.108567	408	JB913	HAL	3/7/43	Cologne	Belgium	Fr, Sp, Gib	11/10/43	12/10/43	Lyneham	3315 1460	Helped by "Service EVA" until 8 September 1943. Helped by Anne Brusselmans. Comet 145. Sailed from Seville for Gibraltar on Norwegian ship *Sneland I* on 8 October 1943
Dunseith	S	F/S	CAN	R.191859	300	LM178	LA	24/7/44	Stuttgart	France	Fr	18/8/44	18/8/44	NK	3324 2554	Wounded. Sherwood. Treated in hospital in le Mans
Durber	WE	SGT		1578491	630	LM269	LA	18/8/44	Bordeaux	France	Fr			NK	3350 1330	Interviewed 10 September 1944. Report IS9/WEA/MB/1330
Durham	AN	W/O	AUS	A.413305	514	DS822	LA	7/6/44	Massy-Palaiseau	France				NK	3349	
Durland	EG	SGT		1582432	514	LM180	LA	12/8/44	Rüsselsheim	Belgium	Bel	7/9/44	7/9/44	Newbury	3323 2364	Broke ankle. Handed himself over to Germans on 13 August 1944. To St Gilles prison hospital. "Ghost Train" 3 September 1944
Duval	HP	P/O	CAN	63092	258	Z3346	HUR	8/7/41	Circus 39	France	Sp, Gib	26/8/41	26/8/41	Calshot	3305 489	Burgundy line. Flown back by Sunderland. MiD (11/6/42). Killed in action on 27 April 1942 in Spitfire AA834, 403 (RCAF) Squadron. French-Canadian from Quebec
Dyer	FSW	P/O	AUS	A.417820	233	KG399	DAK	21/9/44	Supply drop	Holland	Hol			NK	5415 2025	Report IS9/WEA/2/578/2025
Dyer	WH	SGT		1381730	99	X9761	WE	28/9/41	Frankfurt	Belgium	Fr, Sp, Gib	4/3/42	10/3/42	Gourock	3308 692	MM (26/5/42). See AIR 2/5684
Dykes	ED	SGT	CAN	R.212033	82 OTU	BJ790	WE	16/8/44	Nickel	France	Fr			NK	3348 279	Interviewed 18 August 1944. Report IS9/WEA/8/504/279
Dyson	DJ	W/O	AUS	A.427309	460	ND674	LA	11/5/44	Hasselt	Belgium	Bel	10/9/44	10/9/44	Northolt	3323 2412	
Eagleson	OD	F/O	NZ	NZ.421689	486	NV722	TEM	2/5/45	Offensive operations	Germany				NK	NF	DFC (8/12/44, warrant officer) awarded for destruction of twenty-one flying bombs
East	TH	SGT		1811467	630	LM262	LA	7/8/44	Secqueville	France				NK	NF	
Easton	GH	SGT		751228	40	R3609	BL	14/8/40	Chartres	France	Sp, Gib	4/7/41	12/7/41	Glasgow	3305 445	Caught pneumonia in March 1941 while at Gibraltar. MiD (11/6/42)
Ebenrytter	EZ	F/L	POL	P.0103	302	ML358	SP	14/10/44	Armed recce	Holland				NK	3348 2306	Captured. Escaped from train taking him to Germany. Interviewed 21 November 1944. Report IS9/WEA/2/1006/2306
Eberley	H	P/O	CAN	J.89727	49	PB568	LA	21/2/45	Gravenhorst	Holland	Hol			NK	3352 2468	With Flight Sergeant M.H. Makofski. Liberated by Irish Guards 1 April 1945. Interviewed 8 April 1945. Report IS9/WEA/1/338/2468

Eckel	CEB	SGT		1394888	247	JP381	TY	15/2/44	Ramrod	France	Fr	4/9/44	5/9/44	Weymouth	3324 2770	Taken to Paris by André Rougeyron. Left Allied beachhead "near Carentan". From the West Indies
Eddy	WEM	F/L		126609	103	ND417	LA	25/2/44	Augsburg	Belgium	Fr, Sp, Gib	26/4/44	27/4/44	Hendon	3319 1889	Comet 269. See his story in *Home Run* (Bickers), Chapter 9, and see *Rendezvous 127*, pp. 120, 122, 123. DSO (16/6/44), DFC (23/3/45)
Edgerley	MW	F/O	AUS	A.417466	467	R5485	LA	18/7/44	Revigny-sur-Ornain	France	Fr	3/9/44	3/9/44	NK	3325 2896	See *Massacre over the Marne*
Edinborough	B	W/O		1382058	90	EF147	ST	5/3/44	SOE	France	Sp, Gib	2/5/44	3/5/44	Hendon	3319 1906	Helped by the Lefèvre family in Juvisy-sur-Orge. Burgundy line. With Flight Sergeant P.A. Tansley. DFC (25/7/44)
Edwards	JKO	F/L		123886	271	KG444	DAK	21/9/44	Arnhem supply drop	Holland	Hol	29/9/44	29/9/44	Down Ampney	NF	Shot down close to British lines. Suffered burns to face. Rescued by Dutch patriots. After treatment for burns in Brussels, hitched a lift in a 48 Squadron Dakota to RAF Down Ampney. DFC (30/1/45)
Edwards	NCM	F/O		52704	297		ALB	28/5/44	Supply drop	France	Fr			NK	3350 1282	Interviewed 17 August 1944. Report IS9/WEA/8/507/1282
Edwards	W	F/O			107	P4905	BL	12/5/40	Bridges	Belgium	Fr			NK	NF	DFC
Eggleston	WH	SGT		1671485	76	MZ531	HAL	7/6/44	Juvisy	France	Fr	31/8/44	31/8/44	NK	3322 2249	
Elder	A	SGT	CAN	R.215179	28 OTU	LN896	WE	20/4/44	Nickel	France	Fr	12/7/44	13/7/44	NK	3320 2029	Aircraft ran out of fuel when directed by German radio to Brittany. Back by MGB 503
Elderton	FE	SGT	CAN	R.128913	429	MZ362	HAL	25/7/44	Stuttgart	France	Fr			NK	NF	
Eldridge	DRG	SGT		1334644	51	HR839	HAL	28/6/43	Cologne	Belgium	Fr, Sp, Gib	4/9/43	5/9/43	Whitchurch	3314 1389	On detachment from 1663 HCU. Comet 126
Eliot	NS	F/O	AUS	A.415242	218	EF259	ST	1/5/44	Chambly	France	Fr	18/8/44	18/8/44	Northolt	3321 2119	Sherwood. Left for UK from B.14 airstrip, Banville
Ellement	CAE	F/O	CAN	J.36347	411	NH380	SP	20/1/45	Armed recce	Holland				NK	NF	Shot down near Zutphen. Also evaded on 21 April 1945
Ellement	CAE	F/O	CAN	J.36347	411	PL283	SP	21/4/45	Armed recce	Germany	Hol			NK	3352 2404	Baled out near Kiel. Interviewed 17 March 1945. Report IS9/WEA/1/311/2404. Also evaded on 20 January 1945
Elliott	FE	F/O	CAN	J.86622	166	NE170	LA	29/8/44	Agenville	France	Fr	7/9/44	7/9/44	NK	3322 2280	
Elliott	JMcP	F/O		134165	57	W4822	LA	3/11/43	Düsseldorf	Belgium	Fr, Sp, Gib	1/1/44	2/1/44	Whitchurch	3317 1662	Comet 223
Elliott	WJ	F/O	CAN	J.25837	424	HX313	HAL	27/5/44	Bourg-Léopold	Belgium	Bel	12/9/44	12/9/44	Heston	3350 1317	"Ghost Train" 3 September 1944 - see M. Muir. Back to UK from Paris. Interviewed 11 September 1944. Report IS9/WEA/MB/1317
Elliotte	JMcG	F/O	NZ	NZ.427969	75	HK567	LA	7/8/44	Mare de Magne	France	Fr	30/8/44	30/8/44	Northolt	3322 2226	
Ellis	CW	F/S	CAN	R.182994	640	LW654	HAL	10/8/44	Dijon	France	Fr			NK	NF	
Ellison	HG	W/O	NZ	NZ.415304	602	NH366	SP	26/8/44	Armed recce	France	Fr			NK	3350 1288	Liberated 1 September 1944. Interviewed 4 September 1944. Report IS9/WEA/1/131/1288
Elmhirst-Baxter	JC	F/L		119545	625	PB126	LA	30/6/44	Vierzon	France	Fr	18/8/44	18/8/44	Northolt	3321 2124	Sherwood. Left for UK from Bayeux - B.14 airstrip, Banville
Elt	KW	SGT		906012	405	DT745	HAL	11/3/43	Stuttgart	France	Sp, Gib	5/8/43	11/8/43	Liverpool	3314 1351	Commissioned (155556) 12 October 1943 (wef 30/8/43). Recommended for MiD but awarded DFM (7/1/44). See *Valley of the Shadow of Death*, pp.91-4
Embling	JRA	W/C		36035	77	W7916	HAL	2/12/42	Frankfurt	France	And, Sp, Gib	7/3/43	8/3/43	Hendon	3312 1108	Captured on landing. Escaped from train same day (4 December 1942). DSO (2/4/43)
Embry	BE	W/C		9252	107	L9391	BL	27/5/40	St Omer	France	Sp, Gib	27/7/40	2/8/40	Plymouth	3299 41a	Back on HMS *Vidette*. ACM Sir Basil GCB, KBE (5/7/45), DSO (13/9/38) & 3 bars (30/4/40, 20/8/40, 20/7/45), DFC (22/6/45), AFC (1/1/26), MiD (24/9/41, 11/6/42, 1/1/46). Author of *Mission Completed*
Emeny	RT	SGT		1383167	207	ND556	LA	3/5/44	Mailly-le-Camp	France	Sp, Gib	24/6/44	25/6/44	Whitchurch	3320 2001	Suffered burns to the head. Briefly with Flight Sergeant Pittwood. Comet 288. See *Not Just Another Milk Run...*, pp. 45-57
Engstrom	VGW	P/O		41687	40	R3692	BL	6/6/40	St Valéry	France	Fr			NK	NF	Shot down in battle zone. Wounded. The other two of his crew became prisoners of war. Admitted to hospital at Uxbridge. Died on 16 February 1943
Evans	AR	SGT		1379093	102	R9528	HAL	27/4/42	Dunkirk	France	Gib	29/8/42	8/9/42	Gourock	3310 836	Machine-gunned as he parachuted down. MM (1/12/42)
Evans	B	F/S		755262	15 OTU	R1791	WE	30/5/42	Cologne	Belgium	Fr, Sp, Gib	18/8/42	19/8/42	Whitchurch	3310 809	DFM (7/4/42, 108 Squadron). Comet 29. Flown back aboard BOAC Dakota. MiD (1/1/43)
Evans	CF	F/O		158560	298	LL407	HAL	6/6/44	Dropping troops	France	Fr	11/6/44	12/6/44	Port of London	3320 1964	Dropping parachutists in support of the D-Day landings
Evans	DA	F/O	CAN	J.27506	106	ME789	LA	7/7/44	St Leu d'Esserent	France	Fr			NK	NF	
Evans	DH	F/L	CAN	J.5478	411	MK462	SP	15/7/44	Armed recce	France	Fr			NK	3349 373	Interviewed 25 August 1944. Report IS9(WEA)/2/193/373
Evans	FEO	F/S	NZ	NZ.422202	138	LL308	HAL	8/8/44	SOE	France	Fr	8/9/44	8/9/44	NK	3323 2362	ss7. See *Night After Night*, pp. 385-8, and *Chronique des Années Noires ...*, Chapter 14
Evans	FO	F/S	AUS	A.417950	625	PB126	LA	30/6/44	Vierzon	France	Fr	18/8/44	18/8/44	Northolt	3321 2123	Sherwood. Left for UK from Bayeux - B.14 airstrip, Banville
Evans	G	SGT		1652049	138	BB340	HAL	12/4/43	SOE	France	Sp, Gib	6/6/43	7/6/43	Hendon	3313 1234	

Evans	JH	F/S		658281	158	HX334	HAL	12/5/44	Hasselt	Belgium	Bel			NK	3350 1140	Marathon. Liberated 4 September 1944. Interviewed 6 September 1944. Report IS9/WEA/MB/1140. See his biography *Airman Missing*
Evans	PJ	SGT		1387533	625	ME697	LA	3/5/44	Mailly-le-Camp	France	Sp, Gib	23/6/44	24/6/44	Lyneham	3320 1992	Burgundy line, with Sergeant J.McK. Alexander. Report states landed UK at "Swindon"
Evans	RC	F/O	CAN	J.27154	161	LL183	HAL	9/5/44	SOE	France	Fr	9/9/44	9/9/44	Tempsford	3323 2413	
Everiss	SF	P/O		126042	90	BK725	ST	16/4/43	Mannheim	France	And, Sp, Gib	27/6/43	28/6/43	Hendon	3313 1271	Damaged collarbone and broke two ribs. Helped by Chauny/Burgundy lines
Ewan	WH	F/S		659033	257	MN713	TY	16/7/44	Armed recce	France	Fr			NK	3348 308	Interviewed 17 August 1944. Report IS9/WEA/2/87/308
Eyre	SH	F/S		650325	207	L7547	LA	14/2/43	Milan	France	Sz, Fr, Sp, Gib	23/2/44	24/2/44	Whitchurch	3318 1783	Left Switzerland 8 January 1944 with seven other internees
Eyton-Williams	R	P/O		78528	82	P6925	BL	13/6/40	Tanks, Forêt de Gault	France	Fr			NK	NF	Possibly not an evader
Ezra	WA	SGT		1602682	640	MZ855	HAL	12/8/44	Rüsselsheim	Belgium	Bel			Hendon	3350 1338	With Belgian Resistance. Commissioned (182818) 26 September 1944 (wef 6/8/44). Interviewed 10 September 1944. Report no. IS9/WEA/MB/1338. See *Bomber Boys*, Chapter 6
Fagan	AFJ	SGT		1822435	207	ME805	LA	7/7/44	St Leu d'Esserent	France	Fr	2/9/44	2/9/44	NK	3322 2260	Left for UK from Évreux
Fairborn	DWR	SGT	CAN	R.108554	429	MZ362	HAL	25/7/44	Stuttgart	France	Fr	18/8/44	18/8/44	Northolt	3321 2089	Sherwood
Faircloth	LJ	SGT		1894767	12	ND424	LA	27/6/44	Vaires	France	Sp, Gib	9/8/44	10/8/44	Whitchurch	3321 2069	
Fairclough	T	W/O		1077120	103	ME449	LA	12/3/45	Mining	Denmark	Dk	29/3/45	29/3/45	NK	3326 2938	On 550 Squadron, attached to 103 Squadron. To Sweden on 23 March 1945. Back to UK from Stockholm
Fairfax	NT	F/O		129938	107	BZ237	BOS	27/8/43	Gosnay power station	France	Sp, Gib	6/11/43	7/11/43	Whitchurch	3316 1536	Comet 160. Crossed Pyrenees in party of 14 - see Pilot Officer R.J.A. Macleod. See *Home Run*, Chapter 7 (Bickers). MiD (8/6/44)
Fairfield	EH	F/L	CAN		443	MJ444	SP	13/1/45	Armed recce	Belgium				NK	NF	Baled out near Liège. Possibly not an evader
Fairweather	P	SGT			7	JA682	LA	12/8/43	Milan	France				NK	NF	Nothing found for this airman
Fajtl	F	S/L	CZ	82544	122	BM210	SP	5/5/42	Circus 157	Belgium	Fr, Sp, Gib	21/8/42	22/8/42	Hendon	3310 814	Flown back to UK by Hudson. DFC (approved 10/11/42) presented to him at RAF Churchstanton on 28 November 1942. Died 4 October 2006. Hendon
Falcon-Scott	C	SGT	AUS	A.391847	75	T2474	WE	22/12/40	Mannheim	France	Sp, Gib	26/8/41	26/8/41	Calshot	3306 499	Wounded. Captured by Germans. Escaped from Paris hospital
Falcus	R	SGT		1479674	78	JD108	HAL	13/7/43	Aachen	Belgium	Fr, Sp, Gib	3/11/43	4/11/43	NK	3316 1554	In Spanish jail with Sergeant D.W.G. Cowell
Falkowski	JP	W/C	POL	P.0493	303	BS281	SP	9/3/45	Armed recce	Holland	Hol			NK	3352 3048	VM, KW, DFC. OC 3 (Polish) Wing. Briefly captured. Escaped by 15 March 1945. Interviewed 9 May 1945. Report IS9/WEA/1/407/3048
Fargher	TP	F/S		1511188	234	AA973	SP	11/7/44	Rhubarb	France	Fr	24/7/44	24/7/44	Dartmouth	3320 2057	Back by MGB 502 from Brittany. See *Spitfire Mark V In Action*, pp. 209-10 (Peter Caygill, Airlife Publishing, Shrewsbury, 2001)
Farmer	WW	SGT		1851445	10	HX295	HAL	26/3/44	Essen	Belgium	Fr			NK	3350 1370	False papers prepared by Ann Brusselmans. Liberated by US troops 11 September 1944. Interviewed 24 September 1944. Report IS9/WEA/2/527/1370.
Farnbank	RM	F/O		152050	158	LK877	HAL	1/6/44	Trappes	France	Fr	28/8/44	28/8/44	Northolt	3321 2203	Liberated on 25 August 1944. Left for UK from Bayeux- B.14 airstrip, Banville
Farr	TW	F/O	CAN	J.26297	427	LV987	HAL	7/6/44	Achères	France	Fr	30/8/44	30/8/44	Heston	3322 2248	
Fay	AE	F/S	CAN	R.61629	78	W1061	HAL	11/8/42	Mainz	Belgium	Fr, Sp, Gib	7/11/42	7/11/42	Portreath	3311 973	Comet 49. Travelled with Flying Officer Rowicki from Brussels to Spain. DFM (5/2/43)
Fearman	GC	SGT		1262356	514	DS815	LA	22/3/44	Frankfurt	France	Fr	19/9/44	20/9/44	NK	3324 2557	Back to UK from Algiers
Feary	KJ	SGT		1813068	115	HK579	LA	8/9/44	Le Havre	France	Fr	13/9/44	13/9/44	NK	3345 672	Captured. Liberated when Fort Tourneville, Le Havre surrendered 12 September 1944. Interviewed 14 September 1944. Report MISC/INT/672
Fedoruk	M	SGT	CAN	R.159150	44	ME672	LA	24/3/44	Berlin	Holland	Hol	13/4/45	13/4/45	NK	3326 2995	ss7. Liberated by Canadians 9 April 1945. See AIR 14/2073
Fee	J	F/L	AUS	A.405578	106	PB359	LA	19/9/44	Mönchengladbach	Germany				NK	NF	Service number?
Feeley	JH	SGT	CAN	R.163474	82 OTU	BJ790	WE	16/8/44	Nickel	France	Fr			NK	3348 281	Interviewed 18 August 1944.Report IS9/WEA/8/506/281
Fell	WE	SGT	CAN	R.118571	428	LK739	HAL	20/1/44	Berlin	France	Sp, Gib	5/5/44	6/5/44	NK	3319 1907	
Fellows	AR	SGT		1818897	61	ME732	LA	23/9/44	Ladbergen	Holland	Hol			NK	3352 2454	Interviewed 8 April 1945. Report IS9/WEA/2/1051/2454
Fenney	S	SGT		591917	44	ME634	LA	7/7/44	St Leu d'Esserent	France				NK	NF	
Ferguson	D	SGT		1021760	7	BK760	ST	10/4/43	Frankfurt	Belgium	Fr, Sp, Gib	21/6/43	22/6/43	Whitchurch	3313 1254	Back by Dakota. Died on 24 November 1943 - circumstances not known. Has no known grave
Ferguson	KD	F/S	AUS	A.423234	626	LM633	LA	20/7/44	Courtrai	Belgium	Fr			NK	NF	
Fernyhough	GW	P/O		169205	10	LV867	HAL	22/4/44	Düsseldorf	Holland	Bel	8/9/44	8/9/44	Northolt	3323 2534	With Squadron Leader J.H. Trobe DFC. Back to UK from Brussels-Evère. DFC (7/11/44)

Feveyear	RA	SGT		1875006	166	JB649	LA	25/7/44	Stuttgart	France	Fr	8/9/44	8/9/44	Middle Wallop	3323 2448	Back from Orléans with 1 SAS
Fiddick	RL	F/O	CAN	J.29707	622	L7576	LA	28/7/44	Stuttgart	France	Fr	2/10/44	2/10/44	Northolt	3324 2631	
Fidler	R	SGT		1549502	100	LM333	LA	23/8/43	Berlin	Holland	Bel, Fr	22/1/44	23/1/44	Falmouth	3318 1717	Helped by "Service EVA" until 22 October 1943. With both Bordeaux and Burgundy lines. Back to UK from Brittany aboard the *Breizh-Izel*
Fidler	RA	F/S		1320670	515	PZ440	MOS	30/9/44	Day Ranger	Switzerland	Fr	31/12/44	31/12/44	Bovingdon	3325 2836	Crossed into Switzerland on 26 October 1944. Escaped to France with several other RAF internees on 22 December 1944. See *Confounding the Reich*, pp. 79-81; *Infringing Neutrality...*, pp.155-64
Fielden	J	SGT		1052822	1 PRU	DK310	MOS	24/8/42	PR, Italy	Switzerland	Fr, Sp, Gib	22/12/42	23/12/42	Whitchurch	3311 1007	No. 1 PRU. Shot down on Belp airfield, near Berne. Repatriated 17 December 1942. KIA 18 September 1944 as 141154 flying officer DFC (15/9/44) on 544 Squadron
Figuiere	G	SGC	FRA		329	NH548	SP	26/8/44	Patrol	France					NF	Wounded, and briefly taken prisoner
Findlay	AC	F/O	AUS	A.415937	467	PB299	LA	19/9/44	Mönchengladbach	Holland	Bel	24/9/44	24/9/44	NK	3324 2570	
Finlay	DD	F/S		1390619	429	LK800	HAL	30/3/44	Nuremberg	Luxembourg				NK	NF	DFM (23/3/45)
Finn	JPT	SGT	EIR	1029363	466	MZ313	HAL	18/7/44	Vaires	France	Fr	18/8/44	18/8/44	Northolt	3321 2104	Sherwood
Firestone	EH	F/S	CAN	R.174494	407		WE	26/9/44	A/S patrol off Norway	Norway	Nor	11/10/44	12/10/44	Scalloway	3324 2660	Came back on the "Shetland Bus" service. *See Shot Down and on the Run*, pp. 141-8
Firth	JW	SGT		1453649	578	MZ563	HAL	22/4/44	Düsseldorf	Holland	Bel			NK	3323 2532	With Sergeant Duchesnay. Back in UK by 7 September 1944
Fisher	AR	F/O	CAN	J.22571	428	LK739	HAL	20/1/44	Berlin	France	Sp, Gib	1/5/44	2/5/44	Whitchurch	3319 1893	Burgundy line?
Fisher	GC	F/L	CAN	J.4690	408	AE197	HN	28/8/42	Saarbrücken	Belgium	Fr, Gib	30/9/42	5/10/42	Greenock	3310 889	Evacuated by *Seawolf* 21 September 1942. Back on HMS *Malaya*. DFC (24/11/42)
Fisher	HHJ	P/O		169870	218	EH942	ST	22/4/44	Laon	France	Fr	6/9/44	6/9/44	Tempsford	3322 2281	Flown back by Hudson of 161 (SD) Squadron with Pilot Officer D.H. Courtenay. Tempsford?
Fisher	JM	SGT		1499791	76	LL116	HAL	20/1/44	Berlin	France				NK	NF	
Fitzgerald	WJ	SGT	NZ	NZ.413875	90	BK725	ST	16/4/43	Mannheim	France	And, Sp, Gib	5/8/43	11/8/43	Liverpool	3314 1350	With Chauny/Burgundy lines
Flather	GEH	SGT		1592448	432	LK807	HAL	27/4/44	Montzen	Belgium	Bel	7/9/44	7/9/44	NK	3322 2272	Marathon. Flown back from France after liberation
Fletcher	IB	SGT		1594462	467	DV171	LA	24/9/44	Calais	France				NK	NF	
Flintoft	JD	F/O	CAN	J.37127	440	PD592	TY	24/2/45	Railways	Holland	Hol	5/4/45	5/4/45	NK	3326 2943	Liberated by British troops 1 April 1945. Back to UK from Belgium
Flower	LN	P/O		184079	161	LK238	ST	6/10/44	SOE Tablejam 104/26B	Denmark	Swe	7/11/44	8/11/44	Leuchars	3324 2755	With Flight Lieutenant W.J. Parks. Left for Sweden on 26 October 1944. DFC (27/3/45)
Flynn	WJ	F/S	AUS	A.424170	460	NE116	LA	22/6/44	Reims	France	Fr			NK	3350 1284	Sherwood. Interviewed 17 August 1944. Report IS9/WEA/8/148/1284
Foden	DR	F/S	AUS	A.428495	78	MZ692	HAL	22/6/44	Laon	France				NK	NF	Report IS9/WEA/**/1498
Foley	AJ	F/S		658426	625	PB126	LA	30/6/44	Vierzon	France	Fr	18/8/44	18/8/44	Northolt	3321 2126	Sherwood. Left for UK from Bayeux - B.14 airstrip, Banville
Foley	LG	F/L		142901	83	JB402	LA	3/5/44	Mailly-le-Camp	France				NK	NF	DFC (26/10/45). See *Shot Down and on the Run*, p. 91
Foley	WE	F/S	AUS	A.421799	582	ND921	LA	28/6/44	Blainville	France	Fr	6/9/44	6/9/44	NK	3323 2370	Left for UK from Bayeux - B.14 airstrip, Banville
Forbes	CRS	SGT		798513	10	W1041	HAL	27/4/42	*Tirpitz*, Norway	Norway	Swe	29/9/42	29/9/42	Leuchars	3310 866	Left from Stockholm
Forbes	RAL	F/O	CAN	J.29395	419	KB731	LA	12/6/44	Cambrai	France	Fr			NK	3350 1372	Interviewed 20 September 1944. Report IS9/WEA/2/498/1372
Forbes	WD	F/O	CAN	J.27497	61	PA162	LA	3/8/44	Trossy-St Maximin	France				NK	NF	ss7
Ford	JA	SGT	AUS	A.410968	576	ND783	LA	6/5/44	Aubigne	France				NK	NF	
Ford	JB	SGT		1217375	90	BK725	ST	16/4/43	Mannheim	France	Sp, Gib	17/7/43	24/7/43	Liverpool	3314 1327	Helped by Chauny/Oaktree/Burgundy lines. Back to UK on *Monarch of Bermuda*
Forde	DN	F/O		41526	145	R7231	SP	23/7/41	Sweep	France	Sp, Gib	12/10/41	12/10/41	Mount Batten	3306 569	Flown back by Catalina. Evaded with Sergeants Lockhart and Mensik. MiD (1/1/43, flight lieutenant), DFC (26/2/43, 72 Squadron). R of R7231 is a guess
Forland	OW	F/S	CAN	R.84207	426	HE905	WE	12/5/43	Duisburg	Belgium	Fr, Sp, Gib	13/7/43	14/7/43	Whitchurch	3314 1300	Flown back after a week aboard TSS *Samaria* in Gibraltar harbour
Forman	CM	F/O	CAN	J.25870	300	LM178	LA	24/7/44	Stuttgart	France	Fr	18/8/44	18/8/44	Northolt	3321 2130	Wounded. Sherwood. His wrist-watch was found by a French farmer and returned to him nearly sixty years later. Northolt?
Forman	JM	F/L	CAN	J.15236	428	LK913	HAL	15/9/43	Montluçon	France	Fr	15/11/43	16/11/43	Tangmere	3316 1571	Leg injured. Back by Lysander on Operation Water Pistol. DFC (17/7/45)
Forster	R	SGT		1053891	142	DF550	WE	16/9/42	Essen	France	Sp, Gib	19/4/43	20/4/43	Hendon	3313 1173	Evaded with Squadron Leader Barnard and Pilot Officer Glensor. Met McBeath in Spain. See *Safe Houses Are Dangerous*, p. 211
Forster	TW	SGT		1567659	15	W4355	LA	15/3/44	Stuttgart	Switzerland	Fr	23/12/44	24/12/44	NK	3325 2833	Departed Switzerland 24 December 1944. Back to UK from Marseille
Forsyth	DA	F/O	CAN	J.24214	625	LM139	LA	10/6/44	Achères	France				NK	NF	
Forsyth	JH	SGT	CAN	R.86422	21 OTU	W5618	WE	1/6/42	Essen	Belgium	Fr			None	None	Killed on 6 June 1942 by express train at Chalon-sur-Saône railway station,

																France
Fortune	W	SGT		1369450	49	JB473	LA	18/7/44	Revigny-sur-Ornain	France	Fr			Dover	NF	Liberated by US forces. Returned from Arromanches in an LCT. See *Massacre over the Marne*
Forwell	EW	F/L		116379	3400	PA870	SP	7/6/44	NK	France	Fr			NK	3350 1076	DFC (1/10/43). Interviewed 5 September 1944. Report IS9/WEA/2/248/1076. Belonged to 34 Wing. Shot down in a 16 Squadron aircraft
Foster	DC	SGT		1490330	149	EE880	ST	28/6/43	Cologne	Belgium	Fr, Sp, Gib	17/9/43	18/9/43	Lyneham	3315 1406	Comet 131. See *Night After Night* pp. 264-6
Foster	DF	WO2	CAN	R.136520	427	LV987	HAL	7/6/44	Achères	France	Fr			NK	3350 1268	Interviewed 1 September 1944. Report IS9/WEA/7/140/1268
Foster	GT	SGT		1583331	138	Z9232	WH	24/8/42	SOE	France	Sp, Gib	30/9/42	5/10/42	Greenock	3310 883	Evacuated by *Seawolf* 21 September 1942. Back on HMS *Malaya*
Foster	K	SGT		1827859	103	ME449	LA	12/3/45	Mining	Denmark	Swe			NK	NF	Made contact with two Danes at Lyne and was soon sent via Ølgod to Sweden
Fowler	CR	SGT		1874701	75	LM268	LA	11/9/44	Mining	Germany	Dk, Swe	27/9/44	27/9/44	Leuchars	3324 2582	Landed near Stettin. Left for UK from Stockholm. Leuchars?
Fox	A	F/S		1539935	514	LL727	LA	7/6/44	Massy-Palaiseau	France				NK	NF	R. Fox?
Fox	CC	SGT		1018963	158	W7750	HAL	6/8/42	Duisburg	Belgium	Fr, Sp, Gib	30/9/42	5/10/42	Greenock	3310 899	Comet 48. Escorted from Paris by Elvire Morelle and Jeanine De Greef. Back on HMS *Malaya*. DFM (5/2/43). Killed in action (146839 flight lieutenant) 24/25 May 1944 (Aachen) still on 158 Squadron
Foy	JH	F/L	CAN	J.15609	405	HR854	HAL	15/7/43	Montbéliard	France	Sp, Gib	9/4/44	10/4/44	Lyneham	3319 1868	DFC (13/8/43), MiD (1/1/45)
Frame	JH	WO2	CAN	R.167560	405	ND526	LA	24/5/44	Aachen	Holland	Hol			NK	3350 1378	Evaded with J. Hooks. Interviewed 23 September 1944. Report IS9/WEA/2/515/1378
Frame	LWA	F/O	CAN	J.28155	419	KB718	LA	4/7/44	Villeneuve-St Georges	France	Fr	25/8/44	25/8/44	Northolt	3349 379	Hidden by Drue Tartière. Liberated by US troops 23 August 1944. Interviewed 26 August 1944. To UK by US Dakota. Report IS9/WEA/8/163/379
Francis	CR	SGT		1321173	103	ME722	LA	21/5/44	Duisburg	Holland				NK	NF	
Franklin	FJ	F/S		1295050	644	LL228	HAL	5/4/44	SOE	France	Sp, Gib	5/6/44	6/6/44	Whitchurch	3320 1945	With Sergeant R.P. Hindle to Spain. Helped by Françoise Dissard in Toulouse
Frankowski	TJ	SGT	POL	782235	305	Z1245	WE	27/8/42	Kassel	Holland	Bel, Fr, Sp, Gib	24/10/42	25/10/42	Mount Batten	3311 939	Comet 62. See *Blue Skies and Dark Nights*, pp. 111-2 et seq
Fraser	JG	F/O	CAN	J.36722	439	MN547	TY	11/11/44	Canal lock gates	Holland	Hol			NK	3326 2965	Liberated by Canadians 14 April 1945. Interviewed 23 April 1945
Fraser	T	F/S		1551981	10	MZ844	HAL	25/8/44	Watten	France	Fr			NK	3350 1479	Interviewed 14 September 1944. Report IS9(WEA)/1/213/1479
Fraser	WG	P/O		173136	106	ND850	LA	26/4/44	Schweinfurt	France				NK	NF	
Frayne	J	F/O		152744	622	LM108	LA	28/5/44	Angers	France	Sp, Gib	9/8/44	10/8/44	Whitchurch	3321 2067	
Freberg	PG	P/O	CAN	J.6659	7	W7630	ST	10/9/42	Düsseldorf	Germany	Hol, Bel, Fr, Sp, Gib	24/10/42	25/10/42	Mount Batten	3311 935	Comet 68. Escorted from Paris by Elvire Morelle and Jeanine De Greef. DFC (8/1/43). Killed in action 11 April 1943 (7 Squadron)
Frew	GS	F/O	CAN	J.85457	50	ED856	LA	25/8/44	Darmstadt	France	Fr	29/8/44	29/8/44	Northolt	3321 2181	
Frink	JD	FT/O	USA	T.223124	100	LM621	LA	30/6/44	Vierzon	France				NK	NF	Note: his rank was the USAAF's flight officer, not the RAF's flying officer
Frost	R	SGT		1383682	150	BJ877	WE	16/9/42	Essen	Belgium	Fr, Sp, Gib	24/10/42	25/10/42	Portreath	3311 937	Comet 65. Escorted from Paris by Elvire Morelle and Jeanine De Greef
Fry	CW	F/O	CAN	J.22493	138	BB378	HAL	10/12/43	SOE	Denmark	Swe	5/1/44	5/1/44	Leuchars	3317 1671	See *Making for Sweden*, pp. 95-8
Fryer	LR	SGT	USA	R.137350	428	LK739	HAL	20/1/44	Berlin	France	Sz, Fr	10/9/44	11/9/44	NK	3322 2292	In Switzerland from 29 January 1944 to 20 August 1944. Flown to Corsica, Naples, Casablanca and then to UK
Fulbrook	SJ	SGT			82	L8830	BL	17/5/40	Gembloux	Belgium				NK	NF	Aircraft abandoned over Rosseignies, north of Charleroi
Fuller	FE	F/S		1390208	48	KG428	DAK	19/9/44	Arnhem supply drop	Holland	Hol	20/4/45	20/4/45	NK	3327 3017	With Pilot Officer V.B. Christie. See *Free to Fight Again*, pp. 201-205
Fuller	FW	F/S			295	LK567	ST	26/4/45	SOE supply drop	Denmark	Dk	16/5/45	16/5/45	NK	3327 3042	On supply drop to Danish underground
Fullmore	P	SGT			48	KG428	DAK	19/9/44	Arnhem supply drop	Holland	Hol			NK	NF	Name from report IS9/WEA/1/286/2378 of Lieutenant B.D. Carr, 1st Airborne Division. Shown as Fulmore in Pilot Officer V.B. Christie's report
Fulton	JDL	F/O	CAN	J.16190	427	LV995	HAL	12/6/44	Arras	France	Fr			NK	3350 1232	Interviewed 10 September 1944. Report IS9/WEA/2/432/1232
Furneaux	RV	F/S	CAN	R.193367	425	LW715	HAL	15/6/44	Boulogne	France	Fr			NK	3350 1328	Interviewed 12 September 1944. Report IS9/WEA/MB/1328
Furniss-Roe	H	P/O		141860	66	W3719	SP	22/8/43	Ramrod	France	Sp, Gib	5/11/43	6/11/43	Portreath	3316 1547	Evaded again January-April 1944
Furniss-Roe	H	F/O		141860	66	EN575	SP	25/1/44	Ramrod	France	And, Sp, Gib	9/4/44	10/4/44	Lyneham	3319 1871	Lyneham? MiD (1/1/45). Author of *Believed Safe*. Also evaded August-November 1943
Fusinski	J	P/O	POL	P.1719	300	Z1276	WE	27/4/42	Cologne	France	Fr, Sp, Gib	19/8/42	25/8/42	Londonderry	3310 818	Helped by Francisco Ponzán network. Back on RN destroyer. MiD. KIA 27/28 May 1943? See *Safe Houses Are Dangerous*, p. 207
Fyfe	JSM	SGT		987709	626	LM633	LA	20/7/44	Courtrai	Belgium	Fr	13/9/44	13/9/44	Hendon	3325 2886	Back to UK via Paris
Gadd	WC	W/O	AUS	A.416946	453	SM244	SP	21/2/45	V2 site/railways	Holland	Hol			NK	3327 3062	Liberated by Canadians 8 May 1945. Interviewed 11 May 1945. Also report IS9/WEA/PLM/195 in WO 208/3348
Gage	GGM	P/O	CAN	172893	431	MZ522	HAL	27/4/44	Montzen	Belgium	Bel		15/9/44	NK	NF	Liberated by US forces 8 September 1944
Gains	JA	SGT		1487389	57	JB370	LA	7/7/44	St Leu d'Esserent	France				NK	NF	Service number? Given as 14873839 on aircraft loss card

Gaisford	RG	SGT		1376850	90	BK725	ST	16/4/43	Mannheim	France	And, Sp, Gib	23/6/43	23/6/43	Portreath	3313 1269	With Chauny/Burgundy lines
Gallay	P	S/LT	FRA		341	PT996	SP	20/10/44	Armed recce	Holland				NK	NF	
Galloway	AD	SGT		979929	78	LW273	HAL	23/9/43	Mannheim	France	Sz, Fr, Sp, Gib			NK	NF	Evaded over Pyrenees. Report Switzerland/53. Sz, Fr, Sp, Gib?
Galt	DT	P/O	AUS	A.400976	460	W4273	LA	22/11/42	Stuttgart	France	Sp, Gib	6/1/43	7/1/43	Mount Batten	3311 1019	DFC (9/2/43)
Gammon	HE	SGT	CAN	R.191887	425	LW390	HAL	20/2/44	Stuttgart	France	Sp, Gib	4/5/44	5/5/44	Whitchurch	3319 1903	
Gandy	KR	SGT		1625002	90	EF509	ST	9/5/44	SOE	France	Fr	18/8/44	18/8/44	Northolt	3321 2086	Co-author/publisher of 7 x X x 90. See *Agents for Escape...*, Chapter 14
Gardiner	EF	SGT		1322805	61	W4236	LA	9/8/43	Mannheim	Belgium	Fr	13/9/43	14/9/43	Tangmere	3315 1403	With the Possum line. Back by Lysander with Flight Sergeant Herbert Pond RNZAF
Gardner	EW	SGT		1568458	44	LM631	LA	7/7/44	St Leu d'Esserent	France	Fr	8/9/44	8/9/44	NK	3323 2469	
Gardner	R	F/S		1380415	10	LV867	HAL	22/4/44	Düsseldorf	Holland	Bel	13/9/44	13/9/44	Hendon	3324 2559	DFM (6/3/45)
Garland	ML	F/O	CAN	J.35853	403	ML183	SP	17/8/44	Armed recce	France	Fr			NK	3350 1006	Captured. Liberated 1 September 1944. Interviewed 5 September 1944. Report IS9/WEA/2/364/1006
Garlick	SM	F/O		137536	12	LM514	LA	3/5/44	Mailly-le-Camp	France				NK	3327 3122	Hit high tension cables on descent - see Shot *Down and on the Run*, pp. 88-93. MBE (10/12/46)
Garrity	RCB	F/O	CAN	J.20923	431	LK837	HAL	16/6/44	Sterkrade	Holland	Bel	6/9/44	6/9/44	Northolt	3323 2530	ss7. Back to UK from Reims
Garvey	K	F/S		1075988	467	JB121	LA	3/11/43	Düsseldorf	Belgium	Fr, Sp, Gib	17/1/44	17/1/44	Portreath	3318 1709	
Gasecki	JS	P/O	POL	P.2115	305	HE347	WE	21/6/43	Krefeld	Belgium	Fr, Sp, Gib	1/9/43	2/9/43	Whitchurch	3314 1384	Came down near Schilde, 10 kms east of Antwerp. Killed in collision over Lincolnshire on 18 September 1944 in 307 Sq Mosquito HK194
Gaskin	DG	SGT		1894546	299	EF267	ST	19/9/44	Supply drop	Holland	Bel	28/9/44	28/9/44	NK	3324 2652	Back to UK from Brussels. Aircraft number is guess
Gaudon	A	P/O	FRA	F.35515	341	PK996	SP	14/8/44	Armed recce	France	Fr			NK	3350 1122	Interviewed 5 September 1944. Report IS9/WEA/MB/1122
Gauley	GA	WO2	CAN	R.90319	24 OTU	AD675	WH	3/11/43	Nickel	France	Sp, Gib	17/1/44	17/1/44	Portreath	3318 1708	Arrived Gibraltar 13 January 1944
Gault	LWF	SGT		1819396	576	ME800	LA	29/8/44	Stettin					NK	3325 2790	
Gay	SF	F/S	CAN	R.209167	106	ME831	LA	7/7/44	St Leu d'Esserent	France	Fr	28/8/44	28/8/44	Northolt	3322 2219	Suffered severe facial burns. Left for UK from "Allied beachhead"
Gay	TM	P/O		87670	53	AM777	HUD	14/9/41	A/S sweep	France	Sp, Gib	27/1/42	6/2/42	Liverpool	3308 674	To UK by corvette HMS *Pelican*. MiD (11/6/42)
Gaze	FAO	F/L	AUS	60096	66	AR281	SP	4/9/43	Ramrod	France	And, Sp, Gib	27/10/43	28/10/43	Portreath	3315 1502	Australian in RAF. DFC (5/8/41) & Bar (19/1/43). Second Bar to DFC (1/6/45, 610 Squadron)
Geca	B	F/O	POL	P.1797	316	BS189	SP	4/4/43	NK	France	Sp, Gib	4/10/43	5/10/43	Whitchurch	3315 1452	Killed as flight lieutenant on 306 Squadron 7 June 1944
Gee	RR	F/L		112388	161	LK238	ST	6/10/44	SOE Tablejam 104/26B	Denmark	Swe	6/11/44	7/11/44	NK	3324 2741	To Sweden on 30 October 1944. DFC (23/3/45)
Geeson	WP	F/O		150239	625	LM139	LA	10/6/44	Achères	France	Fr	1/9/44	1/9/44	NK	3323 2443	In Royal Masonic Hospital, London, until 15 September 1944
Gelfand	R	P/O	CAN	J.90462	432	NA516	HAL	16/6/44	Sterkrade	Holland	Hol			NK	3326 2998	Captured. In PoW camp at Amersfoort. Escaped from train. Liberated 9 May 1945. Listed in *Footprints on the Sands of Time*
Genno	RRJ	W/O		1169626	248	HR288	MOS	14/8/44	Bordeaux area	France (sea)	Fr			NK	3345 639	Shot down in Gironde river. Hid in lighthouse. Found by Germans. Interviewed 3 September 1944. Report MISC/INT/639. Shot down again, 3 April 1945. Interned Sweden. Back in UK 16 April 1945
George	C	F/S	AUS	A.418384	83	ND467	LA	6/6/44	Caen	France	Fr			NK	3348 89	ss7. Captured 8 June 1944. Escaped from lorry on 3 July 1944. Interviewed 12 August 1944. Report IS9/WEA 2/63/89
George	LHJ	F/O		138213	15	LM575	LA	7/6/44	Massy-Palaiseau	France				NK	NF	DFC (19/5/44)
Gerrard	SW	F/O	CAN	J.28293	426	LW198	HAL	28/6/44	Metz	France	Fr			NK	3349 387	Liberated by US troops 28 August 1944. Interviewed 29 August 1944. Report IS9/WEA/8/233/387
Gettings	G	SGT		907306	158	LK875	HAL	1/6/44	Trappes	France	Fr	29/8/44	29/8/44	Northolt	3321 2210	Liberated on 26 August 1944
Getty	RC	F/O	CAN	J.27741	438	MN298	TY	16/6/44	Bombing	France	Fr	25/8/44	25/8/44	Northolt	3321 2140	Left for UK from B.14 airstrip, Banville. Interviewed 26 August 1944
Gibbons	DC	P/O		173329	166	LM388	LA	12/7/44	Revigny-sur-Ornain	France	Fr	6/9/44	6/9/44	NK	3323 2526	See *Massacre over the Marne*
Gibbs	EPP	S/L		32225	616	P8070	SP	9/7/41	Sweep	France	Sp, Gib	16/9/41	17/9/41	Mount Batten	3306 501	Escaped from St Hippolyte-du-Fort on 18 August 1941. Back by Sunderland. DFC (27/1/42), MiD (11/6/42)
Gibbs	JT	F/S	NZ	NZ.425150	115	LM738	LA	27/9/44	Calais	France				NK	NF	ss7. Service number?
Gibson	CF	F/O		39981	105	L5585	BA	14/5/40	Sedan	France	Sp, Gib			NK	NF	Escaped to Spain in 1940. Awarded CdeG avec Palme (18/6/40). Killed in action 14/15 March 1943 as squadron leader DFC (26/3/43) on 138 Squadron
Gibson	R	F/S			183	R8970	TY	17/8/44	NK	France				NK	NF	
Gilbert	RW	SGT		528758	158	LK841	HAL	1/6/44	Trappes	France	Fr	28/8/44	28/8/44	NK	3321 2179	Left for UK from Normandy
Gilby	AEJ	F/O		147121	207	LM129	LA	7/7/44	St Leu d'Esserent	France				NK	NF	
Gilchrist	PA	W/C	CAN	37348	405	W5551	WE	24/7/41	Brest	France	Sz, Sp, Gib	27/1/42	6/2/42	Liverpool	3308 672	DFC (31/5/40). To UK by corvette. Recommended for DSO but got MiD

																(11/6/42). See *The Evaders* (Cosgrove), pp.42, 46; *Winged Diplomat*, pp. 165-8; *We Act With One Accord*, p. 25
Giles	FA	F/S		1332679	77	MZ748	HAL	28/6/44	Blainville	France				NK	NF	Possibly prisoner of war? Initials FL?
Gill	GD	SGT		1247559	15	W4355	LA	15/3/44	Stuttgart	Switzerland	Ger, Fr, Sp, Gib	24/5/44	25/5/44	Whitchurch	3319 1940	Repatriated with German agreement. Back on BOAC Dakota
Gilleade	RH	F/S		1529488	15	LL889	LA	14/6/44	Le Havre	France	Fr			NK	3348 323	With Major Donald W. McLeod USAAF and Maquis group in Normandy. Interviewed 22 August 1944. Report IS9/WEA/1/33/323
Gimbel	EL	P/O	USA	J.15890	403	BS110	SP	4/4/43	Ramrod	France	Sp, Gib	5/8/43	11/8/43	Liverpool	3314 1346	American in RCAF. DFC (23/3/43). Burgundy line. MiD (14/1/44, flying officer)
Gingras	PH	F/S	CAN	R.163539	405	ND352	LA	10/6/44	Versailles	France	Fr			NK	3348 20	Contacted British HQ, Caen, 18 July 1944. Report IS9/WEA 2/13/20. MiD (1/1/45) as pilot officer J.87974. Awarded C de G by French (1945)
Ginter	C	F/S	CAN	R.218606	419	KB814	LA	15/3/45	Hagen	Germany				NK	NF	Prisoner of war?
Glanville	PT	F/L	AUS	A.412428	19	FZ112	MU	17/8/44	Armed recce	France	Fr			NK	3348 274	Interviewed 21 August 1944. Report IS9/WEA/1/14/274
Glensor	RE	P/O	NZ	NZ.403442	142	DF550	WE	16/9/42	Essen	France	Sp, Gib	20/1/43	26/1/43	Gourock	3312 1041	Arrested in Spain - in prison at Saragossa. *See Safe Houses Are Dangerous*, p.211. DFC (6/11/45) as squadron leader on 49 Squadron (though *By Such Deeds*, p.212, states 166 Squadron)
Gnys	W	S/L	POL	P.1298	317	NH365	SP	27/8/44	Armed recce	France	Fr	4/9/44	4/9/44	Wroughton	NF	Wounded. Captured. Rescued by maquisards. Author *First Kill* (Kimber, 1981). Date back is a guess based on *First Kill*
Goddard	AG	SGT		1590299	640	MZ855	HAL	12/8/44	Rüsselsheim	Belgium	Bel			Hendon	3350 1340	Fought with Belgian Resistance. Interviewed 10 September 1944. Report IS9/WEA/MB/1340. See *Bomber Boys*, Chapter 6
Goddard	G	F/L		158895	635	ND811	LA	4/8/44	Trossy-St Maximin	France	Fr			NK	3350 1016	Interviewed 5 September 1944. Report IS9/WEA/2/316/1016. His pilot was Squadron Leader Bazalgette VC
Goddard	RG	SGT		1333556	78	JB873	HAL	13/5/43	Bochum	Belgium	Fr, Sp, Gib	8/7/43	9/7/43	Hendon	3314 1297	On British collier *Great Hope* from Seville to Gibraltar, 4/5 July 1943. DFM (17/8/43). See *Valley of the Shadow of Death*, pp.290-1
Godfrey	CR	F/O		146099	635	ND811	LA	4/8/44	Trossy-St Maximin	France	Fr			NK	3350 1017	Interviewed 2 September 1944. Report IS9/WEA/2/317/1017. DFC (27/3/45) & Bar (21/9/45). His pilot was Squadron Leader Bazalgette VC
Godfrey	SJ	F/S		987171	50	LM480	LA	3/5/44	Mailly-le-Camp	France	Fr			NK	None	Killed 24 June 1944 when Germans attacked Maquis camp
Goggin	JA	F/O		146355	644	LL403	HAL	5/10/44	Supply drop, Dodex III	Holland	Hol			NK	3352 2373	Interviewed 15 February 1945. Report IS9/WEA/1/282/2373
Gold	C	SGT		1458498	90	LM111	LA	7/8/44	Mare de Magne	France	Fr	25/8/44	25/8/44	Northolt	3321 2161	Left for UK from Bayeux - B.14 airstrip, Banville
Goldberg	D	F/L	CAN	J.4242	403	MJ356	SP	8/3/44	Ranger	France	Sp, Gib	5/5/44	6/5/44	Whitchurch	3319 1910	Joined up with Flying Officer R.G. Crosby in Paris. DFC (20/3/45). See *Silent Heroes*, pp. 26, 32
Goldingay	LD	SGT		968161	9	R1244	WE	11/1/41	Turin	France	Sp, Gib	9/5/41	16/5/41	Liverpool	3304 349	To UK on *Monarch of Bermuda*. DFC (21/4/44). Killed in action as flight lieutenant (130244) on 27/28 April 1944 (7 Squadron). See *Bombers First and Last*, pp. 41 etc. See AIR 2/5684
Goldsmith	BF	SGT		1287042	149	W7508	ST	5/6/42	Essen	Belgium	Fr, Sp, Gib	21/7/42	30/7/42	Gourock	3309 791	Comet 27
Goodman	CE	SGT		1604311	630	LM269	LA	18/8/44	Bordeaux	France	Fr			NK	3350 1336	Interviewed 10 September 1944. Report IS9/WEA/MB/1336
Goodman	DE	F/S		1322826	248	HR288	MOS	14/8/44	Bordeaux area	France (sea)	Fr			NK	3345 640	Shot down in Gironde river. Hid in lighthouse. Found by Germans. Interviewed 3 September 1944. Report MISC/INT/640. Shot down again, 3 April 1945. Interned Sweden. Back in UK 16 April 1945
Gordon	D	F/S		1821434	61	NF914	LA	24/9/44	Calais	France	Fr	29/9/44	29/9/44	NK	3324 2632	Escaped from Calais hospital on 25 September 1944. Flown back from an airfield near St Omer
Gordon	RB	F/O		151794	21	LR404	MOS	8/2/44	Noball site	France	Fr			NK	3348 190	Sherwood. Interviewed 19 August 1944. Report IS9/WEA 2/151/190
Gordon	RT	SGT	CAN	R.181524	576	PB265	LA	24/7/44	Stuttgart	France	Fr			NK	NF	Sherwood
Gordon	WH	F/L	CAN	J.5695	400	AG661	MU	2/6/43	Rhubarb	France	Sz			NK	NF	MiD (1/1/43). In Switzerland 7 July 1943. To UK by C-47 in autumn 1944
Gornall	LJ	F/O		52164	138	LW275	HAL	7/2/44	SOE	France	Sp, Gib	4/5/44	5/5/44	Whitchurch	3319 1900	On his 48th operation. See *Free to Fight Again*, pp. 77-81. DFC (15/9/44). Killed in action 27 February 1945 (still on 138 Squadron)
Gouinlock	J	F/O	CAN	J.24556	432	LK811	HAL	27/5/44	Bourg-Léopold	Holland	Bel	17/9/44	17/9/44	NK	NF	Liberated in Liège on 7 September 1944. Flew back to 'London' aboard a C-47. See *The Evaders* (Cosgrove), pp.146-62
Gould	G	F/S		1580304	630	ME739	LA	10/4/45	Leipzig	Germany	Ger		30/4/45	NK	3327 3069	'Hid' in British army work camp with Flight Sergeant G.G.E. Bourner. Liberated by US Army 19 April 1945. See also Flight Sergeant J.W. Tovey
Gradwell	RS	P/O		170949	9	JA690	LA	7/7/44	St Leu d'Esserent	France	Fr			NK	3350 1061	With Flying Officer R.B. Atkinson. Liberated by British troops. Interviewed 2 September 1944. Report IS9/WEA/2/314/1061. See *Bombers First and Last*,

																pp. 246-52, 271 etc
Graham	AH	SGT		946016	53	AM777	HUD	14/9/41	A/S sweep	France	Sp, Gib	30/12/41	5/1/42	Gourock	3307 644	Back to UK on Polish ship *Batory*. (DFM 3/9/43, 224 Squadron?)
Graham	GT	P/O	CAN	J.14729	419	LW240	HAL	16/9/43	Modane	France	And, Sp, Gib	27/10/43	28/10/43	Portreath	3316 1511	Met Flight Lieutenant F.A.O. Gaze in Paris
Graham	HW	W/O		1376158	7	JA682	LA	12/8/43	Milan	France	Sp, Gib	16/1/44	17/1/44	NK	3318 1712	Crossed Pyrenees 22/23 December 1943. Left Seville by boat 10 January 1944.
Graham	KW	P/O	CAN	J.85879	407		WE	26/9/44	A/S patrol off Norway	Norway	Nor	11/10/44	12/10/44	Scalloway	3324 2658	Came back on the "Shetland Bus" service. See *Shot Down and on the Run*, pp. 141-8
Grandy	GE	W/O	CAN	R.115449	407		WE	26/9/44	A/S patrol off Norway	Norway	Nor	11/10/44	12/10/44	Scalloway	3324 2659	Came back on the "Shetland Bus" service. See *Shot Down and on the Run*, pp. 141-8
Grannum	C	F/L		155216	12	JB650	LA	27/1/44	Berlin	Belgium	Sz			NK	NF	In Switzerland 9 May 1944. DFC (15/8/44 wef 27/1/44)
Grant	DA	SGT	CAN	R.252538	630	LM117	LA	18/7/44	Revigny-sur-Ornain	France	Fr	2/9/44	2/9/44	NK	3349 453	Liberated by US forces 29 August 1944. Report IS9/WEA/MB/453. See *Massacre over the Marne*
Grantham	FA	F/L		104542	174	MN577	TY	14/8/44	Enemy troops	France					None	Killed by shellfire on 16 August 1944
Gray	WJ	SGT		1461487	50	PD237	LA	13/8/44	Bordeaux	France	Fr			NK	3345 644	Captured. Liberated from hospital in Angoulême 1 September 1944. Interviewed 3 September 1944. Report MI9/S/PG/MISC/INT/644. See *D-Day Bombers...*, pp. 241-5
Greatrex	BR	W/O	AUS	A.413758	61	LL775	LA	25/2/44	Augsburg	France	Fr	12/10/44	12/10/44	Northolt	3324 2654	ss7. With the maquis. Got through to the American lines
Greatz	EH	F/S	AUS	A.419264	44	ME694	LA	25/7/44	Stuttgart	France	Fr			NK	3348 289	Sherwood. Interviewed 27 August 1944. Report IS9/WEA/2/102/289
Green	PCN	F/S	RHO	710092	266	MN600	TY	9/8/44	NK	France	Fr	24/9/44	24/9/44	NK	3324 2577	Captured 16 August 1944. Escaped 7 September 1944. Left for UK from Ypres. Killed in action on 25 December 1944
Green	PE	F/S		1482151	90	EF509	ST	9/5/44	SOE	France	Fr			NK	3352 2886	Helped by André Rougeyron. See *Agents for Escape...*, Chapter 14
Greenaway	FH	F/O	AUS	NZ.42296	21	HX961	MOS	4/1/44	Rocket site, Abbeville	France	Sp, Gib	9/4/44	10/4/44	Lyneham	3319 1870	RNZAF though born in Toowoomba, Australia on 2 March 1909. Escaped from his four German guards in Paris. Burgundy line? MBE (28/11/44). Mosquito HX954?
Greenburgh	L	F/O	CAN	49803	514	LL727	LA	7/6/44	Massy-Palaiseau	France	Fr			NK	3348 321	Canadian in RAF. DFC (14/3/44). Sherwood. Interviewed 18 August 1944. Report IS9/WEA/2/149/321. Bar to DFC (31/10/44)
Greene	WA	SGT	CAN	R.200862	419	HX189	HAL	22/4/44	Laon	France	Sp, Gib	23/6/44	24/6/44	Lyneham	3320 1990	Lyneham?
Greenwell	FA	F/S		1505082	57	JB565	LA	24/2/44	Schweinfurt	France	Sp, Gib	23/6/44	24/6/44	Hendon	3320 1993	In Toulouse 12-14 May 1944. Helped by Françoise Dissard. See *The Freedom Trail*, pp. 66-70
Greenwood	RE	F/S		1581933	103	PA999	LA	12/7/44	Revigny-sur-Ornain	France	Fr	8/9/44	8/9/44	NK	3323 2537	ss7. See *Massacre over the Marne*
Griffith	RE	SGT		1457278	75	LJ442	ST	19/11/43	Leverkusen	Belgium	Fr, And, Sp, Gib	3/2/44	4/2/44	Whitchurch	3318 1744	Briefly met Sergeants N.B. Cufley and J. Harvey in France. With Sergeant K. Skidmore over Pyrenees. Recommended for MiD
Griffiths	A	F/O		131642	26	AB240	SP	13/6/44	Patrol, battle area	France	Fr				NF	Rejoined squadron two days later. Shot down again on 23 June and taken prisoner. Sent to Stalag Luft I (Barth)
Griffiths	FC	S/L		37967	138	JD180	HAL	14/8/43	SOE	France	Sz, Fr, Sp, Gib	29/11/43	29/11/43	Lyneham	3316 1588	DFC (21/1/44), AFC (2/6/43). ss7. In Switzerland 19 August 1943. Left 19 October 1943. Flown in a Warwick to Lyneham. Author of *Winged Hours*. Died March 1996
Griffiths	JL	SGT		1379633	102	W7677	HAL	8/9/42	Frankfurt	Luxembourg	Fr, Sp, Gib	6/11/42	6/11/42	Hendon	3311 991	Comet 77. DFM (5/2/43)
Griffiths	RE	SGT		755779	220	P5146	HUD	2/4/41	Crossover patrol	France	Sp, Gib	8/8/41	14/8/41	Gourock	3305 480	Escaped to Spain from St Hippolyte in June 1941 with Sergeant F.H. Miller and four army escapers
Griffiths	WR	SGT		1212974	61	R5613	LA	2/6/42	Essen	Belgium	Fr, Sp, Gib	21/7/42	30/7/42	Gourock	3309 793	ss7. Comet 25. MiD (1/1/43)
Grimer	JA	F/O		138336	77	LK710	HAL	22/4/44	Laon	France	Fr	1/9/44	1/9/44	NK	3345 801	Wounded in right leg. Gangrene set in. Liberated from American Memorial Hospital, Reims on 30 August 1944. Interviewed 18 November 1944. Report MISC/INT/801
Grimsey	MFC	F/O	CAN	J.21464	432	NP687	HAL	25/7/44	Stuttgart	France	Fr			NK	3348 310	Sherwood. Interviewed 17 August 1944. Report IS9/WEA/2/105/310
Grisdale	E	F/S		1039861	626	NE118	LA	22/5/44	Dortmund	Holland	Bel	13/9/44	13/9/44	Hendon	3324 2558	Author of *One of Many*
Grottick	AJ	F/L		136572	611	KH728	MU	22/4/45	Armed patrol	Germany	Ger			NK	NF	Landed near Minden on a wooded hillside. Possibly not an evader - may have landed in Allied lines. MiD (1/1/46)
Grout	JE	F/S		1375129	138	LW281	HAL	18/10/43	SOE	Belgium	Fr, Sp, Gib	11/12/43	12/12/43	Whitchurch	3317 1616	Comet 204. With Staff Sergeant Alfred R. Buinicky USAAF
Grove	WG	SGT		921996	214	BK653	ST	16/4/43	Mannheim	France	Sp, Gib	17/7/43	24/7/43	Liverpool	3314 1318	Oaktree. Back to UK on *Monarch of Bermuda?* KIA (flight lieutenant, 15 Squadron) on 24/25 March 1944 (Berlin)

Groyecki	Z	P/O	POL	P.0325	300	R1705	WE	7/11/41	Mannheim	France	Sp, Gib	20/1/42	21/1/42	Plymouth	3307 667	MiD recommended 29/5/42. Possibly helped by Francisco Ponzán network.
Guild	H	F/S		1126298	429	LV973	HAL	10/6/44	Versailles	France	Fr	18/8/44	18/8/44	Northolt	3321 2102	Sherwood
Gunnell	AF	SGT			115	DS834	LA	29/12/43	Berlin	Holland				NK	NF	In Marathon camp in the Ardennes. Liberated by US forces 8 September 1944
Gurney	JL	SGT		1836527	630	LM269	LA	18/8/44	Bordeaux	France				NK	NF	
Haberlin	MF	SGT		1802303	635	JB728	LA	15/6/44	Lens	France	Fr	6/9/44	6/9/44	NK	3322 2273	
Hagan	A	P/O		135880	77	JD205	HAL	21/6/43	Krefeld	Holland	Hol	26/7/43	30/7/43	Sheerness	3314 1330	With Pilot Officer J.B.M. Haye. Picked up by HMS *Garth* 30 July 1943. DFC (7/9/43). See *Shot Down and on the Run*, p. 108
Hagen	E	2LT	NOR		332	NH597	SP	8/4/45	Offensive operations	Germany				NK	NF	Baled out twenty-five kilometres north of Oldenburg
Hagen	FD	F/O	CAN	J.26861	425	LW715	HAL	15/6/44	Boulogne	France	Fr			NK	3350 1322	Interviewed 12 September 1944. Report IS9/WEA/MB/1322
Haig	T	SGT		1821449	620	LJ830	ST	21/9/44	Arnhem supply drop	Holland	Hol			NK	3350 1409	Liberated 23 September 1944. Interviewed 25 September 1944. Report IS9/WEA/2/563/1409. Aircraft and date are a guess
Haine	RC	P/O		43147	600	L1514	BL	10/5/40	Waalhaven airfield	Holland (sea)	Hol	12/5/40	13/5/40	Harwich	NF	Back aboard HMS *Hereward*. DFC (9/7/40)
Haines	AR	F/O	CAN	J.8601	102	W7916	HAL	2/12/42	Frankfurt	France	Sp, Gib	24/2/43	24/2/43	Portreath	3312 1107	Sailed from Seville for Gibraltar aboard the *Saltwick* on 20 February 1943
Halcrow	AF	F/L	CAN	J.6795	411	MJ899	SP	18/8/44	Armed recce	France	Fr		24/8/44	London	3348 227	Captured. Escaped 20 August 1944. Interviewed 22 August 1944. Report IS9/WEA/1/18/227. DFC (8/12/44)
Hale	XX	SGT			139	P4923	BL	12/5/40	Enemy troops	Belgium	Fr			NK	NF	
Haley	VG	SGT		1251661	218	R1511	WE	10/10/41	Bordeaux	France	Sp, Gib	4/3/42	10/3/42	Gourock	3308 691	Crossed Pyrenees without a guide. MM (26/5/42). See FO 371/28285/Z10066, and AIR 2/5684
Halhead	AJ	SGT	CAN	R.159498	44	LM631	LA	7/7/44	St Leu d'Esserent	France	Fr	6/9/44	6/9/44	NK	3323 2371	
Hall	GB	F/S	AUS	A.452110	466	HX337	HAL	22/4/44	Düsseldorf	Belgium				NK	NF	Service number?
Hall	HB	P/O		138326	35	HR798	HAL	11/11/43	Cannes	France	Sp, Gib	5/2/44	6/2/44	Whitchurch	3318 1747	See *We Act With One Accord*, p.151
Hall	J	SGT		911341	214	BK653	ST	16/4/43	Mannheim	France	Sp, Gib	17/7/43	24/7/43	Liverpool	3314 1320	Oaktree. Back to UK on *Monarch of Bermuda?*
Hallett	CL	SGT		1585043	10	MZ630	HAL	2/6/44	Trappes	France	Fr	18/8/44	18/8/44	Northolt	3321 2079	Sherwood. Left for UK from B.14 airstrip, Banville
Hamilton	CT	SGT	NZ	NZ.411240	408	HR656	HAL	11/3/43	Stuttgart	France	Sz, Fr			NK	NF	
Hamilton	W	SGT		1126345	218	BF514	ST	16/4/43	Mannheim	France	Sz			NK	NF	In Switzerland 28 April 1943. See *Strike Hard*, pp 98-9 - J.B. Hilling
Hammond	AH	F/S		1585538	426	NA510	HAL	12/6/44	Cambrai	France	Fr	11/9/44	11/9/44	Broadwell	3323 2408	Back to UK from Vitry-en-Artois
Hammond	JA	SGT	CAN	R.81832	408	HR656	HAL	11/3/43	Stuttgart	France	Sz, Fr	10/9/44	10/9/44	Hendon	3324 2602	To Switzerland 1 March 1944. Left 4 September 1944
Hammond	WG	F/S		1154252	626	ND952	LA	30/6/44	Vierzon	France	Fr			NK	3345 817	Wounded. Liberated from Paris hospital c. 24 August 1944. Interviewed 17 January 1945. Report MISC/INT/817
Hampton	R	SGT		2211450	50	LL842	LA	24/7/44	Stuttgart	France	Fr	18/8/44	18/8/44	Northolt	3321 2115	Sherwood? Left for UK from Bayeux - B.14 airstrip, Banville
Hancock	DJ	F/S		1451570	640	LW654	HAL	10/8/44	Dijon	France	Fr			NK	NF	
Hand	G	SGT		1591980	432	LW594	HAL	8/5/44	Haine-St Pierre	Belgium	Fr			NK	3348 312	Sherwood. Interviewed 19 August 1944. Report IS9/WEA/2/160/312
Hannah	W	SGT		1820064	10	MZ844	HAL	25/8/44	Watten	France	Fr	10/9/44	10/9/44	NK	3324 2669	Back to UK from Rouen
Hannam	TB	F/S		1321273	222	MH390	SP	27/9/43	Ramrod	France	Sp, Gib	23/12/43	23/12/43	Portreath	3317 1643	Burgundy line? Over Pyrenees with Flight Sergeants J.D. Bawden RCAF and W. Booth
Hanson	SE	F/S		1582306	207	NN724	LA	7/2/45	Ladbergen	Holland	Hol			NK	3352 2434	Author of *Underground out of Holland*
Hanstock	TA	SGT		640500	460	W4273	LA	22/11/42	Stuttgart	France	Sp, Gib	28/3/43	5/4/43	Liverpool	3312 1146	
Hanton	JN	SGT		1321092	57	PD212	LA	28/7/44	Stuttgart	France				NK	NF	
Hanwell	HP	SGT		958800	101	X3472	WE	19/5/42	Mannheim	France	Sz, Fr, Gib	24/7/42	30/7/42	Greenock	3309 796	Evacuated by *Tarana* 14 July 1942. To UK on *Llanstephan Castle*. DFM (18/9/42). See *Shot Down and On the Run*, pp. 50-4
Hardisty	WJ	SGT		1592421	106	ND339	LA	4/7/44	St Leu d'Esserent	France	Fr			NK	3350 1055	Interviewed 1 September 1944. Report IS9/WEA/2/299/1055
Hargreaves	AV	F/O	CAN	J.18032	122	FB107	MU	25/7/44	Bombing	France	Fr			NK	3349 370	Liberated by US troops 25 August 1944. Interviewed 27 August 1944. Report IS9(WEA)/2/244/370
Harkin	BF	F/S	AUS	A.418747	640	MZ855	HAL	12/8/44	Rüsselsheim	Belgium	Bel			Hendon	3350 1339	Landed in a dung heap. Fought with Belgian Resistance. Interviewed 10 September 1944. Report IS9/WEA/MB/1339. See *Bomber Boys*, Chapter 6
Harkins	J	F/S		655208	428	LK931	HAL	4/10/43	Frankfurt	Germany	Bel, Fr, Sp, Gib	23/12/43	23/12/43	Portreath	3317 1642	Comet 219
Harmel	LJG	F/S	BEL	1299917	350	AD314	SP	20/12/43	Ramrod 377	France	Fr	26/2/44	27/2/44	Dartmouth	3318 1807	Belgian in RAF. Evacuated by MGB 503 in Operation Bonaparte II
Harmsworth	F	SGT		2201333	622	LL828	LA	15/3/44	Stuttgart	France	Sp, Gib	22/5/44	23/5/44	Whitchurch	3319 1928	
Harpell	AR	SGT	CAN	R.67205	49	JB473	LA	18/7/44	Revigny-sur-Ornain	France	Fr	3/9/44	3/9/44	NK	3326 2901	See *Massacre over the Marne*
Harper	CH	F/O		153382	464	NT138	MOS	25/7/44	Patrol	France	Fr	23/8/44	23/8/44	Northolt	3321 2156	Left for UK from Le Mans. Interviewed 24 August 1944. See *Massacre over the Marne*, p. 122. MiD (14/6/45)

Harrington	RK	F/O		188947	235	RS619	MOS	5/4/45	Anti-shipping strike	Denmark	Swe	2/5/45	2/5/45	Leuchars	3327 3085	Reached Sweden on 24 April 1945. Flown back by DC-3 Dakota
Harris	HR	SGT		1581276	102	MZ289	HAL	14/6/44	NK	France	Fr	18/6/44	20/6/44	NK	3320 2060	Liberated by US troops 17 June 1944
Harris	SB	F/S		1380154	74	MK672	SP	22/5/44	Ramrod	Belgium	Bel	11/9/44	11/9/44	NK	3322 2296	Captured. St Gilles. "Ghost train" 3 September 1944
Harris	WH	SGT		560630	218	P2183	BA	12/5/40	Bouillon	France				NK	NF	MiD. No Report found. Killed 17 December 1943 in collision on return from Berlin, as warrant officer on 100 Squadron
Harrison	D	P/O	CAN	C.85357	431	MZ529	HAL	27/4/44	Montzen	Belgium	Bel	12/9/44	12/9/44	NK	3326 2976	Marathon
Harrison	GT	P/O	AUS	A.420749	166	ME749	LA	3/5/44	Mailly-le-Camp	France	Fr			NK	NF	Briefly with Sergeant J. Marsden until Maquis camp in which he was hiding was attacked by Germans on 15 May 1944. Liberated 20 August 1944 by US troops
Harrison	JJ	SGT		1457009	77	LW270	HAL	23/4/44	Mining	Denmark	Swe	7/5/44	8/5/44	Leuchars	3319 1913	Back to UK from Stockholm
Harrison	RH	S/L		103504	151	PZ218	MOS	22/7/44	Ranger	France	Fr			NK	NF	DFC (2/6/44). Injured. Taken to hospital in Toulouse, where liberated 18 August 1944. See Flight Lieutenant E.P.A. Horrex
Harrop	E	SGT		1494660	100	LM621	LA	30/6/44	Vierzon	France	Fr	23/8/44	23/8/44	NK	3324 2638	Burgundy line?
Harrowing	J	SGT		618316	635	ND965	LA	11/6/44	Nantes	France	Fr			NK	3350 1226	Aircraft returned to base. With Flight Lieutenant R.A. Boddington. Interviewed 1 September 1944. Report IS9/WEA/2/302/1226
Hart	HJ	W/O	AUS	A.410597	299	LJ942	ST	2/4/45	SOE Tablejam 283	Denmark	Swe	11/5/45	11/5/45	NK	3327 3112	Came down in an inlet on island of Zeeland
Hart	TP	SGT		1015299	50	PD237	LA	13/8/44	Bordeaux	France	Fr			NK	3345 649	Captured. Liberated from hospital in Angoulême 1 September 1944. Interviewed 3 September 1944. Report MI9/S/PG/MISC/INT/649. See *D-Day Bombers...*, pp. 241-5
Hart	XX	SGT			21	L9269	BL	13/6/40	La Mare	France	Fr			NK	NF	Possibly not an evader
Hartman	L	F/S		1601174	196	LJ810	ST	21/9/44	Arnhem supply drop	Holland	Hol			NK	3350 1367	Interviewed 25 September 1944. Report IS9/WEA/2/532/1367
Hartwig	GA	W/O	AUS	A.412313	90	NE177	LA	10/6/44	Dreux	France	Fr	28/8/44	28/8/44	NK	3322 2232	Left for UK from Bayeux - B.14 airstrip, Banville
Harvell	TH	SGT		1890339	514	LM206	LA	28/7/44	Stuttgart	France	Fr			NK	NF	Joined the FFI at Neufchâteau. Also helped liberate the town of Pierrefontaine-les-Varans (Doubs)
Harvey	J	SGT		1455636	77	JD247	HAL	18/11/43	Mannheim	France	Fr	29/1/44	29/1/44	Dartmouth	3318 1729	Chauny. Back to UK by MGB 503 from Brittany on Bonaparte I
Harvey	SA	F/S	CAN	R.285180	514	LL692	LA	28/7/44	Stuttgart	France	Fr		17/8/44	NK	NF	Sherwood
Harvey	WS	F/L	CAN		402	RM906	SP	25/2/45	Armed patrol	Holland	Hol			NK	NF	Taken prisoner. Escaped six weeks later. Liberated by Allied troops
Haslam	FR	SGT		1580859	207	LL973	LA	21/6/44	Wesseling	Belgium	Bel			NK	3350 1394	Liberated after thirteen weeks in hiding. Report IS9/WEA/2/486/1394. WO 208/3350 ?
Hatchett	DJ	SGT		1834626	61	EE186	LA	4/7/44	St Leu d'Esserent	France	Fr	9/9/44	9/9/44	NK	3326 2922	See AIR 14/464 and AIR 14/2073
Hatfield	JE	P/O		40474	264	L6969	DF	13/5/40	EA, The Hague beach	Holland			14/5/40	NK	NF	Killed in action on 28 May 1940
Hatter	CC	SGT		1870681	57	LM580	LA	21/6/44	Wesseling	Belgium	Bel			NK	3350 1240	Stayed with a Madame Wendelen until liberated. Interviewed 13 September 1944. Report IS9/WEA/2/464/1240
Hawken	SA	F/S	AUS	A.418663	630	ME796	LA	18/7/44	Revigny-sur-Ornain	France	Fr	7/9/44	7/9/44	NK	3323 2374	See *Massacre over the Marne*
Hawkins	BLG	P/O		88874	245	Z3470	HUR	26/10/41	Rhubarb	France	Gib	30/9/42	5/10/42	Greenock	3310 879	Escaped from Fort de la Revère 23 August 1942. Evacuated by sea 21 September 1942. Back on HMS *Malaya*. MiD (14/1/44)
Hawkins	GE	F/S		658717	115	HK579	LA	8/9/44	Le Havre	France	Fr			NK	NF	
Hawkins	R	F/O		70802	103	R3916	BL	14/6/40	Troops, Evreux	France	Sp, Gib	7/10/40	8/10/40	Mount Batten	3299 77	Flown to UK by Sunderland. MC (17/3/41). Killed as squadron leader MC, AFC (2/4/43) on 5 October 1943 in Typhoon JP733
Haxton	RB	SGT	CAN	R.190579	432	LW594	HAL	8/5/44	Haine St Pierre	Belgium				NK	NF	
Hay	DF	F/O	CAN	J.28983	429	MZ302	HAL	28/6/44	Metz	France	Fr			NK	NF	
Hay	EAG	SGT		1880401	207	ME805	LA	7/7/44	St Leu d'Esserent	France	Fr	28/8/44	28/8/44	Northolt	3321 2208	Left for UK from Normandy
Hay	RE	W/O	NZ		644	NA672	HAL	26/4/45	SOE Tablejam 353	Denmark	Dk	19/5/45	19/5/45	NK	NF	Flown back to UK over Hamburg by DC-3 Dakota
Hay	TM	SGT		1392504	61	ED722	LA	15/8/43	Milan	France	Sp, Gib	5/11/43	6/11/43	Portreath	3316 1549	Helped by Raymond Picourt. With Warrant Officer R.A. Scott in Paris
Haydon	JPM	F/L	AUS	A.402352	158	W7750	HAL	6/8/42	Duisburg	Belgium	Fr, Sp, Gib	30/9/42	5/10/42	Greenock	3310 898	Comet 46. Escorted from Paris by Elvire Morelle and Jeanine De Greef. Back on HMS *Malaya*. DFC (5/2/43)
Haye	JBM	P/O	HOL	142599	57	ED667	LA	13/5/43	Pilsen	Holland	Hol	26/7/43	30/7/43	Sheerness	3314 1331	Lieutenant in Royal Dutch Air Force. With Pilot Officer Hagan. Picked up by HMS *Garth* 30 July 1944. See Shot *Down and on the Run*, pp. 103-110
Haynes	FL	SGT		1319432	77	LW270	HAL	23/4/44	Mining	Denmark	Swe	9/5/44	9/5/44	Leuchars	3319 1916	Back to UK from Stockholm
Haynes	RH	SGT		1321909	166	ME749	LA	3/5/44	Mailly-le-Camp	France	Fr			NK	3349	Liberated 20 August 1944 by US troops
Hayward	DF	SGT		1332324	156	ND449	LA	6/5/44	Mantes-la-Jolie	France	Fr	29/8/44	29/8/44	Northolt	3322 2213	DFM (23/5/44, 103 Squadron)

Heal	PC	SGT		1604298	149	LJ621	ST	5/6/44	SOE supply drop	France	Fr	12/8/44	12/8/44	NK	3345 836	Broken leg and burnt hands. Captured. Liberated from Rennes hospital 4 August 1944. Interviewed 22 March 1945. Report MISC/INT/836
Healey	JP	SGT	CAN	R.179472	138	LW281	HAL	18/10/43	SOE	Belgium	Bel	17/9/44	17/9/44	NK	3323 2441	Fought with Belgian Resistance forces. Went to Brussels on 15 September 1944. See *The Evaders* (Lavender/Sheffe), pp. 242-243
Heap	ET	SGT	AUS	A.405053	102	W7677	HAL	8/9/42	Frankfurt	Luxembourg	Fr, Sp Gib	31/10/42	1/11/42	Portreath	3311 949	Comet 67. Escorted from Paris by Elvire Morelle and Jeanine De Greef. DFM (5/2/43)
Hearn	EHE	F/L		131973	50	LL922	LA	7/8/44	Secqueville	France	Fr	31/8/44	31/8/44	NK	3322 2228	DFC (23/7/43). Left for UK from Normandy. Bar to DFC (16/1/45)
Heath	GS	F/O	AUS	A.429808	102	NA502	HAL	28/6/44	Blainville	France	Fr	3/9/44	3/9/44	NK	3322 2254	
Heaton	EC	F/O	NZ	NZ.428817	487	HP931	MOS	31/8/44	SS HQ, Vincy	France	Fr			NK	3350 1348	Report IS9/WEA/MB/1348. Interviewed ? See also Warrant Officer K.G. Mason RNZAF
Heaton	GW	SGT		1621017	158	LK877	HAL	1/6/44	Trappes	France	Fr	29/8/44	29/8/44	NK	3321 2187	
Hedley	TJ	F/S		1265222	88	BZ359	BOS	16/8/43	Denain	France	Fr	24/10/43	25/10/43	Penzance	3315 1497	Back by boat
Helean	JA	F/S	NZ	NZ.414288	486	JP845	TY	21/12/43	Ramrod	France	Fr	8/9/44	8/9/44	NK	3323 2395	
Hemingway	JA	P/O		40702	85	L1979	HUR	11/5/40	Patrol	Holland				NK	NF	DFC (1/7/41). MiD (24/9/41). No Report found
Hempstead	JN	SGT		540151	158	HR720	HAL	13/7/43	Aachen	Holland	Bel, Fr, Sp, Gib	24/10/43	25/10/43	NK	3316 1512	With Sergeant R.A. Smith
Henderson	R	SGT		1291378	83	ED313	LA	11/3/43	Stuttgart	France	Sp, Gib	24/5/43	25/5/43	Hendon	3313 1216	Evaded with Flight Lieutenant A.M. Ogilvie DFC. DFM (23/7/43). Killed on operations 22/23 November 1943 (Berlin), as pilot officer
Henderson	WJ	SGT		2202738	90	LM111	LA	7/8/44	Mare de Magne	France	Fr	25/8/44	25/8/44	Northolt	3321 2163	Left for UK from Bayeux - B.14 airstrip, Banville
Henry	EA	LT	FRA	F.003854	347	LW642	HAL	24/7/44	NK	France	Fr	17/8/44	17/8/44	NK	3321 2084	Liberated by US troops on 15 August 1944
Herbert	PR	SGT		959970	15	R1080	WE	26/4/41	Transit	Mediterranean	Fr, Sp, Gib	30/12/41	4/1/42	Gourock	3307 629	Interned by the French, imprisoned by the Spanish
Herd	A	SGT		1821324	158	LK863	HAL	7/6/44	Versailles	France	Fr			NK	NF	Hidden in Paris with Sergeant R.A. Diver until its liberation
Herfjord	KM	LT	NOR	F.P.658	332	TA838	SP	4/1/45	Armed recce	Holland	Hol			NK	3352 2445	Interviewed 8 April 1945. Report IS9/WEA/1/334/2445
Heslop	R	SGT		547843	83	ND966	LA	7/7/44	St Leu d'Esserent	France	Fr	9/9/44	9/9/44	NK	3322 2302	
Hesselden	T	F/S		1138706	97	JB367	LA	18/11/43	Berlin	Belgium	Fr, Sp, Gib	17/1/44	17/1/44	Portreath	3318 1710	Comet 238
Hewitt	I	P/O		119344	35	W1048	HAL	27/4/42	*Tirpitz*, Norway	Norway	Swe	15/6/42	15/6/42	Leuchars	3309 747	Left from Stockholm. DFC (4/8/42). See *Making for Sweden*, pp. 33-5. Bar to DFC (23/5/44, flight lieutenant)
Heyworth	C	SGT		976348	428	LK913	HAL	15/9/43	Montluçon	France	Fr	15/11/43	16/11/43	Tangmere	None	Flown back by Lysander, terminally ill. Died 25 November 1943 as pilot officer (157454) wef 20 August 1943 (gazetted 2/11/43)
Hibbert	G	AC1		538174	None	None	None	17/6/40	None	France	Sp, Gib	4/9/41	5/9/41	Oban	3306 493	Groundcrew. Repatriated on medical grounds. MM (13/3/42)
Hickey	J	F/S			233	KG399	DAK	21/9/44	Supply drop	Holland	Hol			NK	NF	Report IS9/WEA/2/577/*
Hickton	HI	SGT	NZ	NZ.403004	101	R1699	WE	10/9/41	Turin	France	Gib	30/9/42	5/10/42	Greenock	3310 894	Evacuated by *Seawolf* 5 September 1942. Back to UK on HMS *Malaya*. See *Safe Houses are Dangerous*, pp. 164-6; *Night After Night*, pp. 365-6; and *Wait For The Dawn*
Higginson	FW	F/L		44630	56	Z2575	HUR	17/6/41	Circus 14	France	Gib	30/9/42	5/10/42	Greenock	3310 872	DFM (30/7/40). Interned by Vichy. Escaped 23 August 1942. Evacuated by *Seawolf*. Back on HMS *Malaya*. DFC (9/2/43). See *Home Run*, Chapter 4
Hilborne	RA	SGT		1896903	630	LM537	LA	18/7/44	Revigny-sur-Ornain	France	Fr	7/9/44	7/9/44	NK	3322 2270	See *Massacre over the Marne*
Hiley	E	SGT		1433123	100	ND595	LA	25/2/44	Augsburg	Switzerland	Ger, Fr, Sp, Gib	24/5/44	25/5/44	Whitchurch	3319 1939	Repatriated with German agreement. Back on BOAC Dakota
Hill	AF	F/L		123999	582	ND817	LA	7/8/44	Mare de Magne	France				NK	NF	MiD (8/6/44). DFC (4/12/45, squadron leader)
Hill	FD	F/O		132036	158	LW298	HAL	3/11/43	Düsseldorf	Belgium	Fr, Sp, Gib	5/2/44	6/2/44	Whitchurch	3318 1755	With Pilot Officer F.T. Williams DFM. Comet 263. Whitchurch?
Hill	HG	SGT		1836287	166	JB649	LA	25/7/44	Stuttgart	France	Fr	8/9/44	8/9/44	Middle Wallop	3323 2451	Back from Orléans with 1 SAS
Hill	JB	W/O		950389	502	JP164	HAL	29/8/44	Anti-shipping, Loire	France (sea)	Fr	7/12/44	7/12/44	NK	3345 792	ss9. Shot down and rescued by intended victim. In POW camp at St Nazaire. Escaped 19/20 November 1944. Interviewed 8 December 1944. Report MISC/INT/792. JP164?
Hill	JH	W/O		578630	161	LL248	HAL	4/8/44	SOE	France				NK	NF	ss7. Despatcher on Operation BOB166. Back by Hudson from near Caen. Author of *Escape from a Halifax*. Service no?
Hill	JM	F/L	CAN	J.7761	431	MZ522	HAL	27/4/44	Montzen	Belgium	Bel		15/9/44	NK	NF	Liberated by US forces on 8 September 1944
Hills	RA	W/O		1600614	299	LJ942	ST	2/4/45	SOE Tablejam 283	Denmark	Swe	11/5/45	11/5/45	Leuchars	3327 3018	Back by air. Leuchars?
Hillyard	EG	SGT		747947	150	L5541	BA	15/6/40	Troops, Chartres	France	Sp, Gib	14/2/41	23/2/41	Gourock	3302 266	Right arm amputated. MiD (11/6/42)
Hinder	CH	F/S		1221913	620		ST	21/9/44	Supply drop	Holland	Hol			NK	3351 2267	Interviewed 23 October 1944. Report IS9/WEA/2/615/2267
Hindle	RP	SGT		900799	644	LL228	HAL	5/4/44	SOE	France	Sp, Gib	5/6/44	6/6/44	Whitchurch	3320 1946	With Flight Sergeant J. Franklin to Spain. Helped by Françoise Dissard in Toulouse

Hinds	AMcC	SGT	CAN	R.205106	138	LL416	HAL	7/6/44	SOE	France	Fr	22/9/44	22/9/44	Northolt	3324 2550	ss7
Hirst	GH	SGT		1493738	158	JD298	HAL	27/8/43	Nuremberg	Luxembourg	Fr, Sp, Gib			NK	NF	With Sergeant E.W. Brearley. UK September 1944. Report CSDIC/CMF/SKP/3759. See *In Brave Company* pp. 96-8
Hirst	H	SGT		1673523	57	PD212	LA	28/7/44	Stuttgart	France				NK	NF	
Hitchman	SW	SGT		1582327	149	EF202	ST	25/11/43	Mining	France	Fr		11/9/44	NK	3348 35	Report IS9/WEA/8/42/35
Hoad	DJ	F/S		1576247	44	ND520	LA	25/2/44	Augsburg	France	Sp, Gib	24/6/44	25/6/44	Whitchurch	3320 2002	Helped by Françoise Dissard in Toulouse 24 May 1944. Whitchurch?
Hoare	RG	P/O		53948	12	JB650	LA	27/1/44	Berlin	Belgium	Fr, Sp, Gib	24/6/44	25/6/44	Whitchurch	3320 2003	Whitchurch?
Hobday	HS	F/O		119291	617	JB144	LA	15/9/43	Ladbergen	Holland	Bel, Fr, Sp, Gib	5/12/43	6/12/43	Portreath	3317 1603	DFC (28/5/43) for the Dams raid
Hobler	JF	S/L		34060	142	P2246	BA	14/5/40	Sedan	Belgium	Fr			None	NF	Badly burnt in face. Taken to hospital by French. Belgium? Later, air vice-marshal CB, CBE (1/1/45), MiD (1/1/43, 2/6/43 & 8/6/44)
Hodder	W	WO1	CAN	R.104153	432	LW616	HAL	12/6/44	Cambrai	France	Fr	7/9/44	7/9/44	NK	3323 2354	
Hodge	RA	F/S	NZ	NZ.413756	149	BF530	ST	3/7/43	Cologne	Belgium	Fr, Sp, Gib	4/10/43	5/10/43	Whitchurch	3315 1453	Comet 137
Hodges	LM	F/O		33408	49	P1347	HN	4/9/40	Stettin	France	Sp, Gib	13/6/41	14/6/41	Mount Batten	3304 345	MiD (11/6/42). Air Chief Marshal Sir Lewis Hodges KCB, CBE, DSO (19/10/43, 161 Squadron) & Bar (19/10/45, 357 Squadron), DFC (26/5/42) & Bar (25/5/43, 161 Squadron). Died 4 January 2007
Hodgson	CL	SGT		1356440	297	EB297	WH	19/2/43	NK	France	Sp, Gib	5/4/43	12/4/43	Liverpool	3312 1161	Left Madrid with Pilot Officer Spittal, Sergeant J.G. Dawson and Marine Sparks. Commissioned (178766) wef 20 June 1944. MiD [not found]
Hogg	EL	F/O		135755	106	ND680	LA	6/6/44	Coutances	France	Fr			NK	3345 654	Sprained ankle and broken arm. Captured 9 June 1944. Liberated from Stalag 221 (Rennes) 4 August 1944. Interviewed 5 September 1944. Report MI9/S/P.G./MISC/INT/654
Hogg	TC	SGT		3020140	10	LV870	HAL	28/6/44	Blainville	France	Fr			NK	3350 1275	Interviewed 4 September 1944. Report IS9/WEA/7/182/1275
Holland	FE	F/L		89070	184	MN667	TY	7/6/44	NK	France	Fr	20/8/44	20/8/44	Northolt	3321 2111	Left for UK from Bayeux - B.14 airstrip, Banville. Author of *D-Day Plus One*
Hollick	GD	F/S		1583264	570	LJ638	ST	12/4/45	SOE supply drop	Holland	Hol			NK	3348 201	In a house attacked by Germans on 29 April 1945. Interviewed 11 May 1945. Report IS9/WEA/PLM/201
Holliday	HL	F/L		66492	138	Z9232	WH	24/8/42	SOE	France	Gib	30/9/42	5/10/42	Greenock	3310 881	DFC (21/11/41, 214 Squadron). Evacuated by *Seawolf* 21 September 1942. Back on HMS *Malaya*
Hollocks	RA	SGT		1626068	578	LW675	HAL	12/6/44	Amiens	France	Fr	15/9/44	15/9/44	NK	3325 2888	Interviewed 12 September 1944. Report IS9/WEA/MB/1321 (see WO 208/3350)
Holmes	APR	F/O	CAN	J.25018	432	LK807	HAL	27/4/44	Montzen	Belgium	Bel			NK	3350 1319	Received forty-eight splinter wounds when aircraft hit. Interviewed 12 September 1944. Report IS9/WEA/MB/1319. DFC (16/11/45)
Holmes	GEJ	F/S		1579355	296	V1605	ALB	6/6/44	NK	France	Fr	7/6/44	8/6/44	Portsmouth	3320 1973	Left for UK from Allied beachhead
Holroyd	SG	SGT		1194036	158	HR740	HAL	12/6/43	Bochum	Holland	Bel, Fr, Sz	17/9/44	18/9/44	NK	3323 2444	To Switzerland on 9 July 1943. Left on 6 September 1944. Back to UK from Casablanca
Holt	HR	SGT		1576238	90	NE177	LA	10/6/44	Dreux	France	Fr	27/8/44	27/8/44	NK	3322 2235	Liberated 23 August 1944. Left for UK from Bayeux - B.14 airstrip, Banville. See website f4bscale.worldonline.co.uk/sgtharry.htm
Homolle	J	LT	FRA		340	MK234	SP	27/6/44	Sweep	France			28/6/44	NK	NF	
Hood	L	F/S		1499246	582	ND921	LA	28/6/44	Blainville	France	Fr			Northolt	3349 435	Liberated at Livry-Gargan, north-east Paris, by Americans on 29 August 1944. Report IS9/WEA/7/97/435
Hooks	J	SGT	CAN	R.185557	51	LK885	HAL	24/5/44	Aachen	Holland				NK	3350 1380	Evaded with WO2 J.H. Frame. Interviewed 23 September 1944. Report IS9/WEA/2/516/1380
Hooper	GJ	P/O	NZ	NZ.413231	486	EJ787	TEM	2/2/45	Armed patrol	Germany				NK	NF	Shot down near Kirchdorf. Briefly taken prisoner. DFC (14/9/45)
Hooper	RN	F/O	AUS	A.425851	463	LM597	LA	24/6/44	Prouville	France	Fr			NK	NF	
Hooper	RWJ	F/L		81075	161	V9548	LYS	16/11/43	SOE	France	Fr	17/12/43	17/12/43	Tangmere	3317 1625	DFC (14/5/43). Lysander bogged down after landing in France. DSO (14/1/44 - not specifically for evasion)
Hopkins	J	LAC		358338	None	None	None	4/7/40	None	France	Sp, Gib	26/8/41	26/8/41	Calshot	3308 716	Groundcrew at No. 5 Air Stores Park, Verzenay, France. Repatriated on a Medical Board
Horn	VE	SGT		1238498	158	LW298	HAL	3/11/43	Düsseldorf	Belgium	Fr, Sz, Fr	4/9/44	5/9/44	Lyneham	3323 2369	Helped by Anne Brusselmans. Returned to UK from St Tropez, France, via Algiers and Casablanca
Horne	LW	SGT			76	DT515	HAL	7/11/42	Genoa	France	Sz			NK	NF	In Switzerland 17 February 1943. Report Switzerland/31
Hornsey	DG	F/L		65789	76	LK932	HAL	3/11/43	Düsseldorf	Belgium	Fr, Sp, Gib	9/12/43	10/12/43	St Mawgan	3317 1610	Comet 207. Through France with Sergeant George Gineikis USAAF (Comet 209). DFC (4/12/45). Author of *The Pilot Walked Home*

Horrex	EPA	F/L		121093	151	PZ218	MOS	22/7/44	Ranger	France	Fr	6/9/44	6/9/44	NK	3345 811	DFC (2/6/44). Wounded. Captured. Taken to hospital in Toulouse, where liberated 18 August 1944. Interviewed 9 January 1945. Report M.I.9/S/P.G./MISC/INT/811. See Squadron Leader R.H. Harrison
Horsley	HW	S/L		68786	61	LM718	LA	23/9/44	Ladbergen	Holland				NK	3350 1403	Interviewed 27 September 1944. Report IS9/WEA/2/540/1403. KIA 1 February 1945 (Siegen)
Horsley	RM	P/O		120849	50	L7301	MAN	30/5/42	Cologne	Belgium	Fr, Sp, Gib	6/7/42	12/7/42	Gourock	3309 771	Comet 18. Back on the *Narkunda*. DFC (6/10/42). See *Silent Heroes* pp.35, 64, and *Free To Fight Again* pp. 140-64
Hortie	RH	SGT	CAN	R.184340	619	W4127	LA	20/4/44	La Chapelle	France	Fr			NK	3321 2144	ss7. Sherwood. Interviewed 19 August 1944
Horton	S	SGT		1035423	103	ED751	LA	5/9/43	Mannheim	France	Fr	17/9/43	18/9/43	Falmouth	3315 1409	To UK by fishing boat. MiD (8/6/44). Date left for UK is a guess. See *Evader*, pp. 243-44, and *Free To Fight Again*, pp. 182-6
Hoskisson	RT	SGT		961858	61	LM718	LA	23/9/44	Ladbergen	Holland	Hol			NK	3350 1419	Report IS9/WEA/2/539/1419. KIA 1 February 1945 (Siegen)
Houghton	KHL	F/S		580451	207	L7373	MAN	13/10/41	Cologne	Belgium	Fr, Sz, Fr, Sp, Por	24/7/42	24/7/42	Poole	3309 788	DFM (22/11/40, 83 Squadron). Left by Sunderland from Lisbon. Bar to DFM (1/9/42). Killed 2 August 1945 in Liberator KN826 in the Middle East
Houghton	SJ	SGT		745228	220	P5146	HUD	2/4/41	Crossover patrol	France	Sp, Gib	4/7/41	13/7/41	Glasgow	3304 373	Back with Sgt N.J. Ingram
Hourigan	E	F/O	AUS	A.420882	466	LV943	HAL	6/5/44	Mantes-la-Jolie	France	Fr	18/8/44	18/8/44	Northolt	3321 2081	Sherwood. Left for UK from B.14 airstrip, Banville. DFC (9/3/45)
House	CRA	F/L			613	HR251	MOS	18/8/44	Gestapo HQ	France					NF	The target was a former school building at Égletons
Houston	AJ	P/O	CAN	J.35002	28 OTU	LN896	WE	20/4/44	Nickel	France	Fr	12/7/44	13/7/44	NK	3320 2026	Aircraft ran out of fuel when directed by German radio to Brittany. Burgundy line? Back by MGB 503
Howard	DR	SGT		655165	7	R9149	ST	9/3/43	Munich	France	Sp, Gib	17/7/43	24/7/43	Liverpool	3314 1329	Oaktree. Back to UK on SS *Monarch of Bermuda?*
Howard	ND	W/O	AUS	A.409307	1	JP483	TY	2/3/44	Ramrod	Belgium	Fr			NK	3322 2322	Liberated 2 September 1944
Howe	AEA	F/O		154343	61	PD199	LA	2/11/44	Düsseldorf	Germany				NK	5415	Came down near Zweifall, Germany
Howell	E	F/O		144194	138	BB378	HAL	10/12/43	SOE	Denmark	Swe	5/1/44	5/1/44	Leuchars	3317 1672	See *Making for Sweden*, pp. 95-8. DFC (8/12/44, flight lieutenant)
Howells	D	SGT		1836626	44	LM654	LA	5/3/45	Böhlen	Germany				NK		Other six crew taken prisoner of war. Germany?
Howells	JD	F/S		1530990	65	FB223	MU	27/7/44	Sweep	France	Fr			NK	3348 322	Liberated by British forces 16 August 1944. Interviewed 17 August 1944. Report IS9/WEA/2/150/322
Hoyle	K	SGT		1592460	166	LL896	LA	12/7/44	Revigny-sur-Ornain	France	Fr	4/9/44	4/9/44	Hendon	3323 2462	Back to UK from Paris. See *Massacre over the Marne*
Hrbacek	H	S/L	CZ	87618	310	MJ798	SP	21/5/44	Ramrod 905	France	Fr		19/8/44	NK	3348 293	Liberated 17 August 1944. Report IS9/WEA/2/147/293
Huckins	H	SGT			21	L8743	BL	11/6/40	La Mare	France	Fr			NK	NF	Possibly not an evader. 581016 HGU Huckins, later commissioned and DFC (11/8/42, 18 Sq)?
Hudson	HJ	P/O		143810	7	ED595	LA	24/6/43	Wuppertal	Holland	Bel, Fr, Sp, Gib	5/11/43	6/11/43	Whitchurch	3316 1534	DFM (12/3/43). Comet 172
Hughes	M	SGT		1836300	190		ST	21/9/44	Arnhem supply drop	Holland				NK	3350 1402	Interviewed? Report IS9/WEA/2/526/1402
Hughes	S	SGT		1127645	9	ED480	LA	9/7/43	Gelsenkirchen	France	Sp, And, Gib	1/9/43	2/9/43	Whitchurch	3314 1387	Burgundy?
Hughes	T	SGT		2210561	576	LM122	LA	2/11/44	Düsseldorf	Belgium				NK	NF	
Hughes	W	SGT		1074684	102	JB840	HAL	8/3/43	Nuremberg	France	Sp, Gib	20/8/43	21/8/43	Portreath	3314 1365	DFM (1/10/43)
Humphris	RHP	SGT		755447	15	R1080	WE	26/4/41	Transit	Mediterranean	Fr, Sp, Gib	1/10/41	6/10/41	Scapa Flow	3306 566	Interned by the French, escaped, and imprisoned by the Spanish
Hunt	W	SGT		1818270	630	LM269	LA	18/8/44	Bordeaux	France	Fr			NK	3350 1335	Interviewed 10 September 1944. Report IS9(WEA)/MB/1335. See also WO 208/5415
Hunter	AW	SGT		1214904	10	LV882	HAL	1/6/44	Trappes	France	Fr			NK	5415 2045	ss7. Interviewed 28 September 1944. Report IS9(WEA)/6/360/2045
Hunter	K	F/S		1434946	83	JB402	LA	3/5/44	Mailly-le-Camp	France	Fr	6/9/44	6/9/44	Hendon	3325 2887	Back to UK via Paris
Hunter	RI	F/S	AUS	A.426882	467	JA901	LA	3/5/44	Mailly-le-Camp	France	Fr	13/9/44	13/9/44	NK	3345 690	Badly burnt. Suffered gangrene. In hospital under German supervision. Liberated 28 August 1944. Interviewed 26 September 1944. Report MISC/INT/690
Hunter	RO	SGT	CAN	R.102359	161	DK119	HAL	22/7/43	SOE	France	Fr	15/11/43	16/11/43	Tangmere	3316 1574	Back by Lysander on Operation Water Pistol.
Huntley	CO	WO1	CAN	R.87187	207	PB295	LA	21/2/45	Gravenhorst	Holland	Hol			NK	3352 2418	In Holland with Flying Officers F.H. Dell and J.A. Strickland. Interviewed 31 March 1945. Report IS9/WEA/1/321/2418
Huston	HT	F/O	CAN	J.13071	405	HR854	HAL	15/7/43	Montbéliard	France	Sp, Gib	29/11/43	30/11/43	Whitchurch	3316 1591	With Squadron Leader Lambert. Burgundy line. Flown back to UK by DC3. Whitchurch?
Hutchinson	AR	SGT	CAN	R.192337	433	HX353	HAL	4/7/44	Villeneuve-St Georges	France	Fr		30/8/44	NK	3321 2198	Betrayed, captured but escaped when column bombed by US B-26 Marauders on 19 August 1944
Hutchinson	JT	P/O		141812	138	BB313	HAL	12/5/43	SOE	France	Sp, And, Gib	5/8/43	6/8/43	Hendon	3314 1332	With Sergeant W.H. Marshall of same crew. DFC (2/11/43)
Hutton	JW	SGT		1378696	101	R1703	WE	31/8/41	Cologne	Belgium	Fr, Sp, Gib	4/3/42	10/3/42	Gourock	3308 688	Comet 12. MiD (1/1/43). Warrant Officer Hutton DFC (19/9/44) was killed in

															action on 31 July 1944 on 617 Squadron. See *Rendez-vous 127*, photo facing p. 49
Hutton	TH	SGT		1108958	12	W4366	LA	16/4/43	Pilsen	Belgium	Fr, Sp, Gib	17/7/43	24/7/43	Liverpool	3314 1322	Baled out in error - aircraft returned to base. See *Free to Fight Again*, pp.165-70. Back to UK on SS *Monarch of Bermuda?*
Hyde	DB	F/S	CAN	R.149472	622	LL828	LA	15/3/44	Stuttgart	France	Fr			NK	3349 366	Sherwood. Interviewed 19 August 1944. Report IS9/WEA/2/158/366
Hyde	TE	SGT		580579	139	L9416	BL	12/5/40	Enemy troops	Belgium	Fr			NK	NF	Killed on 3 June 1941, still a sergeant on 139 Squadron. Buried at Tripoli War Cemetery
Hyde	WJ	SGT		1895228	75	ND756	LA	28/7/44	Stuttgart	France	Fr	7/9/44	7/9/44	NK	3323 2375	Left for UK from Paris
Hyland	PJ	F/S		566484	12	NE134	LA	22/5/44	Dortmund	Germany	Hol, Bel			NK	3351 2309	Report IS9(WEA)/2/1011/2309
Ibbotson	DT	F/O	AUS	A.415808	44	ME694	LA	25/7/44	Stuttgart	France	Fr			NK	3348 309	Sherwood. Interviewed 17 August 1944. Report IS9/WEA/2/86/309
Inglis	AC	F/S	AUS	A.428916	274	EJ781	TEM	23/4/45	Armed patrol	Germany				NK	NF	Shot down 3 enemy aircraft before being shot down himself. Commissioned and awarded the DFC (14/9/45)
Ingram	NJ	SGT	NZ	580400	82	V5977	BL	13/5/41	St Nazaire	France	Sp, Gib	4/7/41	13/7/41	Glasgow	3304 375	New Zealander in RAF. DFM (5/11/40, 150 Squadron). Captured by Vichy French. Escaped. Commissioned (50185) wef 24 October 1942. DFC (29/6/45) as flight lieutenant on 21 Squadron
Innes	IRC	F/S	AUS	A.423016	78	MZ692	HAL	22/6/44	Laon	France	Fr	6/9/44	6/9/44	NK	3323 2525	MM (12/6/45). See *Massacre over the Marne*, pp. 128-31 & 135-6
Inverarity	T	SGT	CAN	R.170349	434	LW433	HAL	16/6/44	Sterkrade	Holland				NK	NF	
Irvine	SH	F/O			226	FV924	MCL	1/9/44	Enemy troops	France					NF	
Irwin	RP	SGT	EIR	1797758	432	MZ601	HAL	12/6/44	Cambrai	Belgium	Bel			NK	3350 1325	Marathon camp Ardennes. Liberated by US forces 8 September 1944. Interviewed 11 September 1944. Report IS9/WEA/MB/1325
Isherwood	R	F/O		48429	78	LW273	HAL	23/9/43	Mannheim	France	And, Sp, Gib	27/10/43	28/10/43	Portreath	3315 1503	
Ives	JL	SGT	CAN	R.62735	51	Z6569	WH	18/8/41	Cologne	Belgium	Fr, Sp, Gib	30/12/41	5/1/42	Gourock	3307 632	Comet 6. Reached Spain 10 December 1941. To UK on Polish ship *Batory*. MiD (1/1/43). Killed in action on 28 April 1945 in Dakota KG406, 271 Squadron
Jacks	WA	F/O		145426	77	LK710	HAL	22/4/44	Laon	France	Sp, Gib	5/6/44	6/6/44	Whitchurch	3320 1947	Comet 282. DFC (5/9/44)
Jackson	AV	F/S		1377495	514	DS815	LA	22/3/44	Frankfurt	France	Sp, Gib	24/6/44	25/6/44	Whitchurch	3320 1995	In Toulouse 20 May 1944. Helped by Françoise Dissard
Jackson	JH	F/O		105241	109	LR499	MOS	2/12/43	Bochum	Holland				NK	NF	Service number?
Jackson	KE	SGT		1336192	75	HK553	LA	10/6/44	Dreux	France	Fr	26/8/44	26/8/44	Northolt	3321 2147	ss7. Left for UK from Bayeux - B.14 airstrip, Banville. Northolt?
Jackson	RT	F/O		133673	74	NH461	SP	26/8/44	Armed recce	France				NK	NF	Service number?
James	DE	F/S	CAN	R.92762	214	BK653	ST	16/4/43	Mannheim	France	Sp, Gib	17/7/43	24/7/43	Liverpool	3314 1317	Oaktree. Back to UK on *Monarch of Bermuda*?
James	RAV	F/O		149988	97	ND840	LA	6/8/44	Bois de Cassan	France	Fr	6/9/44	6/9/44	Hendon	3324 2757	DFC (10/12/43, 106 Squadron). ss8. Briefly captured in Paris on 23 August. See *Achieve Your Aim*, p. 242
Jannsen	MJ	P/O	HOL		322	RK897	SP	1/4/45	Offensive operations	Holland				NK	NF	Wounded. Baled out near Zutphen
Jarvis	JH	LAC		506616	152	None	HUR	20/5/40	None	France	Sp, Gib	11/3/41	17/3/41	Greenock	3302 236	Groundcrew. Injured helping to put out fire in bomber. Repatriated on medical grounds
Jeffrey	HT	SGT		1392693	158	LW723	HAL	10/4/44	Tergnier	France	Fr	10/9/44	10/9/44	NK	3323 2490	Captured when about to cross Pyrenees. Severely beaten. To Fresnes, Paris. Escaped from train on 2 August 1944. MM (9/2/45)
Jeffrey	JS	WO2	CAN	R.141406	411	NH341	SP	2/7/44	Patrol	France	Fr			NK	NF	With Major Donald W. McLeod USAAF and Maquis group in Normandy. To UK August 1944. Report IS9/WEA/1/26/2344
Jeka	J	F/L	POL	780836	308	ML254	SP	21/5/44	Rhubarb	France	Fr	11/9/44	11/9/44	NK	3322 2290	DFM (306 Squadron), VM. Polish Service number P.1654
Jenkins	CA	SGT		1601485	622	LM108	LA	28/5/44	Angers	France	Fr			NK	3348 287	Liberated by US troops 14 August 1944. Interviewed 17 August 1944. Report IS9/WEA/2/88/287
Jenkins	TJ	SGT		1379417	149	W7572	ST	24/8/42	Frankfurt	Belgium	Fr, Gib	18/10/42	19/10/42	Poole	3311 916	Evacuated by *Seawolf* 12 October 1942
Jenkins	WJ	SGT		1316316	158	HR779	HAL	16/4/43	Mannheim	France	Sz			NK	NF	To Switzerland 12 May 1943. Left c. 16 September 1944. Report Switzerland/32
Jennings	DA	F/O		142451	57	LM580	LA	21/6/44	Wesseling	Belgium	Bel	17/9/44	17/9/44	Hendon	NF	Back by Dakota from Paris, Author of *Jump or Die*
Jennings	DR	WO2	CAN	R.153179	214	SR382	FT	21/6/44	Bomber support	Holland				NK	3350 1481	Splinters in leg. Escaped from Dutch hospital disguised as policeman. Report IS9(WEA)/1/219/1481. DFC (17/11/44)
Jennings	DR	F/S	AUS	A.423542	115	LM166	LA	8/8/44	Lucheux	France	Fr	6/9/44	6/9/44	NK	3322 2277	
Jennings	HJ	F/S	CAN	R.85952	405	BB250	HAL	11/3/43	Stuttgart	France	Sp, Gib	19/4/43	20/4/43	Hendon	3313 1175	MiD (1/1/43). Commissioned during evasion (J.16817). DFC (6/7/43). See *Valley of the Shadow of Death*, pp.94-8

Jezzard	P	SGT		1501713	622	LL828	LA	15/3/44	Stuttgart	France	Sp, Gib	22/5/44	23/5/44	Whitchurch	3319 1929	DFM (2/1/45)
John	HC	SGT	CAN	R.172872	180	FW175	MCL	9/8/44	Forges-les-Eaux	France	Fr	5/9/44	6/9/44	NK	3323 2463	Target was a fuel dump. Back to UK from Bayeux - B.14 airstrip, Banville
Johns	AH	SGT		942751	460	W4988	LA	3/9/43	Berlin	Denmark	Swe	20/9/43	21/9/43	Leuchars	3315 1412	Stole a boat on night of 11 September 1943 at Aalsgaarde, Denmark. Landed in Sweden at Mölle, 0600 hours 12 September 1943
Johnson	D	P/O		178782	640	LW654	HAL	10/8/44	Dijon	France				NK	NF	DFM (19/9/44). Shot down as flight sergeant (1458103) he was commissioned wef 30 June 1944 (gazetted 15/8/44)
Johnson	EC	F/O		119126	617	JB144	LA	15/9/43	Ladbergen	Holland	Bel, Fr, Sp, Gib	20/12/43	21/12/43	Whitchurch	3317 1639	DFC (28/5/43) for the Dams raid. Comet 216. Died, aged ninety, on 1 October 2002
Johnson	G	P/O	AUS	A.414801	467	LM376	LA	30/3/44	Nuremberg	Belgium	Bel		9/9/44	NK	3327 3097	Evaded with Curl. Liberated by US army
Johnson	KH	SGT		634994	295	LJ618	ST	20/9/44	Arnhem supply drop	Holland	Hol	22/9/44	22/9/44	Harwell	NF	Operation Market IV. Returned to base within fifty hours. Surname possibly Johnston
Johnson	RE	F/S		1575340	77	LK710	HAL	22/4/44	Laon	France	Fr	1/9/44	1/9/44	NK	3345	Captured. Right leg amputated below knee. Interviewed 7 February 1945. Report MISC/INT/823
Johnson	RN	F/O	AUS	A.423243	101	DV288	LA	10/4/44	Aulnoye	France	Fr	4/9/44	4/9/44	NK	3322 2261	Left for UK from Bayeux - B.14 airstrip, Banville
Johnson	RVC	SGT		1545885	75	EH938	ST	30/8/43	Mönchengladbach	Belgium	Fr	16/11/43	17/11/43	Tangmere	3316 1579	ss7. Possum. Flown back by Lysander from France on Operation Magdalen II (with Americans Maddox and Murray)
Johnson	SC	F/L			21	NS965	MOS	31/8/44	Interdiction	France					NF	Took off early on 1 September
Johnson	TG	SGT		364844	102	R9528	HAL	27/4/42	Dunkirk	France	Gib	24/7/42	30/7/42	Gourock	3309 790	Evacuated by *Tarana* 14 July 1942. To UK on *Llanstephan Castle*. MiD (1/1/43). Pilot officer (51690) wef 5 April 1943
Johnson	W	SGT		1690722	50	LL922	LA	7/8/44	Secqueville	France	Fr	3/9/44	3/9/44	NK	3322 2263	
Johnson	WG	SGT		524728	467	PB234	LA	18/7/44	Revigny-sur-Ornain	France	Fr	9/9/44	9/9/44	NK	3325 2889	Joined RAF on 1 October 1935. See *Massacre over the Marne*
Johnston	CC	F/L		81926	619	ME745	LA	7/7/44	St Leu d'Esserent	France				NK	NF	
Johnstone	W	SGT		1697226	425	LW390	HAL	20/2/44	Stuttgart	France	Fr			NK	3350 1387	Interviewed 17 September 1944. Report IS9/WEA/2/512/1387
Jolly	SD	F/S	AUS	A.426606	467	JA901	LA	3/5/44	Mailly-le-Camp	France	Fr			NK	3350 1272	Interviewed 1 September 1944. Report IS9/WEA/7/144/1272. See *Silent Heroes*, p. 46
Jones	A	SGT		1523137	76	MZ539	HAL	28/6/44	Blainville	France				NK	NF	
Jones	DL	SGT		1440300	51	DT690	HAL	16/4/43	Pilsen	France	Sp, Gib	14/8/43	15/8/43	Hendon	3314 1357	Landed on Laon-Athies airfield. Recommended for MiD but awarded DFM (1/10/43)
Jones	E	SGT		999682	161	LL183	HAL	9/5/44	SOE	France	Fr	9/9/44	9/9/44	Tempsford	3323 2414	
Jones	ER	F/S	CAN	R.211833	514	LL692	LA	28/7/44	Stuttgart	France	Fr		17/8/44	NK	3321 2109	Sherwood
Jones	HB	LAC		536398	218	P2183	BA	12/5/40	Bouillon	France				NK	NF	MiD (1/1/41). No Report found
Jones	HTS	SGT		1851549	10	NR189	HAL	21/2/45	Worms	Germany	Ger			NK	3352 2400	Other six crew taken prisoner of war. DFM (15/6/45). Liberated by US troops. Interviewed 7 March 1945. Report IS9/WEA/2/1024/2400
Jones	JR	F/L	AUS	A.402462	78	LW273	HAL	23/9/43	Mannheim	France	Sz			NK	NF	DFC (29/12/42). On 2nd tour of ops. Reached Switzerland 8 October 1943. Left 4 October 1944. Report Switzerland/21
Jones	PV	F/O		151230	156	ND449	LA	6/5/44	Mantes-la-Jolie	France	Sp, Gib	24/6/44	25/6/44	Whitchurch	3320 1996	With Flight Sergeant G.M.G. Meer. To UK by Dakota flown by a Frenchman. DFC (23/5/44)
Jones	RA	WO1	CAN	R.121359	431	LK967	HAL	25/11/43	Frankfurt	France	Fr	22/1/44	23/1/44	Falmouth	3318 1719	With both Bordeaux and Burgundy lines. To UK from Brittany aboard the *Breizh-Izel*
Jones	RW	F/L	CAN	J.11270	3	EJ895	TEM	8/2/45	Sweep	Holland	Hol			NK	3327 3000	See *Fighter Command Losses Volume 3*, p. 144, where he is listed as prisoner of war
Jones	SB	SGT	CAN	R.197072	158	LK877	HAL	1/6/44	Trappes	France	Fr	29/8/44	29/8/44	Northolt	3322 2223	Left for UK from Bayeux - B.14 airstrip, Banville
Jones	T	F/S		1489924	295	LK567	ST	26/4/45	SOE supply drop	Denmark	Dk	16/5/45	16/5/45	NK	3327 3043	On supply drop for Danish underground
Jones	WF	F/O	CAN	J.26302	630	PB244	LA	18/8/44	L'Isle-Adam	France	Fr			NK	3323 2383	Liberated 31 August 1944. Back in UK by 6 September 1944
Jones	WL	F/O		131952	158	LK877	HAL	1/6/44	Trappes	France	Fr	29/8/44	29/8/44	NK	3321 2188	
Jopling	RH	P/O	AUS	A.410065	460	ND654	LA	20/7/44	Courtrai	Belgium	Fr		12/9/44	NK	3327 3109	Baled out near Dixmude. Taken to France on 28 July 1944. With Sergeant K.G. Butler. Liberated 7 September 1944 in Halluin. Went to Lille with Butler on 10 September 1944
Jowsey	ME	S/L	CAN	J.6366	442	PT725	SP	22/2/45	Enemy troops	Holland	Hol	5/4/45	5/4/45	NK	3326 2942	DFC (1/10/43). Shot down by own ricochets!
Jubb	RV	P/O	AUS	A.426609	462	LL610	HAL	2/11/44	Düsseldorf	Germany				NK	3348 2293	DFC (2/2/45)
Judson	WG	F/L	NZ	NZ.413425	487	HP933	MOS	6/8/44	Intruder	France	Fr	29/9/44	29/9/44	NK	3324 2734	Shot down by flak. Badly wounded to head. Reached Allied lines one month

																later. DFC (17/4/45). Mosquito HP933 or NT125? – see Flight Lieutenant Coombs
Justason	BR	F/S	CAN	R.174951	432	NP687	HAL	25/7/44	Stuttgart	France	Fr	15/8/44	15/8/44	NK	3321 2098	Left for UK from A22 airstrip near Rennes
Kaminek	A	W/O	POL	788122	310	MA226	SP	5/9/44	Barges	Holland	Hol			NK	3351 2319	Interviewed 14 December 1944. Report IS9/WEA/2/166/2319
Kanakos	TJ	SGT	CAN	R.144074	161	DK119	HAL	22/7/43	SOE	France	Fr	15/11/43	16/11/43	Tangmere	3316 1575	Back by Lysander on Operation Water Pistol. See website www.torontoaircrew.com
Kannengeiser	RD	SGT	FRA	C.3783	347	NA572	HAL	16/1/45	Magdeburg	Germany	Ger	10/3/45	10/3/45	NK	3326 2923	Captured. Escaped when train strafed. Worked as a driver for Germans in Cologne. Walked to Allied lines 1 March 1945. Used nom de guerre "Renet"
Kay	R	F/O		53358	550	ME840	LA	16/6/44	Sterkrade	Holland				NK	NF	ss7
Kaye	PA	SGT	CAN	R.174945	83	PB362	LA	18/8/44	L'Isle-Adam	France	Fr	6/9/44	6/9/44	NK	3323 2466	
Kearins	TSF	F/S	NZ	NZ.404877	485	EN573	SP	15/7/43	Rodeo	France	Fr	24/10/43	25/10/43	Penzance	3315 1498	Back by boat. Croix de Guerre with Silver Star (French) (5/6/46)
Kellett	AF	SGT		1258269	15	EF348	ST	22/6/43	Mülheim	Holland	Bel, Fr, Sp, Gib	5/12/43	6/12/43	Portreath	3317 1602	Comet 173
Kellow	RGT	P/O	AUS	A.411453	617	JB144	LA	15/9/43	Ladbergen	Holland	Bel, Fr, Sp, Gib	2/12/43	3/12/43	St Mawgan	3316 1597	DFM (15/6/43, 50 Squadron). Comet 165. With Sergeant W.F. Catley
Kelly	DV	F/S	AUS	A.418751	467	R5485	LA	18/7/44	Revigny-sur-Ornain	France	Fr	6/9/44	6/9/44	NK	3322 2303	See *Massacre over the Marne*
Kelly	WJ	WO2	CAN	R.100664	419	KB726	LA	12/6/44	Cambrai	France	Fr	6/9/44	6/9/44	NK	3323 2397	In same crew as Mynarski VC
Kemley	HJS	F/L		128489	432	NP687	HAL	25/7/44	Stuttgart	France	Fr			NK	3348 229	Sherwood. Interviewed 17 August 1944. Report IS9/WEA/2/104/229. DFC (26/1/46) wef 25 July 1944
Kemp	AF	F/O	CAN	J.25975	630	PB244	LA	18/8/44	L'Isle-Adam	France	Fr			NK	3323 2382	Liberated 31 August 1944. Back in UK by 6 September 1944
Kennedy	IF	S/L	CAN	J.15273	401	MK311	SP	26/7/44	Rodeo	France	Fr		24/8/44	NK	3349 375	DFC (6/7/43, 249 Squadron) & Bar (5/9/44). Liberated 22 August 1944. Interviewed 25 August 1944. Report IS9/WEA/2/206/375. Author of *Black Crosses off My Wingtip*
Kennedy	JF	F/O	CAN	J.28862	429	MZ302	HAL	28/6/44	Metz	France	Fr			NK	3348 296	Sherwood. Interviewed 17 August 1944. Report IS9/WEA/2/82/296
Kennedy	JL	F/L	CAN	C.1476	24 OTU	AD675	WH	3/11/43	Nickel	France	Sp, Gib	28/12/43	29/12/43	Whitchurch	3317 1658	Comet 210. Sailed from Seville on the *Tudor Prince* c. 21 December 1943 with Flying Officer R.S. Clements and Sergeant R.C. Morley
Kennedy	RS	P/O	CAN	J.19469	426	NP683	HAL	28/6/44	Metz	France	Fr	29/8/44	29/8/44	NK	3322 2231	Left for UK from Bayeux - B.14 airstrip, Banville
Keveren	AJ	SGT		571090	12	ND650	LA	24/3/44	Berlin	Germany	Hol, Bel			NK	3350 1485	With Sergeant Duchesnay. Interviewed 14 September 1944. Report IS9/WEA/MB/1485
Kidd	RM	SGT	NZ	NZ.412700	75	R9248	ST	23/1/43	Lorient	France	Sp, Gib	17/5/43	18/5/43	Mount Batten	3313 1207	ss7
Kiddie	HM	F/S	CAN	R.203424	90	LM111	LA	7/8/44	Mare de Magne	France	Fr	25/8/44	25/8/44	Northolt	3321 2164	Left for UK from Bayeux - B.14 airstrip, Banville
Kieruczenko	W	SGT	POL	784887	138	JD312	HAL	16/8/43	SOE	France	And, Sp, Gib	25/10/43	26/10/43	Lyneham	3315 1492	
Kilpatrick	AW	F/O		125463	193	MN535	TY	7/8/44	Armed recce	France	Fr			NK	3348 290	Liberated by French troops 14 August 1944. Inrerviewed 17 August 1944. Report IS9/WEA/2/119/290. DSO (26/1/45, 197 Squadron)
King	CC	F/O		157923	620	LJ830	ST	21/9/44	Arnhem supply drop	Holland	Hol			NK	3350 1407	Liberated 23 September 1944. Interviewed 25 September 1944. Report IS9/WEA/2/541/1407. Aircraft and date are a guess
King	DAS	F/S		1323677	75	HK594	LA	29/8/44	Stettin	Sweden				NK	NF	ss7. Sweden?
King	FEW	SGT	CAN	R.208361	88	BZ416	BOS	10/9/44	NK	France	Fr	26/9/44	26/9/44	NK	3345 810	Shot in back when on ground. Captured. Liberated from field hospital 21 September 1944. Interviwed 8 January 1945. MISC INT
King	PN	SGT		1586576	207	ND556	LA	3/5/44	Mailly-le-Camp	France				NK	3349	Met up with ill-fated 'D' Squadron, 1 SAS (Fenwick) on 24 July 1944
King	SE	SGT		1304730	50	L7301	MAN	30/5/42	Cologne	Belgium	Fr, Sp, Gib	6/7/42	12/7/42	Gourock	3309 775	Comet 22. Back on the *Narkunda*. See *Free To Fight Again* pp. 140-64
King	WJE	W/O	AUS	A.417084	625	PB126	LA	30/6/44	Vierzon	France	Fr	18/8/44	18/8/44	Northolt	3321 2127	Sherwood. Left for UK from Bayeux - B.14 airstrip, Banville
Kinsella	E	F/O	EIR	50190	88	BZ351	BOS	16/8/43	Denain	France	Sp, Gib	4/10/43	5/10/43	Whitchurch	3315 1444	Comet 138. Guided by Jean-François Nothomb. DSO (3/12/43). See *Heavenly Days*, pp. 211-4
Kirby	RG	P/O		134555	75	BK646	ST	14/6/43	Mining	France	Sp, Gib	7/9/43	8/9/43	Whitchurch	3314 1392	Reached Toulouse on 22 July 1943. To Auch on 23 July 1943. Contracted jaundice
Kirk	AC	F/S	NZ	NZ.425845	75	ND756	LA	28/7/44	Stuttgart	France	Fr	5/9/44	5/9/44	Hendon	3323 2420	His pilot, Pilot Officer I.E. Blance, stayed at the controls to allow crew to escape. Left for UK from Paris by Dakota
Kirk	EE	F/O	CAN	J.23788	425	LW715	HAL	15/6/44	Boulogne	France	Fr			NK	NF	
Kirk	P	LAC		550733	226		BA	13/6/40	German tanks	France	Fr			NK	NF	Rejoined squadron. See Sergeant Asker. DFM (23/12/41)
Kirkwood	FG	F/O	AUS	A.422577	51	LV880	HAL	10/4/44	Tergnier	France	Fr			NK	3352 2361	Liberated 20 August 1944 by US troops. Interviewed 22 August 1944. Report IS9/WEA/8/529/2361
Kitto	RVT	SGT		563186	142	P2246	BA	14/5/40	Sedan	Belgium	Fr			NK	NF	Belgium? DFM (31/5/40). Shot down again 13 June 1940. Returned to UK via

																St Malo. See *The Colours of the Day* pp. 242-3, 246. Commissioned (49721) wef 24 January 1943
Klucha	LJ	F/S	POL	704558	300	JA683	LA	12/6/44	Gelsenkirchen	Germany	Ger			NK	NF	Murdered in woods near Radevormwald two days after shot down
Knaggs	WR	SGT		1559141	106	LL975	LA	24/6/44	Pommerval	France	Fr			NK	3349 465	Interviewed 4 September 1944. Report IS9(WEA)/MB/465. Author *The Easy Trip*
Knowlton	WR	F/O	CAN	J.22596	431	MZ529	HAL	27/4/44	Montzen	Belgium	Bel	10/9/44	10/9/44	Blake Hill Farm	3323 2509	Back to UK from Brussels
Knox	PE	F/S	AUS	A.418433	619	ME846	LA	21/6/44	Wesseling	Belgium	Bel			NK	NF	Later taken prisoner. Report IS9/WEA/MB/1494. Service number A.418435?
Koc	T	F/L	POL	P.0696	308	BL977	SP	3/2/43	Circus 258	France	Sp, Gib	20/2/43	20/2/43	Portreath	3312 1090	
Korpela	OG	F/L	CAN	J.24402	50	ME700	LA	23/9/44	Ladbergen	Holland	Hol	4/4/45	4/4/45	NK	3326 2941	Met Flight Sergeant W.L. Randall. Flown back from Belgium. See AIR 14/2073
Korpowski	B	F/O	POL	P.0982	138	BB340	HAL	12/4/43	SOE	France	Sp, Gib	1/6/43	2/6/43	Hendon	3313 1232	DFC
Kosinski	W	W/O	POL	792587	138	JD312	HAL	16/8/43	SOE	France	And, Sp, Gib	25/10/43	26/10/43	Lyneham	3315 1493	
Kowalski	M	SGT	POL	782276	305	W5593	WE	5/8/41	Frankfurt	Belgium	Fr, Sp, Gib	30/12/41	5/1/42	Gourock	3307 631	Comet 5. To UK on Polish ship *Batory*. MiD (recommended 29/5/42)
Kozik	R	SGT	POL	794282	138	JD312	HAL	16/8/43	SOE	France	And, Sp, Gib	25/10/43	26/10/43	Lyneham	3315 1494	
Kramer	HW	F/O	CAN	J.18965	411	ML295	SP	30/7/44	Armed recce	France	Fr	28/8/44	28/8/44	NK	3350 1052	Captured, briefly, on 20 August 1944. Report IS9/WEA/2/263/1052
Kramer	M	P/O		77345	600	L1514	BL	10/5/40	Waalhaven airfield	Holland (sea)	Hol	12/5/40	13/5/40	Harwich	None	Back aboard HMS *Hereward*. DFC (9/7/40). Killed in action as flight lieutenant 21 May 1941. Commemorated on Runnymede Memorial, Panel 29
Krawczyk	S	F/O	POL	P.1347	305	Z8599	WE	5/5/42	Stuttgart	Belgium	Fr, Sp, Gib	6/7/42	12/7/42	Gourock	3309 779	Helped by Ponzán network. Back on the *Narkunda*. MiD (recommended 23/8/42; approved 22/10/42). KIA 1 November 1942 (304 Squadron)
Kropf	LE	P/O	CAN	J.7931	405	W7770	HAL	16/9/42	Essen	Belgium	Fr, Sp. Gib	31/10/42	1/11/42	Portreath	3311 950	Comet 71. DFC (5/2/43). Flew further twenty operations on 432 Squadron
Kroschel	CH	F/S	AUS	A.418435	166	LL896	LA	12/7/44	Revigny-sur-Ornain	France	Sz, Fr			Croydon	NF	To Switzerland on 24 July 1944. Left 4 October 1944. Flown back from Lyons. Report … 4257? See *Massacre over the Marne*
Kryskow	EJC	F/O	CAN	J.22366	156	JA921	LA	19/2/44	Leipzig	Holland	Hol			NK	3326 2990	Hurt foot landing. Liberated 10 May 1945
Krzehlik	J	F/O	POL	P.1889	138	JD312	HAL	16/8/43	SOE	France	And, Sp, Gib	22/10/43	23/10/43	Poole	3315 1485	Says landed "Bournemouth" in his MI9 report
Kubiak	W	WO2	CAN	R.132761	405	PA970	LA	8/9/44	Le Havre	France	Fr	13/9/44	13/9/44	NK	3345 677	Captured. Liberated when Fort Tourneville, Le Havre surrendered 12 September 1944. Interviewed 14 September 1944. Report MISC/INT/677
Kula	F	SGT	POL	782693	305	N1480	WE	28/8/42	Saarbrücken	Belgium	Fr, Gib	30/9/42	5/10/42	Greenock	3310 901	Solo to Marseilles. Evacuated by *Seawolf* 21 September 1942. Back on HMS *Malaya*. MM?
Kydd	TB	F/S		1398182	227	PB690	LA	21/2/45	Gravenhorst	Holland	Hol			NK	3352 3042	Liberated 1 April 1945 by British troops. Interviewed 5 April 1945. Report IS9/WEA/2/1043/3042
Lagowski	J	S/L	POL	P.0899	305	NS873	MOS	11/7/44	Patrol	France	Fr	9/9/44	9/9/44	NK	3322 2307	Shot down by flak
Laidlaw	AF	P/O	CAN	J.85994	50	PA996	LA	7/7/44	St Leu d'Esserent	France	Fr			NK	3322 2331	ss7. Back in UK by 6 September 1944
Laing	JN	F/S		710119	266	MN807	TY	19/11/44	Armed recce	Holland				NK	3348	Interviewed 14 December 1944
Lakomoy	E	W/O	POL	780883	317	MK943	SP	16/9/43	Enemy ground forces	Holland	Hol			NK	3348 2236	
Lamb	DP	S/L		112530	65	FB129	MU	9/9/44	Patrol	Holland					NF	DFC (11/8/44), 19 Squadron
Lamb	NGM	F/O	CAN	J.28492	297		ALB	29/5/44	Supply drop	France	Fr			NK	3348 320	Liberated 16 August 1944. Interviewed 18 August 1944. Report IS9/WEA/2/126/320
Lamb	WA	SGT	CAN	R.224512	44	LM638	LA	12/7/44	Culmont-Chalindrey	France	Fr	8/9/44	8/9/44	NK	3323 2538	See *Massacre over the Marne*
Lambert	A	S/L	CAN	J.1326	405	HR854	HAL	15/7/43	Montbéliard	France	Sp, Gib	29/11/43	30/11/43	Whitchurch	3316 1590	DFC (22/9/42). Burgundy line. Flown back to UK by DC3. Bar to DFC (21/4/44). Born Grimsby, England, in 1914. Whitchurch?
Lambert	GF	F/O		63419	35	DT806	HAL	10/4/43	Frankfurt	France	Sz, Fr, Sp, Gib	23/2/44	24/2/44	Whitchurch	3318 1785	Left Switzerland 8 January 1944 with seven other internees. Reached Barcelona 16 February 1944. Killed in action on 4/5 July 1944 as squadron leader DFC (16/6/44)
Lambert	J	S/LT	FRA	F.30697	340	AR363	SP	30/7/42	Ramrod	France	Sp, Gib	25/9/43	26/9/43	Whitchurch	3315 1422	Croix de Guerre
Lamus	GH	F/O		121779	408	HR656	HAL	11/3/43	Stuttgart	France	Sz	23/9/44	23/9/44	Heston	3324 2573	In Switzerland 18 March 1943. Appointed Assistant Air Attaché, Switzerland. See *Winged Diplomat*, p.185
Lane	RF	F/O	CAN	J.27277	640	LW654	HAL	10/8/44	Dijon	France	Fr			Northolt	NF	With Flight Sergeant H. Webb. Flown to UK in an Anson. Back at base 8 days after being shot down
Lang	RJ	F/O	CAN	J.25389	434	LW436	HAL	4/8/44	Bois de Cassan	France				NK	NF	
Langford	AB	SGT		581228	107	R3685	BL	9/6/40	Enemy columns, Poix	France	Fr			NK	NF	Possibly not an evader. Killed in action 30 June 1940
Langley	LW	F/S		1394855	9	LL901	LA	23/9/44	Munster	Holland	Hol			NK	3352 2466	ss7. With Sergeant J.G. Miller. Liberated by Candian Army 6 April 1945.

																Interviewed 8 April 1945. Report IS9/WEA/1/337
Lapierre	GJJB	P/O	CAN	J.86146	408	DS726	LA	12/6/44	Cambrai	France	Fr			NK	3348 283	DFC (13/6/44). Mid-under gunner. Liberated 16 August 1944. Interviewed 17 August 1944. Report IS9/WEA/8/139/283
Lapka	SH	S/L	POL	P.76702	306	FZ156	MU	7/6/44	Ramrod 980	France	Fr	26/8/44	26/8/44	Northolt	3321 2142	Left for UK from "Allied beachhead". Interviewed 27 August 1944
Larritt	RD	SGT		1291715	630	PB244	LA	18/8/44	L'Isle-Adam	France	Fr			NK	3350 1001	Interviewed 3 September 1944. Report IS9/WEA/2/353/1001
Lashbrook	WI	S/L		45895	102	HR663	HAL	16/4/43	Pilsen	Belgium	Fr, Sp, Gib	21/6/43	22/6/43	Whitchurch	3313 1264	DFM (18/4/41), MiD (2/6/43). Baled out at 1000 feet. Comet 110. Back by Dakota. DFC (23/7/43). AFC (14/6/45). See Report in AIR 40/2467; *It's Suicide*..., pp.85-8
Lastuk	W	F/O	CAN	J.24731	426	LW198	HAL	28/6/44	Metz	France	Fr	6/9/44	6/9/44	NK	3322 2350	
Latus	TJ	F/L		117473	619	ME745	LA	7/7/44	St Leu d'Esserent	France				NK	3349	
Lavoie	JGY	F/O	CAN	J.22704	428	LK739	HAL	20/1/44	Berlin	France	Sp, Gib	1/5/44	2/5/44	Whitchurch	3319 1892	Burgundy line. MiD (14/6/45)
Law	EA	P/O	AUS	A.422207	115	HK548	LA	7/6/44	Chevreuse	France				NK	NF	
Lawrence	FN	P/O		144693	10	JD368	HAL	27/8/43	Nuremberg	Belgium	Fr, Sp, Gib	10/11/43	11/11/43	Whitchurch	3316 1569	Comet 174. DFC (17/11/44)
Lawrence	JWE	SGT		1087496	158	HR779	HAL	16/4/43	Mannheim	France	Sp, Gib	22/6/43	29/6/43	Liverpool	3313 1280	With Sergeant W.J. Barber. Helped by Roger le Légionnaire and by Jean-Claude Camors. DFM (10/8/43)
Lawrence	ST	WO2	CAN	R.156978	158	LV921	HAL	1/6/44	Trappes	France	Fr	18/8/44	18/8/44	Northolt	3321 2087	ss7. Sherwood
Lawrie	WG	SGT		1819040	35	ME620	LA	8/5/44	Haine St Pierre	Belgium				NK	NF	ss7. Surname Laurie?
Laws	WR	SGT		745880	102	HR663	HAL	16/4/43	Pilsen	Belgium	Fr, Sp, Gib	24/5/43	25/5/43	Hendon	3313 1215	Comet 97. Evaded with Group Captain J.R. Whitley. DFM (6/7/43)
Lawton	R	F/O		139304	190		ST	19/9/44	Arnhem supply drop	Holland	Bel	29/9/44	29/9/44	NK	3324 2629	Back to UK from Brussels
Le Bouvier	JD	F/O		139593	190	LJ982	ST	21/9/44	Arnhem supply drop	Holland	Hol			Fairford	3324 2580	Contacted British troops on 24 September 1944. Back to UK from Brussels. DFC (USA) (13/5/45)
Lear	KF	F/S	AUS	A.414913	149	EH883	ST	23/9/43	Mannheim	Germany	Sz, Fr, Sp			NK	NF	In Switzerland 1 October 1943. Left 4 October 1944. Repatriated via Annecy, France
Leary	W	F/S		1670235	630	ME796	LA	18/7/44	Revigny-sur-Ornain	France	Fr			NK	NF	Back in UK mid-September 1944. See *Massacre over the Marne*
Ledford	WH	SGT	CAN	R.98963	419	DF665	WE	28/8/42	Saarbrücken	Belgium	Fr, Sp, Gib	31/10/42	1/11/42	Portreath	3311 948	ss5. Comet 66. Escorted from Paris by Elvire Morelle and Jeanine De Greef. DFM (5/2/43). Killed in action 23 August 1943 (434 Squadron)
Lee	J	SGT		1089783	620	BK690	ST	6/8/43	Mining	France	And, Sp, Gib	10/10/43	11/10/43	Chivenor	3315 1464	Crossed into Spain 10 September 1943 with two Americans and Sergeant D.B. McMillan. Burgundy? Chivenor?
Lee	NW	SGT			428	LK931	HAL	4/10/43	Frankfurt	Germany	Bel, Fr			NK	NF	With Sergeant Eric Brearley. Author (with Geoffrey French) of *Un Grand Bordel*
Lee	RHA	F/L		33208	85	N2388	HUR	11/5/40	Patrol	Holland	Bel, Fr			NK	NF	Killed in action on 18 August 1940. DSO (31/5/40); DFC (8/3/40), MiD (1/1/41)
Lefèvre	PW	S/L		40719	616	BS114	SP	16/4/43	Ramrod	France	Sp, Gib	13/7/43	14/7/43	Whitchurch	3314 1301	DFC (12/12/41). Assisted by Oaktree from Brittany to Spain. Killed in action on 6 February 1944 (CO of 266 Squadron) in Typhoon JP846
Legarde	F	SGT	FRA		340	PL142	SP	20/8/44	Patrol	France				NK	NF	
Leigh	CC	F/O	CAN	J.22279	182	MN913	TY	19/8/44	Enemy transport	France	Fr			NK	3349 376	Briefly captured. Interviewed 26 August 1944. Report IS9/WEA/2/227/376
Leishman	LW	F/O	CAN	J.25550	158	LK863	HAL	7/6/44	Versailles	France	Fr	31/8/44	31/8/44	NK	3322 2251	In Paris when it was liberated. Interviewed 2 September 1944
Leith	CR	F/O	AUS	A.411790	453	PL313	SP	25/7/44	Armed recce	France	Fr		22/8/44	NK	3350 1453	Liberated by Canadian troops 22 August 1944. Report IS9/WEA/1/61/1453. DFC (26/1/45)
Lennie	DA	F/O	CAN	J.24617	161	LL183	HAL	9/5/44	SOE	France	Fr	6/9/44	6/9/44	Tempsford	3345 655	Captured. Liberated from St Michel prison, Toulouse 19 August 1944. Back in Hudson of 161 Squadron. Interviewed 7 September 1944. Report MISC/INT/655
Lents	GR	LT	FRA	F.30803	341	JL347	SP	3/10/43	Ramrod 258	France	Sp, Gib	6/11/43	7/11/43	London	3316 1567	Left arm injured by splinters. Burgundy line. Back with Captain R.H. Bridgeman-Evans, 2 SAS. London = Hendon? KIA 20 December 1944?
Leslie	SM	F/O	CAN	J.26786	429	LW415	HAL	1/5/44	St Ghislain	Belgium	Bel			NK	3350 1499	ss7. Blown out of aircraft. Captured & liberated. On "Ghost Train". Interviewed 14 September 1944. See *The Evaders* (Cosgrove), p.109-145
Levi	JA	F/L	CAN	J.16908	414	AG548	MU	27/7/44	Recce	France	Fr	5/9/44	5/9/44	NK	3345 808	Wounded. Captured. Liberated 26 August 1944 from Paris hospital. Interviewed 29 November 1944. Report MISC/INT/808. AG548?
Levy	AJD	F/O	AUS	A.422210	218	LJ448	ST	20/4/44	Chambly	France	Fr			NK	3350 1037	Interviewed 30 August 1944. Report IS9/WEA/2/276/1037
Lewis	BG	SGT	CAN	R.153491	619	JB186	LA	18/7/44	Revigny-sur-Ornain	France	Fr		10/9/44	NK	NF	ss7. See *Massacre over the Marne*
Lewis	DE	SGT		1294559	298	LL407	HAL	6/6/44	Dropping troops	France	Fr	11/6/44	12/6/44	Port of London	3320 1965	Dropping parachutists in support of the D-Day landings

Lewis	FE	P/O	CAN	J.10317	7	R9262	ST	21/12/42	Munich	France	Sp, Gib	27/3/43	28/3/43	Portreath	3312 1130	DFC (4/6/43)
Lewis	JH	F/O		145176	76	MZ578	HAL	22/4/44	Düsseldorf	Holland				NK	NF	
Lewis	LA	SGT		1649201	166	LM388	LA	12/7/44	Revigny-sur-Ornain	France	Fr		7/9/44	NK	3350 1138	Interviewed 6 September 1944. Report IS9/WEA/MB/1138. See *Massacre over the Marne*
Lewis	RW	F/O		142873	138	LW275	HAL	7/2/44	SOE	France	Sp, Gib	11/4/44	12/4/44	Lyneham	3319 1880	DFC (14/9/43, 214 Squadron). On 41st operation. See *Free to Fight Again*, pp. 77-81; *Love and War in the Pyrenees*, pp. 209-11. Later, Bomber Command Association treasurer
Lewis	XX	P/O			40	R3693	BL	14/6/40	Merville airfield	France	Fr			NK	NF	Possibly not an evader
Leyne	JL	P/O	CAN	J.85172	431	MZ522	HAL	27/4/44	Montzen	Belgium	Bel	8/9/44	8/9/44	NK	3323 2363	Flown back from France after liberation
Liby	SK	2LT	NOR	FP.12024	118	EP126	SP	16/8/43	Ramrod	France	Fr	24/10/43	25/10/43	Penzance	3315 1488	Escorting US Marauders to bomb airfield near Paris. Back from France by boat
Lindsay	MS	SGT	CAN	R.203549	424	LV910	HAL	28/6/44	Metz	France	Fr	17/9/44	18/9/44	Gosport	3345 779	Wounded. Liberated in French hospital 29 August 1944. Interviewed 20 October 1944. Report MISC/INT/779
Lindsay	PR	F/S	CAN	R.161450	419	HX189	HAL	22/4/44	Laon	France	Fr	5/9/44	5/9/44	NK	3323 2356	
Linton	NW	SGT		1586045	166	NE170	LA	29/8/44	Agenville	France	Fr			NK	3345 651	Captured on landing. Handed over to gendarme 2 September 1944. Liberated 4 September 1944. Interviewed 10 September 1944. Report MISC/INT/651
Little	J	SGT		658501	158	HR752	HAL	15/7/43	Montbéliard	France	Sz, Fr	11/9/44	11/9/44	NK	3322 2294	Crossed into Switzerland on 25 August 1943. Left on 20 August 1944 with Sergeant L.R. Fryer and three others. Back to UK from Casablanca
Littlejohn	DJH	F/O		157918	57	PD212	LA	28/7/44	Stuttgart	France				NK	NF	
Lloyd	DA	SGT		1585587	158	HX334	HAL	12/5/44	Hasselt	Belgium	Bel			NK	NF	Marathon
Lockhart	WG	SGT		748117	74	W3717	SP	6/7/41	Circus 35	France	Sp, Gib	21/10/41	21/10/41	Mount Batten	3307 577	See also Squadron Leader Lockhart. Evaded with Flying Officer Forde from 7 August 1941. MiD (11/6/42). Spitfire serial no. possibly W3317
Lockhart	WG	S/L		112728	161	V9597	LYS	1/9/42	SOE	France	Gib	13/9/42	13/9/42	NK	None?	DFC (5/6/42). Back by felucca on Operation Leda. DSO (9/10/42). Killed on operations 27 April 1944 on 97 Squadron as wing commander DFC & Bar (6/6/44, 692 Squadron)
Lofts	KT	S/L		90483	66	MJ182	SP	21/5/44	Ranger	France	Fr			NK	3348 19	DFC (22/10/40). Met up with Canadians 19 July 1944. Report IS9/WEA/2/14/19. CO of 66 Squadron. Bar to DFC (26/1/45)
Logan	LE	S/L	CAN	C.1359	405	BB250	HAL	11/3/43	Stuttgart	France	Sp, Gib	19/4/43	20/4/43	Hendon	3313 1174	DFC (6/7/43). Shot down and taken prisoner of war on 27/28 September 1943. See *Valley of the Shadow of Death*, pp.94-8
Logan	PNJ	F/L	CAN	J.17678	426	NP683	HAL	28/6/44	Metz	France	Fr			NK	3348 273	Sherwood. Interviewed 18 August 1944. Report IS9/WEA/1/8/273
Loneon	BF	F/S	AUS	A.421741	61	PB436	LA	28/8/44	Königsberg	Denmark	Swe	16/9/44	17/9/44	Leuchars	3323 2433	From Copenhagen to Malmö, Sweden, by boat. Flown to UK in a Mosquito - see *Free to Fight Again*, pp.249-53
Lonsdale	RW	SGT		755548	107	R3916	BA	10/7/40	Amiens	France	Sp, Gib	4/4/41	11/4/41	Belfast	3303 278	Prisoner of Germans in France. Escaped to Marseilles and then Spain. MM (13/3/42). See AIR 2/5684. Commissioned (127169, wef 1/6/42). DFC (14/4/44) on 88 Squadron
Lorimer	GA	WO2	CAN	R.143080	405	ND347	LA	8/5/44	Haine St Pierre	Belgium	Fr			NK	3325 2875	Interviewed 9 September 1944. Report IS9/WEA/MB/1118 in WO 208/3350
Lorimer	PDA	F/S	AUS	A.424773	50	PD237	LA	13/8/44	Bordeaux	France	Fr			NK	NF	Reported by other six crew as having been killed, but survived. See *D-Day Bombers...*, pp. 241-5
Lorne	GF	P/O		138901	218	BK650	ST	30/8/43	Mönchengladbach	Holland	Bel, Fr, Sp, Gib	5/2/44	6/2/44	Whitchurch	3318 1750	Comet 249. See *Rendez-vous 127*, photo facing p. 49 & pp. 100-3
Loudon	JA	F/O	CAN	J.28474	226	FW238	MCL	1/9/44	Enemy troops	France	Fr			NK	3350 1457	Interviewed 9 September 1944. Report IS9/WEA/1/190/1457
Lovegrove	YRW	F/L		47640	299	EF267	ST	19/9/44	Arnhem supply drop	Holland				NK	NF	DFC (26/9/44). MiD (8/6/44). Interviewed 23 October 1944. EF267? His first name was Ypres
Lowe	T	F/O		148903	168	MN265	TY	2/2/45	Armed patrol	Germany				NK	NF	Shot down near Paderborn
Lucas	CD	F/O		153271	50	ME700	LA	23/9/44	Ladbergen	Holland	Hol	3/4/45	3/4/45	NK	3327 3059	With Flight Sergeant H. MacFarlane, Flight Lieutenant J.A. Cote RCAF, and 2nd Lt R.P. Fuller USAAF. Liberated 1 April 1945 - see AIR 14/2073
Lucas	HA	SGT		1818663	514	DS784	LA	18/11/43	Mannheim	Belgium	Bel	17/9/44	17/9/44	NK	3323 2484	Liberated in Brussels 3 September 1944
Lucchesi	Y	P/O	FRA	F.35012	342	BZ388	BOS	3/10/43	Chevilly-Larue, Paris	France	Sp, Gib	7/11/43	8/11/43	Whitchurch	3316 1552	Burgundy line. Crossed Pyrenees with party of American airmen
Lusk	GWP	F/S	AUS	A.425862	466	MZ368	HAL	9/8/44	Coquereaux	France	Bel	9/9/44	9/9/44	NK	3345 807	Captured unconscious. Liberated from a house in Antwerp on 3 September 1944. Interviewed 30 November 1944. Report MISC/INT/807
Lussier	KE	SGT	CAN	R.204124	408	DS845	LA	25/2/44	Augsburg	France	Fr	24/3/44	24/3/44	Dartmouth	3319 1860	Evacuated from Brittany by MGB503 on Operation Bonaparte V. See *The Evaders* (Lavender/Sheffe) p.111

Lusted	RB	F/S	AUS	A.419880	466	MZ368	HAL	9/8/44	Coquereaux	France				NK	NF	
Lyall	R	W/O	AUS	A.409160	453	NH274	SP	12/7/44	Armed recce for MT	France	Fr			NK	3348 288	Liberated by US troops 13 August 1944. Interviewed 17 August 1944. Report IS9/WEA/2/98/288
Lyle	KK	SGT	CAN	R.184814	429	MZ302	HAL	28/6/44	Metz	France				NK	NF	
Lynch	KJ	F/S	AUS	A.420968	218	EF259	ST	1/5/44	Chambly	France	Fr	15/8/44	15/8/44	NK	3322 2216	Sherwood. Injured when lorry overturned on its way to Le Mans after liberation. In several hospitals in UK
Lynch	T	SGT		2204739	9	JA690	LA	7/7/44	St Leu d'Esserent	France	Fr			NK	NF	See *Bombers First and Last*, pp. 246-52
Lyons	AR	SGT		1397284	514	LL692	LA	28/7/44	Stuttgart	France	Fr		17/8/44	NK	3348 56	Sherwood. Liberated by Americans 2 August 1944. Report IS9/WEA 8/45/56
MacCallum	D	SGT		817203	83	X3132	HN	20/3/41	Mining	France	Sp, Gib	4/7/41	13/7/41	Glasgow	3304 374	Crossed Pyrenees with L/Sgt W.H. Batho, RA. See AIR 2/5684. DFM (21/11/41), MiD (11/6/42)
MacDonald	DC	W/O	CAN	R.90369	432	LW592	HAL	27/4/44	Montzen	Belgium				NK	NF	Interviewed 14 September 1944. Report IS9(WEA)/MB/1489. Report in AIR 5420?
MacDonald	JAS	WO2	CAN	R.151905	429	LW680	HAL	15/3/44	Stuttgart	France	Sz, Fr	14/9/44	15/9/44	St Merryn	3323 2535	Switzerland 20 March 1944. To France 4 September 1944. Flown from Lyons to Naples, to Casablanca and to UK
MacDonald	JKF	W/C	CAN	C.890	432	NP687	HAL	25/7/44	Stuttgart	France	Fr	20/8/44	20/8/44	NK	3349 348	Allied lines 14 August 1944. Back from airfield T2. Report IS9/WEA/2/167/348. DFC (19/1/45). See 168 *Jump Into Hell*, p.168-169
MacDonald	K	F/L		54181	90	EF294	ST	2/6/44	SOE	France	Fr			NK	5420 1003	Liberated in France. Interviewed 4 September 1944. Report IS9(WEA)/2/358/1003
MacFarlane	H	SGT		1822137	50	ME700	LA	23/9/44	Ladbergen	Holland	Hol	3/4/45	3/4/45	NK	3327 3063	With Flying Officer C.D. Lucas. Liberated 1 April 1945. See AIR 14/2073
MacGillivray	DK	F/S	CAN	R.152382	428	LK956	HAL	19/11/43	Leverkusen	Holland	Bel, Fr, Sp	13/1/44	14/1/44	Whitchurch	3317 1697	Comet 251. Later commissioned (J.48290). MiD (1/1/45). Interviewed 14 January 1944. Report also in AIR 40/1533
MacGregor	G	SGT		1377432	405	HR854	HAL	15/7/43	Montbéliard	France	Sp, Gib	1/10/43	2/10/43	Whitchurch	3315 1443	Whitchurch? MiD (8/6/44). Canadian in RAF?
MacInnes	DA	F/S	CAN	R.164670	426	LW198	HAL	28/6/44	Metz	France	Fr			NK	3349 391	Liberated by US troops 25 August 1944. Interviewed 29 August 1944. Report IS9/WEA/8/232/391
MacIntosh	AV	SGT	CAN	R.165655	434	LK990	HAL	19/11/43	Leverkusen	Germany	Hol			NK	5415 1108	Captured. Escaped from prison in Germany 20/21 November 1943 and walked to Holland. Interviewed 9 September 1944. Report IS9/WEA/MB/1108. See *Rendez-Vous 127 Revisited*, p. 155
MacIntyre	DP	F/O	CAN	J.5998	35	W1048	HAL	27/4/42	*Tirpitz*, Norway	Norway	Swe	15/6/42	15/6/42	Leuchars	3309 746	Left from Stockholm. DFC (4/8/42). See *Making for Sweden*, pp. 33-5. Later AFC (14/8/45, No. 5 OTU), DFC (US) (13/3/43, 160 Squadron), MiD (14/1/44, 178 Squadron)
Mackay	W	P/O		174141	61	PD199	LA	2/11/44	Düsseldorf	Germany				NK	5415 2296	Came down near Zweifall, Germany. Report IS9/WEA/7/281/2296
Mackenzie	G	P/O		54660	582	PB123	LA	8/9/44	Le Havre	France	Fr	13/9/44	13/9/44	NK	3345 673	Captured. Liberated when Fort Tourneville, Le Havre surrendered 12 September 1944. Interviewed 14 September 1944. Report MISC/INT/673. DFC (12/12/44)
MacKenzie	NW	SGT		910402	109	T2565	WE	5/11/41	Special Duties	France	Sp, Gib	4/3/42	10/3/42	Gourock	3308 699	MiD (1/1/43, warrant officer)
Mackenzie	RM	F/O	AUS	A.413242	168	FD489	MU	7/9/43	Tac/R	France	Sp, Gib	5/11/43	6/11/43	Portreath	3316 1564	Reached Spain on his own initiative. MBE (28/4/44)
Mackinnon	A	F/O		137207	157	MM629	MOS	21/11/44	Bomber support	Holland				NK	NF	Shot down by Mosquito of own squadron. DFC (21/9/45)
MacKinnon	RG	SGT	CAN	R.178188	419	KB719	LA	24/7/44	Stuttgart	France	Fr	1/9/44	1/9/44	NK	3322 2265	
MacKnight	J	SGT		612753	97	JA716	LA	10/8/43	Nuremberg	Belgium	Bel	5/9/44	5/9/44	NK	3323 2384	Marathon. Interviewed 2 September 1944. See also report IS9/WEA/7/133/1161 in WO 208/5415
Maclachlan	CD	F/S	CAN	R.130948	408	DS704	LA	20/12/43	Frankfurt	Belgium	Bel	11/9/44	11/9/44	Northolt	3323 2410	
MacLean	DL	SGT	CAN	R.153260	433	HX353	HAL	4/7/44	Villeneuve-St Georges	France				NK	NF	
MacLean	JA	F/L	CAN	C.1107	405	W7708	HAL	8/6/42	Essen	Holland	Bel, Fr, Sp, Gib	29/8/42	8/9/42	Gourock	3310 837	Comet 39. DFC (16/10/42), MiD (1/1/43). See *The Evaders* (Cosgrove), pp. 11-40, and *Free to Fight Again*, pp. 193-7
MacLennan	NG	F/L		119576	198	JR306	TY	10/8/44	St Quentin area	France	Fr			None	3348 172	Landed in middle of artillery duel. Interviewed 12 August 1944. Report IS9/WEA 2/65/172. See also WO 208/5415. Returned to his squadron in France
Macleod	A	P/O		42013	264	L6965	DF	13/5/40	EA, The Hague beach	Holland	Bel		17/5/40	Folkestone	NF	Returned to UK by destroyer from Antwerp. Killed in action on 28 May 1940
Macleod	RJA	F/S	CAN	1319522	107	BZ237	BOS	27/8/43	Gosnay power station	France	Sp, Gib	6/11/43	7/11/43	Whitchurch	3316 1537	Comet 157. With Flying Officer N.T. Fairfax. Commissioned (155116) wef 29 June 1943 (gazetted 21/9/43). MiD (8/6/44), DFC (29/6/45). See *Home Run* (Bickers), Chapter 7. Died 18 January 1977

MacNicol	JW	F/S	CAN	R.185934	106	LM641	LA	7/8/44	Secqueville	France	Fr	28/8/44	28/8/44	Northolt	3321 2207	Back to UK from Normandy
MacPherson	NH	SGT		1590729	462	LL604	HAL	9/10/44	Bochum	Holland				NK	5420 2143	Interviewed 23 October 1944. Report IS9(WEA)/2/638/2143
MacPherson	WB	WO2	CAN	R.104310	432	LK807	HAL	27/4/44	Montzen	Belgium	Bel			NK	3350 1253	Wounded in arm. With Ann Brusselmans. Interviewed 15 September 1944. Report IS9/WEA/2/480/1253. See also WO/208/5415
Macrae	MET	SGT		1567360	103	ME799	LA	28/7/44	Stuttgart	France				NK	5420 2110	Interviewed 16 October 1944. Report IS9(WEA)/6/400/2110
Maddock-Lyon	R	SGT		2205669	10	MZ793	HAL	14/2/45	Mining	Denmark	Swe	27/2/45	28/2/45	Leuchars	3325 2898	Boarded the SS *Carl* on 19 February 1945. Taken to Sweden by the Swedish pilot on 20 February 1945. Leuchars
Madgett	GEA	F/O		134190	138	LW281	HAL	18/10/43	SOE	Belgium	Fr, Sp, Gib	9/12/43	10/12/43	St Mawgan	3317 1606	Comet 206. Commissioned wef 21 August 1942 (from flight sergeant 976526)
Magee	FB	WO2	CAN	R.109371	625	ND641	LA	24/3/44	Berlin	Holland				NK	5420 1238	ss7. Interviewed 13 September 1944. Report IS9(WEA)/2/458/1238
Maile	R	SGT		1493596	156	ND449	LA	6/5/44	Mantes-la-Jolie	France	Fr	29/8/44	29/8/44	Northolt	3322 2214	See also report IS9/WEA/2/251/1212 in WO 208/5415
Makofski	MH	F/S		1378441	49	PB568	LA	21/2/45	Gravenhorst	Germany	Hol		8/4/45	NK	3327 3088	Walked from Germany (fifty kms NE of Gronau) to Holland. With Pilot Officer H. Eberley. Liberated by Irish Guards 1 April 1945
Malecki	A	SGT	POL	793809	300	Z1276	WE	27/4/42	Cologne	France	Sp, Gib	6/7/42	12/7/42	Gourock	3309 776	Back on the *Narkunda*. MM (recommended 23/8/42; approved 22/10/42)
Malinowski	B	W/O	POL	P.3036	302	AA928	SP	8/9/43	Ramrod S41	Belgium	Fr, Sp, Gib	23/12/43	23/12/43	Portreath	3317 1640	RAF service number 782059
Malkin	A	AC1			53	L4861	BL	18/5/40	Enemy troops	Belgium	Fr			NK	NF	
Mallet	EL	F/L	CAN	J.6186	424	HX313	HAL	27/5/44	Bourg-Léopold	Belgium	Bel			NK	3350 1358	Marathon, Ardennes. Liberated by US forces 8 September 1944. Interviewed 11 September 1944. Report IS9(WEA)/MB/1358, See also WO 208/5420
Mallory	LA	SGT	CAN	R.265262	433	MZ807	HAL	2/12/44	Hagen	France	Fr	19/1/45	19/1/45	Croydon	3325 2867	In hospital in Paris
Mamoutoff	G	F/O	RUS	147939	141	HJ708	MOS	25/3/44	Bomber support	France	Fr			NK	None	Killed 20 June 1944 during evasion
Mann	EA	F/S	CAN	R.180431	103	LL964	LA	31/10/44	Cologne	Belgium				NK	NF	
Manning	LES	SGT		1892872	57	JB318	LA	18/7/44	Revigny-sur-Ornain	France	Fr	5/9/44	5/9/44	NK	3323 2401	Interviewed 5 September 1944. See also report IS9/WEA/MB/1137 in WO 208/5415. See *Massacre over the Marne*
Mansford	ARJ	SGT		1393197	102	JB840	HAL	8/3/43	Nuremberg	France	Sp, Gib	1/9/43	2/9/43	Whitchurch	3314 1385	MiD (14/1/44). Commissioned (170265) wef 4 January 1944. See *Jump for It!*, pp.139-46. Burgundy?
Manstoff	A	F/S		1615909	77	MZ748	HAL	28/6/44	Blainville	France	Fr	30/8/44	30/8/44	Northolt	3321 2201	Left for UK from Bayeux - B.14 airstrip, Banville. DFM (10/11/44)
Mantle	RP	P/O		147695	138	LW281	HAL	18/10/43	SOE	Belgium	Fr, Sp, Gib	9/12/43	10/12/43	St Mawgan	3317 1607	Comet 200
Maples	FA	SGT		1895293	115	LM166	LA	8/8/44	Lucheux	France	Fr	6/9/44	6/9/44	NK	3322 2276	Bordeaux-Loupiac line
March	RD	F/L	CAN		443	SM383	SP	21/4/45	Armed recce	Germany				NK	NF	Shot down by flak while attacking a train near Borkow
Marchant	G	F/S		1339607	299		ST	27/11/44	NK	Norway	Swe	27/2/45	28/2/45	Leuchars	3325 2899	Taken to Stromstad, Sweden by fishing boat on 5/6 February 1945. Leuchars?
Marion	BH	P/O	CAN	J.22552	166	BK361	WE	8/4/43	Duisburg	France	Sp, Gib	24/5/43	25/5/43	Hendon	3313 1213	Helped by Rosine Witton and Raymonde Coache. With Flight Sergeant D.A. Sibbald. Comet 100. See *On Wings of War. A History of 166 Squadron*, pp. 22-4
Marpole	J	F/L		139292	15	LM575	LA	7/6/44	Massy-Palaiseau	France	Fr			NK	NF	DFC (22/5/45)
Marriott	ME	F/S		1393297	257	MN405	TY	13/7/44	Verneuil rail yards	France	Fr	6/9/44	7/9/44	NK	3324 2643	Fractured spine. Back from Arromanches on hospital ship. Interviewed 24 August 1944. See also report 1/65/2329 in WO 208/5420
Marsden	J	SGT		1591984	166	ME749	LA	3/5/44	Mailly-le-Camp	France	Fr	23/8/44	23/8/44	NK	NF	Wounded and captured in gunfight. To Sens hospital. Rescued 15 June 1944. Liberated by Americans 22 August 1944. Four years in hospital. See *Not Just Another Milk Run...* pp. 31-9
Marsh	L	SGT		968674	7	R9149	ST	9/3/43	Munich	France	Sp, Gib	5/2/44	6/2/44	Whitchurch	3318 1754	In German hands 24-25 September 1943. Possum line. Also listed in *Footprints on the Sands of Time*. Whitchurch?
Marshall	WF	SGT	AUS	A.450996	467	R5485	LA	18/7/44	Revigny-sur-Ornain	France	Fr	3/9/44	3/9/44	NK	3349 457	Report IS9/WEA/MB/457. In Paris on 2 September 1944. Service no given as 650996? See *Massacre over the Marne*
Marshall	WH	SGT		1004784	138	BB313	HAL	12/5/43	SOE	France	Sp, And, Gib	5/8/43	6/8/43	Hendon	3314 1333	With Pilot Officer J.T. Hutchinson of same crew. DFM (2/11/43). DFC (15/8/44, flying officer 170177)
Martin	A	F/O		120240	102	HR663	HAL	16/4/43	Pilsen	France	Sp, Gib	21/6/43	22/6/43	Whitchurch	3313 1265	Comet 111. Flown home by Dakota. See Squadron Leader Lashbrook. DFC (23/7/43). See *Silent Heroes*, pp.52-3
Martin	CHT	SGT		1315761	9	LM361	LA	18/4/44	Juvisy	France	Fr	20/8/44	20/8/44	NK	3349 371	Sherwood. Interviewed 19 August 1944. Report IS9/WEA/2/159/371
Martin	GE	SGT		1625906	514	LL678	LA	12/6/44	Gelsenkirchen	Holland	Hol	14/4/45	14/4/45	NK	3326 2947	Liberated by Canadians 9 April 1945. See also report IS9/WEA/1/368/2481 in WO 208/5420
Martin	GKE	W/O	AUS	A.14221	609	MN697	TY	6/6/44	Anti-tank	France	Fr			NK	NF	Broken leg. Wounded by gunfire on ground. With 2/Lt G.I. Tripp USAAF. Commissioned. DFC (17/11/44)

Martin	JR	SGT		1397310	640	MZ677	HAL	2/6/44	Trappes	France	Fr	26/8/44	26/8/44	NK	3326 2910	Shown wreckage of Halifax HX271 (466 Squadron). See also report IS9/WEA/8/534/2362 in WO 208/5420
Martin	JS	F/S		1366175	429	LW680	HAL	15/3/44	Stuttgart	France	Sz	4/9/44	4/9/44	NK	3324 2605	Left Switzerland 27 August 1944
Martin	LF	SGT	CAN	R.80349	419	LW240	HAL	16/9/43	Modane	France	Sp, Gib	17/1/44	17/1/44	Whitchurch	3318 1704	Evaded over Pyrenees. No report in TNA file WO 208/3318. Interviewed on 18 January 1944. DFM (27/6/44). Commissioned (C.42277)
Martin	R	SGT		1076885	35	W7885	HAL	13/2/43	Lorient	France	Sp, Gib	17/7/43	24/7/43	Liverpool	3314 1315	Oaktree. Back to UK on SS *Monarch of Bermuda?*
Marulli de Barletta	G	SGT	FRA	F.30659	342	BZ388	BOS	3/10/43	Chevilly-Larue, Paris	France	Sp, Gib	20/12/43	20/12/43	Lyneham	3317 1626	Burnt about face and hands. Lyneham ? Recommended for MM
Mason	DB	F/L		115761	622	LL885	LA	28/7/44	Stuttgart	France	Fr	23/8/44	23/8/44	Northolt	3321 2158	Left for UK from Le Mans. See *Massacre over the Marne*, p. 122
Mason	EB	F/L	CAN	J.7777	428	LK913	HAL	15/9/43	Montluçon	France	Fr	19/9/44	20/9/44	NK	3323 2522	Flown from Toulouse on a Stirling to Algiers, and from there to UK. Interviewed 11 September 1944. Report IS9/WEA/MB/1348
Mason	KG	W/O	NZ	NZ.416138	487	HP931	MOS	31/8/44	SS HQ, Vincy	France	Fr			NK	3350 1348	Interviewed 11 September 1944. Report IS9/WEA/MB/1348. See also Flying Officer E.C. Heaton RNZAF, and file WO 208/5420
Mason	W	SGT		1590704	75	LL921	LA	18/7/44	Aulnoye	Belgium	Bel	6/9/44	6/9/44	Northolt	3324 2623	Betrayed to Germans. St Gilles prison, Brussels. "Ghost Train" 3 September 1944
Massey	JR	SGT		590895	217	L4463	BFT	17/12/40	Bordeaux	France	Sp, Gib	23/5/41		None	None	Killed 23 May 1941 when Catalina AH560 of the Overseas Aircraft Delivery Flight crashed off Portugal on way back to UK
Matheson	OR	F/L		84010	83	R5610	LA	24/8/42	Frankfurt	Belgium	Fr, Gib	18/10/42	19/10/42	Poole	3311 927	DFC (2/5/41). Evacuated by *Seawolf* 12 October 1942. Bar to DFC (24/9/43)
Matich	NJ	P/O	NZ	NZ.414658	35	HR907	HAL	27/9/43	Hanover	Germany	Hol, Bel, Fr, Sp, Gib	13/1/44	14/1/44	Whitchurch	3317 1699	DFM (10/9/43). Comet 254. Whitchurch? See AIR 14/464; see *We Act With One Accord*, p.147; see *Night After Night*, pp.335-7. DSO (19/5/44)
Matsham	RAW	F/S		1604454	405	PA970	LA	8/9/44	Le Havre	France	Fr			NK	NF	
Matthews	AB	SGT		1336562	644	LL228	HAL	5/4/44	SOE	France	Fr	16/9/44	16/9/44	Tempsford	3323 2481	Fought with Maquis until liberation. Back to UK from Limoges. See *Home Run* (Bickers), Chapter 10. Tempsford? Aircraft number is a guess
Matthews	AW	F/S	AUS	A.418756	463	DV229	LA	10/6/44	Orléans	France	Fr			NK	3348 147	Interviewed 13 August 1944. Report IS9/WEA/2/24/147
Matthews	H	SGT		2209198	158	LK877	HAL	1/6/44	Trappes	France	Fr	28/8/44	28/8/44	Northolt	3322 2222	Left for UK from "Allied beachhead". Interviewed 27 August 1944. See also report IS9/WEA/1/179/2326 in WO 208/5420
Matthews	PV	SGT		658607	61	W5002	LA	15/8/43	Milan	France	Fr	12/11/43	12/11/43	Tangmere	3316 1559	ss7. Back by Lysander on Operation Oriel
Mattock	GR	SGT		1607073	15	W4355	LA	15/3/44	Stuttgart	Switzerland	Fr	4/11/44	4/11/44	Croydon	3324 2723	To France with Sergeant K.A. Reece on 26 January 1944. Back to UK from Paris
Maunsell	JR	F/O		138134	57	LM115	LA	21/6/44	Wesseling	Belgium	Bel			NK	3350 1361	Interviewed 27 September 1944. Report IS9(WEA)/2/559/1361 - see also WO 208/5420. DFC (21/9/45)
Maxwell	JGK	F/L		126559	296	V1605	ALB	6/6/44	NK	France	Fr	7/6/44	8/6/44	Portsmouth	3320 1963	Left for UK from Allied beachhead
Maxwell	PG	F/O		147629	12	LM514	LA	3/5/44	Mailly-le-Camp	France	Fr			NK	NF	
Maxwell	TJ	SGT		1548296	622	LL828	LA	15/3/44	Stuttgart	France	Sp, Gib	22/5/44	23/5/44	Whitchurch	3320 1941	Burgundy line?
May	SH	F/S	AUS	A.412602	41	MB800	SP	19/9/43	Ramrod	Belgium	Fr, Sp, Gib	10/11/43	11/11/43	Whitchurch	3316 1546	Comet 176
May	SN	F/L	CAN		418	PZ220	MOS	17/10/44	Ranger	Balkans				NK	NF	With Russian partisans until April 1945. Balkans?
Mazurkiewicz	J	F/O	POL	P.2318	308	NH186	SP	11/9/44	Armed recce	Holland				NK	5420 2153	Shot by machine-guns as he came down. To Allied lines 30 October 1944. Interviewed 31 October 1944. Report IS9(WEA)/1/249/2153
McAuley	VC	S/L	CAN	J.4761	7	BF379	ST	11/12/42	Turin	Italy	Fr, Sp	8/6/43	9/6/43	Poole	3313 1245	DFC (6/11/42). Escaped to the Vatican City, Rome, and repatriated. Bar to DFC (17/8/43). See Sergeant F.K. Nightingale
McBeath	HL	SGT	CAN	R.128527	7	R9262	ST	21/12/42	Munich	France	Sp, Gib	19/4/43	20/4/43	Hendon	3313 1172	Met with Sergeant R. Forster in Spain. DFM (6/7/43)
McCallum	J	SGT		626278	10	JD368	HAL	27/8/43	Nuremberg	Belgium	Fr, Sp, Gib	27/10/43	28/10/43	Portreath	3315 1504	Burgundy line. Evaded over Pyrenees. MiD (8/6/44)
McCarthy	NJ	SGT		1455735	429	LV973	HAL	10/6/44	Versailles	France	Fr			NK	3348	Sherwood. Interviewed 20 August 1944. Report IS9/WEA/2/179
McCauley	AJ	F/S		1361166	103	JB732	LA	10/4/44	Aulnoye	France				NK	3349	
McConnell	RJ	F/O		39421	82	L8830	BL	17/5/40	Gembloux	France	Fr			NK	NF	Shot down again 10/11 February 1941 (21 Squadron). Prisoner of war
McCormick	DR	F/O	CAN	J.24223	424	LW121	HAL	14/6/44	Cambrai	France	Fr	25/8/44	25/8/44	Northolt	3321 2146	Liberated 20 August 1944 by US troops. Back to UK from Orléans. Northolt?
McCoy	DA	F/O	CAN	J.35656	432	LW592	HAL	27/4/44	Montzen	Belgium	Bel			NK	3350 1257	Interviewed 14 September 1944. Report IS9/WEA/2/484/1257
McCoy	J	SGT		2210780	50	W4824	LA	6/8/44	Bois de Cassan	France	Fr	5/9/44	5/9/44	NK	3323 2399	Back to UK from Paris
McCoy	KLD	SGT	USA	R.143248	626	ND964	LA	21/5/44	Duisburg	Belgium	Fr			NK	3349 425	American in RCAF. Marathon. Interviewed 1 September 1944. Report IS9/WEA/8/267/425. Killed in action 3 March 1945 (mining) on 153 Squadron
McCrea	JE	SGT		1385745	51	DT690	HAL	16/4/43	Pilsen	France	Sp, Gib	1/9/43	2/9/43	Whitchurch	3314 1383	

McCreight	VW	F/O	CAN	J.28361	424	LV910	HAL	28/6/44	Metz	France	Fr	5/9/44	5/9/44	NK	3323 2355	
McCubbin	RC	F/S	CAN	R.156217	424	LW121	HAL	14/6/44	Cambrai	France	Fr	8/9/44	8/9/44	NK	3323 2377	
McDonald	AJ	F/O	CAN	J.26034	441	ML213	SP	2/7/44	Patrol	France	Fr			NK	3348 222	With Major Donald W. McLeod USAAF and Maquis group in Normandy. Liberated 17 August 1944. Interviewed 19 August 1944. Report IS9/WEA/1/11/222
McDonald	GA	F/O	CAN		443	SM314	SP	31/3/45	Offensive operations	Holland				NK	NF	Baled out a dozen kilometres north-east of Deventer
McDougall	J	SGT		1821992	158	LW634	HAL	30/3/44	Nuremberg	Luxembourg	Bel		13/9/44	NK	NF	Interviewed 15 September 1944. Report IS9(WEA)/2/470/1244
McDougall	JB	SGT	CAN	R.58807	405	HR854	HAL	15/7/43	Montbéliard	France	Sp, Gib	1/10/43	2/10/43	Whitchurch	3315 1442	Whitchurch? Later commissioned (C.18114). MiD (8/6/44)
McDowell	AM	F/S	NZ	NZ.426070	75	NG449	LA	21/3/45	Münster	Germany				NK	NF	Service number? Initial J?
McDuff	DM	F/L	CAN	J.11967	442	ML152	SP	19/8/44	Armed recce	France	Fr			NK	3349 377	Captured. Escaped same night. Interviewed 28 August 1944. Report IS9(WEA)/2/246/377
McElroy	LR	P/O	CAN	J.87223	432	NA516	HAL	16/6/44	Sterkrade	Holland	Hol			NK	3327 3010	Captured near Amerongen. Escaped near Kootwijk. Also listed in *Footprints on the Sands of Time*
McEwan	RA	SGT	CAN	R.6190 A	431	HE374	WE	14/4/43	Stuttgart	Switzerland	Fr	28/6/43	29/6/43	Lyneham	3313 1276	Repatriated 29 June 1943 in exchange with Germans. KIA 28/29 June 1944 (Metz) in Halifax MZ591 as pilot officer on 432 Squadron
McFarlane	VT	SGT		569019	None	None	None	14/6/40	None	France	Sp, Gib	5/6/41	14/6/41	Gourock	3308 715	RAF groundcrew attached to 12 Squadron. Wounded. Not interviewed until 29 April 1942. MM (18/8/42)
McGeachin	WG	W/O			644	LL403	HAL	5/10/44	Supply drop, Dodex III	Holland	Hol			NK	NF	
McGechie	W	P/O	CAN	J.87025	298	LL293	HAL	14/10/44	Supply drop	Zuider Zee	Hol	25/4/45	25/4/45	NK	3326 2966	Aircraft came down in the sea. Liberated 15 April 1945
McGee	WE	F/S	NZ	NZ.427902	75	ME752	LA	20/7/44	Homberg	Holland	Bel			NK	3350 1491	Interviewed 14 September 1944. See *Night After Night*, pp. 426-8
McGourlick	DF	F/O	CAN	J.13457	106	DV196	LA	7/8/43	Milan	France	Fr	24/10/43	25/10/43	Penzance	3315 1489	Back via 'Shelburne' boat. Journey arranged from 9 August 1943. DFC (14/11/44)
McGowen	LW	F/S	AUS	A.424274	467	R5485	LA	18/7/44	Revigny-sur-Ornain	France	Fr	6/9/44	6/9/44	NK	3322 2309	See *Massacre over the Marne*
McGown	WL	P/O		174120	514	DS822	LA	7/6/44	Massy-Palaiseau	France	Fr	6/9/44	6/9/44	NK	3323 2487	Left for UK from Paris. DFC (28/11/44)
McGrath	EK	SGT	CAN	R.280735	419	KB752	LA	8/4/45	Hamburg	Germany				NK	NF	Only one to bale out. Service number?
McGregor	EW	SGT	CAN	R.197908	429	LW127	HAL	18/7/44	Mondeville	France	Fr			NK	3348 17	Contacted Winnipeg troops 19 July 1944. Acted as escort to two German deserters 20 July 1944. Report IS9/WEA 2/11/17
McGregor	NR	F/O	CAN	J.14675	428	JP113	HAL	20/4/44	Lens	Belgium	Fr			NK	3326 2974	Baled out as ordered. Back in UK sometime in September 1944
McKay	WG	F/O	CAN	J.22050	51	LW498	HAL	24/5/44	Aachen	Holland				NK	NF	
McKean	RP	F/O	CAN	J.22102	51	LV783	HAL	27/4/44	Montzen	Belgium	Fr	9/9/44	9/9/44	NK	3323 2393	ss7. Liberated in Lille 7 September 1944
McKechnie	F	SGT		1681229	76	MZ539	HAL	28/6/44	Blainville	France				NK	NF	
McKee	LM	SGT		903288	616	W3514	SP	14/8/41	Sweep	France	Sp, Gib	17/12/41	18/12/41	Mount Batten	3307 608	Evaded with Flight Lieutenant Winskill
McKenzie	JW	W/O	NZ	NZ.412077	1	MK744	SP	17/8/44	Ramrod 1211	France	Fr	5/9/44	5/9/44	NK	3323 2402	MiD (1/1/46) as pilot officer. Reached British lines 2 September 1944
McKenzie	WA	SGT		1563940	106	ND850	LA	26/4/44	Schweinfurt	France				NK	NF	
McKinnon	AWD	SGT		1558104	10	MZ584	HAL	1/7/44	St Martin l'Hortier	France	Fr	4/9/44	4/9/44	NK	3324 2616	ss7. DFM (27/3/45)
McLaughlin	JG	P/O	AUS	A.420242	609	JR375	TY	14/1/44	Sweep	Holland	Bel, Fr, Sp, Gib	10/4/44	11/4/44	Whitchurch	3319 1872	His target was rocket installations near Abbeville. Helped by Dutch-Paris
McLean	L	SGT		948851	15	R1080	WE	26/4/41	Transit	Mediterranean	Fr, Sp, Gib	1/10/41	6/10/41	Scapa Flow	3306 567	Interned by the French, escaped, and imprisoned by the Spanish
McLean	W	SGT		996639	7	R9259	ST	6/12/42	Mannheim	Belgium	Sp, Gib	7/1/43	8/1/43	Mount Batten	3311 1020	ss7. Comet 78. By ship from Seville to Gibraltar. DFM (2/3/43)
McLellan	JPW	SGT		1457829	463	LM375	LA	6/10/44	Bremen	Germany				NK	3327 3099	Landed in pond near Papenburg, Germany. Walked west
McLeod	CA	WO2	CAN	R.113455	426	NA510	HAL	12/6/44	Cambrai	France	Fr	4/9/44	4/9/44	Hendon	3323 2458	Back to UK from Paris
McLernon	RA	S/L	CAN	C.1637	434	DK261	HAL	23/8/43	Berlin	Denmark	Swe	21/9/43	21/9/43	Leuchars	3315 1420	Reached Varberg, Sweden on 16 September 1943 aboard fishing boat FN 101 Stanley of Frederikshavn. MiD (1/1/45)
McMahon	AF	F/O			620	LJ849	ST	6/6/44	Supplies to Normandy	France	Fr	8/6/44	9/6/44	Gosport	NF	DFC? Left Normandy from Allied beachhead. No MI9/IS9 report listed. LJ849?
McManus	J	F/S		1529838	644	LL403	HAL	5/10/44	Supply drop, Dodex III	Holland	Hol			NK	3351 2308	Interviewed 21 November 1944. Report IS9/WEA/2/1004/2308
McMillan	DB	SGT	CAN	R.84436	9	ED480	LA	9/7/43	Gelsenkirchen	France	Sp, Gib	10/10/43	11/10/43	Chivenor	3315 1457	Sprained ankles and briefly captured near Le Cateau. Escaped by hitting guard on head with a stone. See also Sergeant J. Lee. Burgundy? See *Bombers First and Last*, pp.140-1
McNaughton	OJ	F/S	CAN	R.140936	106	ME832	LA	4/7/44	St Leu d'Esserent	France	Fr	5/9/44	5/9/44	NK	3323 2379	ss7
McNeilage	DG	F/S	CAN	R.209169	44	PD222	LA	14/8/44	Brest	France	Fr	22/9/44	22/9/44	NK	3345 687	Captured. Liberated from camp at Roscanvel on 18 September 1944. Flown back to UK from Rennes. Interviewed 23 September 1944. Report

																MISC/INT/687
McPhee	AJ	WO2	CAN	R.130527	218	EH942	ST	22/4/44	Laon	France	Sp, Gib	10/7/44	11/7/44	Whitchurch	3320 2019	Burgundy line
McSweeney	KW	P/O	AUS	A.420705	207	LL776	LA	22/5/44	Brunswick	Germany	Hol, Bel	10/9/44	10/9/44	Hendon	3324 2600	On the "Ghost Train" ?
McTrach	J	WO2	CAN	R.131101	76	LL116	HAL	20/1/44	Berlin	France	Fr			NK	3350 1072	Liberated 3 September 1944. Interviewed 5 September 1944. Report IS9/WEA/2/420/1072. See *To See the Dawn Breaking*, pp. 132-3
McWilliams	JH	F/S		1265235	617	ED886	LA	10/12/43	SOE	France	Sp, Gib	23/2/44	24/2/44	Whitchurch	3318 1788	Crossed into Spain with three Americans on 31 January 1944. Boarded a ship at Huelva which sailed on 19 February 1944 for Gibraltar (20 February)
Meanley	R	SGT		1520572	75	NE148	LA	28/7/44	Stuttgart	France	Fr	16/8/44	16/8/44	Northolt	3321 2092	Sherwood? Left for UK from Cherbourg. Northolt?
Medcalf	BT	F/O		143848	100	ND595	LA	25/2/44	Augsburg	Switzerland	Ger, Fr, Sp, Gib	24/5/44	25/5/44	Whitchurch	3319 1933	Repatriated with German agreement. Back on BOAC Dakota
Medland	HD	F/O	CAN	J.24931	161	LL183	HAL	9/5/44	SOE	France	Sp, Gib	5/9/44	6/9/44	NK	3323 2388	With Flying Officer Coldridge. Left Paris 18 July 1944. Arrested in Spain. MiD (14/6/45)
Meer	GMG	F/S		1094376	156	ND449	LA	6/5/44	Mantes-la-Jolie	France	Sp, Gib	24/6/44	25/6/44	Whitchurch	3320 1997	With Flying Officer P.V. Jones. DFM (26/5/44)
Melcombe	DE	P/O	CAN	J.86023	405	ND344	LA	11/6/44	Tours	France	Fr			NK	NF	
Mellor	AA	F/L		86666	139	DZ519	MOS	20/10/43	Berlin	Holland	Bel, Fr, Sp, Gib	1/1/44	2/1/44	Lyneham	3317 1663	Comet 229. MiD (8/6/44)
Mellor	GH	F/S		929433	103	W1216	HAL	5/10/42	Aachen	Belgium	Fr, Sp, Gib	31/10/42	1/11/42	Portreath	3311 951	Comet 69. Evaded with RAF collaborator Michael Joyce. Commissioned (172802) wef 15 February 1944 (11/4/44)
Men_ík	JK	SGT	CZ	787663	312	Z5060	HUR	8/7/41	Circus 39	France	Sp, Gib	21/10/41	21/10/41	Mount Batten	3307 578	5 years pre-war in Czech Air Force. Killed as a flying officer on 22 April 1943
Merchant	JF	F/S	CAN	R.104847	9	JA679	LA	15/7/43	Bologna/Genoa	Italy	Sz, Fr	10/9/44	10/9/44	St Mawgan	3323 2416	DFM (12/11/43). In Switzerland 13 October 1943 - 20 August 1944. Back to UK from Casablanca, via Italy and Morocco
Meredith	AR	F/S	CAN	R.179671	50	LL922	LA	7/8/44	Secqueville	France	Fr	3/9/44	3/9/44	NK	3323 2352	
Merlin	EHR	SGT		700710	175	JP577	TY	16/8/43	Ramrod	France	Sz, Fr	15/9/44	15/9/44	Northolt	3323 2432	In Switzerland 11 November 1943 - 24 April 1944. Back to UK from Brussels. Commissioned (188935) wef 7 November 1944 (23/1/45)
Merrill	EJD	SGT		1579444	102	MZ644	HAL	28/6/44	Blainville	France	Fr			NK	3350 1308	Interviewed 14 September 1944. Report IS9/WEA/MB/1308. See *Massacre over the Marne*, pp. 134-38
Mescall	JM	SGT		105884*	644	LL403	HAL	5/10/44	Supply drop, Dodex III	Holland	Hol			NK	3348 2304	Escaped across the Rhine 20 November 1944 on Pegasus II. See *Bomber Boys* (Chapter 15). Interviewed 20 November 1944. Report IS9/WEA/2/1003/2304. Service number?
Metcalfe	AEB	SGT		1592457	207	ME805	LA	7/7/44	St Leu d'Esserent	France	Fr			NK	NF	
Michaud	JAE	SGT	CAN	R.189956	425	LW591	HAL	24/4/44	Karlsruhe	Luxembourg	Bel			NK	3350 1355	Marathon. Interviewed 10 September 1944 (with Sergeant A. Best). Report IS9/WEA/MB/1355.
Michelmore	D	F/S	AUS	A.423809	467	DV171	LA	24/9/44	Calais	France	Fr			NK	NF	
Michie	NH	SGT	CAN	R.194268	428	LK956	HAL	19/11/43	Leverkusen	Holland	Bel	17/9/44	17/9/44	Northolt	3323 2436	Report also in AIR 40/1533
Milburn	WR	SGT		1536321	103	ED751	LA	5/9/43	Mannheim	France	Sz			NK	NF	In Switzerland 18 September 1943?
Mill	BB	F/L		61997	138	LL287	HAL	30/3/44	SOE	Holland	Bel			NK	NF	DFC (2/3/45, wef 30/3/44). See *After the Battle*, Number 36, p. 37
Millar	G	F/S	CAN	R.160497	432	LK807	HAL	27/4/44	Montzen	Belgium	Fr	7/9/44	7/9/44	NK	3323 2376	
Millar	JB	SGT	CAN	1259997	431	MZ522	HAL	27/4/44	Montzen	Belgium	Bel		15/9/44	NK	NF	Broke leg on landing. Liberated by US forces 8 September 1944. See *The Evaders* (Lavender/Sheffe), p. 243
Millard	PWW	F/S			198	PD618	TY	3/5/45	Armed patrol	Germany				NK	NF	Shot down south-west of Neustadt
Millard	RS	WO2	CAN	R.129923	15	W4355	LA	15/3/44	Stuttgart	Switzerland	Fr	31/12/44	31/12/44	Bovingdon	3325 2835	Perforated lung. To Cadolles hospital, Neuchâtel - see *Infringing Neutrality*, p. 112. Left Switzerland 31 December 1944. At the time of his report he was commissioned J.85642
Miller	AD	W/O	AUS		130	RN196	SP	1/4/45	Offensive operations	Germany				NK	NF	
Miller	FH	SGT		758068	82	V5997	BL	13/5/41	St Nazaire	France	Sp, Gib	8/8/41	14/8/41	Gourock	3305 482	Captured by Vichy French. Escaped from St Hippolyte in June 1941. Miranda de Ebro. AFM (1/1/43), MiD (1/1/43). See AIR 2/5684
Miller	JA	SGT		1583459	102	NA502	HAL	28/6/44	Blainville	France	Fr			NK	3349 386	Met Pilot Officer W.C. Reed, who was told that Miller was evacuated by air c. 7 August. Interviewed 28 August 1944. Report IS9/WEA/8/215/386
Miller	JG	SGT		2212940	61	ED470	LA	23/9/44	Munster	Holland	Hol		10/4/45	NK	3352 2465	Interviewed 8 April 1945. Report IS9/WEA/1/340. See BBMF magazine Autumn 2001, p.27
Miller	LA	F/L		169725	15	LL801	LA	27/4/44	Friedrichshafen	France	Sz, Fr	5/9/44	5/9/44	NK	3323 2506	DFC (22/2/44). Arrested by Swiss on 2 May 1944. Crossed back into France on 13 August 1944. See Flight Sergeant C.A. Campbell
Miller	WL	F/L	NZ	NZ.402208	486	EJ750	TEM	8/2/45	Patrol	Holland	Hol			NK	3352 3005	Interviewed 16 April 1945. Report IS9/WEA/2/1057. DFC (11/12/45)

Millett	TF	F/S		1454685	166	LM388	LA	12/7/44	Revigny-sur-Ornain	France	Fr	8/9/44	8/9/44	Middle Wallop	3323 2366	See *Massacre over the Marne*
Mills	AMcF	SGT		972986	50	L7301	MAN	30/5/42	Cologne	Belgium	Fr, Sp, Gib	6/7/42	12/7/42	Gourock	3309 774	Comet 21. Back on the *Narkunda*. DFM (6/10/42). See *Free To Fight Again*, pp. 140-64
Mills	AW	SGT		926726	103	X9794	WE	7/11/41	Mannheim	France	Gib	18/10/42	19/10/42	Poole	3311 929	Captured by Vichy French. Evacuated by *Seawolf* 12 October 1942
Mills	HL	F/S		1579147	10	MZ793	HAL	14/2/45	Mining	Denmark	Dk	10/3/45	10/3/45	NK	3326 2909	Interviewed 11 March 1945
Mills	WH	SGT		1190001	19	AD551	SP	24/3/42	Abbeville	France	Sp, Gib	10/6/42	15/6/42	Plymouth	3309 745	MiD (1/1/43)
Milne	JR	SGT		658498	429	BK162	WE	16/4/43	Mannheim	France	Sp, Gib	16/8/43	17/8/43	Hendon	3314 1360	ss6. Sailed on the SS *Esneh* from Seville to Gibraltar 11-13 August 1943 with Flying Officer R.E. Barckley and Sergeant H. Riley
Milton	RAE	F/L		42866	65	FB102	MU	11/6/44	Recce (Caen area)	France	Fr			NK	3348 54	Captured by Germans near Caen. Escaped from train 7/8 July 1944. Contacted US forces 6 August 1944. Report IS9/WEA 8/30/54. MC (1/12/44). See *Free to Fight Again*, pp. 124-8
Milton	RAE	P/O		42866	220	P5146	HUD	2/4/41	Crossover patrol	France	Sp, Gib	20/1/43	26/1/43	Gourock	3312 1039	MiD (2/6/43). Shot down again on 10 June 1944. See *Free to Fight Again*, pp. 124-8
Miniakowski	S	SGT	POL	792238	300	Z1276	WE	27/4/42	Cologne	France	Gib	24/7/42	30/7/42	Gourock	3309 797	Evacuated by *Tarana* 14 July 1942. To UK on *Llanstephan Castle*. MiD (recommended 17/9/42). Also shot down over Sweden 9/10 October 1943
Misseldine	JE	SGT		1291166	611	BM303	SP	8/6/42	Circus 191	France	Gib	29/8/42	8/9/42	Gourock	3310 838	Evacuated by *Tarana* 15 August 1942 Evacuated by *Tarana* 15 August 1942 with Pilot Officer Perdue. MID (1/1/43). Commissioned wef 5/11/42 (134227). MiD (8/6/44, as flying officer). See *Silent Heroes*, p.100
Mitchell	HAS	F/O	AUS	A.433608	103	ME449	LA	12/3/45	Mining	Denmark	Swe		16/4/45	NK	3327 3094	With Pilot Officer M.H. Bertie. Crossed to Sweden by boat on 3 April 1945. Flown to UK by BOAC
Mitchell	PK	SGT			266	MN264	TY	7/6/44	NK	France				NK	NF	Possibly Southern Rhodesian, and commissioned (S.R.194008)
Mitchell	R	SGT		1805696	640	LW654	HAL	10/8/44	Dijon	France				NK	NF	
Mitchell	RJ	SGT		943315	49	JB679	LA	26/4/44	Schweinfurt	France	Sz		6/9/44	NK	NF	In Switzerland 20 June 1944
Mitchell	TA	SGT		1549611	576	ME811	LA	6/6/44	Vire	France	Fr			NK	3349 347	Liberated by Welsh Guards. Interviewed 20 August 1944. Report IS9/WEA/2/157/347
Mizener	JL	F/O	CAN	J.23378	65	FB390	MU	20/8/44	Sweep	France	Fr	31/8/44	31/8/44	Heston	3322 2246	
Moffat	J	F/O	CAN	J.27919	427	LV923	HAL	30/3/44	Nuremberg	Belgium	Bel, Fr	15/9/44	15/9/44	NK	3350 1080	ss8. Fought with the maquis. Liberated by Americans 8 September 1944. Interviewed? Report IS9/WEA/2/455/1080
Moffett	T	SGT		1716269	166	ME775	LA	19/5/44	Orléans	France	Fr	26/8/44	26/8/44	Northolt	3321 2178	Left for UK from Bayeux - B.14 airstrip, Banville. See *On Wings of War. A History of 166 Squadron*, pp. 79-80
Moffitt	R	F/S	AUS	A.419198	460	ND654	LA	20/7/44	Courtrai	Belgium				NK	NF	
Mollett	WV	F/O	RHO	80448	266	JR387	TY	15/2/44	Rodeo	France	Fr	26/2/44	27/2/44	Dartmouth	3318 1793	From Southern Rhodesia. Evacuated by Var line in MGB 502 on Operation Easement II. See *Secret Flotillas, Volume I*, p. 323
Mollison	JJ	P/O	CAN	J.86296	429	LV973	HAL	10/6/44	Versailles	France	Fr	18/8/44	18/8/44	Northolt	3321 2105	Sherwood
Molnar	EJ	SGT	CAN	R.168366	550	JA712	LA	27/5/44	Aachen	Belgium	Bel	8/9/44	8/9/44	NK	3322 2274	Flown back from France after liberation
Moloney	PJ	P/O		173441	161	LK238	ST	6/10/44	SOE Tablejam 104/26B	Denmark	Swe	6/11/44	7/11/44	NK	3324 2743	DFM (15/10/43, flight sergeant, 466 Squadron). To Sweden on 30 October 1944. MiD (14/6/45)
Monaghan	AS	P/O	AUS	A.420840	106	ME831	LA	7/7/44	St Leu d'Esserent	France	Fr	28/8/44	28/8/44	NK	3321 2185	See *Silent Heroes*, p.60
Moore	SJ	SGT		1387099	7	BK760	ST	10/4/43	Frankfurt	Belgium	Fr, Sp, Gib	21/6/43	22/6/43	Whitchurch	3313 1253	Back by Dakota
Moore	WJ	F/L			175	MN983	TY	11/9/44	NK	Holland				NK	NF	
Moorhead	P	F/O		152653	35	ND731	LA	4/7/44	Villeneuve-St Georges	France	Fr			NK	3350 1267	Interviewed 1 September 1944. Report IS9/WEA/7/139/1267
Mora	CMM	SGT	NZ	NZ.404652	15	BK657	ST	26/4/43	Duisburg	Holland	Hol	5/5/43	6/5/43	Harwich	3313 1191	Back from Holland by boat. See *Valley of the Shadow of Death*, p.242
Morawski	J	P/O	POL	P.1096	304	W5627	WE	27/4/42	Cologne	France	Sp, Gib	19/8/42	27/8/42	Londonderry	3310 820	Back on RN destroyer. MiD (1/1/43). KIA as flight lieutenant, 12/13 July 1943 in Halifax JD155, 138 Squadron. See *Safe Houses Are Dangerous*, p. 207
Morder	AG	F/O	CAN	J.27151	115	HK550	LA	15/6/44	Valenciennes	France				NK	NF	
More	I	SGT		978951	101	NN705	LA	25/8/44	Rüsselsheim	France				NK	NF	ss9
Morement	HA	LAC		541877	73	None	None	22/6/40	None	France	Sp, Gib	6/6/41	14/6/41	Glasgow	3304 380	Nursing orderly. Captured by Germans on 22 June 1940. Escaped from prisoner-of-war camp near Alençon 10 August 1940. MM (13/3/42)
Moreton	R	F/S		1332943	35	LV861	HAL	15/2/44	Berlin	Holland	Bel	7/9/44	7/9/44	NK	3322 2271	Marathon. Flown back from France after liberation. See *We Act With One Accord*, p.168

Morgan	B	SGT		1890108	460	LM531	LA	3/5/44	Mailly-le-Camp	France	Fr	2/9/44	3/9/44	Locking	3325 2800	Suffered severe malnutrition whilst evading. Left for UK from Chartres. Flown by USAAF to US airbase
Morgan	GR	F/L	CAN	J.6223	169	DD616	MOS	20/4/44	Bomber support	Belgium	Bel			NK	3350 1136	Liberated at a Marathon camp in the Belgian Ardennes. Interviewed 6 September 1944. Report IS9/WEA/MB/1136
Morice	WF	F/S	NZ	NZ.415708	75	BF461	ST	4/11/43	Mining	Denmark	Swe	28/12/43	29/12/43	Leuchars	3317 1659	To Sweden November 1943. MiD (8/6/44). See *Making for Sweden*, pp. 94-5
Morley	HF	S/L		70473	515	PZ440	MOS	30/9/44	Day Ranger	Switzerland	Fr	28/10/44	28/10/44	Hartington	3324 2691	Shot down by Swiss AA guns. Injured and hospitalised. Escaped to France on 19 October 1944. See *Confounding the Reich*, pp. 79-81; *Infringing Neutrality...*, pp.155-64
Morley	RC	SGT		1230169	467	JB121	LA	3/11/43	Düsseldorf	Belgium	Fr, Sp, Gib	28/12/43	29/12/43	NK	3317 1682	Comet 213. Left Seville on the *Tudor Prince* on 21 December 1943 with Flying Officer R.S. Clements and Flight Lieutenant J.L. Kennedy
Morris	E	SGT		982855	207	DV183	LA	16/7/43	Cislago/Brugherio	Italy				NK	NF	
Morris	G	W/O	AUS	A.420476	190		ST	21/9/44	Arnhem supply drop	Holland	Bel	25/9/44	25/9/44	Fairford	3325 2897	Back to UK from Brussels
Morris	J	F/S	CAN	R.191910	419	KB718	LA	4/7/44	Villeneuve-St Georges	France	Fr			NK	NF	Report IS9/WEA/8/209/429
Morris	JE	F/S		1390161	131	MD166	SP	17/5/44	Shipping recce	France	Fr	28/8/44	29/8/44	NK	3321 2168	Liberated in Paris 28 August 1944. MiD (14/6/45)
Morris	JM	F/O	NZ	NZ.422424	75	NE148	LA	28/7/44	Stuttgart	France	Fr	16/8/44	16/8/44	Northolt	3321 2090	2nd pilot. Sherwood. Left for UK from Cherbourg. See *Night After Night*, pp. 354-5. Northolt?
Morrison	AH	F/O	AUS	A.411168	514	DS816	LA	15/6/44	Valenciennes	France	Fr	8/9/44	8/9/44	NK	3323 2470	ss7. Bordeaux-Loupiac line. Back to UK from Vitry. DFC (19/12/45)
Morrison	HA	W/C	CAN	J.4898	405	PA970	LA	8/9/44	Le Havre	France	Fr			NK	NF	DFC (15/9/44). DSO (27/10/44)
Morrison	JD	SGT		1349715	630	ND788	LA	24/3/44	Berlin	Germany				NK	NF	Service number?
Morrison	LC	P/O	AUS	A.413648	408	DS704	LA	20/12/43	Frankfurt	Belgium	Fr, Sp, Gib	9/5/44	10/5/44	Whitchurch	3319 1918	Comet 271
Morrison	WS	F/S		575024	64	MK775	SP	1/9/44	Sweep	Belgium	Bel			NK	3350 1234	Interviewed 10 September 1944. Report IS9/WEA/2/442/1234
Mortimer	JE	F/O	NZ	NZ.412259	485	MH490	SP	3/10/43	Ramrod	France	Fr	8/9/44	8/9/44	NK	3322 2275	With Resistance for 11 months. DFC (1/6/45)
Morton	WB	SGT		1785374	158	NR251	HAL	5/1/45	Hanover	Holland	Hol			NK	3352 2492	Liberated by Canadian troops on 9 April 1945. Interviewed 12 April 1945. Report IS9/WEA/1/361
Morton	WE	SGT	CAN	R.57899	429	LW680	HAL	15/3/44	Stuttgart	France	Sz, Fr	14/9/44	15/9/44	St Merryn	3323 2536	To Switzerland 20 March 1944. To France on 4 September 1944. Flown from Lyons to Naples, Casablanca and UK
Mosley	RR	SGT		568649	106	ND339	LA	4/7/44	St Leu d'Esserent	France	Fr	6/9/44	6/9/44	NK	3324 2541	Left for UK from B.14 airstrip, Banville
Moss	HW	F/S		1339161	207	ND564	LA	20/4/44	La Chapelle	France	Sp, Gib	5/6/44	6/6/44	Whitchurch	3320 1948	ss7
Motheral	CO	P/O	CAN	J.16283	180	FL190	MCL	30/8/43	V1 site, Watten	France	Sp, Gib	29/11/43	30/11/43	Whitchurch	3316 1592	Burgundy line
Mott	AJ	SGT		748276	78	P4950	WH	28/12/40	Lorient	France	Sp, Gib	13/12/41	15/12/41	Pembroke Dock	3307 607	Pilot. Rest of crew prisoners of war. Flown back in a Sunderland. MiD (1/1/43). MBE (3/11/44) as flight lieutenant (120214)
Mott	GE	F/L	CAN	J.22319	441	MJ419	SP	6/8/44	Armed recce Falaise	France	Fr		9/8/44	None	3348 59	Met Americans 9 August 1944 who took him to his base at airfield B.11 (Longue). Report IS9/WEA 2/20/59
Mounts	DC	SGT	USA	R.101816	150	BJ877	WE	16/9/42	Essen	Belgium	Fr, Sp, Gib	24/10/42	25/10/42	Portreath	3311 938	Comet 61. American in RCAF. See *Bomber Command News* 50th, p.21
Mrozowski	W	F/S	POL	784855	306	FZ144	MU	21/6/44	Ramrod 1027	France	Fr			NK	3349 368	Wounded. Liberated 19 August 1944 by British 7th Armoured Division. Interviewed 22 August 1944. Report IS9(WEA)/2/192/368
Muir	M	SGT		1194501	424	HX313	HAL	27/5/44	Bourg-Léopold	Belgium	Bel	12/9/44	12/9/44	Heston	3325 2885	Betrayed 3 July 1944. St Gilles prison, Brussels. "Ghost Train" 3 September 1944. Commissioned (184469) wef 26 May 1944 (24/10/44)
Muller	MA	F/O	HOL	135760	322	MK684	SP	30/8/44	Strafing	France	Fr	9/9/44	9/9/44	NK	3322 2305	Flying a Spitfire Mk IX
Mulvaney	JGJ	P/O	AUS	A.423422	102	NA502	HAL	28/6/44	Blainville	France	Fr	1/9/44	1/9/44	Northolt	3324 2564	Back to UK from 'Normandy'
Munns	S	SGT		1814550	428	LK956	HAL	19/11/43	Leverkusen	Holland	Bel, Fr, Sp, Gib	13/1/44	14/1/44	Whitchurch	3317 1698	Comet 243. With USAAF evaders Applewhite, Kevil and Wiggins. From Seville on the *Lisbeth*. See *Home Run* (Bickers) Chapter 8
Munro	JS	SGT	CAN	R.191440	625	ME684	LA	24/3/44	Berlin	Holland	Bel		15/9/44	NK	3326 2968	
Munro	LN	F/L	CAN	J.11617	190		ST	21/9/44	Arnhem supply drop	Holland	Bel	25/9/44	25/9/44	Fairford	3324 2590	Back to UK from Brussels
Munro	TW	F/O		128704	192	MZ570	HAL	3/5/44	Bomber support	France	Fr	4/9/44	4/9/44	Hendon	3323 2461	Back to UK from Paris. See *Massacre over the Marne*
Munslow	SE	SGT		2200211	76	MZ539	HAL	28/6/44	Blainville	France	Fr	10/9/44	10/9/44	Hendon	3324 2601	
Murphy	BR	F/O		119286	124	AB498	SP	17/2/43	Circus 269	France	Sp, Gib	14/8/43	15/8/43	Hendon	3314 1356	Comet 115. MiD (14/6/45)
Murphy	D	SGT		1565303	15	W4355	LA	15/3/44	Stuttgart	Switzerland				NK	3324 2636	Fractured spine. Repatriated October 1944
Murphy	DG	F/O	CAN	J.29974	419	KB723	LA	4/7/44	Villeneuve-St Georges	France		25/8/44	25/8/44	Northolt	NF	Hidden by Drue Tartière. To UK by US Dakota. Date back is based on date of Sergeant P.P. Barclay's interview
Murphy	JW	F/S	NZ	NZ.424993	75	LL921	LA	18/7/44	Aulnoye	Belgium	Bel	6/9/44	6/9/44	Northolt	3324 2622	Betrayed to Germans on 25 July 1944. St Gilles prison, Brussels. "Ghost

																Train" 3 September 1944
Murphy	P	SGT		1004461	115	HK548	LA	7/6/44	Chevreuse	France	Fr			NK	3350 1014	With Sergeant A. Russell. Interviewed 1 September 1944. Report IS9/WEA/2/296/1014
Murray	D	P/O	CAN	J.36017	426	NA510	HAL	12/6/44	Cambrai	France	Fr	9/9/44	9/9/44	NK	3323 2489	Back to UK from Vitry
Murray	GB	F/L	CAN	J.15476	401	MJ246	SP	28/6/44	Armed recce	France	Fr			NK	3349 364	DFC (29/9/42). Liberated by US Interviewed 16 August 1944. Report IS9/WEA/2/86/364. Reported in *Fighter Command Losses... Vol 3*, p.60, as having been killed
Murray	GH	SGT		1082668	429	MS487	WE	26/3/43	Duisburg	Holland	Bel, Fr, Sp, Gib	27/6/43	28/6/43	Hendon	3313 1272	
Murray	IR	F/S	AUS	A.419202	44	ME694	LA	25/7/44	Stuttgart	France	Fr			NK	3348 319	Sherwood. Interviewed 17 August 1944. Report IS9/WEA/2/101/319
Murray	JH	F/O	CAN	J.25032	77	LW270	HAL	23/4/44	Mining	Denmark	Swe	7/5/44	8/5/44	Leuchars	3319 1915	Back to UK from Stockholm
Murray	RO	SGT	CAN	R.200740	44	ND976	LA	21/5/44	Duisburg	Belgium				NK	NF	
Murray	WJ	F/S		1821564	620		ST	20/9/44	Supply drop	Holland	Bel	28/9/44	28/9/44	NK	3324 2641	Back to UK from Brussels
Murrie	JD	SGT		1823503	9	JA957	LA	7/7/44	St Leu d'Esserent	France	Fr			NK	NF	ss7
Musgrove	GA	F/O	CAN	J.17952	15	LM575	LA	7/6/44	Massy-Palaiseau	France	Fr	18/8/44	18/8/44	Northolt	3321 2128	Sherwood. Left for UK from B.14 airstrip, Banville. DFC (12/12/44)
Mussett	DS	F/L	CAN	J.8212	21	NS831	MOS	1/8/44	Barracks, Poitiers	France	Fr	16/9/44	16/9/44	Tempsford	3323 2437	Back to UK from Limoges
Nabarro	C	F/O		151161	15	W4355	LA	15/3/44	Stuttgart	Switzerland		8/10/44	8/10/44	Northolt	3324 2650	Broke leg landing. Repatriated October 1944. Flown from Annecy via Lyons to Paris
Naylor	BW	SGT		1386637	50	L7301	MAN	30/5/42	Cologne	Belgium	Fr, Sp, Gib	6/7/42	12/7/42	Gourock	3309 773	Comet 23. Back on the *Narkunda*. DFM (6/10/42). See *Free To Fight Again*, pp. 140-64
Neal	JA	F/O	CAN	J.25125	419	HX189	HAL	22/4/44	Laon	France	Fr			NK	3350 1490	Liberated 1 September 1944 by US troops. Interviewed 16 September 1944. See *The Evaders* (Lavender/Sheffe), Chapter 16. Author of *Lucky Pigeon*
Neal	JFA	F/O		155553	69	JA631	WE	8/8/44	Photo recce	France	Fr			NK	3348 313	Shot down by light flak. Liberated by US troops 17 August 1944. Interviewed 20 August 1944. Report IS9/WEA/2/178/313
Nealey	JA	SGT		1590700	619	LM378	LA	18/7/44	Revigny-sur-Ornain	France	Fr	1/9/44	1/9/44	NK	3322 2264	ss7. Met Flight Sergeant L. Hood in Livry-Gargan on liberation. See *Massacre over the Marne*
Needham	WB	F/L	CAN		412	MK622	SP	7/7/44	Armed recce	France				NK	NF	
Neil	MM	F/L	CAN	J.13270	407		WE	26/9/44	A/S patrol off Norway	Norway	Nor	11/10/44	12/10/44	Scalloway	3324 2655	Came back on the "Shetland Bus" service. See *Shot Down and on the Run*, pp. 141-8
Nelles	BA	SGT	CAN	R.212438	434		HAL	4/8/44	Bois de Cassan	France	Fr	3/9/44	3/9/44	NK	3323 2357	
Nelmes	JM	W/O	CAN	R.92464	428	LK913	HAL	15/9/43	Montluçon	France	Fr	19/9/44	20/9/44	NK	3323 2521	Flown to UK from Algiers
Nelson	RF	SGT		1324538	431	LK967	HAL	25/11/43	Frankfurt	France	Sp, Gib	5/2/44	6/2/44	Whitchurch	3318 1746	
Nesbitt-Dufort	J	S/L		29164	138	T1508	LYS	28/1/42	SOE	France	Fr		1/3/42	Tempsford	NF	DSO (25/11/41). Date of return - see *We Landed By Moonlight*, p.28. Tempsford? Probably no MI9 report on account of Special Duties
Nethery	LA	P/O	CAN	J.19356	405	ND347	LA	8/5/44	Haine St Pierre	Belgium	Fr			NK	3325 2876	Interviewed 9 September 1944. Report IS9/WEA/MB/1125 in WO 208/3350
Newbold	L	SGT		1302201	75	Z1652	WE	24/10/42	Milan	France	Sz, Fr		11/9/44	NK	3323 2471	Crossed into Switzerland on 11 November 1942 with Sergeant E. Worsdale RNZAF. Left 26 August 1944 with Sergeant L.R. Fryer and party. See *Night After Night*, pp. 366-8
Newton	JL	SGT		742570	12	W5421	WE	5/8/41	Aachen	Belgium	Fr, Sp, Gib	13/1/42	14/1/42	Pembroke Dock	3307 649	Comet 9. Received no award, but was commissioned pilot officer (127780) wef 2 July 1942. See his biography *Evader* (Derek Shuff)
Newton	R	F/O	CAN	J.26361	620	LJ830	ST	21/9/44	Arnhem supply drop	Holland	Hol			NK	3350 1408	Liberated 23 September 1944. Interviewed 25 September 1944. Report IS9/WEA/2/562/1408. Aircraft and date are a guess
Nichol	A	F/S		519750	207	LM218	LA	7/7/44	St Leu d'Esserent	France	Fr	9/9/44	9/9/44	Northolt	3324 2548	
Nicholls	WA	F/O		156623	57	PD212	LA	28/7/44	Stuttgart	France	Fr			NK	NF	Completed further 24 ops after return to UK. DFC (1945). Died 3 March 2005
Nicholson	JH	SGT		1592868	166	LL896	LA	12/7/44	Revigny-sur-Ornain	France	Fr	4/9/44	4/9/44	Hendon	3322 2225	See *Massacre over the Marne*
Nickerson	RW	F/L	CAN		421	MJ786	SP	21/5/44	Ramrod 905	France				NK	NF	Liberated by Canadian troops August 1944
Nicolaysen	V	SGT	NOR	F.P.5653	331	PL217	SP	29/12/44	Armed recce	Holland	Hol			NK	3352 2470	Liberated by Canadian Army 8 April 1945. Interviewed 9 April 1945. Report IS9/WEA/1/247
Nielsen	HL	SGT		1077104	106	DV196	LA	7/8/43	Milan	France	Fr	26/12/43	26/12/43	Helford	3317 1649	Back via Bordeaux line. Back on Operation Felicitate, MGB 318. See Sergeant T.H. Adams
Nightingale	FK	SGT		618551	7	BF379	ST	11/12/42	Turin	Italy	Fr, Sp	8/6/43	9/6/43	Poole	3313 1246	Escaped to the Vatican City, Rome, and repatriated. DFM (17/8/43). See Squadron Leader V.C. McAuley RCAF

Nimmo	ND	F/L		67073	101	DV288	LA	10/4/44	Aulnoye	France				NK	NF	DFC (17/7/45, 142 Squadron)
Nind	JAW	SGT	CAN	R.194196	149	LJ621	ST	5/6/44	D-Day support	France	Fr	9/9/44	9/9/44	NK	3322 2336	Captured 8 June 1944. At PoW camp at Rennes. Stuck on a train for 10 days. Cut way out on 23 July 1944 and escaped. MiD (14/6/45). Commissioned (J.89639)
Nitelet	AEJG	P/O	BEL	87699	609	W3254	SP	9/8/41	Circus 68	France	Sp, Gib	25/12/41	25/12/41	Plymouth	3307 613	Shot down on same operation as Douglas Bader. Back to France as radio operator for PAO line, in May 1942. Captured. Released 27 November 1942
Nixon	HJ	F/L	CAN	J.6187	411	MJ857	SP	27/6/44	Patrol	France	Fr				NF	Shot down again one month later to the day
Nixon	HJ	F/L	CAN	J.6187	411	NH344	SP	27/7/44	Armed recce	France	Fr			NK	3350 1123	Liberated 30 August 1944. Interviewed 1 September 1944. Report IS9/WEA/MB/1123. Also shot down 27 June 1944. DFC (29/12/44)
Nixon	JE	F/L	CAN	J.38325	192	NR180	HAL	5/3/45	Bomber support	Poland	Rus			NK	NF	Back via Odessa. See his story in *Descent into Danger*
Noakes	EEG	SGT		1335194	245	MN121	TY	7/6/44	NK	France	Fr	16/8/44	16/8/44	Northolt	3321 2094	Sherwood? Left for UK from "Allied beachhead" - Cherbourg?
Nock	HA	F/O		125420	51	JD262	HAL	3/7/43	Cologne	Belgium	Bel	16/9/44	16/9/44	NK	3324 2549	Fought with Maquis. Back to UK from Florennes. MC (12/6/45). See *The Other Battle*, p.121; *Swift & Sure*, p.324
Nolan	DK	F/S	CAN	R.82650	7	R9278	ST	14/4/43	Stuttgart	France	Sp, Gib	5/8/43	11/8/43	Liverpool	3314 1348	Burgundy line
Nolan	KW	F/O	AUS	A.419426	295	LJ618	ST	20/9/44	Arnhem supply drop	Holland	Hol	22/9/44	22/9/44	Harwell	NF	Operation Market IV. Returned to base within fifty hours
Nordin	GM	SGT	CAN	R.197526	434	LW713	HAL	12/6/44	Arras	France	Fr	8/9/44	8/9/44	NK	3323 2467	Bordeaux-Loupiac line. Back to UK from Vitry
Norfolk	WJ	SGT		962219	76	W1064	HAL	1/6/42	Essen	Belgium	Fr, Sp, Gib	19/8/42	25/8/42	Londonderry	3310 815	With the Brusselmans family. Comet 35. MiD (1/1/43). See *Mission Marathon*, p. 326. Commissioned (149248) wef 14 July 1943. See *Belgium Rendez-Vous 127*, p. 41 etc
Norris	XX	SGT			21	L9269	BL	13/6/40	Tanks, Forêt de Gault	France	Fr			NK	NF	Possibly not an evader
North-Lewis	CD	W/C		45073	124 Wing	RB208	TY	24/3/45	Enemy positions	Germany	Ger			NK	3352 2414	DFC (2/3/43) & Bar (26/9/44). Captured. Sent to Allied lines 25 March 1945. Interviewed 29 March 1945. Report IS9/WEA/2/1027/2414. DSO (1/5/45). Died 25 March 2008
Norwood	JA	P/O	CAN	J.86862	298	LL293	HAL	14/10/44	Supply drop	Zuider Zee	Hol	25/4/45	25/4/45	NK	3326 2967	Aircraft came down in the sea. Liberated 15 April 1945
Nugent	RH	LAC		537353	142	L5238	BA	10/5/40	Enemy troops	France	Fr			NK	NF	Shot down again four days later, and killed, aged thirty-five
Nurse	JR	F/S	AUS	A.427540	115	HK548	LA	7/6/44	Chevreuse	France	Fr			NK	NF	
Oakeby	HE	SGT		928958	432	NP706	HAL	18/7/44	Caen	France	Fr			NK	3349 352	Liberated by British troops 18 August 1944. Interviewed 20 August 1944. Report IS9/WEA/2/174/352
O'Brart	DFR	SGT		1265869	620	BK690	ST	6/8/43	Mining	France	And, Sp, Gib	20/9/43	21/9/43	Lyneham	3315 1411	Burgundy line
O'Brien	PA	F/S		1387488	35	ND701	LA	9/4/44	Lille	France	Sz			NK	NF	See *We Act With One Accord*, p.175
O'Connell	BG	F/S	AUS	A.428820	463	NF977	LA	23/10/44	Walcheren	Holland				NK	NF	
Offer	AW	SGT		1447477	76	MZ736	HAL	28/6/44	Blainville	France	Fr	29/8/44	29/8/44	NK	3322 2348	
Oger	RM	ADJ	FRA	C.3231	347	NA606	HAL	11/9/44	Gelsenkirchen	Germany				NK	NF	ss7. Service number?
Ogg	JS	SGT		1456604	7	JB656	LA	16/12/43	Berlin	Holland	Hol			NK	3348 202	ss7. Interviewed 11 May 1945. Report IS9/WEA/PLM/202
Ogilvie	AMcP	F/L	CAN	120865	83	ED313	LA	11/3/43	Stuttgart	France	Sp, Gib	29/5/43	4/6/43	Gourock	3313 1244	DFC (12/3/43). Evaded with Sergeant R. Henderson. Bar to DFC (27/7/43). MiD (1/1/45). Author of *All the Luck in the World*
O'Grady	LM	F/O	CAN	J.29729	422	LW582	HAL	7/6/44	Achères	France	Fr			NK	3350 1053	Interviewed 31 August 1944. Report IS9/WEA/2/293/1053
O'Hara	HF	F/S		655736	12	LM514	LA	3/5/44	Mailly-le-Camp	France	Fr			NK	3350 1083	Interviewed 1 September 1944. Report IS9/WEA/8/257/1083. See *Shot Down and on the Run*, p. 92
Oldacre	WJ	F/L		86656	9	JA690	LA	7/7/44	St Leu d'Esserent	France	Fr	6/9/44	6/9/44	NK	3322 2346	Commended for valuable service in the air (31/8/43). See *Bombers First and Last*, pp. 246-52, 271 etc
O'Leary	JP	P/O	CAN	R.114680	428	DK257	HAL	13/7/43	Aachen	Holland	Bel, Fr, Sp, Gib	6/10/43	7/10/43	NK	3315 1454	Comet 135
Oliphant	ML	F/S	CAN	R.182121	166	NE170	LA	29/8/44	Agenville	France	Fr			NK	3345 659	Captured on landing. Handed over to gendarme 2 September 1944. Liberated 4 September 1944. Interviewed 10 September 1944. Report MISC/INT/659
Olive	QM	SGC	FRA	F.430	346	NA558	HAL	4/11/44	Bochum	Germany				NK	None	Killed evading
Oliver	JG	F/L		119921	613	LR290	MOS	14/1/44	NK	France	Sp, Gib	22/5/44	23/5/44	Whitchurch	3319 1924	Burgundy line. MiD (1/1/45)
Oliver	RD	F/O		179550	571	ML963	MOS	10/4/45	Berlin	Germany	Ger	16/4/45	16/4/45	NK	3326 2948	Liberated by US troops 15 April 1945
Oliver	T	F/O		135909	190	LJ982	ST	21/9/44	Arnhem supply drop	Belgium	Bel			NK	3350 1404	Interviewed 25 September 1944. Report IS9/WEA/2/561/1404
Olszewski	I	S/L	POL		302	TB250	SP	14/3/45	Armed patrol	Holland				NK	NF	Shot down attacking railway south-west of Zwolle
O'Neil	FH	P/O	AUS	A.420989	218	LJ448	ST	20/4/44	Chambly	France	Fr	27/8/44	27/8/44	Northolt	3322 2238	Met up with ill-fated 'D' Squadron, 1 SAS (Fenwick) on 17 July 1944. Left for UK from Bayeux - B.14 airstrip, Banville

Orange	GE	F/S		1434373	190		ST	21/9/44	Arnhem supply drop	Holland	Bel	22/9/44	22/9/44	Croydon	3324 2633	Aircraft ditched in River Waal. Back to UK from Brussels
Orbin	J	SGT		1066587	460	LM531	LA	3/5/44	Mailly-le-Camp	France	Fr	6/9/44	6/9/44	NK	3322 2347	See *Massacre over the Marne*, footnote to p. 195
Orndorff	WR	SGT	CAN	R.96343	419	X3712	WE	29/7/42	Saarbrücken	Belgium	Fr, Sp, Gib	13/9/42	14/9/42	Whitchurch	3310 857	ss5. Comet 44. MiD (1/1/43)
Orr	MO	P/O	CAN	J.95460	103	LL964	LA	31/10/44	Cologne	Belgium			6/11/44	NK	NF	Killed in action 29 November 1944 on 103 Squadron
Orth	DR	F/S	AUS	A.424209	514	LM180	LA	12/8/44	Rüsselsheim	Belgium	Bel			NK	3322 2323	Liberated 10 September 1944. Back in UK by 11 September 1944. See Chester-Master's report
Osborne	JB	F/L		183736	227	PB690	LA	21/2/45	Gravenhorst	Germany	Hol			NK	3327 3118	Shot down near Rheine. Walked across airfield early evening. Met Flying Officer M. Stoyko RCAF. Liberated by British troops 3 April 1945
Ossendorf	R	W/O	CZ	787590	312	MJ907	SP	21/5/44	Armed recce	France	Fr		13/7/44	NK	3320 2031	Shot in hip in gunfight with Germans on 24 June 1944
Outhwaite	JJ	SGT		565200	21	L8738	BL	14/5/40	Enemy troops	Belgium	Fr			NK	NF	Killed in action on 11 June 1940
Outram	HA	S/L		36246	138	Z9232	WH	24/8/42	SOE	France	Sp, Gib	27/9/42	28/9/42	Mount Batten	3310 864	MiD (24/9/41). Evacuated by *Seawolf* 21 September 1942. See *Safe Houses Are Dangerous*, p. 209
Ovenden	GA	P/O	CAN	J.86218	434	LW713	HAL	12/6/44	Arras	France	Fr	8/9/44	8/9/44	NK	3322 2338	
Ovender	RA	SGT	CAN	R.253193	115	HK579	LA	8/9/44	Le Havre	France				NK	NF	
Overwijn	R	F/S	HOL	16709	320	FR179	MCL	25/11/43	V-2 site, Martinvast	France	Sp, Gib	9/4/44	10/4/44	Lyneham	3319 1875	Lyneham?
Owen	NT	P/O		54653	57	JB370	LA	7/7/44	St Leu d'Esserent	France	Fr	7/9/44	7/9/44	Bognor	3324 2745	
Pack	EH	P/O		175630	635	ND895	LA	5/7/44	Wizernes	France				NK	3350 1461	DFM (11/2/44, 97 Sq). ss7. Interviewed 10 September 1944. Report IS9(WEA)/1/198/1461
Pack	JT	SGT		1375376	35	W7701	HAL	8/6/42	Essen	Germany	Hol, Bel, Fr, Sp, Gib	19/8/42	25/8/42	Londonderry	3310 817	Comet 33. Back to UK on RN destroyer. MiD (1/1/43). Later flew Catalinas on 265 Squadron in India
Page	FJ	SGT	AUS	A.427018	27 OTU	X3966	WE	23/9/43	Nickel	France	Sp, Gib	10/4/44	11/4/44	Whitchurch	3319 1876	Dutch-Paris line
Palamountain	G	F/S		1433141	514	LL678	LA	12/6/44	Gelsenkirchen	Holland	Hol	25/4/45	25/4/45	NK	3327 3015	Flown back from Brussels
Palmer	DW	SGT	CAN	R.205550	433	LV839	HAL	28/6/44	Metz	France	Fr	4/9/44	4/9/44	Hendon	3323 2460	Baled out. Aircraft returned to UK. Back to UK from Paris
Palmer	FJ	SGT		1694278	76	MZ539	HAL	28/6/44	Blainville	France	Fr			NK	3350 1263	Liberated by US forces 29 August 1944. Interviewed 1 September 1944. Report IS9/WEA/7/119/1263
Palmer	W	SGT		1576800	77	JD371	HAL	27/8/43	Nuremberg	Belgium	Fr, Sp, Gib	6/11/43	7/11/43	Whitchurch	3316 1540	Escaped from a Resistance camp in Ardennes attacked by Germans on 19 September 1943. Comet 164. DFM (7/1/44)
Panzer	L	F/O	CAN	J.27423	432	LW583	HAL	8/5/44	Haine St Pierre	Belgium	Bel	8/9/44	8/9/44	Northolt	3323 2418	Captured 1 August 1944. St Gilles prison, Brussels. "Ghost Train" 3 September 1944. MiD (14/6/45)
Parama	WJ	F/O	CAN	J.26704	103	ME738	LA	27/4/44	Friedrichshafen	Germany	Sz, Fr			NK	NF	In Switzerland from 29 April to about 16 September 1944
Parent	P	S/LT	FRA	F.31500	341	NH522	SP	26/8/44	Armed recce	France	Fr			NK	3350 1065	Wounded in arm. Captured by Germans. Escaped from hospital. Interviewed? Report IS9/WEA/2/332/1065
Parker	L	F/L	CAN		184	MN718	TY	7/8/44	Enemy tanks	France	Fr			NK	NF	On first sortie with squadron. Very soon rejoined his squadron
Parker	NN	F/S	AUS	A.413240	75	LJ442	ST	19/11/43	Leverkusen	Belgium	Fr, Sp, Gib	5/2/44	6/2/44	Whitchurch	3318 1745	Comet 250. DFC (8/12/44) and Bar to DFC (22/5/45) (both as squadron leader, 97 Squadron)
Parker	TC	P/O		70812	79	L2065	HUR	12/5/40	Patrol	Belgium	Bel			NK	3298 19	Evaded to Allied lines in Belgium. Rejoined squadron in France. MiD (11/6/42). MiD (1/1/45, wing commander). OBE (1/1/46)
Parkes	SMP	SGT		742649	9	R1244	WE	11/1/41	Turin	France	Sp, Gib	9/5/41	16/5/41	Liverpool	3304 346	To UK on *Monarch of Bermuda*. See AIR 2/5684. Killed 25/26 August 1944 (squadron leader 114010, 97 Squadron). DSO (17/10/44). See *Bombers First and Last*, pp. 41 etc
Parkinson	DR	SGT		994280	103	ED751	LA	5/9/43	Mannheim	France	Fr	17/9/43	18/9/43	Falmouth	3315 1410	To UK by fishing boat. MiD (8/6/44). See *Evader*, pp. 243-44; *Free To Fight Again*, pp. 182-6
Parkinson	JE	SGT		1479296	115	HK548	LA	7/6/44	Chevreuse	France	Fr			NK	3350 1067	Interviewed 3 September 1944. Report IS9/WEA/2/350/1067
Parkinson	JR	F/S		1577381	207	LM218	LA	7/7/44	St Leu d'Esserent	France	Fr	3/9/44	4/9/44	NK	3324 2546	
Parks	WR	F/L	CAN	J.25040	10	MZ826	HAL	15/10/44	Mining	Denmark	Swe	7/11/44	8/11/44	Leuchars	3324 2756	ss7. With Pilot Officer L.N. Flower. Sailed to Sweden on 26 October 1944. Flown back in bomb bay of a Mosquito. DFC (23/3/45)
Parry	JH	F/O		143657	512		DAK	18/9/44	Supply drop	Holland	Bel	28/9/44	28/9/44	NK	3324 2608	Back to UK from Brussels
Parsons	KC	F/O		130602	578	MZ511	HAL	20/7/44	Bottrop	Holland	Hol			NK	3352 2388	Liberated 10 March 1945. Report IS9/WEA/1/297/2388
Pascoe	FE	F/O	AUS	A.421041	190		ST	21/9/44	Arnhem supply drop	Holland				NK	3350 1382	Interviewed? Report IS9/WEA/2/513/1382. DFC (21/11/44)
Pask	RJE	SGT		1320778	90	EF509	ST	9/5/44	SOE	France	Fr			NK	3352 2886	Helped by André Rougeyron. See *Agents for Escape...*, Chapter 14
Passy	CW	S/L		72028	138	LW281	HAL	18/10/43	SOE	Belgium	Fr, Sp, Gib	20/12/43	21/12/43	Whitchurch	3317 1630	DFC (12/2/43, 89 Squadron). Comet 214. OBE (14/6/45)

Paston-Williams	H	F/L		83930	100	LM658	LA	12/8/44	Brunswick	Holland	Hol	10/4/45	10/4/45	Down Ampney	3327 3068	Liberated 3 April 1945 by 43 Division. Interviewed 7 April 1945. Back from Eindhoven by RAF Dakota. Report IS9/WEA/2/1049/2457
Paterson	JL	F/O	CAN	J.25343	196	LK556	ST	20/9/44	Supply drop	Holland				NK	3350 1419	Interviewed 26 September 1944. Report IS9/WEA/2/546/1420
Paterson	JL	SGT		1397946	218	EH884	ST	16/8/43	Turin	France	Sz, Fr, Sp, Gib	19/1/44	20/1/44	NK	3318 1715	See *Aviateurs Piétons vers la Suisse*, p. 335
Paton	JS	SGT	CAN	R.69544	405	W5551	WE	24/7/41	Brest	France	Sp, Gib	30/12/41	5/1/42	Gourock	3307 645	Back to UK on Polish ship *Batory*. MiD (1/1/43)
Patrick	K	F/O	CAN	J.16620	427	LV995	HAL	12/6/44	Arras	France	Fr			NK	3350 1460	See *Silent Heroes* p.59, & *The Evaders* (Lavender/Sheffe), pp. 197-207. Interviewed 10 September 1944. Report IS9(WEA)/1/197/1460
Patterson	DG	SGT		1491419	161	DK119	HAL	22/7/43	SOE	France	Fr	23/8/43	24/8/43	Tangmere	3314 1368	Flown back by SOE Lysander
Patus	JGM	SGT	CAN		416	SM228	SP	24/12/44	Patrol	Belgium				NK	NF	Shot down by US anti-aircraft battery
Paulin	RW	SGT		1321294	161	DK119	HAL	22/7/43	SOE	France	Fr	15/11/43	16/11/43	Tangmere	3316 1573	With Hunter, Crome & Kanakos. Back by Lysander on Operation Water Pistol
Pawlikowski	M	F/S	POL	781181	138	JD312	HAL	16/8/43	SOE	France	And, Sp, Gib	27/10/43	28/10/43	Portreath	3316 1510	Portreath?
Payne	HW	SGT		1317973	158	HR791	HAL	11/11/43	Cannes	France	Fr	8/7/44	9/7/44	Tangmere	3320 2008	With Sergeant A.E. Spencer RCAF. Flown back on Operation Mixer I in a USAAF Dakota from a field near Nantua (Ain) with "Major Xavier" (Richard Heslop)
Pearce	JG	SGT		1163899	550	ND733	LA	3/5/44	Mailly-le-Camp	France	Sp, Gib	23/6/44	24/6/44	Lyneham	3320 1989	He was thirty years of age (born 19 April 1914). Baled out; aircraft crashed at RAF Ford. Lyneham?
Pearce	M	SGT		1313589	10	JD368	HAL	27/8/43	Nuremberg	Belgium	Fr, Sp, Gib	27/10/43	28/10/43	Portreath	3315 1505	Burgundy line. Killed in action as flying officer on 640 Squadron, 13 September 1944 (Gelsenkirchen)
Pearce	RE	SGT	AUS	A.403034	405	W7718	HAL	31/7/42	Düsseldorf	Belgium	Fr, Sp, Gib	13/9/42	14/9/42	Whitchurch	3310 858	Briefly with the Brusselmans family. Comet 42. MiD (1/1/43, pilot officer). See *Belgium Rendez-Vous 127*, pp. 44-5
Pearl	JR	SGT		1898991	207	ME472	LA	10/4/45	Leipzig	Germany	Ger			Down Ampney	NF	Reached US lines on 13 April 1945. Flown back by Dakota from Brussels. Author *We Wanted Wings*
Pearman	L	SGT		1199606	101	T2846	WE	13/10/41	Düsseldorf	Germany	Fr, Gib	18/10/42	19/10/42	Poole	3311 928	Evacuated by *Seawolf* 12 October 1942. MM (17/9/43). Commissioned (180073) wef 10 June 1944. MBE (9/6/55). See *Airmen On The Run*, pp.11-34
Penna	C	SGT		1500020	214	R9194	ST	28/11/42	Turin	France	And, Sp, Gib	25/4/43	2/5/43	Liverpool	3313 1190	PAO line. Frostbitten feet crossing Pyrenees. Home on *Stirling Castle*. DFM (14/9/43). Author of *Escape and Evasion*
Pennie	J	SGT		1347770	158	LK841	HAL	1/6/44	Trappes	France	Fr	28/8/44	28/8/44	NK	3321 2180	Met up with Sergeant R.W. Gilbert. Left for UK from Normandy
Penny	HA	F/O		139204	35	HR878	HAL	31/8/43	Berlin	Holland	Bel, Fr, Sp, Gib	10/11/43	11/11/43	Whitchurch	3316 1560	Comet 175. MiD (8/6/44). See *We Act With One Accord*, p.145. Whitchurch?
Pepall	DRRJ	F/S		1416755	218	LJ448	ST	20/4/44	Chambly	France	Fr			NK	3349 365	Sherwood. Report IS9/WEA/2/103/365
Pepper	APW	F/L		130267	97	JB367	LA	18/11/43	Berlin	Belgium	Fr, Sp, Gib	5/2/44	6/2/44	Whitchurch	3318 1749	DFC (7/12/43). Comet 253. MiD (14/6/45)
Pepper	NEW	F/O		39335	139	L9416	BL	12/5/40	Enemy troops	Belgium	Fr			NK	NF	DFC (20/2/40). Killed on 3 June 1941, as wing commander still on 139 Squadron. No known grave
Percival	GA	F/L		127871	2	FR936	MU	27/9/44	Tac/R	Holland	Hol	28/11/44	28/11/44	Northolt	NF	DFC (27/2/45)
Percival	XX	P/O			82	R3754	BL	8/6/40	Abbeville	France	Fr			NK	NF	Possibly not an evader
Perdue	DJ	P/O		100048	12	W5395	WE	1/4/42	Le Havre	France	Gib	29/8/42	8/9/42	Gourock	3310 839	Evacuated by *Tarana* 15 August 1942 with Sergeant Misseldine. MiD (1/1/43)
Pergantes	PH	P/O	CAN	J.87784	433	HX353	HAL	4/7/44	Villeneuve-St Georges	France	Fr	8/9/44	8/9/44	NK	3345 783	Wounded by US aircraft. Liberated in Tournai hospital 3 September 1944. Discharged from UK hospital 25 October 1944. Interviewed 26 October.
Perry	DL	SGT		908781	35	W1048	HAL	27/4/42	*Tirpitz*, Norway	Norway	Swe	2/4/43	3/4/43	Leuchars	3312 1133	DFM (14/5/43). Bar to DFM (28/5/43). See *Making for Sweden*, pp. 33-5
Petch	RH	F/O		50189	617	NF923	LA	23/9/44	Ladbergen	Holland	Hol			NK	3352 2488	DFC (20/4/43, 76 Squadron). Interviewed 11 April 1945. Report IS9/WEA/1/350
Peter	RG	P/O	AUS	A.415272	35	ND759	LA	27/4/44	Friedrichshafen	Switzerland	Ger, Fr, Sp, Gib	24/5/44	25/5/44	Whitchurch	3319 1934	Repatriated with German agreement. Back on BOAC Dakota
Peterkin	JD	F/L	AUS	77123	141	DZ310	MOS	5/7/44	Bomber support	France	Fr	9/9/44	9/9/44	NK	3322 2308	ss2. Shot down by flak. Captured by three German soldiers. Fainted soon after capture, and escaped
Petley	LVE	F/L		37418	21	L9269	BL	13/6/40	Tanks, Forêt de Gault	France	Fr			NK	NF	Killed on operations 4 July 1941 (wing commander, 107 Sq). MID (24/9/41)
Petre	J	F/S		1090310	10	MZ793	HAL	14/2/45	Mining	Denmark	Swe	7/3/45	7/3/45	NK	3326 2919	Crossed with two actors and an actress of Copenhagen's Theatre Royal from Tuborg docks to Sweden by fishing boat on 1 March 1945
Petsche	J	SGT	CAN	R.216097	434	LW713	HAL	12/6/44	Arras	France				NK	NF	DFM (21/4/44)
Philbin	GB	S/L	CAN	J.13999	425	LL594	HAL	5/8/44	St Leu d'Esserent	France	Fr			NK	3345 662	Aircraft exploded in air. Wounded in face. Two ribs broken. Liberated Paris hospital 26 August 1944. Interviewed 13 September 1944. Report

																MI9/S/P.G./MISC/INT/662. DFC (15/9/44)
Phillips	DL	LAC		545177	150	L5524	BA	13/6/40	Vernon-Poix	France	Sp, Gib	19/11/40	4/12/40	Liverpool	3300 133	Wounded. Escaped from hospital. Back to UK on the SS *Aquila*. MM (7/3/41) Commissioned (52730) wef 19 August 1943
Phillips	JA	F/S	CAN	R.161467	419	KB719	LA	24/7/44	Stuttgart	France	Fr	1/9/44	1/9/44	Northolt	3321 2160	
Phillips	JWB	SGT		561185	54	P9388	SP	24/5/40	Patrol	France	Sp, Gib	13/5/41	14/5/41	Mount Batten	3303 283	Leg broken. Hospital. Escaped. To UK by Sunderland. DFM (11/6/40). Died 25 March 1942, aged thirty-one
Phillips	NV	W/O	RHO	778439	266	RB267	TY	9/4/45	Patrol	Holland	Hol			NK	3352 3046	Interviewed 26 April 1945. Report IS9/WEA/1/401/3046
Phillips	REA	F/O	CAN	J.25522	166	ME720	LA	27/4/44	Friedrichshafen	Switzerland	Fr	22/10/44	22/10/44	NK	3324 2671	Shot down by Swiss flak. To France on 21 October 1944. See *On Wings of War. A History of 166 Squadron*, p. 71
Phillips	WE	SGT	CAN	R.125293	90	BK725	ST	16/4/43	Mannheim	France	And, Sp, Gib	23/6/43	24/6/43	Hendon	3313 1268	With Chauny/Burgundy lines
Philliskirk	GM	SGT		1874051	427	LV987	HAL	7/6/44	Achères	France	Fr			NK	3350 1270	Interviewed 1 September 1944. Report IS9/WEA/7/142/1270
Philo	SJV	SGT		1319259	49	LM337	LA	15/8/43	Milan	France	Sp, And, Gib	15/11/43	16/11/43	Lyneham	3316 1580	With Polish escapers Sergeants Raginis and Bakalarski, and Driver Williamson NZASC. Warrant Officer Philo was killed in action on 3 April 1945 on 196 Squadron
Philpott	HG	F/S		1334255	106	ME831	LA	7/7/44	St Leu d'Esserent	France	Fr	29/8/44	29/8/44	Northolt	3322 2239	Left for UK from Bayeux- B.14 airstrip, Banville
Pickering	JD	F/S		747934	120	AM924	LIB	28/5/42	*Tirpitz* recce	Norway	Swe	31/8/42	1/9/42	Leuchars	3310 833	Came down in the sea sixty miles off Lofoten Islands. Reached Sweden on 30 June 1942. DFM (1/12/42). See *Making for Sweden*, pp. 35-8; *Shot Down and on the Run*, pp. 127-33
Pierre	MAJ	F/L	BEL	133525	158	DT694	HAL	14/2/43	Cologne	Germany	Hol, Bel, Fr, Sp, Gib	19/4/43	20/4/43	Hendon	3313 1171	Comet 90. DFC (25/5/43). Came down approx. five miles NW of Aachen on top of a German fort
Pierre	P	F/S	FRA	F.30732	342	BZ390	BOS	4/8/44	Caen-Falaise	France	Fr			NK	3348 145	Took off at 0230 hours, 5 August. Interviewed 16 August 1944. Report IS9/WEA 2/85/145
Pietrasiak	A	SGT	POL	784763	308	P8318	SP	19/8/41	Circus 82	France	And, Sp, Gib	30/12/41	5/1/42	Gourock	3307 642	VM DFM. Treated by Dr Rodocanachi. MiD (recommended 29/5/42). To UK on Polish ship *Batory*. Killed 29 November 1943 on operations on 308 Squadron
Piggott	AC	F/O	CAN	J.23137	166	ME720	LA	27/4/44	Friedrichshafen	Switzerland	Fr	8/10/44	8/10/44	Northolt	3324 2642	Shot down over Switzerland. Crossed to France with repatriation party on 4 October 1944. See *On Wings of War. A History of 166 Squadron*
Pilgrim	NCH	F/S		1435664	149	EF502	ST	10/4/44	SOE	France	Fr	8/7/44	9/7/44	Tangmere	3320 2010	With Sergeant D.E. Cadge. Flown back on Operation Mixer I in a USAAF Dakota from a field near Nantua (Ain) with "Major Xavier" (Richard Heslop)
Pinkerton	FW	SGT		1028921	12	W4858	LA	29/3/43	Berlin	Holland	Bel, Fr, Sp, Gib	21/6/43	22/6/43	Whitchurch	3313 1266	Back by Dakota. Gave talk to his squadron on 22 July 1943
Pipkin	LC	F/L		62260	103	W1219	HAL	6/9/42	Duisburg	Germany	Hol, Bel, Fr, Sp, Gib	24/10/42	25/10/42	Mount Batten	3311 934	Comet 63. DFC (10/11/42). Report of his lecture tour on return to UK - see AIR 14/2479
Pittwood	J	F/S		1219454	207	ND556	LA	3/5/44	Mailly-le-Camp	France	Sp, Gib	23/6/44	24/6/44	Lyneham	3320 1988	Burgundy line? Lyneham is an educated guess
Playfoot	KG	F/O			576	PD235	LA	24/9/44	Calais	France				NK	NF	ss7
Plummer	LA	F/O	CAN		441	MJ668	SP	28/8/44	Armed recce	France			29/8/44	NK	NF	
Pochailo	P	F/O	CAN	J.27129	166	ND579	LA	21/5/44	Duisburg	Holland	Hol			NK	3327 3001	Liberated 12 May 1945
Polesinski	E	SGT	POL	792693	304	W5627	WE	27/4/42	Cologne	France	Sp, Gib	6/7/42	12/7/42	Gourock	3309 777	Back on the *Narkunda*. MiD. See AIR 2/5684. See *Safe Houses Are Dangerous*, p.207
Pond	HA	F/S	NZ	NZ.416161	97	JA707	LA	27/8/43	Nuremberg	Belgium	Fr	13/9/43	14/9/43	Tangmere	3315 1402	With the Possum line. Back by Lysander with Sergeant E.F. Gardiner. DFM (19/5/44)
Poohkay	WM	F/O	CAN	J.19530	427	LV938	HAL	28/6/44	Metz	France	Fr			NK	3350 1273	Liberated by US forces 5 September 1944 & interviewed same day. Report IS9/WEA/7/154/1273. See *We Fell, We Flew, We Lived* p. 323
Porter	KP	WO2	CAN	R.149473	617	JB139	LA	5/8/44	Brest	France	Fr	18/8/44	18/8/44	NK	3322 2242	Left for UK from Bayeux - B.14 airstrip, Banville
Potentier	RHL	F/S	CAN	R.166677	433	HX292	HAL	24/3/44	Berlin	Belgium	Fr			NK	3348 2026	On first op with crew as rear gunner. Baled out. Aircraft returned to UK. With Sergeant D.S. Beckwith. Liberated 11 September 1944. Interviewed 4 October 1944
Pottage	CAM	F/S	CAN	R.212260	426	NP800	HAL	4/11/44	Bochum	Germany				NK	NF	
Potten	CE	SGT		1832778	90	EF509	ST	9/5/44	SOE	France	Fr			NK	3352 2886	Helped by André Rougeyron. See *Agents for Escape...*, Chapter 14
Powell	EA	WO2	CAN	R.142155	425	LW390	HAL	20/2/44	Stuttgart	France	Sp, Gib	5/6/44	6/6/44	Whitchurch	3320 1952	Burgundy line
Powell	EC	SGT		1580783	149	EF202	ST	25/11/43	Mining	France	Fr	11/9/44	11/9/44	NK	3325 2881	Interrogated by IS9 (WEA) in Paris before being flown back to England
Powell	LAT	F/S		975129	88	BZ359	BOS	16/8/43	Denain	France	Fr	9/9/44	9/9/44	Hendon	3323 2389	With Bordeaux-Loupiac organisation

Power	WA	SGT		1001443	77	LW270	HAL	23/4/44	Mining	Denmark	Swe	7/5/44	8/5/44	Leuchars	3319 1912	Back to UK from Stockholm
Pratt	OL	F/S			193	RB346	TY	16/4/45	Armed patrol	Holland				NK	NF	Force-landed south-west of Apeldoorn
Prentice	KR	F/O		139109	69	MF231	WE	14/6/44	Recce	France	Fr	30/8/44	30/8/44	NK	3321 2195	
Prévot	LO	S/L	BEL	84285	122	BM266	SP	30/7/42	Ramrod	France	Sp, Gib	15/10/42	15/10/42	Mount Batten	3311 910	Comet 64. DFC (30/10/42)
Price	EG	SGT	CAN	R.84592	158	W1215	HAL	5/8/42	Bochum	Holland	Bel, Fr, Sp, Gib	7/11/42	7/11/42	Portreath	3311 972	Comet 50. Back to England by Dakota. DFM (5/2/43)
Price	GA	P/O	NZ	NZ.425779	106	ND339	LA	4/7/44	St Leu d'Esserent	France				NK	NF	
Price	ME	F/O			620	LJ849	ST	6/6/44	Supplies to Normandy	France	Fr	8/6/44	9/6/44	Gosport	NF	Left Normandy from Allied beachhead. No MI9/IS9 report listed. LJ849?
Pritchard	A	SGT		2206806	97	ND764	LA	9/6/44	Etampes	France	Fr			NK	3349	
Pritchard	AH	P/O		177398	428	KB756	LA	4/7/44	Villeneuve-St Georges	France	Fr	30/8/44	30/8/44	Northolt	3322 2224	Left for UK from Bayeux - B.14 airstrip, Banville
Proddow	BF	F/O		119143	174	JP548	TY	14/2/44	Ranger	France	Fr	4/9/44	4/9/44	NK	3323 2486	Hid for six months in a brewery. Shot down again and taken prisoner on 24 February 1945
Prowse	HS	F/O	CAN	J.24017	101	LL750	LA	27/4/44	Friedrichshafen	Switzerland	Fr	8/10/44	8/10/44	Northolt	3324 2637	Blown out of aircraft. Injured. Escaped to France with group of repatriates on 4 October 1944
Pryer	WR	SGT		1652559	44	ME634	LA	7/7/44	St Leu d'Esserent	France	Fr	20/8/44	20/8/44	Northolt	3321 2118	Sherwood
Ptácek	R	SGT	CZ	787437	222	P8244	SP	19/8/41	Circus	France	Sp, Gib	30/12/41	5/1/42	Gourock	3307 643	To UK on Polish ship *Batory*. MiD (recommended 29/5/42). Shot down again 28 March 1942 (602 Squadron). Possibly not killed until 4 April 1942
Punter	RH	F/S	CAN	R.157849	626	NE118	LA	22/5/44	Dortmund	Holland	Bel	13/9/44	13/9/44	Hendon	3324 2561	
Purkis	JB	F/L		158700	263	MN878	TY	16/8/44	Armed recce	France	Fr			NK	3349 369	Liberated by British troops 24 August 1944. Interviewed 25 August 1944. Report IS9/WEA/2/202/369. 1388276. DFC (1/9/44)
Pyle	GF	P/O		172962	129	FB108	MU	10/6/44	Tac/R	France	Fr	14/8/44	14/8/44	Wroughton	3348 285	Liberated 11 August 1944. Report IS9/WEA/2/74/285. Back on RAF DC-3 "ambulance". Wroughton? Author of *Broken Mustang [D-Day 4]*
Queale	LW	F/L	CAN	J.24216	405	PA970	LA	8/9/44	Le Havre	France				NK	NF	DFC (15/9/44) & Bar (8/12/44)
Quinn	J	F/S		1345078	12	JB650	LA	27/1/44	Berlin	Belgium	Sz, Fr	4/9/44	4/9/44	Hendon	3324 2595	Reached Switzerland on 9 May 1944. Left 27 August 1944 with Sergeant H. Simister and Warrant Officer A.W. Bennett
Quirk	ES	F/O	AUS	A.423888	196	LJ925	ST	25/2/45	Supply drop	Norway	Nor			NK	3327 3019	
Rabone	GO	F/O	NZ	NZ.413214	106	LM641	LA	7/8/44	Secqueville	France	Fr	28/8/44	28/8/44	Northolt	3321 2200	Left for UK from Bayeux - B.14 airstrip, Banville
Rabson	KL	F/S		1286410	138	LW281	HAL	18/10/43	SOE	Belgium	Fr, Sp, Gib	5/12/43	6/12/43	Whitchurch	3317 1601	DFM (14/9/43). Comet 201
Racey	RF	F/S			74	TB593	SP	5/4/45	Offensive operations	Holland				NK	NF	Came down near Zwolle
Racine	GG	F/L	CAN	J.5800	263	MN170	TY	31/3/44	Rodeo	France	Fr	16/4/44	16/4/44	Dartmouth	3319 1885	Evacuated from Beg-an-Fry, Brittany, by MGB 502. DFC (29/9/44)
Radcliffe	HK	F/S		1562928	254		BFR	17/1/45	NK	Holland	Hol			NK	3352 2382	Interviewed 7 March 1945. Report IS9/WEA/1/292/2382
Radwanski	W	P/O	POL	P.1006	300	Z1271	WE	7/11/41	Mannheim	France	Sp, Gib	27/4/42	8/5/42	Liverpool	3308 722	Recommended for MBE (24/6/42) but awarded MiD. See *Safe Houses Are Dangerous*, p.206
Rae	AM	F/S		1552248	76	MZ623	HAL	24/5/44	Aachen	Belgium	Bel	6/9/44	6/9/44	NK	3322 2287	Marathon. Flown back from France after liberation
Raeder	JKB	2LT	NOR	F.P.847	332	LZ948	SP	13/5/43	Ramrod 71	France	Sp, Gib	5/8/43	11/8/43	Liverpool	3314 1353	Comet 114. Taken to Paris by Mlle. Marie Henri de Bezien
Rafter	RH	WO1	CAN	R.84923	405	PA988	LA	16/8/44	Stettin	Denmark	Swe	2/9/44	3/9/44	Leuchars	3322 2257	To Sweden by boat. Left for UK from Stockholm
Raftery	BF	F/S	AUS	A.424460	460	ME755	LA	14/7/44	Revigny-sur-Ornain	France	Fr	13/9/44	13/9/44	NK	3323 2480	See *Massacre over the Marne*
Rainsford	JE	SGT		1397881	97	JA707	LA	27/8/43	Nuremberg	Belgium	Fr, Sp, Gib	6/11/43	7/11/43	London	3316 1562	Comet 161. With Sergeant O. Ramsden. Sailed from Seville on 1 November 1944 on SS *Star* (Norwegian). London = Hendon? MiD (8/6/44)
Ramsay	TI	F/S	AUS	A.428124	467	PD230	LA	12/8/44	Rüsselsheim	Belgium	Bel			NK	NF	Interviewed by IS9(WEA) on 13 September 1944. Report .... 2089 ?
Ramsden	O	SGT		647735	97	JA707	LA	27/8/43	Nuremberg	Belgium	Fr, Sp, Gib	6/11/43	7/11/43	London	3316 1563	Comet 162. With Sergeant J.E. Rainsford. Sailed from Seville on 1 November 1944 on SS *Star* (Norwegian). London = Hendon? MiD (8/6/44)
Ranalow	PBO	F/L		130989	35	LV861	HAL	15/2/44	Berlin	Holland	Sz		6/10/44	NK	NF	In Switzerland 25 June 1944. Left 16 September 1944. Shot down again 8 April 1945. Died of injuries 10 April 1945. See *We Act With One Accord*, p.168
Randall	FA	F/O	AUS	A.413896	460	W4988	LA	3/9/43	Berlin	Denmark (sea)	Swe			NK	3315 1426	DFC (23/11/43). Killed 16/17 December 1943 on return from ops to Berlin when JB657 hit a tree in Lincolnshire
Randall	WJ	F/S			271	KG444	DAK	21/9/44	Arnhem supply drop	Holland	Hol			NK	NF	Evaded with his pilot, Flight Lieutenant J.K.O. Edwards
Randall	WL	F/S		1294037	274	EJ611	TEM	27/9/44	Patrol	Holland	Hol			NK	3352 2447	Met Flight Lieutenant O.G. Korpela RCAF. Liberated 4 April 1945 by Canadian troops. Interviewed 6 April 1945. Report IS9/WEA/1/331/2447
Randle	WSO	SGT		1385872	150	BJ877	WE	16/9/42	Essen	Belgium	Fr, Sp, Gib	24/10/42	25/10/42	Portreath	3311 936	Comet 60. DFM (8/12/42). Author *Blue Skies and Dark Nights*. Commissioned (144393). MiD (8/6/44, flying officer). AFC (7/9/45)

Raoul-Duval	CE	LT	FRA	F.30175	341	BS548	SP	17/4/43	Circus 286	France	Sp, Gib	3/10/43	17/10/43	Gourock	3315 1471	Burgundy line. Accompanied over Pyrenees by his wife, Josette (née Devin) - see *L'évadé de la France Libre*, pp. 229-230
Ratchford	CE	F/S	CAN	R.100791	619	LL969	LA	18/7/44	Revigny-sur-Ornain	France	Fr	30/8/44	30/8/44	NK	3349 426	ss7. Interviewed 30 August 1944. Report IS9/WEA/8/246/426. See *Massacre over the Marne*
Ratsoy	JS	SGT	CAN	R.10882	82 OTU	BJ790	WE	16/8/44	Nickel	France	Fr			NK	3348 282	Interviewed 18 August 1944. Report IS9/WEA/8/508/282
Rattner	C	F/S		1386377	61	LM359	LA	24/4/44	Munich	France	Fr			NK	3345 750	ss7. Wounded. Handed over to Germans. Liberated from Paris hospital 28 August 1944. Interviewed 10 October 1944. Report MISC/INT/750
Raynel	WG	F/S	NZ	NZ.424998	75	NE148	LA	28/7/44	Stuttgart	France	Fr	16/8/44	16/8/44	Northolt	3321 2099	Sherwood. Left for UK from Cherbourg. Northolt?
Read	KB	SGT		625743	9	W5703	WE	26/8/41	Cologne	France	Sp, Gib	30/12/41	5/1/42	Gourock	3307 626	With Bufton and Crampton of his crew. To UK on Polish ship *Batory*. MiD (11/6/42). See *Bombers First and Last*, pp. 58-9, and *Fighter Pilot*, pp.167-75
Read	MJ	SGT		916294				11/11/44	NK		Sz, Fr			NK	NF	FTU, Ferry Command. See AIR 40/1552. NB: Date lost entered for statistical purposes
Reader	RF	SGT	NZ	NZ.413792	298	LL407	HAL	6/6/44	Dropping troops D-Day	France	Fr		18/9/44	Gosport	3320 1974	Injured pelvis. In German hospital. Interviewed 20 October 1944. Report also MISC/INT/777
Reading	R	F/S		988635	76	MZ575	HAL	12/5/44	Hasselt	Belgium	Fr	7/9/44	7/9/44	Hendon	3324 2599	Marathon
Reading	SK	SGT		1382453	50	ND874	LA	5/6/44	St Pierre-du-Mont	France	Fr	13/6/44	13/6/44	NK	3321 2166	ss7. Captured 6 June 1944. Persuaded guards to let him go. Liberated by US troops
Reain	FFE	F/S	CAN	R.131517	428	LK739	HAL	20/1/44	Berlin	France	Sp, Gib	4/5/44	5/5/44	Whitchurch	3319 1897	MiD (14/6/45). Later, flying officer (J.86288)
Reavey	J	SGT		1602021	576	LM122	LA	2/11/44	Düsseldorf	Belgium				NK	NF	
Redford	FH	F/S	AUS	A.427743	463	DV229	LA	10/6/44	Orléans	France	Fr			NK	3348 140	Interviewed 13 August 1944. Report IS9/WEA 2/25/140
Reece	KA	SGT		1818908	57	JB474	LA	15/3/44	Stuttgart	Switzerland	Fr	4/11/44	4/11/44	Croydon	3324 2722	ss7. To France on 26 October 1944 with Sergeant G.R. Mattock. Back to UK from Paris
Reed	JS	F/O		145816	138	LW275	HAL	7/2/44	SOE	France	Sp, Gib	11/4/44	12/4/44	Lyneham	3319 1881	DFC (2/1/45). See *Free to Fight Again*, pp. 77-81
Reed	LGA	P/O		49333	161	Z9131	WH	24/9/42	SOE	France	Gib	18/10/42	19/10/42	Poole	3311 924	Evacuated by *Seawolf* 12 October 1942. DFC (8/12/42) & Bar (14/12/43). RVO 5th Class (12/6/47) for services on King's Flight
Reed	WC	P/O		174154	158	LV790	HAL	12/6/44	Amiens	France	Fr	5/9/44	5/9/44	Northolt	3324 2547	DFC (27/3/45)
Reeve	PA	SGT	CAN	R.157637	433	HX353	HAL	4/7/44	Villeneuve-St Georges	France	Fr		30/8/44	NK	3321 2197	Betrayed, captured but escaped when column bombed by US B-26 Marauders on 19 August 1944
Reeves	BC	SGT		1321751	30 OTU	BK559	WE	11/6/43	Nickel	France	And, Sp, Gib	27/10/43	28/10/43	Portreath	3315 1506	
Reid	D	SGT	CAN	R.162843	49	LM572	LA	24/6/44	Pommerval	France	Fr		18/7/44	NK	3348 4	Met English sentry 1 July 1944 at Caen. Report IS9 WEA 2/5/4. See also AIR 14/464
Reid	JB	SGT		1822771	578	LW675	HAL	12/6/44	Amiens	France	Fr		15/9/44	NK	NF	
Reid	JM	SGT		1191521	115	X3393	WE	9/12/42	Turin	France	Sp, Gib	21/1/43	26/1/43	Gourock	3312 1057	Comet 83
Reid	JM	SGT		1195235	102	MZ644	HAL	28/6/44	Blainville	France	Fr	28/8/44	28/8/44	Lyneham	3321 2190	Back on RAF Dakota to UK from Orléans. See *Massacre over the Marne*, pp. 134-42
Remington	JB	SGT		1580259	625	ME684	LA	24/3/44	Berlin	Holland	Bel	17/9/44	17/9/44	NK	3323 2477	Back to UK from Brussels
Renard	MCB	F/O	BEL	159219	349	NH199	SP	30/8/44	Strafing	Belgium	Bel	9/9/44	9/9/44	NK	3323 2419	Back to UK from Brussels
Renner	WL	SGT	CAN	R.161153	419	JD463	HAL	4/10/43	Frankfurt	Belgium	Bel	17/9/44	17/9/44	NK	3323 2435	ss7. Liberated 3 September 1944. Left for UK from Brussels
Rennie	BJA	P/O	SAF	87414	144	AD924	HN	9/7/41	Aachen	Belgium	Fr, Sp, Gib	4/9/41	5/9/41	Oban	3305 492	In Madrid by 28 August 1941. MC (13/3/42). See *Escape & Liberation 1940-1945*, pp.126-134. Died 19 October 1942 at 14 OTU
Renwick	P	SGT		1623675	30 OTU	BJ618	WE	9/5/44	Nickel	France	Fr	29/8/44	29/8/44	Northolt	3322 2217	
Reynolds	AJA	SGT		1196437	428	DK229	HAL	9/7/43	Gelsenkirchen	Germany	Hol, Bel, Fr, Sp, Gib	15/3/44	15/3/44	Whitchurch	3319 1835	In failed FanFan boat operation at Quimper at end of October 1943
Reynolds	TJ	SGT		1807833	408	DS704	LA	20/12/43	Frankfurt	Belgium	Bel	11/9/44	11/9/44	Northolt	3323 2409	
Richards	FH	F/L	CAN	J.15892	412	ML277	SP	20/1/45	Armed recce	Holland	Hol			NK	3352 3006	Met up with Colonel Duncan USAAF. Liberated by Lincolnshire Regiment 14 April 1945. Interviewed 16 April 1945. Report IS9/WEA/2/1056
Richards	PW	SGT		1603266	405	ND347	LA	8/5/44	Haine St Pierre	Belgium				NK	NF	
Richardson	KC	SGT		1535160	149	EF202	ST	25/11/43	Mining	France	Fr		11/9/44	NK	3348 34	
Richardson	W	SGT		1578437	50	LM437	LA	3/5/44	Mailly-le-Camp	France				NK	NF	ss7
Riding	RH	F/O		130563	69	MF231	WE	14/6/44	Recce	France	Fr	27/8/44	27/8/44	Northolt	3321 2199	Met Sergeant J.G. Divers during evasion. Left for UK from Bayeux - B.14 airstrip, Banville
Ridley-Martin	MG	F/L		47442	2	FR924	MU	11/10/44	Tac/R	Holland			28/10/44	NK	NF	DFC (19/5/44, 170 Squadron). He was formerly a captain in the Royal

																Signals. Back from behind enemy lines next day
Ridout	TAF	F/S		1396242	107	NS952	MOS	25/8/44	Enemy train	France	Fr			NK	NF	Shot down attacking immobilised train. Back by 4 October 1944, having been rescued by FFI. His pilot, Flight Lieutenant A.J. Rippon DFC, was killed. MiD (1/1/46, warrant officer)
Riley	H	SGT		1079476	51	DT670	HAL	16/4/43	Pilsen	France	Sp, Gib	16/8/43	17/8/43	Hendon	3314 1359	Oaktree/Burgundy line. Sailed on the SS *Esneh* from Seville to Gibraltar 11-13 August 1943 with R.E. Barckley & J.R. Milne
Rippingale	EG	F/S		1392790	514	LL727	LA	7/6/44	Massy-Palaiseau	France				NK	NF	Service number?
Riseley	AH	F/O		106080	88	BZ359	BOS	16/8/43	Denain	France	Fr	24/10/43	25/10/43	Penzance	3315 1496	Back by boat. DSO (14/1/44). See *Heavenly Days*, pp. 216-7 and *2 Group R.A.F.* (Bowyer), pp. 327-8
Ritch	JD	F/O	CAN		418	PZ220	MOS	17/10/44	Ranger	Balkans				NK	3326 2997	With Russian partisans until April 1945. Balkans?
Ritchie	HP	SGT	CAN	R.172045	630	LM537	LA	18/7/44	Revigny-sur-Ornain	France	Fr	1/9/44	1/9/44	NK	3325 2819	See *Massacre over the Marne*
Robert	L	SGT	BEL	1424879	78	MZ763	HAL	23/9/44	Neuss	Holland				NK	3350 1416	Interviewed 26 September 1944. Report IS9/WEA/2/558/1416. His real name was Pierre Davreux, but he served as Robert in case he was shot down
Roberts	AC	SGT	AUS	A.402007	452	P7562	SP	11/7/41	Sweep	France	Sp, Gib	1/10/41	6/10/41	Gourock	3306 561	Escaped from St Hippolyte-du-Fort on 21 August 1941 with Sergeant J. Burridge and seven soldiers. Crossed Pyrenees with Squadron Leader E.P.P. Gibbs. MiD (1/1/43)
Roberts	BL	SGT		1819407	514	LL739	LA	11/5/44	Louvain	Belgium				NK	NF	Killed in action on 7 October 1944 (Emmerich), still on 514 Squadron
Roberts	F	W/O		1349787	341	TB750	SP	30/3/45	Rail target	Holland	Hol			NK	3331 618	Shot down dive-bombing a train. Liberated by Canadian troops 7 April 1945. Report MI9/S/PG/LIB/618
Roberts	MA	W/O	NZ		644	NA672	HAL	26/4/45	SOE Tablejam 353	Denmark	Dk	19/5/45	19/5/45	NK	NF	Flown back to UK over Hamburg by DC-3 Dakota
Robertson	DW	F/O	CAN	J.24040	434	LW713	HAL	12/6/44	Arras	France	Fr	7/9/44	7/9/44	NK	3322 2344	Back to UK from Vitry-en-Artois. Surname Robersons?
Robertson	FWC	SGT		630958	408	DS788	LA	19/2/44	Leipzig	Holland	Bel			NK	3350 1350	Marathon. Interviewed 11 September 1944. Report IS9/WEA/MB/1350
Robertson	HO	SGT		1114418	76	BB242	HAL	6/12/42	Mannheim	France	And, Sp, Gib	8/3/43	15/3/43	Liverpool	3312 1126	DFM (11/5/43). Author of *Dangerous Landing*
Robertson	WA	F/O	CAN	J.24485	158	HX334	HAL	12/5/44	Hasselt	Belgium	Bel			NK	3350 1373	Interviewed 19 September 1944. Report IS9/WEA/2/514/1373
Robillard	JGL	SGT	CAN	R.54188	145	P8536	SP	2/7/41	Circus 29	France	Sp, Gib	26/8/41	26/8/41	Calshot	3305 491	Claimed to have shot down three of his Me109 attackers. Flown home by Sunderland. DFM (11/11/41). See *Fighter Pilot*, p.165
Robinson	DM	P/O	AUS	A.422707	83	PB362	LA	18/8/44	L'Isle-Adam	France	Fr	6/9/44	6/9/44	NK	3323 2372	
Robinson	GL	SGT		1011435	149	W7572	ST	24/8/42	Frankfurt	Belgium	Fr, Gib	18/10/42	19/10/42	Poole	3311 918	Evacuated by *Seawolf* 12 October 1942. See *The RAF Quarterly* Winter 1962
Robinson	W	SGT		1777532	44	ME699	LA	4/7/44	St Leu d'Esserent	France				NK	NF	
Robinson	WW	F/O	CAN	J.19883	300	LM178	LA	24/7/44	Stuttgart	France	Fr	31/8/44	31/8/44	Membury	3345 805	Injuries to left leg. Treated by German doctors in Paris, where liberated c. 27 August 1944. Interviewed 22 November 1944. Report MISC/INT/805
Robson	G	SGT			110	R3670	BL	8/6/40	Amiens	France	Fr			NK	NF	Possibly not an evader
Rogers	R	P/O			21	L8743	BL	11/6/40	La Mare	France	Fr			NK	NF	Possibly not an evader
Roggenkamp	N	W/O	AUS	A.414598	129	FX959	MU	7/6/44	Enemy in Normandy	France	Fr	30/8/44	30/8/44	Northolt	3322 2227	See *Silent Heroes*, p.40
Rohde	HW	2LT	NOR	F.P.5494	332	PT723	SP	2/4/45	Armed recce	Holland	Hol			NK	3352 3020	Briefly captured. Later with Warrant Officer J.C. Van Rossendaal. Liberated 13 April 1945. Interviewed 16 April 1945. Report IS9/WEA/1/375/3020
Rooks	FD	F/O	CAN	J.27317	431	MZ522	HAL	27/4/44	Montzen	Belgium	Bel		15/9/44	NK	NF	Broke leg on landing. Liberated by US forces on 8 September 1944. Initials CO?
Rooney	AJ	SGT		1522906	149	EF202	ST	25/11/43	Mining	France	Fr		11/9/44	NK	3348 149	Contacted Americans 3 August 1944 at Avranches. Report IS9/WEA/2/19/34 jointly with Sergeant K.C. Richardson
Roper	PDL	F/L		132419	146 Wing	MN125	TY	7/6/44	Anti-AFVs	France		13/8/44	13/8/44	NK	3345 796	20 Section, 146 Wing. In a 486 Squadron aircraft. Wounded. Liberated in Rennes hospital 4 August 1944. Interviewed 20 October 1944. Report MISC/INT/796
Rose	CT	F/S		1557436	166	LM388	LA	12/7/44	Revigny-sur-Ornain	France	Fr	7/9/44	7/9/44	NK	3350 1139	Interviewed 6 September 1944. Report IS9/WEA/MB/1139. See *Massacre over the Marne*
Rose	MJA	P/O		189177	3	NV656	TEM	10/2/45	Armed recce	Germany				NK	NF	Baled out near Paderborn. DFC (18/9/45)
Rosher	J	F/S		1347731	617	JB139	LA	5/8/44	Brest	France	Fr	18/8/44	18/8/44	Grove	3322 2243	Left for UK from Rennes
Rosinski	JM	F/O	POL	P.2244	305	LR313	MOS	22/4/44	Leeuwarden airfield	France	Sp, Gib	10/6/44	11/6/44	NK	3320 1960	Crossed to Spain with Warrant Officer Ciula, Pilot Officer W.F. Dobson and Sergeant D. Shepherd
Roskell	G	SGT		613552	226	None	None	14/6/40	None	France	Sp, Gib	14/2/41	23/2/41	Gourock	3302 234	Groundcrew. Forearm amputated. Passed unfit for military service in Marseille on 14 December 1940. MM (13/3/42)

Ross	AG	F/S	CAN	R.176169	106	ND339	LA	4/7/44	St Leu d'Esserent	France	Fr	6/9/44	6/9/44	NK	3324 2540	Left for UK from B.14 airstrip, Banville. Service number given as R.1776169 on aircraft loss card
Ross	AS	F/L	CAN	C.8323	193	MN700	TY	11/6/44	NK	France	Fr		29/8/44	NK	3327 3056	DFC (25/7/44). Baled out at very low altitude. Briefly in German hands
Ross	DG	P/O		120911	90	BK725	ST	16/4/43	Mannheim	France	And, Sp, Gib	21/6/43	22/6/43	Whitchurch	3313 1255	With Chauny/Burgundy lines. Back by Dakota
Ross	F	F/S		1517239	190		ST	21/9/44	Arnhem supply drop	Holland	Bel	25/9/44	25/9/44	Fairford	3324 2591	Back to UK from Brussels
Ross	JD	F/L		125880	56	NV659	TEM	6/2/45	Armed patrol	Germany				NK	NF	Baled out near Paderborn
Rossely	LG	F/S	AUS	A.419057	460	ND654	LA	20/7/44	Courtrai	Belgium	Bel			NK	3350 1401	Interviewed 18 September 1944. Report IS9/WEA/2/488/1401
Rosser	WJ	F/L		102991	66	PV186	SP	26/9/44	Armed recce	Holland				NK	3348	DFC (23/6/42, 130 Squadron). Interviewed 30 October 1944
Roth	JA	P/O	CAN	J.38285	82 OTU	BJ790	WE	16/8/44	Nickel	France	Fr			NK	3348 278	Interviewed 18 August 1944. Report IS9/WEA/8/503/278
Rowicki	K	F/O	POL	P.0148	305	Z8599	WE	5/5/42	Stuttgart	Belgium	Fr, Sp, Gib	30/9/42	5/10/42	Greenock	3310 888	Comet 52. Travelled with Flight Sergeant Fay RCAF from Brussels to Spain. Back on HMS *Malaya*
Rowland	BD	F/S		1456221	570	LJ638	ST	11/4/45	SOE supply drop	Holland	Hol			NK	3348 189	Wounded in jaw. In house attacked by Germans 29 April 1945. Interviewed 11 May 1945. Report IS9/WEA/PLM/189
Royle	L	SGT		2211825	298	LL332	HAL	10/9/44	Special mission	France	Fr	27/9/44	27/9/44	Heston	3324 2626	In hospital at Epinal-les-Mines 12-24 September 1944. Back to UK from Cherbourg
Rudd	RAW	SGT			305	NT187	MOS	9/4/45	Intruder	Germany				NK	NF	Came down near Olpe
Rudkin	L	SGT		950233	12	W4366	LA	16/4/43	Pilsen	Belgium	Fr, Sp, Gib	17/7/43	24/7/43	Liverpool	3314 1323	Baled out in error - aircraft returned to base. Back to UK on SS *Monarch of Bermuda*? See Free to *Fight Again*, pp.165-70
Rudsdale	WA	W/O		1062700	299	EF267	ST	19/9/44	Supply drop	Holland	Hol	29/9/44	29/9/44	NK	3324 2684	Briefly in Nijmegen casualty clearing hospital. Aircraft number is a guess
Rupert	WA	F/O	CAN	J.27691	617	NF923	LA	23/9/44	Ladbergen	Holland	Hol	4/4/45	4/4/45	NK	3326 2940	Liberated 31 March 1945 by Grenadier Guards. Interviewed 5 April 1945. Flown to UK from Belgium
Russell	A	SGT		1800836	115	HK548	LA	7/6/44	Chevreuse	France	Fr			NK	3350 1224	With Sergeant P. Murphy. Interviewed 1 September 1944. Report IS9/WEA/2/297/1224
Rutherford	DE	F/O	CAN	J.26725	432	LK811	HAL	27/5/44	Bourg-Léopold	Belgium	Bel			NK	NF	Liberated in Liège on 7 September 1944. See *The Evaders* (Cosgrove), p.161
Rutter	DR	W/O	AUS		464	TA372	MOS	23/4/45	Intruder	Germany				NK	NF	Shot down north-north-east of Bremen. Aus?
Ryan	C	SGT		576676	190	LJ982	ST	21/9/44	Arnhem supply drop	Belgium	Bel			NK	3350 1406	Interviewed 25 September 1944. Report IS9/WEA/2/542/1406
Rycroft	DF	F/S	CAN	R.198671	101	ME857	LA	25/8/44	Rüsselsheim	France	Fr	21/9/44	21/9/44	Exeter	3325 2869	Back to UK from Reims
Rytka	M	SGT	POL	P.1574	302	Z2423	HUD	21/5/41	Circus	France	Sp, Gib	8/8/41	14/8/41	Gourock	3305 483	Enlisted in Polish Air Force 1935, and in RAF in September 1940. Helped by PAT line from Lille. MBE (approved 6/11/41)
Sabin	S	SGT		952522	235		BFR	2/6/42	Transit to Gibraltar	Atlantic ocean		18/8/42	19/8/42	Whitchurch	3310 813	Ran out of fuel on flight to Gibraltar
Sage	WA	P/O	CAN	J.39326	8200	BJ790	WE	16/8/44	Nickel	France	Fr			NK	3348 280	Interviewed 18 August 1944. Report IS9/WEA/8/505/280
Sale	DJ	F/L	CAN	J.9929	35	DT801	HAL	12/5/43	Duisburg	Holland	Bel, Fr, And, Sp, Gib	5/8/43	11/8/43	Liverpool	3314 1352	DSO (8/10/43) & Bar (1/2/44). DFC (27/6/44). Died in captivity on 20 March 1944. See *We Act With One Accord*, pp.122-3, and *Shot Down and on the Run*, pp.97-103
Salisbury	GE	SGT		1673116	76	MZ539	HAL	28/6/44	Blainville	France	Fr			NK	NF	With Sergeant H. Brown until 1 September 1944 in Reims, France. Author of *Yesterday's Flight Path*
Salter	H	SGT		1318641	78	JB872	HAL	5/9/43	Mannheim	France	Sp, Gib	5/2/44	6/2/44	Whitchurch	3318 1748	ss8. Helped by Resistance group "Ceux de la Résistance". Evaded over Pyrenees
Sam	KLD	P/O	CAN	J.86208	426	LW198	HAL	28/6/44	Metz	France	Fr	5/9/44	5/9/44	NK	3323 2353	Shot down on last trip of tour. CdeG (Silver Star) from French in 1947 for his help in the liberation of Paris. Fluent in Mandarin Cantonese, Japanese and French
Sampson	NT	F/S	NZ	NZ.421774	75	NE148	LA	28/7/44	Stuttgart	France	Fr			NK	3348 311	Sherwood. Interviewed 17 August 1944. Report IS9/WEA/2/138/311
Samson	RH	F/L	AUS	A.414264	156	NE143	LA	31/5/44	Tergnier	France	Fr		8/9/44	NK	3327 3110	Joined the Resistance with Flight Sergeant A.G. Bryant
Sanders	GH	F/O	NZ	NZ.442424	75	NE148	LA	28/7/44	Stuttgart	France	Fr	16/8/44	16/8/44	Northolt	3321 2091	Sherwood? Left for UK from Cherbourg. Service no? Northolt?
Sanders	SF	F/S		1383523	190	LJ982	ST	21/9/44	Arnhem supply drop	Belgium	Bel			NK	3350 1405	Interviewed 25 September 1944. Report IS9/WEA/2/560/1405
Sanderson	JW	SGT		2212990	50	PD237	LA	13/8/44	Bordeaux	France	Fr			NK	3345 647	Captured. Liberated from hospital in Angoulême 1 September 1944. Interviewed 3 September 1944. Report MI9/S/PG/MISC/INT/647. See *D-Day Bombers...*, pp. 241-5
Sandulak	J	SGT	CAN	R.208898	428	KB740	LA	24/7/44	Stuttgart	France	Fr	18/8/44	18/8/44	Northolt	3321 2120	Sherwood. Left for UK from B.14 airstrip, Banville. See *Canadians in the Royal Air Force*, pp. 36-37
Sandvik	GA	SGT	CAN	R.257511	50	PD237	LA	13/8/44	Bordeaux	France	Fr			NK	3345 648	Captured. Liberated from hospital in Angoulême 1 September 1944.

																Interviewed 3 September 1944. Report MI9/S/PG/MISC/INT/648. See *D-Day Bombers...*, pp. 241-5
Sandvik	SJM	2LT	NOR	F.P.5151	332	LZ898	SP	11/9/43	Ramrod	France	Sp, Gib	1/1/44	2/1/44	Lyneham	3317 1661	Burgundy line
Sankey	J	SGT		1119320	10	DT788	HAL	14/2/43	Cologne	Holland	Bel, Fr, Sp, Gib	17/7/43	24/7/43	Liverpool	3314 1324	Oaktree/Burgundy line. Back to UK on SS *Monarch of Bermuda*. DFM (7/9/43)
Sansoucy	JGF	SGT	CAN	R.66953	75	BK646	ST	14/6/43	Mining	France	Sp, And, Gib	4/10/43	5/10/43	Whitchurch	3315 1451	Marie-Claire line. MiD (1/1/45). Later pilot officer (C.86345)
Sansum	IJ	SGT		1311760	78	DT768	HAL	15/7/43	Montbéliard	France	Sp, Gib	10/11/43	11/11/43	Whitchurch	3316 1561	Badly sprained ankle landing
Sassard	R	CAPT	FRA		345	W3771	SP	10/7/44	Ramrod 1072	France				NK	NF	Killed in action on 6 April 1945
Saunders	AJ	F/L	AUS	A.8687	83	PB362	LA	18/8/44	L'Isle-Adam	France	Fr	6/9/44	6/9/44	NK	3324 2542	
Savill	SE	F/O		156617	613	HR251	MOS	18/8/44	Gestapo HQ	France					NF	The target was a former school building at Égletons
Saxton	RWA	SGT		758174	101	R1699	WE	10/9/41	Turin	France	Gib	30/9/42	5/10/42	Greenock	3310 893	Evacuated by *Seawolf* 5 September 1942. Back on HMS *Malaya*. See *Wait For The Dawn*
Schlebusch	J	LT	SAF	328503v	184	MN864	TY	13/8/44	Armed recce Falaise	France	Fr			NK	3348 138	Interviewed 17 August 1944. Report IS9/WEA 1/7/138
Schloesing	JH	CAPT	FRA	F.30638	340	BS244	SP	13/2/43	Circus 262	France	Sz	8/5/43	8/5/43	Portreath	3313 1192	Helped by Robert Aylé in Paris. Comet 91. Killed in action on 26 August 1944
Schnobb	PA	F/O	CAN	J.12895	433	HX291	HAL	22/4/44	Düsseldorf	Holland	Bel			NK	NF	With the Resistance for five months. Liberated in Liège in September 1944 by American forces. MiD (13/6/46)
Schofield	FD	P/O	CAN	J.19292	19	FB233	MU	20/6/44	Rambouillet m/y	France	Fr	27/8/44	27/8/44	Northolt	3321 2206	
Schubert	KT	F/O	CAN	J.28239	431	MZ521	HAL	8/5/44	Haine St Pierre	Belgium				NK	NF	Liberated in Belgium sometime in September 1944
Schulz	LN	SGT	AUS	A.417524	466	LV943	HAL	6/5/44	Mantes-la-Jolie	France	Sp, Gib	23/6/44	24/6/44	Lyneham	3320 1991	Report states landed UK at 'Swindon'
Schwilk	CW	F/S	AUS	A.422304	460	NE116	LA	22/6/44	Reims	France	Fr			NK	3348 307	Captured. Escaped. Sherwood, arrived 7 August 1944. Interviewed 16 August 1944. Report IS9/WEA/2/81/307
Scott	LR	F/S		1386040	44	ND520	LA	25/2/44	Augsburg	France	Fr	8/9/44	8/9/44	Newhaven	3322 2311	With Maquis in France until liberation. Back to UK by corvette. Author *Parachuting to Danger*
Scott	RA	WO2	CAN	R.78434	138	BB334	HAL	12/8/43	SOE	France	Sp, Gib	5/11/43	6/11/43	Portreath	3316 1566	With Sergeant T.M. Hay in Paris. Burgundy line?
Scott	RW	W/O	AUS	A.418184	462	MZ401	HAL	2/11/44	Düsseldorf	Belgium				NK	NF	
Seddon	IV	P/O	AUS	A.426394	158	LK863	HAL	7/6/44	Versailles	France	Fr	31/8/44	31/8/44	NK	3322 2250	In Paris when it was liberated. Interviewed 2 September 1944
Sellors	JF	P/O		177020	184	MN590	TY	10/9/44	NK	Holland				NK	NF	
Semmerling	B	F/O	POL	P.1804	315	BS515	SP	13/3/43	Ramrod 43	France	Sp, Gib	10/5/43	11/5/43	Hendon	3313 1194	Wounded in right hand and both legs. Awarded MC
Semple	EQ	F/O	CAN	J.14331	233	KG424	DAK	6/6/44	Supply drop	France	Fr	3/7/44	3/7/44	NK	NF	Back to England in 271 Squadron aircraft. Rejoined squadron 3 July 1944. MBE (9/3/45). See *The Evaders* (Cosgrove), pp. 166-196
Shanks	DMcK	F/L	AUS	A.400839	464	NS897	MOS	5/6/44	Recce invasion area	France	Fr	3/9/44	3/9/44	NK	3322 2262	ss2. Took-off shortly after midnight 5/6 June. Shot down by flak
Shannon	RCA	WO2	CAN	R.154049	403	MH928	SP	29/6/44	Recce	France				NK	3348 2332	
Sharp	GE	F/L		127943	570	LJ638	ST	12/4/45	SOE supply drop	Holland	Hol			NK	3348 190	In a house attacked by Germans on 29 April 1945. Interviewed 11 May 1945. Report IS9/WEA/PLM/190. DFC (3/8/45)
Sharp	H	SGT		1055046	49	JB473	LA	18/7/44	Revigny-sur-Ornain	France	Fr	3/9/44	3/9/44	Hendon	3325 2882	See *Massacre over the Marne*
Sharpe	D	SGT		1874700	103	ME722	LA	21/5/44	Duisburg	Holland				NK	NF	
Sharples	T	SGT		1759051	57	ME868	LA	7/7/44	St Leu d'Esserent	France	Fr			NK	3350 1057	Interviewed 1 September 1944. Report IS9/WEA/2/301/1057
Shaugnessy	GJ	SGT	CAN	R.186153	432	LW643	HAL	18/4/44	Noisy-le-Sec	France	Sp, Gib	10/7/44	11/7/44	Whitchurch	3320 2017	Suffered minor injuries. With Flying Officer H.D. Thomas RCAF
Shaw	C	F/S		1542386	103	ME799	LA	28/7/44	Stuttgart	France				NK	NF	Marathon? FG Shaw?
Shaw	JW	F/L		124187	109	ML932	MOS	31/8/44	Cologne					NK	NF	
Shepherd	D	SGT		778968	266	MN181	TY	9/4/44	NK	France	Sp, Gib	23/6/44	24/6/44	Lyneham	3320 1986	Crossed to Spain with Warrant Officer Ciula, Pilot Officer W.F. Dobson and Flying Officer Rosinski. Report states landed UK at 'Swindon'
Shepherd	WC	F/O	CAN	J.24030	635	JB728	LA	15/6/44	Lens	France	Fr	6/9/44	6/9/44	NK	3323 2499	Back to UK from Vitry
Sheppard	AH	SGT		537866	115	DS668	LA	19/6/43	Mining	France	Sp, And, Gib	4/10/43	5/10/43	Whitchurch	3315 1447	With Sergeant C.F. Trott. Helped by Marie-Claire organisation. See *Par Les Nuits les Plus Longues...*, pp. 25, 27, 30
Sheppard	JE	S/L	CAN	J.6289	412	MJ304	SP	2/8/44	Sweep	France	Fr	20/8/44	20/8/44	NK	3321 2135	Sherwood? In hospital until 17 August 1944. DFC (22/8/44)
Sheppardson	KJ	F/O		175261	640	LW464	HAL	24/7/44	Stuttgart	France	Fr			NK	3349 378	Interviewed 28 August 1944. Report IS9/WEA/8/205/378. DFC (10/11/44) & Bar (17/7/45, 608 Squadron)
Sheridan	RK	F/S	CAN	R.187618	106	ME831	LA	7/7/44	St Leu d'Esserent	France	Fr	31/8/44	31/8/44	Northolt	3321 2209	Suffered severe facial burns. Left for UK from Normandy. Service number?
Sherk	RJF	F/O	CAN	J.15237	401	MJ126	SP	15/3/44	Ramrod 655	France	Sp, Gib	1/5/44	2/5/44	Whitchurch	3319 1891	Escaped from captivity in Italy in 1943 - UK 13 November 1943. MiD (1/1/45). See *The Evaders* (Cosgrove), p. 6

Sherwin	GK	F/S	CAN	R.160354	226	FV989	MCL	17/8/44	Mosquito support	France	Fr	26/8/44	26/8/44	Northolt	3321 2143	Liberated by US troops 23 August 1944. Left for UK from B.14 airstrip, Banville
Sherwood	A	SGT			269	P5131	HUD	11/6/40	Trondheim	Norway	Swe			NK	NF	Walked 150 miles to Sweden. Interned. See *RAF Coastal Command Losses…*, p. 40
Sherwood	LD	F/O	CAN	J.15715	443	MJ779	SP	26/9/44	Patrol	Holland				NK	3348 2224	Returned a month later
Shields	WC	F/O	CAN	J.21634	429	LV973	HAL	10/6/44	Versailles	France	Fr	18/8/44	18/8/44	Northolt	3321 2106	Sherwood. DFC (12/12/44)
Shields	WH	SGT		1334523	431	HE374	WE	14/4/43	Stuttgart	Switzerland	Fr	28/6/43	29/6/43	Lyneham	3313 1275	Repatriated 29 June 1943 in exchange with Germans. Killed as flight sergeant in Halifax LW510, 78 Squadron, on 24/25 March 1944 (Berlin)
Shimmons	L	SGT		1321645	514	LL695	LA	21/5/44	Duisburg	Holland	Bel			NK	3350 1425	Interviewed 23 September 1944. Report IS9/WEA/2/521/1425
Shoebottom	AR	WO2	CAN	R.130000	44	ME628	LA	24/6/44	Pommerval	France	Fr	9/9/44	9/9/44	NK	3322 2299	
Shoemaker	WS	P/O	CAN	J.87246	462	LL604	HAL	9/10/44	Bochum	Holland	Hol			NK	3352 2426	Interviewed 4 April 1945. Report IS9/WEA/1/329/2426
Shurvell	JW	F/S	CAN	R.172667	405	PA980	LA	28/6/44	Metz	France	Fr	8/9/44	8/9/44	NK	3322 2343	
Shuttleworth	JC	SGT	CAN	R.68135	460	W4273	LA	22/11/42	Stuttgart	France	Sp, Gib	28/3/43	5/4/43	Liverpool	3312 1147	
Siadecki	E	SGT	POL	792851	305	Z8599	WE	5/5/42	Stuttgart	Belgium	Fr, Sp, Gib	13/7/42	14/7/42	Whitchurch	3309 784	With the Brusselmans in Brussels. See *Belgium Rendez-Vous 127* pp. 39-40. Comet 24
Sibbald	DA	F/S	NZ	NZ.411102	35	W7851	HAL	8/3/43	Nuremberg	France	Sp, Gib	24/5/43	25/5/43	Hendon	3313 1214	Helped by Rosine Witton and Raymonde Coache. With Pilot Officer B.H. Marion. Comet 96. DFM (27/7/43). See *Valley of the Shadow of Death*, pp. 66-67
Siddall	JD	F/O	CAN	J.28796	427	LW166	HAL	4/7/44	Villeneuve-St Georges	France	Fr			NK	NF	Slightly injured
Siddons	WHH	F/L		53552	582	ND921	LA	28/6/44	Blainville	France	Fr			NK	NF	DFC (21/1/44, 57 Squadron)
Sierpina	M	SGT	POL	783359	300	Z1276	WE	27/4/42	Cologne	France	Sz	6/10/44	6/10/44	NK	NF	In Switzerland 19 May 1942. Left Switzerland after 16 September 1944
Sigmont	R	F/O	AUS	A.410820	466	HX337	HAL	22/4/44	Düsseldorf	Belgium	Bel			NK	3350 1241	Interviewed 14 September 1944. Report IS9/WEA/2/465/1241
Silva	G	P/O	AUS	A.402258	24 OTU	BD347	WH	31/7/42	Düsseldorf	Belgium	Fr, Sp, Gib	29/8/42	8/9/42	Gourock	3310 834	Comet 37. DFC (30/10/42). Killed in action 13 June 1943 on 210 Squadron. See *The Evaders* (Cosgrove), pp. 30-37
Silva	GD	LT	SAF	328735v	33	NH375	SP	24/8/44	Rodeo	France	Fr			NK	3350 1027	Interviewed 3 September 1944. Report IS9/WEA/2/342/1027
Sim	KW	F/O	CAN	J.9435	245	JR238	TY	4/1/44	Ramrod	France	Sp, Gib	5/6/44	6/6/44	Whitchurch	3320 1949	Burgundy line. Crashed in Belgium?
Simcock	JB	F/S	AUS	A.417899	463	LM589	LA	24/7/44	St Cyr	France				NK	NF	
Simister	H	SGT		954028	158	JD246	HAL	31/8/43	Berlin	Germany	Hol, Bel, Fr, Sz, Fr	10/9/44	10/9/44	St Eval	3322 2295	To Switzerland with Sergeant R.V. Wallace on 15 October 1943. Left 27/28 August 1944 with Flight Sergeant J. Quinn and Warrant Officer A.W. Bennett. MM (9/2/45). See *Free to Fight Again*, pp. 221-4
Simmonds	DV	SGT		1335450	158	LW634	HAL	30/3/44	Nuremberg	Luxembourg	Bel			NK	NF	
Simpson	AB	F/L	AUS	A.408881	467	LM376	LA	30/3/44	Nuremberg	Belgium	Fr, Sz	16/9/44	16/9/44	NK	3323 2439	DFC (5/11/43). Evaded with Flight Sergeant C.A. Campbell. In Switzerland 2 May 1944. Left 27 August 1944. Back to UK via Naples
Simpson	DA	SGT		1860709	106	ND850	LA	26/4/44	Schweinfurt	France				NK	NF	
Simpson	LR	F/S	AUS	A.**8931	627	DZ479	MOS	2/12/43	Berlin	France	Sz			NK	NF	To Switzerland 22 February 1944. Left 19 June 1944
Simpson	TW	F/O	CAN	J.12681	405	HR854	HAL	15/7/43	Montbéliard	France	Sp, Gib	1/10/43	2/10/43	Whitchurch	3315 1427	Burgundy line. Crossed into Spain with Pilot Officer R.F. Conroy. MiD (8/6/44)
Simpson	W	F/L		37235	12	L4949	BA	10/5/40	Enemy troops	Belgium	Fr, Sp, Por	20/10/41	22/10/41	Whitchurch	3307 592	Very badly burned. In hospitals in France to 6 July 1941. DFC (31/5/40). Relinquished commission (squadron leader) due to ill-health wef 28 June 1944
Simpson	WT	SGT		1890776	299	LJ868	ST	19/9/44	Arnhem supply drop	Holland	Bel	29/9/44	29/9/44	NK	3350 1432	MM (27/3/45) for rescuing crew from aircraft whilst under enemy fire. Report IS9/WEA/2/570/1432. See *Free to Fight Again*, pp. 197-200
Singer	CJ	F/S		1366100	90	EF147	ST	5/3/44	SOE	France				NK	NF	
Skibinski	JT	F/O	POL	P.1622	610	EN896	SP	13/2/43	Rodeo 168	France				NK	NF	MBE
Skidmore	K	SGT		1046337	158	HR791	HAL	11/11/43	Cannes	France	And, Sp, Gib	9/2/44	10/2/44	Lyneham	3318 1767	With Sergeant R.E. Griffith over Pyrenees. Author of *Follow the Man With the Pitcher*. Lyneham?
Slack	TAH	F/O		112428	41	EN233	SP	18/7/43	Ramrod, Abbeville	France	Sp, Gib	23/8/43	24/8/43	Whitchurch	3314 1366	Comet 122. From Seville 20 August 1943 on Norwegian ship *Borgholm*. Shot down 23 August 1944 (PoW, Stalag Luft III). Author of *Happy is the Day…*
Slater	J	SGT		1535622	77	HR949	HAL	19/2/44	Leipzig	France	Fr			NK	3350 1231	Interviewed 5 September 1944. Report IS9/WEA/2/430/1231
Slater	S	S/L		145503	103	ME449	LA	12/3/45	Mining	Denmark	Dk	29/3/45	29/3/45	NK	3326 2937	DSO (28/11/44, 576 Squadron), DFC (23/7/43, 100 Squadron) & Bar (15/9/44, 576 Squadron). To Sweden on 23 March 1945. Completed sixty operations

Slipper	AW	F/L		115768	297	P1400	ALB	27/7/44	SOE 'Harry 41'	France	Fr	1/8/44	1/8/44	Calshot	3321 2062	Returned aboard HMT *Devonshire*
Sloane	ST	F/S	AUS	A.434664	578	LL584	HAL	11/9/44	Gelsenkirchen	Belgium				NK	3350 1426	Interviewed 26 September 1944 - see Williams, EO. Report IS9/WEA/2/556/1426
Smail	TW	F/O		136863	625	LM139	LA	10/6/44	Achères	France				NK	NF	
Smik	O	F/L	CZ	130678	312	ML296	SP	4/9/44	Bomber escort	Holland				NK	NF	Crossed to Allied lines 27 October 1944. Shot down and killed on 28 November 1944, as squadron leader DFC, 127 Squadron
Smith	A	SGT		1102463	90	BK725	ST	16/4/43	Mannheim	France	And, Sp, Gib	5/8/43	11/8/43	Liverpool	3314 1349	With Chauny/Burgundy lines
Smith	AJ	SGT		615794	190		ST	21/9/44	Arnhem supply drop	Holland	Bel	22/9/44	22/9/44	Croydon	3324 2634	Aircraft ditched in River Waal. Back to UK from Brussels
Smith	AJ	F/S	AUS	A.422656	467	DV171	LA	24/9/44	Calais	France				NK	NF	
Smith	DPS	S/L	AUS	A.400495	467	LM475	LA	10/5/44	Lille	France	Fr	5/9/44	5/9/44	NK	3323 2464	ss7. DFC (11/7/44). Blown out of aircraft. Only survivor from twelve Lancasters lost on this raid. Back to UK from Paris
Smith	DV	SGT	CAN	R.70152	7	R9261	ST	20/4/43	Stettin	Denmark	Swe	12/5/43	13/5/43	Dyce	3313 1196	ss8. DFM (6/7/43) His report states return to Leuchars. See *Free to Fight Again*, pp. 240-9
Smith	GJA	P/O		171096	100	ND595	LA	25/2/44	Augsburg	Switzerland	Ger, Fr, Sp, Gib	24/5/44	25/5/44	Whitchurch	3319 1932	Repatriated with German agreement. Back on BOAC Dakota
Smith	GL	F/O		156347	90	LM111	LA	7/8/44	Mare de Magne	France	Fr	25/8/44	25/8/44	Northolt	3321 2162	Left for UK from Bayeux - B.14 airstrip, Banville
Smith	HFE	F/O	CAN	J.14627	419	LW240	HAL	16/9/43	Modane	France	Sp, Gib	20/12/43	21/12/43	Whitchurch	3317 1636	Marie-Claire line. See Flying Officer M.H.F. Cooper. DFC (7/7/44). Service no. J.14626?
Smith	HStJ	F/O		129753	122	SR430	MU	12/7/44	Armed recce	France	Fr			NK	3348 144	Interviewed 15 August 1944. Report IS9/WEA/2/75/144. Service number?
Smith	JA	F/O	AUS	A.413909	9	LM361	LA	18/4/44	Juvisy	France	Sp, Gib	24/6/44	25/6/44	Whitchurch	3320 1998	
Smith	JA	SGT		1232112	214	BK653	ST	16/4/43	Mannheim	France	Sp, Gib	17/7/43	24/7/43	Liverpool	3314 1319	Oaktree. Back to UK on SS *Monarch of Bermuda*?
Smith	JB	F/S		1344857	640	LW654	HAL	10/8/44	Dijon	France				NK	NF	
Smith	JF	SGT		1435866	106	JB612	LA	7/5/44	Salbris	France	Fr	22/9/44	22/9/44	NK	3324 2579	ss7
Smith	JG	F/L		120608	78	JN974	HAL	20/12/43	Frankfurt	Holland	Bel	10/9/44	10/9/44	Northolt	3324 2603	Back to UK from Brussels. MiD (14/6/45)
Smith	M	SGT		1710408	30 OTU	BJ618	WE	9/5/44	Nickel	France	Fr	18/8/44	18/8/44	Northolt	3321 2103	Sherwood?
Smith	PB	SGT		1333883	61	W4236	LA	9/8/43	Mannheim	Belgium	Fr, Sp, Gib	3/11/43	4/11/43	Portreath	3316 1530	Comet 158. In party of fourteen over Pyrenees?
Smith	RA	SGT		1213143	10	JD207	HAL	25/7/43	Essen	Holland	Bel, Fr, Sp, Gib	27/10/43	28/10/43	Portreath	3316 1507	With Sgt J.N. Hempstead
Smith	RG	SGT		1195327	142	BK536	WE	20/11/42	Turin	France	Fr	5/2/43	10/2/43	Salcombe	3312 1074	Back on the Yvonne - see *Secret Flotillas*... Vol. I, p. 336. Shot down again on 214 Squadron, 23-24/9/43 (Mannheim). POW. Repatriated February 1945
Smith	RP	SGT	CAN	R.90805	115	X3393	WE	9/12/42	Turin	France	Sp, Gib	20/1/43	26/1/43	Gourock	3312 1058	Comet 81. By ship from Seville to Gibraltar
Smith	RS	P/O	USA		133	BS447	SP	26/9/42	Circus	France	Sp, Gib		26/1/43	NK	NF	American in "Eagle" squadron. With Barnard, Glensor & Doorly. Back in USAAF B-17. See *Aircraft Down!*, pp. 71-105. UK date is a guess
Smith	RV	F/O	CAN		439	MP136	TY	22/10/44	NK	Holland				NK	NF	
Smitton	FA	P/O	CAN	J.85958	405	PA980	LA	28/6/44	Metz	France	Fr	5/9/44	5/9/44	NK	3323 2381	
Sniec	C	F/O	POL	P.1623	302	AA909	SP	8/9/43	Ramrod S41	France	Sp, Gib	17/1/44	17/1/44	Whitchurch	3318 1703	In Miranda de Ebro prison with L.F. Martin
Soury-Lavergne	G	SGT	FRA	F.37968	346	LW443	HAL	2/11/44	Düsseldorf	Germany	Bel	11/11/44	11/11/44	NK	3324 2747	Liberated at Eupen by US troops. Back at Base 13 November 1944
Souter-Smith	EL	F/O		125710	76	DT556	HAL	1/3/43	Berlin	Belgium	Sz			NK	NF	Helped to Switzerland by Paul Hellemans of the Portemine group. Report Switzerland/12
Southwell	DG	SGT		1255623	35	W7658	HAL	19/5/42	Mannheim	France	Gib	18/10/42	19/10/42	Poole	3311 921	Evacuated by *Seawolf* 12 October 1942. DFM (5/2/43). Commissioned (168720) wef 8 December 1943. See *Airmen on the Run*, pp.54-72
Southworth	J	F/S		1621847	644	NA672	HAL	26/4/45	SOE Tablejam 353	Denmark	Dk	19/5/45	19/5/45	NK	3327 3045	Flown back to UK over Hamburg by DC-3 Dakota
Sparkes	JN	SGT		1534177	101	ED377	LA	27/6/43	Mining	France	Sp, And, Gib	4/10/43	5/10/43	Whitchurch	3315 1446	ss7. Marie-Claire line
Sparkes	S	F/S		658563	578	MZ563	HAL	22/4/44	Düsseldorf	Holland				NK	3350 1417	Commissioned (175160) wef 19 April 1944 (LG 6/6/44). Interviewed 23 September 1944. Report IS9/WEA/2/522/1417
Sparks	ENM	S/L		43633	83	JB402	LA	3/5/44	Mailly-le-Camp	France	Sp, Gib	21/6/44	22/6/44	Whitchurch	3320 1984	Burgundy line. DFC (25/1/46) wef 28 August 1944
Spear	AN	SGT		561369	142	L5238	BA	10/5/40	Enemy troops	France	Fr			NK	NF	Evaded again four days later. See *The Colours of the Day*, pp. 97-8, 242
Spear	AN	SGT		561369	142	P2333	BA	14/5/40	Sedan	France	Fr			NK	NF	ss3. DFM (31/5/40). KIA 22 February 1945 aged 33, as 44361 Squadron Leader Spear, 299 Squadron (Stirlings). See *The Colours of the Day*, pp. 97-8, 243
Speirs	AR	P/O	NZ	NZ.413136	7	ND901	LA	1/5/44	Chambly	France	Fr	16/8/44	16/8/44	Northolt	3321 2132	ss7. Sherwood. Injured in lorry accident. To hospital in England. DFC (17/10/44, wef 30/4/44). Later flew on twenty operations on 128 Squadron (Mosquito). Northolt?

Spellman	PJ	F/O		152252	182	MN472	TY	11/9/44	Armed recce	Holland				NK	3348 2245	Shot down again (in Typhoon RB505) and wounded on 30 March 1945. Landed behind own lines. DFC (5/6/45)
Spencer	AE	SGT	CAN	R.195792	24 OTU	AD675	WH	3/11/43	Nickel	France	Fr	8/7/44	9/7/44	Tangmere	3320 2009	With Sergeant H.W. Payne. Flown back on Operation Mixer I in USAAF Dakota from a field near Nantua (Ain) with "Major Xavier" (Richard Heslop)
Spencer	GL	P/O	CAN	J.16834	405	BB250	HAL	11/3/43	Stuttgart	France	Sp, Gib	9/8/43	10/8/43	Prestwick	3314 1345	Oaktree/Burgundy line. Recommended for MC but MiD (8/6/44)
Spiller	HJ	W/O		580911	103	W1188	HAL	24/10/42	Milan	France	Sp, Gib	20/1/43	26/1/43	Gourock	3312 1042	DFM (21/11/41, 12 Squadron). Comet 82. By ship from Seville to Gibraltar. Author of *Ticket to Freedom*. Commended for valuable service in the air (7/9/45)
Spittal	WS	P/O		126031	297	EB297	WH	19/2/43	NK	France	Sp, Gib	7/4/43	7/4/43	Hendon	3312 1151	Army Co-operation Squadron - see J.G. Dawson and C.L. Hodgson. MiD (2/6/43)
Sprawson	E	S/L		70638	106	ND680	LA	6/6/44	Coutances	France	Fr			NK	3348 6	DFC (16/6/44). Met an NCO of R. Ulster Rifles at Caen 9 July 1944. Interviewed 10 July 1944. Report WEA 2/6/6
Springate	AC	F/S		1705182	298	LL293	HAL	14/10/44	Supply drop	Zuider Zee	Hol			NK	3327 3072	Liberated by Canadian Army on 17 April 1945. Interviewed by IS9(W) on 31 July 1945
Squance	TC	F/S		658973	90	LJ509	ST	10/3/44	SOE	France	Sp, Gib	5/5/44	6/5/44	Whitchurch	3319 1911	ss7. Burgundy line. MiD (1/1/45, as pilot officer 177329)
Squires	H	F/S		1500934	158	LV790	HAL	12/6/44	Amiens	France	Fr			Northolt	NF	Wounded. Released from Fresnes prison 20 August 1944. Back by RAF Dakota. Commissioned (177365) 25 July 1944 wef 15 May 1944. DFC (27/3/45)
Stacey	AG	F/O	CAN	J.20960	434	LL243	HAL	27/4/44	Montzen	Holland	Bel	21/9/44	21/9/44	Northolt	3323 2528	Evaded with Pilot Officer R.H. Taylor. Back to UK from Brussels by Dakota
Stankiewicz	K	SGT	POL	783194	303	BS534	SP	13/10/44	Ranger	Holland	Hol			NK	3352 2396	Interviewed 13 March 1945. Report IS9/WEA/1/304/2396
Stark	LWF	F/L		148445	263	MN527	TY	3/7/44	Ramrod	France	Fr	12/7/44	13/7/44	Dartmouth	3320 2046	DFC (10/3/44, as flying officer, 609 Squadron). Returned by MGB 503 from Brittany. Bar to DFC (3/10/44)
Starling	TP	SGT	CAN	R.159985	622	LL782	LA	31/5/44	Trappes	France	Fr			NK	NF	
Staveley	GS	LT			FIU	DZ680	MOS	22/10/43	Mahmoud	France	Fr			NK	NF	Fighter Interception Unit. In FAA, Royal Navy. Initials GJ?
Stearn	FR	SGT		1872359	50	PD237	LA	13/8/44	Bordeaux	France	Fr			NK	3345 646	Captured. Liberated from hospital in Angoulême 1 September 1944. Interviewed 3 September 1944. Report MI9/S/PG/MISC/INT/646. See *D-Day Bombers...*, pp. 241-5
Steel	MS	F/O		160836	10	LV858	HAL	10/4/44	Tergnier	France	Sp, Gib	21/6/44	22/6/44	Whitchurch	3320 1980	Burgundy line. DFC (27/3/45). See *Free to Fight Again*, pp. 84-8; *The Easy Trip*, pp.77-8
Steele	C	SGT		2216277	83	JB402	LA	3/5/44	Mailly-le-Camp	France	Fr	5/9/44	5/9/44	NK	3322 2300	
Steepe	CAD	F/O	CAN	J.26808	419	KB723	LA	4/7/44	Villeneuve-St Georges	France	Fr	25/8/44	25/8/44	Northolt	NF	Hidden by Drue Tartière. To UK by US Dakota. Date back is based on date of Sergeant P.P. Barclay's interview
Stein	LR	F/O	CAN	J.25740	405	PA980	LA	28/6/44	Metz	France	Fr	6/9/44	6/9/44	NK	3322 2349	
Stephen	HLJ	SGT	CAN	R.165184	57	JB370	LA	7/7/44	St Leu d'Esserent	France	Fr			NK	NF	
Stephen	JSJ	F/S		1560846	12	ND424	LA	27/6/44	Vaires	France	Fr	28/8/44	28/8/44	Northolt	3321 2182	Left for UK from B.14 airstrip, Banville
Sterling	TP	F/S	CAN	R.159985	622	LL782	LA	31/5/44	Trappes	France	Fr	2/9/44	2/9/44	NK	3345 650	Arrested by gendarme. Handed over to Germans. Liberated by FFI from Limoges prison 21 August 1944. Interviewed 3 September 1944. Report MISC/INT/650
Stevens	KJ	F/L	AUS	A.408723	57	JB370	LA	7/7/44	St Leu d'Esserent	France	Fr			NK	NF	DFM (11/6/43)
Stevenson	JM	F/O	CAN	C.27788	419	KB727	LA	4/7/44	Villeneuve-St Georges	France	Fr			NK	NF	Escaped from train taking him to Büchenwald. Awarded Croix de Guerre (French)
Stevenson	WH	SGT		1798194	30 OTU	BJ618	WE	9/5/44	Nickel	France	Fr	29/8/44	29/8/44	NK	3321 2191	
Stewart	CJ	WO2	CAN	R.159028	405	ND343	LA	15/6/44	Lens	France	Fr	6/9/44	7/9/44	NK	3324 2576	ss7
Stewart	NE	SGT	CAN	R.112528	226	FV989	MCL	17/8/44	Mosquito support	France	Fr	30/8/44	30/8/44	Northolt	3321 2159	Left for UK from Bayeux - B.14 airstrip, Banville
Stirling	JW	SGT	CAN	R.211027	630	PB244	LA	18/8/44	L'Isle-Adam	France	Fr			NK	3322 2332	Back in UK by 6 September 1944
Stockburn	RC	P/O		143937	501	AA917	SP	11/7/43	Rhubarb	France	Sp, Gib	10/10/43	11/10/43	Chivenor	3315 1456	Burgundy line. DFC (14/9/45, flight lieutenant, 274 Squadron)
Stockford	NJ	SGT		573015	207	ND556	LA	3/5/44	Mailly-le-Camp	France	Sp, Por	14/7/44	15/7/44	Whitchurch	3320 2030	Flew to UK from Lisbon. Died 18 September 1944, aged 22
Stone	JW	SGT		656855	514	LL739	LA	11/5/44	Louvain	Belgium	Bel			NK	NF	Marathon
Stoner	RA	F/O	AUS	A.417901	464	HP934	MOS	27/11/44	Patrol (night)	Holland	Hol			NK	3352 2406	With Flight Lieutenant J. Craven. Interviewed 17 March 1945. Report IS9/WEA/1/309/2406
Stones	J	SGT		153109*	630	LM537	LA	18/7/44	Revigny-sur-Ornain	France	Fr	6/9/44	6/9/44	NK	3323 2373	Service number? See *Massacre over the Marne*

Storey	RE	F/S		1394916	166	JB649	LA	25/7/44	Stuttgart	France	Fr	8/9/44	8/9/44	Middle Wallop	3323 2447	Back from Orléans with unit of 1 SAS
Stormont	F	SGT		1417034	192	MZ570	HAL	3/5/44	Bomber support	France	Fr	4/9/44	4/9/44	Hendon	3323 2457	Back to UK from Paris. See *Massacre over the Marne*
Stousland	CJ	2LT	NOR	F.P.1462	331	PL258	SP	29/12/44	Armed recce	Holland				NK	3352 2403	Taken to Allied lines 17 March 1945. Interviewed 18 March 1945
Stoyko	MS	SGT	CAN	R.167132	405	PB174	LA	20/7/44	Bottrop	Holland	Hol			NK	3352 2450	ss8. Stayed seven and a half months in same house with Colonel Duncan USAAF. Interviewed 8 April 1945. Report IS9/WEA/2/1046/2450
Straight	WW	S/L		90680	242	Z2096	HUR	31/7/41	Anti shipping	France	Gib	24/7/42	25/7/42	Hendon	3309 787	American by birth. MC (1/1/41), DFC (8/8/41). Evacuated by HMS *Tarana* 14 July 1942. Norwegian War Cross (18/12/42). MiD (1/1/43, air commodore). CBE (8/6/44)
Strange	MB	SGT		1071615	76	JB871	HAL	10/4/43	Frankfurt	France	Sp, Gib	6/6/43	7/6/43	Hendon	3313 1236	Comet 103. DFM (6/7/43)
Street	HT	SGT		940782	78	JD409	HAL	30/8/43	Mönchengladbach	Holland	Bel, Fr, Sp, Gib	5/11/43	6/11/43	Whitchurch	3316 1555	ss7. Comet 171
Strickland	JA	F/O	AUS	A.419231	467	NG455	LA	7/2/45	Ladbergen	Germany	Hol			NK	3327 3121	Captured briefly by German farmer on 10 February 1945. In Holland with six other airmen. Liberated by British troops 30 March 1945
Stronach	MP	F/L	CAN	J.21384	405	ND352	LA	10/6/44	Versailles	France	Fr	30/8/44	30/8/44	NK	3345 793	Severe burns to right arm. Liberated from la Pitié hospital, Paris on 25 August. Interviewed 3 November 1944. Report MISC/INT/793
Struck	WE	SGT	CAN	R.197206	100	LM621	LA	30/6/44	Vierzon	France	Fr	18/8/44	18/8/44	Northolt	3321 2129	Liberated at Montmirail on 13 August. Met the Sherwood group at Busloup. Left for UK from "Allied beachhead"
Sumerson	AK	SGT		568963	150	P5232	BA	14/5/40	Sedan	France	Sp, Gib	11/3/41	17/3/41	Greenock	3302 237	Suffered severe burns to face, hands, back and right leg. Repatriated on medical grounds
Summers	DR	SGT		1862059	166	JB644	LA	12/7/44	Revigny-sur-Ornain	France	Fr	28/8/44	28/8/44	Lyneham	3322 2212	Back on RAF Dakota to UK from Orléans. See *Massacre over the Marne*, pp. 134-42
Sutherland	FE	F/S	CAN	R.113262	617	JB144	LA	15/9/43	Ladbergen	Holland	Bel, Fr, Sp, Gib	5/12/43	6/12/43	Portreath	3317 1604	
Sutton	BJ	F/S	AUS	A.424893	467	LL971	LA	21/6/44	Scholven/Buer	Germany	Hol, Bel			NK	NF	ss7. Aircraft blew up. Came down in Germany 3 miles from Dutch border. Report IS9/WEA/6/240/2092
Sutton	L	SGT		1891077	9	JA690	LA	7/7/44	St Leu d'Esserent	France	Fr			NK	NF	
Sutton	LJW	W/O		1289916	514	LL727	LA	7/6/44	Massy-Palaiseau	France	Fr			NK	3349	Service number?
Swartz	RA	F/L	CAN	J.26343	405	PA970	LA	8/9/44	Le Havre	France	Fr			NK	NF	DFC (15/9/44) & Bar (8/12/44) for completing two tours of operations
Sweatman	KC	WO2	CAN	R.120655	424	HX313	HAL	27/5/44	Bourg-Léopold	Belgium	Bel			NK	NF	In a Marathon camp in the Ardennes when liberated by US forces on 8 September 1944
Swida	S	F/O	POL	P.0464	301	Z1491	WE	28/8/42	Saarbrücken	Belgium	Fr, Sw, Fr, And, Sp	23/11/43	24/11/43	Whitchurch	3316 1584	Burgundy line. Flew to England from Gibraltar. Recommended for MC
Swinley	CF	SGT		574565	106	ME831	LA	7/7/44	St Leu d'Esserent	France	Fr	28/8/44	28/8/44	NK	3321 2186	DFM (25/1/46)
Switzer	WA	F/L	CAN	J.21618	193	MN602	TY	15/8/44	Enemy columns	France	Fr	20/8/44	20/8/44	NK	3324 2774	Flew from B3 airfield, France. Baled out at 500 feet. Captured near Falaise 16 August 1944. Escaped same day. MiD (1/1/46)
Szkuta	A	F/O	POL	P.76625	305	Z8599	WE	5/5/42	Stuttgart	Belgium	Sz, Fr, Sp, Por	24/7/42	24/7/42	Poole	3309 786	In Switzerland 4 June 1942. Left by Sunderland from Lisbon. MiD (recommended 23/8/42; approved 22/10/42)
Sznapka	W	F/S	POL	792281	308	W3404	SP	16/8/43	Ramrod	France	Sp, Gib	10/10/43	11/10/43	Chivenor	3315 1463	Chivenor?
Taggart	WR	F/S	CAN	R.78497	235		BFR	2/6/42	Transit to Gibraltar	Atlantic ocean		18/8/42	19/8/42	Whitchurch	3310 812	Ran out of fuel on flight to Gibraltar
Tanner	TW	SGT		1654203	630	PA992	LA	24/7/44	Stuttgart	France	Fr	16/9/44	16/9/44	NK	3323 2483	Captured after five weeks with Maquis. Escaped when German convoy he was in was attacked by Maquis
Tansley	PA	F/S		1393429	90	EF147	ST	5/3/44	SOE	France	Sp, Gib	4/5/44	5/5/44	Whitchurch	3319 1902	Helped by the Lefèvre family in Juvisy-sur-Orge. Burgundy line. With Warrant Officer B. Edinborough
Tapson	CG	F/O	AUS	144272	107	HR193	MOS	5/10/44	Intruder, Holland	Holland	Hol			NK	3352 2398	Slightly injured. Liberated 14/15 March 1945. Report IS9/WEA/1/305/2398. See *Shot Down and on the Run*, pp.110-18
Taras	M	F/O	POL	P.0118	300	Z1271	WE	7/11/41	Mannheim	France	Sp, Gib	27/4/42	8/5/42	Liverpool	3308 721	Crossed Pyrenees 1/2 March 1942 in group of 6, inc. Major R Challenor RE, with Ponzán network. MiD (recommended 24/6/42). See *Safe Houses Are Dangerous*, p.206
Tate	E	F/S		1614527	295	LK567	ST	26/4/45	SOE supply drop	Denmark	Dk	16/5/45	16/5/45	NK	3327 3051	On supply drop for Danish underground
Taylor	BJ	SGT		1602104	166	JB649	LA	25/7/44	Stuttgart	France	Fr	8/9/44	8/9/44	Middle Wallop	3323 2449	Back from Orléans with unit of 1 SAS
Taylor	CO	F/L		120030	619	ED978	LA	11/6/43	Düsseldorf	Belgium	Fr, Sp, Gib	4/9/43	5/9/43	Whitchurch	3314 1391	
Taylor	DA	F/L		42909	21	NS965	MOS	31/8/44	Strasbourg	France	Fr	21/9/44	21/9/44	NK	3324 2578	DFC (25/7/41, 84 Squadron) & Bar (11/8/44). Back to UK from Verdun
Taylor	FJD	SGT		1896922	57	JB318	LA	18/7/44	Revigny-sur-Ornain	France	Fr	1/9/44	1/9/44	NK	3321 2167	See *Massacre over the Marne*
Taylor	FV	S/L	CAN	J.15177	420	HE550	WE	14/4/43	Stuttgart	France	Sz, Fr, Sp, Gib	23/2/44	24/2/44	Whitchurch	3318 1787	Left Switzerland 8 January 1944 with seven other internees. DFC (13/10/44)

Taylor	H	P/O		172574	101	LL863	LA	30/6/44	Vierzon	France	Fr	7/9/44	7/9/44	NK	3322 2284	ss8
Taylor	R	P/O		130843	1409	LR501	MOS	14/6/43	Special task	France	Fr	23/6/43	24/6/43	Tangmere	3313 1270	1409 Flight. Back to UK with SOE agent Richard Heslop in a 161 Squadron Lysander on Operation Curator/Acolyte. Tangmere? DFC (7/9/43)
Taylor	RH	P/O		141793	12	JB650	LA	27/1/44	Berlin	Belgium	Bel			Northolt	3350 1486	Evaded with Flying Officer A.G. Stacey. Liberated by US troops 10 September 1944. Back by Dakota. Interviewed 11 September 1944. DFC (8/6/45)
Taylor	SD	F/O	CAN	J.14635	218	EF504	ST	1/5/44	Chambly	France	Fr	19/8/44	19/8/44	Northolt	3321 2134	Sherwood. Left for UK from "Allied beachhead"
Taylor	WB	F/O	CAN		298	LL293	HAL	14/10/44	Supply drop	Zuider Zee	Hol			NK	3326 2994	
Teague	WG	W/O		1184692	83	JB402	LA	3/5/44	Mailly-le-Camp	France	Fr	5/9/44	5/9/44	NK	3322 2301	DFM (20/4/43)
Teare	TDG	SGT		1438430	103	ED751	LA	5/9/43	Mannheim	France	Fr			NK	3351 2050	Liberated in France after one year in hiding. Flown back by Dakota. Author *Evader*
Templeman	T	F/S	CAN	R.61012	7	R9324	ST	16/6/42	Essen	France	Sp, Gib	5/10/42	6/10/42	Hendon	3311 930	Broke ankle on landing. Solo to Spain (and prisons). Recommended for DCM but awarded DFM (4/12/42) by Bomber Command
Tetlow	F	SGT		1592792	158	LK863	HAL	7/6/44	Versailles	France	Fr	31/8/44	31/8/44	NK	3322 2253	In Paris when it was liberated. Interviewed 2 September 1944
Tew	WR	F/L	CAN	J.7597	401	MJ231	SP	24/7/44	Armed recce	France	Fr		24/8/44	London	NF	Reached US lines 24 August 1944. DFC (20/7/45)
Thom	N	SGT		1397971	100	DV192	LA	27/4/44	Friedrichshafen	France	Sz, Fr			NK	3322 2333	Captured near Vittel 28 April 1944. Escaped Nancy barracks after hitting guard with iron bar on 30 April 1944
Thomas	CA	2LT	USA	T.233104	419	HX189	HAL	22/4/44	Laon	France	Fr			NK	NF	See *The Evaders* (Lavender/Sheffe), p. 155 - pilot named as Jack Kupisiak USAAF
Thomas	DD	LT	SAF		602	MJ398	SP	15/8/44	Patrol	France					NF	Shot down by USAAF P-51. Shot in knee whilst evading
Thomas	EWF	P/O		185723	247	SW408	TY	1/4/45	Offensive operations	Germany				NK	NF	Baled out 6 kilometres north-west of Emsbüren. Report IS9/WEA/2/1041/2436
Thomas	HD	F/O	CAN	J.21187	218	EH942	ST	22/4/44	Laon	France	Sp, Gib	10/7/44	11/7/44	Whitchurch	3320 2018	With Sergeant G.J. Shaughnessy RCAF. Whitchurch? See website http://groups.msn.com/cahsregina/rafescapingsociety.msnw
Thomas	JC	F/O	USA		35	W7885	HAL	13/2/43	Lorient	France	Sz			NK	NF	American in RCAF. Reached Switzerland 13 March 1943. Left on or after 16 September 1944
Thomas	SR	P/O		42029	264	L6958	DF	13/5/40	EA, The Hague beach	Holland			14/5/40	NK	NF	ss2. DFC (29/5/42). AFC (2/6/43). Shot down 5 September 1943 as acting squadron leader (3 Squadron) in Typhoon JP585. Prisoner of War (Stalag Luft III)
Thompson	CG	F/O	CAN	J.16603	627	DZ482	MOS	29/6/44	Beauvoir	France	Fr	11/9/44	11/9/44	Broadwell	3323 2431	With Sergeant Merlin from 22 August to 11 September 1944
Thompson	N	SGT		750816	51	LW498	HAL	24/5/44	Aachen	Holland				NK	NF	
Thompson	WF	F/S		1323997	158	LK841	HAL	1/6/44	Trappes	France	Fr	29/8/44	29/8/44	Northolt	3321 2155	Left for UK from Bayeux - B.14 airstrip, Banville
Thomson	HW	P/O		175967	7	JB455	LA	15/6/44	Lens	Belgium	Fr	12/9/44	12/9/44	NK	3325 2871	ss7. DFC (22/5/45). MC (2/10/45) (both as flight lieutenant)
Thomson	WJL	F/O	CAN	J.35076	419	KB723	LA	4/7/44	Villeneuve-St Georges	France	Fr			NK	NF	
Thorn	EE	SGT		1607735	405	PA980	LA	28/6/44	Metz	France	Fr	5/9/44	5/9/44	NK	3322 2314	
Thorn	RC	F/L		70675	30 OTU	BJ618	WE	9/5/44	Nickel	France	Fr	28/8/44	28/8/44	Northolt	3321 2153	Left for UK from Bayeux - B.14 airstrip, Banville
Thorogood	JD	F/O		148183	609	JR386	TY	30/5/44	Railway rocket strike	France	Fr			NK	3350 1025	Interviewed 3 September 1944. Report IS9/WEA/2/339/1025
Thorpe	KW	SGT		1803660	78	LW273	HAL	23/9/43	Mannheim	France	Sz			NK	NF	In Switzerland on 30 October 1943 with Pilot Officer Wares and Sergeant Barlow. Left some time after 16 September 1944. Report Switzerland/19
Threlkeld	J	SGT		1508714	298	LL334	HAL	5/8/44	SOE	France	Fr	13/9/44	13/9/44	NK	3324 2544	See *Massacre over the Marne*
Thring	GH	F/L	CAN	J.7913	620	LJ849	ST	6/6/44	Supplies to Normandy	France	Fr	8/6/44	9/6/44	Gosport	3320 1959	Left for UK from "Allied beachhead near Caen". LJ849? DFC (8/9/44)
Thurmeier	JJ	F/O	CAN	J.14165	429	LK995	HAL	25/11/43	Frankfurt	France	Bel			NK	3350 1114	"Ghost Train" 3 September 1944. Interviewed ? Report IS9/WEA/MB/1114. See *Rendez-vous 127*, photo facing p. 49 & pp. 113-4
Tideman	TG	F/L		37027	139	P4923	BL	12/5/40	Enemy troops	Belgium	Fr			NK	NF	Promoted squadron leader with seniority 1 January 1942 on 27 March 1942
Tidy	CA	P/O		161395	3	MN188	TY	6/3/44	Ramrod	France	Fr		20/9/44	NK	NF	
Till	AT	W/O	AUS	A.410756	635	ND694	LA	12/8/44	Rüsselsheim	Belgium	Bel			NK	None	Killed 21 August 1944 in gunfight with German troops after failed ambush
Tindall	JW	F/L		141410	83	JB403	LA	3/5/44	Mailly-le-Camp	France	Fr	3/9/44	3/9/44	NK	3345 784	DFM (18/7/41, 58 Squadron). Wounded in left ankle. Liberated from the American Memorial Hospital, Reims on 29 August 1944. Interviewed 30 October 1944. Report MISC/INT/784
Tippett	J	CPL		538806	110	R3670	BL	8/6/40	Amiens	France	Fr			NK	NF	DFM (30/1/40) as leading aircraftman. Possibly not an evader
Titman	G	F/S		643957	158	LV790	HAL	12/6/44	Amiens	France	Fr	31/8/44	31/8/44	Hendon	3323 2455	Back to UK from Paris. DFM (27/3/45)
Titman	R	SGT		1877165	298	LL333	HAL	20/9/44	Supplies to Germany	France	Fr	5/10/44	5/10/44	NK	3324 2630	Back to UK from Paris

Tobin	LP	WO2	CAN	R.159974	44	LM434	LA	21/6/44	Wesseling	Holland	Bel	16/9/44	16/9/44	NK	3323 2516	Back to UK from Paris
Todd	W	SGT		1366260	27 OTU	X3966	WE	23/9/43	Nickel	France	Sp, Gib	19/12/43	20/12/43	Lyneham	3317 1634	Comet 185
Tomicki	S	SGT	POL	782361	305	W5593	WE	5/8/41	Frankfurt	Belgium	Fr, Sp, Gib	30/12/41	5/1/42	Gourock	3307 630	Comet 4. To UK on Polish ship *Batory*. MiD (recommended 29/5/42). Killed in action on 8/9 April 1943 (Duisburg) in Wellington HE148 (300 Squadron)
Tomlinson	GC	S/L		5214	17	N2547	HUR	11/5/40	Patrol	Holland	Fr			NK	NF	He and Flight Lieutenant R.H.A. Lee were probably the first RAF fighter-pilot evaders of the Second World War. DFC (11/6/40)
Tonkin	EW	F/O	AUS	A.436014	453	SM233	SP	18/3/45	V2 site, The Hague	Holland	Hol	11/5/45	11/5/45	NK	3326 2979	Liberated in Holland
Toogood	RA	SGT		1602076	630	PA992	LA	24/7/44	Stuttgart	France	Sz, Fr			NK	NF	In Switzerland on 6 August 1944
Tooke	JRH	2LT	SAF		74	NH367	SP	11/8/44	Armed recce	France	Fr			NK	NF	
Toombs	LW	SGT	CAN	R.152718	158	LK841	HAL	1/6/44	Trappes	France	Fr	27/8/44	27/8/44	Northolt	3322 2220	Liberated by US troops. Left for UK from 'Allied beachhead'
Topham	JB	F/O		178865	514	LL716	LA	3/8/44	Bois de Cassan	France	Fr	7/10/44	8/10/44	Southampton	3324 2651	Aircraft hit by bombs at 15,000 feet. Came back to UK aboard hospital ship (an old Boston ferry boat). DFC (6/2/45)
Tourans	J	W/O		1126191	582	ND817	LA	7/8/44	Mare de Magne	France	Fr			NK	NF	
Tovey	JW	F/S		743793	35	PB377	LA	14/4/45	Potsdam	Germany	Ger			NK	3327 3083	"Hid" in British PoW camp for four days. Liberated by US First Army c. 26 April 1945. See also Sergeant G.G.E. Bourner and Flight Sergeant Gould
Townsend	AEJ	SGT		1130563	12	LM514	LA	3/5/44	Mailly-le-Camp	France	Fr	7/9/44	8/9/44	Newhaven	3324 2746	
Townsley	ED	F/S		1684322	515	NS993	MOS	30/9/44	Day Ranger	Switzerland	Fr	31/12/44	31/12/44	Bovingdon	3325 2837	Flight Lieutenant A.E. Callard's navigator. Back with Flight Sergeant R.A. Fidler. See *Confounding the Reich*, pp. 79-81; *Infringing Neutrality…*, pp.155-64
Tracey	MB	P/O	CAN	J.85387	429	MZ362	HAL	25/7/44	Stuttgart	France	Fr	22/8/44	23/8/44	NK	3324 2645	Back to UK from Arromanches
Treacy	WPF	F/L	EIR	37617	74	K9875	SP	27/5/40	Patrol	France	Sp, Por	29/1/41	30/1/41	Chivenor	3301 175	Flown back from Lisbon to 'Barnstaple'. Killed in action on 20 April 1941 as squadron leader on 242 Squadron. DSO (13/3/42, wef 27 March 1941)
Trend	JM	SGT		1397945	15	LM465	LA	12/6/44	Gelsenkirchen	Holland	Bel	13/9/44	13/9/44	Hendon	3324 2560	ss7. Evaded with Flight Sergeant E. Grisdale
Trnobranski	J	SGT	POL	782743	308	EN916	SP	22/9/43	Ramrod	France	Sp, Gib	15/3/44	16/3/44	Bristol	3319 1844	With Dutch-Paris line
Trobe	JH	S/L	AUS	A.416468	10	LV867	HAL	22/4/44	Düsseldorf	Holland	Bel	8/9/44	8/9/44	Northolt	3323 2533	DFC (3/12/43). With Pilot Officer G.W. Fernyhough. Back to UK from Brussels-Evère
Trotman	DA	F/O		124478	50	ED691	LA	16/4/43	Pilsen	France	Sz			NK	NF	Walked 300 kilometres on his own before crossing into Switzerland on night of 26/27 April 1943. Left circa September/October 1944. Back in England during October 1944
Trott	CF	SGT		577112	115	DS668	LA	19/6/43	Mining	France	Sp, And, Gib	4/10/43	5/10/43	Whitchurch	3315 1448	With Sergeant A.H. Sheppard. Helped by Marie-Claire organisation. See *Par Les Nuits les Plus Longues…*, pp. 25, 27, 30
Trottier	EJ	SGT	CAN	R.169012	28 OTU	LN896	WE	20/4/44	Nickel	France	Fr	12/7/44	13/7/44	NK	3320 2027	Aircraft ran out of fuel when directed by German radio to Brittany. Back by MGB 503
Trottner	C	F/S		1386377	61	LM359	LA	24/4/44	Munich	France	Fr			NK	NF	ss7
Truche	A	CAPT	FRA	F.721	346	NR181	HAL	4/11/44	Bochum	Germany				NK	NF	
Trueman	KW	F/S		1217929	640	MZ855	HAL	12/8/44	Rüsselsheim	Belgium	Bel			Hendon	3350 1341	Fought with Belgian Resistance. Interviewed 10 September 1944. Report IS9/WEA/MB/1341. See *Bomber Boys*, Chapter 6
Trull	JC	F/L	CAN	J.6989	403	MJ944	SP	20/2/44	Ramrod 567	Belgium	Fr	8/8/44	8/8/44	Tempsford	3321 2068	Flown back by Hudson of 161 (SD) Squadron with Sergeant R.W. Watson RAAF. Tempsford?
Truscott	A	SGT		1159715	100	ND595	LA	25/2/44	Augsburg	Switzerland	Ger, Fr, Sp, Gib	24/5/44	25/5/44	Whitchurch	3319 1937	Repatriated with German agreement. Back on BOAC Dakota
Trusty	JGA	SGT		519071	138	BB334	HAL	12/8/43	SOE	France	Sp, Gib	4/10/43	5/10/43	Whitchurch	3315 1449	Burgundy line. DFM (3/10/44)
Tuck	WMD	W/O			56	EJ526	TEM	3/4/45	Offensive operations	Germany				NK	NF	Came down south of Diepholz
Turenne	ER	SGT	CAN	R.86205	35	W7885	HAL	13/2/43	Lorient	France	Sp, Gib	17/7/43	24/7/43	Liverpool	3314 1314	Oaktree. Back to UK on SS *Monarch of Bermuda*?
Turner	AC	SGT	CAN	R.62322	419	DT646	HAL	5/3/43	Essen	Holland	Bel, Fr, Sp, Gib	27/6/43	28/6/43	Hendon	3313 1273	MiD (8/6/44). Later, pilot officer (C.17697)
Turner	DI	P/O		133580	15	EF348	ST	22/6/43	Mülheim	Belgium				NK	NF	
Turner	GR	SGT		1400098	635	ND811	LA	4/8/44	Trossy-St Maximin	France	Fr	31/8/44	31/8/44	Hendon	3323 2456	Back to UK from Paris
Turner	RTF	F/L		114982	299	LK545	ST	20/9/44	Arnhem supply drop	Holland				NK	3350 1379	DFC (1/10/43, 120 Squadron). Interviewed 25 September 1944. Report IS9/WEA/2/531/1379. MC (13/7/45)
Turton	HJF	SGT		1624015	77	NA524	HAL	16/6/44	Sterkrade	Holland			22/9/44	NK	NF	
Tutty	EB	F/L		135616	166	NE112	LA	31/8/44	Agenville	France	Fr	5/9/44	5/9/44	NK	3345 819	(Pilot officer 9/3/43, from Leading Aircraftman 1435325). Seriously injured. Captured. Liberated from Abbeville hospital. Interviewed 26 January 1945.

Tweed	JC	SGT		1333469	138	BB313	HAL	12/5/43	SOE	France	Fr		18/9/43	Tangmere	3315 1407	Report MISC/INT/819 Flown back by 161 Squadron Lysander - see *Shot Down and on the Run*, pp. 74-80. Tangmere?
Tweedy	P	F/S		985105	635	ND819	LA	21/5/44	Duisburg	Belgium	Bel	8/9/44	8/9/44	NK	3322 2289	DFM (14/9/43, 76 Squadron). Marathon. Evaded at some point with Flight Sergeants A.M. Rae and R. Reading
Tyrrell	HW	F/O	HOL		608	KB273	MOS	28/2/45	Berlin	Germany				NK	NF	His surname was Hoyt. See *Strike Hard*, pp.104-5
Tyszko	J	P/O	POL	P.1693	301	Z1491	WE	28/8/42	Saarbrücken	Belgium	Fr, Sp, Gib	30/9/42	5/10/42	Greenock	3310 871	Solo to Spain. Had to swim River Bidassoa as all bridges were guarded. Back on HMS *Malaya*. Recommended for MC
Ullestad	O	CAPT	NOR		80	EJ691	TEM	2/3/45	Armed patrol	Germany				NK	NF	Came down at Hörsten, Dreierwalde. Probably briefly a prisoner of war at some point - see TNA file WO 235/82
Upton	JH	SGT	CAN	R.168613	24 OTU	AD675	WH	3/11/43	Nickel	France	Sp, Gib	4/5/44	5/5/44	Whitchurch	331 1898	Burgundy line. Crossed Pyrenees with Sergeant W.T. Banner and large group of Americans. He got left behind during the crossing
Van den Bok	R	F/O		83004	408	AE197	HN	28/8/42	Saarbrücken	Belgium	Fr, Sp, Gib	2/10/42	3/10/42	Mount Batten	3310 867	DFC (4/8/42). Comet 55. Escorted from Paris by Andrée de Jongh and Jeanine De Greef. Bar to DFC (24/11/42), Second Bar to DFC (26/10/45, 214 Squadron)
Van den Plassche	FED	F/O	BEL	132973	141	HJ708	MOS	25/3/44		France	Sp, Gib	1/5/44	2/5/44	Whitchurch	3319 1896	Belgian in RAF
Van der Heyden	AR	F/O	BEL	162081	349	PT730	SP	5/10/44	Armed recce	Holland			22/10/44	NK	NF	Had to hide in ice-cold water up to his neck for four hours to avoid searching enemy patrols. Met up with British paratrooper with whom he crossed the Rhine near Arnhem. MiD (14/6/45)
Van der Heyden	RPM	CPL	HOL		320	FR149	MCL	12/6/44	Forèt de Grimbosq	France					NF	
Van Eendenburg	LCM	F/L	HOL	108814	322	PL288	SP	1/9/44	Armed recce	Belgium	Fr	9/9/44	9/9/44	Northolt	3323 2391	Came down three kms SE of Mametz. Dutchman in RAF
Van Maarion	JW	F/O	CAN	J.27583	426	LK883	HAL	12/5/44	Louvain	Belgium	Bel	9/9/44	9/9/44	NK	3322 2304	Back to UK from France after liberation
Van Molkot	J	F/S	BEL	1814824	349	MK363	SP	6/6/44	Patrol invasion beach	France	Fr			NK	3348 139	Taken POW. Told Germans his name was Clark and a South African.Liberated 4 August 1944. Interviewed 10 August 1944. Report WEA 2/21/139
Van Roosendaal	JC	W/O	HOL	1692496	322	TB907	SP	1/4/45	Armed recce	Holland	Hol			NK	3352 3022	DFC. Briefly captured. Later with 2nd Lieutenant H.W. Rohde. Liberated 13 April 1945. Interviewed 16 April 1945. Report IS9/WEA/1/376
Varley	CR	SGT		1213445	10	JD315	HAL	16/9/43	Modane	France	Sp, Gib	31/1/44	1/2/44	Whitchurch	3318 1734	Baled out as ordered - aircraft returned to Base
Vass	JR	SGT		1383826	35	HR798	HAL	11/11/43	Cannes	France	Sp, Gib	10/4/44	11/4/44	Whitchurch	3319 1877	Helped by Dutch-Paris
Vassiliades	BM	F/S		1388657	19	FB116	MU	11/8/44	Bombing	France	Fr			NK	3349 392	Interviewed 28 August 1944. Report IS9(WEA)/2/247/392. DFM (5/9/44). KIA 25 March 1945 as flying officer on 3 Squadron in Tempest EJ755
Verge	JE	P/O	CAN	J.36056	82 OTU	BJ790	WE	16/8/44	Nickel	France	Fr			NK	NF	Broke leg on landing
Vernon	JE	F/O	NZ	36145	150	L5459	BA	26/5/40	Roumont	France	Fr			NK	NF	DFC (16/7/40). Killed in action 7 June 1940. From New Zealand. Buried with his two crew at Vergies (Somme)
Vickerman	WK	F/O	CAN	J.26925	432	LW582	HAL	7/6/44	Achères	France	Fr	18/8/44	18/8/44	Northolt	3321 2097	Sherwood. Northolt?
Vidler	AE	F/O		137146	218	LJ448	ST	20/4/44	Chambly	France	Fr			NK	3349	Met up with ill-fated 'D' Squadron, 1 SAS (Fenwick) on 24 July 1944. Report IS9(WEA)/8/526/*
Violett	WT	SGT		1322169	166	LL743	LA	3/5/44	Mailly-le-Camp	France	Fr			NK	3349	Liberated 20 August 1944 by US troops
Virgo	CG	SGT		1812279	166	ME639	LA	25/2/44	Augsburg	France	Sp, Gib	24/6/44	25/6/44	Whitchurch	3320 1999	Burgundy line. In Toulouse 24 May 1944. Helped by Françoise Dissard
Vivian	R	SGT		905339	9	R1244	WE	11/1/41	Turin	France	Sp, Gib	5/6/41	14/6/41	Greenock	3308 713	To UK on HMS *Argus*. Not interviewed until 29 April 1942. DFM (26/5/42). See *Bombers First and Last*, pp. 41 etc
Vlielander Hein	BM	S/LT	HOL		139	MM146	MOS	7/7/44	Berlin	Sweden	Nor, Swe	6/9/44	7/9/44	Leuchars	3323 2453	Royal Neth. Air Service. Crossed into Norway on 22 July 1944. Captured. Escaped immediately and returned to Sweden. DFC (24/9/45)
Wacinski	JT	P/O	POL	P.0400	304	W5627	WE	27/4/42	Cologne	France	Sp, Gib	19/8/42	25/8/42	Londonderry	3310 819	Helped by Francisco Ponzán network. Back on RN destroyer. MiD. See *Safe Houses Are Dangerous*, p. 207
Waddell	G	F/O		155561	157	MM629	MOS	21/11/44	Bomber support	Holland				NK	NF	Shot down by Mosquito of own squadron
Waddell	GMcT	F/O	CAN	J.24600	427	LV987	HAL	7/6/44	Achères	France	Fr			NK	3350 1269	Interviewed 1 September 1944. Report IS9/WEA/7/141/1269
Wade	D	SGT		1593056	460	ME755	LA	14/7/44	Revigny-sur-Ornain	France	Fr	6/9/44	6/9/44	NK	3322 2313	See *Massacre over the Marne*
Wærner	TA	F/L	NOR	F.P.122	332	W3125	SP	1/11/42	Ramrod	France	Sp, Gib	21/1/43	26/1/43	Gourock	3312 1056	
Wainwright	JE	F/S		1435555	44	ME699	LA	4/7/44	St Leu d'Esserent	France				NK	3350 1070	Report IS9/WEA/2/361/1070
Walker	BJI	SGT		950785	77	DT734	HAL	9/3/43	Munich	Belgium	Fr, Sp, Gib	17/5/43	18/5/43	Mount Batten	3313 1208	DFM (6/7/43)
Walker	CA	F/L	CAN	J.4552	418	HX812	MOS	22/3/44	Intruder	France	Fr	7/9/44	7/9/44	NK	3323 2360	

Walker	DF	F/O		151314	514	LL695	LA	21/5/44	Duisburg	Holland				NK	3350 1427	Interviewed 23 September 1944. Report IS9/WEA/2/520/1427
Walker	KA	SGT		1583707	630	ND530	LA	15/3/44	Stuttgart	France	Fr	10/9/44	10/9/44	Hendon	3325 2883	Back to UK via Paris. Interviewed 9 September 1944. Report IS9/WEA/MB/1128 in WO 208/3350
Walker	PW	SGT		1232561	627	DZ479	MOS	2/12/43	Berlin	France	Sz	17/9/44	19/9/44	St Mawgan	3323 2514	Switzerland 22 February 1944. Left 1 September 1944 with Cunliffe. To Naples by boat 8 September 1944. See *At First Sight*, pp. 9-10 (Webb)
Walker	W	SGT		1458025	61	W4236	LA	9/8/43	Mannheim	Belgium	Fr, Sz, Fr, Sp, Gib	5/6/44	6/6/44	Whitchurch	3320 1953	To Switzerland with Sergeant J.C. Whitley. Left with Warrant Officer Blumer and Sergeant Merlin
Wallace	JR	F/S	AUS	A.423364	466	LV956	HAL	18/4/44	Tergnier	France	Sp, Gib	24/6/44	25/6/44	Whitchurch	3320 2004	Helped by Françoise Dissard in Toulouse 24 May 1944
Wallace	P	F/O	CAN	J.18244	411	MK776	SP	27/6/44	Vehicles	France	Fr			NK	3345 651	Injured ankle. Captured. Liberated from hospital at Châlons-sur-Marne 29 August 1944. Interviewed 3 September 1944
Wallace	RV	SGT		1392870	102	JN909	HAL	31/8/43	Berlin	Germany	Hol, Bel, Fr, Sz, Fr	10/9/44	10/9/44	St Eval	NF	Switzerland 15 October 1943 with Sergeant H. Simister. Left c. 16 September 1944. Report Switzerland/3
Wallington	WF	S/L		43339	487	HX938	MOS	9/10/43	A/c engine factory	France	Sp, Gib	20/12/43	21/12/43	Whitchurch	3317 1638	The target was located at Woippy near Metz. Comet 197. DFC (3/11/44)
Walls	A	SGT		1116339	115	HK579	LA	8/9/44	Le Havre	France	Fr	13/9/44	13/9/44	NK	3345 747	Captured. Liberated when Fort Tourneville, Le Havre surrendered 12 September 1944. Interviewed 14 September 1944. Report MISC/INT/747
Walmsley	AH	F/O		142330	101	DV287	LA	14/1/44	Brunswick	Holland	Bel			NK	3350 1353	Marathon. ss9. Interviewed 10 September 1944. Report IS9/WEA/MB/1353
Walmsley	CW	F/S	CAN	R.162645	90	EF147	ST	5/3/44	SOE	France	Fr			NK	3349 390	Interviewed 27 August 1944. Report IS9/WEA/8/190/390
Walmsley	H	SGT		1114164	10	W1041	HAL	27/4/42	*Tirpitz*, Norway	Norway	Swe	24/5/42	24/5/42	Leuchars	3309 742	Left from Stockholm. DFM (16/6/42)
Walsh	DS	SGT		754104	15	R1080	WE	26/4/41	Transit	Mediterranean	Fr, Sp, Gib	18/10/42	19/10/42	Poole	3311 915	Interned by the French. Escaped 5 September 1942. Dates back and Poole?
Walsh	JG	F/S	AUS	A.8955	467	LM219	LA	7/7/44	St Leu d'Esserent	France	Fr	2/9/44	2/9/44	NK	3322 2259	To UK from Évreux
Walsh	MR	SGT	CAN	R.203336	166	LM388	LA	12/7/44	Revigny-sur-Ornain	France	Fr	23/8/44	23/8/44	Northolt	3321 2148	Left for UK from "Normandy". See *Massacre over the Marne*
Walter	BH	P/O	CAN	J.85018	405	PA988	LA	16/8/44	Stettin	Denmark	Swe	2/9/44	3/9/44	Leuchars	3322 2258	To Sweden by boat. Left for UK from Stockholm
Walton	JRC	F/O	AUS	A.414530	464	NT138	MOS	25/7/44	Patrol	France	Fr	23/8/44	23/8/44	Northolt	3321 2157	Left for UK from Le Mans. Interviewed 24 August 1944. See *Massacre over the Marne*, p. 122.
Walton	R	F/O		43117	120	AM924	LIB	28/5/42	*Tirpitz* recce	Norway	Swe	31/8/42	1/9/42	Leuchars	3310 828	Also 2nd Lieutenant (74863), RA. MC (1/12/42). AFC (232 Squadron). See *Making for Sweden*, pp. 35-8 & *Shot Down...Run*, pp. 127-33, & *Air Mail* Jan-Mar 2004, p.33
Walton	WM	F/L		156103	97	NE124	LA	24/6/44	Prouville	France	Fr			NK	3322 2319	DFC (17/3/44, 57 Squadron). Liberated 3 September 1944. Back in UK by 6 September 1944
Walz	DM	F/L	CAN	C.12586	443	MK605	SP	16/6/44	Sweep	France	Fr		17/8/44	NK	3348 91	Interviewed 13 August 1944. Report IS9/WEA/2/70/91. See also AIR 40/2305. Shot down again 24 February 1945. Prisoner of war
Wandzilak	S	F/L	POL	P.0506	308	PL279	SP	26/8/44	Armed recce	France	Fr			NK	3350 1064	Interviewed 3 September 1944. Report IS9/WEA/2/331/1064
Warburton	LA	SGT		992847	101	R1703	WE	31/8/41	Cologne	Belgium	Fr, Sp, Gib	4/3/42	10/3/42	Gourock	3308 687	Comet 13. MiD (1/1/43). Pilot officer (153856) wef 15 October 1943. See *Rendez-vous 127*, photo facing p. 49
Ward	GH	F/O		52500	138	LW281	HAL	18/10/43	SOE	Belgium	Fr, Sp, Gib	20/12/43	21/12/43	Whitchurch	3317 1631	DFM (6/7/43, 89 Squadron). Comet 211. DFC (3/10/44)
Ward	RD	F/L		130411	644	LL403	HAL	5/10/44	Supply drop, Dodex III	Holland	Hol			NK	3327 3064	Wounded on Operation Prgasus II, November 1944. Escaped from hospital. MiD (1/1/45). DFC (9/2/45). See *Bomber Boys* (Chapter 15) and *Home Run* (Nichol/Rennell). Died 16 June 2008
Ward	RH	F/S		927261	296	V1605	ALB	6/6/44	NK	France	Fr	8/6/44	9/6/44	Portsmouth	3320 1978	
Wardzinski	E	F/L	POL	P.1581	3	JP921	TY	29/2/44	Ramrod	Holland				NK	3348 2086	Holland? Evaded again 20 March 1945
Wardzinski	E	F/L	POL	P.1581	308	TB734	SP	20/3/45	Armed patrol	Holland				NK	NF	Second evasion - see 29 February 1944
Wares	D	P/O		156068	49	ED426	LA	7/10/43	Stuttgart	France	Sz			NK	NF	Reached Switzerland on 30 October 1943 with Sergeant R. Barlow
Warnock	JC	F/O		127325	168	AL979	MU	19/7/44	Tac/R	France	Fr	9/9/44	9/9/44	NK	3324 2730	Captured by Germans. In PoW camps at Alençon & Chartres. Jumped from train on 13 August 1944. MiD (14/6/45)
Wasiak	A	SGT	POL	784188	301	Z1491	WE	28/8/42	Saarbrücken	Belgium	Fr, Sp, Gib	5/10/42	6/10/42	Hendon	3310 870	Wounded. Comet 53. Escorted from Paris by Andrée de Jongh and Jeanine De Greef
Wasik	WP	P/O	POL	P.0840	300	Z1276	WE	27/4/42	Cologne	France	Sz, Fr, Sp, Gib	7/11/42	7/11/42	Portreath	3311 971	Also evaded in 1944 - see WO 208/3324 2589
Wasik	WP	F/L	POL	P.0840	300	PA163	LA	29/8/44	Stettin	Denmark	Swe	27/9/44	27/9/44	Leuchars	3324 2589	ss7. Came down in sea off Denmark. Taken on the Laura to Sweden by skipper Jens Jensen. Also evaded in 1942 (see WO 208/3311 971)
Wasylkow	RJ	SGT	CAN	R.189046	429	MZ362	HAL	25/7/44	Stuttgart	France	Fr			NK	3349 351	Liberated by US troops 17 August 1944. Interviewed 20 August 1944. Report

																IS9/WEA/2/173/351
Watelet	GL	SGT	BEL	1299840	609	JR191	TY	17/11/43	Rhubarb	France	Sp, Gib	12/3/44	13/3/44	Lyneham	3319 1831	Belgian in RAF. Tried but failed to cross to Switzerland. Spent weeks in Marseille before getting help from a sailor going home on leave to cross to Spain on 30/31 January 1944
Waterman	FCE	F/L	CAN	J.6362	109	ML985	MOS	31/8/44	Leverkusen					NK	NF	DFC (4/12/42, 40 Squadron - baled out behind enemy lines after raid on Tobruk on 9 August 1942)
Waters	FRW	SGT		1876128	44	PB266	LA	28/7/44	Stuttgart	Germany				NK	NF	
Watkins	TJ	SGT		565841	82	P4904	BL	17/5/40	Gembloux	France	Fr		1/6/40	NK	NF	Commissioned (44735) wef 5 October 1940, he was an acting flight lieutenant, still on 82 Squadron, when awarded the DSO (15/8/41) after being severely wounded in June 1941 attacking a ship in the Mediterranean
Watkins	WE	P/O		162644	263	JR309	TY	13/2/44	Rodeo	France	Sp, Gib	5/5/44	6/5/44	Whitchurch	3319 1909	MiD (14/6/44)
Watlington	JH	F/O	BER	J.8381	400	AG641	MU	22/6/43	Intruder	France	Sp, Gib	22/5/44	23/5/44	Whitchurch	3319 1925	Bermudian in the RCAF. Helped by Dutch-Paris. On Le Hénaff's failed boat operation 2/3 February 1944. Reached Spain on 28 March 1944. See *The Freedom Trail*, pp. 82-3
Watson	E	SGT		967923	40	R3609	BL	14/8/40	Chartres	France	Sp, Gib	19/11/40	4/12/40	Liverpool	3300 132	MM (7/3/41)
Watson	JH	P/O	CAN	J.7802	419	X3359	WE	16/6/42	Essen	Belgium	Fr, Sp, Gib	15/10/42	15/10/42	Mount Batten	3311 911	Comet 32. MiD (2/6/43)
Watson	PD	F/S		1810086	158	NR251	HAL	5/1/45	Hanover	Holland	Hol			NK	3352 2483	With Flight Sergeant R.H.Dickson. Liberated by Canadians on 9 April 1945. Interviewed 12 April 1945. Report IS9/WEA/369/2483
Watson	RR	SGT		1600909	115	LM166	LA	8/8/44	Lucheux	France	Fr	6/9/44	6/9/44	NK	3322 2278	Bordeaux-Loupiac line
Watson	RW	SGT	AUS	A.418600	166	ME749	LA	3/5/44	Mailly-le-Camp	France	Fr	8/8/44	8/8/44	NK	3321 2065	Flown back by Hudson of 161 (SD) Squadron with J.C. Trull. See *On Wings of War. A History of 166* Squadron, pp. 73-4
Watson	SJ	SGT		1895727	625	LM139	LA	10/6/44	Achères	France				NK	NF	
Watson	WC	F/O	CAN	J.29526	419	KB718	LA	4/7/44	Villeneuve-St Georges	France	Fr			Northolt	3349 382	Hidden by Drue Tartière. Interviewed 26 August 1944. Report IS9/WEA/8/165/382. To UK by US Dakota. Northolt?
Watton	PWC	F/S			33	NV783	TEM	12/4/45	Offensive operations	Germany				NK	NF	Shot down west of Uelzen
Watts	GL	F/S		1527439	405	LM345	LA	27/9/43	Brunswick	Holland	Bel, Fr, Sp, Gib	10/4/44	11/4/44	Whitchurch	3319 1874	Dutch-Paris line. DFC (12/12/44, warrant officer)
Waudby	WN	F/S		951052	245	JP971	TY	8/1/44	Ramrod	France	And, Sp, Gib	9/4/44	10/4/44	Lyneham	3319 1873	Lyneham? Commissioned (179586) wef 2 July 1944 (gazetted 29/8/44). DFC (2/2/45)
Waugh	JA	SGT		1591662	102	MZ644	HAL	28/6/44	Blainville	France	Fr			NK	3350 1492	See *Massacre over the Marne*, pp. 133-38
Weare	WTB	SGT		1607656	10	HX326	HAL	26/4/44	Essen	Belgium	Bel			NK	3350 1392	Liberated 14 September 1944. Interviewed 17 September 1944. Report IS9/WEA/2/487/1392. See *Free To Fight Again*, pp. 170-4
Webb	DC	SGT		1393633	65	FZ109	MU	24/6/44	Armed recce	France	Fr	27/8/44	27/8/44	Northolt	3321 2205	Liberated by US troops 23 August 1944
Webb	DJ	SGT	CAN	R.110337	428	ED209	HAL	13/7/43	Aachen	Belgium	Fr, Sp, Gib	10/9/43	10/9/43	Whitchurch	3314 1400	Comet 127. DFM (29/8/44)
Webb	H	F/S		634568	640	LW654	HAL	10/8/44	Dijon	France	Fr			Northolt	NF	With Flying Officer R.F. Lane RCAF. Flown to UK in an Anson. Back at base eight days after being shot down
Webb	JG	SGT		568540	44	PD222	LA	14/8/44	Brest	France	Fr	20/9/44	20/9/44	NK	3345 781	Wounded. Captured 14 August 1944. Liberated 18 September 1944 in Roscanvel with McNeilage. In hospital until 8 October 1944. Interviewed 22 October 1944. Report MI9/S/P.G./MISC/INT/781
Weber	GR	F/O	CAN	J.29725	403	NH232	SP	17/8/44	Armed recce	France	Fr		27/8/44	NK	3350 1030	Interviewed 27 August 1944. Report IS9/WEA/2/233/1030
Weeden	RA	P/O		159888	467	LM376	LA	30/3/44	Nuremberg	Belgium	Bel	7/9/44	7/9/44	Hendon	3322 2315	Marathon. Liberated by US 102nd Cavalry on 6 September 1944. Flown back from Paris
Weight	FGA	SGT		914890	7	R9278	ST	14/4/43	Stuttgart	France	Sp, Gib	5/8/43	11/8/43	Liverpool	3314 1347	Burgundy line. Commissioned (196322) wef 11 March 1945 (15/5/45). DFC (20/7/45).
Weir	CF	SGT		1569288	218	EF259	ST	1/5/44	Chambly	France	Fr	18/8/44	18/8/44	Northolt	3321 2114	Sherwood. Left for UK from "Allied beachhead" - Cherbourg?
Wells	FA	F/S		1868305	44	ME694	LA	25/7/44	Stuttgart	France	Fr			NK	3348 318	Sherwood. Interviewed 17 August 1944. Report IS9/WEA/2/100/318
Wensley	RL	SGT		1624141	90	EF147	ST	5/3/44	SOE	France	Fr	11/9/44	11/9/44	NK	3322 2325	
Wentworth	CW	SGT	CAN	R.185519	434	LK801	HAL	16/6/44	Sterkrade	Holland				NK	NF	POW?
West	JW	F/O	CAN	J.20716	405	ND344	LA	11/6/44	Tours	France	Fr	26/8/44	26/8/44	NK	3321 2141	
Western	WCL	SGT		1586571	626	ND985	LA	27/5/44	Aachen	Belgium	Bel			NK	NF	In a Marathon camp in the Ardennes when liberated by US forces on 8 September 1944
Whalen	WBP	SGT	CAN	R.171362	425	LW591	HAL	24/4/44	Karlsruhe	Luxembourg				NK	3348 2049	

Whaley	HH	P/O	CAN	J.18716	432	LW592	HAL	27/4/44	Montzen	Belgium	Fr	12/9/44	12/9/44	Northolt	3323 2417	
Wharton	L	SGT		1685044	44	LM638	LA	12/7/44	Culmont-Chalindrey	France	Fr	8/9/44	8/9/44	Middle Wallop	3323 2367	See *Massacre over the Marne*
Wheeler	H	F/S			266	MN184	TY	15/8/44	Ground targets	France	Fr			NK	NF	Briefly captured, with Flying Officer Kramer, on 20 August 1944
Wheler	TR	F/O	CAN	J.18199	411	MK941	SP	7/8/44	Armed recce	France	Fr			NK	3350 1219	Captured. Escaped during night of 23/24 August 1944. Interviewed 28 August 1944. Report IS9/WEA/2/250/1219. DFC (8/12/44). MBE (14/9/45)
Whicher	AJ	SGT		1168872	24 OTU	BD347	WH	31/7/42	Düsseldorf	Belgium	Fr, Sp, Gib	29/8/42	8/9/42	Gourock	3310 835	Comet 38. Commissioned pilot officer (181120) 27 June 1944 wef 29 April 1944
Whincop	G	F/O	NZ	NZ.415806	487	LR332	MOS	12/6/44	NK	France	Fr	31/8/44	31/8/44	NK	3322 2229	Left for UK from Bayeux - B.14 airstrip, Banville. Croix de Guerre (French) (9/10/46)
White	AG	F/S		1323084	100	ND675	LA	9/4/44	Mining	Denmark	Swe	7/5/44	8/5/44	Leuchars	3319 1914	Reached Sweden on 26 April 1944. Flown back in Mosquito
White	F	W/O	AUS	A.425252	467	PD230	LA	12/8/44	Rüsselsheim	Belgium	Bel	14/9/44	14/9/44	Fairford	3323 2515	Liberated on 11 September 1944. Back to UK from Brussels
White	FK	F/S	AUS	A.437607	467	PB234	LA	18/7/44	Revigny-sur-Ornain	France	Fr			NK	3351 2043	Back in UK late September 1944. See *Massacre over the Marne*
White	JK	F/O	CAN	J.28083	426	MZ690	HAL	7/6/44	Versailles	France	Fr			NK	3322 2317	Aircraft returned to UK. Liberated 1 September 1944. Back in UK by 6 September 1944. Versailles?
White	LSM	F/S	NZ	NZ.413919	485	BS543	SP	22/8/43	Ramrod 212	France	Sp, Gib	4/10/43	5/10/43	Whitchurch	3315 1450	Captured. Escaped within 45 minutes. Back on a Liberator. MiD (8/6/44). DFC (29/12/44) as flight lieutenant. See his biography *Pilot on the Run*
White	TW	F/S		1323132	44	ME628	LA	24/6/44	Pommerval	France	Fr	9/9/44	9/9/44	NK	3322 2298	
Whitecross	JA	F/O	CAN	41888	50	AD834	HN	28/4/41	Mining	France	Sp, Gib	4/7/41	12/7/41	Greenock	3304 379	Crossed Pyrenees with Captains McPartland and Plant (both RAMC). DFC (28/7/42). Killed on operations 15 August 1941. Canadian in RAF
Whitehead	GGA	P/O		161399	76	LL116	HAL	20/1/44	Berlin	France	Sp, Gib	1/5/44	2/5/44	Whitchurch	3319 1895	Burgundy line. DFC (16/6/44)
Whiteman	WE	SGT		755039	82	V5997	BL	13/5/41	St Nazaire	France	Sp, Gib	8/8/41	14/8/41	Gourock	3305 481	Captured by Vichy French. Commissioned (133516) wef 23 October 1942. MiD (14/1/44, flying officer). DFC (23/3/45, flight lieutenant, 7 Squadron). See AIR 2/5684
Whitley	JC	F/O		155499	61	W4236	LA	9/8/43	Mannheim	Belgium	Fr, Sz	12/9/44	14/9/44	Newquay	3323 2519	Switzerland 20 December 1943, with Sergeant W. Walker. To France 30 August 1944. Flown to UK via Naples
Whitley	JR	G/C		24002	76	JB871	HAL	10/4/43	Frankfurt	France	Sp, Gib	24/5/43	25/5/43	Hendon	3313 1211	AFC (1/2/37). Station CO RAF Linton-on-Ouse. Comet 98. Evaded with Sergeant W.R. Laws. DSO (9/7/43). AOC 4 Group 12 February 1945. CBE (14/6/45)
Whitmore	HNC	F/S		1535794	156	NE143	LA	31/5/44	Tergnier	France	Fr			NK	NF	Joined the Resistance. DFC (20/7/45, warrant officer)
Whitmore	WE	P/O			257	PD598	TY	20/1/45	Armed recce	Holland				NK	NF	Baled out south-west of Utrecht
Whitnall	P	SGT	CAN	R.85965	296	BD534	WH	17/4/43	Transformer, Mezidon	France	Sp, And, Gib	4/10/43	5/10/43	Whitchurch	3315 1445	Army Co-operation Squadron. Marie-Claire line
Whittaker	PL	F/S		1587036	617	NF923	LA	23/9/44	Ladbergen	Holland	Hol			NK	3352 2448	Liberated by British forces 31 March 1945. Interviewed 2 April 1945. DFM (7/12/45)
Whyte	JHF	F/S	NZ	NZ.412522	207	L7547	LA	14/2/43	Milan	France	Sz, Fr, Sp, Gib	9/2/44	10/2/44	Lyneham	3318 1768	On return, completed a second tour of operations on 50 Squadron. DFC (9/11/44)
Wicks	BJ	F/O		40774	56	N2431	HUD	22/5/40	Patrol	France			3/6/40	NK	NF	Killed in action 12 October 1942, as squadron leader DFC (6/6/41) commanding 126 Squadron on Malta
Wiens	RC	F/O	CAN	J.27503	405	PA988	LA	16/8/44	Stettin	Denmark	Swe	8/9/44	9/9/44	Leuchars	3323 2386	Copenhagen to Trelleborg on a coal steamer. See *We Flew, We Fell, We Lived*, pp. 348-54
Wilby	TR	F/O	CAN	J.15138	78	W7856	HAL	11/12/42	Turin	France	Sp, Gib	24/5/43	25/5/43	Hendon	3313 1212	Rear gunner - broke leg in turret as he struggled to get out. Comet 92. DFC (6/7/43)
Wilkie	EJ	P/O	CAN	J.86476	426	LW198	HAL	28/6/44	Metz	France	Fr	6/9/44	6/9/44	NK	3323 2351	
Wilkinson	JS	F/O	NZ	NZ.4211042	75	HK567	LA	7/8/44	Mare de Magne	France	Fr			NK	3348 137	Met British troops on 14 August 1944. Interviewed 16 August 1944. Report WEA 1/5/137. Shot down again, on 15 Squadron, on 3/4 February 1945 (Dortmund). POW. MiD (14/6/45)
Wilkinson	R	SGT		1524176	44	LM631	LA	7/7/44	St Leu d'Esserent	France	Fr	8/9/44	8/9/44	NK	3322 2342	
Wilkinson	RC	S/L		44125	174	BE674	HN	3/5/42	Ramrod	France	Sp, Gib	1/7/42	1/7/42	Mount Batten	3309 750	OBE (6/10/42), DFM & Bar (both 31/5/40, sergeant 564450). See *Free to Fight Again*, pp.46-50
Williams	A	F/O			65	FX926	MU	3/9/44	Patrol	France					NF	
Williams	CJ	F/O		158991	233	KG424	DAK	6/6/44	Supply drop	France	Fr	3/7/44	3/7/44	NK	NF	Back to England in 271 Squadron aircraft. Rejoined squadron 3 July 1944. See *The Evaders* (Cosgrove), pp. 166-196

Williams	EO	SGT		1830460	578	LL584	HAL	11/9/44	Gelsenkirchen	Belgium				NK	3350 2017	Interviewed 26 September 1944. Report IS9/WEA/2/557/2017. See Flight Sergeant S.T. Sloane RAAF
Williams	FT	P/O		159702	97	JB367	LA	18/11/43	Berlin	Belgium	Fr, Sp, Gib	24/1/44	24/1/44	NK	3318 1721	DFM (10/12/43). With Flying Officer F.D. Hill. Comet 259
Williams	H	SGT		993644	149	W7572	ST	24/8/42	Frankfurt	Belgium	Fr, Gib	18/10/42	19/10/42	Poole	3311 920	Evacuated by *Seawolf* 12 October 1942. DFM (5/2/43)
Williams	LH	SGT		1396975	460	LM531	LA	3/5/44	Mailly-le-Camp	France	Fr	6/9/44	6/9/44	NK	3323 2539	
Williams	LKG	SGT	CAN	R.181002	101	LL862	LA	20/7/44	Courtrai	France	Fr			NK	NF	
Williams	MF	SGT		1653064	578	MZ563	HAL	22/4/44	Düsseldorf	Holland	Bel			NK	3323 2531	Back in UK 7 September 1944
Williams	RT	F/S		1317608	65	FZ110	MU	17/5/44	Ranger	Denmark	Swe	30/6/44	1/7/44	Leuchars	3320 1975	To Sweden by boat *Laura* on 5/6 June 44 - see *Shot Down and on the Run*, pp. 120-5. To UK by Mosquito. DFM (3/10/44). Died 5 March 2008
Williams	SF	SGT	CAN	R.197190	514	LL678	LA	12/6/44	Gelsenkirchen	Holland	Hol	23/9/44	23/9/44	Croydon	3324 2555	
Williams	WE	SGT		1890975	576	ME811	LA	6/6/44	Vire	France	Fr			NK	NF	Briefly met Pilot Officer G.F. Pyle while evading
Williamson	GR	SGT		1568572	50	ND953	LA	3/5/44	Mailly-le-Camp	France	Fr			NK	3348 284	Liberated in Paris 15 August 1944. Interviewed 17 August 1944. Report IS9/WEA/8/142/284
Willis	FG	SGT		937660	75	T2474	WE	22/12/40	Mannheim	France	Sp, Gib	4/9/41	5/9/41	Oban	3306 494	Arrived in Gibraltar 1 September 1941 - see AIR 40/1545
Willis	L	SGT	CAN	R.92498	75	R9316	ST	13/2/43	Lorient	France	Sp, Gib	19/4/43	20/4/43	Hendon	3313 1176	Solo to Spain from Brittany
Willis	LR	SGT		742172	9	R1244	WE	11/1/41	Turin	France	Sp, Gib	5/6/41	14/6/41	Greenock	3308 712	To UK on HMS *Argus*. Not interviewed until 29 April 1942. MM (18/8/42). See *Bombers First and Last*, pp. 41 etc. Too ill on return to resume flying duties
Wilson	D	SGT	CAN	R.214308	49	JB473	LA	18/7/44	Revigny-sur-Ornain	France	Fr	4/9/44	4/9/44	NK	3326 2975	See *Massacre over the Marne*
Wilson	EL	P/O	CAN	J.195*1	427	LV995	HAL	12/6/44	Arras	France				NK	NF	Service number?
Wilson	G	P/O		191391	635	PB949	LA	4/4/45	Harburg	Germany	Hol			NK	3327 3026	DFC (20/7/45)
Wilson	GL	F/O		127148	296	V1605	ALB	6/6/44	D-Day glider tow	France	Fr	7/6/44	8/6/44	Portsmouth	3320 1962	Left for UK from Allied beachhead. DFC (14/7/44)
Wilson	HF	SGT		1815032	218	EF259	ST	1/5/44	Chambly	France	Fr	16/9/44	16/9/44	NK	3323 2442	Back to UK from Amiens
Wilson	HR	SGT	CAN	R.58184	51	Z6874	WH	24/10/41	Frankfurt	France	Sp, Gib	27/1/42	6/2/42	Liverpool	3308 673	Across Pyrenees with J. Budzynski, W.H. Dyer, and Z. Groyecki. To UK by corvette. MiD (1/1/43). KIA 27/28 January 1944 (408 Squadron, Lancaster DS710) as flying officer (J.23525)
Wilson	HWD	SGT		1398595	61	PB436	LA	28/8/44	Königsberg	Denmark	Swe	16/9/44	17/9/44	Leuchars	3323 2434	From Copenhagen to Malmo, Sweden, by boat. Flown to UK in a Mosquito. See *Free to Fight Again*, pp.249-53
Wilson	KA	F/O	AUS	A.414449	453	NH557	SP	27/9/44	Arnhem, patrol	Holland				NK	3348 2233	
Wilson	L	P/O		127028	138	Z9232	WH	24/8/42	SOE	France	Gib	30/9/42	5/10/42	Greenock	3310 880	On attachment from 161 Squadron. Evacuated by *Seawolf* 21 September 1942. Back on HMS *Malaya*
Wilson	RHD	SGT		633143	35	W1048	HAL	27/4/42	*Tirpitz*, Norway	Norway	Swe	8/4/43	9/4/43	Leuchars	3312 1152	DFM (25/5/43). See *Making for Sweden*, pp. 33-5
Wilsonshaw	BD	SGT		1861240	419	KB731	LA	12/6/44	Cambrai	France				NK	NF	Surname?
Windiate	JW	SGT	CAN	R.131765	106	DV196	LA	7/8/43	Milan	France	Sz, Fr			NK	NF	In Switzerland 1 October 1943. Left after 16 September 1944
Windsor	C	SGT		2210667	158	LK863	HAL	7/6/44	Versailles	France	Fr	31/8/44	31/8/44	NK	3322 2252	In Paris when it was liberated. Interviewed 2 September 1944
Windsor	KD	SGT	CAN	R.106450	403	BS383	SP	20/6/43	Circus	France	Sp, Gib	23/8/43	24/8/43	Whitchurch	3314 1367	Comet 119. From Seville 20 August 1943 on Norwegian ship *Borgholm* with Flying Officer T.A.H. Slack
Wingham	ST	F/O		156389	76	MZ578	HAL	22/4/44	Düsseldorf	Holland	Bel	13/9/44	13/9/44	Northolt	NF	On 3rd op of 2nd tour. In farmhouse early September 1944 where Germans wanted to set up HQ. Escaped to meet US troops. Dakota from Orly
Winskill	AL	F/L		84702	41	W3447	SP	14/8/41	Sweep	France	Sp, Gib	22/11/41	23/11/41	Pembroke Dock	3307 600	DFC (6/1/42). Bar to DFC (27/7/43). CBE (11/6/60). KCVO (31/12/79). See *Fighter Pilot*, p.165-6; *Secret Sunday*, pp. 20, 89, 92
Winterbottom	JA	SGT		1304749	78	W7782	HAL	8/9/42	Frankfurt	Belgium	Fr, Sp, Gib	15/10/42	16/10/42	Hendon	3311 912	Comet 57. Via Aldermaston for Hendon. DFM (5/2/43)
Winwood	AE	F/S		1582475	235	RS619	MOS	5/4/45	Anti-shipping strike	Denmark	Swe	2/5/45	2/5/45	Leuchars	3327 3080	Coastal Command. Reached Sweden on 24 April 1945. Flown back by DC-3 Dakota. Interviewed by IS9(W) on 12 September 1945
Wiome	M	F/O	CAN	J.29979	433	LW120	HAL	4/7/44	Villeneuve-St Georges	France	Fr	18/8/44	18/8/44	Northolt	3321 2088	Sherwood. Evacuated from camp on 13 August 1944
Witham	S	SGT		1622656	166	ME839	LA	3/8/44	Trossy-St Maximin	France	Fr	8/9/44	8/9/44	NK	3323 2368	
Withecombe	AB	F/O		137231	138	LW275	HAL	7/2/44	SOE	France	Sp, Gib	4/5/44	5/5/44	Whitchurch	3319 1901	See *Free to Fight Again*, pp. 77-81
Witheridge	CH	P/O	CAN	J.18680	49	LM337	LA	15/8/43	Milan	France	Sp, Gib	1/1/44	2/1/44	Whitchurch	3317 1665	Comet 230. Burgundy line? Whitchurch?
Witrylak	Z	F/S	POL	782327	300	PB252	LA	25/7/44	Stuttgart	France	Fr	20/8/44	20/8/44	Northolt	3321 2112	Sherwood? Left for UK from Bayeux - B.14 airstrip, Banville. Northolt?
Wood	DL	W/O		1316023	578	LL584	HAL	11/9/44	Gelsenkirchen	Belgium	Bel	28/9/44	28/9/44	NK	3324 2584	Back to UK from Brussels. Commissioned (189210 wef 19/12/44). DFC (15/6/45)

Wood	EK	F/O	CAN	J.28692	630	PA992	LA	24/7/44	Stuttgart	France	Sz, Fr			NK	NF	Service number?
Wood	ERW	P/O		48814	138	Z9232	WH	24/8/42	SOE	France	Gib	30/9/42	5/10/42	Greenock	3310 882	DFM (23/12/41). Evacuated by *Seawolf* 21 September 1942. Back on HMS *Malaya*
Wood	G	F/S		1067675	570	LJ913	ST	18/9/44	Arnhem supply drop	Holland	Hol			NK	3348 2029	Liberated 6 October 1944. Interviewed 7 October 1944. LJ913? See *The Evaders* (Leo Heaps), pp. 162-4
Wood	GA	F/S		1334647	263	P7113	WW	23/9/43	Ramrod 239	France	Fr	30/10/43	31/10/43	Plymouth	3316 1525	Shot down by flak dive-bombing Morlaix airfield. Back on the *Requin* from Brittany
Woodgate	GJ	F/S	AUS	A.434073	578	LL584	HAL	11/9/44	Gelsenkirchen	Belgium	Bel	28/9/44	28/9/44	NK	3324 2585	Back to UK from Brussels
Woodham	SC	F/O		148803	161	LK238	ST	6/10/44	SOE Tablejam 104/26B	Denmark	Swe	6/11/44	7/11/44	NK	3324 2742	To Sweden on 30 October 1944. MiD (14/6/45)
Woodhouse	KB	F/O	CAN	J.18080	401	MJ119	SP	16/3/44	Ramrod 661	France	Fr	24/3/44	24/3/44	Dartmouth	3319 1858	Evacuated from Brittany by MGB503 in Operation Bonaparte V. See *The Evaders* (Lavender/Sheffe), Chapter 11
Woodland	DA	W/O		1380842	83	JB402	LA	3/5/44	Mailly-le-Camp	France	Fr	7/9/44	7/9/44	NK	3326 2934	Liberated by US troops 28 August 1944. See AIR 14/2073
Woodward	HGM	SGT		1423654	158	LK863	HAL	7/6/44	Versailles	France				NK	3352 2360	With Sergeants A. Herd and R.A. Diver. Interviewed 28 August 1944
Wooll	GR	F/L	CAN	42734	1 PRU	DK310	MOS	24/8/42	PR, Italy	Switzerland	Fr, Sp, Gib	22/12/42	23/12/42	Whitchurch	3311 1006	Canadian in RAF. No. 1 PRU. Shot down on Belp airfield, near Berne. Repatriated 17 December 1942
Woollard	LC	SGT		1332301	617	JB144	LA	15/9/43	Ladbergen	Holland	Bel, Fr	22/1/44	23/1/44	Falmouth	3318 1718	Helped by "Service EVA" until 22 October 1943. With both Bordeaux and Burgundy lines. Back to UK from Brittany aboard the *Breizh-Izel*
Wootton	KB	F/S		1151817	149	EF202	ST	25/11/43	Mining	France	Fr	11/9/44	11/9/44	NK	3325 2884	Interrogated by IS9 (WEA) in Paris. Report IS9/WEA/MB/1496 also in WO 208/3350
Worby	JR	SGT		909969	101	R1699	WE	10/9/41	Turin	France	Sp, Gib	30/12/41	5/1/42	Gourock	3307 633	Crossed Pyrenees with Lieutenant R.E.H. Parkinson and Sergeant G. Campbell. To UK on Polish ship *Batory* MiD (1/1/43)
Worrall	JRW	SGT		1591618	44	ME694	LA	25/7/44	Stuttgart	France	Fr			Northolt	3348 317	Sherwood. Interviewed 17 August 1944. Report IS9/WEA/2/99/317. Author *Escape from France*
Worsdale	E	SGT	NZ	NZ.412919	75	Z1652	WE	24/10/42	Milan	France	Sz, Fr, Sp, Gib	10/7/44	11/7/44	Whitchurch	3320 2016	Walked to Switzerland with Sergeant L. Newbold. Left on 5 June 1944. MiD (1/1/45). See *Night After Night*, pp. 366-8
Wozniak	B	SGT	POL	792865	304	W5627	WE	27/4/42	Cologne	France	Sp, Gib	23/9/42	24/9/42	NK	3310 859	Helped by Francisco Ponzán network. (Flight Sergeant, 138 Sq)? See *Safe Houses Are Dangerous*, p. 207; and WO 208/3320 1972
Wright	AL	SGT	CAN	548615	61	R5787	MAN	31/1/42	Brest	France	Sp, Gib	30/9/42	5/10/42	Greenock	3310 895	Canadian. Enlisted in the RAF in 1937. Helped by Ponzán network. Back to UK on HMS *Malaya*. See *Safe Houses Are Dangerous*, p. 207, and *The Evaders* (Cosgrove), pp. 62-108
Wright	EW	SGT		1813283	218	EF504	ST	1/5/44	Chambly	France	Fr	18/8/44	18/8/44	Northolt	3321 2080	Sherwood. Left for UK from B.14 airstrip, Banville
Wright	KFH	P/O		159515	10	LV867	HAL	22/4/44	Düsseldorf	Holland	Bel			NK	3350 1391	Interviewed 18 September 1944. Report IS9/WEA/2/489/1391
Wright	P	SGT		1186627	76	W1064	HAL	1/6/42	Essen	Belgium	Fr, Sp, Gib	19/8/42	25/8/42	Londonderry	3310 816	Comet 34. MiD (1/1/43)
Wroblewski	J	F/O	POL	P.1583	138	JD312	HAL	16/8/43	SOE	France	And, Sp, Gib	25/10/43	26/10/43	Lyneham	3315 1490	
Wyatt	JH	SGT		754237	49	P1347	HN	4/9/40	Berlin	France	Sp, Gib	4/4/41	11/4/41	Belfast	3303 280	MiD (11/6/42). Shot down again, on 11/12 August 1942 on 78 Squadron, and taken prisoner of war
Wziatek	K	W/O	POL	792662	300	PB252	LA	25/7/44	Stuttgart	France				NK	NF	
Yarwood	HC	F/O		145375	90	EH906	ST	4/3/44	SOE	France	Sp, Gib	22/5/44	23/5/44	Whitchurch	3319 1926	Burgundy line. DFC (4/8/44)
Yates	RE	W/O	AUS	A.410409	12	ND424	LA	27/6/44	Vaires	France	Fr	4/9/44	4/9/44	NK	3322 2321	
Yates	WS	F/S		1295363	428	KB756	LA	4/7/44	Villeneuve-St Georges	France	Fr			NK	3350 1056	Interviewed 31 August 1944. Report IS9/WEA/2/300/1056
Young	AH	P/O		189427	170	ME307	LA	16/3/45	Nuremberg	Germany				NK	NF	DFC (17/10/44 as warrant officer 1424699, 576 Squadron)
Young	LM	F/S	AUS	A.439521	571	ML963	MOS	10/4/45	Berlin	Germany	Ger	18/4/45	18/4/45	NK	3326 2970	Baled out NW of Berlin. Liberated by US troops 14 April 1945. Flew back from Brussels
Young	RF	W/O		1070385	192	NR180	HAL	5/3/45	Bomber support	Poland	Rus			NK	NF	Back via Odessa. See *Descent into Danger* for his story
Young	RW	F/O		55283	207	NN724	LA	7/2/45	Ladbergen	Holland	Hol			NK	3352 2428	Liberated by Grenadier Guards 31 March 1945. Interviewed 2 April 1945. Report IS9/WEA/2/1037/2428
Young	TC	F/S		1581692	61	ND867	LA	7/7/44	St Leu d'Esserent	France	Fr			NK	NF	
Young	TD	SGT		1822876	514	LM180	LA	12/8/44	Rüsselsheim	Belgium				NK	NF	See *Free to Fight Again*, pp. 174-8
Zacharuk	A	WO2	CAN	R.159388	432	NP706	HAL	18/7/44	Caen	France	Fr			NK	3324 2661	MiD (1/1/46)
Zankowski	K	F/O	POL	P.1972	138	JD312	HAL	16/8/43	SOE	France	And, Sp, Gib	25/10/43	26/10/43	Lyneham	3315 1491	
Zawodny	M	SGT	POL	792065	301	Z1333	WE	10/4/42	Essen	Holland	Bel, Fr, Sp, Gib	18/8/42	19/8/42	Whitchurch	3310 811	Comet 31. MiD

Ziendalski	J	F/L	POL		302	NH608	SP	14/8/44	Patrol	France					NF	
Zuk	N	WO2	CAN	R.140655	166	JB649	LA	25/7/44	Stuttgart	France	Fr	8/9/44	8/9/44	Middle Wallop	3323 2446	Back from Orléans with 1 SAS
Zulikowski	J	P/O	POL	P.0715	306	AP516	SP	28/6/41	Circus 26	France	Sp, Gib	30/12/41	5/1/42	Gourock	3307 641	To UK on Polish ship *Batory*. MiD (recommended 29/5/42)

APPENDIX II

List of Comet evaders: 1941–1944

Names and details of the 288 Allied military personnel passed by the Comet line to Spain, 1941-1944

Note: Column headings are as follows:

1. Num - Number given by Comet in its records.
2. DOP - Date over the Pyrenees.
3. Name - Surname of person.
4. Init - Initials.
5. Rank - Rank held at time of escape/evasion.
6. Service - Force in which serving.
7. Sq - Squadron on which serving at time of escape/evasion.
8. A/C num - Serial number of aircraft in which lost, if relevant.
9. Date s/d - Date when shot down/lost, if relevant.
10. WO 208 - Number of person's MI9/IS9 report in TNA file in WO 208 series (where applicable).
11. Comments - Any relevant comments, e.g. name of aircraft

Num	DOP	Name	Init	Rank	Service	Sq	A/C num	Date s/d	WO 208	Comments
1	20/08/1941	Cromar	J	PTE	Army		Nil		3306 514	Comet's first British serviceman. Back in UK 6 October 1941
2	17/10/1941	Conville	R	PTE	Army		Nil		3307 658	Taken over Pyrenees 17/10/41 by "Dédée". UK 4 January 1942
3	17/10/1941	Cowan	A	SGT	Army		Nil		3307 656	Taken over Pyrenees 17/10/41 by "Dédée". UK 4 January 1942
4	10/11/1941	Tomicki	S	SGT	PAF	305	W5593	05/08/1941	3307 630	First airman over Pyrenees with Ives and Kowalski
5	10/11/1941	Kowalski	MR	SGT	PAF	305	W5593	05/08/1941	3307 631	First airman over Pyrenees with Ives and Tomicki
6	10/11/1941	Ives	JL	SGT	RCAF	51	Z6569	18/08/1941	3307 632	First airman over Pyrenees with Kowalski and Tomicki
7	10/12/1941	Birk	HE	SGT	RAAF	99	X9761	28/09/1941	3308 695	
8	10/12/1941	Carroll	HB	P/O	RAF	207	L7321	13/10/1941	3307 666	
9	10/12/1941	Newton	JL	SGT	RAF	12	W5421	05/08/1941	3307 649	
10	26/12/1941	Day	AD	SGT	RCAF	77	Z6826	05/08/1941	3308 693	
11	26/12/1941	Cox	GT	SGT	RAF	207	L7321	13/10/1941	3308 694	
12	26/12/1941	Hutton	JW	SGT	RAF	101	R1703	31/08/1941	3308 688	
13	26/12/1941	Warburton	LA	SGT	RAF	101	R1703	31/08/1941	3308 687	
14	19/01/1942	Sim	TJ	FUS	Army		Nil		3308 700	
15	01/02/1942	Hogan	NJ	CPL	Army		Nil		3308 698	With Belgians Paul Henri de la Lindi and Lieutenant Osselaer. DCM (12/5/42)
16	27/03/1942	McCairns	JA	F/S	RAF	616	P8500	06/07/1941	3308 717	DFC, MM. Prisoner of war. Escaped from Stalag IXC on 22 January 1942
17	13/05/1942	Carr	LW	F/S	RAF	102	W7653	27/04/1942	3309 749	
18	10/06/1942	Horsley	RM	P/O	RAF	50	L7301	30/05/1942	3309 771	DFC
19	10/06/1942	De Mone	HE	SGT	RCAF	16 OTU	DV763	01/06/1942	3309 778	
20	10/06/1942	Baveystock	LH	SGT	RAF	106	L7301	30/05/1942	3309 772	
21	20/06/1942	Mills	AMcF	SGT	RAF	50	L7301	30/05/1942	3309 774	
22	20/06/1942	King	SE	SGT	RAF	50	L7301	30/05/1942	3309 775	
23	20/06/1942	Naylor	BW	SGT	RAF	50	L7301	30/05/1942	3309 773	
24	20/06/1942	Siadecki	A	SGT	PAF	305	Z8599	05/05/1942	3309 784	
25	01/07/1942	Griffiths	WR	SGT	RAF	61	R5613	02/06/1942	3309 793	
26	01/07/1942	Collins	RJ	SGT	RAAF	15 OTU	W5586	30/05/1942	3309 792	
27	01/07/1942	Goldsmith	BF	SGT	RAF	149	W7508	05/06/1942	3309 791	
28	01/07/1942	Czekalski	W	SGT	PAF	305	Z8599	05/05/1942	3309 794	
29	20/07/1942	Evans	B	F/S	RAF	15 OTU	R1791	30/05/1942	3310 809	
30	20/07/1942	Angers	JAA	SGT	RCAF	419	X3359	16/06/1942	3310 810	
31	20/07/1942	Zawodny	M	SGT	PAF	301	Z1333	10/04/1942	3310 811	
32	19/07/1942	Watson	JH	P/O	RCAF	419	X3359	16/06/1942	3311 911	
33	31/07/1942	Pack	JT	SGT	RAF	35	W7701	08/06/1942	3310 817	Was due to have crossed on 18/19 July 1942 but delayed due to "trouble"
34	31/07/1942	Wright	P	SGT	RAF	76	W1064	01/06/1942	3310 816	Was due to have crossed on 18/19 July 1942 but delayed due to "trouble"
35	31/07/1942	Norfolk	WJ	SGT	RAF	76	W1064	01/06/1942	3310 815	Was due to have crossed on 18/19 July 1942 but delayed due to "trouble"
36	31/07/1942	MacFarlane	W	PTE	Army	None	Nil		3310 821	7th A & SH. Escaped from Germany 20 March 1942 with J. Goldie. DCM
37	17/08/1942	Silva	G	P/O	RAAF	24	BD347	31/07/1942	3310 834	24 OTU
38	17/08/1942	Whicher	AJ	SGT	RAF	24	BD347	31/07/1942	3310 835	24 OTU
39	17/08/1942	MacLean	JA	F/L	RCAF	405	W7708	08/06/1942	3310 837	MiD and DFC
40	17/08/1942	Goldie	JML	PTE	Army	None	Nil		3310 840	7th A & SH. Escaped from Germany 20 March 1942 with Private MacFarlane.DCM
41	22/08/1942	Bennett	JT	SGT	RAF	35	W1147	25/07/1942	3310 854	DFM

42	22/08/1942	Pearce	RE	SGT	RAAF	405	W7718	31/07/1942	3310 858	MiD
43	22/08/1942	Black	JBR	SGT	RAF	24 OTU	BD347	31/07/1942	3310 855	MiD
44	22/08/1942	Orndorff	WR	SGT	RCAF	419	X3712	29/07/1942	3310 857	MiD
45	04/09/1942	Beber	AA	SGT	RAF	158	W7750	06/08/1942	3310 900	
46	04/09/1942	Haydon	JPM	F/L	RAAF	158	W7750	06/08/1942	3310 898	
47	04/09/1942	Davies	IH	F/O	RAAF	158	W7750	06/08/1942	3310 896	See *A Quiet Woman's War*, p. 28. First evader at 162 Avenue Voltaire, Brussels
48	04/09/1942	Fox	CC	SGT	RAF	158	W7750	06/08/1942	3310 899	
49	08/09/1942	Fay	AE	F/S	RCAF	78	W1061	11/08/1942	3311 973	Travelled with Flying Officer Kazimierz Rowicki from Brussels to Spain
50	08/09/1942	Price	EG	SGT	RCAF	158	W1215	05/08/1942	3311 972	
51	08/09/1942	Broom	TJ	W/O	RAF	105	DK297	25/08/1942	3310 897	
52	08/09/1942	Rowicki	K	P/O	PAF	305	Z8599	05/05/1942	3310 888	Travelled with Flight Sergeant Fay from Brussels to Spain
53	19/09/1942	Wasiak	A	SGT	PAF	301	Z1491	28/08/1942	3310 879	
54	19/09/1942	Cope	JE	SGT	RAF	115	X3675	28/08/1942	3310 869	
55	19/09/1942	Van nen Bok	R	F/O	RCAF	408	AE197	28/08/1942	3310 867	DFC
56	19/09/1942	Costello-Bowen	EA	F/L	RAF	105	DK297	25/08/1942	3310 868	
57	24/09/1942	Winterbottom	JA	SGT	RAF	78	W7782	08/09/1942	3311 912	DFM. Changed name to Winterton
58	24/09/1942	Brown	R	SGT	RAF	78	W7782	08/09/1942	3311 926	
59	24/09/1942	Bradshaw	E	SGT	RAF	49	R5763	02/09/1942	3311 940	
60	29/09/1942	Randle	WSO	SGT	RAF	150	BJ877	16/09/1942	3311 936	
61	29/09/1942	Mounts	DC	SGT	RCAF	150	BJ877	16/09/1942	3311 938	American
62	29/09/1942	Frankowski	TJ	SGT	PAF	305	Z1245	27/08/1942	3311 939	
63	29/09/1942	Pipkin	LC	F/L	RAF	103	W1219	06/09/1942	3311 934	
64	29/09/1942	Prévot	LO	S/L	RAF	122	BM266	30/07/1942	3311 910	Belgian
65	05/10/1942	Frost	R	SGT	RAF	150	BJ877	16/09/1942	3311 937	
66	05/10/1942	Ledford	WH	SGT	RCAF	419	DF665	28/08/1942	3311 948	ss5. Killed in action 23 August 1943 (434 Squadron)
67	05/10/1942	Heap	ET	SGT	RAAF	102	W7677	08/09/1942	3311 949	
68	05/10/1942	Freberg	PG	P/O	RCAF	7	W7630	10/09/1942	3311 935	Killed in action 11 April 1943
69	15/10/1942	Mellor	GH	F/S	RAF	103	W1216	05/10/1942	3311 951	
70	15/10/1942	Joyce	MJ	SGT	RAF	61	P4324	26/08/1940	3311 947	Prisoner of war. Escaped after collaborating with the Germans
71	15/10/1942	Kropf	LE	P/O	RCAF	405	W7770	16/09/1942	3311 950	
72	15/10/1942	Stadnik	AE	SGT	SovAF	None	NK	13/09/1942	3311 946	Escaped Russian airman – see also Pinchuk (No. 76)
73	19/10/1942	Fuller	RJ	CAPT	Army	None	Nil		3311 976	Prisoner of war. Escaped from Oflag VIB on 30/31 August 1942
74	19/10/1942	Coombe-Tennant	AHS	CAPT	Army	None	Nil		3311 975	Prisoner of war. Escaped from Oflag VIB on 30/31 August 1942. Died 3 February 1988
75	19/10/1942	Arkwright	ASB	MAJ	Army	None	Nil		3311 974	Prisoner of war. Escaped from Oflag VIB on 30/31 August 1942
76	19/10/1942	Pinchuk	PK	SGT	SovAF	None	NK	13/09/1942	3311 979	Escaped Russian airman – see also Stadnik (No. 72)
77	12/11/1942	Griffiths	JL	SGT	RAF	102	W7677	08/09/1942	3311 991	DFM
78	20/12/1942	McLean	W	SGT	RAF	7	R9259	06/12/1942	3311 1020	ss7
79	20/12/1942	Brazill	W	SGT	RAF	150	BJ877	16/09/1942	3311 1014	
80	20/12/1942	Hartin	FD	2 LT	USAAF	423	41-24495	09/11/1942	NONE	Comet's first American airman. 306th BG/423rd BS. Target: St Nazaire (see AIR 20/9159)
81	25/12/1942	Smith	RP	SGT	RCAF	115	X3393	09/12/1942	3312 1058	
82	25/12/1942	Spiller	HJ	W/O	RAF	103	W1188	24/10/1942	3312 1042	DFM. Author *Ticket to Freedom*
83	02/01/1943	Reid	JM	SGT	RAF	115	X3393	09/12/1942	3312 1057	
84	02/01/1943	Williams	JE	LT	USAAF	360	41-24585	12/12/1942	NONE	Report in TNA file AIR 20/9159
85	02/01/1943	Schowalter	GT	1 LT	USAAF	360	41-24585	12/12/1942	NONE	Report in TNA file AIR 20/9159
86	02/01/1943	McKee	JR	1 LT	USAAF	367	41-24495	20/12/1942	NONE	B-17F Rose O'Day. Report in TNA file AIR 20/9159
87	14/02/1943	Spence	JW	LT	USAAF	359	41-24603	23/01/1943	NONE	
88	14/02/1943	Devers	S	SGT	USAAF	359	41-24603	23/01/1943	NONE	
89	14/02/1943	Chaster	JB	SGT	RCAF	207	W4134	03/01/1943	3312 1125	
90	02/04/1943	Pierre	MAJ	F/L	RAF	158	DT694	14/02/1943	3313 1171	Belgian
91	15/04/1943	Schloesing	JH	CAPT	FAF	340	BS244	13/02/1943	3313 1192	French. Killed in action 26 August 1944
92	30/04/1943	Wilby	TR	F/O	RAF	78	W7856	11/12/1942	3313 1212	DFC
93	30/04/1943	Curry	JH	SGT	RAF	165	BM518	09/02/1943	3313 1210	Killed in action 25 July 1943
94	30/04/1943	Fegette	IL	SGT	USAAF	360	41-24585	12/12/1942	NONE	
95	30/04/1943	Whitman	WA	SGT	USAAF	360	41-24585	12/12/1942	NONE	
96	10/05/1943	Sibbald	DA	F/S	RNZAF	35	W7851	08/03/1943	3313 1214	
97	10/05/1943	Laws	WR	SGT	RAF	102	HR663	16/04/1943	3313 1215	
98	10/05/1943	Whitley	JR	G/C	RAF	76	JB871	10/04/1943	3313 1211	AFC. Later DSO
99	10/05/1943	Brownhill	GI	SGT	RAF	207	W4172	09/03/1943	3314 1295	
100	10/05/1943	Marion	BM	P/O	RCAF	166	BK361	08/04/1943	3313 1213	
101	23/05/1943	Bolton	KJ	F/O	RAF	102	HR663	16/04/1943	3313 1231	

102	23/05/1943	Crowther	GC	F/O	RCAF	420	HE550	14/04/1943	3313 1230	DFC
103	23/05/1943	Strange	MB	SGT	RAF	76	JB871	10/04/1943	3313 1236	
104	23/05/1943	Davies	MAT	SGT	RAF	76	JB871	10/04/1943	3313 1235	
105	23/05/1943	César	M	CPL	Army	None	Nil		3313 1237	Commando. Left Gibraltar 29/5/43. Arrived Gourock 4/6/43. Recommended for MM
106	31/05/1943	Canter	WL	SGT	RCAF	408	JB909	14/04/1943	3314 1294	DFM
107	31/05/1943	McTaggart	EE	CAPT	USAAF	83	41-6382	14/05/1943	NONE	P-47C
108	31/05/1943	Walls	RE	SGT	USAAF	368	41-24465	05/04/1943	NONE	B-17F Montana Power
109	31/05/1943	Wemheuer	JE	2 LT	USAAF	365	42-29647	13/05/1943	NONE	Met Pilot Officer S.F. Everiss and Sergeant J.B. Ford in Paris
110	04/06/1943	Lashbrook	WI	S/L	RAF	102	HR663	16/04/1943	3314 1264	DFC, DFM
111	04/06/1943	Martin	A	F/O	RAF	102	HR663	16/04/1943	3313 1265	DFC
112	04/06/1943	Hoehn	DC	2 LT	USAAF	322	42-5406	13/05/1943	NONE	
113	19/07/1943	David	JAA	P/O	RAF	76	JB871	10/04/1943	3314 1336	
114	19/07/1943	Raeder	B	LT	RNAF	332	LZ948	13/05/1943	3314 1353	
115	24/07/1943	Murphy	BR	F/O	RAF	124	AB498	17/02/1943	3314 1356	
116	24/07/1943	Koenig	BH	T/SGT	USAAF	358	42-5792	04/07/1943	NONE	B-17F The Mugger
117	24/07/1943	Berckley	RE	F/O	RAF	3	EK227	02/06/1943	3314 1361	Typhoon pilot
118	24/07/1943	Conroy	RT	2 LT	USAAF	333	42-3190	14/07/1943	NONE	B-17F Mr Five by Five
119	10/08/1943	Windsor	KD	SGT	RCAF	403	BS383	20/06/1943	3314 1367	
120	10/08/1943	Hunt	THE	2 LT	USAAF	544	42-30031	26/06/1943	NONE	
121	10/08/1943	Aguiar	W	SGT	USAAF	544	42-30031	26/06/1943	NONE	
122	10/08/1943	Slack	TAH	F/O	RAF	41	EN233	18/07/1943	3314 1366	
123	13/08/1943	Crowe	WF	S/SGT	USAAF	453	41-34706	31/07/1943	NONE	B-26 engineer/tail gunner
124	13/08/1943	Hager	JM	S/SGT	USAAF	453	41-34706	31/07/1943	NONE	B-26 Marauder crew shot down near Poix
125	20/08/1943	Donaldson	LG	SGT	RAF	78	JD108	13/07/1943	3314 1390	
126	20/08/1943	Eldridge	DRG	SGT	RAF	51	HR839	28/06/1943	3314 1389	
127	30/08/1943	Webb	DJ	SGT	RCAF	428	ED209	13/07/1943	3314 1400	
128	30/08/1943	Clarke	R	SGT	RAF	90	EE873	13/07/1943	3314 1401	ss8
129	30/08/1943	Nekrasov	VI	PTE	USSR	None	Nil		3315 1405	Soviet Army. Escaped from German POW camp on night of 21/22 January 1943. With Flight Lieutenant Brinn to UK
130	30/08/1943	Brinn	WG	F/L	RAF	88	BZ242	16/08/1943	3315 1404	DFM
131	02/09/1943	Foster	DC	SGT	RAF	149	EE880	28/06/1943	3315 1406	
132	02/09/1943	White	J	SGT	USAAF	334	42-30274	17/08/1943	NONE	
133	02/09/1943	Funk	LA	SGT	USAAF	335	42-30176	17/08/1943	NONE	B-17F Assassin
134	02/09/1943	Gallerani	BM	T/SGT	USAAF	548	42-5886	17/08/1943	NONE	
135	18/09/1943	O'Leary	JP	P/O	RCAF	428	DK257	13/07/1943	3315 1454	
136	18/09/1943	Harkins	FX	2 LT	USAAF	569	42-3306	15/08/1943	NONE	B-17F Phoenix collided in mid air
137	22/09/1943	Hodge	RA	F/S	RNZAF	149	BF530	03/07/1943	3315 1453	
138	22/09/1943	Kinsella	E	F/O	RAF	88	BZ351	16/08/1943	3315 1444	
139	22/09/1943	Robertson	AL	2 LT	USAAF	350	42-30050	10/07/1943	NONE	Co-pilot of B-17F Judy D shot down on raid to le Bourget airfield
140	22/09/1943	Maher	WP	2 LT	USAAF	358	42-29635	31/08/1943	NONE	B-17F Auger Head
141	24/09/1943	Bailey	WG	SGT	RCAF	429	HZ355	11/06/1943	3316 1541	
142	24/09/1943	Geyer	BG	SGT	USAAF	331	42-30389	17/08/1943	NONE	B-17F Dear Mom
143	27/09/1943	Duffee	GWH	SGT	RAF	78	JB855	22/06/1943	3315 1465	
144	27/09/1943	Bridge	EA	SGT	RCAF	428	ED209	13/07/1943	3315 1462	
145	27/09/1943	Dungey	EB	SGT	RCAF	408	JB913	03/07/1943	3315 1460	
146	27/09/1943	Bowlby	AT	F/S	RCAF	408	JB913	03/07/1943	3315 1459	DFM
147	27/09/1943	Allison	JC	F/O	RAF	107	BZ237	27/08/1943	3315 1461	Same crew as Flying Officer Fairfax and Flight Sergeant R.J.A. Macleod
148	27/09/1943	Baker	G	SGT	RAF	10	JD368	27/08/1943	3316 1586	
149	03/10/1943	Hooker	WJ	2 LT	USAAF	563	42-30202	30/07/1943	NONE	
150	03/10/1943	Aquino	JM	S/SGT	USAAF	335	42-30176	17/08/1943	NONE	B-17F Assassin
151	03/10/1943	Bennett	CA	LT	USAAF	323	42-29559	17/08/1943	NONE	Pilot of B-17F Stup-n-takit shot down on Schweinfurt mission
152	03/10/1943	Walters	JJ	SGT	USAAF	535	42-3225	17/08/1943	NONE	B-17F Chug A-Lug Lulu
153	03/10/1943	Fahncke	KF	SGT	USAAF	327	42-3435	17/08/1943	NONE	B-17F
154	06/10/1943	Cole	CE	MAJ	USAAF	335	42-30194	12/08/1943	NONE	
155	06/10/1943	Claytor	R	1 LT	USAAF	350	42-5867	17/08/1943	NONE	B-17F Alice from Dallas
156	06/10/1943	Cowherd	FC	T/SGT	USAAF	323	42-29559	17/08/1943	NONE	B-17F Stup-n-takit
157	13/10/1943	Macleod	RJA	F/S	RAF	107	BZ237	27/08/1943	3316 1537	Same crew as Flying Officers Fairfax and Allison
158	13/10/1943	Smith	PB	SGT	RAF	61	W4236	09/08/1943	3316 1530	
159	13/10/1943	Buise	JF	T/SGT	USAAF	331	42-3071	14/07/1943	NONE	
160	13/10/1943	Fairfax	NT	F/O	RAF	107	BZ237	27/08/1943	3316 1536	Same crew as Flight Sergeant R.J.A. Macleod and Flying Officer Allison
161	17/10/1943	Rainsford	JE	SGT	RAF	97	JA707	27/08/1943	3316 1562	
162	17/10/1943	Ramsden	O	SGT	RAF	97	JA707	27/08/1943	3316 1563	
163	17/10/1943	Beard	AW	SGT	RAF	77	JD371	27/08/1943	3316 1539	
164	17/10/1943	Palmer	W	SGT	RAF	77	JD371	27/08/1943	3316 1540	
165	24/10/1943	Kellow	RGT	P/O	RAAF	617	JB144	15/09/1943	3316 1597	DFM
166	24/10/1943	Fleszar	M	T/SGT	USAAF	407	42-29725	03/09/1943	NONE	B-17F Hi-lo Jack

167	24/10/1943	Muir	RD	S/SGT	USAAF	407	42-29725	03/09/1943	NONE	B-17F Hi-lo Jack
168	24/10/1943	Catley	WP	SGT	RAF	77	JD371	27/08/1943	3316 1598	
169	27/10/1943	Judy	LG	S/SGT	USAAF	322	42-2990	17/08/1943	NONE	
170	27/10/1943	Diminno	AT	SGT	USAAF	322	42-2990	17/08/1943	NONE	
171	27/10/1943	Street	HT	SGT	RAF	78	JD409	30/08/1943	3316 1555	
172	27/10/1943	Hudson	HJ	P/O	RAF	7	ED595	24/06/1943	3316 1534	DFM
173	30/10/1943	Kellett	AF	SGT	RAF	15	EF348	22/06/1943	3317 1602	
174	30/10/1943	Lawrence	FN	P/O	RAF	10	JD368	27/08/1943	3316 1569	
175	30/10/1943	Penny	HA	F/O	RAF	35	HR878	31/08/1943	3316 1560	
176	30/10/1943	May	SH	SGT	RAAF	41	MB800	19/09/1943	3317 1546	
177	03/11/1943	Berry	JL	S/SGT	USAAF	327	42-3435	17/08/1943	NONE	
178	03/11/1943	Dix	JHJ	SGT	RAF	158	JD298	27/08/1943	3317 1600	
179	03/11/1943	Clary	JT	2 LT	RCAF	434	DK259	29/09/1943	3317 1595	USAAF. Serving on Canadian squadron
180	03/11/1943	Shipe	P	SGT	USAAF	534	42-3227	17/08/1943	NONE	
181	06/11/1943	Dench	RLH	F/S	RAF	182	JP552	19/08/1943	3317 1576	
182	06/11/1943	Cook	WF	F/O	RCAF	421	BS532	03/10/1943	3317 1577	
183	06/11/1943	MacElroy	JD	2 LT	USAAF	413	42-30372	20/10/1943	NONE	B-17F Shack Rabbit III
184	06/11/1943	Czerwinski	A	F/O	PAF	308	AA935	23/09/1943	3317 1578	
185	09/11/1943	Todd	W	SGT	RAF	27 OTU	X3966	23/09/1943	3317 1634	
186	09/11/1943	Shaver	TC	SGT	USAAF	366	41-24591	06/09/1943	NONE	
187	09/11/1943	Allen	J	SGT	USAAF	322	42-2990	17/08/1943	NONE	With Sergeant R.W. Cornelius in Belgium
188	09/11/1943	Clark	J	F/O	RCAF		NK			Not found
189	12/11/1943	Sarnow	HP	2 LT	USAAF	334	42-30274	17/08/1943	NONE	
190	12/11/1943	Douthett	LF	2 LT	USAAF	358	42-29571	20/10/1943	NONE	
191	12/11/1943	Minnich	MG	2 LT	USAAF	334	42-30274	17/08/1943	NONE	
192	12/11/1943	Hartigan	W	LT	USAAF	358	42-29571	20/10/1943	NONE	
193	15/11/1943	Cornelius	RW	SGT	RAF	1663 HCU	JD368	27/08/1943	3317 1632	Flying with 10 Squadron when lost
194	15/11/1943	DePape	RAG	SGT	RCAF	431	LK925	03/10/1943	3317 1633	With Sergeant R.W. Cornelius in Belgium
195	15/11/1943	Metlen	R	S/SGT	USAAF	413	42-30372	20/10/1943	NONE	B-17F Shack Rabbit III. With Sergeant R.W. Cornelius in Belgium
196	18/11/1943	Sheets	HT		USAAF	413	42-30372	20/10/1943	NONE	B-17F Shack Rabbit III. With Sergeant R.W. Cornelius in Belgium
197	18/11/1943	Wallington	WF	S/L	RAF	487	NK	09/10/1943	3317 1638	Born 14 January 1908. Died 25 December 1974
198	18/11/1943	Smith	RD	2 LT	USAAF	349	42-30035	03/09/1943	NONE	B-17F Torchy on raid to Renault works, Paris
199	18/11/1943	Booth	WH	2 LT	USAAF	349	42-30035	03/09/1943	NONE	B-17F Torchy on raid to Renault works, Paris
200	21/11/1943	Mantle	RP	P/O	RAF	138	LW281	18/10/1943	3317 1607	
201	21/11/1943	Rabson	KL	F/S	RAF	138	LW281	18/10/1943	3317 1601	DFM
202	21/11/1943	Connell	JL	T/SGT	USAAF	559	41-31721	21/09/1943	NONE	B-26 Cactus Jack
203	21/11/1943	Wright	DG	S/SGT	USAAF	368	42-30163	06/09/1943	NONE	
204	21/11/1943	Grout	JE	F/S	RAF	138	LW281	18/10/1943	3317 1616	With Staff Sergeant Alfred R. Buinicky USAAF
205	21/11/1943	Frazer	LF	S/SGT	USAAF	556	41-31684	27/09/1943	NONE	B-26
206	27/11/1943	Madgett	GEA	F/O	RAF	138	LW281	18/10/1943	3317 1606	
207	27/11/1943	Hornsey	DG	F/L	RAF	76	LK932	03/11/1943	3317 1610	DFC. Met up with Sergeant G Gineikis USAAF
208	27/11/1943	Macdonald	LE	SGT	USAAF	349	42-30088	05/11/1943	NONE	
209	27/11/1943	Gineikis	G	SGT	USAAF	349	42-30088	05/11/1943	NONE	Met up with Flight Lieutenant D.G. Hornsey
210	03/12/1943	Kennedy	JL	F/L	RCAF	24 OTU	AD675	03/11/1943	3317 1658	
211	03/12/1943	Ward	GH	F/O	RAF	138	LW281	18/10/1943	3317 1631	DFM
212	03/12/1943	Pope	HL	T/SGT	USAAF	349	42-30088	05/11/1943	NONE	
213	03/12/1943	Morley	RC	SGT	RAF	467	JB121	03/11/1943	3317 1682	
214	06/12/1943	Passy	CW	S/L	RAF	138	LW281	18/10/1943	3317 1630	
215	06/12/1943	Mills	DO	2 LT	USAAF	413	42-3439	20/10/1943	NONE	
216	06/12/1943	Johnson	EC	F/O	RAF	617	JB144	15/09/1943	3317 1639	DFC
217	06/12/1943	Clements	RS	F/O	RCAF	57	W4822	03/11/1943	3317 1657	
218	09/12/1943	Malinowski	B	W/O	PAF	302	AA928	08/09/1943	3317 1640	
219	09/12/1943	Harkins	J	F/S	RAF	428	LK931	04/10/1943	3317 1642	
220	09/12/1943	Johnson	HC	SGT	USAAF	563	42-30789	05/11/1943	NONE	B-17F Flak Suit
221	09/12/1943	Watt	G	S/SGT	USAAF	563	42-30789	05/11/1943	NONE	B-17F Flak Suit. Fought in the Spanish Civil War against the Fascists
222	12/12/1943	Maiorca	JJ	LT	USAAF	563	42-30789	05/11/1943	NONE	B-17F Flak Suit
223	12/12/1943	Elliott	JMcP	F/O	RAF	57	W4822	03/11/1943	3317 1662	
224	12/12/1943	Burgin	JW	T/SGT	USAAF	350	42-5867	17/08/1943	NONE	Shot down in B-17F Alice from Dallas on Regensburg raid
225	12/12/1943	Nutting	RJ	2 LT	USAAF	350	42-5867	17/08/1943	NONE	B-17F Alice from Dallas on Regensburg raid
226	15/12/1943	Justice	JK	1 LT	USAAF	349	42-3229	10/10/1943	NONE	Shot down in Holland in B-17F Pasadena Nena on Munster raid
227	15/12/1943	Spicer	CL	2 LT	USAAF	350	42-30818	08/10/1943	NONE	B-17 Salvo Sal
228	15/12/1943	Smith	CN	2 LT	USAAF		NK		NONE	No details

229	15/12/1943	Mellor	AA	F/L	RAF	139	DZ519	20/10/1943	3317 1663	
230	17/12/1943	Witheridge	CH	SGT	RAF	49	LM337	15/08/1943	3317 1665	
231	17/12/1943	Davies	VW	SGT	RAF	10	JD368	27/08/1943	3317 1664	
232	17/12/1943	Norris	HK	SGT	USAAF	410	42-37821	26/11/1943	NONE	Tail gunner. Sole survivor
233	20/12/1943	Whitlow	WB	1 LT	USAAF	550	42-3539	10/10/1943	NONE	
234	20/12/1943	House	WL	T/SGT	USAAF	546	41-24507	06/09/1943	NONE	B-17F Yankee Raider
235	20/12/1943	Ashcraft	JT	SGT	USAAF	550	42-3539	10/10/1943	NONE	
236	20/12/1943	Combs	TE	T/SGT	USAAF	349	42-30035	03/09/1943	NONE	B-17F Torchy on raid to Renault works, Paris
237	21/12/1943	Garvey	K	F/S	RAF	467	JB121	03/11/1943	3318 1709	
238	21/12/1943	Hesselden	T	F/S	RAF	97	JB367	18/11/1943	3318 1710	
239	23/12/1943	Stanford	KLA	2 LT	USAAF	550	42-3539	10/10/1943	NONE	See *The Freedom Line*
240	23/12/1943	Grimes	RZ	2 LT	USAAF	413	42-30372	20/10/1943	NONE	B-17F Shack Rabbit III. See *The Freedom Line* and *Women in the Resistance*, p. 59
241	23/12/1943	Horning	AJ	2 LT	USAAF	401	42-37737	10/10/1943	NONE	B-17F Tennessee Toddy, Munster raid. See *The Freedom Line.* Back in UK on 30/1/44
242	23/12/1943	Burch	JF	2 LT	USAAF	550	42-3539	10/10/1943	NONE	Drowned crossing the Bidassoa, 23/24 December 1943. See *The Freedom Line*
243	28/12/1943	Munns	S	SGT	RAF	428	LK956	19/11/1943	3317 1698	
244	28/12/1943	Applewhite	TB	2 LT	USAAF	548	42-30795	11/11/1943	NONE	B-17F The Wild Hare
245	28/12/1943	Wiggins	TB	SGT	USAAF	364	42-29952	14/10/1943	NONE	B-17F Sizzle
246	28/12/1943	Kevil	EF	SGT	USAAF	365	42-37751	08/10/1943	NONE	
247	30/12/1943	Laming	PB		NONE	None	Nil		NONE	Civilian. Son of Major Richard Laming, first chief of SOE's Dutch Section
248	30/12/1943	Fry	DA	1 LT	USAAF	350	42-8513	14/10/1943	NONE	P-47D Eager Beaver
249	30/12/1943	Lorne	GF	F/O	RAF	218	BK650	30/08/1943	3318 1750	
250	30/12/1943	Parker	NN	F/S	RAAF	75	LJ442	19/11/1943	3318 1745	
251	03/01/1944	MacGillivray	DK	SGT	RCAF	428	LK956	19/11/1943	3317 1697	
252	03/01/1944	Billows	CJ	F/S	RAF	97	JB367	18/11/1943	3318 1711	
253	03/01/1944	Pepper	APW	F/L	RAF	97	JB367	18/11/1943	3318 1749	
254	03/01/1944	Matich	NJ	P/O	RNZAF	35	HR907	27/09/1943	3317 1699	DFM
255	06/01/1944	Lindsay	AG	2 LT	USAAF	554	41-34971	22/08/1943	NONE	B-26 Pay Off
256	06/01/1944	Gilchrist	RC	2 LT	USAAF	412	42-3317	30/11/1943	NONE	
257	06/01/1944	Alukonis	S	2 LT	USAAF	366	42-37750	14/10/1943	NONE	B-17F Mary T
258	06/01/1944	Covington	WI	F/L	RAF	97	JA716	10/08/1943	3318 1707	DFC
259	09/01/1944	Williams	FT	P/O	RAF	97	JB367	18/11/1943	3318 1721	DFM
260	09/01/1944	Gregory	PE	2 LT	USAAF	412	42-3317	30/11/1943	NONE	
261	09/01/1944	Nield	RC	SGT	USAAF	613	42-39840	01/12/1943	NONE	B-17G The Lopin' Lobo. Baled out in error – aircraft returned to base
262	09/01/1944	Sheehan	RE	1 LT	USAAF	63	42-7975	07/11/1943	NONE	P-47D
263	10/01/1944	Hill	FD	F/O	RAF	158	LW298	03/11/1943	3318 1755	
264	10/01/1944	McConnell	PH	2 LT	USAAF	533	42-29928	04/07/1943	NONE	
265	10/01/1944	Hinote	GL	S/SGT	USAAF	333	42-3538	04/10/1943	NONE	B-17G Ten Knights In A Bar Room
266	10/01/1944	Krawszynski	S	S/SGT	USAAF	366	42-37750	14/10/1943	NONE	B-17F Mary T
267	13/01/1944	Wilson	LG	SGT	USAAF	364	42-30807	14/10/1943	NONE	B-17F Katy
268	13/01/1944	Dalinsky	JJ	S/SGT	USAAF	331	42-30389	17/08/1943	NONE	B-17F Dear Mom
269	07/04/1944	Eddy	WEM	F/L	RAF	103	ND417	25/02/1944	3319 1889	See Home Run, Chapter 9
270	22/04/1944	Mattson	WR	T/SGT	USAAF	579	42-7484	29/01/1944	NONE	B-24 Sally Ann
271	22/04/1944	Morrison	LC	P/O	RAAF	408	DS704	20/12/1943	3319 1918	
272	03/05/1944	Brewer	A	S/SGT	USAAF	547	42-29768	01/12/1943	NONE	B-17F Winsome Winn II
273	03/05/1944	Dzwonkowski	HJ	S/SGT	USAAF	67	42-7544	01/12/1943	NONE	B-24 4-Q-2/Seed of Satan II
274	03/05/1944	Wernersbach	RF	2 LT	USAAF	535	42-3540	01/12/1943	NONE	B-17G Bacta-th'-Sac
275	03/05/1944	Wolff	WE	S/SGT	USAAF	360	42-39795	30/12/1943	NONE	B-17G Women's Home Companion
276	03/05/1944	Martin	BT	1 LT	USAAF	357	42-8610	29/01/1944	NONE	P-47D Ready For Action
277	06/05/1944	Teitel	A	1 LT	USAAF	68	42-7501	21/01/1944	NONE	B-24E Bing's Big Box
278	06/05/1944	Reeves	RP	T/SGT	USAAF	68	42-7635	21/01/1944	NONE	B-24E Ramit-Damit. An extra crew member
279	26/05/1944	Miller	JD	LT	USAAF	366	42-31430	20/02/1944	NONE	305th BG
280	26/05/1944	Leslie	CR	S/SGT	USAAF	547	42-30033	01/12/1943	NONE	B-17F Little America
281	26/05/1944	Campbell	N	2 LT	USAAF	360	42-39795	30/12/1943	NONE	B-17G Women's Home Companion
282	26/05/1944	Jacks	WA	F/O	RAF	77	LK710	22/04/1944	3320 1947	
283	26/05/1944	Sheppard	MA	1 LT	USAAF	527	42-31040	29/01/1944	NONE	B-17G Duffy's Tavern
284	04/06/1944	Hubbard	TH	LT COL	USAAF	355	42-7944	13/11/1943	NONE	P-47D Lil' Jo. 355th FG HQ
285	04/06/1944	Willis	DK	MAJ	USAAF	55	42-68077	10/04/1944	NONE	P-38J
286	04/06/1944	Cornett	JD	2 LT	USAAF	375	42-75219	27/04/1944	NONE	P-47D
287	04/06/1944	Barnes	LA	P/O	RAF	630	ND530	15/03/1944	3320 2000	
288	04/06/1944	Emeny	RT	SGT	RAF	207	ND556	03/05/1944	3320 2001	

APPENDIX III

Evaders and escapers evacuated by sea from France and The Netherlands, July 1942 – July 1944

14 July 1942 – HMS *Tarana* from St Pierre-Plage on Operation BLUEBOTTLE I (8 personnel)

Name	Initials	Rank	Sqdn / Regiment	Location prior to evacuation
Beecroft	J.	Sergeant	101	Safe house
Deane-Drummond	A.J.	Lieutenant	Royal Corps of Signals	Safe house
Hanwell	J.P.	Sergeant	101	Safe house
Johnson	T.G.	Sergeant	102	Safe house
Knight	C.G.	Private	Dorset Regiment	Hospital
Miniakowski	S.	Sergeant	300	Hospital
Simon	A.	Flight Lieutenant	Special Operations Executive	Safe house
Straight	W.W.	Squadron Leader	242	Hospital

15 August 1942 – HMS *Tarana* from Canet-Plage on Operation BLUEBOTTLE II (2)

Name	Initials	Rank	Sqdn / Regiment	Location prior to evacuation
Misseldine	J.E.	Sergeant	611	Safe house
Perdue	D.J.	Pilot Officer	12	Safe house

4 September 1942 – *Seadog* from St Pierre-Plage on Operation LEDA II (1)

Name	Initials	Rank	Sqdn / Regiment	Location prior to evacuation
Lockhart	G.	Squadron Leader	161	Safe house

21 September 1942 – *Seawolf* from Canet-Plage on Operation TITANIA (24)

Name	Initials	Rank	Sqdn / Regiment	Location prior to evacuation
Baird	T.	Corporal	Seaforth Highlanders	Revère II
Barnett	M.G.	Flight Lieutenant	485	Revère I
Browne	P.S.F.	Sergeant	485	Revère II
Charman	E.R.	Sergeant	174	Safe house
Dalphond	M.H.J.	Sergeant	405	Revère II
Donnelly	R.	Driver	Royal Army Service Corps	Revère II
Fisher	C.G.	Flight Lieutenant	408	Safe house
Foster	G.T.	Sergeant	138	Safe house
Goulden	J.	Private	East Lancashire Regiment	Revère II
Hawkins	B.L.G.	Flying Officer	245	Revère I
Hickton	H.T.	Sergeant	101	Revère I
Higginson DFM	F.W.	Flight Lieutenant	56	Revère I
Holliday	H.L.	Flight Lieutenant	138	Safe house
Joly*	G.	Private	Les Fusiliers Mont-Royal	Safe house
Kula	F.	Sergeant	305	Safe house
Lafleur*	C.	Private	Les Fusiliers Mont-Royal	Safe house
Nabarro	D.D.W.	Sergeant	10	Revère I
Outram	H.A.	Squadron Leader	138	Safe house
Owen	T.	Lance Corporal	Welsh Fusiliers	Revère II
Saxton	R.W.A.	Sergeant	101	Revère II
Vanier*	R.	Private	Les Fusiliers Mont-Royal	Safe house
Wilkie	J.	Lance Corporal	Royal Army Medical Corps	Safe house
Wilson	L.	Pilot Officer	161	Safe house
Wood	R.E.W.	Pilot Officer	138	Safe house

12 October 1942 – *Seawolf* from Canet-Plage on Operation ROSALIND (32)

Name	Initials	Rank	Sqdn / Regiment	Location prior to evacuation
Andrews	L.	Private	Gordon Highlanders	Revère II
Baker	D.A.	Sergeant	149	Safe house
Berthelsen	F.J.	Sergeant	149	Safe house
Blyth	C.A.	Sergeant	161	Safe house
Boothby	D.C.	Pilot Officer	161	Safe house
Cameron	R.McD.	Private	Queen's Own Cameron Highlanders	Revère II
Croucher	C.W.	Driver	Australian Army Service Corps	Revère II
Daft	G.	Sergeant	35	Safe house
Donnelly	M.	Private	Gordon Highlanders	Revère II
Dumais*	L.A.	Company Sergeant-Major	Les Fusiliers Mont-Royal	Safe house
Griffin	K.H.	Driver	Australian Army Service Corps	Revère II
Howarth	A.	Corporal	Grenadier Guards, No.2 Commando	Revère II
Jenkins	T.J.	Sergeant	149	Safe house
Lines	L.L.	Sapper	Royal Engineers	Revère II
Livingstone	D.	Private	Seaforth Highlanders	Revère II
MacDonald	E.	Private	Glasgow Highlanders	Revère II
MacKay	T.	Private	Seaforth Highlanders	Revère II
Matheson DFC	A.R.	Flight Lieutenant	83	Safe house
McFarlane	F.	Driver	Royal Army Service Corps	Revère II
McLaren	J.	Private	Glasgow Highlanders	Safe house
Mills	A.W.	Sergeant	103	Revère II
Moran	J.	Driver	Royal Army Service Corps	Revère II
Parker	J.W.	Private	Royal Army Service Corps	Revère II
Pearman	L.	Sergeant	101	Revère II
Reed	L.G.A.	Pilot Officer	161	Safe house

Name	Initials	Rank	Sqdn / Regiment	Location prior to evacuation
Robinson	G.E.	Sergeant	149	Safe house
Smith	J.J.	Private	The Buffs	Revère II
Southwell	D.G.	Sergeant	35	Safe house
Wallis	A.H.	Driver	Royal Army Service Corps	Revère II
Walsh	D.S.	Sergeant	15	Revère II
Watson	R.	Private	Loyal Regiment	Fort de la Duchère
Williams	H.	Sergeant	149	Safe house

Note: *Canadian Army – escaped prisoners of war from the Dieppe raid, 19 August 1942.

5-7 February 1943 – *L'Yvonne* from Carantec (3)
RAF (1)
Sergeant R.G. Smith

USAAF (2)
2nd Lieutenant Mark L. McDermott – 303rd BG/427th BS – B-17F 41-24584 Susfu – lost 23 January 1943 #12
Staff Sergeant Sebastian L. Vogel[2003] – 303rd BG/427th BS – B-17F 41-24584 Susfu – lost 23 January 1943 #13

Note: The # symbol here and below followed by a number, e.g. #12, indicates the number of the USAAF E&E Report for that airman.

30 March 1943 – *Jean* from Carantec (1)
USAAF
Sergeant Ernest T. Moriarty – 306th BG/368th BS – B17F 41-24514 – lost 8 March 1943

7-9 April 1943 – *Dalc'h-Mad* from Tréboul (1)
RAF
Flying Officer G.H.F. Carter RCAF

5-6 May 1943 – motor boat from The Netherlands (1)
RAF
Sergeant C.M.M. Mora RNZAF

30 May 1943 – *Météore* from Carantec (1)
USAAF
Staff Sergeant Harold E. Tilbury – 305th BG/364th BS – B17F 42-29663 – lost 17 May 1943

26 July 1943 – motor boat from The Netherlands (2)
RAF
Pilot Officer A. Hagan
Pilot Officer J.B.M. Haye RNethAF

23-24 August 1943 – *Moïse* from Pors Lanvers (Beuzec) (1)
USAAF
[name not known, but the passenger was 'an English airman' according to website http://personal.georgiasouthern.edu/~etmcmull/ESCAPE.htm]

18-20 September 1943 – *Ar-Voualc'h* from Rosmeur harbour, Douarnenez (4)
RAF (2)
Sergeant S. Horton
Sergeant D.R. Parkinson

USAAF (2)
2nd Lieutenant John W. George – 388th BG/560th BS – B17F 42-3293 *Slightly Dangerous* – lost 6 September 1943 #102
Sergeant C.E. Bell – C47 42-92061 – lost 11 August 1943

Note: Bell was the sole survivor of this transport aircraft shot down near Pleuven. See website http://personal.georgiasouthern.edu/~etmcmull/ESCAPE.htm.

2 October 1943 – *La Pérouse* from Douarnenez (2)
USAAF (2)
Staff Sergeant James T. Cimini – 92nd BG/327th BS – B17F 42-5890 – lost 6 September 1943
Staff Sergeant Michael G. Zelenak – 92nd BG/327th BS – B17F 42-5890 – lost 6 September 1943

23-25 October 1943 – *Suzanne-Renée* from Camaret-sur-Mer (19)
RAF (6)
Squadron Leader J.M. Checketts DFC RNZAF
Flight Lieutenant T.J. Hedley
Flying Officer D.F. McGourlick RCAF
Flying Officer A.H. Riseley
2nd Lieutenant S.K. Liby RNorAF
Flight Sergeant T.S.F. Kearins RNZAF

USAAF (13)
1st Lieutenant Demetrius Kamezis – 388th BG/560th BS – B17F 42-3293 *Slightly Dangerous* – lost 6 September 1943 #126
1st Lieutenant Alfred Kramer – 388th BG/563rd BS – B17F 42-30222 *Lone Wolf* – lost 6 September 1943 #128
2nd Lieutenant John W. Bieger jr – 94th BG/331st BS – B17F 42-3071 – lost 14 July 1943 #133
2nd Lieutenant Richard N. Cunningham – 388th BG/563rd BS – B17F 42-3425 *In God We Trust* – lost 6 September 1943 #131
2nd Lieutenant Wayne S. Rader – 379th BG/536th BS – B17F 42-30001 *Mary Ann* – lost 16 August 1943 #137
2nd Lieutenant Jack E. Ryan – 379th BG/536th BS – B17F 42-30001 *Mary Ann* – lost 16 August 1943 #136
2nd Lieutenant Arthur M. Swap – 388th BG/563rd BS – B17F 42-30222 *Lone Wolf* – lost 6 September 1943 #127

Flight Officer Warren E. Graff – 78th FG/82nd FS – P47C 41-6391 – lost 30 July 1943 #130
Technical Sergeant Edwin R. Myers – 381st BG/525th BS – B17F 42-29789 *Bigtime Operator* – lost 3 September 1943 #135
Staff Sergeant Marius L. Brohard – 388th BG/563rd BS – B17F 42-3425 *In God We Trust* – lost 6 September 1943 #132
Staff Sergeant Frank Kimotek – 303rd BG/358th BS – B17F 42-29635 *Augerhead* – lost 31 August 1943 #134
Staff Sergeant Herschell L. Richardson – 92nd BG/327th BS – B17F 42-30000 – lost 6 September 1943 #176
Staff Sergeant William H. Vickless – 388th BG/563rd BS – B17F 42-30222 *Lone Wolf* – lost 6 September 1943 #129

30-31 October 1943 – *Requin* from Carantec (1)
RAF (1)
Flight Sergeant G.A. Wood

1-2 December 1943 – MGB 318 from Ile-Tariec on Operation ENVIOUS IIB (8)
USAAF (8)[2004]
2nd Lieutenant Russell M. Brooke – 305th BG/366th BS – B17F *Rigor Mortis* 42-24591 – lost 6 September 1943 #241
2nd Lieutenant Henry Cabot Rowland – 388th BG/361st BS – B17F 42-30362 *Wee Bonnie II* – lost 9 September 1943 #243
2nd Lieutenant Harold E. Thompson – 388th BG/361st BS – B17F 42-30362 *Wee Bonnie II* – lost 9 September 1943 #242
2nd Lieutenant Merle E. Woodside – 96th BG/337th BS – B17F 42-3348 *Dottie J III* – lost 14 October 1943 #244
Technical Sergeant Clayton H. Burdick – 386th BG/554th BS – B26 41-34971 – lost 22 August 1943 #240
Staff Sergeant Floyd M. Carl – 92nd BG/327th BS – B17F 42-30000 – lost 6 September 1943 #246
Staff Sergeant Duane J. Lawhead – 305th BG/366th BS – B17F *Rigor Mortis* 42-24591 – lost 6 September 1943 #245
Sergeant Joseph F. Quirk jr – 446th BG/707th BS – B24H 42-7640 – lost 18 November 1943 #247

26 December 1943 – MGB 318 from Ile-Tariec on Operation FELICITATE (19)
RAF (2)
Sergeant T.H. Adams
Sergeant H.L. Neilsen

USAAF (11)[2005]
2nd Lieutenant Charles P. Bronner – 96th BG/337th BS – B17F 42-30040 *Wabbit Twacks III* – lost 14 October 1943 #292
2nd Lieutenant Raymond F. Bye – 96th BG/337th BS – B17F 42-3348 *Dottie J III* – lost 14 October 1943 #287
2nd Lieutenant Vernon E. Clark – 96th BG/337th BS – B17F 42-30040 *Wabbit Twacks III* – lost 14 October 1943 #290
Lieutenant Lionel E. Drew jr – 306th BG/423rd BS – B17 – baled out on 26 June 1943 when alarm bell sounded in aircraft #288
2nd Lieutenant Walter Hargrove – 303rd BG/358th BS – B17F 42-29635 *Augerhead* – lost 31 August 1943 #293
2nd Lieutenant Herman A. Schafer jr – 446th NG/707th BS – B24H 42-7640 – lost 18 November 1943 #291
Technical Sergeant William H. Dunning jr – 96th BG/337th BS – B17F 42-30040 *Wabbit Twacks III* – lost 14 October 1943 #296
Technical Sergeant Merle E. Martin – 388th BG/563rd BS – B17F 42-30222 *Lone Wolf* – lost 6 September 1943 #294
Technical Sergeant Allen J. Priebe – 388th BG/563rd BS – B17F 42-30222 *Lone Wolf* – lost 6 September 1943 #295
Staff Sergeant James G. Wilson – 92nd BG/407th BS – B17F 42-30010 – lost 6 September 1943 #289
Staff Sergeant William W. Rice – 92nd BG/407th BS – B17F 42-30010 – lost 6 September 1943 #297

ROYAL NAVY (6)
Sub-Lieutenant M.J. Pollard RNVR
Petty Officer J. Cole RN
Able Seaman R. Bartley RN
Able Seaman C.J.C. Sanders RN
Able Seaman D.E.J. Shepherd RN
Able Seaman V.E. Williams RN

Note: These six Royal Naval personnel had been left behind on Operation ENVIOUS IIB.

22-23 January 1944 – *Breizh-Izel* from Tréboul (14)
RAF (4)
Warrant Officer R.A. Jones RCAF
Sergeant J.D.H. Carleton
Sergeant R. Fidler
Sergeant L.C. Woollard

USAAF (10)
2nd Lieutenant James E. Armstrong – 384th BG/546th BS – B17E 41-24507 *Yankee Raider* – lost 6 September 1943 #339
Technical Sergeant Robert C. Giles – 100th BG/350th BS – B17F 42-30604 *Badger Beauty V* – lost 4 October 1943 #333
Technical Sergeant Carroll F. Haarup – 100th BG/350th BS – B17F 42-30604 *Badger Beauty V* – lost 4 October 1943 #334
Technical Sergeant Thomas R. Moore – 381st BG/535th BS – B17F 42-3225 *Chug-a-lug Lulu* – lost 17 August 1943
Staff Sergeant Harry H. Horton jr – 381st BG/534th BS – B17F 42-3227 – lost 17 August 1943
Staff Sergeant Joseph M. Kalas – 384th BG/546th BS – B17F 42-3459 – lost 23 September 1943
Staff Sergeant Leonard J. Kelly – 384th BG/546th BS – B17F 42-3459 – lost 23 September 1943
Staff Sergeant Edward F. Sobolewski – 381st BG/534th BS – B17F 42-3227 – lost 17 August 1943
Sergeant Ardell H. Bollinger – 384th BG/546th BS – B17F 42-3459 – lost 23 September 1943 #335

Note: The tenth USAAF airman has not yet been identified.

28-29 January 1944 – MGB 503 from Sous-Kéruzeau on Operation BONAPARTE I (16)
RAF (3)
Flying Officer S.P.J. Blackwell
Sergeant N.B. Cufley
Sergeant J. Harvey

USAAF (13)
1st Lieutenant Donald J. Heskett – 44th BG/66th BS – B24H 42-7548 *Bull o' the Woods* – lost 30 December 1943 #347
1st Lieutenant Richard M. Smith – 95th BG/336th BS – B17F 42-30674 *Kathy Jane III* – lost 30 December 1943 #349
2nd Lieutenant William H. Booher – 95th BG/336th BS – B17F 42-30674 *Kathy Jane III* – lost 30 December 1943 #350

2nd Lieutenant Sidney Casden – 384th BG/546th BS – B17F 42-30058 – lost 26 June 1943 #355
2nd Lieutenant Morton B. Shapiro – 309th BG/564th BS – B24D 42-63973 – lost 30 December 1943 #353
Technical Sergeant Andrew F. Hathaway – 100th BG/349th BS – B17G 42-31215 – lost 26 November 1943 #346
Technical Sergeant Alphonse M. Mele – 95th BG/336th BS – B17F 42-30674 *Kathy Jane III* – lost 30 December 1943 #351
Staff Sergeant Walter E. Dickerman – 447th BG/711th BS – B17G 42-31173 *Maid To Please* – lost 30 December 1943 #354
Staff Sergeant Jerry Eshuis – 95th BG/36th BS – B17F 42-30674 *Kathy Jane III* – lost 30 December 1943 #352
Staff Sergeant James A. King – 305th BG/365th BS – B17F 42-29530 *Boom Town Jnr* – lost 27 August 1943 #343
Staff Sergeant Walter J. Sentkoski – 390th BG,569th BS – B17F 42-3306 *Phoenix* – lost 15 August 1943 #348
Sergeant Fred T. Schmidt – 392nd BG/578th BS – B24H 42-7588 – lost 30 December 1943 #344
Sergeant John L. Sullivan jr. – 392nd BG/578th BS – B24H 42-7588 – lost 30 December 1943 #345

2-3 February 1944 – *Le Jouet-des-Flots* failed evacuation (8)
RAF (2)
Flying Officer J.G. Pilkington – 161 Squadron – Halifax EB129 – lost 10/11 November 1943 (SOE operations)
Flying Officer J.H. Watlington RCAF (see list in Appendix I)

Note: Pilkington was taken prisoner of war and sent to Stalag Luft III (Sagan) and, late in January 1945, to Stalag IIIA (Luckenwalde).

USAAF (4)
2nd Lieutenant Roy G. Davidson Jr – 94th BG/333rd BS – B17F 42-30453 *Thunderbird* – lost 14 October 1943
Technical Sergeant Ralph Hall – 94th BG/331st BS – B17G 42-31212 – lost 5 January 1944
Staff Sergeant Lee C. Gordon – 305th BG/365th BS – B17F 41-24623 – lost 26 February 1943
Staff Sergeant Fred C. Krueger – 94th BG/333rd BS – B17F 42-30453 *Thunderbird* – lost 14 October 1943

Note: Davidson was captured and sent to Stalag Luft III in April 1944. Krueger was captured along with Davidson. Hall remained undetected in Douarnenez until liberated by his fellow countrymen on 22 August 1944. Gordon returned to Paris. He had escaped from Stalag VIIA (Moosburg), and was possibly the only American airmen to escape from a prisoner-of-war camp and to make a "home run". He made two failed escape attempts from Stalag VIIA, including one on a bicycle while yelling the only German he knew, 'Heil, Hitler!' He finally escaped after exchanging identification with an Australian prisoner of war. Getting on a work detail outside the camp he bribed guards with coffee and cigarettes and hid in a bathroom stall until dark. He then jumped a fence when a guard's back was turned and walked out of the camp. He caught a goods train to France, where he made contact with a Resistance group, and returned to England on Operation BONAPARTE II (see below).[2006]

Royal Indian Army Service Corps (2)
Sergeant Shahzaman, escaped prisoner of war
Cook Buland Khan, escaped prisoner of war

Note: Shahzaman had been caught when his papers failed to satisfy an inquisitive gendarme. Sent to a stalag in France again, he escaped on 1 September 1944, and was liberated shortly afterwards by the Americans. Khan, whose papers had satisfied the policeman, came back on Operation BONAPARTE IV (see below).

26-27 February 1944 – MGB 503 from Sous-Kéruzeau on Operation BONAPARTE II (17)
RAF (1)
Flight Sergeant L.J.G. Harmel

USAAF (16)
2nd Lieutenant Milton L. Church – 94th BG/331st BS – B17G 42-31212 – lost 5 January 1944 #423
2nd Lieutenant Louis Feingold – 95th BG/336th BS – B17F 42-30674 *Kathy Jane III* – lost 30 December 1943 #419
2nd Lieutenant Ernest H. Hugonnet – 94th BG/410th BS – B17F 42-30200 *Solo Time Sally* – lost 5 January 1944 #425
2nd Lieutenant James A. Schneider – 91st BG/324th BS – B17F 42-29895 *The Black Swan* – lost 31 December 1943 #432
2nd Lieutenant Warren C. Tarkington – 95th BG/336th BS – B17F 42-30674 *Kathy Jane III* – lost 30 December 1943 #420
Technical Sergeant Kenneth O. Blye – 94th BG/331st BS – B17G 42-31212 – lost 5 January 1944 #424
Technical Sergeant James N. Quinn – 91st BG/324th BS – B17F 42-29895 *The Black Swan* – lost 31 December 1943 #433
Staff Sergeant Lee C. Gordon – 305th BG/365th BS – B17F 41-24623 – lost 26 February 1943 #434
Staff Sergeant Donald D. McLeod – 94th BG/410th BS – B17F 42-30200 *Solo Time Sally* – lost 5 January 1944 #426
Staff Sergeant Harry L. Minor – 379th BG/525th BS – B17F 42-29876 *Battlin' Bobbie* – lost 16 September 1943 #421
Staff Sergeant Mike Olynik – 96th BG/337th BS – B17F 42 3348 *Dottie J III* – lost 14 October 1943 #431
Staff Sergeant John P. Semach – 379th BG/524th BS – B17F 42-29893 *El Diablo* – lost 16 September 1943 #422
Sergeant Harold O. Gilley – 94th BG/410th BS – B17F 42-30200 *Solo Time Sally* – lost 5 January 1944 #428
Sergeant Marion A. Hall – 94th BG/410th BS – B17F 42-30200 *Solo Time Sally* – lost 5 January 1944 #427
Sergeant Robert A. Schwartzburg – 94th BG/410th BS – B17F 42-30200 *Solo Time Sally* – lost 5 January 1944 #429
Sergeant Robert C. Southers – 94th BG/410th BS – B17F 42-30200 *Solo Time Sally* – lost 5 January 1944 #430

26-27 February 1944 – MGB 502 from Beg-an-Fry on Operation EASEMENT II (1)
RAF (1)
Flying Officer W.V. Mollett

16-17 March 1944 – MGB 502 from Sous-Kéruzeau on Operation BONAPARTE III (24)
RAF (1)
Sergeant D. Brown

USAAF (23)
2nd Lieutenant Shirley D. Berry – 389th BG/567th BS – B24D 42-40747 *Heavy Date* – lost 7 January 1944 #456
2nd Lieutenant Joseph A. Birdwell – 390th BG/569th BS – B17F 42-3306 *Phoenix* – lost 15 August 1943 #471
2nd Lieutenant William T. Campbell – 94th BG/333rd BS – B17G 42-37815 *Miss Lace* – lost 26 November 1943 #473
2nd Lieutenant Philip A. Capo – 385th BG/548th BS – B17G 42-31380 – lost 8 February 1944 #459
2nd Lieutenant Edward J. Donaldson – 379th BG/527th BS – B17F 42-29963 *Judy* – lost 30 December 1943 #460
2nd Lieutenant Jack McGough – 94th BG/331st BS – B17G 42-31212 – lost 5 January 1944 #475
2nd Lieutenant Ralph K. Patton[2007] – 94th BG/331st BS – B17G 42-31212 – lost 5 January 1944 #476
2nd Lieutenant Manuel M. Rogoff – 389th BG/567th BS – B24D 42-40747 *Heavy Date* – lost 7 January 1944 #455
2nd Lieutenant William H. Spinning – 351st BG/509th BS – B17F 42-29863 *Kentucky Babe* – lost 11 February 1944 #477

2nd Lieutenant Dean W. Tate – 379th BG/526th BS – B17F 42-29633 – lost 8 February 1944 #467
2nd Lieutenant Charles B. Winkelman – 100th BG/349th BS – B17F 42-30035 *Torchy* – lost 3 September 1943 #468
Technical Sergeant John T. Amery – 100th BG/351st BS – B17F 42-5997 *Heaven Can Wait* – lost 30 December 194 #469
Technical Sergeant Kenneth P. Christian – 384th BG/544th BS – B17G 42-39784 *Cabin In The Sky* – lost 8 February 1944 #472
Technical Sergeant William C. Lessig – 379th BG/526th BS – B17F 42-29633 – lost 8 February 1944 #466
Technical Sergeant Harold R. Vines – 389th BG/567th BS – B24D 42-63977 *Los Angeles City Limits* – lost 7 January 1944 #457
Staff Sergeant Robert K. Fruth – 93rd BG/328th BS – B24H 42-7614 – lost 7 January 1944 #462
Staff Sergeant Frank J. Moast – 94th BG/333rd BS – B17G 42-37815 *Miss Lace* – lost 26 November 1943 #474
Staff Sergeant Russell L. Paquin – 389th BG/567th BS – B24D 42-40747 *Heavy Date* – lost 7 January 1944 #458
Staff Sergeant Everett E. Stump – 92nd BG/326th BS – B17G 42-37984 – lost 8 February 1944 #463
Sergeant Charles W. Creggor – 44th BG/66th BS – B24H 42-7548 *Bull o' The Woods* – lost 30 December 1943 #470
Sergeant Carl W. Mielke – 305th BG/364th BS – B17G 42-40020 *Good Pickin'* – lost 8 February 1944 #465
Sergeant Neelan B. Parker – 379th BG/527th BS – B17F 42-29963 *Judy* – lost 30 December 1943 #461
Sergeant Carlyle A. Van Selus – 92nd BG/326th BS – B17G 42-37984 – lost 8 February 1944 #464

19-20 March 1944 – MGB 503 from Sous-Kéruzeau on Operation BONAPARTE IV (17)
USAAF (16)
1st Lieutenant Francis P. Hennesy – 388th BG/363rd BS – B17F 42-3285 *Mary Ellen* – lost 29 January 1944 #496
1st Lieutenant Glenn B. Johnson – 94th BG/331st BS – B17G 42-31212 – lost 5 January 1944 #494
1st Lieutenant Earl J. Wolf jr – 306th BG/423rd BS – B17G 42-31388 – lost 11 February 1944 #487
2nd Lieutenant Robert L. Costello – 452nd BG/730th BS – B17G 42-31325 – lost 8 February 1944 #490
2nd Lieutenant Norman R. King – 94th BG/410th BS – B17F 42-30200 *Solo Time Sally* – lost 5 January 1944 #493
2nd Lieutenant Robert O. Lorenzi – 452nd BG/730th BS – B17G 42-31325 – lost 8 February 1944 #489
2nd Lieutenant John A. McGlynn – 7th PRG/13th PRS – F5 – lost 14 February 1944 #502
2nd Lieutenant Paul E. Packer – 452nd BG/730th BS – B17G 42-31325 – lost 8 February 1944 #491
2nd Lieutenant Clyde C. Richardson – 388th BG/363rd BS – B17F 42-3285 *Mary Ellen* – lost 29 January 1944 #497
2nd Lieutenant Richard F. Schafer – 309th BG/564th BS – B24D 42-63973 – lost 30 December 1943 #499
Technical Sergeant Elmer D. Risch – 44th BG/66th BS – B-24H 42-7548 *Bull O' The Woods* – lost 30 December 1943 #498
Staff Sergeant Leonard F. Bergeron – 306th BG/423rd BS – B17G 42-31388 – lost 11 February 1944 #488
Staff Sergeant Paul F. Dicken – 309th BG/564th BS – B24D 42-63973 – lost 30 December 1943 #500
Staff Sergeant William J. Scanlon – 92nd BG/326th BS – B17G 42-37984 – lost 8 February 1944 #501
Staff Sergeant Edward J. Sweeney – 452nd BG/730th BS – B17G 42-31325 – lost 8 February 1944 #492
Staff Sergeant Isadore C. Viola – 94th BG/331st BS – B17G 42-31212 – lost 5 January 1944 #495

Royal Indian Army Service Corps (1)
Cook Buland Khan, escaped prisoner of war.

23-24 March 1944 – MGB 503 from Sous-Kéruzeau on Operation BONAPARTE V (26)
RAF (5)
Flying Officer R.E. Barnlund RCAF
Flying Officer G.C. Brickwood
Pilot Officer R.W. Daniel RAAF
Sergeant K.E. Lussier RCAF
Flying Officer K.B. Woodhouse RCAF

USAAF (21)
1st Lieutenant William B. Lock – 92nd BG/326th BS – B-17G 42-31175 *Trudy* – lost 11 January 1944 #531
1st Lieutenant Milton L. Rosenblatt – 44th BG/68th BS – B24E 42-7501 *Bing's Big Box* – lost 21 January 1944 #520
1st Lieutenant Milton V. Shevchik – 92nd BG/326th BS – B17G 42-37984 – lost 8 February 1944 #527
2nd Lieutenant Alfred T. Coffman jr – 381st BG/525th BS – B17G 42-40025 *Touch the Button Nell* – 6 February 1944[2008] #533
2nd Lieutenant William A. Hoffman III – 92nd BG/326th BS – B17G 42-31387 – lost 8 February 1944 #530
2nd Lieutenant Robert V. Laux – 381st BG/532nd BS – B17G 42-31099 *Tenabuo* – lost 11 February 1944 #521
2nd Lieutenant James M. Thorson – 92nd BG/326th BS – B17G 42-37984 – lost 8 February 1944 #528
2nd Lieutenant Phlemon T. Wright – 381st BG/532nd BS – B17G 42-31099 *Tenabuo* – lost 11 February 1944 #522
Technical Sergeant Robert J. Rujawitz – 93rd BG/409th BS – B24 42-100345 – lost 2 March 1944 #534
Staff Sergeant John F. Bernier – 379th BG/526th BS – B17F 42-29633 – lost 8 February 1944 #537
Staff Sergeant George P. Buckner – 92nd BG/326th BS – B17G 42-31387 – lost 8 February 1944 #539
Staff Sergeant David G. Helsel – 379th BG/526th BS – B17F 42-29633 – lost 8 February 1944 #538
Staff Sergeant Charles H. Mullins – 92nd BG/326th BS – B-17G 42-31175 *Trudy* – 11 January 1944 #532
Staff Sergeant Keith W. Sutor – 389th BG/567th BS – B24D 42-40747 *Heavy Date* – lost 7 January 1944 #536
Staff Sergeant Robert H. Sweatt – 389th BG/566th BS – B24D 42-41013 *Trouble 'n Mind* – lost 7 January 1944 #535
Sergeant Rudolph Cutino – 381st BG/532nd BS – B17G 42-31099 *Tenabuo* – lost 11 February 1944 #525
Sergeant Thomas J. Glennan – 381st BG/532nd BS – B17G 42-31099 *Tenabuo* – lost 11 February 1944 #523
Sergeant Richard C. Hamilton – 381st BG/532nd BS – B17G 42-31099 *Tenabuo* – lost 11 February 1944 #526
Sergeant Abe A. Helfgott – 381st BG/532nd BS – B17G 42-31099 *Tenabuo* – lost 11 February 1944 #524
Sergeant Francis C. Wall – 92nd BG/326th BS – B17G 42-37984 – lost 8 February 1944 #529
Sergeant David Warner – 92nd BG/326th BS – B17G 42-31387 – lost 8 February 1944. #540
Note: Also returning on MGB 503 were French agent Le Bourhis and Jean Tréhiou, Resistance worker for the Shelburne line.

15-16 April 1944 – MGB 502 from Beg-an-Fry on Operation SCARF (3)
RAF (1)
Flying Officer G.G. Racine RCAF

USAAF (2)
1st Lieutenant K.R. Williams[2009] – 355th FG/354th FS – P47D 42-8443 *Hell's Angels II* – lost 26 March 1944 #555
Sergeant Richard J. Faulkner – 100th BG/330th BS – B17G 42-39830 *Berlin Playboy* – lost 18 March 1944 #556

Note: Also brought back on this operation were Suzanne Warenghem and Blanche Charlet (see Chapter 8).

12-13 July 1944 Operation – MGB 503 from Sous-Kéruzeau on Operation CROZIER I (13)
RAF (6)
Flight Lieutenant L.W.F. Stark DFC
Flying Officer H.J. Brennan RCAF
Pilot Officer A.J. Houston RCAF
Sergeant A. Elder
Sergeant R.J. Dickson
Sergeant E.J. Trottier RCAF

USAAF (4)
1st Lieutenant Richard J. Gordon – 362nd FG/379th FS – P47D 42-26111 – lost 17 June 1944 #830
1st Lieutenant Frank L. Lee jr – 362nd FG/379th FS – P47D 42-25304 – lost 17 June 1944[2010] #831
2nd Lieutenant William C. Hawkins – 4th FG/335th FS – P51B 43-6316 – lost 21 March 1944 #832
2nd Lieutenant Joseph A. Lilly – 354th FG/355th FS – P51 43-6441 – lost 26 April 1944. #833

Royal Navy (3)
Sub Lieutenant M.I.G. Hamilton RNVR
Leading Seaman A.H. Dellow RNVR
Ordinary Seaman H.D. Rockwood RNVR

Note: These three Royal Naval personnel had mistakenly been left behind in France on Operation REFLEXION, 15/16 April 1944.

24-25 July 1944 – MGB 502 from Sous-Kéruzeau on Operation CROZIER II (5)
RAF (2)
Squadron Leader P.H. Smith (see end of Chapter 8)
Flight Sergeant T.P. Fargher

USAAF (1)
Major William A. Jones – 367th FG/393rd FS – P38J 42-104277 – lost 24 May 1944 #834

SAS (2)
Major O.A.J. Cary-Elwes (Lincolnshire Regiment)
Serjeant E. Mills.

APPENDIX IV

Marathon: 1944

Names of some of the Allied personnel held in camps in (a) Fréteval Forest, France from June to August 1944 (Operation Sherwood), and (b) in camps in the Belgian Ardennes during September 1944 (Marathon).

(A) Sherwood

RAF (34)

Berry, L.F., Flight Lieutenant
Blakey, J., Sergeant
Brakes, B.E., Flight Sergeant
Brown, W.C., Sergeant
Chamberlain, H., Pilot Officer
Charman, A.F., Sergeant
Clay, L.N., Flight Sergeant
Dickens, J.D., Sergeant
Dickie, K.J.A., Flying Officer
Donaldson, W.A., Sergeant
Elmhirst-Baxter, J.C., Flight Lieutenant
Evans, J.H., Flight Sergeant
Finn, J.P.T., Sergeant
? Fisher, J.M., Sergeant
Foley, A.J., Flight Sergeant
Gordon, R.B., Flying Officer
Guild, H., Flight Sergeant
Hallett, C.L., Sergeant
Hampton, R., Sergeant
Hand, G., Sergeant
Holland, F.E., Flight Lieutenant
Kemley, H.J.S., Flight Lieutenant
Lyons, A.R., Sergeant
Martin, C.H.T., Sergeant
McCarthy, N.J., Sergeant
? Meanley, R., Sergeant
? Noakes, E.E.G., Sergeant
Pepall, D.R.R.J., Flight Sergeant
Pryer, W.R., Sergeant
Smith, M., Sergeant
Weir, C.F., Sergeant
Wells, F.A., Flight Sergeant
Worrall, J.R.W., Sergeant
Wright, E.W., Sergeant

RAAF (11)

Andrews, K.G., Sergeant
Eliot, N.S., Flying Officer
Evans, F.O., Flight Sergeant
Flynn, W.J., Flight Sergeant
Greatz, E.H., Flight Sergeant
Hourigan, E., Flying Officer
Ibbotson, D.T., Flying Officer
King, W.J.E., Warrant Officer
Lynch, K.J., Flight Sergeant
Murray, R.I., Flight Sergeant
Schwilk, C.W., Flight Sergeant

Belgian Air Force (1)

Croquet, J.L.J., Pilot Officer

RCAF (31)

Agur, P.G., Flying Officer
Banks, R.H., Sergeant
Beauchesne, N.E., Sergeant
Bender, W.F., Flying Officer
Bester, J.F., Flying Officer
Binnie, N., Sergeant
Brayley, W.E.J., Warrant Officer 2nd Class
Calderbank, J.R., Flying Officer
Campbell, E.A., Flight Lieutenant
Chapman, J.E., Flying Officer
Chapman, T.B., Sergeant
Cowan, R.E., Sergeant
Dunseith, S., Flight Sergeant
Fairborn, D.W.R., Sergeant
Forman, C.M., Flying Officer
Gordon, R.T., Sergeant
Greenburgh, L., Flying Officer
Grimsey, M.F.C., Flying Officer
Harvey, S.A., Flight Sergeant
Hortie, R.H., Sergeant
Hyde, D.B., Flight Sergeant
Jones, E.R., Flight Sergeant
Kennedy, J.F., Flying Officer
Logan, P.N.J., Flight Lieutenant
Mollison, J.J., Pilot Officer
Musgrove, G.A., Flying Officer
Sandulak, J., Sergeant
Shields, W.C., Flying Officer
Taylor, S.D., Flying Officer
Vickerman, W.K., Flying Officer
Wiome, M., Flying Officer

RNZAF (4)

Morris, J.M., Flying Officer
Raynel, W.G., Flight Sergeant
Sanders, G.H., Flying Officer
Speirs, A.R., Pilot Officer

Polish Air Force (1)

Witrylak, Z., Flight Sergeant

South African Army (2)

Adams, E., Private
Hoover, R., Private

USAAF (58)

Allen, Eacott G.; 2/Lt; P; P-51B; 42-106823; 489th FG/847th FS; 8 June 1944.
Andersen, Eugene C.; Sgt; BTG; B-24H; 42-9433; 489th BG/846th BS; 2 June 1944. E&E #1451.[2011]
Barr, Stuart K.; F. O.; CP; B-24H; 42-64447; 448th BG/712th BS; 20 March 1944.
Bies, Walter E.; S/Sgt; TG; B-24J; 42-100294; 93rd BG/328th BS; 24 June 1944.
Blair, Clara A.; Sgt; RWG; B-24H; 42-95310; 491st BG/852nd BS; 2 June 1944. E&E #1008.
Boggan, ; 2/Lt; NK.
Bone, Emmett W.; S/Sgt; LWG; B-17G; 42-31380; 385th BG/548th BS; 8 February 1944. E&E #1011.
? Clark, Paul R.; S/Sgt; RO; B-17G; 42-31594; 457th BG/751st BS; 27 May 1944.
Claytor, Andrew G.; 2/Lt; P; B-17F; 42-3511; 381st BG/535th BS; 25 April 1944. E&E #1021.
Connable, Joseph M.; Sgt; RWG; B-17F; 42-3511; 381st BG/535th BS; 25 April 1944. E&E #1025.
Couture, Robert D.; 2/Lt; P; P-51B; 43-6895; 355th FG/354th FS; 7 June 1944. E&E #997.
Davis, William M.; NK; P; P-38J; 43-28464; 370th FG/NK; 7 July 1944. E&E #1039.

Derling, Clifford G.; NK
Dibetta, Geno; 1/Lt; P; B-17G; 42-31388; 306th BG/423rd BS; 11 February 1944. E&E #962.
Dillon, William T.
Duer, Walter A.; 2/Lt; B; B-24H; 41-29468 *Peg o' My Heart*; 487th BG/838th BS; 11 May 1944.
Eckley, Malcolm K; S/Sgt; LWG; B-17G; 42-97859; 100th BG/418th BS; 25 June 1944. E&E #1004.
Gleason, F; T/Sgt; TTG; B-17G; 43-37788; 447th BG/709th BS; 13 July 1944. E&E #1065.
Goan, John F.; S/Sgt; TG; B-24H; 42-95280; 445th BG/702nd BS; 27 June 1944. E&E #1020.
Goff, Marvin T.; 2/Lt; B; B-24J; 42-110087; 448th BG/713th BS; 1 April 1944. E&E #999.
Golden jr, Guy H.; S/Sgt; RWG; B-17G; 42-31388; 306th BG/423rd BS; 11 February 1944. E&E #1000.
Gorrano, Joseph F.; T/Sgt; TTG; B-17G; 42-31380; 385th BG/548th BS; 8 February 1944. E&E #1010.
Hall, Ralph L.; 2/Lt; CP; B-24H; 42-95280; 445th BG/702nd BS; 27 June 1944. E&E #1019.
Harrell, Max; 2/Lt; P; P-51B; 43-6886; 355th FG/357th FS; 7 June 1944.
Hewitt, C. Edward; T/Sgt; RO; B-17G; 42-31388; 306th BG/423rd BS; 11 February 1944. E&E #1058.
Hjelm, Rex P.; 1/Lt; P; P-38J; 42-68102; 55th FG/343rd FS; 11 June 1944. E&E #992
Hoilman, Donald F.; S/Sgt; TG; B-17G; 42-31380; 385th BG/548th BS; 8 February 1944. E&E #1052.
Holt, Alfred I.; Sgt; TTG; B-25H; 42-97188; 384th BG; 544th BS; 14 June 1944.
Houghton, Kenneth L.; P; B-17G; 42-97859; 100th BG/418th BS; 25 June 1944. E&E #1003.
Johnson, Joseph; NK
Kaplan, William; 2/Lt; P; B-24H; 42-52579; 493rd BG/862nd BS; 22 June 1944. E&E #1105.
Kellerman, William M.; NK
Klemstine, Kenneth P.; CP; B-24H; 42-52579; 493rd BG/862nd BS; 22 June 1944. E&E #1104.
Knight, Marion; Sgt; TG; B-17G; 42-31387; 92nd BG/326th BS; 8 February 1944.
Krol, Theodore J.; 2/Lt; B; B-17G; 42-38033; 401st BG/612th BS; 20 March 1944. E&E #1017.
Lane, Joshua D.; T/Sgt; TTG; B-17G; 42-31568; 457th BG/748th BS; 14 June 1944.
Lay, Beirne; 2/Lt; B; B-24H; 41-29468 *Peg o' My Heart*; 487th BG/838th BS; 11 May 1944.
Lewis, Donald M.; NK
Loring, Warren E.; 2/Lt; P; P-38J; 42-67876; 55th FG/343rd FS; 30 June 1944. E&E #993.
Middleton, Charles D.; S/Sgt; B; B-17F; 42-3511; 381st BG/535th BS; 25 April 1944. E&E #1023.
Pearson, Jonathan; Lt; N; B-17G; 42-31565; NK/NK; 4 March 1944.
Peloquin, Joseph O.; S/Sgt; TTG; B-24H; 42-94999; 44th BG/506th BS; 11 May 1944. E&E #1054.
Peterson, Edward I.; 2/Lt; CP; B-17G; 42-31648 *Ensign Mary*; 379th BG/526th BS; 16 June 1944.
Reedy, Edward F.; S/Sgt; – ;B-24H; 42-95310; 491st BG/852nd BS; 2 June 1944. E&E #1007.
Rice, Roy J.; 2/Lt; CP; B-17F; 42-3511; 381st BG/535th BS; 25 April 1944. E&E #1022.
Richards, Lawrence C.; Sgt; LWG; B-24H; 42-94999; 44th BG/506th BS; 11 May 1944.
Schilling, Kenneth W.; Capt; B; B-24J; 42-100294; 93rd BG/328th BS; 24 June 1944. E&E #1029.
Sidders, Robert E.; S/Sgt; RO; B-17G; 42-37984; 92nd BG/326th BS; 8 February 1944. E&E #1056.
Solomon, George; T/Sgt; RO; B-17G; 42-31380; 385th BG/548th BS; 8 February 1944. E&E #1217.
Souder, David W.; Sgt; BTG; B-17F; 42-3511; 381st BG/535th BS; 25 April 1944. E&E #1024.
Spinks, Heyward C.; 2/Lt; P; P-51B; 43-6985; 357th FG/ 364th FS; 20 June 1944. E&E #963.
Tickner, Russell E.; 2/Lt; B; B-24H; 42-95310; 491st BG/852nd BS; 2 June 1944. E&E #1006.
Vitkus, Ray D.; Sgt; TG; B-17F; 42-3511; 381st BG/535th BS; 25 April 1944. E&E #1026.
Weseloh, E.C.; S/Sgt; TG; B-17G; 42-31388; 306th BG/423rd BS; 11 February 1944. E&E #1001.
Wiseman, Abraham; 2/Lt; N; B-25H; 42-97188; 384th BG/544th BS; 14 June 1944.
Wright, Norman; S/Sgt; RWG; B-24J; 42-100294 *Victory Belle*; 93rd BG/328th BS; 24 June 1944.
Yankus, Thomas L.; Cpl; RO; B-17G; 42-31565; NK/NK; 4 March 1944. E&E #1064.
? Yanzek, William J.; T/Sgt; LWG; B-17G; 42-97454; 381st BG/533rd BS; 19 May 1944.

Notes:
(1) USAAF personnel details are given in the following sequence: Name, initials; Rank; Crew position; Aircraft type; Aircraft number (and name, if any); Bomb or Fighter Group/Squadron; Date lost.
(2) Ranks are (in seniority): Capt – Captain; 1/Lt – 1st Lieutenant; 2/Lt – 2nd Lieutenant; FO – Flight Officer; T/Sgt – Technical Sergeant; S/Sgt – Staff Sergeant; Sgt – Sergeant; Cpl – Corporal.
(3) Crew positions are: P – Pilot; CP – Co-pilot; N – Navigator; B – Bombardier; RO – Radio Operator; BTG – Ball turret gunner; TTG – Top turret gunner; TG – Tail gunner; LWG/RWG – Left/Right waist gunner.
(4) E&E # indicates the number of the USAAF airman's report.
(5) A question mark ("?") in front of the name indicates that it is not clear that that person was on Shewood.

(B) Some of the airmen held in Marathon camps, Belgian Ardennes, September 1944

RAF (23)	**Camps (where known)**
Barton, A.E.J.	Beffe, Acremont, Porcheresse
Best, A.	Villance, Acremont
Bleddin, R.	[not found]
Burton, J.T.H.	Hidden at Waterloo for 4 months with Sergeant Lester Miller Hutchinson USAAF
Dawson, R.	Beffe, Bellevaux, Acremont
Dumbrell, A.G.	Hidden at Wavre and Brussels
Evans, J.H.	Beffe, Acremont, Porcheresse, Bohan-sur-Semois
Flather, G.E.H.	Acremont, Daverdisse
Gunnell, A.F.	Bellevaux
Irwin, R.P.	Bellevaux, Acremont
Lloyd, D.A.	Beffe, Acremont, Porcheresse, Villance, Bohan-sur-Semois
MacKnight, J.	Porcheresse
McCoy, K.L.D.	
Moreton, R.	Beffe, Acremont, Porcheresse, Villance
Rae, A.M.	
Reading, R.	
Robertson, F.W.C.	Beffe, Acremont, Porcheresse
Shaw, F.G.	
Stone, J.W.	Porcheresse
Tweedy, P.	
Walmsley, A.H.	Acremont

Weeden, R.A.	Beffe, Porcheresse
Western, W.C.L.	Beffe, Bellevaux, Acremont

RCAF (9)

Barzelle, C.S.	
Congreve, G.H.	
Doyle, K.J.	Beffe, Porcheresse
Harrison, D.	Bellevaux, Acremont
Leslie, S.M.	
Mallet, E.L.	Bellevaux, Acremont
Michaud, J.A.E.	Villance, Acremont
Morgan, G.R.	Acremont, Porcheresse, Bohan-sur-Semois
Sweatman, K.G.	Bellevaux, Acremont

USAAF (82)

Allen, S.	Bellevaux
Alpoos, D.R.	
Ashman, H.E.	Bellevaux, Porcheresse
Blakely, M.E.	Beffe, Porcheresse
Bowman, C.S.	Bellevaux, Acremont
Bradley, J.J.	
Brammer	Porcheresse
Brennecke, G.E.[2012]	Porcheresse
Brown, J.	
Cargile, D.M.[2013]	
Cochran, Jnr, J.M.	Porcheresse, Bohan-sur-Semois
Colt, Jnr, H.	Bellevaux, Acremont
Cox, H.G.	Bellevaux, Acremont
Davis, R.E.	Bellevaux, Acremont
Dehon, W.B.	Villance, Acremont
Deihl, D.D.	Porcheresse
Dobson, K.	Villance
Earnhart, C.B.	Bellevaux, Acremont
Elsberry, W.E.	Beffe, Porcheresse
Engelman, A.	Villance
Freudenberger, A.T.	Beffe, Acremont, Villance
Gecks, R.H.	Beffe
Gladys, H.H.	Beffe, Acremont, Porcheresse
Godwin, L.B.	Bellevaux
Goewey, P.M.	Bellevaux?
Goldfeder, M.M.	Bellevaux, Acremont
Goldstein, P.	Villance
Goodling, P.	Villance
Griesel, K.C.	Beffe, Acremont, Porcheresse
Griffis, H.C.[2014]	Villance, Acremont
Grip, G.A.	Villance
Hermanski, L.V.	Bellevaux, Acremont
Hincewicz, C.B.	
Hokinson, L.V.	Villance, Acremont
Hutchinson, L.M.	Hidden at Waterloo with Sergeant J.T.H. Burton
Joney, J.L.	Acremont
Kasza, P.A.	Bellevaux, Acremont, Villance
Kilmer, H.F.	Beauraing
Kindig, R.J.	Beffe, Porcheresse
Kite, A.S.	Villance, Acremont
Koch, R.	Porcheresse
Kramer, D.C.	Porcheresse
Kucherenko, A.	Villance, Acremont, Bellevaux
Kuhn, A.E.	Villance, Acremont
Lambert, E.S.	Liberated at Liège
Lincoln, J.W.	Bellevaux, Acremont
MacGilvary, R.	
Martin, R.	
Maupin, H.P.	Acremont, Porcheresse, Villance
Milar, G.	Porcheresse
Mitchell, C.R.	Porcheresse
Monterse, V.	Villance
Pratt, K.	
Petterson, M.	Villance
Pritchett, R.G.	Acremont
Rickey, R.W.	Acremont
Riddle, E.M.	
Robbin, H.	
Roberts, A.D.	Beffe, Porcheresse
Rye, D.E.	Bellevaux
Saleh, M.	Bellevaux
Sandersen, T.	Beffe
Schleichkorn, S.G.	Acremont, Porcheresse
Shaddix, W.C.	Beffe
Sheahan, W.	Acremont

Sherwood, J.S.	Bellevaux, Acremont, Villance
Shimansky, W.	Villance
Simmons, T.S.	Beffe, Porcheresse
Slomowicz, R.A.	
Stinnet, M.J.	
Sullivan, D.	Villance
Sweeney, H.	Porcheresse
Talbot, D.R.	Beffe
Tarleton, W.W.	Bellevaux, Acremont
Thiriot, R.V.	Bellevaux, Acremont, Villance
Tuttle, F.A.	Beffe, Bellevaux, Acremont
Viafore, D.	
Vogle, G.W.	Beffe, Porcheresse
Votzella, C.J.	Bellevaux, Acremont
Weymouth, C.L.	Beffe, Porcheresse
Willis, A.L.	Beffe, Acremont, Porcheresse
Woodrout, T.	Bellevaux

Note: Many names and camp details are taken from *Downed Allied Airmen and Evasion of Capture: The Role of Local Resistance Networks in World War II*, Appendix VI, pp. 177-181, and also from section D of the Comet website *http://www.cometeline.org/cometaviateurpasse.html.*
The village of Porcheresse lies six kilometres from Daverdisse, and the Porcheresse camp is sometimes known by both names.

APPENDIX V

MI9, IS9, and IS9(WEA)

During the First World War the War Office Intelligence Directorate created a small bureau, MI1a, whose remit was to look into how to effect secret communications with officer prisoners of war in Germany, and 'to handle also anything that could be secured from British prisoners in Germany.' Apparently no startling results were obtained,[2015] but MI1a was still in business at the outbreak of war in 1939, when it established a small Combined Services Detailed Interrogation Centre at the Tower of London.

Following the perceived need for some official body to deal with the possibility 'that there might be hundreds of thousands of prisoners in the next war… and that there might well be hundreds or even thousands of evaders as well, loose in the enemy's rear areas and in need of guidance',[2016] the Joint Intelligence Committee recommended the formation of a new unit to deal with these men. The result of their recommendation was the establishment of a small department of the War Office, MI9, on 23 December 1939 in room 424 of the Metropole Hotel, Northumberland Avenue, London. MI9 moved to Wilton Park, east of Beaconsfield, in October 1940. Wilton Park was designated Camp 20, Beaconsfield.

With First World War soldier Major N.R. Crockatt DSO, MC[2017] as its chief, its objectives were:

'(a) To facilitate escapes of British prisoners of war, thereby getting back service personnel and containing additional enemy manpower on guard duties.
(b) To facilitate the return to the United Kingdom of those who succeeded in evading capture in enemy occupied territory.
(c) To collect and distribute information.
(d) To assist in the denial of information to the enemy.
(e) To maintain morale of British prisoners of war in enemy prison camps.'[2018]

In April 1940 the section of MI1a that 'was responsible for Intelligence work connected with enemy prisoners of war and internees in the UK was incorporated in MI9 as MI9(a), the side which dealt with British prisoners of war and internees in enemy and neutral countries being thenceforward known as MI9(b), which as a further commitment was responsible for intelligence aspects of persons arriving in the UK on repatriation from enemy countries.'[2019]

With an increase in the work in 1940 and 1941, a Deputy Directorate of Military Intelligence (Prisoners of War) was established at the end of 1941, with MI9(a) becoming MI19 (Enemy Prisoners of War Intelligence), and MI9(b) becoming MI9 (British Prisoners of War Intelligence). Furthermore, a new Intelligence section, IS9 (Intelligence School 9), was created to take over the executive work of MI9.

There was yet a further re-organisation with effect from 1 January 1942, when MI9 was split 'into two sub-sections, MI9(b) and MI9(d), the former dealing with general questions, co-ordination, distribution of information and liaison with other services and government departments and overseas commands, the latter, MI9(d), being responsible for organising preventive training (instruction in evasion and escape) to combattant personnel of the three services in the United Kingdom and for the issue of evasion and escape equipment and information to units at home and MI9 organisations overseas.'[2020]

MI9(d) arranged to give a series of lectures on escape and evasion to RAF units, but owing to the limited numbers of lecturers available to cover the ever-expanding RAF it was decided to institute RAF Intelligence Course "B", 'and in due course every operational RAF station and OTU in the United Kingdom possessed at least one Intelligence Officer qualified to instruct in MI9 subjects. This instruction was supplemented by lectures from officers on the staff of MI9(d), who visited Group, etc. as required, and by visits from recent evaders and escapers.'

The following table gives an idea of the number of training lectures given by MI9(d) officers only during the period 1 January 1942 to 25 August 1945. The figures 'are conservative and are exclusive of lectures given under local arrangements by officers who qualified at RAF Intelligence Course "B".

Service	**No. of lectures**	**Estimated number of personnel who attended**
Royal Navy	608	90,000
Royal Marines	102	20,000
Army	1,090	346,000
Royal Air Force	1,450	290,000.'[2021]

Other sub-sections of IS9 of MI9(d) were formed as 'work expanded and progressed'. These were IS9(W), IS9(X), IS9(Y), IS9(Z), IS9(D)/P.15, and, later, IS9(AB).

IS9(W) dealt with the interrogation of escapers, evaders and repatriated service personnel. It also prepared all reports (including appendices) made by these persons. It had originated in MI9(b) but, when the other sections were separated from the War Office branch on the formation of IS9 in January 1942, continued in MI9(b) until March 1943, when it was brought into the "School". There was, despite its new establishment, effectively no change in the interrogation of escapers and evaders which had begun under MI9(b). The purpose of interrogations is dealt with below, as are the types of reports.

IS9(X) dealt with escape and evasion planning; location of prisoner-of-war camps; collection of material for MI9 *Bulletin*; selection, recording and co-ordination of despatch of escape material to POW camps; preparation of escape and evasion maps.

IS9(Y) looked after the preparation of coded messages to prisoner-of-war camps; liaison with outside secret departments with regard to special cases; correspondence with prisoner-of-war camps; liaison with selected relatives of prisoners of war; decoding, editing and passing to MI9 of information received from all POW camps; maintenance of camp records, names of attempted escapers, helpers, code users, etc; dealing with censorship slips; dealing with special questionnaires from Reception Camps; interviewing "special" repatriated prisoners of war; preparation of an historical record of each prisoner-of-war camp.

IS9(Z) was responsible for experimental work; production of escape and evasion equipment (including the Aids Box); preparation of prisoner-of-war parcels; distribution of gadgets and special clothing for IS9(D)/P15 agents etc; weekly and monthly stock sheets; despatch of supplies to all theatres on MI9 indents; records, indents, despatch notes, packing, etc.

The Aids Box was designed to 'give the evader sufficient nourishment for 48 hours and so enable him to lie up or move from his original location without the necessity of obtaining food.' Its contents were: 'compressed food, Chewing Gum, Halazone, Benzadrine, Matches, Safety Razor and Soap, Needle and Thread, Surgical Tape, Fishing Line and Hook, Water Bottle and Small Compass.'[2022]

IS9(Z) also issued purses, containing 'normally about £12 in notes of the currency of the country or countries in which the recipient might find himself cut off, appropriate silk maps, a small compass and hacksaw.'

IS9(D)/P15 was concerned with the employment and training (under the auspices of the SIS) of agents sent to enemy occupied countries of Western Europe to assist escapers and evaders to return to the United Kingdom; preparation of plans for the evacuation of escapers and evaders from France, Belgium and Holland; communication with IS9 agents in those countries.

IS9(AB) was set up to interview helpers of British and American escapers and evaders in France, Belgium, Holland and Denmark; to investigate and settle financial claims; and to make recommendations for awards to helpers. (This work was carried out in close co-operation with the Americans and the Intelligence services of the countries concerned).

To assist with the interrogations that it was charged to undertake, IS9(W) was, unofficially, provided with rooms at the London District Assembly Centre (LDAC), from the windows of which one could look out 'on the architectural opulence of Kensington Palace Gardens',[2023] London. 'Personnel of all three Services were interrogated at the L.D.A.C. and accommodated there as long as it was convenient, or necessary, to retain them.'[2024] In the early days it was unusual for the person being interrogated to have to spend more than one night there but, as numbers of RAF evaders and escapers coming through increased, the Air Ministry 'furnished a dormitory and provided an RAF orderly, who also kept the interrogating rooms and conducted men to outside interviews.' With the huge influx of men coming from France in the autumn of 1944 the Air Ministry provided an officer and two orderlies for administration at the LDAC.

The aims of the interrogations carried out by IS9(W) were:

(1) To obtain information for MI9 lectures and the MI9 *Bulletin*;
(2) To obtain information which might be of use to IS9(X) in their planning of escapes;
(3) To supply MI9 with information whereby they could make recommendations for awards to escapers and helpers, settle claims for expenses incurred and pay compensation etc;
(4) To help MI9(d)/P15 to keep in touch with the progress of MI9 organisations on the Continent;
(5) To obtain and make available to the three services and other Government departments information on conditions in enemy and enemy-occupied countries and on military and specialist subjects;
(6) To keep MI5 informed of matters of security interest affecting prisoners of war and evaders and to enable them to interrogate personnel whose cases were regarded as doubtful from the security point of view.

Interrogations were at first carried out by giving the escaper or evader a questionnaire, a sheet of paper and a pencil and asking him to write down his answers. Despite none of the interrogating officers in the early stages having had any training in this field, the system worked tolerably well in the case of those who had escaped from the column of march or who had evaded capture in Belgium and France immediately after the Dunkirk evacuations. As time passed, however, it was thought that the information supplied on the questionnaire was insufficient, and that more was needed to acquire a clearer picture of an escape or evasion.

Getting personnel to write down their account was not always easy, a number of men proving to be virtually illiterate. It was a surprise to discover that near-illiteracy was not confined, as might have been expected, to other ranks only. Experience showed that to get a man to write his own story produced results of limited usefulness and that there was no substitute for a proper interrogation. Where numbers of those waiting to be interrogated were large, as would be the case, for example, after the liberation of northern France in August and September 1944, it was found expedient to issue the men with questionnaires and ask them to fill in their personal details and answer as many of the other questions as they could.

The finished reports were designated MI9/S/PG, the last three letters standing for 'Secret/Prisoners. Germany'. These letters were retained even though an escaper or evader had not come from Germany. The very first such report, MI9/S/PG (B) 1, was made by Captain A.R. Trench, 1st/6th Queens. The numeral 1 at the end signified that his was the first officially numbered report (numbering thereafter was more or less chronological), and the "(B)" that he had been a prisoner in Belgium. Some of the other letters used to denote the country in which an escaper had been imprisoned were CZ, FB, F, G, H, IT, LX, N, and P, for Czechoslovakia, France/Belgium, France, Germany, Holland, Italy, Grand Duchy of Luxembourg, Norway, and Poland, respectively.

The main, other designations used apart from MI9/S/PG were as follows:

IS9/WEA	for prisoners of war liberated by the Allies.
S/PG/LIB	for prisoners of war liberated from Germany.
S/PG/MISC/INT	for miscellaneous intelligence information obtained from prisoners of war liberated from Germany or elsewhere.

Other, less common designations were:

PW/EX/SWITZ	for escapers from Italy to Switzerland.[2025]
CSDIC/CMF/SKP and	
CSDIC/ME/SKP	for escapers from Italy to Allied lines.
UDF/PW/INT/UK	for South African escapers.

The reports themselves were in five parts – the main report (originally MOST and TOP SECRET and later just SECRET); and Appendices A (TOP SECRET); B (TOP SECRET, later SECRET); C (TOP SECRET); and D (TOP SECRET, later SECRET).

The main part of the report contained information on an escape or evasion up to the point where the escaper or evader came into the hands of an escape line (such as Comet or Burgundy). No helpers were named and no descriptions given which might have identified these helpers.

Appendix A contained names and addresses of helpers where known, and dates. This information was mainly provided to assist IS9(D)/P15 and, later, IS9(AB) as a means of cross-checking names.

Appendix B was distributed to Service departments and other interested bodies, as it contained information of a military nature.

Appendix C continued the escape or evasion story from the point where the evader/escaper came into the hands of the organisation/escape line. Names and addresses of helpers (if known), and their description (where necessary), were also included. In many cases this information was duplicated by that in Appendix A.

Appendix D provided details as to the use, or otherwise, of escape aids, such as the Aids Box or the purse containing foreign currency.

Following the invasion of the near Continent in June 1944, MI9 were given the task of forming a new unit to be known as Intelligence School 9 (Western European Area), or IS9(WEA). It was to be a joint British and American unit to undertake MI9 work in the field with 21 Army Group, First US Army Group, 2 Tactical Air Force (British), Ninth USAAF, and the Allied naval forces. Notionally formed at Wilton Park on 14 January 1944, it moved to nearby Fulmer Hall on 1 May 1944. The role of its staff was to maintain close contact with all departments of HQ SHAEF that might in any way be affected by escapers, evaders or prisoners of war in Germany. Staff would also 'be responsible, in conjunction with P15 and the organisations in France, Belgium and Holland, for the continuation of escape and evasion until the war in the west is over.' They were also to 'set up reception and interrogation centres for all escapers and evaders and arrange for the dissemination of all intelligence information and the onward transmission of the men to the United Kingdom.'[2026]

Another of its duties was to 'organise collection and return to their units or to UK of British and American Service personnel of all three Services who may find themselves in enemy occupied territory and cut off from their units, but in a position to evade capture or escape from enemy hands.'[2027] Another of its duties was to direct clandestine organisations to hide personnel as close behind enemy lines as was practicable, for later collection, or, if possible, to guide them through enemy lines. Failing that, then organisations were asked to guide the men to Spain or Switzerland.

The Air Ministry issued further instructions, on 15 February 1945, on the *Disposal of Personnel escaping from enemy captivity or evading capture behind enemy lines on the Continent*. These stated that personnel who had been absent from their 'units for less than two months' were, 'after interrogation by IS9 (WEA) or AIS(CMF)', to be returned direct to their units via No. 107 Personnel Dispersal Centre (PDC) in the case of units based in the United Kingdom. Where units were based on the Continent personnel were 'to be returned [to the UK] direct.' And 'Any person who has been absent from his unit for less than two months will be provided by IS9 (WEA), AIS(CMF) or MI9 with a special report for the information of his CO where special treatment is considered desirable on account of his having been subjected to special danger or hardship.'[2028]

By war's end, to cope with the interrogation of the flood of escapers, evaders and former prisoners of war, IS9(WEA) had established sections of its staff in a number of places in Austria, Germany, Belgium and France – Salzburg, Lübeck, Westertimke, Markt Pongau, Brussels, Namur, Reims, Epinal and Paris. Heading its Advance HQ was Lieutenant-Colonel J.M. Langley, attached to HQ 21 Army Group, and head of MI9's IS9(d), War Office, was Major A.M.S. Neave, with Captain P.J.S. Windham-Wright, and a Captain E.W. Zundel.[2029]

APPENDIX VI

The unusual evasion of Sergeant Edwin Harold Robert Merlin RAF

Harold Merlin was born to British parents in 1920 in Athens, Greece, where his father was an engineer. The family then emigrated to the USA for eight years, before moving to Paris and returning to Greece in 1936. Harold was then sent to the École Nouvelle, *a school in Lausanne, Switzerland. Early in the Second World War, a fluent French and German speaker, he became a journalist for the* Chicago Tribune *newspaper, and was in Paris in June 1940 when the Germans arrived. He escaped to Greece, but was again trapped by the Germans following their invasion of that country in April 1941. Managing to reach Crete, he was evacuated to Cairo, Egypt, where he enlisted in the RAF, with service number 700710. Having undergone basic training in South Africa, he returned to Britain in September 1942, and on completion of his advanced training was posted to 175 Squadron.*[2030]

Shot down by flak near Auxi-le-Château on 16 August 1943 (see Chapter 8) and having been briefly knocked-out, he regained consciousness, still in his aircraft, to find that members of the flak battery who had shot him down were firing at him. Thus prompted to jump out of his Typhoon he ran off into nearby woods. Making his way to the villages of Grouches-Luchuel near Doullens he was given a suit of overalls before being escorted to Frévent. There he was interrogated by Monsieur Hetroit, who then took him to a house in nearby Sibiville. He was still there in September when he was asked to meet a man who was regarded with suspicion by the Resistance.

'On 10 September M. Hetroit, Frévent, whom I had met in August asked me whether I would be willing to contact M. Joseph Becker, Auxi-le-Château, who was reputed to have information which would be useful to the Allies. The patriots had refused to contact Becker as he is a naturalised German, and was under suspicion at the time. Becker owned Stauback Transport Enterprise and was working for the Germans.[2031]

'I agreed to contact Becker in order to discover what his activities were. Becker was unaware that I spoke German or that I was being sent in order to check up on him. He was aware that I was a British airman.

'I went to Becker on 10 September and stayed at his home until 26 October. After a few days observation I concluded that Becker was reliable from the Allied point of view. He obtained information about aerodromes, aircraft, Flak-battery positions, and vague information about V1, in my presence from German officers. He later related this information to me in French as he was still unaware that I understood German. I became friendly with members of the German Feldgendarmerie, the N.C.O. i/c the various transport enterprises in the Auxi-le-Château area, during the first week of my stay with Becker.

'About 17 September I became the driver of Becker's private car. This enabled me to visit various German installations including 32 V1 and V2 sites.[2032]

'From 18 to 25 September I sent detailed information regarding German installations to M. Hetroit, Frévent, and from 25 September to 26 October I delivered it to a café opposite the church in Fortel on Hetroit's instructions. Becker gave me every facility for working in preparing my reports etc. He was fully aware of my activities. He made no attempt to impress me with the importance of any particular piece of information which he passed on to me.

'From 18 September to 26 October I helped approximately 40 Allied aircrew personnel. Until the time of my arrival no organisation for assisting evaders existed in this area. About the end of September a Pole (naturalised Frenchman) named Emile, c/o Librairie du Sacré Coeur, Lille, who was the organiser of Allied aircrew assistance in N. France and Belgium, came to see me at Becker's house. I agreed to take charge of the Auxi-le-Château-Abbeville area. I made the necessary arrangements for accommodation of the airmen and supply of identity cards. Emile arranged their journey from my area.'[2033]

Squadron Leader Checketts (see Chapter 8) was one of the airmen to benefit from Merlin's assistance at this time: 'While in the Auxi-le-Château district I met Sgt Merlin, an American pilot…, who is working with an organisation there. He speaks fluent French, mixes freely with the Germans, and is doing good espionage work. He has been there since 16 August, and was coming out by the next boat organised by the people who sent us over.'[2034] Merlin, however, 'insisted that S/Ldr. Checketts should take my place in the party for the UK' as the squadron leader 'had been badly burned'.[2035]

Though Merlin may have been mixing freely with the Germans, on 15 October 'two German counter-espionage officials arrived in Auxi-le-Château from Paris. They interrogated Becker and me for two days. At the end of this time the two officials were convinced that we were good German collaborators, and they returned to Paris with a quantity of champagne, brandy and meat. The result of this was that the patriots in Auxi-le-Château were convinced that Becker and I were collaborators and the collaborators were convinced we were patriots. In order to render my position more secure I started numerous conflicting rumours about myself.

'On 26 October I escorted 11 Allied airmen (including P/O Haddock, RAF)[2036] to Paris. We travelled by car to Amiens and then by train (second class) to Paris where I made arrangements for the accommodation of nine of them. I arranged contact on their behalf with an organisation. Two of the party:- P/O Haddock and an American S/Sgt were accommodated with a friend of mine:- Mme. Mireille Combas, 17 Rue Des Accacias, Paris, and M. Marcus Celli, Bar Possoz, Place Possoz, Metro Muetto, Paris.

'I stayed at various hotels in Paris, posing as a Frenchman, from 26 October until 7 November.

'I had important information which I wished to get to the UK as quickly as possible. I decided to travel to Switzerland. I had no contact which could help me get away quickly. I arranged with P/O Haddock and the American S/Sgt that should I succeed in getting into Switzerland I would make arrangements for them to follow me.

'M. Celli supplied me with 8,000 francs, and he gave approximately 12,000 francs in Paris for sheltering Allied airmen.

'On 4 November I met Oberleutnant Gerhard Davidt of the German Naval HQ at St. Assisses near Paris. We were introduced by M. Tellier, 10 Boulevard des Invalides, Paris. After a few meetings Davidt gave me a copy of the cypher used by submarines in the North Sea and the telephone cypher used between German naval bases in the Mediterranean. I passed this information to the air attaché in Switzerland on my arrival there.

'I learned from M.Tellier in March 1944 that Davidt had been killed. German Gestapo patrol had opened fire on Davidt's car in the Boulevard des Invalides, Paris in March 1944.

'On 7 November 1943 I left Paris escorted by M. Toni Viviani, Rue Vercingetorix, Paris. All my secret papers were concealed in a loaf of bread in my suitcase. We travelled by train (first class) to Annecy. On this journey our papers were examined on seven occasions by German controls. We then walked to Les Praz where we met M. Pablos, Les Praz, who stated that it was too late in the season to cross the Alps. Toni then returned to Paris with instructions for P/O Haddock and the American S/Sgt to the effect that they were to remain in Paris until they received further instructions from me or from the British Authorities in Switzerland.

'On 8 November I returned to St. Gervais and stayed at a hotel until 9 November when I travelled by bus to Annecy. I then walked to St. Julien where I arrived on the morning of 11 November. I was stopped by French Militia and arrested as my papers were not in order for that area. I was being taken to the Militia HQ when I broke away from my escort and hid in a farmhouse on the outskirts of St. Julien about 50 yards from the Swiss frontier. The farmer, M. Sevaz, was friendly and he gave me a special pass which he had obtained from the German authorities in order to enable him to cross the frontier as part of his farm is in Switzerland. I put my loaf of bread etc. in a sack which I placed in a farm wagon loaned to me by M. Sevaz. He also loaned me a suit of overalls. I drove the wagon to the gate in the fence where I produced my pass to the sentry and was allowed to go through. A few minutes after I was safely on Swiss territory M. Sevaz dashed up to the gate and complained that someone had stolen his wagon and his pass. This was pre-arranged. I had abandoned the wagon a few yards inside the frontier and removed the overalls within sight of the German guard.

'M. Sevaz had given me the name of a friend – Captain Rochat, Swiss Guard. When the Swiss guards at the frontier arrived to arrest me

I stated that I was a Swiss agent and that I must see Captain Rochat at once.[2037] The guards telephoned Captain Rochat who came from Geneva to see me. He took me on his motorcycle to Geneva. He then proposed that I should give some of my information to him before being allowed to contact the British Legation. He claimed to be working in conjunction with British agents. I told him a fairy-tale which was published in the Swiss newspapers the following day. My reason for telling him a story was that he threatened to hand me over to the Swiss guards if I refused. This would have meant the discovery of my secret documents.

'Captain Rochat took me to Mr Farrell, the British Vice Consul at Geneva. I was then interrogated by a member of the British Legation Staff. The loaf of bread containing my secret documents was opened in the presence of Mr Farrell and the man who interrogated me.

'On 12 November I was handed over to the Swiss Authorities and put in prison in Berne on 13 November after being interrogated by a Swiss Colonel who appropriated my French identity card. I remained in prison until 20 November when I was sent to the quarantine in Berne. From 24 November I was interrogated daily for eight days by Air Commodore West and W/Cdr [R.D.] Jones.[2038] On 11 December F/Lt Chinchen, RAAF,[2039] and I went to a party in the British Legation. We were arrested by the Swiss Authorities in the early hours of 12 December for breaking quarantine and were put in prison for thirty-eight hours. I remained in Berne until 14 December when I was sent to Arosa Internment Camp where I remained until 18 January 1944.

'On 24 December Air Commodore West visited Arosa and showed me a cable from the Air Ministry which stated that all the V1 emplacements pin-pointed by RAF 700710 had been attacked successfully.

'On 27 December Air Commodore West sent for me at Arosa and admonished me because my fairy-tale had been published in the Swiss press; also because stories concerning the Albanian front had been discovered amongst my personal possessions at Lydd RAF Station. These stories written between October 1940 and April 1941 were carbon copies of my contributions to my newspaper – *The Chicago Tribune*.

'Air Commodore West then asked me whether I would be willing to undertake an unspecified mission in France. I agreed to carry out his instructions. Air Commodore West made it clear that this work would be entirely voluntary.

'On 19 January 1944 Air Commodore West sent for me and I travelled to Berne. He asked me to obtain information regarding German aerodromes in N. France. I agreed to undertake this mission. On 26 January Air Commodore West received a cablegram from the Foreign Office pointing out that the Hague Convention stipulated that active members of military forces may not be employed on espionage work in enemy territory. Air Commodore West sent a cable to the Air Ministry requesting that the Foreign Office ruling be set aside. He received a reply to the effect that it could not. On 27 January Air Commodore West informed me that my services could not be employed at that time, but should any opportunity arise to employ me, he would get in touch with me. He also informed me that I must regard myself as an internee and stay at Arosa until I should receive further instructions. I returned to Arosa and stayed there until 22 April.'

At the beginning of April 1944 Merlin began planning his escape from Switzerland to France. On 15 April he handed a letter to Wing Commander Peter Bragg, SBO at Arosa. It was addressed to Air Commodore West and stated that he had information regarding a possible means of escape from Switzerland. Merlin also requested permission to use the method outlined. As he had not received a reply a week later he decided to escape. He knew that Sergeant Walter Walker and Sergeant R.A.B. "Red" Blumer RAAF were also planning to escape, but thought that their plan would not succeed. He nevertheless agreed to escort them to France, but refused to include in the party two others – Sergeant Jean Privé FAF and Sergeant J.B. King (see Chapter 11) – whom he considered to be 'unsuitable'.

The three of them, therefore – Merlin, Walker and Blumer – set off on 22 April. After two nights in a wood they crossed the frontier into France approximately 1½ kilometres south of the Villars-lès-Blamont to Damvant road. Walker and Blumer were without papers of any sort, but Merlin carried a British passport and the pass issued by the Swiss authorities to him for the journey from Arosa to Berne (though he had substituted Pruntrut for Berne). Never apparently having been searched by the Swiss all the time that he was in their country he also had with him an automatic pistol that Monsieur Hetroit had given him in September 1943.

Once in France, however, Merlin found himself in need of the gun. Blumer, Merlin said, 'had been very careless during the journey and he refused to obey my instructions. I was forced to threaten to shoot him if he continued to endanger the escape.' Though in Merlin's opinion Blumer was ill, he was not called upon to shoot the Australian. Obtaining bicycles from a Monsieur Schorp of 1, rue de la Prairie, Montbéliard, they cycled to a monastery where, on 27 April, Schorp brought them 'identity cards and carte de travail', enabling then to catch the train to Belfort. Merlin, who clearly had other plans, sent Walker and Blumer 'to Dijon en route for Perpignan' on 28 April. Reaching Spain, the two were flown back from Gibraltar on the night of 5/6 June 1944.

Merlin, meanwhile, put his pistol and passport in an attaché case, and sent them under an assumed name to the luggage office at the Gare de l'Est, Paris while he went first class. It was fortunate that he had taken the precaution of sending the case separately, for all passengers on the train were thoroughly searched by the SD. Arriving in Paris on the morning of 28 April 1944 he went to the Lion de Belford hotel[2040] at 10, rue Boulard, Denfert Rochereau, Paris 14, where he had stayed previously. There he met Toni Viviani, who informed him that Pilot Officer Haddock and the American staff sergeant had been taken by a Victor Toronelli to the Hôtel Clauzet at 33, rue des Martyrs, Paris at the end of November 1943. A few days later Toronelli 'passed them on to the Black Panther, a woman who claimed to help evaders to get to Spain in return for 25,000 francs per head. This woman lived in the cul-de-sac portion of the street south of the rue du Simplon and west of the rue Boinod, Poissonniers, Paris.'

On 3 May Merlin met Toronelli and asked him what had happened to Haddock and the American, only to be told 'that they had been taken care of by the Black Panther.' Toronelli's wife then took Merlin to the Black Panther's home, and was duly informed by the landlady that the Black Panther had been arrested by the Gestapo and had been shot. Furthermore, there was no trace of either airman.[2041] Merlin, who thought that the landlady had been expecting a visit from him, was then put on his guard by Toronelli asking to be reimbursed for the 50,000 francs that he, Toronelli, claimed to have paid to the Black Panther before her arrest. Merlin refused to pay him.[2042] Subsequent information provided by Toronelli proved to be false, and at the end of May he disappeared, claiming that the Gestapo were after him. His brother, Noël, told Merlin that Victor had gone to Montluçon.

From early May Merlin and Viviani had been distributing 'Allied propaganda leaflets to French people in the streets of Paris', and Merlin had also been organising small bands 'of patriots who lived in the vicinity of the Hotel de Lion de Belford' to ambush Germans at night for their weapons. Merlin had also tried to recover his attaché case from the Gare de l'Est but, when he asked for it, the French officials to whom he spoke 'made a move towards two German soldiers who were in the office. I walked out of the station. I arranged for my case to be stolen from the luggage office that night. When I regained possession of it I discovered that the locks had been forced open, but the contents were intact although disturbed.' Fortunately there was no photograph of him in the case, but he nevertheless took the precaution of obtaining a new false identity card.

Further worrying news was given to him on 15 May when he met up with Mitzi Jansen, whose address was the same as that of Mireille Combas. Merlin knew Mitzi from his time in Auxi-le-Château, in October 1943, and she apparently 'owned a transport enterprise in Paris. She informed me that M. Joseph Becker had been arrested by the Gestapo in November 1943, charged with stealing petrol from the Germans and selling it to the French.' He was taken to Lille for interrogation, and also charged with having worked with an American agent to whom he had given information about the V1 sites. Becker had, however, escaped from prison in May 1944, but it was Mitzi's impression that he had been released so that he could act as a German agent. His girl friend, Madame Briet, had then been taken into custody as a hostage. She also stated to Merlin that Becker was working with a M. Georges Terrier, 12 rue Amsterdam, Place Clichy, Paris 12, whom he had asked to contact Mitzi so that she could in turn contact Merlin. Merlin told Mitzi that he did not want Becker to know of his whereabouts.

Learning from a French policeman that the Milice and Gestapo intended to raid the Hôtel de Lion de Belford, Merlin moved on 14 June to another hotel, the Hôtel du Maine, rue du Maine, Paris 14, and 'stayed with a Mademoiselle Yvonne Coullet'.[2043]

A man known to Merlin only as Joseph approached him on 17 June for money to support two British airmen who were being sheltered by him in a rented apartment, as his organisation had broken down. Merlin met him again on 3 July, and was now told that Joseph had succeeded in contacting the rest of his organisation, who now had eight Allied airmen in their charge. In the middle of June Merlin had been put in touch with a French major, who was supposedly working for the Allies. When Merlin asked the major for help with the evaders, it was refused, but a few days later the major approached him with an extraordinary proposal. He, the major, knew of two Frenchmen who had a pre-war French transport aircraft concealed in a church on the outskirts of Paris. This, said the major, could be used to fly the eight airmen, and Merlin, back to England!

After several meetings and discussions, Merlin was informed on 15 July 'that the scheme must be abandoned. They refused to offer any explanation for their change of attitude. I then saw the major, who told me that he could not trust me, and that he did not want to have any dealings with the eight evaders.' On 18 July the major asked Merlin for his pistol 'as he wanted to shoot a German. I gave it to him. On 20 July I asked him to return it to me. He said that I was a nuisance and that I did not deserve to have a pistol. He did not return it.' The major then told Merlin that he could put him 'in touch with the Maquis in Belgium, but I told him I had no desire to go to Belgium. He then said that he would report me as a deserter to the War Office.'

On 22 July Merlin decided to leave Paris. Hitch-hiking his way back to Frévent (Pas-de-Calais) he was put in touch with Lieutenant Pierre Caron (a member of the FFI), and was put 'in charge of the patriots organisations in the St Pol-Arras-Doullens area'. Merlin 'also tried to organise the care of Allied airmen who were evading in that area. I distributed the supplies which were dropped by parachute, and instructed the patriots in their uses.' Quite an army was established, with a strength of 350 men, plus 47 gendarmes, though their arsenal amounted only to 'three M.G.s, 35 Tommy guns, 25 rifles, 30 pistols, 3,000 rounds of M.G. ammunition and 10,000 rounds of Tommy gun ammunition… From the beginning of August until 2 September the patriots sabotaged 12 trains by explosives, several hundred motor trucks by destroying their tyres, and blew up 20 bridges at strategic points.'

On 2 August Lieutenant Caron, Merlin and two other maquisards, one of whom was a Maurice Lefebvre, dressed as workmen and went in a truck to St Pol to pick up 'four unexploded Allied bombs which were lying approximately 100 yards from the German HQ. The bombs were unguarded, but the sentry was standing in front of the HQ and in sight of the bombs.' When an alert German NCO saw them, he called out the guard, but as the four "workmen" were being led off to the Germans' HQ Lieutenant Caron 'punched the NCO on the jaw and the four of us ran in different directions. The German NCO fired at us with his pistol'. The other Germans opened fire with their rifles, wounding Maurice Lefebvre in the left arm, while two bullets passed through Merlin's clothes without touching him. All four, though, made it to safety.

Three days later Merlin was 'stopped by eight German patrols' as he and a Jean Masseron cycled to the village of Oeuf. Somehow the Germans failed to discover the pistol that was hidden about Merlin's person. Further close calls followed when he hid in a farmhouse that was twice searched by the Germans. Undeterred at '21.45 hours I left the house and walked to a V1 launching site on the outskirts of the village.' He hid barely 25 yards from the launch ramp for some six hours, making observations which he later passed on to Lieutenant Caron. But when he tried to get back to Oeuf he found that he 'was completely cut off by German patrols and sentries.' Just before dawn he made a run for it, but though seen and shot at, he made it safely back to the house in the village. This was itself later searched and, yet again, Merlin was not detected.

Indulging in further sabotage – blowing up a railway bridge with three 500lb bombs; putting tintacks on major roads to cause punctures – Merlin faced a different challenge on about 11 August when a German soldier in civilian clothes was brought to him. The German claimed that he was Obergefreiter Friedrich König, 572nd Infantry Regiment[2044] and a deserter from the Normandy front. Merlin searched him, but found no papers, though interrogation revealed that his wife, their two children, and the wife's sister had been killed in the Hamburg bombings in 1941. Searching his bags on the following day, however, Merlin discovered 'a German Luftwaffe officer's shirt, pantaloons and dress cap', and a letter addressed to Karl, dated 26 June 1944. Posted from Hamburg by his wife, it stated that she and the children were well.

Two days later Merlin was informed that a German deserter who had been staying with the maquisards for two months had disappeared. His description fitted that of the man claiming to be König. Confronted with the evidence, König confessed that he was a deserter, but from the Russian front. On 15 August, though, a M. Boucly brought further damning evidence against the German. The man had threatened the household in which he had been staying by saying that if any harm were to come to him he would have the whole village wiped out. As the German was too much of a liability, Merlin decided that he would have to be exterminated and so, lured into a field, he was shot dead by two maquisards. A note was left on his body which would lead the Gestapo, who collected the body on the following day, to believe that he had been shot as a deserter by the German military police. Merlin 'learned subsequently from gendarmes that the German had been a Lieutenant of the Luftwaffe.'

Shortly after this episode, it was the maquisards' turn to execute one of their own countrymen, a 'Roger Faniez, owner of a garage in Arras, and a member of the Arras Militia [Milice].'[2045] They knew that he had been giving information to the Germans, and Faniez (Fagniez?) admitted that he had done so. 'He refused to answer further questions. Lt. Caron shot him. His body was left on the road and was found next day by the gendarmerie who knew what had occurred.'

Merlin busied himself for the next few days, organising and giving orders to the various Maquis units in the St Pol area, but on 22 August he 'met P/O [sic] Thompson, RAF, at a house in Boucquemaison'. Flying Officer C.G. Thompson RCAF, navigator, and his pilot had been lost after marking the target (Beauvoir) in their Mosquito on 29 June 1944. As two Russians who had been with Thompson had disappeared a day or two earlier, Merlin took him to his house in Berles.

On 24 August Merlin and Thompson cycled to Berles and stayed at the home of M. Malvoisin. Later that night the two airmen, Caron, Lefebvre and Adolphe Bouglie 'laid two mines on the railway track near Bailleulmont.'[2046] According to Merlin the "mines" were '40 lb. bombs which were part of a store of 26 bombs which had been salvaged from a 1939 British bomb dump near Louvencourt.' At noon on 25 (or 26) August 'a German locomotive (130 German tons) was derailed and the two coaches which had preceded the locomotive were totally destroyed. Approximately 10 German railway engineers, who were in the coaches, were killed.'

The day following the train wrecking Thompson met two American airmen who had been hiding with Madame Bouglie at Bailleulmont for approximately six months, and the three of them hid in nearby woods until 1 September.

The German Army was now well and truly on the retreat, and skirmishing continued throughout the area for several days, in the course of which many reprisals were taken by angry Frenchmen on unarmed German prisoners of war. Some fifty of them, though guarded by maquisards, were shot in cold blood by what Merlin called 'terrorists'. Thompson remembered 'that a group of about 80 terrorists in the area of St. Pol-Doullens-Arras were endeavouring to steal money and valuables from German P/W who were being guarded by French patriots until they could be collected by the Allied forces. These terrorists succeeded in killing nine German officers at Berles on 3 September and in stealing all their valuables. We were also informed that these terrorists had threatened to shoot P/O Merlin, Lt. Caron, and myself on sight because we had been engaged in protecting the interests of the German P/W.'[2047]

Thompson was introduced to Becker on 8 September, and three days later Merlin took Thompson 'to Vitry and gave him Becker's message to pass it on to the British Intelligence there.' Merlin had met Joseph Becker at Auxi-le-Château on the previous day, and Becker had wanted Merlin to inform British Intelligence 'that he had information about the Siegfried Line in the Trier area, and that he was in contact with revolutionary elements in South Germany.' Thompson was flown home immediately.

On 14 September Merlin went by car to Vitry where he contacted his squadron 'and was identified'. He was then taken to Brussels by the Station Intelligence Officer, where he was briefly interrogated by IS9 (WEA) and to whom he passed on Becker's message. 'I was then sent by air to the UK', where his interrogation lasted for three days, 16-18 September, an unusually long time.

Rejoining his squadron Merlin, now a warrant officer, was shot down again on Christmas Day when his Typhoon, JP918, was hit by flak while on an "armed reconnaissance". Crashing in flames near Malmédy he was flung out, and suffered serious enough injuries to require lengthy hospitalisation.

On 23 January 1945 he was commissioned as a pilot officer with effect from 7 November 1944, and on 3 August 1945 he was promoted to flying officer with effect from 7 May 1945.

APPENDIX VII

Operation Frankton: December 1942

The objective of this audacious raid (see Chapter 7) was to sink six to twelve ships in the Bassens-Bordeaux area of France by attaching limpet mines to their hulls. It was to be carried out by twelve men of the Royal Marine Boom Patrol Detachment under the command of Major H.G. Hasler OBE, who would be dropped by submarine off the mouth of the River Gironde in south-west France, together with six two-man Cockle Mark II canoes. Two to each canoe, they would then paddle for some 120 kilometres (75 miles) up the river until reaching their target. Once the operation had been completed the marines were instructed, rather vaguely, to make for Ruffec, 150 kilometres to the north, and to contact an organisation that would arrange for their escape overland to Spain.

The twelve-strong party and their six canoes were ferried by HM Submarine *Tuna* (Lieutenant-Commander R.P. Raikes DSO, RN) to a point approximately 15 kilometres from the Cordouan Light off the mouth of the Gironde. The operation began badly when, as one of the canoes was being brought out of the submarine, it 'fouled the sharp corner of the hatch clamp and tore a long hole in her canvas side.'[2048] Marines Ellery and Fisher, who were almost in tears, were not to know how fortunate they were when Major Hasler told them that they would have to return with *Tuna*. As Major Hasler left 'he asked Raikes to book a table for them both at the Savoy on April 1. "Not bloody likely", replied Raikes, "but I'll do it for the second."'[2049]

The remaining five cockles and their ten marines were disembarked from the submarine by 2100 hours on 7 December 1942, and paddled off into the night. Three nights later only two cockles, those of Hasler/Sparks and of Corporal A.F. Laver/Marine W.H. Mills, had reached their goal. The first of the three cockles to be lost was destroyed by the forces of nature. Unexpectedly coming upon a fierce tidal-race, Sergeant S. Wallace and Marine R. Ewart lost contact with the others, and at approximately 0400 hours on 8 December were capsized by heavy surf near the Pointe de Grave lighthouse. Swimming ashore they were taken prisoner by members of a nearby flak battery, and handed over to the German Navy. Four days later, at 0030 hours on 12 December 1942, they were murdered in the grounds of Château Magnol.[2050]

The four surviving cockles then came upon a second tidal-race. All made it through, though that of Corporal G.J. Sheard/Marine D. Moffatt was badly damaged. Unable to continue, Major Hasler told them to swim ashore and head for Spain. They never made it. Moffatt's body was washed up on a beach many miles to the north. Sheard's was never found.[2051]

Hasler pressed on with the three surviving canoes, but at 2100 hours on 10 December, after they had become detached from the others, Lieutenant J.W. Mackinnon and Marine J. Conway hit a submerged object, which wrecked their canoe. Having swum ashore they made off inland as best they could, with Frenchmen helping them on their way. At la Réole, 65 kilometres south-east of Bordeaux, having been admitted to a civilian hospital, they were betrayed to the Germans.

At last the four remaining marines saw their targets – the fast blockade-runners that were such a vital link in the supply of raw materials to the German war industry. While Laver and Mills laid their eight delayed-action limpets on two ships, Hasler and Sparks did likewise on four ships. The job done, the two pairs made their way ashore independently. Laver and Mills, however, captured by French police on 14 December 1942, were handed over to the Germans. They, together with Mackinnon and Conway, on the signed order of Generalfeldmarschall Wilhelm Keitel, Chief of the High Command of the German Armed Forces, were murdered, probably in Paris, on 23 March 1943 in accordance with Hitler's *Kommando-Befehl* of 18 October 1942.[2052]

On the morning of 12 December 1942, as they made their way north to Ruffec, Hasler and Sparks, the only ones to survive, heard the limpet mines exploding, though they were not then to know that one ship was sunk and three others damaged to some degree, though repairable.

APPENDIX VIII

Statistical tables

The prime source for the statistics in the tables below is the reports made by evaders to MI9 and IS9 (WEA) from 1940-1945 which, with some exceptions, may now be found in the WO 208 series of files at The National Archives. The information that these reports contain varied over the months and years. Some, for example, gave date and place of return to the UK while others did not; others gave full name and service number while others did not. The result is an incomplete picture, and the statistics in the tables below should *not*, therefore, be taken as absolute and final. In the circumstances, the total of just under 2.200 evaders is as good as can be obtained but, inevitably, it will be found that some of those listed should not have been and that there will be some who should have been listed.

Table I – Evaders by rank

Rank	**1940**	**1941**	**1942**	**1943**	**1944**	**1945**	**TOTAL**
Aircraftman 1st Class	3	-	-	-	-	-	**3**
Aircraftman 2nd Class	1	-	-	-	-	-	**1**
Adjutant (FRA)	-	-	-	-	1	-	**1**
Captain (FRA, NOR)	-	-	-	1	2	1	**4**
Corporal	2	-	-	-	1	-	**3**
Flight Lieutenant	6	4	10	23	119	15	**177**
Flight Officer (USA)	-	-	-	-	2	-	**2**
Flight Sergeant	-	1	9	55	254	32	**351**
Flying Officer	11	3	12	54	307	18	**405**
Group Captain	-	-	-	1	-	-	**1**
Leading Aircraftman	9	-	-	-	-	-	**9**
Lieutenant (FAA, FRA, RN, SAF)	-	-	-	3	6	2	**11**
2nd Lieutenant (NOR, SAF, USA)	-	-	-	4	3	2	**9**
Pilot Officer	15	12	21	40	102	16	**206**
Squadron Leader	2	3	8	11	21	4	**49**
Sub-Lieutenant (FRA, HOL)	-	-	1	-	3	-	**4**
Sergeant	41	54	92	196	441	16	**840**
Sergent-Chef (FRA)	-	-	-	-	2	-	**2**
Warrant Officer	-	-	2	7	40	23	**72**
Warrant Officer 1st Class (CAN)	-	-	-	1	2	1	**4**
Warrant Officer 2nd Class (CAN)	-	-	-	2	32	-	**34**
Wing Commander	1	1	2	-	4	2	**10**
TOTAL	**91**	**78**	**157**	**398**	**1342**	**132**	**2198**

Table II – Numbers of RAF airman evaders shot down each month

	Jan	**Feb**	**Mar**	**Apr**	**May**	**Jun**	**Jul**	**Aug**	**Sep**	**Oct**	**Nov**	**Dec**	**TOTAL**
1939	-	-	-	-	-	-	-	-	-	-	-	-	**-**
1940	-	-	-	-	46	34	2	3	2	-	-	4	**91**
1941	6	-	1	9	4	2	13	16	13	8	6	-	**78**
1942	2	-	1	25	25	14	9	31	23	4	8	15	**157**
1943	2	17	29	60	8	24	41	73	53	24	47	20	**398**
1944	26	43	64	119	152	307	253	186	129	33	24	6	**1342**
1945	19	30	27	50	6	-	-	-	-	-	-	-	**132**
TOTAL	**55**	**90**	**122**	**263**	**241**	**381**	**318**	**309**	**220**	**69**	**85**	**45**	**2198**

Table III – Evaders by nationality

Country	**1940**	**1941**	**1942**	**1943**	**1944**	**1945**	**TOTAL**
Australia	1	3	11	15	132	15	**177**
Belgium	-	1	2	3	6	-	**12**
Bermuda	-	-	-	1	-	-	**1**
Canada	-	10	26	85	399	24	**544**
Czechoslovakia	-	2	1	-	3	-	**6**
Eire	1	-	-	1	3	-	**5**
France	-	-	1	5	14	3	**23**
Holland	-	-	-	2	4	3	**9**
New Zealand	1	2	5	17	25	8	**58**
Norway	-	-	1	3	3	5	**12**
Poland	-	9	20	19	20	4	**72**
Rhodesia	-	-	-	-	3	1	**4**
Russia	-	-	-	-	1	-	**1**
Seychelles	-	-	-	1	-	-	**1**
South Africa	-	1	-	1	5	-	**7**
United Kingdom	87	49	87	242	717	69	**1251**
USA	-	1	3	3	7	-	**14**
TOTAL	**91**	**78**	**157**	**398**	**1342**	**132**	**2198**

Table IV – Evader losses by aircraft type per year

Type	1940	1941	1942	1943	1944	1945	TOTAL
Albemarle	-	-	-	-	9	-	**9**
Battle	21	-	-	-	-	-	**21**
Beaufighter	-	-	2	-	2	3	**7**
Beaufort	1	-	-	-	-	-	**1**
Blenheim	40	3	-	-	-	-	**43**
Boston	-	-	1	11	3	-	**15**
Dakota	-	-	-	-	12	-	**12**
Defiant	4	-	-	-	-	-	**4**
Fortress	-	-	-	-	1	-	**1**
Halifax	-	-	41	167	370	17	**595**
Hampden	2	3	4	-	-	-	**9**
Hudson	2	7	-	-	-	-	**9**
Hurricane	6	5	1	-	-	-	**12**
Lancaster	-	-	6	84	607	34	**731**
Liberator	-	-	4	-	-	-	**4**
Lysander	1		2	1	1	-	**5**
Manchester	-	3	6	-	-	-	**9**
Mitchell	-	-	-	3	6	-	**9**
Mosquito	-	-	4	8	50	7	**69**
Mustang	-	-	-	3	28	2	**33**
Spitfire	3	16	11	38	87	30	**185**
Stirling	-	-	15	48	86	14	**163**
Tempest	-	-	-	-	2	12	**14**
Typhoon	-	-	-	7	53	13	**73**
Wellington	2	38	49	20	24	-	**133**
Whitley	2	3	11	7	-	-	**23**
Whirlwind	-	-	-	1	-	-	**1**
(none)	7	-	-	-	-	-	**7**
(unknown)	-	-	-	-	1	-	**1**
TOTAL	**91**	**78**	**157**	**398**	**1342**	**132**	**2198**

Table V – Country/place in which evader landed

Although it is unclear as to the countries in which some of the evader airmen landed, it is clear that just under two-thirds (63 per cent) landed in France, that just over a quarter (27 per cent) landed in Belgium/Holland/Luxembourg, and that around one in fourteen (7 per cent) came down in either Germany, Denmark or Norway.

	1940	1941	1942	1943	1944	1945	TOTAL
Atlantic Ocean	-	-	2	-	-	-	**2**
Balkans	-	-	-	-	2	-	**2**
Belgium	16	14	60	80	141	1	**311**
Boden Zee	-	-	-	-	2	-	**2**
Denmark	-	-	-	7	18	23	**48**
Denmark (sea)	-	-	-	2	-	-	**2**
France	63	59	67	250	938	-	**1358**
France (sea)	-	-	-	-	5	-	**5**
Germany	-	1	4	9	23	50	**87**
Holland	9	-	5	40	161	53	**268**
Holland (sea)	2	-	-	-	-	-	**2**
Italy	-	-	2	2	-	-	**4**
Luxembourg	-	-	2	3	8	-	**13**
Mediterranean Sea	-	4	-	-	-	-	**4**
North Sea	-	-	-	-	-	2	**2**
Norway	1	-	13	-	10	1	**25**
Poland	-	-	-	-	-	2	**2**
Sweden	-	-	-	-	2	-	**2**
Switzerland	-	-	2	5	24	-	**31**
Zuider Zee	-	-	-	-	5	-	**5**
(unknown)	-	-	-	-	3	-	**3**
TOTAL	**91**	**78**	**157**	**398**	**1342**	**132**	**2198**

Notes to Chapters

1 From http://www.100thbg.com/mainmenus/ee/history/history_02.htm.
2 Information mostly taken from Keith Janes's website at www.conscript-heroes.com.
3 See *El Camino de la Libertad*, p. 137.
4 Full title is d'Oultremont de Wegimont et de Warfusée.
5 From website http://users.skynet.be/bs281548/cometorgnamedumonaline.htm.
6 Also drowned on the same crossing was 2nd Lieutenant James F. Burch USAAF.
7 Service EVA was a Belgian organisation in Brussels that specialised in the interrogation of airmen and in the production of false papers etc., safe houses and civilian clothing, before passing on the airmen to the Comet line.
8 *MI6. British Secret Intelligence Service Operations 1909-45*, p. 84.
9 Also killed in the barracks were two other prisoners – Le Lieutenant Parachutiste Leopold Vande Meerssche, and Louis Pelet.
10 The two airmen, who were sent to prisoner-of-war camps in Germany, were Flying Officer O.J. Wells and Sergeant S.S. Ramsden RCAF, who was accidentally killed by an RAF Mosquito on 22 April 1945.
11 DSO gazetted 18 October 1945; OBE 12 June 1947, having been MBE 30 August 1945; MC and Mentioned 12 May 1942 (for his escape).
12 Guérisse explained the choice of the name to Edmund Cosgrove. SOE told him that he had to have a cover name in case of capture, so, as his English was not too good, he chose the surname of a French-Canadian school friend. When SOE suggested that O'Leary was an Irish name and could not possibly be French-Canadian, Guérisse told them of his friend. SOE acquiesced, but said that if he were to adopt the name O'Leary then his Christian name should be Patrick. See footnote in *The Evaders*, p. 59.

Preface

13 *Rendez-vous 127*, p. 13. General Spaatz was commander of the US Army's Eighth Air Force in England and then, from January 1944, commander of the US Strategic Air Forces in Europe. Born on 28 June 1891, he died on 14 July 1974.
14 For the purposes of this book, "Western Europe" may be considered to be, from north to south and west, Norway, Denmark, Germany, The Netherlands (Holland), Belgium, the Grand Duchy of Luxembourg, and France.
15 See *MI9*, pp. 310-11.
16 See *The Strategic Air Offensive against Germany 1939-1945*, Volume IV, Appendix 41, p. 440 (HMSO, London, 1961).
17 It is presumed that this total includes *all* theatres of war.
18 *Saturday at MI9*, p. 20. The italics are mine – Author.
19 *Wire and Worse...*, p. 26, Charles Rollings (Ian Allan Publishing Ltd, Hersham, 2004).
20 *The Politics of Resistance in France, 1940-1944*, p. 10, John F Sweets (Northern Illinois University Press, DeKalb, USA, 1976).
21 *The Real Enemy*, p. 9.
22 Quoted in *The Politics of Resistance in France, 1940-1944*, pp. 33-4, Sweets, op. cit.
23 CEGES-SOMA, the Centre for Historical Research and Documentation on War and Contemporary Society in Brussels, is a public, federal research institution which collects documentation and carries out research on the wars and conflicts of the twentieth century and their impact on Belgium.
24 *Second Bureau*, p. 49, Philip John Stead (Evans Brothers Ltd, London, 1959).
25 *Colonel Henri's Story*, p. 27, edited by Ian Colvin (William Kimber and Co. Ltd, London, 1954 and 1968).
26 Michael Moores LeBlanc, researcher of Resistance and evasion for over twenty years, in an email to author, 17 May 2006.
27 *Marianne in Chains. In Search of the German Occupation of France 1940-45*, p. 307 – Robert Gildea (Pan Macmillan Ltd, London, 2002). A short account of the raid may be found in *Low Attack*, pp. 101-106, Wing Commander J. de L. Wooldridge DFC and Bar, DFM (Sampson Low, Marston & Co. Ltd, London, no date, but circa 1944).
28 Appendix C, Mrozohski's report IS9 (WEA)/2/192/368 in TNA file WO 208/5583. It should be noted that on this day, 24 July, ground haze had prevented several USAAF B-17 formations from bombing their targets (officially the Periers/St Lô area – way off the north-west). Some of their bombs were accidentally released over their own troops on the ground, killing twenty and wounding sixty.
29 The majority of these reports may be found in the WO 208 series of files at The National Archives (TNA), Kew.
30 The late Sergeant Albert Ernest De Bruin.
31 TNA file AIR 2/5684.

Introduction

32 Lieutenant-Colonel J.M. Langley, *Fight Another Day*, p. 192.
33 Following the fall of France, John Standish Surtees Prendergast Vereker, 6th Viscount Gort VC, GCB, DSO & 2 Bars, MVO, MC became Governor and Commander-in-Chief, Gibraltar 1941-1942, and Governor and Commander-in-Chief, Malta 1942-1944. He was promoted to field marshal in 1943. Born on 10 July 1886, he died on 31 March 1946.
34 As an air commodore Blount had recently been AOC No. 4 (Bomber) Group. He won his MC as a captain in the Royal West Surrey Regiment in the Great War. Born in 1893 he was killed on 23 October 1940 when the aircraft in which he was flying crashed on the edge of Hendon airfield.
35 The ACFF became known later as the Royal Air Force Component, British Expeditionary Force. It comprised four squadrons of Hurricanes (Nos. 1, 73, 85, and 87); four of Lysanders for army co-operation (Nos. 2, 4, 13, and 26), and four of Blenheims for reconnaissance (Nos. 18, 53, 57, and 59).
36 Playfair, a lieutenant attached to No.9 (Wireless) Squadron in 1914, won his MC as a captain in the Royal Artillery in the First World War. He became a KBE in July 1940. Sent to India as AOC-in-C, he was later Commandant of Eastern Region as air marshal KBE, CB, CVO, MC. Born on 22 November 1889, he died on 23 November 1974.
37 Air Marshal Barratt (born 25 February 1891) was created a KCB after the evacuation from France and appointed to Army Co-Operation Command. He died on 4 November 1966.
38 Thorvald August Marius Stauning, born 26 October 1873, had been Danish prime minister from 1924-26, and again from 1929 until his death on 3 May 1942.
39 General Ruge (1882-1961) was later a prisoner of the Germans, and did much to alleviate the awful conditions experienced by Allied prisoners of war at Stalag IIIA (Luckenwalde), near Berlin, as the war drew to a close.
40 One of the legionnaires was Scotsman Ned Callander, a *caporal*, who earned the Croix de Guerre for his bravery on 13 May 1940. Two years later, having joined the RAF and won the DFM, Callander was shot down and taken prisoner of war. He escaped but, having been re-captured, was executed at Mauthausen on 7 March 1944. For an excellent account of his short life see *Fighter! Fighter!*, John Brenan & Richard Frost (Redbek, Whitehaven, 2008).
41 Major-General B.C.T. Paget DSO, MC was appointed a CB for his handling of the Norwegian expedition.
42 Casualties in the Norwegian campaign amounted to 1,335 Norwegians, 1,869 British, and 533 French and Polish troops killed or wounded. It cost the Germans 5,660 killed or wounded, 1,317 of whom were killed on land (with 1,604 wounded and 2,375 missing) and some 2,500 at sea.
43 Admiral of the Fleet Sir Roger John Brownlow Keyes (1872-1945), 1st Baron Keyes of Zeebrugge and Dover.
44 See *The Royal Air Force Medical Services, History of the Second World War, Volume III* Campaigns, p. 48, ed. Squadron Leader S.C. Rexford-Welch (HMSO, London, 1958).
45 A short, contemporary, account of the evacuation by John Masefield was published in March 1941 by William Heinemann Limited

(London).
46 The Historical Section of the Admiralty published a revised total in 1949 – 338,226, of whom 239,446 were rescued from Dunkirk harbour, and 98,780 from the beaches of Malo, Bray, and La Panne to the east of the town.
47 Official figures for British prisoners of war in German hands, issued in November 1940, were: 43,023 Army; 758 RAF; 685 Royal Navy. TNA file WO 193/346.
48 Marshal Henri-Philippe Pétain had replaced Paul Reynaud as premier of France.
49 Of the three signatories only Badoglio lived his natural span. Born on 28 September 1871, he died on 1 November 1956. Charles Léon Clément Huntziger, born 25 June 1880, died on 12 November 1941 when the aircraft in which he was returning to France after a tour of North African colonies crashed into a mountain in fog. Keitel, born 22 September 1882, was tried as a war criminal at Nuremberg in 1945-46 and executed on 16 October 1946.
50 The French government which had been in power up to the armistice had decamped from Paris to the châteaux around Tours and then to Bordeaux. Vichy lies 350 kilometres south of Paris and a similar distance north of Marseille.
51 Appendix C Vallely's report M.I.9/S/P.G. (-) 2620 in TNA file WO 208/3353.
52 The two RAF evaders were Sergeant J.F. Clinton and Flying Officer R. Farnbank, both of whom were shot down in June 1944.
53 For details of one tragic attempt, see *Footprints on the Sands of Time*, p. 42.
54 The population of Marseille in 1939 was 795,000, whereas that of Paris was 2,785,000. Foreign sea-borne trade in and out of Marseille in 1938 amounted to 9957.3 million tons.
55 In 1939 France measured some 213,000 square miles, with a population of 42 million. Spain, on the other hand, had a population of 26.5 million in an area of 197,000 square miles, while Great Britain's 51 million inhabitants squeezed into only 89,000 square miles.
56 *Detachment W*, p. 21.
57 The German army later used the fort as an ammunition dump. Shortly before abandoning Marseille in August 1944 they blew up the nearby Pont Transbordeur (transporter-bridge) that spanned the two sides of the old port, and caused major damage to the fort.
58 *Second Bureau*, p. 9, Philip John Stead (Evans Brothers Ltd, London, 1959).
59 Ibid, p. 22.
60 *Entreprise General de Travaux Ruraux* translates roughly as "Rural Works Company". The name "Cambronne" was chosen after the French colonel of that name who, when called upon by the British at Waterloo to surrender a regiment of Guards, allegedly replied "Merde!" History suggests, however, that this is pure fiction, for by the time the Guards were asked to give up their arms Cambronne was already a prisoner of the British.
61 *The Night Will End*, p. 15, Henri Frenay, translated from the French *La Nuit Finira* by Dan Hofstadter (McGraw-Hill Book Company, New York, 1976). The Canebière is one of Marseille's main thoroughfares, running inland from the Vieux Port.
62 *The Night Will End*, pp. 18-19.
63 *Second Bureau*, p. 56. Colonel Louis Baril had succeeded Colonel Gauché as chief of the Deuxième Bureau in 1940.

Chapter 1

64 *The Bristol Blenheim. A Complete History*, p. 197. Both pilot officers were awarded the DFC, gazetted on 9 July 1940.
65 *The Colours of the Day*, p. 97. Spear rose to the rank of squadron leader, on 299 Squadron flying Stirlings, before he was killed on 22 February 1945 at the age of 33. He is buried in Reichswald Forest War Cemetery, Germany.
66 Both were awarded the DFM, gazetted barely a fortnight after their adventure.
67 *The Colours of the Day*, p. 97.
68 Also on 11 May, a third Hurricane pilot, Pilot Officer J.A. Hemingway, 85 Squadron, was shot down by flak in no-man's land.
69 *Combat Report*, p. 60, Hector Bolitho (B.T. Batsford Ltd, London, 1943). Flight Lieutenant Lee DSO, DFC was killed in action on 18 August 1940.
70 33242 Flight Lieutenant R.S.J. Edwards is believed to have resumed flying duties on 9 Squadron, winning the DFC (21/11/41) and surviving the war.
71 Parker's diary, TNA file WO 208/3298. The line astern formation was Fighter Command's textbook Fighting Area Attack No. 1.
72 Parker op. cit.
73 Parker survived the war, and was released from the RAF as a wing commander in 1945. He was appointed OBE in the New Year's Honours, 1946. Alfred Whitby retired from the RAF in June 1962, aged 50, with the rank of squadron leader. It is believed that Flight Lieutenant Roberts also survived the war. He was posted from 79 Squadron to No. 6 OTU, Sutton Bridge, as an instructor on 17 June 1940.
74 *Valiant Wings*, p. 105.
75 *Valiant Wings*, pp. 104-5.
76 This and previous quotes from Clifford's report M.I.9/S/P.G. (F) 58 in TNA file WO 208/3299.
77 Phillips' report M.I.9(b)/S/P.G. (F) 283 in TNA file WO 208/3303.
78 Phillips op. cit.
79 Archive YPX 207, Cumbria Records Office, Whitehaven.
80 Phillips op. cit.
81 It is wondered whether this young French lad was Roland Lepers – see this chapter below.
82 Phillips op. cit.
83 *Failed to Return...*, p. 16 (Nesbit).
84 *Failed to Return...*, p. 18.
85 590895 Flight Sergeant J.R. Massey, who joined the RAF in 1934, has no known grave, and is commemorated on Panel 37 of The Runnymede Memorial.
86 On 26 May Embry had been notified of his appointment as CO of RAF West Raynham and of his promotion to acting group captain. Norman Franks recounts that Flight Lieutenant H.P. Pleasance, who was flying with 107 Squadron on 27 May, was probably one of the very few who saw his commanding officer (Embry) hand over command of the squadron to his successor (Squadron Leader L.R. Stokes) in the air! (*Valiant Wings*, p. 207). Born on 28 February 1902, Air Chief Marshal Sir Basil Embry GCB, KBE, DSO and three Bars, DFC, AFC, MiD (three times) died on 8 December 1977.
87 On 19 July 1940 Guderian was promoted for his great successes to *generaloberst*, a rank second only to the highest in the Wehrmacht – *generalfeldmarschall*. Born on 17 June 1888, he died on 14 May 1954.
88 *Mission Completed*, p. 176.
89 For those who are not squeamish the full, gory details of how Embry dealt with his guards may be found in *Wingless Victory*, pp. 135-6.
90 *Mission Completed*, p. 183.
91 This and previous quote from *Mission Completed*, p. 184.
92 *Wingless Victory*, p. 233.
93 *Wingless Victory*, p. 245.
94 Embry was rewarded with a second Bar to his DSO (gazetted 20/8/40). Bird was recommended for the DCM, but this was downgraded to the "standard" award of the MM (29/11/40).
95 Treacy's report M.I.9/S/P.G. (F) 175 in TNA file WO 208/3301.
96 Treacy op. cit.
97 From Dothie's report MI9/S/P.G. (F) 35 in TNA file WO 208/3298.
98 Dothie op. cit.

99 The only vessel by the name of *Aquamarine* found in *Jane's Fighting Ships 1944-5* was in the US Navy. She was, co-incidentally, a patrol vessel (yacht), of 250 tons, and had been built in 1925.
100 Hulls' report MI9/S/P.G. (F) 23 in TNA file WO 208/3298. Hulls, an old soldier, had won the MC in the First World War while serving in the Machine Gun Corps. For his latest exploit he received a Bar to his MC (29/11/40). Commander Elkins, who before the war had been serving on HMS *Cumberland* as the Fleet (Gunnery) Officer on the China station, was Mentioned in Despatches (9/8/40) for 'courage and resource in escaping from the enemy.'
101 Treacy op. cit. He may have been watching Heinkels of Kampfgeschwader 53, then based at Lille-Nord, which lost fifteen of its Heinkels to various causes from 18-29 August 1940.
102 Treacy op. cit.
103 Berry's report MI9/S/P.G. (F) 296 in TNA file WO 208/3303.
104 Phillips' report MI9/S/P.G. (F) 133 in TNA file WO 208/3300.
105 This massive wall at the prisoner-of-war camp at Doullens may well have been part of the old Citadelle, on the south-west corner of the town, which guarded the crossing point of the River Authie.
106 This camp was primarily for German internees, twenty-two of whom were imprisoned there at the time. Sometime during the next three weeks they were removed by a German Mission.
107 Stuart-Menteith's report MI9/S/P.G. (F) 78 in TNA file WO 208/3299.
108 The *Ossian* (Captain Rattray), 1514 gross tons, had been damaged off Lundy Island by enemy aircraft on 25 August 1940.
109 Whereas Stuart-Menteith was only Mentioned in Despatches (31/1/41), both Witton and Phillips received the MM (7/3/41).
110 Barrett's report MI9/S/P.G. (F) 14 in TNA file WO 208/3298.
111 In *Valiant Wings*, pp. 251-5, author Norman Franks mentions this brief but glorious episode involving attacks by the other squadrons on the forest.
112 Barrett op. cit. Marjorie Juta was a South African journalist.
113 Barrett op. cit. Penelope Ellison Phillips CBE, née Otto, (born 5 June 1915, died 10 February 2007), was awarded the French Croix de Guerre on her return to England, with Marjorie Juta, from the Atlantic port of Arcachon. [See the *Daily Telegraph* obituary 13 March 2007].
114 Penelope Otto (231808) and Sheila Angus (231810) were later (May 1942) granted commissions in the Women's Auxiliary Territorial Services.
115 In the words of the Official Report (*London Gazette*, 14 August 1947) 'this operation was a direct daylight assault upon an important objective strongly held by the first army of Europe.'
116 *The Greatest Air Battle*, Norman L.R. Franks (Grub Street, 1992), pp. 107-8. *The London Gazette* of 2 October 1942 also announced that the decoration was for gallantry in connection with the Dieppe raid on 19 August 1942.
117 First incarcerated at Oflag IXA (Spangenberg Castle) he then went to Oflag VIB (Dosel bei Warburg), Stalags Luft I (Barth) and III (Sagan).
118 Hawkins' report MI9/S/P.G. (F) 77 in TNA file WO 208/3299.
119 It is presumed that he did not search the whole 130 kilometres of this stretch of the coast.
120 Hawkins op. cit. Carteret is some 200 kilometres west of Le Havre.
121 Hawkins op. cit. The Germans first landed on Jersey on 1 July 1940.
122 Hawkins op. cit. He does not say how he covered the 600 kilometres to Vichy, but he must have gone much of the way by train.
123 Theoretically the French Unoccupied Zone was free of Germans but, in their own interests, they kept a close eye on their colleagues nevertheless. In his report of 14 March 1941 Pierre Dupuy (see following chapter) noted: 'The presence of 52 German members of the Armistice Control Commission in Casablanca is not considered by Marshal Pétain, Huntziger and Nogues as representing a danger of infiltration.'
124 Waters' report MI9/S/P.G. (F) 89 in TNA file WO 208/3299.
125 Attacks on the Algerian harbours of Oran and Mers-el-Kebir resulted in the deaths of 1,297 French sailors. The Royal Navy's losses were provisionally assessed as two wounded and two missing.
126 James Hugh Hamilton Dodds (1880-1956) had fought in the Boer Wars, and been decorated with The Queens Medal and Africa General Star. From 1911 until his retirement in 1941 he was British Consul in, successively, Abyssinia, Tripoli, Palermo, Nice and finally, Marseille. He and Dean, who had escorted the Duke and Duchess of Windsor from the French riviera to safety in Spain, were to play a useful behind-the-scenes role in Marseille before being asked to leave France, which they did on 11 June 1941.
127 TNA file FO 371/28227 Z1231.
128 Three days later the Church of Scotland also received a cable from the British ambassador to Spain, Sir Samuel Hoare, informing them of Caskie's whereabouts. (Most of the information on Caskie has been taken from *Detachment W*. I am indebted to its author, Derek Richardson, for his kind permission to use his material – Author).
129 In *The Tartan Pimpernel* Caskie refers to the address as 46, rue de Forbin, an error repeated in other eminent works.
130 *The Tartan Pimpernel*, pp. 34-5. It will be remembered that in the previous chapter Clifford met torpedoed American seamen at the mission.
131 TNA file FO 371/28227 Z1231. Equally generous were Polish soldiers stranded in Marseille, who gave freely of their own, limited food rations.
132 It was possibly no coincidence that it was also on 25 July that Potts and Besley were escorted to Fort St Jean.
133 *Detachment W*, p. 24.
134 Besley's report S/P.G. (F) 121 in TNA file WO 208/3300.
135 Besley himself received three payments of £5 for July to September plus a £2 clothing allowance.
136 TNA file FO 371/28277 Z559. Hunter was Mentioned in Despatches (2/5/41) for his own evasion. He was later awarded the MC (16/9/41).
137 Hawkins op. cit.
138 Hogg's report MI9/S/P.G. (F) 80 in TNA file WO 208/3299. "Reds" were communists.
139 A major in the West Yorkshire Regiment during the First World War, William Wyndham Torre Torr was known to his friends as "Bunny" (*American Pimpernel*, p. 176).
140 202 Squadron was engaged on convoy patrols, reconnaissance and intelligence-gathering work.
141 Awarded the Military Cross, Hawkins' luck ran out three years later when, as a squadron leader MC, AFC, he was killed in his 3 Squadron Typhoon on operations on 5 October 1943 near Ghent, Belgium.
142 Recommended for the MBE, Potts was awarded the MC (7/3/41). Waters, Lennon and Hogg were each Mentioned in Despatches (31/1/41), though Hogg had been recommended for the MC.
143 Benjamin and Armstrong returned to their squadron later in the month.
144 The house was later requisitioned by the Gestapo for their HQ.
145 Quotes from *Valiant Wings*, p. 262. Sergeant Dowling is buried in Sougé-sur-Braye Communal Cemetery, together with three leading aircraftmen, all of whom were also killed on 15 June 1940 – R.P. Godfray; M.D.J. Thompson; and H.R. Ward.
146 McFarlane's report MI9/S/P.G. (F) 715 in TNA file WO 208/3308.
147 Roskell's report MI9/S/P.G. (F) 234 in TNA file WO 208/3302.
148 McFarlane op. cit.
149 Roskell op. cit.
150 St Hippolyte-du-Fort (Gard) is approximately fifty kilometres (thrity miles) west-north-west of Nîmes, which is itself some 110

kilometres (seventy miles) north-west of Marseille.
151 *Safe Houses are Dangerous*, p. 37.
152 Though Georges' parents were both Greek they had become British subjects, and Georges was therefore born British too. Despite his British citizenship he was not permitted to join the British army during the First World War, and so became a naturalised Frenchman and served gallantly with the French instead.
153 *Detachment W*, p. 28.
154 Morement's report MI9/S/P.G. (F) 380 in TNA file WO 208/3304.
155 Morement op. cit.
156 Morement op. cit.
157 Hartley's report MI9/S/P.G. (F) 147 in TNA file WO 208/3300.
158 A Royal Navy destroyer of 1,760 tons.
159 He was recommended for, and received, the MM (7/3/41).
160 Morement op. cit.
161 He, too, was recommended for, and eventually received, the MM (13/3/42) in recognition of his outstanding courage and perseverance.
162 Watson's report MI9/S/P.G. (-) 132 in TNA file WO 208/3300. Parker was taken prisoner, and spent the rest of the war in Oflag IXA, Oflag VIB and Stalag Luft III.
163 Both 4th Queen's Own Cameron Highlanders, 152nd Brigade, 51st (Highland) Division.
164 Quotes, as above, from Watson op. cit. Captain Johnson left Gibraltar on 9 October 1940 and was back in England (Barrow-in-Furness) on 27 October, with Hogg and Waters.
165 McKenzie received no award, though McAngus and Tull received the MM (7/3/41).
166 Willis' report MI9/S/P.G. (F) 494 in TNA file WO 208/3306.
167 Willis op. cit. Captain G was Captain Ian Garrow.
168 The other aircraft that failed to return was Hampden X3141, 50 Squadron. One of its five crew was taken prisoner of war, and the other four killed.
169 This and previous quote from Sergeant A.J. Mott's report MI9/S/P.G. (-) 607 in TNA file WO 208/3307.
170 M. Hevin was later arrested by the Germans and shot on 22 October 1941 (*Free to Fight Again*, p. 120).
171 *Free to Fight Again*, p. 121.
172 Mott's report op. cit.
173 *Free to Fight Again*, p. 122.
174 Parkes' report MI9(b)/S/P.G. (-) 346 in TNA file WO 208/3304.
175 As Wing Commander Healy was CO of 9 Squadron from 24 July 1940 to 16 January 1941, the letter presumably went to his successor.
176 Parkes op. cit.
177 Parkes op. cit. Amazingly, Parkes still had his service revolver with him, but gave it to Captain Murchie before he, Parkes, left for Spain.
178 Parkes op. cit.
179 Information on the Masos kindly supplied by François Maso's grandson via Keith Janes (email 28 February 2008).
180 Bratley's report MI9/S/P.G. (-) 351 in TNA file WO 208/3304.
181 Willis/Vivian/Blaydon joint reports MI9/S/P.G. (-) 712, 713, 714 in TNA file WO 208/3308.
182 Ibid.
183 Blaydon's report, op. cit.
184 Ibid.

Chapter 2

185 *MI6*, p. 114.
186 *Secret Sunday*, p. 17.
187 *Secret Sunday*, p. 19.
188 Born on 15 October 1907, he died on 13 September 1967.
189 This was a Boeing 314A four-engined flying boat airliner. It crashed at Lisbon on 22 February 1943.
190 Hôtel Suisse reference from *American Pimpernel*, p. 104. The Splendide was a superior hotel of 'très belle apparence, avec grand confort moderne.' *(Guide de pneu Michelin 1939).*
191 *Surrender on Demand*, p. 36.
192 A former Italian politician and now a refugee on account of his being a leading figure of the anti-Fascist movement *Giustizia e Libertà* (Justice and Liberty), his story is told by his wife, Joyce Lussu Salvadori, in *Freedom Has No Frontier*.
193 *Surrender on Demand*, p. 72. Cap Croisette is a promontory only a couple of kilometres south of Marseille.
194 Quoted in *American Pimpernel*, p. 177.
195 TNA file FO 371/28277 Z559. Hopkinson was, post war, Minister of State in the Colonial Office. (Italics are the author's).
196 Both quotes from TNA file FO 371/28277 Z559.
197 *Detachment W*, p. 32.
198 Sillar had escaped with Fitch from a German prisoner-of-war camp near Tournai on 12/13 July 1940. The pair later met Captain B.C. Bradford and Captain A.M.K. Martin, Durham Light Infantry, but decided to split up as a group of four was thought to be too unwieldy.
199 *Surrender on Demand*, p. 106.
200 This and previous quote from *Surrender on Demand*, pp. 110 and 108.
201 *American Pimpernel*, p. 219.
202 *Surrender on Demand*, p. 113.
203 Windsor-Lewis' report MI9/S/P.G. (B) 159 in TNA file WO 208/3300. The other British officer was Captain A.M.K. Martin.
204 This and the three previous quotes from Windsor-Lewis op. cit.
205 Windsor-Lewis op. cit. The Dakar incident had taken place on 8 July 1940. It involved Lieutenant-Commander R.H. Bristowe RN taking a motor boat into Dakar harbour and laying explosive charges under the steering gear and propellers of the French battleship *Richelieu* to prevent her moving. Once this daring feat had been accomplished, the way was clear for aircraft of the Fleet Air Arm to torpedo her as she lay at anchor.
206 *Detachment W*, p. 41.
207 Lang was awarded the MC (21/3/41), and was later Mentioned in Despatches (16/9/41).
208 Later commanding officer of No. 161 (Special Duties) Squadron, he ended a distinguished career as Air Chief Marshal Sir Lewis Hodges KCB, CBE, DSO and Bar, DFC and Bar, and President of the RAF Escaping Society. He died on 4 January 2007.
209 *Free to Fight Again*, p. 33. Sir Brooks Richards says that altogether there were some forty stowaways aboard the *Ville de Verdun* (*Secret Flotillas* Vol.II, p. 11).
210 *American Pimpernel*, p. 116. Bohn had also been sent to Marseille (he had a room at the Hôtel Splendide), by the American Federation of Labor, 'to extract various labor leaders, union officials, and democratic politicians whose lives were now endangered.' *American Pimpernel*, p. 114.
211 *Freedom Has No Frontier*, p. 27.
212 *Freedom Has No Frontier*, p. 28.
213 *Freedom Has No Frontier*, p. 60.

214 Born 4 December 1890, Lussu died in Rome on 5 March 1975. Gioconda (Joyce) Salvadori, born 8 May 1912, died on 4 November 1998.
215 *Freedom Has No Frontier*, p. 61. In 1943 and 1944 Heslop would feature in the evasions of several airmen in eastern France.
216 *Xavier*, pp. 42-3.
217 *Secret Sunday*, pp. 19-20.
218 TNA file HS 6/1000. "Esc." are *escudos*, the Portuguese currency.
219 TNA file HS 6/1000.
220 See website http://en.wikipedia.org/wiki/Calouste_Gulbenkian. Born on 23 March 1869, Calouste Gulbenkian died on 20 July 1955.
221 Both quotes *Pantaraxia*, p. 198.
222 *Detachment W*, p. 45. The officer was Flight Lieutenant W.P.F. Treacy, and one of the sergeants was Sergeant R.W. Lonsdale.
223 *Secret Sunday*, p. 27. According to Darling, however, Parker was to provide useful intelligence of the area.
224 *Secret Sunday*, p. 21.
225 From the ambassador's report of 4 June 1941 in TNA file FO 371/28281 Z5212.
226 The mountains inland from Banyuls and along the Spanish border rise from 540 metres/1,755 feet to the 716 metres/2,327 feet Pic du Col d'el Tourn, some eight kilometres from the coast.
227 *Ambassador On Special Mission*, p. 230. In 1941/1942 the exchange rate was reckoned to be 46.55 pesetas to the pound.
228 Having served in the RAF Technical branch, Mesopotamian Wing, Middle East Area, with effect from 15 September 1920, Charles Plowman Murchie was posted as a supernumerary flying officer to RAF Depot, Uxbridge, with effect from 10 November 1921, and was put on the class "B" list of the Reserve of Air Force Officers with effect from 2 August 1922.
229 Private H.H. Kimble's report MI9/S/P.G./MISC/INT/668 in TNA file WO 208/3345.
230 Kimble op. cit.
231 Murchie's report MI9/S/P.G. (-) 681 in TNA file WO 208/3308. Three of the "RASC" were Privates H.H. Kimble, M. Allen, and C. Camgee who, having been arrested by three German officers, were to spend the next four years in the civilian internment camp at St Denis, near Paris. Two others were Sergeant T. Boyle RASC, who was back by the spring of 1941, and Private R.E. Knight RASC, who ended up in Laghouat, the Vichy French camp in North Africa, and who did not return to the UK until the end of 1942.
232 Clayton's report MI9/S/P.G. (G) 701 in TNA file WO 208/3308. It is possible that the 'pro-British organisation' was the one established in the Lille area by the mercenary Harold Cole.
233 TNA file FO 371/26949 C10338. The reader will note Murchie's use of "I" and "me" rather than "us" and "we".
234 The 1st Glasgow Highlanders were one of the two battalions of the 157th Brigade (Brigadier Sir John Laurie Bt.), which was itself one of the three brigades forming the 52nd (Lowland) Division (Major-General J.S. Drew).
235 Garrow's report MI9/S/P.G. (F) 1075 in TNA file WO 208/3312. Other officers present at Bélâbre were Lieutenant H.S.M. Hogg RE; Captain P.P. Raikes RE; and Lieutenant W. Sillar RAMC who, as seen, was posted to Banyuls to help evaders across the Pyrenees.
236 From a letter to his mother, delivered by Captain James Langley on his repatriation [TNA file AIR 40/1545].
237 Hopkins' report MI9/S/P.G. (-) 716 in TNA file WO 208/3308.
238 O'Shea was not so fortunate. Transferred to an Italian prisoner-of-war camp on 6 December 1942, he went to Germany in late 1943.
239 MacDonald's report MI9/S/P.G. (-) 959 in TNA file WO 208/3311. MacDonald would eventually reach Britain on 1 November 1942.
240 Rennie's report MI9/S/P.G. (-) 492 in TNA file WO 208/3305.
241 Rear gunner Sergeant T.H. Marquiss and wireless operator Sergeant E.R. Berkey RCAF are buried in Dilsen churchyard, Belgium.
242 Rennie op. cit.
243 Rennie op. cit.
244 For their evasions Hibbert was awarded the MM and Rennie the MC (both 13/3/42). Willis got nothing. Rennie was never to return to his native South Africa, for he was killed in an accident on 19 October 1942 as a flight lieutenant pilot instructor at No. 14 OTU (Cottesmore).
245 *Saturday at MI9*, p. 78. Garrow is also described in *Nancy Wake*, p. 27, as being 'very tall, strongly built, clean-shaven and good-looking – a Scot of great charm and considerable cunning.'
246 *Detachment W*, p. 39.
247 *Safer Than a Known Way*, p. 36. Major Newman had himself been left behind on 2 June with the 12th CCS. He escaped from the Heilag (repatriation camp) at Rouen on 16 February 1942, and reached Spain. He sailed from Gibraltar on 4 May 1942, reaching Gourock eight days later. He added an MC to his DSO.
248 Tachon had belonged to 23 Field Regiment, RA, attached to 51 (H) Division. He, too, escaped from the hospital on 5 October 1940, but served with the Resistance until October 1944.
249 Langley's report MI9/S/P.G. (B) 213 in TNA file WO 208/3301.
250 *Fight Another Day*, p. 101. The officers' parole, generous though it may have been, was not extended to the other ranks, but Dodds and Dean, from their office at the US Consulate, were able to provide them with suitable 'comforts'.
251 *Fight Another Day*, p. 103.
252 *Fight Another Day*, p. 105. Langley describes "Maloney" as being 'over six feet tall with a mop of fair curly hair and a wide open face'. At a *maison de rendezvous* couples could rent a room for the purpose of enjoying intimate relations.
253 *Turncoat*, p. 68.
254 Appendix C, Garrow's report MI9/S/P.G. (-) 1075 in TNA file WO 208 5582.
255 *Safe Houses Are Dangerous*, p. 22.
256 *Freedom the Spur*, p. 222.
257 Ibid, p. 228. In his book *Freedom the Spur* Instone more or less claims that he was the driving force in the escape. At the very end of his report – MI9/S/P.G. (F) 268 in TNA file WO 208/3303 made to MI9 on 13 April 1941 – he himself suggests that things may have been somewhat different: 'My subsequent journey through Spain was made under the leadership of Sgt. Jackson.' Whilst so engaged Instone was posing as a sergeant.
258 *Freedom the Spur*, p. 230.
259 Lonsdale's story is related in *Free to Fight Again*, pp. 30-32. Instone has a fuller account in his book *Freedom the Spur*.
260 Instone wrote that it was 'decided that the 31st December would be the ideal night' for their escape, when the 'guards would undoubtedly be celebrating New Year's Eve and would be far less vigilant than usual' – *Freedom the Spur*, p. 231.
261 HMT *Empire Trooper*, 13,994 tons, was originally the German ship *Cap Norte*, built in 1922. She was captured off the Faroe Islands on 9 October 1939 by HMS *Belfast*. The re-named *Empire Trooper* ironically suffered severe damage at the hands of a German raider on 25 December 1940.
262 Though Lonsdale (13/3/42) and Instone (15/7/41) were both awarded the MM, Jack Wyatt was only Mentioned in Dispatches (11/6/42).
263 Flown from Lisbon Treacy was back in England on 1 February. He was to be killed on operations as a squadron leader DSO on 20 April 1941.
264 *Turncoat*, p. 62.
265 *Detachment W*, p. 67.
266 Appendix C, Hewit's report MI9/S/P.G. (-) 1063 in TNA file WO 208/5582.
267 See *Detachment W*, pp. 50-56.
268 TNA file FO 371/28277 Z888.
269 Langley's report MI9/S/P.G. (B) 213 in TNA file WO 208/3301.
270 Hodges' report MI9/S/P.G. (-) 345 in TNA file WO 208/3304.

271 TNA file FO 371/26949A C6013.
272 Ibid.
273 TNA file FO 371/26949A C6013.
274 TNA file FO 371/26949A C6764.
275 TNA file FO 371/28285 Z5713.
276 The strength of Detachment W had risen to 253 by the middle of April 1941 – see *Detachment W*, pp. 68 and 86.
277 TNA file FO 371/28281 Z5617.
278 TNA file FO 371/28281 Z5630.
279 TNA file FO 371/28281 Z5841.
280 TNA file FO 371/28281 Z5629.
281 TNA file FO 371/28285 Z9365. In French the order read: 'Les sentinelles sont autorisées à tirer, après trois sommations et deux coups tirés en l'air, sur ceux des militaires britanniques internés qui tenteraient de s'évader.'
282 Appendix C, Parkinson's report MI9/S/P.G. (-) 611 in TNA file WO 208/5582.
283 Hewit's report MI9/S/P.G. (-) 1063 in TNA file WO 208/3312. See also Chapter 4 for Hewit and Milton's escape attempt.
284 Presumably the compass was thrown out by the storm and the Hudson ran out of fuel having flown in the wrong direction.
285 Milton's report MI9/S/P.G. (-) 1039 in TNA files WO 208/3312 and AIR 20/9159.
286 TNA file FO 371/26949B C13164.
287 See TNA file FO 371/26949B C13164: 'Minne himself made six or seven expeditions to the Lille area and each time brought down a party safely.' Murchie, however, said that Minne 'made five journeys from Lille, bringing five British soldiers or officers each time.' TNA file FO 371/26949A C10338.
288 TNA file FO 371/26949A C10338.
289 TNA file FO 371/26949A C10338.
290 TNA file FO 371/28281 Z5301.
291 It is not known when or how André Minne and the others returned to England, but Minne would return to France in due course as a radio operator for Georges Broussine and his Burgundy network (see Chapter 8). Minne was caught at work by the Germans in August 1943 (see *L'évadé de la France Libre*, p. 169) and deported to Buchenwald, happily surviving the war.
292 The six were Sergeant James Chalmers, Privates F. Drayton, James McDonagh, Robert Osborne, Sam Thompson and T.S. Turner, from No. 13 Platoon, "C" Company. Dodd was from "D" Company.
293 *The Long Way Round*, p. 61.
294 *Secret Sunday*, p. 30.
295 Quotes from *The Real Enemy*, p. 13.
296 St Marthe, the French military HQ in Marseille, was also a prison for serving *légionnaires*.
297 *The Long Way Round*, p. 132.
298 La Comtesse Lili Pastré (1891-1974) was to hide many people, including Jews, in her home as they tried to escape from France during the war.
299 Joint report MI9(b)/S/P.G. (-) 284-290 in TNA file WO 208/3303. In *The Long Way Round*, p. 133, Broad 'waved a piece of blank paper at the Senegalese sentry, shouted a cheerful French phrase or two, and walked out with Private Rankine of the 4th Seaforths, who possessed a genuine pass.'
300 Ibid.
301 Appendix C, Garrow's report MI9/S/P.G. (-) 1075 in TNA file WO 208/5582.
302 *The Long Way Round*, p. 135.
303 Report MI9(b)/S/P.G. (-) 284-290 in TNA file WO 208/3303. Illingworth was not an officer but was 6896836 Lance-Corporal N.R. Illingworth, Queen Victoria's Rifles. He had gone to Cassis-sur-Mer to stay with his uncle, Lieutenant-Colonel Crothers, before returning to Marseille in February 1941. He made his way to Spain later that month with Captain L.A. Wilkins, and was in the Miranda de Ebro camp with Wilkins and Lieutenant Broad for a while. Illingworth died on 29 March 1944, and is buried at Woking (St John's) Crematorium. He was mentioned on 20 September 1945, along with others of his regiment, 'in recognition of gallant and distinguished services in the Defence of Calais in May, 1940.'
304 See http://www.dfait-maeci.gc.ca/department/history/Dupuy-en.asp.
305 Interestingly, Mr Dupuy's summary of his latest findings in Vichy dated 14 March 1941, made on his return to London, referred, inter alia, to the problems surrounding French merchant shipping, for example: '(11) The recent seizure of French merchant ships [by the Germans] has caused great dissatisfaction with French Admiralty, as reason of blockade could not be given because a certain number of these ships were empty. (12) The Germans accused French Admiralty of permitting their ships to be seized by the British in order to replace British ships sunk by U-boats. (13) The Germans have menaced French with cancelling their permission to use their mercantile marine, if proper orders were not given to protect it from being seized.'
306 Note the similarity between this scheme and the Fitch/Fry one referred to earlier in this chapter. If indeed it were a "Swiss" ship, then it may well have been on hire to the International Red Cross for ferrying prisoner-of-war parcels from Lisbon to Marseille, a route that had only opened in January 1941.
307 Whether this was true or not is unclear, but Margaret Palmer was certainly a go-between for Varian Fry and Jay Allen. Allen had gone to Vichy to hopefully interview Marshal Pétain (but failed to get the meeting).
308 *The Long Way Round*, p. 138. This room was in the building at 13, rue des Phocéens – see above, this chapter.
309 Broad's report MI9/S/P.G. (-) 284 in TNA file WO 208/3303.
310 Murphy says (*Turncoat*, p. 74) that Elizabeth Haden-Guest was a 'Jew and Communist militant of Baltic origins' and that she was, according to Dr Rodocanachi, 'devoted body and soul to Ian Garrow'.
311 Quotes from pages 4-7 of a report in TNA file WO 208/3303 collated from reports MI9(b)/S/P.G. (-) 284-290.
312 Finally released from Miranda de Ebro in August 1941 Jean-Pierre Nouveau joined the Free French Forces, and fought with distinction for the remainder of the war, which he survived.
313 Broad was rewarded with the MC (15/7/41) for, as was the usual official wording involving an evasion, 'distinguished services in the field'.
314 Murphy says that two million francs went missing (*Turncoat*, p. 72). William Moore says that it was only 700,000 francs and that they had been procured by Tom Kenny 'from a friend in Cannes as a loan to be repaid by the British Government.' (*The Long Way Home*, p. 141).
315 See *Detachment W*, pp. 65-6.
316 TNA file FO 371/26949A C10338.
317 The Langley quotes are from his report MI9/S/P.G. (B) 213 in TNA file WO 208/3301.
318 *The Tartan Pimpernel*, p. 51.
319 With an exchange rate at the time of approximately 176 French francs to the pound, £5,000 equates to 880,000 francs.
320 *Safe Houses Are Dangerous*, pp. 57-8. Lieutenant Broad noted, however, that Nouveau gave 60,000 francs to the cause.
321 *Secret Sunday*, p. 119.
322 *Safe Houses Are Dangerous*, p. 59.
323 Nancy and Henri were married on 30 November 1939 'to the dismay of his Catholic family'. (*Warriors*, p. 285).
324 *Warriors*, p. 286.
325 *Nancy Wake*, p. 21.

326 From website http://www.64-baker-street.org/agents/agent_fany_nancy_wake_news_04.html.
327 *Nancy Wake*, p. 27.
328 Information on Dowding is taken from Peter Dowding's account on Christopher Long's website.
329 Dodds departed for Spain on 11 June 1941.
330 On his return to England, after a spell in Miranda de Ebro's camp, Anthony Brooks joined SOE's F Section. By war's end he was a major with the DSO and MC. Born on 4 April 1922, he died on 19 April 2007. See his obituary in the *Daily Telegraph*, 15 May 2007.
331 *The Tartan Pimpernel*, p. 103.
332 *The Tartan Pimpernel*, p. 114. Caskie also wrote in his book that he was ordered to close down the mission. The large university town of Grenoble (population then of 90,000) lies some 275 kilometres to the north of Marseille.
333 *The Tartan Pimpernel*, p. 189.
334 *The Tartan Pimpernel*, pp. 201-2.
335 *Le Rhin*, 2,456 tons, was British-built in 1920.
336 Born in Hanoi, Tong-King (French Indo-China, today Vietnam), on 7 April 1908.
337 *Secret Flotillas*, p. 16, Volume II.
338 *Claude and Madeleine*, p. 116.
339 British merchant ships commanded by an officer of the Royal Naval Reserve (RNR), and having in the ship's complement not less than seven other officers and men of the RNR, were entitled to fly the Blue Ensign from the ship while the RNR officer was in command. As for the White Ensign, adopted in 1864 as the sole Ensign of the fleet, only ships of the Royal Navy were entitled to fly it. In the case of *Le Rhin* not a few rules were broken!
340 *Claude and Madeleine*, quoted on p. 126.
341 From website http://www.rafinfo.org.uk/rafescape/guerisse.htm.
342 Madeleine Victorine Bayard was born in Paris on 21 February 1911.
343 *Claude and Madeleine*, p. 158.
344 *Claude and Madeleine*, p. 162.
345 *F Section SOE*, p. 11. Egbert Victor Hector Rizzo was appointed OBE (17 July 1945) for his 'brave conduct'.
346 In 1961 Roman Garby-Czerniawski, the founder and head of Interallié, published the story of this network in his book *The Big Network*.
347 *Claude and Madeleine*, p. 172.
348 HMS *Fidelity*, p. 136.
349 It was not uncommon for Frenchmen to assume false names. Had they kept their original French name – Fergusson's was Fourcade, and he came from nearby le Barcarès – they could have been condemned to death in *absentia* by a Vichy court-martial. Furthermore, they would be hated by the Gaullists for not joining the Fighting Free French. One of *Fidelity*'s crew to survive its sinking was Jean-Jacques Gilbert. He first took the surname Allen but changed it yet again, possibly after a stay in Cornwall, to Tremayne – see *The Last Piece of England*, p. 167.
350 According to Sir Brooks Richards (*Secret Flotillas*, p. 18, Volume II) the evacuation was to have been from Cerbère, some twenty kilometres south of Collioure.
351 *Fidelity* completed only one other operation in the Mediterranean, on the night of 19/20 September 1941, when four SOE agents were landed at le Barcarès for the Autogiro/Urchin network. Refitted for work in the Far East, in convoy ONS 154 on 29 December 1942 she was torpedoed by U-435 (Lieutenant Siegfried Strelow) and lost with all hands. The story of this 'Q' ship has been told in HMS *Fidelity* (1957). A more detailed account appears in *Claude and Madeleine* (2005).
352 *Turncoat*, p. 109. Nîmes is approximately fifty kilometres from St Hippolyte.
353 *Turncoat*, p. 109.

Chapter 3

354 Lieutenant H.L. Farquhar, Coldstream Guards, won his MC in the First World War.
355 *The Second World War*, Vol. II, pp. 459-60. Winston S. Churchill (Cassell, London, 1949; Penguin, London, 1985).
356 Born on 4 December 1892, Franco probably died on 19 November 1975, though officially his death was announced as having occurred on 20 November.
357 Churchill op. cit. p. 459.
358 *The Second Great War. A Standard History*, edition No. 80, p. 3154 (September 1945).
359 In his article in the *Daily Mail* of 4 February 2006, Andrew Roberts suggests that up to 'one million people perished in the civil war, including 200,000 shot on General Franco's orders after his victory in April 1939.'
360 *Ambassador on Special Mission*, p. 14. The appointment with effect from 1 June 1940 of 'The Right Honourable Sir Samuel John Gurney Hoare, Bart., GCS.I, GBE, CMG, to be His Majesty's Ambassador Extraordinary and Plenipotentiary on Special Mission to the Spanish State' was published in *The London Gazette* of 2 August 1940.
361 *Ambassador on Special Mission*, p. 31. Nigel West, in *MI6*, p. 109, makes it clear that Sir Samuel did not help matters on arrival in Madrid. He had 'a number of prejudices against SIS [MI6] and imposed severe restrictions on the activities of the local head of station, Mr Hamilton-Stokes.' As a result the 'Madrid Station virtually ceased to operate', and thereafter great reliance was placed upon the Americans.
362 Súñer, born on 12 September 1901, died on 1 September 2003.
363 *The Trial of German Major War Criminals*, Part 4, p. 92 (HMSO, London, 1946).
364 TNA files FO 371/24517, C11790 and FO 800/323. Beigbeder, born 31 March 1888, died on 6 June 1957.
365 *Ambassador on Special Mission*, p. 77.
366 TNA files FO 371/28281 Z5212.
367 MacCallum op. cit.
368 MacCallum's report MI9/S/P.G. (-) 374 in TNA file WO 208/3304.
369 Their MMs were gazetted on 26 May 1942. As the DCM was at that time deemed to be an "army" medal it could not be given to an airman.
370 Information on Whittinghill from *Women in the Resistance*, pp. 37-8.
371 Captured on 13 June 1940 in the fighting at St Valéry-en-Caux in northern France, Batho escaped ten days later.
372 Appendix C, MacCallum's report MI9/S/P.G. (-) 374 in TNA file AIR 40/1545.
373 The author is unclear as to whether or not this prison was also the *Prisión de Partido de Figueras*.
374 TNA file FO 371/28285 Z9357.
375 TNA file FO 371/28285 Z9357.
376 *No Banners*, p. 71.
377 Southgate relinquished his (honorary) commission with effect from 16 June 1945, on appointment to the RAF Volunteer Reserve.
378 *Freedom the Spur*, p. 242.
379 *Freedom the Spur*, p. 243.
380 TNA file FO 371/28281 Z5212.
381 *Ambassador On Special Mission*, p. 233. Sir Samuel Hoare states that at one time relief for Miranda prisoners was costing the embassy over £1,000 per day, though some of this was defrayed by the Red Cross.
382 Both quotes from a minute dated 26 November 1941 in TNA file FO 371/26949B C13265.
383 Report by Brigadier Torr dated 1 May 1942 in TNA file FO 371/31226 C5280.
384 Ibid.

385 Torr's report op. cit. Brigadier Torr was ably assisted by Lieutenant-Colonel Drummond-Wolff. Sir Samuel Hoare gave credit where it was due when he reported: 'Without their unceasing efforts I do not believe that we should have got more than a mere handful of the men through Spain.' FO 371/28281 Z5212.
386 TNA file FO 371/28281 Z5212.
387 TNA file FO 371/26949B C13310.
388 TNA file FO 371/26949A C10338.
389 TNA file FO 371/31224 C140. It is to be wondered what might have happened had such important matters of state not been resolved satisfactorily.
390 *Fighter Pilot*, p. 175. Barclay had arrived at the embassy on 11 November 1941, and left on 7 December.
391 From Collie's report MI9/S/P.G. (F) 807 in TNA files WO 208/3310 and WO 208/3242.
392 Aston wrote of his adventures in *Nor Iron Bars a Cage*.
393 These men were probably Sergeants B. Evans, J.T. Pack, W.J. Norfolk, and P. Wright of the RAF, and Private W. MacFarlane, 7th Argyll & Sutherland Highlanders, 51st (Highland) Division.
394 Collie's report op. cit. In due course Collie was appointed MBE (29/9/42) 'in recognition of gallant and distinguished services in the field.'
395 *Ambassador on Special Mission*, p. 232.
396 *They Have Their Exits*, p. 143.
397 Besley op. cit.
398 Besley op. cit.
399 Major Charles Robert Ingram Besley MBE, MC, 9th Bn. Royal Northumberland Fusiliers, died aged thirty-four on 14 February 1942. He was buried in Kranji War Cemetery, Singapore. Though appointed MBE on 7 March 1941 his MC was not gazetted until 11 October 1945.
400 Sir Samuel Hoare to Foreign Office in a message dated 17 January 1941 in TNA file FO 371/26949B C666. There was no airman by the name of "Bob Wilson" evading at this time. The only British serviceman of that name at this time was Sergeant R.L. Wilson RAMC.
401 *Ambassador on Special Mission*, p. 78. Cardigan, born 26 January 1904, wrote of his experiences in *I Walked Alone*. He became 7th Marquess of Ailesbury in 1961, and died on 15 July 1974. He was also the 29th Hereditary Warden of Savernake Forest.
402 *I Walked Alone*, p. 127. 1,000 francs was the equivalent of approximately £6.
403 Ibid, p. 152.
404 Ibid, p. 175.
405 Both were Mentioned in Despatches, as was the Earl of Cardigan (31/1/41).
406 *Ambassador on Special Mission*, p. 78.
407 TNA file FO 371/28281 Z5212.
408 TNA file FO 371/26949A C428.
409 TNA file FO 371/28281 Z5301.
410 The previous Secretary of State for Foreign Affairs, Lord Halifax, had been appointed ambassador to the USA following the death, on 12 December 1940, of the then ambassador, Philip Henry Kerr, 11th Marquess of Lothian.
411 TNA file FO 371/28281 Z5212.
412 TNA file FO 371/28281 Z5516.
413 TNA file FO 371/28281 Z5516.
414 Report dated 19 June 1941, in TNA file FO 371/28281 Z5516. What these activities were of Darling's is not clear.
415 *Secret Sunday*, p. 21.
416 *Within Two Cloaks*, p. 88. PIDE (Polícia Internacional e de Defesa do Estado) were the Portuguese International and State Defence Police. Strictly speaking, PIDE did not come into being until 1945. Until then it was the PVDE (Polícia de Vigilância e de Defesa do Estado) – State Defence and Surveillance Police.
417 TNA file FO 371/28281 Z5212.
418 TNA file FO 371/28281 Z5516.
419 Lieutenant Michael Duncan recalls that the car in which he was being driven from Barcelona to Madrid in May 1942 suffered no fewer than three punctures. See *Underground from Posen*, p. 188.
420 TNA file FO 371/31224 C2509/41. With an exchange rate of 46.55 pesetas to the £1, total expenditure amounted to almost £8,800.
421 Farquhar was fulsome in his praise of his two assistants: 'Their unfailing devotion to duty and readiness to undertake any task at any hour have contributed largely to the success of the activities' described. TNA file FO 371/31224 C2509/41.
422 TNA file FO 371/31224 C2509/41.
423 TNA file HS 6/968.
424 TNA file FO 371/31225 C1394.
425 TNA file FO 371/31226 C8014.
426 TNA file FO 371/31226 C8014.
427 TNA file FO 371/31226 C8014. Farquhar clearly had little appreciation of the value of trained aircrew vis-à-vis machines.
428 TNA file FO 371/31226 C11236.
429 TNA file FO 371/31226 C11659.
430 See *The Big Network*, p. 28.
431 TNA file HS 6/968.
432 Guillén was executed by the Franco regime on 24 April 1945.
433 This and two previous quotes from *Secret Sunday*, p. 35.
434 37943 Squadron Leader George Forbes Rodney was a Canadian, from Calgary, who had enlisted in the RAF in 1936. Involved in experimental flying prior to the Second World War he had been awarded the AFC (gazetted 2/1/39) while serving on 148 Squadron.
435 Rodney's report in TNA file AIR 40/1545.
436 Sir Samuel Hoare, 2 August 1941, to Foreign Office, in TNA file FO 371/26929 C8706. The other two officers were Rodney's second pilot, Flying Officer the Honourable M. Child-Villiers (related to the Earls of Jersey), and Flying Officer E.I.J. Bell. Three of the eleven other-ranks airmen were from Rodney's crew, five from Bell's, and three from Sergeant Bryant's Blenheim.
437 Ibid. HMS *Malvernian*, an ocean boarding vessel of 3,133 tons, was abandoned on 19 July 1941 after it was bombed off the Spanish coast. Thirty-two of the fifty-seven crew reached Corunna on 21 July, with the other twenty-five landing at Vigo on the following day.
438 Later promoted wing commander, Rodney was appointed CO of 626 (B) Squadron in 1944, ending his career as a group captain DFC (16/1/45), AFC, MiD (14/1/44). He died on 16 January 1971.
439 TNA file AIR 40/1545.
440 It is not absolutely clear whether Sergeant Bryant spoke to the vice-consul at Corunna or to the pro-consul. The former was Henry Guyatt, OBE, the latter, there at the same time, Henry J. Guyatt. There was also a third Guyatt on the diplomatic staff in Spain at this time – C.H. Guyatt, one of the two vice-consuls at Bilbao.
441 Bryant's report MI9/S/P.G. (-) 731 in TNA file WO 208/3308. Soria lies some 220 kilometres north-east of Madrid.
442 Bryant was killed in a night-flying accident on 11 December 1942 when Wellington X3961, 27 OTU, crashed soon after take-off.
443 Graham Warner states in *The Bristol Blenheim. A Complete History*, p. 480, (Crécy Publishing Ltd, Manchester, 2002) that Z7366 was Sergeant Bryant's aircraft. James J. Halley, however, in *Royal Air Force Aircraft X1000 to X9999 Z1000 to Z9999* (Air-Britain [Historians]

Ltd, Tonbridge, 1984) confirms 'Force-landed near Faro… 20.7.41'.
444 TNA file AIR 40/1545.
445 The 4,019-ton *Briarwood* had been damaged by bombs off Portland on 4 July 1940. She survived the war.
446 Auamara lies between Larache and Alcazarquivir, and very close to the border with French Morocco.
447 TNA file FO 371/26929 C8881.
448 QDM stands for Question Direction Magnetic – what is my magnetic compass bearing? The reply to a QDM is a QDR.
449 Sergeant H.J. King's report to the officer commanding RAF Watton, 16 August 1941, in TNA file AIR 40/1545.
450 Ibid.
451 Sir Samuel Hoare to Foreign Office 30 July 1941, in TNA file FO 371/26929 C8881.
452 In view of the date of their arrival back at Watton it is tempting to believe that the King crew also returned to Britain aboard the *Pasteur* with the Williams crew.
453 Posted to 158 Squadron, and still only twenty-one years of age, Webber was killed in action on the night of 3/4 April 1943 (Essen) when Halifax DT795 crashed into a dyke in Holland. There were no survivors.
454 Nine months later, having joined 630 Squadron, Flight Lieutenant Perrers and his three sergeants (now flight sergeants), together with three new crew members were lost when Lancaster JB236 was shot down on a raid to Berlin (23/24 November 1943). Only Crowe and Mutum survived, as prisoners of war.
455 The Wellingtons were HX597 (lost 3 October), HX680 (9 October), and HX775 (23 October). Blenheim BA738, 18 Squadron, was lost on 10 November, and Blenheim BA807, 1 OADU, on 17 November.
456 Copy of letter via Matt Poole.
457 They were shot down by two Nakajima Ki-43 single-engine fighters flown by Bunichi Yamaguchi (nineteen kills in the war) and Hiroshi Takiguchi (nine kills) of the Japanese Army Air Force's 204th Sentai (flying regiment). A second Liberator from 159 Squadron, BZ926, was also shot down by these two. (Information kindly supplied by Matt Poole.) Bernard Clifton's DFM was gazetted on 6 June 1941 (58 Squadron).

Chapter 4

458 'Friend, if you should fall, another friend will come from the shadows to take your place.' From *Le Chant des Partisans*. Words by J. Kessel and M. Druon; set to music by A. Marly, London, 1943.
459 Gibbs crossed to Spain with Sergeant J. Burridge, Sergeant A.C. Roberts RAAF, Driver R. McClelland RA, and Gunner W. Liddle RA.
460 Appendix C, Parkinson's report MI9/S/P.G. (-) 611 in TNA file WO 208/5582.
461 Appendix C, Parkinson's report, op. cit. They had in fact scaled the aptly named Pic de l'Homme Mort, 2,636 metres/8,567 feet above sea level, and had indeed been on track for Andorra, their goal.
462 Parkinson reported that Tremargat was one of the French crew of HMS *Fidelity*. Sir Brooks Richards (*Secret Flotillas*, Volume II, p. 18) says that one of the three French crewmen was called Lalande. Edward Marriott names none of the three Frenchmen in *Claude and Madeleine*.
463 Worby/Campbell reports MI9/S/P.G. (-) 633 and 634 in TNA file WO 208/3307.
464 Lieutenant Parkinson was appointed MBE (12/5/42), while Worby and Campbell were Mentioned in Despatches. Captain Richard Edward Hope Parkinson MBE was killed in action on 4 November 1942, and is buried in El Alamein War Cemetery.
465 Herbert's report MI9/S/P.G. (-) 629 in TNA file WO 208/3307. Neither of the two gunners, both twenty-four years of age, has a known grave. Sergeant R.W. Channer is commemorated on Panel 41 of the Runnymede Memorial and Sergeant J. Golding on Panel 43.
466 Humphris and McLean joint reports MI9/S/P.G. (-) 566 & 567 in TNA file WO 208/3306. Herbert, however, says in his report that they were picked up at 2000 hours on 5 May 1941, not 6 May.
467 Again, Herbert has a different date, stating that they arrived at Marseille on 9 May.
468 The attack was not a complete waste of time, for one hit was scored on a 2,000-ton ship. Report on Ingram from TNA file AIR 40/1545. Miller's journey to Spain is recounted in the previous chapter. Another Blenheim, V6430, was shot down into the Atlantic with no survivors.
469 See Chapter 2.
470 This and previous quote from Humphris/McLean joint report op. cit.
471 Papers of M.O.A. Baudot de Rouville, Archive YDX 207/14, p. 7.
472 *Safe Houses Are Dangerous*, p. 95. It was to this bar in April 1942 that Airey Neave and Hugh Woollatt were sent from Switzerland after their escapes from Germany – see Chapter 3. For Neave's description of le Petit Poucet see *They Have Their Exits*, pp. 125-6.
473 With Darke were doctors Captain J.J. McPartland RAMC, and Captain F.W.M. Plant RAMC. Also there, as a patient, was Second Lieutenant K.W. Spreckley, 1st Lothians and Border Yeomanry.
474 Chantier de la Jeunesse was an organisation set up by the Vichy government to provide facilities for the youth of France.
475 Tobin's report MI9/S/P.G. (F) 532 in TNA file WO 208/3306.
476 *In Trust and Treason*, p. 45.
477 *In Trust and Treason*, p. 49.
478 *Safe Houses Are Dangerous*, p. 95.
479 Lockhart's report MI9/S/P.G. (-) 577 in TNA file WO 208/3307. The 80,000 francs seems rather generous in view of the proclamation of 22 September 1941 by General von Stülpnagel, military governor of France, that up to 10,000 francs would be paid to anyone contributing to the capture of enemy airmen.
480 Forde's report MI9/S/P.G. (-) 569 in TNA file WO 208/3306.
481 Forde's report op. cit. Their false papers were provided by the Abbé Carpentier.
482 Lockhart's report op. cit.
483 Mensik's report MI9/S/P.G. (-) 578 in TNA file WO 208/3307. He actually crossed the Demarcation Line at Verdelais (Gironde), twenty kilometres west of la Réole.
484 Who can forget the classic line in the film *Reach for the Sky*: 'Crowley-Milling has a pen-knife!'?
485 Information on Schmid from *Conscript Heroes*, p. 221.
486 Ptácek's report MI9/S/P.G. (-) 643 in TNA file WO 208/3307. Again, in the film *Reach for the Sky* who can forget the moment when Kenneth More, as Bader, who had been shot down on 9 August 1941, escapes from the hospital down a rope of knotted sheets, and is caught in an outhouse.
487 Ptácek had joined the French Foreign Legion in September 1939, but was soon released to join the French Air Force. On 16 May 1940 he was posted to a fighter squadron near Chartres, flying the Morane-Saulnier M.S.406. He damaged a German bomber on 3 June, but was himself shot down. Following the defeat of France he made his way to England, joined the RAF, and was posted to 43 Squadron on 4 October 1940.
488 Gibbs' report MI9 (b)/S/P.G. (-) 501 in TNA file WO 208/3306.
489 Ptácek op. cit. The flat above the salon was also one of Paul Cole's safe houses.
490 Pietrasiak said in Appendix C to his report that the group numbered eleven – Cole; Lepers; Crowley-Milling, Ptácek; Pietrasiak; Stachura; and five other ranks. He does not, however, name the five ORs.
491 Pietrasiak's report MI9/S/P.G. (-) 642 in TNA file WO 208/3307.
492 *Conscript Heroes*, p. 167.
493 *Conscript Heroes*, pp. 169-70.
494 *Conscript Heroes*, p. 170.

495 *Conscript Heroes*, p. 176.
496 *Conscript Heroes*, p. 181.
497 Letter of 7 October 1941 from Arthur Yencken to the Rt. Hon. Anthony Eden. TNA file FO 371/26949A C11527.
498 TNA file FO 371/26949A C11527.
499 Winskill's report MI9/S/P.G. (-) 600 in TNA file WO 208/3307. On his return to England, Winskill was given command of 232 Squadron. Shot down in his Spitfire off the Tunisian coast on 18 January 1943 he swam ashore behind enemy lines, and managed to evade capture for a second time. Air Commodore Sir Archibald Winskill KCVO CBE DFC & Bar, Extra Equerry to the Queen (and, on 15 February 1968, appointed Captain of the Queen's Flight), died on 9 August 2005 aged eighty-eight.
500 *Turncoat*, p. 112.
501 Note Pietrasiak's "Belgian pilot".
502 Pietrasiak op. cit.
503 *Turncoat*, p. 90.
504 From Smith's repatriation report (via Linda Ralph), and see *Turncoat*, p. 91.
505 Smith op. cit. "Lady Elizabeth" was Elizabeth Haden-Guest (see Chapter 2). As the first Polish RAF evader of the war was Rytka, this airman may have been in the Polish Air Force rather than the RAF.
506 Duval's report MI9/S/P.G. (-) 489 in TNA file WO 208/3305.
507 Crabtree's report MI9/S/P.G. (F) 490 in TNA file WO 208/3305.
508 Crabtree op. cit.
509 Robillard's report MI9/S/P.G. (-) 491 in TNA file WO 208/3305.
510 From a conversation with Sergeant D.B. Crabtree's son, N. Crabtree, 29 April 2006.
511 Duval op. cit. Loches lies some thirty kilometres south of St Martin-le-Beau.
512 Information via Linda Ralph, and Alexander Garrow and Allan Fraser from Keith Janes' *Conscript Heroes* website. A Zuchthaus was a correctional prison. Smith's well-deserved Military Medal was gazetted on 16 April 1946.
513 *Safe Houses Are Dangerous*, quoted p. 87.
514 There is some doubt as to the surname of François Despretz. "Duprez" is used by many leading authors (Airey Neave in *Saturday at M.I.9*, for example), while Helen Long (*Safe Houses are Dangerous*) uses "Dupré". "Despretz", however, is taken from Maud Baudot de Rouville's account of her time working with the organisation in Lille – Archive YPX 207/14 at the Cumbria Record Office, Whitehaven.
515 The hospital was named after Michel Levy, director of the military medical school at Val-de-Grace, Paris, from 1856 to 1872.
516 Appendix C, Garrow's report MI9/S/P.G. (-) 1075 in TNA file WO 208/5582.
517 Braddon has Garrow's sentence as ten years (*Nancy Wake*, p. 35), but Murphy says twenty years (*Turncoat*, p. 198).
518 *Saturday at M.I.9*, p. 112. Several books incorrectly mention that Garrow was imprisoned at Meauzac, see *Fight Another Day*, p. 184; *Nancy Wake*, p. 39; *Safe Houses Are Dangerous*, p. 109; *The Way Back*, p. 133; and *Turncoat*, p. 198. Mauzac (Dordogne), on the river Dordogne itself and some thirty kilometres east of Bergerac, is the correct spelling, although, to confuse the issue further, there is a Meuzac several kilometres south of Limoges in the Haute-Vienne *département* (and see Airey Neave's comment that Francis Blanchain was arrested in Limoges, many kilometres north of Mauzac). To add even further to the confusion Donald Darling (*Secret Sunday*, p. 102) calls the place Meaujac.
519 Georges Bégué had had a lucky escape when the house in Knightsbridge, London, in which he and three other trainee agents were lodging was destroyed by a bomb. Two of the fellow trainees were killed. Raymond Roche and three others – Lieutenant François Basin; Lieutenant Robert Leroy; and Jean Georges Duboudin – had been landed at Barcarès, near Perpignan, on the night of 19/20 September 1941 from HMS *Fidelity*.
520 He was to receive the DSO (21/6/45) for his 'gallant and distinguished services in the field'.
521 For more on this escape see: http://home.ca.inter.net/~hagelin/georges-begue/archives.html; *SOE in France*, p. 203; *Knights of the Floating Silk*, pp. 160-70 – George Langelaan (Hutchinson, London, 1959); and *The Wolves at the Door*, pp. 103-4, 126-29.
522 After the war Hayes was awarded the MC (21/6/45) and appointed MBE.
523 Groome had been landed at Port Miou (Bouches-du-Rhône), near Cassis, on the night of 3/4 November 1942 from the Polish-manned boat *Seadog* (Lieutenant Buchowski).
524 *Saturday at M.I.9*, p. 112. The exchange rate at the time was roughly 200 French francs to £1. According to Brome (*The Way Back*, p. 133), M. Peyrot 'lived in a small house at Sarlat, some distance from the prison'.
525 The excitable Russell Braddon (*Nancy Wake*, p. 49) suggests that Peyrot's price was 500,000 francs.
526 Blanchain was to make 'a spectacular escape' from captivity. A wanted man, he was obliged to leave for England, which he reached in early 1943. There he married Paula Spriewald, who had herself worked for O'Leary until she, too, had had to leave France in 1942 (*Saturday at M.I.9*, p. 112). See Chapter 6 this book.
527 Note that Helen Long says (*Safe Houses Are Dangerous*, p. 174) that O'Leary watched Garrow 'stroll nonchalantly through the gates amongst the night shift coming off-duty at dawn on 6th December 1942.'
528 See also *The Way Back*, pp. 139-40: 'Towards sundown they reached M. Belin's small, red-brick house at Bergerac.'
529 Appendix C, Inglis' report M.I.9/S/P.G. (F) 1076 in TNA file WO 208/5582. Inglis and his two comrades sailed from Gibraltar aboard the SS *Letitia* on 5 February 1943, arriving at Gourock, Scotland six days later.
530 *Women in the Resistance*, p. 32.
531 They were respectively ball-turret gunner and navigator of B-17F 41-24510, 306th BG/367th BS, shot down on 9 October 1942 on a raid to Lille-Fives.
532 On 15 September 1942, whilst seven cables from the North Mole Light, Gibraltar, the SS *Ravens Point*, 1,787 gross tons, was damaged by a limpet mine attached by men of the Italian Decima Flottiglia MAS (Decima Flottiglia Mezzi d'Assalto, also known as La Decima or Xª MAS – "10th Assault Vehicle Flotilla"), a commando frogman unit.
533 Bufton, Crampton and Read were three of the six-man crew of a Wellington bomber that ran out of engines on the way back from Cologne on the night of 26/27 August. The other three of their crew were taken prisoner.
534 *In Trust and Treason*, p. 71.
535 In a letter dated 30 October Carpentier wrote a warning letter to Suzanne Warenghem: 'Paul [Cole] came through here yesterday with his whole team of footballers (fifteen in all including the "supporters")... One of my cousins was recently very alarmed. Her neighbour Madame Deram [the woman with whom Cole was currently co-habiting] was disturbed by the Gestapo, nobody knows why... I wonder what is going on in the north... for there have been several consecutive arrests or mysterious departures...' Quoted *In Trust and Treason*, p. 69.
536 *Aircraft Down!*, pp. 43-44.
537 *Aircraft Down!*, p. 47.
538 *Fighter Pilot. A Self-Portrait*, p. 174. P.H. Dorchy was one of the vice-consuls at Barcelona.
539 Groyecki's report MI9/S/P.G. (-) 667 in TNA file WO 208/3307.
540 On this Mannheim raid, Polish bomber squadrons lost four Wellingtons. Remarkably, none of the twenty-four crew was killed – one was interned; four (including Groyecki and Budzynski) evaded capture; and nineteen became prisoners of war.
541 Groyecki op. cit.
542 Budzynski's report MI9/S/P.G. (-) 686 in TNA file WO 208/3308.
543 The "hat shop" may have been Jeannine Voglimacci's hair-dressing salon.
544 Wilson's report MI9/S/P.G (-) 673 in TNA file WO 208/3308. Records suggest, however, that Wilson's Whitley crashed in the opposite direction from Calais, at Pihen-lès-Guînes ten kilometres to the south-west of Calais.

545 Romerée is a dozen kilometres south-east of Philippeville (Belgium) and ten or so west of Givet (France).
546 Dyer's report MI9/S/P.G. (-) 692 in TNA file WO 208/3308.
547 Dyer op. cit.
548 Dyer op. cit. "Gustave" has not been identified.
549 Dyer op. cit. The actions of the guide bear all the hallmarks of the traitor Harold "Paul" Cole, a man with few scruples, who would steal money from anyone to fund his luxurious life style. If the guide *were* Cole, then, given the time and place, it is quite possible that the Frenchwoman was Suzanne Warenghem.
550 Dyer op. cit. Gustave was held in custody, and later taken to the prison at St Hippolyte-du-Fort.
551 Wilson op. cit.
552 *Turncoat*, p. 140. Haupsturmführer is equivalent in rank to an army captain, a Royal Navy lieutenant or a flight lieutenant in the British armed forces.
553 These were no doubt the events that caused the postponement of the large convoy on 22 October.
554 *Turncoat*, p. 153.
555 Held in Loos prison until 5 August 1942, Despretz was then deported to Germany. He died of exhaustion in April 1944 in the infirmary of the Sonnenburg concentration camp.
556 *Turncoat*, p. 158.
557 All bar James Smith were executed in a Dortmund prison on 30 June 1943.
558 Born on 4 June 1911 in Paris, Postel-Vinay died in the city of his birth on 11 February 2007.
559 Papers of M.O.A. Baudot de Rouville, Archive YDX 207/14, pp. 13-14.
560 *The Way Back*, pp. 46-7.
561 *The Way Back*, p. 49.
562 *Turncoat*, p. 128. After the war Monsieur Durand was one of those to identify the body of Harold 'Paul' Cole in a Paris morgue.
563 *Secret Sunday*, p. 55.
564 *The Way Back*, p. 74.
565 *The Way Back*, p. 78.
566 *Fight Another Day*, p. 172.
567 *We Landed by Moonlight* (Crécy edition), p. 45.
568 *Safe Houses are Dangerous*, p. 207. From Marseille, Dr Vourc'h took passage on the *Gouverneur Général Lépine* for Tunisia, safe from the Gestapo.
569 Dicks' report MI9/S/P.G. (-) 696 in TNA file WO 208/3308.
570 TNA file FO 371/26949B C13449. (Is "Lion" a not-too subtle reference to someone in Lyon?)
571 Blair was to have a distinguished career in the army, becoming Lieutenant-General Sir Chandos Blair KCVO, OBE, MC.
572 Each of these four escapers, and Stewart, were awarded the MC (12/2/42) 'in recognition of distinguished services in the field'.
573 Thirty-eight-year-old Whigham now lies in Lesneven Communal Cemetery, twenty-four kilometres north-east of Brest, the only airman among thirteen soldiers and three Merchant Navy seamen.
574 This was the second time that Gilchrist had been shot down. Returning from Le Havre on the night of 10/11 March 1941, his 35 Squadron Halifax was attacked by an RAF night-fighter and crashed in Surrey, killing four of the six crew. Fifty-five years later the cigarette lighter of one of the dead, Sergeant R. Lucas, was recovered from the crash site and returned to his family.
575 Dalphond's report MI9/S/P.G. (-) 907 in TNA file WO 208/3311.
576 Dalphond op. cit. The "organisation" was, presumably, the Garrow/O'Leary network.
577 Gilchrist's report MI9/S/P.G. (-) 672 in TNA file WO 208/3308.
578 This and previous quote from *Winged Diplomat*, p. 167.
579 TNA file FO 371/26949B C13449.
580 TNA file FO 371/26949B C13449. The "mairie" stamps would have authenticated the false papers as coming from the particular place indicated by the stamp. *Mairie* was, literally, the mayor's office in a town hall.
581 Dicks' report op. cit. "St Lorenzo di Corda" was possibly Santa Léocadia, a village to the south of Figueras.
582 Birk's story is told in Chapter 6. The other seven evaders were Sergeants J. Budzynski; G.T. Cox; A.D. Day; V.G. Haley; J.W. Hutton; N.W. MacKenzie; and L.A. Warburton.
583 Neave was the first of the six British servicemen to make a "home run" from the notorious Colditz Castle in Saxony. He and Luteyn had had to force their way through deep snowdrifts before reaching Ramsen, Switzerland early on the morning of 9 January.
584 They left by ship on 4 May 1942, arriving at Gourock eight days later. Back in England, Neave went to work for MI9, but Major Hugh Austin Woollatt, aged twenty-seven, was killed in action in Normandy on 17 July 1944.
585 At his interview on 21 January 1943, following his repatriation from France, Lieutenant Commander R.M. Prior RN stated that 'the Germans were aware of the Café au Petit Pouce [*sic*], Nouveau, and the Hotel de Paris Toulouse.' Appendix C, Prior's report MI9/S/P.G. (F) 1037 in TNA file WO 208/5582.
586 See also Douglas and Harding, two other evaders from the St Nazaire raid, in the following chapter.
587 Appendix C, Wheeler's report MI9/S/P.G. (-) 740 in TNA file WO 208/5582.
588 Wheeler op. cit. Note that their meeting with Paul Ulmann was eight months before the Garrow escape referred to earlier in this chapter.
589 Wheeler op. cit. *Libération* (first published in Lyon in July 1941) was the newspaper of the Resistance group Libération-Sud, which was set up by the distinguished Frenchman Émmanuel d'Astier de la Vigerie (born 9 January 1900, died 12 June 1969). It is just possible that Monsieur "B" *was* d'Astier de la Vigerie, who used the alias "Bernard". Wheeler also gives an extraordinary description of Monsieur "B" 'who is easily recognisable on account of his ginger beard, long hair, pallid face, heavy horn-rimmed glasses, and large trilby hat.'
590 Blanchain was one of those arrested at the Noailles hotel (one of the top five hotels in Marseille) in July 1941, and held at Fort St Nicholas. For details of these arrests, and of all the goings-on in Marseille, see Keith Janes' authoritative website at www.conscript-heroes.com.
591 See *Underground from Posen*, p. 167.
592 The two Poles may have been two men who are later listed as having been guests numbers 72 and 87 at the Nouveaus' Marseille apartment – Lieutenant Marian Kozubski and Aviation Cadet Wladislaw Tucholko. See *Safe Houses Are Dangerous*, pp. 206 and 207.
593 Stewart's report MI9/S/P.G. (Italy) 636 in TNA file WO 208/3307.

Chapter 5

594 Wilkinson, now commanding 174 Squadron, had been a sergeant pilot on 3 Squadron when his DFM & Bar were gazetted on 31 May 1940. Soon the most experienced pilot on his squadron, he was made an acting flight lieutenant and, briefly, acting squadron commander all in the space of a month.
595 Wilkinson's report MI9/S/P.G. (-) 750 in TNA file WO 208/3309.
596 This could have been Lancaster L7548, 44 Squadron, but it had crashed a good many kilometres away to the north. The three crew may have been Miller, Cobb, and Dowty (see below, this chapter), though they had been arrested by police at Loches on 1 May.
597 Wilkinson op. cit.
598 *The Wolves at the Door*, p. 19.
599 *The Wolves at the Door*, quoted on p. 24.
600 Born of a French father and a British mother in Cardiff on 6 April 1907, his full name was Jacques Théodore Paul Marie Vaillant de

Guélis. He died at Burntwood Hospital on 7 August 1945 after a car accident in Germany.
601 *The Wolves at the Door*, p. 160.
602 Laussucq, a sixty-two-year-old commercial artist from Pittsburgh, USA, returned to London on 11 September 1944. He died in New York in 1975 at the age of ninety-three.
603 In 1950 Virginia Hall married OSS agent Lieutenant Paul Goillet, whom she had met on active service in the field. She died on 12 July 1982.
604 *Safe Houses Are Dangerous*, p. 207. Roy was guest number eighty-three at the Nouveaus'. Virginia Hall was already known to the Nouveaus by the name Marie Jambe de Bois, having stayed at their flat in March 1942.
605 Shot down off Corfu on 17 April 1942, Stanenkovich had escaped from the Italians. He was guest number eight-two at the Nouveaus' flat in Marseille.
606 Z1276: Five evaders, one prisoner of war; W5627: four evaders, one prisoner of war.
607 For the return of the two Polish officers Wasik and Szkuta to England, see the following chapter.
608 Fusinski's report MI9/S/P.G. (-) 818 in TNA file WO 208/3310.
609 Appendix C, Fusinski's report MI9/S/P.G. (-) 818 in TNA file WO 208/5582.
610 See *Official Secret*, pp. 62-4, Clayton Hutton (Max Parrish & Co Ltd, London, 1960). The Gigli saw (so named after its inventor) hidden in the laces could cut through a one-inch steel bar.
611 Polesinski's report MI9/S/P.G. (-) 777 in TNA file WO 208/3309.
612 Appendix C, Rowicki's report MI9/S/P.G. (-) 888 in TNA file WO 208/5582. The four airmen have not been identified, though it is presumed that two of them were Warrant Officer T.J. Broom and Sergeant E.G. Price RCAF, with whom they are known to have crossed the Pyrenees.
613 Rowicki op. cit. No doubt the farm was that of Francia Usandizaga.
614 Morawski's report MI9/S/P.G. (-) 820 in TNA file WO 208/3310.
615 Taken to Verdun hospital, Lipski was removed, after a brief spell at Stalag Luft III (Sagan), to the NCO camp at Stalag IVB (Mühlberg).
616 Wacinski's report MI9/S/P.G. (-) 819 in TNA file WO 208/3310.
617 They were respectively numbers 77, 78, 79, 84, 85, 86, 90 and 101. See *Safe Houses are Dangerous*, pp. 204-11, for details of the full list.
618 Appendix C, Malecki's report MI9/S/P.G. (-) 776 in TNA file WO 208/3309.
619 Wilkinson's report MI9/S/P.G. (-) 750 in TNA file WO 208/3309.
620 After his return to England, Krawczyk was awarded the Polish Virtuti Militari (5th Class) for his selfless act. He lost his life on operations in November 1942 attacking a U-boat.
621 Appendix C, Wozniak's report MI9/S/P.G. (-) 859 in TNA file WO 208/5582. Prendergaast's DCM was gazetted on 10 November 1942.
622 *The Evaders* [Cosgrove], p. 99.
623 *The Evaders* [Cosgrove], p. 101.
624 Ainger's report M.I9/S/P.G. (-) 863 in TNA file WO 208/3310.
625 Appendix C, Prendergast's report MI9/S/P.G. (G) 865 in TNA file WO 208/5582.
626 Out of Ainger, Barker, Wozniak and Wright, only Barker was rewarded, his DFM being gazetted on 20 October 1942 for his 'operational missions against the enemy', not specifically for his evasion.
627 Templeman's report MI9/S/P.G. (-) 930 in TNA files WO 208/3311 and AIR 40/1533.
628 *The Evaders* [Cosgrove], p. 105.
629 Brigadier Roupell, 1st Battalion The East Surrey Regiment, was a lieutenant when he won his VC, gazetted 23 June 1915, for his actions on Hill 60, Belgium, on 20 April 1915. Born in Tipperary on 7 April 1892, he died in Surrey on 4 March 1974.
630 As seen in the previous chapter, only five commandos evaded capture – Douglas; Harding; Wheeler; Sims; and Lance-Corporal A. Howarth. Four were awarded the Military Medal, but Howarth was only Mentioned in Despatches. He escaped from Fort de la Revère on 5 September 1942, and was evacuated by sea to Gibraltar (see below, and Appendix III).
631 Douglas/Harding reports MI9/S/P.G. (-) 822 and 823 in TNA file WO 208/3310. As leader of the Commando force Lieutenant-Colonel Newman was awarded the Victoria Cross, though not gazetted until 19 June 1945. Born on 19 August 1904, Newman died on 26 April 1972.
632 Appendix C, Mills' report MI9/S/P.G. (-) 745 in TNA file WO 208/5582.
633 Mills op. cit. Private D.R. Edwards RAOC had escaped from Germany. He was to receive the DCM for his fine effort.
634 From Roupell's report MI9/S/P.G. (-) 803 in TNA file WO 208/3309.
635 *Secret Sunday*, p. 60.
636 Ibid. The "Pink List" was so called because of its pink cover, the same colour as the RAF's top secret documents.
637 *The Secret Navies*, p. 17. For more on Slocum see *MI6*, pp. 79-80, 94, 112 etc.
638 *On Hazardous Service*, p. 215.
639 HMS *Tarana*, p. 23.
640 *The Way Back*, p. 81. The Hôtel du Tennis, conveniently close to the beach, was to be used on a number of occasions for the temporary accommodation of escapers and evaders who were awaiting a boat to take them away.
641 The transmitter/receiver set was a 'Type 3, Mark II, built into a small leather suitcase, and weighing 32¾ lbs' – Helen Long, *Safe Houses Are Dangerous*, p. 147.
642 *Secret Sunday*, p. 58. O'Leary would find out later that Ferière had volunteered to return to France only so that he could be re-united with his wife, Mimi. A few weeks later the couple were evacuated from France and out of harm's way on the *Tarana*.
643 *Safe Houses Are Dangerous*, p. 153.
644 *We Landed by Moonlight* (Crécy revised 2nd edition, 2000), p. 49.
645 31 Field Regiment, RA, 4th Indian Division, captured on 27 May 1941 at Halfaya Pass ("Hellfire Pass"), North Africa.
646 Parrott's report MI9/S/P.G./LIB/245 in TNA file WO 208/3328.
647 Captain J.M. Ratcliffe, Middlesex Regiment, was captured. He was to be awarded the George Medal (gazetted 21 February 1946) 'in recognition of conspicuous gallantry in carrying out hazardous work in a very brave manner, while a prisoner of war'. He won it for disposing of bombs that had been dropped by B-24s of the USAAF's 2nd Bomb Division on 24 August 1944 on Oflag 79, a prisoner-of-war camp near Brunswick, Germany. Three prisoners were killed by the bombing. A further seven were badly wounded and thirty more slightly. The target was a nearby airfield.
648 He was liberated from Oflag 79 by American troops on 12 April 1945.
649 The first British officer to whom John Mott was presented for interrogation on reaching Italy again was, amazingly, his younger brother whom he had not seen since 1937! Having been Mentioned in Dispatches for his 1940/41 evasion John was now appointed MBE 'for his great fortitude and determination to return to active duty'. See the *Daily Telegraph* obituary published on 31 May 2002 for details of Arnold John Mott, who died on 9 May 2002.
650 *Fight Another Day*, p. 173.
651 *Fight Another Day*, p. 177.
652 It is not clear whether the caller was a *garde-forestier*, a *garde-champêtre* (rural policeman) or a *garde-chasse* (gamekeeper).
653 Archive YDX 207/14, p. 17.
654 *The Way Back*, p. 130.
655 *On Hazardous Service*, p. 217. Other, reliable, sources state that *Seadog* was Spanish and that *Seawolf* was Moroccan.
656 Kadulski's *nom de guerre* was "Marian Krajewski", but he was known to Donald Darling as "Mischa".

657 Buchowski's trips to North Africa had been carried out in another boat, the *Dogfish*. He assumed command of *Seawolf* sometime around June 1942. Both Kadulski and Buchowski were to be awarded the DSO. Buchowski 'died in a London flat in a lover's quarrel' (Donald Darling, *Secret Sunday*, p. 91), a grubby death for a brave man. 'On 12 April 1943, the newly promoted Lt/Cdr Jan Buchowski was shot dead in the Pimlico flat of Lt Lubomir Chienski, a fellow Polish officer – and jealous husband.' (http://www.conscript-heroes.com/Art31-SeawolfSeadog.html).
658 Quoted by M.R.D. Foot in *SOE in France*, p. 67.
659 *Secret Sunday*, p. 62.
660 *The Way Back*, p. 70. Air Commodore Straight CBE, MC, DFC was later appointed AOC No. 216 (Transport Command) Group at Heliopolis in the Middle East. American-born on 6 November 1912, he became a naturalised Briton in 1936, and died on 5 April 1979.
661 *Saturday at M.I.9*, p. 87.
662 This successful attack took place on the night of 3/4 March 1942.
663 *Detachment W*, p. 133.
664 From his report MI9/S/P.G. (-) 787 in TNA file WO 208/3309. Brome's account of the hospital escape (*The Way Back*, pp. 70-73), namely that the two guards in the hospital were drugged, appears to be somewhat fanciful in the light of Straight's report.
665 Keith Janes, however, believes that the three escapers went directly to Nîmes, and did NOT go via Dr Lévy.
666 Johnson mentions only Straight and Miniakowski in his report MI9/S/P.G. (-) 790 in TNA file WO 208/3309.
667 This and Daladier quote from *SOE in France*, p. 201. Édouard Daladier (1884-1970), a former prime minister of France and Minister of War in 1939, was arrested by the Vichy government in 1940. Interned by the Germans in 1942, he was not liberated until 1945.
668 This small commando force was named 'X' Troop, 11 SAS Battalion, though the number 11 was in fact a corruption of the Roman II (2). This was also the first occasion on which the term Special Air Service was used. The commandos had already been known as Special Service troops in some official circles, but for Colossus they were referred to as II Special Air Service.
669 HM Submarine *Triumph* (Lieutenant J.S. Huddart RN) left Alexandria on 26 December 1941 to land a party of commandos ashore and then patrol the Aegean. Four days later she signalled that the party had been successfully landed but, due to return to pick up the commandos on 9 January 1942, she failed to make the rendezvous. Nothing further was heard of her and, as no axis power claimed her destruction, it is believed that she struck a mine and was sunk with all hands.
670 Deane-Drummond published his story of the affair in *Return Ticket*. For his 'gallant and distinguished services in the field' he was awarded the MC (29/9/42), the same date as Private C.G. Knight was 'Mentioned in recognition of gallant and distinguished services in the field'.
671 Bradley's body was later recovered and buried in la Chaux-de-Fonds Communal Cemetery, but now rests in Vevey Cemetery, Switzerland.
672 Appendix C, Beecroft/Hanwell reports MI9/S/P.G. (-) 795 and 796 in TNA file WO 208/3309 and WO 208/5582. For "PEO" read "PAO"?
673 Beecroft/Hanwell op. cit.
674 *Return Ticket*, p. 176. Perhaps Deane-Drummond fell asleep and missed much of the journey but their destination, Béziers, is some 145 miles (230 kilometres) from Marseille.
675 "Joseph" was a name used by Pat O'Leary.
676 From Johnson's report op. cit. Seymour may well have been Simon, no record being found of a "Seymour". If "Simon" is spoken with a strong French accent it could well be mistaken for Seymour.
677 *Xavier*, p. 43.
678 *On Hazardous Service*, p. 228.
679 *Return Ticket*, p. 182. The record time for repainting the *Tarana* was six hours, and that was in darkness. Perhaps this was the record occasion?
680 Also on the *Llanstephan Castle* was Private Charles Knight. Deane-Drummond was awarded the MC (29/9/42) 'in recognition of gallant and distinguished services in the field'.
681 From Malta came Squadron Leader P.B. "Laddie" Lucas, ex CO of 249 Squadron, his two flight commanders – Flight Lieutenants W.R. Daddo-Langlois and N.W. Lee – and Pilot Officer M.A. Graves of 126 Squadron. Also going home on this Sunderland, from Lisbon, were evaders Flying Officer A. Szkuta PAF, and Flight Sergeant K.H.L Houghton DFM (see Chapter 6).
682 Appendix C, Perdue's report MI9/S/P.G. (-) 839 in TNA file WO 208/5582.
683 Appendix C, Misseldine's report MI9/S/P.G. (-) 838 in TNA file WO 208/5582.
684 Appendix C Evans' report MI9/S/P.G. (-) 836 in TNA file WO 208/5582.
685 Higginson had been shot down on 17 June 1941, with thirteen victories to his credit.
686 *Wait For the Dawn*, pp. 156 & 157. 700 metres (2,275 feet) above sea level in the hills near the village of la Turbie, overlooking the Corniche Inférieure and the Mediterranean Sea, Fort de la Revère lay a few kilometres from Nice to the west and Monte Carlo to the east, with the Italian border barely twenty kilometres beyond Monte Carlo.
687 Pilot Officer Brian Hawkins (88874) is not to be confused with Flying Officer Ronald Hawkins (70802), 103 Squadron (see Chapter 1).
688 Tony Friend was a member of the Monaco police – see *Free to Fight Again*, p. 41, where he is described as 'an Australian Inspector of Police', and also *Wait for the Dawn*, p. 202, where Nabarro says: 'Our friend the Australian at Headquarters…'
689 *The Tartan Pimpernel*, p. 138. Caskie's story of the breakout on pages 142-145 is not, however, to be relied upon for accuracy of detail.
690 Barnett's report MI9/S/P.G. (-) 887 in TNA file WO 208/3310.
691 Barnett op. cit.
692 According to Derrick Nabarro (in Appendix A of his report in TNA file WO 208/3242) she had 'done three months in prison for assisting escapers.' She was awarded the King's Commendation for services to the Allied cause on 23 May 1946. The tea house was also known as the Villa Flor Palace.
693 Private T.J. Kelly, Gordon Highlanders, in his report MI9/S/P.G./LIB/255 in TNA file WO 208/3336.
694 Miller's report in TNA file AIR 40/1533.
695 Miller was liberated at Stalag 357 (Fallingbostel), Germany, on 16 April 1945 by 7th Armoured Division. Six days later he was flown back to the UK from Brussels.
696 Mort's report MI9/S/P.G./LIB/1727 in TNA file AIR 40/1533. Mort, 174 Squadron, shot down in his Hurricane fighter on 2 June 1942, ended the war as a prisoner of the Germans.
697 *The Evaders*, p. 58 (Cosgrove).
698 Appendix C, Pearman's report MI9/S/P.G. (-) 928 in TNA file WO 208/5582.
699 The RAF officers were: Flight Lieutenant H.H. Haszard RCAF, the senior officer of the party; Pilot Officer J. Ester; Pilot Officer D. King; Flying Officer E.V. Lawson; Flying Officer R.A.E. Milton; Pilot Officer A.J. Mott; and Flying Officer T. Wawerski PAF.
700 *Adventures of a Secret Agent*, p. 150.
701 *Adventures of a Secret Agent*, p. 162.
702 Milton's report MI9/S/P.G. (-) 1039 in TNA file WO 208/3312 (and AIR 20/9159).
703 Allen's report MI9/S/P.G. (F) 1128 in TNA file WO 208/3312. Foster, however, in his report mentions that he crossed to Spain with a Captain Greer, Nitelet, Allen, and Nardin. "Greer" was a stage name used by Rake before the war, but who was Nardin? Rake later received the MC (21/6/45).
704 *Wait for the Dawn*, p. 204. "Owens" was probably Lance Corporal T. Owen, Welsh Fusiliers, who had escaped from Fort de la Revère on 5/6 September. Derrick Nabarro was to be awarded the DCM (19/1/43) 'in recognition of gallant and distinguished service'.

705 Vanier was almost certainly the 'wounded Canadian (from the Dieppe raid)' mentioned in Krajewski's report. For Vanier's further exploits see Chapter 8, and see the Possum/Martin section at the end of Chapter 9 for Lafleur's further exploits.
706 Lafleur/Vanier/Joly combined reports MI9/S/P.G. (F) 884, 885, 886 in TNA file WO 208/3310. Each was awarded the MM (22/12/42).
707 This port could have been Sainte Marie.
708 *Secret Flotillas*, Volume II, pp. 185-86.
709 Ibid., p. 186. The "wounded airman" was certainly one of the 138 Squadron crew.
710 Paula Spriewald was German. Born in 1909 in Ennepetal, near Essen, her anti-Hitler father was forced to flee first to Holland and then to Paris. In 1940 Paula and a number of other German women were rounded-up by the French and interned in a camp at Gurs, in the Pyrenees. The commandant, appreciating what would happen should they fall into German hands, did the decent thing and released them.
711 *Secret Flotillas*, pp. 186-7, Volume II. The *G.G. Grévy* was named after Gouverneur-Général Albert Grévy (1824-1899), governor of Algeria from 1879-81. After serving as the German hospital ship *Göttingen* in May 1944, the ship was scuttled at Marseille on 21 August 1944.
712 *Secret Flotillas*, p. 193, Volume II.
713 *The Way Back*, p. 112. "Chouquette" was Madame Lebreton.
714 Dumais told his story in *The Man Who Went Back*, (though here the reader should beware of problems with his chronology).
715 *Secret Flotillas*, Volume II, p. 193.
716 *Secret Flotillas*, Volume II, pp. 193-4. The Polish priest was Father Myrda, but the identity of the Frenchman is not known.
717 The three ration quotes are from *The Man Who Went Back*, p. 94.
718 The Polish authorities had not been happy at having to use one of their precious boats to rescue British personnel, but felucca operations were closed down in January 1943 'with the arrival of Axis guards on the Mediterranean coast' (*S.O.E. in France*, p. 210).
719 This and previous two quotes from TNA file KV4/320.
720 Barnard's report MI9/S/P.G. (-) 1040 in TNA file WO 208/3312, (and AIR 20/9159).
721 Forster's report MI9/S/P.G. (-) 1173 in TNA file WO 208/3313
722 According to Squadron Leader Barnard, the word was that Sergeant Buckell had been betrayed by the mayor of Bayenghem, 'whose house and crops were consequently burned by local people. Later I heard that patriots had shot this Mayor.' – Barnard's report MI9/S/P.G. (-) 1040 in TNA file WO 208/3312.
723 Once back in England, Barnard at first refused to hand over his poster, and this caused quite a stir in high circles before it found its way into official hands.
724 Glensor is shown as having arrived at the Nouveaus' apartment on 23 October, together with Barnard, Forster, Wissenback, and Gise – see *Safe Houses are Dangerous*, p. 211.
725 This was Maud Baudot de Rouville, alias Thérèse Martin.
726 Dick Adams was the pilot of B-17F 41-24472, 306th BG/369th BS, lost on 8 November 1942. For more on his evasion see Chapter 9.
727 Appendix C Barnard's report MI9/S/P.G. (-) 1040 in TNA file WO 208/5582.
728 *Aircraft Down!*, p. 84.
729 Bromwell's report MI9/S/P.G. (F) 1193 in TNA file WO 208/3313.
730 Appendix C Bromwell's report MI9/S/P.G. (F) 1193 in TNA file WO 208/5582.
731 *Aircraft Down!*, p. 83.
732 Doorly's report MI9/S/P.G. (-) 1129 in TNA file WO 208/3312.
733 Ibid.
734 Extraordinarily, another evader, Pilot Officer R.G. Kirby, also went to Auch in the summer of 1943 and there, too, contracted jaundice. Both may have contracted hepatitis A, which normally has a recovery time of less than three weeks and which can be brought on by contaminated water.
735 *Aircraft Down!*, p. 71.
736 Bromwell's report op. cit.
737 TNA file WO 208/5582. It should not be forgotten that Brigadier Roupell VC and his aide-de-camp, Captain Gilbert, took just as long to get home. It is left to the reader's judgement as to the fairness or otherwise of the Intelligence Officer's comments.
738 This small spa town is approximately 115 kilometres from Saragossa and 200 from Madrid. Many airmen were to be accommodated in this hotel in Alhama on their way to Gibraltar, having been very well treated by Spanish Air Force officers.
739 *Aircraft Down!*, p. 95.
740 McBeath had been shot down on 21/22 December 1942.
741 Appendix C Glensor's report MI9/S/P.G. (-) 1041 in TNA file WO 208/5582. Dick Cooper says that the 'twenty other people' were 'a party of a dozen Belgians' *Adventures of a Secret Agent*, p. 173.
742 Glensor, op. cit. This is a good illustration of the mercenary behaviour of some of the more unscrupulous guides.
743 *Adventures of a Secret Agent*, p. 175.
744 Hewit was appointed MBE (4/5/43). Of the airmen, only Milton was rewarded, with a Mention in Despatches (2/6/43).

Chapter 6

745 Arthur Dean, Vice-Consul at Bilbao, in TNA file AIR 2/5904.
746 From information brought back to England from Belgium, in a note dated 10 March 1942 in TNA file HS6/223. Note the mis-spelling of "Jongh".
747 Second Lieutenant Leslie C. Hunt, East Surrey Regiment, *The Prisoners' Progress* (Hutchinson and Co. (Publishers) Ltd., London, no date).
748 The Cameronians, together with the 2nd and 4th Battalions The Seaforth Highlanders, formed the 152nd Brigade (Brigadier H.W.V. Stewart DSO), one of the three infantry brigades of the 51st (Highland) Division (Major-General V.M. Fortune CB, DSO).
749 Arrested on 3 October 1941, she was deported, and died in Auschwitz-Birkenau, probably in September 1944.
750 Captured at Dunkirk, Jones had escaped from a German prisoner-of-war camp at St Valéry-en-Caux and, reaching Brussels, had been persuaded to stay on there. Arrested on 28 October 1941 at the house of Mlle. Thiry, 18 Fossé-aux-Loups, Brussels he died, according to Belgian records, whilst in captivity.
751 Deppé has, erroneously, been called "de Pée" by several well-known authors.
752 From the website of John Clinch. The author is most indebted to John, grandson of Marceline Deloge, for the information relating to the escapes and evasions of the six Scotsmen. Anne Marie lived at 141, rue Stevin, Brussels.
753 Greig's report MI9/S/P.G. (B) 657 in TNA file WO 208/3307.
754 The guide Jean was, apparently, later arrested and executed by the Germans. The Basques, who live on both sides of the western Pyrenees, consider themselves to be neither French nor Spanish, and have their own language.
755 Nestor Bodson also managed to reach England and, after being trained as a wireless operator, was parachuted back into his native Belgium on 27 August 1942 for an SOE operation. Immediately arrested, he was executed by the Germans on 5 December 1943.
756 Quotes from *Secret Sunday*, p. 33.
757 Pierlot was born on 23 December 1883 and died on 13 December 1963.
758 Full name Georges Emmanuel Louis Jules Lechein, born 24 December 1886.
759 A lace seller, she lived at 115, Boulevard Emile Jacqmain, Brussels.
760 De Craen tried to get to England but, arrested in Barcelona, was sent back to Belgium a fortnight later. He was arrested at the end of

February 1942.
761 William Halot, married to the mother of the head of SOE's Belgian Section, Jocelyn Clark, was arrested on 28 February 1942. The five last named all died in German camps. On Halot's arrest, Verhulst escaped to England.
762 Henri Georges Louis De Bliqui, born 30 April 1907, was sent to Germany where, on 11 November 1942, he was executed. (Information on De Bliqui gratefully received from Belgian historian Philippe Connart).
763 *Silent Heroes*, p. 121.
764 Anglet is on the south side of the River Adour, across from Bayonne, and is barely twenty-five kilometres from the Spanish border.
765 I am most grateful to that most diligent researcher, Philippe Connart, for this and other information on the embryonic Comet line – Author.
766 *Little Cyclone*, p. 19. Miss Richards' real name was Mademoiselle Dupuich. [Information via John Clinch].
767 This and the two previous quotes from *Six Faces of Courage*, p. 94.
768 Captured on 11 June 1940 after being wounded at St Valéry-en-Caux, Jim Cromar escaped fourteen days later. Some authors – see, for example, Foot and Langley, *MI9*, pp. 79-80; Nichol and Rennell, *Home Run*, p. 63 – have mistakenly called him Colin Cupar. Donald Darling even called him Cromer. The cost of Cromar's journey, 6,000 BF, was paid for by a man called Weber through a Portemine contact to Octave Delcroix, who gave 2,000 BF to Frédéric de Jongh on 18 August 1941 and the rest three days later. (This information via Philippe Connart.)
769 Cromar's report MI9/S/P.G. (B) 514 in TNA file WO 208/3306.
770 *El Camino de la Libertad*, p. 138. It is common in Spain to add the mother's maiden-name after the father's, e.g. Anabitarte Zapirain.
771 *El Camino de la Libertad*, p. 138. Aracama's address was given as 7, Calle Aguirre Miramón, San Sebastián in TNA file HS 6/223.
772 The Bilbao Consul, fifty-six-year-old W.C. Graham, was assisted by vice-consuls Vyvyan Pedrick, G.H. Guyatt, A.S. Dean, and L. Vallis.
773 The actual expenditure for each man was 10,000 French francs (FF), or 6,500 Belgian francs – 1,000 FF for the journey from Brussels to Spain, a further 1,000 FF for the crossing of the Somme by boat, and 8,000 FF for the guide. Appendix C, Cowan's report MI9(b)/S/P.G. (B) 656 in TNA file WO 208/5582.
774 The eight were: Conville and Cowan; Kowalski, Tomicki, and Ives; Day, Birk, and Carroll.
775 *Secret Sunday*, p. 34.
776 TNA file HS 6/223.
777 *Saturday at M.I.9*, p. 137. St Jean-de-Luz, a dozen kilometres from the Spanish border on the Atlantic coast of France, was then a small town of 7,000 inhabitants. Bayonne's population was, by contrast, c. 27,000.
778 Conville's report MI9/S/P.G. (B) 658 in TNA file WO 208/3307. Bettley and McCubbin survived the war, but twenty-five-year-old Slavin was shot dead on 14 October 1944 during an attempt to escape from Stalag 344 (Lamsdorf).
779 *Little Cyclone*, p. 39.
780 Ibid.
781 Cowan's report MI9/S/P.G. (B) 656 in TNA file WO 208/3307. Villiers was probably Villers-Bretonneux, which is barely four kilometres south of Corbie (where many clandestine crossing were to be made in the months to come).
782 *Saturday at M.I.9*, p. 129.
783 This information comes from a note in TNA file HS 6/223 by "TJ", dated 17 March 1942.
784 Brigitte d'Oultremont, email to author 5 March 2007. For the purposes of this book, however, the line will be referred to as the Comet line, but it should not be forgotten that the line was not Dédée's alone – she was but one of its important links.
785 Information from Philippe Connart, by email 2 July 2008. Drew was a British attempt to organise evasion lines in Belgium and the Low Countries.
786 Appendix C, Wilby's report MI9/S/P.G. (F) 1212 in TNA file WO 208/5582. Wilby had been shot down six months earlier. Suffering a broken leg as he struggled to extricate himself from the rear turret of his doomed Halifax, it was not until 30 April/1 May that he crossed into Spain, by which time he had already been in Comet's hands for several weeks.
787 Information gratefully received via Fred Greyer.
788 In Anne's diary for December 1940 one entry read: 'Our first war Christmas. I hope there won't be many of them. British soldiers are still hiding in Brussels. Some are wounded, others are waiting for the nice weather to start to travel south.' *Rendez-vous 127*, p. 48.
789 *Rendez-vous 127*, p. 49.
790 In *Rendez-vous 127*, pp. 53-4, there is an entry for 3 September 1941 which records the arrival of John, a Canadian, on the previous evening, i.e. 2 September. As will be seen elsewhere in this chapter (see Hutton and Warburton), the reliability of the diary is questionable, and dates given therein are not always to be trusted.
791 Three others of their crew were killed. Flying Officer M. Saferna was found in a tree with his parachute deployed, having probably been hit by one of the Wellington's wings as he drifted to earth. Flying Officer J.J.S. Sukiennik jumped without his parachute. Sergeant W. Rybak was found dead in the remains of the aircraft. The pilot, Squadron Leader S. Scibior, was taken prisoner in Brussels, probably having been betrayed to the Germans. He survived the war, only to be executed in Warsaw in 1952.
792 Tomicki's report MI9/S/P.G. (-) 630 in TNA file WO 208/3307.
793 Quotes from Kowalski's report MI9/S/P.G. (-) 631 in TNA file WO 208/3307.
794 Again, there are two different dates for the departure. Ives says 6 November, while Kowalski gives the improbably earlier 10 October.
795 *Little Cyclone*, p. 43. A *passierschein* allowed the bearer to pass freely within the area stated on it.
796 This was probably the Australians' First World War cemetery near Villers-Bretonneux. See Cowan and Conville, above this chapter.
797 Ives' quotes are from his report MI9/S/P.G. (-) 632 in TNA file WO 208/3307.
798 *Little Cyclone*, p. 50.
799 Possibly Francisco Ponzán or one of his assistants.
800 McLarnon's report MI9/S/P.G./LIB/628 in TNA file WO 208/3331.
801 Newton's report MI9./S/P.G. (-) 649 in TNA file WO 208/3307.
802 St Roch is a small village a few kilometres south-east of Comblain-au-Pont, between the Ourthe and Amblève rivers.
803 Carroll's report MI9/S/P.G. (-) 666 in TNA file WO 208/3307. The tobacconist at whose shop Carroll spent the night was Jean Van Den Hove.
804 Appendix C, Carroll's report MI9/S/P.G. (-) 666 in TNA file WO 208/5582.
805 This account of Albert Day's treatment came from Albert himself. Colonel Rémy, however, says in *Réseau Comète* that a Doctor Raymond Kraekels visited Albert twice a day until he was well again. I am grateful to John Clinch for assisting with these details – Author.
806 Hutton/Warburton combined report MI9/S/P.G. (-) 687, 688 in TNA file WO 208/3308.
807 This was Sergeant H. Fraser, whose Whitley aircraft, shot down on the night of 17/18 May 1941, came down near Maaseik, forty kilometres north-east of Hasselt. Caught in Liège, actually on 4 July 1941, he spent the rest of the war as a prisoner of the Germans.
808 Anne Brusselmans's diary (*Rendez-vous 127*, p. 50) gives the date of 'Jack's arrival at the Brusselmans' apartment as 15 July 1941, though this is clearly impossible given that he and Len Warburton were not shot down for another six weeks.
809 Sim's report MI9/S/P.G. (B) 700 in TNA file WO 208/3308.
810 Returning to Belgium later in 1942 to set up an organisation in Liège, de la Lindi was arrested by the GFP on 18 February 1943, and executed on 31 May 1943 together with six other Belgians – Paul Brouha; Louis Malmendier; Joseph Renkin; Gabriel Debouny; René Lorent; and Pierre Thomas. His story is told in *Une Mission Tres Secrète*.
811 Georges Franz Louis Gustave Osselaer was born in Louvain on 15 October 1907.
812 TNA file HS 6/223.
813 Ibid. Actually, Elvire Morelle was then aged thirty-three. Andrée was twenty-five.

814 This may have been the Villa Marijanie, the home of Madame Gabrielle Lagnau, on the Route de la Barre, which Dédée sometimes used, but was probably the De Greef's house.
815 TNA file HS 6/223. The insulting remarks about Florentino's physical appearance were doubly worse for calling him Spanish. He was Basque, and proud of it.
816 *The Freedom Line*, pp. 95-6.
817 Gaucheret is given as Gauchard in *Little Cyclone*, p. 36.
818 *Saturday at M.I.9*, p. 134. He was possibly in Valenciennes meeting with Charles Morelle, whose home town it was.
819 Jean Ingels was executed at the Tir National, Brussels, on 20 October 1943.
820 This might have been Octave Delcroix, who was the first Brussels-Paris guide until replaced at the end of December 1941 by Andrée Dumon.
821 TNA file HS 6/968. Any information as to the identity of either Octave (Delcroix?) or Lacquer would be most welcome – Author.
822 For his special duties flying McCairns was later promoted to flight lieutenant, and earned a DFC (16/4/43) and Bar (13/8/43) to go with his Military Medal (18/8/42). See Chapter 9.
823 *Jump For It!*, p. 148.
824 *Jump For It!*, p. 151.
825 Carr's report MI9/S/P.G. (-) 749 in TNA file WO 208/3309. Fernande was her Christian name (see her photo in *Shot Down and on the Run*, p. 61).
826 Ibid.
827 Carr's report gives the chief's name as 'M. Michely (?)'. *See Silent Heroes*, p. 128.
828 Re Bruycker-Roberts, see page 112.
829 Both went to Stalag VIIIB (Lamsdorf, later re-named Stalag 344), with Raiston going on to Stalag Luft III (Sagan).
830 Carr's report op. cit.
831 Lance-Corporal Sir Peter Norton-Griffiths, Bt. (175974) was commissioned 2nd Lieutenant in the Intelligence Corps (7/4/41) wef 7 March 1941.
832 Appendix C, Horsley's report MI9/S/P.G. (-) 771 in TNA file WO 208/3309.
833 Naylor/Mills joint report MI9/S/P.G. (-) 773/774 in TNA file WO 208/3309.
834 Rademecker was caught by the Germans in December 1942 and shot in March 1943. (Information courtesy of John Clinch, 12 June 2006).
835 Letter dated 10 September 1981 from Les Baveystock to J.T. Pack. I am most grateful to Jeff Pack for allowing me to see his father's letter – Author.
836 Baveystock letter op. cit. All that is except Leslie Manser, killed, and the navigator, Pilot Officer R.J. Barnes, who was taken prisoner of war.
837 *Wavetops at My Wingtips*, p. 99. "This girl" may have been the 'indomitable' Madame Laurentie.
838 *Little Cyclone*, p. 72. Ed Cosgrove wrote in *The Evaders*, p. 32, that the 'villa was a venerable building with a huge garden, surrounded by a high wall screening it from the street.' Located at 6 Avenue des Erables, St Maur-des-Fossés.
839 *Little Cyclone*, p. 73. Forty-year-old Aimable was executed by the Germans at Mont Valérien, Paris on 28 March 1944. One evader to use Aimable's flat was Flying Officer G.C. Crowther RCAF in May 1943.
840 *Little Cyclone*, p. 73.
841 *Little Cyclone*, p. 71. Robert Aylé, aged forty-five in the summer of 1942, was 'typically French. He had dark brown hair brushed back from a fine, high forehead. His face was compelling and genial.' (ibid.).
842 p. 101 *Wavetops at My Wingtips*.
843 De Mone's report MI9/S/P.G. (-) 778 in TNA file WO 208/3309.
844 It is not known if the wireless set belonged to Comet or to another organisation, see *Fight Another Day*, p. 169: 'The constant refusal of members of Comet to accept a radio and operator in Brussels, on the excuse that it would give us [the British] control, was always a very sore point.'
845 M. van Steenbeck was also head of Service Luc, a clandestine Belgian organisation which had been active since September 1940 and was in contact with London. Luc had been sending couriers to England since March 1941.
846 Naylor/Mills report op. cit. The Englishman may well have been Albert Johnson.
847 Siadecki's report MI9/S/P.G. (-) 784 in TNA file WO 208/3309. The organisation was, of course, Comet.
848 Szkuta's report MI9/S/P.G. (-) 786 in TNA file WO 208/3309.
849 Szkuta's report op. cit.
850 Ernest Demuyter, born in 1893, was six times winner of the Gordon Bennett Cup. He died on 7 February 1963. Roger Anthoine states that the fourth Belgian was Pierre van Biest (*Aviateurs Piétons vers la Suisse…*, p. 231).
851 Szkuta's report MI9/S/P.G. (-) 786 in TNA file WO 208/3309.
852 Houghton's pilot, Pilot Officer L.A. Paskell DFM, and four others of the seven-man crew were killed. One other became a prisoner of war.
853 Houghton's report MI9/S/P.G. (-) 788 in TNA file WO 208/3309.
854 Houghton op. cit. The café was the Petit Pouce (confirmed in the addendum to Appendix C of his report).
855 *Safe Houses Are Dangerous*, p. 83.
856 Quotes from the addendum to Appendix C of Houghton's report, in TNA file WO 208/5582.
857 Ibid. The two sergeants were probably Beecroft and Hanwell. They left for England on the same day as Houghton, who was back six days before them!
858 Houghton's report op. cit.
859 Addendum to Appendix C of Houghton's report op. cit.
860 Pilot Officer Wasik was to evade again (from Denmark to Sweden in August/September 1944).
861 Siadecki's report op. cit. "Didi" was Andrée Dumon and "Didi (2)" Andrée de Jongh.
862 In their report Naylor and Mills say that 'the father of Didi took us to his flat, and met two Poles serving in the RAF – one called Edward Chudyecki. There the party split again. Sergeant King and a Pole were taken to Asnières, where they were sheltered by a Mrs Thomas (French), who had a grocer's shop.' Naylor/Mills report op. cit.
863 Naylor/Mills report op. cit.
864 Siadecki's report op. cit.
865 This and previous quote from Naylor/Mills report op. cit.
866 Naylor/Mills report op. cit.
867 Also on the *Narkunda* were Baveystock, Horsley, De Mone, Sergeants Malecki and Polesinski, and Flying Officer Krawczyk. The *Narkunda*, 16,632 gross tons, was sunk by German aircraft on 18 November 1942 in the western Mediterranean.
868 Peggy Mitchell has not been identified.
869 Goldsmith/Collins/Griffiths/Czekalski report MI9/S/P.G. (-) 791/792/793/794 in TNA file WO 208/3309. This was also another example of Operation Water Closet.
870 Czekalski was killed on operations on 10 April 1944.
871 Pack's report MI9/S/P.G. (-) 817 in TNA file WO 208/3310.
872 Pack op. cit. Maeseyck is today Maaseik.

873 Pack op. cit. The chief of police was Commissioner Louis Rademecker.
874 Pack op. cit. Joe Pack may possibly also have been at the home of the van Steenbeck family at 16, Palais de Justice apartments, Brussels – see King, Naylor and Mills above, this chapter.
875 Watson was shot down on 16/17 June 1942. Evans, another victim of the 1,000-bomber raid to Cologne, crossed with three others (Comet 29-32) in the group before Joe Pack's.
876 Pack op. cit.
877 Appendix C, Evans' report MI9/S/P.G. (-) 809 in TNA file WO 208/5582.
878 Evans op. cit. Evans notes that this 'was not the original farmhouse from which parties left, as the man there had been shot in the leg while crossing the mountains, and his sister refused to have any further dealings with parties.' Tomás Anabitarte Zapirain, born on 8 June 1912, was the first guide to take Andrée de Jongh over the Pyrenees in 1941. He died in Ciboure, France on 8 June 1994. (*El Camino…*, p. 138).
879 MacFarlane followed a day later, reaching Greenock on 26 August. He was awarded the DCM for his escape, as was Goldie (Comet 40) who crossed the Pyrenees three weeks behind MacFarlane.
880 The navigator, Flying Officer J.C. Wernham RCAF, and one of the sergeants were betrayed on 9 June 1942 by a little Dutch boy. Almost two years later Wernham would be murdered by the Gestapo after his "great escape" from Stalag Luft III (Sagan).
881 This and previous quote from *The Evaders*, p. 21 (Cosgrove). For full details of MacLean's evasion see *The Evaders*, Chapter Two, and *Free to Fight Again*, pp. 193-7.
882 Appendix C, Silva's report MI9/S/P.G. (-) 834 in TNA file WO 208/5582.
883 Silva op. cit.
884 Frédéric Wittek, and his brother Martin, were the two sons of Paul Wittek, who had married Andrée de Jongh's sister Suzanne.
885 In terms of Comet getting Allied servicemen into Spain only October, November, and December 1943 were busier, with twenty-eight, thirty-three and forty-one men respectively.
886 Frankowski's report MI9/S/P.G. (-) 939 in TNA file WO 208/3311.
887 This and preceding quotes also from Frankowski's report.
888 Only one of the six crew was taken prisoner. Randle, later group captain, DFM (gazetted 8/12/42), was appointed chairman of the RAF Escaping Society in 1974.
889 See Chapter 9 for details of the disaster that was to strike the Maréchal family, and the Comet organisation in Brussels, in November 1942.
890 Leon Prévot was actually born in Tours, France, on 6 January 1916. He died on 28 April 1994. (Information kindly provided by Marc Artiges).
891 Pipkin's report MI9/S/P.G. (-) 934 in TNA file WO 208/3311. Squadron Leader Pipkin died in a shooting accident on 30 August 1944.
892 Ibid. One of his anonymous Comet helpers, Gertrude Moors, who kept a safe house in Maastricht, was arrested on 18 June 1943. After months of torture, she was condemned to death on 2 July 1944, and died in Auschwitz. Details are from Colin Pateman on John Clinch's website.
893 Freberg's report MI9/S/P.G. (-) 935 in TNA file WO 208/3311. One of the crew survived to become a prisoner of war, but Barr and five others were killed. As for Freberg, he was killed in action on 10/11 April 1943 (Frankfurt), still on 7 Squadron.
894 Freberg op. cit.
895 Stadnik's report MI9/S/P.G. (G) 946 in TNA file WO 208/3311. The PoW camp may have been Stalag VIIIF (Lamsdorf).
896 Stadnik op. cit. Namur was a collection point for Comet "parcels" on their way to Brussels.
897 This and previous quote from *A Quiet Woman's War*, p. 50.
898 See *Footprints on the Sands of Time*, pp. 183-185.
899 His report, made in July 1945, may be found in TNA file AIR 2/13438.
900 *The Loss of Halifax Aircraft PM-Q*, p. 1.
901 Ibid.
902 *The Loss of Halifax Aircraft PM-Q*, p. 3.
903 *The Loss of Halifax Aircraft PM-Q*, p. 3.
904 The C-47 Skytrain was the military version of the DC-3 airliner.
905 For fuller details of Joyce's rise and fall in the RAF see *Footprints on the Sands of Time*, pp. 183-5, but in short he was hailed as a hero, given a medal and commissioned. It was not until evidence came to light in 1945, especially from former Luftwaffe officers, that he was a collaborator that he was stripped of his commission and the Military Medal. Due to the passage of time, however, he could not be tried for any offence under the Air Force Act.
906 Coombe-Tennant, then a major, returned to France on 15 August 1944 as leader of the three-man Jedburgh team Andrew.
907 Appendix C, Arkwright/Coombe-Tennant/Fuller joint reports MI9/S/P.G. (G) 974–976 in TNA file WO 208/5582.

Chapter 7

908 *No Drums…No Trumpets* p. 13.
909 Ibid. For her service the French awarded her the Croix de Guerre avec Palme.
910 Sauveterre-de-Béarn, then a small town of under 1,000 people, lies some 750 kilometres south-west of Paris but, conveniently, only sixty kilometres north of the Spanish border.
911 *No Drums…No Trumpets* pp. 48-9.
912 Ibid. p. 50.
913 Ibid. p. 51. Funds for the escapers and evaders were, at this time, provided out of Mary's own pocket.
914 Von Stülpnagel was appointed *Militärbefehlshaber* (military commander) of France on 25 October 1940. Born on 16 June 1878, he committed suicide (second attempt) on 6 February 1948 in the Cherche-Midi prison, Paris.
915 *No Drums…No Trumpets* p. 49. The Ritz was an expensive hotel on the Place Vendôme 'offrant un confort princier' ('princely comfort'), the highest Michelin rating.
916 *Mission Completed* p. 180.
917 *No Drums…No Trumpets* p. 60.
918 This and subsequent two quotes from Windsor-Lewis' report MI9/S/P.G. (B) 159 in TNA file WO 208/3300. The hotel on the rue Alger was probably the Oxford et Cambridge – 'très confortable, avec agencement moderne ou modernisé' according to the 1939 Michelin guide. The Crillon, on the other hand, centrally situated at 10, Place Concorde, was as good as Parisian hotels got.
919 J.C.Windsor-Lewis DSO, MC was to become commanding officer of the 2nd Battalion (Armoured), Welsh Guards, from December 1943 until May 1946. By the end of the Second World War he was a brigadier, and post-war was Regimental Lieutenant Colonel from 1 May 1951-30 June 1954.
920 *No Drums…No Trumpets* p. 81.
921 Colonel Shaw was sentenced to death, but the sentence was never carried out. He nevertheless spent four years in Fresnes prison.
922 *No Drums…No Trumpets* p. 124.
923 *No Drums…No Trumpets* p. 147.
924 For some inexplicable reason Langley gave Tom Groome the alias Georges de Milleville, though Barry Wynne records that Mary discovered that the name was Maurice de Milleville, the identical name to her elder son. Apparently she never forgave Langley for his 'unpardonable error'. (*No Drums…No Trumpets* p. 148). See also *Fight Another Day*, pp. 188-9, for Langley's meeting with her at an evasion

reunion in Holland in the 1960s.
925 *Escape and Evasion*, p. 99 (Ian Dear).
926 *No Drums...No Trumpets* p. 158. Gaston Denivelle was, or had been, a major in the French army, though was now an antiques dealer. His wife, Renée, was the local dentist.
927 *No Drums...No Trumpets* p. 161. Monsieur Goupille was also arrested and deported, but his fate is not known.
928 Dr Martinez was kept in prison for three months before being released by the Gestapo, after they realised that they could find no proof that he had been treating the Comtesse de Milleville.
929 Appendix C, Robertson/Canter report MI9/S/P.G. (-) 1126-1127 in TNA file WO 208/5582.
930 Robertson/Canter report op. cit.
931 For the next stage of their evasion see Wing Commander Embling and party's story in Chapter 10.
932 *No Drums...No Trumpets*, p. 169.
933 *Cockleshell Heroes* p. 198.
934 *After the Battle*, Number 118, p. 19.
935 *Cockleshell Heroes* p. 205.
936 Hasler op. cit. "Mr Carter" was almost certainly Pat O'Leary himself.
937 Hasler op. cit. For Markin read Martin.
938 For details of the evasion of de Merode and Dawson up to the point where they arrived at the Martins see the Embling story in Chapter 10.
939 They were probably escorted by Pat himself on what would have been his final errand for the PAO line, for on 2 March he was arrested in Toulouse.
940 *Cockleshell Heroes*, p. 166.
941 *No Drums...No Trumpets*, p. 180. Ferdinand Rodriguez returned to England by SOE Lysander on 15/16 August 1943.
942 *No Drums...No Trumpets*, p. 195.
943 Barbie had yet to earn for himself the soubriquet "Butcher of Lyons".
944 *Daily Telegraph*, 10 February 1983. Barbie, born on 25 October 1913, was responsible for the deaths of thousands of Frenchmen, and was extradited from Bolivia in February 1983 to stand trial in France for crimes against humanity. The trial began on 11 May 1987 and ended on 3 July 1987 when he was found guilty of the charges without extenuating circumstances. Sentenced to life imprisonment, he was locked up in Fort Montluc, Lyon, where so many of his victims had suffered, and died there of cancer on 25 September 1991.
945 *No Drums... No Trumpets*, p. 185.
946 *No Drums... No Trumpets*, p. 188.
947 *Women in the Resistance* p. 42. Pauline, born Pauline Gabrielle Gaillard on 9 April 1895, died in Ravensbrück concentration camp on 23 March 1945. Her husband, Marie Henri Barré de Saint-Venant, born on 4 January 1881, had died on 5 October 1933. They had a daughter, Marie-Jacqueline, who was born on 18 February 1920.
948 *No Drums... No Trumpets*, p. 197.
949 *Women in the Resistance*, p. 43.
950 Appendix C, Whitnall's report MI9/S/P.G. (-) 1445 in TNA file WO 208/5582. The location of the farm has not been identified, but it may well have been that of the Debreuilles at Marvaud, St Couton, twenty kilometres east of Ruffec.
951 Appendix C, Sansoucy's report MI9/S/P.G. (-) 1451 in TNA file WO 208/5582.
952 Whitnall op. cit.
953 Appendix C, Raginis' report MI9/S/P.G. (Poland) 1589 in TNA file WO 208/5582.
954 Raginis op. cit. The Hôtel Claridge is listed in the 1939 Michelin Guide as a modest, fourth-grade hotel offering 'un bon confort moyen'. At this time Mary was in Switzerland, asking for funds, of which her organisation was now extremely short.
955 Philo's report MI9/S/P.G. (-) 1580 in TNA file WO 208/3316.
956 Raginis' report MI9/S/P.G. (Poland) 1589 in TNA file WO 208/3316.
957 Raginis op. cit.
958 This was a tragic end to a generous and brave Kiwi soldier, who told Philo that he would have been thirty-nine on or about 27 October. Williamson is now buried in the Mazargues War Cemetery, Marseille. His official date of death is given as 25 October 1943.
959 After waiting for several days for a guide, Ballinger decided to carry on alone on 30 October 1943, and managed to reach Andorra, though in poor shape. He returned to England on 3 December. (*Achtung! Achtung! Die Flugfestungen Kommen!*, p. 44).
960 The author is grateful to Warren B. Carah for permission to use this information from *Achtung! Achtung! Die Flugfestungen Kommen!*, p. 44, and from emails on 13 March 2007.
961 Bakalarski's report MI9/S/P.G. (Poland) 1570 in TNA file WO 208/3316.
962 Appendix C, Philo's report MI9/S/P.G. (-) 1580 in TNA file WO 208/5582.
963 Sergeant Kenneth R. Moore was the tail gunner of B-17F 42-5890, 92nd BG/327th BS, shot down by flak on 6 September 1943 and crashed forty kilometres north-west of Paris, near Poissy.
964 Cooper, from Kenya, had had a charmed life. Shot down on a Ramrod to St Omer on 30 July 1942, he baled out over the Channel and was rescued. Two months later he was shot down again, on 2 October, this time being fished out of the water by an Air Sea Rescue Walrus.
965 Appendix C, Cooper's report MI9/S/P.G. (-) 1635 in TNA file WO 208/5582. It is tempting to believe that Bordeaux was not the man's real name, but that he was a member of Jean-Claude Camors' Bordeaux organisation – see following chapter – though this is unlikely.
966 *One of The Many*, p. 37.
967 Appendix C, Tsoucas' report MI9/S/P.G. (G) 1886 in TNA file WO 208/5583.
968 Tsoucas op. cit.
969 Tsoucas op. cit. The further story, possibly fanciful, is that Mary believed that Pauline posed such a threat to the line that she contemplated having her shot. The suggestion is, however, that it would have been too messy to have had Pauline shot and that instead she was paid the 80,000 francs due to her for expenses and told never to set foot in the Charente department for the rest of the war. See *No Drums... No Trumpets*, pp. 199-203.
970 *No Drums... No Trumpets*, pp. 197-8. One should, however, be aware of that book's somewhat doubtful chronology.
971 *One of The Many*, p. 40.
972 *One of The Many*, p. 42.
973 *One of The Many*, p. 43.
974 Tsoucas op. cit.
975 Tsoucas op. cit.
976 *Women in the Resistance*, p. 43.
977 Appendix C, Furniss-Roe's report MI9/S/P.G. (-) 1871 in TNA file WO 208/5583. Pauline was forty-eight years of age when she met Furniss-Roe!
978 Appendix C, Overwijn's report MI9/S/P.G. (-) 1875 in TNA file WO 208/5583. Tucker was shot down on a Ramrod to Evreux on 5 February 1944 in Typhoon JP385, 175 Squadron.
979 See Chapters 10 and 11. "George" [*sic* – Georges] was the alias of Gabriel Nahas.
980 Goldstein and Casey were pilot and co-pilot respectively of B-17F 42-3186, 92nd BG/407th BS, shot down by flak near Jauriac on 31 December 1943. They crossed into Spain near Andorra on 8 March 1944 and reached Gibraltar on 22 March. They were flown back to Prestwick.

981 Tsoucas was awarded the MC (gazetted 3/8/44) for his exploits.
982 Appendix C, McSweyn's report MI9/S/P.G. (G) 1629 in TNA file WO 208/5582.
983 *One of The Many*, p. 50.
984 McSweyn op. cit.
985 Quote from McSweyn's account in *Free to Fight Again*, p. 220.
986 Quote from McSweyn's account in *Free to Fight Again*, p. 221. 47880 "Buck" Palm, 94 (SAAF) Squadron, was awarded the DSO (22/8/44) 'in recognition of distinguished services'.
987 Appendix C, Martin's report MI9/S/P.G. (-) 1704 in TNA file WO 208/5582.
988 *No Drums... No Trumpets*, p. 203. In the spring, after the missing guide's wife had reported his absence to the authorities, a German patrol found the body of the dead guide. Martinez was arrested and deported. It is tempting to think that this incident related to the McSweyn and party's crossing, even though the facts do not agree – Author.
989 *Women in the Resistance*, p. 41.
990 This man may well have been SS Sturmbannführer Hans Joseph Kieffer who was head of the Abwehr's Section IIIF in France, not of the Gestapo, and was in charge of counter-intelligence work in France. Section IIIF was based at 84 Avenue Foch, Paris. Gestapo HQ were at 11, rue des Saussaies.
991 *No Drums... No Trumpets*, p. 216.
992 *Women in the Resistance*, p. 43.
993 Violette Szabo, parachuted into France on 6/7 June 1944, was captured on 10 June in a gunfight with soldiers of the SS *Das Reich* Division. Lilian Rolfe, flown to France by Lysander on the night of 4/5 April 1944, was arrested in July. Denise Bloch ("Danielle Williams") had entered France in the same way, on the night of 2/3 March 1944, and was arrested on 19 June. She and Lilian Rolfe were Jewish.
994 *No Drums... No Trumpets*, p. 258.
995 Barry Wynne writes that Marie Odile 'was awarded a Commendation for bravery by HM Government in 1947', (see *No Drums... No Trumpets*, footnote to p. 224).
996 *A Life in Secrets. The Story of Vera Atkins and the Lost Agents of SOE*, p. 98 – Sarah Helm (Little, Brown, London, 2005).
997 See *Women in the Resistance*, p. 44.
998 See website www.marcolowe.com/vrmsr/chauny_escape_line/chauny_escape_line.
999 Appendix C, Pilot Officer D.G. Ross's report MI9/S/P.G. (-) 1255 in TNA file WO 208/5582. Dromas was born on 17 December 1911.
1000 Chauny was the largest town in the immediate area with some 8,600 inhabitants. M. Logeon also became a radio operator for the Resistance, and it was one of his messages to London on 8 August 1944 that was responsible for the destruction of a German ammunition train transporting munitions to the front line. His garage was designated an historic monument of Chauny Resistance operations of the Second World War.
1001 Ross op. cit.
1002 Appendix C, Ross op. cit. Mme Ansard was indeed a member of the Dromas organisation.
1003 She was, however, known to British Intelligence as "Leslie", and had already helped Flight Sergeants W.G. Allen and D.R. Bradley, same crew lost on 16/17 April 1943 (Pilsen), and Sergeants S.J. Moore and D. Ferguson, also same crew lost 10/11 April 1943 (Frankfurt). She had an apartment at 16, Avenue du Colonel Bonnet, Paris XVI.
1004 Appendix C, Smith/Fitzgerald joint reports MI9/S/P.G. (-) 1349–1350 in TNA file WO 208/5582.
1005 Smith/Fitzgerald op. cit. The park was possibly the adjacent Jardin des Plantes. Note that Ross says that they met on 24 May.
1006 Ross op. cit.
1007 Appendix C, Everiss' report MI9/S/P.G. (-) 1271 in TNA file WO 208/5582. 2nd Lieutenant J.E. Wemheuer, bombardier/front gunner of B-17F 42-29647, 305th BG/365th BS, was shot down by fighters on 13 May 1943.
1008 Everiss op. cit. Goddard and Murray had also stayed, for six days, with Dr Bohn in Paris. 2nd Lieutenant Homer Contapidis and Sergeant Walter R. Minor were co-pilot and tail gunner respectively of B-17F Midnight 42-29627, 94th BG/410th BS, shot down by fighters and flak on 17 May 1943.
1009 The rear gunner, Flight Sergeant J.R. Couper RCAF, did not survive, possibly falling into a river (the Waal) or a "meer", and has no known grave. Five of the other six became prisoners of war.
1010 Turner's report MI9/S/P.G. (-) 1273 in TNA file WO 208/3313.
1011 This canal runs east from the North Sea at Ijmuiden to the Ij-meer, to the north of Amsterdam.
1012 Turner op. cit. The E-boat, or *Schnellboote*, came in several sizes. Its length varied from ninety to 100 feet, displacing from sixty to eight-five tons. Heavily armed, it was capable of reaching speeds in excess of thirty knots, and was more than a match for the Royal Navy's MGBs.
1013 Nearer Culemborg to the north there is also the River Lek, but Turner would first have come upon the canal.
1014 He later learned from a doctor that he must have displaced one of the vertebrae in his back on landing, and that it was this that was causing him so much distress.
1015 Turner op. cit. He does not give his exact location, but he was now probably in the area of Holland south of Maastricht.
1016 This Vandenhove is not to be confused with the tobacconist from Brussels – see Chapter 6.
1017 Turner op. cit.
1018 Appendix C, Sankey's report MI9/S/P.G. (-) 1324 in TNA file WO 208/5582.
1019 TNA file KV4/321.
1020 Via Michael Moores Leblanc.
1021 See website www.marcolowe.com/vrmsr/chauny_escape_line/chauny_escape_line.
1022 *Flee the Captor*, p. 58.
1023 *Flee the Captor*, p. 98.
1024 Quotes from *Flee the Captor*, p. 170.
1025 Appendix C, Hargest's report MI9/S/P.G. (Italy) 1587 in TNA file WO 208/3242. Hargest may have mis-heard "Prontas", for Nahas was known as "Georges Brantès". He was, however, almost certainly the guide "Georges" whom several evaders met on their way home from Switzerland.
1026 Hargest op. cit.
1027 Brigman was pilot of B-17G 42-39759 Sarah Jane, 390th BG/571st BS, shot down on 30 December 1943. Of the ten crew, eight (including three gunners) evaded capture, and two were taken prisoner of war.
1028 Appendix C, McLaughlin's report MI9/S/P.G. (-) 1872 in TNA file WO 208/5583.
1029 McLaughlin op. cit.
1030 Robert V. Krengle was bombardier of B-24D 42-63973, 389th BG/564th BS, shot down by fighters on 30 December 1943. He crossed to Spain on 30/31 March 1944. E&E #646.
1031 1st Lieutenant Elwood D. Arp and 2nd Lieutenant Howard Sherman were pilot and co-pilot respectively of B-17F 42-5763 Bomb Boogie, 91st BG/401st BS, shot down by fighters on 6 September 1943.
1032 *The Bermuda Historical Quarterly* via Scott Goodall. The "Belgian" pilot was the escaping Dutchman Flight Lieutenant Bram van der Stok.
1033 Henri Queuille (31 March 1884 – 15 June 1970) was allegedly descended from King Jean de Brienne of Jerusalem.
1034 *The Freedom Trail*, p. 83.
1035 Bram van der Stok was born on 13 October 1915 on the island of Sumatra, where his father was a Shell engineer. The other two to

make a "home run" were Sergeant Per Bergsland and Pilot Officer Jens Muller, both Norwegians.
1036 Appendix C, van der Stok's report MI9/S/P.G. (G) 2032 in TNA file WO 208/5583. 1st Lieutenant Joel W. McPherson, 352nd FG HQ, was pilot of P-47 42-75532. 2nd Lieutenant Gilbert M. Stonebarger was co-pilot of B-24 42-95019, 453rd BG/732nd BS, shot down on 25 April 1944.
1037 Appendix C, Thomas' report MI9/S/P.G. (-) 2018 in TNA file WO 208/5583.
1038 See also *La Filière du Rail*, pp. 240-1.
1039 *MI9 Escape and Evasion 1939-1945*, p. 209, and *Shot Down and On the Run*, p. 96. Some of the Dutch-Paris members were: Jacques Rens; Edmond Chait; Jef Lejeune; Hermann Laastman; Paul Veerman; Benno Nykerk; Hans Wisbrun; Father Aan de Stegge. Others (first name only) were: Françoise; Okkie; Anne-Marie; Lucy; Simone; Jacqueline. (See Christopher Long's website).
1040 Quoted in *Flee the Captor*, p. 365. The citation for the medal was dated 16 May 1946.
1041 Born in Reims on 18 July 1910.
1042 Fell's report MI9/S/P.G. (-) 1907 in TNA file WO 208/3319.
1043 Banner's report MI9/S/P.G. (-) 1851 in TNA file WO 208/3319.
1044 The story of the gross negligence and incompetence of SOE's Dutch Section is well told by Nicholas Kelso in *Errors of Judgement*.
1045 Trix Terwindt had escaped from Holland to Switzerland and England in March 1942. After capture, she was sent to the Seminarium prison at Haaren, Holland, and then to the concentration camps at Ravensbrück and Mauthausen, which she survived.
1046 *Saturday at M.I.9*, p. 280.
1047 Both quotes from *Saturday at M.I.9*. p. 281.
1048 Appendix C, Grout's report MI9/S/P.G. (-) 1616 in TNA file WO 208/5582. Lili was indeed wanted by the Gestapo, being forced to leave for Spain on 5 January 1944.
1049 Frazer was shot down on 27 September 1943 (see Appendix II). Buinicky was ball turret gunner of B-17F 42-29635 Auger Head, 303rd BG/358th BS, shot down on 31 August 1943 (Amiens-Glisy).
1050 *Footsteps of a Flying Boot*, p. 189.

Chapter 8

1051 *L'Émigrant* was captured by the Germans on 19 April 1941 when ten kilometres off shore, and was towed into Cherbourg.
1052 419 Flight was re-designated 1419 (Special Duties) Flight on 1 March 1941.
1053 Sibiril's boatyard lay on the River Penzé. Between them, he and his father, Alain, 'organised from their boatyard between February 1942 and February 1944' the passage to England of 140 personnel. Ernest was himself to escape by boat to England on 31 October 1943.
1054 Appendix C Smith's report MI9/S/P.G. (-) 1074 in TNA file WO 208/5582.
1055 McDermott and Vogel respectively co-pilot and radio operator of B-17F 41-24584 Susfu, 303rd BG/427th BS, shot down by Fw190 fighters on 23 January 1943.
1056 For details of this prisoner-of-war exchange, and others, see *Footprints on the Sands of Time*, pp. 170-80.
1057 *Saturday at M.I.9*, p. 217.
1058 *Fight Another Day*, pp. 192-3. It was Bouryschkine ("Williams") who had helped with the escapes from Fort de la Revère and who had himself only been brought out of France by boat in the autumn of 1942.
1059 Neave, *Saturday at M.I.9*, p. 221, has the date as 28 February 1943.
1060 Co-ordinates for the Oaktree drop zone were 48° 35′ 45″ N, 01° 50′ 15″ E, and those for Dido 46° 58′ 25″N, 01° 45′ 20″E.
1061 *Saturday at M.I.9*, p. 222.
1062 Betty was born Roberta Laurie in Scotland on 24 September 1891. Her father was 'a Scottish gardener who had emigrated to the United States.' She later became, as did her father, a naturalised citizen of the USA (*Women in the Resistance*, pp. 214-5). Her husband, Henri (1897-1974), governor of Chad, had been brought to England by Lord Louis Mountbatten aboard HMS *Kelly* in January 1941.
1063 Quotes from *Secret Flotillas*, Volume I, p. 236.
1064 The parachute of the twenty-two-year-old rear gunner, Flying Officer W.J. Freeman RCAF, 'stuck as he was leaving the aircraft. He struck the ground and died twenty minutes later.' For the evasion of the navigator and the mid-upper gunner see towards the end of this chapter.
1065 Also staying here on her flight from Belgium was Maud Olga Baudot de Rouville, who would do good work later in Marseille.
1066 After a time in Fresnes prison, Young was sent to German prisoner-of-war camps for the rest of the war.
1067 *Aviateurs Piétons vers la Suisse...*, pp. 23-4, and '*We Act With One Accord*', pp. 103-6.
1068 Lévêcque is the same man as the one from 19, rue d'Orléans, Paris.
1069 Appendix C, Lefèvre's report MI9/S/P.G. (-) 1301 in TNA file WO 208/5582.
1070 Robinson was top turret gunner of B-17F 42-5175, 306th BG/367th BS, shot down by flak and fighters on 16 February 1943.
1071 Greene was ball turret gunner of B-17F Greenhornet 41-24603, 303rd BG/359th BS, shot down by fighters and flak on 23 January 1943. Jack Orcutt Luehrs was radio operator of B-17F Available Jones 42-5232, 305th BG/364th BS, shot down by fighters on 4 April 1943.
1072 For the strange story of British soldier Ron Jeffery, who helped them, and who had also escaped from a prisoner-of-war camp, see Jeffery's book *Red Runs the Vistula*.
1073 Two others of the crew were taken prisoner of war. Rear gunner Sergeant E.M. Lee, however, was killed in action.
1074 Appendix C, James, Grove, Smith, Hall, Adams joint report MI9/S/P.G. (-) 1317–1321 in TNA file WO 208/5582.
1075 Kononenko, who had escaped earlier in 1943, had been in hiding in the Mons area of France for about four months. In Paris he met Val Williams and Elizabeth Barbier, who sent him to St Brieuc.
1076 Appendix C, Dennison's report MI9/S/P.G. (-) 1325 in TNA file WO 208/5582. (Was the countess Geneviève de Poulpiquet?)
1077 Appendix C, Dennison's report MI9/S/P.G. (-) 1325 in TNA file WO 208/5582.
1078 Lefèvre op. cit.
1079 *Samaria*, a Cunard liner of 19,602 gross tons, had been built by Vickers in Barrow in 1921.
1080 There were at least sixteen airmen aboard: Dennison; Adams; Bulman; Cox; Sergeant J.B. Ford; Grove; Hall; Howard; Sergeant T.H. Hutton; James; Martin; McDonald; Sergeant L. Rudkin; Sergeant J. Sankey; Smith; and Turenne.
1081 *Saturday at M.I.9*, p. 223.
1082 Appendix C, Raoul-Duval's report MI9/S/P.G. (-) 1471 in TNA file WO 208/5582.
1083 "Bill", probably one of the gunners, has not been identified, but 1st Lieutenant Theodore M. Peterson and Technical Sergeant John M. Scott were pilot and radio operator respectively of Lady Godiva, 42-29878, 379th BG/526th BS. Bill and the other seven of the crew were taken prisoner.
1084 Raoul-Duval op. cit. The Russian was probably A.S. Kononenko. Roger Huguen says that Madame Cellarié hid, amongst others, a Russian (Abraham) who had twice escaped from a prisoner-of-war camp in Germany before being brought to Brittany – *Par les Nuits...*, p. 257.
1085 Apparently the two Poles were from 138 Squadron and known as "George" and "Kut". Warrant Officers R. Urbanski and L. Zaborowski, both of whom were captured near the Pyrenees at this time, are likely candidates, shot down on 12/13 April 1943 over Normandy, France.
1086 Raoul-Duval op. cit.
1087 Desoubrie was also responsible for the arrest of Frédéric de Jongh at the Gare du Nord, Paris on 7 June.
1088 Houghton and Brown were respectively ball-turret gunner and radio operator of B-17F 42-30058, 384th BG/546th BS, shot down by fighters on 26 June 1943.

1089 Appendix C, Kononenko's report MI9/S/P.G. (F) 1455 in TNA file WO 208/5582. It is not known when Jack Luehrs USAAF headed south, but he may have been one of the five Americans in Kononenko's group.
1090 The five Americans were: 1st Lieutenant Louis L. Haltom (pilot); Technical Sergeant Glen Wells (radio operator); and Staff Sergeants Niles G. Loudenslager (right waist gunner), Roy A. Martin (ball turret gunner) and William C. Martin (left waist gunner). They had been shot down by fighters on a raid to Lorient in their B-17F 42-29767 Boothill, 96th BG/338th BS. Note that in *Women in the Resistance*, p. 219, Technical Sergeant Herman L. Marshall (top turret gunner) is shown instead of Loudenslager. It is believed that Marshall became a prisoner of war.
1091 The countess survived her imprisonment, some of it at Ravensbrück concentration camp and ten months in a munitions factory near Leipzig working twelve-hour shifts day after day.
1092 Labrosse himself is credited with having helped twenty-seven airmen evaders reach Spain.
1093 Manresa appears to have been recommended by Burgundy at this time as the town to make for.
1094 From Appendix C, Hutchinson/Marshall joint report MI9/S/P.G. (-) 1332/1333 in TNA file WO 208/5582.
1095 *Saturday at M.I.9*, p. 226.
1096 In September 1943 Jimmy Langley left Room 900 to go to MI9b. Airey Neave then became head of the section and filling his place was another one-armed officer, Patrick Joseph Stewart Windham-Wright MC.
1097 There appears to be some conflict over the spelling of "Shelburne", apparently so named after the eponymous county in Ontario, Canada. As contemporary wartime documents (and Airey Neave) use "Shelburne" it is used here. Shelburne or Shelburn? A rose by any other name…
1098 McCairns won his MM for his escape from German prisoner-of-war camp Stalag IXC (Bad Sulza) on 22 January 1942. He was back in England on 30 April 1942.
1099 James McAllister McBride was killed when he crashed in fog near Tangmere on his return from an operation on 16/17 December 1943. Flight Lieutenant S. Hankey, another Lysander pilot, was also killed on that night. For details of these Lysander operations see Chapter 10.
1100 See the account of the Possum/Martin line in Chapter 9.
1101 For details of the 16/17 November pickup see Chapter 10.
1102 *Saturday at M.I.9*, p. 230. Labrosse was occasionally assisted by Dorré's daughter (whom he was to marry after the war).
1103 See *The Man Who Went Back*, p. 143.
1104 *Secret Flotillas*, Volume 1, p. 242. MGBs 502 and 503, 117 feet in length with a beam of 20 feet 3 inches and a mean draught of 4 feet 1 inch, 'displaced 95 tons and were powered by three Davey Paxman diesels of 1,000 hp each which gave a maximum speed of 28 knots'. They 'were armed with a 2-pounder Pom-Pom in power turret forward, a twin .5 inch machine-gun in power turrets on either side of the bridge, a twin 20mm Oerlikon in power turret amidships, a 6-pounder hand operated aft, and two twin .303inch machine-guns.' (Bryan Cooper, *The E-Boat Threat*, p. 79, Macdonald and Jane's, London, 1976).
1105 *Saturday at M.I.9*, p. 232.
1106 Appendix C, Blackwell's report MI9/S/P.G. (F) 1727 in TNA file WO 208/5583.
1107 Lowther was the right waist gunner of B-17F 42-29571 Charlie Horse, 303rd BG/358th BS, shot down by fighters on 20 October 1943 (Duren).
1108 Appendix C, Griffith's report MI9/S/P.G. (-) 1744 in TNA file WO 208/5583.
1109 *Saturday at M.I.9*, p. 241.
1110 His MC (gazetted 4/8/42) was 'for gallant and distinguished services in the Middle East'.
1111 *Saturday at M.I.9*, p. 245.
1112 Appendix C, Harmel's report MI9/S/P.G. (-) 1807 in TNA file WO 208/5583.
1113 See *Fight Another Day*, p. 193.
1114 Quotes from *Saturday at M.I.9*, p. 233. Val Williams, honoured with the BEM for his services, died in August 1968.
1115 *Saturday at M.I.9*, p. 248.
1116 Appendix C, Brown's report MI9/S/P.G. (-) 1848 in TNA file WO 208/5583. The street where he stayed was Daumesnil, not Dominil.
1117 Cregger was left waist gunner on B-24H 42-7548 Bull O' The Woods, 44th BG/66th BS, shot down near Vic-sur-Aisne on 30 December 1943.
1118 A walkie-talkie set originally devised for SOE operations enabling aircraft and ground reception committees to talk to each other at close range.
1119 Numbers vary from twenty-four to thirty, but Neave correctly says 'twenty-four airmen… nearly all of them Americans' – *Saturday at M.I.9*, p. 236.
1120 Khan's report MI9/S/P.G. (F) 1852 in TNA file WO 208/3319.
1121 In *Par Les Nuits Les Plus Longues…* p. 346, the number of airmen is given, incorrectly, as nineteen.
1122 *The Man Who Went Back*, p. 174. The fighter pilot was Leo Harmel who had gone out on Bonaparte II in February.
1123 *Secret Flotillas*, p. 250, Volume I.
1124 Neave, however, reckoned that 'by March 30th, 118 airmen had returned to their bases.' *Saturday at M.I.9*, p. 237. The author's calculations agree with Slocum's total of 111, the numbers going on operations Bonaparte I-V being 19, 20, 25, 17, and 30 respectively. For their part in Shelburne, Dumais was promoted to captain, and Labrosse to lieutenant, and each awarded the MC (16/8/45 and 9/11/44 respectively). Captain Windham-Wright received a Bar to his MC (15/11/45).
1125 The Var line was 'conceived, designed and worked out' (*SOE in France*, p. 70) by Peter J. Harratt DSO, MC, 'an Englishman who had lived for a long time in south-west France in the 1930s and Erwin Deman ("Paul Dent"), a cosmopolitan Jew born in Vienna in 1921.' (*The Secret War from the River Dart*, p. 23). Harratt was seventeen years Deman's senior.
1126 Appendix C, Racine's report MI9/S/P.G. (-) 1885 in TNA file WO 208/5583.
1127 Racine op. cit.
1128 Sir Brooks Richards notes, *Secret Flotillas*, Volume I, p. 324, that Racine was evacuated on Operation Septimus on the night of 17/18 March 1944. This is hardly possible, as Racine was not shot down until 31 March.
1129 For details of Suzanne's return see *In Trust and Treason*, pp. 170-177. See Chapter 5 this book for her earlier exploits. Once in England she joined SOE, and assumed the codename "Charise".
1130 From the official report, quoted in *The Secret War from the River Dart*, p. 30. The seaman killed was twenty-year-old Able Seaman William Alfred Sandalls, who was buried in Charlbury cemetery, Oxfordshire.
1131 *One Foot on the Ground. A Pilot's Memoirs of Aviators & Aviation*, p. 65, Paul Roxin (ATC Press, Rochester, NY, USA, 1998).
1132 Stark's report MI9.S/P.G. (-) 2046 in TNA file WO 208/3320.
1133 Appendix C, Stark's report MI9.S/P.G. (-) 2046 in TNA file WO 208/5583. The French lieutenant was almost certainly Jean Robert – see *Par Les Nuits Les Plus Longues*, p. 358.
1134 Appendix C, Stark op. cit.
1135 Appendix C, Stark op. cit. This was almost certainly *not* the commanding officer of 4th French Parachute Battalion, Commandant Bourgoin (see Chapter 11).
1136 Appendix C, Brennan's report MI9/S/P.G. (-) 2025 in TNA file WO 208/5583.
1137 Guy Hamilton, born 11 September 1922, later directed four of the *James Bond* films. He also co-wrote the film script for *The Colditz Story* (1955).
1138 Lilly and Hawkins were pilots of P51 Mustangs lost on 26 April and 21 March 1944 respectively.
1139 Brennan op. cit.

1140 The Frederick team were: Major A.W. Wise (British); Captain P. Bloch-Auroch (French); and Sergeant K. Kehoe (American).
1141 Robert Kehoe, from website www.cia.gov/csi/studies/winter98_99/art03.
1142 See *Women in the Resistance*, pp. 96-97, and Airey Neave's '128 airmen and seven agents' – *Saturday at M.I.9*, p. 237.
1143 Zetland appears against Yves de Henaff's name in a list of organisations in TNA file WO 208/3242, the potted history of MI9. There is, however, no mention of Curaçao.
1144 He was born on 23 October 1914 at Penhars (Finistère), His family owned a canning plant near Quimper (Finistère).
1145 Appendix C Matthews' report MI9/S/P.G. (-) 1559 in TNA file WO 208/5582.
1146 Dalinsky was taken over the Pyrenees by Comet on 13 January 1944. He was number 268.
1147 Appendix C, Reynolds' report MI9/S/P.G./(-) 1835 in TNA file WO 208/5583. Reynolds eventually crossed the Pyrenees with a party of Americans and refugees on 26/27 January 1944, following the by now well-worn path into Spain that led to Uztarroz and Isaba – and to a police station. Reynolds finally reached Gibraltar on 10 March 1944. For further on Fidler and Woollard see this chapter, below.
1148 Matthews op. cit.
1149 "Felix", otherwise Charles Gueulette, a Belgian, who had parachuted into Belgium in late July 1943, was "burned" in January 1944. He escaped to England in April 1944, though many members of his group were arrested, and some did not return from Germany. Alfred George Albert Blondeel, a man with several other aliases (A. Bakker; Charles George Peeters; Captain Bernard; Pierre Dupuis) was born on 12 December 1914.
1150 This may have been Operation Envious scheduled for 3 November 1943, but which was aborted by MGB 318 due to the would-be passengers having gone to the wrong island for evacuation.
1151 John Watlington, *The Bermuda Historical Quarterly*, via Scott Goodall.
1152 *Secret Flotillas*, Volume I, p. 340.
1153 *The White Rabbit*, p. 92.
1154 An asymptote, from the Greek *asumptotos* (not falling together), is a line that gets nearer and nearer to a given curve but never meets it within a finite distance. Yeo-Thomas specifically chose this codename.
1155 The HQ of the SD are not to be confused with those of the Gestapo at 11, rue des Saussaies, Paris.
1156 He became a wing-commander GC (15/2/46), MC (14/3/44) and Bar (16/5/44), Légion d'Honneur and Croix de Guerre (both French), and the Polish Gold Gross of Merit.
1157 Prisoners' cells were on the fifth (top) floor of 84, Avenue Foch, where there was also an interpreter's office and a guardroom. Located on the floor below were the office and private quarters of SS Sturmbannführer Josef Kieffer, head of the SD in Paris, and also the office of his deputy.
1158 *Saturday at M.I.9*, p. 237.
1159 For a list of the Burgundy names see *L'Evadé de la France Libre*, pp. 296-303.
1160 Appendix C, Fidler/Woollard reports MI9/S/P.G. (-) 1717-1718 in TNA file WO 208/5582.
1161 Fidler/Woollard op. cit.
1162 Carter was born on 1 June 1923 in Paris, of English parents, but the family moved to Bronxville, New York, USA when he was still in his teens. He cut short his studies to join up in Canada on 8 July 1941.
1163 Carter's report MI9/S/P.G. (-) 1155 in TNA file WO 208/3312.
1164 Carter op. cit.
1165 Appendix C, Carter's report MI9/S/P.G. (-) 1155 in TNA file WO 208/5582.
1166 Wilson was top-turret gunner of B-17F 42-5717, 306th BG/423rd BS, shot down by fighters on 16 February 1943.
1167 *Secret Flotillas*, Volume I, p. 317. It was partly in consequence of this failed operation that the Oaktree mission was sent to Brittany.
1168 The Père Supérieur and the Père Hôtelier, the only two members of the monastery who were allowed to speak, were later arrested. They were deported to Germany, where they died in a concentration camp.
1169 Biggs was co-pilot of B-17F Skylark 42-5378, 306th BG/367th BS, shot down by fighters on 6 March 1943.
1170 Carter op. cit.
1171 Appendix C, Carter's report, op. cit.
1172 Ibid.
1173 Appendix C, Carter's report, op. cit.
1174 Denys Teare wrote an excellent account of his long evasion in *Evader*.
1175 *Evader*, pp. 246-7. After almost three months in Fresnes prison, George Thomas spent the next eighteen at Stalag IVB (Mühlberg), Germany, having arrived there circa December 1943.
1176 Horton/Parkinson reports MI9/S/P.G. (F) 1409/1410 in TNA file WO 208/3315.
1177 Appendix C, Horton/Parkinson reports MI9/S/P.G. (F) 1409/1410 in TNA file WO 208/5583.
1178 In *Johnny Checketts: The Road to Biggin Hill*, pp. 115-117, the Suzanne-Renée is called the Suzette.
1179 Checketts' report MI9/S/P.G. (-) 1495 in TNA file WO 208/3315.
1180 Checketts op. cit. Marcel le Conte would celebrate his 26th birthday while Checketts was there.
1181 For Merlin's extraordinary evasion see Appendix VI.
1182 Kearins' report MI9/S/P.G. (-) 1498 in TNA file WO 208/3315.
1183 This and previous quote are from *Spitfire Strikes. A New Zealand Fighter Pilot's Story*, pp. 150 and 151, Johnnie Houlton DFC (John Murray (Publishers) Ltd, London, 1985).
1184 2 Group RAF *A Complete History, 1936-1945*, p. 327, Michael J.F. Bowyer (Faber & Faber, London, 1974 and 1979).
1185 Ibid, p. 328.
1186 For his actions Riseley was awarded the DSO (14/1/44). Merlin also took vital V1 information to Switzerland 'concealed in a loaf of bread' (see Appendix VI). (Was this coincidence, or was it Merlin who took Riseley's information with him?)
1187 Appendix C, Liby's report MI9/S/P.G. (-) 1488 in TNA file WO 208/5582.
1188 Jean Claude was probably Jean-Claude Camors, the organiser of the boat operation, an agent working on behalf of the BCRA and MI9. The French barrister may well have been Paul Campinchi ("François").
1189 Liby is described in Vincent Orange's biography of Checketts as being 'a big, blond man and – as Johnny later learned – "very uncouth."' *Johnny Checketts: The Road to Biggin Hill*, p. 103.
1190 Checketts said, correctly, that it was 'probably on the road to Morgat' some ten kilometres from Châteaulin.
1191 There is a conflict as to the exact date of arrival. Checketts says 25 October, but Riseley's 24 October is preferred. The crossing, so Riseley says, took eighteen hours, the distance from Camaret to Penzance being approximately 250 kilometres. De-briefing interviews of the airmen evaders were held on 26 and 27 October.
1192 Appendix C, Wood's report MI9/S/P.G. (-) 1525 in TNA file WO 208/5582.
1193 HMT *Loch Park*, pennant number FY.1835, 248-tons and built in 1917, had been commissioned in June 1940. She survived the war.
1194 Colonel Scheidhauer's son, Bernard, was one of the fifty executed after The Great Escape from Stalag Luft III (Sagan).
1195 Appendix C, Barber/Lawrence joint report MI9/S/P.G. (-) 1279/1280 in TNA file WO 208/5582.
1196 Barber/Lawrence op. cit.
1197 Barber/Lawrence op. cit. It was not until over a year later that Roger met his deserved fate at the hands of the Resistance. It is probable that Camors and his airmen companions were allowed to go free on this occasion because Roger le Légionnaire was hoping to hook more and bigger fish once he had fully penetrated the Bordeaux line.
1198 Barber/Lawrence op. cit. Durant was indeed hit and captured. He spent the rest of the war as a prisoner of war at Stalag Luft VI

(Heydekrug) and Stalag 357 (Fallingbostel).
1199 Barber/Lawrence op. cit. Apart from Cox (see following chapter), the other names may well have been false.
1200 This information comes from website www.ordredelaliberation.fr/fr_compagnon/173.html. Roger le Neveu had insinuated himself into Resistance networks in Brittany with conspicuous success. See *L'évadé de la France Libre*, pp. 204-5.
1201 In fact, Dumont, Poirier and Depesme stayed on the roof for thirty-six hours before deciding that it was safe to go down.
1202 Information on the café incident and gunfight from website http://assoc.orange.fr/memoiredeguerre/biogr/camors.htm.
1203 In view of the similarity of dates it is presumed that Bordeaux-Loupiac had a hand in the *Breizh-Izel* evacuation.
1204 Appendix C, Nielsen/Adams' joint report MI9/S/P.G. (-) 1649/1650 in TNA file WO 208/5582.
1205 Jean Bougier's name from *We Landed by Moonlight* (revised edition), p. 206.
1206 The story of this incident is told in *Wings of Night*, pp. 99-101.
1207 Lamirault, born 12 June 1918, was arrested in Paris on 15 December 1943. On 15 May 1944 he was transferred from Fresnes prison to Compiègne, and on 2 July 1944 to Dachau. Liberated on 14 April 1945, he was killed in a motor accident in Orléans on 27 May 1945. Lamirault had met Pierre Hentic when both were serving in the 27eme Bataillon de chasseurs alpins in 1936-37.
1208 *The Secret War from the River Dart* p. 6.
1209 Nielsen/Adams op. cit. The name of the island, Guennoc, may also be written as Guenioc (see modern French maps, e.g. Michelin).
1210 MGB 329, borrowed from Coastal Forces for this operation, was not on the strength of 15th MGB Flotilla.
1211 Appendix C, Pollard and five others' composite report MI9/S/P.G. (-) 1651-1656 in TNA file WO 208/5582. The full story of this night's dramatic events may be found in *Secret Flotillas*, Volume I, pp. 187-93.
1212 These RN sailors were, from MGB 329's surfboat, Acting Petty Officer J. Cole; and Able Seamen D.E.J. Sheppard and V.E. Williams; and from MGB 318; Pollard, Able Seamen R. Bartley and C.J.C. Sanders.
1213 The proposed airlift was possibly the Lysander Operation Snowdrop (Flight Lieutenant S.A. Hankey) scheduled for the night of 10/11 December but which had had to be aborted due to bad weather.
1214 Pollard etc op. cit.
1215 *Secret Flotillas*, Volume I, p. 197.
1216 *Secret Flotillas*, Volume I, p. 208. The total number of passengers makes sense if the two women are included as agents.
1217 *The Last Piece of England...*, p. 161. John Garnett was the father of Virginia Bottomley, former Conservative Secretary of State for Health.
1218 From website http://freepages.military.rootsweb.ancestry.com/~hfhm/Roster/images/hargrove_w_story.doc.

Chapter 9

1219 According to Roger Anthoine their victor was probably Hauptmann Walter Ehle, but may have been Oberleutnant Bietman – see *Aviateurs-Piétons vers la Suisse*, p. 232.
1220 Swida's report MI9/S/P.G. (-) 1584 in TNA file WO 208/3316.
1221 This division, operating with French troops in the Belfort area of eastern France, was engaged in heavy fighting from 17-19 June 1940. When the French retreated, the Poles, though virtually surrounded by the Germans, were able to break through to Switzerland. The 15,830 men of this division were, as of 15 June 1940, part of the 84,461 Polish soldiers in France, some 45,000 of whom had escaped from Poland.
1222 Appendix C, Swida's report MI9/S/P.G. (-) 1584 in TNA file WO 208/5582.
1223 Tyszko's report MI9/S/P.G. (-) 871 in TNA file WO 208/3310.
1224 Wasiak's report MI9/S/P.G. (-) 870 in TNA file WO 208/3310.
1225 Appendix C, Wasiak's report MI9/S/P.G. (-) 870 in TNA file WO 208/5582.
1226 Ibid. See also Sergeant Joe Pack's experience at the Ministry of Justice in Chapter 6.
1227 Costello-Bowen's report MI9/S/P.G. (-) 868 in TNA file WO 208/3310. Westmalle is more east-north-east of Antwerp than north-east.
1228 Ibid.
1229 Van den Bok's report MI9/S/P.G. (-) 867 in TNA file WO 208/3310. The body of Wing Commander Twigg now lies in Gosselies Communal Cemetery, Belgium.
1230 Cope's report MI9/S/P.G. (-) 869 in TNA file WO 208/3310. In the event, only one other of his crew survived, and was taken prisoner. 115 Squadron lost four Wellingtons on this raid, with a fifth crashing on its return to England but without loss of life. Of the twenty aircrew in these four aircraft Cope was the only one of eight survivors to evade capture.
1231 Ron Douglas (Sergeant R.C.A. Douglas), *Intercom, Autumn 1990* (the official quarterly magazine of The Aircrew Association), p. 57.
1232 Those killed were Walkington, Sergeant J. Law (flight engineer), and Sergeant L.C. Molloy (rear gunner).
1233 Embling's report MI9/S/P.G. (F) 1108 in TNA file WO 208/3312 (and also in AIR 20/9160).
1234 Embling op. cit. None of the other airmen managed to escape, and spent the rest of the war as prisoners of war of the Germans.
1235 Embling op. cit.
1236 Embling op. cit.
1237 Chauny lies five or six kilometres to the east of Beaugies, and 120 or so north-east of Paris.
1238 Trost was the bombardier/front gunner of B-17F 42-5071, 306th BG/367th BS, lost on 20 December 1942.
1239 Appendix C, de Merode's report MI9/S/P.G. (-) 1131 in TNA file WO 208/5582. As Roubaix was practically part of Lille, it is presumed that the organisation was PAT/PAO.
1240 Roper was the navigator of B-17E 41-9018, 92nd BG/327th BS, shot down by fighters on 9 October 1942.
1241 Embling op. cit.
1242 *Dangerous Landing*, pp. 144-5.
1243 See Chapter 5. His name only appears in Embling's report, but Cyril Penna refers to him as Captain Dick Adams in *Escape and Evasion*, p. 85.
1244 *Escape and Evasion*, p. 82. The French [*sic*] boy Louis was Letory.
1245 *Dangerous Landing*, p. 153.
1246 *Escape and Evasion*, p. 83.
1247 Robertson writes that two Americans died during that awful climb.
1248 At the age of forty-six, and as an air-vice marshal CBE, DSO, and AOC 12 Group, Fighter Command, Embling was killed at RAF Leconfield on 15 July 1959 when his Meteor jet crashed on the runway.
1249 Christie was the only one of the eight aboard BF379 to lose his life. He is buried in Milan War Cemetery. His DFM had been gazetted on 24 December 1940, when on 58 Squadron.
1250 McAuley's report MI9/S/P.G. (Italy) 1245 in TNA file WO 208/3313.
1251 Nightingale's report MI9/S/P.G. (Italy) 1246 in TNA file WO 208/3313.
1252 The Regina Coeli (Queen of Heaven) became a prison in 1881-1885, its buildings having originally formed the monastery of *Chiesa conventuale di Santa Maria Regina Coeli*, which was founded in 1654. The prison, taken over by the Gestapo, was 'a large forbidding building which dominates the north bank of the River Tiber, not far from the Collegio Teutonicum.' (*Special Commando*, p. 161, Rex Woods, William Kimber & Co. Ltd., London, 1985).
1253 McAuley/Nightingale reports op. cit.
1254 Twenty-three-year-old John Rattray Chalmers Stewart is commemorated on Face 33, Medjez-el-Bab Memorial.
1255 Cook's report MI9/S/P.G. (Italy) 1247 in TNA file WO 208/3313.
1256 Appendix C, joint report McAuley/Nightingale/Cook MI9/S/P.G (Italy) 1245, 1246, 1247 in TNA file WO 208/5582.

1257 Seaton was a member of the crew of H.M. Submarine *Oswald*, 1,475 tons, which had been rammed and sunk fifteen kilometres/ten miles south-east of Spartivento Bay in the Mediterranean Sea by an Italian destroyer on 1 August 1940.
1258 Though covering an area of only 108 acres, the Vatican City was, and is, a neutral country in its own right and as such any escaped prisoner of war who gained entry to the city was entitled to be repatriated as if he had entered, say, Switzerland or Sweden.
1259 Joseph Ender, the Swiss guard who received the escapers, had a brother, Anthony, who lived at 362 Maxwell Road, Glasgow.
1260 *The Rome Escape Line*, p. 45, Major Sam Derry, (George G. Harrap & Co. Ltd., London, 1960).
1261 Born 2 March 1876, Eugenio Maria Giuseppe Giovani Pacelli, Pope Pius XII, was elected to office on 2 March 1939. He died on 9 October 1958.
1262 *The Rome Escape Line*, p. 228, op.cit.
1263 Born on 28 February 1898, O'Flaherty died on 30 October 1963.
1264 *Scarlet Pimpernel of the Vatican*, p. 26, J .P. Gallagher (Souvenir Press Ltd, London, 1967).
1265 Any police work, on the other hand, was carried out by the Vatican gendarmerie, all of whom were Italians and had to be of a minimum height of 5 feet 9 inches.
1266 Kidd's report MI9/S/P.G. (-) 1207 in TNA file WO 208/3313. The rest of his crew, six young sergeants, all perished.
1267 Kidd op. cit. The village of Poullaouen is thirty-six and a half kilometres (twenty-three miles) by road from Morlaix. It is a further ten and a half kilometres (six and a half miles) to Carhaix-Plouger.
1268 Jones was the radio operator of B-17F 41-24603 Green Hornet, 303rd BG/359th BS, lost on 23 January 1943.
1269 Cox, top-turret gunner, was shot down in B-24D 41-23678 Ball of Fire, 93rd BG/330th BS, on 9 October 1942.
1270 Wilson, 4 Squadron, was shot down by several Fw190s on a photo reconnaissance on 18 January 1943.
1271 Kidd op. cit. The Canadian, yet to be identified, was probably one of those freed by Françoise Dissard as seen below in this chapter.
1272 See website http://www.93rdbombardmentgroup.com/history.htm.
1273 "Bernard" may have been Bernard Gohon, 'once a French Air Force pilot and a new member of the line' – *Safe Houses are Dangerous*, p. 176. Philippe Franc was almost certainly Philippe Valat, the BCRA radio operator who had taken over from Alex Nitelet and who had recently been "sprung" from Castres.
1274 She joined SOE and went back to France, earning the George Medal (gazetted 17 July 1945) for her outstanding work with the Resistance.
1275 Haines' report MI9/S/P.G. (-) 1107 in TNA file WO 208/3312. The reference was probably to Haines' Halifax, though, as seen, only three of its crew were killed.
1276 Appendix C, Haines' report MI9/S/P.G. (-) 1107 in TNA file WO 208/5582.
1277 The *Saltwick*, 3,775 gross tons, was to be sunk on 21 October 1943 by a torpedo launched from an aircraft.
1278 In June 1943 the London District Transit Camp became the London District Assembly Centre.
1279 McCrea also evaded capture, but the other four of the crew became prisoners of war.
1280 Jones/Alderdice joint report MI9/S/P.G. (-) 1357/1358 in TNA file WO 208/3314.
1281 As no one by that name appears to have evaded it is feared that he became a prisoner of war of the Germans.
1282 Also included in this joint citation was evader Sergeant William Hughes, 102 Squadron, who had returned to England on 20/21 August 1943.
1283 Appendix C, Schloesing's report MI9/S/P.G. (-) 1192 in TNA file WO 208/5582.
1284 Names of the two guides very kindly provided by Jeanine de Greef via Chris and Ann Lyth.
1285 Schloesing, flown to England on 8 May 1943, was to lose his life on operations on 26 August 1944.
1286 *Saturday at M.I.9*, p. 116.
1287 *Saturday at M.I.9*, p. 117. It was also to the Hôtel de Paris that Airey Neave and Woollatt had been taken in April 1942 on their way to the Spanish frontier with Francis Blanchain.
1288 Archive YDX 207/14. p. 19: 'De plus, Georges étais arrêté à Toulouse sur dénonciation d'un juif de Montauban pour 20,000 Frs.'
1289 Charles Cheramy and his English wife, "Pat", were sent to concentration camps in Germany. On her return from Ravensbrück concentration camp, Pat was reunited with her son.
1290 See *Safe Houses Are Dangerous*, p. 183.
1291 Hogg's report MI9/S/P.G./LIB/1811 in TNA file AIR 40/1533. Paul was most probably Paul Ulmann, and "Jane" his wife Imelda.
1292 2nd Lieutenant Dominic Lazzaro was the navigator of B-17F 42-5058 Hun Hunter, shot down by fighters on 16 February 1943. Of the ten crew, only he and the pilot survived.
1293 *Nancy Wake*, p. 75. "Gaston" was Gaston Nègre, who had been caught in the farcical drop near his home. One of those to be freed was the Canadian on 7 Squadron who was mentioned by Sergeant Kidd.
1294 *The Way Back*, p. 171.
1295 Also held in St Pierre were Dr Rodocanachi before going to Germany, and Henri Fiocca (who was to die there).
1296 Also at Natzweiler in September 1944, and later at Dachau, was Flying Officer H.R. Weller RCAF, who had been brutally tortured by the Gestapo after his capture in France on 30 August 1944.
1297 *War Crimes Trials, Volume V – The Natzweiler Trial*, p. 17, edited by Anthony M. Webb (William Hodge and Company, Limited, London, 1949).
1298 *Archive YDX 207/14*, p. 21: 'Graces au petites Martin qui lui avaient crié "Sauvez-vous Albert, les Boches sont la" il avait filé a toutes jambes…'
1299 *All the Luck in the World*, p. 15.
1300 Appendix C, Henderson's report MI9/S/P.G. (-) 1216 in TNA file WO 208/5582.
1301 *All the Luck in the World*, p. 38.
1302 *SOE in France*, p. 217.
1303 Henderson op. cit. Ogilvie remembers, probably erroneously however, that it was Pertschuk himself who took them to La Ville-Dieu.
1304 According to "Freddie" West VC, air attaché in Switzerland, Farrell 'did a wonderful job' organising the escape route to Spain – *Winged Diplomat*, pp. 186-7.
1305 The families of Fabien and Antoine received letters addressed to them from Weimar, Germany. Maurice Wilson spent a week (13–20 June) in Perpignan's citadel before enduring six months in Fresnes prison, Paris. In January 1944 he was sent to Stalag Luft III (Sagan), Germany.
1306 *Winged Hours*, p. 108.
1307 Appendix C, Griffiths' report MI9/S/P.G. (-) 1588 in TNA file WO 208/5582.
1308 Peter B. Seniawsky was lost in B-17 42-29870 Big Moose, 384th BG/545th BS.
1309 Foley and Grauerholtz were co-pilot and navigator respectively of B-17G 42-31164 Lucky Lady, 96th BG/337th BS, lost 5 January 1944.
1310 Appendix C, McWilliams' report MI9/S/P.G. (-) 1788 in TNA file WO 208/5583.
1311 *The Freedom Trail*, p. 67. See also p. 266.
1312 See Chapter 6, footnote 95.
1313 *A Quiet Woman's War*, p. 37.
1314 Ibid, p. 56.
1315 Ibid, p. 57.
1316 *Little Cyclone*, pp. 96-7.

1317 Hope, 540 Squadron, was shot down in Mosquito DZ358 on 8 December 1942 (photo recce to Austria). Greaves, 142 Squadron, was lost in Wellington BK536 on 20/21 November 1942, and Ross in Stirling R9262, 7 Squadron, on 21/22 December 1942.
1318 In *The Freedom Line*, p. 6, author Peter Eisner says that the French police were German troops. Donato, he adds, had once been tried out as a guide over the Pyrenees, but Dédée did not trust him, and he had never been used again. The loyal, steadfast Florentino was the preferred choice.
1319 In this ancient prison prominent French politicians Édouard Daladier and Georges Mandel had also been incarcerated for a time.
1320 For more on this sad episode see *Home Run* (Nichol/Rennell, 2007) pp. 164-71.
1321 Spence and Devers were respectively navigator and top-turret gunner in the same crew as T/Sergeant M.B. Jones USAAF – see above this chapter.
1322 This and previous quote from Chaster's report MI9/S/P.G. (-) 1125 in TNA file WO 208/3312.
1323 Neave gives two conflicting dates for the crossing. In *Little Cyclone* (p. 140) he says that Franco returned with Johnson on 13 March, but in *Saturday at M.I.9* (p. 165) he says that Franco crossed to Spain a week after Johnson, on 20 March. The list of evaders in Cécile Jouan's book *Comète*, however, shows no Americans, or anyone else come to that, being taken to Spain on any date in March 1943.
1324 *Rendez-vous 127*, p. 75.
1325 See the notes on him page xvi.
1326 Tony Goodenough, email to author, 20 September 2007.
1327 I am grateful to Jean-Claude Rasquine, who works at the local authority offices at Oupeye, for information that Monsieur and Madame Cilissen, and a Monsieur Jean-Claude Carens were killed by the falling wreckage. M. Carens, however, lived in the neighbouring village of Herstal. It is reported that two of JD168's engines are still buried under rue Sondeville – Author.
1328 Tony Goodenough op. cit.
1329 This and previous three quotes from Tony Goodenough op. cit.
1330 Tony Goodenough op. cit.
1331 Appendix C, Moore/Ferguson joint report MI9/S/P.G. (-) 1253/1254 in TNA file WO 208/5582.
1332 *Saturday at M.I.9*, p. 166.
1333 Letter dated 28 February 1944 from Airey Neave to Captain Delloye of the Belgian Secret Service in London (via Fred Greyer).
1334 Captain Dominique Edgard Antoine Potier was born on 2 November 1903.
1335 Emile Belva was a member of this group, which was run by Madeleine Kinsbergen.
1336 On the recommendation of Raymond Gallet, Camille Beuré, a self-employed electrician, agreed to shelter Lafleur.
1337 From the unpublished account by Fred Gardiner, the wireless operator.
1338 This and previous two quotes by Fred Gardiner op. cit.
1339 This and previous quote by Fred Gardiner op. cit.
1340 This and previous two quotes by Fred Gardiner op. cit. Only two of JA707's crew were killed. Two more became prisoners of war, and three, including Herbert Pond, evaded capture.
1341 Fred Gardiner op. cit.
1342 In total, Paul Frerlet took twenty-two airmen (British and American) as well as political refugees from Belgium to France before he was arrested by the Germans and deported to a concentration camp, from which he later returned.
1343 They may have stayed at the home of M. and Mme. Bulard at 4, rue de la Liberté, Reims. Madame Bulard in particular, 'chef de gîte' of the Reims area, took a very active role in arranging board and lodging for airmen.
1344 Fred Gardiner op. cit.
1345 *We Landed by Moonlight* (Crécy), p. 200.
1346 Bruce Marshall in *The White Rabbit*, pp. 194-6, says 9 September. Whatever, they were put to death in a most horrible and bestial way, 'hung by the neck on hooks embedded in the wall of the crematorium furnace. They died slowly, strangled by their own weight. Then they were burned.' Extract from *Histoire de la Résistance dans la Region de Florenville (1940-1944)*, p. 19, Alfred Dubru, translated by Gerald and Helen Hauser.
1347 Whalen and Browning, 94th BG/332nd BS, were shot down on 4 October 1943. Desrochers and Klein, 384th BG/544th BS, were shot down on 17 August 1943.
1348 Breuer and Chichester, 94th BG/333rd BS, were bombardier and co-pilot respectively of B-17F 42-30453 Thunderbird, lost 14 October 1943. Murray, 387th BG/556th BS, was lost on 27 September 1943, and Maddox was from the Whalen/Browning crew.
1349 He remained in charge until 23 December 1943, when he went off to help with the organisation of the Marathon camps.
1350 Johnson's report MI9/S/P.G. (-) 1579 in TNA file WO 208/3316. Johnson was the only survivor.
1351 Ibid. Despite the violent explosion Stirling EH938 crashed near Lommel, in Belgium, approximately thirty kilometres west of Weert (Holland).
1352 Ibid. No doubt the doctor was Doctor Pierre.
1353 D'Oultremont had brought with him a money-belt containing three million francs, which was deposited by Potier with Jean-Pierre Mallet, Comet's banker, at 37 rue d'Anjou, Paris. When de Blommaert was forced to return to England his wireless operator, Albert LeMaitre, spent a few days at Nesles-la-Vallée with Philippe and Virginia d'Albert-Lake and with Marcel Renaud (see Chapter 12).
1354 *Saturday at M.I.9*, pp. 246-7.
1355 Madame Mondet, born 1897, was arrested by the Gestapo and deported to Ravensbrück on 20 June 1944, where she died in February 1945.
1356 He was the same doctor who had cared for him on his evasion after the Dieppe raid in August 1942.
1357 For his actions Lafleur was awarded the DCM (15/6/44) 'in recognition of gallant and distinguished services in the field'.
1358 The wretched Gestapo even gouged out one of his eyes.
1359 *Saturday at M.I.9*, p. 261.
1360 *168 Jump Into Hell*, p. 105.
1361 He died on 22 January 1987 in Brussels.

Chapter 10

1362 Willis' report MI9/S/P.G. (-) 1176 in TNA file WO 208/3313.
1363 Later, when he was in Spain, Willis heard that 'the householder had been arrested by the Germans'.
1364 For his outstanding heroism Tomlinson, who was buried in Elan churchyard in the French Ardennes, received no award.
1365 Marsh's report MI9/S/P.G. (F) 1754 in TNA file WO 208/3318.
1366 Appendix C, Whitley's report MI9/S/P.G. (-) 1211 in TNA file WO 208/5582. Confusingly, lost on the same crew as Brownhill was Sergeant Richard Brown. Both Whitley and Marion confusingly refer to Brownhill as "Brown", who *was* a Canadian though not, as Marion says, in the RCAF.
1367 Appendix C, Marion's report MI9/S/P.G. (-) 1213 in TNA file WO 208/5582.
1368 This was Halifax BB311, 408 Squadron, two of whose six survivors – Canadians Parkinson and MacDonald – would meet Neil McKinnon of Taylor's crew. All three, though, were destined to become prisoners of war. See Chapter 7.
1369 Appendix C, Taylor's report MI9/S/P.G. (-) 1787 in TNA file WO 208/5583.
1370 Appendix C, Avery's report MI9/S/P.G. (-) 1274 in TNA file WO 208/5582.
1371 Avery op. cit. Avery and two others of his crew were killed before war's end. Flight Sergeant Avery lost his life on the night of 1/2 March 1944 when Wellington LN614, 15 OTU, suffered a major electrical failure on a night bombing exercise and plunged into the ground.

1372 Billie Stephens, captured on the St Nazaire raid (March 1942), escaped from Colditz Castle on the night of 14/15 October 1942 with Major R.B. "Ronnie" Littledale 60th Rifles, KRRC (killed in Normandy on 1 September 1944), Captain P.R. "Pat" Reid RASC, and Flight Lieutenant H.D. "Hank" Wardle. Reid and Wardle reached Switzerland twenty-six hours before the other two.
1373 This was 1046183 Brown from the same 207 Squadron crew as Sergeant G.I. Brownhill. Brown had reached Switzerland in only nine days. See endnote 1366.
1374 Bruce was pilot of B-17F 42-29725 Hi-Lo Jack, 92nd BG/407th BS, shot down on 3 September 1943. Carah was co-pilot of B-17F 42-29928, 381st BG/533rd BS, lost 4 July 1943.
1375 Taylor op. cit. Stephens eventually got away on 5 June 1944.
1376 2nd Lieutenant Bruce reported that he 'had a German-made 7.65 [mm] gun which he had purchased in Bern', while Carah 'had a Luger that he had purchased himself and the remainder of the party had Lugers and Browning automatics given to them by the British Legation.' *Achtung! Achtung! Die Flugfestungen Kommen!*, pp. 85-6, from Bruce's E&E Report No. 224.
1377 Taylor op. cit. The youth organisation was les Compagnons de France.
1378 *Full Moon to France*, p. 198.
1379 *Xavier*, p. 147.
1380 *Xavier*, p. 224.
1381 This and previous two quotes from *Achtung! Achtung! Die Flugfestungen Kommen!*, p. 30.
1382 Taylor op. cit.
1383 Lieutenant George Reid Millar became well-known for his books *Maquis* (published 1945), *Horned Pigeon* (1946), and for his autobiography *Road to Resistance* (1979). Born on 19 September 1910 Millar died in January 2005.
1384 Appendix C, Millar's report MI9/S/P.G. (G) 1716 in TNA file WO 208/5582.
1385 *Road to Resistance*, p. 267.
1386 Millar op. cit.
1387 Millar op. cit. Heslop, by then lieutenant-colonel, was to be awarded the DSO on the same date (22/3/45) as George Reid Millar who was awarded the MC (27/4/44) for his escape, and would later be awarded the DSO (22/3/45) for further SOE activities. Heslop would also receive the Medal of Freedom with Bronze Palm from the Americans (23/5/47).
1388 Schrieber was from the 379th BG; Howell was tail gunner on the same crew as John Carah. Bruzewski, 381st BG/535th BS, was lost on 17 August 1943. Mulholland was co-pilot of B-17F 42-5865 Janie, 100th BG/351st BS, lost on 3 September 1943. Miller was right-waist gunner of B-17F 42-30362 Wee Bonnie II, 388th BG/561st BS, shot down by flak on 9 September 1943.
1389 *The Freedom Line*, p. 193, and *Footsteps of a Flying Boot*, p. 123.
1390 Millar op. cit.
1391 Lashbrook and crew were Altendorf's seventeenth victim. Altendorf, who was flying with II./NJG4, had also flown in the Battle of Britain and, remarkably, survived the war.
1392 Website http://www.geocities.com/CapeCanaveral/Runway/9601/uk.html. Much of the information on Squadron Leader Lashbrook is from this site, with the kind permission of Ken Arnold.
1393 Williams' George Medal was gazetted on 6 January 1942, after he, then a leading aircraftman, and 1122529 Aircraftman 1st Class Kenneth Bland helped to remove a burning ammunition tank after it had caught fire one day in June 1941. Bland was also awarded the George Medal.
1394 Website http://www.geocities.com/CapeCanaveral/Runway/9601/uk.html.
1395 Hoehn was bombardier of B-17F 42-5406, 91st BG/322nd BS, shot down by fighters on 13 May 1943 twenty-five kilometres north of Amiens. Records show that seven of the crew died in the incident, and that two were taken prisoner of war. Doug Hoehn was the only evader.
1396 Quotes from Ken Arnold website op. cit. In 1978 Wally Lashbrook received the MBE to add to the DFC, AFC and DFM already won. Alfred Martin also later received the DFC.
1397 With him were seven other evaders: Sergeant K.W. Elt; Sergeant W.J. Fitzgerald; Pilot Officer E.L. Gimbel; Flight Sergeant D.K. Nolan; Second Lieutenant J.K.B. Raeder; Sergeant A. Smith; and Sergeant F.G.A. Weight.
1398 His first DSO was gazetted on 8 October 1943, the second on 1 February 1944.
1399 Appendix C, Taylor's report MI9/S/P.G. (-) 1270 in TNA file WO 208/3313.
1400 This and previous quote from *Xavier*, pp. 138-9. In his book Heslop refers to Robert Taylor as 'Phillip Miller'.
1401 *We Landed by Moonlight*, p. 95.
1402 Appendix C, Mora's report MI9/S/P.G. (-) 1191 in TNA file WO 208/5582.
1403 This boat and others were specially built for him by a boatbuilder called Meyer, who lived just outside The Hague.
1404 Appendix C, Haye's report MI9/S/P.G. (-) 1331 in TNA file WO 208/5582. The daughter's name was Elly.
1405 Appendix C Hagan's report MI9/S/P.G. (-) 1330 in TNA file WO 208/5582.
1406 Martin Gutterling's twin brother was another to go to England with Mora and Bernard Reijnders.
1407 Hagan op. cit. It should be remembered that by this time the Dutch were already suffering from a chronic food shortage, and were being slowly starved to death by the Germans. By the end of the war nettle and dandelion "soup" was a delicacy.
1408 Haye op. cit.
1409 TNA file KV4/321.
1410 Letter of 6 October 1943 (courtesy of Mrs Winifred Hagan).
1411 From the letter in the possession of Mrs Winifred Hagan. Tony gave his address as 47, Princes Way, Wimbledon (tel. Putney 7970).
1412 From the letter of 6 October 1943 in the possession of Mrs Winifred Hagan, who kindly allowed its, and the others, partial reproduction here.
1413 Born on 9 November 1917 in Sorabaja in the Dutch East Indies, Schrader died in The Hague on 8 November 2000. Details kindly supplied by Wilco Vermeer, who helps with the most informative Dutch website www.ww2awards.com.
1414 Letter of 29 November 1945 (courtesy of Mrs Winifred Hagan). It is not known if the penicillin, the new wonder drug, was ever sent.
1415 *Shot Down and on the Run*, p. 109.
1416 They were two of six to evade capture, the seventh being taken prisoner of war.
1417 *Valley of the Shadow of Death*, p. 529. It is not clear whether or not they were the last, for others crossed before the New Year.
1418 Conroy's report MI9/S/P.G. (-) 1429 in TNA file WO 208/3315. Conroy was the only survivor of Wellington HE593, 429 (RCAF) Squadron, shot down on the night of 11/12 June 1943. The other three evaders from Halifax HR854 were Flight Lieutenant J.H. Foy DFC, RCAF; and Sergeants G. MacGregor and J.B. McDougall, RCAF. The seventh member of the crew, Flight Sergeant A.O. Prior RCAF, was taken prisoner.
1419 Sansum's report MI9/S/P.G. (-) 1561 in TNA file WO 208/3316.
1420 Ibid. It is interesting to speculate as to which 'organisation' arranged the rest of his journey for him, for his name does not appear on Comet's list. This was at the time when other lines such as Burgundy, Brandy or Oaktree were moving evaders south, and the redoubtable Françoise Dissard, following the collapse of the PAO line, had established her own network from Toulouse.
1421 Sergeant Ablett must have applied for a commission before his last operation, for he ended the war as a flying officer in Stalag Luft III (Sagan).
1422 Butterfield's report MI9/S/P.G. (-) 1542 in TNA file WO 208/3316.
1423 Ibid. Butterfield had left his flying boots with his first helpers.
1424 Ibid. The Demarcation Line passed just to the south of Dompierre. Its significance had, however, diminished following the German take-over of the whole of France in November 1942.

1425 Butterfield op. cit. It is tempting to believe that somehow Gabriel Nahas was involved, and that the railwaymen were members of the Résistance Fer, who also helped Brigadier Hargest.
1426 What happened to the American, Low, thereafter is not known.
1427 Gunning, 'a flight commander of high standing and affection' was taken prisoner of war. *2 Group RAF A Complete History, 1936-1945*, p. 327, Michael J.F. Bowyer (Faber and Faber, London, 1974).
1428 These three were probably Sergeants J.D. Duncan RCAF, G. Bartley and S. Hughes, whose Lancaster had crashed near Cambrai on 9/10 July 1943. They were in the hands of the Chauny organisation by 14 July, and in Paris a week later.
1429 Appendix C, Brinn's report MI9/S/P.G. (-) 1404 in TNA file WO 208/5582. Forty-nine-year-old Germaine Bajpai was one of the three chiefs of the safe-house system set up by "Jerome" in Paris at around this time, August 1943.
1430 In Appendix C to his report Webb gives firm dates for his and Clarke's journey to Paris and Bordeaux. If both his and Brinn's dates *are* accurate, then Webb and Clarke must have waited in Bordeaux for eight days before setting off with Brinn and Nekrasov. In view of Comet's records, which state that the four men crossed the Pyrenees on 30 August 1943, Webb's dates seem to be at fault, and he must have lost one whole week somewhere on his travels.
1431 On the night of 21/22 January 1943 a small force of seventy-nine Lancasters and three Mosquitos was sent to bomb Essen, twenty-five kilometres west of Duisburg. Bombs were dropped blindly through 10/10ths cloud cover.
1432 Nekrasov's report MI9/S/P.G. (G) 1405 in TNA file WO 208/3315. Born on 22 March 1922 he was a former law student from Morozovo, Kalinin.
1433 *2 Group RAF A Complete History, 1936-1945*, p. 328, op. cit.
1434 Fairfax/Macleod joint report MI9/S/P.G. (-) 1536/1537 in TNA file WO 208/3316.
1435 Fairfax/Macleod op. cit. The young Frenchman was René Gerrault, who 'lived with his wife, Paulette, and two small children' (*Home Run* [Bickers] p. 83) in a large farmhouse owned by his uncle, who was also living there.
1436 Allison's report MI9/S/P.G. (-) 1461 in TNA file WO 208/3315.
1437 Ibid.
1438 Appendix C, Allison's report MI9/S/P.G. (-) 1461 in TNA file WO 208/5582. The War Graves employee may have been a M. Eley, whose wife also helped Flight Lieutenant W.G. Brinn, DFM.
1439 Baker's report MI9/S/P.G. (-) 1586 in TNA file WO 208/3316. Of the eight men aboard, the nineteen-year-old rear gunner, Flight Sergeant G.R.M. Warren RCAF was killed, and the mid-upper gunner, Sergeant G.R. Darvill, was taken prisoner. The remainder evaded.
1440 Ibid. The Frydryk family were 'Polish immigrants who had a small wooden house along the road to Villers-Saint-Ghislain.' (10 Squadron Association 2006 Newsletter No. 36). George Baker returned to operations, but was killed as a flying officer with all his 101 Squadron crew on 3/4 May 1944.
1441 Bridge's report MI9/S/P.G. (-) 1462 in TNA file WO 208/3315.
1442 Duffee's report MI9/S/P.G. (-) 1465 in TNA file WO 208/3315.
1443 From website www.bowlby.pbwiki.com/Unexpected%20Adventure%20in%20Europe.
1444 Seville is 540 kilometres/340 miles south of Madrid. The Guadalquivir flows for 100 kilometres from Seville into the Atlantic Ocean.
1445 On the evening of 7 May 1945 *Sneland I* was sailing as No. 2 in the starboard column of outward-bound convoy EN 91 from Methil in the Firth of Forth, Scotland, when she was torpedoed by U-2336 (Klusmeier) and sunk approximately one and a half miles south-east of May Island. *Sneland I* and another ship also sunk in the same convoy, SS *Avondale Park*, were the last two merchantmen to be sunk in the European war.
1446 Buise was top-turret gunner of B-17F 42-3071, 94th BG/331st BS, shot down by fighters on 14 July 1943.
1447 Smith's report MI9/S/P.G. (-) 1530 in TNA file WO 208/3316. For more on Whitley's evasion see following chapter.
1448 This may have been the Café Larre in Sutar, Anglet, which was being used as an overnight base at this time.
1449 From *Home Run*, (Bickers), p. 99.
1450 Built in 1922 D/S *Borgholm*, 1,561 gross tons, sailed from Gibraltar on 26 August 1943 in Convoy MKS22 and arrived at Liverpool on 6 September. She survived the war. Hunt and Aguiar were respectively bombardier and ball-turret gunner of B-17F, 42-30031, The Bad Penny, 384th BG/544th BS, shot down by fighters and flak on 26 June 1943. Of the ten crew, three evaded and seven were taken prisoner.
1451 Appendix C, Slack's report MI9/S/P.G. (-) 1366 in TNA file WO 208/5582. Slack was absolutely correct. Balfe's MM was gazetted on 17 September 1917, and his regimental number was indeed 4512.
1452 Slack op. cit. No doubt the café was the Café Pierre.
1453 Schuhart permitted the crew to leave their ship before sinking her. Nine days later he and the U-29 sank the Royal Navy's aircraft carrier HMS *Courageous* (22,500 tons).
1454 William is buried in Bristol (Canford) Cemetery.
1455 Cornelius' report MI9/S/P.G. (-) 1632 in TNA file WO 208/3317.
1456 Appendix C, Cornelius' report MI9/S/P.G. (-) 1632 in TNA file WO 208/5582.
1457 Allen was top-turret gunner of B-17F 42-2990 Dame Satan, 91st BG/322nd BS, lost on 17 August 1943.
1458 De Pape's report MI9/S/P.G. (-) 1633 in TNA file WO 208/3317. It is likely that De Pape's aircraft was shot down by the night-fighter.
1459 Of the other seven, four were taken prisoner (including the pilot) and three killed. The crew that Ray De Pape had left behind in England then teamed up with Flight Sergeant F.F.E. Reain RCAF, and were lost on *their* first operation, 20/21 January 1944. Six, including Reain, evaded capture, with the seventh being taken prisoner. See p. 57 *The Evaders* (Lavender & Sheffe).
1460 De Pape was heading west, not south-east, which would have taken him deeper into Germany rather than into Belgium.
1461 *The Evaders*, p. 63 (Lavender/Sheffe).
1462 They were respectively ball-turret gunner and right waist gunner on B-17F 42-30372 "Shack Rabbit III", 96th BG/413rd BS, lost on 20 October 1943.
1463 Again, was this the Café Pierre? Or the Café Larre, in Sutar, Anglet?
1464 *The Evaders*, p. 66 (Lavender/Sheffe). Research by Bruce Bolinger suggests that this inn may have been run by a British couple, and may have been called the Martutene.
1465 Men of the *División Azul* (Blue Division), which had been fighting on the Russian front, were ordered back to Spain by Franco on 10 October 1943.
1466 Simister's report MI9/S/P.G. (-) 2295 in TNA file WO 208/3322.
1467 Simister op. cit.
1468 Simister op. cit.
1469 Simister op. cit.
1470 *Free to Fight Again*, p. 223.
1471 A route not dissimilar to that taken by Sergeant R.V.C. Johnson – see Chapter 9.
1472 *Winged Diplomat*, p. 186.
1473 Neame, O'Connor and Boyd escaped in January 1944.
1474 Brigadier Miles was buried in Figueras municipal cemetery. Air Commodore West suggests that Miles' departure from Switzerland had been known to the Gestapo, who alerted their agents in Barcelona 'and they must have caught up with him'. (*Winged Diplomat*, p. 198).
1475 Colonel H.A. Cartwright MC, then a captain in the Middlesex Regiment, had been a prisoner of the Germans for almost four years during the First World War, and had made some twenty escape attempts before finally succeeding shortly before the armistice. "Alan Smith" was Allen Dulles (1893-1969), first civilian director, and longest serving (1953-1961), of the USA's CIA.
1476 Contrast Hargest's crossing with that of Palm, Cooper, McSweyn and Martin (Chapter 7) which was undertaken at more or less the

ame time.
477 Also lost, in Spitfire BS279, was Captain Marion E. Jackson, 4th FG/336th FS, who was taken prisoner of war.
478 Gaze's report MI9/S/P.G. (-) 1502 in TNA file WO 208/3315.
479 From Malins' own account published in *Silk and Barbed Wire* (editor Brian Walley; Sage Pages, Warwick, Western Australia, 2000). Also taken prisoner was the second pilot, Pilot Officer E.N. Bell RCAF – see page 240.
480 Information from Stephen Hathaway, grandson of Stan Hathaway, from website
www.wartimememories.co.uk/airfields/tempsford.html. Allen's journey is not known, but was no doubt similar to Stan Hathaway's.
481 Heyworth's commission as a pilot officer (157454) with effect from 20 August 1943 was announced in *The London Gazette* on 2 November 1943.
482 Mason's report MI9/S/P.G. (-) 2522 in TNA file WO 208/3323.
483 Nelmes' report MI9/S/P.G. (-) 2521 in TNA file WO 208/3323. Giat (Put-de-Dôme) is some sixty kilometres west of Clermont-Ferrand.
484 Forman' report MI9/S/P.G. (-) 1571 in TNA file WO 208/3316.
485 Bell was later taken prisoner, and ended up at Stalag Luft III (Sagan).
486 *They Shall Grow Not Old*, p. 185.
487 Mason op. cit. Dmytruk now lies in the communal cemetery at les Martres-de-Veyre (Puy-de-Dôme). Auzat-sur-Allier is some forty kilometres south-south-east of Clermont-Ferrand.
488 Appendix C, Forman, op. cit.
489 Forman can be forgiven for believing that it was on an island, for at the point in question the Charente forms a prodigious "U" bend, the landing ground being between the two arms of the "U".
490 Twenty-six-year-old Pilot Officer Charles Heyworth is commemorated on Panel 2, Brighton (Woodvale) Borough Crematorium.
491 Appendix C, Hooper's report MI9/S/P.G. (-) 1625 in TNA file WO 208/5582.
492 On this same, foul night, two other Lysander pilots, Hankey and McBride, crashed and were killed as they attempted to land on their return. Also lost in the two Lysanders, V9367 and V9674, were two of the four agents on their way back from France. This was also the foggy night on which some thirty RAF Bomber Command aircraft crashed on their return from Berlin, also with considerable loss of life.
493 Mason op. cit.
494 In *Un Grand Bordel* Norman Lee confesses on page 84 that he could not confirm either that he had been at Dillingen or Medernach.
495 *Un Grand Bordel*, p. 101.
496 Little is known of the evasion of either Brearley or Hirst, as no MI9/IS9 report has been found for either man – Author.
497 Probably via what was known as an S-Phone – a walkie-talkie system enabling communication between the ground and an aircraft.
498 Possibly a Stirling of 75 Squadron, which lost one of its aircraft on 4/5 March 1944 (Operation Trainer 124) in a crash near Rochefort-Montagne (Puy-de-Dôme), some twenty kilometres south-west of Clermont-Ferrand.
499 *Un Grand Bordel*, p. 148.
500 *Special Forces in the Invasion of France*, p. 270 – Paul Gaujac, Histoire & Collections, Paris, 1999.
501 *Un Grand Bordel*, p. 146.
502 This man may have been Staff Sergeant Alfred E. Wendt, tail gunner of B-17F 42-30386, 305th BG/364th BS, shot down by flak on 7 January 1944 and which ditched in the sea off Calais.
503 *Un Grand Bordel*, pp. 143-4.
504 Mason's report op. cit.
505 *Hauptverbindestab* translates as Signals/Liaison Staff.
506 Information on the German attacks from *Special Forces in the Invasion of France*, op. cit., pp. 273-4.
507 When he returned to England in 1945 from prisoner-of-war camps Stalag Luft VII (Bankau) and Stalag IIIA (Luckenwalde), Columbus married the sister of his pilot before returning to Canada. Herbert Campbell was the right waist gunner of B-17G 42-97199, 91st BG/324th BS, shot down by flak on 28 April 1944.
508 *Un Grand Bordel*, p. 171.
509 Ibid, p. 177.
510 *Special Forces in the Invasion of France*, op. cit., pp. 273-4.
511 Mason op. cit.
512 There are two places called Cussac in more or less the same area – one, in the Cantal *département* a dozen kilometres south-west of Flour, the other, a further twenty kilometres or so south-west of the first, in Aveyron.
513 Mason op. cit. Flight Sergeant Buchanan RAAF was in Mason's party.

Chapter 11

514 From Jim Mortimer's unpublished account of his flying career.
515 At the same time as Bellows, the fiercely-contested Operation Pedestal was under way, delivering life-giving stores to Malta.
516 Jim Mortimer's unpublished account of his flying career, p. 8.
517 Ibid, p. 14
518 If indeed Jim Mortimer was at le Tréport, then he would probably have been swept through the *Avant Port* and on up the River Bresle.
519 As the crow flies, Sailly-Flibeaucourt is approximately thirty kilometres north-east of le Tréport. To get to it from le Tréport Jim would have had to have crossed the Canal de la Somme, or the River Somme itself. He makes no mention of either, however, and it is possible that he mistook le Tréport for either St Valery-sur-Somme or le Crotoy, which lie on the south and north sides respectively of the Somme estuary.
520 "Cinq Quent On" is otherwise known as St Quentin.
521 One of the Americans was J.R. Struejen (not identified).
522 A likely candidate for this US pilot was 1st Lieutenant Karl J. Goethal, 55th FG/343rd FS, who was shot down in his P-38J 43-28388 on 11 June 1944 while bombing Compiègne station.
523 Jim Mortimer op. cit.
524 From Ray Barlow's unpublished account, by kind permission of his widow, Peggy. As to the delayed take-off of ED426 official records show that it took off at more or less the same time as the other aircraft on the operation. In the 49 Squadron history *Beware of the Dog at War*, p. 261, the author notes that ED426 was lost on its 45th trip.
525 Ray Barlow op. cit.
526 Ray Barlow op. cit.
527 Ray Barlow op. cit.
528 Ray Barlow op. cit.
529 *Official Secret*, p. 64.
530 These two survivors were the gunners, Attwood and Fitzgerald. Actually only lightly injured, they had been taken to l'Amerique farm, but were captured two days later. After two months in Fresnes prison, Paris, they were removed to prisoner-of-war camps in Germany.
531 Barlow op. cit. Ray gives the date of entering Switzerland as 30 October, but Roger Anthoine says 29 October in *Aviateurs Piétons…*, p. 101.
532 Ibid. Ray and Peggy Barlow had been married only ten days before Ray went missing.
533 All five of the crew succeeded in evading capture.
534 Spencer's report MI9/S/P.G. (-) 2009 in TNA file WO 208/3320.
535 Ibid.

1536 Ibid.
1537 Heslop was never captured, and was awarded the DSO for more than two years' work in France (see also Chapters 5 and 10).
1538 On the night of 6/7 June 1944, a team of Ain maquisards led by La Brosse managed to destroy fifty-one of the fifty-two locomotiv at the Ambérieu sheds and marshalling yards while Capitaine Chabot and his men kept the Germans at bay. Ambérieu was an importa section of the railway line from Lyon to the Bourg-Culoz line, which ultimately leads on south-east to Italy via Modane.
1539 Appendix C, Payne's report MI9/S/P.G. (-) 2008 in TNA file WO 208/5583. The "police" may well have been *miliciens*.
1540 *SOE in France*, p. 373. GMR – Groupe Mobile de Réserve – was a paramilitary force created by Vichy in 1941.
1541 Payne op. cit.
1542 *The Bedford Triangle*, p. 127.
1543 This was Captain James Estes USAAF.
1544 Raymond's surname was Samuel but, as he was Jewish, changed it to Aubrac to avoid further persecution.
1545 Moulin was so badly tortured by Klaus Barbie and his Gestapo thugs that he died from his injuries on 8 July 1943.
1546 Rooney's report IS9/WEA/2/19/34 in TNA file WO 208/3348.
1547 According to Rooney op. cit, Leray 'was a fellow around 5' 10", had a small black "Hitler" moustache, also a non-smoker.'
1548 Rooney op. cit.
1549 According to the very observant Rooney the gendarme 'was wearing civilian clothes, clean shaven, wore thick horn rimmed glasse quite a well built man around thirty. He did not actually work in Le Temple.'
1550 *The Next Moon*, p. 119. It will be noted that Rooney described Bourgoin as missing his left arm.
1551 Quoted in *Special Forces in the Invasion of France*, p. 133.
1552 Quoted by M.R.D. Foot *SOE in France*, p. 406, from R. Leroux's book *Le Combat de Saint-Marcel*.
1553 *The Next Moon*, p. 129.
1554 *The Next Moon*, p. 139.
1555 I can find no details of a USAAF raid on Nantes during May 1944, but there was a heavy attack on that town by B-17 bombers of t 1st and 3rd Bomb Divisions on 7 June 1944, with the loss of one B-17. Treillières is some ten kilometres north of Nantes, and Saffré son forty kilometres north of Nantes. – Author.
1556 Rooney op. cit.
1557 The "Battle of Berlin" is the name given to RAF Bomber Command's attempts to destroy the German capital in sixteen heavy, nig raids during the winter of 1943-44 – four in November 1943, four in December, six in January 1944, and one each in February and Marc
1558 *At First Sight*, p. 9 – Alan B. Webb (Alan B. Webb, c/o The Mosquito Aircraft Museum, London Colney, 1991).
1559 *At First Sight*, p. 9.
1560 Walker's report MI9/S/P.G. (-) 2514 in TNA file WO 208/3323.
1561 *At First Sight*, p. 9.
1562 *At First Sight*, p. 9.
1563 Walker op. cit.
1564 Trent was co-pilot of B-17F 42-30604 Badger Beauty V, 100th BG/350th BS, hit by flak (and running out of fuel) on 4 October 194 Drew Willingham was co-pilot of B-17F 42-30837 Ole Bassar, 388th BG/561st BS, shot down by flak on 5 December 1943. The le common rank of flight officer was given to someone who had graduated from flying training but who had not yet qualified for promotion the rank of 2nd Lieutenant.
1565 1st Lieutenant Hilbert W. Phillippe (not Phillipi) was bombardier in the same crew as Trent.
1566 Walker op. cit.
1567 They were not shot, but sent to prisoner-of-war camps.
1568 Tempting though it may be to believe that the supposed British captain was a German spy infiltrating the French resistance, he w almost certainly the very active Richard Heslop ("Xavier").
1569 Walker op. cit.
1570 Ibid. Cunliffe had been shot down on 15/16 March 1944, and had crossed into Switzerland on the evening of 22 March. King, 72 (Squadron, shot down over Sicily on 12 July 1943 and captured by the Italians, had escaped by hiding in the roof of a hut at Campo 73 (Car when the guards left on 13 September 1943. Working his way north, he reached Switzerland on 6 January 1944.
1571 The date of Simpson's return is not known.
1572 The Typhoon flight sergeant may have been Flight Sergeant G.L. Renshaw, 175 Squadron, shot down in JR190 on 6 January 1944.
1573 Fryer's report MI9/S/P.G. (-) 2292 in TNA file WO 208/3322. Six of the seven crew were to evade capture. The seventh – Sergea W.R. Wynveen RCAF – was captured by the Germans.
1574 Quotes from Fryer op. cit.
1575 Merchant's DFM was actually gazetted while he was a prisoner of the Italians, on 12 November 1943.
1576 Appendix C, Bell's report MI9/S/P.G. (-) 1878 in TNA file WO 208/5583.
1577 These were possibly 2nd Lieutenant Harold Freeman and Staff Sergeant John C. McLaughlin both shot down in different B-17s on December 1943. Some of the other Americans may have been from McLaughlin's crew.
1578 They were flown back in a Hudson of 161 Squadron on 3/4 May 1944. Thackthwaite, by now promoted to major, was later award the OBE.
1579 The author is grateful to website http://www.militarymuseum.org/Ortiz.html for much on this extraordinary soldier.
1580 Blott's report MI9/S/P.G. (-) 1930 in TNA file WO 208/3319.
1581 Blott op. cit. Sergeant Ruth was an American airman.
1582 Blott op. cit.
1583 Wodehouse (born 15 October 1881; died 14 February 1975) was thought by many to have been a Nazi sympathiser and, worse collaborator. He was no more than a victim of circumstance, naïvely caught up in the swift German advance into France in May/June 19 following which he spent forty-nine weeks in German internment camps. He became a KBE shortly before his death.
1584 W.W. Farmer, p. 1, unpublished manuscript, *WWII Experiences*, 2 May 1995. Copy of manuscript courtesy of Tom Harvell.
1585 Louis Volbert later joined the Belgian Air Force, but was killed in an aircrash in the Belgian Congo.
1586 p. 3 Farmer op. cit.
1587 Farmer's report IS9/WEA/2/527/1370 in TNA file WO 208/3350.
1588 Some three kilometres south-west of Givet.
1589 The broken line may well have been Comet.
1590 Robert C. Augustus, 445th BG/703rd BS, was shot down on 12 April 1944 in B-24 41-29118 Nine Yanks and a Jerk. Peter M. Cla tail-turret gunner of B-24 42-7601 Sin Ship, 445th BG/702nd BS, was also shot down on 12 April 1944.
1591 Glassman and Stinnett were from B-17 42-30360 Lady Millicent, 96th BG/338th BS, which was shot down by flak and fighters o April 1944.
1592 Appendix C, Potentier's report IS9/WEA/2/579/2026 in TNA file WO 208/3348.
1593 Beckwith's report MI9/S/P.G. (-) 2279 in TNA file WO 208/3322. Note that this report is not altogether reliable as to dates.
1594 *Special Forces in the Invasion of France*, p. 21.
1595 The American's Harrington airbase was home to their black-painted B-24 bombers flying clandestine missions to Europe on behalf their OSS and the Bristish SOE. "Carpetbagger" was a codename 'which someone had lifted from the annals of the American Civil W For a fuller story of the Harrington airbase and its operations see *The Bedford Triangle* (Martin W. Bowman; Patrick Stephens Limit

1988).
1596 The Ukrainians 'probably came from the *Freiwillingen (Ost) Stamm-Regiment 4*, which had settled in Namur since February 1944 and had become a training station for Russian and Ukrainian volunteers from the Eastern troops.' *Special Forces in the Invasion of France*, p. 31, fn. 14.
1597 *Special Forces in the Invasion of France*, p. 32. Captain Desmond Ellis Hubble (109634), Intelligence Corps, was removed to Germany and executed at Buchenwald concentration camp on 13 September 1944. He has no known grave, and is remembered on the Bayeux Memorial. [Note: His official date of death is shown as 11 September 1944]. He was "Mentioned" in *The London Gazette* (6/6/46) 'in recognition of gallant and distinguished services in the field'.
1598 Apart from those killed in action, estimated by Layton to be forty or so, the Germans captured 106 partisans. Their torture and death by machine-gun fire were witnessed by several wood-cutters. The bodies were buried in the Bear Pit, near Linchamps – *Special Forces in the Invasion of France*, p. 31.
1599 Farmer op. cit, p. 5. Farmer's later account does not tally with the report that he made on 24 September 1944, and the many inconsistencies may, perhaps, be explained by the passage of time. He stated, for example, in the later account that he had been in the thick of the fighting on 12 June, but makes no mention of his participation in the battle in his 1944 report.
1600 In those five days they had covered an estimated 125 kilometres/eighty miles through Montherme, Villers, Donchery and Grandpré (Ardennes).
1601 Smitton and Thorn were liberated by the Americans on 31 August at Neuville-sur-Ornain. They went via Paris (1 September) to England (5 September).
1602 Farmer op. cit, p. 10.
1603 Farmer op. cit, p. 8.
1604 4th Armored, together with the 35th (Major-General P.W. Baade) and 80th (Major-General H. L. McBride) Divisions, comprised XII Corps (Major-General Manton S. Eddy), US Third Army (General George S. Patton, Jr).
1605 Farmer op. cit. p. 13.
1606 Farmer op. cit. p. 14.
1607 The XVth Corps comprised the 79th Infantry Division (Major General I.T. Wyche) and the French 2nd Armoured Division (Major General LeClerc).
1608 LM647, 550 Squadron, was the Lancaster to fall at Vignory on 12/13 July 1944, while the other was almost certainly Lancaster LM206, 514 Squadron, that crashed seven kilometres north-west of Neufchâteau on 28/29 July 1944. Five of its crew were killed, one was injured and taken prisoner of war, and one, Sergeant T.H. Harvell, evaded.
1609 Identified as Lancaster ND767, 622 Squadron, in *RAF Bomber Command Losses of the Second World War 1944*, p. 154, and *The Nuremberg Raid*, Martin Middlebrook, p. 336 & p. 341.
1610 Moffat's report IS9/WEA/2/455/1080 in TNA file WO 208 3350. He came down, of course, on 31 March, not 1 April.
1611 All of the Lancaster crew and five of the Halifax crew are buried in Hotton War Cemetery, forty-eight kilometres south-east of Namur.
1612 Vital was thirty-seven years of age, Albert twenty-eight (born on 7 June 1915).
1613 Bill Jones was wireless operator of Halifax LW634, 158 Squadron.
1614 Jim Moffat says in his report that the date of the attack was 15 May. '17 May' is from *Behind Enemy Lines*, p. 149.
1615 Bill Jones survived the war, only to die of lung cancer in 1971, ten years after Vital Paul, who suffered a fatal heart-attack.
1616 *Behind Enemy Lines*, p. 86.
1617 Moffat's report op. cit.
1618 *Behind Enemy Lines*, p. 138.
1619 Quinzy is Quincy-Landzécourt, four kilometres south-west of Montmédy.
1620 *Behind Enemy Lines*, pp. 169-70.
1621 *After the Battle*, Number 36, p. 37, Battle of Britain Prints International Ltd, London, 1982.
1622 Beale was sent to Stalag Luft I (Barth).
1623 I am also indebted to Stefaan Calus for obtaining much of this information from the *Turfsteker*, dated 15 August 2004, the monthly magazine of the Zelzate local historical society, "Selsaete".
1624 Appendix C, Brown's report MI9/S/P.G. (-) 2285 in TNA file WO 208/5583.
1625 *SOE in France*, p. 284. Starr had, in fact, 'studied mining at London University'. *Das Reich*, p. 68, Max Hastings (Michael Joseph Ltd, London, 1981). Max Hastings also says that the mayor of Castelnau-sous-l'Auvignon, Roger Laribeau, appointed Starr as his deputy.
1626 Griffin also ended up as a prisoner of war at Stalag Luft I (Barth).
1627 Brown op. cit. "Lanne Maignan" has not been identified, but may have been the two villages, close to each other, of Lannes and Mézin.
1628 They were ball-turret gunner and radio operator respectively of B-17G 42-38009, 381st BG/534th BS, shot down by flak on 15 June 1944 The entire crew evaded capture.
1629 Dubé is buried in Olizy communal cemetery.
1630 Montgomery was pilot of P-38J 42-68036, shot down while on bomber support on 11 February 1944. E&E #746.
1631 The story of their crossing is briefly told in *The Freedom Trail*, pp. 68-70.
1632 Appendix C, Jackson's report MI9/S/P.G. (-) 1995 in TNA file WO 208/5583. Francis, Cavanaugh, Hotaling and Woodard were all from B-17 42-97070, 457th BG/750th BS. Ross was lost in B-24 42-100430, 448th BG/715th BS.
1633 Both were from B-17 42-30782, 306th BG/368th BS.
1634 Jackson op. cit.
1635 They appear to have been taken prisoner of war. Swanson was the pilot of B-17 42-31946, 94th BG/309th BS, lost on 20 April 1944 attacking a V1 site.
1636 Co-pilot of B-24 42-28763, 389th BG/564th BS, Hamby was shot down on 1 April 1944.
1637 Burgess was lost in B-26 42-95845, 391st BG/575th BS. His E&E report was #756.
1638 Appendix C, Virgo's report MI9/S/P.G. (-) 1999 in TNA file WO 208/5583.
1639 Appendix C, Alexander's report MI9/S/P.G. (-) 1987 in TNA file WO 208/5583. Staff Sergeant Ned A Daugherty USAAF, 445th BG/703rd BS, had been shot down on 18 March 1944..
1640 Miller was tail gunner of B-24H 42-7548 Bull O' The Woods, 44th BG/66th BS, shot down near Vic-sur-Aisne on 30 December 1943. He had been wounded in the arm and had been in hospital in Paris. His E&E report was #847.
1641 McPhee's report MI9/S/P.G. (-) 2015 in TNA file WO 208/3320.
1642 Ibid. There are a number of caves in the woods near St Cristophe-à Berry, a kilometre or two north-east of Vic-sur-Aisne.
1643 None of the other seven crew aboard ND508 survived.
1644 Appendix C, McPhee's report MI9/S/P.G. (-) 2019 in TNA file WO 208/5583.
1645 Knopp was right-waist gunner of B-17F 42-30040 Wabbit Twacks II, 96th BG/337th BS, shot down by fighters on 14 October 1943. His E&E report is #1526.
1646 McPhee op. cit.
1647 Pilot Officer D.N. Thompson had been shot down on 1/2 January 1944. Miller was co-pilot of B-17F 42-30249 El Sabo, 385th BG/551st BS, shot down by fighters and flak on 30 December 1943.
1648 From Jeffrey's report MI9/S/P.G. (F) 2490 in TNA file WO 208/3323.
1649 Ibid. Forster [*sic*] was Flight Lieutenant W.W. Foster RCAF, 169 Squadron, shot down in his Mosquito on 15/16 March 1944 (bomber support), who became a prisoner of war, as did Pilot Officer D.R. Murphy, 12 Squadron, shot down 27/28 January 1944. Foster and Murphy

had been captured together in Tarbes on 12 May 1944.
1650 Five others of Lennie's crew evaded. The seventh became a prisoner of war.
1651 Dubois and a second of the Belgians, who was calling himself Sergeant Viermulen, had both been working under cover in Belgium as wireless operators using the codenames "Wig" and "Jacqueline" respectively. Mission completed, they were making their way back to the UK.
1652 Jeffrey's report op. cit.
1653 See particularly Squadron Leader Jack Currie's *Battle Under the Moon* (AirData Publications Ltd, Wilmslow, 1995), and Lionel Lacey-Johnson's *Point Blank and Beyond*, Chapter 15 (Airlife Publishing Ltd, Shrewsbury, 1991).
1654 TNA file AIR 27/2037.
1655 Alexander's report MI9/S/P.G. (-) 1987 in TNA file WO 208/3320.
1656 TNA file KV4/322.
1657 TNA file KV4/322. Ferrières (Loiret) is twelve kilometres north of Montargis and ninety-seven south of Paris.
1658 TNA file KV4/322. This action by Benito was also typical of Florentino Goïcoechea, just as the route was typical of that used by Comet.
1659 Addendum to Appendix C, Ossendorf's report MI9/S/P.G. (-) 2031 in TNA file WO 208/5583.
1660 Ossendorf op. cit.
1661 Hyland's report IS9 (WEA)/2/1011/2309 in TNA file WO 208/5415.
1662 Hyland, op. cit. Nijmegen lies on the River Waal, not the Rhine.
1663 Unfortunately no Appendix C has been found for Hyland but, judging by his report number, it is possible that he remained in Holland or Belgium until the liberation.

Chapter 12

1664 *Saturday at M.I.9.* p. 241.
1665 Ibid. p. 242.
1666 Ibid. p. 241.
1667 Ibid. p. 264.
1668 Information re the Lili Dumon/Pierre Boulain episode is taken from *The Freedom Line*, pp. 269-77.
1669 *Saturday at M.I.9.* pp. 253-4.
1670 Omer Jubault ("André"), born 8 November 1903, was the military commander of the Châteaudun sector of the underground movement Libération-Nord, and thus a man of some local importance. A gendarme in Cloyes for eight years, he went into hiding on 10 January 1944 to avoid arrest by the Germans, who suspected him of Resistance activities.
1671 The population of Cloyes-sur-le-Loir was 1,439 in 1939, while that of Châteaudun, 130 kilometres west of Paris, was 6,205.
1672 For a full list of helpers from Châteaudun see *The Extraordinary Adventure of the Forest of Fréteval May-August 1944*, which shows the French view of affairs in the forest.
1673 The two Americans were radio operator and navigator respectively of a B-17 that had been shot down on 4 March 1944 at St Symphorien, Belgium, whilst on operations to Germany.
1674 Brayley's report IS9/WEA/2/148/188 in TNA file WO 208/3348.
1675 Pepall's report IS9/WEA/2/103/365 in TNA file WO 208/3349. The secret equipment in Pepall's aircraft was "G-H", a blind-bombing device that had first been used on operations on 3/4 November 1943. G-H allowed an aircraft to transmit a signal which was re-radiated to the aircraft by two ground beacons, thus enabling the navigator to receive an accurate "fix" of his aircraft's position.
1676 Ibid. Neither Doolan nor the flight engineer, Sergeant C.T. Bishop, survived. According to German sources the pilot was found dead at the controls.
1677 In his report Pepall's actual words were: 'I slept with Boubony and his wife in their one room in the basement…'.
1678 Pepall op. cit.
1679 Berry's report IS9/WEA/2/79/143 in TNA file WO 208/3348. Clearly, the Ju88 pilot was exceptionally skilled.
1680 Brayley remembered the shop as a florist's, but Berry as a bicycle shop.
1681 At this time there were twenty-nine Comet helpers active in Paris, twenty-one of whom were women – see *Women in the Resistance*, p. 206.
1682 Born Virginia Roush at Dayton, Ohio, on 4 June 1910, she and Philippe had married on 1 May 1937 at St Petersburg, Florida, USA.
1683 The apartment belonged to Philippe d'Albert-Lake's mother. The family were apparently obliged to sell it later for financial reasons.
1684 See *An American Heroine in the French Resistance*, pp. 91-4. The baker's name is given as Renard by Virginia d'Albert-Lake. The airmen of 384th BG/546th BS were from B-17F 41-24507 Yankee Raider, lost over Normandy on 6 September 1943. Their pilot, 2nd Lieutenant J.E. Armstrong USAAF, was one of those to return to England from Brittany on the *Breiz-Izel* – see Chapter 8 and Appendix III.
1685 Note the similarity between this incident and the one in Chapter 8 involving the arrest of Marie-Claire and company at Pau station on 23 November.
1686 Max and Daniel were, probably, Max Roger, the French guide between Bordeaux and St Jean-de-Luz, who is mentioned by airmen as a man with a scar on the nose, and Albert Ancia who was then with Jean de Blommaert for Marathon/Sherwood. (Information from Philippe Connart).
1687 Brayley op.cit.
1688 Both Hallouin and his wife were, according to Peter Berry, 'magnificent throughout' the life of the camp.
1689 Knight was tail gunner of B-17G 42-31387, 92nd BG/326th BS, shot down by fighters on 8 February 1944. Hoilman and Solomon were tail gunner and radio operator respectively of B-17G 42-31380, 385th BG/548th BS, which was hit by flak and ran out of fuel on the same operation.
1690 Berry op. cit. "Es. and Es." were Escapers and Evaders. Lucien was Squadron Leader Lucien Boussa.
1691 Gorrano was top-turret gunner in the same crew as Hoilman and Solomon.
1692 Berry op. cit.
1693 Berry op. cit. The three sixteen-man tents are marked on Pepall's sketch as "Large tents".
1694 *Free to Fight Again*, p. 90. Weir had been shot down on 1/2 May 1944.
1695 Berry op. cit. Having spoken to other members of the camp over sixty years after the event it is clear to the author that Berry was prone to exaggeration. As to the food, there was usually so little available that men would not have been permitted to have eaten as and when they chose.
1696 Croquet, a Belgian fighter pilot shot down on 11 February 1944, had arrived at the camp on 14 June 1944 with Americans Stuart K. Barr and Robert Sidders, and with Flight Sergeant Larry Clay (see p. 282).
1697 Berry op. cit., and previous six quotes. Sergeant Cliff Hallett, who arrived at the camp a fortnight or so after it had opened, has no recollection of any such camp meeting, let alone it being called a "Bitch Session".
1698 Pepall op. cit.
1699 Berry op. cit.
1700 Berry op. cit.
1701 Adams' report UDF/PW/INT/UK/2 in TNA file WO 208/3346.
1702 Hoover's report UDF/PW/INT/UK/1 in TNA file WO 208/3346.
1703 Hoover op. cit.
1704 Wiseman was navigator of B-25H 42-97188, 384th BG/544th BS, shot down by fighters and flak on 14 June 1944.

1705 McCarthy's report IS9/WEA/2/179 in TNA file WO 208/3348.
1706 The small lake was possibly l'Étang de la Verrerie.
1707 Dibetta was the pilot of B-17G 42-31388, 306th BG/423rd BS, shot down by flak and fighters on 11 February 1944.
1708 Brayley op. cit. "Gilbert" was Pierre Guillaumin.
1709 Hyde's report IS9/WEA/2/156/366 in TNA file WO 208/3349.
1710 Krol was bombardier of B-17G 42-30833, 401st BG/612th BS, shot down by fighters on 20 March 1944.
1711 Gordon's report IS9/WEA/2/151/190 in TNA file WO 208/3348.
1712 Wickman was navigator of B-17G 42-39962, 384th BG/547th BS, shot down eighteen kilometres south of Dieppe on 11 February 1944.
1713 Gordon op. cit.
1714 *An American Heroine in the French Resistance*, p. 110.
1715 Hyde op. cit.
1716 Martin believed their downfall to have been caused by an exploding flak shell. It is possible, however, that it was their own photoflash detonating prematurely, as they were prone to do if there was a faulty fuse.
1717 Martin's report IS9/WEA/2/159/371 in TNA file WO 208/3349.
1718 During his evasion Martin was told by the police in Paris that Light 'had just left Sens en route for Spain', but he was one of those unfortunate airmen to endure several weeks at Buchenwald concentration camp before being sent to Stalag Luft III (Sagan) in October 1944.
1719 Martin's report op.cit. Barr was co-pilot of B-24H 42-64447 The Comanche, 448th BG/712th BS, shot down by flak on 20 March 1944. Sidders was radio operator of B-17G 42-37984, 92nd BG/326th BS, shot down by fighters on 8 February 1944. Flying Officers Bender and Gordon came across Robert Sidders on 5 April.
1720 Berry's report op. cit.
1721 McCarthy op. cit.
1722 Plateau, a farmer, lived in the house at la Touche where Emile Zola wrote his novel *La Terre*. Plateau's ultimate fate is not known.
1723 *Escape from France*, p. 56.
1724 Berry op. cit. Cliff Hallett recalls that the Russian – he never knew his name – stayed with them all the way to Dinard. (Interview with author, 17 March 2006.)
1725 Berry op. cit. Berry does not explain what the trouble was between the two, nor why Boussa distrusted Toussaint. This was, in fact, a fiction on Berry's part. The two men, Boussa and Toussaint, were separated for obvious security reasons. There was no "trouble" between them.
1726 Quoted from a report made by Philippe d'Albert-Lake, National Archives and Records Administration, RG 498, Records of Headquarters, European Theater of Operations, United States Army (World War II), MIS-X, reproduced in *An American Heroine in the French Resistance*, pp. 247-251.
1727 The single runway at Woodbridge was 3,000 yards long. Between 15 November 1943 and 30 June 1945 4,120 emergency landings were made.
1728 *Canadians in the Royal Air Force*, p. 36.
1729 Chamberlain's report IS9 (WEA)/8/46/36 in TNA file WO 208/3350.
1730 This, it must be said, was a common address for operational/serving airmen to give. Berry was not alone in this therefore.
1731 Gordon op. cit.
1732 *Free to Fight Again*, p. 93.
1733 Schwilk's report IS9/WEA/2/81/307 in TNA file WO 208/3348.
1734 Agur's report IS9/WEA/2/83/316 in TNA file WO 208/3348.
1735 MacVean, Hurley, Pace and Williams were pilot, co-pilot, top-turret gunner, and left waist gunner respectively of B-24H 42-50344 Red Sox, 448th BG/714th BS, shot down on 27 June 1944. Sergeant Watkins was arrested on 10 August. He had been shot down on 28/29 June 1944, but was caught when he was being escorted to the camp at Fréteval. He went instead to a camp in east Germany.
1736 Schwilk op. cit. The American was Staff Sergeant Orion H. Shumway (not Chumley), right waist gunner of B-17G 42-31568, 457th BG/748th BS, shot down on 14 June 1944. Fisher may have been Flight Sergeant J.E. Fisher, 207 Squadron, who was captured on 7 August.
1737 Agur op. cit. Sergeant W.C. Brown had been shot down on 22/23 June 1944. Technical Sergeant Fred D. Gleason was top-turret gunner of B-17G 43-37788, 447th BG/709th BS, lost on 13 July 1944.
1738 Spinks was the pilot of P-51B Mustang 43-6985, 357th FG/364th FS, shot down by flak on a strafing mission near Paris on 20 June 1944. Lane was top-turret gunner in the same crew as Shumway.
1739 For John Watkins' brief account see *It's Suicide But It's Fun*, pp. 123-4.
1740 *Escape from France*, p. 58.
1741 *Saturday at M.I.9*, p. 265.
1742 A modest establishment at 14, Rue du Bourg-Belé, classified by Michelin in happier times as a simple but well-kept hotel.
1743 Dunhill's objective was to establish a recconnaisance party south-east of Vitre to report enemy movement in the Rennes–Laval area. Due to the Americans' advance, however, Greville-Bell and his men were too late.
1744 Berry op. cit. In his report Berry states that Baker arrived at "Bouchards farm", but this was probably a typing error for Fouchard, a family farming at Bellande. Berry also states that Baker arrived on 'Thursday evening 10 August 44'. Airey Neave is clear that Baker set off for the forest on 11 August, and dates in reports by other Sherwood campers tie in with the later date.
1745 Martin op. cit. Individuals' chronologies vary.
1746 Norman Wright was the right-waist gunner of B-24J 42-100294, 93rd BG/328th BS, shot down by flak on 24 June 1944.
1747 Martin op. cit. General Irwin was probably Major General S. LeRoy Irwin, later XII Corps commander, US Third Army.
1748 This and two previous quotes from *Escape from France*, pp. 58-9.
1749 *Saturday at M.I.9*, pp. 260-70.
1750 SAS Log Book in TNA file WO 218/198.
1751 Cliff Hallett, letter to author 25 February 2006.
1752 *Saturday at M.I.9*, p. 271
1753 *Saturday at M.I.9,* p. 278. Despite Comet's apparent lack of enthusiasm and suspicion of Ancia's identity, the head of Comet himself, Gaston Matthys, was to play a major part in helping with the Ardennes camps after he had been obliged to leave Brussels rather hurriedly. Furthermore, it is recorded that he did indeed meet Albert Ancia – see *Mission Marathon*, p. 340.
1754 According to Michael Moores LeBlanc, an authority on Second World War evaders in Western Europe, Comet had by this time become, in practice, two separate organisations, one headed by Michou Dumon, the other by Michiels. There was, apparently, 'no love lost between them' (communication with author, 17 May 2006).
1755 This Porcheresse, some thirty-five kilometres south-east of Dinant, is not to be confused with the Porcheresse thirty kilometres south-east of Namur.
1756 'Nous eûmes recours à un subterfuge qui consistait à les faire passer d'un camp à l'autre pour tromper leur impatience…' *Mission Marathon*, p. 333.
1757 In January 1944 Emile the Plumber was called to a rendezvous at a house only to discover that he had walked into a Gestapo trap. Coolly explaining that he had come to fix the plumbing, he was allowed to leave (see http://users.skynet.be/bs281548/cometorgnameEmileRoiseux.htm).
1758 Brailsford's report IS9/WEA/MB/1306 in TNA file WO 208/3350.
1759 Appendix C, Barnes' report MI9/S/P.G. (-) 2000 in TNA file WO 208/5583.

1760 Nos 44, 49 and 619 Squadrons each lost six; 57 Squadron lost five plus one ditched; 207 Squadron lost five; and 630 Squadron lost four with a fifth crashing in England on its return.
1761 Frank Haslam, via email from his son, also Frank Haslam, 25 May 2004. Wiemismeer is three or four kilometres east of Genk and a similar distance north of the Albert canal, in the north-east of Belgium.
1762 Frank Haslam op. cit.
1763 Via Frank Haslam jnr, editor 207 Squadron Newsletter and website.
1764 Frank Haslam jnr op. cit.
1765 Ron Dawson had been shot down on the fateful Nuremberg raid on 30/31 March 1944, and Bill Robertson on 19/20 February 1944.
1766 From *In Pursuit of Freedom.*
1767 *Airman Missing*, p. 56. I am greatly indebted to John Evans and to author Greg Lewis for permission to quote from their book – Author.
1768 *Mission Marathon*, p. 345 – '… les Allemands n'étaient venus à Beffe que pour y mendier du ravitaillement'.
1769 From *In Pursuit of Freedom.*
1770 John Evans, *Airman Missing*, p. 57.
1771 Barton op. cit.
1772 John Evans, *Airman Missing*, p. 58.
1773 Samuel G. Schleichkorn, pilot of B-24 41-29118, 445th BG/703rd BS, crashed near Perwex, Brabant, Belgium on 12 April 1944. Howard P. Maupin, pilot of P-47 42-22535 Kathleen Ann, 356th FG/360th FS, crashed near Neerwinden, Belgium on 20 March 1944 (details via Keith Janes).
1774 Morgan's report IS9/WEA/MB/1136 in TNA file WO 208/3350. Nestor Bodson writes that when 'it was learned that the enemy was looking for a man accused of killing one of their foresters, Father Arnould closed the site.' *Downed Allied Airmen…*, p. 62.
1775 Barton op. cit.
1776 According to Rémy (*Mission Marathon*, p. 347) it was 'un des plus important carrefours des Ardennes', one of the most important crossroads in the Ardennes, and 'les Allemands n'avaient pas manqué d'y établir un barrage dans lequel it était à tous égards préférable de ne pas se jeter', the Germans had not forgotten to put a checkpoint there which it was best not to come upon.
1777 Barton op. cit.
1778 Barton op. cit.
1779 See *Mission Marathon*, pages 333-4.
1780 Barton op. cit.
1781 F.W. Brown, letter of 14 June 2004.
1782 F.W. Brown op. cit.
1783 The three Americans were from B17G 42-38055 "K", 457th BG/748th BS, which crashed at Moerbeke-Waas (Belgium) on 27 May 1944.
1784 F.W. Brown op. cit. Curiously, the Bohan camp was also called "Robinson", but it was some twenty kilometres south-west of Porcheresse.
1785 *Airman Missing*, p. 64.
1786 Ibid.
1787 *Airman Missing*, p. 67.
1788 This hotel had, briefly, been the headquarters of the German Governor of Paris, General Dietrich von Choltitz. Appointed to that office on 7 August, he took up his post two days later but, contrary to Hitler's orders to destroy the city, surrendered with 17,000 of his men to the French on 25 August 1944. Born on 9 November 1894, Choltitz died of wounds sustained during the war on 4 November 1966.
1789 Of the thirty-one 431 Squadron aircrew shot down fifteen were killed, seven were taken prisoner and nine, including Harrison, evaded capture.
1790 Harrison's report MI9/S/P.G. (-) 2976 in TNA file WO 208/3326.
1791 Sergeant Irwin's report for some reason states that he was on 139 Squadron not, as it should have, 432 (RCAF) Squadron.
1792 Harrison, op. cit.
1793 Irwin's report IS9 (WEA)/MB/1325 in TNA file WO 208/3350.
1794 Harrison also names nine of the Americans who were at the Bellevaux camp: Charles Amerson; Charles B. Earnhart; Paul P. Kassa; Fred Tuttle; Carmen J. Vozzella; Woodrow W. Tarleton; Lloyd Hermanski; Roy Davies; Walton Goldfuler.
1795 Mallet's report IS9 (WEA)/MB/1358 in TNA file WO 208/3350.
1796 Mallet's report says that they stayed at 'Ghed (no trace)'. It was, in fact, Geel, fourteen kilometres west of Balen and twenty-four south of Turnhout.
1797 Mallet op. cit.

Chapter 13

1798 TNA file AIR 14/2145.
1799 Thring's report MI9/S/P.G. (-) 1959 in TNA file WO 208/3320.
1800 Ibid. Mathieu is, in fact, barely two kilometres west of Périers.
1801 TNA file KV4/322. A "hard" is a man-made berth, the opposite of a "soft" berth, e.g. a sandy beach.
1802 This account is taken from Canadian Air Force files.
1803 His award appeared in *The London Gazette* of 9 April 1945 and in AFRO 625/45 dated 13 April 1945. Recommendation for award dated 5 December 1944, in TNA file Air 2/9231.
1804 Parkinson's report in TNA file WO 208/3350. Washbourne is commemorated on The Runnymede Memorial as one 'of those who fell and have no known grave.' His date of death is shown in *The Runnymede Memorial Register* 7 Part XIV, p. 67, as 8 June 1944 but, according to Parkinson's testimony, he survived until the following day at least.
1805 From website http://monsite.wanadoo.fr/vivre_larcay/page4.html. 'This is the heavy bill paid by a family of the Resistance which always refused to lie down before Nazism and Pétainism'. See also *L'évadé de la France libre*, pp. 289-90.
1806 From *The Day the Chain Broke*, an account by members of Dave Arundel's usual crew. Excerpts are here reproduced with Dave Arundel's kind permission, via Mrs Pat MacGregor, whose father, Sergeant L.M. Byrne, was the flight engineer in Bill Reed's crew.
1807 *The Day the Chain Broke*.
1808 *The Day the Chain Broke*. "Tom" may have been 2nd Lieutenant Thomas L. Lemond USAAF, co-pilot of B-17 42-37913, 100th BG/418th BS, which was shot down at La Ferté-Saint-Samson, barely fifteen kilometres west of Villers-Vermont, on 18 March 1944.
1809 *The Day the Chain Broke*.
1810 *The Day the Chain Broke*.
1811 *The Day the Chain Broke*.
1812 The story of their extraordinary battle for survival is told in *Nachtjagd*, pp. 176-180, Theo Boiten (The Crowood Press, Ramsbury, 1997); and in *In Brave Company*, pp. 149-151, W.R. Chorley (P.A. Chorley, Sixpenny Handley, 1990).
1813 There was cloud from 200–3,000 feet and another, solid, layer from 10,000 feet upwards.
1814 Brown's report IS9/WEA/2/73/268 in TNA file WO 208/3348. The late daylight was the result of British Double Summer Time.
1815 Brown op. cit.
1816 Brown op. cit.
1817 Brown op. cit.

1818 Quoted in *Special Forces in the Invasion of France*, p. 176.
1819 The other two members of Francis were Lieutenant Guy le Borgne (French, "Durance") and Sergeant A.J. Dallow RAC (British, "Groat").
1820 Moydon was quite possibly one of the French SAS engaged on Operation Samwest.
1821See *Special Forces in the Invasion of France*, pp. 174-5.
1822 Major-General Troy H. Middleton, commander of VIII Corps, US Third Army.
1823 *War As I knew It*, p. 97.
1824 As a result of George Brophy's testimony, Pilot Officer Mynarski was awarded a posthumous Victoria Cross (11 October 1946), unaware that his promotion had come through the previous day.
1825 Of the twenty-one crewmen, three were killed, eleven were taken prisoner, and seven evaded capture. Flying Officer J.M. Stevenson RCAF, pilot of KB727, was to escape from the train that was taking him and many other aircrew from Paris to Buchenwald in August 1944.
1826 Barbizon, population 690 in 1939, became famous in the 19th Century for the Barbizon School of painters, which flourished from circa 1830 to 1870. Some of its artists were recognised as the forerunners of the Impressionist movement, and in due course the town 'became an elegant country retreat and a place of artistic pilgrimage.' Michelin *Paris Green Guide*, 1959.
1827 Born on 12 June 1903 at Kenosha, Wisconsin, USA, Drue was raised on a Mexican ranch. Under her screen name of Drue Leyton, she made ten films between 1934 and 1939, and starred in two Broadway productions in 1937. She died on 8 February 1997 at Corona Del Mar, California, USA.
1828 See www.bbc.co.uk/ww2peopleswar/stories/11/a4151611.shtml. The Grand and the smaller Ermitage (150 rooms) were the two best hotels in the spa town.
1829 *The House near Paris*, p. 145.
1830 Technical Sergeants Robert C. Giles, Carroll F. Haarup, and Staff Sergeant Thomas Mezynski, respectively top-turret gunner, radio operator, and ball-turret gunner, were three of the four evaders from 100th BG/350th BS, B-17F 42-30604 Badger Beauty V, that crashed a few kilometres south of Caen on 4 October 1943. The other six crew members were taken prisoner – see Chapter 11.
1831 Olga Christol is credited by Drue Tartière as having hidden thirty-nine airmen evaders in her Paris flat (see also p. 270).
1832 The author is indebted to website http://www.thememoryproject.com/digital-archive/profile.cfm?collectionid=324&cnf=wwII for the information on Flying Officer Frame.
1833 Descriptions of Steepe and Murphy from *The House near Paris*, pp. 262 and 263.
1834 *The House near Paris*, p. 272, also previous quote.
1835 From Appendix 'C' of his report, IS9 (WEA)/8/162/381 in TNA file WO 208/3349. Date of interview: 26 August 1944.
1836 See *Women in the Resistance*, p. 46.
1837 Ibid.
1838 This and previous quote are from Phil Barclay's account written in 1993 for H.O. Dovey (see list in Bibliography).
1839 Donaldson's report IS9 (WEA)/2/37/1023 in WO 208/3350. He was one of only nine wing commanders to evade capture during the war.
1840 Given that he landed near St Pol, the other V1 target *may* have been at Flers, half a dozen kilometres south-west of St Pol.
1841 Boness' report IS9/WEA/MB/1346 in WO 208/3350.
1842 Appendix C, Davies' report MI9/S/P.G. (-) 2059 in TNA file WO 208/5583.
1843 Bulbasket was to prove a disaster for the SAS. Attacked by the Germans on 3 July 1944 the troop suffered thirty-seven casualties, thirty-three of whom were captured and executed. Also executed with them was American airman Lincoln Bundy.
1844 Appendix C Nixon's report IS9/WEA/MB/1123 in TNA file WO 208/3350.
1845 Baskette was co-pilot of B-17G 42-102464, 457th BG/750th BS, shot down by flak on 14 June 1944.
1846 Having reported to the squadron in April 1944 to become familiarized with bomber operations, MacDonald flew his first operation on 9 April, but was not appointed squadron commander until 30 May 1944.
1847 The navigator, Flight Lieutenant H.J.S. Kemley, reported that they were jumped by a Ju88 from Châteaudun airfield. Kemley's report S9/WEA/2/104/229 in TNA file WO 208/3348.
1848 Appendix C, MacDonald's report IS9/WEA/2/167/348 in TNA file WO 208/3349.
1849 See *168 Jump Into Hell*, p. 167.
1850 *Destination: Buchenwald*, p. 41. Colin Burgess (Kangaroo Press Pty Ltd, Kenthurst, NSW, Australia, 1995).
1851 Madame Orsini was later shot in the chest by Desoubrie, probably to stop her giving evidence against him, but she survived to stand ial in May 1946 for her collaboration. She was acquitted for lack of evidence due to the absence of key witnesses for the prosecution.
1852 *168 Jump into Hell*, p. 168.
1853 Not wishing to cause undue loss of life, some Luftwaffe night-fighter pilots aimed for the bomber's engines. Not only would this estroy the bomber but it would also, hopefully, allow the crew to bale out. The night-fighter crews also wished to avoid blowing up the ombs – and themselves! Rökker survived the war with sixty-four victories.
1854 Of the 350 or so Ukrainian deserters who survived the war, 230 stayed with the French Foreign Legion. Others emigrated to North merica or to Australia. The 116 who returned to the Ukraine suffered twenty years' imprisonment in Siberia.
1855 The five airmen and eight SAS soldiers lie in Graffigny-Chemin Communal Cemetery (Haute-Marne). See *Massacre over the Marne*, p. 162-3.
1856 Appendix C, Pilot Officer F.H. O'Neill's report MI9/S/P.G. (-) 2238 in TNA file WO 208/5583.
1857 Top-turret gunner Hines, 801st BG/850th BS, was lost in B-24 42-95317 on 4 July 1944. Note: On 5 August 1944 the 801st became e 492nd BG.
1858 His date of death is officially given as 8 August 1944. He is commemorated on the Bayeux Memorial, Panel 18, Column 2.
1859 *The Brereton Diaries*, p. 332, Lewis H. Brereton (William Morrow & Co., New York, 1946).
1860 Appendix C of the Reeve/Hutchinson joint report M.I9/S/P.G. (F) 2197/2198 in TNA file WO 208/5583.
1861 Green's report MI9/S/P.G. (F) 2577 in TNA file WO 208/3324.
1862 According to Pergantes, Major Feld 'subsequently died in hospital in Rouen'.
1863 After visits to two American hospitals, Pergantes was taken to Paris before being flown to England on 8 September. There he 'was sent 140 American Hospital and subsequently to the King Edward VII Sanatorium', from which he was discharged on 25 October.
1864 Green, op cit.
1865 This American and a British paratrooper sergeant prisoner of war who was also on the train kept the German guards informed of the isoners' conversations, and were, not surprisingly, regarded with great suspicion by Green and the others.
1866 Till was shot down in a Lancaster of 635 Squadron. The rest of his crew were killed. The circumstances of the Lancaster's loss are not own, but as Till was the bomb aimer and thus nearest to the front escape hatch he was probably the first – and maybe the only – of the ew to bale out.
1867 From the joint Ezra/Goddard/Harkins/Trueman report in TNA file WO 208/3350.
1868 Ibid. Till was 'buried by the nuns at Dinant', but his body now rests in Hotton War Cemetery, Belgium.
1869 Ibid.
1870 Parent's report in TNA file WO 208/3350.
1871 Ibid.
1872 See website http://www.lesdeportesdutrainfantome.org/, and the article by Nicholas Farrell in the *Sunday Telegraph*, 19 April 1992.
1873 *Gruppenführer* was an SS rank equivalent to *Generalleutnant* in the Wehrmacht (German Army) and to *lieutenant-general* in the British

Army.
1874 *Belgium Rendez-Vous 127 Revisited*, p. 116.
1875 From Verheggen's own account as published in the book *Ein klein dorp, een zware tol* ("A little village, a heavy burden") by Jozef and Frans Craeninckx with Steffan van Laere (date and place not known). Kindly translated for me by Stefaan Calus – Author.
1876 Ibid.
1877 Wachsmuth was an anti-Nazi. In 1935 he had taken the dangerous stance of refusing to join the Nazi Party so, to get him out of harm's way, a professor at Bonn University persuaded him to join the German Army.
1878 Ibid.
1879 Mason's report MI9/S/P.G. (-) 2623 in TNA file WO 208/3324.
1880 Ibid.
1881 Cunningham's report MI9/S/P.G. (-) 2621 in TNA file WO 208/3324. Muir reported that he was taken to 'the Luftwaffe Secret Police headquarters on the Avenue Louise, Brussels', which was the location of the Gestapo HQ in Brussels.
1882 Panzer's report MI9/S/P.G. (-) 2418 in TNA file WO 208/3323.
1883 Brown's report MI9/S/P.G. (-) 2286 in TNA file WO 208/3322.
1884 Panzer op. cit.
1885 Muir's report MI9/S/P.G. (-) 2885 in TNA file WO 208/3325.
1886 Elliott's report IS9/WEA/MB/1317 in TNA file WO 208/3350. Sergeant Elsliger had baled out in error on the night of 27/28 May 1944, but had not been captured until 16 June. He was taken away to Stalag Luft VII (Bankau) prisoner-of-war camp.
1887 Flying Officer Panzer was on the waiting list for the "black cell", but was never called to endure its horrors. He says that one American spent twenty-nine days in the cell.
1888 Murphy's report MI9/S/P.G. (-) 2622 in TNA file WO 208/3324.
1889 The full, tragic story of Squadron Leader Blenkinsop, a man surely destined for high rank in the RCAF, is told in *One Who Almost Made it Back*.
1890 See especially *One Who Almost Made It Back*, p. 234; and see website http://www.lancastermuseum.ca:80/s,blenkinsop.html. Squadron Leader Blenkinsop is commemorated on the Runnymede Memorial, Panel 278.
1891 *Rendez-vous 127*, p. 113.
1892 Thurmeier's report IS9/WEA/MB/1114 in TNA file WO 208/3350. The Tedesco couple both died in Germany.
1893 The B-24 was serial 42-40550 SA "C for Charlie", 801st BG (Provisional)/406th BS. The crew for a "Carpetbagger" aircraft was eight as opposed to a bomber B-24's crew of nine or ten, but on this night Wolcott's crew were taking along a second navigator, Lieutenant Carmen T. Vozzella, for training purposes.
1894 Virgil R. Marco's account *Victims of Luftwaffe (Part 3)*.
1895 Could the "dog house" have been at 19, Rue Forestière, Brussels, where Flying Officer Elliott and Sergeant Muir were taken?
1896 Virgil R. Marco op. cit.
1897 Two others from the Ghost Train to avail themselves of a barge, the *Irwin*, for the night were Americans 2nd Lieutenant Alfred Sanders, a B-24 pilot, and 1st Lieutenant John J. Bradley, a B-17 navigator, who had been on the train with Flying Officer Stuart Leslie RCAF and another American, Sergeant Royce McGillivray.
1898 Only Lawrie lost his life. Durland and the other five of his crew survived to evade capture.
1899 July 15, 2004 Volume 46, No.12 "Air Force", the official newspaper of the RAAF. See also *Night After Night*, pp. 432-4.
1900 Durland's report MI9/S/P.G. (B) 2564 in TNA file WO 208/3323.
1901 This and two previous quotes from TNA file WO 219/339.
1902 *Evader*, p. 183.
1903 *The Evaders*, (Cosgrove), p. 147. The two gunners – Pilot Officer H.H. Rodgers RCAF, and Sergeant T.F. McClay RAF – were, Jack Gouinlock was later to discover, apparently *not* murdered. Though McClay was believed to have perished in the crash, the author is not aware of the circumstances of their deaths. Neither has a known grave, and both are commemorated on The Runnymede Memorial. Their pilot Pilot Officer H.J. Menzies, was one of those unsung heroes who remained at the controls of a doomed aircraft to save the lives of their crews.
1904 *The Evaders*, (Cosgrove), p. 152.
1905 *The Evaders*, (Cosgrove), p. 155.
1906 Robert, a Belgian, had served for one year in the Belgian Army before enlisting in the RAF.
1907 Robert's report IS9/WEA/2/558/1416 in TNA file WO 208/3350.
1908 TNA file AIR 14/2073.
1909 Warren and Thorne were escaped prisoners of war, as was, possibly, Granat (see *Footprints on the Sands of Time*, pp. 92-3). On 2[illegible] September Lieutenants James and Guthrie, captured at Arnhem on 25 and 17 September 1944 respectively, had jumped off the train that was taking them to Germany.
1910 See *Footprints on the Sands of Time*, p. 94.
1911 Thorne died on 2 February 1945 and was laid to rest in Doetinchem (Loolaan) General Cemetery.
1912 Appendix C, Rupert's report MI9/S/P.G. (-) 2940 in TNA file WO 208/5583.
1913 Appendix C, Carey's report IS9/WEA/ 2/550/1424 in TNA file WO 208/3350.
1914 *MI9*, p. 224. For more on the Pegasus operations see *Saturday at M.I.9*, Chapter 24.
1915 Appendix C, Mahoney's report MI9/S/P.G. (H) 2712 in TNA file WO 208/5583.
1916 Mahoney op. cit.
1917 Tovey's report MI9/S/P.G. (-) 3083 in TNA file WO 208/3327.

Chapter 14

1918 Appendix C, Sergeant K.G. Butler's report MI9/S/P.G. (-) 2880 in TNA file WO 208/5583. This happened to Marthe Nollet in 1944.
1919 See http://www.flensted.eu.com/, the comprehensive website of Søren C. Flensted, Danish air historian, for whose generous assistance I am most grateful – Author.
1920 The Me110 of 7./NJG 3 was flown by Unteroffizier Berg, with Unteroffizier Krebs as his *Funker* (radar/radio operator).
1921 At 1.55 a.m. on 21 April the remains of Stirling R9261 fell approximately 500 metres north-west of Kelstrup, near Slagelse on the we[st] coast of the island.The seven who perished were laid to rest in Svinø cemetery on 24 April 1943. The extra crew member was Squadro[n] Leader W.A. Blake, who was acting as second pilot.
1922 Appendix C, Smith's report MI9/S/P.G. (-) 1196 in TNA file WO 208/5582.
1923 The Germans were well aware of the traffic of enemy personnel from Bromma, and kept a close eye on the airport. Two aircraft flyi[ng] from it during the war were shot down.
1924 Williams' report MI9/S/P.G. (-) 1975 in TNA file WO 208/3320.
1925 Vlielander Hein's report MI9/S/P.G. (N) 2453 in TNA file WO 208/3323.
1926 Vlielander Hein op. cit.
1927 Count Folke Bernadotte of Wisborg (born 2 January 1895) was chosen after the war to be the UN Security Council's mediator in th[e] Arab-Israeli conflict of 1947-48. He was assassinated on 17 September 1948 by the underground Jewish group Lehi.
1928 *War As I Knew It*, p. 97.
1929 Ibid., p. 105.
1930 Hunter's report MI9/S/P.G./MISC/INT/690 in TNA file WO 208/3345. In the event, of the seven crew, only Hunter and Flight Sergea[nt]

S.D. Jolly RAAF survived, Jolly also evading.
1931 Mutter had been shot down in Mustang FB119, 65 Squadron, on 30 April 1944. He was captured in Paris on 22 July 1944, and was one of the unfortunate airmen to spend several weeks in Buchenwald concentration camp before being released to Stalag Luft III (Sagan) in October 1944.
1932 *Not Just Another Milk Run...*, p. 39. I am most grateful to Molly Burkett for permission to quote from her book and to use Jack Marsden's story.
1933 Going with Hammond to Paris were two of his crew, Warrant Officer II B.A.J. Solberg RCAF and Sergeant C.E.F. Fisher. Less seriously injured, after only two days in Paris they were sent by Red Cross train to Germany, being imprisoned at Stalag Luft VII in Silesia.
1934 Philbin's report MI9/S/P.G./MISC/INT/662 in TNA file WO 208/3345.
1935 Major General Philippe Leclerc (1902–1947), born Philippe François Marie, Comte de Hauteclocque, commanded the French 2nd Armoured Division.
1936 Von Choltitz, born on 9 November 1894, was released from Allied captivity in 1947 and died on 4 November 1966 in hospital at Baden-Baden, Germany due to an old war illness.
1937 Brown's report MI9/S/P.G./MISC/INT/752 in TNA file WO 208/3345.
1938 Lusk's report MI9/S/P.G./MISC/INT/807 in TNA file WO 208/3345.
1939 In fierce street fighting on 26 June the Americans captured Lieutenant General Karl-Wilhelm von Schlieben, commander of the German forces in Cherbourg, and also Rear-Admiral Hennecke, Sea Defence Commandant for Normandy. The last strongpoint in the naval arsenal surrendered on the following day. The north of the Cotentin peninsula was finally cleared of German forces on 1 July 1944.
1940 Gordon's report MI9/S/P.G. (F) 2632 in TNA file WO 208/3324.
1941 Two of the crew of a C-47 that was off course and shot down over St Nazaire on 30 October 1944.
1942 Captain Foot's report IS9/WEA/6/57/59 in TNA file WO 208/3348.
1943 Gray's report MI9/S/P.G./MISC/INT/644 in TNA file WO 208/3345.
1944 Sanderson's report MI9/S/P.G./MISC/INT/647 in TNA file WO 208/3345. Sanderson was well-advanced in years for aircrew, being thirty-five. Gray was also thirty-five, and Hart was thirty-two. The other three were all only twenty.
1945 Zerstörergeschwader 1 with its Ju88 aircraft had left its base at Bordeaux-Mérignac for Germany on 16 July.
1946 Gray op. cit.
1947 From the crew's joint report MI9/S/P.G. (-) 2655-2660 in TNA file WO 208/3324.
1948 Ibid.
1949 From the excellent and informative website www.shetland-heritage.co.uk. The submarine chasers were probably from the US Navy's "Wooden Type" series, which was undertaken from 1941-1943. The General Motors' engines were of the "pancake diesel" type and were unknown to the Norwegian mechanics. For his work on them Senior Petty Officer Angelveidt, Royal Norwegian Navy, was recommended for an award.
1950 *The Shetland Bus*, p. 5.
1951 *The Shetland Bus*, p. 119.
1952 Larsen was later able to add the DSO to his impressive array of gallantry awards. For a fuller account of the rescue of the Biddle crew see *Shot Down and on the Run*, pp. 141-8.
1953 1st Canadian Army along the coast itself; British 2nd Army on its right flank; US Ninth Army on 2nd Army's right flank.
1954 *A Full Life*, p. 207, Lieutenant-General Sir Brian Horrocks (Collins, London, 1960).
1955 *Six of the Best*, p. 180, Jimmy Edwards (Robson Books Ltd, London, 1984).
1956 Edwards' report in TNA file AIR 27/1574.
1957 Both were captured.
1958 Edwards' report in TNA file AIR 27/1574.
1959 Edwards was awarded the DFC for his actions, the short citation in *The London Gazette* (2/2/45) merely saying: 'In air operations, this officer has displayed skill, courage and fortitude of a very high order.'
1960 The NSB, co-founded in 1931 by Anton Mussert (born 11 May 1894) and Cornelis van Geelkerken (born 19 March 1901), sided with the Nazis during the Second World War. Mussert was arrested after the war, and executed on 7 May 1946. Van Geelkerken was also arrested. Sentenced to life imprisonment he was released in 1959, and died on 29 March 1979.
1961 Appendix C, Goggin's report IS9/WEA/1/282/2373 in TNA file WO 208/3352.
1962 Ward's report MI9/S/P.G. (H) 3064 in TNA file WO 208/3327.
1963 Goggin op. cit.
1964 *Travel by Dark. After Arnhem*, p. 146, Graeme Warrack (Harvill Press Ltd, London, 1963).
1965 The Scots major *may* have been Major J.S.A'D Coke, KOSB, att. 7th (Airborne) Battalion. Though John Coke was with Graeme Warrack most of the way to the river crossing on 23 November, Coke's death officially occurred on 18 November 1944.
1966 *Saturday at M.I.9*, p. 296. "O'Casey" (glider pilot?) has not been identified – Author.
1967 Donmall's report IS9/WEA/6/716/2599 in TNA file WO 208/3352.
1968 The Germans had prepared a forest of cunningly-disguised pillboxes in this area, through which the US Third Army was to attack. Its commander, General Patton, noted that one pillbox was camouflaged like a wooden barn. 'When you opened the door through which the hay was supposed to be put, you came to a concrete wall nine feet thick with an 88 mm. gun sticking out. Another was built inside an old house…' *War As I Knew It*, p. 242.
1969 General Patton also noted that on 22 December 1944 'the 5th Infantry Division had driven the enemy back to the Sauer River in its front, and killed quite a few when they tried to escape across the river.' *War As I Knew It*, pp. 202-3.
1970 The RAF Bomber Command loss card for Halifax NA572 shows Renet's name as Kannengeiser. Renet is the name given on his report in TNA file WO 208/3326. (See Appendix I.)
1971 Jones' report IS9/WEA/2/1024/2400 in TNA file WO 208/3352. All the other six of his crew became prisoners of war.
1972 The date on which the first patient to be successfully treated with penicillin was 14 March 1942. By the time of the Normandy landings in June 1944 2.3 million doses of penicillin had been produced.
1973 Website www.army.mod.uk/para/history/rhine.htm.
1974 North-Lewis' report IS9/WEA/2/1027/2414 in TNA file WO 208/3352.
1975 540 US Dakota aircraft carried twelve parachute battalions – five British, one Canadian and six American – closely followed by 1,300 tugs and gliders packed with troops.
1976 Rohde's report IS9/WEA/1/375/3020 in TNA file WO 208/3352.
1977 Flying Officer Bert Wolters was killed on 16 September 1944 when his Spitfire, MJ460, collided with another of his squadron, MK208, in cloud over Kent. The other pilot, Flying Officer C.R.R. Mandes, baled out.
1978 Van Roosendaal's report IS9/WEA/1/376/3022 in TNA file WO 208/3352.
1979 Foster, 4th FG/334th FS, had been shot down on 31 March 1945 in P51-D Buffalo Bertie, 44-11336.
1980 During this period they were looked after by "Jans" (J. Van Veen), who was head of the local underground movement, and who provided the airmen with civilian clothing, tobacco, and food, even managing to obtain bread coupons from local farmers.
1981 Dr Kentgens, a dentist by profession, lived at "Tandarts", Zoetermeer.
1982 The lodge was the property of Mynheer E. van Romunde of Westeringkade 69, Den Haag.
1983 Rowland's report IS9/WEA/PLM/189 in TNA file WO 208/3348.
1984 Anderson's report IS9/WEA/PLM/197 in TNA file WO 208/3348.

1985 Annette Tison's account on website http://www.b24.net/, with her kind permission.
1986 McCormick was waist gunner of B-24 42-29421, 392nd BG/578th BS, shot down on 22 February 1945.
1987 Annette Tison op. cit.
1988 Annette Tison op. cit.
1989 In their MI9 reports filed on 11 May 1945, Rowland, Anderson, Bell, Hollick, and Sharp all mention "The Jolly Duck" by name, almost certainly a reference to the hunting lodge – "Het jachthuis". There is some debate today, however, as to whether or not "The Jolly Duck" was the name of McCormick's B-24, but most of its crew can recall seeing neither such a name nor a yellow duck painted on its nose.
1990 He was a member of the Nazi paramilitary organisation *Nationalsozialistisches Kraftfahrkorps* (NSKK), or the *National Socialist Drivers Corps*.
1991 Hollick's report IS9/WEA/PLM/201 in TNA file WO 208/3348. Kentgens, who had been shot through the head, survived.
1992 It is presumed that she and her son, who was also in The Jolly Duck during the fighting, were arrested, for none of the airmen mention the fact of their escape in their reports. It is possible, however, that the "Joe" mentioned in his report by Sharp was the van Rijs' son.
1993 Annette Tison op. cit.
1994 Annette Tison op. cit.
1995 Annette Tison op. cit.
1996 Robertson's report, dated 9 July 1945, to his commanding officer (via Annette Tison).
1997 Boyd's report MI9/S/P.G. (-) 3076 in TNA file WO 208/3327.
1998 When the Germans got to the wreckage, they threw McBeath's body into a ditch at Værløse airfield. Not located until after the war, McBeath was laid to rest by the Reverend O.E.L. Christiansen at Værløse cemetery on 9 June 1945.
1999 The author gratefully acknowledges the help of Søren Flensted in providing these details. See his website www.flensted.eu.com/1945036.shtml.
2000 Hart's report MI9/S/P.G. (-) 3112 in TNA file WO 208/3327.
2001 Hart op. cit.
2002 The author is grateful to Søren Flensted for permission to use this information from his website www.flensted.eu.com.

Appendix III

2003 Broke a bone in his foot – see TNA file AIR 20/9160.
2004 I am indebted to Claude Hélias for these names – Author.
2005 I am, again, indebted to Claude Hélias for the names of the USAAF airmen – Author.
2006 Thanks to Edouard Renière for the details of the escape.
2007 Later Chairman of the Air Forces Escape and Evasion Society.
2008 Coffman's B-17 was badly damaged but, after Coffman and two others had baled out, the pilot flew it back to England.
2009 See websites http://www.conscript-heroes.com:80/Art34-Ken-Williams.html, and http://www.littlefriends.co.uk/355thfg.
2010 Gordon and Lee were forced to bale out when their fighters ran out of fuel 50 kilometres south-east of Plouha.

Appendix IV

2011 Eugene Andersen was one of those injured when the truck taking the evaders to a Normandy airstrip overturned.
2012 Staff Sergeant Glen E. Brennecke, 96th BG, was shot down on 4 March 1944.
2013 Staff Sergeant Daniel M. Cargile was one of the two waist gunners of a B-17G "Pathfinder" attached to 100th BG which was lost on 20 July 1944. He and five others evaded, while six others were taken prisoner.
2014 Captain Henry C. Griffis was the radar operator aboard the same B-17 as Cargile.

Appendix V

2015 *MI9* (Foot and Langley), p. 30.
2016 Ibid, p. 32.
2017 Crockatt was awarded the MC (1/1/1917) and the DSO (12/12/1919) whilst serving in the Royal Scots.
2018 TNA file WO 208/3242.
2019 TNA file WO 208/3242.
2020 Ibid.
2021 Ibid.
2022 For the full story of aids for operational airmen see *Official Secret*, Clayton Hutton (Max Parrish & Co. Ltd, London, 1960).
2023 Lieutenant-Colonel A.P. Scotland, OBE, *The London Cage*, p. 123, (Evans Brothers Limited, London, 1957).
2024 TNA file WO 208/3242.
2025 It should be noted, however, that, even though he had escaped from Italy to Switzerland, Brigadier Hargest's report was numbered MI9/S/P.G. (Italy) 1587 to denote his escape from Italy.
2026 *MI9 Escape and Evasion 1939-1945*, p. 216.
2027 TNA file WO 208/3246.
2028 From TNA file AIR 14/464.
2029 For the full 'battle order' of places and personnel employed by IS9 (WEA) in April 1945 see TNA file WO 208/3246.

Appendix VI

2030 Details taken from *Aviateurs Piétons vers la Suisse*…, pp. 160-1.
2031 Becker was one of the five sector leaders of the Resistance organisation Bordeaux-Loupiac, which was headed by René Guittard. For more information on this group see website http://www.conscript-heroes.com/Resistance TernoisAppxENG.html#appx2.
2032 The existence of the V1 (its German military designation was *FZG. 76*) and of the V2 (A-4) were not known at this time, and Merlin is clearly commenting with the benefit of hindsight.
2033 This and much of what follows is taken from Appendix C of Merlin's report in MI9/S/P.G. (-) 2342 in TNA file WO 208/5583.
2034 Appendix C, Checketts' report MI9/S/P.G. (-) 1495 in TNA file WO 208/5582.
2035 Merlin's report MI9/S/P.G. (-) 2432 in TNA file WO 208/3323.
2036 Haddock, shot down on 15 July 1943, had also been on. 175 Squadron.
2037 "Captain Rochat" was the alias of Paul de Saugy (see *Aviateurs Piétons vers la Suisse*…, p. 164).
2038 Air Commodore Freddie West VC makes no direct mention in his book *Winged Diplomat* (see p. 206) to such a seemingly important incident. All he says, à propos a defecting German rocket scientist being passed over to the RAF in Paris in September 1944, is: 'German rocket and flying-bomb technique had come into our purview some time earlier…', a hint possibly to this being the information brought by Merlin. Wing Commander R.D. Jones was assistant air attaché at the British Legation.
2039 Flight Lieutenant Geoffrey T. Chinchen was shot down by flak over Libya in a Kittyhawk of 3 (RAAF) Squadron on 14 June 1942. He was awarded the DFC on 18 September 1942.
2040 This must have been a cheap hotel, for it is not listed in the 1939 Michelin guide.
2041 It is almost certain that Pilot Officer E.A. Haddock and his American co-evader were arrested in Paris on 17 December 1943.
2042 This begs the question: Did Merlin have sufficient funds to pay such a large sum and, if so, how did he come by them? From the British

in Switzerland, perhaps (though he makes no mention of this)?
2043 Again, this hotel does not feature in the 1939 Michelin Guide.
2044 This regiment was a component unit of the 302nd Infanterie Division, which was reliably identified in northern France in early 1942, but which was transferred to the southern sector of the Russian front early in 1943.
2045 The 1939 Michelin Guide lists the garage in Arras as 'Roger et Fagniez, 22 r. Doullens', dealers in Peugeot cars.
2046 Appendix C, Thompson's report MI9/S/P.G. (-) 2431 in TNA file WO 208/5583. Bailleulmont is probably Bailleul-aux-Cornailles.
2047 Thompson op. cit.

Appendix VII

2048 *Cockleshell Heroes*, p. 118.
2049 From the *Daily Telegraph* obituary of Lieutenant-Commander Raikes, 28 June 2005, who died on 5 May 2005, aged 93.
2050 *Cockleshell Heroes*, p. 236.
2051 David Moffatt and George Jellicoe Sheard are commemorated on Panels 103 and 74 respectively of the Plymouth Naval Memorial.
2052 This *Kommando-Befehl* ("Commando Order") 'dealt with the classes of persons who were to be excluded from the protection of the Geneva Convention and were not to be treated as prisoners of war, but when captured were to be handed over to the S.D.' Once in the hands of the SD the enemy "commandos" – those excluded from the protection of the Geneva Convention – were to be shot.

Selected Bibliography, Magazines and Manuscripts

168 Jump Into Hell – Arthur G. Kinnis & Stanley Booker (Arthur G. Kinnis, Victoria, Canada, 1999)
2nd Tactical Air Force. Volume One. Spartan to Normandy June 1943 to June 1944 – Christopher Shores and Chris Thomas (Ian Allan Publishing Ltd, Hersham, 2004)
– *Volume Two. Breakout to Bodenplatte July 1944 to January 1945* (2005)
– *Volume Three. From the Rhine to Victory* (2006)
"7 x X x 90" (The Story of a Stirling Bomber and Its Crew) – Charles Potten (K. Gandy and C. Potten, Ely and Hove, 1986)
Achtung! Achtung! Die Flugfestungen Kommen! – Lt. Col. John M. Carah, USAF (ret.) Edited by Warren B. Carah (Elbow Lane Books, Brighton, Michigan, USA, 1990 & 2006)
Adventures of a Secret Agent – Captain Dick Cooper (Frederick Muller Ltd, London, 1957)
After the Battle, Number 118 – Editor-in-Chief Winston G. Ramsey (Battle of Britain International Ltd., London, 2002)
Agents for Escape. Inside the French Resistance 1939-1945 – André Rougeyron (Louisiana State University Press, Baton Rouge, USA, 1996)
Aircraft Down! Evading Capture in WWII Europe – Philip D. Caine (Brassey's, Dulles, Virginia, USA, 2000)
Air Forces Escape & Evasion Society – Ralph K. Patton & Lt. Col. Clayton C. David (Ret.) (Turner Publishing Company, Paducah, Kentucky, USA, 1992)
Airman Missing – Greg Lewis (Newman Books, Stratford-upon-Avon, 2008)
Airmen On the Run – Laurence Meynell (Odhams Press Ltd, London, 1963)
All the Luck in the World – Allan M. Ogilvie (Creative Publishers, St Johns, Newfoundland, Canada, 1994)
Ambassador On Special Mission – Sir Samuel Hoare (Collins, London, 1946)
American Pimpernel – Andy Marino (Hutchinson, London, 1999; Arrow Books, London, 2000)
An Affair of Chances – Ian McGeoch (Imperial War Museum, London, 1991)
An American Heroine in the French Resistance. The Diary and Memoir of Virginia D'Albert-Lake – Judy Barrett Litoff (editor) (Fordham University Press, New York, USA, 2006)
A Prisoner's Duty. Great Escapes in U.S. Military History – Robert C. Doyle (Naval Institute Press, Annapolis, USA, 1997)
A Quiet Woman's War – William Etherington (Mousehold Press, Norwich, 2002; reprint 2006)
A Shaky Do. The Skoda works raid 16/17th April 1943 – Peter Wilson Cunliffe (Accycunliffes Publications, Lostock Hall, Preston, 2007)
A Talent to Survive – Rex Woods (William Kimber & Co Ltd, London, 1982)
Aviateurs-Piétons vers la Suisse 1940-1945 – Roger Anthoine (Editions Secavia, Geneva, Switzerland, 1997)
Bale Out! – Alfie Martin (Colourpoint Books, Newtownards, 2005)
Battle of France Then and Now, The – Peter D. Cornwell (Battle of Britain International Ltd, Old Harlow, 2007)
Behind Enemy Lines. A Memoir of James Moffat – Mary Thomas (Mary Thomas, Belleville, Ontario, Canada, 2001)
Belgium Rendez-Vous 127 – Revisited – Yvonne Daley-Brusselmans (Sunflower University Press, USA, 2001)
Believed Safe – Bill Furniss-Roe (William Kimber & Co Ltd, London, 1987)
Big Network, The – Roman Garby-Czerniawski (George Ronald, London, 1961)
Black Crosses off my Wingtip – Squadron Leader I.F. Kennedy DFC & Bar (The General Store Publishing House, Burnstown, Ontario, Canada, 1994)
Blue Skies and Dark Nights – Bill Randle (Independent Books, Bromley, 2002)
Bomber Boys – Mel Rolfe (Grub Street, London, 2004; reprinted in paperback 2007)
Bombers First and Last – Gordon Thorburn (Robson Books, London, 2006)
Bristol Blenheim, The. A Complete History – Graham Warner (Crécy Publishing Limited, Manchester, 2002)
Broken Mustang [D-Day 4] – George F. Pyle (Blaisdon Publishing, Hornby, Bedale, 2001)
By Such Deeds. Honours and Awards in the Royal New Zealand Air Force 1923-1999. Group Captain C.M. Hanson, OBE, RNZAF (Rtd) (Volplane Press, Christchurch, New Zealand, 2001)
Canadians in the Royal Air Force – Les Allison (Les Allison, Roland, Manitoba, Canada, 1978)
Claude and Madeleine – Edward Marriott (Picador, London, 2005)
Colours of the Day, The – P.A. Chapman (Country Books, Bakewell, 1999)
Comet Connection, The. Escape from Hitler's Europe – George Watt (The University Press of Kentucky, Lexington, USA, 1990; reprinted in paperback 1994)
Conscript Heroes – Peter Scott Janes (Paul Mould Publishers, Boston, 2004)
Dangerous Landing – Henry Ord Robertson DFM (Patrick Stephens Limited, Wellingborough, 1989)
Destination Buchenwald – Colin Burgess (Kangaroo Press Pty Ltd, Kenthurst, NSW, Australia, 1995)
Detachment W – Derek Richardson (Paul Mould Publishing UK, Boston, 2004)
D-Day Bombers: The Veterans' Story – Stephen Darlow (Grub Street, London, 2004; Bounty Books, London, 2007)
D-Day Plus One – Frank 'Dutch' Holland with Adam Wilkins (Grub Street, London, 2007)
Downed Allied Airmen and Evasion of Capture: The Role of Local Resistance Networks in World War II – Herman Bodson (McFarland & Company, Inc, Jefferson, USA, 2005)
Easy Trip, The – Bill Knaggs (Perth & Kinross Libraries, Perth, 2001)
El Camino de la Libertad – Juan Carlos Jiménez de Aberásturi
Errors of Judgement. SOE's Disaster in the Netherlands, 1941-44 – Nicholas Kelso (Robert Hale Limited, London, 1988)
Escape! – Lieutenant Colonel James Edwin Armstrong USAFR (Honoribus Press, Spartanburg, USA, 2000)
Escape and Evasion – Ian Dear (Arms and Armour Press, London, 1997)
Escape and Evasion – Cyril Penna, DFM (United Writers Publications, Penzance, 1987)
Escape and Liberation 1940-1945 – A.J. Evans (Hodder and Stoughton Ltd, London, 1945)
Escape From a Halifax Bomber – J.H. Hill (The Book Guild Ltd, Lewes, 1983)
Escape from Enemy-Occupied Europe – Terry Bolter (private, no date)
Escape from France – Raymond Worrall (Silver Quill Publications, Catterick, 2004)
Escape from Montluc – André Devigny (Dobson Books Ltd, London, 1957)
Escaping Club, The – A. J. Evans (Jonathan Cape, London, 1921; Florin Books, London, 1936)
Evader – Derek Shuff (Spellmount Ltd, Staplehurst, 2003)
Evader – T.D.G. Teare (Hodder and Stoughton, London, 1954; Air Data Publications Ltd, Wilmslow, 1996)
Evaders, The – Ed Cosgrove (Clarke, Irwin & Co Ltd, Toronto, Canada, 1970; paperback 1976)
Evaders, The – Emerson Lavender & Norman Sheffe (McGraw Hill Ryerson Ltd, Ontario, Canada, 1992)
Extraordinary Adventure of the Forest of Fréteval May-August 1944, The – Cécile Jubault (no publisher, 1967)
Failed to Return. Mysteries of the Air 1939-1945 – Roy Conyers Nesbit (Patrick Stephens Ltd, Wellingborough, 1988)
Farewell Campo 12 – Brigadier James Hargest, CBE, DSO**, MC (Michael Joseph Ltd, London, 1945)
Fight Another Day – Lt. Colonel J.M. Langley MBE, MC (Collins, London, 1974)
Fighter Pilot. A Self-Portrait by George Barclay – Humphrey Wynn (editor) (William Kimber & Co Ltd, London, 1976)

Fire From the Forest. The SAS Brigade in France, 1944 – Roger Ford (Cassell, London, 2003)
Flee the Captor – Herbert Ford (Southern Publishing Association, Nashville, USA, 1966)
Flight Most Secret – Gibb McCall (William Kimber & Co Ltd, London, 1981)
Follow the Man With the Pitcher – Kenneth Skidmore (Countrywise, Birkenhead, 1996)
Footprints on the Sands of Time – Oliver Clutton-Brock (Grub Street Publishing, London, 2003)
Freedom Has No Frontier – Joyce Lussu (trans. William Clowes) (Michael Joseph Ltd, London, 1969); (Casa Editrice Gius. Laterta & Figli, Bari, Italy, 1967)
Freedom Line, The – Peter Eisner (William Morrow, New York, USA, 2004)
Freedom the Spur – Gordon Instone, MM (Burke Publishing Co Ltd, London, 1953)
Freedom Trail, The – Scott Goodall (Inchmere Design, Great Britain, 2005)
Free to Fight Again. RAF Escapes and Evasions 1940-45 – Alan W.Cooper (William Kimber & Co Ltd, Wellingborough, 1988)
F Section SOE. The Story of the Buckmaster Network – Marcel Ruby (Leo Cooper Ltd, London, 1988)
Full Moon to France – Devereaux Rochester (Robert Hale Ltd, London, 1978)
Guide du Pneu Michelin 1939 – Michelin (Michelin et Cie, Clermont-Ferrand, 1939)
Happy is the Day. A Spitfire Pilot's Story – Tom Slack (United Writers Publications Ltd, Cornwall, 1987)
Highland Division, The – Eric Linklater (HMSO, London, 1942)
HMS Fidelity – Marcel Jullian (Souvenir Press Ltd, London, 1957)
HMS Tarana. In at the Deep End – Ron Stephens, Sue and Andy Parlour (Serendipity Publishers, Darlington, 2007)
Home Run: Escape from Nazi Europe – John Nichol and Tony Rennell (Penguin Books Ltd, London, 2007)
Home Run. Great RAF Escapes of World War II – Richard Townshend Bickers (Leo Cooper, London, 1992)
House near Paris, The – Drue Tartière with M.R. Werner (Simon and Schuster Inc, New York, USA, 1946)
Hugh Dormer's Diaries – Hugh Dormer (Jonathan Cape, London, 1947)
Infringing Neutrality. The RAF in Switzerland 1940-45 – Roger Anthoine (Tempus Publishing Ltd, Stroud, 2006)
In Lands Not My Own. A Wartime Journey – Reuben Ainsztein (Random House, Inc, New York, USA, 2002)
In Pursuit of Freedom – Arthur Barton (privately, 1993)
Intelligence and National Security, Vol.11, No.2 (April 1996) – H.O. Dovey (Frank Cass, London, 1996)
In the Footsteps of a Flying Boot – Art Horning (Carlton Press, Inc, New York, USA, 1994)
In the Shadows of War – Thomas Childers (Henry Holt & Co LLC, New York, USA, 2003)
In Trust and Treason. The Strange Story of Suzanne Warren – Gordon Young (Studio Vista Ltd, London, 1959)
It's Further via Gibraltar – Patrick Gibbs (Faber and Faber, London, 1961)
It's Suicide But It's Fun… – Chris Goss (Crécy Books, Bristol, 1995)
I Walked Alone – The Earl of Cardigan (Routledge & Kegan Paul Ltd, London, 1950)
Johnny Checketts: The Road to Biggin Hill – Vincent Orange (Grub Street, London, 2007)
Jump or Die – Douglas Jennings (Tucann Books, Lincoln, 2005)
La Filière du Rail – Gabriel Nahas (Éditions France-Empire, Paris, 1982)
La Maison des Otages – André Frossard (Éditions Famot, Geneva, 1976)
Last Piece of England, The. The story of a private island – Richard Barber (islandrace.com, Saltash, 2008)
L'évadé de la France Libre. Le réseau Bourgogne – Georges Broussine (Éditions Tallandier, Paris, 2000)
Little Cyclone – Airey Neave (Hodder and Stoughton, London, 1954; Coronet Books, London, 1973)
Lone Evader – Ted Coates (Australian Military History Publications, Loftus, 1995 & 1998)
Long Way Round, The. An Escape Through Occupied France – William Moore (Leo Cooper in association with Secker and Warburg Ltd, London, 1986)
Loss of Halifax Aircraft PM-Q, The – Gordon Mellor (private, no date)
Love and War in the Pyrenees – Rosemary Bailey (Weidenfeld & Nicolson, London, 2008)
Love is in the Air. The Wartime Letters and Memories of Joe Pack & Margaret Dillon. Edited by Jeff Pack (Woodfield Publishing Ltd, Bognor Regis, 2008)
'Making for Sweden...' Part 1 – The RAF 1939 to 1945 – Rolph Wegmann and Bo Widfeldt (Air Research Publications, Walton-on-Thames, 1997)
Man Who Went Back, The – Lucien Dumais (Leo Cooper, London, 1975)
Massacre over the Marne – Oliver Clutton-Brock (Patrick Stephens Ltd, Sparkford, 1994)
Mémoires Résistantes. Histoire du Réseau Jade-Fitzroy 1940-1944 – Alya Aglan (Les Éditions du Cerf, Paris, 1994)
MI6. British Secret Intelligence Service Operations 1909-45 – Nigel West (George Weidenfeld & Nicolson Ltd, London, 1983)
MI9. Escape and Evasion 1939-1945 – M.R.D. Foot & J.M. Langley (The Bodley Head, London, 1979)
Missing Presumed Dead – Stanley A. Hawken, OBE (Hill of Content Publishing, Melbourne, Australia, 1989)
Mission Completed – Air Chief Marshal Sir Basil Embry, GCB, KBE, DSO***, DFC, AFC (Methuen & Co Ltd, London, 1957)
Mission Marathon – Rémy [Gilbert Renault] (Librairie Académique Perrin, Paris, 1974)
Nancy Wake – Russell Braddon (Cassell & Co Ltd, London, 1956; Pan Books Ltd, London, 1958)
Next Moon, The – André Hue and Ewen Southby-Tailyour (Viking/Penguin Books Ltd, London, 2004)
Night After Night. New Zealanders in Bomber Command – Max Lambert (HarperCollinsPublishers [New Zealand] Limited, Auckland, New Zealand, 2007)
No Banners – Jack Thomas (W.H. Allen & Co. Ltd, London, 1955)
No Drums, No Trumpets – Barry Wynne (Arthur Barker, London, 1961)
Nor Iron Bars a Cage – W.H. Aston, MM (Macmillan & Co Ltd, London, 1946)
Not Just Another Milk Run… – Molly Burkett and Geoff Gilbert (Barny Books, Hough on the Hill, Grantham, 2004)
Official Secret – Clayton Hutton (Max Parrish & Co Ltd, London, 1960)
One Hundredth Airman, The – Reg Stead & Murray Straker (published by the authors in Canada, 2000)
One of Many – Eric Grisdale (privately? No details given)
One of The Many – Mike Cooper (J & KH Publishing, Hailsham, 1997)
One Who Almost Made It Back – Peter Celis (Grub Street Publishing, London, 2008)
On Hazardous Service – A. Cecil Hampshire (William Kimber & Co Ltd, London, 1974)
On Wings of War. A History of 166 Squadron – Jim Wright (166 Squadron Association, Kirkby Park, 1996)
Operation Skua – Major R.T. Partridge, DSO, (Fleet Air Arm Museum, Yeovilton, 1983)
Our Personal War – Jan Tickner (Eakin Press, Austin, Texas, USA, 2000)
Pantaraxia – Nubar Gulbenkian (Hutchinson & Co Ltd, London, 1965)
Parachuting to Danger – Lionel Scott (Robert Hale, London, 1988; published as 'I Dropped In', 1959)
Par les nuits les plus longues: Réseaux d'évasion d'aviateurs en Bretagne, 1940-1944 – Roger Huguen (Coop Breizh, Spezet, France, 1993 – 10th edition 2003)
Peter Five – Freddie Clark (Independent Books, Bromley, 1993)
Pilot on the Run – Errol Braithwaite (Century Hutchinson New Zealand, Auckland, 1986)
Politics of Resistance in France, 1940-1944, The – John F. Sweets (Northern Illinois University Press, DeKalb, USA, 1976)

Real Enemy, The – Pierre d'Harcourt (Longmans, Green and Co Ltd, London, 1967)
Red Runs the Vistula – Ron Jeffery (Nevron Associates, Auckland, New Zealand, 1985)
Rendez-vous 127 – Anne Brusselmans (Ernest Benn Ltd, London, 1954)
Réseau Comète (1) – Jules Rémy (1966)
Return Ticket – Anthony Deane-Drummond (Collins, London, 1953)
Return to St Valéry – Derek Lang (Leo Cooper Ltd, London, 1974)
Road to Resistance. An Autobiography – George Millar (The Bodley Head Ltd, London, 1979)
Royal Air Force Coastal Command Losses of the Second World War Volume 1 1939-1941 – Ross McNeill (Midland Publishing, Hinckley, 2003)
Royal Air Force Fighter Command Losses of the Second World War Volume 1 1939-1941 – Norman L R Franks (Midland Publishing Ltd, Earl Shilton, 1997)
– *Volume 2 1942-1943* (Midland Publishing Ltd, Earl Shilton, 1998)
– *Volume 3 1944-1945* (Midland Publishing Ltd, Earl Shilton, 2000)
Royal Air Force Quarterly, The (Winter 1942)
Safe Houses are Dangerous – Helen Long (William Kimber & Co Ltd, London, 1985)
Safer Than a Known Way – Philip Newman (William Kimber & Co Ltd, London, 1983)
Saturday at M.I.9 – Airey Neave (Hodder and Stoughton Ltd, London, 1969)
Scarlet Pimpernel of the Vatican, The – J.P. Gallagher (Souvenir Press Ltd, London, 1967)
Secret Flotillas. Volume I: Clandestine Sea Operations to Brittany 1940-1944 and *Secret Flotillas. Volume II: Clandestine Sea Operations in the Mediterranean, North Africa and the Adriatic 1940-1944* – Sir Brooks Richards (Frank Cass Publishers, London, 2004). Note: These two volumes were originally published in one volume under the title *Secret Flotillas. The clandestine sea lines to France and French North Africa 1940-1944* (HMSO, London, 1996)
Secret Navies, The – A. Cecil Hampshire (William Kimber & Co Ltd, London, 1978)
Secret Sunday – Donald Darling (William Kimber & Co Ltd, London, 1975)
Secret War from the River Dart, The – Lloyd Bott, CBE, DSC (The Dartmouth History Research Group in association with the Dartmouth Museum, Dartmouth, 1997)
Shetland Bus, The – David Howarth (Thomas Nelson and Sons Ltd, London, 1951)
Shot Down and on the Run – Air Commodore Graham Pitchfork (The National Archives, Kew, 2003)
Silent Heroes – Sherri Greene Ottis (The University Press of Kentucky, Lexington, USA, 2001)
Six Faces of Courage – M.R.D. Foot (Eyre Methuen Ltd, London, 1978)
SOE in France – M.R.D. Foot (HMSO, London, 1966)
Special Forces in the Invasion of France – Paul Gaujac (Histoire & Collections, Paris, 1999)
*Squadron Leader Tommy Broom DFC**. The Legendary Pathfinder Mosquito Navigator* – Tom Parry Evans (Pen & Sword, Barnsley, 2007)
Sunday at Large – Donald Darling (William Kimber & Co Ltd, London, 1977)
Surrender on Demand – Varian Fry (Random House Inc, New York, 1945; Johnson Books, Boulder, USA, 1997)
Tartan Pimpernel, The – Donald C. Caskie (Oldbourne Book Co Ltd, London, 1957)
They Have Their Exits – Airey Neave (Hodder and Stoughton Ltd, London, 1953)
Those Who Dared. A Comprehensive List of World War II Allied Escapers – G.A. Brown FRSA (Battleline Books 1983)
Ticket to Freedom – H.J. Spiller (William Kimber & Co Ltd, Wellingborough, 1988)
Undercover Sailors – A. Cecil Hampshire (William Kimber & Co Ltd, London, 1981)
Underground from Posen – Michael Duncan (William Kimber & Co Ltd, London, 1954)
Under the St. Andrew's Cross: Russian & Cossack Volunteers in World War II 1941-1945 – Peter J. Huxley-Blythe (Europa Books Inc, New York, USA, 2004)
Une Mission Tres Secrète. Paul Henri de la Lindi – Hervé Gérard (Editions J.M. Collet, Brussels, no date)
Valiant Wings – Norman L.R. Franks (Crécy Books, Manchester, 1994; first published by William Kimber & Co Ltd, London, 1988)
Valley of the Shadow of Death. The Bomber Command Campaign March–July 1943 – J. Alwyn Phillips (Air Research Publications, New Malden, 1992)
War As I Knew It – George S. Patton, Jr. (Houghton Mifflin Company, Boston, USA, 1947)
Warriors – Max Hastings (HarperCollins Publishers, London, 2005)
Wavetops at My Wingtips – Flight Lieutenant Leslie Baveystock DSO, DFC*, DFM (Airlife Publishing Ltd, Shrewsbury, 2001)
Way Back, The. The Story of Lieutenant-Commander Pat O'Leary G.C., D.S.O., R.N. – Vincent Brome (Cassell and Co Ltd, London, 1957)
We Flew We Fell We Lived – Philip LaGrandeur (Vanwell Publishing Limited, St Catherines, Ontario, Canada, 2006)
We Landed by Moonlight. Secret RAF Landings in France 1940-1944 – Hugh Verity (Ian Allan Ltd, Shepperton, 1978; Revised 2nd Edition by Crécy Publishing Ltd, Manchester, 2000)
We Wanted Wings – John Pearl (Lancfile Publishing, Boston, 2007)
Where Bleed the Many – George Dunning, DCM (Elek Books Ltd, London, 1955)
White Rabbit, The – Bruce Marshall (Evans Brothers Limited, London, 1952)
Winged Diplomat. The Life Story of Air Commodore 'Freddie' West, V.C. – P.R. Reid (Chatto and Windus Ltd, London, 1962)
Winged Hours – Frank Griffiths (William Kimber & Co Ltd, London, 1981)
Wingless Victory – Anthony Richardson (Odhams Press Ltd, London, 1950)
Wings of Night. The Secret Missions of Group Captain Pickard, DSO and two bars, DFC – Alexander Hamilton (William Kimber & Co. Ltd, London 1977)
Within Two Cloaks – Philip Johns (William Kimber & Co Ltd, London, 1979)
Wolves at the Door, The: The True Story of America's Greatest Female Spy – Judith L. Pearson (The Lyons Press, Guilford, Connecticut, USA, 2005)
Women in the Resistance – Margaret L. Rossiter (Praeger Publishers, New York, USA, 1986)
YDX 207/14, Papers of M.O.A. Baudot de Rouville (held at the Cumbria Record Office and Local Studies Library [Whitehaven], no date)
Yesterday's Flight Path – Geoffrey Salisbury (The Book Guild, Lewes, 1988)
Xavier – Richard Heslop (Rupert Hart-Davies Ltd, London, 1970)

Index

Abbott, George M, 12, 34, 37
Abeille, Valentine, 147
Ablett, Sgt P.D., 228
"Achille", see Blanchain, Francis
Adams DCLI, Pte, 21
Adams, Pte Ebrehim, 278-80
Adams SAAF, Capt R.D., 107, 193-4
Adams, Sgt R.W., 163-4
Adams, Sgt T.H., 182-3, 185
Adons, Vicaire, 132
Affleck, P/O J., 219, 251
Aguiar USAAF, S/Sgt W., 233
Agur RCAF, F/O P.G., 284-5
Ainger, Sgt S.R.J., 91-2
Alain Divanac'h, see le Hénaff
Albinet, Cmdt, 28
Alderdice, Sgt J., 199, 200
Aldridge USAAF, Capt H., 268
Alexander, Sgt J. McK., 267, 270
Alianza Española Democratica, 59
Allen, Sgt E.A., 239
Allen, Jay, US journalist, 38
Allen USAAF, T/Sgt J., 234-5
Allen, P/O P.F., 105
Allen, F/S W.G., 218
Allen, Sgt W.H., 103
Allison, F/O J.C., 230-3
Alliston, F/O A.W., 267
Ancia, Albert, xii, 221, 273-4, 288-9, 296
Anderson, F/O D.W., 339-40
Angers RCAF, Sgt J.A.A.A.B., 128
Anne-Marie, (*convoyeuse*), 276, 280
Antwis, Sgt P., 330
Appert, Jean, 114
Aracama, Bernardo 115, 121, 123, 127
Arathoon, May and June, 102
Archibald RNZAF, F/O J., 328
Ardenois, Georges, 284
Arkwright, Maj A.S.B., 133
Armée Blanche, 264, 291
Armée Secrète Ardennes, 263
Armstrong, Sgt, 14
Armstrong USAAF, 2/Lt J.E., 177
Armstrong, Robert, 163
Arnold, Sgt G.G., 255
Arnould, Georges ("Albert le Pâtissier"), 288, 292-3
Arnould, Abbé, 291-2
Arp USAAF, 1/Lt Elwood D., 154, *454*
Arseneaut RCAF, W/O J.D.H., 231
Arundel, Sgt D.R., 300-1
Ar-Voualc'h, 175, 180
Ashton, P/O J.F., 120
Asker, Sgt H.A., 10-11
Astley, Pte C., 160
Aston, Sgt W.H., 51, 52
Athen, 344-5
Atkins, Vera, 88
Attwood, Sgt G., 246
Aubert, Henri, 182
Aubrac, Raymond, 251
Auda USAAF, Lt R.F., 318
Augustus USAAF, S/Sgt Robert C., 258-9
Autphene, Mme. Germaine, 264
Avery, Sgt J.V., 219
Avons, Marguérite, 219-20
Avons, Serge, 220-2
Axford, Sgt J.L., 135
Ayers, F/Sgt J., 343-4
Aylé, Robert, xii, 124, 132, 163, 200-1

Babcock USAAF, 2/Lt F., 317-8
Bach, Jean, 162
Backhouse, Sgt E., 329
Badoglio, Marshal Pietro, xxxi, *437*
Bailey USAAF, 2/Lt H., 141-2
Baillergeon, Marcel, 75
Baird, F/L R.B., 335
Bajpai, Germaine, xii, 230-1
Bakalarski PAF, Sgt P., 140-2
Baker, Sgt G., 231-4
Baker, Capt P., 286
Bakewell, Sgt L., 150
Balcon, Jean-Marie, 183
Balfe, Joe, 233
Balfour, Sgt A., 310
Ball, William R., 24-5
Ballinger USAAF, 1/Lt Olof M., 141
Bangos USAAF, 2/Lt, 268
Banks RCAF, Sgt R.H., 274, 289
Banner, Sgt W.T., 157-8
Barber, Sgt W.J., 184
Barbie, Klaus, 88, 139
Barbier, Elizabeth, xii, 163, 165
Barbrooke, Cpl D.J., 1
Barckley, F/O R.E., 233
Barclay, Sgt P.P., 306-7
Barclay, F/L R.G.A., 51, 77-8
Bardoux, Mme, 204
Barker, Sgt F.A., 91-2
Barker, F/L B.D., 163-4
Barlow USAAF, T/Sgt A.R., 144-5
Barlow, Sgt R., 246-8
Barnard, S/L D.B., 107-11
Barnes, P/O L.A., 288-9
Barnes, P/O R.J., *451*
Barnett RNZAF, F/L M.G., 101, 105
Barnlund RCAF, F/O R.E., 171
Barr, F/L L.R., 130
Barr USAAF, Flt/O S.K., 282
Barra, Cmdt, 252
Barratt, AM A.S., xxix, 436
Barré de St Venant, Pauline ("Marie Odile", "Mme Laroche"), 139-40, 143-4, 147-8
Barrett, F/L F.O., 10, 14
Barrett RNZAF, F/L R., 326
Barry RCAF, F/S J.N., 163-4, 177-9
Barton, Sgt A.E.J., 289-93
Baseden, Yvonne, 147-8
Baskette USAAF, 2/Lt Theodore R., 308-9, *469*
Bathgate RNZAF, F/O J.R.G., 167, 175, 240
Batho, L/Sgt W.H., 46, 48, 55, *442*
Batory (ship), 66, 118
Batterbury, P/O F.W., 336
Baudot de Rouville, Maud Olga Andrée, xii, 4-5, 67, 81, 192-4, 198, 201, 203-5, *455*
Baumgarten, Gert 325
Bauset, F/O P, 306-7
Baveystock, Sgt L.H., 123-4

Bayard, Madeleine "Barclay", 12, 42
Bazalgette, P/O F.S., 3
Beale, F/L D., 265
Beattie RCAF, F/O R.L., 256
Beaujolin, Gilbert, 152
Becker, Joseph, 181-2, 430-2
Beckett, Sgt L.A., 18
Beckwith, Sgt D.S., 258-60
Beecroft, Sgt J., 97-9
Bégué, Georges, 75
Beigbeder y Atienza, Col Juan, 46
Beleir, Lt Gilbert, 265
Belitta, Mme., 230
Bell, Mr, 152
Bell, F/O E.I.J., 59-60
Bell RCAF, P/O E.N., 240, 256
Bell, L/Sgt J.K., 21, 34, 38
Bell RCAF, Sgt P., 311
Bell, Sgt P.H., 77
Bell, Cpl W.A., 21
Bell, F/Sgt W.H., 339-40
Belva, Emile, 210
Bender RCAF, F/O W.F., 280, 284
Benjamin, P/O, 14
Benjoin, 242
Bennett, S/L D.E., 60
Bennett, P/O G., 59
Bennett, Ursula Lloyd, 10
Benting, P/O A.W., 321
Bernadotte, Count Folke, 327
Berry, Sgt H., 9
Berry, F/L L.F. "Peter", 274-9, 282, 284, 286-7
Berthet, Guy, 75-6, 197
Besley, Capt C.R.I., 11-13, 40, 52-3
Best, Sgt A., 266
Bettley, Cpl Enoch, 112, 115, *450*
Beure, Raymonde, 214-5
Bezault, Lucien, 274, 281
Biddle, F/O G.A., 332-3
Bienfait, Yvonne, 288, 294
Biggs USAAF, 1/Lt Robert E., 178
Binns, Lt Wallace, 220
Bird, L/Bdr A.E., 6-7
Birk RAAF, Sgt H.E., 80, 82, 84, 118-20
Bisher USAAF, 1/Lt H.E., 266
Bitner, 42-3
Blackwell, F/O S.J.P., 168
Blair, Lt C., 82-4
Blakely USAAF, S/Sgt C.W., 144
Blanc, Charles Clément 219-22
Blanc, Mme Laurence, 219-22
Blanchain, Francis, xii, 75, 85, 88, 91, 97, 105, 126
Blanchard, Sgt L.S., 209
Blanchebarbe, Abbé, 139, 144
Blaydon, Sgt R.W., 19-22
Blaylock USAAF, Lt, 144
Bleicher, Sgt Hugo, xvii
Blenkinsop RCAF, S/L E.W., 317
Bleu et Jonquille, 157
Bloch, Denise (SOE), 148, *454*
Bloch, Gaby, 75
Bloch, Pierre, 75
Bloch-Auroch, Capt, 252
Blondeel, Alfred "Pointer", 176-7
Bloom, Lt Marcus, 204-5
Blott, F/L W., 257
Blount, AVM C.H.B., xxix, *436*
Blücher, xxix
Blythe USAAF, Maj Leon W., 144
Board, Sgt L.E., 271
Bodineau, Roger, 202, 299-300
Bodnar, Sgt John P. (US Marines), 257
Bodson, Nestor, 112
Body RCAF, F/O R., 304
Boggan USAAF, 2/Lt, 286-7
Bohn, Dr Frank, 25
Bold, Sgt P.F., 59
Bollaert, Emile, 176-7
Boness, Sgt L.F., 308
Boon, F/Sgt P.C., 327
Boorer, W/O W.G., 344-5
Boorn Brothers, The – see Newton, Alfred/Henry
Bordeaux, 142, 174, 183, 185
Bordeaux line, 177
Bordeaux-Loupiac *réseau*, 183
Boreham SAS, Pct R., 311
Borgholm, 233
Borrel, Andrée, 203
Bossick, F/Sgt H., 267-8
Bougaiev, Ivan, 166, 169-70
Bougier, Jean ("Jeannot"), 185-6, *457*
Boulain, Pierre, see Desoubrie, Jean-Jacques
Boulanger, Renée, 114
Bourgogne, 174, 202, 266
Bourgoin, Cmdt Pierre, 252, 271-2
Bouryschkine, Vladimir "Val Williams", xii, 101, 161-6, 169
Boussa, S/L Lucien "Daniel Mouton", xiii, 274, 277-9, 282, 285-6, 288
Bouteloupt, Madeleine, xiii, 223
Bowen-Morris, F/O U.B., 323
Bowlby RCAF, F/S A.T., 231-2
Bowman USAAF, Sgt C.S., 295
Boyd, AM O.T., 237
Boyd RAAF, F/O D.L., 341
Bradford, Capt B.C., 28
Bradley, F/S D.R., 218
Bradley, Sgt S., 98
Brailsford, F/O R.F., 288
Brakes, F/S B.E., 284
Brandy, 151, 174, 202
Bratley, Sgt H.W., 19-21
Brayley RCAF, W/O II W.E.J., 274-7, 279
Brearley, Sgt E.W., 241-3
Bréaux, Lt Gérard, 259
Brégi, Jean, 76
Brégi, Philippe, 205
Breizh-Izel, 177, 185
Brennan RCAF, F/O H.J., 173
Bresmal, Jacques, 294
Brett, W/O P., 344-5
Brettel, F/L E.G., 108
Breuer USAAF, 2/Lt Charles, 213, *460*
Briarwood, 61
Brice, Stefan, 163
Brickwood, F/O G.C., 171
Bridge, RCAF, Sgt E.A., 231-2
Bridger, P/O J., 136
Bridier, Henri, 206
Brierley, Loyal Regt, 228
Brifaut, Lt Pierre, 199
Brigade Blanche, 231
Brigman Jnr USAAF, 2/Lt Campbell, 153-4, *454*
Brinn, F/L W.G., 229-30

British Seamen's Institute, 116, 118
Broad, 2/Lt R.L., 22, 36-9
Broadley, F/O J., 239
Bromwell, LAC A.V., 108-10
Bronner USAAF, 2/Lt, 182
Brookes, Sgt J., 1
Brooks, Anthony, 41, *441*
Brooks USAAF, S/Sgt H.C., 266
Broom, W/O T.J., 190
Brophy RCAF, F/O G.P., 304
Brossolette, Pierre, 176-7
Brough, Sgt J.F.Q., 251
Broussine, Georges ("Burgundy", "Jean Pierre"), xiii, 165-7, 174, 177, 202
Brown, Sgt D., 170
Brown RCAF, F/O E., 329
Brown, Sgt. F.W., 294
Brown USAAF, S/Sgt L., 165
Brown, F/Sgt L.J.S., 265-6
Brown, Sgt R., 106, 218-9
Brown, Sgt R.C., 315-6
Brown RCAF, F/L R.G., 301-4
Brown, Sgt W., 285, 287
Browne RNZAF, Sgt P.S.F., 102
Brownhill, Sgt G., 218
Browning USAAF, T/Sgt H.M., 213, *460*
Bruce, Sgt J., 159
Bruce USAAF, 2/Lt Ralph, 219, 222
Brugère, Nicole, 97
Brun, Louis, 220-22
Brusselmans, Anne, xiii, 117, 120, 208, 231, 317
Bruycker-Roberts, Anne-Marie, 112, 122, *449*
Bruzewski USAAF, T/Sgt Otto F., 221
Bryant, Sgt F.T.J., 60-1
Buchan, Sgt W., 297
Buchanan RAAF, F/Sgt J.E.G., 242
Buchowski, Lt Jan, 96
Budzynski PAF, Sgt Janek, 78, 80, 119
Bufton, S/L H.E., 77-8, *445*
Bugg, F/O, Embarkation Officer, 297
Buinicky USAAF, S/Sgt Alfred R., 159, *455*
Buise USAAF, Sgt John F., 232
Bulman RCAF, F/S E.L., 163-4
Bulmer, F/Sgt S.T., 306
Burch USAAF, 2/Lt J.F., 221, *436*
Bureau, Roger, 153-4
Burgess USAAF, Capt M.K., 267, *465*
Burgundy (line), see Broussine, Georges, and 149, 206, 220-1, 266, 273, 306
Burgwal family, 225-6
Burney, Lt Christopher, 49
Burrell, Sgt H.J.E., 118
Burridge, Sgt J., 34
Burrows, Sgt D.E., 209
Butterfield, S/L W.R., 228-9
Buttke USAAF, Capt Robert L., 283

Cadge, Sgt D.E., 249
Café Baroux, 114
Café du Brabant, 114
Café du Soleil, 97
Calderwood, F/O W., 309-10
Camard, M., 162-3
Camard, Jean, 162
Cameron, F/L D., Asst Air Attaché, 61
Cammaerts, Francis, 257
Camors, Jean-Claude, xiii, 174, 182-5
Camp de Chambaran, 76, 89, 95, 103, 110
Campbell USAAF, Sgt Alfred M., 266, 268
Campbell RCAF, F/L E.A., 283
Campbell, Sgt G., 65
Campbell USAAF, S/Sgt Herbert A., 242, *463*
Campinchi, Paul, 160, 162, 166-9
Campinchi, Thérèse, 160
Canaris, Admiral Wilhelm, xxvi, 45
Cancellucia, Contessa, 96
Canet-Plage, 42-3, 71, 94-5, 103-6, 198, 205
Canning, Sgt L.W., 255
Cant, W/O R.G., 179
Canter, Sgt H.J.B., 137, 193-4
Cap Arcona, 344-5
Carah USAAF, 2/Lt John M., 219, 222
Cardigan, Earl of, 53-4
Cardozo, Maj Frederick, 242
Carey, P/O J.C.L., 322
Cariou, Abbé, 179
Carleton, Sgt J.D.H., 177
Carnell, Cpl B., 29, 32
Carpentier, Abbé Pierre, xiii, 30, 69-73, 77-81
Carr, F/S L.W., 122-3
Carr, Lt Brian, 336
Carrière, Capt, 259
Carroll, P/O H.B., 80, 118-20
Carson USAAF, Sgt Kenneth, 154
Cartelet, Louis, 221-2
Carter RCAF, F/O G.H.F., 177-9
Cartwright, Col Henry, 138, 237
Cary-Elwes SAS, Maj O., 173
Casey RCAF, F/O G.A., 11
Casey USAAF, 2/Lt Shirley V., 145
Caskie, Rev. Donald Currie, xiii, 12-3, 15, 23-4, 31, 33, 37, 40-1, 48, 66, 68, 101, 103, 134
Castillo de San Fernando prison, 17, 46
Cato, 234
Cattrell, Pte A., 28, 32
Cautley, Miss, 36, 56
Cavanaugh USAAF, Capt A.T., 266
CEGES-SOMA, xxvi, *436*
Cellarier, Mme, 163-4
Cellerie, Mme, 166
Ceux De La Libération, 158
Chait, Salomon (Edmund), 154-6
Chamberlain, P/O H., 283, 309
Chamberlain, Prime Minister Neville, xxix
Champ USAAF, Flt/O Frank A., 266
Channer, Sgt R.W., 66
Chappell RAMC, Maj, 4
Charlet, Blanche, 172
Charman, Sgt A.F., 238
Charneau, Andrée, 164-6
Chaster RCAF, F/S J.B., 208
Chauny Escape Line, 148
Chaveau, Dr, 274, 282
Checketts RNZAF, S/L J.M., 181-3, 245
Cheramy, Maud Eleanor, xiii, 100, 201
Chester-Master RAAF, F/S R.C., 319
Chichester USAAF, 2/Lt Stanley R., 213, *460*
Chisholm RAAF, Sgt K.B., 163
Chouquette, see Lebreton
Christensen, Sgt J.R.W., 105
Christie, P/O Brock, 336
Christie, F/L W.T., 195
Christol, Olga, 270, 306, *469*
Church USAAF, 2/Lt Milton L., 169

Churchill, Prime Minister Winston, xxx, 1, 45, 326
Citronelle mission, 259
Clapham, Gnr John H., 77
Clark RNR, Lt-Cdr E.B., 94, 99
Clark USAAF, S/Sgt P.M., 258, 260, *464*
Clarke, Sgt H.N., 214
Clarke, Sgt R.,230
Clay, F/S L.N., 282
Clayton, Sgt H.K., 27-8, 35-6, 38
Clement RCAF, F/O J., 299-300
Clifford, AC2 R., xxviii, 3-4, 6
Clifton, F/Sgt B., 63
Clonts Jr USAAF, 1/Lt C.R., 268
Coache, Raymonde, xiv, 132
Coache, René Gustave, xiv, 127-9
Cobb, Sgt I.A., 102
Cochran USAAF, 2/Lt, James M., 294
Coen, P/O O.H., 77-8
Cogneau, Daniel, 280-1
Cohen RN, Cdr Kenneth, 160
Coke, Maj John, 323
Cole, Harold, xiv, 4, 12, 32, 67-72, 74, 77, 80-1, 100, 172, 266
Colhoun, Sgt H., 219
Collie RASC, Capt G.F., 51
Collins RAAF, Sgt R.J., 94, 127
Collins, Sgl W., 74
Columbus RCAF, W/O G.P., 241-2
Combe, Brig J., 237
Comet, Comète, 57, *passim*
Conroy RCAF, F/Sgt R.F., 228
Contopodis USAAF, 2/Lt Homer, 149, 151, *454*
Conville, Pte R., 112, 116-8
Conway, Marine J., 433
Cook, F/S P., 329-30
Cook, Q/Sgt W., 195-6
Cooke, S/L T.C.S., 256
Coombe-Tennant, Capt A.H.S., 133, *452*
Cooper, Capt A.R. 103, 110
Cooper, F/O M.H.F., 142-3, 145-6, *453*
Cope, Sgt J.E., 190-1
Copley, F/Sgt R.A., 119
Corbet RCAF, F/Sgt C.M., 283
Corby RCAF, F/Sgt R.C., 258-60
Cornelius, Sgt R.W., 159, 233-5
Cornelius, A/S W., 234
Cornett USAAF, 2/Lt Jack D., 288-9
Costello-Bowen, F/L E.A., 190
Courtenay, P/O D.H., 267-8
Cowan, Sgt A.G., 112, 116-8
Cox USAAF, T/Sgt A.B., 184, 197-8
Cox RCAF, Sgt D.M., 163-4
Cox, Sgt G.T., 80, 118-20
Cox, LAC, 2
Cozzens USAAF, Lt Wallis O., 318
Crabtree, Sgt D.B., 18, 72-3
Craig RASC, Dvr Albert, 160
Crampton, Sgt W.F., 77-8, *445*
Craven, F/O Jack, 335
Crawshay, Capt W.R. ("Crown"), 308
Cregger USAAF, S/Sgt Charles W., 170, *456*
Creswell, Michael Justin, xiv, 33, 50, 81, 121, 164, 205, 273, 283
Crichton, Sgt A., 98
Crilly, Sgt A.C., 269
Crockatt, Norman Richard, xiv, 23, 75, 97
Cromar, Pte Jim, 57, 114
Crome, Sgt D.A., 239-40
Croquet, P/O J.L.J., 277, 282, 286, *466*
Cross, Sgt W., 251
Crowe, Sgt F.C., 63
Crowley-Milling, F/L D., 69-72
Crowther RCAF, F/O G.C., 218
Csete, Bdr W., 34
Cufley, Sgt N.B., 168-9
Cunliffe, F/O F., 254-5
Cunningham RCAF, F/O W., 315-6
Curaçao, 174
Curator/Acolyte circuit, 225
Curran SAS, Cpl, 311
Cybulski, Maurice, 19
Czarnecki PAF, Sgt L., 90
Czekalski PAF, Sgt W., 90, 94, 125-7

d'Albert-Lake, Philippe, xiv, 276-7, 279-80, 283, 285, 289
d'Albert-Lake, Virginia, xiv, 276, 280
d'Allendre, M., 163
d'Andleau, Charles A., 200
d'Harcourt, Pierre, xvi, xxvi, 36-8, 105
d'Oultremont, Count Edouard, xvii, 121
d'Oultremont, Count Georges, xvii, 121, 129, 167, 213-4
d'Oultremont, Comtesse Paul, 288
d'Ursel, Count Antoine, xviii, 221
Dahlia, 175
Daily Telegraph, *The*, 333, *438*
Daladier, Édouard, 97, *448*
Dalc'h-Mad, 179
Daley RE, Capt G.F.K., 97
Dalinsky USAAF, Sgt J.J., 175, *456*
Dalphond RCAF, Sgt M.H.J., 83, 101-2
Daman, Hortense, xiv
Damerment, Madeleine, 71, 77, 80
Daniel RAAF, P/O R.W., 171
Dansey, Claude Edward Marjoribanks, xiv, 81, 116, 169
Darke RAMC, Capt Geoffrey, 68
Darling, Donald, xiv, 23-4, 26-7, 55, 59, 81, 94, 106, 113, 115-6, 162, 164, 219, 286, 345
Darnand, Joseph, xiv, 156
Dassié, Jean, 208
Daugherty USAAF, S/Sgt Ned A., 267, *465*
Davenport RCAF, F/L R.M., 154
Davidson RAAF, F/Sgt N.M., 328
Davies, F/O A.G., 336
Davies, Sgt H.D., 308
Davies, Sgt M.A.T., 217-8
Davis, Sgt J., 1
Davreux, Béatrice, 294
Davy, Marie-Madeleine, 306
Dawson, Sgt J.G., 138, 192-3, 197
Dawson, F/Sgt Ron, 290, 296
Dax, W/O E.A., 342-4
Day RCAF, Sgt A.D., 118-21
Day, F/Sgt R.S., 342-4
De Beer, F/O A.G., 329
de Bizien, Christine, 149, 209
De Bliqui, Henri, 113, *449*
de Blommaert de Soye, Baron Jean, xv, 214, 273-4, 276-7, 279, 282-3, 286, 288
de Bollardière, Cmdt J.P., 259-60
de Breyne RCAF, F/O A., 304
de Ceret, Lt J., 25
De Colvenaer, Albert, 265

de Cortes, Fabien, 75-6, 204-5
de Courcy, Vicomte, 37
de Gaulle, General Charles, xxxi
De Grasse, 29
De Greef, Elvire, xv, 114-6, 125, 128, 201, 207-8, 273-4
De Greef, Fernand, xv, 114-5
De Greef, Freddy, xv, 114
De Greef, Jeanine, xv, 114, 118, 125, 132, 190, 235
de Guélis, Jacques, 88, *446*
de Jong family, 226-7
de Jongh, Andrée "Dédée", xv, 90, 112-6, 118-25, 127-9, 132-3, 190, 206-08, 223
de Jongh, Frédéric "Paul", "Kiki", 90, 113, 115-7, 120-1, 125-9, 133, 149, 151, 163, 207, 209, 218
de Kegal, M., 223
de la Lindi, Maj Paul H., 120, *450*
de la Marnierre, Mme., 185-6
De la Olla, Jean, xv, 81, 201, 204
de Lange USAAF, Sgt, 335-6
de Lestang-Parade, Hugues, 202
de Ligne, Elisabeth Marie, xv
de Mauduit, Comtesse Betty, 162-3, *455*
de Menten de Horne, xv, 129, 208
de Merode, F/O Prince W.P.M.G., 138, 192-3, 197
de Milleville, Barbé, xvi, 134
de Milleville, Comtesse Mary, xv, 134-5, 137-8, 140, 145, 147-8, 192
de Milleville, Maurice, xvi, 134-40, 143, 145, 147
de Milleville, Octave, xvi, 134, 136
De Mone RCAF, Sgt H.E., 124
DePape RCAF, Sgt R.A.G., 159, 234-5
de Poulpiquet, Comtesse Geneviève, 82, 178, *455*
de Suzannet, la Comtesse Hélène, 162-3
De Veuster, Claire, 288, 294
de Vomécourt, Philippe A.C., 75, 82
de Wiart VC, Maj-Gen A. Carton, 237
Dean, Arthur S., 5, 11-12, 28, 37, 39-40, *438*, *440*
Deane-Drummond, Lt A., 97-8
Death, F/O G.F., 332
Debreuille, Amélie, 135
Debreuille, Armand, 135, 137-9
Dechaumont, Maurice, 80
Deihl USAAF, T/Sgt D.D., 318
Dellow RNVR, L/S A.H., 173
Deloge, Mme Marceline, 112, *449*
Delpy, Emile (guide),141
Deman, Erwin ("Paul Dent"), 172
Denivelle, Gaston, 136-7, 139
Denivelle, Renée, 136-7
Dennis, L/Sgt, 98
Dennison RCAF, P/O B.C., 163-4
Depesme, Claude P., 184
Depourque, Mme Jeanne, 112, 120
Deppé, Arnold Louis Camil, xvi, 112-5
Deprez, Lt R. ("Lucullus"), 265
Dereniuk RCAF, P/O H., 239
Déricourt, Henri, 99-100, 225
Deronne, Insp Jo, 136
Desforges, René, 280
Desoubrie, Jean-Jacques, xvi, 103, 165, 210, 273-4, 288, 310
Despretz, François, xvi, 74, 77, 80
Desrochers USAAF, T/Sgt John M., 213, *460*
Deutschland, 344-5
Devers USAAF, T/Sgt S., 208, *459*
Devigne, Kay, 305-6
Devin, Josette, 165-6
Devin, Marceau, 258-60
Dewavrin, Col ("Passy"), 162
Dezitter, Prospère Valère, xvi, 113, 159, 208-10, 273, 318
Dibetta USAAF, 1/Lt Geno, 279, *466*
Dickson RCAF, Sgt A.F., 119
Dickson, F/Sgt G., 179
Dickson RCAF, Sgt R.J., 173
Dilling USAAF, Capt D.K., 144
Dillon, P/O C.T., 342
Dimes, L/Bdr E.W., 77
Dimitru, Boris (moneylender), 39
Dings, Flore, xvi, 122
Disbrow USAAF, 2/Lt Robert C., 266
Dissard, Marie-Louise ("Françoise"), xvii, 76, 85, 147, 198, 201, 203-6, 266, 269
Dmytruk RCAF, Sgt P., 240
Dodds, Maj J.H.H., 11-13, 24-5, 37, 40, 41, *438*, *440*, *441*
Donaldson RAAF, W/C D.R., 307-8
Donaldson, Sgt W.A., 283
Donmall, P/O N.E., 336-7
Donny, Baron Jacques, xvii, 112-3, 120
Doolan RAAF, F/L G.McG., 275, *466*
Doorly, F/O E.,108-10
Dorchy, P.H. (vice-consul), 21, 30, 51-2, 76, 78, 110, 194
Dothie, 2/Lt W.H., 8
Douglas, L/Cpl E., 93-4
Douglas, Sgt R.C.A., 191
Dowding, Cpl K. Bruce, xvii, 40, 48, 68, 72, 77, 80-1, 105
Dowty, Sgt B.A., 102
Drechsler RCAF, F/Sgt W.W., 199
Drew USAAF, Lt Lionel E., 182, 185
Drew mission, 116
Dromas, Etienne, xvii, 148-9, 152, 168, 192, *454*
Drummond-Wolff, Col (military attaché), 39
Dubé RCAF, P/O H.E., 266
Dubois, Drotais, 80
Dubreuil, Guy, 178
Duchêne, Mme Ann, 112, 116
Duchesnay RCAF, F/O A.A.H.J.N.A., 269
Duff, Lt A.G., 54
Duffee, Sgt G.W.H., 231-2
Duffy SAS, Cpl Bill, 311
Dufour, Maurice, 74
Dufournier, Denise, xvii
Dumais, Lucien A., xvii, 106-7, 167-74, 214
Dumon, Aline Lili ("Michou", "Micheline", "Lili du Chaila"), xviii, 159, 234, 273, 276
Dumon, Andrée ("Nadine"), xvii, 115, 121, 124-5, 128, 159, 206, 234, 273, 276, 288
Dumon, Eugène, xvii
Dumon, Françoise, xvii, 288
Dumont, Pierre, 184
Duncan, Lt M.G., 82-5
Dunderdale RN, Cdr W.H., 160
Dungey RCAF, Sgt E.B., 231-2
Dunkley SAS, Serj F.W., 311
Dupuy, Pierre, Canadian *chargé d'affaires*, 37
Durant, Sgt E., 184
Durland, Sgt E.G., 319
Durski, Lt-Cdr (Free Polish Navy), 96
Dutch-Paris line, 152 *et seq.*
Dutour, Capitaine, 74

Duval, P/O H.P., 18, 72-3

Easton, Sgt G.H., 17-18, 21
Eccles, F/L G.B., 330
Eden, Anthony (Secretary of State), 24, 50-1, 54-5, 57
Edgar RSC, Sgl T., 68
Edman USAAF, Sgt Bruno, 276
Edwards, Pte D.R., 93, *447*
Edwards, F/L J.K.O., 333-4, 346
Edwards, W/O K.F., 131
Edwards, F/L R.S.J., 2
Eidsheim, Skipper Ingvald, 332
Eisenhower, Gen Dwight D., 319-20, 338
Elder RCAF, Sgt A., 173
Eliot RAAF, F/O N.S., 284
Elkin USAAF, Sgt, 153-4
Elkins RN, Cdr R.F., 8
Ella, 345
Elliott RCAF, F/O W.J., 316-7
Elsliger RCAF, Sgt J.H., 317, *470*
Embling, W/C J.R.A., 148, 191-4, 198
Embry, W/C B.E., 6-7, 134
Emden, xxix
Emeny, Sgt R.T., 288-9
Erasquin, Martin (guide), 221
Ernest, Odette, 155-6
Escrenier, Alphonse, xviii
Evans, Sgt A.R., 100
Evans, F/Sgt B., 128
Evans, Sgt P.J., 270
Evans, F/Sgt J.H., 271, 290-1, 294-5
Evendon, Pte G., 72
Everiss, P/O S.F., 149, 151-2
Eyre, Sgt S.H., 219
Ezra, Sgt W.A., 313

Fairfax, F/O N.T., 230, 232
Falconer, M.D.M. (vice-consul), 61
Falcon-Scott RAAF, Sgt C., 18
Falkingham, F/S O., 195
FanFan, Fan-Fan, see Hénaff, Yves le
Fantini, Sgt L.C., 191
Fargher, F/S T.P., 173-4
Farmer, F/Sgt H.J., 342
Farmer, Sgt W.W., 258-61, 310
Farnsworth, Dvr L., 15
Farquhar MC, H.L. (consul-general), 45, 55-7, 81, 136
Farrell, Victor, xviii, 48, 82, 84, 98, 138, 144, 147, 205, 219
Faure, Henri, 250-1
Favbre, Ginette, 139-40, 142, 147-8
Fay RCAF, F/Sgt A., 90, 190
Fearman, Sgt G.C., 242
Feary, Sgt K.J., 329
Feld USAAF, Maj Nathan, 312
Felippe, Pierre (guide), 154
Fell RCAF, Sgt W.E., 157
Fenwick SAS, Maj I., 311
Ferguson, Sgt D., 209-10, 224
Fergusson, (French sailor), 43, *442*
Ferière, Jean, 81, 94-5
Féron, Baron Henri, 248
Ferrani USAAF, 2/Lt, 153-4
Ferrusola, Joseph (guide), 220, 222
Fiat Libertas, 159
Fidler, Sgt R., 175, 177
Figueras, 5, *passim*
Fillerin, Gabriel, 68
Fillerin, Geneviève, xviii, 68, 107
Fillerin, Marguerite, xviii, 68
Fillerin, Norbert, xviii, 68, 74, 77, 107, 201-2, 233
Finney USAAF, Sgt Robert, 154
Fiocca, Henri, xviii, 31, 39, 40
Fiocca, Nancy, xviii, 31, 33, 38, 40, 75, 192, 197-8, 203-4
Firestone, F/Sgt E.H., 331
Firth, Sgt J.W., 269
Fisher RCAF, F/O A.R., 157
Fisher, Sgt C.E.F., *471*
Fisher USAAF, 1/Lt D.A., 177
Fisher RCAF, F/L G.C., 191
Fisher, P/O H.H.J., 267-8
Fisher, F/S J.E., 285, *467*
Fitch, Capt F., 24-5, 28, 31
Fitzgerald RAAF, F/O A., 246
Fitzgerald RNZAF, Sgt W.J., 149
Flack RASC, Dvr E., 51-2
Flynn RAAF, F/S W.J., 284
Foley USAAF, 2/Lt William M., 206
Fonteneau, Madame and Pierre, 252-3
Foot SAS, Capt M.R.D., 330-1
Ford RNVR, Lt Basil, 94
Ford, Sgt J.B., 149, 151-2, 154
Forde, F/O D.N., 68-9
Forland RCAF, F/Sgt O.W., 164
Forman RCAF, F/L J.M., 239-40
Forster, L/Cpl H.L., 39
Forster, Sgt R., 107-10
Forster, Sgt T.W., 257
Forster RCAF, F/L W., 268
Forsyth RCAF, Sgt J.H., xxv
Fort de la Duchère, 95, 103
Fort de la Revère, 67, 83, 89, 95, 101-5, 119
Fort St Jean, 12, 15-6, 18, 21, 24-5, 28-32, 36, 40, 44, 53
Foster, F/L, 266
Foster, Sgt G.F., 104
Foster, Sgt H.J., 103
Foster USAAF, 2/Lt Kenneth E., 338
Fouquerel, Aimable, xviii, 124, 218
Frame RCAF, F/O L.W.A., 304, 306-7
Franc, Philippe (*convoyeur*), 197-8
Francis USAAF, Maj Roderick L., 266
Francis, Jedburgh team, 303
Franco, Generalissimo Francisco, 45-6, 55
"Franco", see Nothomb, Jean-François
Frankowski PAF, Sgt T.J., 129-30
Frans Hals, see Kragt, Dick
Fraser, Pte A.C., 70, 72
Fraser, Sgt H., 120, *450*
Fraser, Sgt S.J., 17-18, 21, *439*
Fraysse, Jean (*Paris Mondiale*), 305
Frazer USAAF, S/Sgt Lloyd E., 159, *455*
Freberg RCAF, P/O P.G., 130-1
Frederick, Jedburgh team, 173, 252
Freeman USAAF, 2/Lt Harold, 256
Freeman RCAF, F/O W.J., *455*
Frenay, Henri, xxxii
Frerlet, Paul, 212, *460*
Friday RCAF, Sgt J.W., 304
Friend, Tony, 101, 107, *448*
Frost, Sgt R., 130-1
Fry, Varian Mackey, 23-6, 31, *439*
Frydryk family, 231

Fryer, Gnr H., 71
Fryer RCAF, Sgt L.R., 255
Fuller, Capt H.J., 133
Fuller, F/Sgt F., 336, 343-4
Fullerton, Hugh (US consul-general), 15, 40
Furniss-Roe, F/O H., 144-5
Fusinski PAF, P/O J., 89-91, 94

G.G. Grévy, 105, *448*
Gaisford, Sgt R.G., 149
Gallet, Raymond, 211, 214
Gardiner, Sgt E.F., 211-3
Gardner, Cpl W.F., 67, 71-2, 226
Garel, Francis, 75
Garnett, John (Royal Navy), 186
Garrow, Captain I.G., xviii, 28, 30-2, 34, 37-8, 40-1, 43-4, 54-5, 59, 66-8, 71-2, 74-7, 81, 105, 201
Gasior, (Polish doctor), 71-2
Gaze, F/L F.A.O., 238
Geelen, Pierre "Grand Pierre", 210, 213-4
Genistat FAF, Cdt Marcel, 19-20
Georges, Madame, 167-8
Gerard, René, 184, 253, 289-90
Gibbs, S/L E.P.P., 65, 69, *444*
Gicquel, Jean, 168, 173-4
Gilbert, Capt C.H., 91, 93-4
Giles USAAF, T/Sgt Robert C., 302-3, 305, *469*
Gill, Sgt F.D., 257-8
Gillet, Abbé Pierre, 158
Gimbel RCAF, P/O E.L., 149
Giroulle, A. ("Troilus"), 265
Gise USAAF, 2/Lt William J., 76, 107, 445
Giskes, Maj Herman, 158
Gladys USAAF, Hank, 291
Glass, Insp Georges, 231
Glassman USAAF, 2/Lt Carl I., 258-9
Glaze USAAF, 1/Lt Ivan E., 266
Gleason USAAF, Sgt F., 285
Glensor RNZAF, P/O R.E., 107, 110-1
Goddard, Sgt A., 313
Goddard, Sgt R.G., 149, 151-2, *454*
Godfrey RCAF, WO II S.E., 265
Goggin, F/O J.A., 335
Goïcoechea, Florentino, xviii, 118-21, 123, 125, 127-9, 132-3, 190, 201, 218, 221, 223, 232-3, 235
Goiunlock RCAF, F/O J., 320-1
Goldie, Pte J.M.L., 127, 129
Golding, Sgt J., 66
Goldingay, Sgt L.D., 19-22
Goldsmith, Sgt B.F., 94, 127
Goldstein USAAF, 2/Lt Coleman, 145
Good RCAF, P/O R.E., 283
Goodman, F/L G.M., 254-5
Gordon, F/O D., 329-30
Gordon USAAF, S/Sgt Lee C., 176
Gordon, F/O R.B., 280, 284
Gordon-Stables, Capt B., 297
Gorrano USAAF, T/Sgt Joseph I., 277
Gort VC, General Viscount, xxix, *436*
Gosling, Walter (civilian), 107, 110
Goss RE, Capt, 330
Graham MiD, F/O C.E.M., 321
Graham RCAF, P/O G.T., 238
Graham, P/O K., 331
Granat, Pte J., 322
Grandy, W/O G.E., 331
Grauerholtz USAAF, 2/Lt Larry E., 206, *459*
Gray, S/L R.W.H., 270
Gray, Sgt W.J., 330
Greaves, Sgt W.G.J., 207, *459*
Green, F/Sgt P.C.N., 311-2
Greenaway RNZAF, F/O F.H., 255
Greenburgh RCAF, F/O L., 282
Greene USAAF, Sgt Frank, 163, 165, *455*
Greene RCAF, Sgt W.A., 267
Greenheart circuit, 49
Greenwell, F/S F.A., 206, 266
Greig, Pte Duncan, 112-3, 116, 118
Greindl, Baron Albert, xviii, 208
Greindl, Baron Jean ("Nemo"), xix, 116, 121, 133, 206-8
Greville-Bell DSO, SAS, Capt A., 286-7
Grew, F/O W.T., 321
Griesel USAAF, Ken, 291
Griffin, P/O C.G., 265
Griffin, Sgt R.E., 61
Griffith, Sgt R.E., 168-9
Griffiths, S/L F.C., 205-6
Griffiths, Sgt R.E., 34, 67
Griffiths, Sgt R.V., 82
Griffiths, Sgt W.R., 94, 123, 127
Grimar, José, 288
Grimsey RCAF, F/O M.F.C., 283, 309
Groome, Thomas Gilmour ("Georges"), xix, 75-6, 96, 136, 192, 201, 203-4, 345
Grout, F/S J.E., 159
Grove, Sgt W.G., 163-4
Grow US, Maj-Gen R.W., 303-4
Guérisse, Albert-Marie, see O'Leary, Pat
Guillot, P.M.F.C. ("Pernod"), 174
Gulbenkian, Calouste, 26
Gulbenkian, Nubar, 26-7
Gulley, P/O A.R., 9
Gunnell, Sgt A.F., 296
Gunning, S/L R.S., 229, *461*
Guthrie, Lt D.R., 322
Gutterling, Maarten, 226-7

Haarup USAAF, T/Sgt Carroll F., 305, *469*
Haddock, P/O E.A., 181
Haden-Guest, Elizabeth, xix, 38
Hagan, P/O A., 216, 226-7
Haig, Sgt T., 322
Haine, P/O R.C., 1
Haines RCAF, F/O A.R., 191, 198-9
Haislip US, Lt-Gen Wade H., 262, 286
Halifax, Lord, 37, 45
Hall Sgt J., 163-4
Hall, Virginia, 75, 82, 87-8
Hallett, Sgt C., 278, 286-7
Hallouin family, 274, 277, 279, 286
Halot, Alexander, 21
Halot, William, xix, 112-3
Hamby USAAF, 1/Lt Jesse M., 267, *465*
Hamilton RNVR, Sub-Lt M.I.G., 173, *456*
Hammond RCAF, Sgt J.A., 255
Hammond, F/S W.G., 328, *471*
Hand, Sgt G., 274, 289
Hankey, F/S S.A., 175
Hanwell, Sgt H.P, 97-8
Harding, Pte V., 93-4
Harding-Smith RNZAF, P/O D., 216
Hargest, Brig James, 153, 206, 237, 238, *454*
Hargrove USAAF, 2/Lt Walter, 182, 186

Harkin RAAF, F/S B.F., 313
Harmel, F/Sgt L.J.G., 169-70, *456*
Harper, Sgt R., 215
Harris, ACM Sir Arthur, xxviii, 124, 247
Harris, Sgt W.H., 3, 153
Harrison RCAF, P/O D., 295, 296
Harrison, P/O G.T., 328
Hart USAAF, 2/Lt, 268
Hart RAAF, W/O H.J., 341
Hart, Sgt T.F., 330
Hartin USAAF, 2/Lt F.D., 133
Hartley, Spr L., 16
Harvell, Sgt T.H., 310-1
Harvey, Sgt J., 168-9
Haslam, Sgt F.R., 289
Hasler, Maj H.G. "Blondie", xxx, 137-8, 192-3, 433
Hathaway, Sgt S.F., 239
Havouis, Mme Renée, 143
Hawkins, F/O B.L.G., 100-2
Hawkins, F/O R., 11, 13-14
Hawkins USAAF, S/Sgt Richard G., 318
Hawkins USAAF, 2/Lt W. "Bill", 173
Hawthorn, F/S R., 132
Haye RNethAF, P/O (Lt) J.B.M., 226-7
Hayes, Lt Jack Beresford, 75
Haywood USAAF, T/Sgt Joseph R., 144-5
Heal, Sgt P.C., 327
Healy, W/C E.A., 20
Heap RAAF, Sgt E.T., 131
Heather, L/Bdr J., 71
Hecht, Christian, 223
Heckler circuit, 82, 88
Hedley, F/Sgt T.J., 181-3
Heflin USAAF, Col Clifford J., 250
Heldman USAAF, 2/Lt Henry, 144-5
Le Hénaff, Yves ("FanFan"), 155, 174-7, 180
Henderson, Sgt R., 204-5
Henry USAAF, T/Sgt., 268
Hentic, Pierre, 185-6
Heraux, Madame, 305-6
Herbert, Sgt P.R., 66-7, 71-2
Hernandez, Claude, 179
Heslop, Richard ("Xavier"), 26, 99, 103, 219-21, 225, 249-50, *461*
Hessa, 332-3
Hewit, Lt W.M., 32-4, 65, 103, 110-1
Hewitt USAAF, Lt, 319
Heyworth, Sgt C., 239-40, *462*
Hibbert, AC1 G., 28-9
Hickman, Sgt G.P., 163
Hickton RNZAF, Sgt H.I., 101, 104-5
Higgins, Maj (Ret'd), 134
Higginson, F/L F.W., 72, 100-1, 104, *448*
Hill, AC1, 3
Hill, W/O J., 330-1
Hills, W/O R.A., 342
Hillyard, LAC E.G., 14
Hines USAAF, T/Sgt Frank E., 311, *469*
Hirst, Sgt G.H., 241
Hitchman, Sgt S.W., 251-3
Hitra, 332
Hjelm USAAF, 1/Lt Rex P., 283
HMS *Argus*, 22, 123
HMS *Fidelity*, 42-3
HMS *Furious*, 31, 244
HMS *Garth*, 227
HMS *Hereward*, 1
HMS *Kelvin*, 16
HMS *Malaya*, 90, 92, 105
HMS *Minna*, 105
HMS *Prince of Wales*, 67
HMS *Tarana*, 26, 94-100
HMT *Empire Trooper*, 31
HMT *Pasteur*, 61
Hoad, F/Sgt D.J., 267
Hoare, P/O R.G., 266
Hoare, Sir Samuel, xix, 23-4, 27, 39, 45-63, *442*
Hobler, S/L J.F., 1
Hochepied, Charmaine, 232
Hodges, Andrew, US Red Cross, 330
Hodges, F/O (later W/C) L.M., 25, 28, 33, 40, 175, 239, 241
Hoehn USAAF, 2/Lt Douglas C., 223
Hogan, Cpl N.J., 120-1
Hogg, F/O E.L., 328
Hogg, Lt H.S.M., 14
Hogg, F/O R.C., 202-3
Hoilman USAAF, S/Sgt Donald F., 277, *466*
Holdsworth RNVR, Lt-Com G., 160
Hollemans, Paul, 112
Hollender, Denis, 157
Hollick, F/Sgt G.D., 339-40
Holliday, F/L H.L., 104
Holroyd, Sgt S.G., 214
Holz USAAF, 1/Lt Raymond K., 267
Hooper, F/L R.W.J., 167, 175, 240-1
Hoorn, Jan, 340-1
Hoover, Pte Rudolph, 278-80
Hope, F/S S.F., 207, *459*
Hopkins, LAC J., 18, 28-9
Hopkinson, Henry (SIS), 24
Hore-Belisha, Leslie, xxix
Horsley, P/O R.M., 123-5
Hortie RCAF, Sgt R.H., 274
Horton, Sgt S., 179-80
Hoste, Charles, xix
Hotaling, 1/Lt Monroe J., 266, *465*
Houghton, Sgt S.J., 34, 66
Houghton, Sgt K.H.L., 126
Houghton USAAF, S/Sgt John H., 165, *455*
Houston RCAF, P/O A.J., 173
Hovelacque, Patrick ("Kumel"), 174
Howard, Sgt D.R., 163-4
Howarth, Cpl A., 103, 107, *447*
Howell USAAF, S/Sgt William C., 221
Hubbard, Cpl A.V., 38
Hubbard USAAF, Lt-Col Thomas H., 288-9
Hubble, Capt D.E., 259, *464*
Hue, André, 252-3
Huet, Pierre, 169
Hugh, (Jedburgh), 308
Hughes, Sgt W., *459*
Hugill, P/O F., 11
Hulls, Capt L.R., 8
Humphris, Sgt R.H.P., 66-7
Hunt, Sgt C.S., 59
Hunt USAAF, 2/Lt Tom J.E., 233
Hunt SAS, Tpr, 311
Hunter, Lt C.D., 13, *438*
Hunter RAAF, Sgt R.I., 327
Hunter RAAF, Sgt R.O., 239-40
Huntziger, General Charles, xxx, xxxi, xxxii, 13, 34, *437*
Hurley, John P. (US consul-general), 12, 24

Iurley USAAF, 2/Lt John E., 285, *467*
Iuston RCAF, F/O H.T., 227
Iutchinson RCAF, Sgt A.R., 312
Iutchinson, P/O J.T., 166-7
Iutton, Sgt J.W., 80, 118, 120
Iutton, Clayton, 247
Iyde RCAF, F/Sgt D.B., 280-1
Iyde, Sgt T.E., 3
Iyland, F/Sgt P.J., 272

alamoff SAS, Cpl, 33
ngels, Jean 115, 121, *450*
nglis, Pte P.F., 76
ngram, Sgt N.J., 66-7
nstone, Gnr G., 7, 31, 49
rwin, Sgt R.P., 295-6
sherwood, F/O R., 238
tterbeek, Raymond, xix
ves RCAF, Sgt J.L., 117-8, 120

acks, F/O W.A., 289
ackson, F/Sgt A.V., 266-7
ackson, Sgt S.T., 31
acob, Raymonde and Alice, 171-2
acques, René, 274
acquet, Fernand, 296
ade-Fitzroy *réseau*, 185
ames RCAF, F/S D.E., 163-4
ames, Lt E.A., 322
ames, Sgt H.M., 107
ames, Sgt O.B., 47
ane Henriette, 199
anes, Pte P.S., 70, 72
arvis, LAC J.H., 32
ean-Marie resistance network, 142
eanson, Pierre ("Sarol"), 185-6
effrey, F/Sgt H.T., 268-9
effrey, F/Sgt J.G., 195
eunet, Raymond, 214-5
ockey circuit, 5, 256
ohann van Oldervarnebilt, 244
ohns RN, Cdr Philip, 55
ohnson, Albert Edward ("B"), xix, 90, 118, 123, 128, 132-3, 190, 208
ohnson, Herschel (US *Chargé d'Affaires*), 24
ohnson, Capt Denis ("Paul"), 219
ohnson, Sgt H., 191
ohnson, Capt J.R., 17, 54
ohnson, Sgt R.V.C., 167, 213-5
ohnson, Sgt T.G., 97-8
ohnstone, Sgt, 339-40
oly, Pte Guy, 104
ones, LAC H.B., 3
ones, Cpl A., 112
ones, Sgt D.L., 199-200
ones RCAF, Sgt E.R., 283
ones, Sgt H.T.S., 336
ones USAAF, T/Sgt M.B., 197-8
ones, F/O R., 310
ones RCAF, WO R.A., 177
ones, W/C R.D., 257
ones, F/Sgt T., 342-4
ones, Sgt W., 263
ones USAAF, Maj W.A., 173
ouanjean, Georges, 162, 165, 178-9
oy, Dr Charles, 24
oyce, Sgt M.J., 131-2, 452

Jubault, Omer ("André"), 274, 276-7, 279, 282, 288
Jumeau, Clément (SOE 'F'), 75
Justason RCAF, F/S B.R., 309-10

Kadulski, Lt Marian (Polish Navy), 96, 104-5, *447*
Kanakos RCAF, Sgt T.J., 239-40
Katsaros USAAF, Sgt John, 267
Kay, Sgt N., 61
Kearins RNZAF, F/Sgt T.S.F., 181
Kehoe US, Sgt Robert R., 173, 252
Keller USAAF, 1/Lt, 330
Kelly, F/O G.W., 230-1
Kelly RCAF, W/O W.J., 304
Kemley, F/L H.J.S., 283, 309
Kemp, Spr D., 67
Kennedy RCAF, F/O J.F., 285
Kennedy RCAF, F/L J.L., 249
Kennedy, S/L J.S., 11
Kenny, Tom, xix, 31-2, 37
Kentgens, Dr Joop, 339-40
Keveren, Sgt A.J., 269
Keyes, Admiral Sir Roger, xxx, *436*
Khan, Cook Buland, 170-1
Kidd RNZAF, Sgt R.M., 197-8
Kimpton, F/S G.W., 265
King, F/O C.C., 323
King, Sgt H.J., 62
King, Sgt J.B., 254
King, Sgt P.N., 311
King, Sgt S.E., 123, 125-7
King, Sgt W.J., 62
Kingsford-Smith RAAF, P/O P., 202-3
Kirk, LAC P., 10
Kitto, Sgt R.V.T., 1
Klein USAAF, Sgt Alfred M., 144-5
Klein USAAF, S/Sgt Ellis H., 213, *460*
Kliks, Robert, 102
Klooster family, 335
Knapp, Georgina, 36
Knight, Pte C.G., 97
Knight, F/S D.C., 222-3
Knight, F/O F.T., 325
Knight USAAF, Sgt Marion, 277, 284, *466*
Knopp USAAF, S/Sgt L.W., 268
Knott, Mynheer L., 340
Knox, Capt B.M.W. ("Kentucky"), 302-3
Koch USAAF, T/Sgt Raymond, 294
Kok, A.G., 339
Kononenko SovAF, Sgt A.S., 163-5, *455*
Kool, Kees, 226
Kowalski PAF, Sgt M., 117
Kozubski, Lt Marian, 88
Kraay, Suzy, 153, 156
Kragt, Dignus ("Dick", "Frans Hals"), xx, 158, 335-6
Krajewski, see Kadulski
Kramer, P/O M., 1
Krasevac USAAF, T/Sgt Albert L., 250
Krawczyk PAF, F/O S., 90-1, *447*
Krengle USAAF, 1/Lt Robert V., 154, *454*
Kresser, Samuel L., 48
Krol USAAF, 2/Lt Theodore J., 280, *467*
Kropf RCAF, P/O L.E., 131-2
Krulicki RCAF, F/Sgt L.J., 325
Kubiak RCAF, W/O W., 329
Kylius USAAF, 2/Lt Robert E., 178

l'Armée Blanche, 258, 292

L'Émigrant, 160
L'Épingle Noire, 123
l'équipe DDD, 113
L'Yvonne, 160-1, 183
la Bouline, 26
La Libération, 144, 238
la ligne Dédée, 116, 119
la ligne Félix, 176
La Nouette, 252-3
La Pérouse, 175, 180
Laatsman, Herman, 153
Labourer circuit, 213
Labrosse, Raymonde, xx, 161-2, 165-8, 170, 172-4, 214
Lafleur, Conrad, xx, 104, 210-2, 214, 276
La-Horaine, 176
Laing, F/Sgt C.V., 342
Laird RCAF, S/L G.J., 262
Lambert RCAF, S/L A., 227
Lambert, F/L G.F., 219
Lamirault, Claude ("Fitzroy"), 185, *457*
Lane Jr USAAF, T/Sgt Joshua D., 285
Lang, Capt D.B., 25
Lang AIF, Pte D., 93
Langdon, F/O, 182
Langelaan, Lt George, 75
Langley, Lt (later Lt-Col) James M., xx, 30-2, 37, 39-40, 50, 59, 76, 81, 94-5, 106, 109, 113, 121-2, 136, 161, 168, 201, 219
Langlois, F/L R.B., 118-9
Lanvers, Pierrot, 99
Lapprand, Jean (Doubs FFI), 311
Laroche, Madame, see Barré de St Venant, Pauline
Larsen, Leif, 332-3
Lart, W/C E.C. de V., 47
Lashbrook, S/L W.I, 222-3
Lathbury, Brig Gerald, 323
Laussucq, Henri ("Aramis"), 88, *446*
Lavallee RCAF, P/O L.M., 239
Lavoie RCAF, F/O J.G.Y., 157
Lawhead USAAF, S/Sgt Duane J., 182
Lawrence, Sgt J.W.E., 184
Lawrie RNZAF, P/O J., 319, *470*
Laws, Sgt W.R., 217-8
Layton USAAF, 1/Lt Victor J., 259
Lazzaro USAAF, 2/Lt Dominic, 202-3
le Blond, Capt, 303-4
Le Bouvier, F/O J.D., 333
le Calvez, Marie-Thérèse, 169, 173
le Cornec, François, 161, 167-9, 173
le Contre, Brigitte, 88
le Cun, Georges, 168
le Duc, Dr, 171-2, 183
le Harivel, J.P. (SOE 'F'), 75
le Janne, Dr, 171
le Jouet-des-Flots, 155, 171, 176
le Neveu, Roger ("le Légionnaire"), 165-6, 183-4, 201, 203-4
Le Rhin, 42
le Rousset, M., 300
le Train Fantôme, 313
Lebel, Capt P., 302-3
Lebon, Nicole, 147
Lebreton, Mme "Chouquette", 95, 106, 198, 205
Lechein, Georges, xxv, 113-4
Leclerc, Maj-Gen P., 328, *471*
Leçuyras, Albert, 203-5
Ledford RCAF, Sgt W.H., 131
Le-Dinan, 160
Ledru, Simone, 214-5
Lee, Sgt B.A., 228
Lee, Sgt G.H., 122
Lee, Sgt N.W., 241-3
Lee, F/L R.H.A.,1
Lefèvre, S/L P.W., 163-4
Legge, Brig-Gen Barnwell Rhett, 219
Le Grelle, Count Jacques, xx, 210
Leigh, Vera (SOE), 203
Lennie RCAF, F/O D.A., 268
Lennon, 2/Lt J.D., 11, 13-4
Lepers, Roland, 32, 67, 70-1, 77, 80
Lepper, CQMS D., 31
Letory, Louis (PAO guide), 192-4
Levi RCAF, F/L J.A., 328
Levy USAAF, 2/Lt, 316
Lévy, Dr, 97
Lewis, P/O L.W.C., 312
Lewis, F/O R.W., 256
l'Helgouach, Capt L. (Jed team Hugh), 308
Liby RNorAF, 2/Lt S.K., 181-3
Liégeois, Constance Elisabeth, *452*
Liewer, Philippe, 75
Light RAAF, F/O K.W., 282
Lilly USAAF, Lt Joe, 173
Lindell, Mary, see de Milleville, Comtesse Mary
Lindsay USAAF, 2/Lt Andrew G., 175
Linklater, 2/Lt J.P.T., 32-3
Lipski, Sgt B., 90, *447*
Lissette RNZAF, W/O L.H., 270
Lister RN, ERA D., 219
Little, Sgt J., 255
Llanstephan Castle, 99
Llewellyn-Jones, L/Cpl, 52
Lloyd, Sgt D.A., 290
Lloyd, F/S T.A., 269
Loch Park, 183
Lockhart, 68-9
Lombert, Georges "Gregoose", 261
Lonsdale, Sgt R.W., 13, 31, *440*
Lorgé, Jean Pierre, 211-2, 215
Lorimer RAAF, F/S P.D.A., 330
Loring USAAF, 2/Lt Warren E., 283
Loucks USAAF, T/Sgt D.S., 318
Loudon, P/O J.B.T., 18
Louis, Serge, 261-2
Love, Sgt J.P., 98
Low USAAF, F.D., 229
Lowther USAAF, S/Sgt John W., 168, *456*
Lucas, see Michalkiewicz
Luckhurst, Pte J.N., 102
Luctor et Emergo/Fiat Libertas, 159
Luehrs USAAF, T/Sgt Jack O., 163-5, *455*
Lukasz, see Michalkiewicz
Lusk RAAF, F/S G., 329
Lussier RCAF, Sgt K.E., 171
Lussu, Emilio ("M. Dupont"), 23-6, 99
Luther, Sgt T.W.C., 226
Lynch RAAF, F/S K.J., 287
Lyon, Robert (SOE 'F'), 75
Lyons, Sgt A.R., 283

Maca, Henri, xx, 158-9, 288
Maca, Maria, xx, 159
Maca, Paul, 159
MacCallum, Sgt D., 46-8, 55

MacDonald, Pte E., 28-9
MacDonald, F/Sgt I.A., 195
MacDonald RCAF, Sgt I.R., 148-9, 152
MacDonald, P/O J., 152
MacDonald, Sgl L.R., 67
MacDonald RCAF, W/C J.K.F., 309-10
MacFarlane, Pte W., 127-8
Mackenzie, P/O G., 329
MacLean RCAF, F/L J.A., 129
Macleod, F/Sgt R.J.A., 230, 232-3
MacVean USAAF, 2/Lt Peter D., 285, *467*
Maddox USAAF, T/Sgt Harold B., 213, *460*
Maderson, Sgt A.A., 47
Magnant, Guy, 199
Magrath, Sgt W.J.Q., 47, *442*
Maguire, Maj Hugh, 335
Mahoney, Sgt P.J., 323
Mainguy, Joseph, 169, 173
Maitland, F/L I., 191
Malecki PAF, Sgt A., 89-91
Malins, P/O R.O., 239
Mallet RCAF, F/L E.L., 296
Malraison, Col, 103
Mandel USAAF, T/Sgt, 153-4
Mandinaud, Yvonne, 138
Manos USAAF, S/Sgt Joseph E., 205-6
Manser VC, P/O L., 123
Marcus family, 307
Marec, Louis, 179
Maréchal, Elsie Jeanette, xx, 206
Maréchal, Elsie Mary, xx, 113, 130-1, 206-7
Maréchal, Georges, xx, 206-7
Maréchal, Robert, 206-7
Marie-Claire, see de Milleville, Comtesse Mary
Mariette Pasha, 25
Marion RCAF, P/O B.H., 218
Marksman circuit, 219
Marriott USAAF, 2/Lt Paul A., 144
Marsal, Joseph, xxi, 220
Marsden, Sgt J., 328
Marsh, Sgt L., 214, 217
Marshall RNVR, Lt R.M., 169-73
Marshall, Sgt W.H., 166-7,
Martell, Christian ("Brandy"), 174
Martin, F/O A., 223
Martin, Capt A.M.K., 25, 40
Martin, Sgt C.H.T., 281-2, 286-7, *467*
Martin RCAF, Sgt L.F., 142-3, 145-6, 162, 164
Martin USAAF, Merle, 186
Martin, Thérèse – see Baudot de Rouville, Maud
Martinez, Dr, 137, *452*
Martinez, Angel (guide), 146-7
Marzin family, 171, 183
Masaryk, Jan (Czech Foreign Minister), 33
Maso, François (taxi driver), 21, 27
Mason RCAF, F/L E.B., 239-43
Mason, P/O F., 119
Mason SANF(V), Lt J. McQ., 185
Mason, Sgt W., 315-6
Massey, Sgt J.R., 5
Masson, Jean, see Desoubrie, Jean-Jacques
Matthews, Sgt P.V., 167, 174-5
Matthys, Gaston, xxi, 293, 295-6, *467*
Mattock, Sgt G.R., 257
Maupin USAAF, Flt/O Howard P., 292, *468*
Maxwell, P/O D.C.H., 272
Mayes, Gnr W., 74
McAngus, Dvr E.A., 17-8
McAuley DFC, S/L V.C., 194-6
McBeath RCAF, Sgt H.L., 110, *449*
McBeath RCAF, P/O T.A., 341
McBride, F/O J.McA., 167, 240, 456, *463*
McCairns, F/Sgt (later F/O) J.A., 121-2, 167, 175, 213-4, *456*
McCann, Pte, 254
McCarthy, Sgt N.J., 279, 282, 286-7
McCormick USAAF, S/Sgt John E., 339-40, *471*
McCrea, Sgt J.E., 199, *459*
McCubbin, Pte John, 112, 116, *450*
McDermott USAAF, 2/Lt Mark L., 161, *455*
McDonald RCAF, Sgt C.E., 163-4
McDonald USAAF, 1/Lt William, 153
McFarlane, Dvr F., 103
McFarlane, Sgt V.T., 15, 21, 39
McGeachin, W/O W.G., 334
McGlasson, Pte T.F., 76
McGlinchy USAAF, 2/Lt Frank, 153
McGourlick RCAF, F/O D.F., 181-3, 185
McGregor RNZAF, F/L S.M., 317
McKay RCAF, P/O W., 83, 102
McKee, Sgt L.M., 71-2
McKenzie, Pte D., 17-8, *439*
McKinnon, Sgt H.N., 149, 152, 218
McLain USAAF, 1/Lt Charles J., 267
McLaren, Pte J., 67, 72
McLarnon, Sgt J.W., 102, 118
McLaughlin USAAF, Sgt John C., 256, *464*
McLaughlin RAAF, P/O J.G., 153-4
McLean, Sgt L., 66-7
McLean, Sgt W., 133
McLear, QMSgt M.J., 31
McLeod, P/O A., 2
McMillan, Sgt A.J., 18-19
McMullen, Pte W., 102
McPhee RCAF, WO2 A.J., 267-9, *465*
McPherson USAAF, 1/Lt Joel W., 155, *454*
McSweeney RAAF, P/O K., 317
McSweyn RAAF, P/O A.F., 140, 142-3, 145-6
McWilliams, F/Sgt J.H., 206
McWilliams, F/L O.G.E., 11
Meeus, Albert, xxvi, 113
Melcombe RCAF, P/O D.E., 299
Meldrich USAAF, 2/Lt Walter A., 266
Melis, Eliseo, 59
Mellisson, Germaine ("Annie"), 276, 280
Mellor, F/Sgt G.H., 131-3
Menginou SAS, L/Cpl, 311
Mensik CzAF, Sgt J., 69
Menzies, Col Stewart, xxi, 160, 320
Merchant, F/Sgt J.F., 255-6, *464*
Merlin, Sgt E.H.R., 181, 430-2
Metlen USAAF, Sgt Robert, 235, *462*
Meyer, Lt R. ("Yonne"), 308
Mezynski USAAF, S/Sgt Thomas, 305, *469*
Michalkiewicz, Lt Marian ("Lukasz", "Lucas"), 105-6
Michand RCAF, Sgt J.A.E., 266
Michel Lévy Military Hospital, 15-16, 66, 74
Michelli, Henri, xxi, 121-2
Michiels, Yvon, xxi, 113, 207, 288, 293
Middleton, Sgt H., 329
Milburn, Sgt W.R., 180
Miles, Brig Reginald, 237, *462*
Mill, F/L B., 265
Millar, Lt G.R., 220-2, *461*

Millard, F/Sgt P.W.W., 344
Miller, Sgt F.H., 66-7
Miller USAAF, S/Sgt George R., 267, 268, *465*
Miller, Sgt J., 102
Miller USAAF, 2/Lt Richard M., 268, *465*
Miller USAAF, S/Sgt Rosswell, 221-2, *461*
Mills, Sgt A.McF., 123, 125-7
Mills, Sgt A.W., 102-3
Mills SAS, Serj E., 173
Mills, Sgt W.H., 85, 93
Milner-Gibson RN, Lt-Cdr Jasper, 42
Milton, P/O (later F/L) R.A.E., 34, 65-7, 103, 110-1
Miniakowski PAF, Sgt S., 89-90, 97
Minne, André, 35, *441*
Minor USAAF, Sgt Walter R., 150, 152, *454*
Miranda de Ebro, 5, *passim*
Misseldine, Sgt J.E., 99-100
Mithridate, 162, 164-5
Moffat RCAF, F/O J., 262-3, *465*
Mollett, F/O W.V., 171
Mondet, Mme Fernande, 214-5, *460*
Monin, Marie, 88
Montet, Maurice ("Brandy" line),174, 202
Montgomery, Hugh, 196
Montgomery USAAF, Lt-Col Robert F., 266, *465*
Moore USAAF, Sgt Kenneth R., 142, *453*
Moore, Sgt S.J., 209-10, 224
Moore USAAF, T/Sgt T.R., 177
Mora RNZAF, Sgt C.M.M., 225-6
Morawski PAF, P/O J., 58, 89-91, 94
Morelle, Charles, xxi, 114-5, 122, 132, 206
Morelle, Elvire, xxi, 115, 117-8, 121, 124-5, 127-9, 207
Morement, LAC H.A., 16
Morgan RCAF, F/L G.R., 292
Morrison DFC, F/O John, 262
Mort, Sgt C.R., 102, *448*
Mortimer RNZAF, F/O J.E., 244, *463*
Mosley, Col (Barcelona consulate), 55
Mott, Sgt (later F/L) A.J., 18-19, 95-6, 185, *447*
Moulin, Jean, 251, *464*
Mounts RCAF, Sgt D.C., 130
Mouvement de Libération Nationale, 184
Mowat, Pte J.A., 72-4
Moydon SAS, (French), 303, *468*
Mrozohski, F/Sgt W., xxvii, *436*
Muelle, Willy, 112
Muir, Sgt M., 316-7
Mulette, Lucienne, 214-5
Mulholland USAAF, 2/Lt Eugene V., 221-2, *461*
Müller, SS-Gruppenführer Heinrich, xxvi
Murchie, Capt Charles P., 5, 20, 27-8, 30, 32, 34-40, 49, 55, *439*
Murphy, Sgt D., 257
Murphy RCAF, F/O D.G., 306-7
Murphy, P/O D.R., 266, 268
Murphy RNZAF, F/Sgt J.W., 315-7
Murphy, Sgt P., 299
Murray USAAF, T/Sgt Fred L., 213, *460*
Murray, Sgt G.H., 149, 151-2
Mussolini, Benito, 45-6
Mutin, 160, 187
Mutter, F/O N.E.S., 327, *470*
Mutum, Sgt R.B., 63, 444
Mynarski VC, WO II A.C., 304, *469*
Myrda, Father, xxi, 101, *449*

Nabarro, F/O C., 257
Nabarro, Sgt D.D.W., 101, 104
Nahas, Gabriel, xxi, 145, 153, 156, 206, 237
Narkunda, 91, 127
Naylor, Sgt B.W., 123, 125-7
Neave, Maj A.M.S., xxi, 52, 84-5, 97, 136, 158, 161, 171, 174, 177, 201, 208, 210, 215, 273-4, 286-8, 296, 323, 335-6
Nederlandse Binnenlandse Strijdkrachten, 339
Nègre, Gaston, xxi, 65, 77, 93, 95-7, 100, 105, 126
Neil, F/L M.M., 331
Neill, Pte A., 77
Neill RAAF, P/O F.H., 311
Neill, Sgt L., 222-3
Nekrasov, Pte V.I. (Soviet Army), 230, *461*
Nelmes RCAF, W/O J.M., 239-43
Newbold, Sgt L., 255
Newman, Lt-Col A.C., 93, *447*
Newman RAMC, Maj Philip, 30
Newton, Alfred W.O., 49
Newton, Henry G.R., 49
Newton, Sgt J.L., 118-20
Newton RCAF, F/O R., 322
Nice USAAF, T/Sgt K.H., 268
Nielsen, Sgt H.L., 182-3, 185-6
Nieslierewiez, Jan, 253
Nightingale, F/Sgt F.K., 194-6
Niox, Mme Ghislaine, 186
Nitelet, P/O Alex, xxi, 77-8, 95-6, 101, 103, 185
Nixon RCAF, F/L H.J., 308-9
Noble USAAF, 1/Lt Richard, 266
Nolan RCAF, F/Sgt D.K., 149
Norelius USAAF, Flt/O, 330
Norfolk, Sgt W.J., 128
Norm USAAF, Sgt, 341
North-Lewis, W/C C.D., 338
Nothomb, Jean-François, xxii, 159, 162, 200-1, 208-10, 221, 223, 230-3
Nouët, Franz, 184
Nouveau, Jean-Pierre "Bedard", 39, *441*
Nouveau, Louis, xxii, 31, 39-40, 47, 66-7, 70, 77, 82, 84-6, 88-90, 93, 96-100, 105, 161, 165, 192, 201-2
Nouveau, Renée, xxii, 47, 66-7, 70, 77, 82, 84-6, 88-90, 93, 97-8, 198, 203-4
Nugent, LAC R.H., 1
Nykerk, Benno, 153
Nys, Henri (*convoyeur*), 288-9

O'Brien, Sgt J., 251
O'Connor, Lt-Gen R.N., 237
O'Flaherty, Hugh, 196
O'Leary, Pat "Joseph" (Guérisse, Albert-Marie), xix, xxii, 41-4, 48, 59, 65, 67, 74-7, 79, 81-2, 85, 91, 93-103, 105-6, 137-8, 161, 165, 167, 174, 192, 194, 197-8, 201-5, *436*
O'Neill RAAF, P/O F.H., 311
O'Shea, Pte Jack, 29
O'Sullivan, Capt H.B., 82-3, 85, 93
O'Sullivan, F/Sgt J.L, 63
Ogden-Smith, Maj C.M. (Jed Francis), 303
Ogilvie RCAF, F/L A.M., 204, 205
Olav Tryggvason, xxix
Oliver, F/O T., 333
Olschanesky, Sonia (SOE), 203
Olsen, Alfred, 342
Operations:-
Abloom, 94
Achilles, 136

Bellows, 244
Bludgeon, 251
Bluebottle, 98-9
Bonaparte I-V, 168-73
Brasenose, 213
Bulbasket, 308
Bull, 99
Buttercup 2, 202
Colossus, 97, 222
Cooney, 252
Crozier, 172-4
Dido, 161
Dongson/Grog, 252
Director 24, 202
Dunhill, 286
Dynamo, xxx
Easement II, 174
Envious, 174, 185
Envious IIA, 185-6
Envious IIB, 174, 182, 186
Falstaff, 104
Felicitate, 174, 182, 185-6
Frankton, 137-8, 433
Gain, 311
Helm, 219
Husky, 164
John 13, 251
Magdalen, 167, 213
Marathon, 273
Market/Garden, 322, 333
Mirfield, 178
Mixer I, 250
Nectarine, 104
Oaktree, 161-3, 165-7, 174
Octave, 122
Oriel, 175
Osric 53, 318
Pampas, 185
Pegasus I, 323
Pegasus II, 323, 335
Reflexion, 173
Rob Roy I, 297
Rosalind, 105, 107, 167
Rupert, 311
Saint, 88
Samwest, 173, 252, 302
Scarf, 172, 174
Scenery, 241
Shakespeare, 286
Shelburne, 167, 169, 171, 174, 273
Sherwood, 273, 274, 286, 288
Titania, 104, 105
Trojan Horse, 239
Varsity, 338
Water Closet, 118, 123
Water Pistol, 167, 240
Yolande, 161
Organisation Todt, 270
Organizzazione di Vigilanza Repressione dell'Antifascismo, 194
Ormerod, Sgt, 317
Orsini, Mme, 310
Ortiz US, Capt P.J. (Marines), 256-7
Osborne, Pte, 36, 38
Osselaer, Lt Georges, 120, *450*
Ossendorf, W/O R., 271-2
Ossian, 10
Outram, S/L H.A., 104
Overwijn, F/S R., 144-5
Owen, L/Cpl T., 104
Owens USAAF, S/Sgt Francis E., 141-2

Pace Jr USAAF, T/Sgt Harry G., 285
Pack, Sgt J.T., 127-9
Page, Sgt F.J., 154
Paillole, Capt P., xxxi
Pallett RCAF, W/O II C.G., 152
Palm SAAF, Capt R.B., 143, 145-6, 157, *453*
Palmer, Miss Margaret, 38
Panzer RCAF, F/O L., 316, *470*
Papillon, Abbé , 200
Parayre, Michael ("Parker"), 27, 67, 70
Parent, Raoul, 173
Parent, Sous/Lt P., 313
Parish, F/L C.W., 325
Parker, P/O T.C., 2
Parker, P/O G., 17
Parker AIF, Cpl J.A., 93, 102
Parkes, Sgt S.M.P., 19-22, *439*
Parkinson, Sgt D.R., 179-80
Parkinson RCAF, P/O G.M., 148-9, 152
Parkinson, F/Sgt J.E., 299
Parkinson, 2/Lt R.E.H., 20-1, 32, 34, 65-6
Parrott, Capt R.F., 95-6, *467*
Parsons, P/O J.R.B., 82
PAT/PAO line, 47, 76, 78-82, *passim*
Patch US, Lt-Gen A., 311
Patching, Bandsman J.H., xxxi
Patterson, Sgt D.G., 239
Patton Jnr, Gen George S., 285-6, 303, 327
Paul, Albert, 263
Paul, Cécile, 263
Paul, Desiré, 263
Paul, Louis, 264
Paul, Vital, 263
Paulin, Sgt R.W., 239
Pavot, 113
Payne, Sgt H.W., 249-50
Pearce, F/L F.O.J., 255
Pearce, Sgt J.G., 267, 269
Pearl, Sgt J., xxv
Pearman, Sgt L., 102-3
Pearson RASC, Sgt G.E., 256
Pearson USAAF, Lt Jonathan, 274, 276, *466*
Pedrick, Vyvyan (vice-consul, Bilbao), 115
Penna, Sgt C., 192-4
Pepall, F/S D.R.R.J., 274-7
Pepper, F/O N.E.W., 3
Perdue, P/O D.J., 99-100
Pergantes RCAF, P/O P.H., 312
Péri, Lt de Vaisseau C.A.M., 42-3, *442*
Pertschuk, Maurice ("Eugène", SOE), 204-5
Pétain, Maréchal Henri-Philippe, xxii, xxxi, 113
Peter, P/O R.G., 257
Peterson USAAF, 1/Lt Theodore M., 165, *455*
Petit Poucet, (Marseille café), 68, 71, 84-6, 103
Peyraud, Lt (gendarme, Ruffec), 143
Peyrot, (prison warder at Mauzac), 75-6
Philbin RCAF, S/L G.B., 328
Phillippe USAAF, 1/Lt Hilbert W., 254, *464*
Phillips, LAC D.L., 9-10, 14, 152
Phillips, Sgt J.W.B., 4-5, 9, 69
Phillips, Pte W., 65
Phillips RCAF, Sgt W.E., 149

Phillips SAS, Trooper, 311
Philo, Sgt S.J.V., 140-2
Philomène, 88
Phythian, Pte Ellis, 200
Pic de Rulle, 141
Pickard, W/C Percy, 185
Picourt, Raymond A.E., 310
Pierlot, Hubert (head of Belgian govt in exile), 113
Pierre, F/L M.A.J., 163
Pietrasiak PAF, Sgt A., 70-2
Piette, Maxime (radio operator), 300
Pilgrim, F/S N.C.H., 249-50
Pinchuk SovAF, Sgt P.K., 131, 133, 206
Pink List, The, 94
Pinkerton, Sgt F.W., 224
Pipkin, F/L L.C., 130, *452*
Pirlot, Ferdinande ("Pochette"), 122
Pitch and Toss, 96
Pittwood, F/S J., 267
Plasket USAAF, T/Sgt William B., 141-2
Playfair, AVM P.H.L., xxix, *436*
Poirier, André, 184
Pol III, xxix
Polesinski PAF, Sgt E., 58, 89-91
Pollard RNVR, Sub/Lt M.J., 186
Ponchet, (stoker, Belgian Ghost Train), 314
Pond RNZAF, F/S H.A., 212-3
Ponzán Vidál, Francisco, xxii, 58-9, 88, 90
Portemine group, 113
Porteous RNZAF, Sgt R.D., 102, 118
Possum/Martin *réseau*, 210-1, 214, 276
Postel-Vinay, André, xxii, 77, 80, 105
Potentier RCAF, F/Sgt R.H.L., 258-9
Potier, Capt D.E. ("Possum/Martin"), 167, 210-1, 213-5, 276
Potts, Maj W.C.W., 11-12, 14
Poupard, Roger, 274, 280-1
Pow, Pte Andrew, 77
Powell, F/S, 182
Powell, Sgt E.C., 251-3
Prassinos, Mario, xxii, 73, 77, 81, 84, 86, 91, 93, 96, 100, 104, 108-110, 126
Prendergast, Sgt J., 91-2
Prévot, Georges (Paris policeman), 267
Prévot, S/L L.O., 130, *452*
Price, Jurgens (Unilever), 40
Price RCAF, Sgt E.G., 190, *447*
Prior RN, Lt-Com R.M., 103
Prisión Cellular, Figueras, 14
Prontas, see Nahas, Gabriel
Prosper circuit, 113, 159, 209-10, 273
Prunus circuit, 204
Ptáček, Sgt Rudolf, 69-70, 72

Queen Mary, 265
Quinn USAAF, Sgt William N., 175

Racine RCAF, F/L G.G., 171
Rademecker, Louis (chief of police), 123-4, *451*
RAF Boat No. *360*, 187
Raginis PAF, Sgt W., 140-2, 189
Raikes, Capt P.P., 14, 54
Raikes DSO, RN, Lt-Cdr R.P., 433
Rainwater, Pte 1/C, 260
Raiston RCAF, F/S J.W., 122
Ramsay USAAF, Flt/O, 266
Randall, F/L F.R., 275
Randall, F/S W. "Bill", 334
Randle, Sgt W.S.O., 130, *452*
Randolet, Lt Emile, 264
Raoul Caulaincourt, 184
Raoul-Duval FAF, Lt Claude, 165-6
Rapley, Mr (consular official, Spain), 14, 49
Ratcliffe, Capt J.M., 95-6
Rattner, F/S C., 328
Rea RCAF, P/O H.D., 240
Read, Sgt K.B., 77, *445*
Reain RCAF, Sgt F.F., 157-8
Reddé, Edith, 198, 201
Reed, F/O J.S., 256
Reed, F/L L.G.A., 239
Reed, P/O W.C., 300
Reeve RCAF, Sgt P.A., 312
Reeves, Sgt B.C., 238
Regent Tiger, 234
Reid, Capt Pat, 219
Reid, Spr R., 77
Reijnders, Edward, 226-7
Reilly USAAF, S/Sgt T.P., 335
Rejern, Henriette, 143, 147
Renaud, Marcel (baker), 276
Renault, Gilbert ("Rémy), 289
Rendle, Howard (coxswain MGB 318), 186
Renet FAF, Sgt R.D., 336, *471*
Rennie, P/O B.J.A., 29-30
Rens, Jacques, 153-4, 156
Requin, 183
Résistance Fer, 206, 237-8
Reynolds, Sgt A.J.A., 175, 456
Richards, Mlle Dupuich, 114, *449*
Richardson, Sgt K.C., 251-3
Rieu, Jules, 157
Riley, Sgt H., 164-5
Riou, Mme and Julien, 252-3
Riquet, Father Michel, 307
Riseley, F/O A.H., 181-3
Risler US, Sgt Jack R. (Marines), 257
Ritschdorf, Matilda and Jeannine, 131-3
Rizzo, E.V.H., 42-3, *442*
Robb, Sgt I.A., 215
Robert, Sgt L., 321
Roberts USAAF, 2/Lt, 153
Roberts USAAF, Alvis D., 291
Roberts, F/L C.L.C., 2
Robertson RAMC, Col, 4
Robertson, Sgt F.W.C., 290-1, 293
Robertson, Sgt H.O., 137, 193-4
Robertson, F/L J.S., 340
Robillard RCAF, Sgt J.G.L., 18, 72-3
Robinette USAAF, Lt, 341
Robins RNZAF, F/L J.D., 326-7
Robinson, S/Sgt Allen H., 163, *455*
Robinson, Sgt C., 275
Robinson, Sgt G., 310
Robinson RCAF, F/O W.W., 328
Roby, Eugènie, 155
Roche, R.B., 75
Rochester, Deveraux "Elizabeth", 219-20
Rockwood RNVR, Ord/Sn, H.D., 173
Rodney, S/L G.F., 59-60, *443*
Rodocanachi, Fanny, xxii, 44, 67, 70-1, 74, 79, 107-9
Rodocanachi, Dr Georges, xxii, 15, 38, 44, 67, 70-1, 74, 78-9, 93, 97, 102, 107-9, 202
Rodriguez, Ferdinand, 136, 138

Rodriguez, José (guide), 140-1, 143
Roger, Jacques, xxii
Roger, Max, 209
Rogers, (French sailor), 43
Rohan, M., 168
Rohde RNorAF, 2/Lt H.W., 338-9
Roiseux, Emile "le Plombier", 288, 294-5, *467*
Rolfe, Lilian (SOE), 148, *454*
Rollin, Lt Leo (FFI), 330-1
Rooney, Sgt A.J., 251-3
Roper USAAF, 2/Lt Grady W., 192-3, 198, *458*
Roper, F/L P.D.L., 327
Rosenblatt USAAF, T/Sgt Alvin A., 144
Rosher, F/S H.S., 329-30
Roskell, Sgt G., 15
Ross, P/O D.G., 149
Ross, Pte Joseph, 77
Ross, Sgt P.G.E., 207-8, 224, *459*
Ross USAAF, 1/Lt William O., 266
Ross RCAF, P/O W.D.F., 231
Rouillon, François, 136, 139
Roupell VC, Brig G.R.P., 91, 93-4, *447*
Roure, Rémy, 184
Rowan-Hamilton, 2/Lt A.D., 82-5
Rowden, Diana (SOE), 203
Rowicki PAF, F/O K., 90, 116, 190
Rowland, F/S B.D., 339-40
Ruge, Col Otto, xxx, *436*
Rullier, Mme Martha, 135-6
Rupert RCAF, F/O W.A., 321-2
Russell USAAF, French M, 250
Russell, Sgt W., 299
Ruth USAAF, Sgt, 257
Rutherford RCAF, F/O D.E., 321
Ryan RAAF, Sgt A., 62
Ryan, Sgt C., 333
Ryckman USAAF, Lt W.G., 318
Rytka PAF, P/O M., 67, 72

Sale RCAF, F/L (later S/L) D.J., 179, 224-5, 238
Salez, Victor, 175
Salvadori, Joyce, 26, 99
Samaria, 164
Sanctuaire de Notre-Dame-de-Laghet, 103
Sanderson, Sgt J.W., 330
Sandulak RCAF, Sgt J., 283
Sandvik RCAF, Sgt G.A., 330
Sankey, Hon. H.A.A., 33
Sankey, Sgt J., 149, 151-2
Sansoucy RCAF, Sgt J.G.F., 139
Sansum, Sgt I.J., 228
Saunders, F/Sgt S.F., 333
Savinos, Leoni, xxii, 77, 99
Sawyer, Col, 40
Saxton, Sgt R.W.A., 102, 104-5
Scapa Flow, 67, 94
Scheidhauer, Col Michel, 183, 186, *457*
Schleichkorn USAAF, 1/Lt Samuel G., 292, *468*
Schloesing FAF, Capt (S/L) J.H., 200-1
Schneider USAAF, Sgt, 153-4
Schoenmaker, Paul, 128
Scholar circuit, 147
Schrader, Anton "Toni", 225-7
Schrieber USAAF, Lt D., 221
Schwilk RAAF, F/S C.W., 284-5
Schyns, Pastor, 117
Scott USAAF, T/Sgt John M., 165, *455*
Seadog, 96, *467*
Seamen's Mission, Marseille, 3, *passim*
Seaton RNVR, Ldg/Smn F., 196, *458*
Seawolf, 26, 96, 99, 104-6, *467*
Seddon RNVR, Lt R., 172, 174
Semple RCAF, F/O E.Q., 297-9
Seniawski USAAF, S/Sgt Pete, 206
Serein, Maurice, 274, 281
Service Luc, 8, 206
Sevenster, Arie, 152
Seymour, F/S, 98
Shahzaman, Sgt, 170-1
Sharp, F/L G.E., 339-41
Shaughnessy RCAF, F/S G.J., 155
Shaw, Col Cecil, 6, 134-5, *452*
Sheets USAAF, Sgt Harold T., 235, *462*
Sheppard, Sgt A.H., 139
Sherman USAAF, 2/Lt Howard, 154, *454*
Sherriff, Maj Gordon, 335
Shetland Bus, The, 332
Shoebridge, Sgt R.B., 122
Shumway USAAF, S/Sgt Orion H., 285, *467*
Siadecki PAF, Sgt E., 90, 125-7
Sibbald, F/S D.A., 218
Sibiril, Ernest, 160, 178, 183, *455*
Sibiril, Léon, 183
Sidders USAAF, Sgt Robert E., 282, *467*
Sierpina PAF, Sgt M., 89
Sikorski, Gen Wladyslaw, 96
Sillar RAMC, Lt W., 24, *439*
Silva RAAF, P/O G., 129
Sim, Fus T.J., 120-1
Simister, Sgt H., 235-7
Simmons, Dvr H.C.D., 72-4
Simmons, P/O R.A., 258
Simon, André (SOE), 97, 99
Simoniz USAAF, 2/Lt Aubert, 200
Simpson RAAF, F/L A.B., 254-5
Simpson RAAF, F/Sgt L.R., 254
Simpson RCAF, F/O P.W., 228
Sims RAAF, F/Sgt E.A., 226
Sims, L/Cpl R.W., 84-5, 93
Slack, F/O T.A.H., 233
Slavin, Pte S., 112, 115
Slocum RN, Capt F.A., 42, 94, 160, 164-5, 171
Small, F/Sgt E.G., 275
Small, Pte E.J., 22
Smets, Mary and Golly, 320-1
Smit, Karst, 159
Smith, Sgt A., 149
Smith RCAF, Sgt D.V., 325-6
Smith, W/C D.W.M., 239
Smith, F/O H.F.E., 142-3, 145-6
Smith, Gnr H.W., 76
Smith, Pte James, 72-4, 80
Smith RAAF, F/O J.A., 266, 281-2
Smith, Sgt J.A., 163-4
Smith, Sgt P.B., 211, 232
Smith, S/L P.H., 173
Smith, Sgt R.G., 160
Smith RCAF, Sgt R.P., 133
Smith, P/O R.S., 108-10, 238
Smith RAAF, F/S R.V., 255
Smitton RCAF, P/O F.A., 260
Sneland I, 232
Śnieć PAF, F/O C., 146
Solberg RCAF, W/O II B.A.J., *471*

Solly, P/O C.J., 289-90
Solomon USAAF, T/Sgt G., 277, 279, *466*
Soulié, Geneviève, xxiii
Southgate, S/L Maurice, 49
Sowden RNR, 1/Lt D.W., 94
Spaatz, Lt Gen Carl A., xxv, *436*
Sparkes, Sgt J.N., 139
Sparks, S/L E.N.M., 267
Sparks, Marine W.E., 137-8, 192-3, 433
Spear, Sgt A.N., 1
Spence USAAF, 2/Lt John W., 208, *459*
Spencer RCAF, Sgt A.E., 249-50
Spencer RCAF, F/Sgt G.L., 163-5
Spiller, Sgt H.J., 133
Spinks USAAF, 2/Lt Hayward C., 285
Spriewald, Paula, 96, 102, 105
Squires, F/Sgt H., 300-1
Saltwick, 199, *459*
St Gilles Prison, 116 *passim*
St Hippolyte-du-Fort, 15, *passim*
Stachura, Cadet Henryk, 70-2
Stadnik SovAF, Sgt A.E., 131-3, 206
Stanenkovich, Lt M., 88, 91, *446*
Stanko USAAF, Lt M.N., 294, *468*
Stapel USAAF, Capt Wilmer, 250
Stark, F/L L.W.F., 172-3
Starr, George "Hilaire", 265
Stauning, Prime Minister Thorvald, xxix, *436*
Stead USAAF, Sgt Jack W., 267
Stearn, Sgt F.R., 330
Stearns USAAF, 1/Lt C.A., 335
Steel, F/O M.S., 267
Steepe RCAF, F/O C.A.D., 306-7
Stein USAAF, Lt, 319
Stephens, A/B Ron, 95, 99
Stephens RNVR, Lt-Cdr L.W. "Billie", 219, 269
Stephenson, Gnr G., 39
Stewart, Lt H.E., 82-5, 88, 90
Stewart, Capt J.R.C., 195, *458*
Stinnett USAAF, 2/Lt Myrle J., 258-9, *464*
Stirling Castle, 194
Stockford, Sgt N.J., 270
Stone, Sgt J.W., 294
Stonebarger USAAF, 2/Lt Gilbert M., 155, *454*
Stoner USAAF, 2/Lt Robert, 276
Stoner RAAF, F/O Ross A., 335
Stout, F/L G.S., 321
Strachan, Dvr J., 71-2
Straight, S/L W.W., 34, 65, 96-9, 101
Strange, Sgt M.B., 217-8
Stronach RCAF, F/L M.P., 328
Stuart-Menteith, Capt W.G., 9-10
Stülpnagel, General von, 137, *452*
Sumerson, Sgt A.K., 32
Summers, F/O, 10
Súñer, Ramon Serrano, 46
Surridge, Cpl H.W.C., 22
Suzanne-Renée, 180, 182-3
Swanson USAAF, 1/Lt Donald E., 266
Swanson, F/O J.R.S., 321
Sweatman RCAF, WO II K.C., 296
Swida PAF, F/O S., 141, 188-9
Szabo, Violette (SOE), 148, *454*
Szkuta PAF, F/O A., 89-90, 125-6

Tachon, Cpl S.F., 30, *440*
Tack, Sgt Gordon H., 302
Tait, W/C J.B., 97, 321
Tanguy, Claude 186
Tante Go, see Elvire De Greef
Tarleton USAAF, Woodrow, 295
Tartière, Mme Dorothy "Drue", 305-7
Tate, F/Sgt E., 343-4
Taylor, LAC J.H., xxv, 15
Taylor RCAF, S/L F.V., 218-20, 222, 229
Taylor, P/O R., 225
Taylor, F/O S.D., 280
Teare, Sgt T.D.G., 180, 320
Tedder, AM Sir Arthur, 319
Teer USAAF, Maj Charles R., 250
Teitel USAAF, Lincoln, 280
Templeman, F/Sgt T., 92
Templewood, Viscount, see Hoare, Sir Samuel
Terwindt, Beatrix, 158, *455*
Thacker USAAF, Lt Bud, 267
Thackthwaite, Capt H.H.A., 256, *464*
Thielbek, 344, 345
Thomas, P/O, 2
Thomas, Sgt G.F., 180, 267
Thomas, F/O H.D., 155
Thomas RCAF, F/O J.C., 162
Thomas USAAF, Capt Maurice S., 178
Thomé, Monique, 235
Thompson RCAF, P/O D.N., 268, *465*
Thompson, Pte G., 15
Thompson, Sgt P.M., 60
Thorn, Sgt E.E., 260
Thorne, Sgt P.S.C., 322
Thorpe, Sgt K.W., 248
Thring RCAF, F/L G.H., 297
Thurmeier RCAF, F/O J.J., 317-8
Till RAAF, W/O A.T., 313
Tissier, Pierre ("Pierrot"), 186
Tobin, Pte J., 68
Todd, Sgt W., 235
Tomicki PAF, Sgt S., 117
Tomlinson RCAF, P/O F.M., 217
Tomlinson, S/L G.C., 1
Torr, Brigadier W.W.T., 14, 23-4, 48-50, 56, 71
Toussaint, François, xxiii, 113, 274, 282-3, 285
Tovey, F/Sgt J.W., 323-4
Townshend, Mr Edmund, 333
Treacy, F/L W.P.F., 6-9, 30-1
Tréhiou, Jean, 171, 173
Tremargat RNVR, Lt (Frenchman), 65
Trenchard, Miss Eve Sarah, 102, 107
Trent USAAF, Flt/O Hubert E., 254
Tresemer USAAF, Maj Edward C., 250
Tromelin, Jean (*passeur*), 162
Trost USAAF, 2/Lt John, 192-4, *458*
Trotobas, Michael, 75
Trott, Sgt C.F., 139
Trottier RCAF, Sgt E.J., 173
Trueman, F/S/ K.W., 313
Trythall, Capt H.R., 54
Tsoucas SBS, Capt George, 143-5, *453*
Tucholko, Av-Cad W., 88
Tuck, Gnr F., 74
Tucker RAAF, P/O C., 144-5
Tull, Dvr F., 17-18, *439*
Turberville, Daniel (SOE), 75
Turenne RCAF, Sgt E.R., 162-4, 179
Turner RCAF, Sgt A.C., 149-52
Tuttle USAAF, S/Sgt F.A., 318

Twigg RCAF, W/C J.D., 191
Tyszko PAF, P/O J., 188-90

Ugeux, Pierre, xviii
Ulmann, Paul, xxiii, 75-6, 85, 108-10, 192-3, 197, 203-5
Unsworth, P/O J., 119
Usandizaga, Françoise (Francia, Frantxia), xxiii, 118-9, 123, 125, 127, 129, 132, 207, 218, 223, 235

Vallely, Sgt J.D., xxxi
Valy, Pierre, 178
van Belle, Henriette, xxvi, 113
van der Stok, F/L Bram, 155-6
van der Weerd, Gerard ("Wodka"), 174
van Lier, Peggy, xxiii, 90, 121-2, 207
van Muylem, René, xxiii, 316
van Niftrik, Baron J.G., 237
van Roosendaal, W/O J.C., 338
van Rosenthal, 153
van Steenbeck, M., 125, *451*
van Tricht, General, 237
Vandenhove, Jean-François, 113
Vanier, Robert, 104, 175, *468*
Vanlierde, Louis, 291-2
Var line, 171-2, 255
Vass, Sgt J.R., 154
Veerman, Paul, 156-7
Verhague, Mme, 308-9
Verheggen, Louis (engine driver), 314-5
Verhulst, Roger ("Cyrano"), 112-3
Verity, S/L H., 167, 213-4, 225
Verloop, Cornelius, xxiii, 77, 80
Viallet, Julien, 220
Vidal, Francisco Ponzán, 58-9, 88, 90, *450*
Vidler, F/O A.E., 311
Vigars, Sgt R.E., 304
Vigra, 332, 333
Villa Anita, 71
Ville de Verdun, 25
Vincer, G/C, 200
Violette, Capt and Mme, 126-7, 190
Virgo, Sgt C.G., 267
Virmoux, Robert (*passeur*), 177
Viron, Etienne (baker), 285-6
Visser 't Hooft, Dr W.A., 153, 279
Vivian, Sgt R., 19-22, 39
Vogel USAAF, S/Sgt Sebastian L., 161, *455*
Voglimacci, Mme Jeannine, 4-5, 70
Volbert, Louis, 258, *464*
von Choltitz, Gen Dietrich, 329
von Ribbentrop, Joachim, 46
Vozzella USAAF, Lt Carmen T., 318, *470*

Wacinski PAF, F/O J., 58, 89-91, 94
Wærner RNorAF, F/L T.A., 107, 110-1
Wagland, S/L J.C.W., 241
Wake, Nancy, see Fiocca, Nancy
Walker, Sgt P.W., 254-5
Walker, "Whiz", 211
Walkington, S/L J.G.G., 191
Wallace RAAF, F/S J.R., 267
Wallace, Sgt R.V., 236-7
Walls, Sgt A., 329
Walsh, Sgt D.S., 66-7, 102-3
Warburton, Sgt L.A., 80, 118, 120
Ward, Sgt K., 235
Ward, F/L R.D., 335
Warenghem, Suzanne, xxiii, 68, 77, 80, 172
Wares, P/O D., 246-8
Warnon, Elisabeth, *452*
Warren RNVR, Sub-Lt 94
Washbourne RAAF, F/S G., 299
Wasiak PAF, Sgt A., 188, 190
Wasik PAF, P/O W.P., 89, 125-6
Waters, Capt C.D., 11, 13-14
Watkins, Dvr C.F., 21
Watkins, Sgt J.C., 285
Watlington RCAF, F/O J.H., 154-5, 175-6
Watson, Sgt E., 17-18
Watson RCAF, P/O J.H., 128, *451*
Watson RCAF, F/O W.C., 306-7
Watson, F/O G.S., 336
Wattebled, Alex ("Jacques"), xxiii, 85, 102, 204
Watts, F/S G.L., 153-4
Waucquez, Gérard ("Brichamart"), 113, 119, 122
Waudby, F/Sgt W.N., 144-5
Wawerski PAF, F/O T., 89
Webb RCAF, Sgt D.J., 230-1
Webber RCAF, Sgt R., 63
Weidner, Gabrielle, xxiii, 156
Weidner, Johan Hendrik, xxiii, 152-3, 156-7, 307
Weight, Sgt F.G.A., 149
Weir, Sgt C.F., 277, 284
Weir RAAF, W/O J., 265
Wemheuer USAAF, 2/Lt J.E., 149, *454*
Wendelen, "Tybalt", 175-6
Wendt USAAF, Sgt P., 242
West VC, A/Cdre Freddie, 84
West USAAF, Lt, 266
Westburg, Sgt R.H., 83
Western, Sgt W.C.L., 296
Whalen USAAF, S/Sgt Arthur T., 213, *460*
Whalen RCAF, Sgt W.B.P., 266
Wheelwright circuit, 265
Whicher, Sgt A.J., 129
Whinney, Lt Patrick, 42
Whipple USAAF, 1/Lt Charles, 307
Whitby, Sgt A.W., 2
White, Sgt J.F., 63,
White, P/O P.D., 149
Whitehead, F/L George, 259-60
Whiteman, Sgt W.E., 66-7
Whitfield, J.G. (vice-consul), 17, 20, 35, 39, 51, 56, 67, 71
Whiting, F/O T.A., 6
Whiting RNVR, Sub-Lt H.P., 94-5, 99
Whitley, Sgt J., 211
Whitley, Sgt J.C., 232, 254
Whitley, G/C J.R., 217-8
Whitnall RCAF, Sgt P., 139
Whittaker, F/S P.L., 321-2
Whittinghill, George (US vice-consul), xxiii, 48, 82, 87, 89, 136
Wickman USAAF, 2/Lt Alfred L., 280-1
Wilby RCAF, F/O T.R., 116
Wilkins, Capt L.A., 31, 37
Wilkinson, Cpl F., 70, 72
Wilkinson, S/L R.C., 87-9, 91, 93,
Wilkinson, F/O E. ("Alexandre", SOE), 103
Williams, Val – see Bouryschkine, Vladimir
Williams, F/O C.J., 298-9
Williams, F/O G.G., 222
Williams RNZAF, Sgt G.K., 61-2

Williams USAAF, Lt Ken, 172
Williams USAAF, Sgt L., 285
Williams, Sgt M.F., 269
Williams RNVR, Lt P., 170-4
Williams, Sgt R.A., 216
Williams, F/S R.T., 326
Williamson, Dvr F.G., 140-2
Williamson, Pte T., 67, 71-2
Willingham USAAF, 2/Lt Clarence D., 254
Willis USAAF, Maj D.K., 288
Willis, Sgt F.G., 18, 29
Willis RCAF, Sgt L., 216-7
Willis, F/S L.R., 19-22, 39
Williston RCAF, F/S R.O., 231
Willmann, Mlle G., 304
Wilmet, Maurice, 122
Wilmore, Sgt E.W., 18
Wilson USAAF, T/Sgt Claiborne W., 178, *457*
Wilson RCAF, Sgt H.R., 78-80
Wilson USAAF, S/Sgt James G., 182
Wilson, P/O L., 104
Wilson F/O M.H.G., 197-8, 205, *459*
Windham-Wright, Capt Patrick J.S., xxiv, 169-71
Windsor RCAF, Sgt K.D., 233
Windsor-Lewis, Maj J.C., 25, 134-6, *452*
Winskill, F/L A.L., 71-2
Wise, Maj A.W., 236, 252
Wiseman USAAF, 2/Lt Abraham, 279
Wissenback USAAF, T/Sgt Erwin D., 76, 107, *445*
Wittek, Fred, 129, *452*
Wittek, Suzanne (née de Jongh), xxiv, 121
Witton, Pte J., 9-10, 152
Witton, Rosine, xxiv, 163, 223
Wolcott USAAF, Lt H.W., 318
Wolf, Mme Jeanie, 112
Wolters, L.D., 338, *471*
Wood, P/O E.R.W., 104
Wood, F/Sgt G., 323
Wood, F/S G.A., 183
Woodard USAAF, 1/Lt Earl E., 266, *465*
Woodhouse RCAF, F/O K.B., 171
Woollard, Sgt L.C., 175, 177
Wootton, Sgt K.B., 251-3
Worby, Sgt J.R., 65
Workman USAAF, Sgt Ralph J., 266
Worrall, Sgt J.R.W., 282, 287
Wozniak PAF, Sgt B., 58, 90-92
Wright, Sgt A.L., 81-2, 91-2
Wright AFC, S/L C., 297
Wright, Sgt E.W., 280
Wright USAAF, S/Sgt Norman, 286, *467*
Wright, Sgt P., 128-9
Wright, F/O S.P., 309
Wuyts-Denis, Vincent and Ghislaine, 291
Wyatt, Sgt J.H., 28, 31

"Xavier", see Heslop, Richard

Yankus USAAF, Sgt Tom, 274, 276-7
Yarwood, F/O H.C., 306
Yaternick RCAF, F/O E., 269
Yee USAAF, 2/Lt Wilbert K., 276
Yeo-Thomas, W/C F.F.E., 176-7, *457*
Young, Sgt D.C., 162
Young, Sgt T., 319
Younger, K.G. (MI5), 133

Zapirain, Tomas Anabitarte, 114
Zarifi, Georges, xxiv, 105, 205
Zawodny PAF, Sgt M.,128
Zetland, 175
Zielenkiewicz USAAF, 1/Lt Adolph, 144
Zucaralli, Joseph, 75